Lecture Notes in Computer Science   10587

Commenced Publication in 1973
Founding and Former Series Editors:
Gerhard Goos, Juris Hartmanis, and Jan van Leeuwen

More information about this series at http://www.springer.com/series/7409

Claudia d'Amato · Miriam Fernandez
Valentina Tamma · Freddy Lecue
Philippe Cudré-Mauroux · Juan Sequeda
Christoph Lange · Jeff Heflin (Eds.)

The Semantic Web – ISWC 2017

16th International Semantic Web Conference
Vienna, Austria, October 21–25, 2017
Proceedings, Part I

 Springer

Editors
Claudia d'Amato (iD)
University of Bari
Bari
Italy

Miriam Fernandez
KMi, The Open University
Milton Keynes
UK

Valentina Tamma
University of Liverpool
Liverpool
UK

Freddy Lecue
Accenture Technology Labs
Dublin
Ireland

Philippe Cudré-Mauroux
University of Fribourg
Fribourg
Switzerland

Juan Sequeda
Capsenta, Inc.
Austin, TX
USA

Christoph Lange (iD)
Universität Bonn
Bonn
Germany

Jeff Heflin
Lehigh University
Bethlehem, PA
USA

ISSN 0302-9743   ISSN 1611-3349   (electronic)
Lecture Notes in Computer Science
ISBN 978-3-319-68287-7   ISBN 978-3-319-68288-4   (eBook)
DOI 10.1007/978-3-319-68288-4

Library of Congress Control Number: 2017955717

LNCS Sublibrary: SL3 – Information Systems and Applications, incl. Internet/Web, and HCI

Printed on acid-free paper

This Springer imprint is published by Springer Nature
The registered company is Springer International Publishing AG
The registered company address is: Gewerbestrasse 11, 6330 Cham, Switzerland

Preface

The International Semantic Web Conference (ISWC) is the premier forum for Semantic Web researchers and practitioners from around the world to gather and share ideas and discoveries. The conference continues to bring together a diverse set of individuals with skills and interests ranging from artificial intelligence to information systems and Web systems. We continue to see steadily increasing adoption of semantic technologies, although more often than not, their use is invisible to consumers.

This volume contains the proceedings of ISWC 2017 with all the papers accepted to the main conference tracks: the Research, Resources, and In-Use Tracks. In addition to the long-standing Research and In-Use Tracks, we have continued the Resources and Journal Tracks that were introduced last year. We also brought back an Industry Track and hope that this will encourage even more cross-fertilization between practitioners and researchers.

The Research Track is home to the most ground-breaking results in the field. This year, we received 197 full submissions, of which 44 were accepted for publication in this volume and presentation at the conference. A large team of reviewers, including 423 Program Committee (PC) members and 23 Senior Program Committee (SPC) members, was carefully selected to ensure a wide coverage of expertise. Each paper was assigned to five reviewers and to an SPC member. The assignment process was based on a bidding phase where PC and SPC members selected papers to review based on their expertise. PC members received a maximum of three papers to review, while SPC members received a maximum of nine papers. A specific form was designed by the Research Track chairs to facilitate the reviewing process and to ensure that all important aspects of the papers were examined. As per the usual process, we included a rebuttal period where authors could respond to the initial reviews. SPC members oversaw the reviews and discussion for each paper in order to resolve disagreements when possible and ensure constructive feedback. Discussions for the papers took place before and after the rebuttal phase to ensure that the authors could answer the key concerns highlighted by the reviewers and that the provided answers were debated, acknowledged, and considered for the final recommendation. Over the course of five days, the SPC members and Research Track chairs held discussions to assess all papers and to make a final decision on which papers to select. During this process, additional reviews were requested for controversial papers. Meta-reviews were written to summarize these discussions and the final recommendation for each paper. While the names of PC members were not visible to the authors, or to each other, during the reviewing period, PC members were given the opportunity to sign their reviews and discussions before the final decision was sent to the authors.

The purpose of the Resources Track is to share resources and best practices for developing them, as we strongly believe that this is crucial in order to consolidate research material, ensure reproducibility of results, and in general gain new scientific insights. The term "resource" can refer to: datasets, ontologies, vocabularies, workflows, evaluation benchmarks or methods, replication studies, services, APIs, and software frameworks that have contributed to the generation of novel scientific work. One of the requirements of this track is that the resources were published with a permanent URI in order to guarantee future access. This year, our publisher piloted a dedicated infrastructure for publishing snapshots of resources to facilitate this process. The track received 76 submissions and accepted 23 of them; seven of these, as well as three of the Research Track, made use of the dedicated resource publishing facility, as can be seen from the respective references in these papers. Each paper received four reviews, and an SPC member provided a meta-review. Similar to the Research Track, there was a rebuttal phase, which was then followed by further discussion among the reviewers and managed by the SPC member who summarized all views in a recommendation to the Resource Track chairs. The final decisions were determined through discussions between the track chairs and the SPC members and were based on the overall views expressed by the reviewers, the meta-reviews and the lively discussions that occurred before and after the rebuttal phase.

The In-Use Track provides a forum for the community to explore the benefits and challenges of applying semantic technologies in concrete, practical applications, in contexts ranging from industry to government and science. This year, the track required that papers provide evidence that there is use of the proposed application or tool by the target user group, preferably outside the group that conducted the development. We received 29 submissions, and accepted nine. Each submission was assigned four reviewers.

Traditionally, ISWC has a different keynote speaker to kick off each day of the main conference. This year we had three exciting keynote talks delivered by Nada Lavrac (Jozef Stefan Institute), Deborah L. McGuinness (Rensselaer Polytechnic Institute), and Jamie Taylor (Google). The titles and abstracts of these talks are included in this volume.

There were many important activities at ISWC 2017 that are not represented in these proceedings. The two days prior to the main conference involved many smaller sessions: workshops, tutorials, and the doctoral consortium. Aidan Hogan and Valentina Presutti were our workshops and tutorials chairs, and selected seven tutorials and 19 workshops for the program. The doctoral consortium was chaired by Lora Aroyo and Fabien Gandon. In all, 26 PhD students submitted papers, and after review by the PC, 13 were accepted to the event.

The Journal Track provided the authors of papers recently published in Semantic Web journals the opportunity to present their papers to the conference community. The editors of the *Journal of Web Semantics* and the *Semantic Web Journal* selected a total of 12 papers published in the previous year (but never presented at ISWC).

The first day of the main conference included an Industry Track and a Posters and Demonstrations Session. The Industry Track was chaired by Achille Fokoue and Peter Haase with the goal of presenting the state of adoption of semantic technologies in industrial applications, whether it be specific industries or as a horizontal technology. This track received 30 submissions and accepted 18 for presentation. The Posters and Demonstrations Track was chaired by Nadeschda Nikitina and Dezhao Song.

This year saw the return of a reinvigorated Semantic Web Challenge. Led by Dan Bennett, Axel Ngonga, and Heiko Paulheim, this year's challenge involved two measurable tasks, i.e., knowledge graph population and knowledge graph validation.

In recognition of the maturing of the field, we added two new events to the conference. In order to reach out to the general public, we featured an event supported by the Vienna Business Agency for the local community in the form of a combined local business lounge and Semantic Web meet-up, co-located with the Posters and Demonstration Track. In addition, this year ISWC celebrated its first Job Fair, bringing together job candidates with open positions in both industry and academia.

The success of a large conference like ISWC also depends on a number of people whose contribution is not directly reflected in the program. We would like to thank our sponsorship chairs Michel Dumontier, Sabrina Kirrane, and Harald Sack, for their efforts in securing external funding to help offset the fixed costs of the conference. We would like to thank our student coordinators Lalana Kagal and Gianluca Demartini for managing the student travel fellowships and organizing the mentoring lunch. Stefan Dietze and Davide Taibi provided the valuable service of collecting and organizing our metadata; an essential task for a community that places so much value on semantics. Our publicity chair Anna Lisa Gentile did a fantastic job of getting the word out on multiple platforms. And of course, the proceedings you are reading today (whether in "old-school" paper form or electronically) would not have been possible without the diligent efforts of our proceedings chair, Christoph Lange.

Last, but certainly not least, we would like to give a big thank you to our local chairs Axel Polleres and Elmar Kiesling. Few people realize the amount of work that goes into the logistics of a conference of this scale, and often the local chairs are invisible unless something goes horribly wrong. Axel, Elmar, and their team have worked countless hours over the course of two years to ensure that everything runs smoothly.

October 2017

Claudia d'Amato
Miriam Fernandez
Valentina Tamma
Freddy Lecue
Philippe Cudré-Mauroux
Juan Sequeda
Jeff Heflin

Organization

Organizing Committee

General Chair

Jeff Heflin Lehigh University, USA

Local Chairs

Axel Polleres WU Wien, Austria
Elmar Kiesling TU Wien, Austria

Research Track Chairs

Claudia d'Amato University of Bari, Italy
Miriam Fernandez KMi, The Open University, UK

Resources Track Chairs

Valentina Tamma University of Liverpool, UK
Freddy Lecue Accenture, Dublin, Ireland/Inria, Sophia Antipolis, France

In-Use Track Chairs

Philippe Cudré-Mauroux University of Fribourg, Switzerland
Juan Sequeda Capsenta, Austin, USA

Workshop and Tutorial Chairs

Aidan Hogan Universidad de Chile, Chile
Valentina Presutti Institute of Cognitive Sciences and Technologies,
CNR, Italy

Poster and Demo Track Chairs

Nadeschda Nikitina University of Oxford, UK
Dezhao Song Thomson Reuters, Eagan, USA

Journal Track Chairs

Abraham Bernstein University of Zurich, Switzerland
Pascal Hitzler Wright State University, USA
Steffen Staab University of Koblenz, Germany

Industry Track Chairs

Achille Fokoue IBM Yorktown, USA
Peter Haase metaphacts, Germany

Doctoral Consortium Chairs

Lora Aroyo	Vrije Universiteit Amsterdam, The Netherlands
Fabien Gandon	Inria Sophia Antipolis, France

Semantic Web Challenge Chairs

Dan Bennett	Thomson Reuters, Eagan, USA
Axel Ngonga	University of Paderborn, Germany
Heiko Paulheim	University of Mannheim, Germany

Proceedings Chair

Christoph Lange	University of Bonn and Fraunhofer IAIS, Germany

Metadata Chairs

Stefan Dietze	L3S, Leibniz University, Germany
Davide Taibi	Institute for Educational Technology, CNR, Italy

Sponsorship Chairs

Michel Dumontier	Maastricht University, The Netherlands
Sabrina Kirrane	WU Wien, Austria
Harald Sack	FIZ Karlsruhe, KIT Karlsruhe, Germany

Student Coordinators

Lalana Kagal	Massachusetts Institute of Technology, USA
Gianluca Demartini	University of Queensland, Australia

Publicity Chair

Anna Lisa Gentile	IBM Research Almaden, USA

Local Committee

Bettina Bauer	SBA Research, Vienna, Austria
Fajar J. Ekaputra	TU Wien, Austria
Javier D. Fernández	WU Wien, Austria
Yvonne Poul	SBA Research, Vienna, Austria
Doris Wyk	WU Wien, Austria

Program Committee

Senior Program Committee – Research Track

Harith Alani	Knowledge Media Institute, Open University, UK
Abraham Bernstein	University of Zurich, Switzerland
Kalina Bontcheva	University of Sheffield, UK
Philipp Cimiano	Bielefeld University, Germany

Oscar Corcho	Universidad Politécnica de Madrid, Spain
Mathieu D'Aquin	Insight Centre, National University of Ireland Galway, Ireland
Fabien Gandon	Inria, France
Jose Manuel Gomez-Perez	Expert System, Spain
Jorge Gracia	Universidad Politécnica de Madrid, Spain
Claudio Gutierrez	Universidad de Chile, Chile
Olaf Hartig	Linköping University, Sweden
Pascal Hitzler	Wright State University, USA
Craig Knoblock	University of Southern California, USA
Vanessa Lopez	IBM Research, USA
Thomas Lukasiewicz	University of Oxford, UK
H. Sofia Pinto	Instituto Superior Tecnico, Portugal
Uli Sattler	University of Manchester, UK
Stefan Schlobach	Vrije Universiteit Amsterdam, The Netherlands
Steffen Staab	Institut WeST, University of Koblenz-Landau, Germany and WAIS, University of Southampton, UK
Vojtěch Svátek	University of Economics, Prague, Czech Republic
Tania Tudorache	Stanford University, USA
Maria Esther Vidal	Universidad Simon Bolivar, Venezuela
Denny Vrandečić	Google, USA

Program Committee – Research Track

Maribel Acosta	Institute AIFB, Karlsruhe Institute of Technology, Germany
Alessandro Adamou	Knowledge Media Institute, The Open University, UK
Nitish Aggarwal	IBM Watson, USA
Guadalupe Aguado-De-Cea	Universidad Politécnica de Madrid, Spain
Panos Alexopoulos	Textkernel B.V., The Netherlands
Jose Julio Alferes	Universidade Nova de Lisboa, Portugal
Muhammad Intizar Ali	Insight Centre for Data Analytics, National University of Ireland, Galway
Marjan Alirezaie	Orebro University, Sweden
Faisal Alkhateeb	Yarmouk University, Jordan
Tahani Alsubait	Umm Al-Qura University, Saudi Arabia
José Luis Ambite	University of Southern California, USA
Pramod Anantharam	Bosch Research and Technology Center, USA
Renzo Angles	Universidad de Talca, Chile
Grigoris Antoniou	University of Huddersfield, UK
Kemafor Anyanwu	North Carolina State University, USA
Manuel Atencia	University of Grenoble Alpes and Inria, France
Ioannis N. Athanasiadis	Wageningen University, The Netherlands
Medha Atre	IIT Kanpur, India

Christian Chiarcos	Universität Frankfurt am Main, Germany
Michael Cochez	Fraunhofer Institute for Applied Information Technology FIT, Germany
Pieter Colpaert	Ghent University, Belgium
Simona Colucci	Politecnico di Bari, Italy
Sam Coppens	Autodesk, USA
Olivier Corby	Inria, France
Paulo Costa	George Mason University, USA
Luca Costabello	Fujitsu Ireland, Ireland
Fabio Cozman	Universidade de Sao Paulo, Brazil
Isabel Cruz	University of Illinois at Chicago, USA
Philippe Cudré-Mauroux	University of Fribourg, Switzerland
Bernardo Cuenca-Grau	University of Oxford, UK
Edward Curry	Insight Centre for Data Analytics, NUI Galway, Ireland
Olivier Curé	Université Paris-Est LIGM, France
Aba-Sah Dadzie	KMi – The Open University, UK
Enrico Daga	The Open University, UK
Florian Daniel	Politecnico di Milano, Italy
Laura Daniele	TNO/Netherlands Organization for Applied Scientific Research, The Netherlands
Jérôme David	Inria Rhône-Alpes, France
Victor de Boer	VU University Amsterdam, The Netherlands
Gerard de Melo	Rutgers University, USA
Jeremy Debattista	ADAPT Centre, School of Computer Science and Statistics, Trinity College Dublin, Ireland
Thierry Declerck	DFKI GmbH, Germany
Jaime Delgado	Universitat Politecnica de Catalunya, Spain
Daniele Dell'Aglio	University of Zurich, Switzerland
Emanuele Della Valle	DEIB Politecnico di Milano, Italy
Gianluca Demartini	University of Queensland, Australia
Elena Demidova	L3S Research Center, Germany
Ronald Denaux	Expert System, Spain
Tommaso Di Noia	Politecnico di Bari, Italy
Ian Dickinson	Epimorphics Ltd., UK
Dennis Diefenbach	Jean Monnet University, France
Stefan Dietze	L3S Research Center, Germany
Ying Ding	Indiana University, USA
Leigh Dodds	Leigh Dodds, UK
John Domingue	KMi – The Open University, UK
Derek Doran	Wright State University, USA
Mauro Dragoni	Fondazione Bruno Kessler – FBK-IRST, Italy
Michel Dumontier	Maastricht University, The Netherlands
Maud Ehrmann	EPFL DHLAB, Switzerland
Thomas Eiter	Vienna University of Technology, Austria
Henrik Eriksson	Linköping University, Sweden
Vadim Ermolayev	Zaporizhzhya National University, Ukraine

Jérôme Euzenat	Inria and University of Grenoble Alpes, France
James Fan	HelloVera.ai, USA
Nicola Fanizzi	Università di Bari, Italy
Catherine Faron-Zucker	Université Nice Sophia Antipolis, France
Anna Fensel	Semantic Technology Institute (STI) – University of Innsbruck, Austria
Alberto Fernandez	University Rey Juan Carlos, Spain
Javier D. Fernández	Vienna University of Economics and Business WU Wien, Austria
Sebastien Ferre	University of Rennes 1, France
Besnik Fetahu	L3S Research Center, Germany
Tim Finin	University of Maryland Baltimore County, USA
Valeria Fionda	University of Calabria, Italy
Lorenz Fischer	Sentient Machines, UK
Fabian Flöck	GESIS Cologne, Germany
Antske Fokkens	VU University Amsterdam, The Netherlands
Muriel Foulonneau	Luxembourg Institute of Science and Technology, Luxembourg
Enrico Franconi	Free University of Bozen-Bolzano, Italy
Flavius Frasincar	Erasmus University Rotterdam, The Netherlands
Fred Freitas	Universidade Federal de Pernambuco (UFPE), Brazil
Adam Funk	University of Sheffield, UK
Aldo Gangemi	Université Paris 13 and CNR-ISTC, Italy
Shen Gao	University of Zurich, Switzerland
José Maria García	University of Seville, Spain
Raúl García Castro	Universidad Politécnica de Madrid, Spain
Andrés García-Silva	Expert System, Spain
Claire Gardent	CNRS/LORIA Nancy, France
Daniel Garijo	Information Sciences Institute, University of Southern California, USA
Anna Lisa Gentile	IBM Research Almaden, San Jose, CA, USA
Chiara Ghidini	FBK-irst, Italy
Alain Giboin	Inria Sophia Antipolis/Méditerranée, France
Rafael S. Gonçalves	Stanford University, USA
Gregory Grefenstette	Biggerpan, France
Ruediger Grimm	University of Koblenz Landau, Germany
Paul Groth	Elsevier Labs, The Netherlands
Tudor Groza	The Garvan Institute of Medical Research, Australia
Alessio Gugliotta	Innova, Italy
Cathal Gurrin	Dublin City University, Ireland
Christophe Guéret	Accenture, Ireland
Olaf Görlitz	Chefkoch GmbH, Germany
Peter Haase	metaphacts, Germany
Armin Haller	Australian National University, Australia
Harry Halpin	World Wide Web Consortium, UK
Karl Hammar	Jönköping University, Sweden

Siegfried Handschuh   University of Passau, Germany
Andreas Harth   AIFB, Karlsruhe Institute of Technology, Germany
Oktie Hassanzadeh   IBM Research, USA
Tom Heath   Open Data Institute, UK
Johannes Heinecke   Orange Labs, France
Andreas Herzig   IRIT-CNRS, France
Stijn Heymans   Amazon, USA
Aidan Hogan   DCC Universidad de Chile, Chile
Laura Hollink   Centrum Wiskunde & Informatica, The Netherlands
Matthew Horridge   Stanford University, USA
Katja Hose   Aalborg University, Denmark
Andreas Hotho   University of Würzburg, Germany
Geert-Jan Houben   TU Delft, The Netherlands
Wei Hu   Nanjing University, China
Yingjie Hu   University of Tennessee Knoxville, USA
Ioana Hulpus   University of Mannheim, Germany
Eero Hyvönen   University of Helsinki and Aalto University, Finland
Ignacio Iacobacci   Sapienza Università di Roma, Italy
Yazmin Angelica   Vienna University of Technology, Austria
   Ibanez-Garcia
Luis-Daniel Ibáñez   University of Southampton, UK
Oana Inel   VU University Amsterdam, The Netherlands
Valentina Ivanova   Linköping University, Sweden
Krzysztof Janowicz   University of California Santa Barbara, USA
Mustafa Jarrar   Birzeit University, Palestine
Ernesto Jimenez-Ruiz   University of Oslo, Norway
Clement Jonquet   University of Montpellier LIRMM, France
Martin Kaltenböck   Semantic Web Company, Austria
Mark Kaminski   University of Oxford, UK
Pavan Kapanipathi   IBM T.J. Watson Research Center, USA
Md. Rezaul Karim   Fraunhofer Institute for Applied Information
     Technology FIT, Germany
Marcel   Springer Nature
   Karnstedt-Hulpus
Tomi Kauppinen   Aalto University School of Science, Finland
Takahiro Kawamura   Japan Science and Technology Agency, Japan
Maria Keet   University of Cape Town, South Africa
Mayank Kejriwal   Information Sciences Institute, University of Southern
     California, USA
Kristian Kersting   TU Darmstadt, Germany
Carsten Keßler   Aalborg University, Denmark
Haklae Kim   Samsung, South Korea
Hong-Gee Kim   Seoul National University, South Korea
Sabrina Kirrane   Vienna University of Economics and Business WU Wien,
     Austria
Matthias Klusch   DFKI, Germany

Matthias Knorr	Universidade Nova de Lisboa, Portugal
Magnus Knuth	Hasso Plattner Institute, University of Potsdam, Germany
Boris Konev	University of Liverpool, UK
Stasinos Konstantopoulos	NCSR Demokritos, Greece
Roman Kontchakov	Birkbeck, University of London, UK
Jacek Kopecky	University of Portsmouth, UK
Manolis Koubarakis	National and Kapodistrian University of Athens, Greece
Adila Krisnadhi	Wright State University, USA and Universitas Indonesia, Indonesia
Udo Kruschwitz	University of Essex, UK
Tobias Kuhn	VU University Amsterdam, The Netherlands
Benedikt Kämpgen	Empolis Information Management GmbH, Germany
Patrick Lambrix	Linköping University, Sweden
Steffen Lamparter	Siemens AG Corporate Technology, Germany
Christoph Lange	University of Bonn and Fraunhofer IAIS, Germany
David Laniado	Eurecat - Technology Centre of Catalonia, Spain
Ken Laskey	The MITRE Corporation, USA
Agnieszka Lawrynowicz	Poznan University of Technology, Poland
Danh Le Phuoc	Technische Universität Berlin, Germany
Maxime Lefrançois	MINES Saint-Etienne, France
Maurizio Lenzerini	University of Rome La Sapienza, Italy
Chengkai Li	University of Texas at Arlington, USA
Juanzi Li	Tsinghua University, China
Wenwen Li	Arizona State University, USA
Giorgia Lodi	DigitPA, Italy
Nuno Lopes	TopQuadrant Inc., Ireland
Chun Lu	Université Paris-Sorbonne and Sépage, France
Markus Luczak-Roesch	Victoria University of Wellington, New Zealand
Carsten Lutz	Universität Bremen, Germany
Ioanna Lytra	Enterprise Information Systems, Institute of Applied Computer Science, University of Bonn and Fraunhofer IAIS, Germany
Alexander Löser	Beuth Hochschule für Technik Berlin, Germany
Frederick Maier	Institute for Artificial Intelligence, USA
Maria Maleshkova	AIFB, Karlsruhe Institute of Technology, Germany
Claudia Marinica	ETIS/ENSEA UCP CNRS, France
David Martin	Nuance Communications, USA
Trevor Martin	University of Bristol, UK
Mercedes Martinez-Gonzalez	University of Valladolid, Spain
Miguel Martinez-Prieto	University of Valladolid, Spain
Wolfgang May	Universität Göttingen Germany, Germany
Diana Maynard	University of Sheffield, UK
John McCrae	National University of Ireland Galway, Ireland
Fiona McNeill	Heriot Watt University, UK

Lionel Médini	LIRIS/University of Lyon, France
Eduardo Mena	University of Zaragoza, Spain
Robert Meusel	SAP SE, Germany
Franck Michel	Université Côte d'Azur, CNRS, I3S, France
Nandana Mihindukulasooriya	Universidad Politécnica de Madrid, Spain
Peter Mika	Schibsted, Norway
Alessandra Mileo	INSIGHT Centre for Data Analytics, Dublin City University, Ireland
Daniel Miranker	Institute for Cell and Molecular Biology, The University of Texas at Austin, USA
Riichiro Mizoguchi	Japan Advanced Institute of Science and Technology, Japan
Dunja Mladenic	Jozef Stefan Institute, Slovenia
Marie-Francine Moens	KU Leuven, Belgium
Pascal Molli	University of Nantes/LS2N, France
Gabriela Montoya	Aalborg University, Denmark
Federico Morando	Nexa Center for Internet and Society, Politecnico di Torino, Italy
Luc Moreau	King's College London, UK
Yassine Mrabet	National Library of Medicine, USA
Paul Mulholland	The Open University, UK
Raghava Mutharaju	GE Global Research, USA
Ralf Möller	University of Lübeck, Germany
Claudia Müller-Birn	Freie Universität Berlin, Germany
Hubert Naacke	UPMC, France
Amedeo Napoli	LORIA Nancy (CNRS - Inria - Université de Lorraine), France
Axel-Cyrille Ngonga-Ngomo	University of Paderborn, Germany
Matthias Nickles	Digital Enterprise Research Institute, National University of Ireland Galway, Ireland
Nadeschda Nikitina	Oxford University, UK
Andriy Nikolov	metaphacts GmbH, Germany
Malvina Nissim	University of Groningen, The Netherlands
Lyndon Nixon	MODUL Technology GmbH, Austria
Andrea Giovanni Nuzzolese	STLab ISTC-CNR, Italy
Leo Obrst	MITRE, USA
Francesco Osborne	KMi, The Open University, UK
Raul Palma	Poznan Supercomputing and Networking Center, Poland
Matteo Palmonari	University of Milano-Bicocca, Italy
Jeff Pan	University of Aberdeen, UK
Rahul Parundekar	Toyota Info-Technology Center, USA
Bibek Paudel	University of Zurich, Switzerland
Heiko Paulheim	University of Mannheim, Germany

Terry Payne	University of Liverpool, UK
Tassilo Pellegrini	University of Applied Sciences St. Pölten, Austria
Laura Perez-Beltrachini	University of Edinburgh, UK
Silvio Peroni	University of Bologna, Italy
Catia Pesquita	LaSIGE, Universidade de Lisboa, Portugal
Rafael Peñaloza	Free University of Bozen-Bolzano, Italy
Reinhard Pichler	Vienna University of Technology, Austria
Emmanuel Pietriga	Inria, France
Giuseppe Pirrò	Institute for High Performance Computing and Networking (ICAR-CNR), Italy
Vassilis Plachouras	Thomson Reuters, UK
Dimitris Plexousakis	Institute of Computer Science FORTH, University of Crete, Greece
Simone Paolo Ponzetto	University of Mannheim, Germany
Mike Pool	Goldman Sachs Group, USA
Livia Predoiu	University of Oxford, UK
Laurette Pretorius	University of South Africa, South Africa
Cédric Pruski	Luxembourg Institute of Science and Technology, Luxembourg
Guilin Qi	Southeast University, China
Yuzhong Qu	Nanjing University, China
Jorge-Arnulfo Quiané-Ruiz	QCRI, Qatar
Filip Radulovic	Sépage Paris, France
Dnyanesh Rajpathak	General Motors, Operations Research R&D, USA
Ganesh Ramakrishnan	IIT Bombay, India
Maya Ramanath	IIT Delhi, India
David Ratcliffe	CSIRO Data61 and Australian National University, Australia
Dietrich Rebholz-Schuhmann	Insight Centre for Data Analytics, National University of Ireland Galway, Ireland
José Luis Redondo-García	Amazon Research, UK
Georg Rehm	DFKI, Germany
Achim Rettinger	Karlsruhe Institute of Technology, Germany
Juan Reutter	Pontificia Universidad Catòlica, Chile
Martin Rezk	Rakuten Inc., Japan
German Rigau	IXA Group – UPV/EHU, Spain
Carlos Rivero	Rochester Institute of Technology, USA
Giuseppe Rizzo	ISMB, Italy
Mariano Rodríguez Muro	IBM Research, USA
Marco Rospocher	Fondazione Bruno Kessler, Italy
Camille Roth	CNRS, Germany
Marie-Christine Rousset	University of Grenoble Alpes, France
Ana Roxin	University of Burgundy UMR CNRS, France

Audun Stolpe   Norwegian Defence Research Establishment (FFI),
                               Norway
Umberto Straccia   ISTI-CNR, Italy
Markus Strohmaier   RWTH Aachen and GESIS, Germany
Heiner Stuckenschmidt   University of Mannheim, Germany
Gerd Stumme   University of Kassel, Germany
Fabian Suchanek   Télécom ParisTech University, France
Jing Sun   The University of Auckland, New Zealand
York Sure-Vetter   Karlsruhe Institute of Technology (KIT), Germany
Marcin Sydow   PJIIT and ICS PAS Warsaw, Poland
Pedro Szekely   USC/Information Sciences Institute, USA
Mohsen Taheriyan   Google, USA
Hideaki Takeda   National Institute of Informatics, Japan
Kerry Taylor   Australian National University, Australia
Annette Ten Teije   VU University Amsterdam, The Netherlands
Andrea Tettamanzi   University of Nice Sophia Antipolis, France
Kia Teymourian   Rice University, USA
Dhavalkumar Thakker   University of Bradford, UK
Matthias Thimm   Universität Koblenz-Landau, Germany
Allan Third   The Open University, UK
Krishnaprasad   Wright State University, USA
  Thirunarayan
Ilaria Tiddi   KMi, The Open University, UK
Ramine Tinati   University of Southampton, UK
Thanassis Tiropanis   University of Southampton, UK
Konstantin Todorov   LIRMM/University of Montpellier, France
David Toman   University of Waterloo, Canada
Nicolas Torzec   Yahoo, USA
Farouk Toumani   Limos Blaise Pascal University Clermont-Ferrand, France
Yannick Toussaint   LORIA, France
Sebastian Tramp   eccenca GmbH, Germany
Cassia Trojahn   UT2J and IRIT, France
Raphaël Troncy   EURECOM, France
Dmitry Tsarkov   Google, Switzerland
Anni-Yasmin Turhan   Technische Universität Dresden, Germany
Jürgen Umbrich   Vienna University of Economy and Business (WU),
                               Austria
Jörg Unbehauen   University of Leipzig, Germany
Jacopo Urbani   Vrije Universiteit Amsterdam, The Netherlands
Alejandro Vaisman   Instituto Tecnològico de Buenos Aires, Argentina
Herbert Van De Sompel   Los Alamos National Laboratory Research Library, USA
Marieke van Erp   KNAW Humanities Cluster, The Netherlands
Willem Robert van Hage   Netherlands eScience Center, The Netherlands
Jacco van Ossenbruggen   CWI and VU University Amsterdam, The Netherlands

Ruben Verborgh	Ghent University – imec, Belgium
Daniel Vila-Suero	Ontology Engineering Group UPM, Spain
Serena Villata	CNRS, Laboratoire d'Informatique Signaux et Systèmes de Sophia Antipolis, France
Marta Villegas	Barcelona Supercomputing Center, Spain
Piek Vossen	VU University Amsterdam, The Netherlands
Domagoj Vrgoc	Pontificia Universidad Catòlica de Chile, Chile
Holger Wache	University of Applied Science and Arts Northweastern Switzerland, Switzerland
Claudia Wagner	GESIS-Leibniz Institute for the Social Sciences, Germany
Simon Walk	Graz University of Technology, Austria
Haofen Wang	Shenzhen Gowild Robotics Co. Ltd., China
Kewen Wang	Griffith University, Australia
Shenghui Wang	OCLC Research, The Netherlands
Zhichun Wang	Beijing Normal University, China
Paul Warren	KMi, The Open University, UK
Grant Weddell	University of Waterloo, Canada
Rigo Wenning	W3C, France
Erik Wilde	CA Technologies, Switzerland
Cord Wiljes	CITEC, Bielefeld University, Germany
Gregory Todd Williams	Rensselaer Polytechnic Institute, USA
Jiewen Wu	Accenture Tech Labs, Ireland
Marcin Wylot	TU Berlin, Germany
Josiane Xavier Parreira	Siemens AG Österreich, Austria
Yong Yu	Shanghai Jiao Tong University, China
Fouad Zablith	American University of Beirut, Lebanon
Ondřej Zamazal	University of Economics Prague, Czech Republic
Benjamin Zapilko	GESIS, Leibniz Institute for the Social Sciences, Germany
Amrapali Zaveri	Maastricht University, The Netherlands
Sergej Zerr	L3S Research Center, Germany
Qingpeng Zhang	City University of Hong Kong, China
Ziqi Zhang	Nottingham Trent University, UK
Jun Zhao	University of Oxford, UK
Antoine Zimmermann	École des Mines de Saint-Étienne, France

Additional Reviewers – Research Track

Ahn, Jinhyun	Binns, Reuben
Anelli, Vito Walter	Blume, Till
Ara, Safina Showkat	Bosque-Gil, Julia
Atencia, Manuel	Bourgaux, Camille
Bader, Sebastian	Brank, Janez
Bakhshandegan Moghaddam, Farshad	Calleja, Pablo
Basile, Valerio	Čerāns, Kārlis
Batsakis, Sotiris	Charalambidis, Angelos

Charron, Bruno
Chen, Jiaoyan
Chernushenko, Iurii
Ciortea, Andrei
Collarana, Diego
Comerio, Marco
Dehghanzadeh, Soheila
Di Francescomarino, Chiara
Dimitrov, Dimitar
Donadello, Ivan
Feier, Cristina
Frank, Matthias
Freitas, Andre
Galkin, Mikhail
Gao, Shen
Gao, Yimei
Giboin, Alain
Giménez-García, José M.
Gottschalk, Simon
Hanika, Tom
Hildebrandt, Marcel
Janke, Daniel
Jiaoyan, Chen
Kaefer, Tobias
Kamdar, Maulik R.
Kasper, Patrick
Keppmann, Felix Leif
Keskisärkkä, Robin
Kilias, Torsten
Kling, Christoph
Kondylakis, Haridimos
Koopmann, Patrick
Laforest, Frederique
Lee Sungin
Lima, Rinaldo
Liu, Qian
Mehdi, Gulnar
Mihindukulasooriya, Nandana
Mireles, Victor
Molinari, Andrea
Moodley, Kody

Mossakowski, Till
Musto, Cataldo
Nanni, Federico
Narducci, Fedelucio
Niebler, Thomas
Nishioka, Chifumi
Novalija, Inna
Osmani, Aomar
Padia, Ankur
Patkos, Theodore
Pham, Le Thi Anh Thu
Piao, Guangyuan
Plu, Julien
Qiu, Lin
Rettig, Laura
Revenko, Artem
Ringsquandl, Martin
Rokicki, Markus
Saeef, Mohammed Samiul
Sarker, Md Kamruzzaman
Schneider, Patrik
Setty, Vinay
Shivaprabhu, Vivek
Simkus, Mantas
Smirnova, Alisa
Soru, Tommaso
Steinmetz, Nadine
Suchanek, Fabian M.
Tachmazidis, Ilias
Thoma, Steffen
Thost, Veronika
Tommasini, Riccardo
Usbeck, Ricardo
Van Harmelen, Frank
Wang, Xin
Wang, Zhe
Xiao, Guohui
Xu, Kang
Yimei, Gao
Zaraket, Fadi
Zhang, Gensheng

Senior Program Committee – Resources Track

Mauro Dragoni	Fondazione Bruno Kessler – FBK-IRST, Italy
Daniel Garijo	Information Sciences Institute, University of Southern California, USA
Alasdair Gray	Heriot-Watt University, UK
Matthew Horridge	Stanford University, USA
Ernesto Jimenez-Ruiz	University of Oslo, Norway
Bijan Parsia	University of Manchester, UK
Stefan Schulte	Vienna University of Technology, Austria

Program Committee – Resources Track

Muhammad Intizar Ali	Insight Centre for Data Analytics, National University of Ireland, Galway, Ireland
Elena Cabrio	Université Côte d'Azur, CNRS Inria I3S, France, France
Mari Carmen Suárez-Figueroa	Universidad Politécnica de Madrid, Spain
David Carral	TU Dresden, Germany
Tim Clark	Massachusetts General Hospital/Harvard Medical School, USA
Francesco Corcoglioniti	Fondazione Bruno Kessler, Italy
Daniele Dell'Aglio	University of Zurich, Switzerland
Ying Ding	Indiana University, USA
Mohnish Dubey	Computer Science Institute, University of Bonn, Germany
Fajar J. Ekaputra	Vienna University of Technology, Austria
Diego Esteves	University of Bonn, Germany
Stefano Faralli	University of Mannheim, Germany
Mariano Fernández López	Universidad San Pablo CEU, Spain
Aldo Gangemi	Université Paris 13 and CNR-ISTC, Italy
Alejandra Gonzalez-Beltran	University of Oxford, UK
Rafael S. Gonçalves	Stanford University, USA
Christophe Guéret	Accenture, Ireland
Amelie Gyrard	Ecole des Mines de Saint Etienne, France
Pascal Hitzler	Wright State University, USA
Robert Hoehndorf	King Abdullah University of Science and Technology, Saudi Arabia
Aidan Hogan	DCC, Universidad de Chile, Chile
Antoine Isaac	Europeana and VU University Amsterdam, The Netherlands
Chen Jiaoyan	GIScience, Heidelberg University, Germany
Simon Jupp	European Bioinformatics Institute, UK
Maria Keet	University of Cape Town, South Africa, South Africa
Elmar Kiesling	Vienna University of Technology, Austria

Christoph Lange   University of Bonn and Fraunhofer IAIS, Germany,
                           Germany
Steffen Lohmann   Fraunhofer IAIS, Germany
Phillip Lord   Newcastle University, UK
Maria Maleshkova   AIFB, Karlsruhe Institute of Technology, Germany
Nicolas Matentzoglu   University of Manchester, UK
Fiona McNeill   Heriot Watt University, UK
Nandana   Universidad Politécnica de Madrid, Spain
  Mihindukulasooriya
Raghava Mutharaju   GE Global Research, USA
Giulio Napolitano   Fraunhofer IAIS and University of Bonn, Germany
Vinh Nguyen   Kno.e.sis Center, Wright State University, USA
Alessandro Oltramari   Bosch Research and Technology Center, USA
Tommaso Pasini   Sapienza University of Rome, Italy
Heiko Paulheim   University of Mannheim, Germany
Silvio Peroni   University of Bologna, Italy
María Poveda-Villalón   Universidad Politécnica de Madrid, Spain
Mariano Rico   Universidad Politécnica de Madrid (UPM), Spain
German Rigau   IXA Group, UPV/EHU, Spain
Giuseppe Rizzo   ISMB, Italy
Mariano Rodríguez   IBM Research, USA
  Muro
Marco Rospocher   Fondazione Bruno Kessler, Italy
Edna Ruckhaus   Universidad Politécnica de Madrid
Anisa Rula   University of Milano-Bicocca, Italy
Michele Ruta   Politecnico di Bari, Italy
Satya Sahoo   Case Western Reserve University, USA
Cristina Sarasua   Institute for Web Science and Technologies (WeST),
                           Universität Koblenz-Landau, Germany
Marco Luca Sbodio   IBM Research, Ireland
Jodi Schneider   University of Illinois Urbana Champaign, USA
Hamed Shariat Yazdi   University of Siegen, Germany
Stian Soiland-Reyes   The University of Manchester, UK
Krishnaprasad   Wright State University, USA
  Thirunarayan
Cassia Trojahn   UT2J and IRIT, France
Raphaël Troncy   EURECOM, France
Federico Ulliana   University of Montpellier II, France
Natalia   University of Texas at El Paso, USA
  Villanueva-Rosales
Serena Villata   CNRS, Laboratoire d'Informatique, Signaux et Systèmes
                           de Sophia Antipolis, France
Simon Walk   Graz University of Technology, Austria
Peter Wetz   TIPCO, Austria
Amrapali Zaveri   Maastricht University, The Netherlands
Jun Zhao   University of Oxford, UK

Additional Reviewers – Resources Track

Amini, Reihaneh
Atemezing, Ghislain Auguste
Bianchi, Federico
Bosque-Gil, Julia
Byamugisha, Joan
Chakraborty, Nilesh
Daquino, Marilena
Francis, Jonathan
Gracia, Jorge
Halilaj, Lavdim
Hu, Wei
Kastler, Leon
Lehrig, Sebastian
Mader, Christian
Mulligan, Natasha
Navas-Loro, María

Nayyeri, Mojtaba
Poggi, Francesco
Priyatna, Freddy
Radulovic, Filip
Sarker, Md Kamruzzaman
Sarntivijai, Sirarat
Sazonau, Viachaslau
Shimizu, Cogan
Spahiu, Blerina
Tommasi, Pierpaolo
Wadkar, Sudarshan
Warrender, Jennifer
Weller, Tobias
Wiens, Vitalis
Zhou, Lu

Program Committee – In-Use Track

Jean-Paul Calbimonte	University of Applied Sciences and Arts Western Switzerland HES-SO, Switzerland
Christophe Guéret	Accenture, Ireland
Mauro Dragoni	Fondazione Bruno Kessler, FBK-IRST, Italy
Oshani Seneviratne	Massachusetts Institute of Technology, USA
Tudor Groza	The Garvan Institute of Medical Research, Australia
Stefan Dietze	L3S Research Center, Germany
Héctor Pérez-Urbina	Google, USA
Tim Clark	Massachusetts General Hospital/Harvard Medical School, USA
Anna Lisa Gentile	IBM Research Almaden, USA
Dezhao Song	Thomson Reuters, USA
Prateek Jain	BlackRock, USA
Brian Davis	Insight Centre for Data Analytics, Galway, Ireland
Andriy Nikolov	metaphacts GmbH, Germany
Raphaël Troncy	EURECOM, France
Pedro Szekely	USC/Information Sciences Institute, USA
Harald Sack	FIZ Karlsruhe, Leibniz Institute for Information Infrastructure and KIT Karlsruhe, Germany
Daniel Garijo	Information Sciences Institute, University of Southern California, USA
Achille Fokoue	IBM Research, USA
Matthew Horridge	Stanford University, USA
Irene Celino	CEFRIEL, Italy
Jérôme Euzenat	Inria and University of Grenoble Alpes, France
Boris Motik	University of Oxford, UK

Maria Sokhn	University of Applied Sciences of Western Switzerland, Switzerland
Raghava Mutharaju	GE Global Research, USA
Peter Mika	Schibsted, Norway
Ruslan Mavlyutov	University of Fribourg, Switzerland
Varish Mulwad	GE Global Research, USA
Jose Manuel Gomez-Perez	Expert System, Spain
Jerven Bolleman	Swiss Institute of Bioinformatics, Switzerland
Giuseppe Rizzo	ISMB, Italy
Thomas Steiner	Google, Germany
Paul Groth	Elsevier Labs, The Netherlands
Vanessa Lopez	IBM Research, Ireland
Craig Knoblock	University of Southern California, USA
Oscar Corcho	Universidad Politécnica de Madrid, Spain
Peter Haase	metaphacts GmbH, Germany
Steffen Lamparter	Siemens AG, Corporate Technology, Germany

Additional Reviewers – In-Use Track

Alrifai, Ahmad
Biswas, Russa
Garijo, Daniel
Gentile, Anna Lisa

Palumbo, Enrico
Tudorache, Tania
Türker, Rima

Sponsors

Platinum Sponsors

http://www.ibm.com/

http://www.elsevier.com/

Gold Sponsors

https://www.semantic-web.at/

metaphacts

http://www.metaphacts.com/

BIG DATA EUROPE
Empowering Communities with Data Technologies

https://www.big-data-europe.eu/

http://www.oracle.com/

SIEMENS
Ingenuity for life

http://siemens.at/

https://data.world/

 THOMSON REUTERS®

http://www.thomsonreuters.com/

http://www.ontoforce.com/

 OИTOFORCE   EVERYBODY A DATASCIENTIST

http://ontotext.com/

exchange ideas & share knowledge

http://www.videolectures.net/

Bronze Sponsors

https://www.inria.fr/centre/sophia/

Google

http://www.google.com/

Student Travel Award Sponsors

https://www.nsf.gov/

http://swsa.semanticweb.org/

WiFi Sponsor

https://www.kapsch.net/

Supporters

Supported by

http://swsa.semanticweb.org/

https://viennabusinessagency.at/

https://www.w3.org/

https://www.eurai.org/

http://www.iospress.nl/

http://www.springer.com/

Organizers

WU WIRTSCHAFTS UNIVERSITÄT WIEN VIENNA UNIVERSITY OF ECONOMICS AND BUSINESS

https://www.wu.ac.at/en/

https://www.tuwien.ac.at/en/

https://www.sba-research.org/

Abstracts of Invited Talks

From Relational to Semantic Data Mining

Nada Lavrač[1,2,3]

[1] Jožef Stefan Institute, Ljubljana, Slovenia
nada.lavrac@ijs.si
[2] Jožef Stefan International Postgraduate School, Ljubljana, Slovenia
[3] University of Nova Gorica, Nova Gorica, Slovenia

Abstract. Relational Data Mining (RDM) addresses the task of inducing models or patterns from multi-relational data. One of the established approaches to RDM is propositionalization, characterized by transforming a relational database into a single-table representation. The talk provides an overview of propositionalization algorithms, and a particular approach named wordification, all of which have been made publicly available through the web-based ClowdFlows data mining platform. The focus of this talk is on recent advances in Semantic Data Mining (SDM), characterized by exploiting relational background knowledge in the form of domain ontologies in the process of model and pattern construction. The open source SDM approaches, available through the ClowdFlows platform, enable software reuse and experiment replication. The talk concludes by presenting the recent developments, which allow to speed up SDM by data mining and network analysis approaches.

Ontologies for the Modern Age

Deborah L. McGuinness

Rensselaer Institute for Data Exploration and Applications, USA
dlm@cs.rpi.edu

Abstract. Ontologies are seeing a resurgence of interest and usage as big data proliferates, machine learning advances, and integration of data becomes more paramount. The previous models of sometimes labor-intensive, centralized ontology construction and maintenance do not mesh well in today's interdisciplinary world that is in the midst of a big data, information extraction, and machine learning explosion. In this talk, we will provide some historical perspective on ontologies and their usage, and discuss a model of building and maintaining large collaborative, interdisciplinary ontologies along with the data repositories and data services that they empower. We will give a few examples of heterogeneous semantic data resources made more interconnected and more powerful by ontology-supported infrastructures, discuss a vision for ontology-enabled future research and provide some examples in a large health empowerment joint effort between RPI and IBM Watson Health.

Applied Semantics: Beyond the Catalog

Jamie Taylor

Google, USA
jamietaylor@google.com

Abstract. A decade ago a number of semantic catalogs started appearing. These catalogs gave identifiers to things, assigned them categories and asserted facts about them. Dubbed knowledge graphs, the intent is to describe the world in a machine readable way.

These catalogs have proved incredibly useful, allowing publishers to organize their content management systems, powering machines that can win game shows and allowing search engines to guide users by interpreting their queries as being about "things not strings."

While useful, these catalogs are semantically limited. The connections entities participate in are sparse, requiring human understanding when decoding relationships and categorical membership. Entities are frequently identified by lucky linguistic matches rather than constraints against semantic intent.

If machines are to understand our world and react intelligently to requests about it, knowledge graphs need to grow beyond catalogs, encoding things which stretch the notion of "fact" and act as semantic APIs for the real world.

Contents – Part I

Contents – Part II

In-Use Track

Research Track

Multi-label Based Learning for Better Multi-criteria Ranking of Ontology Reasoners

Nourhène Alaya[1,2]([⊠]), Myriam Lamolle[1], and Sadok Ben Yahia[2]

[1] LIASD EA4383, IUT of Montreuil, University of Paris 8, 93520 Saint-Denis, France
{n.alaya,m.lamolle}@iut.univ-paris8.fr
[2] LIPAH LR11ES14, Faculty of Sciences of Tunis,
University of Tunis El-Manar, 2092 Tunis, Tunisia
sadok.benyahia@fst.rnu.tn

Abstract. A growing number of highly optimized reasoning algorithms have been developed to allow inference tasks on expressive ontology languages such as OWL(DL). Nevertheless, there is broad agreement that a reasoner could be optimized for some, but not all the ontologies. This particular fact makes it hard to select the best performing reasoner to handle a given ontology, especially for novice users. In this paper, we present a novel method to support the selection ontology reasoners. Our method generates a recommendation in the form of reasoner ranking. The efficiency as well as the correctness are our main ranking criteria. Our solution combines and adjusts multi-label classification and multi-target regression techniques. A large collection of ontologies and 10 well-known reasoners are studied. The experimental results show that the proposed method performs significantly better than several state-of-the-art ranking solutions. Furthermore, it proves that our introduced ranking method could effectively be evolved to a competitive meta-reasoner.

Keywords: Ontology · Reasoner · Multi-label classification · Multi-target regression · Multi-criteria · Ranking · Advising · Meta-reasoning

1 Introduction

A growing number of highly optimized ontology reasoners [10] have been developed to allow inference tasks on expressive ontology languages such as OWL(DL) [6]. Nevertheless, it is well accepted that a reasoner could be optimized for some but not all the ontologies. Indeed, the respective authors of [5,18] have outlined that, often in practice, reasoners tend to exhibit unpredictable behaviours when dealing with real world ontologies. They noticed that the reasoner performances can considerably vary across the ontologies, even when the size or/and the expressivity of these ones are fixed. Furthermore, Gardiner et al. [4] and more recently Lee et al. [9] pinpointed out that reasoners may disagree over inferences or query answers, computed from the same input ontology. All of the aforementioned authors offered different explanations of these phenomena: bottlenecks in the ontology design [5]; interactions between reasoning optimisation techniques

© Springer International Publishing AG 2017
C. d'Amato et al. (Eds.): ISWC 2017, Part I, LNCS 10587, pp. 3–19, 2017.
DOI: 10.1007/978-3-319-68288-4_1

[4]; or even reasoner implementation bugs [9]. Given all of these findings, it is obvious that for a typical OWL user, deciding the most performing reasoner to handle a given ontology is not a trivial task. Recently, we conducted a preliminary study [2] on designing a system to support users in reasoner selection task for the classification of OWL ontologies. The proposed system, called *Rak-SOR*, automatically ranks a set of candidate reasoners based on their predicted robustness. The ranked list gathers relevant reasoners, those capable to achieve the reasoning task within a fixed time limit and to deliver *correct* results. It also includes the irrelevant ones. Such configuration allows users to figure out which reasoners to select and the ones to avoid. To put this specification into practice, we defined a set of preference rules based on bucket order principal [3], a special case of partial order. Our method showed good ranking prediction quality comparing to our baseline method[1]. Nevertheless, we admit that the prediction accuracy of RakSOR depends heavily on the accuracy of the robustness predictive model of each examined reasoner. This dependency makes it difficult to further improve the effectiveness of its results. Furthermore, both the RakSOR learning and prediction process are time consuming and highly complex. Finally, RakSOR supports only reasoners specifically tuned for the OWL 2 DL profile.

In a continuous improvement outlook, in this paper, we present a novel accuracy boosted solution for reasoner ranking, based on multi-label learning paradigm [16,20]. We also demonstrate that this method could be used as the core component of a very competitive meta-reasoner [8]. The novel solution, called **Multi-RakSOR**, uses reasoner efficiency and result correctness as main ranking criteria. It reuses our previous reasoner preference rules and order principals [2], but also considers the ontology OWL profile as an additional reasoner ranking criteria. Indeed, it supports both OWL 2 DL and EL profiles. Subsequently, it has two seperated sets of alternative reasoners. Multi-RakSOR maps the feature values describing an input ontology into a complete ranking over a set of alternative reasoners. It also indicates the expected relevance[2] of each of the ranked reasoners. To achieve this end, the introduced ranking solution combines, in a *consistent* way, multi-label classification [20] and multi-target regression [14] techniques. The ontology features as well as the ranking predictions can efficiently be computed in a polynomial time with respect to the size of the input. Thanks to the various optimization efforts, a novel meta-reasoner was built upon the Multi-RakSOR ranking solution.

The main contributions of this paper can be summarized as follows:

1. The design description of a novel multi-label based solution for the multi-criteria ranking of ontology reasoners.
2. The summary of a large scale experimental evaluations covering 10 well known reasoners and 1954 unique ontologies, collected from the corpus of the latest Ontology Reasoner Evaluation Workshop (ORE'2015) [13].

---

[1] It is a trivial solution which outputs the same reasoner ranking regardless of the ontology under study.

[2] This refers to the success or the failure of the ontology classification task.

3. The depiction of a comparative study which includes several multi-label learning algorithms. The obtained results show that Multi-RakSOR performs significantly better than state-of-the-art multi-label solutions, in terms of accuracy in ranking and relevance prediction.
4. The characterization of a meta-reasoner based on the introduced multi-label ranking solution of ontology reasoners. Evaluation results prove that the novel meta-reasoner can outperform all of the examined reasoners, in terms of result correctness. Evaluations also highlight that, at average, the meta-reasoner can significantly boost the reasoning efficiency on OWL DL ontologies, but it is less capable when headling OWL EL ontologies.

2 Background and Related Works

2.1 Key Notions of Multi-label Learning Paradigm

In the multi-label learning context [14, 16, 20], each input instance is characterized by a d-dimensional feature vector $\mathbf{X}^{(i)} = (x_1^i, x_2^i, \ldots, x_d^i)$, associated with a set of m output labels $\mathbf{Y}^{(i)} = (y_1^i, y_2^i, \ldots, y_m^i)$. Let $\mathcal{X}$ be the space domain of the input features and let $\mathcal{Y}$ be the domain of the output labels, also called the target variables space. The task of multi-label learning is to train a model, i.e. a function $h : \mathcal{X} \rightarrow \mathcal{Y}$. The model is capable to predict the proper output label vector $\widehat{Y} = (\widehat{y_1}, \widehat{y_2}, \ldots, \widehat{y_m})$, given the feature vector $X \in \mathcal{X}$ of an unseen input instance. The model is learned from a dataset $\mathcal{D} = \{(X^{(1)}, Y^{(1)}), \ldots, (X^{(n)}, Y^{(n)})\}$, which assembles n training examples.

2.2 Multi-label Learning Techniques for Algorithm Selection

In our context, an input instance stands for the vector of feature values which describes a user ontology. On the other hand, each target variable stands for a reasoner. More precisely, a target label depicts a reasoner rank or any other score value. Indeed, the target labels could be real-valued, binary, ordinal, categorical or even of mixed types. Each form of target labels has specific multi-label learning task. In this paper, we are interested in three of these tasks. They are mainly:

- **Multi-Label Classification** task (MLC) [20]. It is concerned with learning a model that outputs a bipartition of the output labels into relevant label set P_x and irrelevant label set N_x, where $P_x \cap N_x = \emptyset$ and $P_x \cup N_x = \mathcal{Y}$. Literally, the outputs are binary labels, i.e. $\mathcal{Y} = \{0, 1\}^m$, with 0 means irrelevant target. This approach was used by Olmo et al. [12] to introduce a recommendation system of relevant machine learning algorithms.
- **Label Ranking** task (LR) [20]. It is concerned with learning a model that outputs an ordering of the labels according to their relevance to the input instance. Hence, the h function maps every instance $X \in \mathcal{X}$ to a total strict order, $\prec$, over the set of the output labels. A ranking over $\mathcal{Y}$ can conveniently be represented by a permutation σ of the set of indices $\{1, \ldots, m\}$, where $\sigma(i)$ stands for the rank value of the target variable y_i. LR techniques are the

building blocks of various algorithm selection systems: meta-learning solutions [15], SAT solver portfolios [11] and the ontology meta-reasoner R_2O_2 [8].

- **Multi-target Regression** task (MTR) [14]. It is also known as the multi-variate or multi-output regression task. It is the most general form of multi-label learning task. Indeed, MTR techniques are designed to predict multiple real-valued target variables, whether they are binary ones (MLC case), permutations (LR case) or float values. Formally, the MTR output space has the following form: $\mathcal{Y} \equiv \mathbb{R}^m$. To best of our knowledge, no previous work have employed MTR techniques to rank algorithms.

Based on this review, it seems that label ranking (LR) techniques are promising solutions for the automatic selection of ontology reasoners. Indeed, they simplify the ranking process, i.e. just one predictive model to train and they are known to be highly accurate. Nevertheless, we are convinced that they cannot satisfy all of our requirements. Actually, all of the reviewed works employ single ranking criterion. Besides, they output the rank values of the alternatives without any indication of their relevance. In fact, the computed rankings follow strict total order, with the assumption that all the alternatives are relevant ones. This is a quite different specification from what we need to fulfil. As previously explained, we are interested in ranking relevant and irrelevant reasoners by applying partial order rules. The real challenge is to find a way to incorporate our multi-criteria preference rules in a multi-label learning method without any precision or information lost. Details of the proposed solution to overcome this challenge are outlined in the forthcoming sections.

2.3   Ontology Features

In our previous work [1], we proposed a rich set of ontology features, qualitative and quantitative ones, covering a broad range of structural and syntactic attributes of OWL ontologies. These features were put forward to thoroughly describe the ontology design complexity. Our collection gathers a lot of well known state-of-art metrics, some of them are already used reasoner prediction solutions and in ontology quality evaluation systems. Our features are arranged into four categories: (1) *size description* features, which characterize the amount of knowledge explicitly asserted in the ontology; (2) *expressivity description* features, which mainly includes the OWL profile and the description logic family name; (3) *structural features*, which outline the design of named class and property respective inheritance hierarchies; (4) *syntactic features*, which delineate the main characteristic of the OWL grammar. To compute feature values, any full translation of the OWL ontology to particular kind of graph representation is avoided. In this paper experimentations, we discarded the metrics with high-computing cost, like the tree depth of named class hierarchy. This left us with 123 ontology feature values to be measured.

3 Novel Multi-label Learning Method for Multi-criteria Ranking of Ontology Reasoners

In this section, we introduce the **Multi-RakSOR** method. We give a short specification of its reasoner ranking rules, before outlining its learning mechanism.

3.1 Reasoner Ranking Criteria and Preference Rules

A ranking represents a *preference function* over a set of alternatives. In our context, the alternatives are some set of ontology reasoners considered as promising candidates. This set is denoted by $\mathcal{R}$. In [1,2], we stressed on the importance of considering not only the runtime of reasoners but also the correctness of their derived results, as comparison criteria. We also highlighted the need to specify particular reasoner robustness judgement constraints, like the range of ontologies, the reasoning task and the success/failure respective states.

In this paper, our study concerns the classification task of OWL DL and OWL EL ontologies within a tight time schedule. We apply the Gardiner et al. [4] reasoner correctness checking method. Accordingly, results delivered by a reasoner are either correct or unexpected. Subsequently, we can specify a first ordinal criterion which split up the set of reasoners into four groups according to their termination state: (1) **S**uccess, when the reasoner terminates the task within a fixed time-limit and delivers correct results; (2) **U**nexpected, in case of an achieved task within the time limit, but has unexpected results, i.e. incorrect; (3) **T**imeout, when the fixed time lapse is exceeded; and (4) **H**alt, when the reasoner crashes and do not terminate the task. Given this specification, we can formally describe the preference rules over ontology reasoners using bucket order principals [3]. In short, a bucket is a set of equally ranked alternatives. Initially, four buckets are defined each of them corresponds to a specific termination state (S,U,T,H). A strict total order over the buckets is also decided: $\mathcal{B}_S \prec \mathcal{B}_U \prec \mathcal{B}_T \prec \mathcal{B}_H$. Clearly, reasoners belonging to $\mathcal{B}_S$ bucket are the most preferred ones. The $\mathcal{B}_U$ reasoners can terminate the reasoning task but the correctness of their results is not approved by our correctness checking method. In our opinion, they are much preferred than reasoners falling in the $\mathcal{B}_T$ bucket, which can not release any results within the fixed time lapse. Of course, the worse reasoners are in $\mathcal{B}_H$ bucket. Seeking more precision, a second ranking criterion standing for the efficiency of the reasoner over the *correctly* classified ontologies is applied. Accordingly, reasoners within the *success* bucket $\mathcal{B}_S$ are linearly sorted in an increasing order w.r.t their reasoning runtime. The final ordered bucket partition over the set of the alternative reasoners, i.e. $\mathcal{R}$, has the following form: $\mathbf{B} = B_1 \prec \ldots \prec B_k \prec \mathcal{B}_U \prec \mathcal{B}_T \prec \mathcal{B}_H$, where $k = |\mathcal{B}_S|$. Reasoner ranks are computed by following these rules. Subsequently, ties may appear in the list of ranks. Indeed, tied reasoners imply that they did not succeed to classify the ontology for the same failure cause.

Multi-RakSOR considers a further important criterion. This is the OWL profile of the input ontology. It is widely known that some reasoners are specifically tuned to particular OWL profiles. For instance, ELK is a highly performing OWL

EL specialised reasoner. On the other hand, there is no proof of the correctness of its results when applied to OWL DL ontologies. In short, it is absurd to advise an EL reasoner to handle a DL ontology. Given this fact, Multi-RakSOR splits the set of alternative reasoners into DL and EL specialised subsets, i.e. $\mathcal{R}_{DL}$ and $\mathcal{R}_{EL}$. Once the profile of an input ontology is identified, the above usual ranking rules are applied over the corresponding set of reasoners.

3.2   Specification of the Novel Multi-label Ranking Method

In the Multi-RakSOR system, the ranks of reasoners are computed prior to any learning step, by applying to afore-described rules on actual results of reasoner evaluations. The produced ranks together with the metrics describing the studied ontologies are then, provided to the learning component. Afterwards, a multi-label predictive model is trained, to be able to predict these ranks for future unseen ontologies. We assert that providing only the reasoner ranks might be misleading for the users. This is because the ranked list might include some, or even only, reasoners expected to fail the classification of the input ontology. Hence, it is important not only to predict the ranks but also to outline the successful/unsuccessful reasoners.

To satisfy all of these requirements, we introduce a novel multi-label ranking method applied to ontology reasoners. The learning process involves two equally important subsequent goals. The first is to produce the bipartition of set of the output labels $\mathcal{Y}$ into relevant label set P_x and irrelevant label set N_x, with $P_x \cup N_x = \mathcal{Y}$ and $P_x \cap N_x = \emptyset$. The second is a ranking over $\mathcal{Y}$ which respects the previously introduced preference rules. Specially, the ranking should be consistent, this means to satisfy the following couple of conditions:

- There should be no irrelevant labels ranked higher than relevant ones and vice versa. Formally, whenever $\forall y_i \in P_x$ and $\forall y_j \in N_x$, then $y_i \prec y_j$. In other words, y_i is preferred to y_j and it is ranked lower $\sigma(i) < \sigma(j)$.
- The relevant labels must form a strict total ordered set. Formally, $\forall y_i, \forall y_j \in P_x$ with $i \neq j$, then either y_i is preferred to y_j or y_j is preferred to y_i. The irrelevant labels are allowed to have equal ranks.

3.3   Multi-RakSOR Learning and Prediction Steps

To put the above specification into practice, a transformation of the multi-label ranking process is proposed. Indeed, the key idea of our solution is to learn a separate multi-label model for each of the following sub-problems: *(i)* a model to predict the ranking with ties of the alternative reasoners, denoted by $h_r()$ and *(ii)* a model to predict the relevance of each reasoner, denoted by $h_b()$. Afterwards, at the prediction time, the computed relevance bipartition and ranking of reasoners for an input ontology, are synchronized by checking their consistency and probably correcting their values. A further issue is about predicting a ranking with ties using multi-label learning techniques. We previously highlighted the lack of multi-label based solutions to predict a ranking which involves a partial order. To overcome this absence, multi-target regression (MTR) techniques [14] are employed. The latter ones can handle different kinds of learning problems provided that the domain of the output variables is within $\mathbb{R}^m$. In other words, no matter whether the rank values are strict or tied, the MTR model will try to predict the closest possible values to the real ones. Now, we can list the required steps to train the Multi-RakSOR predictive model.

Training time. the Multi-RakSOR model h_{mlti} is comprised of 2 sub-models: a multi-label classification (**MLC**) model, $h_b : \mathcal{F}^d \rightarrow \{0,1\}^m$, which predicts the relevance of the output labels, and a multi-target regression (**MTR**) model, $h_r : \mathcal{F}^d \rightarrow \mathbb{R}^m$, which predicts the ranking with ties of these labels. Each of these models is learned independently from dedicated datasets, respectively $\mathcal{D}_b$ and $\mathcal{D}_r$. The latter ones share the same input vectors, which describes the features of the ontologies. It is important to note that the training datasets are profile specific ones. In other terms, for each supported OWL profile, a dataset is assembled and a dedicated Multi-RakSOR predictive model is trained.

Prediction time. During this online stage, to compute the ranking for a new introduced ontology, our system operates in five steps. Firstly, the feature values of the introduced ontology are computed and provided to the prediction component. Afterwards, the Multi-RakSOR predictive model which corresponds to the ontology OWL profile is invoked. Then, the MLC sub-model is applied to get the predicted relevance of each reasoner. Similarly, the MTR model is addressed to get the predicted ranks. Finally, the consistency of the computed ranks are checked and probably adjusted. More details about our ranking checking method are provided in the upcoming subsection.

3.4   Ranking Consistency Checking Method

Based on the specification provided in Subsect. 3.2, the ranking checking method must ensure that: *(1)* the rank values of the relevant labels form a strict total ordered set of natural numbers; and *(2)* no irrelevant reasoner is ranked lower than a relevant one. If one of these rules is broken, then the ranking is adjusted. Algorithm 1 shows the steps achieved by *rankingCheckingMethod()*. The procedure takes as input the matrix $\widehat{\mathbf{Y}}$, which encodes the different computed predictions. We design by $max_{\sigma}^{P_x}$ the maximal rank value of the relevant output labels. Known that the ranks take values in $\mathbb{N}^*$ and they are expected to be linearly sorted in an increasing strict order, then we can assert that $max_{\sigma}^{P_x} = |P_x|$. Through the first loop of Algorithm 1, the $max_{\sigma}^{P_x}$ value is computed. The rank values corresponding to the relevant labels are stored in the R_x array. The cells of this array corresponding to irrelevant reasoners are set to 0. The resulting R_x array is then handled by *rankOrderTransformation()*. The main role of this function is to ensure the application of our 1st consistency rule. This idea behind this function is quite straightforward. The ranks in the R_x array are seen as numerical scores. By consequence, the function computes the strict total order of their values. Potential ties of the relevant reasoners rank values are arbitrary

---

Algorithm 1: The ranking consistancy checking method

1 **Function rankingCheckingMethod($\widehat{\mathbf{Y}} \in M_{m \times 2}(\mathbb{R})$)**
2 $\mathbf{R}_x \leftarrow [0, \ldots, 0]$; // $\mathbf{R}_x$ is of size m
3 $max_\sigma^{P_x} \leftarrow 0$;
4 **for** $i \leftarrow 1$ **to** $|\widehat{\mathbf{Y}}|$ **do**
5   **if** $\widehat{\mathbf{Y}}[i][1] = 1$ **then**
6          $\mathbf{R}_x[i] \leftarrow \widehat{\mathbf{Y}}[i][2]$;
7          $max_\sigma^{P_x} \leftarrow max_\sigma^{P_x} + 1$;
8   **end**
9 **end**
10 $\mathbf{R}_x \leftarrow rankOrderTransformation(\mathbf{R}_x)$;
11 **for** $i \leftarrow 1$ **to** $|\widehat{\mathbf{Y}}|$ **do**
12   **if** $\widehat{\mathbf{Y}}[i][1] <> 0$ **then** // Relevant label, update the rank
13          $\widehat{\mathbf{Y}}[i][2] \leftarrow \mathbf{R}_x[i]$;
14   **else if** $\widehat{\mathbf{Y}}[i][2] \leq max_\sigma^{P_x}$ **then** // Irrelevant label, Inconsistency case
15          $updateIrrelevantRanks(\widehat{\mathbf{Y}}, max_\sigma^{P_x}, i)$;
16   **end**
17 **end**
18 **return** $\widehat{\mathbf{Y}}$;

---

broken. For instance, let $[1, 3, 3, 3, 5, 4]$ be the predicted ranks of 6 reasoners and $[1, 0, 1, 1, 1, 0]$ their predicted relevance. By substituting the ranks of the irrelevant reasoners by 0, the resulting R_x array is equal to $[1, 0, 3, 3, 5, 0]$. It is clear that these are non consistent rank values[3]. In this case, *rankOrderTransformation()* function ignores the 0 values and considers the remaining values as scores to be ranked. It finally returns $[1, 0, 2, 3, 4, 0]$. Afterwards, the inconsistencies w.r.t. the second rule are caught by simply verifying whether an irrelevant label has a rank lower than $max_\sigma^{P_x}$ (see Algorithm 1, Line 14). If this is the case, then the first inconsistent rank is set to $(max_\sigma^{P_x} + 1)$, and subsequently, all the remaining rank values of irrelevant reasoners are updated. Our solution is intuitive and inexpensive one, capable at least to fix the inconsistencies. As a matter of fact, in our opinion, the exact ranking of the irrelevant reasoners is less important for the user. In this example, the final adjusted ranking is equal to $[1, 5, 2, 3, 4, 6]$.

4   Data Collection

To build up the Multi-RakSOR system, data describing the empirical performances of reasoners are required. Therefore, a large scale evaluations of an important number of reasoners is conducted using the evaluation tools employed in the

---

[3] The ranking contains ties and is not linear.

latest Ontology Reasoner Evaluation Workshop (ORE 2015) [13]. This includes the evaluation Framework[4] and the ontology corpus.

Ontologies. This includes 1967 ontology collected from the ORE 2015 corpus [13]. 1920 of them are sampled from three different source corpora[5] and 47 are user submitted ontologies[6]. At first, the OWL profiles of the ontologies are checked. The process revealed that 11 user submitted ontologies do not fit to any of the standard OWL profiles. It was also impossible to load 2 other ontologies. This left us with 1954 validated ontologies, 1191 are within the OWL DL profile and the remaining 763 are OWL EL ones. Afterwards, the selected ontologies are arranged into 2 different collections, based on their profiles.

Reasoners and evaluations. To build up our advising system, we selected a representative subset of popular and efficient ontology reasoners. More precisely, we picked up the 10 best ranked reasoners[7] in both the DL and EL classification challenges of ORE 2015. Then, we assigned them to 2 groups: OWL DL and OWL EL specialised reasoners. In the first group, we can find **Konclude**, **HermiT**[8], **MORe**[9], **TrOWL**, **FaCT++**, **JFact**, **Racer** and finally **Pellet**[10]. The second group has the same reasoners as the first one, in addition to, **ELK** and **ELepHant**. Description and references to these systems could be found in [13]. By following the ORE competition processing steps, two classification challenges (DL and EL) are set up. Each challenge puts the selected reasoners into comparison when attempting to classify the ontology collection that corresponds to their group. To conduct these evaluations, we run the ORE Framework in the sequential mode on a machine equipped with an Intel Core I7, CPU running at 3.4 GHz and having 32 GB RAM, where 10 GB were made available for each reasoner. We set the condition of 3 min time limit to classify an ontology by a reasoner, where only 150 s were allowed for reasoning and 30 s could be used for parsing and writing results. In the ORE Framework, the times are measured in wall clock time instead of CPU time. Figure 1 summarizes the results of the carried out challenges[11]. For each OWL profile and for every reasoner, the percentage of ontologies classified with success is illustrated, together with the failure percentage. Figure 1 details also the different cases of failure (Unexpected, Timeout and Halt). Worth to be noted, the reasoners are ordered according to their success rate. Furthermore, Fig. 2 depicts the average runtime exhibited by every reasoner over the correctly classified ontologies, i.e. the success cases, and for each ontology collection. We can notice that Konclude is the most robust

---

[4] ORE Framework is available at https://github.com/andreas-steigmiller/ore-2014-competition-framework/.

[5] Available at https://zenodo.org/record/18578#.WReUzlXyjcc.

[6] Available at https://zenodo.org/record/50737#.WReW01Xyjcc.

[7] Reasoners are available at https://zenodo.org/record/50738#.WRhPVVXyjcc.

[8] Specifically, it is the HermiT implementation based on OWL API 4 (HerimT-OA4).

[9] This is exactly the MOReHermiT implementation.

[10] We used the Pellet implementation based on OWL API 4 (Pellet-OA4).

[11] Evaluation results produced by ORE for the 10 reasoners are available at https://github.com/Alaya2016/OntoClassification-Results2017/.

reasoner over the DL ontologies, while ELK outperforms all the system over the EL Ontologies. Konclude is rated the 3rd on the EL classification challenge. In general, the success rates of the different reasoners are very close when considering EL ontologies, but they are quiet distinct in the case of DL ones. Indeed, there is a much important failure rate in the DL classification challenge. This is due to the high expressivity of the OWL 2 DL profile. By closely looking to Fig. 2, we can remark that the Hermit system, which has the 2nd best success rate, achieved the worst reasoning average runtime over the correct cases. Several other systems showed similar behaviours. Overall, we can pinpoint that reasoner ranks computed based on correctness does not completely meet their ranks based on efficiency. Based on these facts, it is obvious that defining general rules to select *"best"* reasoner for any ontology is not a trivial task and might not be effective in practice.

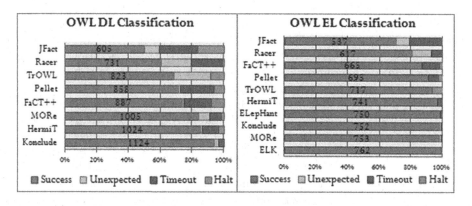

Fig. 1. Summary of reasoner evaluation results of the classification track over DL and EL respective ontology collections.

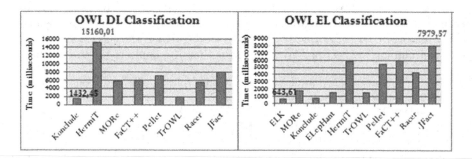

Fig. 2. Comparison of reasoner average runtime for correctly classified ontologies (success cases, time in millisconds) over the DL and the EL respective ontology collections.

Training and testing datasets. For learning evaluation purpose, we split up the ontology collection into training and testing sets. The decomposition respects, in the best possible way, the distribution of ontologies over the size bins. We selected 654 test ontologies, i.e. 391 DL and 263 EL. This selection is hold out to later assess the quality of predictions. The remaining 800 DL and 500 EL ontologies are gathered in the training set to build up the Multi-RakSOR predictive models. As final step, the features values of the selected ontologies are measured (c.f. Subsect. 2.3). Then, the reasoner ranking and relevance vectors are computed. Hence, OWL profile based datasets are created by incorporating the feature vectors and their corresponding relevance and rank vectors.

5   Experimental Evaluation of Multi-RakSOR

Multi-RakSOR[12] is realised with Java. It has a generic design and three main building blocks: the ontology profiler, the multi-learner and the multi-predictor components. In this paper experiments, Multi-RakSOR uses the Binary Relevance (BR) algorithm [7] as the base MLC learner and the Ensemble of Regressor Chains (ERC) algorithm [14] as the base MTR learner. Mulan[13] [17], the Java multi-label learning API, allowed the access to these state-of-art algorithms. We recall that 654 ontologies were held out to evaluate the prediction quality of Multi-RakSOR. Given a test ontology, the predicted reasoner relevance and ranking values are compared to the ideal ones. These are the actual correct relevance values and ordering of the reasoners given the ontology under examination. Afterwards, the agreement between the predicted and the ideal values are assessed using the metrics, we describe in the following. Our results are then compared against existing multi-label learning solutions.

5.1   Evaluation Metrics

A two-step evaluation procedure is designed to adjudge the prediction quality of Multi-RakSOR. First, the accuracy of the predicted reasoner relevance bipartition is checked. For this kind of evaluations, the assessment metrics of binary multi-label classification models [20] are employed. In particular, the F1-Measure for each test case is computed and then, averaged over the whole test set. Similarly, the **Hamming loss** (HM-Loss) score is measured and averaged across all the test cases. This metric computes the percentage of misclassified labels. Generally speaking, a good MLC model should maximize its F1-Measure value, while minimizing its HM-Loss value. Later on, the quality of the produced rankings is assessed using 4 metrics falling in 2 categories. We already employed these metrics in [2]. The main purpose of the first metric category is to show to what extent a predicted ranking is correlated to the *ideal* one. It is composed of the average value of the generalized *Kendall Tau correlation coefficient*, denoted by

---

[12] A demo application reproducing the evaluations of Multi-RaKSOR is available at https://github.com/Alaya2016/Multi-RakSORDemo/.

[13] Mulan is available at http://mulan.sourceforge.net/download.html.

KendalTauX and the average value of the *Spearman rank correlation coefficient*, denoted by *SpearmanRho*. The second category is made up from *information retrieval* based metrics. They examine how well we are ranking the reasoners at the top of the list, i.e. at the Kth position. To get an overall idea of precision considering the whole test set, the *Mean Average Precision* is computed and denoted by MAP@K. Two particular values are retained: MAP@1 and MAP@3.

5.2   Multi-label Learning Methods

We compare the quality of Multi-RakSOR relevance prediction against 4 well known MLC solutions [20]: (1) the neural network approach for the multi-label classification task (*BP-MLL*); (2) the Random K-Labelsets method (RA*K*EL); (3) the adaptive boosting algorithm for multi-label learning *(AdaBoost.MH)*; and (4) the multi-label k-Nearest Neighbor (*ML-kNN*) algorithm. In a second stage, we compare the quality of Multi-RakSOR predicted rankings to those produced by 4 *label ranking* (LR) solutions [15]: (1) the K-Nearest Neighbor approach for label ranking (*LR-kNN*); (2) the predictive clustering trees for ranking (*PCTR*); (3) the label ranking trees (*LRT*); and (4) the ranking by pairwise comparison algorithm (*RPC*). It is worth to be noted that these algorithms predict only the ranks of the target labels and do not separate them into relevant/irrelevant ones. However, they are the building blocks of the meta-reasoner[14] R_2O_2 [8]. For each learning task (MLC, MTR) and for every training dataset (DL, EL), we train the predictive models of all of the aforementioned learning solutions. Then, we assess their predictive quality over our testing datasets.

5.3   Relevance Prediction Assessment Results

Figure 3 depicts the assessment results of the reasoner relevance bipartition predictions achieved by the the studied solutions. For both the DL and the EL

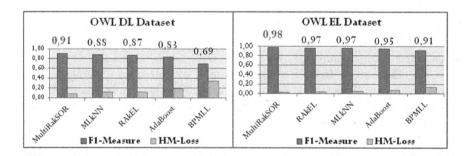

Fig. 3. Comparison summary of relevance prediction quality achieved by the examined works over each of the OWL profile based test datasets.

---

[14] It is to be considered that we didn't get access to R_2O_2 running executable. Hence, we were enable to establish any comparison with this system.

datasets, Multi-RakSOR showed very high prediction capabilities, characterized by a score of F1-measure above 0.91 and low Hamming Loss (HM-Loss) value. It outperformed all the other MLC solutions and rated the first over the two datasets. We can also remark that predicting the relevance bipartition over EL test cases seems to be more easier than over DL cases. Actually, Multi-RakSOR has achieved a close to optimum F1-Measure. This could be explained that all of the studied reasoners has showed closer performances when classified EL ontologies. Hence, their performance are almost predictable on this kind of ontologies.

5.4   Ranking Prediction Assessment Results

Figure 4 sketches the assessment results of the ranking quality achieved by the examined MTR methods over the DL and EL testing datasets. First, it can be noted that in both the datasets and according to the different assessment metrics, Multi-RakSOR have outperformed its base MTR leaner, the ERC algorithm. This observation pinpoints the positive impact of our proposed ranking correction step (c.f. Subsect. 3.4). Accordingly, we can assert that checking the consistency of the predicted ranks w.r.t. the predicted relevance of reasoners is effective and can contribute to the overall improvement of the ranking quality. Multi-RaKSOR can identify the top most performing reasoner, regarding both the correctness and the efficiency criteria, with a precision of more than 88%, for both DL and EL ontologies. According to Kendall TauX, Multi-RaKSOR is also capable to predict the ties across the irrelevant reasoners and produce rankings that are at 94% positively correlated to the real ones.

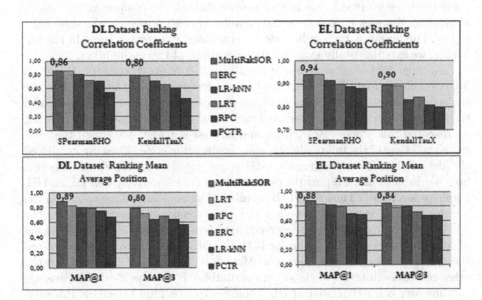

Fig. 4. Comparison summary of the ranking prediction quality achieved by the examined works over each of the OWL profile based test datasets.

More interestingly, Multi-RakSOR method have overpassed all of its counterparts, LR-KNN, RPC, PCTR and LRT, w.r.t. the different assessments measures. This result is important since these are well recognized algorithms in the field of label ranking. Besides, they are part of R_2O_2, the only existing reasoner ranking system. These empirical results could be explained by the fact that none of these algorithms is originally designed to predict a ranking which includes ties. Even that they can handle such ranking, they are not particularly optimized for. Once again, these findings show that our proposed Multi-RakSOR method adds good multi-label ranking abilities to the existing solutions. Despite the challenges, these results proves that it was worthwhile to investigate time and effort in exploring and accommodating multi-label learning techniques for better automatic ranking of ontology reasoners.

6   Experimental Evaluation of Meta-RakSOR

The main purpose of this set of evaluations is to investigate the effectiveness of building a meta-reasoner upon our multi-label ranking solution. A meta-reasoner has various common treats with SAT algorithm portfolio approach [11,19]. The portfolio aims to take advantage of the complementarity of the algorithms by combining them. Roughly speaking, a portfolio could be built in by gathering a set of performing algorithms, together with an intelligent selector capable to decide the most performing one to any input instance. Multi-RakSOR ranking method could be seen as an intelligent selector by only considering the reasoner on the top of the ranked list. From a theoretical perspective, Multi-RakSOR could easily be evolved into a meta-reasoner. Indeed, the computing algorithms of ontology features have polynomial complexity with respect to the size of the inputs. Furthermore, the predictions are computed in constant time. In the following, we experimentally examine the worthiness of this assumption.

The upgraded version of our system is called **Meta-RakSOR**. Given an input ontology, Meta-RakSOR computes its feature vector then, predicts the ranks of the available reasoners using the approach described in Sect. 3. Finally, the reasoner with the lowest predicted rank value is invoked. In our experiments, we repeated this process for each EL and DL test ontology. We stored the computational time of the full prediction and classification steps. Then, we compared the Meta-RakSOR achieved results to those computed by the other reasoners (c.f. Sect. 4). Tables 1 and 2 report the evaluation results respectively over DL and EL ontology test sets[15]. They report the number of success and failure cases and the average runtime in milliseconds over the correctly classified ontologies (i.e. the AVG. Time column). It can be observed that Meta-RakSOR has the highest level of correctly processed ontologies for both the DL and EL ontologies. It is rated the first on both challenges. However, Meta-RakSOR has not outperformed the other reasoners in terms of classification runtime. It has the 2nd lowest average runtime over correctly classified DL ontologies, just behind Konclude. However,

---

[15] Meta-RakSOR can handle both DL and EL profiles.

Table 1. Results summary of the **OWL DL** classification challenge (Test Set).

Reasoner	Success	Failure			AVG. time
		#U	#T	#H	
M-RakSOR	367	12	8	4	1545.69
Konclude	366	12	11	2	1358.43
HermiT	334	3	42	12	14243.19
MORe	326	26	35	4	6428.77
FaCT++	295	4	69	23	4509.77
Pellet	287	4	84	16	2157.61
TrOWL	274	84	0	33	2157.61
Racer	245	67	75	4	4813.06
JFact	196	39	94	62	8258.99

Table 2. Results summary of the **OWL EL** classification challenge (Test Set).

Reasoner	Success	Failure			AVG. time
		#U	#T	#H	
M-RakSOR	263	0	0	0	2166.13
ELK	262	0	0	1	635.68
Konclude	259	4	0	0	817.01
MORe	259	3	1	0	1807.03
ELepHant	258	1	4	0	1179.67
HermiT	256	0	7	0	6418.43
TrOWL	243	0	0	20	1116.69
Pellet	242	1	16	4	6081.54
FaCT++	232	0	29	2	6092.75
Racer	214	31	18	0	3994.49
JFact	186	24	52	1	5767.34

it is placed the 6th by considering the average runtime over EL ontologies. Nevertheless, for this set of ontologies, it showed better performance than known reasoners, like FaCT++, HermiT and Pellet. In overall, the achieved results are very encouraging ones. It proves the potential benefits of Meta-RakSOR, especially in terms of result correctness. Still, we assert that using a meta-reasoner for light-weighted and inexpressive ontologies is not worthwhile, since the time overhead due to the prediction steps may overpass the actual classification time. Based on this observation, Meta-RakSOR could be improved by fixing a default reasoner to be applied for *easy* cases without needing any prediction effort.

7 Conclusion

In this paper, we introduced an automatic ranking mechanism of ontology reasoners. It combines multi-label classification and multi-target regression techniques. It achieves both reasoner ranking and reasoner relevance prediction in a consistent way. The proposed system considers the correctness and the efficiency of reasoners in the ranking process. We studied separately OWL DL and OWL EL specific reasoners. We achieved high ranking prediction quality and outperformed existing solutions. We also examined the feasibility of employing our ranking solution as the key component of a novel meta-reasoner. The experimental results of the latter one showed the potential of our proposals. It also revealed that more optimisation steps are required to improve its efficiency. For future work, we are intending to examine more reasoner evaluation criteria, such as the energy and memory consumption. We are also planning to study different reasoning tasks, like consistency checking and realisation. Actually, our ultimate goal is to conduct different reasoner evaluation campaigns under a variety of machine, time and memory configurations and for different reasoning tasks. Once these data is gathered, a larger scale multi-criteria ranking system of ontology reasoners could be established.

References

1. Alaya, N., Yahia, S.B., Lamolle, M.: What makes ontology reasoning so arduous? Unveiling the key ontological features. In: Proceedings of the 5th International Conference on Web Intelligence, Mining and Semantics, pp. 4:1–4:12 (2015)
2. Alaya, N., Yahia, S.B., Lamolle, M.: RakSOR: ranking of ontology reasoners based on predicted performances. In: Proceedings of the 28th IEEE International Conference on Tools with Artificial Intelligence, pp. 1076–1083 (2016)
3. Fagin, R., Kumar, R., Mahdian, M., Sivakumar, D., Vee, E.: Comparing partial rankings. SIAM J. Discrete Math. **20**, 628–648 (2006)
4. Gardiner, T., Tsarkov, D., Horrocks, I.: Framework for an automated comparison of description logic reasoners. In: Cruz, I., Decker, S., Allemang, D., Preist, C., Schwabe, D., Mika, P., Uschold, M., Aroyo, L.M. (eds.) ISWC 2006. LNCS, vol. 4273, pp. 654–667. Springer, Heidelberg (2006). doi:10.1007/11926078_47
5. Gonçalves, R.S., Parsia, B., Sattler, U.: Performance heterogeneity and approximate reasoning in description logic ontologies. In: Cudré-Mauroux, P., et al. (eds.) ISWC 2012. LNCS, vol. 7649, pp. 82–98. Springer, Heidelberg (2012). doi:10.1007/978-3-642-35176-1_6
6. W.O.W. Group: OWL 2 Web Ontology Language: Document Overview. W3C Recommendation, 27 October 2009. http://www.w3.org/TR/owl2-overview/
7. Ioannou, M., Sakkas, G., Tsoumakas, G., Vlahavas, I.P.: Obtaining bipartitions from score vectors for multi-label classification. In: Proceedings of the 22nd International Conference on Tools with Artificial Intelligence, ICTAI, pp. 409–416. IEEE Computer Society (2010)
8. Kang, Y.-B., Krishnaswamy, S., Li, Y.-F.: R_2O_2: an efficient ranking-based reasoner for OWL ontologies. In: Arenas, M., et al. (eds.) ISWC 2015. LNCS, vol. 9366, pp. 322–338. Springer, Cham (2015). doi:10.1007/978-3-319-25007-6_19
9. Lee, M., Matentzoglu, N., Parsia, B., Sattler, U.: A multi-reasoner, justification-based approach to reasoner correctness. In: Arenas, M., et al. (eds.) ISWC 2015. LNCS, vol. 9367, pp. 393–408. Springer, Cham (2015). doi:10.1007/978-3-319-25010-6_26
10. Matentzoglu, N., Leo, J., Hudhra, V., Sattler, U., Parsia, B.: A survey of current, stand-alone OWL reasoners. In: Proceedings of the 4th International Workshop on OWL Reasoner Evaluation, pp. 68–79 (2015)
11. Oentaryo, R.J., Handoko, S.D., Lau, H.C.: Algorithm selection via ranking. In: Proceedings of Twenty-Ninth AAAI Conference on Artificial Intelligence, pp. 1826–1832 (2015)
12. Olmo, J.L., Romero, C., Gibaja, E., Ventura, S.: Improving meta-learning for algorithm selection by using multi-label classification: a case of study with educational data sets. Int. J. Comput. Intell. Syst. **8**(6), 1144–1164 (2015)
13. Parsia, B., Matentzoglu, N., Gonçalves, R.S., Glimm, B., Steigmiller, A.: The OWL Reasoner Evaluation (ORE) 2015 resources. In: Groth, P., Simperl, E., Gray, A., Sabou, M., Krötzsch, M., Lecue, F., Flöck, F., Gil, Y. (eds.) ISWC 2016. LNCS, vol. 9982, pp. 159–167. Springer, Cham (2016). doi:10.1007/978-3-319-46547-0_17
14. Spyromitros-Xioufis, E., Tsoumakas, G., Groves, W., Vlahavas, I.: Multi-target regression via input space expansion: treating targets as inputs. Mach. Learn. **104**(1), 55–98 (2016)
15. Sun, Q., Pfahringer, B.: Pairwise meta-rules for better meta-learning-based algorithm ranking. Mach. Learn. **93**(1), 141–161 (2013)

16. Tsoumakas, G., Katakis, I., Vlahavas, I.P.: Mining multi-label data. In: Data Mining and Knowledge Discovery Handbook, 2nd edn., pp. 667–685 (2010)
17. Tsoumakas, G., Spyromitros-Xioufis, E., Vilcek, J., Vlahavas, I.: Mulan: a Java library for multi-label learning. J. Mach. Learn. Res. **12**, 2411–2414 (2011)
18. Wang, T.D., Parsia, B.: Ontology performance profiling and model examination: first steps. In: Aberer, K., et al. (eds.) ASWC/ISWC 2007. LNCS, vol. 4825, pp. 595–608. Springer, Heidelberg (2007). doi:10.1007/978-3-540-76298-0_43
19. Xu, L., Hutter, F., Hoos, H.H., Leyton-Brown, K.: Satzilla: portfolio-based algorithm selection for sat. J. Artif. Int. Res. **32**, 565–606 (2008)
20. Zhang, M., Zhou, Z.: A review on multi-label learning algorithms. IEEE Trans. Knowl. Data Eng. **26**(8), 1819–1837 (2014)

The Efficacy of OWL and DL on User Understanding of Axioms and Their Entailments

Eisa Alharbi$^{(\boxtimes)}$, John Howse, Gem Stapleton, Ali Hamie,
and Anestis Touloumis

University of Brighton, Brighton, UK
{e.alharbi2,John.Howse,g.e.stapleton,a.a.hamie,
a.touloumis}@brighton.ac.uk

Abstract. OWL is recognized as the de facto standard notation for ontology engineering. The Manchester OWL Syntax (MOS) was developed as an alternative to symbolic description logic (DL) and it is believed to be more effective for users. This paper sets out to test that belief from two perspectives by evaluating how accurately and quickly people *understand* the informational content of axioms and derive *inferences* from them. By conducting a between-group empirical study, involving 60 novice participants, we found that DL is *just as effective* as MOS for people's understanding of axioms. Moreover, for two types of inference problems, *DL supported significantly better task performance than MOS*, yet MOS never significantly outperformed DL. These surprising results suggest that the belief that MOS is more effective than DL, at least for these types of task, is unfounded. An outcome of this research is the suggestion that ontology axioms, when presented to non-experts, may be better presented in DL rather than MOS. Further empirical studies are needed to explain these unexpected results and to see whether they hold for other types of task.

Keywords: Ontologies · OWL · DL · Manchester OWL Syntax · Usability

1 Introduction

This paper sets out to provide evidence to support the untested belief that the Manchester syntax [6] for OWL [2] is more effective for users than Description Logic (DL) [3]. Research efforts have focused on the usability of OWL itself, demonstrating the importance placed on effectively supporting ontology engineers and other stakeholders [4,14,17]. In light of this, it is equally as important to determine whether OWL, or more specifically the Manchester OWL Syntax (MOS), is an effective choice of notation. After all, MOS is widely employed and was developed with the intention of being usable by people [6]. Surprisingly, however, in this paper we found no evidence that MOS is superior to DL but instead that DL was sometimes more effective than MOS.

© Springer International Publishing AG 2017
C. d'Amato et al. (Eds.): ISWC 2017, Part I, LNCS 10587, pp. 20–36, 2017.
DOI: 10.1007/978-3-319-68288-4_2

To probe deeply into the relative usability of notations, it is necessary to consider the tasks for which they are to be used. In the context of ontology engineering, notations are used to write axioms which must then be understood. Inferences are derived from those axioms and, ideally, ontology engineers would at least be able to accurately identify when sound inferences hold. Of course, numerous other activities are performed, such as debugging and repair [8,12], but in this paper, we focus on relative usability from the perspective of understanding axioms and deriving inferences from them. The specific questions we address, via an empirical study, represent the first steps towards determining the relative efficacy of MOS as compared to DL and are as follows:

1. Does MOS support significantly more accurate understanding of axioms than DL? We found MOS to be no more effective than DL.
2. Does MOS support significantly more accurate identification of sound inferences than DL? We found that MOS does not and, sometimes, DL is more effective than MOS.
3. Does MOS lead to significantly fewer unsound inferences than DL? We found that MOS does not and, sometimes, DL is more effective than MOS.

Given the surprising answers to these questions, particularly with respect to MOS not significantly outperforming DL, additional research is needed. In particular, future empirical studies should evaluate MOS and DL to determine the extent to which DL can outperform MOS and to identify tasks for which MOS outperforms DL. A key take-away message is that it is not clear-cut that MOS is a more usable notation.

The paper is set out as follows. Section 2 provides an overview of related work, focusing on the usability of MOS. In Sect. 3, we illustrate the nature of task that users were required to perform in our empirical study. The hypotheses to be tested are given in Sect. 4 and the experiment design is described in Sect. 5, together with the statistical methods employed. The results obtained are given in Sect. 6 and discussed in Sect. 7. We identify threats to validity in Sect. 8 and conclude in Sect. 9. The experiment materials and data collected are at https:// sites.google.com/site/eisamalharbi/owlanddlefficiency.

2   Background

Ontology engineering has become a major activity with many stakeholders involved in producing ontologies. The W3C OWL working group devised several different syntaxes – e.g. RDF/XML and a functional style syntax – designed to serve different purposes. However "none of them ... are designed for ease of use by humans when building or analyzing ontologies" [6]. Given the diversity of expertise held by different stakeholders, it is important to ensure the efficacy of notations used for ontology engineering.

The Manchester syntax was created with a view that it "would be easier to write and understand, particularly for non-logicians" [6]. This is supported by the official W3C working group documentation: "The Manchester syntax is a user-friendly compact syntax for OWL 2 ontologies"[1]. Indeed, the Manchester syntax is the de facto standard notation used for ontology engineering and various tools support its use, such as Protégé [11]. It is believed that because the Manchester syntax uses short and intuitive English words instead of logical symbols, such as those employed by DL, usability is improved [6].

Despite these beliefs, it is known that some users find interpreting OWL difficult. Warren et al. provide insight into the relative efficacy of different Manchester OWL constructs, with a focus on drawing sound inferences from given axioms [17]. Whilst this study revealed that users were "prone to certain misconceptions" it did not compare the Manchester syntax with DL or other notations. An evaluation by Sarker et al. [15] reported that ROWLtab, a Protégé plugin that allows users to enter OWL axioms by way of rules, " is much quicker than the standard interface, while at the same time, also less prone to errors for hard modeling tasks." Others have also considered the understandability of OWL, such as [14], and Horridge et al. [4] provided insight into the relative cognitive complexity of OWL justifications, but again not in comparison to DL.

In summary, insight has been gained about the relative understandability of different Manchester OWL axioms, particularly within the context of inference problems. However, the perceived superiority of the Manchester syntax has not been rigorously tested by empirical studies that aim to understand its relative cognitive advantages over DL. In this paper we present the first such empirical study, revealing unexpected results.

3   Tasks: Understanding Axioms and Inference

When presented with an ontology, users need to understand the informational content of axioms as well as derive insights from them. Consider the following:

1. Demon SubClassOf Elf
2. Korrigan SubClassOf Demon
3. Mermaid SubClassOf Spirit
4. Elf DisjointWith Nisse
5. Demon SubClassOf hates only Goblin
6. Elf SubClassOf chases some Spirit
7. Halfling SubClassOf watches some Fairy
8. guides Domain Mermaid

Each of these axioms needs to be *understood*. For example, axiom 2 indicates class subsumption and is taken to mean 'All Korrigans are Demons'. Axiom 4 asserts class disjointness: 'No Elf is a Nisse'. More complex axioms involve quantifiers, such as axiom 7 which tells us that 'Halflings watch at least one Fairy'.

The derivation of inferences requires people to *reason* about their informational content. Reasoning is clearly a harder task than understanding axioms, since the axioms must be understood in order to make sound inferences from them. Considering the axioms above, many inferences can be drawn, such as:

- 'No Demon is a Nisse': from axiom 1 we know 'All Demons are Elves' and from axiom 4 we see that 'No Elf is a Nisse'; so 'No Demon is a Nisse'.
- 'Korrigans hate only Goblins': follows from axioms 2 and 5.
- 'Demons chase at least one Spirit': follows from axioms 1 and 6.

In each case, two axioms have been used to derive the conclusions; more complex reasoning can also occur, but we focus on inferences drawn from two axioms.

It is also important that people do not make incorrect inferences. Examples of statements that are not semantically entailed by the axioms above include: 'No Halfling is a Spirit', 'Fairies track only Elves', and 'Things scare only Halflings.' It would be unsound to deduce any of these three statements. In summary, it is important that ontology engineers and end-users understand axioms correctly, draw sound inferences from them, and do not make unsound inferences. The study we design covers all three aspects.

4   Main Hypotheses

There is a belief that the Manchester syntax is usable, in that it is easy to read (i.e. understandable) and write, as exemplified by Sect. 2. A possible reason for this is the use of text rather than symbols. For instance, contrast Goblin SubClassOf Imp with Goblin ⊑ Imp: both express 'all goblins are imps'. The MOS is likely to be easier for people to understand than the DL even though it requires people to understand what is meant by SubClassOf.

DL, by contrast to MOS, exploits purely syntactic conventions whose semantics are defined in a stipulative way; the symbols do not immediately correspond to a natural language interpretation of the axioms. Therefore, DL's syntactic objects are further removed from their semantics than those of MOS. This means that DL could provide an additional cognitive burden on users, as there is a need to learn how to read the symbols in addition to then deriving an understanding of the axioms. This suggests that users of DL need to be more conscious of semantic conventions than users of MOS. Consequently, we expect an increased cognitive load for DL users which could be a deterrent to their performance when understanding and reasoning about axioms.

Given the above discussion, we identify the following hypotheses:

- People more accurately *understand* axioms using MOS than DL.
- People identify *sound inferences* more accurately using MOS than DL.
- People make fewer *unsound inferences* using MOS than DL.
- People perform tasks more quickly *overall* using MOS than DL.

With regard to the first three hypotheses, we will present a fine-grained statistical analysis that inspects performance with respect to understanding different types of axioms and different styles of inference task. Regarding the last hypothesis, time data was collected for each question, which involved all three types of task (i.e. *understanding*, *sound inference* and *unsound inference*). This design decision was to reduce the impact of fatigue effect on the data, since fewer questions and, thus, fewer sets of axioms needed to be presented to participants; if we collected time data at the fine-grained level, participants would need to answer nine times as many questions - given our design - which is not feasible. Consequently, there was no time data specifically for measuring the understanding of different types of axioms or for different styles of inference task.

5   Empirical Study Design

In order to determine whether MOS or DL most effectively helped people understand and reason about ontologies, we focused on six axiom types:

1. simple class subsumption: C_1 SubClassOf C_2 and $C_1 \sqsubseteq C_2$,
2. simple class disjointness: C_1 DisjointWith C_2 and $C_1 \sqcap C_2 \sqsubseteq \bot$,
3. complex class subsumption, involving all values from constraints: C_1 SubClassOf R only C_2 and $C_1 \sqsubseteq \forall R.C_2$,
4. complex class subsumption, involving some values from constraints: C_1 SubClassOf R some C_2 and $C_1 \sqsubseteq \exists R.C_2$,
5. domain: R Domain C_1 and $\exists R.\top \sqsubseteq C_1$,
6. range: R Range C_1 and $\top \sqsubseteq \forall R.C_1$,

where the C_i are primitive concepts. These were chosen because they are commonly occurring, especially simple class subsumption and complex class subsumption involving some values from which are prominent in biomedical ontologies. It was deemed important that participants had no prior knowledge of the information contained in the axioms, so that they could not work out the answers without reading the MOS or DL. Equally, the use of abstract-style axioms, such as in the enumerated list above, could be off-putting to participants. Therefore, the axioms presented information about mythical creatures to give some context to the questions. A between-group design was used, with participants being exposed to one of the two notations[1]. We measured relative efficacy through accuracy and time performance data. Accuracy was taken to be the primary performance indicator: one notation was more effective than another if people performed tasks significantly more accurately with it. To establish whether significant performance differences existed, we designed an empirical study that required participants to answer questions that required a set of checkboxes to be selected, corresponding to understanding the axioms and deriving sound inferences from the axioms. Further checkboxes were included that related to information that could not be deduced from the axioms. The nature of these checkboxes will be further explained below.

5.1   Designing Questions for the Study

A screenshot of a question used in the study is given in Fig. 1. There is a list of 14 axioms, presented in DL in this case. Participants are asked one question: 'Which of the following statements hold?' This is followed by a list of nine checkbox statements, given in natural language. Therefore, each question can be viewed as comprising nine tasks: for each checkbox, determine whether the information conveyed by the associated statement is necessarily true. Figure 1 will be used as a running example where we describe the question design process. The next three subsections consider factors that informed the question design.

---

[1] The study included a third group which saw a diagrammatic representation of the axioms. We do not report on that group in this paper.

Banshee ⊑ Spirit
Gnome ⊑ Dwarf
Imp ⊑ Troll
Pixie ⊑ Spirit
Gnome ⊓ Fiend ⊑ ⊥
Imp ⊓ Dwarf ⊑ ⊥
Dwarf ⊑ ∀frightens.Pixie
Elf ⊑ ∀watches.Halfling
Fiend ⊑ ∃scares.Elf
Spirit ⊑ ∃annoys.Fiend
∃guides.⊤ ⊑ Elf
∃helps.⊤ ⊑ Elf
⊤ ⊑ ∀chases.Halfling
⊤ ⊑ ∀likes.Banshee

Fig. 1. Screenshot of a DL question.

Understanding Axioms. As discussed earlier, an axiom can be understood through a natural language statement. For example, Gnome ⊑ Dwarf, given in Fig. 1 is understood as 'All Gnomes are Dwarfs'. The axiom types and their representations in MOS and DL are given in Table 1 together with their associated natural language interpretation written in an abstract form; we call these interpretations *statement styles* which will be used in the context of inference as well as understanding. To obtain a sufficient number of data points to statistically analyse accuracy performance, each axiom type was tested for understandability three times, in three different questions. Since there are six axiom types, we had a total of 18 tasks (resp. 18 checkboxes) relating to understanding axioms. These 18 tasks were distributed evenly across the questions: each question included three.

Table 1. Representing axioms

Axiom type	MOS	DL	Statement style
Simple class subsumption	C_1 SubClassOf C_2	$C_1 \sqsubseteq C_2$	All C_1 are C_2
Simple class disjointness	C_1 DisjointWith C_2	$C_1 \sqcap C_2 \sqsubseteq \bot$	No C_1 is a C_2
Complex class subsumption: all VF	C_1 SubClassOf p only C_2	$C_1 \sqsubseteq \forall p.C_2$	C_1 p only C_2
Complex class subsumption: some VF	C_1 SubClassOf p some C_2	$C_1 \sqsubseteq \exists p.C_2$	C_1 p at least one C_2
Domain	p Domain C	$\exists p.\top \sqsubseteq C$	Only C p things
Range	p Range C	$\top \sqsubseteq \forall p.C$	Things p only C

Making Sound Inferences from Axioms. From Banshee $\sqsubseteq$ Spirit and Spirit $\sqsubseteq$ $\exists$annoys.Fiend in Fig. 1 we can deduce Banshee $\sqsubseteq$ $\exists$annoys.Fiend, which is interpreted as 'Banshees annoy at least one Fiend'. We tested inferences that involved only two axioms and, in each case, one of the axioms was simple class subsumption. To give a controlled variety of inference tasks, simple class subsumption axioms were paired with each of the six axiom types we are considering. Such a pairing resulted in an inference whose interpretation is one of the six statement styles given in Table 1. Each such pairing was used to give three inference tasks for each statement style and 18 sound inference tasks overall. These 18 tasks were distributed evenly across the questions: each question included three sound inference tasks.

Making Unsound Inferences from Axioms. To test the ability of each notation to reduce the likelihood of unsound reasoning, tasks were included that corresponded to statements that were not semantically entailed by the axioms. For example, in Fig. 1, the statement Things chase only Imps cannot be inferred from the axioms. To ensure the unsound inference tasks were non-trivial, we used statements that contained classes and properties that were present in the axiom list. For consistency with the other two test types and to facilitate the statistical analysis we produced three statements that were unsound inferences from the axioms for each of the six statement styles. This gave a total of 18 statements that are unsound inferences from the axioms, again distributed evenly across the questions: each question included three unsound inference tasks.

Generating Axioms for Questions. Overall, we required participants to perform 54 tasks: 18 each for understanding axioms, sound inferences, unsound inferences. Each question had nine checkboxes, so we required six questions. Each question needed a set of axioms from which three statements could be understood, three sound inferences made, and three unsound inferences identified.

It was important to have tasks of sufficient complexity to reveal statistically significant differences – should they exist – and, therefore, a reasonable number of axioms was required for each question. However, if too many axioms were involved, participants may have found the tasks too difficult to perform with minimal training. Informal experimentation indicated that providing two axioms of each type was appropriate. As discussed, the sound inference tasks involved just two axioms, one of which was always simple class subsumption. Hence to include, for each question, three sound inference tasks and, for half the questions, a simple class subsumption understanding task - each question contained four simple class subsumption axioms. So each of the six questions involved a list of 14 axioms: four simple class subsumption axioms and two of each other type.

Each set of 14 axioms was randomly generated in order to avoid selection bias, using ten named classes and eight named properties; in total 27 different class names and 15 different property names were used across the six questions. Each class name started with a different letter to avoid potential misreading, the same was true for property names. The axioms were ordered according to axiom type: simple class subsumption, simple class disjointness, followed by complex class subsumption involving all values from, some values from constraints, domain, and, lastly, range. Within these axiom types the axioms were ordered alphabetically; see Fig. 1. The checkbox statements were generated randomly by statement style and task type, whilst ensuring the required distribution of checkboxes. The statements for each question were presented in fixed random order, see Fig. 1. The presentation of each question (i.e. order of axioms, order of checkbox statements, position of items on the screen), was identical for each participant, except for the use of MOS and DL.

Summary. The six questions were designed to test participants' ability to understand axioms, to make sound inferences, and to recognize unsound inferences. Each question involved a list of 14 axioms and nine checkbox statements. The 14 axioms consisted of four simple class subsumption axioms and two each of the other axiom types. The nine checkbox statements involved three statements testing axiom understanding, three testing sound inference and three testing unsound inference. In total participants were required to consider 54 checkbox statements. To be answered correctly, the axiom understanding statements and sound inference statements boxes should be checked, but the unsound inference statements boxes should be unchecked.

5.2 Experiment Phases

The experiment had three phases: paper-based training, software-based training, and the main study. The paper-based training taught participants how to understand axioms. This consisted of one A4 sheet containing one training axiom for each of the six axiom types. They were written using the mythical creatures scenario and presented alongside English language explanations, like those in Sect. 3. For example, the MOS group were shown the statement Boggart SubClassOf scares only Midget (among others) and were told this meant 'Boggarts scare only Midgets'; the DL group saw Boggart $\sqsubseteq$ $\forall$scares.Midgets alongside the same meaning. Participants retained their training sheet throughout the study.

In the second phase of the study, participants were taught how to answer the questions using the software that collected performance data, familiarizing them with the user interface. This involved participants answering questions similar to those designed for the main study. The training material was identical for each group, except that the notation used was different. They were told that some of the possible answers required inferences to be made from the axioms presented. The participants attempted the training questions, then the experiment facilitator told them the correct answers and explained why they were correct.

The third phase collected performance data based on the six questions described in Sect. 5.1. Participants were told that the information presented in each question was independent of the information in the other questions, so inferences should only be made from the axioms on the screen. They could not re-attempt questions but were able to refer to the single side of A4 paper training material from phase 1. To reduce the impact of learning effect, the questions were presented in a random order generated separately for each participant. After the answers to a question were submitted, the software showed a pause screen, allowing participants to decide when to start the next question. This feature was designed to reduce fatigue effect and to ensure that the time recorded to answer each question was appropriate; the recorded time was the duration from when the question was displayed until an answer was submitted, not the time taken to select individual checkboxes as this would not be meaningful. No time limit was imposed on the participants, allowing them to spend as long as they needed to answer each question.

5.3 Experiment Execution

Participants were recruited by word-of-mouth and were all students, studying a variety of subjects, at the University of Brighton, none associated with the authors' research group. Some participants were not native English speakers but all had proficiency in English. Participants were randomly divided into groups, one for MOS the other for DL. A pilot study was conducted to test the experiment design, the software used to display the questions, and the data collection process. Ten participants (6F, 4M, ages 18–38) took part in the pilot, five per group. No changes were required after the pilot study. A further 50 participants (18F, 32M, ages 18–45) took part in the main study, 25 in each group.

The experiment was performed in a usability laboratory, providing a quiet environment without interruption. Participants were treated equally with the same environment, equipment, materials and procedures. They performed the experiment individually, and were provided with full details about the purpose of their role by an experiment facilitator. Upon completion, each participant was provided with a debrief summary, telling them how to access the study's results. Participants were offered a £6 canteen voucher for their time spent in the study (approximately 30 min).

5.4 Statistical Methods

Statistical analysis was based on the Generalized Estimation Equations (GEE) method [10] implemented in the R package geepack [18]. In addition, the function ComparisonStats was used to evaluate the statistical significance of the desired comparisons for the accuracy data. The notation type (participant group), the axiom type, and checkbox type were used as explanatory variables that are linearly connected with the probability of providing a correct answer. The significance of the explanatory variables and their interaction will be assessed to determine whether they affect the probability of correctly performing a task. The following model was fitted to the accuracy data:

$$
\log\left[\frac{\Pr(Y_{ij}=1)}{1-\Pr(Y_{ij}=1)}\right] = \beta_0 + \beta_1 x_{ij1} + \beta_2 x_{ij2} + \beta_3 x_{ij3} + \beta_4 x_{ij4} + \beta_5 x_{ij5} + \beta_6 x_{ij6}
$$
$$
+ \beta_7 x_{ij7} + \beta_8 x_{i8} + \beta_9 x_{ij1}x_{ij6} + \beta_{10}x_{ij2}x_{ij6}
$$
$$
+ \beta_{11}x_{ij3}x_{ij6} + \beta_{12}x_{ij4}x_{ij6} + \beta_{13}x_{ij5}x_{ij6} + \beta_{14}x_{ij1}x_{ij7}
$$
$$
+ \beta_{15}x_{ij2}x_{ij7} + \beta_{16}x_{ij3}x_{ij7} + \beta_{17}x_{ij4}x_{ij7} + \beta_{18}x_{ij5}x_{ij7}
$$
$$
+ \beta_{19}x_{ij1}x_{i8} + \beta_{20}x_{ij2}x_{i8} + \beta_{21}x_{ij3}x_{i8} + \beta_{22}x_{ij4}x_{i8}
$$
$$
+ \beta_{23}x_{ij5}x_{i8} + \beta_{24}x_{ij6}x_{i8} + \beta_{25}x_{ij7}x_{i8} + \beta_{26}x_{ij1}x_{ij6}x_{i8}
$$
$$
+ \beta_{27}x_{ij2}x_{ij6}x_{i8} + \beta_{28}x_{ij3}x_{ij6}x_{i8} + \beta_{29}x_{ij4}x_{ij6}x_{i8}
$$
$$
+ \beta_{30}x_{ij5}x_{ij6}x_{i8} + \beta_{31}x_{ij1}x_{ij7}x_{i8} + \beta_{32}x_{ij2}x_{ij7}x_{i8}
$$
$$
+ \beta_{33}x_{ij3}x_{ij7}x_{i8} + \beta_{34}x_{ij4}x_{ij7}x_{i8} + \beta_{35}x_{ij5}x_{ij7}x_{i8}
$$

where $\Pr(Y_{ij}=1)$ is the probability for participant i to answer checkbox j correctly (i.e. ticked for understanding and sound inference tasks, not ticked for unsound inference tasks) and

- x_{ij1} is the indicator for the *simple class disjointness* statement style,
- x_{ij2} is the indicator for the *domain* statement style,
- x_{ij3} is the indicator for the *range* statement style,
- x_{ij4} is the indicator for the *simple class subsumption* statement style,
- x_{ij5} is the indicator for the complex class subsumption statement style involving *some values from*,
- x_{ij6} is the indicator for the unsound inference task type,
- x_{ij7} is the indicator for the sound inference task type,
- x_{i8} is the indicator for the *MOS* group,

for $i = 1,\ldots,60$, corresponding to the individual participants, and $j = 1,\ldots,54$, corresponding to the individual checkboxes. The βs are coefficients of the model computed using the data. ComparisonStats uses the βs to produce the p-value and the confidence interval for the contrast under study. Using this GEE-based model, we could determine whether the odds of providing a correct answer for any one combination statement style and task type is significantly different between groups (i.e. notation); this model also takes into account the expected correlation among the responses provided by each individual participant.

The regression model $\log(Z_{ik}) = \gamma_0 + \gamma_1 x_{i8}$ was fitted to the time data where Z_{ik} is the time needed for participant i to answer question k, x_{i8} is the indicator for the *MOS* group, for $i = 1,\ldots,60$ and $k = 1,\ldots 6$. This GEE-based model allowed us to determine whether the time taken to answer questions for one notation was significantly different from the other.

6 Results

The following results are based on the data collected from 60 participants (30 per group); as no changes were made after the pilot study, we carried forward the data when performing the statistical analysis. Each participant answered six questions providing a total of 3240 accuracy observations: 1620 for each group, 1080 for task type and 540 for each statement style. For each statistical comparison, arising from the 18 combinations of task type and statement style, there were 180 accuracy observations (90 each group). For the time data there were $60 \times 6 = 360$ observations, 180 for each group. Throughout, results were taken to be statistically significant at the 5% level.

6.1   Understanding Tasks

We present a full explanation for understanding tasks where the statement style was All C_1 are C_2; the remaining cases are similar and are in Table 2. Both treatments yielded a mean accuracy rate of 90.00%. Using the GEE-based model, the odds of providing a correct answer in the OWL group are 1.00 times that in the DL group, with a 95% confidence interval of $(0.40, 2.52)$ and p-value of 1.00. Therefore, there is no significant difference between MOS and DL when understanding simple class subsumption axioms. No significant differences were found between MOS and DL for any of the understanding tasks.

Table 2. Results for understanding tasks.

Statement Style	MOS	DL	Odds	CI	p-value	Significant
All C_1 are C_2	90.00%	90.00%	1.00	$(0.40, 2.52)$	1.00	$\times$
No C_1 are C_2	82.22%	83.33%	0.93	$(0.34, 2.53)$	0.88	$\times$
C_1 p only C_2	87.78%	92.22%	0.61	$(0.21, 1.76)$	0.36	$\times$
C_1 p at least one C_2	85.56%	93.33%	0.42	$(0.31, 1.33)$	0.14	$\times$
Only C p things	84.44%	80.00%	1.36	$(0.58, 3.18)$	0.48	$\times$
Things p only C	81.11%	83.33%	0.32	$(0.32, 2.33)$	0.76	$\times$

6.2   Sound Inference Tasks

We present a full explanation for sound inference tasks where the statement style was Things p only C since this case yielded a significant result; the remaining cases are given in Table 3. MOS and DL yielded mean accuracy rates of 58.89% and 83.33%. Using the GEE-based model, the odds of providing a correct answer in the MOS group are 0.29 times that in the DL group, with a 95% confidence interval of $(0.13, 0.61)$ and a p-value <0.005. Therefore, there is a significant difference between MOS and DL when performing sound inference tasks for this statement style: DL better supports sound reasoning using a simple class subsumption axiom with a complex class subsumption axiom involving range. In terms of effect size for this task type, on average we would expect 24 more correct answers per 100 tasks when people use DL instead of MOS.

Table 3. Results for sound inference tasks.

Statement Style	MOS	DL	Odds	CI	p-value	Significant
All C_1 are C_2	78.89%	63.33%	2.16	$(0.84, 5.60)$	0.11	×
No C_1 are C_2	70.00%	56.67%	1.78	$(0.90, 3.53)$	0.10	×
C_1 p only C_2	67.78%	82.22%	0.45	$(0.20, 1.04)$	0.06	×
C_1 p at least one C_2	71.11%	80.00%	0.62	$(0.31, 1.20)$	0.16	×
Only C p things	64.44%	67.78%	0.86	$(0.40, 1.87)$	0.71	×
Things p only C	58.89%	83.33%	0.29	$(0.13, 0.61)$	0.00	✓

6.3 Unsound Inference Tasks

We present the case for unsound inference tasks where the statement style was All C_1 are C_2; the remaining cases are given in Table 4. MOS and DL yielded mean accuracy rates of 93.33% and 100.00%. Using the GEE-based model to compare MOS and DL for this task, we obtained a p-value <0.005. Therefore, there is a significant difference between MOS and DL when identifying unsound inference tasks for this statement style: DL better prevents unsound reasoning. In terms of effect size for this task type, on average we would expect 7 more correct answers per 100 tasks when people use DL instead of MOS.

Table 4. Results for unsound inference tasks.

Statement Style	MOS	DL	Odds	CI	p-value	Significant
All C_1 are C_2	93.33%	100.00%	0.00	$(0.00, 0.00)$	0.00	✓
No C_1 are C_2	77.78%	77.78%	1.00	$(0.41, 2.47)$	1.00	×
C_1 p only C_2	90.00%	90.00%	1.00	$(0.30, 3.32)$	1.00	×
C_1 p at least one C_2	91.11%	91.11%	1.00	$(0.30, 3.30)$	1.00	×
Only C p things	90.00%	92.22%	0.76	$(0.26, 2, 23)$	0.62	×
Things p only C	88.89%	81.11%	0.91	$(0.91, 3.81)$	0.09	×

6.4 Time Performance

The fastest mean time was for DL, where participants answered questions in 2 minutes 22.46 s, on average, which increased to 2 min 37.88 s for MOS. Using the regression model for the time data, no significant differences were found, with $p = 0.075$. Therefore, we have not found evidence that using OWL supports significantly improved task performance, with respect to time.

7 Discussion

The participants were not familiar with MOS or DL, so by that measure they were novices. They were trained to understand the axioms types in the appropriate notation (MOS or DL) by considering a natural language form. They were also trained to perform the inference tasks used in the study. We hypothesized that participants using MOS would perform significantly better than those using DL. The results of this empirical study are surprising: there were few significant differences between MOS and DL and, where there were significant differences, it was DL that performed better. This result does, however, chime with Keet [9] who reported that non-English language modellers preferred Protégé v3 with a symbolic DL interface over Protégé v3 using MOS.

7.1 Understanding Axioms

The success rates for understanding the axioms were high for both notations, indicating that participants had a strong understanding of their meaning. Participants using MOS achieved between 81.11% (range) and 90.00% (simple class subsumption) accuracy, with the DL group achieving between 80.00% (domain) and 93.33% (complex class subsumption involving some values from). We hypothesized that MOS would, however, outperform DL due to its textual nature: MOS appears more closely aligned with its natural language interpretation, potentially placing a lower cognitive burden on users. The lack of significant differences show, at least for tasks of this type, no difference in cognitive burden. The axioms considered in this study were chosen due to their simple form and their frequent use in ontologies but future work should consider more complex axioms to determine whether MOS brings performance benefits.

7.2 Sound Inferences

We expected the sound inference tasks to be cognitively more demanding than understanding tasks for both notations. This is confirmed by the accuracy rates which are higher for understanding axioms than for sound inference. Participants using MOS achieved between 58.89% ('range' statement styles) and 78.89% ('simple class subsumption' statement styles), with the DL group achieving between 56.67% ('disjointness' statement styles) and 82.22% ('complex class subsumption involving all values' from statement styles). These lower accuracy rates are consistent with Warren et al. [17] who found "users are prone to certain misconceptions. These include confusion ... about the inheritance of property characteristics," although the sound inference tasks in the study involved class inheritance only. Despite increased difficulty, we still expected the OWL group to perform significantly better, in part due to the expected improved understanding that did not materialize. Since the accuracy rates reduced, as compared to the understanding tasks, we can be sure that the sound inference tasks required reasonable cognitive effort to perform. As cognitive effort was demonstrably required, we cannot readily attribute lack of significant differences - found in five of the six cases - to triviality of the inference tasks. Thus, we suggest that our hypothesis is not supported: MOS does not support more accurate inferences to be made. DL can, in fact, sometimes outperform MOS. Further work needs to consider more complex inference tasks to reinforce, or otherwise, these results.

The evidence for cognitive burden arising from the task difficulty further supports the significant difference found in the 'range' statement style case, i.e. 'Things p only C'. The 'range' statement style is expressed as p Range C in MOS and $\top \sqsubseteq \forall p.C$ in DL, an example is in Fig. 1. The checkbox statement 'Things like only Spirits' can be inferred from the axioms $\top \sqsubseteq \forall like.Banshee$ (like Range Banshee) and Banshee $\sqsubseteq$ Spirit (Banshee SubClassOf Spirit). Of the participants using DL, 25 out of 30 correctly made this inference against, surprisingly, only 13 out 30 for MOS users. It is not immediately clear why there is a significant difference only in this case. One possible explanation is that participants may be misunderstanding Range to mean the image of the relation (as is the case in some languages such as Z [16]) implying that two different classes cannot be the range. So participants interpreting Range in this way would only partially understand range axioms, leading to lack of ability to make sound inferences. If this conjecture is correct, it indicates a problem with using natural language in notations: some people may interpret natural language in a reasonable but incorrect way; a case of a little knowledge being a dangerous thing.

7.3 Unsound Inferences

The success rates for the unsound inference tasks were high for both notations, indicating that they were effective. Again, we expected MOS to outperform DL, but this was not the case. Interestingly, the DL group performed significantly better than the MOS group for unsound inferences involving 'simple class subsumption' style statements that were unsound inferences. Further work is needed to understand why these results were obtained.

8   Threats to Validity

Threats to validity are categorized as internal, construct and external [13]. With respect to internal validity, a major consideration related to carry-over effect which can arises when the measure of one treatment is affected by the measurement of another treatment. Using a between-group design ensured that each participant was only exposed to one notation and this threat was eliminated.

Construct validity focuses on dependent variables (accuracy rate, false negatives, and time) and independent variables (questions and treatments). Errors could arise if the axioms were ordered in such a way that cognition was hindered (this could also increase time taken). To manage this effect, all axioms were carefully ordered, ensuring that simple class subsumption axioms appeared first and so forth, minimizing unwanted variation between questions. The classes and properties in each question did not share a common first letter in an attempt to reduce false negatives due to misreading. Careful consideration was paid to the time taken to submit an answer: the inclusion of a pause screen between each question ensured that the question was only displayed when the participant was ready and they used the same PC with no applications running in the background. These steps were taken to ensure that the time to answer the questions was measured accurately, so far as is reasonably possible.

Lastly, we focus on external validity, by examining the limitations of the results and the extent to which they can be generalized. We observe the following. The questions involved three types of task: understanding axioms, drawing sound inferences from them, and identifying unsound inferences. Thus, our results are for these types of task only and exclude, for example, writing axioms or identifying incoherence and subsequently repairing the ontology (see [7]). Moreover, the sound inference tasks only required two axioms to be used to make the desired inference. More complex reasoning tasks were not considered.

Our tasks were limited in that each question involved 14 axioms of six commonly occurring types. Other styles of axioms may yield different results. In terms of inference, we realise that, in practice, ontologies can contain thousands of axioms. This makes the task of identifying axioms from which inferences can be made more difficult. Horridge et al. [5] identify minimal sets of axioms from which entailments holds, making inference tasks closer in cognitive complexity to the tasks in our study. Despite being able to focus on only the axioms involved in an entailment, it is important to extend our findings to inference tasks involving more than two axioms; the authors of [4] stated that "fewer than 10" axioms can still give rise to "difficult justifications" from the perspective of cognition.

The participants were all novices and were (minimally) trained in the notations. With ontologies being developed in a range of areas, where stakeholders need not have expertise in MOS or DL, our results are particularly relevant. We might obtain different results for expert participants who are familiar with one of DL and MOS. Ultimately, our results should be taken to be valid within the constraints imposed by the study design and execution.

9   Conclusion

The belief that the Manchester syntax for OWL is more usable than competing notations is widespread. Our findings suggest that for a range of task types - understanding axioms, deriving sound inferences from them, and preventing unsound reasoning - the Manchester syntax for OWL is *not* more effective than DL. This result itself is surprising, but our study also suggests that DL can sometimes better support users than the Manchester syntax. These results begin to challenge the belief that the Manchester syntax is easier for people to use.

Further work is needed to determine the extent to which DL better supports task performance than the Manchester syntax and our research raises more questions than it answers. For instance, for more complex versions of the three task types considered in our study, does the Manchester syntax support more accurate understanding than DL or other notations? Other types of task were not considered, such as writing axioms and ontology debugging and repair: does the

Manchester syntax support more accurate task performance than DL, or other notations, for these other tasks? Would we see similar results if our study was re-run with expert users? Answering these questions could yield exciting new insights into the relative cognitive complexity of competing notation choices and the different types of task that ontology engineers must perform. Indeed, not only are such answers important for ontology engineers and end-users, but also more widely in that they could impact the design of future notations. Beyond this, our major takeaway message is that it is not clear-cut that the Manchester syntax for OWL is a more usable notation than competing alternatives.

Acknowledgement. Gem Stapleton was funded by a Leverhulme Trust Research Project Grant (RPG-2016-082).

References

1. OWL 2 Web Ontology Language Manchester Syntax, 2nd edn. W3C WG Note 11. https://www.w3.org/TR/owl2-manchester-syntax/. Accessed May 2017
2. The OWL 2 Web Ontology Language (2016). http://www.w3.org/TR/owl2-overview/. Accessed Apr 2016
3. Baader, F., Calvanese, D., McGuinness, D., Nadi, D., Patel-Schneider, P.F. (eds.): The Description Logic Handbook. Cambridge University Press, Cambridge (2003)
4. Horridge, M., Bail, S., Parsia, B., Sattler, U.: The cognitive complexity of OWL justifications. In: Aroyo, L. et al. (eds.) ISWC 2011. LNCS, vol. 7031, pp. 241–256. Springer, Heidelberg (2011). doi:10.1007/978-3-642-25073-6_16
5. Horridge, M., Parsia, B., Sattler, U.: Laconic and precise justifications in OWL. In: Sheth, A., Staab, S., Dean, M., Paolucci, M., Maynard, D., Finin, T., Thirunarayan, K. (eds.) ISWC 2008. LNCS, vol. 5318, pp. 323–338. Springer, Heidelberg (2008). doi:10.1007/978-3-540-88564-1_21
6. Horridge, M., Patel-Schneider, F.: Manchester syntax for OWL 1.1. In: 4th International Workshop OWL: Experiences and Directions (2008)
7. Hou, T., Chapman, P., Blake, A.: Antipattern comprehension: an empirical evaluation. In: FOIS, pp. 211–224. IOS Press (2016)
8. Kalyanpur, A., Parsia, B., Sirin, E., Hendler, J.: Debugging unsatisfiable classes in OWL ontologies. Web Semant. **3**(4), 268–293 (2005)
9. Keet, C.M.: The use of foundational ontologies in ontology development: an empirical assessment. In: Antoniou, G., Grobelnik, M., Simperl, E., Parsia, B., Plexousakis, D., Leenheer, P., Pan, J. (eds.) ESWC 2011. LNCS, vol. 6643, pp. 321–335. Springer, Heidelberg (2011). doi:10.1007/978-3-642-21034-1_22
10. Liang, K., Zeger, S.: Longitudinal data analysis using generalized linear models. Biometrika **73**, 13–22 (1986)
11. Musen, M.: The Protégé project: a look back and a look forward. AI Matters **4**(1), 4–12 (2015)
12. Neuhaus, F., Vizedom, A., Baclawski, K., Bennett, M., Dean, M., Denny, M., Grueninger, M., Hashemi, A., Longstreth, T., Obrst, L.: Towards ontology evaluation across the life cycle. Appl. Ontol. **8**(3), 179–194 (2013)
13. Purchase, H.: Experimental Human Computer Interaction: A Practical Guide with Visual Examples. Cambridge University Press, Cambridge (2012)

14. Rector, A., Drummond, N., Horridge, M., Rogers, J., Knublauch, H., Stevens, R., Wang, H., Wroe, C.: OWL pizzas: practical experience of teaching OWL-DL. Engineering Knowledge in the Age of the SemanticWeb. LNCS, vol. 3257, pp. 63–81. Springer, Berlin, Heidelberg (2004). doi:10.1007/978-3-540-30202-5_5

15. Sarker, M.K., Krisnadhi, A., Carral, D., Hitzler, P.: Rule-Based OWL Modeling with ROWLTab Protégé Plugin. In: Blomqvist, E., Maynard, D., Gangemi, A., Hoekstra, R., Hitzler, P., Hartig, O. (eds.) ESWC 2017. LNCS, vol. 10249, pp. 419–433. Springer, Cham (2017). doi:10.1007/978-3-319-58068-5_26

16. Spivey, J.: The Z Notation: A Reference Manual. Prentice Hall, Upper Saddle River (1989)

17. Warren, P., Mulholland, P., Collins, T., Motta, E.: The usability of description logics. In: Presutti, V., d'Amato, C., Gandon, F., d'Aquin, M., Staab, S., Tordai, A. (eds.) ESWC 2014. LNCS, vol. 8465, pp. 550–564. Springer, Cham (2014). doi:10.1007/978-3-319-07443-6_37

18. Yan, J., Fine, J.: Estimating equations for association structures. Stat. Med. **23**, 859–880 (2004)

A Decidable Very Expressive Description Logic for Databases

Alessandro Artale, Enrico Franconi[✉], Rafael Peñaloza, and Francesco Sportelli

KRDB Research Centre, Free University of Bozen-Bolzano, Bolzano, Italy
{artale,franconi,penaloza,sportelli}@inf.unibz.it

Abstract. We introduce $\mathcal{DLR}^+$, an extension of the n-ary proposition-ally closed description logic $\mathcal{DLR}$ to deal with attribute-labelled tuples (generalising the positional notation), projections of relations, and global and local objectification of relations, able to express inclusion, functional, key, and external uniqueness dependencies. The logic is equipped with both TBox and ABox axioms. We show how a simple syntactic restriction on the appearance of projections sharing common attributes in a $\mathcal{DLR}^+$ knowledge base makes reasoning in the language decidable with the same computational complexity as $\mathcal{DLR}$. The obtained $\mathcal{DLR}^{\pm}$ n-ary description logic is able to encode more thoroughly conceptual data models such as EER, UML, and ORM.

1 Introduction

We introduce the description logic (DL) $\mathcal{DLR}^+$ extending the n-ary DL $\mathcal{DLR}$ [6], in order to capture database oriented constraints. While $\mathcal{DLR}$ is a rather expressive logic, tailored for conceptual modelling and ontology design, gener-alising many aspects of classical description logics and OWL, it lacks a number of expressive means relevant for database applications that can be added with-out increasing the complexity of reasoning—when used in a carefully controlled way. The added expressivity is motivated by the increasing use of description logics as an abstract conceptual layer (an *ontology*) over relational databases. For example, the $\mathcal{DLR}$ family of description logics is used to formalise and per-form reasoning in the ORM conceptual modelling language for database design (adopted by Microsoft in Visual Studio) [8,15].

We remind that a $\mathcal{DLR}$ knowledge base, as defined in [6], can express axioms with (i) propositional combinations of concepts and (compatible) n-ary relations – as opposed to just binary roles as in classical description logics and OWL, (ii) concepts as unary projections of n-ary relations – generalising the exis-tential operator over binary roles in classical description logics and OWL, and (iii) relations with a selected typed component.

C. d'Amato et al. (Eds.): ISWC 2017, Part I, LNCS 10587, pp. 37–52, 2017.
DOI: 10.1007/978-3-319-68288-4_3

As an example of $\mathcal{DLR}$, in a knowledge base where `Pilot` and `RacingCar` are concepts and `DrivesCar`, `DrivesMotorbike`, `DrivesVehicle` are binary relations, the following statements:

$$\texttt{Pilot} \sqsubseteq \exists[1]\sigma_{2:\texttt{RacingCar}}\texttt{DrivesCar}$$

$$\texttt{DrivesCar} \sqcup \texttt{DrivesMotorbike} \sqsubseteq \texttt{DrivesVehicle}$$

assert that a pilot drives a racing car and that driving a car or a motorbike implies driving a vehicle.

The language we propose here, $\mathcal{DLR}^+$, extends $\mathcal{DLR}$ in the following ways.

– While $\mathcal{DLR}$ instances of n-ary relations are n-tuples of objects—whose components are identified by their position in the tuple—instances of relations in $\mathcal{DLR}^+$ are *attribute-labelled tuples* of objects, i.e., tuples where each component is identified by an attribute and not by its position in the tuple (see, e.g., [11]). For example, the relation `Employee` may have the signature:

$$\texttt{Employee(firstname, lastname, dept, deptAddr)},$$

and an instance of `Employee` could be the tuple:

$$\langle\texttt{firstname : John, lastname : Doe, dept : Purchase, deptAddr : London}\rangle.$$

– Attributes can be *renamed*, for example to recover the positional attributes:

$$\texttt{firstname, lastname, dept, deptAddr} \ \rightleftarrows\ 1, 2, 3, 4.$$

– *Relation projections* allow to form new relations by projecting a given relation on some of its attributes. For example, if `Person` is a relation with signature `Person(name, surname)`, it could be related to `Employee` as follows::

$$\pi[\texttt{firstname, lastname}]\texttt{Employee} \sqsubseteq \texttt{Person},$$

$$\texttt{firstname, lastname} \ \rightleftarrows\ \texttt{name, surname}.$$

– The *objectification* of a relation (also known as *reification*) is a concept whose instances are unique *object identifiers* of the tuples instantiating the relation. Those identifiers could be unique only within an objectified relation (*local objectification*), or they could be uniquely identifying tuples independently on the relation they are instance of (*global objectification*). For example, the concept `EmployeeC` could be the *global* objectification of the relation `Employee`, assuming that there is a global 1-to-1 correspondence between pairs of values of the attributes `firstname, lastname` and `EmployeeC` instances:

$$\texttt{EmployeeC} \equiv \textcircled{\circ}\, \exists[\texttt{firstname, lastname}]\texttt{Employee}.$$

Consider the relations with the following signatures:

$$\texttt{DrivesCar(name, surname, car)}, \quad \texttt{OwnsCar(name, surname, car)},$$

and assume that anybody driving a car also owns it: DrivesCar $\sqsubseteq$ OwnsCar. The *locally* objectified events of driving and owning, defined as

$$\text{CarDrivingEvent} \equiv \textcircled{\cdot}\,\text{DrivesCar}, \quad \text{CarOwningEvent} \equiv \textcircled{\cdot}\,\text{OwnsCar},$$

do not imply that a car driving event by a person is the owning event by the same person and the same car: CarDrivingEvent $\not\sqsubseteq$ CarOwningEvent. Indeed, they are even disjoint: CarDrivingEvent $\sqcap$ CarOwningEvent $\sqsubseteq \perp$.

It turns out that $\mathcal{DLR}^+$ is an expressive description logic able to assert relevant constraints typical of relational databases. In Sect. 3 we will consider *inclusion dependencies, functional and key dependencies, external uniqueness* and *identification* axioms. For example, $\mathcal{DLR}^+$ can express the fact that the attributes firstname, lastname play the role of a multi-attribute key for the relation Employee:

$$\pi[\text{firstname}, \text{lastname}]\text{Employee} \sqsubseteq \pi^{\leqslant 1}[\text{firstname}, \text{lastname}]\text{Employee},$$

and that the attribute deptAddr functionally depends on the attribute dept within the relation Employee:

$$\exists[\text{dept}]\text{Employee} \sqsubseteq \exists^{\leqslant 1}[\text{dept}]\,(\pi[\text{dept}, \text{deptAddr}]\text{Employee}).$$

While $\mathcal{DLR}^+$ turns out to be undecidable, we show how a simple syntactic condition on the appearance of projections sharing common attributes in a knowledge base makes the language decidable. The result of this restriction is a new language called $\mathcal{DLR}^\pm$. We prove that $\mathcal{DLR}^\pm$, while preserving most of the $\mathcal{DLR}^+$ expressivity, has a reasoning problem whose complexity does not increase w.r.t. the computational complexity of the basic $\mathcal{DLR}$ language.

We also present in Sect. 6 the implementation of an API for the reasoning services in $\mathcal{DLR}^\pm$.

2 The Description Logic $\mathcal{DLR}^+$

We start by introducing the syntax of $\mathcal{DLR}^+$. A $\mathcal{DLR}^+$ *signature* is a tuple $\mathcal{L} = (\mathcal{C}, \mathcal{R}, \mathcal{O}, \mathcal{U}, \tau)$ where $\mathcal{C}$, $\mathcal{R}$, $\mathcal{O}$ and $\mathcal{U}$ are finite, mutually disjoint sets of *concept names, relation names, individual names,* and *attributes,* respectively, and τ is a *relation signature* function, associating a set of attributes to each relation name $\tau(RN) = \{U_1, \ldots, U_n\} \subseteq \mathcal{U}$, with $n \geqslant 2$.

$$
\begin{aligned}
C &\;\to\; CN \mid \neg C \mid C_1 \sqcap C_2 \mid \exists^{\geqslant q}[U_i]R \mid \textcircled{\odot}\,R \mid \textcircled{\cdot}\,RN \\
R &\;\to\; RN \mid R_1 \backslash R_2 \mid R_1 \sqcap R_2 \mid R_1 \sqcup R_2 \mid \sigma_{U_i:C}R \mid \pi^{\leqslant q}[U_1,\ldots,U_k]R \\
\varphi &\;\to\; C_1 \sqsubseteq C_2 \mid R_1 \sqsubseteq R_2 \mid CN(o) \mid RN(U_1{:}o_1,\ldots,U_n{:}o_n) \mid o_1 = o_2 \mid o_1 \neq o_2 \\
\vartheta &\;\to\; U_1 \rightleftarrows U_2
\end{aligned}
$$

Fig. 1. The syntax of $\mathcal{DLR}^+$.

The syntax of concepts C, relations R, formulas φ, and attribute renaming axioms ϑ is given in Fig. 1, where $CN \in \mathcal{C}$, $RN \in \mathcal{R}$, $U \in \mathcal{U}$, $o \in \mathcal{O}$, q is a positive integer and $2 \leqslant k < \text{ARITY}(R)$. The *arity* of a relation R is the number of the attributes in its signature; i.e., $\text{ARITY}(R) = |\tau(R)|$, with the relation signature function τ extended to complex relations as in Fig. 2. Note that it is possible that the same attribute appears in the signature of different relations.

$$
\begin{aligned}
\tau(R_1 \backslash R_2) &= \tau(R_1) \\
\tau(R_1 \sqcap R_2) &= \tau(R_1) && \text{if } \tau(R_1) = \tau(R_2) \\
\tau(R_1 \sqcup R_2) &= \tau(R_1) && \text{if } \tau(R_1) = \tau(R_2) \\
\tau(\sigma_{U_i : C} R) &= \tau(R) && \text{if } U_i \in \tau(R) \\
\tau(\pi^{\lessgtr q}[U_1, \ldots, U_k] R) &= \{U_1, \ldots, U_k\} && \text{if } \{U_1, \ldots, U_k\} \subset \tau(R) \\
\text{undefined} &&& \text{otherwise}
\end{aligned}
$$

Fig. 2. The signature of $\mathcal{DLR}^+$ relations.

As mentioned in the introduction, the $\mathcal{DLR}^+$ constructors added to $\mathcal{DLR}$ are the *local* and *global objectification* ($\odot\, RN$ and $\circledcirc\, R$, respectively); *relation projections* with the possibility to count the projected tuples ($\pi^{\lessgtr q}[U_1, \ldots, U_k] R$), and *renaming axioms* over attributes ($U_1 \rightleftarrows U_2$). Note that local objectification ($\odot\, R$) can be applied to relation names, while global objectification ($\circledcirc\, RN$) can be applied to arbitrary relation expressions. We use the standard abbreviations:

$$
\bot = C \sqcap \neg C, \quad \top = \neg \bot, \quad C_1 \sqcup C_2 = \neg(\neg C_1 \sqcap \neg C_2), \quad \exists[U_i] R = \exists^{\geqslant 1}[U_i] R,
$$

$$
\exists^{\leqslant q}[U_i] R = \neg(\exists^{\geqslant q+1}[U_i] R), \quad \pi[U_1, \ldots, U_k] R = \pi^{\geqslant 1}[U_1, \ldots, U_k] R.
$$

A $\mathcal{DLR}^+$ *TBox* $\mathcal{T}$ is a finite set of *concept inclusion* axioms of the form $C_1 \sqsubseteq C_2$ and *relation inclusion* axioms of the form $R_1 \sqsubseteq R_2$. We use $X_1 \equiv X_2$ as a shortcut for the two axioms $X_1 \sqsubseteq X_2$ and $X_2 \sqsubseteq X_1$. A $\mathcal{DLR}^+$ *ABox* $\mathcal{A}$ is a finite set of *concept instance* axioms of the form $CN(o)$, *relation instance* axioms of the form $RN(U_1 : o_1, \ldots, U_n : o_n)$, and *same/distinct individual* axioms of the form $o_1 = o_2$ and $o_1 \neq o_2$, with $o_i \in \mathcal{O}$. Restricting ABox axioms to concept and relation names only does not affect the expressivity of $\mathcal{DLR}^+$ due to the availability of unrestricted TBox axioms. A $\mathcal{DLR}^+$ *renaming schema* $\mathfrak{R}$ is a finite set of renaming axioms of the form $U_1 \rightleftarrows U_2$. We use the shortcut $U_1 \ldots U_n \rightleftarrows U_1' \ldots U_n'$ to group many renaming axioms with the meaning that $U_i \rightleftarrows U_i'$ for all $i = 1, \ldots, n$. A $\mathcal{DLR}^+$ knowledge base (KB) $\mathcal{KB} = (\mathcal{T}, \mathcal{A}, \mathfrak{R})$ is composed by a TBox $\mathcal{T}$, an ABox $\mathcal{A}$, and a renaming schema $\mathfrak{R}$.

The renaming operator $\rightleftarrows$ is an equivalence relation over the attributes $\mathcal{U}$, $(\rightleftarrows, \mathcal{U})$. The partitioning of $\mathcal{U}$ into equivalence classes induced by a renaming schema is meant to represent the alternative ways to name attributes in the knowledge base. A unique *canonical representative* for each equivalence class is chosen to replace all the attributes in the class throughout the knowledge base. From now on we assume that a knowledge base is consistently rewritten by substituting each attribute with its canonical representative. After this rewriting, the renaming schema does not play any role in the knowledge base. We allow only *arity-preserving* renaming schemas, i.e., there is no equivalence class containing two attributes from the same relation signature.

As shown in the introduction, the renaming schema is useful to reconcile the named attribute perspective and the positional perspective on relations. It is also important to enforce *union compatibility* among relations involved in relation inclusion axioms, and among relations involved in ⊓- and ⊔-set expressions. Two relations are *union compatible* (w.r.t. a renaming schema) if they have the same signature (up to the attribute renaming induced by the renaming schema). Indeed, as it will be clear from the semantics, a relation inclusion axiom involving non union compatible relations would always be false, and a ⊓- and ⊔-set expression involving non union compatible relations would always be empty.

The semantics of $\mathcal{DLR}^+$ uses the notion of *labelled tuples* over a countable potentially infinite domain Δ. Given a set of labels $\mathcal{X} \subseteq \mathcal{U}$ an $\mathcal{X}$-*labelled tuple over* Δ (or *tuple* for short) is a *total* function $t\colon \mathcal{X} \to \Delta$. For $U \in \mathcal{X}$, we write $t[U]$ to refer to the domain element $d \in \Delta$ labelled by U. Given $d_1, \ldots, d_n \in \Delta$, the expression $\langle U_1\colon d_1, \ldots, U_n\colon d_n \rangle$ stands for the tuple t defined on the set of labels $\{U_1, \ldots, U_n\}$ such that $t[U_i] = d_i$, for $1 \leqslant 1 \leqslant n$. The *projection* of the tuple t over the attributes $U_1, \ldots, U_k$ is the function t restricted to be undefined for the labels not in $U_1, \ldots, U_k$, and it is denoted by $t[U_1, \ldots, U_k]$. The relation signature function τ is extended to labelled tuples to obtain the set of labels on which a tuple is defined. $T_\Delta(\mathcal{X})$ denotes the set of all $\mathcal{X}$-labelled tuples over Δ, for $\mathcal{X} \subseteq \mathcal{U}$, and we overload this notation by denoting with $T_\Delta(\mathcal{U})$ the set of all possible tuples with labels within the whole set of attributes $\mathcal{U}$.

A $\mathcal{DLR}^+$ *interpretation* is a tuple $\mathcal{I} = (\Delta, \cdot^\mathcal{I}, \imath, L)$ consisting of a nonempty countable potentially infinite *domain* Δ specific to $\mathcal{I}$, an *interpretation function* $\cdot^\mathcal{I}$, a *global objectification function* $\imath$, and a family L containing one *local objectification function* ℓ_{RN_i} for each named relation $RN_i \in \mathcal{R}$. The global objectification

$$(\neg C)^\mathcal{I} = \top^\mathcal{I} \backslash C^\mathcal{I}$$
$$(C_1 \sqcap C_2)^\mathcal{I} = C_1^\mathcal{I} \cap C_2^\mathcal{I}$$
$$(\exists^{\geqslant q}[U_i]R)^\mathcal{I} = \{d \in \Delta \mid \, |\{t \in R^\mathcal{I} \mid t[U_i] = d\}| \geqslant q\}$$
$$(\text{\textcircled{o}}\,R)^\mathcal{I} = \{d \in \Delta \mid d = \imath(t) \wedge t \in R^\mathcal{I}\}$$
$$(\text{\textcircled{$\cdot$}}\,RN)^\mathcal{I} = \{d \in \Delta \mid d = \ell_{RN}(t) \wedge t \in RN^\mathcal{I}\}$$
$$(R_1 \backslash R_2)^\mathcal{I} = R_1^\mathcal{I} \backslash R_2^\mathcal{I}$$
$$(R_1 \sqcap R_2)^\mathcal{I} = R_1^\mathcal{I} \cap R_2^\mathcal{I}$$
$$(R_1 \sqcup R_2)^\mathcal{I} = \{t \in R_1^\mathcal{I} \cup R_2^\mathcal{I} \mid \tau(R_1) = \tau(R_2)\}$$
$$(\sigma_{U_i\colon C}R)^\mathcal{I} = \{t \in R^\mathcal{I} \mid t[U_i] \in C^\mathcal{I}\}$$
$$(\pi^{\leqslant q}[U_1, \ldots, U_k]R)^\mathcal{I} = \{\langle U_1\colon d_1, \ldots, U_k\colon d_k \rangle \in T_\Delta(\{U_1, \ldots, U_k\}) \mid$$
$$1 \leqslant |\{t \in R^\mathcal{I} \mid t[U_1] = d_1, \ldots, t[U_k] = d_k\}| \lessgtr q\}$$

Fig. 3. The semantics of $\mathcal{DLR}^+$ expressions.

function is an injective function, $\imath : T_\Delta(\mathcal{U}) \to \Delta$, associating a *unique* global identifier to each tuple. The local objectification functions, $\ell_{RN_i} : T_\Delta(\mathcal{U}) \to \Delta$, are associated to each relation name in the signature, and as the global objectification function they are injective: they associate an identifier—which is guaranteed to be unique only within the interpretation of a relation name—to each tuple.

The interpretation function $\cdot^{\mathcal{I}}$ assigns a domain element to each individual, $o^{\mathcal{I}} \in \Delta$, a set of domain elements to each concept name, $CN^{\mathcal{I}} \subseteq \Delta$, and a set of $\tau(RN)$-labelled tuples over Δ to each relation name RN, $RN^{\mathcal{I}} \subseteq T_\Delta(\tau(RN))$. Note that the unique name assumption is not enforced. The interpretation function $\cdot^{\mathcal{I}}$ is unambiguously extended over concept and relation expressions as specified in Fig. 3. Notice that the construct $\pi^{\geq q}[U_1, \ldots, U_k]R$ is interpreted as a classical projection over a relation, thus including only tuples belonging to the relation.

The interpretation $\mathcal{I}$ satisfies the concept inclusion axiom $C_1 \sqsubseteq C_2$ if $C_1^{\mathcal{I}} \subseteq C_2^{\mathcal{I}}$, and the relation inclusion axiom $R_1 \sqsubseteq R_2$ if $R_1^{\mathcal{I}} \subseteq R_2^{\mathcal{I}}$. It satisfies the concept instance axiom $CN(o)$ if $o^{\mathcal{I}} \in CN^{\mathcal{I}}$, the relation instance axiom $RN(U_1 : o_1, \ldots, U_n : o_n)$ if $\langle U_1 : o_1^{\mathcal{I}}, \ldots, U_n : o_n^{\mathcal{I}} \rangle \in RN^{\mathcal{I}}$, and the axioms $o_1 = o_2$ and $o_1 \neq o_2$ if $o_1^{\mathcal{I}} = o_2^{\mathcal{I}}$, and $o_1^{\mathcal{I}} \neq o_2^{\mathcal{I}}$, respectively. $\mathcal{I}$ is a *model* of the knowledge base $(\mathcal{T}, \mathcal{A}, \Re)$ if it satisfies all the axioms in the TBox $\mathcal{T}$ and in the ABox $\mathcal{A}$, once the knowledge base has been rewritten according to the renaming schema.

Example 1. Consider the relation names R_1, R_2 with $\tau(R_1) = \{W_1, W_2, W_3, W_4\}$, $\tau(R_2) = \{V_1, V_2, V_3, V_4, V_5\}$, and a knowledge base with the renaming axiom $W_1 W_2 W_3 \rightleftarrows V_3 V_4 V_5$ and a TBox $\mathcal{T}_{\mathsf{exa}}$:

$$\pi[W_1, W_2]R_1 \sqsubseteq \pi^{\leq 1}[W_1, W_2]R_1 \tag{1}$$

$$\pi[V_3, V_4]R_2 \sqsubseteq \pi^{\leq 1}[V_3, V_4](\pi[V_3, V_4, V_5]R_2) \tag{2}$$

$$\pi[W_1, W_2, W_3]R_1 \sqsubseteq \pi[V_3, V_4, V_5]R_2. \tag{3}$$

The axiom (1) expresses that W_1, W_2 form a multi-attribute key for R_1; (2) introduces a functional dependency in the relation R_2 where the attribute V_5 is functionally dependent from attributes V_3, V_4, and (3) states an inclusion between two projections of the relation names R_1, R_2 based on the renaming schema axiom. □

KB satisfiability refers to the problem of deciding the existence of a model of a given knowledge base; *concept satisfiability* (resp. *relation satisfiability*) is the problem of deciding whether there is a model of the knowledge base with a non-empty interpretation of a given concept (resp. relation). A knowledge base *entails* (or *logically implies*) an axiom if all models of the knowledge base are also models of the axiom. For instance, it is easy to see that the TBox in Example 1 entails that V_3, V_4 are a key for R_2:

$$\mathcal{T}_{\mathsf{exa}} \models \pi[V_3, V_4]R_2 \sqsubseteq \pi^{\leq 1}[V_3, V_4]R_2,$$

and that axiom (2) is redundant in $\mathcal{T}_{\mathsf{exa}}$. The decision problems in $\mathcal{DLR}^+$ can be all reduced to KB satisfiability.

Lemma 2. *In $\mathcal{DLR}^+$, concept and relation satisfiability and entailment are reducible to KB satisfiability.*

3   Expressiveness of $\mathcal{DLR}^+$

$\mathcal{DLR}^+$ is an expressive description logic able to assert relevant constraints in the context of relational databases, such as *inclusion dependencies* (namely inclusion axioms among arbitrary projections of relations), *equijoins*, *functional dependency* axioms, *key* and *foreign key* axioms, *external uniqueness* axioms, *identification* axioms, and *path functional dependencies*.

An *equijoin* among two relations with disjoint signatures is the set of all combinations of tuples in the relations that are equal on their selected attribute names. Let R_1, R_2 be relations with signatures $\tau(R_1) = \{U, U_1, \ldots, U_{n_1}\}$ and $\tau(R_2) = \{V, V_1, \ldots, V_{n_2}\}$; their equijoin over U and V is the relation $R = R_1 \underset{U=V}{\bowtie} R_2$ with signature $\tau(R) = \tau(R_1) \cup \tau(R_2) \setminus \{V\}$, which is expressed by the $\mathcal{DLR}^+$ axioms:

$$\pi[U, U_1, \ldots, U_{n_1}]R \equiv \sigma_{U:(\exists[U]R_1 \sqcap \exists[V]R_2)}R_1$$
$$\pi[V, V_1, \ldots, V_{n_2}]R \equiv \sigma_{V:(\exists[U]R_1 \sqcap \exists[V]R_2)}R_2$$
$$U \rightleftarrows V.$$

A *functional dependency* axiom $(R : U_1 \ldots U_j \to U)$ (also called *internal uniqueness* axiom [9]) states that the values of the attributes $U_1 \ldots U_j$ uniquely determine the value of the attribute U in the relation R. Formally, the interpretation $\mathcal{I}$ satisfies this functional dependency axiom if, for all tuples $s, t \in R^{\mathcal{I}}$, $s[U_1] = t[U_1], \ldots, s[U_j] = t[U_j]$ imply $s[U] = t[U]$. Functional dependencies can be expressed in $\mathcal{DLR}^+$, assuming that $\{U_1, \ldots, U_j, U\} \subseteq \tau(R)$, with the axiom:

$$\pi[U_1, \ldots, U_j]R \sqsubseteq \pi^{\leqslant 1}[U_1, \ldots, U_j](\pi[U_1, \ldots, U_j, U]R).$$

A special case of a functional dependency are *key* axioms $(R : U_1 \ldots U_j \to R)$, which state that the values of the key attributes $U_1 \ldots U_j$ of a relation R uniquely identify tuples in R. A key axiom can be expressed in $\mathcal{DLR}^+$, assuming that $\{U_1 \ldots U_j\} \subseteq \tau(R)$, with the axiom:

$$\pi[U_1, \ldots, U_j]R \sqsubseteq \pi^{\leqslant 1}[U_1, \ldots, U_j]R.$$

A *foreign key* is the obvious result of an inclusion dependency together with a key constraint involving the foreign key attributes.

The *external uniqueness* axiom $([U^1]R_1 \downarrow \ldots \downarrow [U^h]R_h)$ states that the join R of the relations $R_1, \ldots, R_h$ via the attributes $U^1, \ldots, U^h$ has the joined attribute functionally dependent on all the others [9]. This can be expressed in $\mathcal{DLR}^+$ with the axioms:

$$R \equiv R_1 \underset{U^1=U^2}{\bowtie} \cdots \underset{U^{h-1}=U^h}{\bowtie} R_h$$
$$R : U_1^1, \ldots, U_{n_1}^1, \ldots, U_1^h, \ldots, U_{n_h}^h \to U^1$$

where $\tau(R_i) = \{U^i, U^i_1, \ldots, U^i_{n_i}\}, 1 \le i \le h$, and R is a new relation name with $\tau(R) = \{U^1, U^1_1, \ldots, U^1_{n_1}, \ldots, U^h_1, \ldots, U^h_{n_h}\}$.

Identification axioms as defined in $\mathcal{DLR}_{ifd}$ [4] (an extension of $\mathcal{DLR}$ with functional dependencies and identification axioms) are a variant of external uniqueness axioms, constraining only the elements of a concept C; they can be expressed in $\mathcal{DLR}^+$ with the axiom:

$$[U^1]\sigma_{U_1:C} R_1 \downarrow \ldots \downarrow [U^h]\sigma_{U_h:C} R_h.$$

Path functional dependencies—as defined in the description logics family $\mathcal{CFD}$ [16]—can be expressed in $\mathcal{DLR}^+$ as identification axioms involving joined sequences of functional binary relations. $\mathcal{DLR}^+$ also captures the *tree-based identification constraints (tid)* introduced in [5] to express functional dependencies in $DL\text{-}Lite_{RDFS,tid}$.

The rich set of constructors in $\mathcal{DLR}^+$ allows us to extend the known mappings in description logics of popular conceptual database models, and to provide the foundations for their reasoning tasks. The EER mapping as introduced in [1] can be extended to deal with multi-attribute keys (by using identification axioms) and named roles in relations; the ORM mapping as introduced in [8,15] can be extended to deal with arbitrary subset and exclusive relation constructs (by using inclusions among global objectifications of projections of relations), arbitrary internal and external uniqueness constraints, arbitrary frequency constraints (by using projections), local objectification, named roles in relations, and fact type readings (by using renaming axioms); the UML mapping as introduced in [3] can be fixed to deal properly with association classes (by using local objectification) and named roles in associations.

Aside from conceptual modelling, $\mathcal{DLR}^+$ could be studied in relation to other tasks relevant for database scenarios, such as query answering [6], constraint checking with respect to a partially closed world (i.e., with DBoxes [13]), inconsistent database repairing, etc. In this paper, we focus just on the basic consistency and entailment reasoning tasks.

4   The $\mathcal{DLR}^{\pm}$ Fragment of $\mathcal{DLR}^+$

Since a $\mathcal{DLR}^+$ knowledge base can express inclusions and functional dependencies, the entailment problem is undecidable [7]. Thus, in this section we present $\mathcal{DLR}^{\pm}$, a decidable syntactic fragment of $\mathcal{DLR}^+$ limiting the coexistence of relation projections in a knowledge base.

Given a $\mathcal{DLR}^+$ knowledge base $\mathcal{KB} = (\mathcal{T}, \mathcal{A}, \mathfrak{R})$, we define the *projection signature of* $\mathcal{KB}$ as the set $\mathscr{S}$ containing the signatures $\tau(RN)$ of all relations $RN \in \mathcal{R}$, the singleton sets associated with each attribute name $U \in \mathcal{U}$, and the relation signatures that appear explicitly in projection constructs in some axiom from $\mathcal{T}$, together with their implicit occurrences due to the renaming schema. Formally, $\mathscr{S}$ is the smallest set such that (i) $\tau(RN) \in \mathscr{S}$ for all $RN \in \mathcal{R}$; (ii) $\{U\} \in \mathscr{S}$ for all $U \in \mathcal{U}$; and (iii) $\{U_1, \ldots, U_k\} \in \mathscr{S}$ for all $\pi^{\le q}_{\ge}[V_1, \ldots, V_k]R$ appearing as sub-formulas in $\mathcal{T}$ and $V_i \in [U_i]_{\mathfrak{R}}$ for $1 \le i \le k$.

The *projection signature graph* of $\mathcal{KB}$ is the directed acyclic graph corresponding to the Hasse diagram of $\mathcal{T}$ ordered by the proper subset relation $\supset$, whose sinks are the attribute singletons $\{U\}$. We call this graph $(\supset, \mathcal{T})$. Given a set of attributes $\tau = \{U_1, \ldots, U_k\} \subseteq \mathcal{U}$, the *projection signature graph dominated by* τ, denoted as $\mathcal{T}_\tau$, is the sub-graph of $(\supset, \mathcal{T})$ with τ as root and containing all the nodes reachable from τ. Given two sets of attributes $\tau_1, \tau_2 \subseteq \mathcal{U}$, PATH$_{\mathcal{T}}(\tau_1, \tau_2)$ denotes the set of paths in $(\supset, \mathcal{T})$ between τ_1 and τ_2. Note that, PATH$_{\mathcal{T}}(\tau_1, \tau_2) = \varnothing$ both when a path does not exist and when $\tau_1 \subseteq \tau_2$. The notation CHILD$_{\mathcal{T}}(\tau_1, \tau_2)$ means that τ_2 is a child (i.e., a direct descendant) of τ_1 in $(\supset, \mathcal{T})$. We now introduce $\mathcal{DLR}^{\pm}$ as follows.

Definition 3. *A $\mathcal{DLR}^{\pm}$ knowledge base is a $\mathcal{DLR}^{+}$ knowledge base that satisfies the following syntactic conditions:*

1. *the projection signature graph $(\supset, \mathcal{T})$ is a multitree: i.e., for every node $\tau \in \mathcal{T}$, the graph $\mathcal{T}_\tau$ is a tree; and*
2. *for every projection construct $\pi^{\leq q}[U_1, \ldots, U_k]R$ and every concept expression of the form $\exists^{\geq q}[U_1]R$ appearing in $\mathcal{T}$, if $q > 1$ then the length of the path PATH$_{\mathcal{T}}(\tau(R), \{U_1, \ldots, U_k\})$ is 1.*

The first condition in $\mathcal{DLR}^{\pm}$ restrict $\mathcal{DLR}^{+}$ in the way that multiple projections of relations may appear in a knowledge base: intuitively, there cannot be different projections sharing a common attribute. Moreover, observe that in $\mathcal{DLR}^{\pm}$ PATH$_{\mathcal{T}}$ is necessarily functional, due to the multitree restriction. By relaxing the first condition the language becomes undecidable, as we mentioned at the beginning of this Section. The second condition is also necessary to prove decidability of $\mathcal{DLR}^{\pm}$; however, we do not know whether this condition could be relaxed while preserving decidability.

Figure 4 shows that the projection signature graph of the knowledge base from Example 1 is indeed a multitree. Note that in the figure we have collapsed

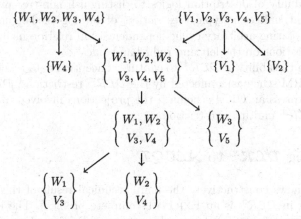

Fig. 4. The projection signature graph of Example 1.

equivalent attributes in a unique equivalence class, according to the renaming schema. Furthermore, since all its projection constructs have $q = 1$, this knowledge base belongs to $\mathcal{DLR}^{\pm}$.

$\mathcal{DLR}$ is included in $\mathcal{DLR}^{\pm}$, since the projection signature graph of any $\mathcal{DLR}$ knowledge base is always a degenerate multitree with maximum depth equal to 1. Not all the database constraints as introduced in Sect. 3 can be directly expressed in $\mathcal{DLR}^{\pm}$. While functional dependency and key axioms can be expressed directly in $\mathcal{DLR}^{\pm}$, equijoins, external uniqueness axioms, and identification axioms introduce projections of a relation which share common attributes, thus violating the multitree restriction. For example, the axioms for capturing an equijoin between two relations, R_1, R_2 would generate a projection signature graph with the signatures of R_1, R_2 as projections of the signature of the join relation R sharing the attribute on which the join is performed, thus violating condition 1.

However, in $\mathcal{DLR}^{\pm}$ it is still possible to reason over both external uniqueness and identification axioms by encoding them into a set of saturated ABoxes (as originally proposed in [4]) and check whether there is a saturation that satisfies the constraints. Therefore, we can conclude that $\mathcal{DLR}_{ifd}$ extended with unary functional dependencies is included in $\mathcal{DLR}^{\pm}$, provided that projections of relations in the knowledge base form a multitree projection signature graph. Since (unary) functional dependencies are expressed via the inclusions of projections of relations, by constraining the projection signature graph to be a multitree, the possibility to build combinations of functional dependencies as the ones in [4] leading to undecidability is ruled out.

Note that the *non-conflicting keys* sufficient condition guaranteeing the decidability of inclusion dependencies and keys of [12] is in conflict with our more restrictive requirement: indeed [12] allow for overlapping projections, but the considered datalog language is not comparable to $\mathcal{DLR}^{+}$. In general, description logic based languages, such as $\mathcal{DLR}^{+}$, and datalog based languages, such as the language proposed in [12], are incomparable in terms of expressiveness, due to the inability of description logics to distinguish non-tree models in the TBox. Note that, unlike the typical restrictions of datalog-like languages, there is no problem in stating arbitrary cyclic dependencies in relation inclusion axioms involving projections on the left and right hand sides.

Concerning the ability of $\mathcal{DLR}^{\pm}$ to capture conceptual data models, only the mapping of ORM schemas is affected by the $\mathcal{DLR}^{\pm}$ restrictions: $\mathcal{DLR}^{\pm}$ is able to correctly express an ORM schema if the projections involved in the schema satisfy the $\mathcal{DLR}^{\pm}$ multitree restriction.

5 Mapping $\mathcal{DLR}^{\pm}$ to $\mathcal{ALCQI}$

This section shows constructively the main technical result of this paper, i.e., that reasoning in $\mathcal{DLR}^{\pm}$ is an EXPTIME-complete problem. The lower bound is clear by observing that $\mathcal{DLR}$ is a sublanguage of $\mathcal{DLR}^{\pm}$. More challenging is the upper bound obtained by providing a mapping from $\mathcal{DLR}^{\pm}$ knowledge bases to $\mathcal{ALCQI}$ knowledge bases—a propositionally complete description logic with qualified number restrictions $\exists^{\geqslant q} R.\, C$, and inverse roles R^- (see [2] for more details). We adapt and extend the mapping presented for $\mathcal{DLR}$ in [6], with the modifications proposed by [10] to deal with ABoxes without the unique name assumption.

We recall that the renaming schema $\Re$ does not play any role since we assumed that a $\mathcal{DLR}^{\pm}$ knowledge base is rewritten by choosing a single canonical representative for each equivalence class of attributes induced by $\Re$. Thus, we consider $\mathcal{DLR}^{\pm}$ knowledge bases as pairs of TBox and ABox axioms.

$$
\begin{aligned}
(\neg C)^{\dagger} &= \neg C^{\dagger} \\
(C_1 \sqcap C_2)^{\dagger} &= C_1^{\dagger} \sqcap C_2^{\dagger} \\
(\exists^{\geqslant q}[U_i]R)^{\dagger} &= \begin{cases} \exists^{\geqslant q}\big(\mathrm{PATH}_{\mathscr{G}}(\tau(R),\{U_i\})^{\dagger}\big)^-.\, R^{\dagger}, & \text{if } \mathrm{PATH}_{\mathscr{G}}(\tau(R),\{U_i\}) \neq \varnothing \\ \bot, & \text{otherwise} \end{cases} \\
(\circledcirc R)^{\dagger} &= R^{\dagger} \\
(\odot RN)^{\dagger} &= A_{RN}^{l} \\[4pt]
(R_1 \backslash R_2)^{\dagger} &= R_1^{\dagger} \sqcap \neg R_2^{\dagger} \\
(R_1 \sqcap R_2)^{\dagger} &= R_1^{\dagger} \sqcap R_2^{\dagger} \\
(R_1 \sqcup R_2)^{\dagger} &= \begin{cases} R_1^{\dagger} \sqcup R_2^{\dagger}, & \text{if } \tau(R_1)=\tau(R_2) \\ \bot, & \text{otherwise} \end{cases} \\
(\sigma_{U_i:C}R)^{\dagger} &= \begin{cases} R^{\dagger} \sqcap \forall \mathrm{PATH}_{\mathscr{G}}(\tau(R),\{U_i\})^{\dagger}.\, C^{\dagger}, & \text{if } \mathrm{PATH}_{\mathscr{G}}(\tau(R),\{U_i\}) \neq \varnothing \\ \bot, & \text{otherwise} \end{cases} \\
(\pi^{\leqslant q}[U_1,\dots,U_k]R)^{\dagger} &= \begin{cases} \exists^{\geqslant 1,\leqslant q}\big(\mathrm{PATH}_{\mathscr{G}}(\tau(R),\{U_1,\dots,U_k\})^{\dagger}\big)^-.\, R^{\dagger}, \\ \qquad\qquad \text{if } \mathrm{PATH}_{\mathscr{G}}(\tau(R),\{U_1,\dots,U_k\}) \neq \varnothing \\ \bot, \qquad\qquad \text{otherwise} \end{cases}
\end{aligned}
$$

Fig. 5. The mapping to $\mathcal{ALCQI}$ for concept and relation expressions.

We first introduce a mapping function $\cdot^{\dagger}$ from $\mathcal{DLR}^{\pm}$ concepts and relations to $\mathcal{ALCQI}$ concepts. The function $\cdot^{\dagger}$ maps each concept name CN and each relation name RN appearing in the $\mathcal{DLR}^{\pm}$ KB to the $\mathcal{ALCQI}$ concept names CN and A_{RN}, respectively. The latter can be informally understood as the "global" reification of RN. For each relation name RN, the $\mathcal{ALCQI}$ signature also includes a concept name A_{RN}^{l} and a role name Q_{RN} to capture local objectification. The mapping $\cdot^{\dagger}$ is extended to concept and relation expressions as illustrated in Fig. 5, where the notation $\exists^{\geqslant 1,\leqslant q} R.\, C$ is a shortcut for the conjunction $\exists R.\, C \sqcap \exists^{\leqslant q} R.\, C$.

The mapping crucially uses the projection signature graph to map projections and selections, by accessing paths in the projection signature graph $(\supset, \mathscr{T})$ associated to the $\mathcal{DLR}^{\pm}$ KB. If there is a path $\mathrm{PATH}_{\mathscr{G}}(\tau,\tau') = \tau, \tau_1, \dots, \tau_n, \tau'$

from τ to τ' in $\mathscr{T}$, then the $\mathcal{ALCQI}$ signature contains role names $Q_{\tau'}, Q_{\tau_i}$, for $i = 1, \ldots, n$, and the following role chain expression is generated by the mapping:

$$\mathrm{PATH}_{\mathscr{T}}(\tau, \tau')^{\dagger} = Q_{\tau_1} \circ \ldots \circ Q_{\tau_n} \circ Q_{\tau'},$$

In particular, the mapping uses the following notation: the inverse role chain $(R_1 \circ \ldots \circ R_n)^-$, for R_i a role name, stands for the chain $R_n^- \circ \ldots \circ R_1^-$, with R_i^- an inverse role, the expression $\exists^{\leq 1} R_1 \circ \ldots \circ R_n.C$ stands for the $\mathcal{ALCQI}$ concept expression $\exists^{\leq 1} R_1. \ldots .\exists^{\leq 1} R_n.C$ and $\forall R_1 \circ \ldots \circ R_n.C$ for the $\mathcal{ALCQI}$ concept expression $\forall R_1. \ldots .\forall R_n.C$. Thus, since $\mathcal{DLR}^{\pm}$ restricts to $q = 1$ the cardinalities on any path of length strictly greater than 1 (see condition 2 in Definition 3), the above notation shows that we remain within the $\mathcal{ALCQI}$ syntax when the mapping applies to cardinalities. If, e.g., we need to map the $\mathcal{DLR}^{\pm}$ cardinality constraint $\exists^{\leq q}[U_i]R$ with $q > 1$, then, to stay within the $\mathcal{ALCQI}$ syntax, U_i must not be mentioned in any other projection in such a way that $|\mathrm{PATH}_{\mathscr{T}}(\tau(R), \{U_i\})| = 1$. Finally, notice that the mapping introduces a concept name $A_{RN}^{\tau_i}$ for each projected signature τ_i in the projection signature graph dominated by $\tau(RN)$, i.e., $\tau_i \in \mathscr{T}_{\tau(RN)}$, informally to capture the global reifications of the various projections of RN in the given KB. We also use the shortcut A_{RN} which stands for $A_{RN}^{\tau(RN)}$.

Intuitively, each node in the projection signature graph associated to a $\mathcal{DLR}^{\pm}$ KB denotes a relation projection and the mapping reifies each of these projections. The target $\mathcal{ALCQI}$ signature resulting from mapping the $\mathcal{DLR}^{\pm}$ KB of Example 1 is partially presented in Fig. 6, together with the projection signature graph (showed in Fig. 4). Each node of the graph is labelled with the corresponding global reification concept $(A_{R_i}^{\tau_j})$, for each $R_i \in \mathcal{R}$ and each projected signature

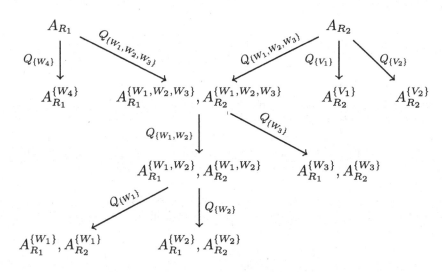

Fig. 6. The $\mathcal{ALCQI}$ signature generated by $\mathcal{T}_{\mathsf{exa}}$.

τ_j in the projection signature graph dominated by $\tau(R_i)$, while the edges are labelled by the roles (Q_{τ_i}) needed for the reification.

To better clarify the need for the path function in the mapping, notice that each $\mathcal{DLR}^\pm$ relation is reified according to the decomposition dictated by the projection signature graph it dominates. Thus, to access, e.g., an attribute U_j of a $\mathcal{DLR}^\pm$ relation R_i it is necessary to follow the path through the projections that use the attribute. Such a path, from the node denoting the whole signature of the relation, $\tau(R_i)$, to the node denoting the attribute U_j is returned by the PATH$_{\mathscr{G}}(\tau(R_i), U_j)$ function. For example, considering the example in Fig. 6, to access the attribute W_1 of the relation R_2 in the expression $(\sigma_{W_1:C} R_2)$, the mapping of the path PATH$_{\mathscr{G}}(\tau(R_2), \{W_1\})^\dagger$ is equal to the role chain $Q_{\{W_1,W_2,W_3\}} \circ Q_{\{W_1,W_2\}} \circ Q_{\{W_1\}}$, so that $(\sigma_{W_1:C} R_2)^\dagger = A_{R_2} \sqcap \forall Q_{\{W_1,W_2,W_3\}} . \forall Q_{\{W_1,W_2\}} . \forall Q_{\{W_1\}} . C$. Similar considerations can be done when mapping cardinalities over relation projections.

Figures 7 and 8 present in details the mapping of a $\mathcal{DLR}^\pm$ KB into a KB in $\mathcal{ALCQI}$. Let $\mathcal{KB} = (\mathcal{T}, \mathcal{A})$ be a $\mathcal{DLR}^\pm$ KB with signature $(\mathcal{C}, \mathcal{R}, \mathcal{O}, \mathcal{U}, \tau)$. The mapping $\gamma(\mathcal{KB})$ is assumed to be unsatisfiable (i.e., it contains the axiom $\top \sqsubseteq \bot$) if the ABox contains the relation assertion $RN(t)$ with $\tau(RN) \neq \tau(t)$, for some relation $RN \in \mathcal{R}$ and some tuple t. Otherwise, $\gamma(\mathcal{KB}) = (\gamma(\mathcal{T}), \gamma(\mathcal{A}))$ defines the mapped $\mathcal{ALCQI}$ KB.

Intuitively, γ_{dsj} ensures that relations with different signatures are disjoint, thus, e.g., enforcing the union compatibility. The axioms in γ_{rel} introduce classical reification axioms for each relation and its relevant projections. The axioms in γ_{lobj} make sure that each local objectification differs from the global one while each role Q_{RN} defines a bijection.

To translate the ABox, we first map each individual $o \in \mathcal{O}$ in the $\mathcal{DLR}^\pm$ ABox $\mathcal{A}$ to an $\mathcal{ALCQI}$ individual o. Each tuple in relation instance axioms occurring in $\mathcal{A}$ is mapped via an injective function ξ to a distinct individual. That is,

$$\gamma(\mathcal{T}) = \gamma_{dsj} \cup \bigcup_{RN \in \mathcal{R}} \gamma_{rel}(RN) \cup \bigcup_{RN \in \mathcal{R}} \gamma_{lobj}(RN) \cup$$

$$\bigcup_{C_1 \sqsubseteq C_2 \in \mathcal{KB}} C_1^\dagger \sqsubseteq C_2^\dagger \cup \bigcup_{R_1 \sqsubseteq R_2 \in \mathcal{KB}} R_1^\dagger \sqsubseteq R_2^\dagger$$

$$\gamma_{dsj} = \{A_{RN_1}^{\tau_i} \sqsubseteq \neg A_{RN_2}^{\tau_j} \mid RN_1, RN_2 \in \mathcal{R},$$

$$\tau_i \in \mathscr{T}_{\tau(RN_1)}, \tau_j \in \mathscr{T}_{\tau(RN_2)}, |\tau_i| \geqslant 2, |\tau_j| \geqslant 2, \tau_i \neq \tau_j\}$$

$$\gamma_{rel}(RN) = \bigcup_{\tau_i \in \mathscr{T}_{\tau(RN)}} \bigcup_{\text{CHILD}_{\mathscr{G}}(\tau_i, \tau_j)} \{A_{RN}^{\tau_i} \sqsubseteq \exists Q_{\tau_j} . A_{RN}^{\tau_j}, \exists^{\geqslant 2} Q_{\tau_j} . \top \sqsubseteq \bot\}$$

$$\gamma_{lobj}(RN) = \{A_{RN} \sqsubseteq \exists Q_{RN} . A_{RN}^l, \exists^{\geqslant 2} Q_{RN} . \top \sqsubseteq \bot,$$
$$A_{RN}^l \sqsubseteq \exists Q_{RN}^- . A_{RN}, \exists^{\geqslant 2} Q_{RN}^- . \top \sqsubseteq \bot\}.$$

Fig. 7. The mapping into a $\mathcal{ALCQI}$ KB.

$$\gamma(\mathcal{A}) = \{CN^\dagger(o) \mid CN(o) \in \mathcal{A}\} \cup \tag{4}$$

$$\{o_1 \neq o_2 \mid o_1 \neq o_2 \in \mathcal{A}\} \cup \{o_1 = o_2 \mid o_1 = o_2 \in \mathcal{A}\} \cup \tag{5}$$

$$\{A_{RN}^{\tau_i}(\xi(t[\tau_i])) \mid RN(t) \in \mathcal{A} \text{ and } \tau_i \in \mathscr{T}_{\tau(RN)}\} \cup \tag{6}$$

$$\{Q_{\tau_j}(\xi(t[\tau_i]), \xi(t[\tau_j])) \mid RN(t) \in \mathcal{A}, \tau_i \in \mathscr{T}_{\tau(RN)} \text{ and } \text{CHILD}_\mathscr{G}(\tau_i, \tau_j)\} \cup \tag{7}$$

$$\{Q_o(o) \mid o \in \mathcal{O}\} \cup \tag{8}$$

$$\{Q_t(o_1) \mid t = \langle U_1{:}o_1, \dots, U_n{:}o_n \rangle \text{ occurs in } \mathcal{A}\}. \tag{9}$$

Fig. 8. The mapping $\gamma(\mathcal{A})$

$\xi : T_\mathcal{O}(\mathcal{U}) \to \mathcal{O}_{\mathcal{ALCQI}}$, with $\mathcal{O}_{\mathcal{ALCQI}} = \mathcal{O} \cup \mathcal{O}^t$ being the set of individual names in $\gamma(\mathcal{KB})$, $\mathcal{O} \cap \mathcal{O}^t = \varnothing$ and

$$\xi(t) = \begin{cases} o \in \mathcal{O}, & \text{if } t = \langle U{:}o \rangle \\ o \in \mathcal{O}^t, & \text{otherwise.} \end{cases}$$

Following [10], the mapping $\gamma(\mathcal{A})$ in Fig. 8 introduces a new concept name Q_o for each individual $o \in \mathcal{O}$ and a new concept name Q_t for each relation instance t occurring in $\mathcal{A}$, with each Q_t restricted as follows:

$$Q_t \sqsubseteq \exists^{\leqslant 1}\big(\text{PATH}_\mathscr{G}(\tau(t), \{U_1\})^\dagger\big)^-.$$
$$\exists\big(\text{PATH}_\mathscr{G}(\tau(t), \{U_2\})^\dagger\big).Q_{o_2} \sqcap \dots \sqcap \exists\big(\text{PATH}_\mathscr{G}(\tau(t), \{U_n\})^\dagger\big).Q_{o_n}$$

Intuitively, (6) and (7) reify each relation instance axiom occurring in $\mathcal{A}$ using the projection signature of the involved tuple itself. The Formulas (8) and (9) together with the axioms for concepts Q_t guarantee that there is exactly one $\mathcal{ALCQI}$ individual reifying a given tuple in a relation instance axiom. Clearly, the size of $\gamma(\mathcal{KB})$ is polynomial in the size of $\mathcal{KB}$ under the same coding of the numerical parameters.

We are now able to state our main technical result.

Theorem 4. *A $\mathcal{DLR}^\pm$ knowledge base $\mathcal{KB}$ is satisfiable iff the $\mathcal{ALCQI}$ knowledge base $\gamma(\mathcal{KB})$ is satisfiable.*

As a direct consequence of this theorem and the fact that $\mathcal{DLR}$ is a sublanguage of $\mathcal{DLR}^\pm$, we obtain the following corollary.

Corollary 5. *Reasoning in $\mathcal{DLR}^\pm$ is ExpTime-complete.*

6   Implementation of a $\mathcal{DLR}^\pm$ API

We have implemented the framework discussed in this paper. DLRtoOWL is a Java library fully implementing $\mathcal{DLR}^\pm$ reasoning services. The library is based on the tool ANTLR4 to parse serialised input, and on OWLAPI4 for the OWL2 encoding, and it includes the OWL reasoner JFact. DLRtoOWL provides a Java

$\mathcal{DLR}$ API package to allow developers to create, manipulate, serialise, and reason with $\mathcal{DLR}^{\pm}$ knowledge bases in their Java-based application, extending in a compatible way the standard OWL API with the $\mathcal{DLR}^{\pm}$ TELL and ASK services.

During the development of this new library we strongly focused on performance. Since the OWL encoding is only possible if we have already built the $\mathcal{ALCQI}$ projection signature multitree, in principle the program should perform two parsing rounds: one to create the multitree and the other one to generate the OWL mapping. We faced this issue using dynamic programming: during the first (and only) parsing round we store in a data structure each axiom that we want to translate in OWL and, after building the multitree, by the dynamic programming technique we build on-the-fly a Java class which generates the required axioms.

We have used the $\mathcal{DLR}^{\pm}$ API within a plugin for general ontology reasoning for conceptual design tools based on languages such as EER, UML (with OCL), and ORM (with derivation rules) [14]. This plugin supports the detection of inconsistencies, redundancies, complete derivations of the strictest implicit constructs and unexpected behaviours. Reasoning helps the modeller to detect relevant formal properties of the ontology that may be undetected during the modelling phase, which give rise to design quality degradation and/or increased development times and costs. The system is still at an early stage of completion, but it has been proved to be highly effective and efficient: indeed, it computes derivations in real time in the background while the ontology is being designed.

7 Conclusions

We have introduced the very expressive $\mathcal{DLR}^{+}$ description logic, which extends $\mathcal{DLR}$ with database oriented constraints. $\mathcal{DLR}^{+}$ is expressive enough to cover directly and more thoroughly the EER, UML, and ORM conceptual data models, among others. Although reasoning in $\mathcal{DLR}^{+}$ is undecidable, we show that a simple syntactic constraint on KBs restores decidability. In fact, the resulting logic $\mathcal{DLR}^{\pm}$ has the same complexity (EXPTIME-complete) as the basic $\mathcal{DLR}$ language. In other words, handling database constraints does not increase the complexity of reasoning in the logic. To enhance the use and adoption of $\mathcal{DLR}^{\pm}$, we have developed an API that fully implements reasoning for this language, and maps input knowledge bases into OWL. Using a standard OWL reasoner, we are able to provide a variety of $\mathcal{DLR}^{\pm}$ reasoning services.

We plan to investigate the problem of query answering under $\mathcal{DLR}^{\pm}$ ontologies and to check whether the complexity for this problem can be lifted from known results in $\mathcal{DLR}$ to $\mathcal{DLR}^{\pm}$.

References

1. Artale, A., Calvanese, D., Kontchakov, R., Ryzhikov, V., Zakharyaschev, M.: Reasoning over extended ER models. In: Parent, C., Schewe, K.-D., Storey, V.C., Thalheim, B. (eds.) ER 2007. LNCS, vol. 4801, pp. 277–292. Springer, Heidelberg (2007). doi:10.1007/978-3-540-75563-0_20

2. Baader, F., Calvanese, D., McGuinness, D., Nardi, D., Patel-Schneider, P.F. (eds.): The Description Logic Handbook: Theory Implementation and Applications. Cambridge University Press, New York (2003)
3. Berardi, D., Calvanese, D., De Giacomo, G.: Reasoning on UML class diagrams. Artif. Intell. **168**(1–2), 70–118 (2005)
4. Calvanese, D., De Giacomo, G., Lenzerini, M.: Identification constraints and functional dependencies in description logics. In: Proceedings of the Seventeenth International Joint Conference on Artificial Intelligence, IJCAI 2001, pp. 155–160. Morgan Kaufmann (2001)
5. Calvanese, D., Fischl, W., Pichler, R., Sallinger, E., Simkus, M.: Capturing relational schemas and functional dependencies in RDFS. In: Proceedings of the 28th AAAI Conference on Artificial Intelligence (AAAI), pp. 1003–1011. AAAI Press (2014)
6. Calvanese, D., Giacomo, G.D., Lenzerini, M.: Conjunctive query containment and answering under description logic constraints. ACM Trans. Comput. Logic **9**(3), 22:1–22:31 (2008)
7. Chandra, A.K., Vardi, M.Y.: The implication problem for functional and inclusion dependencies is undecidable. SIAM J. Comput. **14**(3), 671–677 (1985)
8. Franconi, E., Mosca, A., Solomakhin, D.: ORM2: formalisation and encoding in OWL2. In: International Workshop on Fact-Oriented Modeling (ORM 2012), pp. 368–378 (2012)
9. Halpin, T., Morgan, T.: Information Modeling and Relational Databases, 2nd edn. Morgan Kaufmann, San Francisco (2008)
10. Horrocks, I., Sattler, U., Tessaris, S., Tobies, S.: How to decide query containment under constraints using a description logic. In: Parigot, M., Voronkov, A. (eds.) LPAR 2000. LNAI, vol. 1955, pp. 326–343. Springer, Heidelberg (2000). doi:10. 1007/3-540-44404-1_21
11. Kanellakis, P.C.: Elements of relational database theory. In: Meyer, A., Nivat, M., Paterson, M., Perrin, D., van Leeuwen, J. (eds.) The Handbook of Theoretical Computer Science, vol. B, Chap. 17, pp. 1075–1144. North Holland (1990)
12. Lukasiewicz, T., Cali, A., Gottlob, G.: A general datalog-based framework for tractable query answering over ontologies. Web Semant. Sci. Serv. Agents World Wide Web **14**, 57–83 (2012)
13. Patel-Schneider, P.F., Franconi, E.: Ontology constraints in incomplete and complete data. In: Cudré-Mauroux, P., et al. (eds.) ISWC 2012. LNCS, vol. 7649, pp. 444–459. Springer, Heidelberg (2012). doi:10.1007/978-3-642-35176-1_28
14. Sportelli, F.: NORMA: A software for intelligent conceptual modeling. In: Proceedings of the Joint Ontology Workshops 2016 (JOWO-2016) (2016). http://ceurws.org/Vol-1660/demo-paper3.pdf
15. Sportelli, F., Franconi, E.: Formalisation of ORM derivation rules and their mapping into OWL. In: Debruyne, C., Panetto, H., Meersman, R., Dillon, T., Kühn, E., O'Sullivan, D., Ardagna, C.A. (eds.) OTM 2016. LNCS, vol. 10033, pp. 827–843. Springer, Heidelberg (2016)
16. Toman, D., Weddell, G.E.: Applications and extensions of PTIME description logics with functional constraints. In: Proceedings of the 21st International Joint Conference on Artificial Intelligence, IJCAI 2009, pp. 948–954 (2009)

Improving Visual Relationship Detection
Using Semantic Modeling of Scene Descriptions

Stephan Baier[1(⊠)], Yunpu Ma[1,2], and Volker Tresp[1,2]

[1] Ludwig Maximilian University, 80538 Munich, Germany
stephan.baier@campus.lmu.de
[2] Siemens AG, Corporate Technology, Munich, Germany
{yunpu.ma,volker.tresp}@siemens.com

Abstract. Structured scene descriptions of images are useful for the automatic processing and querying of large image databases. We show how the combination of a statistical semantic model and a visual model can improve on the task of mapping images to their associated scene description. In this paper we consider scene descriptions which are represented as a set of triples (*subject, predicate, object*), where each triple consists of a pair of visual objects, which appear in the image, and the relationship between them (e.g. *man-riding-elephant, man-wearing-hat*). We combine a standard visual model for object detection, based on convolutional neural networks, with a latent variable model for link prediction. We apply multiple state-of-the-art link prediction methods and compare their capability for visual relationship detection. One of the main advantages of link prediction methods is that they can also generalize to triples which have never been observed in the training data. Our experimental results on the recently published Stanford Visual Relationship dataset, a challenging real world dataset, show that the integration of a statistical semantic model using link prediction methods can significantly improve visual relationship detection. Our combined approach achieves superior performance compared to the state-of-the-art method from the Stanford computer vision group.

Keywords: Visual relationship detection · Knowledge graph · Link prediction

1   Introduction

Extracting semantic information from unstructured data, such as images or text, is a key challenge in artificial intelligence. Semantic knowledge in a machine-readable form is crucial for many applications such as search, semantic querying and question answering.

Novel computer vision algorithms, mostly based on convolutional neural networks (CNN), have enormously advanced over the last years. Standard applications are image classification and, more recently, also the detection of objects

© Springer International Publishing AG 2017
C. d'Amato et al. (Eds.): ISWC 2017, Part I, LNCS 10587, pp. 53–68, 2017.
DOI: 10.1007/978-3-319-68288-4_4

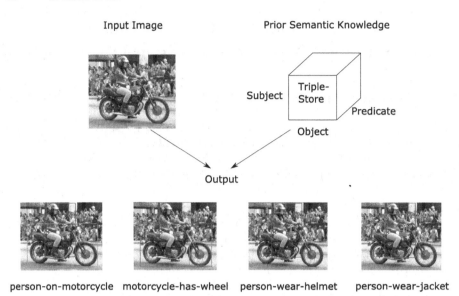

person-on-motorcycle   motorcycle-has-wheel   person-wear-helmet   person-wear-jacket

Fig. 1. The input to the model is a raw image. In combination with a semantic prior we generate triples, which describe the scene.

in images. However, the semantic expressiveness of image descriptions that consist simply of a set of objects is rather limited. Semantics is captured in more meaningful ways by the relationships between objects. In particular, visual relationships can be represented by triples of the form (*subject, predicate, object*), where two entities appearing in an image are linked through a relation (e.g. *man-riding-elephant, man-wearing-hat*).

Extracting triples, i.e. visual relationships, from raw images is a challenging task, which has been a focus in the Semantic Web community for some time [2–4,27,32,38] and recently also gained substantial attention in main stream computer vision [6,7,18,25]. First approaches used a single classifier, which takes an image as input and outputs a complete triple [7,25]. However, these approaches do not scale to datasets with many object types and relationships, due to the exploding combinatorial complexity. Recently, [18] proposed a method which classifies the visual objects and their relationships in independent preprocessing steps, and then derives a prediction score for the entire triple. This approach was applied to the extraction of triples from a large number of potential triples. In the same paper, the first large-scale dataset for visual relationship extraction was published.

The statistical modeling of graph-structured knowledge bases, often referred to as knowledge graphs, has recently gained growing interest. The most popular approaches learn embeddings for the entities and relations in the knowledge graph. Based on the embeddings a likelihood for a triple can be derived. This approach has mainly been used for link prediction, which tries to predict missing triples in a knowledge graph. A recent review paper can be found in [20].

In the approach described in this paper, statistical knowledge base models, which can infer the likelihood of a triple, are used to support the task of visual link prediction. For example if the visual model detects a motorbike, it is very likely that the triple *motorbike-has_part-wheel* is true, as all motorbikes have wheels. We suggest that integrating such prior knowledge can improve various computer vision tasks. In particular, we propose to combine the likelihood from a statistical semantic model with a visual model to enhance the prediction of image triples.

Figure 1 illustrates our approach. The model takes as input a raw image and combines it with a semantic prior, which is derived from the training data. Both types of information are fused, to predict the output, which consists of relevant bounding boxes and a set of triples describing the scene.

For combining the semantic prior with the visual model we employ a probabilistic approach which can be divided into a semantic part and a visual part. We show how the semantic part of the probabilistic model can be implemented using standard link prediction methods and the visual part using recently developed computer vision algorithms.

We train our semantic model by using absolute frequencies from the training data, describing how often a triple appears in the training data. By applying a latent variable model, we are able to also generalize to unseen or rarely seen triples, which still have a high likelihood of being true, due to their similarity to other likely triples. For example if we frequently observe the triple *person-ride-motorcycle* in the training data we can generalize also to a high likelihood for *person-ride-bike* due to the similarity between *motorcycle* and *bike*, even if the triple *person-ride-bike* has not been observed or just rarely been observed in the training data. The similarity of *motorcycle* and *bike* can be derived from other triples, which describe, for example, that both have a *wheel* and both have a *handlebar*.

We conduct experiments on the Stanford Visual Relationship dataset recently published by [18]. We evaluate different model variants on the task of predicting semantic triples and the corresponding bounding boxes of the subject and object entities detected in the image. Our experiments show, that including the semantic model improves on the state-of-the-art result in the task of mapping images to their associated triples.

The paper is structured as follows. Section 2 gives an overview of the state-of-the-art link prediction models, the employed computer vision techniques and related work. Section 3 describes the semantic and the visual part of our model and how both can be combined in a probabilistic framework. In Sect. 4 we show a number of different experiments. Finally, we conclude our work with Sect. 5.

2   Background and Related Work

Our proposed model joins ideas from two areas, computer vision and statistical relational learning for semantic modeling. Both fields have developed rapidly in recent years. In this chapter we discuss relevant work from both areas.

2.1   Statistical Link Prediction

A number of statistical models have been proposed for modeling graph-structured knowledge bases often referred to as knowledge graphs. Most methods are designed for predicting missing links in the knowledge graph. A recent review on link prediction can be found in [20]. A knowledge graph $\mathcal{G}$ consists of a set of triples $\mathcal{G} = \{(s, p, o)_i\}_{i=1}^N \subseteq \mathcal{E} \times \mathcal{R} \times \mathcal{E}$. The entities $s, o \in \mathcal{E}$ are referred to as *subject* and *object* of the triple, and the relation between the entities $p \in \mathcal{R}$ is referred to as *predicate* of the triple.

Link prediction methods can be described by a function $\theta : \mathcal{E} \times \mathcal{R} \times \mathcal{E} \to \mathbb{R}$, which maps a triple (s, p, o) to a real valued score. The score of a triple $\theta(s, p, o)$ represents the likelihood of the triple being true. Most recently developed link prediction models learn a latent representation, also called embedding, for the entities and the relations. In the following we describe the link prediction methods, which are used in paper.

DistMult: DistMult [35] scores a triple by building the tri-linear dot product of the embeddings, such that

$$\theta(s, p, o) = \langle a(s), r(p), a(o) \rangle = \sum_j a(s)_j r(p)_j a(o)_j \tag{1}$$

where $a : \mathcal{E} \to \mathbb{R}^d$ maps entities to their latent vector representations and similarly $r : \mathcal{R} \to \mathbb{R}^d$ maps relations to their latent representations. The dimensionality d of the embeddings, also called rank, is a hyperparameter of the model.

ComplEx: ComplEx [33] extends DistMult to complex valued vectors for the embeddings of both, relations and entities. The score function is

$$\begin{aligned}
\theta(s, p, o) = Re(\langle a(s), r(p), \overline{a(o)} \rangle) = & \langle Re(a(s)), Re(r(p)), Re(a(o)) \rangle \\
& + \langle Im(a(s)), Re(r(p)), Im(a(o)) \rangle \\
& + \langle Re(a(s)), Im(r(p)), Im(a(o)) \rangle \\
& - \langle Im(a(s)), Im(r(p)), Re(a(o)) \rangle
\end{aligned} \tag{2}$$

where $a : \mathcal{E} \to \mathbb{C}^d$ and $r : \mathcal{R} \to \mathbb{C}^d$; $Re(\cdot)$ and $Im(\cdot)$ denote the real and imaginary part, respectively, and $\bar{\cdot}$ denotes the complex conjugate.

Multiway NN: The multiway neural network [8, 20] concatenates all embeddings and feeds them to a neural network of the form

$$\theta(s, p, o) = \left(\beta^T \tanh \left(A \left[a(s), r(p), a(o) \right] \right) \right) . \tag{3}$$

where $[\cdot, \cdot, \cdot]$ denotes the concatenation of the embeddings $a(s), r(p), a(o) \in \mathbb{R}^d$. A is a weight matrix and β a weight vector.

RESCAL: The tensor decomposition RESCAL [21] learns vector embeddings for entities and matrix embeddings for relations. The score function is

$$\theta(s, p, o) = a(s) \cdot R(p) \cdot a(o) \qquad (4)$$

with $\cdot$ denoting the dot product, $a : \mathcal{E} \to \mathbb{R}^d$ and $R : \mathcal{R} \to \mathbb{R}^{d \times d}$.

Typically, the models are trained using a ranking cost function [20]. For our task of visual relationship detection, we will train them slightly differently using a Poisson cost function for modeling count data, as we will show in Sect. 3.2. Another popular link prediction method is TransE [5], however it is not appropriate for modeling count data; thus we are not considering it in this work.

2.2 Image Classification and Object Detection

Computer vision methods for image classification and object detection have improved enormously over the last years. Convolutional neural networks (CNN), which apply convolutional filters in a hierarchical manner to an image, have become the standard for image classification. In this work we use the following two methods.

VGG: The VGG-network is a convolutional neural network, which has shown state-of-the-art performance at the Imagenet challenge [28]. It exists in two versions, i.e. the VGG-16 with 16 convolutional layers and VGG-19 with 19 convolutional layers.

RCNN: The region convolutional neural network (RCNN) [11] proposes regions, which show some visual objects in the image. It uses a selective search algorithm for getting candidate regions in an image [31]. The RCNN algorithm then rejects most of the regions based on a classification score. As a result, a small set of region proposals is derived. There are two extensions to RCNN, which are mainly faster and slightly more accurate [10,23]. However, in our experiments we use the original RCNN, for a fair comparison with [18]. Our focus is on improving visual relationship detection trough semantic modeling rather than on improving computer vision techniques.

2.3 Visual Relationship Detection

Visual relationship detection is about predicting triples from images, where the triples consist of two visual objects and the relationship between them. This is related to visual caption generation, which recently gained considerable popularity among the deep learning community, where an image caption, consisting of natural text, is generated given an image [16,17,34]. However, the output in visual relationship detection is more structured (a set of triples), and thus it is more appropriate for further processing, e.g. semantic querying. Related work on relational reasoning with images can also be found in visual question answering [1,15,26,39] and has also been subject to neural symbolic reasoning [27,38].

The extraction of semantic triples has also been successfully applied to text documents, e.g. the Google Knowledge Vault project for improving the Google Knowledge Graph [8].

Some earlier work on visual relationship detection was concerned with learning spatial relationships between objects, however with a very limited set of only four spatial relations [9,12]. Other related work attempted to learn actions and object interactions of humans in videos and images [13,19,22,24,36,37]. Full visual relationship detection has been demonstrated in [6,7,25], however, also with only small amounts of possible triples. In [6], an ontology over the visual concepts is defined and combined with a neural network approach to maintain semantic consistency.

The Stanford computer vision group proposed a scalable model and applied it to a large-scale dataset, with 700,000 possible triples. In their work, entities of the triples were detected separately and a joint score for each triple candidate was computed [18]. The visual module in [18] uses the following computer vision methods, which we will also use in our approach. An RCNN for object detection is used to derive candidate regions. Further, a VGG-16 is applied to the detected regions for obtaining object classification scores for each region. Finally, a second VGG, which classifies relationships, such as *taller-than*, *wears*, etc., is applied to the union of pairs of regions. The model also contains a language prior, which can model semantic relationships to some extend based on word embeddings. The language prior allows the model to generalize to unseen triples. However, our experiments show that integrating state-of-the-art link prediction methods for modeling semantics is more appropriate for improving general prediction and generalization to unseen triples.

3   Modeling Visual Relationships

In the following we describe our approach to jointly modeling images and their corresponding semantics.

3.1   Problem Description

We assume data consisting of images and corresponding triple sets. For each *subject s* of a triple (s, p, o) there exists a corresponding region i_s in the image. Similarly, each *object o* corresponds to an region i_o, and each *predicate p* to an

Fig. 2. The subject and object of the triple relate to two regions in the image, and the predicate relates to the union of the two regions.

Fig. 3. The pipeline for deriving a ranked list of triples is as follows: The image is passed to a RCNN, which generates region candidates. We build pairs of regions and predict a score for every triple, based on our ranking method. The visual part is similar to [18], however the ranking method is different as it includes a semantic model.

region i_p, which is the union of the regions i_s and i_o. Thus, one data sample can be represented as a six-tuple of the form (i_s, i_p, i_o, s, p, o). Figure 2 shows an example of a triple and its corresponding bounding boxes. During training, all triples and their corresponding areas are observed. After model training the task is to predict the most likely tuples (i_s, i_p, i_o, s, p, o) for a given image. Figure 3 shows the processing pipeline of our method, which takes a raw image as an input, and outputs a ranked list of triples and bounding boxes.

3.2   Semantic Model

In contrast to typical knowledge graph modeling, we do not only have one global graph $\mathcal{G}$, but an instance of a knowledge graph $\mathcal{G}_i$ for every image i. Each triple which appears in a certain image can be described as a tuple (s, p, o, i). The link prediction model shall reflect the likelihood of a triple to appear in a graph instance, as a prior without seeing the image. By summing over the occurrences in the i-th dimension, we derive the absolute frequency of triples (s, p, o) in the training data, which we denote as $y_{s,p,o}$. We aim to model $y_{s,p,o}$ using the link prediction methods described in Sect. 2.1. As we are dealing with count data, we assume a Poisson distribution on the model output $\theta(s, p, o)$. The log-likelihood for a triple is

$$\log p(y_{s,p,o}|(s,p,o), \Theta) = y_{s,p,o} \log \eta(\theta(s,p,o)) - \eta(\theta(s,p,o)) - \log(y_{s,p,o}!), \quad (5)$$

where Θ are the model parameters of the link prediction method and η is the parameter for the Poisson distribution, namely

$$\eta(\theta(s,p,o)) = \exp(\theta(s,p,o)). \quad (6)$$

We train the model by minimizing the negative log-likelihood. In the objective function the last term $\log(y_{s,p,o}!)$ can be neglected, as it does not depend on the model parameters. Thus the cost function for the whole training dataset becomes

$$cost = \sum_{(s,p,o)} \eta(\theta(s,p,o)) - y_{s,p,o} \log \eta(\theta(s,p,o)). \quad (7)$$

Using this framework, we can train any of the link prediction methods described in Sect. 2, by plugging the prediction into the cost function and minimizing the cost function using a gradient-descent based optimization algorithm. In this work we use Adam, a recently proposed first-order gradient-based optimization method with adaptive learning rate [14].

3.3 Visual Model

Our visual model is similar to the approach used in [18]. Figure 3 shows the involved steps. An image is first fed to an RCNN, which generates region proposals for a given image. The region proposals are represented as bounding boxes within the image. The visual model further consists of two convolutional neural networks (CNNs). The first CNN which we denote as CNN_e takes as input the subregion of the image defined by a bounding box and classifies entities from the set $\mathcal{E}$.

The second CNN, which we denote as CNN_r takes the union region of two bounding boxes as an input, and classifies the relationship from the set $\mathcal{R}$. While training, both CNNs use the regions (bounding boxes) provided in the training data.

For new images, we derive the regions from the RCNN. We build all possible pairs of regions, where each pair consists of a region i_s and i_o. We apply CNN_e to the regions, to derive the classification scores $CNN_e(s|i_s)$ and $CNN_e(o|i_o)$. Then the union of the regions i_s and i_o is fed to CNN_r to derive the score $CNN_r(p|i_p)$, where $i_p = union(i_s, i_o)$. Figure 2 shows an example of the bounding boxes of the *subject* and the *object*, as well as the union of the bounding boxes, which relates to the *predicate* of the triple.

3.4 Probabilistic Joint Model

In the last step of the pipeline in Fig. 3, which we denote as ranking step, we need to combine the scores from the visual model with the scores from the semantic model. For joining both, we propose a probabilistic model for the interaction between the visual and the semantic part. Figure 4 visualizes the joint model for all variables in a probabilistic graphical model. The joint distribution factors as

$$p(s, p, o, i_s, i_p, i_o) \propto \tilde{p}(s, p, o) \cdot \tilde{p}(i_s|s) \cdot \tilde{p}(i_p|p) \cdot \tilde{p}(i_o|o) \qquad (8)$$

with $\tilde{p}$ denoting unnormalized probabilities. We can divide the joint probability of Eq. (8) into two parts. The first part is $\tilde{p}(s, p, o)$, which models semantic triples. The second part is $\tilde{p}(i_s|s) \cdot \tilde{p}(i_p|p) \cdot \tilde{p}(i_o|o)$, which models the visual part given the semantics.

Following [29,30] we derive the unnormalized joint probability of the triples $\tilde{p}(s, p, o)$ using a Boltzmann distribution. With the energy function $E(s, p, o) = -\log \eta(\theta(s, p, o))$ the unnormalized probability for the triples becomes

$$\tilde{p}(s, p, o) = \eta(\theta(s, p, o)). \qquad (9)$$

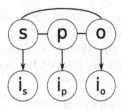

Fig. 4. The probabilistic graphical model describes the interaction between the visual and the semantic part for a given image. We assume the image regions i_s, i_p and i_o to be given by the RCNN and infer the underlying s, p, o triples.

The visual modules described in the previous section, model the unnormalized probabilities $\tilde{p}(s|i_s)$, $\tilde{p}(p|i_p)$, and $\tilde{p}(o|i_o)$. By applying Bayes rule to Eq. (8) and assuming equal probabilities for all image regions we get

$$p(s,p,o,i_s,i_p,i_o) \propto \tilde{p}(s,p,o) \cdot \frac{\tilde{p}(s|i_s) \cdot \tilde{p}(p|i_p) \cdot \tilde{p}(o|i_o)}{\tilde{p}(s) \cdot \tilde{p}(p) \cdot \tilde{p}(o)}. \tag{10}$$

The additional terms of the denominator $\tilde{p}(s)$, $\tilde{p}(p)$, $\tilde{p}(o)$ can be derived through marginalization of $\tilde{p}(s,p,o)$.

For each image, we derive the region candidates i_s, i_p, i_o from the RCNN. We do not have to normalize the probabilities as we are finally interested in a ranking of the most likely six-tuples (i_s, i_p, i_o, s, p, o) for a given image. The final unnormalized probability score on which we rank the tuples is

$$\tilde{p}(s,p,o,i_s,i_p,i_o) = \eta(\theta(s,p,o))\frac{CNN_e(s|i_s) \cdot CNN_r(p|i_p) \cdot CNN_e(o|i_o)}{\tilde{p}(s) \cdot \tilde{p}(p) \cdot \tilde{p}(o)}. \tag{11}$$

4   Experiments

We evaluate our proposed method on the recently published Stanford Visual Relationship dataset [18]. We compare our proposed method against the state-of-the-art method from [18] in the task of predicting semantic triples from images. As in [18] we will divide the setting into two parts: First an evaluation on how well the methods perform when predicting all possible triples and second only evaluating on triples, which did not occur in the training data. This setting is also referred to as zero-shot learning, as the model has not seen any training images containing the triples which are used for evaluation.

4.1   Dataset

The dataset consists of 5000 images. The semantics are described by triples, consisting of 100 entity types, such as *motorcycle, person, surfboard, watch*, etc. and 70 relation types, e.g. *next_to, taller_than, wear, on*, etc. The entities correspond to visual objects in the image. For all *subject* and *object* entities the corresponding regions in the image are given. Each image has in average 7.5 triples, which describe the scene. In total there are 37993 triples in the dataset. The dataset is split into 4000 training and 1000 test images. The data split is identical to the split in [18], thus we can directly compare our results. There are 1877 triples, which only occur in images from the test set but not in the training set.

4.2   Visual Relationship Detection

Experimental Setting. For doing visual relationship detection, we consider four different types of settings. Three of them are identical to the experimental settings in [18]. We add a fourth setting, which eliminates the evaluation of correctly detecting the bounding boxes, and solely evaluates the predicted triples. The four settings are as follows.

Phrase Detection: In phrase detection the task is to give a ranking of likely triples plus the corresponding regions for the *subject* and *object* of the triple. The bounding boxes are derived from the RCNN. Subsequently, we apply our ranking function (see Eq. (11)) to the pairs of objects, as shown in Fig. 3. A triple with its corresponding bounding boxes is considered correctly detected, if the triple is similar to the ground truth, and if the union of the bounding boxes has at least 50% overlap with the union of the ground truth bounding boxes.

Relationship Detection: The second setting, which is also considered in [18] is relationship detection. It is similar to phrase detection, but with the difference that it is not enough when the union of the bounding boxes is overlapping by at least 50%. Instead, both the bounding box of the *subject* and the bounding box of the *object* need at least 50% of overlap with their ground truth.

Triple Detection: We add a setting, which we call triple detection, which evaluates only the prediction of the triples. A triple is correct if it corresponds to the ground truth. The position of the predicted bounding boxes is not evaluated.

Predicate Detection: In predicate detection, it is assumed that *subject* and *object* are given, and only the correct *predicate* between both needs to be predicted. Therefore, we use the ground truth bounding boxes with the respective labels for the objects instead of the bounding boxes derived by the RCNN. This separates the problem of object detection from the problem of predicting relationships.

For each test image, we create a ranked list of triples. Similar to [18] we report the recall at the top 100 elements of the ranked list and the recall at top 50. Note, that there are 700000 possible triples, out of which the correct triples need to be ranked on top.

When training the semantic model, we hold out 5% of the nonzero triples as a validation set. We determine the optimal rank for the link prediction methods based on that hold-out set. For the visual model (RCNN and VGG) we use a pretrained model provided by [18].

Table 1. Results for visual relationship detection. We report recall at 50 and 100 for four different validation settings.

Task evaluation	Phrase det.		Rel. det.		Predicate det.		Triple det.	
	R@100	R@50	R@100	R@50	R@100	R@50	R@100	R@50
Lu et al. V [18]	2.61	2.24	1.85	1.58	7.11	7.11	2.68	2.30
Lu et al. full [18]	17.03	16.17	14.70	13.86	47.87	47.87	18.11	17.11
RESCAL	19.17	18.16	16.88	15.88	52.71	52.71	20.23	19.13
MultiwayNN	18.88	17.75	16.65	15.57	51.82	51.82	19.76	18.53
ComplEx	19.36	18.25	17.12	16.03	53.14	53.14	20.23	19.06
DistMult	15.42	14.27	13.64	12.54	42.18	42.18	16.14	14.94

Results. Table 1 shows the results for visual relationship detection. The first row shows the results, when only the visual part of the model is applied. This model performs poorly, in all four settings. The full model in the second row adds the language prior to it and also some regularization terms during training, which are described in more detail in [18]. This drastically improves the results. As expected the recall at top 100 is better than at top 50, however the difference is rather small, which shows that most of the correctly ranked triples are ranked quite high. The results for predicate detection are much better than for the other settings. This shows that one of the main problems in visual relationship detection is the correct prediction of the entities. In the last four rows we report the results of our method, which adds a link prediction model to the visual model. We compare the results for the integration of the four link prediction methods described in Sect. 2.1. We see that with all link prediction methods the model performs constantly better than the state-of-the-art method proposed by [18], except for *DistMult*. For *Relationship detection*, which is the most challenging setting, *ComplEx* works best, with a recall of 17.12 and 16.03 for the top 100 and top 50 results respectively. *RESCAL* performs slightly better than the *Multiway Neural Network* in all evaluation settings. For the setting of *Triple Detection* the scores are higher for all methods, as expected, as the overlap of the bounding

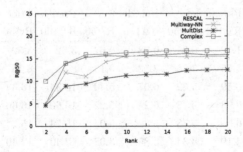

Fig. 5. Recall at 50 as a function of the rank

boxes is not taken into account. However, the relative performance between the methods does not vary much.

Figure 5 shows the recall at 50 on the test set for our different variants as a function of the rank. We see that the performances of *ComplEx* and *RESCAL* converge relatively quickly to a recall of around 16. The *Multiway Neural Network* converges a bit slower, to a slightly smaller maximum. *DistMult* converges slower and to a much smaller maximum recall of 12.5.

4.3   Zero-Shot Learning

Experimental Setting. We also include an experimental setting, where we only evaluate on triples, which had not been observed in the training data. This setting reveals the generalization ability of the semantic model. The test set contains 1877 of these triples. We evaluate based on the same settings as in the previous section, however for the recall we only count how many of the unseen triples are retrieved.

Results. Table 2 shows the results for the zero-shot experiments. This task is much more difficult, which can be seen by the huge drop in recall. However, also in this experiment, including the semantic model significantly improves the prediction. For the first three settings, the best performing method, which is the *Multiway Neural Network*, almost retrieves twice as many correct triples, as the state-of-the-art model of [18]. Especially, for the *Predicate Detection*, which assumes the objects and subjects to be given, a relatively high recall of 16.60 can be reached. In the zero-shot setting for *Predicate Detection* even the integration of the worst performing semantic model *DistMult* shows significantly better performance than the state-of-the-art method. These results clearly show that our model is able to infer also new likely triples, which have not been observed in the training data. This is one of the big benefits of the link prediction methods.

Table 2. Results for the zero shot learning experiments. We report recall at 50 and 100 for four different validation settings.

Task evaluation	Phrase det.		Rel. det.		Predicate det.		Triple det.	
	R@100	R@50	R@100	R@50	R@100	R@50	R@100	R@50
Lu et al. V [18]	1.12	0.95	0.78	0.67	3.52	3.52	1.20	1.03
Lu et al. full [18]	3.75	3.36	3.52	3.13	8.45	8.45	5.39	4.79
RESCAL	6.59	5.82	6.07	5.30	16.34	16.34	6.07	5.30
MultiwayNN	6.93	5.73	6.24	5.22	16.60	16.60	6.24	5.22
ComplEx	6.50	5.73	5.82	5.05	15.74	15.74	5.82	5.05
DistMult	4.19	3.34	3.85	3.08	12.40	12.40	3.85	3.08

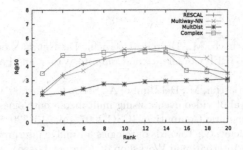

Fig. 6. Recall at 50 as a function of the rank for the zero-shot setting.

Figure 6 shows the recall at 50 on the zero-shot test set as a function of the rank. As expected, the models start to overfit in the zero-shot setting if the rank is to high. With a limited rank the models have less freedom for explaining the variation in the data; this forces them to focus more on the underlying structure, which improves the generalization property. *ComplEx*, which has more parameters due to the complex valued embeddings, performs best with small ranks and reaches the maximum at a rank of around 8. *Multiway Neural Network* reaches the maximum at a rank of 10 and *RESCAL* at a rank of 14. The highest recall is achieved by *RESCAL* at 5.3.

5   Conclusion

We presented a novel approach for including semantic knowledge into visual relationship detection. We combine a state-of-the-art computer vision procedure with latent variable models for link prediction, in order to enhance the modeling of relationships among visual objects. By including a statistical semantic model, the predictive quality can be enhanced significantly. Especially the prediction of triples, which have not been observed in the training data, can be enhanced through the generalization properties of the semantic link prediction methods. The recall of the best performing link-prediction method in the zero-shot setting is almost twice as high as the state-of-the art method. We proposed a probabilistic framework for integrating both the semantic prior and the computer vision algorithms into a joint model. This paper shows how the interaction of semantic and perceptual models can support each other to derive better predictive accuracies. The developed methods show great potential also for broader application areas, where both semantic and sensory data is observed. For example, in an industrial setting it might be interesting to model sensor measurements from a plant jointly with a given ontology. The improvement over the state-of-the-art vision model shows that performance improvement does not only rely on better computer vision models but also on improvements in the semantic modeling. As part of future work, we will explore more expressive ontologies, for example by integrating external information from publicly available knowledge graphs, to further improve the results.

References

1. Andreas, J., Rohrbach, M., Darrell, T., Klein, D.: Neural module networks. In: Proceedings of the IEEE Conference on Computer Vision and Pattern Recognition, pp. 39–48 (2016)
2. Bagdanov, A.D., Bertini, M., Del Bimbo, A., Serra, G., Torniai, C.: Semantic annotation and retrieval of video events using multimedia ontologies. In: International Conference on Semantic Computing, ICSC 2007, pp. 713–720. IEEE (2007)
3. Bannour, H., Hudelot, C.: Towards ontologies for image interpretation and annotation. In: 2011 9th International Workshop on Content-Based Multimedia Indexing (CBMI), pp. 211–216. IEEE (2011)
4. Bloehdorn, S., et al.: Semantic annotation of images and videos for multimedia analysis. In: Gómez-Pérez, A., Euzenat, J. (eds.) ESWC 2005. LNCS, vol. 3532, pp. 592–607. Springer, Heidelberg (2005). doi:10.1007/11431053_40
5. Bordes, A., Usunier, N., Garcia-Duran, A., Weston, J., Yakhnenko, O.: Translating embeddings for modeling multi-relational data. In: Advances in Neural Information Processing Systems, pp. 2787–2795 (2013)
6. Chen, N., Zhou, Q.Y., Prasanna, V.: Understanding web images by object relation network. In: Proceedings of the 21st International Conference on World Wide Web, pp. 291–300. ACM (2012)
7. Choi, W., Chao, Y.W., Pantofaru, C., Savarese, S.: Understanding indoor scenes using 3d geometric phrases. In: Proceedings of the IEEE Conference on Computer Vision and Pattern Recognition, pp. 33–40 (2013)
8. Dong, X., Gabrilovich, E., Heitz, G., Horn, W., Lao, N., Murphy, K., Strohmann, T., Sun, S., Zhang, W.: Knowledge vault: a web-scale approach to probabilistic knowledge fusion. In: Proceedings of the 20th ACM SIGKDD International Conference on Knowledge Discovery and Data Mining, pp. 601–610. ACM (2014)
9. Galleguillos, C., Rabinovich, A., Belongie, S.: Object categorization using co-occurrence, location and appearance. In: IEEE Conference on Computer Vision and Pattern Recognition, CVPR 2008, pp. 1–8. IEEE (2008)
10. Girshick, R.: Fast R-CNN. In: Proceedings of the IEEE International Conference on Computer Vision, pp. 1440–1448 (2015)
11. Girshick, R., Donahue, J., Darrell, T., Malik, J.: Rich feature hierarchies for accurate object detection and semantic segmentation. In: Proceedings of the IEEE Conference on Computer Vision and Pattern Recognition, pp. 580–587 (2014)
12. Gould, S., Rodgers, J., Cohen, D., Elidan, G., Koller, D.: Multi-class segmentation with relative location prior. Int. J. Comput. Vis. 80(3), 300–316 (2008)
13. Gupta, A., Kembhavi, A., Davis, L.S.: Observing human-object interactions: using spatial and functional compatibility for recognition. IEEE Trans. Pattern Anal. Mach. Intell. 31(10), 1775–1789 (2009)
14. Kingma, D., Ba, J.: Adam: A method for stochastic optimization. arXiv preprint arXiv:1412.6980 (2014)
15. Krishna, R., Zhu, Y., Groth, O., Johnson, J., Hata, K., Kravitz, J., Chen, S., Kalantidis, Y., Li, L.J., Shamma, D.A., et al.: Visual genome: connecting language and vision using crowdsourced dense image annotations. Int. J. Comput. Vis. 123(1), 32–73 (2017)
16. Kulkarni, G., Premraj, V., Ordonez, V., Dhar, S., Li, S., Choi, Y., Berg, A.C., Berg, T.L.: Babytalk: understanding and generating simple image descriptions. IEEE Trans. Pattern Anal. Mach. Intell. 35(12), 2891–2903 (2013)

17. LeCun, Y., Bengio, Y., Hinton, G.: Deep learning. Nature **521**(7553), 436–444 (2015)
18. Lu, C., Krishna, R., Bernstein, M., Fei-Fei, L.: Visual relationship detection with language priors. In: Leibe, B., Matas, J., Sebe, N., Welling, M. (eds.) ECCV 2016. LNCS, vol. 9905, pp. 852–869. Springer, Cham (2016). doi:10.1007/978-3-319-46448-0_51
19. Maji, S., Bourdev, L., Malik, J.: Action recognition from a distributed representation of pose and appearance. In: 2011 IEEE Conference on Computer Vision and Pattern Recognition (CVPR), pp. 3177–3184. IEEE (2011)
20. Nickel, M., Murphy, K., Tresp, V., Gabrilovich, E.: A review of relational machine learning for knowledge graphs. Proc. IEEE **104**(1), 11–33 (2016)
21. Nickel, M., Tresp, V., Kriegel, H.P.: A three-way model for collective learning on multi-relational data. In: Proceedings of the 28th International Conference on Machine Learning (ICML 2011), pp. 809–816 (2011)
22. Ramanathan, V., Li, C., Deng, J., Han, W., Li, Z., Gu, K., Song, Y., Bengio, S., Rosenberg, C., Fei-Fei, L.: Learning semantic relationships for better action retrieval in images. In: Proceedings of the IEEE Conference on Computer Vision and Pattern Recognition, pp. 1100–1109 (2015)
23. Ren, S., He, K., Girshick, R., Sun, J.: Faster R-CNN: towards real-time object detection with region proposal networks. In: Advances in Neural Information Processing Systems, pp. 91–99 (2015)
24. Rohrbach, M., Qiu, W., Titov, I., Thater, S., Pinkal, M., Schiele, B.: Translating video content to natural language descriptions. In: Proceedings of the IEEE International Conference on Computer Vision, pp. 433–440 (2013)
25. Sadeghi, M.A., Farhadi, A.: Recognition using visual phrases. In: 2011 IEEE Conference on Computer Vision and Pattern Recognition (CVPR), pp. 1745–1752. IEEE (2011)
26. Santoro, A., Raposo, D., Barrett, D.G., Malinowski, M., Pascanu, R., Battaglia, P., Lillicrap, T.: A simple neural network module for relational reasoning. arXiv preprint arXiv:1706.01427 (2017)
27. Serafini, L., Donadello, I., Garcez, A.d.: Learning and reasoning in logic tensor networks: theory and application to semantic image interpretation. In: Proceedings of the Symposium on Applied Computing, pp. 125–130. ACM (2017)
28. Simonyan, K., Zisserman, A.: Very deep convolutional networks for large-scale image recognition. arXiv preprint arXiv:1409.1556 (2014)
29. Tresp, V., Esteban, C., Yang, Y., Baier, S., Krompaß, D.: Learning with memory embeddings. arXiv preprint arXiv:1511.07972 (2015)
30. Tresp, V., Ma, Y., Baier, S., Yang, Y.: Embedding learning for declarative memories. In: Blomqvist, E., Maynard, D., Gangemi, A., Hoekstra, R., Hitzler, P., Hartig, O. (eds.) ESWC 2017. LNCS, vol. 10249, pp. 202–216. Springer, Cham (2017). doi:10.1007/978-3-319-58068-5_13
31. Uijlings, J.R., Van De Sande, K.E., Gevers, T., Smeulders, A.W.: Selective search for object recognition. Int. J. Comput. Vis. **104**(2), 154–171 (2013)
32. Uren, V., Cimiano, P., Iria, J., Handschuh, S., Vargas-Vera, M., Motta, E., Ciravegna, F.: Semantic annotation for knowledge management: sequirements and a survey of the state of the art. J. Web Semant. Sci. Serv. Agent World Wide Web **4**(1), 14–28 (2006)
33. Welbl, J., Riedel, S., Gaussier, E., Bouchard, G.: Complex embeddings for simple link prediction. In: Proceedings of the 33rd International Conference on Machine Learning (2016)

34. Xu, K., Ba, J., Kiros, R., Cho, K., Courville, A., Salakhudinov, R., Zemel, R., Bengio, Y.: Show, attend and tell: Neural image caption generation with visual attention. In: International Conference on Machine Learning, pp. 2048–2057 (2015)
35. Yang, B., Yih, W.t., He, X., Gao, J., Deng, L.: Embedding entities and relations for learning and inference in knowledge bases. arXiv preprint arXiv:1412.6575 (2014)
36. Yao, B., Fei-Fei, L.: Grouplet: A structured image representation for recognizing human and object interactions. In: 2010 IEEE Conference on Computer Vision and Pattern Recognition (CVPR), pp. 9–16. IEEE (2010)
37. Yao, B., Fei-Fei, L.: Modeling mutual context of object and human pose in human-object interaction activities. In: 2010 IEEE Conference on Computer Vision and Pattern Recognition (CVPR), pp. 17–24. IEEE (2010)
38. Yilmaz, Ö., Garcez, A.S.d., Silver, D.L.: A proposal for common dataset in neural-symbolic reasoning studies. In: NeSy@ HLAI (2016)
39. Zhu, Y., Lim, J.J., Fei-Fei, L.: Knowledge acquisition for visual question answering via iterative querying (2017)

An Empirical Study on How the Distribution of Ontologies Affects Reasoning on the Web

Hamid R. Bazoobandi[✉], Jacopo Urbani, Frank van Harmelen, and Henri Bal

Department of Computer Science, Vrije Universiteit Amsterdam,
Amsterdam, The Netherlands
h.bazoubandi@vu.nl, {jacopo,frank.van.harmelen,bal}@cs.vu.nl

Abstract. The Web of Data is an inherently distributed environment where ontologies are located in (physically) remote locations and are subject to constant changes. Reasoning is affected by these changes, but the extent and significance of this dependency is not well-studied yet. To address this problem, this paper presents an empirical study on how the distribution of ontological data on the Web affects the outcome of reasoning. We study (1) to what degree datasets depend on external ontologies and (2) to what extent the inclusion of additional ontological information via IRI de-referencing and the *owl:imports* directive to the input datasets leads to new derivations.

We based our study on many RDF datasets and on a large collection of RDFa, and JSON-LD data embedded into HTML pages. We used both Jena and Pellet in order to evaluate the results under different semantics. Our results indicate that remote ontologies are often crucial to obtain non-trivial derivations. Unfortunately, in many cases IRIs were broken and the *owl:imports* is rarely used. Furthermore, in some cases the inclusion of remote knowledge either did not yield any additional derivation or led to errors. Despite these cases, in general, we found that inclusion of additional ontologies via IRIs de-referencing and *owl:imports* directive is very effective for producing new derivations. This indicates that the two W3C standards for fetching remote ontologies have found their way into practice.

Keywords: RDF · RDFa · JSON-LD · OWL · Reasoning · Web of data

1 Introduction

The Web contains large volumes of semantically annotated data encoded in RDF [21] or similar formats. Often, this data contains expressive ontologies that machines can leverage to perform reasoning and derive valuable implicit information. Since information re-usage is a corner stone of the Semantic Web [18], many datasets reuse ontologies that are already available rather than creating their own

This work is partially funded by the Dutch public-private research community COM-MIT/ and NWO VENI project 40 639.021.335.

© Springer International Publishing AG 2017
C. d'Amato et al. (Eds.): ISWC 2017, Part I, LNCS 10587, pp. 69–86, 2017.
DOI: 10.1007/978-3-319-68288-4_5

ones. These ontologies are distributed across the Web and the W3C standardized two mechanisms to retrieve them: IRIs de-referencing [7] and *owl:imports* [18].

The number and correctness of new derivations that reasoners produce depend on the availability and quality of these external ontologies. Therefore, it is crucial that reasoners can successfully retrieve them and that the union of external ontologies is still consistent. Unfortunately, the Web is an inherently distributed and uncoordinated environment where several factors may preclude the fetching and reusage of remote data. For example, remote ontologies might silently disappear or move to other locations, or independent authors may publish ontologies that contain syntactic and/or semantic mistakes [14]. All these possibilities can heavily affect the output of reasoning or even make reasoning impossible.

Although much effort has already been invested on studying the quality and accessibility of resources on the Web of Data (WoD) [5–7], to the best of our knowledge no work has ever studied how the distribution of ontological data on the web affects reasoning. The goal of this paper is to study this from a purely empirical perspective. To that end, we conduct a number of experiments and analyse the output of reasoning over a wide range of documents to offer a first preliminary answer to the following questions: *(a)* how many derivations can reasoners derive from individual documents? *(b)* To what extent do documents link to external ontologies and how accessible are such links? *(c)* How many new derivations can reasoners derive after external ontologies are included and how can we characterize such derivations? *(d)* To what extent does the inclusion of additional ontological data endanger reasoning? This paper presents a number of experiments to answer these questions.

As the input for our experiments, we took samples from *LODLaundromat (LODL)* [5], which is a large crawl of RDF documents from the WoD, and *Web Data Commons (WDC)* [27], which contains extracted RDFa, MicroData, and JSON-LD graphs embedded in the HTML pages. We conducted our experiments using Jena [24] and Pellet [29], two widely used reasoners, and performed two types of analyses: a quantitative analysis, which focuses on the number of derived triples; and a qualitative analysis, which looks into the relevance of derived triples with the input document.

We summarise below some key outcomes of our experiments. These will be discussed in the remainder of this paper with more details:

- In the majority of the cases, reasoning on a single document produces a small number of derivations that are mostly RDF or OWL axioms;
- Only a small number of IRIs were de-referencable. However, when IRIs could have been accessed, the inclusion of additional knowledge allowed reasoners to derive new triples. This finding highlights the importance of maintaining functioning links in the WoD;
- The directive *owl:imports* is used only in a very small number of documents (less than 0.2% documents of LODL and only on 121 graphs out of 500M in WDC). In the documents that use it, the (recursive) inclusion of the remote

ontologies led to a significant increase of the number of derived triples. This demonstrates the potential of this mechanism;
- In a non-negligible number of cases, the inclusion of remote ontologies did not lead to the derivation of new triples. Also, we observed cases where the inclusion of external ontologies led to conflicts that made Pellet fail. Additionally, in some cases Jena did not finish reasoning within 72 h (despite the fact that on average the number of statements in input was fairly small).

In general, our findings are encouraging because they indicate that remote knowledge (fetched either with IRI de-referencing or via *owl:imports*) does lead to new valuable derivations. However, we have also witnessed several problems that show further research is still very much needed.

This paper is structured as follows: Sect. 2 reports on the experimental settings; Sect. 3 presents the results of the experiments where reasoning was applied without fetching remote ontologies, Sect. 4 presents the results after we de-referenced IRIs and Sect. 5 after we imported ontologies via *owl:imports*. Finally, Sect. 6 reports on related work while Sect. 7 concludes the paper. An extended version of this paper is available as technical report at http://hbi250. ops.few.vu.nl/iswc2017/survey/iswc2017_tr.pdf.

2   Experimental Setup

Inputs. On the Web, semantically-annotated data are primarily encoded either as RDF knowledge graphs (which are serialized in a number of files) or be embedded in HTML pages. Therefore, we considered two large collections of both types: *LODLaundromat* (LODL) [5] and the *Web Data Commons* (WDC) dataset [27]. LODL contains a collection of RDF files that were either crawled from online archives or submitted to the system. At the time we conducted this study, the collection consisted of 500K RDF files from more than 600 domain names. The WDC dataset contains RDFa, Microdata, Microformat, and JSON-LD data extracted from HTML pages. We use the 2015 crawl which provides about 541M named graphs from more than 2.7M domain names. We chose these two datasets because they are, to the best of our knowledge, the largest available collections of semantically-annotated data available on the Web. We must stress, however, that neither of these two collections offers any guarantee of representativeness. As far as we know, no crawled collection from the Web can make such a claim. They simply represent the best approximation that we have available.

In this paper, we refer to sets of triples which are locally available as *documents*. For LODL, a document corresponds to a RDF file. For WDC, a document corresponds to the set of triples in a named-graph (the named graph is the URI of the webpage from which the triples were extracted). We refer to the number of triples contained in a document as its *size*. We used two reasoners, *Pellet* [29] (version 2.3.1) and the *OWLMiniReasoner* of Jena [24] (version 3.1.0), to evaluate reasoning under different computational logic. We use these two reasoners (instead of, for instance, more scalable solutions like RDFox [26], VLog [30] or

WebPIE [31]) because they are well-tested implementations and work under different semantics. The *OWLMiniReasoner* reasoner in Jena works under the RDF semantics and supports an incomplete fragment of OWL Full that omits the forward entailments of *minCardinality/someValuesFrom* restrictions (detailed list of the supported constructs is available online[1]). In contrast, Pellet supports a sound but incomplete OWL DL reasoning (i.e., SROIQ(D)) [29] and we use it to perform ABox DL reasoning[2]. Once again, we refer to the online documentation for a detailed list of the supported constructs. Each reasoner is launched with the default settings. The only modification is that we disabled the automatic *owl:imports* inclusion for both reasoners in all experiments.

We refer to the terms and axioms defined in the RDF [21], RDFS [8], OWL [18], and XSD [13] specifications as *standard terms* and *standard axioms* respectively. A standard predicate is a standard term that appears as predicate in a triple. We assume that standard terms and axioms are locally available (but not part of the input document) because in practice the reasoners have stored a local copy.

Reasoning. In this paper, reasoning is used to derive new conclusions. The reasoning procedure is simple and equivalent for both reasoners: First, we load a set of triples G into the reasoner. We refer to the set G as the *input* of the reasoning process. In some experiments, G equals to a document while in others it will include also some remotely fetched triples. Then, we query the reasoner with the SPARQL query SELECT ?s ?p ?o { ?s ?p ?o }, which is meant to retrieve all the triples the reasoner can derive. Each answer returned by the reasoner is translated into a RDF triple $\langle ?s\ ?p\ ?o \rangle$. Let G' be the set of all returned triples. We call every triple $t \in G' \setminus G$ a *derived* triple and refer to the set $G' \setminus G$ as the *set of derived triples* or *derived triples*, or in short *derivations*. Clearly, this set will be different depending on the used reasoner. We would like to stress that the purpose of our experiments is *not* to compare the output of two reasoners but to analyse their output w.r.t. the inclusion/exclusion of remote ontological information.

Categorization of Derivations. In order to perform a more fine-grained analysis of the derived triples, we categorize them based on the complexity of reasoning process that produces them into the following four disjoint categories:

- **Type1** derivations are derivations that contain *only standard terms*. Typically, triples in this category are the tautologies extracted from these languages (e.g., $\langle rdf{:}subject\ rdf{:}type\ rdf{:}Property \rangle$).
- **Type2** derivations contain exactly one non-standard term that appears in one or more triples in the input set (e.g., $\langle {:}resource\ rdf{:}type\ rdf{:}Resource \rangle$).

---

[1] https://jena.apache.org/documentation/inference/#owl.
[2] TBox and ABox are terms from Description Logics. TBox triples encode 'schema' information which is crucial for reasoning while ABox triples encode assertional information.

- **Type3** derivations contain two non-standard terms that appear in the same input triple (e.g., if the input contains the triple ⟨*:ClassA owl:equivalentClass :ClassB*⟩ then a *Type3* derivation could be ⟨*:ClassB rdfs:subClassOf :ClassA*⟩).
- **Type4** derivations contain two or more non-standard terms that never appeared in the same input triple (e.g., if the input contains the triples ⟨*:resource rdf:type :ClassA*⟩ and ⟨*:ClassA rdfs:subClassOf :ClassB*⟩ then a *Type4* triple could be ⟨*:resource rdf:type :ClassB*⟩).

The reason behind such classification is that *Type1* derivations should be easy to return. *Type2* and *Type3* derivations are less easy because they require one pass on the data (*Type3* have the additional complexity that the reasoner might need to change the ordering of the terms). The derivation of *Type4* derivations usually requires a join between multiple triples, and thus their derivation is computationally more demanding. Most non-trivial implicit knowledge that reasoners derive are usually of *Type2*, *Type3* or *Type4*.

Failures. In some experiments, the reasoners were unable to complete the reasoning process. Causes for failure varied between a limited scalability of the algorithms/implementation, syntactic errors [6], and ontological inconsistencies [28]. Please note that the notion *ontological inconsistency* usually includes *unsatisfiability*, *incoherence*, or *inconsistency*. However, because reasoners do not crash as a result of *unsatisfiability* and *incoherence*, in this paper we ignore them, and whenever we use the term *ontological inconsistency* or in short *inconsistency*, we refer to conflicting assertions (ABox) or axioms (TBox) that make reasoning impossible and cause reasoner to abort the process.

A complete analysis of the failures is beyond the scope of this paper. Here, we say that a reasoner *failed* (or that a *failure* occurred) when the reasoner did not terminate successfully the reasoning process. We classify failures either as *exceptions*, which occurred when the reasoner had prematurely terminated (e.g., because of an inconsistency or a syntactic error in the input), or as *timeouts* in case the reasoner did not conclude the inference within 72 h.

Computing Infrastructure. Many experiments required several hours to finish, thus, we launched several of them in parallel using the DAS4 [3] cluster. Each machine in the cluster has 24G of memory and two quad-core 2.4 GHz CPUs.

Data and Source Code. All data, source code to run the experiments, and all derived triples are available at http://hbi250.ops.few.vu.nl/iswc2017/survey/.

3 Local Reasoning

First, we intend to evaluate how many new derivations the reasoners can derive from local data. But what can be considered as "local" in the Web of Data? One possibility is to consider all the RDF datasets that are stored on the same website as local. Unfortunately, there are several repositories that contain datasets from several other locations. Another possibility is to assume that local data is stored in files that share the same prefix (e.g. *dbpedia-01.gz*, *dbpedia-02.gz*), but this is a rather weak heuristic which does not always hold in practice. For the LODL dataset, we eventually concluded that the best solution was to consider as "local" only the triples that are contained in a single document (i.e., a RDF file for LODL and a named graph for WDC), because documents are the minimal storage units that are always entirely available on the same physical location. Thus, we will compute how many new triples reasoners can derive from single documents.

Data Collection. In our context, performing reasoning on every document is neither feasible nor desirable. The infeasibility is due to the large number of documents in LODL and WDC. We estimated that even if we could use all machines of our cluster it would take months to finish the computation. The undesirability comes from the fact that more than two thirds of the documents in LODL are fetched from two sources – *sonicbanana.cs.wright.edu* and *worldbank.270a.info* – while in the WDC dataset there is a significant difference between the number of documents from popular domain names such as http://wordpress.com and the ones from less popular sources.

With such large skew in terms of provenance, aggregations over the entire datasets will be strongly biased towards a few sources. While a simple random sampling strategy would be enough to reduce the input to a manageable size, it would be ineffective in removing the bias. To avoid this second problem, we first perform a random sampling over domain names with the sample size determined by the Cochram's formula [9] with a confidence level of 95%, and less than 0.5% margin of error. Then, from every selected domain name, we randomly picked as many documents as the logarithmic transformation of number of documents from that domain. This is a well-known methodology for sampling from skewed sources [19]. We call $LODL_1$ the sample extracted from LODL, and WDC_1 the sample extracted from WDC. Statistics about them are reported in Table 1.

One surprising number in Table 1 is the relatively small number of documents in $LODL_1$. In fact, 673 documents are indeed only a small fraction of all documents in the LODL collection. Such aggressive reduction is due to the relatively low number of domains in the collection and the extreme skew in the distribution of files among them. With such input, we are forced to select only a few documents per domain, otherwise we would be unable to construct a sample without skew. We believe this is the fairest methodology in order to present results which are most representative (i.e., cover the largest number of sources). If the reader is interested in biased results, we report in the TR the results obtained with a larger randomly selected sample.

Table 1. Statistics about the samples of $LODL_1$ and WDC_1 used for local reasoning.

	#Domains	#Documents	#Documents per domain				#Triples per documents			
			Max	Average	Median	Min	Max	Average	Median	Min
$LODL_1$	510	673	7	1.3	1	1	5.2M	80.9K	70	1
WDC_1	67K	74K	8	1.35	1	1	10.6K	20.5	6	1

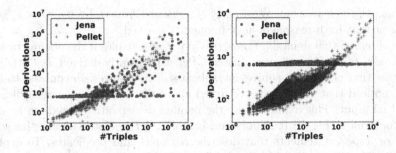

Fig. 1. Number of derived triples w.r.t document size on LODL$_1$ (left) and WDC$_1$ (right).

Reasoning Results. We launched Pellet and Jena over both samples, and report in Fig. 1 the number of derivations in relation with the size of the documents. We can draw a few interesting considerations from these results: First, the number of Pellets' derivations is proportional to the size of the input documents. This occurs both with LODL$_1$ and WDC$_1$. The number of the derivations produced by Jena was instead more constant. It only starts to grow proportionally with the largest LODL$_1$ documents.

Figure 2a shows the percentage of documents that yielded triples in each of the four categories outlined in Sect. 2. We see that all documents led to *Type1* and *Type2* derivations, regardless of the reasoner used. We inspected samples of the triples in each category and found that most *Type1* triples are RDFS and OWL axioms, while most of the *Type2* derivations are triples that describe resources or predicates, e.g., both reasoners always derive that predicates are instances of *rdf:Property*. In general, almost all documents have also led to *Type3* derivations. The only exception was WDC$_1$ in combination with Jena since in this case almost 20% of the documents did not return any *Type3* derivation. We manually inspected a sample of *Type3* derivations and found that they resemble to *Type2* information in the sense that they also describe predicates and resources.

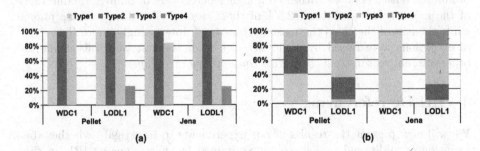

Fig. 2. (a) Percentage of documents that yielded derivations of each type. (b) Ratio of each derivation type w.r.t total number of derivations.

For example, the statement "a property is a *rdfs:subPropertyOf* itself" is a *Type3* statement that both reasoners have frequently derived.

We observed that Jena did not derive any *Type3* triples if the document contained only standard predicates. Instead, Pellet frequently derived *Type3* triples that state that classes are equivalent/subclass of themselves. In contrast to Pellet, we noticed that Jena always returned about 600 *Type1* triples regardless of the actual input. This explains why the number of derivations tends to be constant for Jena in Fig. 1: It mainly consists of 600 *Type1* statements plus some *Type2* or *Type3* statements that describe resources and predicates. To explain this more clearly, we show in Fig 2b the ratio of each derivation type against total number of derivations in the samples. We see from the figure that Jena on WDC_1 only produces *Type1* derivations, thus the total number of derivations tends to remain constant for each document. The situation is different for $LODL_1$ where the sizes of documents vary considerably. There, a smaller number of all derivations is of *Type1* which indicates that Jena derives significantly more derivations of other types. Interestingly, we notice from Fig. 2a that all WDC_1 documents derive *Type2* triples and about 80% of them derive *Type3* derivations with Jena. However, in Fig. 2b we see that these triples are fewer than *Type1* triples. This means that each document led to only few *Type2* and *Type3* statements while the largest number of derivations is of *Type1*.

Finally, we observed that neither reasoner was able to derive *Type4* triples from WDC_1, while for $LODL_1$ only 24% of the documents yielded such derivation. This suggests that in general most of the derivations that we can obtain from single documents are sort of "descriptions" of the terms in the dataset (e.g., a predicate is an instance of *rdfs:Property*, a class is an instance of *rdfs:Class*, etc.).

Failures. *Type2* and *Type3* derivations should be easy to calculate since they can be typically derived with a single pass on the data. Unfortunately, we still witnessed a number of failures with both reasoners. These failures were rare in WDC_1 (i.e., less than 0.1% for both reasoners, and all these cases were *exceptions* caused by syntax errors). With $LODL_1$, Jena successfully finished for more than 99.9% of the input documents. When it did not, *timeout* was the primary cause of failure. With Pellet we witnessed a higher percentage of failures (about 12% of the inputs). In more than 72.5% of these cases, Pellet threw an *exception*, while the rest of the cases the reasoner *timed out*. Interestingly, more than 92% of exceptions were raised by inconsistencies while the rest were raised due to other internal reasons (e.g. *Unknown concept type exception*).

4   IRI De-referencing

We will now present the results of our experiments to investigate whether the inclusion of additional remote content obtained by de-referencing IRIs in the documents leads to more derivations. To this end, we considered all documents of $LODL_1$ and WDC_1 for which local reasoning succeeded. Given the low failure rate, these samples are roughly equivalent to the original $LODL_1$ and WDC_1 datasets. In this section, we refer to these two subsets as $LODL_2$ and WDC_2 respectively.

Unfortunately, de-referencing every IRI in each document is not technically feasible due to high latencies and limited bandwidth. To reduce the workload, first, we avoided de-referencing IRIs that were part of standard vocabularies (RDF, RDFS, OWL, XSD) since that content is typically already known by the reasoner. Second, we limited de-referencing to only two subsets of IRIs: *predicate IRIs* and *Class IRIs*. The firsts are IRIs that appear as predicates of triples. These IRIs (excluding those from standard vocabularies) appear in 99.7% of the $LODL_2$ documents and 83.4% of the WDC_2 documents. The seconds are IRIs that were either explicitly defined as instances of *rdfs:Class* or appeared as subjects or objects of predicates that we knew their domains or ranges were instances of *rdfs:Class* (e.g., the object of the *rdf:type* predicate). De-referencing class IRIs was not always possible: in fact, only 67.63% of documents in $LODL_2$ and 71.79% of documents in WDC_2 contain class IRIs. Table 2 reports statistics about the number of distinct predicates and classes in the $LODL_2$ and WDC_2 datasets.

Table 2. Statistics of predicate/classes IRIs per document in each sample.

	$LODL_2$				WDC_2			
	Max	Average	Median	Min	Max	Average	Median	Min
Predicate	432	14.3	6	0	67	3.6	3	0
Predicate domains	11	2.5	2	0	5	1.4	1	0
Class	496	7.9	1	0	14	1.3	2	0
Class domains	11	1.5	1	0	4	0.7	1	0

Furthermore, not all IRIs could be accessed: Only 4.7% of predicates and 35.9% of the class IRIs in WDC_2 were de-referencable. The $LODL_2$ dataset presented a significantly different situation: There, roughly 73% of predicates and 74.5% of class IRIs were accessible. We analyzed the inaccessible predicate IRIs in WDC_2 and found that more than 84.6% of them pointed to non-existent resources on http://schema.org. We reported the full list of accessible and inaccessible IRIs in the public repository of this study.

Experimental Procedure. We proceeded as follows: First we performed reasoning only on the single document (see Sect. 3). Then, we repeated the process only considering the remotely-fetched triples, and finally considering the document plus its remotely-fetched triples. We counted as *new* only those derivations that could have been derived in this last step (document plus the remote triples). In other words, we only count the derivations that were impossible to derive without adding external content to the input.

4.1   Experimental Results

Based on the number of new derivations, we divided the input documents into three groups: Those that yielded new derivations (*Deriving*), those that produced

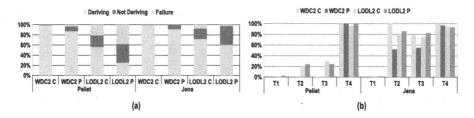

Fig. 3. After de-referencing predicate (P) and class (C) IRIs: Ratio of *Deriving*, *Not Deriving* and *Failed* reasoning processes (a). Ratio of documents that derive each derivation type (b).

no new derivations (*Not-Deriving*), and those for which the reasoning process failed (*Failure*). Figure 3a shows the percentage of documents in each group. The figure shows that a relatively large percentage of documents in LODL$_2$ derived no additional information after remote triples were added. Furthermore, documents in WDC$_2$ are more likely to yield new derivation after de-referencing IRIs than documents in LODL$_2$. Moreover, the figure also suggests that de-referencing class IRIs is more likely to produce additional derivations than de-referencing predicate IRIs. This is interesting because documents often contain more predicate IRIs than class IRIs.

***Deriving* Documents.** To study how the de-referencing of IRIs affects the number of derivations, Fig. 4 shows a comparison between the size of the input documents and the number of new derivations. The figure shows that for WDC$_2$, regardless the type of IRI that is de-referenced and irrespective of the reasoner, the number of new derived triples is proportional to the size of input document. This is similar to the local reasoning results (see Fig. 1). On the contrary, the reasoning for LODL$_2$ is different from local reasoning results, especially with Jena.

In order to gain more insights, we classified the newly derived triples into the four categories defined in Sect. 2. Figure 3b reports the ratio of documents that derive each specific derivation type (*T1–T4*) after de-referencing predicate (P) or class (C) IRIs. Figure 3b shows a different situation than in the local case (Fig. 2b). If we perform only local reasoning, then only a rather small percentage

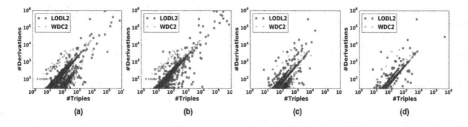

Fig. 4. Number of derivations vs input size after de-referencing: classes with Jena (a), predicates with Jena (b), classes with Pellet (c), predicates with Pellet (d).

of LODL$_1$ documents derived *Type4* triples. Instead, after we de-reference IRIs, the majority of documents in both datasets did derive *Type4* triples.

Also, while every document in the local reasoning experiments derived *Type1* triples, such new derivation is almost non-existent after IRIs are de-referenced. The absence of *Type1* new derivations was expected because *Type1* triples are most often RDFS and OWL axioms that reasoners can derive anyway, thus they are not considered as *new* derivation. Aside from that, Fig. 3b shows that Jena derived many more *Type2* and *Type3* derivations than Pellet. Our manual inspection of these new *Type2* and *Type3* triples revealed that these derivations are mostly basic statements such as "an entity is of type *owl:Thing*", or "resource is different from another resource". Pellet is usually capable of concluding such derivation without additional data; hence, for this reasoner these statements are not counted as new derivations. This is not the case for Jena, and therefore it can derive them after external triples are included.

Finally, we observed that with WDC$_2$ documents the number of all *Type2*, *Type3*, and *Type4* derivations tends to be proportional to the size of input document. This situation is different for larger LODL$_2$ documents because these documents tend to use richer OWL ontologies which trigger more reasoning. Consequently, the number of derived triples is no longer proportional to the input size.

Not Deriving Documents. Figure 3a also shows that there are cases where both reasoners did not derive any new triples. We scrutinized each *Not Deriving* document and the corresponding remotely-fetched triples, and found two main reasons for this: First, in some cases these triples only stated comments, labels, and descriptions intended for human interpretation. Reasoners can only conclude a limited number of derivations from such data. Second, the remote ontologies are dependent on yet more external ontologies, and so the inclusion of the remote data without its dependencies leads to no new derivation. Figure 3a also shows a larger number of *Not Deriving* and *Failure* cases with LODL$_2$ than with WDC$_2$. This was surprising to us since we expected that IRI de-referencing was more effective in native RDF datasets than in datasets embedded in HTML pages.

Failures. Figure 3a reports a non-negligible number of cases where the inclusion of remote triples led to a failure of the reasoning process. Note that in this experiment the input samples only contain documents for which local reasoning had succeeded. Therefore, the failures we refer to are caused by the inclusion of external ontologies. Pellet had the largest proportion of failed cases over LODL$_2$ documents (20–40%). From our execution traces, we noticed that Pellet almost always failed due to inconsistencies (this accounts for 99% of the cases with predicates, and almost 94% with classes). Sometimes these inconsistencies were caused by conflicts introduced between triples fetched from different sources, while sometimes the conflict was between the external knowledge and the input document. Jena failed less times, but this is due to the fact that it is less stringent about consistency. Whenever Jena failed, it was because it timed out.

Further inspections indicated that inconsistencies are exacerbated when triples are included from more sources. When Pellet failed due to inconsistencies over LODL$_2$, on average we de-referenced predicates from more than 18 sources (median 9), and classes from more than 11 sources (median 6). The average is significantly lower if we consider the cases where Pellet did not fail: predicates were from 5 sources (median 2), and classes from around 7 sources (median 2). This indicates that an excessive linking to multiple sources increases the chances of stumbling into inconsistencies.

5 OWL Imports

Data Collection. The directive *owl:imports* is another standard mechanism to link the document to external ontologies. In this section, we study how such inclusion affects the outcome of the reasoning process. This directive is used in less than 0.2% (939 documents) of the whole LODL dataset and in only 121 documents of the WDC dataset. Therefore, we do not sample them but instead use all of them. First, we executed local reasoning on them and filtered out all the documents for which this process failed. This reduced our input to 554 LODL documents (83 sources) while the size of the WDC documents remained unchanged: 121 documents from 16 different sources. In this section, we refer to these subsets of documents as LODL$_3$ and WDC$_3$ respectively.

The *owl:imports* directive defines a transitive process, i.e., an imported ontology may itself import additional ontologies [1]. The documents in WDC$_3$ only import the *goodrelations*[3] ontology, which is accessible and does not contain links to any other ontology. On the other hand, the documents in LODL$_3$ import 221 distinct ontologies from 62 different domain names. 76.9% of such imported ontologies were accessible, and only 52 of the documents imported ontologies with nested *owl:imports* statements. We found that the maximum length of transitive *owl:imports* chain is 4. Table 3 provides more information about the documents and the imported ontologies they mention. In the public repository, we report also the list of all inaccessible ontologies and more details on the ones that we fetched.

Experimental Procedure. We proceeded in a similar way to Sect. 4, namely, we performed three reasoning processes: one over the documents without the imported ontologies, one over only the set of imported ontologies, and one over the document and its imported ontologies combined. Also in this case, we count as *new* derivation only those triples that are exclusively present in the last step (i.e., triples that are impossible to derive without importing external ontologies).

5.1 Experimental Results

Similarly to Sect. 4.1, we categorized documents into the three groups of *Deriving*, *Not-Deriving*, and *Failure*, and present the collected statistics in Fig. 5a. The figure shows that both reasoners derived new triples from every document in WDC$_3$. However, we also see that for a significant number of documents in LODL$_3$

---

[3] http://purl.org/goodrelations/v1.

Table 3. Number of triples and number of imported links per document.

	# Triples				# Imported ontologies			
	Max	Average	Median	Min	Max	Average	Median	Min
LODL₃	4.3M	51.7K	397	2	48	4.5	4	1
WDC₃	281	31.1	29	22	1	1	1	1

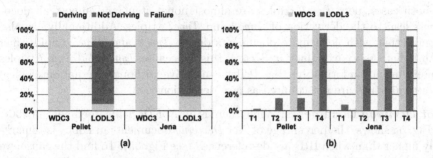

Fig. 5. (a) Ratio of documents in Derived/Not Derived/Failed groups. (b) Ratio of documents that derived each type of derivations.

both reasoners were not able to derive any new triple. This was surprising to us since these documents were explicitly pointing to the external ontologies so we assumed that the import process would lead to at least some new derivations.

Deriving Documents. Figure 6 reports the number of new derived triples against the number of triples in the input document. We observe no proportional relation between the number of derived triples and the size on input document in LODL₃ and the outcome with the two reasoners is different. This is in contrast with WDC₃ because here both reasoners derived roughly an equal number of derivations. Furthermore, each reasoner in WDC₃ derived almost the same number

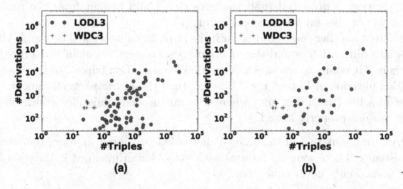

Fig. 6. Number of new derivations vs the document size after importing ontologies using Jena (a), and Pellet (b).

of triples per document (dots overlay each other in the figure). There are two reasons behind such regularity on WDC$_3$: *First*, as Table 3 shows, documents in WDC$_3$ tend to be of similar size; *second*, all documents in WDC$_3$ import the same ontology (goodrelations).

Similarly as before, we classified the newly derived triples into our four categories and report the results in Fig. 5b. We notice that the type of new derivations is akin to what reasoners derived when IRIs were de-referenced (see Fig. 3b). In both cases, new *Type1* triples are almost nonexistent and almost all documents lead to the derivation of *Type3* and *Type4* triples. Additionally, we also observe that with Jena more documents derive *Type2* and *Type3* triples than with Pellet. As we explained in Sect. 4, this is because *Type2* and *Type3* triples usually include information that Pellet can derive without external ontological data (and hence are not counted as new derivations).

***Not Deriving* Documents.** While there is no *Not Deriving* document in WDC$_3$, as Fig. 5a shows, the percentage of *Not Deriving* documents in LODL$_3$ is remarkably higher than when IRIs are de-referenced (see Fig. 3a). To find the cause, we studied the connections between the documents and the ontologies they import. In some cases, we found that the ontological information included from external sources was either already in the document or reasoners were able to derive it from the triples in the document itself. In other cases (which were the majority), we found that the *owl:imports* statement was the only link between the document and the imported ontology. In other words, no term from the directly or indirectly imported ontologies was used in triples of the input document.

We can only speculate on the possible reasons behind the lack of links between the documents and the imported ontologies. One possible explanation could be that publishers put the *owl:imports* statements at the beginning of a large file (as a sort of "header") even though the remote knowledge was relevant for triples that were serialized much later on. Then, the large file was split in smaller ones without replicating the *owl:imports* statement on each file. In such a case, the only file that would contain the *owl:imports* statement is the first split, but this split does not contain any relevant triple for the remote ontology and hence no new derivation is produced (and the ones that could benefit from the remote content do not contain a link to the ontology).

Similarly, another case could occur if the publisher stores the *TBox* and *ABox* triples into different files and the *owl:imports* statement is put in the TBox file even though it points to relevant information for the ABox triples. In this case, if the ABox files do not import the TBox file, then the *owl:imports* statement will appear in a file (the TBox one) where it is not needed while files which might need it are not properly linked.

Failures. In about 18% of the cases, Pellet failed and threw an exception about inconsistency. There were no failures with WDC$_3$. Jena timed out in only ∼0.3% of the cases. Pellet never timed out.

6   Related Work

Various aspects of Linked Open Data have been extensively studied in the last decade. Studies span a wide range of subjects including the quality of data [5,22,25], inconsistencies in the schema [2], the utilization of the standard vocabularies, and the depth and quality of the ontologies [11,12,32]. In [12], the authors provide some statistics about the utilization of ontologies and vocabularies. Bechhofer et al. [4] analyze a number of ontologies on the Web and find that the majority are OWL Full, mostly because of the syntactic errors or misuse of the vocabulary. Wang et al. [32] present similar finding and also report the frequency of the OWL language constructs and the shape of class hierarchies in the ontologies. Authors of [16] processed a large number of ontologies with various reasoners and show that most OWL reasoners are robust against the web.

As part of their research, authors of [10] report that only a small percentage of graphs on the Web uses *owl:imports*, a claim that our results confirm. The authors of [17] introduce ϵ-Connections to provide modelers with suitable means for developing Web ontologies in a modular way, and to provide an alternative to *owl:imports*.

More recently, Glimm et al. [15] discuss the current availability of OWL data on the Web. They report a detailed analysis on the number of used RDFS/OWL terms and highlight that the *owl:sameAs* triples are very popular. Similarly, Matentzoglu et al. [23] present another evaluation of the OWL landscape on the Web and a method to build an OWL DL corpus for evaluation of OWL engines. There have also been extensive studies on quality assessments and consistency of graphs on the Web. For instance, Zaveri et al. [33] provide a framework for linked data assessment. Feeney et al. [14] found string interdependencies between vocabularies and provide a tool to combine common linked data vocabularies into a single local logical model. Furthermore, they suggest a set of recommendation for linked data ontology design. None of these methods evaluate the interplay between data distribution and reasoning as we do. Therefore, we believe our results are a natural complement to all the above works.

7   Conclusions

The goal of this paper was to better understand how the distribution and reuse of ontologies affect reasoning on the Web of data. To this end, we analyzed several samples from LODLaundromat, which is a large crawl of RDF documents, and from Web Data Commons, which contains knowledge graphs that are embedded in HTML pages. We selected samples from hundreds of different domains in order to be as representative as possible. We compared the derivations produced by Pellet and Jena with and without remote external ontologies to understand, both from a quantitative and qualitative perspective, which are the major changes in terms of new derivations.

What have we learned? If we do not include any remote ontology, then reasoning tends to be rather trivial in the sense that it mainly returns RDFS and OWL axioms or description of the terms used in the document (e.g. that a property is an instance of *rdfs:Property*). However, if we do include remote ontologies, either by IRI de-referencing or *owl:imports*, then reasoners are able to derive many more non-trivial derivations.

Next to these positive findings, our analysis highlights some important problems:

- Reasoning on single documents is not always possible. In fact, we observed a number of failures (0.1–12%) during the reasoning process with both reasoners. These failures are due to either syntax errors, timeouts or inconsistencies;
- There are a non-negligible number of cases where the inclusion of the remote ontologies did not lead to any new derivation. Also, there are cases where the inclusion of remote ontologies breaks the reasoning process since it causes inconsistencies;
- The *owl:imports* directive is rarely used. Furthermore, it seems in many cases it is not used correctly (e.g., if the dataset is split in multiple files, the *owl:imports* statement is not replicated on each file) and this greatly reduces its potential;
- A significant number of IRIs are not accessible anymore. This is an important problem because the Semantic Web encourages ontological reuse as a basic principle, and if an ontology becomes unavailable then all documents that link to it will be unable to access its knowledge.

Some of these issues are already being studied in the community (for instance the rare usage of *owl:imports* is shown in [10], and the problem of non-accessible IRIs is well-known [20]) while others are not well-studied yet. Possible directions for future work could aim at researching techniques to selectively pick the "best" remote ontologies to avoid stumbling in errors. Also, it would be interesting to design methods to try to recover from situations where the documents do not point to any remote ontology by considering, for instance, ontologies that were linked for similar data. All these techniques could be potentially useful to make the Semantic Web more resilient to adverse situations. With this paper, we provided a first snapshot of the current state of reasoning on the Web of Data. Our findings are encouraging, and our hope is that they stimulate the community to reflect on the adoption of current semantic technologies.

References

1. Antoniou, G., van Harmelen, F.: Web ontology language: OWL. In: Staab, S., Studer, R. (eds.) Handbook on Ontologies. IHIS, pp. 91–110. Springer, Heidelberg (2009). doi:10.1007/978-3-540-92673-3_4
2. Baclawski, K., Kokar, M.M., Waldinger, R., Kogut, P.A.: Consistency checking of semantic web ontologies. In: Horrocks, I., Hendler, J. (eds.) ISWC 2002. LNCS, vol. 2342, pp. 454–459. Springer, Heidelberg (2002). doi:10.1007/3-540-48005-6_40
3. Bal, H., Epema, D., de Laat, C., van Nieuwpoort, R., Romein, J., Seinstra, F., Snoek, C., Wijshoff, H.: A medium-scale distributed system for computer science research: infrastructure for the long term. Computer **49**(5), 54–63 (2016)

4. Bechhofer, S., Volz, R.: Patching syntax in OWL ontologies. In: McIlraith, S.A., Plexousakis, D., van Harmelen, F. (eds.) ISWC 2004. LNCS, vol. 3298, pp. 668–682. Springer, Heidelberg (2004). doi:10.1007/978-3-540-30475-3_46

5. Beek, W., Rietveld, L., Bazoobandi, H.R., Wielemaker, J., Schlobach, S.: LOD Laundromat: a uniform way of publishing other people's dirty data. In: Mika, P., Tudorache, T., Bernstein, A., Welty, C., Knoblock, C., Vrandečić, D., Groth, P., Noy, N., Janowicz, K., Goble, C. (eds.) ISWC 2014. LNCS, vol. 8796, pp. 213–228. Springer, Cham (2014). doi:10.1007/978-3-319-11964-9_14

6. Behkamal, B., Kahani, M., Bagheri, E., Jeremic, Z.: A metrics-driven approach for quality assessment of linked open data. J. Theor. Appl. Electron. Commer. Res. 9(2), 64–79 (2014)

7. Berners-Lee, T.: Linked data-design issues (2006). http://www.w3.org/DesignIssues/LinkedData.html

8. Brickley, D., Guha, R.V.: RDF Schema 1.1. W3C Recommendation (2014)

9. Cochran, W.G.: Sampling Techniques. Wiley, New York (2007)

10. Delbru, R., Tummarello, G., Polleres, A.: Context-dependent OWL reasoning in Sindice - experiences and lessons learnt. In: Rudolph, S., Gutierrez, C. (eds.) RR 2011. LNCS, vol. 6902, pp. 46–60. Springer, Heidelberg (2011). doi:10.1007/978-3-642-23580-1_5

11. Ding, L., Kolari, P., Ding, Z., Avancha, S.: Using ontologies in the semantic web: a survey. In: Ontologies, pp. 79–113 (2007)

12. Ding, L., Pan, R., Finin, T., Joshi, A., Peng, Y., Kolari, P.: Finding and ranking knowledge on the semantic web. In: Gil, Y., Motta, E., Benjamins, V.R., Musen, M.A. (eds.) ISWC 2005. LNCS, vol. 3729, pp. 156–170. Springer, Heidelberg (2005). doi:10.1007/11574620_14

13. Fallside, D.C., Walmsley, P.: XML schema part 0: primer. W3C Recommendation (2004)

14. Feeney, K., Mendel-Gleason, G., Brennan, R.: Linked data schemata: fixing unsound foundations. Semant. Web J. Spec. Issue Qual. Manag. Semant. Web Assets 1–23 (2015)

15. Glimm, B., Hogan, A., Krötzsch, M., Polleres, A.: OWL: yet to arrive on the web of data? In: WWW 2012 Workshop on Linked Data on the Web, vol. 937 (2012). http://CEUR-WS.org

16. Gonçalves, R.S., Matentzoglu, N., Parsia, B., Sattler, U.: The empirical robustness of description logic classification. In: Proceedings of the 2013th International Conference on Posters & Demonstrations Track, vol. 1035, pp. 277–280 (2013). http://CEUR-WS.org

17. Grau, B.C., Parsia, B., Sirin, E.: Combining OWL ontologies using ε-connections. J. Web Semant. 4(1), 40–59 (2006)

18. Hitzler, P., Krötzsch, M., Parsia, B., Patel-Schneider, P.F., Rudolph, S.: OWL 2 web ontology language primer. W3C Recommendation (2009)

19. Jackson, S.L.: Research Methods and Statistics: A Critical Thinking Approach. Cengage Learning, Boston (2015)

20. Käfer, T., Abdelrahman, A., Umbrich, J., O'Byrne, P., Hogan, A.: Observing linked data dynamics. In: Cimiano, P., Corcho, O., Presutti, V., Hollink, L., Rudolph, S. (eds.) ESWC 2013. LNCS, vol. 7882, pp. 213–227. Springer, Heidelberg (2013). doi:10.1007/978-3-642-38288-8_15

21. Klyne, G., Carroll, J.J., McBride, B.: RDF 1.1 concepts and abstract syntax. W3C Recommendation (2014)

22. Kontokostas, D., Westphal, P., Auer, S., Hellmann, S., Lehmann, J., Cornelissen, R., Zaveri, A.: Test-driven evaluation of linked data quality. In: Proceedings of WWW (2014)
23. Matentzoglu, N., Bail, S., Parsia, B.: A snapshot of the OWL web. In: Alani, H., et al. (eds.) ISWC 2013. LNCS, vol. 8218, pp. 331–346. Springer, Heidelberg (2013). doi:10.1007/978-3-642-41335-3_21
24. McBride, B.: Jena: a semantic web toolkit. IEEE Internet Comput. 6(6), 55–59 (2002)
25. Mendes, P.N., Mühleisen, H., Bizer, C.: Sieve: linked data quality assessment and fusion. In: Proceedings of Joint EDBT/ICDT Workshops, pp. 116–123. EDBT-ICDT (2012)
26. Motik, B., Nenov, Y., Piro, R., Horrocks, I., Olteanu, D.: Parallel materialisation of datalog programs in centralised, main-memory RDF systems. In: Proceedings of AAAI, pp. 129–137 (2014)
27. Mühleisen, H., Bizer, C.: Web data commons-extracting structured data from two large web corpora. In: Proceedings of the Workshop Linked Data Web, vol. 937, pp. 133–145 (2012)
28. Parsia, B., Sirin, E., Kalyanpur, A.: Debugging OWL ontologies. In: Proceedings of WWW, pp. 633–640 (2005)
29. Sirin, E., Parsia, B., Grau, B.C., Kalyanpur, A., Katz, Y.: Pellet: a practical OWL-DL reasoner. Web Semant. Sci. Serv. Agents World Wide Web 5, 51–53 (2007)
30. Urbani, J., Jacobs, C., Krötzsch, M.: Column-oriented datalog materialization for large knowledge graphs. In: Proceedings of AAAI, pp. 258–264 (2016)
31. Urbani, J., Kotoulas, S., Maassen, J., Van Harmelen, F., Bal, H.: WebPIE: a web-scale parallel inference engine using MapReduce. J. Web Semant. 10, 59–75 (2012)
32. Wang, T.D., Parsia, B., Hendler, J.: A survey of the web ontology landscape. In: Cruz, I., Decker, S., Allemang, D., Preist, C., Schwabe, D., Mika, P., Uschold, M., Aroyo, L.M. (eds.) ISWC 2006. LNCS, vol. 4273, pp. 682–694. Springer, Heidelberg (2006). doi:10.1007/11926078_49
33. Zaveri, A., Rula, A., Maurino, A., Pietrobon, R., Lehmann, J., Auer, S.: Quality assessment for linked data: a survey. Semant. Web 7(1), 63–93 (2015)

Expressive Stream Reasoning with Laser

Hamid R. Bazoobandi[1], Harald Beck[2(✉)], and Jacopo Urbani[1]

[1] Vrije Universiteit Amsterdam, Amsterdam, The Netherlands
h.bazoobandi@vu.nl, jacopo@cs.vu.nl
[2] Institute of Information Systems, Vienna University of Technology, Vienna, Austria
beck@kr.tuwien.ac.at

Abstract. An increasing number of use cases require a timely extraction of non-trivial knowledge from semantically annotated data streams, especially on the Web and for the Internet of Things (IoT). Often, this extraction requires expressive reasoning, which is challenging to compute on large streams. We propose Laser, a new reasoner that supports a pragmatic, non-trivial fragment of the logic LARS which extends Answer Set Programming (ASP) for streams. At its core, Laser implements a novel evaluation procedure which annotates formulae to avoid the re-computation of duplicates at multiple time points. This procedure, combined with a judicious implementation of the LARS operators, is responsible for significantly better runtimes than the ones of other state-of-the-art systems like C-SPARQL and CQELS, or an implementation of LARS which runs on the ASP solver Clingo. This enables the application of expressive logic-based reasoning to large streams and opens the door to a wider range of stream reasoning use cases.

1 Introduction

The Web and the emerging Internet of Things (IoT) are highly dynamic environments where streams of data are valuable sources of knowledge for many use cases, like traffic monitoring, crowd control, security, or autonomous vehicle control. In this context, reasoning can be applied to extract implicit knowledge from the stream. For instance, reasoning can be applied to detect anomalies in the flow of information, and provide clear explanations that can guide a prompt understanding of the situation.

Problem. Reasoning on data streams should be done in a timely manner [11,21]. This task is challenging for several reasons: *First*, expressive reasoning that supports features for a fine-grained control of temporal information may come with an unfavourable computational complexity. This clashes with the requirement of a reactive system that shall work in a highly dynamic environment. *Second*, the continuous flow of incoming data calls for incremental evaluation techniques

---

This work is partially funded by the Dutch public-private research community COMMIT/ and NWO VENI project 639.021.335 and by the Austrian Science Fund (FWF) projects P26471 and W1255-N23.

C. d'Amato et al. (Eds.): ISWC 2017, Part I, LNCS 10587, pp. 87–103, 2017.
DOI: 10.1007/978-3-319-68288-4_6

that go beyond repeated querying and re-computation. *Third*, there is no consensus on the formal semantics for the processing of streams which hinders a meaningful and fair comparison between stream reasoners.

Despite recent substantial progress in the development of stream reasoners, to the best of our knowledge there is still no reasoning system that addresses all three challenges. Some systems can handle large streams but do not support expressive temporal reasoning features [3,5,17,19]. Other approaches focus on the formal semantics but do not provide implementations [14]. Finally, some systems implemented only a particular rule set and cannot be easily generalized [16,27].

Contribution. We tackle the above challenges with the following contributions.

- We present *Laser*, a novel stream reasoning system based the recent rule-based framework LARS [9], which extends Answer Set Programming (ASP) for stream reasoning. Programs are sets of rules which are constructed on formulae that contain window operators and temporal operators. Thereby, Laser has a fully declarative semantics amenable for formal comparison.
- To address the trade-off between expressiveness and data throughput, we employ a tractable fragment of LARS that ensures uniqueness of models. Thus, in addition to typical operators and window functions, Laser also supports operators such as $\Box$, which enforces the validity over intervals of time points, and @, which is useful to state or retrieve specific time points at which atoms hold.
- We provide a novel evaluation technique which annotates formulae with two time markers. When a grounding of a formula φ is derived, it is annotated with an interval $[c, h]$ from a *consideration time* c to a *horizon time* h, during which φ is guaranteed to hold. By efficiently propagating and removing these annotations, we obtain an incremental model update that may avoid many unnecessary re-computations. Also, these annotations enable us to implement a technique similar to the Semi-Naive Evaluation (SNE) of Datalog programs [1] to reduce duplicate derivations.
- We present an empirical comparison of the performance of Laser against the state-of-the-art engines, i.e., C-SPARQL [5] and CQELS [19] using micro-benchmarks and a more complex program. We also compare Laser with an open source implementation of LARS which is based on the ASP solver Clingo to test operators not supported by the other engines.

Our empirical results are encouraging as they show that Laser outperforms the other systems, especially with large windows where our incremental approach is beneficial. This allows the application of expressive logic-based reasoning to large streams and to a wider range of use cases. To the best of our knowledge, no comparable stream reasoning system that combines similar expressiveness with efficient computation exists to date. See [7] for an extended version of this paper.

2   Theoretical Background: LARS

As formal foundation, we use the logic-based framework LARS [9]. We focus on a pragmatic fragment called *Plain LARS* first mentioned in [8]. We assume the reader is familiar with basic notions, in particular those of logic programming. Throughout, we distinguish *extensional atoms* $\mathcal{A}^{\mathcal{E}}$ for input and *intensional atoms* $\mathcal{A}^{\mathcal{I}}$ for derivations. By $\mathcal{A} = \mathcal{A}^{\mathcal{E}} \cup \mathcal{A}^{\mathcal{I}}$, we denote the set of *atoms*. Basic arithmetic operations and comparisons are assumed to be given in form of designated extensional predicates, but written with infix notation as usual. We use upper case letters X, Y, Z to denote variables, lower case letters $x, y, \dots$ are for constants, and p, a, b, q for predicates for atoms.

Definition 1 (Stream). *A stream $S = (T, v)$ consists of a timeline T, which is a closed interval in $\mathbb{N}$, and an evaluation function $v : \mathbb{N} \mapsto 2^{\mathcal{A}}$. The elements $t \in T$ are called time points.*

Intuitively, a stream S associates with each time point a set of atoms. We call S a *data stream*, if it contains only extensional atoms. To cope with the amount of data, one usually considers only recent atoms. Let $S = (T, v)$ and $S' = (T', v')$ be two streams s.t. $S' \subseteq S$, i.e., $T' \subseteq T$ and $v'(t') \subseteq v(t')$ for all $t' \in T'$. Then S' is called a *window* of S.

Definition 2 (Window function). *Any (computable) function w that returns, given a stream $S = (T, v)$ and a time point $t \in \mathbb{N}$, a window S' of S, is called a window function.*

In this work, we focus on two prominent sliding windows that select recent atoms based on time, respectively counting. A sliding time-based window selects all atoms appearing in the last n time points.

Definition 3 (Sliding Time-based Window). *Let $S = (T, v)$ be a stream, $t \in T = [t_1, t_2]$ and let $n \in \mathbb{N}$, $n \geq 0$. Then the sliding time-based window function τ_n (for size n) is $\tau_n(S, t) = (T', v|_{T'})$, where $T' = [t', t]$ and $t' = \max\{t_1, t - n\}$.*

Similarly, a sliding tuple-based window selects the last n tuples. We define the *tuple size* $|S|$ of stream $S = (T, v)$ as $|\{(a, t) \mid t \in T, a \in v(t)\}|$.

Definition 4 (Sliding Tuple-based Window). *Let $S = (T, v)$ be a stream, $t \in T = [t_1, t_2]$ and let $n \in \mathbb{N}$, $n \geq 1$. The sliding tuple-based window function $\#_n$ (for size n) is*

$$\#_n(S, t) = \begin{cases} \tau_{t-t'}(S, t) & \text{if } |\tau_{t-t'}(S, t)| \leq n, \\ S' & \text{else,} \end{cases}$$

where $t' = \max(\{u \in T \mid |\tau_{t-u}(S, t)| \geq n\} \cup \{t_1\})$ and $S' = ([t', t], v')$ has tuple size $|S'| = n$ such that $v'(u) = v(u)$ for all $u \in [t' + 1, t]$ and $v'(t') \subseteq v(t')$.

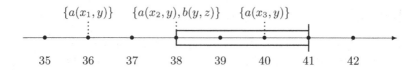

$\{a(x_1,y)\}$ $\{a(x_2,y),b(y,z)\}$ $\{a(x_3,y)\}$

35   36   37   38   39   40   41   42

Fig. 1. A time (resp. tuple) window of size 3 at $t = 41$

We refer to these windows simply by time windows, resp. tuple windows. Note that for time windows, we allow size $n = 0$, which selects all atoms at the current time point, while the tuple window must select at least one atom, hence $n \geq 1$.

Note that we associate with each time point a set of atoms. Thus, for the tuple-based window, if $[t', t]$ is the smallest timeline in which n atoms are found, then in general one might have to delete arbitrary atoms at time point t' such that exactly n remain $[t', t]$.

Example 1. Consider a data stream $D = (T, v_D)$ as shown in Fig. 1, where $T = [35, 42]$ and $v_D = \{36 \mapsto \{a(x_1,y)\}, 38 \mapsto \{a(x_2,y), b(y,z)\}, 40 \mapsto \{a(x_3,y)\}\}$. The indicated time window of size 3 has timeline $[38, 41]$ and only contains the last three atoms. Thus, the window is also the tuple window of size 3 at 40. Notably, $[38, 41]$ is also the temporal extent of the tuple window of size 2, for which there are two options, dropping either $a(x_2,y)$ or $b(y,z)$ at time 38.

Although Definition 4 introduces nondeterminism, one may assume a deterministic function based on the implementation at hand. Here, we assume data is arriving in a strict order from which a natural deterministic tuple window follows.

Window operators $\boxplus^w$. A window function w can be accessed in rules by window operators. That is to say, an expression $\boxplus^w \alpha$ has the effect that α is evaluated on the "snapshot" of the data stream delivered by its associated window function w. Within the selected snapshot, LARS allows to control the temporal semantics with further modalities, as will be explained below.

2.1 Plain LARS Programs

Plain LARS programs as in [8] extend normal logic programs. We restrict here to positive programs, i.e., without negation.

Syntax. We define the set $\mathcal{A}^+$ of *extended atoms* by the grammar

$$a \mid @_t a \mid \boxplus^w @_t a \mid \boxplus^w \Diamond a \mid \boxplus^w \Box a,$$

where $a \in \mathcal{A}$ and $t \in \mathbb{N}$ is a time point. The expressions of form $@_t a$ are called *@-atoms*. Furthermore, if $\star \in \{@_t, \Diamond, \Box\}$, $\star a$ is a *quantified atom* and $\boxplus^w \star a$ a *window atom*. We write $\boxplus^n$ instead of $\boxplus^{\tau_n}$ for the window operator using a time window function, and $\boxplus^{\#n}$ uses the tuple window of size n.

A *rule* r is of the form $\alpha \leftarrow \beta_1, \ldots, \beta_n$, where $H(r) = \alpha$ is the *head* and $B(r) = \{\beta_1, \ldots, \beta_n\}$ is the *body* of r. The head α is of form a or $@_t a$, where

$a \in \mathcal{A}^{\mathcal{I}}$, and each β_i is an extended atom. A *(positive plain) program* P is a set of rules. We say an extended atom β *occurs* in a program P if $\beta \in \{H(r)\} \cup B(r)$ for some rule $r \in P$.

Example 2 (cont'd). The rule $r = q(X, Y, Z) \leftarrow \boxplus^3 \Diamond a(X, Y), \boxplus^{\#3} \Diamond b(Y, Z)$ expresses a query with a join over predicates a and b in the standard snapshot semantics: If for some variable substitutions for X, Y, Z, $a(X, Y)$ holds some time during the last 3 time points and $b(Y, Z)$ at some time point in the window of the last 3 tuples, then $q(X, Y, Z)$ is must be inferred.

We identify rules $\alpha \leftarrow \beta_1, \ldots, \beta_n$ with implications $\beta_1 \wedge \cdots \wedge \beta_n \rightarrow \alpha$, thus obtaining by them and their subexpressions the set $\mathcal{F}$ of *formulae*.

Semantics. We first define the semantics of ground programs, i.e., programs without variables, based on a *structure* $M = \langle S, W, \mathcal{B} \rangle$, where $S = (T, v)$ is a stream, W a set of window functions, and $\mathcal{B}$ a static set of atoms called *background data*. Throughout, we use $W = \{\tau_n, \#_n \mid n \in \mathbb{N}\}$. We define when extended atoms β (and its subformulae) hold in a structure M at a given time point $t \in T$ as follows. Let $a \in \mathcal{A}$ and φ be a quantified atom. Then,

$$
\begin{aligned}
M, t \Vdash a \quad & \text{iff} \quad a \in v(t) \text{ or } a \in \mathcal{B}, \\
M, t \Vdash \Diamond a \quad & \text{iff} \quad M, t' \Vdash a \text{ for some } t' \in T, \\
M, t \Vdash \Box a \quad & \text{iff} \quad M, t' \Vdash a \text{ for all } t' \in T, \\
M, t \Vdash @_{t'} a \quad & \text{iff} \quad M, t' \Vdash a \text{ and } t' \in T, \\
M, t \Vdash \boxplus^w \varphi \quad & \text{iff} \quad M', t \Vdash \varphi, \text{ where } M' = \langle w(S, t), W, \mathcal{B} \rangle.
\end{aligned}
$$

For a data stream $D = (T, v_D)$, any stream $I = (T, v) \supseteq D$ that coincides with D on $\mathcal{A}^{\mathcal{E}}$ is an *interpretation stream* for D, and a structure $M = \langle I, W, \mathcal{B} \rangle$ an *interpretation* for D. Satisfaction by M at $t \in T$ is as follows: For a rule r of form $\alpha \leftarrow \beta_1, \ldots, \beta_n$, we first define $M, t \models B(r)$ iff $M, t \Vdash \beta_i$ for all $i \in \{1, \ldots, n\}$. Then, $M, t \models r$ iff $M, t \Vdash \alpha$ or $M, t \not\models B(r)$; M is a *model* of program P (for D) at time t, denoted $M, t \models P$, if $M, t \models r$ for all $r \in P$; and M is *minimal*, if in addition no model $M' = \langle S', W, \mathcal{B} \rangle \neq M$ of P exists s.t. $S' = (T, v')$ and $v' \subsetneq v$.

Definition 5 (Answer Stream). *An interpretation stream I is an answer stream of program P for the data stream $D \subseteq I$ at time t, if $M = \langle I, W, \mathcal{B} \rangle$ is a minimal model of the reduct $P^{M,t} = \{r \in P \mid M, t \models B(r)\}$.*

Note that using tuple windows over intensional data seems neither useful nor intuitive. For instance, program $P = \{a \leftarrow \boxplus^{\#1} \Diamond b\}$ is inconsistent for a data stream D at time t, where the last atom is b, occurring at time $t-1$: by deriving a for time t, suddenly a would be the last tuple.

Proposition 1. *Let P be a positive plain LARS program that employs only time windows, and tuple window operators only over extensional atoms. Then, P always has a unique answer stream.*

Non-ground programs. We obtain the semantics for non-ground programs in a straightforward way by considering rules with variables as schematic descriptions of respective ground instantiations. Substitutions σ are defined as usual.

Example 3 (cont'd). Consider the ground program P obtained from rule r of Example 2 by replacing variables with constants from the data stream D in Example 1:

$$
\begin{array}{lll}
r_1: & q(x_1, y, z) & \leftarrow \boxplus^3 \Diamond a(x_1, y), \boxplus^{\#3} \Diamond b(y, z) \\
r_2: & q(x_2, y, z) & \leftarrow \boxplus^3 \Diamond a(x_2, y), \boxplus^{\#3} \Diamond b(y, z) \\
r_3: & q(x_3, y, z) & \leftarrow \boxplus^3 \Diamond a(x_3, y), \boxplus^{\#3} \Diamond b(y, z)
\end{array}
$$

At time $t = 41$, the time window $\boxplus^3$ and the tuple window $\boxplus^{\#3}$ are identical, as indicated in Fig. 1, and contain atoms $a(x_2, y)$, $b(y, z)$, and $a(x_3, y)$. Consider rule r_1. Window atom $\boxplus^3 \Diamond a(x_1, y)$ does no hold, since there is not a time point t in the selected window such that $a(x_1, y)$ holds at t. However, the remaining window atoms in P all holds, hence the body of rules r_2 and r_3 hold. Thus, a model of P (for D at time 41) must include $q(x_2, y, z)$ and $q(x_3, y, z)$. We obtain the answer stream $D \cup (T, \{41 \mapsto \{q(x_2, y, z), q(x_3, y, z)\}\})$.

Definition 6 (Output). Let $I = (T, v)$ be the answer stream of program P (for a data stream D) at time t. Then, the output (of P for D at t) is defined by $v(t) \cap \mathcal{A}^\mathcal{I}$, i.e., the intensional atoms that hold at t.

Given a data stream $D = (T, v)$, where $T = [t_1, t_n]$, we obtain an *output stream* $S = (T, v)$ by the output at consecutive outputs, i.e., for each $t' \in T$, $v(t')$ is the output for $(T', v|_{T'})$, where $T' = [t_1, t']$. Thus, an output stream is the formal description of the sequence of temporary valid derivations based on a sequence of answer streams over a timeline. Our goal is to compute it efficiently.

Example 4 (cont'd). Continuing Example 3, the output of P for D at 41 is $\{q(x_2, y, z), q(x_3, y, z)\}$. The output stream $S = (T, v)$ is given by $v = \{t \mapsto \{q(x_1, y, z), q(x_2, y, z) \mid t = 38, 39\} \cup \{t \mapsto \{q(x_2, y, z), q(x_3, y, z)\} \mid t = 40, 41, 42\}$.

3   Incremental Evaluation of LARS Programs

In this section, we describe the efficient output stream computation of Laser. The incremental procedure consists in continuously grounding and then annotating formulae with two time points that indicate when and for how long formulae hold. We thus address two important sources of inefficiency: grounding (including time variables) and model computation.

Our work deliberately focuses on exploiting purely sliding windows. The longer a (potential) step size [9], the less incremental reasoning can be applied. In the extreme case of a tumbling window (i.e., where the window size equals the step size) there is nothing that can be evaluated incrementally. However, as long as the two subsequent windows share some data, the incremental algorithm can be beneficial. We now give the intuition of our approach in an Example.

Example 5 (cont'd). Consider again the stream of Fig. 1, and assume that we are at $t = 36$, where $a(x_1, y)$ appears as first atom in the stream. In rule $r = q(X, Y, Z) \leftarrow \boxplus^3 \Diamond a(X, Y), \boxplus^{\#3} \Diamond b(Y, Z)$, the atom matches the window atom $\alpha = \boxplus^3 \Diamond a(X, Y)$, and we obtain a substitution $\sigma = \{X \mapsto x_1, Y \mapsto y\}$ under which $a(X, Y)$ holds at time 36. However, for α, we can use σ for the next 3 time points due to the size of the window and operator $\Diamond$. That is, we start *considering* σ at time 36 and we have a guarantee that the grounding $\alpha\sigma$ (written postfix) holds until time point 39, which we call the *horizon time*. We thus write $\alpha\sigma_{[36,39]}$ for the *annotated ground formula*, which states that $\boxplus^3 \Diamond a(x_1, y)$ holds at all evaluation $t \in [36, 39]$, i.e., at $t \in [37, 39]$, the neither the grounding nor the truth of $\boxplus^3 \Diamond a(x_1, y)$ needs to be re-derived.

Definition 7. *Let $\alpha \in \mathcal{F}$ be a formula, and $c, h \in \mathbb{N}$ such that $c \leq h$, and σ a substitution. Then, $\alpha\sigma$ denotes the formula which replaces variables in α by constants due to σ; $\alpha\sigma_{[c,h]}$ is called an* annotated formula, c *is called the* consideration time *and h the* horizon time, *and the interval $[c, h]$ the* annotation.

As illustrated in Example 5, the intended meaning of an annotated formula $\alpha\sigma_{[c,h]}$ is that formula $\alpha\sigma$ holds throughout the interval $[c, h]$. Annotations might overlap.

Example 6. Consider an atom $a(y)$ streams at time points 5 and 8. Then, for the formula $\alpha = \boxplus^9 \Diamond a(X)$, we get the substitution $\sigma = \{X \mapsto y\}$ and an annotation $a_1 = [5, 14]$ at $t = 5$, and then $a_2 = [8, 17]$ at $t = 8$. That is to say, $\alpha\sigma = \boxplus^9 \Diamond a(y)$ holds at all time points $[5, 14]$ due to annotation a_1 and at time points $[8, 17]$ due to a_2, and for each $t \in [8, 14]$ it suffices to retrieve one of these annotations to conclude that $\alpha\sigma$ holds at t.

We note that the tuple window can be processed dually by additionally introducing a *consideration count* $c_\#$ and a *horizon count* $h_\#$, i.e., an annotated formula $\alpha\sigma_{[c_\#, h_\#]}$ would indicate that $\alpha\sigma$ holds when the number of atoms received so far is between $c_\#$ and $h_\#$. In essence, the following mechanisms work analogously for time- and tuple-based annotations. We thus limit our presentation to the time-based case for the sake of simplification.

The consideration time allows us to implement a technique similar to semi-naive evaluation (SNE) (see, e.g., VLog [26], RDFox [24], Datalog [1]) which increases efficiency by preventing duplicate derivations. Conceptually, SNE is a method which simply imposes that at least one formula that instantiates the body should be derived during or after the previous execution of the rule, otherwise the rule would surely derive a duplicate derivation. Based on the horizon time, on the other hand, we can quickly determine which formulae should be maintained in the working memory and which ones can be erased because they no longer hold. We delete an annotated formula $\alpha\sigma_{[c,h]}$, as soon as the current time t exceeds h. This way of incrementally adding new groundings and immediately removing outdated is more efficient than processing all possible groundings. In particular, it is more efficient to maintain duplicates with temporal overlaps as in Example 6 than looking up existing groundings and merging their intervals.

Algorithm 1. Evaluation *Eval.* INPUT: Data stream $D=(T, v_D)$, where $T = [t_1, t_n]$; program P. OUTPUT: Output stream of P for D.

---

1 $S_0, I_0 \leftarrow \emptyset$; (set of ground formulae)
2 **for** $t_i \in \langle t_1, \ldots, t_n \rangle$ **do**
3      $\quad S_i \leftarrow S_{i-1} \cup \{ a_{[t_i,t_i]} \mid a \in v_D(t_i) \}$;
4      $\quad I_i \leftarrow S_i \cup \{ a_{[c,h]} \mid a_{[c,h]} \in I_{i-1} \wedge t_i \leq h \}$;
5      $\quad$ **while** *True* **do**
6          $\quad\quad I \leftarrow I_i$;
7          $\quad\quad$ **for** $\alpha \leftarrow \beta_1, \ldots, \beta_n \in P$ **do**
8              $\quad\quad\quad$ **for** $j \in \{1, \ldots, n\}$ **do** $I_i \leftarrow I_i \cup grd(\beta_j, I, t_1, t_i)$;
9              $\quad\quad\quad X \leftarrow \{ \alpha \sigma_{[max(c_1,\ldots,c_n),min(h_1,\ldots,h_n)]} \mid \beta \sigma_{[c_1,h_1]}, \ldots, \beta \sigma_{[c_n,h_n]} \in I_i$
10             $\quad\quad\quad\quad \wedge c_1, \ldots, c_n \leq t_i \wedge \bigvee_{j=1}^{n}(c_j = t_i) \}$;
11             $\quad\quad\quad I_i \leftarrow I_i \cup X \cup \{ \alpha \sigma_{[t_i,t_i]} \mid @_U \alpha(\sigma \cup \{U \mapsto t_i\})_{[t_i,h]} \in I_i \}$;
12         $\quad\quad$ **end**
13         $\quad\quad$ **if** $I_i = I$ **break**;
14     $\quad$ **end**
15     $\quad v(t_i) = \{ a \in \mathcal{A}^{\mathcal{I}} \mid a_{[c,h]} \in I_i \wedge c \leq t_i \leq h \}$; (can be streamed out if needed)
16 **end**
17 **return** $S = (T, v)$

Algorithm 1. We report in Algorithm 1 the main reasoning algorithm performed by the system. Sets $I_1, \ldots, I_n$ contain the annotated formulae at times $t_1, \ldots, t_n$; S_0, I_0 are convenience sets necessary for the very first iteration. At the beginning of each time point t_i we first collect in line 3 all facts from the input stream. Each atom $a \in v(t_i)$ is annotated with $[t_i, t_i]$, i.e., its validity will expire to hold already at the next time point. In line 4, we expire previous conclusions based on horizon times, i.e., among annotated intensional atoms $a_{[c,h]}$ only those are retained where $t_i \leq h$. Note that we do not delete atoms from the data stream.

In lines 5–14, the algorithm performs a fixed-point computation as usual where all rules are executed until nothing else can be derived (line 13). Lines 8–11 describe the physical execution of the rules and the materialization of the new derivations. First, line 8 collects all annotated groundings for extended atoms from the body of the considered rule. We discuss the details of this underlying function *grd* later (see Algorithm 2). In line 9 we then consider any substitution for the body that currently holds ($c_1, \ldots, c_n \leq t_i$). In order to produce a new derivation, we additionally require at least one formula was not considered in previous time points ($\bigvee_{j=1}^{n}(c_j = t_i)$).

The last condition implements a weak version of SNE, which we call *sSNE*. In fact, it only avoids duplicates between time points and not within the same time point. In order to capture also this last source of duplicates, we would need to add an additional internal counter to track multiple executions of the same rule. We decided not to implement this to limit the space overhead.

Algorithm 2. Function grd. INPUT: Formula α, database I, beginning time point t_b, end time point t_e. OUTPUT: Annotated groundings for α.

---

1 **switch** α **do**
2   **case** $p(\mathbf{x})$: **return** $\{\alpha\sigma_{[c,h]} \mid \alpha\sigma_{[c,h]} \in I\}$
3   **case** $\boxplus^n\beta$: $S \leftarrow grd(\beta, I, max(0, t_e - n), t_e)$;
4   **return** $S \cup \{\alpha\sigma_{[c,\min(c+n,h)]} \mid \beta\sigma_{[c,h]} \in S\}$
5   **case** $\Diamond\beta$: $S \leftarrow grd(\beta, I, t_b, t_e)$; **return** $S \cup \{\alpha\sigma_{[c,\infty]} \mid \beta\sigma_{[c,h]} \in S\}$
6   **case** $\Box\beta$: $S \leftarrow grd(\beta, I, t_b, t_e)$;
7   **return** $S \cup \{\alpha\sigma_{[t_e,t_e]} \mid \beta\sigma_{[c_1,h_1]}, \ldots, \beta\sigma_{[c_n,h_n]} \in S \wedge$
8              $c_i \leq c_{i+1}, h_i \geq c_{i+1} \; \forall 1 \leq i < n \wedge$
9              $c_1 \leq t_b \wedge t_e \leq h_n\}\}$
10   **case** $@_U\beta$: $S \leftarrow grd(\beta, I, t_b, t_e)$;
11   **return** $S \cup \{\alpha\sigma_{[c,h]} \mid \alpha\sigma_{[c,h]} \in I\} \cup$
12             $\{\alpha\sigma'_{[c,\infty]} \mid \beta\sigma_{[c,h]} \in S \wedge u \in [c,h] \wedge u \in [t_b, t_e] \wedge \sigma' = \sigma \cup \{U \mapsto u\}\}$
13 **end**

Matching substitutions in line 9 then are assigned to the head, where variables which are not used can be dropped as usual. Notice that consideration/horizon time for the ground head atom is given by intersection of all consideration/horizon times of the body atoms, i.e., the guarantee for the derivations is in the longest interval for which the body is guaranteed to hold. If the head is of form $@_U\alpha$ and holds now, i.e., at t_i, we also add an entry for α to I_i (line 11). After the fixed-point computation has terminated (line 13), we can either stream the output at t_i, i.e., $v'(t_i)$ (line 15), or store it for a later output of the answer stream S after processing the entire timeline (line 17).

Algorithm 2. The goal of function grd is to annotate and return all ground formulae which hold now or in the future. Depending on the input formula α, the algorithm might perform some recursive calls to retrieve annotated ground subformulae. In particular, this function determines the interval $[c, h]$ from a consideration time c to a horizon time h during which a grounding holds. It is precisely this annotation which allows us to perform an incremental computation and avoid the re-calculation of the entire inference at any time point.

Function grd works by a case distinction on the form of the input formula α, similarly as the entailment relation of the LARS semantics (Sect. 2). We explain the first three cases directly based on an example.

Example 7 (cont'd). As in Example 6, assume $\alpha = \boxplus^9\Diamond a(X)$ and input atom $a(y)$ at time 5. Towards annotated groundings of α, we first obtain the substitution $\sigma = \{X \mapsto y\}$ which can be guaranteed only for time point $c = 5$ for atom $a(X)$, i.e., $a(X)\sigma_{[5,5]} = a(y)_{[5,5]}$. Based on this, we eventually want to compute $\alpha\sigma_{[5,14]}$. This is done in two steps. First, the subformula $\beta = \Diamond a(X)$ is agnostic about the timeline, and its grounding $\beta\sigma$ gets an annotation $[5, \infty]$. The intuition behind setting the horizon time to ∞ at this point is that $\Diamond\beta$ will always hold as soon β holds once. The restriction to a specific timeline is then carried out when

$\beta\sigma_{[5,\infty]}$ is handled in case $\boxplus^9\beta$, which limits the horizon to $\min(c+n,\infty) = 14$; any horizon time h received for β that is smaller than 14 would remain.

Thus, the conceptual approach of Algorithm 2 is to obtain the intervals when a subformula holds and adjust the temporal guarantee either by extending or restricting the annotation. Since the operator $\square$ evaluates intervals, we have to include the boundaries of the window. That is, if a formula $\boxplus^n\square p(\mathbf{x})$ must be grounded, we call grd in Algorithm 1 for the entire timeline $[t_1, t_i]$, where t_i is the current evaluation time. Thus, we get $t_b = t_1, t_e = t_i$ initially. However, in order for $\square p(\mathbf{x})$ to hold under a substitution σ within the window of the last n time points, $p(\mathbf{x})\sigma$ must hold at every time point $[t-n, t]$. Thus, the recursive call for $\boxplus^n\beta$ limits the timeline to $[t_e - n, t_e]$. Then, the case $\square\beta$ seeks to find a sequence of ordered, overlapping annotations $[c_1, h_1], \ldots, [c_n, h_n]$ that subsumes the considered interval $[t_b, t_e]$. In this case, $\square\beta$ holds at t_e, but it cannot be guaranteed to hold longer. Thus, when $a\sigma_{[t_e, t_e]}$ is returned to the case for $\boxplus^n$, the horizon time will not be extended.

Example 8 (cont'd). Consider $\alpha' = \boxplus^2\square a(X)$. Assume that in the timeline $[0, 7]$ at time points $t = 5, 6, 7$, we received the input $a(y)$, hence $\boxplus^2\square a(y)$ has to hold at $t = 7$. When we call (in Algorithm 1) $grd(\alpha', I, 0, 7)$, where $I = \{a(y)_{[5,5]}, a(y)_{[6,6]}, a(y)_{[7,7]}\}$, the case for $\boxplus^2\beta$ will call $grd(\square a(X), I, 5, 7)$. The sequence of groundings as listed in I subsumes $[5, 7]$, i.e., the scope given by $t_b = 5$ and $t_e = 7$, and thus the case for $\square$ returns $\square a(y)_{[7,7]}$. The annotation remains for α', i.e., $grd(\alpha', I, 0, 7) = \{\boxplus^2\square a(y)_{[7,7]}\}$. Note when at time 8 atom $a(y)$ does not hold, neither does $\boxplus^2\square a(y)$. Hence, in contrast to $\diamond$, the horizon time is not extended for $\square$.

With respect to the temporal aspect, the case for @ works similarly as the one for $\diamond$, since both operators amount to existential quantification within the timeline. In addition $\diamond$, the @-operator also includes in the time point substitution $U \mapsto u$ where the subformula β holds (line 12). In Line 11, we additionally take from I the explicit derivations for @-atoms derived so far.

Proposition 2. *For every data stream D and program P, Algorithm 1 terminates.*

Theorem 1. *Let P be a positive plain LARS program, D be a data stream with timeline $T = [t_1, t_n]$. Then, S is the output stream of P for D iff $S = Eval(D, P)$.*

Tuple-based windows. As noted earlier, our annotation-based approach based on consideration time c and horizon time h works analogously from the tuple-based window by additionally working with a consideration count $c_\#$ and a horizon count $h_\#$ for every ground formula. Each formula can then hold and expire in only one of these dimensions, or both of them at the same time.

Example 9. Consider again rule r from Example 5. When $b(y, z)$ streams in at time 38 as third atom, we obtain an annotated ground formula $\boxplus^{\#3}\diamond b(y, z)_{[3\#, 5\#]}$. That is, when the fourth and fifth atoms stream in, regardless at which time points, $\boxplus^{\#3}\diamond b(y, z)$ is still guaranteed to hold.

Adding negation. Notably, our approach can be extended for handling negation as well. In plain LARS as defined in [8], extended atoms β from rule bodies may occur under negation. We can, however, instead assume negation to occur directly in front of atoms: Due to the FLP-semantics [13] of LARS [9], where "not" can be identified with $\neg$, we get the following equivalences for both $w \in \{\tau_n, \#_n\}$: $\neg \boxplus^w \Diamond a(\mathbf{x}) \equiv \boxplus^w \Box \neg a(\mathbf{x})$ and $\neg \boxplus^w \Box a(\mathbf{x}) \equiv \boxplus^w \Diamond \neg a(\mathbf{x})$. The case is more subtle for @, since $@_t \neg a(\mathbf{x})$ implies that $a(\mathbf{x})$ is false. However, due to the definition of @, $\neg @_t a(\mathbf{x})$ can also hold if t is not contained in the considered timeline. Thus, the equivalence $\neg \boxplus^w @_t a(\mathbf{x}) \equiv \boxplus^w @_t \neg a(\mathbf{x})$ (necessarily) holds only if the timeline contains t. This assumption is safe when we assume that the timeline always covers all considered time points.

Our approach extends naturally to a variant of plain LARS where negation appears only in front of atoms: In addition to the base case $p(\mathbf{x})$ in Line 2 in Algorithm 2 we must add a case for a negative literal $\ell = \neg p(\mathbf{x})$. Using standard conventions, we then have to consider all possible substitutions σ for variables in $\mathbf{x}$ that occur positively in the same rule r, such that $p(\mathbf{x})\sigma$ does not hold.

We obtain a fragment that is significantly more expressive, but results in having multiple answer streams in general: note that plain LARS essentially subsumes normal logic programs, and the program $a \leftarrow \text{not } b;\ b \leftarrow \text{not } a$ has two answer sets $\{a\}$ and $\{b\}$. Analogously, we get multiple answer streams by allowing such loops through negation. To retain both unique model semantics and tractability, we propose restricting to stratified negation, i.e., allowing negation but no loops through negation. Then, we can add to Algorithm 1 an additional for-loop around lines 6–13 to compute the answer stream stratum by stratum bottom up as usual. In fact, our implementation makes use of this extension.

4   Evaluation

We evaluate the performance of $Laser$[1] on two dimensions: First, we measure the impact of our incremental procedures on several operators by microbenchmarking the system on special single-rule programs. Second, we compare the performance against the state of the art on more realistic programs.

Streams. Unfortunately, we could not use some well-known stream reasoning benchmarks (e.g., *SRBench* [28], *CSRBench* [12] *LSBench* [20], and *CityBench* [2]) because (i) we need to manually change the window sizes and the speed of stream in order to benchmark our incremental approach, but this is not often supported in these benchmarks; (ii) in order to be effective, a micro-benchmark needs to introduce as little overhead as possible; (iii) we needed to make sure that all reasoners return the same results for a fair comparison, and this was easier with a custom data generator that we wrote for this purpose.

State-of-the-art. In line with current literature, we selected *C-SPARQL* [5], and *CQELS* [19] as our main competitors. For LARS operators that are not supported by these engines, we compare Laser with *Ticker* [10], another recent

---

[1] https://github.com/karmaresearch/Laser.

engine for (non-stratified) plain LARS programs.[2] Ticker comes with two reasoning modes, a fully incremental one, and another one that uses an ASP encoding which is then evaluated by the ASP solver Clingo [15]. The incremental reasoning mode was not available at the time of this evaluation. Thus, our evaluation against Ticker concerns only the reasoning mode which is based on Clingo.

Data generation. Unfortunately, each engine has its own routines for reading the input. As a result, we were compelled to develop custom data generators to guarantee fairness. A key problem is that CQELS processes every new data item immediately after the arrival in contrast to Laser and C-SPARQL that process them in batches. Hence, to control the number of triples that stream into CQELS, and make sure that all engines receive equal number of triples at every time point, we configured each data generator to issue a triple at calculated intervals. For this same reason, we report the evaluation results as the average runtime per input triple and not runtime per time point.

Experimental platform. The experiments were performed on a machine with 32-core Intel(R) Xeon(R) 2.60 GHz and 256 G of memory. We used Java 1.8 for C-SPARQL and CQELS and PyPy 5.8 for Laser. We set the initial Java heap size to 20 G and increase the maximum heap size to 80 G to minimize potential negative effects of JVM garbage collection. For Ticker we used Clingo 5.1.0.

Window-Diamond. The standard snapshot semantics employed in C-SPARQL and CQELS selects recent data and then abstracts away the timestamps. In LARS, this amounts to using $\diamond$ to existentially quantify within a window. Here, we evaluate how efficiently each engine can evaluate this case.

We use the rule $q(A, B) \leftarrow \boxplus^n \diamond p(A, B)$, where a predicate of form $r(A, B)$ corresponds to a triple $\langle A, r, B \rangle$. The window size and the *stream rate* (i.e. the number of atoms streaming in the system at every time point) are the experiment parameters. We create a number of artificial streams which produces a series of unique atoms with predicate p at different rates; we vary window sizes from 1 s to 80 s and the stream rate from 200 to 800 triples per second (t/s).

Figure 2(a) reports the average runtime per input triple for each engine. The figure shows that Laser is faster than the other engines. Furthermore, we observe that average runtime of Laser grows significantly slower with the window size as well as with the stream rate. Here, incremental reasoning clearly is beneficial.

Window-Box. The Box operator is not available in C-SPARQL and CQELS. The semantics of $\Box$ (as well as @) may be encoded using explicit timestamps in additional triples but the languages themselves do not directly support it. Therefore, we evaluate the performance of Laser against Ticker. Similar to the experiments with $\boxplus\diamond$, we employ the rule $q(A, B) \leftarrow \boxplus^n \Box p(A, B)$. The experimental settings are similar to the previous experiment and results are reported in Fig. 2(b), showing that Laser was orders of magnitude faster than Ticker. Notice that with $\Box$ we cannot extend the horizon time, therefore the incremental evaluation cannot be exploited. Thus, the performance gain stems from maintaining existing substitutions instead of full recomputations.

---

[2] https://github.com/hbeck/ticker.

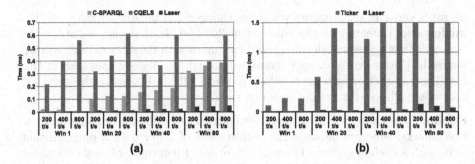

Fig. 2. (a) Avg runtime of ◇ (b) and of □ on multiple window sizes and stream rates.

Data joins. We now focus on a rule which requires a data join. The computation evaluates the rule $q(A, C) \leftarrow \boxplus^n \Diamond p(A, B), \boxplus^n \Diamond p(B, C)$ with different window sizes/stream rates. This program adds the crucial operation of performing a join. From the results reported in Fig. 3(a), we observe the following:

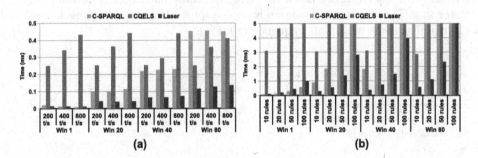

Fig. 3. (a) Avg. runtimes when the rule requires a data join (b) Avg. runtimes with multiple rules.

(i) Laser is significantly faster that CQELS and C-SPARQL with all configurations of window and stream sizes. (ii) The difference becomes bigger for larger window sizes for which the benefit of incremental evaluation increases.

We profiled the execution of Laser with the larger windows and stream sizes and discovered that only about half of the time is spent on the join while half is needed to return the results. We also performed an experiment where we deactivated sSNE and did a normal join instead. We observed that sSNE is slightly slower than the normal join with small window sizes, but as the size of windows and stream rate increase, sSNE is significantly faster. In the best case, the activation of sSNE produced a runtime which was 10 times lower.

Evaluating multiple rules. We now evaluate the performance of Laser in a situation where the program contains multiple rules. In C-SPARQL or CQELS, this translates to a scenario where there are multiple standing queries. To do so, we run a series of experiments where we changed the number of rules and the window sizes (stream rate was constant at 200 t/s). To that end, we utilize the same rule that we used in the *data join* benchmark with the same data generator. Figure 3(b) presents the average runtime (per triple). We see that also in this case Laser outperforms both C-SPARQL and CQELS, except in the very last case where all systems did not finish on time.

Cooling use case. So far we have evaluated the performance using analytic benchmarks. Now, we measure the performance of Laser with a program that deals with a cooling system. The program of Fig. 4 determines based on a water temperature stream whether the system is working under normal conditions, or it is too hot and produces steam, or is too cold and the water is freezing.

The system also reports temperature readings that are either too high or too low. Note that both @ (especially in the rule head) and □ go beyond standard stream reasoning features. It is not possible to directly translate this program into C-SPARQL or CQELS queries, so we can only compare the performance of Laser with Ticker. In this case, the data generator produces a sequence of random temperature readings. Like before, we gradually increased the window size and stream rate. The results, shown in Fig. 5, indicate that Laser is considerably faster than Ticker and can maintain a good response time ($\leq 100\,\mu s$) even when the readings come with high frequency (800 t/s).

$r_1 :$ $@_T\, steam(V) \leftarrow \boxplus^n @_T\, temp(V),\ V \geq 100$

$r_2 :$ $@_T\, liquid(V) \leftarrow \boxplus^n @_T\, temp(V),\ V \geq 1,\ V < 100$

$r_3 :$ $@_T\, isSteam \leftarrow \boxplus^n @_T\, steam(V)$

$r_4 :$ $@_T\, isLiquid \leftarrow \boxplus^n @_T\, liquid(V)$

$r_5 :$ $alarm \leftarrow \boxplus^n \square\, isSteam$

$r_6 :$ $normal \leftarrow \boxplus^n \square\, isLiquid$

$r_7 :$ $freeze \leftarrow not\, alarm, not\, normal$

$r_8 :$ $veryHot(T) \leftarrow \boxplus^n @_T\, steam(V), V \geq 150$

$r_9 :$ $veryCold(T) \leftarrow \boxplus^n @_T\, liquid(V), V = 1$

Fig. 4. Program for a cooling system monitoring.

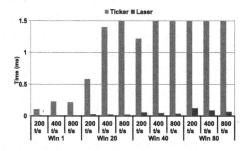

Fig. 5. Average execution time per atom of Lars program in Fig. 4.

5   Related Work and Conclusion

Related Work. The vision of stream reasoning was proposed by Della Valle et al. in [11]. Since then, numerous publications have studied different aspects of stream reasoning such as: extending SPARQL for stream querying [4,19], building stream reasoners [4,19,22], scalable stream reasoning [16], and ASP models for stream reasoning [14]. However, due to lack of standardized formalism for RDF stream processing, each of these engines provide a different set of features, and results are hard to compare. A survey of these techniques is available at [21]. Our work differs in the sense that it is based on LARS [9], one of the first formal semantics for stream reasoning with window operators.

An area closely related to stream processing is incremental reasoning, which has been the subject of a large volume of research [23,27]. In this context, [6] describes a technique to add expiration time to RDF triples to drop them when the are no longer valid. Nonetheless, this approach does not support expressive operations such as □ and @ that our engine supports. In a similar way, [18] proposes another incremental algorithm for processing streams which again boils down to efficiently identifying expired information. We showed that our approach outperforms their work. Next, [8] proposes a technique to incrementally update an answer stream of a so-called s-stratified plain LARS program by extending truth maintenance techniques. While [8] focuses on multiple models, we aim at highly efficient reasoning for use cases that guarantee single models. Similarly, the incremental reasoning mode of Ticker [10] focuses on model maintenance but not on high performance. Stream reasoning based on ASP was also explored in a probabilistic context [25] which however did not employ windows.

Conclusion. We presented Laser, a new stream reasoner that is built on the rule-based framework LARS. Laser distinguishes itself by supporting expressive reasoning without giving up efficient computation. Our implementation, freely available, has competitive performance with the current state-of-the-art. This indicates that expressive reasoning is possible also on highly dynamic streams of data. Future work can be done on several fronts: Practically, our techniques extend naturally to further windows operators such as tumbling windows or tuple-based windows with pre-filtering. From a theoretical perspective, the question arises which variations or more involved syntactic fragments of LARS may be considered that are compatible with the presented annotation-based incremental evaluation. Moreover, our support of stratified negation is prototypical and can be made more efficient. More generally, investigations on the system-related research question of reducing the runtimes even further are important to tackle the increasing number and volumes of streams that are emerging from the Web.

References

1. Abiteboul, S., Hull, R., Vianu, V.: Foundations of Databases, vol. 8. Addison-Wesley, Reading (1995)
2. Ali, M.I., Gao, F., Mileo, A.: CityBench: a configurable benchmark to evaluate RSP engines using smart city datasets. In: Arenas, M., et al. (eds.) ISWC 2015. LNCS, vol. 9367, pp. 374–389. Springer, Cham (2015). doi:10.1007/978-3-319-25010-6_25
3. Anicic, D., Fodor, P., Rudolph, S., Nenad Stojanovic, E.-S.: A unified language for event processing and stream reasoning. In: Proceedings of WWW, pp. 635–644 (2011)
4. Barbieri, D.F., Braga, D., Ceri, S., Valle, E.D., Grossniklaus, M.: C-SPARQL: SPARQL for continuous querying. In: Proceedings of WWW, pp. 1061–1062. ACM (2009)
5. Barbieri, D.F., Braga, D., Ceri, S., Della Valle, E., Grossniklaus, M.: C-SPARQL: a continuous query language for RDF data streams. Int. J. Semant. Comput. 4(1), 3–25 (2010)
6. Barbieri, D.F., Braga, D., Ceri, S., Valle, E., Grossniklaus, M.: Incremental reasoning on streams and rich background knowledge. In: Aroyo, L., Antoniou, G., Hyvönen, E., Teije, A., Stuckenschmidt, H., Cabral, L., Tudorache, T. (eds.) ESWC 2010. LNCS, vol. 6088, pp. 1–15. Springer, Heidelberg (2010). doi:10.1007/978-3-642-13486-9_1
7. Bazoobandi, H.R., Beck, H., Urbani, J.: Expressive Stream Reasoning with Laser. CoRR, abs/1707.08876 (2017)
8. Beck, H., Dao-Tran, M., Eiter, T.: Answer update for rule-based stream reasoning. In: Proceedings of IJCAI, pp. 2741–2747 (2015)
9. Beck, H., Dao-Tran, M., Eiter, T., Fink, M.: LARS: A logic-based framework for analyzing reasoning over streams. In: Proceedings of AAAI, pp. 1431–1438 (2015)
10. Beck, H., Eiter, T., Folie, C.: Ticker: a system for incremental ASP-based stream reasoning. TPLP (2017, to appear)
11. Della Valle, E., Ceri, S., Van Harmelen, F., Fensel, D.: It's a streaming world! reasoning upon rapidly changing information. IEEE Intell. Syst. 24(6), 83–89 (2009)
12. Dell'Aglio, D., Calbimonte, J.-P., Balduini, M., Corcho, O., Della Valle, E.: On correctness in RDF stream processor benchmarking. In: Alani, H., et al. (eds.) ISWC 2013. LNCS, vol. 8219, pp. 326–342. Springer, Heidelberg (2013). doi:10.1007/978-3-642-41338-4_21
13. Faber, W., Leone, N., Pfeifer, G.: Recursive aggregates in disjunctive logic programs: semantics and complexity. In: Alferes, J.J., Leite, J. (eds.) JELIA 2004. LNCS (LNAI), vol. 3229, pp. 200–212. Springer, Heidelberg (2004). doi:10.1007/978-3-540-30227-8_19
14. Gebser, M., Grote, T., Kaminski, R., Obermeier, P., Sabuncu, O., Schaub, T.: Answer set programming for stream reasoning. arXiv preprint arXiv:1301.1392 (2013)
15. Gebser, M., Kaminski, R., Kaufmann, B., Schaub, T.: Clingo = ASP + control: Preliminary report. CoRR, abs/1405.3694 (2014)
16. Hoeksema, J., Kotoulas, S.: High-performance distributed stream reasoning using S4. In: Ordring Workshop at ISWC (2011)
17. Komazec, S., Cerri, D., Fensel, D.: Sparkwave: continuous schema-enhanced pattern matching over RDF data streams. In: DEBS, pp. 58–68 (2012)
18. Le-Phuoc, D.: Operator-aware approach for boosting performance in RDF stream processing. Web Semant. Sci. Serv. Agents World Wide Web 42, 38–54 (2017)

19. Le-Phuoc, D., Dao-Tran, M., Xavier Parreira, J., Hauswirth, M.: A native and adaptive approach for unified processing of linked streams and linked data. In: Aroyo, L., Welty, C., Alani, H., Taylor, J., Bernstein, A., Kagal, L., Noy, N., Blomqvist, E. (eds.) ISWC 2011. LNCS, vol. 7031, pp. 370–388. Springer, Heidelberg (2011). doi:10.1007/978-3-642-25073-6_24

20. Le-Phuoc, D., Dao-Tran, M., Pham, M.-D., Boncz, P., Eiter, T., Fink, M.: Linked stream data processing engines: facts and figures. In: Cudré-Mauroux, P., et al. (eds.) ISWC 2012. LNCS, vol. 7650, pp. 300–312. Springer, Heidelberg (2012). doi:10.1007/978-3-642-35173-0_20

21. Margara, A., Urbani, J., Van Harmelen, F., Bal, H.: Streaming the web: Reasoning over dynamic data. Web Semant. Sci. Serv. Agents World Wide Web **25**, 24–44 (2014)

22. Mileo, A., Abdelrahman, A., Policarpio, S., Hauswirth, M.: StreamRule: a nonmonotonic stream reasoning system for the semantic web. In: International Conference on Web Reasoning and Rule Systems, pp. 247–252 (2013)

23. Motik, B., Nenov, Y., Piro, R., Horrocks, I.: Incremental update of datalog materialisation: the backward/forward algorithm. In: Proceedings of AAAI, pp. 1560–1568 (2015)

24. Nenov, Y., Piro, R., Motik, B., Horrocks, I., Wu, Z., Banerjee, J.: RDFox: a highlyscalable RDF store. In: Arenas, M., et al. (eds.) ISWC 2015. LNCS, vol. 9367, pp. 3–20. Springer, Cham (2015). doi:10.1007/978-3-319-25010-6_1

25. Nickles, M., Mileo, A.: A hybrid approach to inference in probabilistic nonmonotonic logic programming. In: Proceedings of the 2nd International Workshop on Probabilistic Logic, pp. 57–68 (2015)

26. Urbani, J., Jacobs, C., Krötzsch, M.: Column-oriented datalog materialization for large knowledge graphs. In Proceedings of AAAI, pp. 258–264 (2016)

27. Urbani, J., Margara, A., Jacobs, C., Harmelen, F., Bal, H.: DynamiTE: parallel materialization of dynamic RDF data. In: Alani, H., et al. (eds.) ISWC 2013. LNCS, vol. 8218, pp. 657–672. Springer, Heidelberg (2013). doi:10.1007/978-3-642-41335-3_41

28. Zhang, Y., Duc, P.M., Corcho, O., Calbimonte, J.-P.: SRBench: a streaming RDF/SPARQL benchmark. In: Cudré-Mauroux, P., et al. (eds.) ISWC 2012. LNCS, vol. 7649, pp. 641–657. Springer, Heidelberg (2012). doi:10.1007/978-3-642-35176-1_40

Semantics and Validation of Shapes Schemas for RDF

Iovka Boneva[1]([⊠]), Jose E. Labra Gayo[2], and Eric G. Prud'hommeaux[3]

[1] Univ. Lille - CRIStAL, 59000 Lille, France
iovka.boneva@univ-lille.fr
[2] University of Oviedo, Oviedo, Spain
labra@uniovi.es
[3] W3C and Stata Center, MIT, Cambridge, USA
eric@w3.org

Abstract. We present a formal semantics and proof of soundness for shapes schemas, an expressive schema language for RDF graphs that is the foundation of Shape Expressions Language 2.0. It can be used to describe the vocabulary and the structure of an RDF graph, and to constrain the admissible properties and values for nodes in that graph. The language defines a typing mechanism called shapes against which nodes of the graph can be checked. It includes an algebraic grouping operator, a choice operator and cardinality constraints for the number of allowed occurrences of a property. Shapes can be combined using Boolean operators, and can use possibly recursive references to other shapes.

We describe the syntax of the language and define its semantics. The semantics is proven to be well-defined for schemas that satisfy a reasonable syntactic restriction, namely stratified use of negation and recursion. We present two algorithms for the validation of an RDF graph against a shapes schema. The first algorithm is a direct implementation of the semantics, whereas the second is a non-trivial improvement. We also briefly give implementation guidelines.

1 Introduction

RDF's distributed graph model encouraged adoption for publication and manipulation of e.g. social and biological data. Coding errors in data stores like DBpedia have largely been handled in a piecemeal fashion with no formal mechanism for detecting or describing schema violations. Extending uptake into environments like medicine, business and banking requires structural validation analogous to what is available in relational or XML schemas.

While OWL ontologies can be used for limited structural validation, they are generally used for formal models of reusable classes and predicates describing objects in some domain. Applications typically consume and produce graphs composed of precise compositions of such ontologies. A company's human resources records may leverage terms from FOAF and Dublin Core, but only certain terms, composed into specific structures, and subject to additional use-specific constraints. We would no more want to impose the constraints of a single

C. d'Amato et al. (Eds.): ISWC 2017, Part I, LNCS 10587, pp. 104–120, 2017.
DOI: 10.1007/978-3-319-68288-4_7

human resources application suite on FOAF and Dublin Core than we would want to assert that such applications need to consume all ontologically valid permutations of FOAF and Dublin Core entities. Further, open-world constraints on OWL ontologies make it impossible to use conventional OWL tools to e.g. detect missing properties. Shape expression schemas (ShEx 1.0) [6,8] were introduced as a high level language in which it is easy to mix terms from arbitrary ontologies. They provide a schema language in which one can define structural constraints (arc labels, cardinalities, datatypes, etc.) and since version 2.0 (ShEx 2.0)[1], mix them using Boolean connectives (disjunction, conjunction and negation).

A schema language for any data format has several uses: communicating to humans and machines the form of input/output data; enabling machine-verification of data for production, publication, or consumption; driving query and input interfaces; static analysis of queries. In this, ShEx provides a similar role as relational and XML schemas. A ShEx schema validates nodes in a graph against a schema construct called a *shape*. In XML, validating an element against an XML Schema[2] type or element or Relax NG[3] production recursively tests nested elements against constituent rules. In ShEx, validating a node in a graph against a shape recursively tests the nodes which are the object of triples constrained in that shape. An essential difference however is that unlike trees, graphs can have cycles and recursive definitions can yield infinite computation. Moreover, ShEx 2.0 includes a negation operator, and it is well known that mixing recursion with negation can lead to incoherent semantics.

Contributions. In this paper we present *shapes schemas*, a schema language that is the foundation of ShEx 2.0 (Sect. 2). The precise relationship between shapes schemas and ShEx 2.0 is given at the end of Sect. 2. We formally define the semantics of shapes schemas and show that it is sound for schemas that mix recursion and negation in a stratified manner (Sect. 3). We then propose two algorithms for validating an RDF graph node against a shapes schema. Both algorithms are shown to be correct w.r.t. the semantics (Sect. 4). We finally discuss future research directions and conclude (Sect. 5).

Related Work. In [8] we gave semantics for ShEx 1.0. The latter does not use Boolean operators end because of negation, the extension to ShEx 2.0 (and thus to shapes schemas) is non trivial.

Closest to shapes schemas is the SHACL[4] language both in terms of purpose and expressiveness. SHACLalso defines named constraints called shapes to be checked on RDF graph nodes. Unlike ShEx, SHACLis not completely independent from the RDF Schema vocabulary: rdfs:Classes play a particular role there as a shape can be required to hold for all the nodes that are instances of some rdfs:Class. Therefore validation in SHACLrequires partial RDF Schema entailment

---

[1] Shape Expressions Language 2.0. http://shex.io/shex-semantics/index.html.

[2] W3C XML Schema. http://www.w3.org/XML/Schema.

[3] RELAX NG home page. http://relaxng.org.

[4] Shapes Constraint Language (SHACL). https://www.w3.org/TR/shacl/.

in order to discover all rdfs:Classes of a node. Regarding expressiveness, the main differences between SHACLand shapes schemas are that SHACLallows to define constraints based on property paths and for comparison of values; SHACLdoes not have the algebraic operators some-of and each-of and uses Boolean connectives for defining complex shapes; finally SHACLdoes not define the semantics of recursive shapes.

Ontology languages such as OWL, description logics or RDF Schema are not meant to define (complex) constraints on the data and we do not compare shapes schemas with them. Proposals were made for using OWL with a closed world assumption in order to express integrity constraints [5,9]. They associate alternative semantics with the existing OWL syntax and can be misleading for users.

Some approaches use SPARQL to express constraints on graphs (SPIN[5], RDFUnit [3]), or compile a domain specific language into SPARQL queries [2]. SPARQL allows to express complex constraints but does not support recursion. While SPARQL constraints can be validated by standard SPARQL engines, they are harder to write and maintain compared to high-level schemas like ShEx and SHACL.

Description Set Profiles[6] is a constraint language that uses an RDF vocabulary to define templates and constrain the value and cardinality of properties. It does not have any equivalent of the each-of algebraic operator, and was not designed to be human-readable.

Introductory Example. Let is: be a namespace prefix from some ontology, ex: be the prefix used in the example schema and instance, and foaf: and xsd: be the standard FOAF and XSD prefixes, respectively. The schema $\mathbf{S}_0$ is as follows

\<UserShape\>	→ foaf:name @\<StringValue\> ; foaf:mbox @\<IRIValue\> [0;1]
\<ProgShape\>	→ ex:expertise @\<IRIValue\> [0;*] ; ex:experience @\<ExpValueSet\>
\<ClientShape\>	→ ex:clientNbr @\<IntValue\> | ex:clientAffil @\<AnythgShape\>
\<IssueShape\>	→ is:reportedBy @\<ClientAndUser\> ;
	is:reproducedBy @\<ProgShape\> [1;5] ;
	is:relatedTo @\<IssueShape\> [0;*]
\<AnythgShape\>	→ IRI @\<AnythgShape\> [0;*]
\<ClientAndUser\>	→ Def_{Client} ; IRI − {ex:clientNbr, ex:clientAffil} @\<AnythgShape\> [0;*]
	AND Def_{User} ; IRI − {foaf:name, foaf:mbox} @\<AnythgShape\> [0;*]
\<StringValue\>	→ xsd:string
\<IRIValue\>	→ IRI
\<ExpValueSet\>	→ {ex:senior, ex:junior}
\<IntValue\>	→ xsd:integer

where Def_{Client} is the definition of \<ClientShape\>, and similarly for Def_{User}, and − in the definition of \<ClientAndUser\> is the set difference operator. The schema $\mathbf{S}_0$ defines four shapes intended to describe users, programmers, clients and issues, respectively. \<UserShape\> requires that a node has one foaf:name property with string value, and an optional foaf:mbox that is an IRI. The optional mailbox is specified by the cardinality constraint [0;1]. Other

---

[5] SPIN - Modeling Vocabulary. http://www.w3.org/Submission/spin-modeling/.

[6] Description Set Profiles: A constraint language for Dublin Core Application Profiles. http://dublincore.org/documents/dc-dsp/.

cardinality constraints used in $\mathbf{S}_0$ are [0;*] for zero or more, and [1;5] for one up to five. When no cardinality is given, the default is "exactly one". A <ProgShape> node has zero or more ex:expertise properties with values that are IRIs, and one ex:experience property whose value is one among ex:senior and ex:junior. A <ClientShape> has either a ex:clientNbr that is an integer, or a ex:clientAffil(iation) with unconstrained value (i.e. <AnythgShape>), but not both. Finally, an issue (<IssueShape>) is reported by somebody who is client and user, is reproduced by one to five programmers, and can be related to zero or more issues.

The shapes in $\mathbf{S}_0$ whose name contains Value specify the set of allowed values for a node. This can be the set of all values of some literal datatype (e.g. string, integer), the set of all nodes of some kind (e.g. IRI), or an explicitly given set (e.g. <ExpValueSet>). <AnythgShape> is satisfied by every node. It states that the node can have zero or more outgoing triples whose predicates can be any IRI, and whose objects match <AnythgShape>. Finally, <ClientAndUser> uses a conjunction to require that a node has both the client and the user properties. Its definition is a bit technical. The right hand side of the conjunction states that the node must have a foaf:name and an optional foaf:mbox (Def_{User}). Moreover (the ; operator), the node can have any number ([0;*]) of properties that can be any IRI except for foaf:name and foaf:mbox and whose value is unconstrained. The latter is necessary in order to allow the "client" properties required by the left hand side of the conjunction.

Graph $\mathbf{G}_0$ here after is described by schema $\mathbf{S}_0$. Nodes ex:issue1 and ex:issue2 have shape <IssueShape>; ex:fatima and ex:emin are <ClientAndUser>; ex:ren and ex:noa have shape <ProgShape>.

ex:issue1
   is:reportedBy ex:fatima ;
   is:reproducedBy ex:ren , ex:noa ;
   is:relatedTo ex:issue2 .
ex:issue2
   is:reportedBy ex:emin ;
   is:reproducedBy ex:ren ;
   is:relatedTo ex:issue1 .

ex:fatima ex:clientNbr 1 ;
   foaf:name "Fatima Smith" .
ex:ren ex:expertise ex:semweb ;
   ex:experience ex:senior .
ex:noa ex:experience ex:junior .
ex:emin ex:clientAffil "ABC";
   foaf:name "Emin V. Petrov" ;
   foaf:mbox <mailto:evp@example.org> .

The RDF Graph Model. As usual, we assume three disjoint sets: IRI a set of IRIs, Lit a set of literals, and Blank a set of blank nodes. An *RDF graph* is a set of triples over IRI ∪ Blank × IRI × IRI ∪ Lit ∪ Blank. For a triple (s, p, o) in some graph, s is called its subject, p is called its predicate, and o is called its object. We denote $\mathbf{Nodes(G)}$ the set of *nodes* of the graph $\mathbf{G}$, that is, the elements that appear in a subject or object position in some triple of $\mathbf{G}$. The *neighbourhood* of node n in graph $\mathbf{G}$ is the set of triples in $\mathbf{G}$ that have n as subject, and is denoted $neigh_{\mathbf{G}}(n)$ or simply $neigh(n)$ when $\mathbf{G}$ is clear from the context. We use disjoint union on sets of triples, denoted ⊎: if N, N_1, N_2 are sets of triples, $N = N_1 \uplus N_2$ means that $N_1 \cup N_2 = N$ and $N_1 \cap N_2 = \emptyset$.

2   Shapes Schemas

A shapes schema **S** defines a set of named shapes. A shape is a description of the graph structure that can be visited starting from a particular node. It can talk about the value of the node itself and about its neighbourhood. Shapes can use (Boolean combinations of) other shapes and can be recursive.

Formally, a shapes schema **S** is a pair (**L, def**), where **L** is a set of *shape labels* used as names of shapes and **def** is a function that with every shape label associates a shape expression. In examples, we write $L \to S$ as short for **def**$(L) = S$ (for a shape label L and a shape expression S).

Shape Expressions. The grammar for shape expressions is given on Fig. 1a. A *shape expression* (ShExpr) is a Boolean combination of two atomic components: value description and neighbourhood description. A neighbourhood description (NeigDescr) defines the expected neighbourhood of a node and is given by a triple expression (TExpr, see below). A value description (ValueDescr) is a set that declares the admissible values for a node. The set can contain IRIs, literals, and the special constant _b to indicate that the node can be a blank node. ShEx 2.0 proposes concrete syntax for different kinds of value description sets (literal datatypes, regex patterns to be matched by IRIs, intervals, etc.). Here we focus on defining the semantics so the concrete syntax for such sets is irrelevant. A ValueDescr can be an arbitrary set with the unique assumption that it has a finite representation for which membership can be effectively computed.

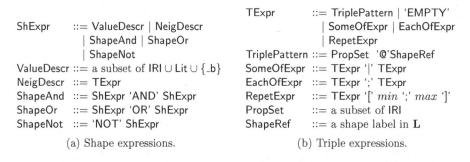

(a) Shape expressions.   (b) Triple expressions.

Fig. 1. The grammar for shape expressions and triple expressions.

Triple expressions. Triple expressions describe the expected neighbourhood of a node. They are inspired by regular expressions likewise DTDs and XML Schema for XML. A triple expression will be matched by the neighbourhood of a node in a graph, similarly to type definitions in XML Schema that are matched by the children of some node. The main difference is that the neighbourhood of a node in an RDF graph is a (unordered) set, whereas the children of a node in an XML document form a sequence.

The grammar for triple expressions (TExpr) is given on Fig. 1b, in which min is a natural, and max is a natural or the special value $*$. The basic triple expression is a triple pattern and it constrains triples. A triple expression composed of each-of (separated by a ';'), some-of (separated by a '|') and repetition operators is satisfied if some distribution of the triples in the neighborhood of a node exactly satisfies the expression. Section 3.1 defines this and draws the analogy with regular expressions. In examples, we omit the braces for singleton PropSets, e.g. we write foaf:name @<StringValue> instead of {foaf:name} @<StringValue>.

Example 1 (Shape expressions, triple expressions). In schema S_0 from the introductory example, the definitions of the five shapes with name ...Shape... are triple expressions and collectively make use of all the operators: each-of (;), some-of (|), repetition. All shapes with name ...Value... are defined by atomic ValueDescrs. The definition of <ClientAndUser> is a ShapeAnd expression.   □

Relationship between Shapes Schemas and ShEx 2.0. Shapes schemas slightly generalizes ShEx 2.0 and thus allows for a more concise definition of syntax and semantics. For readers familiar with ShEx 2.0 we now explain how shapes schemas differ from ShEx 2.0. First, TriplePattern uses a set of properties, whereas the analogous triple constraint in ShEx 2.0 uses a single property. This slight generalization allows to encode the CLOSED and EXTRA constructs of ShEx 2.0. In shapes schemas, triple expressions are always closed (whereas in ShEx 2.0 they are non closed by default) but an expression E can be made non-closed by transforming it into $E; P$ @<AnythgShape>$[0; *]$, where P is the set of all IRIs not mentioned as properties in E, and <AnythgShape> is as defined in the introductory example. The EXTRA modifier is encoded in a similar way, using sets of properties in triple patterns and negation. Second, a ValueDescr is an arbitrary set of values that can be IRIs, literals or blank nodes, whereas the analogous node constraint in ShEx 2.0 defines a set of allowed values using a combination of elementary constraints such as XSD datatypes, facets, numerical intervals, node kinds. Using an arbitrary set of values allows to get rid of unnecessary (w.r.t. defining the semantics) details. Third, ShEx 2.0 allows to use shape labels in shape definitions; this is syntactic sugar and is equivalent to replacing the label by its definition. Finally, in shapes schemas we omit inverse properties which would make the proofs longer without representing any additional challenge w.r.t. the semantics.

3   Semantics of Shapes Schemas

A shape defines the structure of a graph when visited starting from a node that has that shape. In this section we give a precise meaning of the following statement

SHAPES_SEM: node n in graph **G** has shape (or type) L from schema **S**[7]

---

[7] "type" is used as synonym of "shape", esp. in the notion of *typing* to be introduced shortly. The use of "type" must not be confused with rdf:type from RDF Schema. Shapes schemas are totally independent from the RDF Schema vocabulary.

To give a sound definition for SHAPES_SEM is not trivial because of the presence of recursion. It also requires to make a design choice that we explain now.

Example 2 (Simple recursive schema). Let schema $\mathbf{S}_1$ and graph $\mathbf{G}_1$ be:

<IssueSh> → is:reportedBy @<Str> ; is:relatedTo @<IssueSh> [0;*]
<Str>   → xsd:string

<i1> is:reportedBy "Ren" ; is:relatedTo <i2> .
<i2> is:reportedBy "Bob" ; is:relatedTo <i1> .

Example 2 captures the essence of recursion. If <i1> has shape <IssueSh> then <i2> also has shape <IssueSh>. If on the other hand <i1> does not have shape <IssueSh>, then neither does <i2>. This illustrates two important aspects of the semantics of shapes schemas. First, whether a node has some shape cannot be defined independently of the shapes of the other nodes in the graph. The consequence of this apparently simple fact is that we need a global statement about which nodes satisfy which shapes; we call this a typing. A typing must be correct, i.e. coherent with itself. Second, in the above example there is a (design) choice to make. Clearly, there are two acceptable alternatives: either (1) both <i1> and <i2> have shape <IssueSh>, or (2) none of them does. Such choice is well known for recursive languages: (1) corresponds to a maximal solution, and (2) to a minimal solution. Both choices can lead to sound semantics. In shapes schemas we choose the maximal solution. This is justified by applications: in the above example we *do want* to consider <i1> as a valid <IssueSh>. It would not be the case with semantics based on a minimal solution.

3.1   Typing and Correct Typing

The semantics is based on the notion of *typing*: this is a set of couples that associate a node of an RDF graph with a shape label (a type). In the sequel we consider a graph $\mathbf{G}$ and a schema $\mathbf{S} = (\mathbf{L}, \mathbf{def})$.

Definition 1 (node-type association, typing). *A node-type association is a couple (n, L) in* $\mathbf{Nodes}(\mathbf{G}) \times \mathbf{L}$. *A typing of $\mathbf{G}$ by $\mathbf{S}$ is a set of node-type associations.*

Example 3. With $\mathbf{S}_1$ and $\mathbf{G}_1$ from Example 2, the following are typings

$typing_1 = \{(<i1>, <IssueSh>), (<i2>, <IssueSh>), ("Ren", <Str>), ("Bob", <Str>)\}$
$typing_2 = \{("Ren", <Str>), ("Bob", <Str>)\}$
$typing_3 = \{(<i1>, <IssueSh>), (<i2>, <IssueSh>)\}$
$typing_4 = \emptyset.$

A typing is correct if, intuitively, it contains an evidence for every node-type association in it. In the above example $typing_1$ and $typing_2$ are correct, whereas $typing_3$ is not correct as it contains e.g. the association (<i1>, <IssueSh>) but does not contain the association ("Ren", <Str>) that is required for <i1> to have type <IssueSh>. The empty typing ($typing_4$) is always correct.

Definition 2 (correct typing). *Let* $typing \subseteq \mathbf{Nodes(G)} \times \mathbf{S}$. *We say that* $typing$ *is a correct typing if for any* $(n, L) \in typing$, *it holds* $typing, n \vdash \mathbf{def}(L)$, *where* $\vdash$ *is the relation defined on Fig. 2a.*

$$\text{se-value-descr1} \frac{n \in V}{typing, n \vdash V}$$

$$\text{se-value-descr2} \frac{\begin{array}{c} \_b \in V \\ n \in \mathsf{Blank} \end{array}}{typing, n \vdash V}$$

$$\text{se-neig-descr} \frac{typing, neigh(n) \vDash E}{typing, n \vdash E}$$

$$\text{se-shape-and} \frac{\begin{array}{c} typing, n \vdash S_1 \\ typing, n \vdash S_2 \end{array}}{typing, n \vdash S_1 \text{ AND } S_2}$$

$$\text{se-shape-or1} \frac{typing, n \vdash S_1}{typing, n \vdash S_1 \text{ OR } S_2}$$

$$\text{se-shape-or2} \frac{typing, n \vdash S_2}{typing, n \vdash S_1 \text{ OR } S_2}$$

$$\text{se-shape-not} \frac{typing, n \nvdash S}{typing, n \vdash \text{NOT } S}$$

(a) Node satisfies a shape expression.

$$\text{te-tpattern} \frac{\begin{array}{c} N = \{(subj, pred, obj)\} \\ pred \in P \\ (obj, L) \in typing \end{array}}{typing, N \vDash P \, @L}$$

$$\text{te-empty} \frac{N = \emptyset}{typing, N \vDash \mathsf{EMPTY}}$$

$$\text{te-some-of1} \frac{typing, N \vDash E_1}{typing, N \vDash E_1 | E_2}$$

$$\text{te-some-of2} \frac{typing, N \vDash E_2}{typing, N \vDash E_1 | E_2}$$

$$\text{te-each-of} \frac{\begin{array}{c} N = N_1 \uplus N_2 \\ typing, N_1 \vDash E_1 \\ typing, N_2 \vDash E_2 \end{array}}{typing, N \vDash E_1; E_2}$$

$$\text{te-repet} \frac{\begin{array}{c} N = N_1 \uplus \ldots \uplus N_k \\ min \leq k \leq max \\ typing, N_i \vDash E \text{ for all } 0 \leq i \leq k \end{array}}{typing, N \vDash E[min; max]}$$

(b) Set of triples matches a triple expression.

Fig. 2. Definitions of the $\vdash$ and $\vDash$ relations.

Discussion on $\vdash$. For a shape expression S, the definition of $typing, n \vdash S$ on Fig. 2a is by recursion on the structure of S. In Rules se-value-descr, V is a subset of $\mathsf{IRI} \cup \mathsf{Lit} \cup \{\_b\}$ defining a ValueDescr. A node n satisfies the value description V if n belongs to the set V, or if n is a blank node and $\_b$ is in V. The other base case is Rule se-neig-descr, in which E is a TExpr representing a neighbourhood description. A node n satisfies the NeigDescr E if the neighbourhood of n matches the triple expression E. The matching relation $\vDash$ is defined on Fig. 2b and discussed below. The remaining four rules are for the Boolean operators. The rules for AND and OR are as one would expect. Regarding negation, a node satisfies a ShapeNot expression if it does not satisfy its sub-expression, as stated by Rule se-shape-not. The premise of that rule is $typing, n \nvdash S$ and means that (using the inference rules on Fig. 2a) it is impossible to construct a proof for $typing, n \vdash S$.

Discussion on $\vDash$. For a set of triples N, *a typing typing and a* TExpr E, *we say that* N *matches* E *with typing*, and we write $typing, N \vDash E$, as defined recursively on the structure of E on Fig. 2b. Note that the $\vDash$ relation is defined for an arbitrary set of triples N. In practice, N will be (a subset of) the neighbourhood of some node. In the basic Rule te-tpattern, $P@L$ is a TriplePattern with P a set of IRIs and L a shape label. A singleton set of triples $\{(subj, pred, obj)\}$ matches the triple pattern if the predicate $pred$ belongs to P and the object has type L in $typing$. The other basic rule is Rule te-empty: an empty set of triples satisfies the EMPTY triple expression.

The remaining rules are about the composed triple expressions. A set of triples matches a SomeOfExpr if it matches one of its sub-expressions (Rules te-some-of). The semantics of a EachOfExpr is a bit more complex. A set N matches an each-of triple expression $E_1; E_2$ if N is the disjoint union of two sets N_1 and N_2, and N_1 matches the sub-expressions E_1, and N_2 matches the sub-expression E_2. Let us make a parallel between regular expressions and triple expressions. The each-of operator is analogous to concatenation. Recall that a string w matches a regular expression $R_1 \cdot R_2$ (where $\cdot$ is concatenation) whenever w can be "split" into two strings w_1 and w_2 such that their concatenation gives w ($w = w_1 \cdot w_2$), and w_1 matches R_1, and w_2 matches R_2. In the case of triple expressions, the set of triples N is "split" into two disjoint sets N_1 and N_2: disjoint union on sets is analogous to concatenation on words. Following the same analogy, repetition in triple expressions corresponds to Kleene star (the star operator) in regular expressions, with the difference that it allows to express arbitrary intervals for the number of allowed repetitions, whereas Kleene star is always $[0, *]$. So, in Rule te-repet, a set of triples N matches a repetition triple expression $E[min; max]$ if N can be split as the disjoint union of k sets $N_1, \ldots, N_k$ such that k is within the interval bound $[min; max]$ and each of these sets matches the sub-expression E. Note that $k = 0$ is possible only when $N = \emptyset$.

The laws of the Boole algebra can be used to put a shape expression in disjunctive normal form in which only atomic sub-expressions ValueDescr and NeigDescr are negated. From now on we consider only shape expressions in disjunctive normal form. Note also that the each-of and some-of operators are associative and commutative and we use them as operators of arbitrary arity, as e.g. in schema $\mathbf{S}_0$ from the introductory example.

3.2   Stratified Negation

Because of the presence of recursion and negation, the notion of correct typing is not sufficient for defining sound semantics of shapes schemas.

Example 4 (Negation and recursion). Let schema $\mathbf{S}_2$ and graph $\mathbf{G}_2$ below:

```
<L1> → NOT(ex:p <L2>)          <n1> ex:p <n2> .
<L2> → NOT(ex:p <L1>)          <n2> ex:p <n1> .
```

These two typings of $\mathbf{G_2}$ by $\mathbf{S_2}$ are both correct: $typing_5 = \{(<n1>, <L1>)\}$ and $typing_6 = \{(<n2>, <L2>)\}$.   □

The two typings in Example 4 strongly contradict each other. In order to prove that node $<n1>$ has shape $<L1>$ (in $typing_5$), we need to prove that $<n1>$ does **not** have shape $<L2>$. The latter however does hold in $typing_6$. Such strong contradictions are possible only in presence of negation. In comparison, in Example 2 we also have two contradicting typings, but none of them uses in its proof a negative statement that is positive in the other typing.

This problem is well known in logic programming e.g. in Datalog, see Chap. 15 in [1] for an overview. The literature considers several solutions for defining coherent semantics in this case, among which the most popular are negation-as-failure, stratified negation and well-founded semantics. For instance, well-founded semantics would answer *undefined* to the question "does n have shape L" whenever there exist two proofs that contradict each-other on that fact. We exclude this solution for two reasons: it is not helpful for users, and it might require to compute all possible typings which is costly. We opt for stratification semantics instead. It imposes a syntactic restriction on the use of recursion together with negation, so that schemas as the one on Example 4 are not allowed. This is a reasonable restriction because negation in ShEx is expected to be used mainly locally, e.g. to forbid some property in the neighbourhood of a node.

We now define of stratified negation. The *dependency graph* of $\mathbf{S}$ is a graph whose set of nodes is $\mathbf{L}$, and that has two kinds of edges labelled dep^- and dep^+ defined by (recall that shape expressions in disjunctive normal form):

- There is a *negative dependency* edge $dep^-(L_1, L_2)$ from L_1 to L_2 iff the shape label L_2 appears in $\mathbf{def}(L_1)$ under an occurrence of the NOT operator;
- There is a *positive dependency* edge $dep^+(L_1, L_2)$ from L_1 to L_2 iff the shape label L_2 appears in $\mathbf{def}(L_1)$ but never under an occurrence of NOT.

Definition 3 (schema with stratified negation). *A schema* $\mathbf{S} = (\mathbf{L}, \mathbf{def})$ *is with stratified negation if there exists a natural number* k *and a mapping strat from* $\mathbf{L}$ *to the interval* $[1; k]$ *such that for all shape labels* L_1, L_2:

- *if* $dep^-(L_1, L_2)$, *then* $strat(L_1) > strat(L_2)$;
- *if* $dep^+(L_1, L_2)$, *then* $strat(L_1) \geq strat(L_2)$.

The mapping *strat* is called a *stratification* of $\mathbf{S}$. A well known property of stratified negation is that the dependency graph does not have a cycle that goes through a negative dependency edge. This intuitively means that if shape L_1 depends negatively on shape L_2, then L_2 does not (transitively) depend on L_1. Positive interdependence is allowed in an unrestricted manner, as in $\mathbf{S_1}$ from Example 2. $\mathbf{S_2}$ from Example 4 is not with stratified negation because $dep^-(<L1>, <L2>)$ and $dep^-(<L2>, <L1>)$.

Example 5 (Stratification). Let schema $\mathbf{S_3}$ below.

$<L1> \rightarrow$ NOT(ex:a @$<L2>$; ex:b @$<Str>$) $<L3> \rightarrow$ ex:c @$<L2>$
$<L2> \rightarrow$ ex:c @$<L3>$ $<Str> \rightarrow$ xsd:string

The dependency graph contains the edges $dep^-(\text{<L1>}, \text{<L2>})$, $dep^-(\text{<L1>}, \text{<Str>})$, $dep^+(\text{<L2>}, \text{<L3>})$, $dep^+(\text{<L3>}, \text{<L2>})$. The unique loop is around <L2> and <L3> and it goes through positive dependencies only, so the schema is stratified. A stratification should be such that <Str> and <L2> are on stratums strictly lower than <L1>, and <L2> and <L3> are on the same stratum. One possible stratification is <L1> on stratum 2 and the other three shape labels on stratum 1. Another one is <L2> and <L3> on stratum 1, <Str> on stratum 2, and <L1> on stratum 3. The latter is called a most refined stratification as none of the stratums can be split.

3.3   Maximal Correct Typing

Recall from Example 3 that both $typing_1$ and $typing_4$ are correct. Note that <i1> has shape <IssueSh> according to $typing_1$ but not according to $typing_4$. Then what is the correct answer of SHAPES_SEM for <i1> and <IssueSh>? Does <i1> have shape <IssueSh> at the end? This section provides an answer to that question. In one sentence: we trust $typing_1$ because it is greater; actually it is the greatest (maximal) typing. The comparison is based on set inclusion.

The following Lemma 1 establishes that a maximal typing always exists in absence of negation. The proof is based on Lemma 2 in [8] that can be easily extended for the richer schemas we have here.

Lemma 1. *Let* **S** *be a schema that does not use the negation operator* NOT. *Then for all graphs* **G***, there exists a correct typing* $typing_g$ *of* **G** *by* **S** *such that for every* $typing'$*, if* $typing'$ *is a correct typing of* **G** *by* **S***, then* $typing' \subseteq typing_g$.

The typing $typing_g$ can be computed as the union of all correct typings $typing'$.

Let us now define a maximal typing in presence of negation. Let $strat$ be a stratification of **S** that has k strata, with $k \geq 1$. For any $1 \leq i \leq k$, the schema $\mathbf{S}_i$ is the restriction of **S** that uses only the shape labels whose stratum is less than i. Formally, $\mathbf{S}_i = (\mathbf{L}_i, \mathbf{def}_i)$ with $\mathbf{L}_i = \{L \in \mathbf{L} \mid strat(L) \leq i\}$, and their respective definitions $\mathbf{def}_i(L) = \mathbf{def}(L)$. Remark that if **S** is stratified, then $\mathbf{S}_1$ is negation-free.

For a set of labels $\mathbf{L}_i \subseteq \mathbf{L}$, $typing_{|\mathbf{L}_i} = \{(n, L) \in typing \mid L \in \mathbf{L}_i\}$ is the restriction of $typing$ on the labels from $\mathbf{L}_i$.

Definition 4 (stratification-maximal correct typing). *Let* $\mathbf{S} = (\mathbf{L}, \mathbf{def})$ *be a schema,* **G** *be a graph, and* $strat$ *be a stratification of* **S** *with* k *stratums (for* $k \geq 1$*). For any* $1 \leq i \leq k$*, let* $typing_i$ *be the typing of* **G** *by* $\mathbf{S}_i$*, defined by:*

- *$typing_1$ is the maximal correct typing of* **G** *by* $\mathbf{S}_1$*, as defined in Lemma 1;*
- *for any* $1 \leq i < k$*,* $typing_{i+1}$ *is the union of all correct typings* $typing'$ *of* **G** *by* $\mathbf{S}_{i+1}$ *s.t.* $typing'_{|\mathbf{L}_i} = typing_i$.

The stratification-maximal correct typing of **G** by **S** with stratification $strat$ is $Typing(\mathbf{G}, \mathbf{S}, strat) = typing_k$.

Typing($\mathbf{G}, \mathbf{S}, strat$) from the above definition is indeed a correct typing for $\mathbf{G}$ by $\mathbf{S}$, as shown in the following proposition that is the core of the proof of soundness for the semantics of shapes schemas.

Proposition 1. *For any schema* $\mathbf{S}$, *any stratification strat of* $\mathbf{S}$ *and any graph* $\mathbf{G}$, *Typing*($\mathbf{G}, \mathbf{S}, strat$) *is a correct typing of* $\mathbf{G}$ *by* $\mathbf{S}$.

Proof. Goes by induction on the number of stratums. The base case (1 stratum) is Lemma 1. For the induction case and stratum $i + 1$, by induction hypothesis $typing_i$ is correct for $\mathbf{G}$ and $\mathbf{S}_i$. It is enough to show that if $typing'$ and $typing''$ are two correct typings for $\mathbf{G}$ by $\mathbf{S}_{i+1}$ and $typing'_{|\mathbf{L}i} = typing''_{|\mathbf{L}i} = typing_i$, then their union $typing = typing' \cup typing''$ is correct for $\mathbf{G}$ by $\mathbf{S}_{i+1}$. Let $(n, L) \in typing$ and suppose that $(n, L) \in typing'$. Because $typing'$ is correct, we have $typing', n \vdash \mathbf{def}(L)$. We will show that (*) the proof for $typing', n \vdash \mathbf{def}(L)$ can be used as a proof for $typing, n \vdash \mathbf{def}(L)$. If $\mathbf{def}(L)$ does not contain a negation of a triple expression, then (*) easily follows from the definition of $\vdash$.

So suppose $\mathbf{def}(L)$ contains a negation operator on top of the triple expressions $E_1, \ldots, E_l$. That is, (recall that shape expressions are in disjunctive normal form), NOT E_j is a sub-expression of $\mathbf{def}(L)$ for every $1 \leq j \leq l$. Then the proof for $typing', n \vdash \mathbf{def}(L)$ contains applications of Rule se-shape-not for NOT E_j that witness that there does not exist a proof for $typing', n \vdash E_j$, for every $1 \leq j \leq l$. We need to show that a proof $typing, n \vdash E_j$ cannot exist. Suppose by contradiction that P is a proof for $typing, n \vdash E_j$, for some $1 \leq j \leq l$. Let $\mathbf{L}'$ be the set of all shape labels that appear in E_j, then P uses only node-type associations with labels from $\mathbf{L}'$. That is, $typing_{|\mathbf{L}'}, n \vdash E_j$ holds. As E_j is negated in $\mathbf{def}(L)$, we have $\mathbf{L}' \subseteq \mathbf{L}_i$, so $typing_{|\mathbf{L}_i}, n \vdash E_j$ also holds. But $typing_{|\mathbf{L}_i} = typing_i \subseteq typing'$. Contradiction. $\square$

Lemma 2 below establishes that *Typing*($\mathbf{G}, \mathbf{S}, strat$) does not depend on the stratification being chosen. This allows to define the maximal correct typing (Definition 5) and to give a precise meaning of SHAPES_SEM (Definition 6) which was the objective of this section.

Lemma 2. *Let* $\mathbf{S} = (\mathbf{L}, \mathbf{def})$ *be a schema and* $\mathbf{G}$ *be a graph. Let* $strat_1$ *and* $strat_2$ *be two stratifications of* $\mathbf{S}$. *Then Typing*($\mathbf{G}, \mathbf{S}, strat_1$) = *Typing*($\mathbf{G}, \mathbf{S}, strat_2$).

Proof. (Idea) The proof uses a classical technique as e.g. for stratified Datalog. There exists a unique (up to permutation on the numbering of stratums) most refined stratification $strat_{\text{ref}}$ such that for any other stratification $strat'$, each stratum of $strat'$ can be obtained as a union of stratums of $strat_{\text{ref}}$. Then we show that for any stratification $strat'$, *Typing*($\mathbf{G}, \mathbf{S}, strat'$) = *Typing*($\mathbf{G}, \mathbf{S}, strat_{\text{ref}}$).

Definition 5 (maximal correct typing). *Let* $\mathbf{S} = (\mathbf{L}, \mathbf{def})$ *be a schema and* $\mathbf{G}$ *be a graph. The* maximal correct typing *of* $\mathbf{G}$ *by* $\mathbf{S}$ *is denoted Typing*($\mathbf{G}, \mathbf{S}$) *and is defined as Typing*($\mathbf{G}, \mathbf{S}, strat$) *for some stratification strat of* $\mathbf{S}$.

Input: **G**: a graph, **S** = (**L**, **def**): a schema, *strat* a stratification for **S** with *k* strata

Output: *Typing*(**G**, **S**)

```
1  typing ← ∅;
2  for i from 1 to k do
       // Add all node-type associations for stratum i
3      foreach n in Nodes(G) do
4          foreach L in Lᵢ do
5              add (n, L) to typing;
       // Refine w.r.t the types on stratum i
6      changing ← true;
7      while changing do
8          changing ← false;
9          foreach (n, L) in typing s.t. L ∈ Lᵢ do
10             if not typing, n ⊢ def(L) then
11                 remove (n, L) from typing;
12                 changing ← true;
13 return typing
```

Algorithm 1. The algorithm *refine*(**G**, **S**, *strat*).

Definition 6 (shapes_sem). *Let* **S** = (**L**, **def**) *be a schema and* **G** *be a graph. We say that node n (of* **G***) has shape L (from* **S***) if* $(n, L) \in Typing(\mathbf{G}, \mathbf{S})$.

4   Validation

In Sect. 3 we have given a declarative semantics of the shapes language. We now consider the related computational problem. We are again interested by the SHAPES_SEM statement (as defined in Sect. 3), i.e. checking whether a given node has a given shape.

4.1   Refinement Algorithm

Algorithm 1 computes *Typing*(**G**, **S**, *strat*). The *i*-th iteration of the loop on line 2 computes $typing_i$ from Definition 4. The algorithm is correct thanks to Lemma 2 from [8] applied to every stratum *i*. According to that lemma, the maximal typing defined as the union of all correct typings (i.e. $typing_i$) can be computed by iteratively removing unsatisfied node-type associations (done on line 11) until a fixed point is reached (detected when *changing* remains *false*). The advantage of the *refine* algorithm is that once *Typing*(**G**, **S**) is computed, testing whether node *n* has shape *L* is done with no additional cost by testing whether (n, L) belongs to *Typing*(**G**, **S**). The drawback is that it considers all node-type associations which is not always necessary, as shown here after.

Input: n: node in $\mathbf{G}$, L: label in $\mathbf{L}$, Hyp: a stack over $\mathbf{Nodes}(G) \times \mathbf{L}$
Output: *true* if n has label L, *false* otherwise

1 $Hyp = Hyp.\,push((n, L))$;
2 $Dep = \emptyset$;
3 **foreach** (n', L') in $dep(n, L) \setminus Hyp$ **do**
4 $\quad$ **if** $prove(n', L', Hyp)$ **then**
5 $\quad\quad \mid \quad Dep = Dep \cup \{(n', L')\}$;
6 result $= Dep \cup Hyp, n \vdash \mathbf{def}(L)$;
7 $Hyp = Hyp.\,pop()$;
8 **return** result ;

Algorithm 2. $prove(n, L, Hyp)$. Graph $\mathbf{G}$ and schema $\mathbf{S}$ are global variables.

4.2 Recursive Algorithm

Algorithm 2 allows to check whether node n has shape L without constructing $Typing(\mathbf{G}, \mathbf{S})$. The idea is to visit only a sufficiently large portion of $Typing(\mathbf{G}, \mathbf{S})$.

Example 6 (Motivation of the prove algorithm). Considering schema $\mathbf{S}_3$ from Example 5 and graph $\mathbf{G}_3$ below:

ex:n1 ex:a ex:n2   ex:n2 ex:c ex:n3 .
ex:n1 ex:b 4 .   ex:n3 ex:c ex:n2 .

We want to check whether ex:n1 has shape <L1>. Remark that the neighbor nodes of ex:n1 are ex:n2 and 4, whereas the shape labels on which the definition of <L1> depends are <L2> and <Str>. Any correct proof for $typing,$ ex:n1 $\vdash$ <L1> (or for $typing,$ ex:n1 $\nvdash$ <L1>) would have as leaves either applications of Rule se-value-descr that do not depend on $typing$, or applications of Rule te-tpattern that uses node-type associations (n, L) where n is a neighbor of ex:n1 and L' is a label such that $dep^+(\text{<L1>}, L')$ or $dep^-(\text{<L1>}, L')$.

Assume schema $\mathbf{S} = (\mathbf{L}, \mathbf{def})$ and graph $\mathbf{G}$. For a shape label L in $\mathbf{S}$ and a node n in $\mathbf{G}$, we denote $dep(n, L)$ the set of node-type associations (n', L') s.t. n' is a neighbor of n (that is, $(n, p, n') \in neigh(n)$ for some IRI p) and L' appears as a shape reference in $\mathbf{def}(L)$. Algorithm 2 uses this easy to show property: $typing, n \models \mathbf{def}(L)$ iff $typing \cap dep(n, L), n \models \mathbf{def}(L)$. In order to check whether n has shape L, Algorithm 2 will (recursively) check whether n' has shape L' for all (n', L') in $dep(n, L)$. The parameter Hyp is a stack of node-type associations that is also seen (on line 3) as the set of node-type associations it contains. Dep is a set of node-type associations.

Example 7 (Execution trace of the prove algorithm). Here is the tree of recursive calls generated during the evaluation of $prove(\text{ex:n1}, \text{<L1>}, [])$ for graph $\mathbf{G}_3$ and schema $\mathbf{S}_3$, where $[]$ is the empty stack. The returned value is given on the right. $prove(\text{ex:n1}, \text{<L1>}, [])$ generates four recursive calls that correspond to

$dep(\text{ex:n1}, <\text{L1}>)$. The call for ex:n3 and $<\text{L3}>$ does not generate any recursive call: $dep(\text{ex:n3}, <\text{L3}>)$ contains only $(\text{ex:n2}, <\text{L2}>)$ which is on the stack.

$prove(\text{ex:n1}, <\text{L1}>, [])$	$true$
$\vdash prove(\text{ex:n2}, <\text{L2}>, [(\text{ex:n1}, <\text{L1}>)])$	$true$
$\vert \vdash prove(\text{ex:n3}, <\text{L3}>, [(\text{ex:n1}, <\text{L1}>), (\text{ex:n2}, <\text{L2}>)])$	$true$
$\vdash prove(\text{ex:n2}, <\text{Str}>, [(\text{ex:n1}, <\text{L1}>)])$	$false$
$\vdash prove(4, <\text{L2}>, [(\text{ex:n1}, <\text{L1}>)])$	$false$
$\vdash prove(4, <\text{Str}>, [(\text{ex:n1}, <\text{L1}>)])$	$false$

The correctness of the *prove* algorithm is stated by the following:

Proposition 2 (Correctness of the *prove* algorithm). *For any node n and any shape label L, the evaluation of $prove(n, L, [])$ terminates and returns true if $(n, L) \in Typing(\mathbf{G}, \mathbf{S})$ and false otherwise.*

Proof (Sketch). For termination: the recursion cannot be infinite-breadth as *prove* generates a finite number of recursive calls on line 4. Infinite-depth recursion is also impossible because Hyp is a call stack and the condition on line 3 prevents from (recursively) calling *prove* with the same node and label.

The proof of correctness goes by induction on the stratum of L using the most refined stratification *strat*. For every stratum i we show that whenever Hyp contains only node-type associations (n', L') with $strat(L') > i$, and for any L s.t. $strat(L) = i$, $Typing, n \vdash \mathbf{def}(L)$ iff $prove(n, L, Hyp)$ returns true. For the $\Rightarrow$ direction, the main argument is that if $Typing, n \vdash \mathbf{def}(L)$ then also $Typing \cup Hyp, n \vdash \mathbf{def}(L)$. This is not true in general because of negation, but is true if Hyp is on stratum $\geq strat(L)$ as in this case no type in Hyp is negated in $\mathbf{def}(L)$. For the $\Leftarrow$ direction, we need to show that if $prove(n, L, Hyp)$ returns *true* then $(n, L) \in Typing(\mathbf{G}, \mathbf{S})$. The problematic case is when $prove(n, L, Hyp)$ returns *true* whereas n does not have label L. Such error necessarily comes from the fact that on line 6 the algorithm used some $(n', L') \in Hyp \setminus Typing(\mathbf{G}, \mathbf{S})$ in the proof for $Dep \cup Hyp, n \vdash \mathbf{def}(L)$. Consequently, $strat(L) = strat(L')$, and because we consider the most refined stratification, it follows that L and L' mutually depend on each other in the dependency graph of $\mathbf{G}$. Then we need to distinguish two cases. Either all shape labels on stratum i only depend on each others, as for instance $<\text{L2}>$ and $<\text{L3}>$ from Example 5. In that case $prove(n, L, Hyp)$ returns *true* based only on hypotheses in Hyp, which is correct w.r.t. the semantics based on maximal solution: if nothing outside stratum i allows to disprove that n has label L, then it is indeed the case. The other possibility is that a shape label L' on stratum i depends also on shapes from lower stratums, as $<\text{IssueSh}>$ from Example 2 that depends on $<\text{Str}>$. Then the test on line 6 of the call of *prove* with L' will take this dependency into account and return *true* only if all conditions, including those that depend on the lower stratums, are satisfied. $\square$

4.3   On Implementation of the Validation Algorithms

Both algorithms use a test for *typing*, $n \vdash \mathbf{def}(L)$, which non trivial part is the test of the $\vDash$ relation required in Rule se-neig-descr. The latter is equivalent to checking whether a word (a string) matches a regular expression disregarding the ordering of the letters of the word. Here the word is over the alphabet of triple patterns that occur in the triple expression. In [4] we presented an algorithm for this problem based on regular expression derivatives. In [8] we gave another algorithm for so called deterministic single-occurrence triple expressions. That algorithm can be extended to general expressions, and was used in several of the implementations of ShEx available as open source[8].

The *prove* algorithm was presented in a form that is easier to understand but not optimized. An implementation could reduce considerably the search space of the algorithm by exploring only relevant node-shape associations from $dep(n, L)$ For instance, in Example 7 checking 4 against L2 is useless first because 4 is accessible from ex:n1 by ex:b whereas <L2> in the schema is accessible from <L1> by ex:a.

A more involved version of the *prove* algorithm could memorize portion of $Typing(\mathbf{G}, \mathbf{S})$ to be reused. This however should be done carefully: one should not memorize all node-shape associations (n, L) for which the algorithm returned *true*, as some of these can be false positives as discussed in the proof of Proposition 2.

5   Conclusion

In this paper we introduced shapes schemas that formalize the semantics of ShEx 2.0 and we showed that the semantics of ShEx 2.0 is sound. We also presented two algorithms for validating an RDF graph against a shapes schema.

ShEx and the underlying formalism presented here are still evolving, and there are several promising directions some of which are already being explored: introduce operators for value comparison, use property paths in triple patterns, define an RDF transformation language based on ShEx. We also plan to consider several heuristics and optimizations as the ones discussed in Sect. 4.3 in order to accelerate the validation of shapes schemas. These will be validated on examples. Another open problem is error reporting in ShEx: how to give useful feedback for correcting validation errors. We also plan to explore the exact relationship between shapes schemas and SHACLand establish whether shapes schemas can be encoded in SPARQL extended with recursion as the one defined in [7].

Acknowledgments. This work was partially supported by CPER Nord-Pas de Calais/FEDER DATA Advanced data science and technologies 2015–2020, ANR project DataCert ANR-15-CE39-0009.

---

[8] A list of the available ShEx implementations can be found on http://shex.io/.

References

1. Abiteboul, S., Hull, R., Vianu, V.: Foundations of Databases. Addison-Wesley, Reading (1995)
2. Fischer, P.M., Lausen, G., Schätzle, A., Schmidt, M.: RDF constraint checking. In: Proceedings of the Workshops of the EDBT/ICDT 2015 Joint Conference. CEUR-WS.org (2015)
3. Kontokostas, D., Westphal, P., Auer, S., Hellmann, S., Lehmann, J., Cornelissen, R., Zaveri, A.: Test-driven evaluation of linked data quality. In: Proceedings of the 23rd International Conference on World Wide Web (WWW 2014) (2014)
4. Labra Gayo, J.E., Prud'hommeaux, E., Boneva, I., Staworko, S., Solbrig, H.R., Hym, S.: Towards an RDF validation language based on regular expression derivatives. In: Proceedings of the Workshops of the EDBT/ICDT 2015 Joint Conference. CEUR-WS.org (2015)
5. Motik, B., Horrocks, I., Sattler, U.: Adding integrity constraints to OWL. In: OWL: Experiences and Directions 2007 (OWLED 2007) (2007)
6. Prud'hommeaux, E., Labra Gayo, J.E., Solbrig, H.R.: Shape expressions: an RDF validation and transformation language. In: Proceedings of the 10th International Conference on Semantic Systems, SEMANTICS 2014. ACM (2014)
7. Reutter, J.L., Soto, A., Vrgoč, D.: Recursion in SPARQL. In: Arenas, M., et al. (eds.) ISWC 2015. LNCS, vol. 9366, pp. 19–35. Springer, Cham (2015). doi:10.1007/978-3-319-25007-6_2
8. Staworko, S., Boneva, I., Labra Gayo, J.E., Hym, S., Prud'hommeaux, E.G., Solbrig, H.R.: Complexity and expressiveness of ShEx for RDF. In: 18th International Conference on Database Theory (ICDT). Schloss Dagstuhl - Leibniz-Zentrum fuer Informatik (2015)
9. Tao, J., Sirin, E., Bao, J., McGuinness, D.L.: Integrity constraints in OWL. In: Proceedings of the 24th AAAI Conference on Artificial Intelligence. AAAI (2010)

Temporal Query Answering in DL-Lite over Inconsistent Data

Camille Bourgaux and Anni-Yasmin Turhan[(✉)]

Technische Universität Dresden, Dresden, Germany
{camille.bourgaux,anni-yasmin.turhan}@tu-dresden.de

Abstract. In ontology-based systems that process data stemming from different sources and that is received over time, as in context-aware systems, reasoning needs to cope with the temporal dimension and should be resilient against inconsistencies in the data. Motivated by such settings, this paper addresses the problem of handling inconsistent data in a temporal version of ontology-based query answering. We consider a recently proposed temporal query language that combines conjunctive queries with operators of propositional linear temporal logic and extend to this setting three inconsistency-tolerant semantics that have been introduced for querying inconsistent description logic knowledge bases. We investigate their complexity for DL-Lite$_\mathcal{R}$ temporal knowledge bases, and furthermore complete the picture for the consistent case.

1 Introduction

Context-aware systems [3,18] observe their environment over time and are able to detect situations while running in order to adapt their behaviour. They rely upon heterogeneous sources such as sensors (in a broad sense) or other applications that provide them with data. A context-aware system needs to integrate this data and should behave resilient towards erroneous or contradictory data. Since the collected data usually provides an incomplete description of the observed system, the closed world assumption employed by database systems, where facts not present are assumed to be false, is not appropriate. Moreover, it is convenient to use some knowledge about the system to reason with the data and get more complete answers to the queries that capture the situations to be recognized than from the data alone. To address these requirements and facilitate data integration, *ontologies* have been used to implement situation recognition [3,14,18,25].

Ontology-mediated query answering [15] performs database-style query answering over description logic (DL) knowledge bases that consist of an ontology (called a TBox) expressing conceptual knowledge about a domain and a dataset (or ABox) containing facts about particular individuals [5]. An important issue that may arise when querying data through ontology reasoning is the inconsistency of the data w.r.t. the ontology. This is especially true for context-aware systems, since in the applications that need to perform situation recognition, the ABox is usually populated by frequently changing data from sensors

---

Supported by the DFG in CRC 912 (HAEC) and the DAAD.

C. d'Amato et al. (Eds.): ISWC 2017, Part I, LNCS 10587, pp. 121–137, 2017.
DOI: 10.1007/978-3-319-68288-4_8

or other sources. The problem is that under the classical semantics, every query is entailed from an inconsistent knowledge base and thus classical reasoners are rendered useless. Several inconsistency-tolerant semantics have been introduced for DL knowledge bases (see [7] for a survey) to remedy this problem.

A situation is often defined not only w.r.t. the current state of the system but depends also on its history. For instance, a system that operates on a cluster of servers may need the list of servers which have been almost overloaded at least twice in the past ten time units. Likewise in the medical domain a critical situation for a patient can depend on the patient's medical history. That is why research efforts have recently been devoted to temporalizing query answering [4,11] by allowing to use operators of *linear temporal logic* (LTL) [26] in the queries. In this setting, the query is answered over a *temporal knowledge base* consisting of a global TBox and a sequence of ABoxes that represents the data at different time points. The situation previously described can then be recognized by answering the query "$\lozenge^-(\mathsf{AlmostOverloaded}(x) \wedge \bigcirc^- \lozenge^- \mathsf{AlmostOverloaded}(x))$", where $\lozenge^-$ is the LTL operator "eventually in the past" and $\bigcirc^-$ the operator "previous", over the sequence of datasets that correspond to the last ten observations of the system, an ontology defining the concept $\mathsf{AlmostOverloaded}$. A lot of work has been dedicated to the temporalization of DL, combining different temporal logics and DL languages (see [23] for a survey). As efficiency is a primary concern, particular attention has been paid to temporalized DLs of the DL-Lite family [16] (see [2] for different temporal extensions of DL-Lite). The DLs of this family cover an important fragment of the RDF query language SPARQL and underlie the OWL 2 QL profile of the Semantic Web standard [24]. They possess the notable property that query answering can be reduced to evaluation of standard database queries. The construction of temporal queries has also attracted a lot of interest recently [1,19,20], and querying temporal databases has been studied as well (see e.g., [17]). Here, we consider the setting proposed in [11] which does not allow for temporalized concepts or axioms in the TBox but focuses on querying sequences of ABoxes with temporal queries.

This work presents results on lifting inconsistency-tolerant reasoning to temporal query answering. To the best of our knowledge, this is the first investigation of temporal query answering under inconsistency-tolerant semantics. We consider three semantics that have been defined for DL knowledge bases and that we find particularly relevant. They are all based upon the notion of a *repair*, which is a maximal consistent subset of the data. The *AR semantics* [21,22], inspired by consistent query answering in the database setting [6], considers the queries that hold in *every repair*. This semantics is arguably the most natural and is widely accepted to query inconsistent knowledge bases. However, AR query answering is intractable even for DL-Lite, which leads [21,22] to propose a tractable approximation of AR, namely the *IAR semantics*, which queries the *intersection of the repairs*. Beside its better computational properties, this semantics is more cautious since it provides answers supported by facts that are not involved in any contradictions, so it may be interesting in our setting when the system should change its behaviour only if some situation has been recognized with a very high confidence. Finally, the *brave semantics* [9] returns every answer that holds in *some repair*, so is supported by some consistent set of facts. This less cautious semantics may be relevant for context recognition, when critical situations must be handled imperatively.

The contributions of this paper are as follows. In Sect. 3 we extend the AR, IAR and brave semantics to the setting of temporal query answering. We distinguish in our analysis three cases for *rigid predicates*, i.e., whose extensions do not change between time points: no rigid predicates, rigid concepts only, or rigid concepts and roles. We show that when there is no rigid predicate, existing algorithms for temporal query answering and for IAR query answering can be combined to perform IAR temporal query answering. We also show that this method can sometimes be used for AR and provides in any case an approximation of the AR answers. In Sect. 4 we investigate the computational properties of the three semantics, considering both *data complexity* (in the size of the data only), and *combined complexity* (in the size of the whole problem), and distinguishing three different cases regarding the rigid symbols that are allowed. We show that in all cases except for brave semantics with rigid predicates, the data complexity is not higher than in the atemporal setting. In all cases, adding the temporal dimension does not increase the combined complexity. Our complexity analysis also leads us to close some open questions about temporal query answering under the classical semantics in the presence of rigid predicates. In particular, we show that it can often be reduced to the case without rigid predicates.

Detailed proofs of all the results are provided in [13].

2   Preliminaries

We briefly recall the syntax and semantics of DLs, the three inconsistency-tolerant semantics we consider, and the setting of temporal query answering.

Syntax. A DL *knowledge base (KB)* $\mathcal{K}$ consists of an ABox $\mathcal{A}$ and a TBox $\mathcal{T}$, constructed from three countably infinite sets: a set $\mathsf{N_C}$ of *concept names* (unary predicates), a set $\mathsf{N_R}$ of *role names* (binary predicates), and a set $\mathsf{N_I}$ of *individual names* (constants). The *ABox* (dataset) is a finite set of *concept assertions* $A(a)$ and *role assertions* $R(a,b)$, where $A \in \mathsf{N_C}$, $R \in \mathsf{N_R}$, $a, b \in \mathsf{N_I}$. The *TBox* (ontology) is a finite set of axioms whose form depends on the particular DL. In DL-Lite$_{\mathcal{R}}$, TBox axioms are either *concept inclusions* $B \sqsubseteq C$ or *role inclusions* $P \sqsubseteq S$ built according to the following syntax (where $A \in \mathsf{N_C}$ and $R \in \mathsf{N_R}$):

$$B := A \mid \exists P, \quad C := B \mid \neg B, \quad P := R \mid R^-, \quad S := P \mid \neg P$$

Inclusions of the form $B_1 \sqsubseteq B_2$ or $P_1 \sqsubseteq P_2$ are called *positive inclusions* (PI), those of the form $B_1 \sqsubseteq \neg B_2$ or $P_1 \sqsubseteq \neg P_2$ are called *negative inclusions* (NI).

Semantics. An *interpretation* has the form $\mathcal{I} = (\Delta^{\mathcal{I}}, \cdot^{\mathcal{I}})$, where $\Delta^{\mathcal{I}}$ is a non-empty set and $\cdot^{\mathcal{I}}$ maps each $a \in \mathsf{N_I}$ to $a^{\mathcal{I}} \in \Delta^{\mathcal{I}}$, each $A \in \mathsf{N_C}$ to $A^{\mathcal{I}} \subseteq \Delta^{\mathcal{I}}$, and each $R \in \mathsf{N_R}$ to $R^{\mathcal{I}} \subseteq \Delta^{\mathcal{I}} \times \Delta^{\mathcal{I}}$. We adopt the unique name assumption (i.e., for all $a, b \in \mathsf{N_I}$, $a^{\mathcal{I}} \neq b^{\mathcal{I}}$ if $a \neq b$). The function $\cdot^{\mathcal{I}}$ is straightforwardly extended to general concepts and roles, e.g., $(R^-)^{\mathcal{I}} = \{(d,e) \mid (e,d) \in R^{\mathcal{I}}\}$ and $(\exists P)^{\mathcal{I}} = \{d \mid \exists e : (d,e) \in P^{\mathcal{I}}\}$. An interpretation $\mathcal{I}$ satisfies an inclusion $G \sqsubseteq H$ if $G^{\mathcal{I}} \subseteq H^{\mathcal{I}}$; it satisfies $A(a)$ (resp. $R(a,b)$) if $a^{\mathcal{I}} \in A^{\mathcal{I}}$ (resp. $(a^{\mathcal{I}}, b^{\mathcal{I}}) \in R^{\mathcal{I}}$). We call $\mathcal{I}$ a *model* of $\mathcal{K} = \langle \mathcal{T}, \mathcal{A} \rangle$ if $\mathcal{I}$ satisfies all axioms in $\mathcal{T}$ and all assertions in $\mathcal{A}$. A KB is *consistent* if it has a model, and we say that an ABox $\mathcal{A}$ is $\mathcal{T}$-*consistent* (or simply *consistent* for short), if the KB $\langle \mathcal{T}, \mathcal{A} \rangle$ is consistent.

Queries. A *conjunctive query* (CQ) takes the form $q = \exists \boldsymbol{y} \, \psi(\boldsymbol{x}, \boldsymbol{y})$, where ψ is a conjunction of atoms of the forms $A(t)$ or $R(t, t')$, with t, t' individuals or variables from $\boldsymbol{x} \cup \boldsymbol{y}$. A CQ is called *Boolean* (BCQ) if it has no free variables (i.e. $\boldsymbol{x} = \emptyset$). A BCQ q is *entailed* from $\mathcal{K}$, written $\mathcal{K} \models q$, iff q holds in every model of $\mathcal{K}$. Given a CQ q with free variables $\boldsymbol{x} = (x_1, \ldots, x_k)$ and a tuple of individuals $\boldsymbol{a} = (a_1, \ldots, a_k)$, $\boldsymbol{a}$ is a *certain answer* to q over $\mathcal{K}$ just in the case that $\mathcal{K} \models q(\boldsymbol{a})$, where $q(\boldsymbol{a})$ is the BCQ resulting from replacing each x_j by a_j.

Inconsistency-Tolerant Semantics. A *repair* of $\mathcal{K} = \langle \mathcal{T}, \mathcal{A} \rangle$ is an inclusion-maximal subset of $\mathcal{A}$ that is $\mathcal{T}$-consistent. We consider three semantics based on repairs.

A tuple $\boldsymbol{a}$ is an answer to q over $\mathcal{K}$ under

- *AR semantics*, written $\mathcal{K} \models_{\mathrm{AR}} q(\boldsymbol{a})$,
  iff $\langle \mathcal{T}, \mathcal{A}' \rangle \models q(\boldsymbol{a})$ for *every repair* $\mathcal{A}'$ of $\mathcal{K}$;
- *IAR semantics*, written $\mathcal{K} \models_{\mathrm{IAR}} q(\boldsymbol{a})$,
  iff $\langle \mathcal{T}, \mathcal{A}^{\cap} \rangle \models q(\boldsymbol{a})$ where $\mathcal{A}^{\cap}$ is the *intersection of all repairs* of $\mathcal{K}$;
- *brave semantics*, written $\mathcal{K} \models_{\mathrm{brave}} q(\boldsymbol{a})$,
  iff $\langle \mathcal{T}, \mathcal{A}' \rangle \models q(\boldsymbol{a})$ for *some repair* $\mathcal{A}'$ of $\mathcal{K}$.

In DL-Lite$_{\mathcal{R}}$, IAR or brave CQ answering is in P w.r.t. data complexity (in the size of the ABox) and NP-complete w.r.t. combined complexity (in the size of the whole KB and the query), and AR CQ answering is coNP-complete w.r.t. data complexity and Π_2^p-complete w.r.t. combined complexity [9, 21].

Temporal Query Answering. We consider the framework presented in [11].

Definition 1 (TKB). *A* temporal knowledge base *(TKB)* $\mathcal{K} = \langle \mathcal{T}, (\mathcal{A}_i)_{0 \leq i \leq n} \rangle$ *consists of a TBox* $\mathcal{T}$ *and a finite sequence of ABoxes* $(\mathcal{A}_i)_{0 \leq i \leq n}$. *A sequence* $\mathcal{J} = (\mathcal{I}_i)_{0 \leq i \leq n}$ *of interpretations* $\mathcal{I}_i = (\Delta, \cdot^{\mathcal{I}_i})$ *over a fixed non-empty domain* Δ *is a* model *of* $\mathcal{K}$ *iff for all* $0 \leq i \leq n$, $\mathcal{I}_i$ *is a model of* $\langle \mathcal{T}, \mathcal{A}_i \rangle$, *and for every* $a \in \mathsf{N}_\mathsf{I}$ *and all* $1 \leq i \leq j \leq n$, $a^{\mathcal{I}_i} = a^{\mathcal{I}_j}$. Rigid predicates *are elements from the set of* rigid concepts $\mathsf{N}_{\mathsf{RC}} \subseteq \mathsf{N}_{\mathsf{C}}$ *or of* rigid roles $\mathsf{N}_{\mathsf{RR}} \subseteq \mathsf{N}_{\mathsf{R}}$. *A sequence of interpretations* $\mathcal{J} = (\mathcal{I}_i)_{0 \leq i \leq n}$ respects the rigid predicates *iff for every* $X \in \mathsf{N}_{\mathsf{RC}} \cup \mathsf{N}_{\mathsf{RR}}$ *and all* $1 \leq i \leq j \leq n$, $X^{\mathcal{I}_i} = X^{\mathcal{I}_j}$. *A TKB is* consistent *if it has a model that respects the rigid predicates. A sequence of ABoxes* $(\mathcal{A}_i)_{0 \leq i \leq n}$ *is* $\mathcal{T}$-consistent, *or simply* consistent, *if the TKB* $\langle \mathcal{T}, (\mathcal{A}_i)_{0 \leq i \leq n} \rangle$ *is consistent.*

It is sometimes convenient to represent a sequence of ABoxes as a set of assertions associated with timestamps, which we call *timed-assertions*: $(\mathcal{A}_i)_{0 \leq i \leq n}$ becomes $\{(\alpha, i) \mid \alpha \in \mathcal{A}_i, 0 \leq i \leq n\}$. A *rigid assertion* is of the form $A(a)$ with $A \in \mathsf{N}_{\mathsf{RC}}$ or $R(a,b)$ with $R \in \mathsf{N}_{\mathsf{RR}}$. We distinguish three cases in our analysis:

Case 1 with $N_{RC} = N_{RR} = \emptyset$, Case 2 with $N_{RC} \neq \emptyset$ and $N_{RR} = \emptyset$, and Case 3 with $N_{RC} \neq \emptyset$ and $N_{RR} \neq \emptyset$. Note that since rigid roles can simulate rigid concepts, these three cases cover all possibilities. We denote by $N_X^{\mathcal{K}}$ the elements of N_X occurring in $\mathcal{K}$.

Definition 2 (TCQ). *Temporal conjunctive queries (TCQs) are built from CQs as follows: each CQ is a TCQ, and if ϕ_1 and ϕ_2 are TCQs, then so are $\phi_1 \wedge \phi_2$ (conjunction), $\phi_1 \vee \phi_2$ (disjunction), $\bigcirc\phi_1$ (strong next), $\bullet\phi_1$ (weak next), $\bigcirc^-\phi_1$ (strong previous), $\bullet^-\phi_1$ (weak previous), $\Box\phi_1$ (always), $\Box^-\phi_1$ (always in the past), $\Diamond\phi_1$ (eventually), $\Diamond^-\phi_1$ (some time in the past), $\phi_1 U \phi_2$ (until), and $\phi_1 S \phi_2$ (since). Given a TCQ ϕ with free variables $\mathbf{x} = (x_1, \ldots, x_k)$ and a tuple of individuals $\mathbf{a} = (a_1, \ldots, a_k)$, $\phi(\mathbf{a})$ denotes the Boolean TCQ (BTCQ) resulting from replacing each x_j by a_j. The tuple $\mathbf{a}$ is an answer to ϕ in a sequence of interpretations $\mathcal{J} = (\mathcal{I}_i)_{0 \leq i \leq n}$ at time point p $(0 \leq p \leq n)$ iff $\mathcal{J}, p \models \phi(\mathbf{a})$, where the entailment of a BTCQ ϕ is defined by induction on its structure as shown in Table 1. It is a certain answer to ϕ over $\mathcal{K}$ at time point p, written $\mathcal{K}, p \models \phi(\mathbf{a})$, iff $\mathcal{J}, p \models \phi(\mathbf{a})$ for every model $\mathcal{J}$ of $\mathcal{K}$ that respects the rigid predicates.*

Table 1. Entailment of BTCQs

ϕ	$\mathcal{J}, p \models \phi$ iff
$\exists \mathbf{y}\, \psi(\mathbf{y})$	$\mathcal{I}_p \models \exists \mathbf{y}\, \psi(\mathbf{y})$
$\phi_1 \wedge \phi_2$	$\mathcal{J}, p \models \phi_1$ and $\mathcal{J}, p \models \phi_2$
$\phi_1 \vee \phi_2$	$\mathcal{J}, p \models \phi_1$ or $\mathcal{J}, p \models \phi_2$
$\bigcirc\phi_1$	$p < n$ and $\mathcal{J}, p+1 \models \phi_1$
$\bullet\phi_1$	$p < n$ implies $\mathcal{J}, p+1 \models \phi_1$
$\bigcirc^-\phi_1$	$p > 0$ and $\mathcal{J}, p-1 \models \phi_1$
$\bullet^-\phi_1$	$p > 0$ implies $\mathcal{J}, p-1 \models \phi_1$
$\Box\phi_1$	$\forall k, p \leq k \leq n, \mathcal{J}, k \models \phi_1$
$\Box^-\phi_1$	$\forall k, 0 \leq k \leq p, \mathcal{J}, k \models \phi_1$
$\Diamond\phi_1$	$\exists k, p \leq k \leq n, \mathcal{J}, k \models \phi_1$
$\Diamond^-\phi_1$	$\exists k, 0 \leq k \leq p, \mathcal{J}, k \models \phi_1$
$\phi_1 U \phi_2$	$\exists k, p \leq k \leq n, \mathcal{J}, k \models \phi_2$ and $\forall j, p \leq j < k, \mathcal{J}, j \models \phi_1$
$\phi_1 S \phi_2$	$\exists k, 0 \leq k \leq p, \mathcal{J}, k \models \phi_2$ and $\forall j, k < j \leq p, \mathcal{J}, j \models \phi_1$

Thus, TCQ answering is straightforwardly reduced to entailment of BTCQs and we can focus w.l.o.g. on the latter problem.

3   Temporal Query Answering over Inconsistent Data

We extend the three inconsistency-tolerant semantics to temporal query answering. The main difference to the atemporal case is that in the presence of rigid predicates a TKB $\mathcal{K} = \langle \mathcal{T}, (\mathcal{A}_i)_{0 \leq i \leq n} \rangle$ may be inconsistent even if each KB $\langle \mathcal{T}, \mathcal{A}_i \rangle$ is consistent. In this case there need not exist a sequence of interpretations $\mathcal{J} = (\mathcal{I}_i)_{0 \leq i \leq n}$ such that each $\mathcal{I}_i$ is a model of $\langle \mathcal{T}, \mathcal{A}_i \rangle$ and which respects rigid predicates. That is why we need to consider as repairs the $\mathcal{T}$-consistent sequences of subsets of the initial ABoxes that are component-wise maximal.

Definition 3 (Repair of a TKB). *A* repair *of a TKB* $\mathcal{K} = \langle \mathcal{T}, (\mathcal{A}_i)_{0 \leq i \leq n} \rangle$ *is a sequence of ABoxes* $(\mathcal{A}'_i)_{0 \leq i \leq n}$ *such that* $\{(\alpha, i) \mid \alpha \in \mathcal{A}'_i, 0 \leq i \leq n\}$ *is a maximal* $\mathcal{T}$-consistent subset of $\{(\alpha, i) \mid \alpha \in \mathcal{A}_i, 0 \leq i \leq n\}$. *We denote the set of repairs of* $\mathcal{K}$ *by* $Rep(\mathcal{K})$.

The next example shows the influence of rigid predicates on the repairs.

Example 1. Consider the following TKB $\mathcal{K} = \langle \mathcal{T}, (\mathcal{A}_i)_{1 \leq i \leq 2} \rangle$. The TBox expresses that web servers and application servers are two distinct kinds of servers, and the ABoxes provide information about a server a that executes two processes.

$$\mathcal{T} = \{\mathsf{WebServer} \sqsubseteq \mathsf{Server},\ \mathsf{AppServer} \sqsubseteq \mathsf{Server},\ \mathsf{WebServer} \sqsubseteq \neg\mathsf{AppServer}\}$$
$$\mathcal{A}_1 = \{\mathsf{WebServer}(a),\ \mathsf{execute}(a, b)\}$$
$$\mathcal{A}_2 = \{\mathsf{AppServer}(a),\ \mathsf{WebServer}(a),\ \mathsf{execute}(a, c)\}$$

Assume that no predicate is rigid. The TKB $\mathcal{K}$ is inconsistent because the timed-assertions $(\mathsf{AppServer}(a), 2)$ and $(\mathsf{WebServer}(a), 2)$ violate the negative inclusion of $\mathcal{T}$, since $\mathsf{AppServer}(a)$ and $\mathsf{WebServer}(a)$ cannot both be true at time point 2. It follows that $\mathcal{K}$ has two repairs $(\mathcal{A}'_i)_{1 \leq i \leq 2}$ and $(\mathcal{A}''_i)_{1 \leq i \leq 2}$ with $\mathcal{A}'_1 = \mathcal{A}''_1 = \mathcal{A}_1$, and $\mathcal{A}'_2 = \{\mathsf{AppServer}(a), \mathsf{execute}(a, c)\}$ and $\mathcal{A}''_2 = \{\mathsf{WebServer}(a), \mathsf{execute}(a, c)\}$ which correspond to the two different ways of restoring consistency.

Assume now that $\mathsf{AppServer}$ is rigid. There is a new reason for $\mathcal{K}$ being inconsistent: the timed-assertions $(\mathsf{WebServer}(a), 1)$ and $(\mathsf{AppServer}(a), 2)$ violate the negative inclusion of $\mathcal{T}$ due to the rigidity of $\mathsf{AppServer}$ which implies that $\mathsf{AppServer}(a)$ and $\mathsf{WebServer}(a)$ should be both entailed at time point 1. Then $\mathcal{K}$ has two repairs $(\mathcal{A}'_i)_{1 \leq i \leq 2}$ and $(\mathcal{A}''_i)_{1 \leq i \leq 2}$ with $\mathcal{A}'_1 = \{\mathsf{execute}(a, b)\}$, $\mathcal{A}'_2 = \{\mathsf{AppServer}(a), \mathsf{execute}(a, c)\}$, and $\mathcal{A}''_1 = \mathcal{A}_1$, $\mathcal{A}''_2 = \{\mathsf{WebServer}(a), \mathsf{execute}(a, c)\}$. Note that even if $(\mathcal{A}'_i)_{1 \leq i \leq 2}$ is maximal (since adding $\mathsf{WebServer}(a)$ to $\mathcal{A}'_1$ renders the TKB inconsistent), $\mathcal{A}'_1$ is not a repair of $\langle \mathcal{T}, \mathcal{A}_1 \rangle$ since it is not maximal.

Next we extend the semantics AR, IAR, and brave to the temporal case in the natural way by regarding sequences of ABoxes.

Definition 4 (AR, IAR, brave semantics for TCQs). *A tuple* $\boldsymbol{a}$ *is an answer to a TCQ* ϕ *over a TKB* $\mathcal{K} = \langle \mathcal{T}, (\mathcal{A}_i)_{0 \leq i \leq n} \rangle$ *at time point* p *under*

- *AR semantics, written* $\mathcal{K}, p \models_{AR} \phi(\boldsymbol{a})$,
  iff $\langle \mathcal{T}, (\mathcal{A}'_i)_{0 \leq i \leq n} \rangle, p \models \phi(\boldsymbol{a})$ *for every repair* $(\mathcal{A}'_i)_{0 \leq i \leq n}$ *of* $\mathcal{K}$;
- *IAR semantics, written* $\mathcal{K}, p \models_{IAR} \phi(\boldsymbol{a})$,
  iff $\langle \mathcal{T}, (\mathcal{A}^{IR}_i)_{0 \leq i \leq n} \rangle, p \models \phi(\boldsymbol{a})$, *with* $\mathcal{A}^{IR}_i = \bigcap_{(\mathcal{A}'_j)_{0 \leq j \leq n} \in Rep(\mathcal{K})} \mathcal{A}'_i$, $0 \leq i \leq n$;
- *brave semantics, written* $\mathcal{K}, p \models_{brave} \phi(\boldsymbol{a})$,
  iff $\langle \mathcal{T}, (\mathcal{A}'_i)_{0 \leq i \leq n} \rangle, p \models \phi(\boldsymbol{a})$ *for some repair* $(\mathcal{A}'_i)_{0 \leq i \leq n}$ *of* $\mathcal{K}$.

The following relationships between the semantics are implied by their definition:

$$\mathcal{K}, p \models_{\text{IAR}} \phi(a) \quad \Rightarrow \quad \mathcal{K}, p \models_{\text{AR}} \phi(a) \quad \Rightarrow \quad \mathcal{K}, p \models_{\text{brave}} \phi(a)$$

Next, we illustrate the effect of the different semantics in the temporal case.

Example 2 (Example 1 cont'd). Consider the three temporal conjunctive queries:

$$\phi_1 = \Box(\exists y \ \text{execute}(x, y)) \qquad\qquad \phi_2 = \Box(\exists y \ \text{Server}(x) \wedge \text{execute}(x, y))$$
$$\phi_3 = \Box(\exists y \ \text{AppServer}(x) \wedge \text{execute}(x, y))$$

In Case 1 with no rigid predicate, the intersection of the repairs is $(\mathcal{A}_i^{IR})_{1 \leq i \leq 2}$ with $\mathcal{A}_1^{IR} = \mathcal{A}_1$, $\mathcal{A}_2^{IR} = \{\text{execute}(a, c)\}$. Then $\mathcal{K}, 1 \models_{\text{IAR}} \phi_1(a)$, since in every model of the intersection of the repairs a executes b at time point 1 and c at time point 2. For ϕ_2, $\mathcal{K}, 1 \models_{\text{AR}} \phi_2(a)$, since every model of every repair assigns a to WebServer at time point 1 and either to AppServer (in models of $(\mathcal{A}_i')_{1 \leq i \leq 2}$) or to WebServer (in models of $(\mathcal{A}_i'')_{1 \leq i \leq 2}$) at time point 2, but $\mathcal{K}, 1 \not\models_{\text{IAR}} \phi_2(a)$. Finally, $\mathcal{K}, 1 \not\models_{\text{brave}} \phi_3(a)$ because no repair entails AppServer(a) at time point 1.

If AppServer is rigid, the intersection of the repairs is $(\mathcal{A}_i^{IR})_{1 \leq i \leq 2}$ with $\mathcal{A}_1^{IR} = \{\text{execute}(a, b)\}$, $\mathcal{A}_2^{IR} = \{\text{execute}(a, c)\}$. So still $\mathcal{K}, 1 \models_{\text{IAR}} \phi_1(a)$ holds. Since every model of every repair assigns a to Server at time points 1 and 2 (either because a is a web server or an application server), $\mathcal{K}, 1 \models_{\text{AR}} \phi_2(a)$, but $\mathcal{K}, 1 \not\models_{\text{IAR}} \phi_2(a)$. Finally, $\mathcal{K}, 1 \models_{\text{brave}} \phi_3(a)$ because every model of $\langle \mathcal{T}, (\mathcal{A}_i')_{1 \leq i \leq 2} \rangle$ assigns a to AppServer at any time point by rigidity of AppServer, but $\mathcal{K}, 1 \not\models_{\text{AR}} \phi_3(a)$.

We point out some characteristics of Case 1. Since there is no rigid predicate, the interpretations $\mathcal{I}_i$ of a model $\mathcal{J} = (\mathcal{I}_i)_{0 \leq i \leq n}$ of $\mathcal{K}$ that respects the rigid predicates are independent, besides the interpretation of the constants.

Proposition 1. *If* $\mathsf{N_{RC}} = \mathsf{N_{RR}} = \emptyset$*, then* $\mathcal{K} = \langle \mathcal{T}, (\mathcal{A}_i)_{0 \leq i \leq n} \rangle$ *is consistent iff every* $\langle \mathcal{T}, \mathcal{A}_i \rangle$ *is consistent. Moreover, if* $\mathcal{K}$ *is consistent, for every* $0 \leq p \leq n$*,* $\mathcal{I}_p'$ *is a model of* $\langle \mathcal{T}, \mathcal{A}_p \rangle$ *iff there exists a model* $(\mathcal{I}_i)_{0 \leq i \leq n}$ *of* $\mathcal{K}$ *such that* $\mathcal{I}_p = \mathcal{I}_p'$*.*

Proposition 1 has important consequences. First, the repairs of $\mathcal{K}$ are all possible sequences $(\mathcal{A}_i')_{0 \leq i \leq n}$ where $\mathcal{A}_i'$ is a repair of $\langle \mathcal{T}, \mathcal{A}_i \rangle$, so the intersection of the repairs of $\mathcal{K}$ is $(\mathcal{A}_i^{\cap})_{0 \leq i \leq n}$ where $\mathcal{A}_i^{\cap}$ is the intersection of the repairs of $\langle \mathcal{T}, \mathcal{A}_i \rangle$. Second, we show that the entailment (resp. IAR entailment) of a BTCQ from a consistent (resp. inconsistent) DL-Lite$_{\mathcal{R}}$ TKB can be equivalently defined w.r.t. the entailment (resp. IAR entailment) of the BCQs it contains as follows:

Proposition 2. *If* $\mathcal{K}$ *is a DL-Lite$_{\mathcal{R}}$ TKB and* $\mathsf{N_{RC}} = \mathsf{N_{RR}} = \emptyset$*, the entailments shown in Table 2 hold for* $S = \text{classical when } \mathcal{K}$ *is consistent, and for* $S = \text{IAR}$*.*

This is a remarkable result, since it implies that answering temporal CQs under IAR semantics can be done with the algorithms developed for the consistent case [10,11] by replacing classical CQ answering by IAR CQ answering (see [8,22,27] for algorithms). The following example shows that this is unfortunately not true for brave or AR semantics.

Table 2. Entailment under classical or IAR semantics without rigid predicates

ϕ	$\mathcal{K}, p \models_S \phi$ iff
$\exists \boldsymbol{y}\, \psi(\boldsymbol{y})$	$\langle \mathcal{T}, \mathcal{A}_p \rangle \models_S \exists \boldsymbol{y}\, \psi(\boldsymbol{y})$
$\phi_1 \wedge \phi_2$	$\mathcal{K}, p \models_S \phi_1$ and $\mathcal{K}, p \models_S \phi_2$
$\phi_1 \vee \phi_2$	$\mathcal{K}, p \models_S \phi_1$ or $\mathcal{K}, p \models_S \phi_2$
$\bigcirc \phi_1$	$p < n$ and $\mathcal{K}, p+1 \models_S \phi_1$
$\bullet \phi_1$	$p < n$ implies $\mathcal{K}, p+1 \models_S \phi_1$
$\bigcirc^- \phi_1$	$p > 0$ and $\mathcal{K}, p-1 \models_S \phi_1$
$\bullet^- \phi_1$	$p > 0$ implies $\mathcal{K}, p-1 \models_S \phi_1$
$\Box \phi_1$	$\forall k,\, p \leq k \leq n,\, \mathcal{K}, k \models_S \phi_1$
$\Box^- \phi_1$	$\forall k,\, 0 \leq k \leq p,\, \mathcal{K}, k \models_S \phi_1$
$\Diamond \phi_1$	$\exists k,\, p \leq k \leq n,\, \mathcal{K}, k \models_S \phi_1$
$\Diamond^- \phi_1$	$\exists k,\, 0 \leq k \leq p,\, \mathcal{K}, k \models_S \phi_1$
$\phi_1 U \phi_2$	$\exists k,\, p \leq k \leq n,\, \mathcal{K}, k \models_S \phi_2$ and $\forall j,\, p \leq j < k, \mathcal{K}, j \models_S \phi_1$
$\phi_1 S \phi_2$	$\exists k,\, 0 \leq k \leq p,\, \mathcal{K}, k \models_S \phi_2$ and $\forall j,\, k < j \leq p, \mathcal{K}, j \models_S \phi_1$

Example 3. Consider the following TKB $\mathcal{K} = \langle \mathcal{T}, (\mathcal{A}_i)_{1 \leq i \leq n} \rangle$ and TCQ ϕ.

$$\mathcal{T} = \{T \sqsubseteq \neg F\} \qquad \mathcal{A}_i = \{T(a), F(a)\} \text{ for } 1 \leq i \leq n \qquad \phi = \Box^-(T(a) \wedge \bullet^- F(a))$$

Now, $\mathcal{K}, k \models_{\text{brave}} T(a) \wedge \bullet^- F(a)$ for every $0 \leq k \leq n$, but $\mathcal{K}, n \not\models_{\text{brave}} \phi$. This is because the same repair cannot entail $T(a) \wedge \bullet^- F(a)$ both at time point k and $k + 1$, since it would contain both $(T(a), k)$ and $(F(a), k)$ which is not possible. For AR semantics, consider $\phi = T(a) \vee F(a)$ over the TKB $\mathcal{K}$: while ϕ holds under AR semantics at each time point, neither $T(a)$ nor $F(a)$ does.

However, if the operators allowed in the TCQ are restricted to $\wedge, \bigcirc, \bullet, \bigcirc^-, \bullet^-, \Box$, and $\Box^-$, then AR TCQ answering can be done with the algorithms developed for the consistent case by simply replacing classical CQ answering by AR CQ answering (see [8] for algorithms). Moreover, contrary to the brave semantics, this method still provides a *sound approximation* of AR answers even for unrestricted TCQs, since for all operators, the "if" direction from Table 2 is true.

4   Complexity Analysis for DL-Lite$_{\mathcal{R}}$

The complexity of TCQ answering under the classical semantics in DL-Lite$_{\mathcal{R}}$ with *negations* in the query has been shown ALogTime-complete w.r.t. data complexity and PSpace-complete w.r.t. combined complexity, rigid concepts and roles being present or not [12]. In our case, i.e., without negations, CQ evaluation over databases provides a NP lower bound for combined complexity and it has been shown in [10,11] that TCQs in DL-Lite$_{\mathcal{R}}$ are rewritable so that they can be answered over a temporal database—albeit for a restricted setting without rigid roles and with rigid concepts only for TCQs that are rooted. The NP membership of TCQ answering in Case 1 for combined complexity is implied by this latter work as follows: it is possible to guess for each time point i and CQ q from the TCQ either a rewriting q' of q that holds in $\mathcal{A}_i$ together with the rewriting steps that produce q' and the variables assignment that maps q' in $\mathcal{A}_i$, or to guess "false". Checking that q' is indeed a rewriting of q and holds in $\mathcal{A}_i$ can be done in polynomial time and there are polynomially many such pairs of a time point and a CQ to test. Moreover, verifying that the propositional LTL formula obtained by replacing the CQs by propositional variables is satisfied by the sequence of truth assignments that assigns the propositional abstraction of q to false at time point i if "false" has been guessed and to true otherwise is in P since the formula does not contain negation. It follows that TCQ answering is NP-complete w.r.t. combined complexity. To alleviate the limitations imposed in [10,11], we first show that TCQ answering without negations is NP-complete w.r.t. combined complexity even in the presence of rigid concepts and roles, with the restriction that a rigid role can only have rigid sub-roles. Indeed, we show that under this restriction, TCQ answering in Case 3 can be reduced to TCQ answering in Case 1 by adding to every ABox a set of assertions that models rigid consequences of the TKB and is computable in polynomial time.

For the remainder of this section, $\mathcal{K} = \langle \mathcal{T}, (\mathcal{A}_i)_{0 \leq i \leq n} \rangle$ is a DL-Lite$_\mathcal{R}$ TKB and ϕ is a BTCQ. The set of constants of ϕ is denoted by $\mathsf{N}_\mathsf{I}^\phi$. We make use of the following notations: for a role P and two constants or variables x and y, $P^- := S$ if $P = S^-$ and $P(x, y)$ denotes $S(x, y)$ if $P = S$ and $S(y, x)$ if $P = S^-$. We assume w.l.o.g. that no $x \in \mathsf{N}_\mathsf{I}^\mathcal{K}$ is of the form x_w^e where w, e are words built over $\mathsf{N}_\mathsf{I}^\mathcal{K} \cup \mathsf{N}_\mathsf{C}^\mathcal{K} \cup \mathsf{N}_\mathsf{R}^\mathcal{K}$ and $\mathbb{N}$ respectively.

As a first step, we assume that $\mathcal{K}$ is consistent and construct a model $\mathcal{J}_\mathcal{K}$ of $\mathcal{K}$ such that for any Boolean *conjunctive query* $q = \exists \boldsymbol{y} \, \psi(\boldsymbol{y})$ such that $\mathsf{N}_\mathsf{I}^q \subseteq \mathsf{N}_\mathsf{I}^\mathcal{K}$, $\mathcal{K}, p \models q$ iff $\mathcal{J}_\mathcal{K}, p \models q$. We build a sequence of (possibly infinite) ABoxes $(chase_{\mathrm{rig}}^\mathcal{K}(\mathcal{A}_i))_{0 \leq i \leq n}$ similar to the chase presented in [15] for KBs. Let $\mathcal{S}$ be a set of DL-Lite$_\mathcal{R}$ assertions. A PI α is applicable in $\mathcal{S}$ to an assertion $\beta \in \mathcal{S}$ if

- $\alpha = A_1 \sqsubseteq A_2$, $\beta = A_1(a)$, and $A_2(a) \notin \mathcal{S}$
- $\alpha = A \sqsubseteq \exists P$, $\beta = A(a)$, and there is no b such that $P(a, b) \in \mathcal{S}$
- $\alpha = \exists P \sqsubseteq A$, $\beta = P(a, b)$, and $A(a) \notin \mathcal{S}$
- $\alpha = \exists P_1 \sqsubseteq \exists P_2$, $\beta = P_1(a_1, a_2)$, and there is no b such that $P_2(a_1, b) \in \mathcal{S}$
- $\alpha = P_1 \sqsubseteq P_2$, $\beta = P_1(a_1, a_2)$, and $P_2(a_1, a_2) \notin \mathcal{S}$.

Applying a PI α to an assertion β means adding a new suitable assertion β_{new} to $\mathcal{S}$ such that α is not applicable to β in $\mathcal{S} \cup \{\beta_{\mathrm{new}}\}$.

Definition 5 (Rigid chase of a TKB). *Let* $\mathcal{K} = \langle \mathcal{T}, (\mathcal{A}_i)_{0 \leq i \leq n} \rangle$ *be a DL-Lite$_\mathcal{R}$ TKB. Let* $(\mathcal{A}_i')_{0 \leq i \leq n} = (\mathcal{A}_i \cup \{\beta \mid \exists k, \beta \in \mathcal{A}_k \text{ and } \beta \text{ is rigid}\})_{0 \leq i \leq n}$, *let* $\mathcal{T}_p$ *be the set of positive inclusions in* $\mathcal{T}$, *and let* N_i *be the number of assertions in* $\mathcal{A}_i'$. *Assume that the assertions of each* $\mathcal{A}_i'$ *are numbered from* $N_1 + \cdots + N_{i-1} + 1$

to $N_1 + \cdots + N_i$ following their lexicographic order. Consider the sequences of sets of assertions $\mathcal{S}^j = (\mathcal{S}_i^j)_{0 \leq i \leq n}$ defined as follows:

$$\mathcal{S}^0 = (\mathcal{A}_i')_{0 \leq i \leq n} \quad and \quad \mathcal{S}^{j+1} = \mathcal{S}^j \cup \mathcal{S}^{new} = (\mathcal{S}_i^j \cup \mathcal{S}_i^{new})_{0 \leq i \leq n},$$

where $\mathcal{S}^{new}$ is defined in terms of the assertion β_{new} obtained from: let $\beta \in \mathcal{S}_{i_\beta}^j$ be the first assertion in $\mathcal{S}^j$ such that there is a PI in $\mathcal{T}_p$ applicable in $\mathcal{S}_{i_\beta}^j$ to β and α be the lexicographically first PI applicable in $\mathcal{S}_{i_\beta}^j$ to β. If α, β are of the form

- $\alpha = A_1 \sqsubseteq A_2$ and $\beta = A_1(a)$ then $\beta_{new} = A_2(a)$
- $\alpha = A \sqsubseteq \exists P$ and $\beta = A(a)$ then $\beta_{new} = P(a, a_{new})$
- $\alpha = \exists P \sqsubseteq A$ and $\beta = P(a, b)$ then $\beta_{new} = A(a)$
- $\alpha = \exists P_1 \sqsubseteq \exists P$ and $\beta = P_1(a, b)$ then $\beta_{new} = P(a, a_{new})$
- $\alpha = P_1 \sqsubseteq P_2$ and $\beta = P_1(a_1, a_2)$ then $\beta_{new} = P_2(a_1, a_2)$

where a_{new} is constructed from α and β as follows:

- if $a \in \mathsf{N_I^K}$ then $a_{new} = x_{aP}^{i_\beta}$
- otherwise $a \notin \mathsf{N_I^K}$, then let $a = x_{a'P_1...P_l}^{i_1...i_l}$ and define $a_{new} = x_{a'P_1...P_lP}^{i_1...i_l i_\beta}$.

If β_{new} is rigid, then $\mathcal{S}^{new} = (\{\beta_{new}\})_{0 \leq i \leq n}$, otherwise, $\mathcal{S}^{new} = (\mathcal{S}_i^{new})_{0 \leq i \leq n}$ with $\mathcal{S}_{i_\beta}^{new} = \{\beta_{new}\}$ and $\mathcal{S}_i^{new} = \emptyset$ for $i \neq i_\beta$. Let N be the total number of assertions in $\mathcal{S}^j$. If β_{new} is not rigid, β_{new} is numbered by $N + 1$, otherwise for every $0 \leq i \leq n$, the assertion $\beta_{new} \in \mathcal{S}_i^{new}$ added to $\mathcal{S}_i^j$ is numbered by $N + 1 + i$.

We call the rigid chase of $\mathcal{K}$, denoted by $chase_{rig}(\mathcal{K}) = (chase_{rig}^{\mathcal{K}}(\mathcal{A}_i))_{0 \leq i \leq n}$, the sequence of sets of assertions obtained as the infinite union of all $\mathcal{S}^j$, i.e.,

$$chase_{rig}(\mathcal{K}) = (chase_{rig}^{\mathcal{K}}(\mathcal{A}_i))_{0 \leq i \leq n} = \bigcup_{j \in \mathbb{N}} \mathcal{S}^j = (\bigcup_{j \in \mathbb{N}} \mathcal{S}_i^j)_{0 \leq i \leq n}.$$

If $\mathcal{K}$ is consistent, let $\mathcal{J}_{\mathcal{K}} = (\mathcal{I}_i)_{0 \leq i \leq n}$ where $\mathcal{I}_i = (\Delta, \cdot^{\mathcal{I}_i})$ is defined as follows: $\Delta = \mathsf{N_I^K} \cup \Gamma_N$ where Γ_N is the set of individuals that appear in $chase_{rig}(\mathcal{K})$ but not in $\mathcal{K}$, $a^{\mathcal{I}_i} = a$ for every $a \in \Delta$, $A^{\mathcal{I}_i} = \{a \mid A(a) \in chase_{rig}^{\mathcal{K}}(\mathcal{A}_i)\}$ for every $A \in \mathsf{N_C}$, and $R^{\mathcal{I}_i} = \{(a, b) \mid R(a, b) \in chase_{rig}^{\mathcal{K}}(\mathcal{A}_i)\}$ for every $R \in \mathsf{N_R}$. Then:

Lemma 1. $\mathcal{J}_{\mathcal{K}}$ is a model of $\mathcal{K}$ that respects the rigid predicates, and for any BCQ $q = \exists \boldsymbol{y} \psi(\boldsymbol{y})$ such that $\mathsf{N_I^q} \subseteq \mathsf{N_I^K}$, $\mathcal{K}, p \models q$ iff $\mathcal{J}_{\mathcal{K}}, p \models q$ iff $\mathcal{I}_p \models q$.

We want to construct in polynomial time a set of assertions $\mathcal{R}$ that captures all relevant information about rigid concepts and roles for TCQ answering. Without any restriction on the TBox, $\mathcal{R}$ may be infinite. To see this, consider $\mathcal{K}$ with $\mathcal{T} = \{\exists R^- \sqsubseteq \exists R, R \sqsubseteq S\}$ with S rigid, $\mathcal{A}_0 = \{R(a, b)\}$, $\mathcal{A}_i = \emptyset$ for $1 \leq i \leq n$. Since a model of $\mathcal{K}$ that respects rigid predicates is such that $\phi = \exists x_1 \ldots x_{k+1} S(x_1, x_2) \wedge \ldots \wedge S(x_k, x_{k+1})$ holds for any $k > 0$ and at any time point, but can be such that no cycle of S, nor $\exists xy R(x, y)$ holds at some time point $i > 0$, $\mathcal{R}$ has to contain an infinite chain of S. Therefore we assume the restriction that rigid roles only have rigid sub-roles, i.e., $\mathcal{T}$ does not entail any role inclusion of the form $P_1 \sqsubseteq P_2$ with $P_1 := R_1 | R_1^-$, $R_1 \in \mathsf{N_R} \backslash \mathsf{N_{RR}}$ and $P_2 := R_2 | R_2^-$, $R_2 \in \mathsf{N_{RR}}$.

Proposition 3. *Let $\mathcal{R}$ be as follows:*

$$\mathcal{R} = \{A(a) \mid A \in \mathsf{N}^{\mathcal{K}}_{\mathsf{RC}}, a \in \mathsf{N}^{\mathcal{K}}_{\mathsf{I}}, \exists i, \langle \mathcal{T}, \mathcal{A}_i \rangle \models_{brave} A(a)\} \cup$$

$$\{R(a,b) \mid R \in \mathsf{N}^{\mathcal{K}}_{\mathsf{RR}}, a,b \in \mathsf{N}^{\mathcal{K}}_{\mathsf{I}}, \exists i, \langle \mathcal{T}, \mathcal{A}_i \rangle \models_{brave} R(a,b)\} \cup$$

$$\{P(a, x_{aP}) \mid R \in \mathsf{N}^{\mathcal{K}}_{\mathsf{RR}}, P := R|R^-, a \in \mathsf{N}^{\mathcal{K}}_{\mathsf{I}}, \exists i, \langle \mathcal{T}, \mathcal{A}_i \rangle \models_{brave} \exists x P(a, x)\} \cup$$

$$\{A(x_{P_1}) \mid S \in \mathsf{N}^{\mathcal{K}}_{\mathsf{R}} \backslash \mathsf{N}^{\mathcal{K}}_{\mathsf{RR}}, P_1 := S|S^-, A \in \mathsf{N}^{\mathcal{K}}_{\mathsf{RC}},$$

$$\exists i, \langle \mathcal{T}, \mathcal{A}_i \rangle \models_{brave} \exists x y P_1(x, y) \text{ and } \mathcal{T} \models \exists P_1^- \sqsubseteq A\} \cup$$

$$\{P_2(x_{P_1}, x_{P_1 P_2}) \mid S \in \mathsf{N}^{\mathcal{K}}_{\mathsf{R}} \backslash \mathsf{N}^{\mathcal{K}}_{\mathsf{RR}}, P_1 := S|S^-, R \in \mathsf{N}^{\mathcal{K}}_{\mathsf{RR}}, P_2 := R|R^-,$$

$$\exists i, \langle \mathcal{T}, \mathcal{A}_i \rangle \models_{brave} \exists x y P_1(x, y) \text{ and } \mathcal{T} \models \exists P_1^- \sqsubseteq \exists P_2\}$$

The set $\mathcal{R}$ is computable in polynomial time and such that (i) $\mathcal{K}$ is consistent iff $\mathcal{K}_{\mathcal{R}} = \langle \mathcal{T}, (\mathcal{A}_i \cup \mathcal{R})_{0 \le i \le n} \rangle$ is consistent with $\mathsf{N}_{\mathsf{RC}} = \mathsf{N}_{\mathsf{RR}} = \emptyset$, and (ii) for any BTCQ ϕ such that $\mathsf{N}^{\phi}_{\mathsf{I}} \subseteq \mathsf{N}^{\mathcal{K}}_{\mathsf{I}}, \mathcal{K}, p \models \phi$ iff $\mathcal{K}_{\mathcal{R}}, p \models \phi$ with $\mathsf{N}_{\mathsf{RC}} = \mathsf{N}_{\mathsf{RR}} = \emptyset$.

The size of $\mathcal{R}$ is polynomial in the size of $\mathsf{N}^{\mathcal{K}}_{\mathsf{C}}, \mathsf{N}^{\mathcal{K}}_{\mathsf{R}}$, and $\mathsf{N}^{\mathcal{K}}_{\mathsf{I}}$, and since atomic query answering under brave semantics as well as subsumption checking can be done in polynomial time, $\mathcal{R}$ can be computed in P. The first three parts of $\mathcal{R}$ retain information about the participation of individuals of $\mathsf{N}^{\mathcal{K}}_{\mathsf{I}}$ in rigid predicates. The last two witness the participation in rigid predicates of the role-successors w.r.t. non-rigid roles, thus take into account also anonymous individuals that are created in $chase_{rig}(\mathcal{K})$ when applying PIs whose right-hand side is an existential restriction with a non-rigid role. Note that the individuals created in $chase_{rig}(\mathcal{K})$ when applying such a PI with a rigid role are witnessed by the x_{aP} or $x_{P_1 P_2}$ if they do not follow from a rigid role assertion. They do not need to be witnessed otherwise, since the assertion $P_2(x_{P_1}, x_{P_1 P_2})$ is sufficient to trigger all the anonymous part implied by the fact that $x_{P_1 P_2}$ is in the range of P_2.

The key point of the proof for Claim *(i)* in Proposition 3, is that a minimal inconsistent subset of $\mathcal{K}$ of the form $(\alpha, i), (\beta, j)$ with $i \ne j$ entails the violation of a NI that involves a rigid predicate, and that the rigid consequences of α and β are captured by $\mathcal{R}$. For the other direction, the main idea is that a minimal inconsistent subset of $\mathcal{K}_{\mathcal{R}}$ of the form $(\alpha, i), (\beta, i)$ with $\alpha \in \mathcal{R}$ is such that there is some $\alpha' \in \mathcal{A}_j$ that triggered the addition of α in $\mathcal{R}$, and a model of $\mathcal{K}$ that respects the rigid predicates should satisfy both β and the rigid consequences of α' at time point i. To prove Claim *(ii)* of Proposition 3, we first show that for any Boolean *conjunctive query* $q = \exists \boldsymbol{y} \, \psi(\boldsymbol{y})$ such that $\mathsf{N}^q_{\mathsf{I}} \subseteq \mathsf{N}^{\mathcal{K}}_{\mathsf{I}}, \mathcal{J}_{\mathcal{K}}, p \models q$ iff $\mathcal{K}_{\mathcal{R}}, p \models q$ with $\mathsf{N}_{\mathsf{RC}} = \mathsf{N}_{\mathsf{RR}} = \emptyset$ by defining homomorphisms between $\mathcal{I}_p$ and the canonical model of $\langle \mathcal{T}, (\mathcal{A}_p \cup \mathcal{R}) \rangle$.

Lemma 2. *If $q = \exists \boldsymbol{y} \, \psi(\boldsymbol{y})$ is such that $\mathsf{N}^q_{\mathsf{I}} \subseteq \mathsf{N}^{\mathcal{K}}_{\mathsf{I}}$, then $\mathcal{I}_p \models q$ iff $\mathcal{K}_{\mathcal{R}}, p \models q$.*

We then show by induction on the structure of the BTCQ ϕ that if $\mathsf{N}^{\phi}_{\mathsf{I}} \subseteq \mathsf{N}^{\mathcal{K}}_{\mathsf{I}}$, then $\mathcal{K}, p \models \phi$ iff $\mathcal{K}_{\mathcal{R}}, p \models \phi$ with $\mathsf{N}_{\mathsf{RC}} = \mathsf{N}_{\mathsf{RR}} = \emptyset$, so that TCQ answering over $\mathcal{K}$ in Case 3 can be done by TCQ answering over $\mathcal{K}_{\mathcal{R}}$ in Case 1 and pruning answers that contain individual names not from $\mathsf{N}^{\mathcal{K}}_{\mathsf{I}}$. Note that a model of $\mathcal{K}_{\mathcal{R}}$ is a model of $\mathcal{K}$ but does not respect rigid predicates in general. We can reduce BTCQ entailment over $\mathcal{K}$ with rigid predicates to BTCQ entailment over $\mathcal{K}_\mathcal{R}$ without rigid predicates only because our TCQs do not allow LTL operators to be nested in existential quantifications. This prevents existentially quantified variables to link different time points. Otherwise a query as $\exists xy\Box(R(a,x) \wedge R(x,y))$ with $\mathcal{T} = \{B \sqsubseteq \exists R, \exists R^- \sqsubseteq \exists R\}$, $R \in \mathsf{N_{RR}}$ and $\mathcal{A}_i = \{B(a)\}$ would be entailed from $\mathcal{K}$ but not from $\mathcal{K}_\mathcal{R}$ with $\mathsf{N_{RR}} = \emptyset$. Indeed, in this case $\mathcal{R} = \{R(a, x_{aR})\}$, so x_{aR} may have a different R-successor in each interpretation of a model of $\mathcal{K}_\mathcal{R}$ and y cannot be mapped to the same object at every time point.

It follows from Proposition 3 and the NP-completeness of TCQ answering in Case 1 that TCQ answering is NP-complete w.r.t. combined complexity with the lower bound coming from the atemporal case. The following theorem summarizes the known complexity results for the classical semantics.

Theorem 1. *If $\mathcal{T}$ does not entail any role inclusion of the form $P_1 \sqsubseteq P_2$ with $P_1 := R_1|R_1^-$, $R_1 \in \mathsf{N_R}\backslash\mathsf{N_{RR}}$ and $P_2 := R_2|R_2^-$, $R_2 \in \mathsf{N_{RR}}$, then consistency checking is in P w.r.t. combined complexity and TCQ answering is in P w.r.t. data complexity, and NP-complete w.r.t. combined complexity.*

We now turn our attention to the inconsistency-tolerant semantics.

Theorem 2. *The results in Fig. 1 hold.*

	AR	IAR	brave	AR	IAR	brave
Case 1 ($\mathsf{N_{RC}} = \emptyset, \mathsf{N_{RR}} = \emptyset$)	coNP-c	in P	in P	Π_2^p-c	NP-c	NP-c
Case 2 ($\mathsf{N_{RC}} \neq \emptyset, \mathsf{N_{RR}} = \emptyset$)	coNP-c	in P	NP-c	Π_2^p-c	NP-c	NP-c
Case 3* ($\mathsf{N_{RC}} \neq \emptyset, \mathsf{N_{RR}} \neq \emptyset$)	coNP-c	in P	NP-c	Π_2^p-c	NP-c	NP-c

Fig. 1. Data [left] and combined [right] complexity of BTCQ entailment over DL-Lite$_\mathcal{R}$ TKBs under the different semantics. *: only with rigid specializations of rigid roles

In what follows, we present the key ideas underlying Theorem 2. First note that verifying that a sequence of ABoxes $(\mathcal{A}_i')_{0 \leq i \leq n}$ is a repair of $\mathcal{K}$ can be done in P by checking that $\mathcal{A}_i' \subseteq \mathcal{A}_i$ for every i, that $(\mathcal{A}_i')_{0 \leq i \leq n}$ is consistent, and that adding any other timed-assertion of $\mathcal{K}$ renders it inconsistent.

AR Upper Bounds. We show that ϕ does not hold under AR semantics by guessing a repair of $\mathcal{K}$ that does not entail ϕ.

IAR Upper Bounds. We compute the minimal inconsistent subsets of $\mathcal{K}$ in P by checking the consistency of every timed-assertion and pair of timed-assertions, then answer the query over the TKB from which they have been removed. Indeed, if a timed-assertion (α, i) is inconsistent it cannot be in a repair, and if there exists a consistent (β, j) such that $\{(\alpha, i), (\beta, j)\}$ is inconsistent, (α, i) is not in the repairs that contain (β, j). In the other direction, if (α, i) does not appear in some repair $(\mathcal{A}'_i)_{0 \leq i \leq n}$ of $\mathcal{K}$, since the repairs are maximal, $(\mathcal{A}'_i)_{0 \leq i \leq n} \cup \{(\alpha, i)\}$ is inconsistent so (α, i) is in some minimal inconsistent subset of $\mathcal{K}$.

AR and IAR Lower Bounds. Hardness results come from the atemporal case.

Combined Complexity of Brave. We show that ϕ holds under brave semantics by guessing a repair of $\mathcal{K}$ that entails ϕ. Hardness comes from the atemporal case.

Data Complexity of Brave. The data complexity upper bound for brave CQ answering relies on the fact that the size of the minimal sets of assertions that support the query is bounded by the query size, which is not true in the temporal setting (e.g., consider $\phi = \Box A(a)$, which needs n assertions to be entailed). Moreover, while brave BCQ entailment is tractable in the atemporal setting, we show that if rigid concepts are allowed, brave BTCQ entailment is NP-hard.

Proposition 4. *If* $\mathsf{N}_{\mathsf{RC}} \neq \emptyset$, *brave TCQ answering is* NP*-complete w.r.t. data complexity.*

Proof. We show the lower bound by reduction from SAT. Let $\varphi = C_1 \wedge \ldots \wedge C_n$ be a CNF formula over variables $x_1, \ldots, x_m$. We define the following problem of BTCQ entailment under brave semantics over TKB $\mathcal{K}$ with concepts $T, F \in \mathsf{N}_{\mathsf{RC}}$:

$$\mathcal{T} = \{\exists Pos \sqsubseteq Sat, \exists Neg \sqsubseteq Sat, \exists Pos^- \sqsubseteq T, \exists Neg^- \sqsubseteq F, T \sqsubseteq \neg F\}$$
$$\mathcal{A}_i = \{Pos(c, x_j) \mid x_j \in C_i\} \cup \{Neg(c, x_j) \mid \neg x_j \in C_i\} \text{ for } 1 \leq i \leq n$$

Let $\phi = \Box^- Sat(c)$. We show that φ is satisfiable iff $\mathcal{K}, n \models_{\text{brave}} \phi$. Indeed, since T and F are rigid, a repair of $\mathcal{K}$ is such that each x_j has either only Pos or Neg incoming edges in the whole TKB. Thus, each repair defines a valuation such that x_j is true if x_j has no incoming Neg-edge, and false otherwise. A repair of $\mathcal{K}$ that entails ϕ, i.e., that is such that c has an outgoing edge in every ABox, corresponds thus to a valuation of the x_j that satisfies every clause C_i.

It remains to show that in Case 1, brave TCQ answering is in P. We describe a method for brave BTCQ entailment when $\mathsf{N}_{\mathsf{RC}} = \mathsf{N}_{\mathsf{RR}} = \emptyset$ that proceeds by type elimination over a set of tuples built from the query and that represent the TCQs that are entailed at each time point. First, we define the structure on which the method operates. We consider the set $L(\phi)$ of *leaves* of ϕ, that is, the set of all BCQs in ϕ, and the set $F(\phi)$ of *subformulas* of ϕ. In what follows, we identify the BCQs of $L(\phi)$ and the BTCQs of $F(\phi)$ with their *propositional abstractions*: if we write that a KB or a TKB entails some elements of $L(\phi)$ or $F(\phi)$, we consider them as BCQs or BTCQs, and if we write that some elements of $L(\phi)$ or $F(\phi)$ entail others, we consider the elements of $L(\phi)$ as propositional variables and those of $F(\phi)$ as propositional LTL formulas built over these variables.

Definition 6. *A justification structure* J *for* ϕ *in* $\mathcal{K}$ *is a set of tuples of the form* $(i, L_{now}, F_{now}, F_{prev}, F_{next})$, *where* $0 \leq i \leq n$, $L_{now} \subseteq L(\phi)$, $F_{now} \subseteq F(\phi)$, $F_{prev} \subseteq F(\phi)$, *and* $F_{next} \subseteq F(\phi)$.

Note that the size of a justification structure for ϕ in $\mathcal{K}$ is linearly bounded in n and independent of the size of the ABoxes. A tuple $(i, L_{\text{now}}, F_{\text{now}}, F_{\text{prev}}, F_{\text{next}})$ is *justified in* J iff it fulfills all of the following conditions:

(1) $\langle T, \mathcal{A}_i \rangle \models_{\text{brave}} \bigwedge_{q \in L_{\text{now}}} q$

(2) If $i > 0$, there exists $(i - 1, L'_{\text{now}}, F'_{\text{now}}, F'_{\text{prev}}, F'_{\text{next}}) \in J$ such that $F_{\text{prev}} = F'_{\text{now}}$ and $F_{\text{now}} = F'_{\text{next}}$

(3) If $i < n$, there exists $(i + 1, L'_{\text{now}}, F'_{\text{now}}, F'_{\text{prev}}, F'_{\text{next}}) \in J$ such that $F_{\text{next}} = F'_{\text{now}}$ and $F_{\text{now}} = F'_{\text{prev}}$

(4) For every $\psi \in L(\phi)$, if $F_{\text{now}} \models \psi$, then $\psi \in L_{\text{now}}$

(5) For every $\psi \in F(\phi)$, if $F_{\text{now}} \models \psi$, then $\psi \in F_{\text{now}}$

(6) For every $\psi \in F(\phi)$, if $\bigwedge_{q \in L_{\text{now}}} q \wedge \bigcirc^{-}(\bigwedge_{\chi \in F_{\text{prev}}} \chi) \wedge \bigcirc(\bigwedge_{\chi \in F_{\text{next}}} \chi) \models \psi$, then $\psi \in F_{\text{now}}$

(7) For every $\psi, \psi' \in F(\phi)$:

if $\psi \vee \psi' \in F_{\text{now}}$, then either $\psi \in F_{\text{now}}$ or $\psi' \in F_{\text{now}}$

if $\Diamond \psi \in F_{\text{now}}$, then either $\psi \in F_{\text{now}}$ or $\Diamond \psi \in F_{\text{next}}$

if $\Diamond^{-} \psi \in F_{\text{now}}$, then either $\psi \in F_{\text{now}}$ or $\Diamond^{-} \psi \in F_{\text{prev}}$

if $\psi' U \psi \in F_{\text{now}}$, then either $\psi \in F_{\text{now}}$ or $\psi' \in F_{\text{now}}$ and $\psi' U \psi \in F_{\text{next}}$

if $\psi' S \psi \in F_{\text{now}}$, then either $\psi \in F_{\text{now}}$ or $\psi' \in F_{\text{now}}$ and $\psi' S \psi \in F_{\text{prev}}$

(8) If $i = n$,

$\forall \psi \in F(\phi)$ of the form $\bullet \varphi$, $\psi \in F_{\text{now}}$

$\forall \psi \in F(\phi)$ of the form $\bigcirc \varphi$, $\psi \notin F_{\text{now}}$

$\forall \psi \in F(\phi)$ of the form $\Diamond \varphi, \Box \varphi, \varphi' U \varphi$, $\psi \in F_{\text{now}}$ iff $\varphi \in F_{\text{now}}$

(9) If $i = 0$,

$\forall \psi \in F(\phi)$ of the form $\bullet^{-} \varphi$, $\psi \in F_{\text{now}}$

$\forall \psi \in F(\phi)$ of the form $\bigcirc^{-} \varphi$, $\psi \notin F_{\text{now}}$

$\forall \psi \in F(\phi)$ of the form $\Diamond^{-} \varphi, \Box^{-} \varphi, \varphi' S \varphi$, $\psi \in F_{\text{now}}$ iff $\varphi \in F_{\text{now}}$

We give the intuition behind the elements of the tuples fulfilling these conditions. The first element i is the time point considered, L_{now} is a set of BCQs whose conjunction is entailed under brave semantics by $\langle T, \mathcal{A}_i \rangle$ (Condition 1), and F_{now} is the set of formulas that can be entailed together with L_{now}, depending on what is entailed in the previous and next time points, this information being stored in F_{prev} and F_{next}, respectively (Condition 6). Conditions 2 and 3 ensure that there is a sequence of tuples representing every time point from 0 to n such that this information is coherent between consecutive tuples. Condition 4 expresses that L_{now} is precisely the set of BCQs contained in F_{now} and Condition 5 that F_{now} is maximal in the sense that it contains its consequences. Condition 7 enforces that F_{now}, F_{prev} and F_{next} respect the semantics of LTL operators and Conditions 8 and 9 enforce this semantics at the ends of the finite sequence.

A justification structure J is *correct* if every tuple is justified, and ϕ is *justified at time point p by J* if there is $(p, L_{\text{now}}, F_{\text{now}}, F_{\text{prev}}, F_{\text{next}}) \in J$ such that $\phi \in F_{\text{now}}$. We show that ϕ is entailed from $\mathcal{K}$ at time point p under brave semantics iff there is a correct justification structure for ϕ in $\mathcal{K}$ that justifies ϕ at time point p. The main idea is to link the tuples of a sequence $((i, L_{\text{now}}, F_{\text{now}}, F_{\text{prev}}, F_{\text{next}}))_{0 \leq i \leq n}$ to a consistent TKB $\mathcal{K}' = \langle T, (\mathcal{A}'_i)_{0 \leq i \leq n} \rangle$ such that for every i, $\mathcal{A}'_i \subseteq \mathcal{A}_i$ and $\langle T, \mathcal{A}'_i \rangle \models \bigwedge_{q \in L_{\text{now}}} q$. We show that there is such a $\mathcal{K}'$ such that $\mathcal{K}', p \models \phi$ iff there is such a sequence of tuples that is a correct justification structure for ϕ in $\mathcal{K}$ and justifies ϕ at time point p.

The complexity of brave TCQ answering follows from the characterization of brave BTCQ entailment with justification structures.

Proposition 5. *In* Case 1, *brave TCQ answering is in* P *w.r.t. data complexity.*

Proof. We start with a justification structure J for ϕ in $\mathcal{K}$ that contains all possible tuples and remove the unjustified tuples as follows: (i) remove every tuple that does not satisfy Conditions 1, 4–8 or 9, and (ii) repeat the following steps until a fix-point has been reached: iterate over the tuples from time point 0 to n, eliminating those which do not satisfy Condition 3, then from n to 0 eliminating those which do not satisfy Condition 2. We then check whether the resulting justification structure contains a tuple $(p, L_{\text{now}}, F_{\text{now}}, F_{\text{prev}}, F_{\text{next}})$ such that $\phi \in F_{\text{now}}$. Since the size of J is linear in n, this process requires at most quadratically many steps. Verifying that a given tuple is justified is in P w.r.t. data complexity (checking Conditions 3 or 2 is linear in n and only the brave entailment of a BCQ from a DL-Lite$_{\mathcal{R}}$ KB for Condition 1 depends on the size of the ABox), so the complete procedure runs in P w.r.t. data complexity.

5   Conclusion and Future Work

We extended the AR, IAR and brave semantics to the setting of temporal query answering in description logics. We first showed that in the case where rigid predicates are not allowed, TCQ answering under IAR semantics can be achieved by combining algorithms developed for TCQ answering under the classical semantics with algorithms for CQ answering under IAR semantics over atemporal KBs. We also showed that in some cases, the same applies to AR semantics and that in any case, this method provides a sound approximation of AR answers. Since this is not true for brave semantics and we believe that this semantics can be relevant, for instance in the application of situation recognition, it would be useful to characterize the queries for which this method would be correct. Indeed, for many pairs of a TBox and query, the minimal subsets of the TKB such that the query can be mapped into them cannot be inconsistent (e.g., if pairs of predicates that may be needed at the same time point do not appear in any NI entailed by the TBox. If $\mathcal{T} = \{A \sqsubseteq \neg C, B \sqsubseteq \neg C\}$ and $\phi = \exists x A(x) \wedge \Diamond(\exists x B(x) \wedge \bigcirc(\exists x C(x)))$, for ϕ being entailed at time point p, $\exists x A(x)$ should hold at p, $\exists x B(x)$ at time point $i \geq p$ and $\exists x C(x)$ at $i + 1 \geq p$. Thus, there cannot be a conflict between the C and the A or B timed-assertions used to satisfy the different CQs).

Our second contribution is a complexity analysis of the three semantics for DL-Lite$_{\mathcal{R}}$, depending on which predicates are allowed to be rigid. Encouragingly, only brave semantics in the cases with rigid predicates has a higher data complexity than in the atemporal case. In the other cases handling of inconsistencies comes at no extra cost for temporal reasoning in terms of computational complexity. These results rise hope for feasibility of making ontology-based applications in temporal settings resilient against noise in the data.

We also showed that for the classical semantics, rigid predicates can be handled by adding a set of assertions to each ABox of the TKB, proving that disallowing negations in the query makes the combined complexity of TCQ answering drop from PSPACE to NP. However, our approach that adds the set of assertions $\mathcal{R}$ to every ABox to reduce Cases 2 or 3 to Case 1 works only for the classical semantics. Now, practical algorithms still remain to be found for inconsistency-tolerant temporal query answering with rigid predicates.

References

1. Artale, A., Kontchakov, R., Kovtunova, A., Ryzhikov, V., Wolter, F., Zakharyaschev, M.: First-order rewritability of temporal ontology-mediated queries. In: Proceedings of IJCAI (2015)
2. Artale, A., Kontchakov, R., Ryzhikov, V., Zakharyaschev, M.: A cookbook for temporal conceptual data modelling with description logics. ACM Trans. Comput. Log. **15**(3), 25:1–25:50 (2014)
3. Baader, F., Bauer, A., Baumgartner, P., Cregan, A., Gabaldon, A., Ji, K., Lee, K., Rajaratnam, D., Schwitter, R.: A novel architecture for situation awareness systems. In: Giese, M., Waaler, A. (eds.) TABLEAUX 2009. LNCS, vol. 5607, pp. 77–92. Springer, Heidelberg (2009). doi:10.1007/978-3-642-02716-1_7
4. Baader, F., Borgwardt, S., Lippmann, M.: Temporalizing ontology-based data access. In: Bonacina, M.P. (ed.) CADE 2013. LNCS, vol. 7898, pp. 330–344. Springer, Heidelberg (2013). doi:10.1007/978-3-642-38574-2_23
5. Baader, F., Calvanese, D., McGuinness, D., Nardi, D., Patel-Schneider, P.F. (eds.): The Description Logic Handbook: Theory, Implementation and Applications. Cambridge University Press, New York (2003)
6. Bertossi, L.E.: Database Repairing and Consistent Query Answering. Synthesis Lectures on Data Management. Morgan & Claypool Publishers, USA (2011)
7. Bienvenu, M., Bourgaux, C.: Inconsistency-tolerant querying of description logic knowledge bases. In: Pan, J.Z., Calvanese, D., Eiter, T., Horrocks, I., Kifer, M., Lin, F., Zhao, Y. (eds.) Reasoning Web 2016. LNCS, vol. 9885, pp. 156–202. Springer, Cham (2017). doi:10.1007/978-3-319-49493-7_5
8. Bienvenu, M., Bourgaux, C., Goasdoué, F.: Querying inconsistent description logic knowledge bases under preferred repair semantics. In: Proceedings of AAAI (2014)
9. Bienvenu, M., Rosati, R.: Tractable approximations of consistent query answering for robust ontology-based data access. In: Proceedings of IJCAI (2013)
10. Borgwardt, S., Lippmann, M., Thost, V.: Temporal query answering in the description logic *DL-Lite*. In: Fontaine, P., Ringeissen, C., Schmidt, R.A. (eds.) FroCoS 2013. LNCS, vol. 8152, pp. 165–180. Springer, Heidelberg (2013). doi:10.1007/978-3-642-40885-4_11
11. Borgwardt, S., Lippmann, M., Thost, V.: Temporalizing rewritable query languages over knowledge bases. J. Web Semant. **33**, 50–70 (2015)
12. Borgwardt, S., Thost, V.: Temporal query answering in DL-Lite with negation. In: Proceedings of GCAI (2015)
13. Bourgaux, C., Turhan, A.Y.: Temporal query answering in DL-Lite over inconsistent data. LTCS-Report 17–06, Chair for Automata Theory, TU Dresden (2017). https://lat.inf.tu-dresden.de/research/reports.html
14. Calbimonte, J., Jeung, H., Corcho, Ó., Aberer, K.: Enabling query technologies for the semantic sensor web. Int. J. Semant. Web Inf. Syst. **8**(1), 43–63 (2012)

15. Calvanese, D., De Giacomo, G., Lembo, D., Lenzerini, M., Poggi, A., Rodriguez-Muro, M., Rosati, R.: Ontologies and databases: the *DL-Lite* approach. In: Tessaris, S., Franconi, E., Eiter, T., Gutierrez, C., Handschuh, S., Rousset, M.-C., Schmidt, R.A. (eds.) Reasoning Web 2009. LNCS, vol. 5689, pp. 255–356. Springer, Heidelberg (2009). doi:10.1007/978-3-642-03754-2_7

16. Calvanese, D., De Giacomo, G., Lembo, D., Lenzerini, M., Rosati, R.: Tractable reasoning and efficient query answering in description logics: the DL-Lite family. J. Autom. Reason. (JAR) **39**(3), 385–429 (2007)

17. Chomicki, J., Toman, D., Böhlen, M.H.: Querying ATSQL databases with temporal logic. ACM Trans. Database Syst. **26**(2), 145–178 (2001)

18. Endsley, M.R.: Toward a theory of situation awareness in dynamic systems. Hum. Factors **37**(1), 32–64 (1995)

19. Gutiérrez-Basulto, V., Klarman, S.: Towards a unifying approach to representing and querying temporal data in description logics. In: Krötzsch, M., Straccia, U. (eds.) RR 2012. LNCS, vol. 7497, pp. 90–105. Springer, Heidelberg (2012). doi:10.1007/978-3-642-33203-6_8

20. Klarman, S., Meyer, T.: Querying temporal databases via OWL 2 QL. In: Kontchakov, R., Mugnier, M.-L. (eds.) RR 2014. LNCS, vol. 8741, pp. 92–107. Springer, Cham (2014). doi:10.1007/978-3-319-11113-1_7

21. Lembo, D., Lenzerini, M., Rosati, R., Ruzzi, M., Savo, D.F.: Inconsistency-tolerant semantics for description logics. In: Hitzler, P., Lukasiewicz, T. (eds.) RR 2010. LNCS, vol. 6333, pp. 103–117. Springer, Heidelberg (2010). doi:10.1007/978-3-642-15918-3_9

22. Lembo, D., Lenzerini, M., Rosati, R., Ruzzi, M., Savo, D.F.: Inconsistency-tolerant query answering in ontology-based data access. J. Web Semant. **33**, 3–29 (2015)

23. Lutz, C., Wolter, F., Zakharyaschev, M.: Temporal description logics: a survey. In: Proceedings of TIME (2008)

24. Motik, B., Cuenca Grau, B., Horrocks, I., Wu, Z., Fokoue, A., Lutz, C.: OWL 2 web ontology language profiles. W3C Recommendation, 11 December 2012. http://www.w3.org/TR/owl2-profiles/

25. Özçep, Ö.L., Möller, R.: Ontology based data access on temporal and streaming data. In: Koubarakis, M., Stamou, G., Stoilos, G., Horrocks, I., Kolaitis, P., Lausen, G., Weikum, G. (eds.) Reasoning Web 2014. LNCS, vol. 8714, pp. 279–312. Springer, Cham (2014). doi:10.1007/978-3-319-10587-1_7

26. Pnueli, A.: The temporal logic of programs. In: Proceedings of FOCS (1977)

27. Tsalapati, E., Stoilos, G., Stamou, G.B., Koletsos, G.: Efficient query answering over expressive inconsistent description logics. In: Proceedings of IJCAI (2016)

Semantic Wide and Deep Learning for Detecting Crisis-Information Categories on Social Media

Grégoire Burel[(⊠)], Hassan Saif, and Harith Alani

Knowledge Media Institute, The Open University, Milton Keynes, UK
{g.burel,h.saif,h.alani}@open.ac.uk

Abstract. When crises hit, many flog to social media to share or consume information related to the event. Social media posts during crises tend to provide valuable reports on affected people, donation offers, help requests, advice provision, etc. Automatically identifying the category of information (e.g., *reports on affected individuals, donations and volunteers*) contained in these posts is vital for their efficient handling and consumption by effected communities and concerned organisations. In this paper, we introduce Sem-CNN; a wide and deep Convolutional Neural Network (CNN) model designed for identifying the category of information contained in crisis-related social media content. Unlike previous models, which mainly rely on the lexical representations of words in the text, the proposed model integrates an additional layer of semantics that represents the named entities in the text, into a *wide* and *deep* CNN network. Results show that the Sem-CNN model consistently outperforms the baselines which consist of statistical and non-semantic deep learning models.

Keywords: Semantic deep learning · Crisis information processing · Social media

1 Introduction

Social media has become a common place for communities and organisations to communicate and share various information during crises, to enhance their situational awareness, to share requests or offers for help and support, and to coordinate their recovery efforts.

The volume and velocity of this content tend to be extremely high, rendering it almost impossible for organisations and communities to manually analyse and process the content shared during such crises [12,16]. For example, in a single day during the 2011 Japan earthquake, 177 million tweets related to the crisis were sent [5]. In 2013, more than 23 million tweets were posted about the haze in Singapore [22].

Olteanu and colleagues study samples of tweets posts during various crisis situations, and found that crisis-related social tweets tend to bare one of the following general information categories [20]: *affected individuals, infrastructures*

© Springer International Publishing AG 2017
C. d'Amato et al. (Eds.): ISWC 2017, Part I, LNCS 10587, pp. 138–155, 2017.
DOI: 10.1007/978-3-319-68288-4_9

and utilities, donations and volunteer, caution and advice, sympathy and emotional support, other useful information. However, tools to automatically identify the category of information shared during crises are still largely unavailable.

Recent research is mostly focused on processing social media content to determine what documents are related to a crisis and what documents are not (e.g., [20]), or to detect the emergence of major crisis event (e.g., *floods* [26], *wildfires* [29], *earthquakes* [23], *nuclear disasters* [28], etc.). However, the automatic identification of the category or type of information shared about events is still in its infancy [20].

For example, although both of the tweets *'Colorado fire displaces hundreds; 1 person missing.'* and *'If you are evacuating please dont wait, take your pets when you evacuate'* were posted during the 2012 Colorado's wildfire crisis,[1] they bare different information, i.e., while the former tweet reports information on individuals affected by the fire, the latter offers advices to the public. The approach presented in this paper is aimed at classifying such kind of documents to automatically determine which ones provide which category of information. Such a mechanism can help users (e.g., citizens, humanitarian organisation, government officials, police forces) to quickly filter big volumes of crisis-related tweets to only those that provide the types of information they are interested in.

Most current research on identifying crisis information from social media rely on the use of supervised and unsupervised Machine Learning (ML) methods, such as classifiers, clustering and language models [1]. More recently, deep learning has emerged as a new ML technique able to capture high level abstractions in data, thus providing significant improvement over traditional ML methods in certain tasks, such as in text classification [13], machine translation [2,8] and sentiment analysis [10,27].

Applying deep learning to enhance the analysis of crisis-related social media content is yet to be thoroughly explored [4]. In this paper, we hypothesise that the encapsulation of a layer of semantics into a deep learning model can provide a more accurate crisis-information-category identification by better characterising the contextual information, which is generally scarce in short, ill-formed social media messages.

We therefore propose Sem-CNN; a semantically enhanced *wide* and *deep* Convolutional Neural Network (CNN) model, to target the problem above. We also investigate the integration of semantic information in two different methods; (a) using semantic concept labels, and (b) using semantic concept abstracts from DBpedia.[2] Our main contributions in this paper are:

- Generation of a wide and deep learning model (Sem-CNN) to identify the category of crisis-related information contained in social media posts.
- Demonstration of two methods for enriching deep learning data representations with semantic information.
- Evaluation of the approach on three samples of the CrisisLexT26 dataset, which consists around 28,000 labelled tweets.

---

[1] High Park fire Wikipedia article, https://en.wikipedia.org/wiki/High_Park_fire.
[2] DBpedia, http://dbpedia.org.

– Produce an accuracy that outperforms the best baselines by up to +22.6% F-measure (min +0.5%), thus proving the potential of semantic deep learning approaches for processing crisis-related social media content.

The rest of the paper is structured as follows. Section 2 shows related work in the areas of event detection and deep learning. Section 3 describes our proposed deep learning model for event identification. Sections 4 and 5 show our evaluation set up and the results of our experiments. Section 6 describes our reflections and our planned future work. Section 7 concludes the paper.

2   Related Work

Crisis-related data analysis is often divided into three main tasks [20]. First, *crisis-related* posts are separated from *non-related* documents. This allows the filtering of documents that may have used a *crisis-related* term or hashtag, but does not contain information that is relevant to a particular crisis event. Second, the type of events mentioned (e.g., *fires, floods, bombing*) are identified from each remaining post in order to identify the main type of event discussed in a document. Third, the category of information contained in these crisis-related tweets are determined. Olteanu and colleagues observed that there is a small number of information categories that most crisis-related tweets tend to bare [20]. These categories are shown in Table 1 along with examples of tweets related to the Colorado's Wildfires. Crisis-information-category can be used by responders to better asses an event situation as they tend to be more actionable than the more general event categories.

Table 1. Crisis information categories from [20], and tweet examples

Category	Example
Affected individuals	'*Colorado fire displaces hundreds; 1 person missing: Firefighters in Colorado and new mexico are battling wind-fu*'
Caution and advice	'*If you are evacuating please dont wait, take your pets when you evacuate #HighParkFire*'
Donations and volunteering	'*RT @username: we are available to house a displaced kitty or two if needed #flagstafffire cc @username*'
Infrastructure and utilities	'*Homes at risk from Colorado wildfire: Hundreds of families took refuge early Monday at a northern Colorado*'
Sympathy and support	'*Pray for rain! RT @username: #HighParkFire is now at 36,930 acres.*'
Other useful information	'*Photo of the Colorado wildfire from space (via @NASA) URL #HighParkFire*'

In our previous work [4], we showed that the first two tasks can be performed relatively successfully with traditional classification techniques (e.g., SVM), achieving higher than 80% in precision and recall values. However, the automatic identification of crisis information categories proved to be a more challenging task.

Identifying *information categories* from social media is a commonly used step in event detection literature, and several recent works used deep learning for event detection in different contexts. The advantage brought by deep learning models over traditional ML feature-based methods is the lightweight feature engineering they require and their reliance instead on word embeddings as a more general and richer representation of words [18].

Pioneer works in this field include [6,11,18], which address the problem of event detection at the sentence and/or phrase level by first identifying the event triggers in a given sentence (which could be a verb or nominalisation) and classifying them into specific categories. Multiple deep learning models have been proposed to address this problem. For example, Nguyen and Grishman [18] use CNNs [15] with three input channels, corresponding to *word embeddings, word position embeddings*, and *ACE entity type embeddings*[3], to learn a word representation and use it to infer whether a word is an event trigger or not. Contrary to the general DBpedia entities and concepts that we use in our research, ACE entities are limited to only a few concepts and cannot be associated to concept or entity descriptions or abstracts.

We investigated the use of semantics for crises-event detection with deep learning methods in [4], where we added a CNN layer to a traditional CNN model by combining two parallel layers that join word embeddings and semantic embeddings initialised from extracted concepts. Although the model performed well for identifying crisis-related tweets and the general crisis events they mention, its performance in identifying information categories could not outperform the more traditional classification methods such as SVM. This was perhaps due to the training complexity of CNN and the semantic embeddings as the amount of semantics in each document is limited.

The approach introduced in this paper differs from [4] by using a variation of the *wide* and *deep* learning model [7] that is designed for balancing the *richness* of semantic information with the *shallowness* of textual content of documents. In particular, it reuses the strength of CNN models for dealing with textual content and a more traditional linear model for dealing with the richness of semantic information. Contrary to the approach in [4], our new model also considers entity and concept abstracts in its semantic input for allowing a better representation of the document semantics.

---

[3] Automatic Content Extraction (ACE) Entities, http://ldc.upenn.edu/collaborations/past-projects/ace.

3   The Sem-CNN Approach for Identifying Crisis Information Categories

In the context of Twitter,[4] the identification of the category of information contained in crises-related tweets is a text classification task where the aim is to identify which posts contain which category of crisis-related information. In this section we describe our proposed Sem-CNN model, which is a semantically enriched deep learning model for identifying crisis-related information categories on Twitter.

The proposed approach is a *wide* and *deep* learning model [7] that jointly integrates shallow textual information in a *deep* Convolutional Neural Network (CNN) model with semantic annotations in a *wide* generalised linear model.

The pipeline of our model consists of five main phases as depicted in Fig. 1:

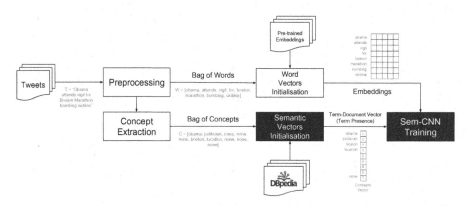

Fig. 1. Pipeline of the proposed semantic Sem-CNN deep learning model for detecting crises information categories.

1. *Text Processing*: A collection of input tweets are cleaned and tokenised for later stages;
2. *Word Vector Initialisation*: Given a bag of words produced in the previous stage and a pre-trained word embeddings, a matrix of word embedding is constructed to be used for model training;
3. *Concept Extraction*: This phase run in parallel with the previous phase. Here the semantic concepts of named-entities in tweets are extracted using an external semantic extraction tool (e.g., TextRazor[5], Alchemy API[6], DBpedia Spotlight [9]);
4. *Semantic Vector Initialisation*: This stage constructs a vector representation for each of the entities and concepts extracted in the previous phase. The vector is either constructed from DBpedia concept labels or from DBpedia concept abstracts;

---

[4] Twitter, http://twitter.com.

[5] TextRazor, https://www.textrazor.com/.

[6] Alchemy API, http://www.ibm.com/watson/alchemy-api.html..

5. *Sem-CNN Training*: In this phase the proposed Sem-CNN model is trained from both, the word embeddings matrix and the semantic term-document vector (concept names or concept abstracts).

In the following subsections we detail each phase in the pipeline.

3.1   Text Preprocessing

Tweets are usually composed of incomplete, noisy and poorly structured sentences due to the frequent presence of abbreviations, irregular expressions, ill-formed words and non-dictionary terms. This phase therefore applies a series of preprocessing steps to reduce the amount of noise in tweets including, for example, the removal of URLs, and all non-ASCII and non English characters. After that, the processed tweets are tokenised into words that are consequently passed as input to the *word embeddings* phase. Although different methods can be used for preprocessing textual data, we follow the same approach used by Kim in the CNN sentence classification model [13].

3.2   Word Vector Initialisation

An important part for applying deep neural networks to text classification is to use word embeddings. As such, this phase aims to initialise a matrix of word embeddings for training the information classification model.

Word embeddings is a general name that refers to a vectorised representation of words, where words are mapped to vectors instead of a one dimension space [3]. The main idea is that semantically close words should have a similar vector representation instead of a distinct representation. Different methods have been proposed for generating embeddings such has Word2Vec [17] and GloVe [21] and they have shown to improve the performance in multiple NLP tasks. Hence, in this work we choose to initialise our model with Google's pre-trained Word2Vec model [17] to construct our word embeddings matrix, where rows in the matrix represent embedding vectors of the words in the Twitter dataset.

3.3   Concept Extraction and Semantic Vector Initialisation

As mentioned in the previous step, using word embeddings for training deep learning classification models has shown to substantially improve classification performance. However, conventional word embedding methods merely rely on the context of a word in the text to learn its embeddings. As such, learning word embeddings from Twitter data might not be as sufficient for training our classifier because tweets often lack context due to their short length and noisy nature.

One possible approach to address this issue is to enrich the training process of our proposed model with the semantic embeddings of words in order to better capture the context of tweets. This approach we pursued in [4] was to add semantic embeddings (i.e., a vectorised representation of semantic concepts) to a two layer

CNN model [4]. However, since tweets are small documents the number of unique concepts available within a corpus of documents is much lower than the number of words present in the corpus. As a consequence, the number of available concepts may not allow the efficient training of the semantic embeddings.

In this context, rather than using semantic embeddings, we propose to use the more traditional vector space model representation of documents where the semantics of each document is represented as a vector that identifies the presence of individual semantic concepts as vector indexes within a concept space. We also represent the presence of individual semantic concepts (or associated abstract words) rather than the frequency of concepts within a tweet since tweets are short textual documents.

Before converting the tweets' semantics into the vector space model representation, we first extract the named-entities in tweets (e.g., *'Oklahoma'*, *'Obama'*, *'Red Cross'*) and map them to their associated semantic concepts (aka semantic types) (e.g., *'Location'*, *'Politician'*, *'Non-Profit Organisation'*) using multiple semantic knowledge bases including DBpedia and Freebase.[7]

We decided to use the TextRazor tool due to its higher accuracy, coverage, and performance in comparison with other entity extraction and semantic linking tools [24].

We use the extracted entities along with their concepts to enrich the training process in the Sem-CNN model. We investigate two different methods for integrating the semantics into the vector space model: (1) the usage of the semantic concepts and entities labels, and; (2) the usage of the DBpedia descriptions of semantic concepts and entities (i.e., concept abstracts). In the following subsections we describe these methods in more detail.

3.3.1   Semantic Concepts Vector Initialisation

The first method for converting the concepts and entities extracted from tweets using the TextRazor tool is to use, when available, their semantic labels (`rdfs:label`) from DBPedia. When such labels are unavailable, the labels that are returned from TextRazor are used directly instead.

The method used for converting a given document using the semantic concepts vector initialisation method is displayed in Fig. 1. For an example document $D = $ '*Obama attends vigil for Boston Marathon bombing victims.*', the concepts and entities labels are extracted and tokenised using a semantic extraction tool and DBpedia so that the words that do not have extracted semantics are converted to a *none* label. Using this method the document D may be tokenised as $T_s = $ ['*obama*', '*politician*', '*none*', '*none*', '*none*', '*boston*', '*location*', '*none*', '*none*', '*none*'] using entity and entity-type tokens. The tokenised version is then converted into the vector space model that the depends on the concept space size $N_s = $ ['*obama*', '*politician*', '*boston*', '*location*', $\cdots$, '*none*'] of size n_s, where n_s represents the total number of concepts and entities in the corpus of documents where D is extracted from. Using the previous concept space, T_s can be converted to the following vector space model $V_s = [1, 1, 1, 1, 0, 0, 0, \cdots, 1]$.

---

[7] Freebase, http://www.freebase.com.

3.3.2   Semantic Abstracts Vector Initialisation

The second method uses, when available, the first sentence of the DBpedia abstracts (dbo:abstract) rather than the semantic labels (rdfs:label). This has the potential advantage of providing richer contextual representation of the semantics contained in the tweets as DBpedia abstracts normally contain additional implicit semantics that are not available in the rdfs:label. In particular, since DBpedia abstracts are extracted from Wikipedia articles,[8] the first sentence of each abstract tends to contain highly descriptive terms that are effectively semantic concepts even though they are not explicitly represented as such (i.e., DBpedia concepts). For example, for the semantic concept dbpedia:Barack_Obama, the first sentence of the dbo:abstract property is 'Barack Hussein Obama II; born August 4, 1961) is an American politician serving as the 44th President of the United States, the first African American to hold the office.'. This sentence contains multiple implicit entities and concepts such as dbo:President_of_the_United_States, dbo:Politician, dbpedia:United_States. As a consequence, by using the dbo:abstract of the concepts and entities found in the documents, we effectively increase the concept space size of the concept vectors and increase the contextual semantics of the document.

The method used for converting the extracted semantics to the vector space model is the same as the one used when doing the semantic concepts vector initialisation except that the concept and entity labels are replaced with the first sentence of the DBpedia abstracts. Effectively, we obtain longer vectors for each documents since the semantic vocabulary space n_a, is larger than the label-only semantic space n_s ($n_a \gg n_s$).

In principle, it is possible to use both the content of abstracts and semantic concepts labels together. However, it does not necessarily increase the amount of semantics found each semantic vector since each dbo:abstract already contains the labels of the extracted concept and entities found in tweets. As a consequence, we focus our research on the semantic concepts vectorisation and the semantic abstracts vectorisation approaches individually.

3.4   A Wide and Deep Semantic CNN Model for Text Classification

This phase aims to train our Sem-CNN model (Fig. 2) from the word embeddings matrices and semantic vectors described in the previous section. Below we describe the *wide* and *deep* CNN model that we propose to tackle the task of identifying fine-grained information within crisis-related documents.

As discussed in Sect. 2, CNN can be used for classifying sentences or documents [13]. The main idea is to use word embeddings coupled with multiple convolutions of varying sizes that extract important information from a set of words in a given sentence, or a document, and then apply a softmax function that predicts its class.

CNN models can be also extended with semantic embeddings in order to use contextual semantics when classifying textual documents [4]. However, there are

---

[8] Wikipedia, http://en.wikipedia.org.

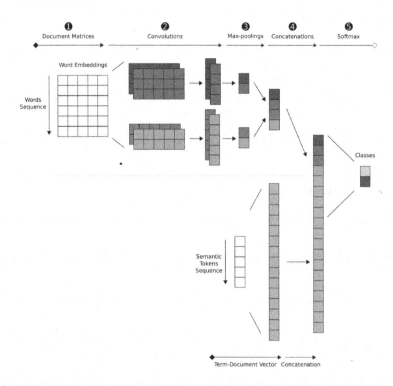

Fig. 2. *Wide* and *Deep* Convolutional Neural Network (CNN) for text classification with word embeddings and semantic document representations: (1) A word embedding matrix is created for a document: (2) Multiple convolutional filters of varying sizes generate features vectors; (3) Max pooling is performed on each features vector; (4) The resulting vectors are concatenated with the semantic vector representation of the document, and; (5) A softmax layer is used for classifying the document.

some drawbacks in simply adding an additional parallel layer of convolutions that integrates these extracted semantic embeddings (Sect. 2).

First, the limited number of available semantics across tweets is low, which limits the usefulness of embeddings since little data is available for training them. Second, the CNN networks takes into account the location of the entities within the tweets. Although this might be beneficial in principle, the number of non-annotated terms in tweets makes this less useful, and make the model more complicated to train.

A potential solution to those problems is to create a deep learning model that takes into account the *richness* and depth of the semantics contained in the entities and concepts extracted from documents (tweets) and the *shallowness* of the textual content.

The *wide* and *deep* learning model [7] is a deep learning model that jointly trains a wide linear model and a deep neural network. This approach can be potentially useful for our particular task where we need to combine *shallow* textual information with the *richer* semantic information. In particular, we can use the deep neural network on the textual part of documents whereas the wide part is trained on the entities extracted from documents. This means that we effectively balance the *shallowness* of textual content with the *richer* information of semantic concepts and entities.

Although in general the Sem-CNN model (Fig. 2) is philosophically similar to the *wide* and *deep* learning model, the proposed model has three major differences:

1. Rather than using a set of fully connected layers for the *deep* part of the model, we use a set of convolutions since this is known to perform well for text classification tasks [4,13].
2. In the standard *wide* and *deep* learning model, the wide and deep layers use the same input features encoded in different formats (i.e., feature embeddings and feature vectors) whereas our model uses two different feature sets for each part of the model (i.e., word embeddings and concept/entity feature vectors).
3. The standard *wide* and *deep* learning model uses cross product transformations for the feature vectors in the *wide* part of the model. In the Sem-CNN model we omit this transformation due to the small size of the semantic vocabulary and the number of semantics extracted in each document.

The design of the Sem-CNN model allows the integration of semantics in different ways as long as the semantic layer is encoded as a vector space model. In particular, Sem-CNN can integrate semantics using the two semantic vectorisation approaches discussed in Sect. 3.3. In the next section, we compare both integration approaches in the particular context of fine-grained information identification in crisis-related tweets.

4   Experimental Setup

Here we present the experimental setup used to assess our event detection model. As described earlier, the aim is to apply and test the proposed model on the task of information-category detection in crisis-related tweets. As such, our evaluation requires the selection of: (1) a suitable Twitter dataset; (2) the identification of the most appropriate semantic extraction tool, and; (3) the identification of baseline models for cross-comparison.

4.1   Dataset

To assess the performance of our model we require a dataset where each tweet is annotated with an information-category label (e.g. *affected individuals, infrastructures*, etc.). For the purpose of this work we use the CrisisLexT26 dataset [19].

CrisisLexT26 includes tweets collected during 26 crisis events in 2012 and 2013. Each crisis contains around 1,000 annotated tweets for a total of around

28,000 tweets with labels that indicate if a tweet is related or unrelated to a crisis event (i.e. *related/unrelated*).

The tweets are also annotated with additional labels, indicating the information categories present in the tweet as listed in Table 1. More information about the CrisisLexT26 dataset can be found on the CrisisLex website.[9]

Note that in our experiments (Sect. 5) we discard the tweets' *related* and *unrelated* labels and keep only the *information type* labels since the task we experiment with focuses on the identification of information categories within crisis-related tweets.

Three data sets are used in this experiment:

- **Full Dataset**: This consists of all the 28,000 labeled tweets mentioned above.
- **Balanced Dataset 1**: Since the annotations tend to be unbalanced, we create a balanced version of our dataset by performing biased random under-sampling using tweets from each of the 26 crisis events present in the CrisisLexT26 dataset. As a result, 9105 tweets (32.6%) are extracted from the full dataset.
- **Balanced Dataset 2**: Besides the previous under-sampled dataset, we also consider an under-sampled dataset where only tweets that contain at least two semantic entities or concepts are extracted. The aim of this dataset is to better understand the availability of semantic annotations on the Sem-CNN dataset. After under-sampling the model with at least two entities and concepts for each tweet, we obtain 1194 tweets (4.3% of the tweets present in the full dataset).

Table 2 shows the total number of tweets and unique words under each of the three dataset subsets.

Table 2. Statistics of the three Twitter datasets used for the evaluation.

Dataset	No. of tweets	No. of words	No. of word embeddings	No. of tweets with extracted entities
Full dataset	27,933	57,563	16,617	18,298
Balanced dataset 1	9,105	26,933	10,429	5,420
Balanced dataset 2	1,194	5,671	3,540	1,194

4.2 Concept Extraction

As mentioned in Sect. 3, the Sem-CNN model integrates both, the entities' semantic concepts and abstracts of these concepts into the training phase of the classifier in order to better capture information-category clues in tweets.

---

[9] CrisisLex T26 Dataset, http://www.crisislex.org/data-collections.html#CrisisLex T26.

Using TextRazor, we extract 4,022 semantic concept and entities and from those concepts and entities, we manage to match them to 3,822 unique abstract.

Looking at the different datasets, we notice that most of the semantics found in our dataset refer either to a type of event (e.g., *Earthquake, Wildfire*) mentioned in the tweets or to the place (e.g., *Colorado, Philippines*) where the event took place. This shows the value of using these types of semantics as discriminative features for event detection in tweets and may be beneficial for the identification of crisis-related information types.

4.3 Baselines

As discussed in Sect. 2, the task of event detection and information category identification in crisis-related documents in social media has been typically targeted by traditional machine learning classifiers (e.g., Naive Bayes, MaxEnt, SVM). Hence, in our evaluation we consider the following baselines for comparison:

- **SVM (TF-IDF):** A linear kernel SVM classifier trained from the words' TF-IDF vectors extracted from our dataset.
- **SVM (Word2Vec):** A linear kernel SVM classifier trained from the Google pre-trained 300-dimensional word embeddings [17].

In order to provide a thorough evaluation for our model, we also consider two additional variations of SVM as baselines: a SVM trained from the semantic concepts of words (SVM-Concepts) as well as a SVM trained from the semantic abstracts (SVM-Abstracts). Note that in [4], SVM was found to outperform other ML methods such as Naive Bayes and CART in various tasks on crisis-related tweets, and hence we focus our comparison here to SVM only.

5 Evaluation

In this section, we report the results obtained from using the proposed Sem-CNN model for identifying crisis-related information categories from social media posts. Our baselines of comparison is the SVM classifiers trained from TF-IDF, Word2Vec (pre-trained word embeddings), semantic concepts, and semantic abstracts features, as described in Sect. 4.3.

We train the proposed Sem-CNN model using 300 long word embeddings vectors with $F_n = 128$ convolutional filter of sizes $F_s = [3, 4, 5]$. For avoiding over-fitting, we use a dropout of 0.5 during training and use the ADAM gradient decent algorithm [14]. We perform 2,000 iterations with a batch size of 256.

Table 3 shows the results computed using 5-fold cross validation for our crisis information category classifiers on the full dataset, the balanced dataset sample, and the two balanced dataset samples. In particular, the table reports the precision (P), recall (R), and F1-measure (F1) for each model and dataset. The table also reports the types of features and embeddings used to train the different classifiers.

Table 3. Crisis information category detection performance of baselines and our proposed Sem-CNN model on the full and under-sampled datasets.

Model	Features	Semantics	Full dataset			Balanced dataset 1			Balanced dataset 2		
			P	R	F1	P	R	F1	P	R	F1
SVM	TF-IDF	-	0.644	0.604	0.617	0.608	0.610	0.607	0.555	0.548	0.540
SVM	Word2Vec	-	0.565	0.499	0.508	0.539	0.548	0.541	0.611	0.618	0.609
SVM	TF-IDF	Concepts	0.644	0.606	0.618	0.612	0.615	0.612	0.549	0.547	0.542
SVM	Word2Vec	Concepts	0.572	0.500	0.509	0.543	0.552	0.544	0.577	0.586	0.576
SVM	TF-IDF	Abstracts	0.633	0.590	0.603	0.595	0.598	0.595	0.499	0.499	0.495
SVM	Word2Vec	Abstracts	0.541	0.455	0.467	0.506	0.517	0.506	0.502	0.511	0.497
SEM-CNN	CNN-Embed	Concepts	0.645	0.600	0.621	0.627	0.625	0.626	0.675	0.601	0.636
SEM-CNN	CNN-Embed	Abstracts	0.646	0.604	0.624	0.628	0.628	0.628	0.676	0.608	0.640

5.1 Baselines Results

From Table 3 we can see that identifying information categories within crisis-related messages is a challenging tasks, where both, the SVM models produce relatively low results that vary between 46.7% and 61.8% in average F_1, based on the type of training features and dataset.

For the full dataset, we notice that SVM trained from Word2Vec features only gives 56.5%, 49.9% and 50.8% in P, R and F_1 measures respectively. However, using SVM with TF-IDF features improves the performance substantially by around +18.83% yielding in 64.4% P, 60.4% R and 61.7% F_1.

A similar performance trend can be observed under the balanced dataset 1, where SVM with TF-IDF gives higher performance than SVM with Word2Vec features although the performance of SVM with either type of feature on this datasets stays similar to the one reported under the full dataset.

For the balanced dataset 2, we notice a different trend. Here, Word2Vec features seem to outperform TF-IDF features by +10.6% in all measures on average. This might be due to the small size of this dataset in comparison with the size of the full dataset and the balanced dataset 1 as shown in Table 2. This issue is further discussed in Sect. 6.

The second part of Table 3 shows the performance of our baselines when semantic features are added to the feature space of the SVM models. Here we can observe that SVM classifiers trained either from concepts or abstract features do not have much impact on the overall performance. In particular, SVMs trained from concept features under both, the full and balanced dataset 1 give up to 61.8% F_1, which is in general similar to F_1 of a SVM trained from TF-IDF features solely. Nonetheless, on the balanced dataset 2 the performance when using concept features with SVM drops. It is also worth noting that using semantic abstracts as features for event information classification yields in more noticeable changes in the classification performance. In essence, the performance in this case drops even further compared with the concept features.

The above results suggest that plainly using semantic concepts or abstracts with traditional machine learning classifiers (SVM in this case) for identifying crises-related information categories has no additional value on the performance of these classifiers and that more complex classifier are necessary in order to integrate semantic concepts and entities efficiently.

5.2 Sem-CNN Results

In general, we observe that the Sem-CNN models needs relatively few steps in order to obtain the best F_1 results with the models converging around 400–600 steps (Fig. 3).

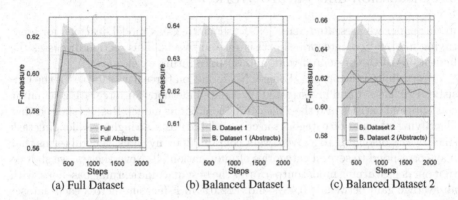

(a) Full Dataset   (b) Balanced Dataset 1   (c) Balanced Dataset 2

Fig. 3. F-measure against the number of training steps for Sem-CNN on each dataset with concept labels and concept abstracts.

The third part of Table 3 depicts the results of the proposed Sem-CNN model. From these results, we notice that Sem-CNN trained either from the concepts or abstract features yields noticeable improvement in the identification performance on all the three datasets. In particular, applying Sem-CNN on the first two datasets (full and balanced dataset 1) increases $P/R/F_1$ on average by +1.19% compared to SVM with TF-IDF and concepts features (the best performing baseline model).

On the balanced dataset 2, we noticed that Sem-CNN gives the highest detection performance with 63.6% F-measure for concepts features and 64% F-measure for the abstracts features. This represents +17.71% F-measure average increase in performance upon using the traditional SVM classifier on this dataset. These results show that our semantic deep learning model is able to use the semantic features of words more efficiently than SVM and find more specific and insightful patterns to distinguish between the different types of event-related information in tweets.

The significance of the results obtained by Sem-CNN against the best semantic baselines (SVM TF-IDF with concepts or abstract) can be compared by performing paired t-tests. We observe that the Sem-CNN with concepts and Sem-CNN with abstracts models mostly significantly outperform their SVM TF-IDF counterparts in term of F-measure (with $p < 0.001$ for Sem-CNN with abstracts for the balanced dataset 1 and 2; $p < 0.01$ for Sem-CNN with concept for the balanced dataset 2, and; $p < 0.05$ for Sem-CNN with concept for the full dataset). The only non-significant cases appears to be Sem-CNN with abstracts on the full dataset ($p = 0.062$) and Sem-CNN with concepts on the balanced dataset 2 ($p = 0.146$). The difference in F-measure for the Sem-CNN with abstract and Sem-CNN with concepts is non-significant ($0.395 < p < 0.092$) meaning that in general both approaches can be used with similar results.

6   Discussion and Future Work

In this paper we presented Sem-CNN, a semantic CNN model designed for identifying information categories in crisis-related tweets. This section discusses the limitations of the presented work and outlines future extensions.

We evaluated the proposed Sem-CNN model on three data samples of the CrisisLexT26 dataset and investigated two related methods for integrating semantic concepts and entities into the *wide* component of our model. Results showed that identifying information categories in crisis-related posts is a highly challenging task since tweets belonging to a given event contain, in many cases, general terms that may correspond to several categories of information [4]. Nevertheless, we showed that our deep learning model outperforms the best machine learning baselines, with an average gain between +0.48% and +22.6% in F-measure across each dataset subset. Compared to the best baselines, the proposed models significantly outperformed the best baselines in 67% of the cases ($p < 0.05$).

When creating our model, we used the DBpedia abstracts (`dbo:abstract`) of concepts in addition to their labels (`rdfs:label`) in order to add additional semantic context to the Sem-CNN model. Results showed a minimal average increase of +0.3% ($0.395 < p < 0.092$) in F-measure when using DBpedia abstracts in comparison with solely using semantic concepts. Despite the non-significance of such improvement, we can speculate that such small increase in F-measure might be attributed to the inclusion of more detailed descriptions of the abstract concepts that are often identified by entity extraction tools. This can be taken as a small demonstration of the potential value of expanding beyond the simple labels of concepts in such analysis scenarios. One obvious next step would be to replace, or extend, these abstracts in our model with semantics extracted from these abstracts. This could help refining and extending the concept labels used in the Sem-CNN model.

The proposed semantic *wide* and *deep* CNN model is built on top of a CNN network and a *wide* generalised linear model. Our model assumes that all inputs (i.e., words and semantic concepts and entities) are loosely coupled with each other. However, it might be the case that the latent clues of the information categories can be determined based on the intrinsic dependencies between the words and semantic concepts of a tweet. Hence, room for future work is to incorporate this information in our detection model, probably by using recurrent neural networks (RNN) [8] due to their ability to capture sequential information in text or by using Hierarchical Attention Network (HAN) [30] in order to allow the model to focus on key semantic concepts and entities. Another direction would be by moving from the back-of-concepts representation used in our model to the back-of-semantic-relations [25]. This can be done by extracting the semantic relations between named-entities in tweets (e.g., $Tsunami < location > Sumatra$, $Evacuation < place > HighPark$) and use them to learn a more effective semantic vector representation similarly.

We also plan to better optimise our model by adding additional layers and performing parameter optimisation. Results could also be improved modifying the size of the model filters as well as the number of filters present in the *deep* part of Sem-CNN. In our experiments, we used the general Google pre-trained 300-dimensions word embeddings. Although previous work showed that not using pre-trained embeddings only slows down the learning phase of similar CNN models, [4] it would be interesting to experiment with embeddings tailored to social media such as pre-trained Twitter embeddings.[10]

In our evaluation we merely relied on SVM as a baseline and a case study of traditional machine learning baseline. This is because in our previous work [4] SVM showed to outperform other ML models (e.g., Naive Bayes, MaxEnt, J48, etc.) in identifying information categories in tweets. Those results are discussed in detail in [4].

We experimented with the SVM model using TF-IDF and Word2Vec features. Results showed that while TF-IDF features outperform Word2Vec features on both, the full and balanced 1 datasets, Word2Vec gives higher performance on the balanced dataset 2. This might be due the small size of the balanced dataset 2. As shown in Table 2, the balanced dataset 2 comprises 4.3% of the tweets in full dataset only, which may have had impact on the performance of these two types of features. We plan to further investigate this issue by extending our experiments to cover more datasets with different sizes and characteristics.

7   Conclusion

Very large numbers of tweets are often shared on Twitter during crises, reporting on crisis updates, announcing relief distribution, requesting help, etc. In this paper we introduced Sem-CNN, a *wide* and *deep* CNN model that uses the conceptual semantics of words for detecting the information categories of crisis-related tweets (e.g., *affected individuals, donations and volunteer, emotional support*).

We investigated the addition of the semantic concepts that appear in tweets to the learning component of the Sem-CNN model. We also showed that using semantic abstracts can marginally (i.e. non-significantly) improve upon semantic labels when integrating semantics into deep learning models.

We used our Sem-CNN model on a Twitter dataset that covers 26 different crisis events, and tested its performance in classifying tweets with regards

---

[10] Twitter Word2Vec model, http://www.fredericgodin.com/software.

to the category of information they hold. Results showed that our model generally outperforms the baselines, which consist of traditional machine learning approaches.

Acknowledgment. This work has received support from the European Union's Horizon 2020 research and innovation programme under grant agreement No. 687847 (COMRADES).

References

1. Atefeh, F., Khreich, W.: A survey of techniques for event detection in Twitter. Computat. Intell. **31**(1), 132–164 (2015)
2. Bahdanau, D., Cho, K., Bengio, Y.: Neural machine translation by jointly learning to align and translate. arXiv preprint (2014). arXiv:1409.0473
3. Bengio, Y., Ducharme, R., Vincent, P., Jauvin, C.: A neural probabilistic language model. J. Mach. Learn. Res. **3**, 1137–1155 (2003)
4. Burel, G., Saif, H., Fernandez, M., Alani, H.: On semantics and deep learning for event detection in crisis situations. In: Proceedings of the workshop on Semantic Deep Learning (SemDeep) at 14th Extended Semantic Web Conference (ESWC), Portoroz, Slovenia (2017)
5. Campanella, T.J.: Urban resilience and the recovery of New Orleans. J. Am. Planning Assoc. **72**(2), 141–146 (2006)
6. Chen, Y., Xu, L., Liu, K., Zeng, D., Zhao, J.: Event extraction via dynamic multi-pooling convolutional neural networks. In: Proceedings of Annual Meeting of the Association for Computational Linguistics (ACL), Beijing, China (2015)
7. Cheng, H.T., Koc, L., Harmsen, J., Shaked, T., Chandra, T., Aradhye, H., Anderson, G., Corrado, G., Chai, W., Ispir, M., et al.: Wide & Deep learning for recommender systems. CoRR abs/1606.07792 (2016)
8. Cho, K., Van Merriënboer, B., Gulcehre, C., Bahdanau, D., Bougares, F., Schwenk, H., Bengio, Y.: Learning phrase representations using RNN encoder-decoder for statistical machine translation. In: Proceedings of Conference on Empirical Methods in Natural Language Processing (EMNLP), Doha, Qatar (2014)
9. Daiber, J., Jakob, M., Hokamp, C., Mendes, P.N.: Improving efficiency and accuracy in multilingual entity extraction. In: Proceedings of the 9th International Conference on Semantic Systems (I-Semantics) (2013)
10. Dos Santos, C.N., Gatti, M.: Deep convolutional neural networks for sentiment analysis of short texts. In: Proceedings of International Conference on Computational Linguistics (COLING), Dublin, Ireland (2014)
11. Feng, X., Huang, L., Tang, D., Qin, B., Ji, H., Liu, T.: A language-independent neural network for event detection. In: Proceedings of Annual Meeting of the Association for Computational Linguistics (ACL), Berlin, Germany (2016)
12. Gao, H., Barbier, G., Goolsby, R.: Harnessing the crowdsourcing power of social media for disaster relief. IEEE Intell. Syst. **26**(3), 10–14 (2011)
13. Kim, Y.: Convolutional neural networks for sentence classification. In: Proceedings of Conference on Empirical Methods in Natural Language Processing (EMNLP). Doha, Qatar (2014)
14. Kingma, D., Ba, J.: Adam: a method for stochastic optimization. In: Proceedings of International Conference on Learning Representations (ICLR). Banff, Canada (2014)

15. LeCun, Y., Bottou, L., Bengio, Y., Haffner, P.: Gradient-based learning applied to document recognition. Proc. IEEE **86**(11), 2278–2324 (1998)
16. Meier, P.: Digital humanitarians: how big data is changing the face of humanitarian response. Taylor & Francis Press, London (2015)
17. Mikolov, T., Chen, K., Corrado, G., Dean, J.: Efficient estimation of word representations in vector space. arXiv preprint (2013). arXiv:1301.3781
18. Nguyen, T.H., Grishman, R.: Event detection and domain adaptation with convolutional neural networks. In: Proceedings of Annual Meeting of the Association for Computational Linguistics (ACL). Beijing, China (2015)
19. Olteanu, A., Castillo, C., Diaz, F., Vieweg, S.: CrisisLex: A lexicon for collecting and filtering microblogged communications in crises. In: Proceedings of International Conference on Weblogs and Social Media (ICWSM). Oxford, UK (2014)
20. Olteanu, A., Vieweg, S., Castillo, C.: What to expect when the unexpected happens: social media communications across crises. In: Proceedings of ACM Conference on Computer Supported Cooperative Work & Social Computing (CSCW). Vancouver, Canada (2015)
21. Pennington, J., Socher, R., Manning, C.D.: Glove: Global vectors for word representation. In: Empirical Methods in Natural Language Processing (EMNLP). Doha, Qatar (2014)
22. Prasetyo, P.K., Ming, G., Ee-Peng, L., Scollon, C.N.: Social sensing for urban crisis management: the case of Singapore haze. In: Proceedings of International Conference on Social Informatics (SocInfo). Kyoto, Japan (2013)
23. Qu, Y., Huang, C., Zhang, P., Zhang, J.: Microblogging after a major disaster in China: a case study of the 2010 Yushu earthquake. In: Proceedings of ACM Conference on Computer Supported Cooperative Work (CSCW). Hangzhou, China (2011)
24. Rizzo, G., van Erp, M., Troncy, R.: Benchmarking the extraction and disambiguation of named entities on the semantic web. In: LREC. Reykjavik, Iceland (2014)
25. Saif, H., Dickinson, T., Leon, K., Fernandez, M., Alani, H.: A semantic graph-based approach for radicalisation detection on social media. In: European Semantic Web Conference. Portoroz, Slovenia (2017)
26. Starbird, K., Palen, L., Hughes, A.L., Vieweg, S.: Chatter on the red: what hazards threat reveals about the social life of microblogged information. In: Proceedings of ACM Conference on Computer Supported Cooperative Work (CSCW). Savannah, Georgia, USA (2010)
27. Tang, D., Qin, B., Liu, T.: Document modeling with gated recurrent neural network for sentiment classification. In: Proceedings of Conference on Empirical Methods in Natural Language Processing (EMNLP). Lisbon, Portugal (2015)
28. Thomson, R., Ito, N., Suda, H., Lin, F., Liu, Y., Hayasaka, R., Isochi, R., Wang, Z.: Trusting tweets: the Fukushima disaster and information source credibility on Twitter. In: Proceedings of International ISCRAM Conference on Vancouver, Canada (2012)
29. Vieweg, S., Hughes, A.L., Starbird, K., Palen, L.: Microblogging during two natural hazards events: what twitter may contribute to situational awareness. In: Proceedings of Conference on Human Factors in Computing Systems (CHI). Atlanta, GA, USA (2010)
30. Yang, Z., Yang, D., Dyer, C., He, X., Smola, A.J., Hovy, E.H.: Hierarchical attention networks for document classification. In: HLT-NAACL, pp. 1480–1489 (2016)

Tractable Query Answering for Expressive Ontologies and Existential Rules

David Carral[(✉)], Irina Dragoste, and Markus Krötzsch

Center for Advancing Electronics Dresden (cfaed), TU Dresden, Dresden, Germany
david.carral@tu-dresden.de

Abstract. The disjunctive skolem chase is a sound and complete (albeit non-terminating) algorithm that can be used to solve conjunctive query answering over DL ontologies and programs with disjunctive existential rules. Even though acyclicity notions can be used to ensure chase termination for a large subset of real-world knowledge bases, the complexity of reasoning over acyclic theories still remains high. Hence, we study several restrictions which not only guarantee chase termination but also ensure polynomiality. We include an evaluation that shows that almost all acyclic DL ontologies do indeed satisfy these general restrictions.

1 Introduction

Answering conjunctive queries (CQs) over knowledge bases is an important reasoning task with many applications in data management and knowledge representation. A flurry of research efforts have significantly improved our understanding of this problem, and led to different solutions for description logics (DL) ontologies [2,6,25] and programs with disjunctive existential rules [1,5]. One such proposed approach is the use of *acyclicity notions* [9,10,19,21]; i.e., sufficient conditions that guarantee termination of the *disjunctive chase algorithm* [3]—a sound and complete materialization-based procedure where all relevant consequences of a knowledge base are precomputed, allowing queries to be directly evaluated over materialized sets of facts. As shown in [9,10], acyclicity notions can be used to determine that the chase will indeed terminate over a large subset of real-world DL ontologies.

Nevertheless, even if a knowledge base is characterized as acyclic, CQ answering still remains a problem of high theoretical complexity: CQ answering over acyclic programs with disjunctive existential rules is coN2ExpTime-complete [7]. For acyclic Horn-$\mathcal{SROIQ}$ ontologies, it is ExpTime-complete [10].

Example 1. Let $\mathcal{R}_n = \{D_{i-1}(x) \rightarrow \exists y_i.L_i(x,y_i) \wedge D_i(y_i), D_{i-1}(x) \rightarrow \exists z_i. R_i(x,z_i) \wedge D_i(z_i) \mid i = 1,\ldots,n\}$. The chase of the program $\mathcal{P} = \langle \mathcal{R}_n, \{D_0(c)\}\rangle$, depicted in Fig. 1, is exponentially large in n. Note that, $\mathcal{P}$ is acyclic with respect to all notions described in [10] and can be expressed in most DL fragments.

M. Krötzsch—The author thanks the competent and friendly staff of trauma surgery ward OUC-S2 at the University Hospital *Carl Gustav Carus*, Dresden, where some of this research has been executed.

© Springer International Publishing AG 2017
C. d'Amato et al. (Eds.): ISWC 2017, Part I, LNCS 10587, pp. 156–172, 2017.
DOI: 10.1007/978-3-319-68288-4_10

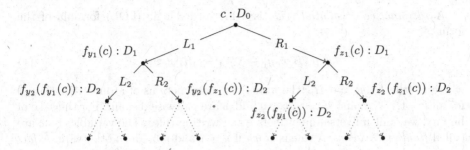

Fig. 1. Graphical representation of the chase of $\mathcal{P}$.

In this paper, we study the limits of tractable reasoning using the chase and propose a series of restrictions that, if combined, prevent the exponential blow-up highlighted in the previous example. Moreover, we define a novel acyclicity notion, namely *tractable acyclicity*, tailored for DL ontologies, which ensures that the size of the chase stays polynomial. In turn, this implies that CQ answering over deterministic "tractably acyclic" ontologies is (theoretically) as hard as solving the same problem over a given set of facts. On the practical side, we assess the generality of tractable acyclicity using two different corpuses of real-world ontologies. As it turns out, our notion does characterize almost all acyclic ontologies, thus showing that CQ answering may be quite efficient in practice.

In summary, our main contributions are as follows:

- We consider five general restrictions on the expressivity of rules and ontologies, and thoroughly study the complexity of CQ answering when combinations of these restrictions are satisfied (Sect. 3).
- Using some of these restrictions, we define tractable acyclicity, a notion specially tailored for DL ontologies which guarantees tractability of reasoning over expressive deterministic ontologies (Sect. 4). To the best of our knowledge, the use of notion is the only approach to guarantee tractable CQ answering over ontologies besides the combined approach [12,17,18,20,25].
- We empirically study the generality of tractable acyclicity on two large corpuses of real-world ontologies with encouraging results (Sect. 5).

2   Preliminaries

Let $\mathbf{P}$, $\mathbf{V}$ and $\mathbf{F}$ be some infinite countable and pairwise disjoint sets of *predicates*, *variables* and *function symbols*, respectively, such that every $S \in \mathbf{P} \cup \mathbf{F}$ is associated with some arity $ar(S) \geq 0$. *Constants* are function symbols of arity 0. *Terms* are built from variables and function symbols as usual. We abbreviate a sequence of terms $t_1, \ldots, t_n$ with $\boldsymbol{t}$, and identify such a sequence with the set $\{\boldsymbol{t}\}$. An *atom* is a formula of the form $P(\boldsymbol{t})$ with P a $|\boldsymbol{t}|$-ary predicate. With $\varphi[\boldsymbol{x}]$ we stress that $\boldsymbol{x}$ are the free variables in the formula φ. We identify a conjunction of formulas with the set of all the formulas in the conjunction and vice-versa.

A *(disjunctive existential) rule* is a first-order logic (FOL) formula of the form

$$\forall \boldsymbol{x}, \boldsymbol{y}.(B[\boldsymbol{x}, \boldsymbol{y}] \rightarrow \vee_{i=1}^{n} \exists \boldsymbol{v}_i.H_i[\boldsymbol{x}, \boldsymbol{v}_i]) \tag{1}$$

where B (the *body*) and H_i (the *heads*) are conjunctions of atoms with $H_i \neq \emptyset$ for all $i = 1, \ldots, n$; and $\boldsymbol{v}_1, \ldots, \boldsymbol{v}_n$, $\boldsymbol{y}$ and $\boldsymbol{x}$ are pairwise disjoint. For the sake of brevity, we omit universal quantifiers when writing rules. The variables in $\boldsymbol{x}$ are called *frontier variables*. A rule is *Horn* if $n = 1$ and *non-Horn* otherwise. A *fact* is a *ground atom*; i.e., an atom without occurrences of variables. An *instance* $\mathcal{I}$ is a finite set of facts only containing constants as terms. A *program* is a pair $\langle \mathcal{R}, \mathcal{I} \rangle$ with $\mathcal{R}$ a rule set and $\mathcal{I}$ an instance. Without loss of generality, we assume that every existentially quantified variable occurs in at most one rule (†).

The main reasoning task we are studying in this paper is CQ answering. Nevertheless, without loss of generality, we restrict our attention to the simpler task of entailment of Boolean conjunctive queries (BCQs). A *BCQ*, or simply a *query*, is a formula of the form $\exists \boldsymbol{y}.Q[\boldsymbol{y}]$ with Q a conjunction of atoms.

A *substitution* is a partial function defined over the set of terms. The *application of a substitution* σ to an atom α, denoted with $\alpha\sigma$, is the atom that results from replacing all occurrences of every term t in the domain of σ with $\sigma(t)$. We denote the substitution $\{(t_1, u_1), \ldots, (t_n, u_n)\}$ with $[t_1/u_1, \ldots, t_n/u_n]$.

The *skolemization* $sk(\rho)$ of a rule ρ as in (1) is the formula $B \rightarrow \bigvee_{i=1}^{n} sk(H_i)$ where, for every $i = 1, \ldots, n$, $sk(H_i)$ is the conjunction that results from replacing every (existentially quantified variable) $v \in \boldsymbol{v}_i$ by the term $f_v(\boldsymbol{x})$ with f_v a fresh function symbol specific to v (which, by assumption (†) and the definition of a rule, is also specific to the i-th disjunct in the head of the rule ρ).

Definition 2. *Consider a rule ρ of the form (1), a substitution σ defined only on $\boldsymbol{x} \cup \boldsymbol{y}$, and a set of facts $\mathcal{F}$. Then, $\langle \rho, \sigma \rangle$ is applicable to $\mathcal{F}$ if $B\sigma \subseteq \mathcal{F}$. In this case, the result of applying $\langle \rho, \sigma \rangle$ to $\mathcal{F}$ is $\{\mathcal{F} \cup sk(H_i)\sigma \mid i = 1, \ldots, n\}$.*

A chase tree of $\langle \mathcal{R}, \mathcal{I} \rangle$ is a (possibly infinite) tree where each node is labeled by a set of facts, such that all of the following conditions hold.

(1) The root is labeled with $\mathcal{I}$.

(2) If a node labeled with $\mathcal{F}$ has n children labeled with $\mathcal{F}_1, \ldots, \mathcal{F}_n$, then there is some rule $\rho \in \mathcal{R}$ and some substitution σ such that $\{\mathcal{F}_1, \ldots, \mathcal{F}_n\}$ is the result of applying $\langle \rho, \sigma \rangle$ to $\mathcal{F}$.

(3) (Fairness) If there is a node α labeled with a set $\mathcal{F}$, a rule $\rho \in \mathcal{R}$, and a substitution σ such that $\langle \rho, \sigma \rangle \in \mathcal{R}$ is applicable to $\mathcal{F}$; then, in all paths starting from α, there is some node β with n children, each of them labeled with a different set in the result of applying $\langle \rho, \sigma \rangle$ to the label of β.

The result of the (Skolem) chase is the (possibly infinite) set of all (possibly infinite) sets of facts obtained as the union of all sets of facts along some path.

Due to the order of rule applications, a program $\mathcal{P}$ may admit many different chase trees but, nevertheless, the result of the Skolem chase of $\mathcal{P}$ is always unique.

Fact 3. *A program $\mathcal{P}$ entails a query $\exists v.Q$ if and only if $\mathcal{F} \models \exists v.Q$ holds for every set of facts $\mathcal{F}$ in the result of the chase of $\mathcal{P}$.*

If the chase terminates for some program, then the result of the chase is the set of all (finite) leaf labels. In this case, Fact 3 leads to an effective decision procedure for BCQ entailment. Therefore, in the subsequent section, we study several restrictions on a set of rules which ensure efficient chase termination.

3   Tractable Reasoning for Disjunctive Existential Rules

In this section we present and study several restrictions, which can ensure tractability of BCQ entailment over rule sets. These insights will be the basis for our investigation of tractable query answering for ontologies in Sect. 4. An important concept for predicting the behaviour of the chase procedure is the *dependency graph* of a rule set:

Definition 4. *The dependency graph $G(\mathcal{R})$ of a rule set $\mathcal{R}$ has the existential variables in $\mathcal{R}$ as nodes, and an edge $y \rightarrow z$ if the skolem chase of some program $\langle \mathcal{R}, \mathcal{I} \rangle$ contains terms of the form $f_z(t)$ and $f_y(s)$ such that $f_y(s) \in t$.*

The key to our tractability results is the notion of a *braid*, which, intuitively speaking, consists of a possibly large number of intertwined paths.

Definition 5. *Consider a directed graph G. A* path *is a sequence of nodes $\alpha_1, \ldots, \alpha_n$ with $\alpha_i \rightarrow \alpha_{i+1} \in G$ for all $i = 1, \ldots, n-1$. The graph G is acyclic if, for every path $\alpha_1, \ldots, \alpha_n$ with $n \geq 2$, $\alpha_1 \neq \alpha_n$. A* simple path *is a path which does not contain two occurrences of the same node. A* braid *is a sequence of nodes $\alpha_1, \ldots, \alpha_n$ such that, for all $i = 1, \ldots, n-1$, there are at least two different simple paths from α_i to α_{i+1}.*

A number of natural conditions on a set of rules $\mathcal{R}$ might be considered in order to reduce the complexity of the chase. We will consider the following five:

(a) The graph $G(\mathcal{R})$ is acyclic.
(f) The arity of all function symbols in $sk(\mathcal{R})$ is at most 1.
(b) The length of the braids in $G(\mathcal{R})$ is bounded.
(w) The treewidth of the rules in $\mathcal{R}$ is bounded.
(p) The arity of the predicates in $\mathcal{R}$ is bounded.

Most of these conditions are self-explanatory and straightforward to check. The treewidth of rules is the treewidth of the graph that has the terms of a rule as nodes, and an undirected edge whenever two terms appear in the same atom [13]. It is a well-known measure for "tree-likeness", which is bounded by the number of terms per rule.[1] Checking if a graph G has treewidth at most k for a given constant k is polynomial in G. Both acyclicity and the maximal braid

---

[1] Readers not familiar with treewidth may safely use this number as a surrogate.

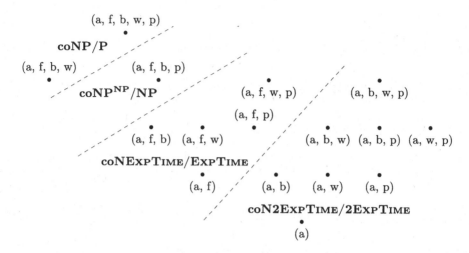

Fig. 2. Complexity of BCQ entailment with respect to the size of the rule set satisfying some combination of (a), (f), (b), (w) and (p). All of the above results are tight and refer to the combined complexity of BCQ entailment over nondeterministic and deterministic rule sets, respectively.

length can be computed efficiently if the dependecy graph is known. We present ways of approximating these conditions efficiently in Sect. 4.

In the remainder of the section, we characterize the (combined) complexity of BCQ entailment over sets of rules satisfying every possible combination of the above restrictions. We summarize our findings in Fig. 2, which only includes cases that satisfy (a), since its omission leads to undecidability (Theorem 11). Moreover, as indicated in Theorem 7, the "coNP/ P" result refers to the complexity regarding the size of the rule set, with the query considered fixed.

Whilst restrictions (a), (f), (w), and (p) have been considered in previous work [10], (b) is a novel notion instrumental to ensure tractability of reasoning. See how the rule set from Example 1 may not satisfy such a restriction.

Example 6. Let $\mathcal{R}_n$ be the set of rules presented in Example 1 and let $G(\mathcal{R}_n)$ be the graph depicted in Fig. 3. Note how, for every every odd $n \geq 1$, there is a braid of length $(n + 1)/2$ in $G(\mathcal{R}_n)$; e.g., $z_1, z_3, \ldots, z_n$ or $y_1, y_3, \ldots, y_n$.

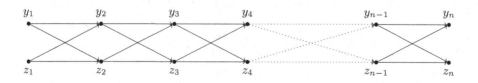

Fig. 3. Dependency graph of the set of rules $\mathcal{R}_n$ from Example 6.

Combining all restrictions allows us to obtain the main result of this section.

Theorem 7. *Deciding BCQ entailment for programs $\langle \mathcal{R}, \mathcal{I} \rangle$ with $\mathcal{R}$ a rule set satisfying (a), (f), (b), and (w) is in coNP provided that the size of the query is fixed. Moreover, if $\mathcal{R}$ is a set of deterministic rules, then it is in P.*

The key for proving this result is a property that relates braid length to the size of the chase. As we will show, if a rule set $\mathcal{R}$ satisfies (f), then every term in the chase of $\langle \mathcal{R}, \mathcal{I} \rangle$ corresponds to some path in $G(\mathcal{R})$ and some constant. In turn, this implies that, if there is a polynomial bound on the number of paths in $G(\mathcal{R})$, then the number of terms introduced during the computation of the chase of $\langle \mathcal{R}, \mathcal{I} \rangle$ is also polynomially bounded. Therefore, we first show that there is indeed such a polynomial upper bound on the number of paths in a graph if the length of the braids in such a graph is fixed. Once this is shown, we can easily verify that, if $\mathcal{R}$ satisfies (b) and (f), then there is a polynomial upper bound on the number of terms that may occur in the chase of a program $\langle \mathcal{R}, \mathcal{I} \rangle$.

Lemma 8. *Consider some directed acyclic graph G with n nodes. If there is a bound k on the length of the braids, then there are at most $3k \cdot n^{3k}$ paths in G.*

Proof. First, we verify the following intermediate result: (∗) Consider two nodes α and β in G. If, for every node γ, the sequence α, γ, β is not a braid in G; then $P_G(\alpha, \beta) \leq 3n^2$ with $P_G(\alpha, \beta)$ the number of paths from α to β.

Let G' be the graph that results from removing every node γ not occurring in a path from α to β. Then, for every node γ in G' with $\gamma \neq \alpha$ and $\gamma \neq \beta$, $P_{G'}(\alpha, \gamma) = 1$ or $P_{G'}(\gamma, \beta) = 1$. Let G'' be the graph obtained from G' via simultaneous application of the following rules to every node γ in G': If $P_{G'}(\alpha, \gamma) = 1$ and $\alpha \rightarrow \gamma \notin G'$, then remove the (only) edge of the form $\delta \rightarrow \gamma \in G'$ and add $\alpha \dashrightarrow \gamma$. If $P_{G'}(\gamma, \beta) = 1$ and $\gamma \rightarrow \beta \notin G'$, then remove the edge of the form $\gamma \rightarrow \delta \in G'$ and add $\gamma \rightarrow \beta$.

The previously presented transformation preserves the number of paths from α to β; i.e., $P_G(\alpha, \beta) = P_{G''}(\alpha, \beta)$. Moreover, the nodes in G'' can be fully distributed into four pairwise disjoint s ets L_1, L_2, L_3 and L_4 such that all of the following hold: $L_1 = \{\alpha\}$; $L_4 = \{\beta\}$; and, for every pair of nodes γ and δ, $\gamma \rightarrow \delta \in G''$ only if (i) $\gamma = \alpha$ and $\delta \in L_2 \cup L_4$, (ii) $\gamma \in L_2$ and $\delta \in L_3 \cup L_4$, or (iii) $\gamma \in L_3$ and $\delta = \beta$. As the sets L_2 and L_3 may contain at most n nodes, then $P_{G''}(\alpha, \beta) \leq n^2 + n + 1 \leq 3n^2$ (as n is at least 2).

We now proceed to show the lemma. Let B_m be the set of paths containing a path p in G iff (i) p contains a braid of length m and (ii) p does not contain a braid of length $m + 1$. Then, every path $p \in B_m$ is of the form $\alpha_1, s_1, \alpha_2, s_2, \ldots, s_{m-1}, \alpha_m$ where $\alpha_1, \ldots, \alpha_m$ is a braid; and, for every $i = 2, \ldots, m - 1$, s_i is a sequence of nodes not containing a node γ such that $\alpha_i, \gamma, \alpha_{i+1}$ is a braid in G (as this would imply that p contains a braid of length $m + 1$). By (∗), there are at most $3n^2$ possible paths in G for every s_i. Moreover, there are at most n^m braids of length m. Therefore, B_m contains at most $n^m \cdot 3n^{2(m-1)} \leq 3n^{3m}$ paths. The number of paths in G is at most $\sum_{i=0}^{k} |B_i| \leq k|B_k|$ (as every B_j with $j > k$ is empty). Hence, the number of paths in G is necessarily less than $3k \cdot n^{3k}$. □

Proof (of Theorem 7). Since $\mathcal{R}$ satisfies (w), we can apply a normalization procedure to compute a conservative extension $\langle \mathcal{R}', \mathcal{I} \rangle$ of $\langle \mathcal{R}, \mathcal{I} \rangle$ with an upper bound on the number of variables per rule [13]. Moreover, this transformation does not modify the dependency graph of $\mathcal{R}$ (i.e., $G(\mathcal{R}) = G(\mathcal{R}')$).

We first determine an upper bound on the maximal number of terms T and atoms A that may occur in the chase of $\langle \mathcal{R}', \mathcal{I} \rangle$. By (f), every term in the chase of $\langle \mathcal{R}', \mathcal{I} \rangle$ is of the form $f_{y_n}(\ldots (f_{y_1}(c)) \ldots)$ with c a constant. Furthermore, such a term occurs in the chase only if $y_1, \ldots, y_n$ is a path in $G(\mathcal{R}')$. Hence, every term in the chase of $\langle \mathcal{R}', \mathcal{I} \rangle$ corresponds to some path in $G(\mathcal{R}')$ and some constant. By Lemma 8 and the fact that $\mathcal{R}'$ satisfies (b), we conclude that the number of paths in $G(\mathcal{R}')$ is polynomial in the number of nodes in $G(\mathcal{R}')$ (which coincides with the number of existentially quantified variables in $\mathcal{R}'$). Therefore, T is polynomially large with respect to $\langle \mathcal{R}', \mathcal{I} \rangle$ and, since the number of variables per rule in $\mathcal{R}'$ is fixed, so is A. If $\mathcal{R}'$ is a set of deterministic rules, then we can compute the only branch on some (arbitrarily chosen) chase tree of $\langle \mathcal{R}', \mathcal{I} \rangle$ to solve BCQ entailment. This branch is a sequence of at most A sets of facts; and, as there is an upper bound on the number of variables per rule in $\mathcal{R}'$, each of these sets can be computed in polynomial time. Moreover, checking if the facts in the branch entail a query is in P if the size of the query is fixed.

In the nondeterministic case, we can guess some sequence of facts and then check whether (i) such a sequence is a complete branch in some chase tree of $\langle \mathcal{R}', \mathcal{I} \rangle$. Then, a query is not entailed by $\langle \mathcal{R}', \mathcal{I} \rangle$ iff (ii) it is not entailed by the facts in this branch. Note that, (i-ii) can be checked in P. □

We proceed by showing the complexity of BCQ answering for any other combination of the restrictions (a), (f), (b), (w), and (p). This shows, in particular, that our chosen set of restrictions is minimal (among these selected conditions) and any other combination leads to intractability.

Theorem 9. *Deciding BCQ entailment for programs $\langle \mathcal{R}, \mathcal{I} \rangle$ with $\mathcal{R}$ a rule set satisfying (a), (f), (b), (w), and (p) is coNP-hard. Moreover, if $\mathcal{R}$ is a set of deterministic rules, then it is P-hard.*

Proof. The results stated in the theorem follow from hardness of SAT and propositional Horn logic entailment, respectively. □

Theorem 10. *Deciding BCQ entailment for programs $\langle \mathcal{R}, \mathcal{I} \rangle$ with $\mathcal{R}$ a rule set satisfying (a), (f), (b), and (p) is in coNP^{NP}-complete. Moreover, if $\mathcal{R}$ is a set of deterministic rules, then it is in NP-complete.*

Proof. To show membership, we can make an analogous argument to the one in the proof of Theorem 7 to show that there is a polynomial upper bound on the number of terms T that may occur during the computation of the chase $\langle \mathcal{R}, \mathcal{I} \rangle$. Moreover, since the arity of the predicates is bounded by some ℓ, the number of atoms in the chase is at most $A = P^{\ell} \cdot T$.

If $\mathcal{R}$ is a set of deterministic rules, then we can guess some sequence of sets $\mathcal{F}_1, \ldots, \mathcal{F}_n$ of facts with $\mathcal{F}_1 = \mathcal{I}$; some sequence $\langle \rho_1, \sigma_1 \rangle, \ldots, \langle \rho_{n-1}, \sigma_{n-1} \rangle$ of pairs of rules and substitutions with $\rho_i \in \mathcal{R}$ for every $i = 1, \ldots, n-1$; and some additional substitution σ. To determine if $\langle \mathcal{R}, \mathcal{I} \rangle$ entails some query Q, we check that, for every $i = 1, \ldots, n-1$, (i) $\mathcal{F}_{i+1}$ is the result of the application of $\langle \rho_i, \sigma_i \rangle$ on $\mathcal{F}_i$; and (ii) $\mathcal{F}_n \models Q\sigma$. Note that, (i-ii) can be verified in polynomial time, and $\mathcal{F}_1, \ldots, \mathcal{F}_n$ may not necessarily be a complete branch in a chase tree of $\langle \mathcal{R}, \mathcal{I} \rangle$.

If $\mathcal{R}$ is a set of nondeterministic rules, then we simply guess some sequence of sets $\mathcal{F}_1, \ldots, \mathcal{F}_n$ of facts with $\mathcal{F}_1 = \mathcal{I}$. To determine that $\langle \mathcal{R}, \mathcal{I} \rangle$ does not entail some query Q, we check that, for every $i = 1, \ldots, n-1$, (i)$\mathcal{F}_{i+1}$ is the result of the application of some rule in $\mathcal{R}$ and some substitution on $\mathcal{F}_i$; (ii) no rule in $\mathcal{R}$ and substitution is applicable to $\mathcal{F}_n$; and (iii)$\mathcal{F}_n \not\models Q$. (i-iii) can be polynomially checked using an NP oracle.

For coNP^{NP}-hardness, we reduce from the valuation problem of quantified Boolean formulas (QBF) of the form $\forall \boldsymbol{X}.\exists \boldsymbol{Y}.\varphi$, where $\boldsymbol{X}, \boldsymbol{Y}$ are lists of propositional variables and φ is in 3CNF, i.e., $\varphi = (L_1^1 \vee L_2^1 \vee L_3^1) \wedge \ldots \wedge (L_1^n \vee L_2^n \vee L_3^n)$, such that the literals L_j^i are variables or negated variables from $\boldsymbol{X} \cup \boldsymbol{Y}$.

We construct a set of nondeterministic without existential variables rules using constants t (true) and f (false). We add two facts $\mathsf{tf}(t)$ and $\mathsf{tf}(f)$. For every $i \in \{1, \ldots, n\}$, we add all (polynomially many) facts of the form $c_i(v_1, v_2, v_3)$ with $v_1, v_2, v_3 \in \{t, f\}$ such that $(L_1^i \vee L_2^i \vee L_3^i)$ is true when assigning the values v_1, v_2, v_3 to the (at most) three variables in the clause. In addition, for each universally quantified $X \in \boldsymbol{X}$, we add a disjunctive fact $\mathsf{val}_X(t) \vee \mathsf{val}_X(f)$. Finally, QBF valuation is encoded in the rule:

$$\bigwedge_{1 \leq i \leq n} c_i(x_1^i, x_2^i, x_3^i) \wedge \bigwedge_{X \in \boldsymbol{X}} \mathsf{val}_X(v_X) \wedge \bigwedge_{Y \in \boldsymbol{Y}} \mathsf{tf}(v_Y) \rightarrow \mathsf{trueQBF} \qquad (2)$$

where each variable has the form v_Z for $Z \in \boldsymbol{X} \cup \boldsymbol{Y}$, and x_j^i denotes v_Z for the propositional variable Z that occurs in L_j^i. Then $\mathsf{trueQBF}$ is entailed iff, for all models (i.e., all assignments of universal variables $X \in \boldsymbol{X}$), there is an assignment for the variables $Y \in \boldsymbol{Y}$, such that each clause in φ is true.

The hardness result for deterministic rules follows when considering QBF without universally quantified variables; i.e., propositional satisfiability. □

Theorem 11. *BCQ entailment for programs $\langle \mathcal{R}, \mathcal{I} \rangle$ with $\mathcal{R}$ a set of deterministic rules satisfying (f), (b), (w), and (p) is undecidable.*

Proof. We use a reduction from a known undecidable problem described as follows (see Sect. 2.5.1 of [16] for a very similar and more detailed argument). A context-free grammar is a tuple $\langle S, P \rangle$ with S a non-terminal, and P a set of production rules of the form $A \rightarrow BC$ or $A \rightarrow a$ where A, B and C are non-terminals and a is a terminal. The language generated by a grammar $\langle S, P \rangle$ is the set of all strings of terminals which can be produced by rewriting S applying the production rules in P. The following problem is undecidable [14]: Given two context-free grammars $G_1 = \langle P_1, S_1 \rangle$ and $G_2 = \langle P_2, S_2 \rangle$, with disjoint sets of non-terminals and common terminal symbols 0 and 1, determine whether there is some word in the intersection of the languages generated by G_1 and G_2.

Consider two binary predicates T_0 and T_1, a specific binary predicate NT_A for every non-terminal A occurring in G_1 or G_2, a unary predicate X, and a constant c. For all $i \in \{1, 2\}$, let $\mathcal{R}_i = \{T_a(x, y) \rightarrow NT_A(x, y) \mid A \rightarrow a \in P_i\} \cup \{NT_B(x, y) \wedge NT_C(y, z) \rightarrow NT_A(x, z) \mid A \rightarrow BC \in P_i\}$. Moreover, let $\mathcal{R} = \mathcal{R}_1 \cup \mathcal{R}_2 \cup \{X(x) \rightarrow \exists y.T_0(x, y) \wedge X(y), X(x) \rightarrow \exists z.T_1(x, z) \wedge X(z)\}$. Then, the intersection of the languages generated by G_1 and G_2 is empty iff $\langle \mathcal{R}, \{X(c)\}\rangle$ does not entail the query $\exists x.NT_{S_1}(c, x) \wedge NT_{S_2}(c, x)$.

The rules in $\mathcal{R}$ satisfy (f), (b), (w), and (p): The arity of all of the symbols in $sk(\mathcal{R})$ (i.e., f_y and f_z) is one, $G(R)$ contains two nodes, and the arity of every predicate is at most two. Moreover, the number of variables per rule is bounded and hence, so is the treewidth.   □

Theorem 12. *Deciding BCQ entailment for programs $\langle \mathcal{R}, \mathcal{I} \rangle$ with $\mathcal{R}$ a rule set satisfying (a) is in coN2EXPTIME. Moreover, if $\mathcal{R}$ is a set of deterministic rules, then it is in 2EXPTIME.*

Proof. We first determine the maximal number of ground (skolem) terms and corresponding facts that may occur in the chase. Let n be the number of skolem functions in $sk(\mathcal{R})$, and let m be the maximal arity of such functions. The maximal nesting depth of ground terms in the chase is n, since every term of greater depth is cyclic and, by (a), such terms may not occur in the chase of $\langle \mathcal{R}, \mathcal{I} \rangle$. Ground terms then correspond to trees of depth at most n, fan-out at most m, and with leaves from the set C of constants in $\langle \mathcal{R}, \mathcal{I} \rangle$. Such trees have most $n \cdot m^n$ nodes in total. As each node is assigned a constant or function symbol, there are at most $T = (|C| + n)^{n \cdot m^n}$ trees, and hence ground terms, overall. Now, if $\langle \mathcal{R}, \mathcal{I} \rangle$ contains k different predicate symbols of arity at most ℓ, then the maximal number of ground facts based on T terms is $A = kT^\ell = k(C_{\mathcal{I}} + n)^{\ell \cdot n \cdot m^n}$. The number of facts A is therefore double exponential in the size of $\langle \mathcal{R}, \mathcal{I} \rangle$ and hence, so is the length of every branch in a chase tree of a program $\langle \mathcal{R}, \mathcal{I} \rangle$.

If $\mathcal{R}$ is a set of deterministic rules, then there is only one branch in every possible chase tree of a program $\langle \mathcal{R}, \mathcal{I} \rangle$ which can be computed in double-exponentially many steps. Then, a query is entailed by $\langle \mathcal{R}, \mathcal{I} \rangle$ iff such query is entailed by the set of facts in the branch. If $\mathcal{R}$ only contains nondeterministic rules, membership in coN2EXPTIME follows from the fact that BCQ non-entailment can be shown by guessing some branch of the tree, and then checking that the set of facts in such branch does not entail the query.   □

Theorem 13. *Deciding BCQ entailment for programs $\langle \mathcal{R}, \mathcal{I} \rangle$ with $\mathcal{R}$ a rule set satisfying (a) and (f) is in coNEXPTIME. Moreover, if $\mathcal{R}$ is a set of deterministic rules, then it is in EXPTIME.*

Proof. We determine that the maximal number of facts that may occur in the chase of $\langle \mathcal{R}, \mathcal{I} \rangle$ is exponential in the size of the program. The remainder of the proof is analogous to that of Theorem 12.

Let n be the number of skolem functions in $sk(\mathcal{R})$ which, by (f), have an arity of at most 1. The maximal nesting depth of ground terms in the chase is n, since every term of greater depth is cyclic and, by (a), such terms may not occur in the chase of $\langle \mathcal{R}, \mathcal{I} \rangle$. Ground terms then correspond to sequences of depth at most n and, since each element in the sequence is assigned a constant or function symbol, there are at most $T = (C + n)^n$ ground terms, overall. In turn, the maximal number of facts in the chase is $A = kT^\ell = k(C + n)^{\ell \cdot n}$ with k the number of predicates and ℓ the maximal arity of a predicate in $\langle \mathcal{R}, \mathcal{I} \rangle$. $\square$

Theorem 14. *Deciding BCQ entailment for programs $\langle \mathcal{R}, \mathcal{I} \rangle$ with $\mathcal{R}$ a rule set satisfying (a), (b), (w), and (p) is coN2ExpTime-hard. Moreover, if $\mathcal{R}$ is a set of deterministic rules, then it is 2ExpTime-hard.*

Proof. For the first result, we present a reduction of the word problem of double-exponentially time-bounded non deterministic Turing machines (TMs) to BCQ non-entailment. Given such reduction, it is clear how to produce a similar reduction to prove the second result stated in the theorem.

Consider a N2ExpTime Turing Machine (TM) M. We simulate the computation of M on an input string I by constructing a program $\langle \mathcal{R}, \mathcal{I} \rangle$ such that $\langle \mathcal{R}, \mathcal{I} \rangle$ does not entail some nullary predicate *Reject* iff M accepts I. To address computation steps and tape cells, we recall a construction by [4] to (deterministically) construct a chain of double exponentially many elements. Let $\mathcal{I} = \{r_0(0), r_0(a), Scc_0(0, 1), Min_0(0), Max_0(a)\}$. For each $i \in \{0, \ldots, n-1\}$, with n the length of the input I, we add the rules in $\{R_i(x) \wedge R_i(y) \rightarrow \exists v_i . S_i(x, y, v_{i+1}) \wedge R_{i+1}(v_{i+1}), S_i(x, y, z) \wedge S_i(x, y', z') \wedge Scc_i(y, y') \rightarrow Scc_{i+1}(z, z'), S_i(x, y, z) \wedge S_i(x', y', z') \wedge Max_i(y) \wedge Min_i(y') \wedge Scc_i(x, x') \rightarrow Scc_{i+1}(z, z'), Min_i(x) \wedge S_i(x, x, y) \rightarrow Min_{i+1}(y), Max_i(x) \wedge S_i(x, x, y) \rightarrow Max_{i+1}(y)\}$ It can be shown, by induction on i, that in any path of any chase tree of $\langle \mathcal{R}, \mathcal{I} \rangle$, the relation r_n contains 2^{2^n} elements, which are linearly ordered by Scc_n.

The remaining TM simulation follows standard constructions (cf. [11]), using elements of the r_n chain to refer to specific time points and tape cells when encoding a run of the TM. Nondeterministic transitions are captured using rules with disjunction. Assuming that the state of M at step s is captured with facts $State_q(s)$ for all states Q, we can complete the simulation by adding rules $State_q(x) \wedge Max_n(x) \rightarrow Reject$ for all non-accepting states q of M. We can assume without loss of generality that M runs for the maximum double-exponential number of steps on all rejecting runs, so that the query *Reject* is entailed iff there are no accepting runs.

The rules in $\mathcal{R}$ satisfy (a), (b), (w), and (p): $G(\mathcal{R})$ is the smallest graph containing $v_i \rightarrow v_{i+1}$ for every $i = 1, \ldots, n$ and hence, this graph is acyclic and does not contain any braids. Also, both the arity of the predicates, and treewidth of the rules in $\mathcal{R}$ is fixed. Finally, it can be checked that the rules added to finalize the reduction (cf. [11]) do not violate (a), (b), (w), nor (p). $\square$

Theorem 15. *Deciding BCQ entailment for programs $\langle \mathcal{R}, \mathcal{I} \rangle$ with $\mathcal{R}$ a rule set satisfying (a), (f), (w), and (p) is coNExpTime-hard. If $\mathcal{R}$ is a set of deterministic rules, then it is ExpTime-hard.*

Proof. We show that, using a set of rules satisfying (a), (f), (w), and (p), we can define a program that, given some n, can generate an exponentially long chain of terms sorted by some binary predicate. The remainder of the proof is analogous to that of Theorem 14.

Let $\mathcal{R}$ be the set containing the rules in $\{S_i(x) \rightarrow \exists y_{i+1}, z_{i+1}.L_i(x, y) \wedge R_i(x, z_{i+1}) \wedge Scc_{i+1}(y_{i+1}, z_{i+1}), R_i(x, z) \wedge Scc_i(x, y) \wedge L_i(y, w) \rightarrow Scc_{i+1}(z, w)\}$ for each $i \in \{0, \ldots, n-1\}$. We can show, by induction on i, that in any path of any chase tree of $\langle \mathcal{R}, \{S_0(c)\}\rangle$, the relation S_n contains 2^n elements, which are linearly ordered by Scc_n.

The rules in $\mathcal{R}$ satisfy (a), (f), (w), and (p): $G(\mathcal{R})$ is the smallest graph containing $y_i \rightarrow y_{i+1}, y_i \rightarrow z_{i+1}, z_i \rightarrow y_{i+1}$, and $z_i \rightarrow z_{i+1}$ for every $i = 1, \ldots, n$, and hence, this graph is acyclic. Also, the arity of every function symbol in $sk(\mathcal{R})$ is 1, and both the arity of the predicates and treewidth of the rules is fixed. $\square$

Theorem 16. *Deciding BCQ entailment for programs $\langle \mathcal{R}, \mathcal{I} \rangle$ with $\mathcal{R}$ a rule set satisfying (a), (f), and (b) is coNExpTime-hard. Moreover, if $\mathcal{R}$ is a set of deterministic rules, then it is ExpTime-hard.*

Proof. The first and second parts of the theorem follow from the hardness of fact entailment over disjunctive and non-disjunctive Datalog [11], respectively. Note that, every (possibly disjunctive) Datalog program—a program containing only deterministic rules without existential variables—satisfies (a), (f) and (b).

$\square$

4   Tractable Reasoning for Ontologies

Across this section we discuss how to employ the chase to reason over DL ontologies and then, using some of the results from the previous section, we define *tractable acyclicity*, an acyclicity condition tailored for DL ontologies which ensures tractability of BCQ entailment.

We consider the $\mathcal{SRI}$ fragment of the description logic $\mathcal{SROIQ}$, which is the logical basis of OWL 2 DL. We present this DL using a normal form close to that of [8]. Note that, in such a normal form, occurrences of the negation logical constructor are normalized into axioms of the form (3) in Fig. 4. Moreover, we do not consider number restrictions nor nominals in our definition of DL, as the use of these logical constructors would require *equality reasoning*. There are well-known techniques to axiomatize the meaning of equality—e.g., singularization [10, 21]—but these are not our focus.

Let $\mathbf{C}$, $\mathbf{R}$, and $\mathbf{I}$ be some infinite countable and pairwise disjoint sets of *concepts*, *roles*, and *individuals*, respectively. Moreover, let $\mathbf{R}^- = \mathbf{R} \cup \{R^- \mid R \in \mathbf{R}\}$; and, for every $R \in \mathbf{R}^-$, $R^{--} = R$. A *TBox axiom* is a formula of one of the forms given on the left hand side of Fig. 4. An *ABox axiom* or *assertion* is a formula of the form $A(a)$ or $R(a, b)$ with $A \in \mathbf{C}$, $R \in \mathbf{R}$ and $a, b \in \mathbf{I}$. A *ontology* is a tuple $\langle \mathcal{T}, \mathcal{A} \rangle$ with $\mathcal{T}$ a set of TBox axioms and $\mathcal{A}$ a set of assertions.

We do not consider any structural restrictions, such as role regularity [15], in our definition of ontologies. These restrictions are unnecessary for preserving correctness when using the chase and hence, we ignore them.

$$\prod_{i=1}^{n} C_i \sqsubseteq \bigsqcup_{i=1}^{m} D_i \;\mapsto\; \bigwedge_{i=1}^{n} C_i(x) \to \bigvee_{i=1}^{m} D_i(x) \tag{3}$$

$$C \sqsubseteq \forall R.D \;\mapsto\; C(x) \wedge R\langle x,y\rangle \to D(y) \tag{4}$$

$$C \sqsubseteq \exists R.Self \;\mapsto\; C(x) \to R\langle x,x\rangle \tag{5}$$

$$\exists S.Self \sqsubseteq D \;\mapsto\; R\langle x,x\rangle \to D(x) \tag{6}$$

$$\prod_{i=1}^{n} S_i \sqsubseteq R \;\mapsto\; \bigwedge_{i=1}^{n} S_i\langle x,y\rangle \to R\langle x,y\rangle \tag{7}$$

$$S_1 \circ \ldots \circ S_n \sqsubseteq R \;\mapsto\; S_1\langle x_0,x_1\rangle \wedge \ldots \wedge S_n\langle x_{n-1},x_n\rangle \to R\langle x_0,x_n\rangle \tag{8}$$

$$C \sqsubseteq \exists R.D \;\mapsto\; C(x) \to \exists y.R\langle x,y\rangle \wedge D(y) \tag{9}$$

Fig. 4. Mapping Ψ. In the above, $C_{(i)}, D \in \mathbf{C}$, $R, S_{(i)} \in \mathbf{R}^-$, and $m, n \geq 1$. Moreover, for every $R \in \mathbf{R}$, $R^-\langle t,u\rangle = R(u,t)$ and $R\langle t,u\rangle = R(t,u)$.

The semantics of ontologies are given by means of a mapping into programs.

Fact 17. *An ontology $\mathcal{O}$ entails some query Q iff $\langle \Psi(\mathcal{R}), \mathcal{I}\rangle \models Q$ with Ψ the function mapping axioms to rules defined in Fig. 4.*

Due to the close correspondence between DL axioms and rules highlighted by the previous result, we identify an axiom α with the rule $\Psi(\alpha)$, a TBox $\mathcal{T}$ with the set of rules $\Psi(\mathcal{R})$, and an ontology $\langle \mathcal{T}, \mathcal{A}\rangle$ with the program $\langle \Psi(\mathcal{R}), \mathcal{A}\rangle$.

By definition, every TBox $\mathcal{T}$ satisfies restrictions (f) and (w) and hence, we only need to determine whether $\mathcal{T}$ satisfies (a) and (b) to guarantee tractability of reasoning over a deterministic ontology $\langle \mathcal{T}, \mathcal{A}\rangle$. Unfortunately, the dependency graph of a TBox—which needs to be checked in order to verify (a) and (b)—cannot be computed in polynomial time.

Lemma 18. *Given a TBox $\mathcal{T}$, the computation of $G(\mathcal{T})$ is ExpTime-hard.*

Proof. The lemma follows from the fact that entailment of concept subsumptions by a TBox (which is ExpTime-hard) can be decided by computing the dependency graph of another TBox $\mathcal{T}'$.

Consider a TBox $\mathcal{T}$ and two concepts C and D. Moreover, let $\mathcal{T}' = \mathcal{T} \cup \{\alpha_1 = C \sqsubseteq \exists R_Y.C \sqcap Y, \alpha_2 = Y \sqcap D \sqsubseteq \exists R_Z.Z\}$ with R_Y and R_Z, and Y and Z some fresh roles and concepts, respectively. Then, $\mathcal{T} \models C \sqsubseteq D$ iff $y \to z \in G(\mathcal{T}')$ with y and z the variables occurring in the rules $\Psi(\alpha_1)$ and $\Psi(\alpha_2)$. $\square$

Since the computation of the dependency graph of a TBox is rather expensive, we define an over-approximation of this graph based on the definition of model-summarizing acyclicity (MSA) [10] which can be computed more efficiently.

Definition 19. *Given a set of rules $\mathcal{R}$, let $\mathcal{R}_S$ be the set of rules that results from replacing every rule $\rho \in \mathcal{R}$ of the form (1) by the following rule.*

$$B \to \bigwedge_{1 \leq i \leq n} \left(H_i \wedge \bigwedge_{x \in \mathbf{x}} \bigwedge_{v \in v_i} Scc(x,v) \right)\theta \tag{10}$$

In the above, Scc is a fresh binary predicate and θ is the substitution mapping every variable in $v \in \boldsymbol{v}_i$ to a fresh constant c_v (which, by (†) and the definition of a rule, is also specific to the i-th disjunct in the head of the rule ρ).

The summarizing dependency graph $G_S(\mathcal{R})$ of a rule set $\mathcal{R}$ is the smallest graph containing an edge $y \rightarrow z$ if $\langle \mathcal{R}_S, \mathcal{I}_\mathcal{R}^\star \rangle \models Scc(c_y, c_z)$ where $\mathcal{I}_\mathcal{R}^\star$ is the critical instance of $\mathcal{R}$; i.e., the set of all facts that can be constructed using the predicates in $\mathcal{R}$ and the special constant $\star$.

Lemma 20. *Consider a rule set $\mathcal{R}$. Then, the summarizing dependency graph of $\mathcal{R}$ is a superset of the dependency graph of $\mathcal{R}$.*

Proof. Consider some chase tree T of a program $\langle \mathcal{R}, \mathcal{I} \rangle$; and a function h mapping every constant to $\star$, and every skolem term of the form $f_y(t)$ to the constant c_y. Then, for every set of facts $\mathcal{F}$ associated to some node α in T, $h(\mathcal{F})$ is contained in the result of the chase of $\langle \mathcal{R}_S, \mathcal{I}_\mathcal{R}^\star \rangle$. The previous claim can be verified by induction on the path from the root of T to α.

Let us assume that there is some edge $y \rightarrow z \in G(\mathcal{R})$. Then, by the definition of the dependency graph, there must be some terms $f_z(t)$ and $f_y(s)$ with $f_y(s) \in t$ occurring in some set of facts $\mathcal{F}$ in some chase tree of a program $\langle \mathcal{R}, \mathcal{I} \rangle$. Let $B[\boldsymbol{x}, \boldsymbol{y}] \rightarrow \bigvee_{i=1}^n \exists \boldsymbol{v}_i . H_i[\boldsymbol{x}, \boldsymbol{v}_i]$ be the only rule in $\mathcal{R}$ containing z in some disjunct in the head. Then, $B[\boldsymbol{x}/t] \subseteq \mathcal{F}$, and hence, $h(B[\boldsymbol{x}/t])$ is contained in the result of the chase of $\langle \mathrm{MSA}(\mathcal{R}), \mathcal{I}_\mathcal{R}^\star \rangle$. Since $B \rightarrow \bigwedge_{i=1}^n (H_i' \wedge \bigwedge_{x \in \boldsymbol{x}} \bigwedge_{v \in \boldsymbol{v}_i} Scc(x, v))\theta \in \mathrm{MSA}(\mathcal{R})$, then $Scc(c_y, c_z)$ is also in the result of the chase of $\langle \mathrm{MSA}(\mathcal{R}), \mathcal{I}_\mathcal{R}^\star \rangle$. In turn, this implies that $y \rightarrow z \in G_S(\mathcal{R})$. $\qquad \square$

We proceed with the definition of tractable acyclicity, and thereafter establish the complexity of checking this condition and reasoning over such ontologies

Definition 21. *A TBox $\mathcal{T}$ is k-tractable acyclic (TA_k) if its summarizing graph is acyclic and the length of every braid in this graph is at most k.*

Theorem 22. *Deciding TA_k membership of a TBox $\mathcal{T}$ is P-complete.*

Proof. To verify membership, we propose a polynomial procedure to determine if $G_S(\mathcal{T})$ is acyclic and then compute the length of the longest braid in $G_S(\mathcal{T})$. Let $\mathcal{P} = \langle \mathcal{R}, \mathcal{I} \rangle$ be the program where $\mathcal{I}$ is the instance containing $E(c_y, c_z)$ for every $y \rightarrow z \in G_S(\mathcal{T})$, and $Neq(c_y, c_z)$ for every pair of nodes y and z in $G_S(\mathcal{T})$ with $y \neq z$; and $\mathcal{R} = \{\rightarrow P(x, x), E(x, y) \rightarrow P(x, y), P(x, y) \wedge P(y, z) \rightarrow P(x, z), P(x, y) \wedge P(y, z) \rightarrow P(x, z), P(x, y) \wedge P(x, z) \wedge Neq(y, z) \wedge E(y, w) \wedge E(z, w) \rightarrow B(x, w), B(x, y) \wedge B(y, z) \rightarrow B(x, z)\}$. Then, there is a braid starting in y and ending in z in $G_S(\mathcal{R})$ if and only if $\mathcal{P} \models B(c_y, c_z)$. Thus, to determine the maximum length of a braid in $G_S(\mathcal{R})$, we simply have to look for the largest path over the binary predicate B in the result of the chase of $\mathcal{P}$. Moreover, $G_S(\mathcal{R})$ is acyclic if and only if $\mathcal{P}$ does not entail the query $\exists x . P(x, x)$. Note that, the program $\mathcal{P}$ can be constructed in polynomial time since the computation of $G_S(\mathcal{T})$ is tractable. Moreover, as the number of variables per rule in $\mathcal{R}$ is at most 4 and the maximum arity of a predicate is 2, the chase of such a program can be computed in polynomial time.

Hardness of the TA_k membership check can be readily ascertained via reduction from propositional horn entailment.   □

Theorem 23. *Deciding BCQ entailment for TA_k ontologies $\langle T, A \rangle$ is coNP-complete provided the size of the query is fixed. Moreover, if T is a deterministic TBox, then it is P-complete.*

Proof. If T is TA_k, then $G_S(T)$ is acyclic and every braid in $G_S(T)$ is of length at most k. In turn, this implies that $G(T)$ is acyclic and every braid in $G(T)$ is of length at most k by Lemma 20. Since the TBox T satisfies restrictions (a), (b), (f), and (w), the theorem follows from Theorems 7 and 23.   □

5   Evaluation

To assess the empirical generality of TA_k, we analyzed ontologies from MOWL-Corp [22] and Oxford Ontology Library,[2] two large corpora of real-world OWL ontologies. These ontologies were transformed into the normal form defined in Fig. 4 using standard normalization techniques [8]. After this step, we disregarded ontologies with nominals and number restrictions; and also ontologies without any axiom of type (9), as these are trivially TA_0. Since the MOWLCorp is rather large, we only considered ontologies in this corpus with up to 1,000 axioms of type (9). The final set contained 1,576 TBoxes from MOWLCorp and 225 TBoxes from the Oxford Ontology Library.

To determine TA_k membership, we first constructed the summarizing dependency graphs of the TBoxes. For this, we transformed axioms to rules using the mapping in Fig. 4 and derived the programs described in Definition 19, over which we reasoned using the RDFox [24] datalog rule engine. Out of the obtained graphs, we found 974 (61.8%) acyclic ones from MOWLCorp and 171 (76%) from Oxford Library. Then, we determined TA_k membership of acyclic graphs by counting the length of their longest braid. We did this by constructing the program defined in Theorem 22, over which we reasoned using RDFox.

As our results show in Table 1, 78.3% of acyclic ontologies from MOWLCorp are TA_1, 90.8% are TA_2, 95.5% are TA_3, 98.8% are TA_4 and 99% are TA_5. In the Oxford Library, 51.4% of the acyclic ontologies are TA_1, 69.5% are TA_2, 81.2% are TA_3, 92.3% are TA_4, 97.6 % are TA_5 and 98.2 % are TA_6. There was only one ontology from the Oxford corpus (00477.owl), containing more than 150,000 rules of type (9), for which computing TA_k membership did not terminate.

Our acyclicity notion is theoretically equivalent to MSA and as general as MFA with respect to the evaluated ontologies: In our test set, there are no MFA ontologies which were not MSA. This validates the claims from [7,10], where it was observed that MFA (the most general known acyclicity criterion for the skolem chase) is not empirically more general than MSA. Moreover, our results show that almost all acyclic ontologies are TA_k with a small k: TA_5 characterizes 97% of the ontologies in both corpora.

---

[2] http://www.cs.ox.ac.uk/isg/ontologies/.

Table 1. Histogram of TA_k on ontologies from MOWL and Oxford corpora, where for TA_k we only count ontologies that do not also belong to TA_j for all $j < k$

MOWLCorp	TA_1	TA_2	TA_3	TA_4	TA_5	TA_{22}	TA_{23}	TA_{25}	Total
	763	122	36	42	2	2	6	1	974
Oxford Onto. Library	TA_1	TA_2	TA_3	TA_4	TA_5	TA_6	TA_{11}	TA_{23}	Total
	88	31	20	19	9	1	1	1	170

6   Conclusions and Future Work

To the best of our knowledge, this is the first systematic study of tractability of CQ answering with disjunctive existential rules. An important application is tractable query answering over OWL ontologies, a task which in general is known to be intractable [25]. We have shown that our restrictions do indeed apply, for small bounds of the related parameters, to many practical ontologies.

Our work therefore suggests a new approach to efficient reasoning that might be applicable to many realistic ontologies, and which might be natural to implement in existing reasoners such as HermiT [23], which use chase-like procedures already. The extension of our work with more general conditions for restricted chase termination, which was recently shown to work well with many OWL ontologies [7], may further help to extend the applicability of this approach.

Acknowledgements. Supported by the DFG within the cfaed Cluster of Excellence, CRC 912 (HAEC), and Emmy Noether grant KR 4381/1-1.

References

1. Baget, J.F., Leclère, M., Mugnier, M.L., Salvat, E.: On rules with existential variables: walking the decidability line. Artif. Intell. **175**(9–10), 1620–1654 (2011)
2. Bienvenu, M., Hansen, P., Lutz, C., Wolter, F.: First order-rewritability and containment of conjunctive queries in Horn description logics. In: Proceedings of 25th International Joint Conference on Artificial Intelligence (IJCAI'16), pp. 965–971. IJCAI/AAAI Press (2016)
3. Bourhis, P., Morak, M., Pieris, A.: The impact of disjunction on query answering under guarded-based existential rules. In: Proceedings of the 23rd International Joint Conference on Artificial Intelligence, Beijing, China, 3–9 August 2013, pp. 796–802. IJCAI/AAAI (2013)
4. Calì, A., Gottlob, G., Pieris, A.: Query answering under non-guarded rules in Datalog+/-. In: Hitzler, P., Lukasiewicz, T. (eds.) RR 2010. LNCS, vol. 6333, pp. 1–17. Springer, Heidelberg (2010). doi:10.1007/978-3-642-15918-3_1
5. Calì, A., Gottlob, G., Kifer, M.: Taming the infinite chase: query answering under expressive relational constraints. J. Artif. Intell. Res. (JAIR) **48**, 115–174 (2013)
6. Calvanese, D., De Giacomo, G., Lembo, D., Lenzerini, M., Rosati, R.: Tractable reasoning and efficient query answering in description logics: the DL-Lite family. J. Autom. Reason. (JAR) **39**(3), 385–429 (2007)

7. Carral, D., Dragoste, I., Krötzsch, M.: Restricted chase (non)termination for existential rules with disjunctions. In: Sierra, C. (ed.) Proceedings of the 26th International Joint Conference on Artificial Intelligence (IJCAI 2017), pp. 922–928 (2017)

8. Carral, D., Feier, C., Cuenca Grau, B., Hitzler, P., Horrocks, I.: $\mathcal{EL}$-ifying ontologies. In: Demri, S., Kapur, D., Weidenbach, C. (eds.) IJCAR 2014. LNCS, vol. 8562, pp. 464–479. Springer, Cham (2014). doi:10.1007/978-3-319-08587-6_36

9. Carral, D., Feier, C., Hitzler, P.: A practical acyclicity notion for query answering over $Horn$-$\mathcal{SRIQ}$ ontologies. In: Groth, P., Simperl, E., Gray, A., Sabou, M., Krötzsch, M., Lecue, F., Flöck, F., Gil, Y. (eds.) ISWC 2016. LNCS, vol. 9981, pp. 70–85. Springer, Cham (2016). doi:10.1007/978-3-319-46523-4_5

10. Cuenca Grau, B., Horrocks, I., Krötzsch, M., Kupke, C., Magka, D., Motik, B., Wang, Z.: Acyclicity notions for existential rules and their application to query answering in ontologies. JAIR **47**, 741–808 (2013)

11. Dantsin, E., Eiter, T., Gottlob, G., Voronkov, A.: Complexity and expressive power of logic programming. ACM Comput. Surv. **33**(3), 374–425 (2001)

12. Feier, C., Carral, D., Stefanoni, G., Grau, B.C., Horrocks, I.: The combined approach to query answering beyond the OWL 2 profiles. In: Yang, Q., Wooldridge, M. (eds.) Proceedings of the Twenty-Fourth International Joint Conference on Artificial Intelligence, IJCAI 2015, Buenos Aires, Argentina, 25–31 July 2015, pp. 2971–2977. AAAI Press (2015). http://ijcai.org/Abstract/15/420

13. Gottlob, G., Pichler, R., Wei, F.: Bounded treewidth as a key to tractability of knowledge representation and reasoning. Artif. Intell. **174**(1), 105–132 (2010)

14. Hopcroft, J.E., Ullman, J.D.: Introduction to Automata Theory, Languages and Computation. Addison-Wesley, Boston (1979)

15. Horrocks, I., Kutz, O., Sattler, U.: The even more irresistible SROIQ. In: Proceedings, Tenth International Conference on Principles of Knowledge Representation and Reasoning, United Kingdom, 2–5 June 2006, pp. 57–67. AAAI Press (2006)

16. Kazakov, Y.: Saturation-based decision procedures for extensions of the guarded fragment. Ph.D. thesis, Universität des Saarlandes, Saarbrücken, Germany (2006)

17. Kontchakov, R., Lutz, C., Toman, D., Wolter, F., Zakharyaschev, M.: The combined approach to query answering in dl-lite. In: Principles of Knowledge Representation and Reasoning: Proceedings of the Twelfth International Conference, KR 2010, Toronto, Ontario, Canada, 9–13 May 2010. AAAI Press (2010) http://aaai.org/ocs/index.php/KR/KR2010/paper/view/1282

18. Kontchakov, R., Lutz, C., Toman, D., Wolter, F., Zakharyaschev, M.: The combined approach to ontology-based data access. In: IJCAI, pp. 2656–2661 (2011)

19. Krötzsch, M., Rudolph, S.: Extending decidable existential rules by joining acyclicity and guardedness. In: Proceedings 22nd IJCAI, pp. 963–968. AAAI Press (2011)

20. Lutz, C., Seylan, İ., Toman, D., Wolter, F.: The combined approach to OBDA: taming role hierarchies using filters. In: Alani, H., Kagal, L., Fokoue, A., Groth, P., Biemann, C., Parreira, J.X., Aroyo, L., Noy, N., Welty, C., Janowicz, K. (eds.) ISWC 2013. LNCS, vol. 8218, pp. 314–330. Springer, Heidelberg (2013). doi:10.1007/978-3-642-41335-3_20

21. Marnette, B.: Generalized schema-mappings: from termination to tractability. In: Proceedings of the 28th ACM SIGMOD-SIGACT-SIGART Symposium on Principles of Database Systems, PODS 2009, June 2009, USA, pp. 13–22. ACM (2009)

22. Matentzoglu, N., Bail, S., Parsia, B.: A snapshot of the OWL web. In: Alani, H., Kagal, L., Fokoue, A., Groth, P., Biemann, C., Parreira, J.X., Aroyo, L., Noy, N., Welty, C., Janowicz, K. (eds.) ISWC 2013. LNCS, vol. 8218, pp. 331–346. Springer, Heidelberg (2013). doi:10.1007/978-3-642-41335-3_21

23. Motik, B., Shearer, R., Horrocks, I.: Hypertableau reasoning for description logics. J. Artif. Intell. Res. (JAIR) **36**(1), 165–228 (2009)
24. Motik, B., Nenov, Y., Piro, R., Horrocks, I., Olteanu, D.: Parallel materialisation of Datalog programs in centralised, main-memory RDF systems. In: AAAI (2014)
25. Stefanoni, G., Motik, B., Krötzsch, M., Rudolph, S.: The complexity of answering conjunctive and navigational queries over OWL 2 EL knowledge bases. J. Artif. Intell. Res. **51**, 645–705 (2014)

Zooming in on Ontologies: Minimal Modules and Best Excerpts

Jieying Chen[1](✉), Michel Ludwig[3](✉), Yue Ma[1](✉), and Dirk Walther[2](✉)

[1] LRI, Univ. Paris-Sud, CNRS, Université Paris-Saclay, Orsay, France
{jieying.chen,yue.ma}@lri.fr
[2] Fraunhofer Institute for Transportation and Infrastructure Systems (IVI),
Zeunerstrasse 38, 01069 Dresden, Germany
dirk.walther@ivi.fraunhofer.de
[3] Beaufort, Luxembourg
michel.ludwig@gmail.com

Abstract. Ensuring access to the most relevant knowledge contained in large ontologies has been identified as an important challenge. To this end, minimal modules (sub-ontologies that preserve all entailments over a given vocabulary) and excerpts (certain, small number of axioms that best capture the knowledge regarding the vocabulary by allowing for a degree of semantic loss) have been proposed. In this paper, we introduce the notion of subsumption justification as an extension of justification (a minimal set of axioms needed to preserve a logical consequence) to capture the subsumption knowledge between a term and all other terms in the vocabulary. We present algorithms for computing subsumption justifications based on a simulation notion developed for the problem of deciding the logical difference between ontologies. We show how subsumption justifications can be used to obtain minimal modules and to compute best excerpts by additionally employing a partial Max-SAT solver. This yields two state-of-the-art methods for computing all minimal modules and all best excerpts, which we evaluate over large biomedical ontologies.

1 Introduction

Knowledge about a complex system represented in ontologies yields a collection of axioms that are too large for human users to browse, let alone to comprehend or reason about it. In this paper, we propose a computational framework to zoom in on large ontologies by providing users with either the necessary axioms that act as explanations for sets of entailments, or fix-sized sub-ontologies containing the most relevant information over a vocabulary.

Various approaches to extracting knowledge from ontologies have been suggested including ontology summarization [23,25,29], ontology modularization [9,14,26–28], ontology decomposition [6,20], and consequence justifications [3,11]. Existing ontology summarization systems focus on producing an abridged version of RDF/S ontologies by identifying the most important nodes

This work is partially funded by the ANR project GoAsQ (ANR-15-CE23-0022).

© Springer International Publishing AG 2017
C. d'Amato et al. (Eds.): ISWC 2017, Part I, LNCS 10587, pp. 173–189, 2017.
DOI: 10.1007/978-3-319-68288-4_11

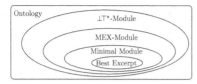

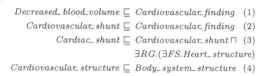

$$Decreased\_blood\_volume \sqsubseteq Cardiovascular\_finding \quad (1)$$
$$Cardiovascular\_shunt \sqsubseteq Cardiovascular\_finding \quad (2)$$
$$Cardiac\_shunt \sqsubseteq Cardiovascular\_shunt \sqcap \quad (3)$$
$$\exists RG.(\exists FS.Heart\_structure)$$
$$Cardiovascular\_structure \sqsubseteq Body\_system\_structure \quad (4)$$

Fig. 1. Zooming in on an ontology **Fig. 2.** Example axioms in Snomed CT (*FS* for *Finding_site*, *RG* for *Role_Group*)

and their links under certain numeric measures, e.g., in/out degree centrality of a node [25]. In contrast, ontology modularization and decomposition developed for Description Logics (DLs) [2] is to identify ontological axioms needed to define the relationships between concept and role names contained in a given signature. Modules are sub-ontologies that preserve all logical consequences over a given signature, and ontology decomposition partitions an ontology into atoms that are never split by different modules. Computing minimal modules is known to be hard. Hence, existing systems are either restricted to tractable DLs [5,13,15] or they compute approximations of minimal modules [6,9,21]. This has resulted in two important module notions: the semantics-based modules computed by the system MEX [13] and the syntactic locality-based ⊥⊤*-modules [22]. Figure 1 shows the set inclusion relationship between these notions, where we focus on MEX-modules, minimal modules and best excerpts (see below) in this paper. A justification for a particular logical consequence is a minimal set of axioms that preserve the entailment. Although computing all justifications is generally a hard task, different approaches have been shown promising for this task [1,10,17,30].

Different module notions and justifications share the property that the number of the axioms they contain is not bounded (besides the size of the entire ontology). Even minimal modules for small signatures may be large rendering human understanding more difficult. To this end, the notion of best excerpts [4] has been introduced as size-bounded subsets of ontologies that preserve as much knowledge about a given signature as possible.

The following real-world example illustrates possible benefits of best excerpts. Suppose a user is concerned with the cardiovascular disease defined in the Snomed CT[1] ontology $\mathcal{T}$ consisting of 317 891 axioms. The user then selects the terms *Cardiovascular_finding*, *Decreased_blood_volume* and *Cardiac_shunt* from $\mathcal{T}$ as her signature Σ of interest. To help the user zoom in on $\mathcal{T}$ for Σ, we can extract, for instance, the ⊥⊤*-module and obtain 51 axioms, or the *smallest* minimal modules, which yields a further reduction down to 15 axioms,[2] among which are the axioms given in Fig. 2. Arguably our user still feels overwhelmed by the amount of 15 axioms. This is where the notion of best k-excerpt steps in. By setting $k = 3$, the user can get a best 3-excerpt $\mathcal{E}_1$ consisting of the axioms 1–3 listed

---

[1] http://www.ihtsdo.org/snomed-ct.

[2] Refer to https://goo.gl/o1QFGm for the whole list and for cases where larger minimal modules appear in practice.

above. By zooming in further, say extracting one-sized excerpts, she obtains $\mathcal{E}_2$ consisting of the first axiom. As a best excerpt, $\mathcal{E}_1$ guarantees all logical entailments over the terms *Cardiac_shunt* and *Decreased_blood_volume*. And the singleton $\mathcal{E}_2$ keeps the complete information over the term *Decreased_blood_volume*. Note that $\mathcal{E}_2$ is returned due to the fact that it needs more than two axioms to preserve the full information for any other concept in Σ. Moreover, axiom 4 is in $\mathcal{M}$ but missing in $\mathcal{E}_1$ and in $\mathcal{E}_2$. This is because they merely serve to provide background knowledge for reasoning over, thus not directly linked to, the user's input terms Σ, which are excluded from best excerpts due to the size restriction. In this way, the user gains control over a large ontology. An approximate approach to computing ontology excerpts based on information retrieval was introduced in [4]. However, it cannot guarantee to compute the best excerpt.

In this paper, we generalise the notion of a justification to *subsumption justification* as a minimal set of axioms needed to define the relationship between a selected term to the remaining terms in a given vocabulary. Inspired by a proof-theoretic solution to the logical difference problem between ontologies [7,18], we develop recursive algorithms to compute subsumption justifications. A minimal module preserving the knowledge about a vocabulary can now be characterised as the union of subsumption justifications, one for each term in the vocabulary. By taking the union of subsumption justification for as many terms as possible without exceeding a given size limitation yields a best excerpt. The algorithm operates in two stages: First, for every term in the vocabulary, all subsumption justifications are computed. Similarly to modules, no bound on the size of such justifications exists. Second, minimal modules are obtained by taking the union of one subsumption justification for every term, and best k-excerpts, for $k > 0$, are obtained by packing a subsumption justification for as many terms as possible into a space of at most k axioms. The latter is solved via an encoding into a partial Max-SAT problem [8]. Note that [4] only considers excerpts based on information retrieval, which provide an approximate solution that can be computed rather quickly, albeit not capturing the knowledge in an optimal way. In this paper, however, we provide an algorithm for computing best excerpts via subsumption justifications. Best excerpts can be used as a benchmark to evaluate the quality of other excerpt or incomplete module notions.

Our contribution is three-fold: (i) We define the notion of subsumption justification and then introduce two of its applications (Sect. 3): computing minimal modules and best excerpts; (ii) moreover, we present algorithms of computing subsumption justifications (Sect. 4); (iii) finally, we evaluate the performance of overall algorithms (Sect. 5). Our algorithm for computing minimal modules outperformed the search-based approach from [5], and as the first best excerpt extraction algorithm, we can obtain the excerpts of a better quality than the excerpts based on information retrieval [4].

2   Preliminaries

Let $\mathsf{N_C}$ and $\mathsf{N_R}$ be mutually disjoint (countably infinite) sets of concept names and role names. We use A, B, X, Y, Z to denote concept names, and r, s for role names. The set of $\mathcal{ELH}$-*concepts* C and the set of $\mathcal{ELH}$-*inclusions* α are built by the following grammar rules: $C ::= \top \mid A \mid C \sqcap C \mid \exists r.C$, $\alpha ::= C \sqsubseteq C \mid C \equiv C \mid r \sqsubseteq s$, where $A \in \mathsf{N_C}$ and $r, s \in \mathsf{N_R}$. An $\mathcal{ELH}$-*TBox* is a finite set of $\mathcal{ELH}$-inclusions (also called axioms).

The semantics is defined using interpretations $\mathcal{I} = (\Delta^{\mathcal{I}}, \cdot^{\mathcal{I}})$, where the domain $\Delta^{\mathcal{I}}$ is a non-empty set, and $\cdot^{\mathcal{I}}$ is a function mapping each concept name A to a subset $A^{\mathcal{I}}$ of $\Delta^{\mathcal{I}}$ and every role name r to a binary relation $r^{\mathcal{I}}$ over $\Delta^{\mathcal{I}}$. The *extension* $C^{\mathcal{I}}$ of a possibly complex concept C is defined inductively as: $(\top)^{\mathcal{I}} := \Delta^{\mathcal{I}}$, $(C \sqcap D)^{\mathcal{I}} := C^{\mathcal{I}} \cap D^{\mathcal{I}}$, and $(\exists r.C)^{\mathcal{I}} := \{x \in \Delta^{\mathcal{I}} \mid \exists y \in C^{\mathcal{I}} : (x, y) \in r^{\mathcal{I}}\}$.

An interpretation $\mathcal{I}$ *satisfies* a concept C, an axiom $C \sqsubseteq D$, $C \equiv D$, or $r \sqsubseteq s$ iff $C^{\mathcal{I}} \neq \emptyset$, $C^{\mathcal{I}} \subseteq D^{\mathcal{I}}$, $C^{\mathcal{I}} = D^{\mathcal{I}}$, or $r^{\mathcal{I}} \subseteq s^{\mathcal{I}}$, respectively. An interpretation $\mathcal{I}$ is a *model* of $\mathcal{T}$ if $\mathcal{I}$ satisfies all axioms in $\mathcal{T}$. An axiom α *follows* from $\mathcal{T}$, written $\mathcal{T} \models \alpha$, if for all models $\mathcal{I}$ of $\mathcal{T}$, it holds that $\mathcal{I}$ satisfies α.

An $\mathcal{ELH}$-*terminology* $\mathcal{T}$ is an $\mathcal{ELH}$-TBox consisting of axioms of the form $A \sqsubseteq C$, $A \equiv C$, $r \sqsubseteq s$, where A is a concept name, r and s are role names, C is an $\mathcal{ELH}$-concept and no concept name A occurs more than once on the left-hand side of an axiom of the form $A \equiv C$. To simplify the presentation we assume that terminologies do not contain any occurrence of $\top$ and no axioms of the form $A \equiv B$ (after having removed multiple B-conjuncts) for concept names A and B. Note that the material presented in the paper can easily be extended to take $\top$ into account. A terminology is said to be *acyclic* iff it can be unfolded (i.e., the process of substituting each concept name A by the right-hand side C of its defining axiom $A \equiv C$ terminates).

We say that a concept name A is *conjunctive in* $\mathcal{T}$ iff there exist concept names $B_1, \ldots, B_n$, $n > 0$, such that $A \equiv B_1 \sqcap \ldots \sqcap B_n \in \mathcal{T}$; otherwise A is said to be *non-conjunctive in* $\mathcal{T}$. An $\mathcal{ELH}$-terminology $\mathcal{T}$ is *normalised* iff it only contains axioms of the forms $A \sqsubseteq B_1 \sqcap \ldots \sqcap B_m$, $A \equiv B_1 \sqcap \ldots \sqcap B_n$, $A \sqsubseteq \exists r.B$ and $A \equiv \exists r.B$, where $m \geq 1$, $n \geq 2$, A, B, B_i are concept names, and each conjunct B_i is non-conjunctive in $\mathcal{T}$. Every $\mathcal{ELH}$-terminology $\mathcal{T}$ can be normalised in polynomial time into a terminology $\mathcal{T}'$ such that for all $\mathcal{ELH}$-inclusions α formulated using concept and role names from $\mathcal{T}$ only, it holds that $\mathcal{T} \models \alpha$ iff $\mathcal{T}' \models \alpha$. Note that each axiom $\alpha \in \mathcal{T}$ is transformed individually into a set of normalised axioms. Moreover, we assume that when $\mathcal{T}$ is normalised, a denormalisation function $\delta_{\mathcal{T}} : \mathcal{T}' \to 2^{\mathcal{T}}$ is computed that maps every normalised axiom $\beta \in \mathcal{T}'$ to a set of axioms $\delta_{\mathcal{T}}(\alpha) \subseteq \mathcal{T}$ that consists of all axioms $\alpha \in \mathcal{T}$ that generated β during their normalisation.

We denote the number of axioms in a TBox $\mathcal{T}$ with $|\mathcal{T}|$. A signature Σ is a finite subset of $\mathsf{N_C} \cup \mathsf{N_R}$. For a syntactic object χ (i.e., a concept, an axiom, or a TBox), $\mathrm{sig}(\chi)$ is the set of concept and role names occurring in χ. We denote with $\mathrm{sig}^{\mathsf{N_C}}(\chi)$ the set of concept names in $\mathrm{sig}(\chi)$. We write $\mathcal{ELH}_{\Sigma}$ to denote the set of $\mathcal{ELH}$-concepts C such that $\mathrm{sig}(C) \subseteq \Sigma$. A subset $M \subseteq \mathcal{T}$ is called a *justification for an $\mathcal{ELH}$-concept inclusion α from* $\mathcal{T}$ iff $M \models \alpha$ and $M' \not\models \alpha$ for every $M' \subsetneq M$. We denote the set of all justifications for an $\mathcal{ELH}$-concept inclusion α from an $\mathcal{ELH}$-terminology $\mathcal{T}$ with $\mathrm{Just}_{\mathcal{T}}(\alpha)$. Note that $\mathrm{Just}_{\mathcal{T}}(\alpha)$ may contain exponentially many justifications in the number of axioms in $\mathcal{T}$.

The logical difference between two $\mathcal{ELH}$-terminologies T_1 and T_2, denoted as $\mathsf{cDiff}_\Sigma(T_1, T_2)$, is the set of all $\mathcal{ELH}$-inclusions α of the form $C \sqsubseteq D$ for $\mathcal{ELH}$-concepts C and D such that $\mathsf{sig}(\alpha) \subseteq \Sigma$, $T_1 \models \alpha$, and $T_2 \not\models \alpha$.

If two terminologies are logically different, the set $\mathsf{cDiff}_\Sigma(T_1, T_2)$ consists of infinitely many concept inclusions. The *primitive witnesses theorems* from [12] allow us to consider only certain inclusions of a simpler syntactic form. It states that if $\alpha \in \mathsf{cDiff}_\Sigma(T_1, T_2)$, where T_1 and T_2 are $\mathcal{ELH}$-terminologies and Σ a signature, then either $A \sqsubseteq D$ or $C \sqsubseteq A$ is a member of $\mathsf{cDiff}_\Sigma(T_1, T_2)$, where $A \in \mathsf{sig}^{\mathsf{Nc}}(\alpha)$ and C, D are $\mathcal{ELH}$-concepts occurring in α. We call such concepts A *witnesses* and denote the set of witnesses with $\mathsf{cWtn}_\Sigma(T_1, T_2)$. It holds that $\mathsf{cWtn}_\Sigma(T_1, T_2) = \emptyset$ iff $\mathsf{cDiff}_\Sigma(T_1, T_2) = \emptyset$.

A k-excerpt of T w.r.t. Σ is a subset $\mathcal{E}$ of T such that $|\,\mathcal{E}\,| \leq k$. Let μ be an incompleteness measure, we say a k-excerpt $\mathcal{E}$ is the best excerpt of T w.r.t. Σ if $\mu(T, \Sigma, \mathcal{E}) = \min\{\mu(T, \Sigma, \mathcal{E}') \mid \mathcal{E}' \text{ is a } k\text{-excerpt of } T\}$. In this paper, we use the size of concept witness $\mathsf{cWtn}_\Sigma(T, \mathcal{E})$ as the incompleteness measure.

3 Application of Subsumption Justification

In this section, we introduce the notion of subsumption justification, and give two applications of this notion. The algorithms for computing subsumption justifications are given separately in Sect. 4.

We assume that T, T_1, and T_2 are acyclic normalised $\mathcal{ELH}$-terminologies, Σ is a signature, $X \in \mathsf{N_C}$ is concept names.

Definition 1. *We say that* $\mathcal{M} \subseteq T$ *is an* $\langle X, \Sigma \rangle$-*subsumee module of* T *iff for every* $C \in \mathcal{ELH}_\Sigma$, $T \models C \sqsubseteq X$ *implies* $\mathcal{M} \models C \sqsubseteq X$. *Similarly, we define the notion of an* $\langle X, \Sigma \rangle$-*subsumer module* $\mathcal{M}$ *of* T *to be a subset of* T *such that for every* $D \in \mathcal{ELH}_\Sigma$, $T \models X \sqsubseteq D$ *implies* $\mathcal{M} \models X \sqsubseteq D$.

Additionally, a set $\mathcal{M}$ *is called an* $\langle X, \Sigma \rangle$-*subsumption module of* T *iff* $\mathcal{M}$ *is an* $\langle X, \Sigma \rangle$-*subsumee and* $\langle X, \Sigma \rangle$-*subsumer module of* T. *An* $\langle X, \Sigma \rangle$-*subsumee (resp. subsumer, subsumption) justification is an* $\langle X, \Sigma \rangle$-*subsumee (resp. subsumer, subsumption) module of* T *that is minimal w.r.t.* $\subsetneq$.

We denote the set of all $\langle X, \Sigma \rangle$-subsumee (resp. subsumer, subsumption) justifications as $\mathcal{J}_T^{\leftarrow}(X, \Sigma)$ (resp. $\mathcal{J}_T^{\rightarrow}(X, \Sigma)$, $\mathcal{J}_T(X, \Sigma)$). Note that there may exist multiple $\langle X, \Sigma \rangle$-(subsumer, subsumee) subsumption justifications.

Example 1. Let $\Sigma = \{A_1, A_2, B\}$ and let $T = \{\alpha_1, \alpha_2, \alpha_3, \alpha_4, \alpha_5, \alpha_6, \alpha_7\}$, where $\alpha_1 = X \equiv Y \sqcap Z$, $\alpha_2 = Y \sqsubseteq B$, $\alpha_3 = Z \equiv Z_1 \sqcap Z_2$, $\alpha_4 = A_1 \sqsubseteq Y$, $\alpha_5 = A_2 \sqsubseteq Z$, $\alpha_6 = A_2 \sqsubseteq Z_1$, and $\alpha_7 = A_2 \sqsubseteq Z_2$. Then the sets $\mathcal{M}_1 = \{\alpha_1, \alpha_3, \alpha_4, \alpha_6, \alpha_7\}$, $\mathcal{M}_2 = \{\alpha_1, \alpha_4, \alpha_5\}$, and T are all $\langle X, \Sigma \rangle$-subsumee modules of T, whereas only $\mathcal{M}_1$ and $\mathcal{M}_2$ are $\langle X, \Sigma \rangle$-subsumee justifications of T. The set $\mathcal{M}_3 = \{\alpha_1, \alpha_2\}$ is an $\langle X, \Sigma \rangle$-subsumer justification of T. Finally, the sets $\mathcal{M}_1 \cup \mathcal{M}_3$ and $\mathcal{M}_2 \cup \mathcal{M}_3$ are $\langle X, \Sigma \rangle$-subsumption justifications of T.

Proposition 1. $\mathcal{M}$ *is an* $\langle X, \Sigma \rangle$-*subsumption module of* T *iff* $X \notin \mathsf{cWtn}_\Sigma(T, \mathcal{M})$.

Proposition 1 follows from the *primitive witnesses theorems* [12] and Definition 1.

3.1   Application 1: Computing Minimal Modules

A module is a subset of an ontology that can act as a substitute for the ontology w.r.t. a given signature. In this paper, we consider the notion of basic modules from [5] for acyclic $\mathcal{ELH}$-terminologies.

Definition 2 (Basic Module [5]). *Let $\mathcal{T}$ be an $\mathcal{ELH}$-terminology, and let Σ be a signature. A subset $\mathcal{M} \subseteq \mathcal{T}$ is called a* basic $\mathcal{ELH}$-module *of $\mathcal{T}$ w.r.t. Σ iff* $\mathsf{cDiff}_\Sigma(\mathcal{T}, \mathcal{M}) = \emptyset$.

To apply subsumption justifications for computing all modules that are minimal w.r.t. $\subsetneq$, we define the operator $\otimes$ to combine subsumption justifications of $\mathcal{T}$ for all Σ-concept names, as follows: Given a set S and $\mathbb{S}_1, \mathbb{S}_2 \subseteq 2^S$, $\mathbb{S}_1 \otimes \mathbb{S}_2 := \{ S_1 \cup S_2 \mid S_1 \in \mathbb{S}_1, S_2 \in \mathbb{S}_2 \}$. For instance, if $\mathbb{S}_1 = \{\{\alpha_1, \alpha_2\}, \{\alpha_3\}\}$ and $\mathbb{S}_2 = \{\{\alpha_2, \alpha_3\}, \{\alpha_4, \alpha_5\}\}$, then $\mathbb{S}_1 \otimes \mathbb{S}_2 = \{\{\alpha_1, \alpha_2, \alpha_3\}, \{\alpha_1, \alpha_2, \alpha_4, \alpha_5\}, \{\alpha_2, \alpha_3\}, \{\alpha_3, \alpha_4, \alpha_5\}\}$. Note that the $\otimes$ operator is associative and commutative.

For a set $\mathbb{M}$ of sets, we define a function $\mathsf{Minimise}_\subseteq(\mathbb{M})$ as follows: $\mathcal{M} \in \mathsf{Minimise}_\subseteq(\mathbb{M})$ iff $\mathcal{M} \in \mathbb{M}$ and there does not exist a set $\mathcal{M}' \in \mathbb{M}$ such that $\mathcal{M}' \subsetneq \mathcal{M}$. Finally, we can use the $\otimes$ operator and the $\mathsf{Minimise}_\subseteq(\mathbb{M})$ function to combine sets of subsumer and sets of subsumee modules to obtain a set of subsumption modules, whose correctness is guaranteed by Proposition 1.

Theorem 1. *Let $\mathbb{M}_\Sigma^\mathcal{T}$ be the set of all minimal basic $\mathcal{ELH}$-modules of $\mathcal{T}$ w.r.t. Σ. Then* $\mathbb{M}_\Sigma^\mathcal{T} := \mathsf{Minimise}_\subseteq(\otimes_{X \in \Sigma \cap \mathsf{N_c}}(\mathcal{J}_X^{\rightarrow}(X, \Sigma) \otimes \mathcal{J}_X^{\leftarrow}(X, \Sigma)))$.

Please note that, given a TBox and a signature, MEX-module is unique [14] but there may exist exponential many minimal basic modules in theory. A relation between basic module and MEX module is given below:

Proposition 2. *Let $\mathcal{M}$ be the MEX-module of $\mathcal{T}$ w.r.t. Σ. It holds that for every minimal basic $\mathcal{EL}$-module $\mathcal{M}'$ of $\mathcal{T}$ w.r.t. Σ, $\mathcal{M}' \subseteq \mathcal{M}$.*

Intuitively, Proposition 1 follows from the fact that MEX-modules are based on a semantic inseparability notion [14], whereas the notion of basic modules uses a weaker, deductive inseparability notion based on $\mathcal{EL}$-inclusions [5]; see, e.g., [19] for more on inseparability.

3.2   Application 2: Computing Best Excerpts

Based on subsumption justifications, in this section, we present an encoding of the best k-excerpt problem in a partial Max-SAT problem, with the aim of delegating the task of finding the best excerpt to a Max-SAT solver. In that way we can leverage the decades of research efforts dedicated to developing efficient SAT solvers for our problem setting. We continue with reviewing basic notions relating to propositional logic and Max-SAT.

Partial Max-SAT is an extension of the Boolean Satisfiability (SAT) to optimization problems. Formally, a partial Max-SAT problem $\mathcal{P}$ is pair $\mathcal{P} = (H, S)$

where H and S are finite sets of clauses, called *hard* and *soft* clauses, respectively. We say that a valuation v is a solution of P iff. v satisfies all the clauses in H and there does not exist a valuation v' that satisfies all the clauses in H and $\sum_{\psi \in S} v'(\psi) > \sum_{\psi \in S} v(\psi)$.

The objective of a partial Max-SAT problem is hence to find a propositional valuation that satisfies all the hard clauses in H and that satisfies a maximal number of the soft clauses in S. Note that a partial Max-SAT problem may nevertheless admit several solutions.

We now describe of our encoding of the best k-excerpt problem into partial Max-SAT. For every axiom $\alpha \in T$, we introduce a fresh propositional variable p_α. Consequently, each solution v to our partial Max-SAT problem yields a best excerpt that consists of all axioms α such that $v(p_\alpha) = 1$.

For a $\langle A, \Sigma \rangle$-subsumption justification $j \in \mathcal{J}_T(A, \Sigma)$, we introduce the formula $F_j := \bigwedge_{\alpha \in j} p_\alpha$. Consequently, F_j is valued 1 iff. p_α is valued 1, equivalently, each axiom in j is selected to be contained in a best excerpt.

For the set of $\langle A, \Sigma \rangle$-subsumption justifications $\mathcal{J} = \mathcal{J}_T(A, \Sigma)$, we define $G_{\mathcal{J}} := \bigvee_{j \in \mathcal{J}} F_j$. For instance, let $T = \{\alpha_1, \alpha_2, \alpha_3, \alpha_4, \alpha_5\}$, $\mathcal{J} = \{\{\alpha_2, \alpha_3\}, \{\alpha_1, \alpha_4\}\}$, and $j = \{\alpha_2, \alpha_3\}$. Then $F_j = p_{\alpha_2} \wedge p_{\alpha_3}$ and $G_{\mathcal{J}} := (p_{\alpha_2} \wedge p_{\alpha_3}) \vee (p_{\alpha_1} \wedge p_{\alpha_4})$.

Definition 3 (Encoding of the Best Excerpt Problem). *For every $A \in \Sigma$, let $\mathcal{J}_A(X, \Sigma)$ be the set of all the $\langle A, \Sigma \rangle$-subsumption justifications of a terminology T, and let q_A be a fresh propositional variable. The partial Max-SAT problem for finding best k-excerpts of T w.r.t. Σ, denoted with $P_k(T, \Sigma)$, is defined as follows. We set $P_k(T, \Sigma) := (H_k(T), S_k(T, \Sigma))$, where*

$$H_k(T) := Card(T, k) \cup \bigcup_{A \in \Sigma \cap N_C} Clauses(q_A \leftrightarrow G_{\mathcal{J}_A}),$$

$$S_k(T, \Sigma) := \{ q_A \mid A \in \Sigma \cap N_C \},$$

and $Card(T, k)$ is the set of clauses specifying that at most k clauses from the set $\{ p_\alpha \mid \alpha \in T \}$ must be satisfied.

In the hard part of our partial Max-SAT problem, the clauses in $Card(T, k)$ specify that the cardinality of the resulting excerpt $\mathcal{E} \subseteq T$ must be equal to k. We do not fix a certain encoding that should be used to obtain $Card(T, k)$, but we note that there exist several techniques that require a polynomial number of clauses in k and in the size of T (see e.g. [24]). Moreover, for every concept name $A \in \Sigma$, the variable q_A is set to be equivalent to the formula $G_{\mathcal{J}}$, i.e. q_A will be satisfied in a valuation iff the resulting excerpt will have the property that the knowledge of A w.r.t. Σ in T is preserved ($A \in Preserved_\Sigma(T, \mathcal{E})$). Finally, the set $S_k(T, \Sigma)$ of soft clauses specifies that a maximal number of q_A must be satisfied, enforcing that the resulting excerpt $\mathcal{E}$ will yield the smallest possible number of difference witnesses (whilst obeying the constraint that $|\mathcal{E}| = k$).

We can now show the correctness of our encoding, i.e. a best k-excerpt can be obtained from any solution to the partial Max-SAT problem $P_k(T, \Sigma)$.

Theorem 2 (Correctness & Completeness). *Let T be a normalised $\mathcal{ELH}$-terminology, let Σ be a signature, and let $0 \leq k \leq |T|$. It holds that $\mathcal{E} \subseteq T$ is a best k-excerpt of T w.r.t. Σ iff there exists a solution v of the partial Max-SAT problem $P_k(T, \Sigma)$ such that $\mathcal{E} = \{\, \alpha \in T \mid v(p_\alpha) = 1 \,\}$.*

Algorithm 1 shows how best excerpts are computed by using partial Max-SAT encoding. In Line 7, the algorithm iterates over every concept name A in Σ and the set of all subsumption justifications $\mathcal{J}_T(A, \Sigma)$ are computed. The formula $G_{\mathcal{J}_A}$ is computed next and stored in a set S. After the iteration over all the concept names A in Σ is complete, the partial Max-SAT problem $P_k(T, \Sigma)$ is constructed with the help of the formulas $G_{\mathcal{J}_A}$ that are stored in S. Subsequently, a solution v of $P_k(T, \Sigma)$ is computed using a partial Max-SAT solver and the best k-excerpt is returned by analysing which variables p_α have been set to 1 in the valuation v.

Our algorithm of computing subsumption justifications given below runs in exponential time in the size of T and Σ. Hence, we have that Algorithm 1 overall requires exponential time in the size of T and Σ in the worst case.

Algorithm 1. Computing Best k-Excerpts

```
1  function ComputeBestExcerpt(T, Σ, k)
2      if k = 0 then
3          return ∅
4      if k = |T| then
5          return T
6      S := ∅
7      for every A ∈ Σ ∩ N_C do
8          Compute ⟨A, Σ⟩-subsumption justifications of T: J_T(A, Σ)
9          Transfer ⟨A, Σ⟩-subsumption justifications of T to its propostional formula  G_{J_A}
10         S := S ∪ {G_{J_A}}
11     Compute P_k(T, Σ) using S
12     Find the set of solutions V of P_k(T, Σ) using partial Max-SAT solver
13     return { α ∈ T | v(p_α) = 1, v ∈ V }
```

---

4   Algorithms of Computing Subsumption Justifications

In the following subsections, we present algorithms for computing subsumer and subsumee justifications. The algorithms use the following notion of a cover of a set of sets. For a finite set S and a set $\mathbb{T} \subseteq 2^S$, we say that a set $\mathbb{M} \subseteq 2^S$ is a *cover of* $\mathbb{T}$ iff $\mathbb{M} \subseteq \mathbb{T}$ and there exists $\mathcal{M}' \in \mathbb{M}$ such that $\mathcal{M}' \subseteq \mathcal{M}$ for every $\mathcal{M} \in \mathbb{T}$. In other words, a cover is a subset of $\mathbb{T}$ containing all sets from $\mathbb{T}$ that are minimal w.r.t. $\subsetneq$. Therefore, a cover of the set of all subsumption modules also contains all subsumption justifications. We will use covers to characterise the output of our algorithms to ensure that all justifications have been computed.

The algorithms expect the input terminologies to be normalised. Thus, we have to normalise our terminologies first if they are not yet normalised (cf. Sect. 2). The denormalisation function δ_T that we obtain from the process of normalisation is then applied to the outputs of the algorithms to obtain the subsumer and subsumee justifications of the original terminology. More precisely, each subsumer or subsumee justification $\mathcal{M} = \{\beta_1, \ldots, \beta_n\}$ of the normalised terminology is transformed into the set $\{\{\gamma\} \mid \gamma \in \delta_{\mathcal{T}}(\beta_1)\} \otimes \ldots \otimes \{\{\gamma\} \mid \gamma \in \delta_{\mathcal{T}}(\beta_n)\}$ to obtain subsumer or subsumee justifications of the original terminology, respectively. In what follows we assume that $\mathcal{T}$, $\mathcal{T}_1$, and $\mathcal{T}_2$ are acyclic normalised $\mathcal{ELH}$-terminologies.

4.1   Computing Subsumer Justifications

The algorithm for computing subsumer justifications relies on the notion of a subsumer simulation between terminologies from [7,18], which we introduce first.

Definition 4 (Subsumer Simulation). *A relation* $S \subseteq sig^{N_C}(\mathcal{T}_1) \times sig^{N_C}(\mathcal{T}_2)$ *is called a Σ-subsumer simulation from $\mathcal{T}_1$ to $\mathcal{T}_2$ if the following conditions hold:*

$(S_1^{\rightarrow})$ *if* $(X_1, X_2) \in S$, *then for every* $B \in \Sigma$ *with* $\mathcal{T}_1 \models X_1 \sqsubseteq B$ *it holds that* $\mathcal{T}_2 \models X_2 \sqsubseteq B$; *and*

$(S_2^{\rightarrow})$ *if* $(X_1, X_2) \in S$, *then for each* $Y_1 \bowtie_1 \exists r.Z_1 \in \mathcal{T}_1$ *with* $\mathcal{T}_1 \models X_1 \sqsubseteq Y_1$, $\mathcal{T}_1 \models r \sqsubseteq s$, $s \in \Sigma$, $\bowtie_1 \in \{\sqsubseteq, \equiv\}$, *there exists* $Y_2 \bowtie_2 \exists r'.Z_2 \in \mathcal{T}_2$ *with* $\mathcal{T}_2 \models X_2 \sqsubseteq Y_2$, $\bowtie_2 \in \{\sqsubseteq, \equiv\}$, $\mathcal{T}_2 \models r' \sqsubseteq s$, *and* $(Z_1, Z_2) \in S$.

We write $sim_{\rightarrow}^{\Sigma}([\mathcal{T}_1, X_1], [\mathcal{T}_2, X_2])$ *iff there is a Σ-subsumer simulation S from $\mathcal{T}_1$ to $\mathcal{T}_2$ with $(X_1, X_2) \in S$; and in the case of $\mathcal{T}_2 \subseteq \mathcal{T}_1$ we write* $sim_{\rightarrow}^{\mathcal{T}_1, \Sigma}(X_1, X_2)$.

A subsumer simulation conveniently captures the set of subsumers in the following sense: If a Σ-subsumer simulation from $\mathcal{T}_1$ to $\mathcal{T}_2$ contains the pair (X_1, X_2), then X_2 entails w.r.t. $\mathcal{T}_2$ all subsumers of X_1 w.r.t. $\mathcal{T}_1$ that are formulated in the signature Σ. Formally, we obtain the following theorem from [18].

Theorem 3. *It holds that* $sim_{\rightarrow}^{\Sigma}([\mathcal{T}_1, X_1], [\mathcal{T}_2, X_2])$ *iff for all* $D \in \mathcal{ELH}_{\Sigma}$: $\mathcal{T}_1 \models X_1 \sqsubseteq D$ *implies* $\mathcal{T}_2 \models X_2 \sqsubseteq D$.

Guided by the subsumer simulation notion, we can device our algorithm for computing subsumer justifications. Algorithm 2 computes the subsumer justifications for an acyclic normalised $\mathcal{ELH}$-terminology $\mathcal{T}$, a signature Σ, and a concept name X. Lines 3–10 of the algorithm compute all $\langle X, \Sigma \rangle$-subsumption modules of $\mathcal{T}$. To ensure that the returned modules are minimal w.r.t. $\subsetneq$, the algorithm calls the function $\text{Minimise}_{\subseteq}(\mathbb{M}_X)$ in Line 11, which removes any set in $\mathbb{M}_X$ that is not minimal.

We illustrate Algorithm 2 (Fig. 3) with the following two examples. First example, let $\mathcal{T} = \{X \sqsubseteq B, X \sqsubseteq Y, Y \sqsubseteq B\}$ and $\Sigma = \{B\}$. Consider the execution of $\text{COVER}_{\rightarrow}(\mathcal{T}, X, \Sigma)$. In Line 4, $\mathbb{M}_X^{\rightarrow}$ is set to $\text{Just}_{\mathcal{T}}(X \sqsubseteq B)$, where $\text{Just}_{\mathcal{T}}(X \sqsubseteq B) = \{\{X \sqsubseteq B\}, \{X \sqsubseteq Y, Y \sqsubseteq B\}\}$. Since there are no axioms of the form $Y \sqsubseteq \exists r.Z \in \mathcal{T}$ or $Y \equiv \exists r.Z \in \mathcal{T}$, the lines 5–10 have no effect. Finally, the algorithm returns $\mathbb{M}_X^{\rightarrow}$ in Line 11.

For the second example, let $\mathcal{T} = \{\alpha_1, \alpha_2, \alpha_3, \alpha_4, \alpha_5\}$ and $\Sigma = \{A, B, s\}$, where $\alpha_1 = X \sqsubseteq \exists r.A$, $\alpha_2 = X \sqsubseteq \exists r.B$, $\alpha_3 = X \sqsubseteq \exists r.Y$, $\alpha_4 = Y \equiv A \sqcap B$, and $\alpha_5 = r \sqsubseteq s$. We consider again the execution of $\text{COVER}_{\rightarrow}(\mathcal{T}, X, \Sigma)$. We

Algorithm 2: Computing a Cover of all Subsumer Justifications

1 **function** COVER$_\rightarrow$ $(\mathcal{T}, X, \Sigma)$
2 $\quad$ $\mathrm{M}_X^\rightarrow = \{\emptyset\}$
3 $\quad$ **for every** $B \in \Sigma \cap \mathsf{N_C}$ *such that* $\mathcal{T} \models X \sqsubseteq B$ **do**
4 $\quad\quad$ $\mathrm{M}_X^\rightarrow := \mathrm{M}_X^\rightarrow \otimes \mathrm{Just}_\mathcal{T}(X \sqsubseteq B)$
5 $\quad$ **for every** $Y \bowtie_1 \exists r.Z \in \mathcal{T}$ $(\bowtie_1 \in \{\sqsubseteq, \equiv\})$ *and* $s \in \Sigma \cap \mathsf{N_R}$ *such that* $\mathcal{T} \models X \sqsubseteq Y$ *and* $\mathcal{T} \models r \sqsubseteq s$ **do**
6 $\quad\quad$ $\mathrm{M}_{\exists s.Z}^\rightarrow := \emptyset$
7 $\quad\quad$ **for every** $Y' \bowtie_2 \exists r'.Z' \in \mathcal{T}$ $(\bowtie_2 \in \{\sqsubseteq, \equiv\})$ *such that* $\mathcal{T} \models X \sqsubseteq Y'$, $\mathcal{T} \models r' \sqsubseteq s$, *and* $\mathrm{sim}_\rightarrow^{\mathcal{T},\Sigma}(Z, Z')$ **do**
8 $\quad\quad\quad$ $\mathrm{M}_{Z'}^\rightarrow := \mathrm{COVER}_\rightarrow(\mathcal{T}, Z', \Sigma)$
9 $\quad\quad\quad$ $\mathrm{M}_{\exists s.Z}^\rightarrow := \mathrm{M}_{\exists r.Z}^\rightarrow \cup (\{\{Y' \bowtie_2 \exists r'.Z'\}\} \otimes \mathrm{M}_{Z'}^\rightarrow \otimes \mathrm{Just}_\mathcal{T}(X \sqsubseteq Y') \otimes \mathrm{Just}_\mathcal{T}(r' \sqsubseteq s))$
10 $\quad\quad$ $\mathrm{M}_X^\rightarrow := \mathrm{M}_X^\rightarrow \otimes \mathrm{M}_{\exists s.Z}^\rightarrow$
11 $\quad$ **return** $\mathrm{Minimise}_\subseteq(\mathrm{M}_X^\rightarrow)$

Algorithm 3: Computing a Cover of all Subsumee Justifications – Conjunctive Case

1 **function** COVER$_\leftarrow^\sqcap$ $(\mathcal{T}_1, X_1, \Sigma, \mathcal{T}_2, X_2)$
2 $\quad$ **let** $\alpha_{X_1} := X_1 \equiv Y_1 \sqcap \ldots \sqcap Y_m \in \mathcal{T}_1$
3 $\quad$ $\mathrm{M}_{(X_1, X_2)}^\leftarrow := \emptyset$
4 $\quad$ **for** $\Gamma \in \mathit{DefForest}_{\mathcal{T}_2}^\sqcap(X_2)$ **do**
5 $\quad\quad$ Let $\delta_\Gamma := \{\mathrm{def}_{\mathcal{T}_2}^\sqcap(X') \mid X' \in \mathrm{leaves}(\Gamma) \cap \mathrm{def}_{\mathcal{T}_2}^\sqcap \}$
6 $\quad\quad$ $\mathrm{M}_\Gamma^\leftarrow := \{\Gamma\}$
7 $\quad\quad$ **for** $X_2' \in \mathrm{leaves}(\Gamma)$ **do**
8 $\quad\quad\quad$ $\mathrm{M}_{X_2'}^\leftarrow := \emptyset$
9 $\quad\quad\quad$ **for every** $X_1' \in \mathit{non\text{-}conj}_{\mathcal{T}_1}(X_1)$ **do**
10 $\quad\quad\quad\quad$ **if** $\mathrm{sim}_\leftarrow^\Sigma([\mathcal{T}_1, X_1'], [\mathcal{T}_2 \setminus \delta_\Gamma, X_2'])$ **then**
11 $\quad\quad\quad\quad\quad$ $\mathrm{M}_{X_2'}^\leftarrow := \mathrm{M}_{X_2'}^\leftarrow \cup \mathrm{COVER}_\leftarrow(\mathcal{T}_1, X_1', \Sigma, \mathcal{T}_2 \setminus \delta_\Gamma, X_2')$
12 $\quad\quad\quad$ $\mathrm{M}_\Gamma^\leftarrow := \mathrm{M}_\Gamma^\leftarrow \otimes \mathrm{M}_{X_2'}^\leftarrow$
13 $\quad\quad$ $\mathrm{M}_{(X_1, X_2)}^\leftarrow := \mathrm{M}_{(X_1, X_2)}^\leftarrow \cup \mathrm{M}_\Gamma^\leftarrow$
14 $\quad$ **return** $\mathrm{M}_{(X_1, X_2)}^\leftarrow$

Algorithm 4: Computing a Cover of all Subsumee Justifications

1 **function** COVER$_\leftarrow$ $(\mathcal{T}_1, X_1, \Sigma, \mathcal{T}_2, X_2)$
2 $\quad$ **if** X_1 *is not* Σ-entailed w.r.t. $\mathcal{T}_1$ **then**
3 $\quad\quad$ **return** $\{\emptyset\}$
4 $\quad$ $\mathrm{M}_{(X_1, X_2)}^\leftarrow := \mathrm{COVER}_\leftarrow^{\mathsf{N_C}}(\mathcal{T}_1, X_1, \Sigma, \mathcal{T}_2, X_2)$
5 $\quad$ **if** X_1 *is not complex* Σ-entailed in $\mathcal{T}_1$ **then**
6 $\quad\quad$ **return** $\mathrm{M}_{(X_1, X_2)}^\leftarrow$
7 $\quad$ **if** $X_1 \equiv \exists r.Y \in \mathcal{T}_1$, *and* r, Y *are* Σ-entailed w.r.t. $\mathcal{T}_1$ **then**
8 $\quad\quad$ $\mathrm{M}_{(X_1, X_2)}^\leftarrow := \mathrm{M}_{(X_1, X_2)}^\leftarrow \otimes \mathrm{COVER}_\leftarrow^\exists(\mathcal{T}_1, X_1, \Sigma, \mathcal{T}_2, X_2)$
9 $\quad$ **else if** $X_1 \equiv Y_1 \sqcap \ldots \sqcap Y_m \in \mathcal{T}_1$ **then**
10 $\quad\quad$ $\mathrm{M}_{(X_1, X_2)}^\leftarrow := \mathrm{M}_{(X_1, X_2)}^\leftarrow \otimes \mathrm{COVER}_\leftarrow^\sqcap(\mathcal{T}_1, X_1, \Sigma, \mathcal{T}_2, X_2)$
11 $\quad$ **return** $\mathrm{Minimise}_\subseteq(\mathrm{M}_{(X_1, X_2)}^\leftarrow)$

Algorithm 5: Computing a Cover of all Subsumee Justifications – Local Case

1 **function** COVER$_\leftarrow^{\mathsf{N_C}}$ $(\mathcal{T}_1, X_1, \Sigma, \mathcal{T}_2, X_2)$
2 $\quad$ $\mathrm{M}_{(X_1, X_2)}^\leftarrow = \{\emptyset\}$
3 $\quad$ **for** *every* $B \in \Sigma \cap \mathsf{N_C}$ *such that* $\mathcal{T}_1 \models B \sqsubseteq X_1$ **do**
4 $\quad\quad$ $\mathrm{M}_{(X_1, X_2)}^\leftarrow := \mathrm{M}_{(X_1, X_2)}^\leftarrow \otimes \mathrm{Just}_{\mathcal{T}_2}(B \sqsubseteq X_2)$
5 $\quad$ **return** $\mathrm{M}_{(X_1, X_2)}^\leftarrow$

Algorithm 6: Computing a Cover of all Subsumee Justifications – Existential Case

1 **function** COVER$_\leftarrow^\exists$ $(\mathcal{T}_1, X_1, \Sigma, \mathcal{T}_2, X_2)$
2 $\quad$ Let $\alpha_{X_1} := X_1 \equiv \exists r.Y_1 \in \mathcal{T}_1$
3 $\quad$ $\mathrm{M}_{(X_1, X_2)}^\leftarrow := \{\mathrm{max\text{-}tree}_{\mathcal{T}_2}^\sqcap(X_2)\}$
4 $\quad$ **for every** $s \in \Sigma \cap \mathsf{N_R}$ *such that* $\mathcal{T}_1 \models s \sqsubseteq r$ **do**
5 $\quad\quad$ $\mathrm{M}_{(X_1, X_2)}^\leftarrow := \mathrm{M}_{(X_1, X_2)}^\leftarrow \otimes \mathrm{Just}_{\mathcal{T}_2}(s \sqsubseteq r)$
6 $\quad$ **for every** $X_2' \in \mathit{non\text{-}conj}_{\mathcal{T}_2}(X_2)$ **do**
7 $\quad\quad$ Let $\alpha_{X_2'} := X_2' \equiv \exists s.Y_2' \in \mathcal{T}_2$
8 $\quad\quad$ $\mathrm{M}_{Y_2'}^\leftarrow := \mathrm{COVER}_\leftarrow(\mathcal{T}_1, Y_1, \Sigma, \mathcal{T}_2, Y_2')$
9 $\quad\quad$ $\mathrm{M}_{(X_1, X_2)}^\leftarrow := \mathrm{M}_{(X_1, X_2)}^\leftarrow \otimes \{\{\alpha_{X_2'}\}\} \otimes \mathrm{M}_{Y_2'}^\leftarrow$
10 $\quad$ **return** $\mathrm{M}_{(X_1, X_2)}^\leftarrow$

Fig. 3. Algorithms of computing subsumer and subsumee justifications

proceed to Line 5 as there are no concept names in Σ entailed by X w.r.t. $\mathcal{T}$. However, the concepts $\exists r.A$, $\exists r.B$ and $\exists r.Y$ are entailed by X w.r.t. $\mathcal{T}$. It holds that $\mathrm{sim}_\rightarrow^{\mathcal{T},\Sigma}(Z, Z')$ for every $(Z, Z') \in \{(A, A), (B, B), (Y, Y), (A, Y), (B, Y)\}$, whereas $\mathrm{sim}_\rightarrow^{\mathcal{T},\Sigma}(Z, Z')$ does not hold for any $(Z, Z') \in \{(A, B), (B, A), (Y, A), (Y, B)\}$. Therefore, for every $Z \in \{A, B, Y\}$ the recursive call $\mathrm{COVER}_\rightarrow(\mathcal{T}, \Sigma, Z)$ is made in Line 8. The following sets are computed in lines 6–10: $\mathrm{M}_A^\rightarrow = \{\emptyset\}$, $\mathrm{M}_B^\rightarrow = \{\emptyset\}$, and $\mathrm{M}_Y^\rightarrow = \{\{\alpha_4\}\}$ as well as

$$\mathrm{M}_{\exists s.A}^{\rightarrow} = (\{\alpha_1, \alpha_5\} \otimes \mathrm{M}_A^{\rightarrow}) \cup (\{\alpha_3, \alpha_5\} \otimes \mathrm{M}_Y^{\rightarrow}) = \{\{\alpha_1, \alpha_5\}, \{\alpha_3, \alpha_4, \alpha_5\}\}$$
$$\mathrm{M}_{\exists s.B}^{\rightarrow} = (\{\alpha_2, \alpha_5\} \otimes \mathrm{M}_B^{\rightarrow}) \cup (\{\alpha_3, \alpha_5\} \otimes \mathrm{M}_Y^{\rightarrow}) = \{\{\alpha_2, \alpha_5\}, \{\alpha_3, \alpha_4, \alpha_5\}\}$$
$$\mathrm{M}_{\exists s.Y}^{\rightarrow} = \{\alpha_3, \alpha_5\} \otimes \mathrm{M}_Y^{\rightarrow} = \{\{\alpha_3, \alpha_4, \alpha_5\}\}$$
$$\mathrm{M}_X^{\rightarrow} = \mathrm{M}_{\exists r.A}^{\rightarrow} \otimes \mathrm{M}_{\exists s.B}^{\rightarrow} \otimes \mathrm{M}_{\exists r.Y}^{\rightarrow} = \{\{\alpha_3, \alpha_4, \alpha_5\}\}.$$

Finally, $\mathrm{COVER}_{\rightarrow}(\mathcal{T}, X, \Sigma)$ returns $\mathrm{Minimise}_{\subseteq}(\mathrm{M}_X^{\rightarrow}) = \{\{\alpha_3, \alpha_4, \alpha_5\}\}$ in Line 11.

The following theorem shows that Algorithm 2 indeed computes the set of subsumer modules, thus producing a cover of subsumer justifications.

Theorem 4. *Let* $\mathrm{M}_X^{\rightarrow} := \mathrm{COVER}_{\rightarrow}(\mathcal{T}, X, \Sigma)$. *Then* $\mathrm{M}_X^{\rightarrow}$ *is a cover of the set of* $\langle X, \Sigma \rangle$*-subsumer justifications of* $\mathcal{T}$.

Observe that $\mathrm{COVER}_{\rightarrow}(\mathcal{T}, X, \Sigma)$ may be called several times during the execution of Algorithm 2. The algorithm can be optimised by caching the return value of the first execution, and retrieving it from memory for subsequent calls.

4.2   Computing Subsumee Justifications

The algorithm for computing subsumee justifications relies on the notion of subsumee simulation between terminologies [7,18]. First we present some auxiliary notions for handling conjunctions on the left-hand side of subsumptions.

We define for each concept name X a so-called *definitorial forest* consisting of sets of axioms of the form $Y \equiv Y_1 \sqcap \ldots \sqcap Y_n$ which can be thought of as forming *trees*. Any $\langle X, \Sigma \rangle$-subsumee justification contains the axioms of a selection of these trees, i.e., one tree for every conjunction formulated over Σ that entails X w.r.t. $\mathcal{T}$. Formally, we define a set of a $\mathrm{DefForest}_{\mathcal{T}}^{\sqcap}(X) \subseteq 2^{\mathcal{T}}$ to be the smallest set closed under the following conditions: $\emptyset \in \mathrm{DefForest}_{\mathcal{T}}^{\sqcap}(X)$; $\{\alpha\} \in \mathrm{DefForest}_{\mathcal{T}}^{\sqcap}(X)$ for $\alpha = X \equiv X_1 \sqcap \ldots \sqcap X_n \in \mathcal{T}$; and $\Gamma \cup \{\alpha\} \in \mathrm{DefForest}_{\mathcal{T}}^{\sqcap}(X)$ for $\Gamma \in \mathrm{DefForest}_{\mathcal{T}}^{\sqcap}(X)$ with $Z \equiv Z_1 \sqcap \ldots \sqcap Z_k \in \Gamma$ and $\alpha = Z_i \equiv Z_i^1 \sqcap \ldots \sqcap Z_i^n \in \mathcal{T}$. Given $\Gamma \in \mathrm{DefForest}_{\mathcal{T}}^{\sqcap}(X)$, we set $\mathrm{leaves}(\Gamma) := \mathrm{sig}(\Gamma) \setminus \{X \in \mathrm{sig}(C) \mid X \equiv C \in \Gamma\}$ if $\Gamma \neq \emptyset$; and $\{X\}$ otherwise. We denote the maximal element of $\mathrm{DefForest}_{\mathcal{T}}^{\sqcap}(X)$ w.r.t. $\subseteq$ with $\mathrm{max\text{-}tree}_{\mathcal{T}}^{\sqcap}(X)$. Finally, we set $\mathrm{non\text{-}conj}_{\mathcal{T}}(X) := \mathrm{leaves}(\mathrm{max\text{-}tree}_{\mathcal{T}}^{\sqcap}(X))$.

For example, let $\mathcal{T} = \{\alpha_1, \alpha_2, \alpha_3\}$, where $\alpha_1 = X \equiv Y \sqcap Z$, $\alpha_2 = Y \equiv Y_1 \sqcap Y_2$, and $\alpha_3 = Z \equiv Z_1 \sqcap Z_2$. Then $\mathrm{DefForest}_{\mathcal{T}}^{\sqcap}(X) = \{\emptyset, \{\alpha_1\}, \{\alpha_1, \alpha_2\}, \{\alpha_1, \alpha_3\}, \{\alpha_1, \alpha_2, \alpha_3\}\}$. We have that $\mathrm{leaves}(\{\alpha_1, \alpha_3\}) = \{Y, Z_1, Z_2\}$, $\mathrm{max\text{-}tree}_{\mathcal{T}}^{\sqcap}(X) = \{\alpha_1, \alpha_2, \alpha_3\}$, and $\mathrm{non\text{-}conj}_{\mathcal{T}}(X) = \{Y_1, Y_2, Z_1, Z_2\}$.

We say that $X \in \mathsf{N_C}$ is *Σ-entailed w.r.t.* $\mathcal{T}$ iff there exists $C \in \mathcal{EL}_\Sigma$ with $\mathcal{T} \models C \sqsubseteq X$. We say that $r \in \mathsf{N_R}$ is *Σ-entailed w.r.t.* $\mathcal{T}$ iff there exists $s \in \Sigma \cap \mathsf{N_R}$ with $\mathcal{T} \models s \sqsubseteq r$. Moreover, we say that X is *complex Σ-entailed w.r.t.* $\mathcal{T}$ iff for every $Y \in \mathrm{non\text{-}conj}_{\mathcal{T}}(X)$ one of the following conditions holds:

(i) there exists $B \in \Sigma$ such that $\mathcal{T} \models B \sqsubseteq Y$ and $\mathcal{T} \not\models B \sqsubseteq X$;
(ii) there exists $Y \equiv \exists r.Z \in \mathcal{T}$ such that r and Z are both Σ-entailed in $\mathcal{T}$.

For example, let $\mathcal{T} = \{X \equiv X_1 \sqcap X_2, B_1 \sqsubseteq X_1, X_2 \equiv \exists r.Z, B_2 \sqsubseteq Z, s \sqsubseteq r\}$. We have that non-conj$_{\mathcal{T}}(X) = \{X_1, X_2\}$, then r is Σ-entailed w.r.t. $\mathcal{T}$; X is complex Σ-entailed w.r.t. $\mathcal{T}$ for $\Sigma = \{B_1, B_2, s\}$; but X is not complex Σ'-entailed w.r.t. $\mathcal{T}$, where Σ' ranges over $\{B_1, B_2\}, \{B_1, s\}, \{B_2, s\}$. Additionally, X is not complex Σ-entailed w.r.t. $\mathcal{T} \cup \{B_1 \sqsubseteq X\}$.

Definition 5 (Subsumee Simulation). *We say that a relation $S \subseteq$ $sig^{\mathsf{N_C}}(\mathcal{T}_1) \times sig^{\mathsf{N_C}}(\mathcal{T}_2)$ is a Σ-subsumee simulation from $\mathcal{T}_1$ to $\mathcal{T}_2$ iff the following conditions are satisfied:*

$(S_1^{\leftarrow})$ *if $(X_1, X_2) \in S$, then for every $B \in \Sigma$ with $\mathcal{T}_1 \models B \sqsubseteq X_1$ it holds that $\mathcal{T}_2 \models B \sqsubseteq X_2$;*

$(S_2^{\leftarrow})$ *if $(X_1, X_2) \in S$ and $X_1 \equiv \exists r.Y_1 \in \mathcal{T}_1$ such that $\mathcal{T}_1 \models s \sqsubseteq r, s \in \Sigma$ and Y_1 is Σ-entailed in $\mathcal{T}_1$, then for every $X_2' \in$ non-conj$_{\mathcal{T}_2}(X_2)$ there exists $X_2' \equiv \exists r'.Y_2 \in \mathcal{T}_2$, such that $(Y_1, Y_2) \in S$ and $\mathcal{T}_2 \models s \sqsubseteq r'$;*

$(S_3^{\leftarrow})$ *if $(X_1, X_2) \in S$ and $X_1 \equiv Y_1 \sqcap \ldots \sqcap Y_n \in \mathcal{T}_1$, then for every $X_2' \in$ non-conj$_{\mathcal{T}_2}(X_2)$ there exists $X_1' \in$ non-conj$_{\mathcal{T}_1}(X_1)$ with $(X_1', X_2') \in S$.*

We write $\mathrm{sim}_{\leftarrow}^{\Sigma}([\mathcal{T}_1, X_1], [\mathcal{T}_2, X_2])$ iff there exists a Σ-subsumee simulation S from $\mathcal{T}_1$ to $\mathcal{T}_2$ with $(X_1, X_2) \in S$. Moreover, we write $\mathrm{sim}_{\leftarrow}^{\mathcal{T}_1, \Sigma}(X_1, X_2)$ iff there exists a Σ-subsumee simulation S from $\mathcal{T}_1$ to $\mathcal{T}_1$ with $(X_1, X_2) \in S$.

Analogously to subsumer simulations, a subsumee simulation captures the set of subsumees as it is made precise in the following theorem from [18].

Theorem 5. *It holds that $\mathrm{sim}_{\leftarrow}^{\Sigma}([\mathcal{T}_1, X_1], [\mathcal{T}_2, X_2])$ iff for every $D \in \mathcal{ELH}_{\Sigma}$: $\mathcal{T}_1 \models D \sqsubseteq X_1$ implies $\mathcal{T}_2 \models D \sqsubseteq X_2$.*

Using the notion of a subsumee simulation, we can device Algorithm 4 for computing a cover of the subsumee justifications for a given $\mathcal{ELH}$-terminology $\mathcal{T}$, a concept name X, and a signature Σ. The correct function call for obtaining the $\langle X, \Sigma \rangle$-subsumee justifications of $\mathcal{T}$ is $\mathrm{COVER}_{\leftarrow}(\mathcal{T}, X, \Sigma, \mathcal{T}, X)$. Note that Algorithms 3, 5, and 6 are called as subroutines in Line 4, 8 and 10 in Algorithm 4. The four different parameters for Algorithm 4 are needed due to the recursive calls in Algorithm 3 (Line 11) and Algorithm 6 (Line 8).

We illustrate Algorithm 4 with the following example. Let $\mathcal{T} = \{X \equiv \exists r.Y, Y \equiv \exists s.Z, Z \equiv A \sqcap Z', A \sqsubseteq B, B \sqsubseteq Z', Z' \sqsubseteq A\}$ be an $\mathcal{EL}$-terminology, and let $\Sigma = \{A, B, r, s\}$ be a signature. It can easily be seen that $\mathcal{T}$ is normalised. Consider the execution of $\mathrm{COVER}_{\leftarrow}(\mathcal{T}, X, \Sigma, \mathcal{T}, X)$. As X is (complex) Σ-entailed, $\mathrm{COVER}_{\leftarrow}^{\mathsf{N_C}}(\mathcal{T}, X, \Sigma, \mathcal{T}, X)$ is called in Line 4. The for-loop in lines 3–4 of Algorithm 5 does not apply as $\mathcal{T} \not\models A \sqsubseteq X$ and $\mathcal{T} \not\models B \sqsubseteq X$. We obtain $\mathrm{COVER}_{\leftarrow}^{\mathsf{N_C}}(\mathcal{T}, X, \Sigma, \mathcal{T}, X) = \{\emptyset\}$ backtracking to Line 4 of $\mathrm{COVER}_{\leftarrow}(\mathcal{T}, X, \Sigma, \mathcal{T}, X)$. The if-statement in Line 7 applies as $\mathcal{T}$ contains an axiom of the form $X \equiv \exists r.Y$, where X and r are each Σ-entailed. We proceed with $\mathrm{COVER}_{\leftarrow}^{\exists}(\mathcal{T}, X, \Sigma, \mathcal{T}, X)$ in Line 8. We obtain $\mathbb{M}_{(X,X)}^{\leftarrow} :=$ $\{\text{max-tree}_{\mathcal{T}}^{\sqcap}(X)\} = \{\emptyset\}$ in Line 3 of Algorithm 6. Since non-conj$_{\mathcal{T}}(X) = \{X\}$ and $X \equiv \exists r.Y \in \mathcal{T}$, the recursive call $\mathrm{COVER}_{\leftarrow}(\mathcal{T}, Y, \Sigma, \mathcal{T}, Y)$ in Line 8 of Algorithm 6 is made.

Then, in Line 8 of Algorithm 4, $\text{COVER}_{\leftarrow}^{\exists}(\mathcal{T}, Y, \Sigma, \mathcal{T}, Y)$ is called as Y is complex Σ-entailed w.r.t. $\mathcal{T}$, $Y \equiv \exists s.Z \in \mathcal{T}$, and s, Z are each Σ-entailed.

Similar to $\text{COVER}_{\leftarrow}^{\exists}(\mathcal{T}, X, \Sigma, \mathcal{T}, X)$, the execution of $\text{COVER}_{\leftarrow}^{\exists}(\mathcal{T}, Y, \Sigma, \mathcal{T}, Y)$ invokes $\text{COVER}_{\leftarrow}(\mathcal{T}, Z, \Sigma, \mathcal{T}, Z)$ from Line 8 of Algorithm 6.

As Z is Σ-entailed w.r.t. $\mathcal{T}$, we have that $\text{COVER}_{\leftarrow}^{\mathsf{Nc}}(\mathcal{T}, Z, \Sigma, \mathcal{T}, Z)$ is executed. The for-loop in Line 3 of Algorithm 5 applies as $\mathcal{T} \models A \sqsubseteq Z$ and $\mathcal{T} \models B \sqsubseteq Z$ so that we have $\mathrm{M}_Z^{\leftarrow} := \text{Just}_{\mathcal{T}}(A \sqsubseteq Z) \otimes \text{Just}_{\mathcal{T}}(B \sqsubseteq Z)$, where $\text{Just}_{\mathcal{T}}(A \sqsubseteq Z) = \text{Just}_{\mathcal{T}}(B \sqsubseteq Z) = \{Z \equiv A \sqcap Z', A \sqsubseteq B, B \sqsubseteq Z', Z' \sqsubseteq A\}$. This finishes the call $\text{COVER}_{\leftarrow}^{\mathsf{Nc}}(\mathcal{T}, Z, \Sigma, \mathcal{T}, Z)$, and we backtract to Line 4 of $\text{COVER}_{\leftarrow}(\mathcal{T}, Z, \Sigma, \mathcal{T}, Z)$. As Z is not complex Σ-entailed, this finishes the call $\text{COVER}_{\leftarrow}(\mathcal{T}, Z, \Sigma, \mathcal{T}, Z)$ with $\mathrm{M}_Z^{\leftarrow} = \{Z \equiv A \sqcap Z', A \sqsubseteq B, B \sqsubseteq Z', Z' \sqsubseteq A\}$.

We backtrack to Line 8 of $\text{COVER}_{\leftarrow}^{\exists}(\mathcal{T}, Y, \Sigma, \mathcal{T}, Y)$ and set $\mathrm{M}_Y^{\leftarrow} := \mathrm{M}_Y^{\leftarrow} \otimes \{\{Y \equiv \exists s.Z\}\} \otimes \mathrm{M}_Z^{\leftarrow}$ which yields $\mathrm{M}_Y^{\leftarrow} = \{\{Y \equiv \exists s.Z, Z \equiv A \sqcap Z', A \sqsubseteq B, B \sqsubseteq Z', Z' \sqsubseteq A\}\}$. This finishes the call $\text{COVER}_{\leftarrow}^{\exists}(\mathcal{T}, Y, \Sigma, \mathcal{T}, Y)$ and it backtracks to Line 8 and ends the call $\text{COVER}_{\leftarrow}(\mathcal{T}, Y, \Sigma, \mathcal{T}, Y)$. We set $\mathrm{M}_X^{\leftarrow} := \mathrm{M}_X^{\leftarrow} \otimes \{\{X \equiv \exists r.Y\}\} \otimes \mathrm{M}_Y^{\leftarrow}$ in Line 9 of Algorithm 6 for $\text{COVER}_{\leftarrow}^{\exists}(\mathcal{T}, X, \Sigma, \mathcal{T}, X)$. Thus $\text{COVER}_{\leftarrow}^{\exists}(\mathcal{T}, X, \Sigma, \mathcal{T}, X)$ returns $\mathrm{M}_X^{\leftarrow} = \{\{X \equiv \exists r.Y, Y \equiv \exists s.Z, Z \equiv A \sqcap Z', A \sqsubseteq B, B \sqsubseteq Z', Z' \sqsubseteq A\}\}$ and we backtrack to Line 10 of Algorithm 4. Finally, all sets that are not minimal w.r.t. $\subsetneq$ are removed from $\mathrm{M}_X^{\leftarrow}$ in Line 11, which ends the execution of $\text{COVER}_{\leftarrow}(\mathcal{T}, X, \Sigma, \mathcal{T}, X)$.

The following theorem shows that Algorithm 4 indeed computes a cover of the set of subsumee modules. Thus every subsumee justification is guaranteed to be among the computed sets of axioms.

Theorem 6. *Let* $\mathrm{M}_X^{\leftarrow} := \text{COVER}_{\leftarrow}(\mathcal{T}, X, \Sigma, \mathcal{T}, X)$. *Then* $\mathrm{M}_X^{\leftarrow}$ *is the set of all* $\langle X, \Sigma \rangle$-*subsumee justifications of* $\mathcal{T}$.

5 Evaluation

We have implemented our algorithms for computing subsumption justifications, minimal (basic) modules, and best excerpts in Java. The performance of the implementation has been evaluated using the $\mathcal{EL}$-fragment of two prominent biomedical ontologies: Snomed CT (version Jan 2016), a terminology consisting of 317 891 axioms, and NCI (version 16.03d),[3] a terminology containing 165 341 axioms. To compute the sets $\text{Just}_{\mathcal{T}}(\alpha)$, we deployed the SAT-based tool BEACON [1], which uses an efficient group-MUS enumerator. To solve our partial Max-SAT problem, we made use of the system Sat4j [16]. All experiments were conducted with a timeout of 10 min on machines equipped with an Intel Xeon Core 4 Duo CPU running at 2.50 GHz and with 64 GiB of RAM.

Computation of all Subsumption Justifications. Table 1 shows the results obtained for computing all subsumption justifications. The first row indicates the ontology used in each experiment. The experiments are divided into four categories according to the numbers of concept and role names included in an

---

[3] http://evs.nci.nih.gov/ftp1/NCI_Thesaurus.

Table 1. The statistics of experiments on computing all subsumption justifications for signatures generated at random, 1000 signatures of each size (minimal/maximal/median/standard deviation)

Ontologies	Snomed CT		NCI	
$(|\Sigma \cap N_C|, |\Sigma \cap N_R|)$	(10,10)	(30,10)	(10,10)	(30,10)
Nb. of all subsumption justifications	1.0/19.0/1.0/0.9	1.0/1328.0/1.0/10.7	1.0/136.0/1.0/3.5	1.0/7008.0/1.0/41.8
Card. of a subsumption justification	0.0/18.0/0.0/1.7	0.0/15.0/0.0/3.2	0.0/15.0/0.0/3.2	0.0/27.0/0.0/8.1
Success rate	88.7%	82.4%	84.8%	91.7%
Computation time (s)	0.2/519.7/0.4/59.2	0.7/576.3/1.6/28.5	0.2/472.4/1.3/66.9	0.2/577.3/7.6/97.0

Table 2. Percentage of computation time consumed by sub-task of the algorithm for computing subsumption justifications

Sub-task	JUST	Reasoner	Simulation check	others
Percentage (%)	94.60	1.79	1.57	2.04

input signature, as specified in the second row. For each category, we generated 1000 random signatures and computed the corresponding subsumption justifications for each concept name in the signature. Row 3 shows that multiple subsumption justifications can exist in real-world ontologies, e.g., there are 1328 subsumption justifications for a random signature consisting of 30 concept and 10 role names in Snomed CT. Meanwhile, Row 4 reports the cardinality of subsumption justifications, e.g., the largest one having 27 axioms for a signature of 30 concept and 10 role names from NCI. Row 5 shows that the subsumption justifications for more than 82.4% of random signatures can be computed within 10 mins, whereas the statics of the actual computation times is given in Row 6. Moreover, Table 2 details how the computation time was spent on different sub-tasks which determined the bottleneck of our tool. Indeed, 94.6% of the computation time was spent by BEACON on computing all justifications for concept name inclusions. Therefore, a considerable boost in performance of our tool can be expected by precomputing such justifications.

Computation of all Minimal Basic Modules. We compare our approach for computing all minimal basic modules with the search algorithm proposed in [5] in terms of computation time, as depicted in Fig. 4. The x-axis stands for the sizes of input ontologies. To obtain different sized input ontologies, we used random signatures to extract their MEX-modules [14], yielding 328 sub-ontologies of sizes ranging from 14 to 2271. Our method (red squares) was generally about 10 times faster than the search-based approach (blue triangles) except for 11 small sized input ontologies. This indicates that our approach is suitable for computing all minimal basic modules, esp. for large ontologies.

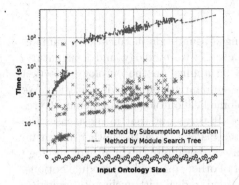

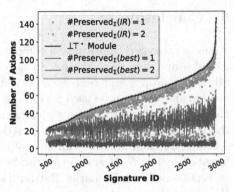

Fig. 4. Time comparison of computing minimal modules by our method (subsumption justification based approach, cf. Theorem 1) and the existing module search tree based approach [5] over different sized input ontologies (Color figure online)

Fig. 5. Comparison of the best excerpts (our approach) and the approximating excerpts (IR approach [4]) over 2500 signatures, each of which consists of a concept name from Snomed CT and its TOP-concept named *SNOMED CT Concept* (Color figure online)

Computation of Best Excerpts. We compare the size of locality based modules with the number of axioms in IR-excerpts [4] and best excerpts needed to preserve the same amount of knowledge. We denote with $\#\text{Preserved}_\Sigma(IR) = n$ and $\#\text{Preserved}_\Sigma(best) = n$, for $n \in \{1, 2\}$, the minimal number of axioms needed to preserve the knowledge of n concept names w.r.t. the signature Σ by an IR-excerpt and best excerpt, respectively. In this experiment, instead of using random signatures, we consider a scenario where a user searches for sub-ontologies of Snomed CT related to a particular concept name. We compute 2 500 different signatures each consisting of a concept name related to diseases, the TOP-concept and all role names of Snomed CT.

In Fig. 5, these 2 500 signatures are ranked increasingly by the sizes of their $\perp\top^*$-local modules (the black line) along the x-axis. The y-axis represents the number of axioms in the module and excerpts for a signature. The red (resp. green) line presents the sizes of best excerpts that preserve the knowledge for one (resp. two) concept names, i.e., $\#Preserved_\Sigma(best) = 1$ (resp. $\#Preserved_\Sigma(best) = 2$); similarly, the blue (resp. orange) dots for IR-excerpts. We can see that the red line is below all blue dots and the green line is below all orange dots. Consequently, the best excerpts are always smaller than IR-based excerpts for preserving same degree of information. In other words, best excerpts provide a more concise way to zoom in on an ontology. Our experiment also shows that our Max-SAT encoding works efficiently. After computing the subsumption justifications for all concept names in a signature, it only takes 0.15 s on average to compute best excerpts.

6   Conclusion

We have presented algorithms of computing subsumption justifications, minimal modules and best excerpts for an acyclic $\mathcal{ELH}$-terminology and a signature. Minimal modules and best excerpts can be applied in the ontology selection process and they can be used for ontology summarization and visualization. We have conducted an evaluation with large biomedical ontologies that demonstrates the viability of our algorithms in practice. It turns out that in most cases the set of all minimal modules can be computed faster than with another algorithm based on search [5]. Best excerpts can be used to evaluate the quality of ontology excerpts based on Information Retrieval or of other (incomplete) module notions. We expect that the algorithms can be extended to deal with cyclic terminologies, domain and range restrictions in order to be applicable for, e.g., linked data summarization by providing small sized basic modules.

References

1. Arif, M.F., Mencía, C., Ignatiev, A., Manthey, N., Peñaloza, R., Marques-Silva, J.: BEACON: an efficient SAT-based tool for debugging $\mathcal{EL}^+$ ontologies. In: Creignou, N., Le Berre, D. (eds.) SAT 2016. LNCS, vol. 9710, pp. 521–530. Springer, Cham (2016). doi:10.1007/978-3-319-40970-2_32
2. Baader, F., Calvanese, D., McGuinness, D.L., Nardi, D., Patel-Schneider, P.F.: The Description Logic Handbook: Theory, Implementation and Applications, 2nd edn. Cambridge University Press, Cambridge (2010)
3. Baader, F., Peñaloza, R., Suntisrivaraporn, B.: Pinpointing in the description logic $\mathcal{EL}^+$. In: Hertzberg, J., Beetz, M., Englert, R. (eds.) KI 2007. LNCS, vol. 4667, pp. 52–67. Springer, Heidelberg (2007). doi:10.1007/978-3-540-74565-5_7
4. Chen, J., Ludwig, M., Ma, Y., Walther, D.: Towards extracting ontology excerpts. In: Zhang, S., Wirsing, M., Zhang, Z. (eds.) KSEM 2015. LNCS (LNAI), vol. 9403, pp. 78–89. Springer, Cham (2015). doi:10.1007/978-3-319-25159-2_7
5. Chen, J., Ludwig, M., Walther, D.: On computing minimal EL-subsumption modules. In: Proceedings of WOMoCoE 2016 (2016)
6. Del Vescovo, C., Peñaloza, R.: Dealing with ontologies using cods. In: Proceedings of DL 2014, pp. 157–168 (2014)
7. Ecke, A., Ludwig, M., Walther, D.: The concept difference for EL-terminologies using hypergraphs. In: Proceedings of DChanges 2013 (2013)
8. Fu, Z.: Extending the Power of Boolean Satisfiability: techniques and applications. Ph.D. thesis, Princeton University (2007)
9. Grau, B.C., Horrocks, I., Kazakov, Y., Sattler, U.: Modular reuse of ontologies: theory and practice. JAIR 31(1), 273–318 (2008)
10. Kalyanpur, A., Parsia, B., Horridge, M., Sirin, E.: Finding all justifications of OWL DL entailments. In: Aberer, K., et al. (eds.) ASWC/ISWC -2007. LNCS, vol. 4825, pp. 267–280. Springer, Heidelberg (2007). doi:10.1007/978-3-540-76298-0_20
11. Kalyanpur, A., Parsia, B., Sirin, E., Hendler, J.A.: Debugging unsatisfiable classes in OWL ontologies. J. Web Semant. 3(4), 268–293 (2005)
12. Konev, B., Ludwig, M., Walther, D., Wolter, F.: The logical difference for the lightweight description logic EL. JAIR 44, 633–708 (2012)

13. Konev, B., Lutz, C., Walther, D., Wolter, F.: Semantic modularity and module extraction in description logics. In: Proceedings of ECAI 2008, pp. 55–59 (2008)
14. Konev, B., Lutz, C., Walther, D., Wolter, F.: Model-theoretic inseparability and modularity of description logic ontologies. Artif. Intell. **203**, 66–103 (2013)
15. Kontchakov, R., Pulina, L., Sattler, U., Schneider, T., Selmer, P., Wolter, F., Zakharyaschev, M.: Minimal module extraction from DL-lite ontologies using QBF solvers. In: Proceedings of DL 2009, pp. 836–841 (2009)
16. Le Berre, D., Parrain, A.: The Sat4j library, release 2.2. J. Satisf. Boolean Model. Comput. **7**(2–3), 59–64 (2010)
17. Ludwig, M.: Just: a tool for computing justifications w.r.t. ELH ontologies. In: Proceedings of ORE 2014, pp. 1–7 (2014)
18. Ludwig, M., Walther, D.: The logical difference for ELHr-terminologies using hypergraphs. In: Proceedings of ECAI 2014, pp. 555–560 (2014)
19. Lutz, C., Wolter, F.: Deciding inseparability and conservative extensions in the description logic EL. J. Symb. Comput. **45**(2), 194–228 (2010)
20. Martín-Recuerda, F., Walther, D.: Fast modularisation and atomic decomposition of ontologies using axiom dependency hypergraphs. In: Mika, P., et al. (eds.) ISWC 2014. LNCS, vol. 8797, pp. 49–64. Springer, Cham (2014). doi:10.1007/978-3-319-11915-1_4
21. Romero, A.A., Kaminski, M., Grau, B.C., Horrocks, I.: Module extraction in expressive ontology languages via datalog reasoning. JAIR **55**, 499–564 (2016)
22. Sattler, U., Schneider, T., Zakharyaschev, M.: Which kind of module should I extract?. In: Proceedings of DL 2009 (2009)
23. Schlicht, A., Stuckenschmidt, H.: Criteria-based partitioning of large ontologies. In: Proceedings of K-CAP 2007, pp. 171–172 (2007)
24. Sinz, C.: Towards an optimal CNF encoding of boolean cardinality constraints. In: Beek, P. (ed.) CP 2005. LNCS, vol. 3709, pp. 827–831. Springer, Heidelberg (2005). doi:10.1007/11564751_73
25. Troullinou, G., Kondylakis, H., Daskalaki, E., Plexousakis, D.: RDF digest: efficient summarization of RDF/S KBs. In: Gandon, F., Sabou, M., Sack, H., d'Amato, C., Cudré-Mauroux, P., Zimmermann, A. (eds.) ESWC 2015. LNCS, vol. 9088, pp. 119–134. Springer, Cham (2015). doi:10.1007/978-3-319-18818-8_8
26. Vescovo, C., Gessler, D.D.G., Klinov, P., Parsia, B., Sattler, U., Schneider, T., Winget, A.: Decomposition and modular structure of bioportal ontologies. In: Aroyo, L., Welty, C., Alani, H., Taylor, J., Bernstein, A., Kagal, L., Noy, N., Blomqvist, E. (eds.) ISWC 2011. LNCS, vol. 7031, pp. 130–145. Springer, Heidelberg (2011). doi:10.1007/978-3-642-25073-6_9
27. Vescovo, C.D., Parsia, B., Sattler, U.: Logical relevance in ontologies. In: Proceedings of DL 2012 (2012)
28. Vescovo, C.D., Parsia, B., Sattler, U., Schneider, T.: The modular structure of an ontology: atomic decomposition. In: Proceedings of IJCAI 2011, pp. 2232–2237 (2011)
29. Zhang, X., Cheng, G., Qu, Y.: Ontology summarization based on RDF sentence graph. In: Proceedings of WWW 2007, pp. 707–716 (2007)
30. Zhou, Z., Qi, G., Suntisrivaraporn, B.: A new method of finding all justifications in OWL 2 EL. In: Proceedings of WI 2013, pp. 213–220 (2013)

Global RDF Vector Space Embeddings

Michael Cochez[1,2,3]($\boxtimes$), Petar Ristoski[4], Simone Paolo Ponzetto[4], and Heiko Paulheim[4]

[1] Fraunhofer FIT, 53754 Sankt Augustin, Germany
michael.cochez@fit.fraunhofer.de
[2] Informatik 5, RWTH University Aachen, Aachen, Germany
[3] Faculty of Information Technology, University of Jyvaskyla, Jyväskylä, Finland
[4] Data and Web Science Group, University of Mannheim, Mannheim, Germany
{petar.ristoski,simone,heiko}@informatik.uni-mannheim.de

Abstract. Vector space embeddings have been shown to perform well when using RDF data in data mining and machine learning tasks. Existing approaches, such as RDF2Vec, use *local* information, i.e., they rely on local sequences generated for nodes in the RDF graph. For word embeddings, global techniques, such as *GloVe*, have been proposed as an alternative. In this paper, we show how the idea of global embeddings can be transferred to RDF embeddings, and show that the results are competitive with traditional local techniques like RDF2Vec.

Keywords: Graph embeddings · Linked open data · Data mining

1 Introduction

While RDF data is graph shaped by nature, most traditional data mining and machine learning software expect data to be in propositional form. Hence, to be used in machine learning and data mining pipelines, RDF data needs to be transformed to propositional feature vectors.

Recently, vector space embeddings have been proposed as a means to create low-dimensional feature vector representations of nodes in an RDF graphs. Inspired by techniques from NLP, such as word2vec [14], they train neural networks for automatically learning the mapping of RDF nodes to feature vectors. Vector space embeddings have been shown to outperform traditional methods for creating propositional feature vectors from RDF [22], e.g., in tasks like content-based recommender systems [24].

Unlike the first models for RDF vector space embeddings, which are based on paths, walks, or kernels, and therefore rely on *local* patterns, in this paper we present an approach in that exploits *global* patterns for creating vector space embeddings, inspired by the Global Vectors (GloVe) [20] approach for learning vector space embeddings for words from a text corpus. We show that using the GloVe approach on the same data as the older RDF2Vec approach does not improve the created embeddings. However, this approach is able to incorporate larger portions of the graph, without substantially increasing the computational

© Springer International Publishing AG 2017
C. d'Amato et al. (Eds.): ISWC 2017, Part I, LNCS 10587, pp. 190–207, 2017.
DOI: 10.1007/978-3-319-68288-4_12

time, leading to comparable results. The main contributions of this paper are this new embedding approach and an approach to approximate all-pairs Personalized PageRank (PPR) computation, which is used to efficiently compute such embeddings.

The rest of this paper is structured as follows. Section 2 presents an overview on related work. In Sect. 3, we explain the basic idea of GloVe embeddings, and show how we transfer that idea to RDF graphs. Section 4 discusses an evaluation in different scenarios. We close with a summary and an outlook on future work.

The source code used in this evaluation can be found from https://github.com/miselico/globalRDFEmbeddingsISWC. Possible further developments will also be on http://users.jyu.fi/~miselico/software/.

2   Related Work

RDF vector space embeddings, i.e., projections of an RDF graph into a low-dimensional, dense vector space, have recently been proposed as a means to make RDF data accessible for propositional machine learning techniques, and shown to outperform traditional feature generation techniques [22].

RDF2Vec [22] is one of the first approaches that uses language modeling approaches for unsupervised feature extraction from sequences of words, and adapts them to RDF graphs. The approach generates sequences by leveraging local information from graph sub-structures, harvested by Weisfeiler-Lehman Subtree RDF Graph Kernels and graph walks, and then learns latent numerical representations of entities in RDF graphs.

The RDF2Vec approach is closely related to the approaches DeepWalk [21] and Deep Graph Kernels [31]. DeepWalk uses language modeling approaches to learn social representations of vertices of graphs by modeling short random-walks on large social graphs, like BlogCatalog, Flickr, and YouTube. The Deep Graph Kernel approach extends the DeepWalk approach, by modeling graph substructures, like graphlets, instead of graph walks. In this paper, we pursue and deepen the idea of random and biased walks since those have proven to be scalable even to large RDF graphs, unlike other transformation approaches, such as graph kernels. Node2vec [7] is another approach very similar to DeepWalk, which uses second order random walks to preserve the network neighborhood of the nodes.

Furthermore, multiple approaches for knowledge graph embeddings for the task of link prediction have been proposed [16], which could also be considered as approaches for generating propositional features from graphs. RESCAL [17] is one of the earliest approaches, which is based on factorization of a three-way tensor. The approach is later extended into Neural Tensor Networks (NTN) [28], which can be used for the same purpose (optionally using multilingual information [10]). One of the most successful approaches is the model based on translating embeddings, TransE [2]. This model builds entity and relation embeddings by regarding a relation as translation from head entity to tail entity. This approach assumes that relationships between words could be computed by their vector difference in the embedding space. However, this approach cannot deal with reflexive, one-to-many, many-to-one, and many-to-many relations. This problem was resolved in the TransH model [30], which models a relation as a hyperplane together with a translation operation on it. More precisely, each relation is characterized by two vectors, the norm vector of the hyperplane, and the translation vector on the hyperplane. While both TransE and TransH, embed the relations and the entities in the same semantic space, the TransR model [13] builds entity and relation embeddings in separate entity space and multiple relation spaces. This approach is able to model entities that have multiple aspects, and various relations that focus on different aspects of entities.

Unlike the first models for RDF vector space embeddings, which are based on paths, walks, or kernels, and therefore rely on *local* patterns, the approach in this paper exploits *global* patterns for creating vector space embeddings, inspired by the Global Vectors (GloVe) [20] approach for learning vector space embeddings for words from a text corpus.

3   Global Vectors from RDF Data

The embedding method which we propose borrows the optimization problem and approach from GloVe [20]. Glove training, however, is based on the creation of a global co-occurrence matrix from text. Consequently, in our approach we need to devise a way to build a co-occurrence matrix from graph data. To this end, we first weigh the edges of the graph and compute approximate personalized PageRank scores starting from each node. The PageRank score for the other nodes (i.e., context nodes) is then used as the absolute frequency in a matrix. This procedure is then repeated on the graph with all edges reversed and the result is added to the co-occurrence matrix. This combined matrix is then subsequently used for training the vectors with the original Glove approach.

3.1   The GloVe Model

GloVe was designed for creating dense word vectors (also known as *word embeddings*) from natural language texts, which have been recently used with much success in a plethora of Natural Language Processing tasks. GloVe follows a distributional semantic view of word meaning in context, which basically relies on the assumption that 'words which are similar in meaning occur in similar contexts' [25] – i.e., meaning can be derived from the context (i.e., the surrounding words) of the word in a large corpus of text.

Consequently, to build a GloVe model a word-word co-occurrence matrix is first built, which contains for each word how often other words occur in its context. Model parameters then include the size of the context window, whether to distinguish left context from right context, as well as a weighting functions to weight the contribution of each word co-occurrence – e.g., a decreasing weighting function, where word pairs that are d words apart contribute $1/d$ to the total co-occurrence count.

After obtaining a co-occurrence matrix, GloVe attempts to minimize the following cost function using Adagrad [5].

$$J = \sum_{i,j=1}^{V} f(X_{ij}) \left(w_i^T \tilde{w}_j + b_i + \tilde{b}_j - \log X_{ij} \right)^2 \tag{1}$$

where $f(X_{ij})$ is a weighting function on co-occurrence counts of word j in the context of word i (X_{ij}), w_i are word vectors, $\tilde{w}_j$ context vectors and b_i and b_j biases. The intuition behind this cost function is the following one. Each summand of the summation represents the amount of error attributed to a count X_{ij} in the co-occurrence matrix. The error consists of a weighing function f, to dampen the effect of very large co-occurrence counts, and a squared error factor. The squared error factor will become smaller when the dot product of word vectors becomes closer to the logarithm of the probability that the words co-occur. Or turned the other way, when two words co-occur often, their vectors' dot product will be relatively high, meaning that the vectors are more similar to make the error factor smaller. The logarithm also causes that ratios of co-occurrence probabilities are associated with differences of vectors. As a result, the embedding contains information useful for determining analogies.

3.2   Building a Co-occurrence Matrix from Graph Data

The co-occurrence matrix for textual data is obtained by linearly scanning through the text and counting the occurrence of context words in the context of each word. However, the graph which we use as input data does not have a linear structure. This problem has been worked around in the past by performing random walks starting from each of the nodes in the graph. Recording the paths of these walks results in a linear sequence of node (and optionally edge) labels, which can then, in turn, be used as a pseudo-text to train a model. This approach is, for example, used in node2vec [7] and RDF2Vec [22]. However, in these approaches, the trained model is different from the GloVe model and it does not use the co-occurrence counts, but rather trains a neural network on the individual context windows directly. In the case of GloVe, only the counts are needed and hence we are looking for a method to obtain these without generating the random walks explicitly.

A possible solution would be to perform a breadth-first search of a certain depth starting from each node in turn, and take all reachable nodes as the context of each start node. Given these kinds of contexts, one could then straightforwardly apply GloVe's co-occurrence weighting and assign a lower weight to co-occurrence counts of nodes which are further away from the focus node. However, this simple approach is problematic in that: (a) there could be nodes reachable through multiple paths at different levels, (b) there could be loops in the graph, making a walk pass through the same node multiple times, and (c) if there is a node with many context nodes at level d, but only few ones at level $d-1$, then the ones at level d will dominate the closer ones in the co-occurrence matrix as there are that many of them.

To solve this problem, we investigate the use of Personalized PageRank [18] to determine how important nodes are in the context of a focus node. In general, PageRank is used to find important nodes in a directed graph. Its first, well-known use is the ranking of web pages, but later PageRank has also been applied in other areas (e.g., peer-to-peer networks [9] and social network analysis [15], among others). At its heart, PageRank works by simulating random walkers over the graph and observing where these random walkers end up. A simplified model which we will elaborate below would be as follows. First, we denote the out degree of a node i as $deg(i)$. Then, if there are n nodes in the graph, construct an $n \times n$ matrix P filled with zeros except for positions i, j, for which there exists an arc $i \rightarrow j$. These positions contain $1/deg(i)$. Now, the simplified page rank problem is solved by finding the stationary solution to (notation from [1] – $p^{(i)}$ is the vector converging to the PageRank value for each page after i iterations.)

$$p^{(k+1)} = P^T p^{(k)}. \tag{2}$$

This simplified version of PageRank can run into a number of problems, namely some pages may have a zero out degree (so called dangling nodes) and there could be groups of pages which form closed cycles. In the first case, PageRank (i.e., random walkers) will get lost from the graph and any node linking directly or indirectly to a zero out-degree node will get a PageRank of zero. In the second case walkers will get trapped and the pages in the cycles will accumulate all PageRank. To amend these problems, the above equation is adapted to include parts which ensure that when a walk ends up in a dangling node, it will continue from another node selected from a distribution v, called the teleportation distribution. Further, to avoid ending in a cycle, a random jump is also performed with probability α to a node selected from the same distribution. Usually, v is chosen to be a uniform distribution, making each node equally likely to be the target of the jump. However, in the case of personalized page rank the distribution is degenerate as the target of these random jumps is always the node for which the rank vector is computed (which we called the focus node). In effect, the Personalized PageRank vector indicated the importance of nodes from the perspective of the focus node.

Computing PageRank (and also the PPR variant) is reasonably scalable. However, as we need to compute PPR for each individual node in turn, in order to build the co-occurrence matrix, the rapidly becomes too expensive. Moreover, the PageRank algorithm assigns a value to all nodes in the graph. If we computed the co-occurrence matrix this way, we would end up with a very large (in our experiments below this would become around 500 TB) dense matrix with many small values, which have little to no impact on the later training. Hence, we designed a faster, approximate all-pairs PPR computation method, which results in a sparse matrix. This algorithm is based on an approximate PPR method which we will introduce next.

3.3   BCA: A Fast Personalized PageRank Approximation

A method for faster computation of Personalized PageRank, called Bookmark-Coloring Algorithm (BCA) was presented by Berkhin [1]. The main idea behind this method is to create an approximation to the standard PPR such that the effort of the algorithm is only used for these nodes which will receive a significant rank. This requires fewer computations and since nodes with no significant PageRank are not assigned a value, a sparse representation is obtained.

An intuitive version of the BCA algorithm is as follows (for full details, see [1]). To compute the PPR vector $p^{(b)}$ for a focus node b, we start by injecting a unit amount of paint, representing the walkers in the standard personal PageRank computation, to b. From this paint an α-portion is retained and added to the value for b in $p^{(b)}$. The remaining $(1 - \alpha)$-portion is distributed uniformly over the out-links. This retain-and-distribute process is then repeated recursively for all nodes which got paint injected. When a node has a zero out degree, the outgoing paint is discarded.

This basic algorithm can be improved by choosing the order in which nodes considered for the retain-and-distribute. It is more efficient to select nodes with a larger amount of paint fist. To achieve this, a max priority queue, with the amount of paint as priorities is maintained. In principle, the queue could contain an entry for each node involved in each distribute step. However, it is more efficient to merge the separate wet paint amounts into one entry. Hence, the queue must allow efficient finding and updating of elements. Finally, when the amount of paint to be distributed becomes negligible (i.e., less than the parameter ϵ) it gets discarded, making the resulting rank vector sparse. All these improvements are described in more detail in the BCA paper [1]. One more technique described in the same paper is reuse of Bookmark-Coloring Vectors (BCV – the equivalent to the PageRank vector) for the computation of other BCVs. This is analyzed further for the case of hubs (i.e., nodes which correspond to a subset of important pages). The BCV is precomputed for these pages and whenever the retain-and-distribute process forwards paint to a page $p^{(h)}$ in the hub, the amount is multiplied with the BCV corresponding to $p^{(h)}$ and added to $p^{(b)}$. This optimization makes sense when many BCVs have to be computed, which is also the case for the co-occurrence matrix. However, since we are interested in computing the BCV for *all* nodes, further enhancements are possible, as we will discuss in the following subsection.

3.4   A Fast All-Pairs PPR Algorithm

The method introduced in the previous subsection speeds up the computation of individual PPR computations. Now, the observation leading to reuse of BCVs for pages in a hub can be adapted to our setting. The main point is that the computation of the BCV of node b can reuse the BCV of nodes reachable through its out links. Especially, it is beneficial if the BCV of nodes one hop away have already been computed. Adopting this viewpoint, we say that computation of the BCV of the node b *depends* on the BCV computation of all one-hop reachable

---

Algorithm 1. Determining the BCV Computation Order

---

function BCVORDER(Graph & $G_{original}$)

    $G \leftarrow G_{original}$ ▷ Copied because G will be modified in the function

    Initialize list $Order$ ▷ The list with the node ordering

    Initialize max priority queue Q_{indeg} ▷ The nodes in ascending in-degree

    Add all nodes to Q_{indeg}

    repeat

        while G has a node n with out-degree 0 **do**

            Add n to $Order$, Remove n from G, Remove n from Q_{indeg}

        end while

        if G is not empty **then**   ▷ There is a cycle which needs to be broken

            $n \leftarrow Q_{indeg}.pop()$

            Add n to $Order$, Remove n from G

            for all d dependent on n **do**

                Update priority of d in Q_{indeg}

            end for

        end if

    until G is empty

    return $Order$

end function

---

nodes and hence b is a *dependent* of these nodes. Now, what we want to achieve is that we only compute the BCV for nodes once the BCVs of all its dependent nodes have been computed. However, this will not always be feasible as the graphs contains cycles. Hence, we want to quickly find an ordering of nodes, such that we can likely reuse as many BCV computations as possible. To achieve this we break cycles and in that case compute the BCV for the node at which we break without being able to count on all dependents being available. We choose the node for breaking the cycle to be the one with the highest in-degree as that one is likely to cause most reuse and break multiple cycles at once. The pseudocode of the Algorithm is shown in Algorithm 1, the actual implementation also includes a couple of indexes and bitmaps to speed up the computation. Now, with the order determined, we can compute each BCV, reusing many previously computed values.

3.5 Biasing the Random Walks

The default PageRank and BCA algorithm assume that a random walker will follow the out edges of a node with equal likelihood. However, one can also create a setup in which given out edges are more likely than others. For BCA, this possibility was already hinted in the original paper [1], but not elaborated much further. This so called biasing can be accomplished by taking into account the out edge weights when distributing the paint over them.

Following our previous work [3], we apply twelve different strategies for assigning these weights to the edges of the graph. These weights will then in turn bias the random walks on the graph. In particular, when a walk arrives in a vertex v with out edges $v_{o1}, \ldots v_{od}$, then the walk will follow edge v_{ol} with a probability computed by

$$\Pr[\text{follow edge } v_{ol}] = \frac{weight(v_{ol})}{\sum_{i=1}^{d} weight(v_{oi})}$$

In other words, the normalized edge weights are directly interpreted as the probability to follow a particular edge. To obtain these edge weights, we make use of the following statistics computed from the RDF data:

Predicate Frequency for each predicate in the dataset, we count the number of times the predicate occurs (only occurrences as a predicate are counted).
Object Frequency for each resource in the dataset, we count the number of times it occurs as the object of a triple.
Predicate-Object frequency for each pair of a predicate and an object in the dataset, we count the number of times there is a statement with this predicate and object.

Besides these statistics, we also use PageRank [18] computed for the entities in the knowledge graph [29]. This PageRank is computed based on links between the Wikipedia articles representing the respective entities. When using the PageRank computed for DBpedia, not each node has a value assigned, as only entities which have a corresponding Wikipedia page are accounted for in the PageRank computation. Examples of nodes which do not have a PageRank include DBpedia types or categories, like http://dbpedia.org/ontology/Place and http://dbpedia.org/resource/Category:Central_Europe. Therefore, we assigned a fixed PageRank to all nodes which are not entities. We chose a value of 0.2, which is roughly the median PageRank in the non-normalized page rank values we used.

We have essentially two types of metrics, those assigned to nodes, and those assigned to edges. The predicate frequency and predicate-object frequency, as well as the inverses of these, can be directly used as weights for edges. Therefore, we call these weighting methods *edge-centric*. In the case of predicate frequency each predicate edge with that label is assigned the weight in question. In the case of predicate-object frequency, each predicate edge which ends in a given object gets assigned the predicate-object frequency. We also use the inverse metrics, where not the absolute frequency is assigned, but its multiplicative inverse.

In contrast, the object frequency, and also the used PageRank metric, assign a numeric score to each node in the graph. Therefore, we call weighting approaches based on them *node-centric*. To obtain a weight for the edges, we either *push* the weight down, meaning that the number assigned to a node is used as the weight of all in edges, or we *split* the number down, meaning that the weight is divided by the number of in edges and then assigned to all these edges. If *split* is not mentioned explicitly in node centric weighting strategies, then it is a push down strategy.

Note that uniform weights are equivalent to using object frequency with splitting the weights. To see why this holds true, we have to follow the steps which will be taken. First, each node gets assigned the amount of times it is used as an object. This number is equal to the number of in edges to the node. Then, this number is split over the in edges, i.e., each in edge gets assigned the number 1. Finally, this weight is normalized, assigning to each out link a uniform weight. Hence, this strategy would result in the same walks as using unbiased random walks over the graph.

So, even if we add unbiased random walks to the list of weighting strategies, we retain 12 unique ones, each with their own characteristics. These strategies, which we further elaborated upon in our earlier work [3], are:

Uniform approach:

1. *Uniform = Object Frequency Split*

Edge-centric approaches:

2. *Predicate Frequency*
3. *Inverse Predicate Frequency*
4. *Predicate-Object Frequency*
5. *Inverse Predicate-Object Frequency*

Node-centric object freq. approaches (See also strategy 1):

6. *Object Frequency*
7. *Inverse Object Frequency*
8. *Inverse Object Frequency Split*

Node-centric PageRank approaches:

9. *PageRank*
10. *Inverse PageRank*
11. *PageRank Split*
12. *Inverse PageRank Split*

3.6 Combining the Pieces

In earlier work on RDF graph embeddings (specifically RDF2Vec [22]), symmetric windows were used on top of generated random walks, which include both node and edge labels. These symmetric windows have the focus word in the middle and the context of the word is both before and after it. This means that the context of a node b consists of the nodes it can reach by following edges, as well as the nodes which can reach b. What this means is that the result RDF2Vec would be the same, independently of whether the original walks would be performed forward or backward. Inspired by this, we investigated the effect of creating the co-occurence matrix as the sum of the normal PPR matrix as described above and the PPR matrix of the graph with all edges reversed. Since a positive effect on the embeddings was obtained (at least for the tasks we used in the evaluation) we chose to use this approach.

RDF2Vec also includes edge labels into the walks and the embedding procedure. We also noticed a positive effect including the edge labels whenever they are traversed by paint with a weight equal to the amount of paint. Because the summation and additions of the label weights might lead to a skew in the values, we normalize each BCV in the co-occurence matrix by removing the value on the diagonal and scaling the remaining values such that their sum is 1. This operation led to improvements in the results and hence we adopted this technique for the overall algorithm. The pseudo code of the Global RDF Vector Space Embedding algorithm can be found in Algorithm 2.

Algorithm 2. Global RDF Vector Space Embedding

---

function CREATEEMBEDDINGS(Graph & G, Weighting Strategy W)

    Weigh G according to W

    $Order \leftarrow BCVOrder(G)$

    Compute all BCV according to $Order$, reusing results

    $G_r \leftarrow ReverseEdges(G)$

    Weigh G_r according to W

    $ReverseOrder \leftarrow BCVOrder(G_r)$

    Compute all BCV according to $ReverseOrder$, reusing results

    Sum the BCVs obtained for the normal and reversed graph and normalize,
               forming the co-occurrence matrix.

    Execute Glove training for the co-occurrence matrix.

    return The resulting vectors

end function

The overall algorithm has several parameters. First, there is the weighting strategy; the options are described above. Second, there are the parameters α and ϵ for the BCA algorithm. We chose the α parameter to be 0.1 and $\epsilon = 0.00001$, which is within the ranges stated by Berkhin [1]. Third, there are the parameters for the GloVe training. There is the vector length, which we choose to be 200, which is in the middle of the sizes used in the original Glove experiments [20]. We use 20 training iterations as we noticed that more iterations did not significantly decrease the cost function. We used the default values for the Adagrad learning rate and damp function.

4 Evaluation

First, we evaluate the different weighting strategies on a number of classification and regression tasks, comparing the results of different feature extraction strategies combined with different learning algorithms. Second, we evaluate the weighting strategies on the task of computing document similarity. We evaluate our approach using DBpedia [12]. We use the English version of the 2016-04 DBpedia dataset, which contains $4,678,230$ instances and $1,379$ mapping-based properties. In our evaluation we only consider object properties, and ignore literals. All the experiments were run using a Linux machine using at most 300 GB RAM and 24 Intel Xeon 2.60 GHz CPUs. For all the weighing strategies the processes took between 6 h for the least demanding strategy, the Predicate Frequency strategy, and up to 48 h for the most demanding strategy, the Predicate-Object Frequency. The runtime for building the related work approaches, using the publicly available code,[1] was more than a week.

---

[1] https://github.com/thunlp/KB2E.

Table 1. Classification results. The best results for each dataset are marked in bold.

Strategy/Dataset	Cities				Metacritic movies				Metacritic albums				AAUP				Forbes			
	NB	KNN	SVM	C4.5	NB	KNN	SVM	C4.5	NB	KNN	SVM	C4.5	NB	KNN	SVM	C4.5	NB	KNN	SVM	C4.5
Uniform	57.32	63.89	67.47	58.32	68.41	68.66	70.65	66.11	62.05	60.44	64.12	58.68	83.64	89.42	29.54	89.98	94.08	79.74	74.51	94.64
Predicate frequency	60.00	59.32	66.39	54.79	58.31	56.22	58.92	58.06	61.73	58.30	61.40	59.27	83.65	89.42	27.75	88.68	91.93	79.74	74.51	94.37
Inverse predicate frequency	49.08	52.16	53.05	41.97	66.32	66.62	69.73	61.63	64.90	62.56	64.52	59.33	83.21	89.42	29.84	89.00	92.48	79.74	74.51	93.70
Predicate object frequency	57.39	61.84	67.89	52.79	64.28	62.85	64.73	64.12	58.11	56.49	60.17	56.68	83.65	89.42	29.51	90.97	93.14	79.74	74.51	93.83
Inv. predicate object freq.	54.37	63.47	60.26	47.53	62.50	65.55	67.34	61.88	61.27	64.38	62.83	59.14	82.45	89.42	29.39	89.87	93.28	79.74	74.51	93.96
Object frequency	61.89	56.32	68.42	46.16	65.65	62.85	65.04	63.97	57.72	55.91	59.20	59.59	84.08	89.42	29.42	90.96	92.87	79.74	74.51	93.43
Inverse object frequency	53.87	56.26	60.76	47.11	62.49	65.50	68.10	63.15	59.01	62.12	63.86	58.43	82.45	89.42	29.03	89.65	93.28	79.74	74.51	94.90
Inverse object freq. split	56.79	54.29	56.26	50.21	60.76	61.27	63.77	61.32	61.35	60.70	61.86	61.73	82.45	89.42	29.60	89.76	93.28	79.74	74.51	93.96
PageRank	63.37	64.95	66.89	59.34	73.56	78.26	77.79	75.09	76.39	78.20	79.69	71.66	81.58	89.42	29.91	93.31	93.93	79.74	74.51	**95.78**
Inverse PageRank	53.29	55.13	69.69	51.61	80.09	80.44	79.69	76.78	71.66	72.24	79.69	66.68	84.30	89.42	29.46	93.21	92.22	80.29	64.69	94.09
PageRank split	54.79	57.71	69.90	51.76	78.66	81.01	79.56	76.67	75.09	72.31	**80.99**	69.53	82.01	89.42	29.39	89.54	90.88	80.29	75.65	93.28
Inverse PageRank split	50.66	54.21	66.99	49.71	71.68	72.13	74.64	71.32	69.85	70.76	72.05	67.78	82.78	89.42	30.70	93.09	93.02	79.74	74.51	94.91
RDF2VecGloVe	64.84	48.18	67.26	53.34	64.25	67.20	69.61	62.69	63.75	66.10	65.21	59.13	73.89	85.66	27.49	92.45	86.98	81.07	74.92	95.42
Best baseline	72.71	60.00	71.70	75.29	78.50	66.90	79.30	70.80	74.25	64.69	77.94	64.50	63.44	91.04	93.44	92.81	67.09	76.49	76.97	76.47
DB_TransE	65.79	75.71	74.63	61.50	65.75	64.17	68.96	61.16	62.81	60.48	64.17	56.86	80.28	84.86	28.95	89.65	92.88	79.98	74.37	95.44
DB_TransH	64.39	72.66	76.66	60.89	63.51	63.25	67.43	60.96	63.97	63.13	65.07	60.23	80.39	84.86	27.55	89.21	93.82	79.98	74.37	93.68
DB_TransR	63.08	67.32	74.50	59.84	64.38	60.16	64.43	52.04	63.56	59.68	66.41	60.39	79.19	84.86	28.95	89.00	93.28	79.98	74.37	93.70
Best RDF2Vec	**89.73**	69.16	84.19	72.25	80.24	78.68	**82.80**	72.42	73.57	76.30	78.20	68.70	75.07	**94.48**	29.11	94.15	88.53	80.58	77.79	86.38

4.1 Machine Learning Tasks

We use the DBpedia entity embeddings on five different datasets from different domains, for the tasks of classification and regression, i.e., *Cities*[2], *Metacritic Movies*[3], *Metacritic Albums*[4], *AAUP*[5] and *Forbes*[6]. Details on the dataset can be found in [23]. We follow the same experimental setup as in our RDF2Vec paper [22], using Naive Bayes, k-Nearest Neighbors, C4.5, and Support Vector Machine for classification, and Linear Regression, M5Rules, and k-Nearest Neighbors for regression, measuring accuracy and root mean squared error (RMSE) in stratified 10-fold cross validation. The results on parameter settings for the algorithms can be found in [22].

Furthermore, from our original RDF2Vec paper [22], we report the *best baseline* and the *best RDF2Vec* performance. As an additional baseline, we use the same set of random walks used in [22] to build a simple GloVe model, and report the results under *RDF2VecGloVe*. Furthermore, we compare our results to the embedding approaches TransE, TransH, and TransR, which have shown to be scalable to large knowledge graphs.

Tables 1 and 3 depict the results for the classification and regression task. We determine the significance in ranking of the approaches using the approach introduced by Demšar [4], as discussed in [22]. The results are depicted in Tables 2 and 4.

We can observe that although RDF2Vec is a very strong competitor, the approach introduced in this paper is capable of producing embeddings which outperform the results achieved with RDF2Vec in specific cases. In particular for classification algorithms which yield inferior results with RDF2Vec. It is also remarkable that TransE, TransH, and TransR are often outperformed by the baselines. Furthermore, we can observe that a naive application of the GloVe approach to walks (RDF2VecGloVe) does not lead to convincing results.

4.2 Document Modeling

Calculating entity similarity lies at the heart of knowledge-rich approaches to computing semantic similarity, a fundamental task in Natural Language Processing and Information Retrieval [32]. As previously mentioned, in the feature embedding space semantically similar entities appear close to each other in the feature space. Therefore, the problem of calculating the similarity between two instances is a matter of calculating the distance between two instances in the given feature space. To do so, we use the standard cosine similarity measure, which is applied on the vectors of the entities.

---

[2] https://www.imercer.com/content/mobility/quality-of-living-city-rankings.html.
[3] http://www.metacritic.com/browse/movies/score/metascore/all.
[4] http://www.metacritic.com/browse/albums/score/metascore/all.
[5] http://www.amstat.org/publications/jse/jse_data_archive.htm.
[6] http://www.forbes.com/global2000/list/.

Table 2. Classification average rank results. The best ranked results for each method are marked in bold. The learning models for which the strategies were shown to have significant difference based on the Friedman test with $\alpha < 0.05$ are marked with *. The single values marked with * mean that are significantly worse than the best strategy at significance level $q = 0.05$

Method	NB	KNN*	SVM*	C4.5*
Uniform weight	7.2	9.4	8.9	8.8
Predicate frequency weight	11.5	13	14.7	12.4
Inverse predicate frequency weight	10.2	11.4	9.9	14.2*
Predicate object frequency weight	10.1	12.1	11.5	10.8
Inverse predicate object frequency weight	11.7	9.2	12.6	11.9
Object frequency weight	9.8	13.1	11.7	11.8
Inverse object frequency weight	12.3	11.2	12.3	11.9
Inverse object frequency split weight	11.5	12.8	12.7	10.9
PageRank weight	**5.2**	6.2	6.6	**2.6**
Inverse PageRank weight	7.4	6.4	7.5	5.8
PageRank split weight	8.8	5.4	4.7	9
Inverse PageRank split weight	9	9.4	7.1	6.2
RDF2VecGloVe	12	9.4	10	8.6
Best baseline	9	8.8	**3.4**	7.2
DB_TransE	9.4	9.8	10.9	9.9
DB_TransH	8.6	9.4	11.2	11.6
DB_TransR	9.7	11.8	11.5	12
Best RDF2Vec	7.6	**2.2**	3.8	5.4

We use the entity similarity approach in the task of calculating semantic document similarity. We follow an approach similar to the one presented in [19], where two documents are considered to be similar if many entities of the one document are similar to at least one entity in the other document. More precisely, we try to identify the most similar pairs of entities in both documents, ignoring the similarity of all the other 1–1 similarities values. The similarity of two documents is then defined as the average maximum similarity for all entities in each document (see [3]).

We evaluate performance on document similarity approach using the LP50 dataset [11]. We follow standard practices and use Pearson's linear correlation coefficient and Spearman's rank correlation plus their harmonic mean as evaluation metrics. In addition to the baselines introduced above, we compare our approach to the following approaches:

Table 3. Regression results. The best results for each dataset are marked in bold.

Strategy/Dataset	Cities			Metacritic Movies			Metacritic Albums			AAUP			Forbes		
	LR	KNN	M5	LR	KNN	M5	LR	KNN	M5	LR	KNN	M5	LR	KNN	M5
Uniform	18.41	18.02	11.20	16.32	23.31	20.50	11.96	13.19	13.35	6.35	57.10	6.45	19.27	20.85	18.01
Predicate frequency	16.10	17.31	19.68	17.63	21.75	18.14	10.98	15.72	13.73	6.36	57.10	6.41	17.58	19.33	17.89
Inverse predicate frequency	21.71	16.42	14.40	20.69	21.88	18.44	12.67	13.44	12.94	6.35	57.10	6.37	18.93	20.58	18.04
Predicate object frequency	16.02	15.78	14.31	20.77	24.33	19.42	12.54	14.00	12.32	6.30	57.10	6.37	19.14	19.50	17.59
Inverse predicate object frequency	14.52	14.24	19.50	18.03	22.62	17.60	**10.79**	13.47	11.28	6.30	57.10	6.36	18.91	19.14	19.25
Object frequency	11.74	16.49	16.77	20.84	22.63	17.83	12.51	14.23	12.12	6.34	57.10	6.41	18.07	20.38	18.92
Inverse object frequency	15.87	18.31	15.40	18.49	22.00	18.49	13.37	14.60	13.38	6.37	57.10	6.44	17.86	19.07	17.00
Inverse object frequency split	15.96	14.01	20.52	21.40	23.32	18.94	11.61	13.20	12.63	6.40	57.10	6.43	19.62	20.31	19.87
PageRank	17.61	**9.50**	14.43	18.08	19.75	19.20	12.56	14.31	12.48	**6.28**	57.10	6.32	18.98	19.40	**16.27**
Inverse PageRank	13.41	13.33	10.47	17.91	20.52	16.63	13.17	13.73	12.72	6.37	57.10	6.46	18.79	18.99	18.93
PageRank split	19.70	20.51	12.44	17.22	19.86	18.84	12.58	12.46	10.93	6.31	57.10	6.32	17.61	20.90	19.22
Inverse PageRank split	17.22	18.63	12.65	17.76	23.09	19.82	12.04	14.17	11.90	6.36	57.10	6.39	17.42	18.93	20.10
RDF2VecGloVe	20.50	20.24	20.57	23.10	26.37	23.04	13.87	15.74	13.93	6.34	57.31	6.37	20.45	21.55	19.18
Best baseline	17.79	18.21	17.04	21.45	21.62	19.19	13.32	13.99	12.81	8.08	34.94	6.36	19.16	19.81	18.20
DB_TransE	14.22	14.45	14.46	20.66	23.61	20.71	13.20	14.71	13.23	6.34	57.27	6.43	20.00	21.55	17.73
DB_TransH	13.88	12.81	14.28	20.71	23.59	20.72	13.04	14.19	13.03	6.35	57.27	6.47	19.88	21.54	16.66
DB_TransR	14.50	13.24	14.57	20.10	23.37	20.04	13.87	15.74	13.93	6.34	57.31	6.37	20.45	21.55	17.18
Best RDF2Vec	11.92	12.67	10.19	**15.45**	17.80	15.50	10.89	11.72	10.97	**6.26**	56.95	6.29	18.35	21.04	16.61

Table 4. Regression average rank results. The best ranked results for each method are marked in bold. The learning models for which the strategies were shown to have significant difference based on the Friedman test with $\alpha < 0.05$ are marked with *. The single values marked with * mean that are significantly worse than the best strategy at significance level $q = 0.05$

Method	LR*	KNN*	M5*
Uniform weight	9.2	9.7	11.4
Predicate frequency weight	6.7	9.5	11.3
Inverse predicate frequency weight	12.2	8.3	8.5
Predicate object frequency weight	9.3	10.1	7.7
Inverse predicate object frequency weight	5.3	6.9	8.4
Object frequency weight	7.1	10.3	9.1
Inverse object frequency weight	10.5	9.7	10.6
Inverse object frequency split weight	12	8.1	12.9
PageRank weight	8.4	6.1	6.3
Inverse PageRank weight	8.9	5.3	8.6
PageRank split weight	7.4	8.9	6.3
Inverse PageRank split weight	7.5	9.3	10
RDF2VecGloVe	15.5*	17.5*	15*
Best baseline	15.2*	7.2	9.2
DB_TransE	10.7	14.1	11.9
DB_TransH	11	11.9	11.2
DB_TransR	11.7	14.1	11
Best RDF2Vec	**2.4**	**4**	**1.6**

- TF-IDF: Distributional baseline algorithm.
- AnnOv: Similarity score based on annotation overlap that corresponds to traversal entity similarity with radius 0, as described in [19].
- Explicit Semantic Analysis (ESA) [6].
- GED: semantic similarity using a Graph Edit Distance based measure [27].
- Salient Semantic Analysis (SSA), Latent Semantic Analysis (LSA) [8].
- Graph-based Semantic Similarity (GBSS) [19].

The results for the related approaches were taken from the respective papers, except for ESA, which was taken from [19], where it is calculated via the public ESA REST endpoint[7]. All results are collected in Table 5. We can see that our approach, using inverse predicate object frequency weights, outperforms the state-of-the-art approaches, as well as the embeddings generated by RDF2Vec.

---

[7] http://vmdeb20.deri.ie:8890/esaservice.

Table 5. Document similarity results - Pearson's linear correlation coefficient (r) Spearman's rank correlation (ρ) and their harmonic mean μ

Approach	r	ρ	μ
Uniform weight	0.537	0.535	0.536
Predicate frequency weight	0.534	0.532	0.533
Inverse predicate frequency weight	0.632	**0.621**	**0.627**
Predicate object frequency weight	0.331	0.323	0.327
Inverse predicate object frequency weight	0.541	0.544	0.542
Object frequency weight	0.346	0.348	0.347
Inverse object frequency weight	0.523	0.547	0.534
Inverse object frequency split weight	0.504	0.513	0.509
PageRank weight	0.488	0.485	0.486
Inverse PageRank weight	0.429	0.481	0.454
PageRank split weight	0.539	0.528	0.533
Inverse PageRank split weight	0.512	0.511	0.512
RDF2VecGloVe	0.569	0.432	0.491
Best RDF2Vec	**0.708**	0.556	0.623
DB_TransE	0.565	0.432	0.490
DB_TransH	0.570	0.452	0.504
DB_TransR	0.578	0.461	0.513
TF-IDF	0.398	0.224	0.287
AnnOv	0.590	0.460	0.517
LSA	0.696	0.463	0.556
SSA	0.684	0.488	0.570
GED	0.630	\	\
ESA	0.656	0.510	0.574
GBSS	0.704	0.519	0.598

5   Conclusion and Outlook

In this paper, we have introduced a novel approach for generating embeddings of RDF graphs, which exploits global instead of local patterns. We have shown that it is possible to outperform local graph embeddings techniques, in particular on document similarity. For most other tasks similar performance can be obtained.

One key finding of this work is that weighting techniques are a crucial factor in the overall performance. In the future, we would like to investigate this point more thoroughly, and analyze the interplay of the dataset, the task, the learning algorithm, and the weighting technique more formally and with more exhaustive experimentation. One way to achieve this is by evaluating the embedding using intrinsic measures such as those suggested in [26]. Besides, we would like to further investigate how the literals in the dataset can be incorporated while learning the embedding. Furthermore, as GloVe embeddings are known to work particularly well for finding analogies, we plan to adapt the approach for predicting missing links in RDF data sets.

Acknowledgements. The work presented in this paper has been partially funded by the Junior-professor funding programme of the Ministry of Science, Research and the Arts of the state of Baden-Württemberg (project "Deep semantic models for high-end NLP application"), and by the German Research Foundation (DFG) under grant number PA 2373/1-1 (Mine@LOD).

References

1. Berkhin, P.: Bookmark-coloring algorithm for personalized pagerank computing. Internet Math. **3**(1), 41–62 (2006)
2. Bordes, A., Usunier, N., Garcia-Duran, A., Weston, J., Yakhnenko, O.: Translating embeddings for modeling multi-relational data. In: NIPS, pp. 2787–2795 (2013)
3. Cochez, M., Ponzetto, S.P., Paulheim, H.: Biased graph walks for RDF graph embeddings. In: WIMS (2017)
4. Demšar, J.: Statistical comparisons of classifiers over multiple datasets. J. Mach. Learn. Res. **7**, 1–30 (2006)
5. Duchi, J., Hazan, E., Singer, Y.: Adaptive subgradient methods for online learning and stochastic optimization. J. Mach. Learn. Res. **12**, 2121–2159 (2011)
6. Gabrilovich, E., Markovitch, S.: Computing semantic relatedness using Wikipedia-based explicit semantic analysis. In: IJCAI, pp. 1606–1611 (2007)
7. Grover, A., Leskovec, J.: Node2vec: scalable feature learning for networks. In: KDD, pp. 855–864 (2016)
8. Hassan, S., Mihalcea, R.: Semantic relatedness using salient semantic analysis. In: AAAI, pp. 884–889 (2011)
9. Kamvar, S.D., Schlosser, M.T., Garcia-Molina, H.: The Eigentrust algorithm for reputation management in P2P networks. In: WWW, pp. 640–651 (2003)
10. Klein, P., Ponzetto, S.P., Glavaš, G.: Improving neural knowledge base completion with cross-lingual projections. In: EACL, vol. 2, pp. 516–522 (2017)
11. Lee, M., Pincombe, B., Welsh, M.: An empirical evaluation of models of text document similarity. Cogn. Sci. Soc. **27**, 1254–1259 (2005)
12. Lehmann, J., Isele, R., Jakob, M., Jentzsch, A., Kontokostas, D., Mendes, P.N., Hellmann, S., Morsey, M., van Kleef, P., Auer, S., Bizer, C.: DBpedia - A large-scale. Multilingual knowledge base extracted from Wikipedia. Semant. Web J. **6**, 167–195 (2013)
13. Lin, Y., Liu, Z., Sun, M., Liu, Y., Zhu, X.: Learning entity and relation embeddings for knowledge graph completion. In: AAAI, pp. 2181–2187 (2015)
14. Mikolov, T., Chen, K., Corrado, G., Dean, J.: Efficient estimation of word representations in vector space. arXiv preprint arXiv:1301.3781 (2013)
15. Mislove, A., Marcon, M., Gummadi, K.P., Druschel, P., Bhattacharjee, B.: Measurement and analysis of online social networks. In: IMC, pp. 29–42 (2007)
16. Nickel, M., Murphy, K., Tresp, V., Gabrilovich, E.: A review of relational machine learning for knowledge graphs. Proc. IEEE **104**(1), 11–33 (2016)
17. Nickel, M., Tresp, V., Kriegel, H.P.: A three-way model for collective learning on multi-relational data. In: ICML, pp. 809–816 (2011)

18. Page, L., Brin, S., Motwani, R., Winograd, T.: The PageRank citation ranking: bringing order to the web. Technical report 1999-66, Stanford InfoLab, November 1999
19. Paul, C., Rettinger, A., Mogadala, A., Knoblock, C.A., Szekely, P.: Efficient graph-based document similarity. In: Sack, H., Blomqvist, E., d'Aquin, M., Ghidini, C., Ponzetto, S.P., Lange, C. (eds.) ESWC 2016. LNCS, vol. 9678, pp. 334–349. Springer, Cham (2016). doi:10.1007/978-3-319-34129-3_21
20. Pennington, J., Socher, R., Manning, C.D.: Glove: global vectors for word representation. In: EMNLP 2014, pp. 1532–1543 (2014)
21. Perozzi, B., Al-Rfou, R., Skiena, S.: DeepWalk: online learning of social representations. In: KDD, pp. 701–710 (2014)
22. Ristoski, P., Paulheim, H.: RDF2Vec: RDF graph embeddings for data mining. In: Groth, P., Simperl, E., Gray, A., Sabou, M., Krötzsch, M., Lecue, F., Flöck, F., Gil, Y. (eds.) ISWC 2016. LNCS, vol. 9981, pp. 498–514. Springer, Cham (2016). doi:10.1007/978-3-319-46523-4_30
23. Ristoski, P., de Vries, G.K.D., Paulheim, H.: A collection of benchmark datasets for systematic evaluations of machine learning on the semantic web. In: Groth, P., Simperl, E., Gray, A., Sabou, M., Krötzsch, M., Lecue, F., Flöck, F., Gil, Y. (eds.) ISWC 2016. LNCS, vol. 9982, pp. 186–194. Springer, Cham (2016). doi:10.1007/978-3-319-46547-0_20
24. Rosati, J., Ristoski, P., Di Noia, T., Leone, R.D., Paulheim, H.: RDF graph embeddings for content-based recommender systems. In: CEUR Workshop Proceedings, vol. 1673, pp. 23–30. RWTH (2016)
25. Rubenstein, H., Goodenough, J.B.: Contextual correlates of synonymy. Commun. ACM 8(10), 627–633 (1965)
26. Schnabel, T., Labutov, I., Mimno, D.M., Joachims, T.: Evaluation methods for unsupervised word embeddings. In: EMNLP, pp. 298–307 (2015)
27. Schuhmacher, M., Ponzetto, S.P.: Knowledge-based graph document modeling. In: WSDM, pp. 543–552 (2014)
28. Socher, R., Chen, D., Manning, C.D., Ng, A.: Reasoning with neural tensor networks for knowledge base completion. In: NIPS, pp. 926–934 (2013)
29. Thalhammer, A., Rettinger, A.: PageRank on Wikipedia: towards general importance scores for entities. In: Sack, H., Rizzo, G., Steinmetz, N., Mladenić, D., Auer, S., Lange, C. (eds.) ESWC 2016. LNCS, vol. 9989, pp. 227–240. Springer, Cham (2016). doi:10.1007/978-3-319-47602-5_41
30. Wang, Z., Zhang, J., Feng, J., Chen, Z.: Knowledge graph embedding by translating on hyperplanes. In: AAAI, pp. 1112–1119 (2014)
31. Yanardag, P., Vishwanathan, S.: Deep graph kernels. In: KDD, pp. 1365–1374 (2015)
32. Zhang, Z., Gentile, A.L., Ciravegna, F.: Recent advances in methods of lexical semantic relatedness - a survey. Nat. Lang. Eng. 19(4), 411–479 (2013)

LDScript: A Linked Data Script Language

Olivier Corby[1]([⊠]) (ID), Catherine Faron-Zucker[2](ID), and Fabien Gandon[1](ID)

[1] Université Côte d'Azur, Inria, CNRS, I3S, Sophia Antipolis, France
{olivier.corby,fabien.gandon}@inria.fr
[2] Université Côte d'Azur, I3S, Inria, CNRS, Sophia Antipolis, France
faron@i3s.unice.fr

Abstract. In addition to the existing standards dedicated to representation or querying, Semantic Web programmers could really benefit from a dedicated programming language enabling them to directly define functions on RDF terms, RDF graphs or SPARQL results. This is especially the case, for instance, when defining SPARQL extension functions. The ability to capitalize complex SPARQL filter expressions into extension functions or to define and reuse dedicated aggregates are real cases where a dedicated language can support modularity and maintenance of the code. Other families of use cases include the definition of *functional* properties associated to RDF resources or the definition of procedural attachments as functions assigned to RDFS or OWL classes with the selection of the function to be applied to a resource depending on the type of the resource. To address these needs we define *LDScript*, a Linked Data script language on top of the SPARQL filter expression language. We provide the formal grammar of the syntax and the Natural Semantics inference rules of the semantics of the language. We also provide a benchmark and perform an evaluation using real test bases from W3C with different implementations and approaches comparing, in particular, script interpretation and Java compilation.

Keywords: SPARQL · Linked Data · Programming · Semantic Web

1 Introduction

RDF is the standard framework recommended by the W3C to represent and exchange Linked Data on the Web. It is associated with RDF Schema and OWL for ontology-based modelling on the semantic Web and with SPARQL for data and ontology querying. The development of the Web of data opens up a wide range of use cases where, in addition to the existing standards, Semantic Web programmers would benefit from having a dedicated programming language enabling them to define functions on RDF terms or RDF graphs. This is the case, for instance, when defining SPARQL extension functions implemented for a special purpose and domain or application dependent. This would also be needed to capitalize a complex SPARQL filter expression or the definition of special purpose extension aggregates to be reused across queries or sub-queries.

© Springer International Publishing AG 2017
C. d'Amato et al. (Eds.): ISWC 2017, Part I, LNCS 10587, pp. 208–224, 2017.
DOI: 10.1007/978-3-319-68288-4_13

Another kind of use cases is the definition of *functional* properties associated to RDF resources, the results of which are computed on demand. For instance, the value of the `surface` property of a rectangular object could be computed as the product of the values of its width and length properties; the age of a person could also be computed from her date of birth. These use cases can also be extended to the definition of procedural attachments as functions assigned to RDFS or OWL classes. The selection of the function to be applied to a resource can then be made dependent on the types (classes) of the resource.

The requirements we propose for a programming language enabling such definitions of functions are:

- The objects of the language are RDF terms (URIs, blank nodes and literals), RDF triples and graphs as well as SPARQL query solutions. This is required to facilitate the access and manipulation of Linked Data in their native model without adding the burden of parsing, encapsulating, mapping, and serializing in other programming languages.
- The statements of the language include SPARQL filter expressions and SPARQL queries (the SELECT and CONSTRUCT query forms). This is required to be able to directly leverage in the program these operations that are tailored to Linked Data access and processing. Again, encapsulating and mapping these operations to other programming paradigms can make them clumsy and inefficient.
- The language provides function definition and function call. This is the core motivation of our proposal to add all the needed primitives to program and execute functions inside RDF frameworks.
- Functions can be exchanged and shared among Semantic Web plaforms and are interoperable.

In this paper, we address the research question: *Can we define a standard-based programming language that meets the above described requirements?* To answer this question, we define *LDScript*, a Linked Data script language on top of the SPARQL filter expression language, taking advantage of the fact that the SPARQL filter expression language potentially enables users to express the definitions of functions. We effectively define a *programming language* on top of SPARQL filter expression language. Syntactically, it consists in a couple of additional statements: a FUNCTION statement enabling users to define functions and a LET statement enabling them to define local variables. We present the syntax and semantics of LDScript as well as an implementation and we illustrate the simplicity as well as the expressive power of this extension with real cases of LDScript functions. We also provide a benchmark and we report the results of an evaluation of LDScript using real test bases from W3C with different implementations and approaches comparing, in particular, script interpretation and Java compilation.

This article is based on an initial research report [4] and presents our scientific contributions with the following plan. In Sect. 2 we present state-of-the-art approaches to define extension functions. In Sect. 3 we introduce LDScript with an overview of this language. In Sect. 4 we formally define the syntax and semantics of LDScript. In Sect. 5 we study several use cases and we show how they can easily be addressed by using LDScript. In Sect. 6 we evaluate the efficiency of different implementations of LDScript on various test cases. In Sect. 7 we conclude and draw some perspectives of our work.

2   Related Work

Although no contribution so far has directly addressed the research question we target in this paper, a number of previous works are somehow related to the issue. SPIN is a W3C member submission which proposes a SPARQL-based rule and constraint language and, additionally, enables one to represent both SPARQL queries (SPIN templates) and SPARQL extension functions (SPIN functions) [6]. SPIN is represented in RDF. In SPIN, a SPARQL extension function is identified by a resource of type sp:Function (with sp the prefix denoting the SPIN namespace) which is linked by property sp:body to its definition as a SPARQL query of the form SELECT or ASK.

Jena provides a java URI scheme for naming and accessing SPARQL extension functions implemented in Java. This enables one to dynamically load the bytecode implementing the function. By convention, the location of the Java class must be found in the Java classpath and the local name of the function must be the name of the Java class implementing it[1]. Here is an example of a SPARQL query using an extension function f:myTest implemented in Java. It filters the RDF triples for which f:myTest returns true when called with the triple's subject and object as parameters:

```
PREFIX f: <java:app.myFunctions.>
SELECT ?x WHERE { ?x ?p ?y FILTER f:myTest(?x, ?y) }
```

When compared to the above stated requirements for a Semantic Web programming language, Jena relies only on Java for extension functions and the code of the function has to deal with mappings from the Linked Data models and syntaxes to the object oriented models and syntax of Java.

G. Williams [9] proposes to implement SPARQL extension functions in JavaScript as an agreed-upon programming language, and to share implementations among query engines by using an embedded JavaScript interpreter. Functions are identified by URLs and their source code may be retrieved at run time by dereferencing their URL. It relies on an RDF schema enabling one to describe a SPARQL extension function and retrieve its source code at run time by dereferencing its URL. Here is an example of RDF statements describing a SPARQL extension function to compute a geographical distance in kilometers. The location of its JavaScript source code is the value of property ex:source (with ex the namespace prefix of the extension function schema) and the function name in the source code that should be called to execute the extension function is the value of property ex:function.

---

[1] https://jena.apache.org/documentation/query/writing_functions.html.

```
<http://example.com/functions/distance> a ex:Function;
  dc:description"Geographic distance in km";
  ex:source <http://example.com/distance.js>;
  ex:function "gdistance" .
```

When compared to our proposed requirements, the code of the function has to deal with mappings from the Linked Data models and syntaxes to the object oriented model and syntax of JavaScript.

M. Atzori [1] proposes to implement SPARQL extension functions based on both a generic extension function wfn:call and the SPARQL SERVICE clause. Function wfn:call is similar to the Lisp *funcall* function and takes the extension function to be evaluated as its first argument. Any occurrence of the wfn:call function is replaced by a SERVICE call to delegate the evaluation of the extension function to the SPARQL endpoint implementing the function. The SPARQL endpoint's IRI is computed from the extension function's IRI, based on a Function-to-Endpoint IRI pattern. When compared to the requirements for a Semantic Web programming language, this proposal does not provide a language but rather an RPC-like hook to call functions that have to be hosted and executed in a separate server process.

When compared to these four state-of-the-art proposals, the key idea of our proposal described in the following is to extend the SPARQL language, and more precisely its filter language, in order to enable the definition of extension functions in the SPARQL filter language *itself* and using its native syntax. With LDScript we propose a self-contained and Linked Data oriented programming language for extension functions.

Relatedly, SPARQL-Generate [7] also extends SPARQL with a few constructs with the specific target of enabling the generation of RDF from heterogeneous sources. It is a template language whereas our proposal is a programming language. In fact we could emulate SPARQL-Generate with LDScript and STTL SPARQL Template Transformation Language [3].

PL/SQL[2] is a programming language that is tightly integrated with the SQL query language for relational databases. LDScript is designed with similar goals but for triple stores.

Finally, it must be noted that Prolog may be worth considered for entailments purpose which is not the topic of this work.

3   Overview of LDScript

Our goal is to define functions, the objects of which are Linked Data entities (URI, RDF literals, RDF triples, etc.) with the main objective of defining SPARQL extension functions and possibly extend SPARQL itself. One possibility is to rely on an existing programming language, e.g. Java, and use the specific API of the SPARQL implementation of the RDF entities. However, this approach has several weaknesses. First, it is not interoperable because other

---

[2] http://www.oracle.com/technetwork/database/features/plsql/.

SPARQL implementations of RDF entities do not use the same API. Hence, the functions cannot be reused across different SPARQL implementations. Second, one does not benefit of SPARQL native function library dedicated to RDF terms (functions isURI, isBlank, isLiteral, datatype, strdt, strlang, langMatch, uri, bnode, etc.) Third, one must switch back and forth from SPARQL to (e.g.) Java environments with their compiler, project management environment, etc., and link the compiled functions to the SPARQL interpreter.

Another possibility would be to design a specific programming language the object of which would be RDF entities with a library implementing SPARQL functions. The weakness of this approach would be that users would have to learn yet another programming language.

We propose LDScript, a third way that reconciles the above two approaches: a programming language whose objects are RDF entities, SPARQL compatible and embedding the complete SPARQL function library.

LDScript primarily relies on the SPARQL filter expression language. A SPARQL filter is either (a disjunction or conjunction of) a relational expression or a call to a built-in or externally defined boolean function. Among the built-in SPARQL functions stands the IF ternary function which evaluates the first argument and returns the value of the second argument if the first argument results in an effective value of true, or else the value of the third argument. A SPARQL filter restricts the solutions of a graph pattern matching to those satisfying the constraint it expresses: the filtered solutions result in the boolean value *true* when substituted into the filter expression.

We propose to define functions by taking advantage of the fact that the SPARQL filter language enables users to define expressions. Handbooks of programming languages explain that typical programming languages include as commands: variables declaration, assignment, call, return, sequential blocks, iterative commands and *if* statements. For this reason, in this section we will introduce the corresponding statements in LDScript. LDScript primitives are also directly descending from the historical definitions of *function* and *function definition* as introduced by John McCarthy [8].

Here are the namespaces and prefixes used in the definitions:

```
prefix xt: <http://ns.inria.fr/sparql-extension/>
prefix us: <http://ns.inria.fr/sparql-extension/user/>
prefix rq: <http://ns.inria.fr/sparql-function/>
prefix dt: <http://ns.inria.fr/sparql-datatype/>
prefix ex: <htp://example.org/>
```

3.1 LDScript Function Definition

In LDScript, a *function definition* starts with the FUNCTION keyword. The first argument of the declaration is the name (a URI) of the function being defined followed by its argument list. The variables in the argument list play the usual role of function arguments. The second argument is the body of the function being defined. It is an LDScript expression or a sequence of expressions. For example, the *factorial* function us:fac is defined as follows, by using the SPARQL IF built-in function and embedding a recursive call:

```
FUNCTION us:fac(?n) {
  IF (?n = 0, 1, ?n * us:fac(?n - 1)) }
```

Here is another example of function definition. A call to the us:status function returns the status (married or single) of the resource given as parameter. Its definition uses the SPARQL built-in IF function and EXISTS operator.

```
FUNCTION us:status(?x) {
IF (EXISTS { ?x ex:hasSpouse ?y } || EXISTS { ?y ex:hasSpouse ?x },
    ex:Married, ex:Single) }
```

A call to a defined function returns the result of the evaluation of its body, with its arguments bound by the function call. In the body, the arguments are *local* variables in the sense that the variable bindings are local to the body of the function and exist only during the execution of the function. For instance, according to its above definition, a call to function us:fac will return the value returned by a call to the IF SPARQL built-in function form, with a given value for variable ?n.

The language for defining the body of a function is LDScript, i.e. the SPARQL filter expression language extended with statements presented in this document. Hence, to define extension functions, LDScript programmers can make use of the expressivity of the whole SPARQL filter expression language. In particular, this includes built-in SPARQL functions, among which the IF function form enabling to consider alternatives, and the EXISTS operator to test the existence of graph patterns. This also includes extension functions defined in LDScript or externally defined in another language (as SPARQL allows it). LDScript provides overloading in the sense that it enables users to define several functions with the same name and a different number of arguments.

For example, the SPARQL query below comprises the definition of function us:fac in a FUNCTION clause and the WHERE clause embeds a call to this function to search the resources whose income is greater or equal to 10! = 3,628,800.

```
SELECT ?x ?i
WHERE { ?x ex:income ?i FILTER (?i >= us:fac(10)) }
FUNCTION us:fac(?n) { IF (?n = 0, 1, ?n * us:fac(?n - 1)) }
```

3.2   Local Variable Declaration

LDScript function definitions can embed *local variable declarations*. These are expressed in a LET statement. Its first argument declares a local variable and its value; its second argument is an expression which is evaluated with the transient binding of the local variable declared. After completion of the expression evaluation, the binding vanishes. The result of a LET statement is the result of its second argument. For instance, the example LET statement below returns the pretty-printing of the current date, e.g. "29/01/2017".

```
LET (?n = now()) { concat(day(?n), "/", month(?n), "/", year(?n)) }
```

A LET statement can also execute a SPARQL query in its first argument and bind the *select* variables with the first query solution. For instance, the following function uses a LET statement to return the first retrieved type of a resource.

```
FUNCTION us:type(?s){ LET (SELECT ?t WHERE {?s a ?t}){ ?t }}
```

An alternative syntax enables users to explicit the (subset of) variables to be bound. The binding of the variables of the LET statement is done by name (not by position).

```
FUNCTION us:type(?s){ LET (((?t)) = SELECT ?t WHERE {?s a ?t}){?t}}
```

3.3   Loop Statements

In order to iterate a statement on the elements of a list of values, LDScript is provided with the FOR loop statement. As an example, the following function iteratively calls the xt:display function on the prime numbers among a given list of natural numbers.

```
FOR (?n IN xt:list(1, 2, 3, 4, 5)) {
  IF (us:prime(?n)) { xt:display(?n) } }
```

The FOR statement can iterate on the results of a SPARQL SELECT or CONSTRUCT query. In the case of a CONSTRUCT query, it iterates on the triples of the graph. For instance, the following function iteratively calls the xt:display function on RDF triples of the form ?x a foaf:Person.

```
FOR ((?s, ?p, ?o) IN CONSTRUCT WHERE { ?x a foaf:Person }) {
  xt:display(?s, ?p, ?o) }
```

Note that there are a lot of possibilities to integrate queries as expressions. We have chosen a generic principle that matches LET/FOR statements and SELECT/CONSTRUCT queries with the same design pattern. In addition this choice has the advantage of being generalizable to other objects such as lists, triples and graphs:

```
FOR ((?fst, ?snd) IN ?listOfPairs)
LET ((?s, ?p, ?o) = ?triple)
```

The model and the implementation take such objects as solution mappings and graphs into account. They are implemented using a pointer datatype, that is a kind of blank node pointing to an object. As a blank node it can pass through all statements. As a pointer, it is exploited by pattern matching expressions like in the above LET and FOR statements.

3.4   Function Evaluation

LDScript is provided with the FUNCALL function to call a function whose name is dynamically computed. For instance, the following example retrieves the name of the appropriate us:surface method and applies it to argument ?x.

```
FUNCALL(us:method(us:surface, ?x), ?x)
```

LDScript is provided with the APPLY function to iteratively call a binary function on a list of arguments. For example, the following function call enables to compute the sum of the elements of a list of numbers with the binary rq:plus function.

```
APPLY(rq:plus, xt:list(1, 2, 3, 4, 5))
```

3.5   List Datatype

LDScript is provided with a dt:list datatype to manage lists of values. A dt:list datatype value is a list whose elements are RDF terms: URIs, literals, blank nodes or sublists of type dt:list. The elements of a list need not be of the same kind, neither of the same datatype. The dt:list datatype comes with a set of predefined functions among which xt:size returns the size of the list, xt:get returns the nth element, xt:sort sorts the list according to the ORDER BY rules of SPARQL, xt:iota returns the list of n first integers, xt:cons adds an element to the head of the list, etc.

The MAPLIST function enables one to apply a function to the elements of a list and return the list of the results. For instance, the call to function MAPLIST shown below returns the list of the results of the calls to function us:fac on the first ten integers.

```
MAPLIST(us:fac, xt:iota(10))
```

There are several variants of the MAPLIST function: MAP applies a function and returns true, MAPSELECT returns the list of elements such that the boolean function returns true.

4   LDScript Formal Definition

The previous section gave an overview of LDScript. In this section we formally define the syntax and semantics of this language.

4.1   LDScript Syntax

LDScript grammar is based on SPARQL[3]. The definition of BuiltInCall is extended with LET, FOR, MAP, FUNCALL and APPLY statements.

---

[3] http://www.w3.org/TR/sparql11-query/#grammar.

```
Function ::= 'FUNCTION' iri ('()' | VarList) Body
Body ::= '{' '}' | '{' Expression (';' Expression)* '}'
VarList ::= '(' Var (',' Var)* ')'
BuiltInCall ::= SPARQL_BuiltInCall | IfThenElse
| 'LET' '(' (Decl (',' Decl) *        | SelectQuery) ')' Body
| 'FOR' '(' (VarOrList 'IN' ExpQuery | SelectQuery) ')' Body
| Map     '(' iri ',' Expression ')'
| 'funcall' '(' Expression (',' Expression)* ')'
| 'apply' '(' iri ',' Expression ')'
IfThenElse ::= 'IF' '(' BuiltInCall ')' Body
  ( 'ELSE' ( Body | IfThenElse ) ) ?
Decl ::= VarOrList2 '=' ExpQuery
VarOrList ::= Var | VarList
VarOrList2 ::= VarOrList | '(' VarList ')'
ExpQuery ::= Expression | SelectQuery | ConstructQuery
Map ::= 'MAP' | 'MAPLIST' | 'MAPSELECT'
```

4.2 LDScript Semantics

As usually done for programming languages, we formally defined the semantics of the core of LDScript by a set of Natural Semantics inference rules [5]. These rules enable us to define the semantics of the evaluation of the expressions of the language in an environment with variable bindings. The bottom of the rule is the conclusion and the top is the condition. The $\vdash$ symbol states that the expression on the right side is evaluated in the environment given on the left side. The $\rightarrow$ symbol represents the evaluation of the expression on the left side into the value on the right side. An environment is a couple (μ, ρ) where μ is the basic graph pattern (BGP) solution mapping and ρ represents local variable bindings. In addition, the environment must contain a reference to the SPARQL dataset, which is not detailed hereafter.

Rule 1 states that local variables are evaluated within ρ which is managed as a stack, latest variable binding first; rule 2 states that global variables are evaluated within μ which is a BGP solution. Rules 3 and 4 specify the evaluation of function calls. The $\Rightarrow$ symbol represents a function definition lookup for the function name on the left side. The solution mapping environment is empty during function body evaluation: there are no global variables. Each function call creates a fresh environment with function parameters (if any) as local variables. Rule 5 specifies the evaluation of the LET clause which declares a local variable to be added to environment ρ. Hence, a declared local variable may hide a function parameter or a BGP variable. BGP variables are accessible in a LET statement (e.g. in a filter), but recall that, inside a function body, the μ environment is empty. Rules 6 & 7 specify the evaluation of a LET clause with a SPARQL query of the SELECT form which binds the variables of the SELECT clause and evaluates the expression. Rule 8 specifies the evaluation of the FOR statement by evaluating the first expression that returns a list of values and then binds the variable successively with each element of this list and evaluates the second expression with each local binding. Since this statement does not compute a result in itself, it always returns *true*. Rules 9, 10, 11, 12, and 13 specify MAP, FUNCALL and APPY statements. Rule 14 specifies the evaluation of an LDScript expression. The semantics is that of standard SPARQL expression evaluation, except that the overall environment comprises an environment for local variables in addition to the standard environment for BGP variables.

$$\overline{\mu, \rho[x = v] \vdash x \to v} \tag{1}$$

$$\frac{x \notin \rho}{\mu[x = v], \rho \vdash x \to v} \tag{2}$$

$$\frac{f() \Rightarrow f() = body \,\wedge\, \emptyset, \emptyset \vdash body \to res}{\mu, \rho \vdash f() \to res} \tag{3}$$

$$\frac{\begin{array}{l} f(e_1, \dots e_n) \Rightarrow f(x_1, \dots x_n) = body \\ \forall i \in \{1..n\}\ \mu, \rho \vdash e_i \to v_i \\ \emptyset, [x_1 := v_1; \dots x_n := v_n] \vdash body \to res \end{array}}{\mu, \rho \vdash f(e_1, \dots e_n) \to res} \tag{4}$$

$$\frac{\mu, \rho \vdash e_1 \to v_1 \,\wedge\, \mu, \rho[x := v_1] \vdash e_2 \to res}{\mu, \rho \vdash let(x = e_1, e_2) \to res} \tag{5}$$

$$\frac{\begin{array}{l} \mu, \rho \vdash query \to \{\mu_1\} \cup \Omega \\ \mu, \rho.\mu_1 \vdash exp \to v \end{array}}{\mu, \rho \vdash let(query, exp) \to v} \tag{6}$$

$$\frac{\begin{array}{l} \mu, \rho \vdash query \to \emptyset \\ \mu, \rho \vdash exp \to v \end{array}}{\mu, \rho \vdash let(query, exp) \to v} \tag{7}$$

$$\frac{\begin{array}{l} \mu, \rho \vdash e \to (v_1, \dots v_n) \\ \forall i \in \{1..n\}\ \mu, \rho[x := v_i] \vdash b \to r_i \end{array}}{\mu, \rho \vdash for(x = e, b) \to true} \tag{8}$$

$$\frac{\begin{array}{l} \mu, \rho \vdash e \to (v_1, \dots v_n) \\ \forall i \in \{1..n\}\ \mu, \rho \vdash f(v_i) \to r_i \end{array}}{\mu, \rho \vdash map(f, e) \to true} \tag{9}$$

$$\frac{\mu, \rho \vdash e \to f \,\wedge\, \mu, \rho \vdash f(e_1, ..e_n) \to v}{\mu, \rho \vdash funcall(e, e_1, ..e_n) \to v} \tag{10}$$

$$\frac{\begin{array}{l} \mu, \rho \vdash e \to (v_1, ..v_n) \\ \mu, \rho \vdash apply(f, (v_1, ..v_n)) \to v \end{array}}{\mu, \rho \vdash apply(f, e) \to v} \tag{11}$$

$$\frac{\mu, \rho \vdash f() \rightarrow v}{\mu, \rho \vdash apply(f, ()) \rightarrow v} \tag{12}$$

$$\begin{array}{c} \mu, \rho \vdash apply(f, (v_2, ..v_n)) \rightarrow r \\ \mu, \rho \vdash f(v_1, r) \rightarrow v \\ \hline \mu, \rho \vdash apply(f, (v_1, ..v_n)) \rightarrow v \end{array} \tag{13}$$

$$\frac{sparql(\mu, \rho \vdash exp \rightarrow v)}{\mu, \rho \vdash exp \rightarrow v} \tag{14}$$

The above described Natural Semantics inference rules defining the semantics of the evaluation of LDScript expressions should be completed with the Natural Semantics inference rules defining the semantics of the evaluation of SPARQL queries within LDScript. These should be written according to Sect. 18.6 of the SPARQL recommendation[4].

5   Examples of Use Cases

In this section, we present the definition of several LDScript extension functions showing the expressive power and usability of the language. Some additional examples can be found at: http://ns.inria.fr/sparql-extension.

5.1   Extended Aggregates

LDScript enables programmers to simply define extended aggregates with a simple extension of the SPARQL interpreter. We introduce the `aggregate` function which is as an additional generic aggregate. This function takes as arguments an expression (e.g. `?v` in the example below) and aggregates the results of the expression into a `dt:list`. Then we can call a custom aggregation function with this list as argument. The example below defines `sort_concat`, a variant of the `group_concat` aggregate which sorts the elements before concatenation occurs. The `rq` prefix and namespace are used to assign a URI to each SPARQL standard function, hence `rq:concat` function is SPARQL `concat` function.

```
SELECT (aggregate(?v) AS ?list) (us:sort_concat(?list) AS ?res)
WHERE { ?x rdf:value/rdf:rest*/rdf:first ?v }
FUNCTION us:sort_concat(?list){ apply(rq:concat, xt:sort(?list)) }
```

---

[4] https://www.w3.org/TR/sparql11-query/#sparqlAlgebraEval.

5.2   Procedural Attachment

LDScript enables programmers to perform procedural attachment to RDF resources. The idea is to annotate the URI of a function to declare that it is a method associated to a class. In the example RDF annotation below, two functions are described, us:surfaceRectangle and us:surfaceCircle which compute surfaces; it states that they implement the method us:surface for us:Rectangle and us:Circle respectively.

```
us:surfaceRectangle a xt:Method ; xt:name us:surface ;
  xt:input (us:Rectangle) ; xt:output xsd:double .
us:surfaceCircle a xt:Method ;  xt:name us:surface ;
  xt:input (us:Circle) ; xt:output xsd:double .
```

Then, the method us:surface can be called on a resource as follows, without mentioning its type:

```
SELECT * (funcall(xt:method(us:surface, ?x), ?x) as ?m)
WHERE { ?x a us:Figure }
```

The xt:method function is defined below. It retrieves the function ?fun implementing the method ?m by finding the type ?t of the resource (line 3) and then finding a method attached to the type, or a superclass of the type (line 4). In the latter case, this implements method inheritance following the rdfs:subClassOf relation.

```
01   FUNCTION xt:method(?m, ?x){
02     LET (SELECT * WHERE {
03       ?x rdf:type/rdfs:subClassOf* ?t .
04       ?fun a xt:Method ; xt:name ?m ; xt:input(?t)})
05     { ?fun } }
```

Finally, the methods us:surfaceRectangle and us:surfaceCircle are defined as follows:

```
FUNCTION us:surfaceRectangle(?x){
  LET (SELECT * WHERE {?x us:width ?w ; us:length ?l})
  { ?w * ?l } }
FUNCTION us:surfaceCircle(?x){
  LET (SELECT * WHERE {?x us:radius ?r})
  { 3.14159 * power(?r, 2) } }
```

Below are some RDF descriptions of figures for which we can now compute the surface using the above defined procedural attachment.

```
us:Circle    rdfs:subClassOf us:Figure .
us:Rectangle rdfs:subClassOf us:Figure .
us:cc a us:Circle ; us:radius 1.5 .
us:rr a us:Rectangle ; us:width 2 ; us:length 3 .
```

5.3   Calendar

We wrote LDScript functions to compute the weekday of a date literal of type xsd:date[5] and functions to generate a calendar given a year[6]. We designed a dynamic Web page generated from DBpedia events where events of a given year are placed into the calendar[7]. The performance of LDScript is such that the Web page is computed and displayed in real time.

5.4   SHACL

As part of a SHACL validator, we wrote an interpreter for W3C SHACL Property Path language[8]. This real use case shows that LDScript enables users to write such programs in a few lines: the function below recursively rewrites a property path shape expression ?pp as an LDScript list.

```
FUNCTION sh:path(?shape, ?pp){
    LET (SELECT ?shape ?pp ?q ?path WHERE {
        GRAPH ?shape {
            # rdf:rest is for a sequence
            values ?q {
                sh:inversePath sh:alternativePath
                sh:zeroOrMorePath sh:oneOrMorePath
                sh:zeroOrOnePath rdf:rest }
            ?pp ?q ?path } } ) {
    IF (! bound(?q)){
        IF (isURI(?pp)){ ?pp } ELSE { error() }}
    ELSE IF (?q = rdf:rest) {
        xt:list(sh:sequence, sh:list(?shape, ?pp)) }
    ELSE { xt:list(?q, sh:path(?shape, ?path)) } } }
```

6   Implementation and Evaluation

We implemented LDScript using the SPARQL interpreter of the Corese Semantic Web Factory [2]. The FUNCTION, LET and other statements are implemented by the SPARQL parser, compiler and interpreter. Should an error occur, function evaluation resumes in error mode, according to the same model as SPARQL evaluation error: in a FILTER, the filter fails; in a SELECT or a BIND clause, *"the variable remains unbound for that solution but the query evaluation continues"*[9].

---

[5] http://ns.inria.fr/sparql-extension/calendar.

[6] http://corese.inria.fr/srv/template?transform=st:calendar.

[7] http://corese.inria.fr/srv/template?profile=st:calendar3.

[8] http://ns.inria.fr/sparql-extension/datashape.

[9] http://www.w3.org/TR/2013/REC-sparql11-query-20130321/#assignment.

6.1   Generic Evaluation and Validation

LDScript has been validated on the functions described in Sect. 5 and extensively used in several STTL transformations on a server available online[10] [3]. We measured the performance of our implementation of LDScript on the execution of (1) a recursive Fibonacci function to test an exponential number of calls, (2) on the Bubble sort algorithms to evaluate loops and (3) on statistics functions for the calculation aspect. We compared with Java and JavaScript implementations which, of course, benefit from many years of optimizations. The goal of this first evaluation was just to show that a direct implementation on top of a SPARQL engine without dedicated optimizations is already usable. The results are shown using a logarithmic scale in Fig. 1. The extension function fib implements the Fibonacci sequence. The computation of fib(35) = 9227465 on a HP EliteBook laptop takes 3650 ms in LDScript, 68.8 ms in JavaScript and 24.9 ms in Java.

```
FUNCTION us:fib(?n) {
  IF (n <= 2, 1, us:fib(?n - 2) + us:fib(?n - 1)) }
```

Bubble sort on an array of 1000 items takes 580.1 ms in LDScript, 6 ms in JavaScript and 9.5 ms in Java. Three statistic functions together (average, median and standard deviation) on an array containing 100000 integer values take 157.1 ms in LDScript, 80.5 ms in JavaScript and 6.9 ms in Java.

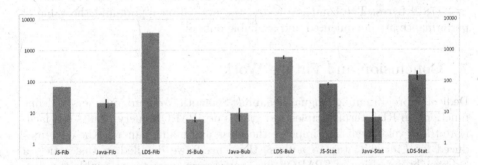

Fig. 1. Comparison of mean times and their mean absolute differences for JavaScript (JS), Java and LDScript (LDS) computing recursive Fibonacci (-Fib in Blue), Bubble sort (-Bub in green) and statistics (-Stat in red) using a logarithmic scale. (Color figure online)

The above described first implementation of LDScript is a proof of concept where we focused on the design and the semantics. Although focusing on performance is future work, we already took the first step of providing and comparing alternative implementations, as described in the following.

---

[10] http://corese.inria.fr.

6.2   Java Compiling and Specific Evaluation

In addition to LDScript interpreter, we have written a compiler from LDScript to Java. This enables us, among other things, to evaluate the performance of the LDScript interpreter compared to the equivalent Java code. We have compared performances on three LDScript programs with different programming characteristics (e.g. recursive calls) as well as a full implementation of the SHACL standard as a real use case. We therefore have four programs for this last evaluation: the recursive Fibonacci function, a calendar function that computes the weekday of a given date, a parser of Roman to Arabic numbers and reverse, and a SHACL validator. As a result, the execution time of the compiled Java code is higher than pure Java because the compiled code operates on RDF terms with XSD datatypes whereas a native Java code would operate on Java datatypes. Our experiments show that the LDScript interpreter can be as fast as the Java code produced by the LDScript compiler and sometimes slightly faster. One exception is the generated Java code for the Fibonacci function which is much more efficient, e.g. by a factor of 20 for fib(35). This is due to the optimized implementation of function call and recursion in Java. For the three other use cases, the performances of the LDScript interpreter and the Java code are equivalent. For the SHACL validator, we have tested it on the 97 SHACL test cases from W3C. The Java code runs in 5.2 s while the LDScript interpreter runs in 4.93 s (average time of ten runs after warmup on an HP laptop). The Java source code is 3220 lines and 37055 bytes, the LDScript source code is 2009 lines and 17819 bytes. The complete codes, the evaluation report and the table of performance are documented and available online[11].

7   Conclusion and Future Work

Dedicated programming language enabling Semantic Web programmers to define functions on RDF terms, triples and graphs or SPARQL query results can facilitate the development and improve the reuse and maintenance of the code produced for Linked Data. To address these needs we detailed in this article a lightweight extension of SPARQL filter expression language to enable the *definition* of extension functions and we defined a Linked Data script language on top of the SPARQL filter expression language. Compared to the state-of-the-art we directly extend the SPARQL language in order to enable the definition of extension functions in the SPARQL language *itself* and using its native syntax, building on a well-known and widely accepted component of the Web of data. The key point of our proposal is that a programming language can easily be integrated in SPARQL to define extension functions.

LDScript has all the features of Turing-complete programming languages: constants, lists, variables, expressions, boolean connectors, if-then-else, iteration, local variable definition, function definition, function call, recursion. LDScript is a programming language where values are RDF terms, hence its use to define

---

[11] http://ns.inria.fr/sparql-extension/example/table.html.

extension functions avoids to cast datatype values from RDF to the target language (e.g. Java) and back. It enables us to associate function definitions directly to a SPARQL query, with no need to compile nor link code. All standard SPARQL functions are natively available in LDScript and can be used directly in a LDScript function definition. LDScript extends the SPARQL filter expression language with several classical programming statements, among which FUNCTION, LET, FOR, FUNCALL and APPLY. The SELECT and CONSTRUCT SPARQL query forms are also statements of LDScript and can be used as well in the definition of functions. In addition, the language provides recursion, hence enabling recursive SPARQL queries: a function can execute a SPARQL query that can call the function. An LDScript interpreter is implemented in the Corese Semantic Web Factory as well as a compiler of LDScript into Java and the performances of the LDScript interpreter have been demonstrated on generic and concrete test cases. We successfully implemented several use cases with LDScript, among which a SHACL validator.

As future work, we will work on type checking function definition. LDScript indeed needs a type analysis because several new constructs have implicit type constraints: for example, the expression argument in Map must be list-valued; the first argument of funcall must be URI-valued. We also intend to extend higher order functions application to predefined functions. In the current version, higher order functions operate only on LDScript user-defined functions. On another note, we will work on the improvement of the performance of our implementation, and plan to provide a second implementation of LDScript on another triple store to validate the language. Finally, we plan to investigate the notion of "Linked Functions" and go further in the definition of a function programming language for SPARQL. The principle would consist in (1) dereferencing a function URI to get the function definition, provided security rules on function namespaces, and (2) annotating function URIs in the spirit of Linked Data.

References

1. Atzori, M.: Toward the Web of functions: interoperable higher-order functions in SPARQL. In: Mika, P., et al. (eds.) ISWC 2014. LNCS, vol. 8797, pp. 406–421. Springer, Cham (2014). doi:10.1007/978-3-319-11915-1_26
2. Corby, O., Faron-Zucker, C.: The KGRAM abstract machine for knowledge graph querying. In: IEEE/WIC/ACM International Conference on Web Intelligence, Toronto, Canada (2010)
3. Corby, O., Faron-Zucker, C., Gandon, F.: A generic RDF transformation software and its application to an online translation service for common languages of linked data. In: Arenas, M., et al. (eds.) ISWC 2015. LNCS, vol. 9367, pp. 150–165. Springer, Cham (2015). doi:10.1007/978-3-319-25010-6_9
4. Corby, O., Faron-Zucker, C., Gandon, F.: LDScript: a Linked Data Script Language. Research report RR-8982, INRIA (2016)
5. Kahn, G.: Natural semantics. In: Brandenburg, F.J., Vidal-Naquet, G., Wirsing, M. (eds.) STACS 1987. LNCS, vol. 247, pp. 22–39. Springer, Heidelberg (1987). doi:10.1007/BFb0039592

6. Knublauch, H.: SPIN - SPARQL Syntax. Member Submission, W3C (2011). http://www.w3.org/Submission/2011/SUBM-spin-sparql-20110222/
7. Lefrançois, M., Zimmermann, A., Bakerally, N.: A SPARQL extension for generating RDF from heterogeneous formats. In: Blomqvist, E., Maynard, D., Gangemi, A., Hoekstra, R., Hitzler, P., Hartig, O. (eds.) ESWC 2017. LNCS, vol. 10249, pp. 35–50. Springer, Cham (2017). doi:10.1007/978-3-319-58068-5_3
8. McCarthy, J.: Recursive functions of symbolic expressions and their computation by machine, part I. Commun. ACM **3**(4), 184–195 (1960)
9. Williams, G.: Extensible SPARQL functions with embedded javascript. In: ESWC Workshop on Scripting for the Semantic Web, SFSW 2007, Innsbruck, Austria. CEUR Workshop Proceedings, vol. 248 (2007)

Practical Update Management
in Ontology-Based Data Access

Giuseppe De Giacomo[1], Domenico Lembo[1(✉)], Xavier Oriol[2],
Domenico Fabio Savo[1], and Ernest Teniente[2]

[1] Sapienza Università di Roma, Rome, Italy
{degiacomo,lembo,savo}@dis.uniroma1.it
[2] Universitat Politècnica de Catalunya, Barcelona, Spain
{xoriol,teniente}@essi.upc.edu

Abstract. Ontology-based Data Access (OBDA) is gaining importance
both scientifically and practically. However, little attention has been paid
so far to the problem of updating OBDA systems. This is an essential
issue if we want to be able to cope with modifications of data both at
the ontology and at the source level, while maintaining the independence
of the data sources. In this paper, we propose mechanisms to properly
handle updates in this context. We show that updating data both at
the ontology and source level is first-order rewritable. We also provide
a practical implementation of such updating mechanisms based on non-
recursive Datalog.

1 Introduction

Ontology Based Data Access (OBDA) is a data integration approach that allows
for querying data sources through a unified conceptual view of the application
domain, expressed as an ontology [17]. In this way, users may ask queries without
being aware of the underlying structure of the data, while considering additional
knowledge provided by the ontology. One interesting feature of OBDA is that
data sources remain independent and only loosely coupled with the ontology
through the use of declarative mappings.

In OBDA, the ontology is usually specified in a lightweight language, like
a Description Logic (DL) of the *DL-Lite* family [4]. *DL-Lite* logics have the
ability of essentially capturing conceptual models such as UML class diagrams,
while being characterized by nice computational properties with respect to query
answering. Indeed, this task in *DL-Lite* based OBDA systems is *first-order (FO)
rewritable*, which means that any conjunctive query over the ontology (or TBox)
can be answered by rewriting it first into a FO-query over a *virtual* set of facts
(or ABox), and then into FO-queries over the data sources, by suitably unfolding
(traversing backward) the mappings [17].

Little attention has been paid so far in OBDA to the problem of updating, which is the main target of this paper. Namely, we consider "write-also
OBDA systems", where a user may change the *extensional level* of the system,
in contrast with "read-only OBDA systems", where this service is not provided.

© Springer International Publishing AG 2017
C. d'Amato et al. (Eds.): ISWC 2017, Part I, LNCS 10587, pp. 225–242, 2017.
DOI: 10.1007/978-3-319-68288-4_14

We recall that updating a logical theory means changing the old beliefs with new ones, through both addition and removal of pieces of information. This is usually accomplished according to the principle of minimal change, i.e., old information contradicting the new one should be removed in a way that the new theory is as close as possible to the previous one [8,9,16,18,21].

Besides guaranteeing the above behaviour, our goal is to allow users to update the data at the ontology level while maintaining the independence of the data sources. This is in contrast with the traditional way to handle updates in databases, since we should not force the update to propagate to the sources, as done in view updating [10,11,19]. Indeed, sources are not under the exclusive control of the ontology, and changing them has a high risk of deeply impacting the contents used by other source clients.

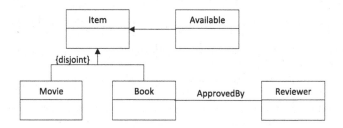

Fig. 1. UML ontology of a library

For example, consider the ontology of a library specified as a UML class diagram in Fig. 1, where books are approved by reviewers, movies and books are items, some of which are available. Obviously, a movie is not a book, and an item is not a reviewer. Such an ontology can be encoded through the following *DL-Lite* axioms:

$$\text{Movie} \sqsubseteq \text{Item} \quad \exists\text{ApprovedBy} \sqsubseteq \text{Book} \quad \exists\text{ApprovedBy}^- \sqsubseteq \text{Reviewer}$$
$$\text{Available} \sqsubseteq \text{Item} \quad \text{Book} \sqsubseteq \text{Item} \quad \text{Book} \sqsubseteq \neg\text{Movie} \quad \text{Item} \sqsubseteq \neg\text{Reviewer}$$

Then, consider an external source whose schema contains the relational tables T_Movie, T_Book, T_Copy, T_Borrow, T_RevAuthor, and T_Rev, and link it to the ontology through the mapping below, which we write as Datalog rules, whose heads (resp. bodies) contain only ontology (resp. database) predicates.

```
Movie(x)    :- T_Movie(x)
Book(x)     :- T_Book(x)
Available(x):- T_Copy(x,y), ¬T_Borrow(y,z)
Reviewer(y) :- T_RevAuthor(r,y)
ApprovedBy(x,y):- T_Rev(x,r,z), z>=5, T_RevAuthor(r,y)
```

Let the following set of facts be a database instance at the sources:

```
T_Movie(Alien), T_Book(Ubik), T_Copy(Ubik,C1), T_Copy(Ubik,C2),
T_Borrow(C1,Bob)
```

It is not difficult to see that the above mapping and database imply the (virtual) ABox { Movie(Alien),Book(Ubik),Available(Ubik)}. Assume now that we want to insert Item(Matrix) and to delete Available(Ubik). Notice that this update does not correspond to any source database update. Indeed, to insert in the database the item 'Matrix', we have to classify it either as a movie or as a book, thus, entailing an unintended fact. The problem is even worse for the case of deleting the availability of 'Ubik', for which we have to either delete the copy 'C2' (and thus deleting an existing copy of the book), or mark it as borrowed by some unknown user of the library (when no borrowing might exist). Moreover, these (unintended) changes in the database affect the contents used by other database clients, whereas we only want to change some ABox assertions for the users of the OBDA system.

To avoid these situations, we materialize the ABox facts that the user of the OBDA system inserts (resp. deletes) and that are not derived (resp. derived) from the data sources. In this way, the requested updates can always be accomplished without affecting the contents of the sources. This is achieved by materializing the *differences* between the current (virtual) ABox (as generated by the data sources through the mappings) and the one desired by the user. To handle these materialized facts, we use some special auxiliary *ins/del* relational tables and suitably extend the mappings. As an example, consider the following new mappings for Item and Available (which replaces the previous one):

```
Item(x)      :- ins_Item(x)
Available(x):- T_Copy(x,y), ¬T_Borrow(y,z), ¬del_Available(x)
```

Now, we can achieve the previous ontology update by materializing the facts ins_Item(Matrix) and del_Available(Ubik).

Let us now consider an update that contradicts previous data. Assume that we want to insert Book(Alien). This contrasts the fact that 'Alien' is already known to be a movie. We manage situations like this through the materialization of additional insertions/deletions that allow us to keep the system consistent, according to a specific minimal change criterion introduced in [7]. In our example, to fully accomplish the update we materialize both ins_Book(Alien) and del_Movie(Alien).

There is a further update scenario of interest in write-also OBDA systems. Since the data sources are autonomous, they in turn can be freely changed by their users. Thus we need to deal with two kinds of updates: *ontology-level* and *source-level*. An ontology-level update is posed over the ontology, and is the update we discussed so far. Instead, a source-level update occurs when a data source is modified.

For the source-level case, our framework detects how the update at the sources is reflected, through the mapping, in ABox insertions/deletions, and based on them it computes the additional insertions/deletions that will maintain the system consistent. As we will show, only ABox insertions induced by a source-level update may cause inconsistency, and to repair it we essentially treat them as if they were ontology-level updates. Note however that, whereas we can expect ontology-level updates directly specified by users to be coherent with the ontology, i.e., they alone do not violate TBox axioms, which is a classical assumption in update theory, this does not necessarily hold for ABox insertions induced by a source-level update. Consider an update at the sources that inserts the facts T_Movie(TheShining) and T_Book(TheShining). This is a legal source-level update, since no constraints are specified on the source database (it can even be possible that tables T_Movie and T_Book belong to different databases). This source-level update induces two ABox insertions, i.e., Movie(TheShining) and Book(TheShining), which together violate the disjointness Book ⊑ ¬Movie. To cope with this problem our framework repairs the induced ontology-level update according to a minimality criterion which allows to filter away the conflicting insertions but to maintain their common consistent logical consequences. In our example, this means that both Movie(TheShining) and Book(TheShining) will be invalidated at the ontology level (i.e., the OBDA system will not infer them), but their common consequence Item(TheShining) will be considered as an ABox insertion induced by the source-level update. We remark that the last form of inconsistency, which we call incoherence, is due to mutually conflicting insertions in the update itself, and should not to be confused with the case when the update is inconsistent with the previous state of the OBDA system, which we discussed before.

The contributions we provide in this paper can be then summarized as follows.

- We define a new formal framework for ontology-level and source-level updates.
- We show that both update mechanisms are first-order rewritable, that is, the new contents of the materialized *differences* when an update occurs can be computed by means of first-order queries. This entails that ontology-level and source-level updates are in AC^0 (i.e., sub-polynomial) in data complexity, which is the usual desired complexity for OBDA tasks.
- We prove these results by computing updates by means of non-recursive Datalog programs, which can be straightforwardly translated into other (relational-algebra equivalent) languages, such as SQL or SPARQL. Thus, we argue that our framework is not only computationally feasible, but also practically embeddable in current OBDA solutions with existing technology, and without affecting the clients working on the source databases.
- We propose variants of update semantics to handle incoherent (in the sense explained above) update specifications, which naturally arise in source-level updates. To the best of our knowledge, incoherent updates have not been studied before, and, as a side contribution, we formalize and study different solutions to this problem.

The rest of the paper is organized as follows. In Sect. 2 we provide some preliminaries on ontologies and read-only OBDA systems. In Sect. 3 we describe how to transform read-only OBDA systems into write-also ones and provide an overview of our techniques to manage both ontology-level and source-level updates. In Sects. 4 and 5 we provide the algorithms to accomplish the two kinds of updates, respectively, and show that both are first-order rewritable. We conclude the paper in Sect. 6.

2   Preliminaries

We assume to have three pairwise disjoint, countably infinite alphabets: N_O for ontology predicates, N_S for relational predicates, and N_I for constants. Moreover, we use standard notions for relational databases [1].

Ontologies. A DL ontology $\mathcal{O}$ is pair $\langle \mathcal{T}, \mathcal{A} \rangle$, where $\mathcal{T}$ is the TBox and $\mathcal{A}$ is the ABox, providing intensional and extensional knowledge, respectively [2]. Roughly, DL ontologies represent knowledge in terms of concepts, denoting sets of objects, and roles, denoting binary relationships between objects. In this paper we focus on ontologies expressed in $DL\text{-}Lite_A$ [17]. A $DL\text{-}Lite_A$ TBox is a finite set of axioms of the form $B_1 \sqsubseteq B_2$, $B_1 \sqsubseteq \neg B_2$, $R_1 \sqsubseteq R_2$, $R_1 \sqsubseteq \neg R_2$, and (funct R), where: R, possibly with subscript, is an *atomic role* P, i.e., a binary predicate in N_O, or its inverse P^-; B_i, called *basic concept*, is an *atomic concept* A, i.e., a unary predicate in N_O, or a concept of the form $\exists R$, which denotes the set of objects occurring as first argument of R; (funct R) denotes the functionality of R, which states that its first argument is a key. Suitable restrictions are imposed on the combination of inclusions among roles and functionalities. A $DL\text{-}Lite_A$ ABox is a finite set of facts of the form $A(c)$ or $P(c, c')$, where $c, c' \in N_I$.

As for the semantics, we denote with $Mod(\mathcal{O})$ the set of models of $\mathcal{O}$. We say that $\mathcal{O}$ is consistent if $Mod(\mathcal{O}) \neq \emptyset$, inconsistent otherwise, and that an ABox $\mathcal{A}$ is $\mathcal{T}$-consistent if $\langle \mathcal{T}, \mathcal{A} \rangle$ is consistent. Moreover, we denote with $\mathcal{O} \models \alpha$ the entailment of a fact or axiom α by $\mathcal{O}$, and with $cl_\mathcal{T}(\mathcal{A})$ the ground closure of $\mathcal{A}$, i.e., set of ABox facts α such that $\langle \mathcal{T}, \mathcal{A} \rangle \models \alpha$. We assume that, for each atomic concept or role N, $\mathcal{T} \not\models N \sqsubseteq \neg N$.

Read-only OBDA systems. An *OBDA specification* is a triple $\mathcal{J} = \langle \mathcal{T}, \mathcal{M}, \mathcal{S} \rangle$, where $\mathcal{T}$ is a DL TBox, $\mathcal{S}$ is a relational schema, called *source schema*, and $\mathcal{M}$ is a *mapping* between $\mathcal{S}$ and $\mathcal{T}$. As usual in OBDA, we assume $\mathcal{M}$ to be a GAV mapping [14], which we represent as Datalog rules, whose head predicates are from N_O and body predicates are from N_S. As usual in Datalog we require such rules to be safe [1]. It is easy to see that $\mathcal{M}$, seen as a program, is non-recursive. Note that OBDA specifications of the above form can be considered *read-only*, since they are not specifically thought to be updated, but are usually only queried by users.

An *OBDA system* is a pair $(\mathcal{J}, D)$, where $\mathcal{J} = \langle \mathcal{T}, \mathcal{M}, \mathcal{S} \rangle$ is an OBDA specification, and D is a *source database*, i.e., a set of facts for $\mathcal{S}$. A representation of a read-only OBDA system is given in Fig. 2(a). The semantics of $(\mathcal{J}, D)$ is given in terms of interpretations of $\mathcal{T}$. To define it, we make use of the *retrieved ABox*, i.e., the set

$$ ret(\mathcal{M}, D) = \{N(t) \mid t \in eval(\varphi(x), D) \text{ and } N(x)\text{:-}\varphi(x) \in \mathcal{M}\} $$

where N is a concept or role in N_O and $eval(\varphi(x), D)$ denotes the evaluation of $\varphi(x)$, seen as a query, over D. Then, a model of $(\mathcal{J}, D)$ is a model of the ontology $\langle \mathcal{T}, ret(\mathcal{M}, D) \rangle$, and the notions of consistency and entailment introduced before naturally extend to an OBDA system. We point out that in OBDA systems the retrieved ABox is usually not really computed. To emphasize this, we often refer to the retrieved ABox as the *virtual ABox* of an OBDA system.

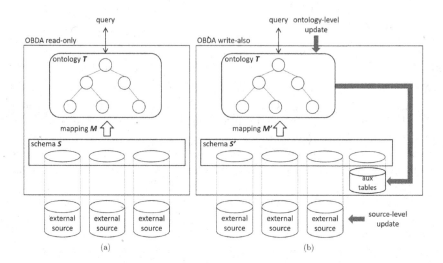

Fig. 2. (a) Read-only OBDA architecture (b) Write-also OBDA architecture.

3   Write-also OBDA Systems

Given a "read-only" OBDA specification $\mathcal{J} = \langle \mathcal{T}, \mathcal{M}, \mathcal{S} \rangle$, our framework extends the source schema $\mathcal{S}$ to be able to materialize some ABox insertions/deletions without affecting the original source database. More in detail, the framework extends the database schema $\mathcal{S}$ to a new schema $\mathcal{S}'$ by considering, for each ontology atomic concept/role N, two additional tables ins_N and del_N, used to trace insertions/deletions of ABox facts for N[1]. Then, the framework systematically changes the mapping $\mathcal{M}$ into a mapping $\mathcal{M}'$ in the following way:

1. For each atomic concept/role N, add the new mapping assertion $N(\boldsymbol{x})$:- $ins\_N(\boldsymbol{x})$. This guarantees that the instances in ins_N belong to the retrieved ABox as instances of N (i.e., as N facts);
2. Replace each mapping assertion of the form $N(\boldsymbol{x})$:- $\phi(\boldsymbol{x})$, with the mapping assertion $N(\boldsymbol{x})$:- $\phi(\boldsymbol{x}) \wedge \neg del\_N(\boldsymbol{x})$. This avoids the entailment of N facts that are stored as deleted through instances of del_N.

We call $\mathcal{J}' = \langle \mathcal{T}, \mathcal{M}', \mathcal{S}' \rangle$ a *write-also OBDA specification*. It is not difficult to realize that the OBDA specifications $\mathcal{J}$ and $\mathcal{J}'$ are equivalent, in the sense that, when the contents of the new tables ins_N/del_N are empty, both OBDA specifications have the same retrieved ABox. Thus, this mapping extension preserves the semantics of the original one, but permits modifying the retrieved ABox through the ins_N/del_N tables without collateral effects. In the following, given a write-also mapping $\mathcal{M}'$, we denote by $\pi(\mathcal{M}')$ the original read-only mapping $\mathcal{M}$.

---

[1] These tables are typically stored in a different database from those containing actual data, but conceptually are part of $\mathcal{S}'$.

We now intuitively illustrate how the framework modifies the contents of the ins_N/del_N tables for accomplishing ontology-level and source-level updates.

Ontology-level update. An ontology-level update refers to the situation where the update is posed over the ontology. It is intended to change the extensional level of the write-also OBDA system, but without modifying the data at the sources. Thus, it does not change the content of source predicates in the original source schema $\mathcal{S}$. It is accomplished by (1) computing the full set of ontological insertions/deletions that are required to satisfy it in a consistent manner, and (2) realizing the previous set of ontological insertions/deletions. The first step is done through a Datalog program computed at compile time (that is, the Datalog rules are fully determined by the OBDA specification, whereas Datalog facts comes from the user requested update and the current database state of the source schema $\mathcal{S}'$). Such program encodes the update semantics presented in [7], which allows for solving possible inconsistencies between the new beliefs implied by the update and the old ones. Such semantics also allow to preserve logical consequences of the old beliefs that are still consistent with the update. Then, the second step manipulates the ins/del tables accordingly, in order to satisfy the previously computed insertions/deletions. Since such tables are not accessible to data source clients, such update is transparent to them.

Source-level update. A source-level update refers to the situation in which the update is posed over the source database. Such kind of update is always applied to the sources as requested. However, it may have effects at the ontological level, since it is propagated by the mapping. To handle source-level updates, the framework: (1) computes which insertions/deletions of ABox facts are caused by the database update (we call such facts *retrieved ABox changes*); (2) computes the set of ontological insertions/deletions that are required to accomplish the changes computed previously in a consistent manner; (3) realizes the previous ontological updates. Step (1) is performed through the adaptation of a technique from the literature on view change computation [20]. Step (2), even though similar in principle to Step (1) for ontology-level updates, presents some further complications. Indeed, even though the modification is coherent at the level of the sources, there are no guarantees that it corresponds to a coherent update at the level of the ontology. For instance, a source-level update might cause the insertion of both the facts $C(o)$ and $D(o)$ in the retrieved ABox, whereas the ontology entails that C and D are disjoint. In this situation, our framework adopts a new update semantics suited for dealing with incoherent updates and, according to it, modifies the content of the ins/del tables in order to reflect the proper changes upon the retrieved ABox. Similarly as before, the first two steps are computed through Datalog programs built at compile time.

4   Ontology-Level Update

We start with some notions on update over ontologies. Following [5,7,15], an *ontology update* $\mathcal{U}$ is a pair of sets of ABox facts $(\mathcal{A}_{\mathcal{U}}^+, \mathcal{A}_{\mathcal{U}}^-)$, where $\mathcal{A}_{\mathcal{U}}^+$ are *insertions* and $\mathcal{A}_{\mathcal{U}}^-$ are *deletions*. We say that an update $\mathcal{U} = (\mathcal{A}_{\mathcal{U}}^+, \mathcal{A}_{\mathcal{U}}^-)$ is *coherent* with a TBox $\mathcal{T}$ if: (i) $Mod(\langle \mathcal{T}, \mathcal{A}_{\mathcal{U}}^{+}\rangle) \neq \emptyset$, i.e., the set of facts we are adding is consistent with $\mathcal{T}$; (ii) $\mathcal{A}_{\mathcal{U}}^{-} \cap \mathrm{cl}_{\mathcal{T}}(\mathcal{A}_{\mathcal{U}}^{+}) = \emptyset$, i.e., the update is not asking for deleting and inserting the same knowledge at the same time. Specifically, we define the result of updating an ontology as follows.

Definition 1 [7]. *Let* $\mathcal{O} = \langle \mathcal{T}, \mathcal{A} \rangle$ *be a consistent DL-Lite$_\mathcal{A}$ ontology and let* $\mathcal{U} = (\mathcal{A}_{\mathcal{U}}^{+}, \mathcal{A}_{\mathcal{U}}^{-})$ *be an update coherent with* $\mathcal{T}$. *The result of updating* $\mathcal{O}$ *with* $\mathcal{U}$, *denoted by* $\mathcal{O} \bullet \mathcal{U}$, *is the ABox* $\mathcal{A}^{\mathcal{U}} = \mathcal{A}' \cup \mathcal{A}_{\mathcal{U}}^{+}$, *where* $\mathcal{A}'$ *is a maximal subset of the closure* $\mathrm{cl}_{\mathcal{T}}(\mathcal{A})$ *such that* $\mathcal{A}' \cup \mathcal{A}_{\mathcal{U}}^{+}$ *is* $\mathcal{T}$-consistent, *and* $\langle \mathcal{T}, \mathcal{A}^{\mathcal{U}} \rangle \not\models \beta$ *for each* $\beta \in \mathcal{A}_{\mathcal{U}}^{-}$.

The above update semantics is syntax-independent, consequence conservative, and the ABox resulting from the update operation is, up to logical equivalence, unique [7].

An ontology-level update over a write-also OBDA system $(\langle \mathcal{T}, \mathcal{M}, \mathcal{S} \rangle, D)$ is an update over the ontology $\langle \mathcal{T}, ret(\mathcal{M}, D) \rangle$. To realize the update, we first compute the ABox facts that should be inserted-to/deleted-from the retrieved ABox $ret(\mathcal{M}, D)$, according to Definition 1. Then, we specify the changes to be performed on the ins/del tables from these ABox facts.

For the first task, we make use of a non-recursive Datalog program able to manage updates over *DL-Lite$_\mathcal{A}$* ontologies, which has been presented in [7]. This program derives the insertions/deletions for a concept/role N as derived literals of the form $ins\_N'(\boldsymbol{x})$ and $del\_N'(\boldsymbol{x})$. To do so, the program uses as base facts the current contents of the database D, together with the requested ontology update. That is, the program has a fact $ins\_N\_ol(\boldsymbol{t})$ for each $N(\boldsymbol{t}) \in \mathcal{A}_{\mathcal{U}}^{+}$, and $del\_N\_ol(\boldsymbol{t})$ for each $N(\boldsymbol{t}) \in \mathcal{A}_{\mathcal{U}}^{-}$. Since the Datalog derivation rules are fully determined by $\mathcal{T}$ and $\mathcal{M}$, we refer to it as *Datalog($\mathcal{T}, \mathcal{M}$)*, and denote the base facts as $D+\mathcal{U}$.

Basically, *Datalog($\mathcal{T}, \mathcal{M}$)* derives insertions/deletions from the requested update, and computes some extra deletions to avoid violating disjoint/functionality axioms in $\mathcal{T}$, and some extra insertions to preserve information, according to the update semantics of Definition 1. We illustrate these ideas by showing some of the rules for our example:

```
del_Movie'(x)  :- T_Movie(x), del_Item_ol(x)
del_Movie'(x)  :- T_Movie(x), ins_Book_ol(x)
ins_Item'(x)   :- del_Movie'(x), ¬del_Item_ol(x)
```

The first rule states that a movie should be deleted if it is deleted as an item. This is required to fully accomplish the deletion since, otherwise, the item would still be implied because of Movie ⊑ Item. The second rule implies the deletion of a movie because of the insertion of a book when the movie is in the database, to avoid violating Book ⊑ ¬Movie. This reflects the principle that information in the update has to be preferred to the old one, in case of contradiction. The third one entails the insertion of an item when it is deleted as a movie for preserving this entailed belief. This reflects the consequence conservative nature of our update semantics (cf. Definition 1).

Algorithm 1. ontology-level-Update($\mathcal{T}, \mathcal{M}, \mathcal{U}, D$)

---

1 $D' \leftarrow D$
2 **foreach** *fact ins_N'(t) derived* by *Datalog($\mathcal{T}$, $\mathcal{M}$)* from $D{+}\mathcal{U}$ **do**
3   **if** *del_N(t)* $\in D$ **then** remove *del_N(t)* from D' **else** insert *ins_N(t)* into D'
4 **foreach** fact *del_N'(t) derived* by *Datalog($\mathcal{T}$, $\mathcal{M}$)* from $D{+}\mathcal{U}$ **do**
5   **if** *ins_N(t)* $\in D$ **then** remove *ins_N(t)* from D' **else** insert *del_N(t)* into D'
6 **return** D'

$Datalog(\mathcal{T}, \mathcal{M})$ is sound and complete to compute the ABox modifications required to accomplish an update [7].

Then, we realize these derived insertions/deletions using the ins/del database tables by means of Algorithm 1. Intuitively, the algorithm tries to insert a fact by first removing its deletion from D' (if any). Indeed, this means that the fact is implied by $\pi(\mathcal{M})$ (i.e., the read-only version of the mapping) and D. If there is no deletion of this fact in D, then, it is recorded as an insertion. The case of deletions is analogous. The following result is a consequence of the correctness of Datalog($\mathcal{T}$, $\mathcal{M}$) and Algorithm 1.

Theorem 1. *Let $(\langle \mathcal{T}, \mathcal{M}, \mathcal{S}\rangle, D)$ be a consistent write-also OBDA system, and $\mathcal{U}$ be an update coherent with $\mathcal{T}$. Algorithm 1 computes D' s.t. $\langle \mathcal{T}, ret(\mathcal{M}, D)\rangle \bullet \mathcal{U} = ret(\mathcal{M}, D')$.*

The above theorem says that Algorithm 1 correctly realizes an ontology-level update. Considering the data complexity of non-recursive Datalog, Theorem 1 immediately implies that computing ontology-level updates is in AC^0 in data complexity, i.e., in the size of $D{+}\mathcal{U}$.

5   Source-Level Update

A source level update is a set of update operations, both insertions and deletions, over the source database. We denote it by $\mathcal{U}_{sl}$. The basic idea is to first use the event rules in [20] to compute the changes over the ABox that are induced by $\mathcal{U}_{sl}$.

ABox changes induced by $\mathcal{U}_{sl}$ are of two kinds: insertion and deletion. More formally, let $(\langle \mathcal{T}, \mathcal{S}, \mathcal{M}\rangle, D)$ be a write-also OBDA system, $\mathcal{U}_{sl}$ a source-level update, and D' the database obtained by applying $\mathcal{U}_{sl}$ to D. The *retrieved ABox changes* derived by D, $\mathcal{M}$ and $\mathcal{U}_{sl}$ are represented as a pair $(\mathcal{A}^+, \mathcal{A}^-)$, where $\mathcal{A}^+ = ret(\pi(\mathcal{M}), D') \setminus ret(\pi(\mathcal{M}), D)$, and $\mathcal{A}^- = ret(\pi(\mathcal{M}), D) \setminus ret(\pi(\mathcal{M}), D')$. $\mathcal{A}^+$ and $\mathcal{A}^-$ are called the retrieved ABox insertions and deletions, respectively.

The deletion of ABox facts cannot make the ontology inconsistent. So, when a new ABox deletion is retrieved, we simply check if such deletion was present in the corresponding del table, and if so, we remove it. In this way, we ensure that del tables only contains deletions of facts currently retrieved by $\pi(\mathcal{M})$. The case of retrieved ABox insertions is more complicated, since adding new ABox facts might make the ontology inconsistent. Hence, besides removing from the ins tables the facts corresponding to the new retrieved insertions (if any), we need to deal with possible inconsistencies. This is similar to what happens for ontology-level updates. However, in this case, retrieved ABox insertions might not be coherent with the TBox (i.e. the newly inserted ABox facts alone might directly contradict the TBox). Thus, we need some further machinery to deal with incoherency.

For ease of exposition, in the following we first discuss the simplified setting in which we assume that the retrieved ABox insertions are coherent with the TBox (although not necessarily consistent with the TBox and the virtual retrieved ABox). Then we tackle the full setting, providing a solution for the case in which retrieved ABox insertions may be incoherent (and inconsistent).

5.1 Coherent Source-Level Updates

Let $\mathcal{J} = \langle \mathcal{T}, \mathcal{M}, \mathcal{S} \rangle$ be a write-also OBDA specification, D a database for $\mathcal{S}$, and $\mathcal{U}_{sl}$ a source-level update (thus, involving source predicates but no auxiliary ins/del predicates in $\mathcal{S}$). We proceed as follows: (1) obtain the retrieved ABox changes $(\mathcal{A}^+, \mathcal{A}^-)$ derived by D, $\mathcal{M}$, and $\mathcal{U}_{sl}$; (2) for that part of $(\mathcal{A}^+, \mathcal{A}^-)$ that is already realized through facts in the ins/del tables (due to previous updates) remove the corresponding ins/del facts that become redundant, (3) for the non-redundant part of $\mathcal{A}^+$ proceed as for ontology-level updates to compute the necessary deletions from the current retrieved ABox for preserving the ontology consistency.

The first step can be performed by exploiting a *view change* computation technique. Indeed, each mapping rule can be seen as a *relational view* by considering the head of the rule as a *relational query*. Specifically, we use the technique described in [20], which has been shown to be sound and complete for computing insertions and deletions of *view contents* in the *view change* computation problem for general first-order queries.

The idea of this technique is to materialize the insertion/deletion operations in an update $\mathcal{U}_{sl}$ over the source database in some ad-hoc *ins_T_Table/del_T_Table*, and compute the resulting retrieved ABox change $(\mathcal{A}^+, \mathcal{A}^-)$ through a Datalog program: for each $N(t)$ fact in $\mathcal{A}^+/\mathcal{A}^-$ the program generates a *ins_N_sl(t)/del_N_sl(t)* fact.

For instance, in our running example, we can detect that an item is inserted as available through the following rules:[2]

```
ins_Avail_sl(x):- ins_T_Copy(x,y), del_T_Borrow(y,z),
            ¬ins_T_Borrow(y,w), ¬T_Borrowed_pre(y), ¬T_Avail(x)
ins_Avail_sl(x):- ins_T_Copy(x,y), ¬T_Borrow(y,w),
            ¬ins_T_Borrow(y,z), ¬T_Avail(x)
ins_Avail_sl(x):- T_Copy(x,y), ¬del_T_Copy(x,y), del_T_Borrow(y,z),
            ¬ins_T_Borrow(y,w), ¬T_Borrowed_pre(y), ¬T_Avail(x)
T_Borrowed_pre(y):- T_Borrow(y,z), ¬del_T_Borrow(y,z)
T_Avail(x):- T_Copy(x,y), ¬T_Borrow(y,z)
```

---

[2] Unsafe rules in the example can be made easily safe using auxiliary predicates.

The first two rules detect that x is newly available when we insert a new copy of it which is not borrowed anymore, or has never been borrowed, respectively (provided that x was not available according to the original mapping $\mathcal{M}$ before the update). The third rule corresponds to the case that a preexisting copy of the item is no longer borrowed. Deletions are computed using similar rules:

```
del_Avail_sl(x):- del_T_Copy(x,y), ¬T_Borrow(y,z),
                  ¬T_Avail_pre(x), ¬ins_Avail_sl(x)
del_Avail_sl(x):- T_Copy(x,y), ¬T_Borrow(y,w), ins_T_Borrow(y, z),
                  ¬T_Avail_pre(x), ¬ins_Avail_sl(x)
T_Avail_pre(x):- T_Copy(x,y), ¬del_T_Copy(x,y), ¬T_Borrowed_pre(y),
                 ¬ins_T_Borrow(y, w)
```

The first rule detects that x is no longer available because we have deleted a copy of it that was not borrowed, being this copy the unique one still available, and without adding any other copy nor deleting a borrowing from another one. Similarly, the second detects that x is no longer available because of borrowing the last available copy without inserting new copies nor deleting previous borrowings.

The computed ins_N_sl/del_N_sl facts are directly derived from the update over the source database and the mapping $\mathcal{M}$. Therefore, if the corresponding ins_N/del_N facts were already present in the OBDA system due to some previous updates, now there is no need to still keep them. Hence, for the sake of non-redundancy, they must be deleted from D if they were part of it. We notice that in this case, we do not have to take care of inconsistencies that may arise due to the update. Indeed, inconsistencies, if any, have been already solved by the accomplishment of previous updates, which required the insertions of the same facts that now are entailed by the source-level update.

However, ins_N_sl facts that do not already have a corresponding ins_N (due to previous updates), may lead to inconsistencies when combined with the current retrieved ABox. Indeed, consider the case that our current retrieved ABox contains *Book(Eat)*, and because of a source-level update we have $ins\_Movie\_sl(Eat)$. Note that *Book(Eat)* is not violating any TBox constraint, neither applying $ins\_Movie\_sl(Eat)$ violates any TBox constraint per se, but the combination of both violates the TBox disjunction assertion between *Book* and *Movie*.

To solve this situation, we have to delete some ABox facts. This deletion is exactly the same we do in the case of ontology-level insertions. Thus, we can compute these extra deletions by directly invoking the ontology-level update algorithm given in Sect. 4 (Algorithm 1: ontology-level-Update). Note that del_N_sl updates cannot lead to inconsistencies, therefore, they can be omitted when invoking the ontology-level-Update.

All this behavior is formally shown in Algorithm 2. Given a write-also OBDA system $(\langle \mathcal{T}, \mathcal{M}, \mathcal{S} \rangle, D)$, the algorithm takes as input $\mathcal{T}$, $\mathcal{M}$, the requested source-level update $\mathcal{U}_{sl}$ (expressed as ins_T_Table/del_T_Table facts[3]) and D. Also, it makes use of $Datalog^{sl}$, the Datalog program encoding the rules discussed

---

[3] These rules can be transparently captured through database triggers.

Algorithm 2. source-level-Update($\mathcal{T}$, $\mathcal{M}$, $\mathcal{U}_{sl}$, D)

---

1 $\mathcal{A}^+ \leftarrow \emptyset$
2 **foreach** *fact ins_N_sl(t) derived* by $Datalog^{sl}$ ($\mathcal{T}$, $\mathcal{M}$) from $\mathcal{U}_{sl} + D$ **do**
3   **if** *ins_N(t)* $\in D$ **then** remove *ins_N(t)* from D **else** include $N(t)$ in $\mathcal{A}^+$
4 **foreach** *fact del_N_sl(t) derived* by $Datalog^{sl}$ ($\mathcal{T}$, $\mathcal{M}$) from $\mathcal{U}_{sl} + D$ **do**
5   **if** *del_N(t)* $\in D$ **then** remove *del_N(t)* from D
6 $D' = \text{apply}(\mathcal{U}_{sl}, D)$
7 **return** ontology-level-Update($\mathcal{T}$, $\mathcal{M}$, $(\mathcal{A}^+, \{\})$, D')

---

above. In the algorithm, apply($\mathcal{U}_{sl}$, D) indicates the application $\mathcal{U}_{sl}$ to the source database D.

5.2 Incoherent Source-Level Update

When the retrieved ABox insertions are not necessarily coherent with the ontology (i.e., they might violate, by themselves, the TBox), we can no longer proceed as done in Sect. 5.1. In particular, we cannot simply invoke, as in Algorithm 2, the algorithm ontology-level-Update, since this algorithm requires the input update to be coherent.

To cope with the above problem, in the following we consider a new kind of ontology-level update, which we call *weakly-coherent*, and study it. Intuitively, a weakly-coherent update is an ABox update whose insertions might directly contradict the TBox, but that cannot contradict its own deletions. More formally, given a consistent ontology $\mathcal{O} = \langle \mathcal{T}, \mathcal{A} \rangle$ and an update $\mathcal{U} = (\mathcal{A}_{\mathcal{U}}^+, \mathcal{A}_{\mathcal{U}}^-)$, we say that $\mathcal{U}$ is *weakly-coherent* with $\mathcal{T}$ if $\mathcal{A}_{\mathcal{U}}^- \cap \text{cl}_{\mathcal{T}}(\mathcal{A}_{\mathcal{U}}^+) = \emptyset$. In other terms, differently from coherent updates, in weakly-coherent ones we do not require that $Mod(\langle \mathcal{T}, \mathcal{A}_{\mathcal{U}}^+ \rangle) \neq \emptyset$. Note that all updates of the form $(\mathcal{A}^+, \emptyset)$, like the ontology-level updates inferred by source-level ones, which we are analyzing in this section, are always trivially weakly-coherent.

Then, our idea is to introduce a new operator for ontology-level weakly-coherent updates, and show that the result of applying such operator can be easily computed by adapting the previous algorithms and Datalog programs for coherent updates.

To this aim, in the following we in fact present and discuss two new semantics for updating a consistent ontology with a weakly-coherent update. Similar to the update semantics given in Definition 1, these new semantics are consequence conservative, that is, they allow to preserve both coherent consequences of incoherent updates, as well as consistent knowledge inferred by the ontology before an inconsistent update is performed. We will show that the result of the update obtained according to the first semantics that we present always contains the result that we obtain with the second semantics, that is, the former is more conservative than the latter. Thus, we will base our algorithmic solution for incoherent source-level updates on the second semantics.

Before proceeding further we need to give some notions. Given an ontology $\mathcal{O} = \langle \mathcal{T}, \mathcal{A} \rangle$ we denote with $HB(\mathcal{O})$ the Herbrand Base of $\mathcal{O}$, i.e. the set of ABox facts that can be built over the ontology alphabet $\mathsf{N_O}$. Moreover, we introduce the notion of *consistent logical consequences* [12] of $\mathcal{A}$ with respect to $\mathcal{T}$ as the set $clc_{\mathcal{T}}(\mathcal{A}) = \{\alpha \mid \alpha \in HB(\mathcal{O})$ and there exists $\mathcal{A}' \subseteq \mathcal{A}$ such that $\mathcal{A}'$ is $\mathcal{T}$-consistent, and $\langle \mathcal{T}, \mathcal{A}' \rangle \models \alpha\}$. Note that, if the ontology $\mathcal{A}$ is $\mathcal{T}$-consistent, then $clc_{\mathcal{T}}(\mathcal{A}) = cl_{\mathcal{T}}(\mathcal{A})$.

The new update semantics we are presenting refer to the notion of *closed ABox repair* [12] of an inconsistent ontology.

Definition 2. *Let $\mathcal{T}$ be a TBox and $\mathcal{A}$ be an ABox. A closed ABox repair (CA-repair) of $\mathcal{A}$ with respect to $\mathcal{T}$ is a $\mathcal{T}$-consistent ABox $\mathcal{A}'$ such that $cl_{\mathcal{T}}(\mathcal{A}')$ is a maximal subset of $clc_{\mathcal{T}}(\mathcal{A})$ that is $\mathcal{T}$-consistent.*

The set of all *CA*-repairs of an ABox $\mathcal{A}$ with respect to $\mathcal{T}$ is denoted by $carSet_{\mathcal{T}}(\mathcal{A})$.

Example 1. Consider the TBox $\mathcal{T}$ of our running example and the following ABox:
$$\mathcal{A}_{inc} = \{\texttt{Movie(Moon)}, \texttt{ApprovedBy(Moon,Pit)}\}.$$
It is easy to see that the ABox $\mathcal{A}_{inc}$ is not $\mathcal{T}$-consistent, since both $\texttt{Movie(Moon)}$ and $\texttt{Book(Moon)}$ follows from $\mathcal{T}$ and $\mathcal{A}_{inc}$. The set $carSet_{\mathcal{T}}(\mathcal{A}_{inc})$ contains the following $\mathcal{T}$-consistent ABoxes:

$\mathcal{A}_{r1} = \{\texttt{Movie(Moon)}, \texttt{Reviewer(Pit)}, \texttt{Item(Moon)}\};$
$\mathcal{A}_{r2} = \{\texttt{Book(Moon)}, \texttt{ApprovedBy(Moon,Pit)}, \texttt{Reviewer(Pit)}, \texttt{Item(Moon)}\}.$ □

Intuitively, our first solution for updating an ontology with a weakly-coherent update consists in first restoring the consistency of the update with respect to the TBox, and then proceeding as in the case of coherent update. Since, given an update $\mathcal{U}$ and an ontology $\mathcal{O} = \langle \mathcal{T}, \mathcal{A} \rangle$, there may exist more then one repair of $\mathcal{A}_{\mathcal{U}}^{+}$ with respect to $\mathcal{T}$, we compute a single update by taking the intersection of all the *CA*-repairs of $\mathcal{A}_{\mathcal{U}}^{+}$ with respect to $\mathcal{T}$, thus following the *When In Doubt Throw It Out* (WIDTIO) principle [21].

Definition 3. *Let $\mathcal{O} = \langle \mathcal{T}, \mathcal{A} \rangle$ be a consistent DL-Lite$_{\mathcal{A}}$ ontology, and let $\mathcal{U}$ be a weakly-coherent update. The operator $\bullet_1$ is the update operator such that $\mathcal{O} \bullet_1 \mathcal{U} = \mathcal{O} \bullet \mathcal{U}_{rep}$, where $\mathcal{U}_{rep} = (\bigcap_{\mathcal{A}_i^r \in carSet_{\mathcal{T}}(\mathcal{A}_{\mathcal{U}}^{+})} cl_{\mathcal{T}}(\mathcal{A}_i^r), \mathcal{A}_{\mathcal{U}}^{-}).$*

We note that $\mathcal{U}_{rep}$ actually coincides with the repair of $\mathcal{A}_{\mathcal{U}}^{+}$ with respect to $\mathcal{T}$ under the *ICAR semantics* presented in [12].

Example 2. Let $\mathcal{O} = \langle \mathcal{T}, \mathcal{A} \rangle$ be a *DL-Lite$_{\mathcal{A}}$* ontology where $\mathcal{T}$ is the TBox of our running example and $\mathcal{A}$ is the ABox $\{\texttt{Movie(Moon)}\}$. Moreover, let $\mathcal{U}$ be the weakly-coherent update $(\mathcal{A}_{inc}, \{\})$, where $\mathcal{A}_{inc}$ is as in Example 1. It is easy to see that $\mathcal{U}_{rep} = cl_{\mathcal{T}}(\mathcal{A}_{r1} \cap \mathcal{A}_{r2}) = \{\texttt{Reviewer(Pit)}, \texttt{Item(Moon)}\}$. Consequently, $\mathcal{O} \bullet_1 \mathcal{U} = \mathcal{O} \bullet \mathcal{U}_{rep} = \{\texttt{Movie(Moon)}, \texttt{Reviewer(Pit)}, \texttt{Item(Moon)}\}$. □

The second update semantics follows a different approach. Instead of computing a coherent update by performing the intersection of all the repairs of the original weakly-coherent update and then using it for updating the ontology as described in Sect. 4, we first update the ontology with each repair separately, and then we apply the WIDTIO principle in order to have a single ABox as result.

Definition 4. *Let $\mathcal{O} = \langle \mathcal{T}, \mathcal{A} \rangle$ be a consistent DL-Lite$_\mathcal{A}$ ontology, and let $\mathcal{U}$ be a weakly-coherent update. The operator $\bullet_2$ is the update operator such that $\mathcal{O} \bullet_2 \mathcal{U} = \langle \mathcal{T}, \mathcal{A}_\cap \rangle$ where $\mathcal{A}_\cap = \bigcap_{\mathcal{A}_i^r \in carSet_\mathcal{T}(\mathcal{A}_\mathcal{U}^+)} cl_\mathcal{T}(\mathcal{O} \bullet (\mathcal{A}_i^r, \mathcal{A}_\mathcal{U}^-))$.*

Example 3. Consider the ontology $\mathcal{O}$ and the update $\mathcal{U}$ of Example 2. The update semantics given in Definition 4 requires, for each repair $\mathcal{A}_{ri}$ of $\mathcal{A}_{inc}$ with respect to $\mathcal{T}$, to compute $\mathcal{O} \bullet \mathcal{A}_{ri}$. Easily, one can see that:

$\mathcal{O} \bullet \mathcal{A}_{r1} = \{\texttt{Movie(Moon)}, \texttt{Reviewer(Pit)}, \texttt{Item(Moon)}\}$
$\mathcal{O} \bullet \mathcal{A}_{r2} = \{\texttt{Book(Moon)}, \texttt{ApprovedBy(Moon,Pit)}, \texttt{Reviewer(Pit)}, \texttt{Item(Moon)}\}$.

Hence, we have that $\langle \mathcal{T}, \mathcal{A} \rangle \bullet_2 \mathcal{U} = cl_\mathcal{T}(\mathcal{O} \bullet \mathcal{A}_{r1}) \cap cl_\mathcal{T}(\mathcal{O} \bullet \mathcal{A}_{r2}) = \{\texttt{Reviewer(Pit)}, \texttt{Item(Moon)}\}$. □

The following result determines the relation between the above update semantics.

Theorem 2. *Let $\mathcal{O} = \langle \mathcal{T}, \mathcal{A} \rangle$ be a consistent DL-Lite$_\mathcal{A}$ ontology, and $\mathcal{U}$ be an update possibly inconsistent with $\mathcal{T}$. Then $cl_\mathcal{T}(\mathcal{O} \bullet_2 \mathcal{U}) \subseteq cl_\mathcal{T}(\mathcal{O} \bullet_1 \mathcal{U})$.*

Proof. Let $\mathcal{A}^\cap = \bigcap_{\mathcal{A}_i^r \in carSet_\mathcal{T}(\mathcal{A}_i^+)} cl_\mathcal{T}(\mathcal{A}_i^r)$. Toward a contradiction, assume that $cl_\mathcal{T}(\mathcal{O} \bullet_2 \mathcal{U}) \not\subseteq cl_\mathcal{T}(\mathcal{O} \bullet_1 \mathcal{U})$. This means that there is at least one ABox assertion $\alpha \in cl_\mathcal{T}(\mathcal{O} \bullet_2 \mathcal{U})$ such that $\alpha \notin cl_\mathcal{T}(\mathcal{O} \bullet_1 \mathcal{U})$. Only two cases are conceivable.

First case: $\mathcal{O} \models \alpha$. Since $\alpha \notin cl_\mathcal{T}(\mathcal{O} \bullet_1 \mathcal{U})$, then there is an assertion $\beta \in cl_\mathcal{T}(\mathcal{A}^\cap)$ such that $\langle \mathcal{T}, \{\beta\} \rangle \models \neg\alpha$. Since for each $\mathcal{A}_i^r \in carSet_\mathcal{T}(\mathcal{A}_\mathcal{U}^+)$ we have that $\mathcal{A}^\cap \subseteq \mathcal{A}_i^r$, then $\beta \in cl_\mathcal{T}(\mathcal{A}_i^r)$. This means that for each ABox $\mathcal{A}_i^{new} = \mathcal{O} \bullet (\mathcal{A}_i^r, \mathcal{A}^-)$, $\beta \in cl_\mathcal{T}(\mathcal{A}_i^{new})$. Therefore $\beta \in cl_\mathcal{T}(\mathcal{O} \bullet_2 \mathcal{U})$, and $\langle \mathcal{T}, \mathcal{O} \bullet_2 \mathcal{U} \rangle \models \neg\alpha$ which is a contradiction.

Second case: $\mathcal{O} \not\models \alpha$. Since $\alpha \in cl_\mathcal{T}(\mathcal{O} \bullet_2 \mathcal{U})$, then for each $\mathcal{A}_i^r \in carSet_\mathcal{T}(\mathcal{A}_\mathcal{U}^+)$, and for each $\mathcal{A}_i^{new} = \mathcal{O} \bullet (\mathcal{A}_i^r, \mathcal{A}^-)$, $\alpha \in cl_\mathcal{T}(\mathcal{A}_i^{new})$. Since $\mathcal{O} \not\models \alpha$, then for each $\mathcal{A}_i^r \in carSet_\mathcal{T}(\mathcal{A}_\mathcal{U}^+)$, $\alpha \in \mathcal{A}_i^r$. Hence, $\alpha \in cl_\mathcal{T}(\mathcal{A}^\cap)$ and so $\langle \mathcal{T}, \mathcal{O} \bullet_1 \mathcal{U} \rangle \models \alpha$ which is a contradiction. □

Interestingly, the converse is not true (cf. Examples 2 and 3). As a consequence, we see that the first semantics is more *conservative* then the second. For this reason (and for lack of space), in the rest of this paper we focus on the first semantics and leave the study of the second for future work.

We now turn back to the management of the case in which the ontology update implied by a source-level update is incoherent. To this aim, we modify step (2) described in Sect. 5.1. In particular, in step (2) we now identify the part of the update that is coherent with the TBox, which has to be realized as before. Also, we repair the remaining part (i.e., the incoherent one) according to Definition 3, that is, by deriving the deletion of all incoherent inserted facts and the insertion of all their coherent consequences. Again, all these computations can be done with a non-recursive Datalog program.

We note that retrieved ABox deletions are always coherent since they cannot contradict the TBox, but an insertion is coherent only if it is not paired to an insertion in a disjoint predicate, or if there is no other insertion that together with it violates a functional role. To compute this we make use of suitable Datalog rules. Namely, for each atomic concept A we pose:

```
ins_A_coherent(x) :- ins_A_sl(x),¬ins_A₁_sl(x),..,¬ins_Aₙ_sl(x),
                     ¬ins_P₁_sl(x,y₁),..,¬ins_Pₘ_sl(x,yₘ),
                     ¬ins_Q₁_sl(z₁,x),..,¬ins_Qₖ_sl(zₖ,x)
```

where each A_i is an atomic concept such that $\mathcal{T} \models A \sqsubseteq \neg A_i$, each P_i is an atomic role such that $\mathcal{T} \models A \sqsubseteq \neg \exists P_i$, and each Q_i is an atomic role such that $\mathcal{T} \models A \sqsubseteq \neg \exists Q_i^-$. We proceed similarly for roles. In this case however, besides disjointnesses, we have also to consider that a role R can be involved in functionality axioms or can be asymmetric, i.e., R is such that $\mathcal{T} \models R \sqsubseteq \neg R^-$. Assuming R functional and not involved in any disjointness (both between concepts and relations), we write the following rules to deal with insertions in R:

```
ins_R_coherent(x,y) :- ins_R_sl(x,y), ¬clash_R(x)
clash_R(x):- ins_R_sl(x,y), ins_R_sl(x,z), y ≠ z
```

Note that the above rules are similar in spirit to those used in [13] for query rewriting.

Next, we deal with the rest of *ins_N_sl*, i.e., those that directly contradict a TBox axiom. For each one of them, we obtain the additional insertions/deletions that must be effectively performed, according to Definition 3, for both solving incoherency and preserving consistent consequences. In explaining this step we consider only inclusions and disjointnesses between atomic concepts. Other forms of axioms are dealt with in a similar way.

We consider two kinds of Datalog rules. The first kind computes the insertions (coherent or not) entailed by insertions clashing with the TBox. That is, for each pair of TBox axioms of the form $A_1 \sqsubseteq A_2$, $A_1 \sqsubseteq \neg A_3$ entailed by $\mathcal{T}$ we have the rule:

```
ins_A₂_closure(x):-ins_A₁_sl(x), ins_A₃_sl(x)
```

The second kind of rules filters these insertions to apply only those not contradicting the TBox. Concretely, for each atomic concept A, we consider a Datalog rule with the form:

```
ins_A_ol(x):-ins_A_closure(x), ¬ins_A₁_sl(x),..,¬ins_Aₙ_sl(x)
```

where each A_i is an atomic concept such that $\mathcal{T} \models A \sqsubseteq \neg A_i$.

Note that we derive a new ontology-level insertion. Indeed, we use such new insertions to invoke the ontology-level-Update algorithm, which will insert these new facts while deleting those currently retrieved ABox facts that clashes with it, so, ensuring the consistency of the ontology. This ontology-level update invocation is performed after applying the source-level update in D, that is, after

---

Algorithm 3. source-level-Update($\mathcal{T}$, $\mathcal{M}$, $\mathcal{U}_{sl}$, D)

---

1 $\mathcal{A}^+ \leftarrow \emptyset$
2 **foreach** *fact ins_N_coherent(t) derived* by $Datalog^{sl}$ $(\mathcal{T}, \mathcal{M})$ from $\mathcal{U}_{sl} + D$ **do**
3   **if** *ins_N(t)* $\in D$ **then** remove *ins_N(t)* from D **else** include $N(t)$ in $\mathcal{A}^+$
4 **foreach** *fact del_N_sl(t) derived* by $Datalog^{sl}$ $(\mathcal{T}, \mathcal{M})$ from $\mathcal{U}_{sl} + D$ **do**
5   **if** *del_N(t)* $\in D$ **then** remove *del_N(t)* from D
6 // Dealing with incoherent insertions
7 **foreach** *fact ins_N_ol derived* by $Datalog^{sl}$ $(\mathcal{T}, \mathcal{M})$ from $\mathcal{U}_{sl} + D$ **do**
8   include $N(t)$ in $\mathcal{A}^+$
9 **foreach** *fact del_N'(t) derived* by $Datalog^{sl}$ $(\mathcal{T}, \mathcal{M})$ from $\mathcal{U}_{sl} + D$ **do**
10   **if** *ins_N(t)* $\in D$ **then** remove *ins_N(t)* from D
11   **else** insert *del_N(t)* into D
12 $D' = \text{apply}(\mathcal{U}_{sl}, D)$
13 **return** ontology-level-Update($\mathcal{T}$, $\mathcal{M}$, $(\mathcal{A}^+, \{\})$, D')

---

inserting/deleting each tuple in the *ins_T_Table/del_T_Table* tables in/from the corresponding *T_Table*.

Finally, we must avoid entailing a clash because of the insertions in the database. Thus, for each $A_1 \sqsubseteq \neg A_2$ assertion entailed by the TBox, where each A_i is a basic concept/role, we consider the rules:

```
del_A₁'(x̄):-ins_A₁_sl(x̄), ins_A₂_sl(x̄)
del_A₂'(x̄):-ins_A₁_sl(x̄), ins_A₂_sl(x̄)
```

Intuitively, these rules are only meant to *cancel* the insertions that cause the clash. The entire general procedure is described by Algorithm 3. Notice that by removing rows 6–11, this algorithm is exactly as Algorithm 2, with the proviso that in line 2 we are using ins_N_coherent in place of ins_N_sl. Indeed, in the general setting we have to add the treatment of facts ins_N_ol, and del_N' produced by the new version of the program $Datalog^{sl}(\mathcal{T}, \mathcal{M})$. We conclude by stating the correctness of the algorithm.

Theorem 3. *Let $(\langle \mathcal{T}, \mathcal{M}, \mathcal{S} \rangle, D)$ be a consistent write-also OBDA system, $\mathcal{U}_{sl}$ an update over D, and $\mathcal{A}^{ret} = (\mathcal{A}^+, \mathcal{A}^-)$ be the retrieved ABox change derived by D, $\pi(\mathcal{M})$, and $\mathcal{U}_{sl}$. Algorithm 3 returns a D' such that $\langle \mathcal{T}, ret(\mathcal{M}, D) \setminus \mathcal{A}^- \rangle \bullet_1 (\mathcal{A}^+, \emptyset) = ret(\mathcal{M}, D')$.*

Intuitively, the retrieved ABox computed from D', in turn obtained by Algorithm 3, is equivalent to realizing the ontology-level update $(\mathcal{A}^+, \emptyset)$ over the ontology $\langle \mathcal{T}, ret(\mathcal{M}, D) \setminus \mathcal{A}^- \rangle$, i.e., over the original retrieved ABox after deleting $\mathcal{A}^-$.

From this theorem we get that computing the result of a source-level update is in AC^0 in data complexity as for ontology-level update.

6   Conclusion

In this paper we have studied write-also OBDA Systems under *ontology-level* and *source-level* updates. We have shown how to handle both updates through non-recursive Datalog programs. Such programs can be easily translated into first-order query languages, and thus we have shown that update computation in our framework is first-order rewritable. We stress that the techniques proposed in this paper are ready-implementable and can be adopted by state-of-the-art tools for OBDA, such as Mastro [6] and Ontop [3]. This will be the subject of our future work.

Acknowledgments. This work has been partially supported by the Ministerio de Economia y Competitividad (under project TIN2014-52938-C2-2-R).

References

1. Abiteboul, S., Hull, R., Vianu, V.: Foundations of Databases. Addison Wesley Publ. Co., Reading (1995)
2. Baader, F., Calvanese, D., McGuinness, D., Nardi, D., Patel-Schneider, P.F. (eds.): The Description Logic Handbook: Theory, Implementation and Applications, 2nd edn. Cambridge University Press, Cambridge (2007)
3. Calvanese, D., Cogrel, B., Komla-Ebri, S., Kontchakov, R., Lanti, D., Rezk, M., Rodriguez-Muro, M., Xiao, G.: Ontop: answering SPARQL queries over relational databases. Semantic Web J. **8**(3), 471–487 (2017)
4. Calvanese, D., De Giacomo, G., Lembo, D., Lenzerini, M., Rosati, R.: Tractable reasoning and efficient query answering in description logics: the DL-Lite family. J. Autom. Reason. **39**(3), 385–429 (2007)
5. Calvanese, D., Kharlamov, E., Nutt, W., Zheleznyakov, D.: Evolution of *DL-Lite* knowledge bases. In: Patel-Schneider, P.F., Pan, Y., Hitzler, P., Mika, P., Zhang, L., Pan, J.Z., Horrocks, I., Glimm, B. (eds.) ISWC 2010. LNCS, vol. 6496, pp. 112–128. Springer, Heidelberg (2010). doi:10.1007/978-3-642-17746-0_8
6. Civili, C., Console, M., De Giacomo, G., Lembo, D., Lenzerini, M., Lepore, L., Mancini, R., Poggi, A., Rosati, R., Ruzzi, M., Santarelli, V., Savo, D.F.: MASTRO STUDIO: managing ontology-based data access applications. Proc. VLDB Endowment **6**(12), 1314–1317 (2013)
7. Giacomo, G., Oriol, X., Rosati, R., Savo, D.F.: Updating DL-Lite ontologies through first-order queries. In: Groth, P., Simperl, E., Gray, A., Sabou, M., Krötzsch, M., Lecue, F., Flöck, F., Gil, Y. (eds.) ISWC 2016. LNCS, vol. 9981, pp. 167–183. Springer, Cham (2016). doi:10.1007/978-3-319-46523-4_11
8. Eiter, T., Gottlob, G.: On the complexity of propositional knowledge base revision, updates and counterfactuals. Artif. Intell. **57**, 227–270 (1992)
9. Flouris, G., Manakanatas, D., Kondylakis, H., Plexousakis, D., Antoniou, G.: Ontology change: classification and survey. Knowl. Eng. Rev. **23**(2), 117–152 (2008)
10. Guessoum, A., Lloyd, J.W.: Updating knowledge bases. New Gener. Comput. **8**(1), 71–89 (1990)
11. Kakas, A.C., Mancarella, P.: Database updates through abduction. In: Proceedings of the 16th International Conference on Very Large Data Bases (VLDB), pp. 650–661 (1990)

12. Lembo, D., Lenzerini, M., Rosati, R., Ruzzi, M., Savo, D.F.: Inconsistency-tolerant semantics for description logics. In: Hitzler, P., Lukasiewicz, T. (eds.) RR 2010. LNCS, vol. 6333, pp. 103–117. Springer, Heidelberg (2010). doi:10.1007/978-3-642-15918-3_9

13. Lembo, D., Lenzerini, M., Rosati, R., Ruzzi, M., Savo, D.F.: Query Rewriting for Inconsistent DL-Lite Ontologies. In: Rudolph, S., Gutierrez, C. (eds.) RR 2011. LNCS, vol. 6902, pp. 155–169. Springer, Heidelberg (2011). doi:10.1007/978-3-642-23580-1_12

14. Lenzerini, M.: Data integration: a theoretical perspective. In: Proceedings of the 21st ACM SIGACT SIGMOD SIGART Symposium on Principles of Database Systems (PODS), pp. 233–246 (2002)

15. Lenzerini, M., Savo, D.F.: Updating inconsistent description logic knowledge bases. In: Proceedings of the 20th European Conference on Artificial Intelligence (ECAI), pp. 516–521 (2012)

16. Olivé, A.: Integrity constraints checking in deductive databases. In Proceedings of the 17th International Conference on Very Large Data Bases (VLDB), pp. 513–523 (1991)

17. Poggi, A., Lembo, D., Calvanese, D., De Giacomo, G., Lenzerini, M., Rosati, R.: Linking data to ontologies. In: Spaccapietra, S. (ed.) Journal on Data Semantics X. LNCS, vol. 4900, pp. 133–173. Springer, Heidelberg (2008). doi:10.1007/978-3-540-77688-8_5

18. Reiter, R.: On specifying database updates. J. Logic Programm. 25(1), 53–91 (1995)

19. Teniente, E., Olivé, A.: Updating knowledge bases while maintaining their consistency. Very Large Database J. 4(2), 193–241 (1995)

20. Urpí, T., Olivé, A.: A method for change computation in deductive databases. In: Proceedings of the 18th International Conference on Very Large Data Bases (VLDB), pp. 225–237 (1992)

21. Winslett, M.: Updating Logical Databases. Cambridge University Press, Cambridge (1990)

Computing Authoring Tests from Competency Questions: Experimental Validation

Matt Dennis[1,2(✉)], Kees van Deemter[1], Daniele Dell'Aglio[1,3], and Jeff Z. Pan[1]

[1] University of Aberdeen, Aberdeen, UK
[2] University of Portsmouth, Portsmouth, UK
matt.dennis@port.ac.uk
[3] University of Zurich, Zurich, Switzerland

Abstract. This paper explores whether Authoring Tests derived from Competency Questions accurately represent the expectations of ontology authors. In earlier work we proposed that an ontology authoring interface can be improved by allowing the interface to test whether a given Competency Question (CQ) is able to be answered by the ontology at a given stage of its construction, an approach known as CQ-driven Ontology Authoring (CQOA). The experiments presented in the present paper suggest that CQOA's understanding of CQs matches users' understanding quite well, especially for inexperienced ontology authors.

Keywords: Ontology authoring · Competency questions

1 Introduction

Ontology Authoring. Formal ontologies have become a widely accepted vehicle for representing knowledge in a range of domains, where they offer precise explanations of key terminologies. Many of these ontologies are formulated in terms of Description Logic (DL, [2]), a family of formalisms based on decidable fragments of First-Order Logic (FOL).

Examples include the medical SNOMED CT ontology[1], and the ontologies of the Open Biomedical Ontologies Consortium (GO [1], MGED [30]). The W3C standard Web Ontology Language (OWL 2) uses DLs as its underpinnings.

However, the precision offered by DL comes at a cost. Despite the existence of sophisticated ontology authoring interfaces such as *Protégé* [17], users and developers frequently fail to comprehend important implications of the information contained in the ontology [8,24]. In some cases, particular DL constructs are to blame (such as DL's use of the universal quantifier); in other cases, the main difficulty is to combine a large number of individually simple propositions and to establish their combined reasoning consequences.

Competency Questions and CQOA. These challenges have led to the notion of a Competency Question (CQ) [12]: a question that, in the opinion of the developer, the finished ontology should be able to answer. Initially, CQs were mainly

---

[1] Cf. http://www.ihtsdo.org/snomed-ct/.

© Springer International Publishing AG 2017
C. d'Amato et al. (Eds.): ISWC 2017, Part I, LNCS 10587, pp. 243–259, 2017.
DOI: 10.1007/978-3-319-68288-4_15

used as a "pencil and paper" tool for ontology authors (henceforth: authors): the idea is to encourage authors to formulate a number of CQs at the start of the authoring process. For example, a CQ for a restaurant domain might ask: "What is the price of asparagus soup?". The idea is that listing such CQs can help to make authors aware of what information they need to encode.

Recently a number of authors have proposed that CQs should become part of the authoring interface.

One approach, which comes to terms with a particularly wide range of CQs, was Ren et al.'s [25], where we proposed CQ-driven Ontology Authoring (CQOA), in which the authoring interface checks continually, during authoring, which of the CQs are *handled correctly* by the ontology.

In formalising what it means to handle a CQ correctly, we draw on a key concept in linguistics, called *presupposition* (e.g., [18]). A presupposition of a *declarative* sentence is a proposition whose truth is a precondition to assessing the truth or falsity of the sentence: if the presupposition does not hold, the sentence is neither true nor false. Applied to a *question*, a presupposition is a proposition that needs to be true in order for the question to have an answer. For example, the question "What is the price of the cutlery?", when asked in a restaurant, presupposes that cutlery is on sale in that restaurant: if it is not, then the question cannot be answered. We argued that the idea of a failed presupposition (i.e., a question presupposing a falsehood) captures what happens when an ontology is unable to answer a CQ.

[25] contains an empirical study into the kinds of CQs that ontology authors tend to ask, yielding a set of CQ *archetypes*, see Table 1 (and their *sub-types*, see Table 2). Next, each type of presuppositions was mapped to some Authoring Tests (ATs), each of which is testable using satisfiability checking or subsumption checking services in the $\mathcal{ALCQ}$ DL. For example, the CQ "Which pizzas contain chocolate?" (called a *Selection Question*) triggers the following ATs:

Positive Presupposition: $Pizza \sqcap \exists contains.Choc$ is satisfiable
Complement Presupposition: $Pizza \sqcap \forall contains.\neg Choc$ is satisfiable

The first formula denotes the set of things that are pizzas and contain chocolate. By using the standard logical notion of satisfiability (e.g., [10]), the *Positive Presupposition* asserts not simply that the above-mentioned set is non-empty, but that the ontology *permits* it to be non-empty (i.e., its emptiness does not follow logically from the ontology). The second formula denotes the set of things that are pizzas and do *not* contain chocolate; the *Complement Presupposition* asserts that the ontology permits this set to be non-empty. If both presuppositions hold, it is possible for the ontology to contain pizzas that contain chocolate and ones that do not. Complement Presuppositions are less often discussed than Positive ones (though see e.g., [32]), suggesting that they might be less firmly associated with the sentences in question; we return to this issue in Sect. 3. CQOA is potentially powerful because it can help ontology authors to understand, at every stage of the authoring process, whether each of the CQs that they have specified is handled *correctly* by the ontology they are constructing.

Use in an Authoring Tool. We are incorporating CQs and the checking of their presuppositions into an ontology authoring tool. This tool uses a natural language-like dialogue as the main mode of interaction, using the controlled natural language OWL Simplified English (OSE) [23].

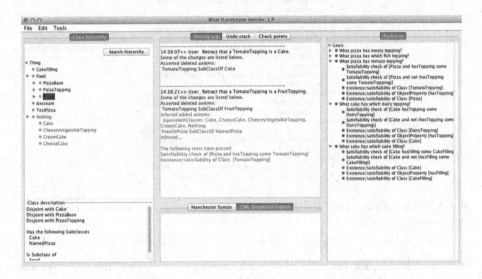

Fig. 1. Our prototype authoring tool

Figure 1 shows the main panel of the authoring tool, which consists of three main regions. On the left is a (clickable) presentation of the hierarchy of named classes in the ontology and a small window which can show a simple verbalisation of the axioms about a given class. In the centre is a history log, which shows the whole past dialogue interaction, and an area where the user can compose their next contribution to the dialogue. The user can choose between using OSE and using Manchester Syntax for DLs [14].

18 out of the 28 types of CQs identified by [25] have wordings that can be incorporated into an extension of OSE. Once the CQ has been entered, its presuppositions are extracted for use as authoring tests. The "task list" (shown in Fig. 2) is expanded to show the new CQ; the authoring tests coming from the CQ are shown indented underneath. From then on, the status of the authoring tests (succeed or fail) from reasoning [22] is indicated by "traffic lights" in front of the tests. When an authoring action (e.g. adding a new axiom) creates a change in the status of one or more authoring tests, this is announced in feedback as part of the main dialogue (the top central panel of Fig. 1). We hope that this kind of dynamic feedback can help authors to understand their progress.

However, CQOA hinges on the accuracy of the mapping from presuppositions to ATs: it hinges on whether a CQOA system's understanding of what it means for a CQ to be "handled correctly" matches the user's understanding.

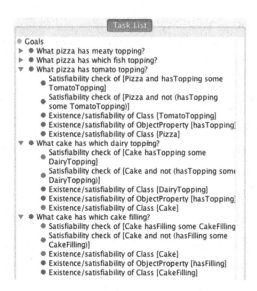

Fig. 2. Task list—the CQs are the top level list elements, with their associated ATs shown below

It is conceivable, for example, that authors who have entered the CQ "Which pizzas contain chocolate?" are happy with an ontology that defines pizzas as not containing chocolate. If so, the Complement Presupposition fails, yet the author might consider the CQ to have been handled correctly: Ren et al.'s mapping would be wrong. In this paper, we present a series of experiments to investigate whether the interpretation of CQs embodied in the mapping from presuppositions to ATs is in accordance with users' understanding.

2   Related Work

Empirical studies of ontology authoring emphasise the complexity of the ontology authoring task both for novice and experienced users [9,24]. These studies suggest that current ontology authoring tools let users control the authoring process while many users prefer to be guided by the system.

A range of solutions has been proposed. Ontology testing is widely used to provide feedback to authors on the quality of the ontology. For example, the *Rabbit* interface [6] and the *Simplified English prototype* [23] test for the presence of incorrect words and syntactically disallowed structures in the ontology. *Protégé* [17] and *OntoTrack* [19] use reasoners to offer basic semantic checking, testing for inconsistency, for example. Systems such as *Roo* [7] intend to advise the user of the consequences of an authoring action. Justification engines [19] explain the feedback given by the system, for example when an inconsistency is detected. Systems such as the *OWL Unit Test Framework* in *Protégé, Tawny-OWL* [20] and *OntoStudio*[2] allow users to define unit tests and run these in the authoring environment.

These techniques have difficulty capturing requirements specific to the ontology in question. CQOA, by contrast, has the potential of capturing requirements that are specific to one ontology and one user. Exploiting CQs for ontology authoring is not a new idea [11,16,27,29]—interesting approaches include the formalisation of CQs into SPARQL queries [31] or DL queries [21]. An algorithm for checking natural language CQs has been developed by [4]. However, most of these studies have focused on simple CQs such as "What is ... ?", "How much ... ?", and on answering CQs, instead of informing the user which CQs *can be* answered, and explaining why this is. An exception is Hofer et al. [13], which evaluates the coverage of biomedical ontologies by checking whether all terminologies in CQs can be mapped to terminologies in a target biomedical ontology. The CQOA approach goes further by addressing a wider range of CQs.

With a feature-based framework, Ren et al. [25] identified 12 archetypes of CQ patterns in their collection (Table 1), where the 2nd and 3rd columns show the pattern and an example from the corpus. The last four columns show the primary features of a pattern. Some archetype patterns have sub-types; subtypes of archetype 1 are shown in Table 2, in which the last three columns are the secondary features of the subtype.

Table 1. CQ Archetypes (from [25]) (PA = Predicate Arity, RT = Relation Type, M = Modifier, DE = Domain-independent Element; obj. = object property relation, data. = datatype property relation, num. = numeric modifier, quan. = quantitative modifier, tem. = temporal element, spa. = spatial element; CE = class expression, OPE = object property expression, DP = datatype property, I = individual, NM = numeric modifier, PE = property expression, QM = quantity modifier)

ID	Pattern	Example	PA	RT	M	DE
1	Which [CE1] [OPE] [CE2]?	Which pizzas contain pork?	2	obj.		
2	How much does [CE] [DP]?	How much does Margherita Pizza weigh?	2	data.		
3	What type of [CE] is [I]?	What type of software (API, Desktop application etc.) is it?	1			
4	Is the [CE1] [CE2]?	Is the software open source development?	2			
5	What [CE] has the [NM] [DP]?	What pizza has the lowest price?	2	data.	num.	
6	What is the [NM] [CE1] to [OPE] [CE2]?	What is the best/fastest/most robust software to read/edit this data?	3	both	num.	
7	Where do I [OPE] [CE]?	Where do I get updates?	2	obj.		spa.
8	Which are [CE]?	Which are gluten free bases?	1			
9	When did/was [CE] [PE]?	When was the 1.0 version released?	2	data.		tem.
10	What [CE1] do I need to [OPE] [CE2]?	What hardware do I need to run this software?	3	obj.		
11	Which [CE1] [OPE] [QM] [CE2]?	Which pizza has the most toppings?	2	obj.	quan.	
12	Do [CE1] have [QM] values of [DP]?	Do pizzas have different values of size?	2	data.	quan.	

---

[2] http://www.semafora-systems.com/en/products/ontostudio/.

Table 2. CQ Sub-types of Archetype 1 (from [25]) (QT = Question Type, V = Visibility, QP = Question Polarity, sel. = selection question, bin. = binary question, cout. = counting question, exp. = explicit, imp. = implicit, sub. = subject, pre. = predicate, pos. = positive, neg. = negative)

ID	Pattern	Example	QT	V	QP
1a	Which [CE1] [OPE] [CE2]?	What software can read a .cel file?	sel.	exp.	pos.
1b	Find [CE1] with [CE2]	Find pizzas with peppers and olives	sel.	imp. pre.	pos.
1c	How many [CE1] [OPE] [CE2]?	How many pizzas in the menu contains meat?	cout.	exp.	pos.
1d	Does [CE1] [OPE] [CE2]?	Does this software provide XML editing	bin.	exp.	pos.
1e	Be there [CE1] with [CE2]?	Are there any pizzas with chocolate?	bin.	imp. pre.	pos.
1f	Who [OPE] [CE]?	Who owns the copyright?	sel.	imp. sub.	pos.
1g	Be there [CE1] [OPE]ing [CE2]?	Are there any active forums discussing its use?	bin.	exp.	pos.
1h	Which [CE1] [OPE] no [CE2]?	Which pizza contains no mushroom?	sel.	exp.	neg.

3   Study Design

Our question is whether the interpretation of CQs embodied in the mapping from presuppositions to ATs is in accordance with users' understanding.

We conducted a series of three experiments mainly for the ATs of occurrence and relation satisfiability. Study 1 used a lay audience with participants recruited from the general population; the ontology and authoring tests were presented in English. Studies 2 and 3 were run with participants who had some experience with Description Logics, so the ontology and authoring tests in these experiments were expressed using DL syntax.

3.1   Participants

Study 1 (English, crowdsourcing). Participants were recruited by Mechanical Turk (www.mturk.com), a crowdsourcing tool. Participants had to have an approval rate of 90% (i.e. 90% of their work was judged by other requesters as of good quality) and pass a Cloze test [28] for English fluency. We recruited 54 participants (50% male, 50% female; 32% aged 18–25, 57% 26–40, and 11% 40–65).

Study 2 (DL, Summer School). The first of the two experiments related to the DL version occurred during the 12th Reasoning Web Summer School (Aberdeen 2016). The event targeted beginner and intermediate DL practitioners, such as PhD students and researchers in the Semantic Web area. Of our 15 participants, 86% were male, 14% female. 33% were aged 18–25 and 66% aged 26–40. 46% of participants were self-assessed novices, 40% were beginners and 14% reported as having intermediate skills; no participants identified as experts. The experiment was conducted during a dedicated 60-minute session of the school. The average time to complete the test was 32 (SD 21) min.

Study 3 (DL, Conference in China). The second DL-based experiment was conducted at the CCKS2016 conference, held in China in September 2016. The conference targeted people interested in learning about semantic technologies; it contained tutorial sessions about DLs and ontology authoring. The experiment was conducted after the tutorial, to ensure that participants were able to understand the proposed DL formulae. 67 participants were recruited. 55% were male, 42% were female, and 3% undisclosed. 36% were aged 18–25, 54% 26–40, 7% 41–65, and 3% undisclosed. 61% were self-assessed novices, 22% beginners, 12% intermediate, 3% experts and 2% undisclosed. The average time to complete the test was 17 (SD 6) min.

3.2   Materials

Ontology. Given that our interest was not in testing people's comprehension of complex ontologies, but in testing the treatment of presuppositions in CQs, we wanted the ontology to be fairly easy to comprehend, in a domain that many people understand, while still containing all the phenomena we are interested in. We therefore created a simple ontology from scratch. The subject was hot drinks, a topic that many people have a good understanding of. The complete ontology is shown in Table 3.

Table 3. The ontology, as presented to participants in the DL and in the English studies reported below.

	DL	Non DL
1	$hasContent \circ hasContent \sqsubseteq hasContent$	The robot understands that things can 'contain' other things, and that this is transitive. Transitive means that, for example, if flour contains gluten, and a loaf of bread contains flour, then the loaf of bread therefore contains gluten
2	$Drink \equiv CoffeeDrink \sqcup TeaDrink$	All drinks are coffee drinks or tea drinks
3	$Coffee \sqsubseteq \exists hasContent.Caffeine$	Coffee beans contain caffeine
4	$CoffeeDrink \equiv \exists hasContent.Coffee$	Coffee drinks contain coffee beans
5	$TeaDrink \equiv \exists hasContent.Tea$	Tea Drinks contain tea leaves
6	$CoffeeDrink \sqcap TeaDrink \sqsubseteq \bot$	Nothing can be both a coffee drink and a tea drink at the same time
7	$Cappuccino \sqsubseteq Drink \sqcap \exists hasContent.SteamedMilk \sqcap \exists hasContent.Coffee$	A cappuccino is a drink that contains steamed milk and coffee beans
8	$Americano \sqsubseteq CoffeeDrink$	An Americano is a coffee drink

Competency Questions. Seven CQs were used. All but one were judged (via their authoring tests) to be non-answerable. In other words, the criteria of [25] assert that the ontology in its current form fails to make all the CQs answerable. Table 4 shows the CQs, their archetype according to the classification proposed in [25], and whether they can be answered: if not, a brief explanation is provided.

Table 4. The competency questions proposed to the participants of the study

	Competency question	Archetype	Answ.	Reason
1	Which are the coffee drinks?	8	Yes	
2	Which coffee drinks contain caffeine?	1	No	All the coffee drinks contain caffeine
3	Which tea drinks contain caffeine?	1	No	The relation between tea drinks and caffeine is undefined
4	Which coffee drinks contain tea leaves?	1	No	No coffee drink contains tea leaves
5	Which coffee drinks contain the most caffeine?	11	No	The answer cannot be computed
6	Which drinks contain coffee beans or tea leaves?	1	No	All drinks contain either beans or tea leaves
7	Which drinks contain coffee beans and tea leaves?	1	No	No drink contains both coffee beans and tea leaves

Most of the CQs are of archetype 1 (see Table 1)—a realistic design choice, as this is the most common type of CQ used by human users [25]. CQs 6 and 7 are more complex than 2, 3 and 4, since they exploit logical connectors between the concepts proposed.

Authoring Tests. Each CQ had a set of ATs associated with it, following the mapping proposed by Ren and colleagues. We focus on four types (from [25]) of AT in this paper, with examples shown in Table 5.

ATs of types 1 and 2 assess the presence in the ontology of concepts and properties, respectively. These tests pass if the concept or property is defined in the ontology. The example AT of type 1 presented in Table 5 is associated with CQs 1, 2, 4 and 5 of Table 4; similarly, the AT example of type 2 is associated with all the CQs except 1.

ATs of types 3 and 4 are Relation Satisfiability tests. They aim at verifying whether relations between classes are possible. For example, the AT proposed (in Table 3) for Relation Satisfiability assesses whether a coffee drink can contain caffeine. If it cannot, the associated CQ is judged to be not answerable.

55 ATs were used in total: 21 fillers (Non-relevant ATs used as an attention check) and 34 non-fillers. Disregarding fillers, there were 16 of type 1, 6 of type 2, 6 of type 3 and 6 of type 4.

Table 5. Authoring test types and examples

Type	DL	Non DL
1. Occurrence (conc.)	$CoffeeDrink$ should occur in the ontology	A coffee drink should be defined
2. Occurrence (prop.)	$hasContent$ should occur in the ontology	It must be possible for something to contain something
3. Relation Satisfiability	$CoffeeDrink \sqcap \exists hasContent.Caffeine$ should be satisfiable in the ontology	It must be possible for a coffee drink to contain caffeine
4. Relation Satisfiability (complement)	$CoffeeDrink \sqcap \neg\exists hasContent.TeaLeaf$ should be satisfiable in the ontology	It must be possible for a coffee drink to not contain tea leaves

3.3 Variables

The independent variable was the type of authoring test. The dependent variable was what we call *relevance*; this records whether a participant judged an authoring test to be relevant to a given CQ (i.e., whether the AT expresses a presupposition of the CQ) or not.

3.4 Procedure

In the DL experiment, we collected information about participants' experience in ontology authoring. Next, participants were given a written scenario to read. The scenario was designed to make sense to people not previously acquainted with the notion of an ontology, and in such a way that the role of the CQs would nonetheless be clear. The scenario read as follows:

Costabucks is a hot drinks company. They are creating a robot that can answer questions from customers about the hot drinks that they sell. The robot's programmers have to tell the robot some facts about hot drinks so that it understands enough to answer the questions. To do this, the robot's designers give the robot "rules" about the world.

Once all of the Customer Questions (CQs) can be answered by the robot, its knowledge of the coffee menu is considered complete, and it can be used in the shop.

*The programmers are using a special **programming tool** which allows them to add possible customer questions to its interface, and the tool can inform them when the questions are able to be answered by the current set of rules.*

*To do this, the tool breaks down the questions into several smaller **authoring tests**, which all must be passed in order for the question to be judged as answerable. The authoring tests are automatically generated by the tool, based on what the customer question is.*

Participants were shown the ontology (set of axioms) shown in Table 3, using one of the two formats (DL or English). Next, a simple example CQ was shown and the types of authoring test that could arise from it. The symbols used to highlight whether the AT 'passed' or not were explained. Following this, participants were shown the 7 CQs, one by one. For each CQ, participants were shown the CQ's associated ATs and asked, in each case, whether they agreed. Participants could give a reason to explain their judgement if they wished; an example is shown in Fig. 3. The list of authoring tests also contained certain non-relevant *fillers* which served as an attention check, and allowed us to gauge the ability of participants to understand the task. For example, for the first CQ: *Which are the coffee drinks?*, we inserted fillers such as *Steamed milk should be defined* and *Tea-leaves should be defined*, which are not relevant to coffee drinks.

Participants were told that as long as all ATs had *passed*, the CQ was considered answerable by the programming tool, and if any ATs were *failing*, then the CQ was judged as non-answerable. Participants were asked whether they agreed with this answerability judgement or not.

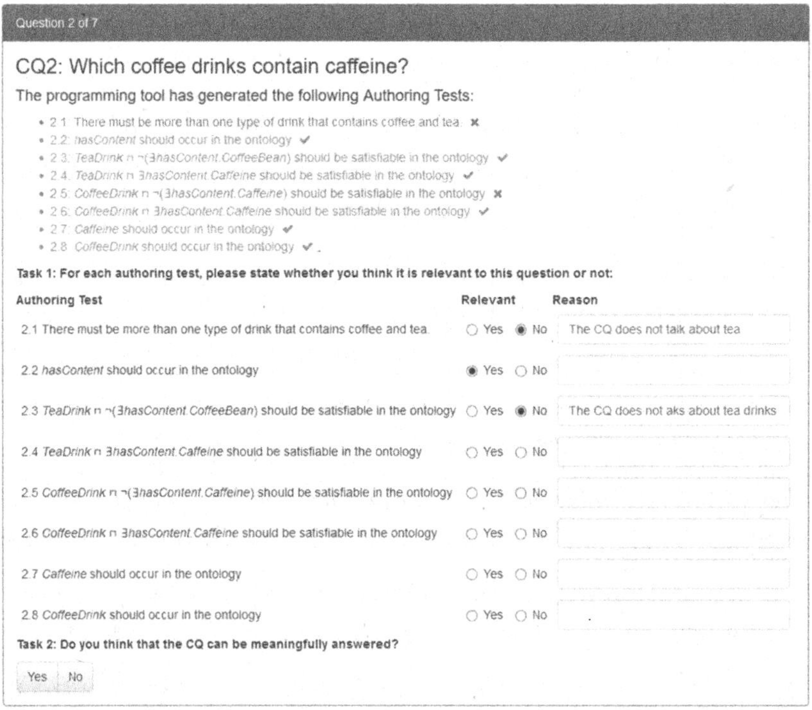

Fig. 3. Screenshot of study 2 showing one experimental participant's judgement of ATs for one CQ. The participant has so far only addressed the first three ATs. In two cases, she has offered a reason.

3.5   Hypotheses

In order to verify the mappings from presuppositions to the 4 types of ATs from [25], we formulated the following hypotheses before conducting our experiments.

H1: occurrence ATs are agreed with more often than disagreed with.

H2: satisfiability ATs that focus on a concept mentioned in a CQ are agreed with more often than disagreed with.

H3: satisfiability ATs that focus on the complement of a concept mentioned in a CQ are agreed with more often than disagreed with.

H4: satisfiability ATs that focus on a concept mentioned in a CQ are agreed with more often than satisfiability ATs that focus on the complement of a concept mentioned in a CQ.

The first three hypotheses are the core of our investigation, making explicit an expectation inherent in the literature. They assert that these ATs proposed in [25] are agreed with more often than disagreed with (separating out three different types of ATs). If linguistic theory is right about presuppositions, then we would expect to see at least the first two of these hypotheses overwhelmingly supported. The fourth hypothesis reflects a more tentative expectation, namely that *positive* presuppositions are more firmly associated with questions of the form "Which ..." than are *complement* presuppositions (cf., Sect. 1).

4   Results

Results are given for all participants, followed by participants who successfully identified at least 50% of the filler ATs (i.e. a 50% *filler threshold*), and finally results for those participants who successfully identified at least 66% of filler ATs. H1, H2 and H3 were assessed by binomial test. Hypothesis H4 was analysed by a χ^2 test of *attype* (authoring test type) × *answer* (relevant or not relevant). In all analyses, a significance threshold of $p < .05$ was used.

Table 6. Results of study 1 (English, crowdsourcing), showing the percentage of times an AT of a particular type was marked as relevant. * indicates significance of binomial test. Here and in Table 5 and 6, *Filler thresholds* indicate the percentage of filler ATs that has to be answered correctly to be counted. Thus, the 66% column shows only results for those who understood ATs quite well, whereas the 0% column shows all.

Filler threshold	0%		50%		66%	
AT type	Relevant	Not relevant	Relevant	Not relevant	Relevant	Not relevant
Occurrence (conc)	96% (830)	4% (34)*	97% (482)	3% (14)*	98% (298)	2% (6)*
Occurrence (prop)	91% (296)	9% (28)*	90% (168)	10% (18)*	84% (96)	16% (18)*
Satisfiability (conc)	76% (245)	24% (79)*	82% (152)	18% (34)*	83% (95)	17% (19)*
Satisfiability (comp)	72% (233)	28% (91)*	71% (132)	29% (54)*	72% (82)	28% (32)*

Study 1 (English, crowdsourcing). As shown in Table 6, H1, H2 and H3 are confirmed with a significant majority of participants agreeing with the generated authoring tests. H4 is not supported.

Study 2 (DL, Summer school, UK). The results from the first description logic experiment are shown in Table 7, for filler thresholds 0 and 50%, H1, H2 and H3 are confirmed with a significant majority agreeing with the generated ATs. However, at a 66% filler threshold, H3 is not supported, with only a small majority of 'satisfiability of complement of concept' ATs being marked as relevant. Once again, H4 is not supported.

Table 7. Results of study 2 (DL, Summer School, UK) showing the percentage of times an AT of a particular type was marked as relevant. * indicates significance of binomial test. Bold - non significance

Filler threshold	0%		50%		66%	
AT type	Relevant	Not relevant	Relevant	Not relevant	Relevant	Not relevant
Occurrence (conc)	95% (227)	5% (13)*	94% (181)	6% (11)*	96% (108)	4% (4)*
Occurrence (prop)	100% (90)	0% (0)*	100% (72)	0% (0)*	100% (42)	0% (0)*
Satisfiability (conc)	78% (70)	22% (20)*	82% (59)	18% (13)*	93% (39)	7% (3)*
Satisfiability (comp)	64% (58)	36% (32)*	62.5% (45)	37.5% (27)*	**55%** (23)	**45%** (19)

Study 3 (DL, Conference in China). The results from the second description logic experiment are shown in Table 8. As before, H1 and H2 are confirmed for all filler thresholds, but this time there is no support for H3: as the filler threshold is increased, more of the 'satisfiability of complement of concept' ATs are marked as non-relevant. For the filler thresholds of 50% and 66% (representing the DL-logically more capable participants), significant majorities marked these ATs as *non-relevant*. For hypothesis H4, a χ^2 test of *ATtype* × *answer* (for both types of satisfiability AT) shows this to be significant for all filler thresholds (0%: $\chi^2 = 31.517$, $p < 0.001$; 50%: $\chi^2 = 44.211$, $p < 0.001$; 66%: $\chi^2 = 34.036$, $p < 0.001$), hence this hypothesis is confirmed.

Table 8. Results of study 3 (DL, Conference in China) showing the percentage of times an AT of a particular type was marked as relevant. * indicates significance of binomial test. Bold - non significance

Filler threshold	0%		50%		66%	
AT type	Relevant	Not relevant	Relevant	Not relevant	Relevant	Not relevant
Occurrence (conc)	83% (893)	17% (179)*	82% (499)	18% (109)*	78% (250)	22% (70)*
Occurrence (prop)	86% (347)	14% (55)*	88% (201)	12% (27)*	79% (95)	21% (25)*
Satisfiability (conc)	70% (280)	30% (122)*	74% (168)	26% (60)*	73% (88)	27% (32)*
Satisfiability (comp)	**50%** (202)	**50%** (200)	**43%** (98)	**57%** (130)	36% (43)	64% (77)*

5   Discussion

We have found that *occurrence* ATs are almost universally agreed with; this was not surprising, since an ontology that does not define a given concept or relation is unable to shed light on any CQ containing it. We also found broad agreement that the key concept involved in a Selection Question must be satisfiable. However, when dealing with the complement of such a concept, participants in study 3 did not agree that this had to satisfiable. Remarkably (cf., the three levels of Filler threshold in Table 6), the better a participant was at identifying relevant ATs, the more this type of ATs was disagreed with. We did not reliably find this declining pattern with the other DL experiment (study 2, the three levels of Filler threshold in Table 5); this could be due to the smaller number of participants or to the type of participants taking part in study 2.

How to explain these findings? Presentation format may have affected CQ interpretation: when an ontology is presented using DL formulas, a less "natural language-like" interpretation of CQs (which were themselves formulated in English in all experiments) may be triggered. It seems possible that participants' exposure to DL formulas in the DL-based experiments activates in their minds a literal interpretation of CQs, which has no presuppositions. For example, according to this literal interpretation, "Which As have a B?" can have "none of the As" and "all of the As" as legitimate answers. If this explanation is correct, one would expect that H2 and H3 are less well supported by the DL experiments than by the non-DL experiment, which was not the case. Conversely, the reasoning above gives one no reason to expect the observed difference between positive and complement presuppositions. Alternative explanations need to be explored.

It might seem plausible that subjects with more experience using formal logic are more likely to use a literal interpretation of these formulas, which has no presuppositions (as explained above). If this is correct, then one should expect that both H2 and H3 are less well supported by participants with a high level of expertise in logic than by subjects with a low level of expertise in logic. To investigate this, we performed a post-hoc analysis on the two DL experiments. We partitioned participants into two groups - those who reported their experience as 'novice' vs. those reporting as 'beginner','intermediate' and 'expert' (because only those reporting as novices had no prior DL experience). We found no significant differences between the two groups. For satisfiability of a concept, 69% were marked as relevant by the novice group and 73% were marked as relevant by the others. For satisfiability of the complement of a concept, 52% of ATs were marked as relevant and 54% for the other group.

A second option is to use the filler ATs (rather than self-reported experience) as a guide to participants' expertise. We split the results into three groups - one for those who identified under 50% of fillers, a second for those who identified over 50% but under 66%, and a third for those who identified over 66% Table 9. For both types of AT, a χ^2 test of *relevant* $\times$ *group* was significant (Satisfiability of Concept: $\chi^2 = 8.955$, $p < 0.02$; Satisfiability of complement of concept: $\chi^2 = 15.053$, $p < 0.001$). Strikingly, the trend differs for the two types of AT. For satisfiability of a concept, more ATs are marked as relevant as the filler threshold

Table 9. Results of the post-hoc test for authoring test relevance across the three groups of participants.

	Filler group	Relevant	Not-relevant
Satisfiability (conc)	<50%	64%	36%
	50–66%	72.5%	27.5%
	Over 66%	78%	22%
Satisfiability (comp)	<50%	61%	39%
	50–66%	56%	44%
	Over 66%	41%	59%

is increased. However, for satisfiability of the complement of a concept, the trend is in the other direction, with fewer of these ATs being marked relevant as the filler threshold is increased.

6   Conclusions

Our experimental findings suggest that the CQ-driven Ontology Authoring (CQOA) approach to testing the answerability of a CQ, as embodied in Ren et al.'s mapping from CQs to ATs, is on the right track: in each of our three experiments, participants agreed with the way in which this mapping decides whether a CQ can be answered by a given ontology.

We consider these findings to be an important milestone towards the goal of improving ontology authoring via CQOA. Our results do not yet prove the *usefulness* of CQs for ontology authoring: it is possible that even an authoring interface that understands perfectly how a user has intended a given set of CQs, and which uses this understanding to tell the user which CQs have yet to be addressed, might still not contribute much to the authoring task, for example because of the manner in which the interface indicates which CQs and ATs have been met (perhaps the "traffic lights" illustrated in Fig. 2 are not understood well enough). We hope to do further experiments, to investigate the effect of CQOA on the speed and accuracy of ontology authoring, and the effect on the user's understanding of, and trust in, the ontology they have authored.

Our studies allowed us to flesh out some additional issues. Intriguing questions arose from the asymmetry between *positive* and *complement* presuppositions, particularly among users with higher DL proficiency. While it is easy to see why these users may have "unlearnt" to assign presuppositions to sentences, it is more difficult to see why this should hold particularly for complement presuppositions. These issues should be investigated further, to find out whether CQOA's usefulness is different for users with different backgrounds and/or aptitudes.

The literature on Linguistic Pragmatics is rich in theories that formalise what the presuppositions of a given sentence type are thought to be [3,18], but there has only been a limited amount of empirical testing of these theories ([26] for an overview; [5,15] for empirical studies). Our findings suggest that the support for many presuppositions is far from universal, where some were supported by as few as 36% of participants. In other words, the idea of "determining the presuppositions of a question" turns out to be a subtle affair. Perhaps the question of what information is presupposed by a given sentence is a matter of degrees, best thought of in terms of an expectation that the sentence can raise in the hearer's mind, where the strength of this expectation can differ. To vary on a classic example, suppose someone asks you "Is the king of France bald?". Traditional approaches can only say that this question does, or does not, presuppose that France has a king; perhaps a more graded approach is preferable, which asserts that the question raises the expectation that France has a king, but the strength of this expectation can differ in strength between different hearers.

Acknowledgments. This research has been funded by the EPSRC project: WhatIf: Answering "What if" questions for Ontology Authoring. EPSRC reference EP/J014176/1.

References

1. Ashburner, M., Ball, C.A., Blake, J.A., Botstein, D., Butler, H., Cherry, J.M., Davis, A.P., Dolinski, K., Dwight, S.S., Eppig, J.T., et al.: Gene ontology: tool for the unification of biology. Nat. Genet. **25**(1), 25–29 (2000)
2. Baader, F.: The Description Logic Handbook: Theory, Implementation and Applications. Cambridge University Press, Cambridge (2003)
3. Beaver, D.: Presupposition. In: van Benthem, J., ter Meulen, A. (eds.) Handbook of Logic and Language, pp. 939–1009. North Holland, Amsterdam (1997)
4. Bezerra, C., Freitas, F., Santana, F.: Evaluating ontologies with competency questions. In: IEEE/WIC/ACM International Joint Conference on Web Intelligence (WI) and Intelligent Agent Technologies (IAT), vol. 3, pp. 284–285. IEEE (2013)
5. Breheny, R., Katsos, N., Williams, J.: Are generalised scalar implicatures generated by default? An on-line investigation into the role of context in generating pragmatic inferences. Cognition **100**, 434–463 (2006)
6. Denaux, R., Dimitrova, V., Cohn, A.G., Dolbear, C., Hart, G.: Rabbit to OWL: ontology authoring with a CNL-based tool. In: Fuchs, N.E. (ed.) CNL 2009. LNCS (LNAI), vol. 5972, pp. 246–264. Springer, Heidelberg (2010). doi:10.1007/978-3-642-14418-9_15
7. Denaux, R., Thakker, D., Dimitrova, V., Cohn, A.G.: Interactive semantic feedback for intuitive ontology authoring. In: FOIS, pp. 160–173 (2012)
8. Dzbor, M., Motta, E., Buil, C., Gomez, J.M., Görlitz, O., Lewen, H.: Developing ontologies in OWL: an observational study. In: OWLED. CEUR Workshop Proceedings, vol. 216. CEUR-WS.org (2006)
9. Dzbor, M., Motta, E., Gomez, J.M., Buil, C., Dellschaft, K., Görlitz, O., Lewen, H.: D4.1.1 analysis of user needs, behaviours & requirements wrt user interfaces for ontology engineering. Technical report, August 2006
10. Enderton, H.B.: A Mathematical Introduction to Logic. Academic Press, San Diego (2001)
11. Fernandes, P.C.B., Guizzardi, R.S.S., Guizzardi, G.: Using goal modeling to capture competency questions in ontology-based systems. JIDM **2**(3), 527 (2011)

12. Grueninger, M., Fox, M.: Methodology for the design and evaluation of ontologies. In: IJCAI Workshop on Basic Ontology Issues in Knowledge Sharing (1995)
13. Hofer, P., Neururer, S., Helga Hauffe, T.I., Zeilner, A., Göbel, G.: Semi-automated evaluation of biomedical ontologies for the biobanking domain based on competency questions. Stud. Health Tech. Inform. **212**, 65–72 (2015)
14. Horridge, M., Drummond, N., Goodwin, J., Rector, A.L., Stevens, R., Wang, H.: The manchester OWL syntax. In: OWLed, vol. 216 (2006)
15. Huang, Y.T., Snedeker, J.: On-line interpretation of scalar quantifiers: insight into the semantic-pragmatics interface. Cogn. Psychol. **58**, 376–415 (2009)
16. Keet, C.M., Lawrynowicz, A.: Test-driven development of ontologies. In: Sack, H., Blomqvist, E., d'Aquin, M., Ghidini, C., Ponzetto, S.P., Lange, C. (eds.) ESWC 2016. LNCS, vol. 9678, pp. 642–657. Springer, Cham (2016). doi:10.1007/978-3-319-34129-3_39
17. Knublauch, H., Fergerson, R.W., Noy, N.F., Musen, M.A.: The Protégé OWL plugin: an open development environment for semantic web applications. In: McIlraith, S.A., Plexousakis, D., Harmelen, F. (eds.) ISWC 2004. LNCS, vol. 3298, pp. 229–243. Springer, Heidelberg (2004). doi:10.1007/978-3-540-30475-3_17
18. Levinson, S.C.: Pragmatics. Cambridge University Press, Cambridge (1983)
19. Liebig, T., Noppens, O.: Ontotrack: a semantic approach for ontology authoring. Web Semant. Sci. Serv. Agents World Wide Web **3**(2), 116–131 (2005)
20. Lord, P.: The semantic web takes wing: programming ontologies with Tawny-OWL. In: OWLED 2013 (2013). http://www.russet.org.uk/blog/2366
21. Malheiros, Y., Freitas, F.: A method to develop description logic ontologies iteratively based on competency questions: an implementation. In: ONTOBRAS, pp. 142–153 (2013)
22. Pan, J.Z., Ren, Y., Zhao, Y.: Tractable approximate deduction for OWL. Artif. Intell. **235**, 95–155 (2016)
23. Power, R.: OWL simplified english: a finite-state language for ontology editing. In: Kuhn, T., Fuchs, N.E. (eds.) CNL 2012. LNCS, vol. 7427, pp. 44–60. Springer, Heidelberg (2012). doi:10.1007/978-3-642-32612-7_4
24. Rector, A., Drummond, N., Horridge, M., Rogers, J., Knublauch, H., Stevens, R., Wang, H., Wroe, C.: OWL pizzas: practical experience of teaching OWL-DL: common errors & common patterns. In: Motta, E., Shadbolt, N.R., Stutt, A., Gibbins, N. (eds.) EKAW 2004. LNCS, vol. 3257, pp. 63–81. Springer, Heidelberg (2004). doi:10.1007/978-3-540-30202-5_5
25. Ren, Y., Parvizi, A., Mellish, C., Pan, J.Z., Deemter, K., Stevens, R.: Towards competency question-driven ontology authoring. In: Presutti, V., d'Amato, C., Gandon, F., d'Aquin, M., Staab, S., Tordai, A. (eds.) ESWC 2014. LNCS, vol. 8465, pp. 752–767. Springer, Cham (2014). doi:10.1007/978-3-319-07443-6_50
26. Sedivy, J.C.: Implicature during real time conversation: a view from language processing research. Philos. Compass **2**(3), 275–496 (2007)
27. Suárez-Figueroa, M.C., Gómez-Pérez, A.: Ontology requirements specification. In: Suárez-Figueroa, M., Gómez-Pérez, A., Motta, E., Gangemi, A. (eds.) Ontology Engineering in a Networked World, pp. 93–106. Springer, Heidelberg (2012). doi:10.1007/978-3-642-24794-1_5
28. Taylor, W.L.: Cloze procedure: a new tool for measuring readability. Journal. Q. **30**, 415–433 (1953)
29. Uschold, M., Gruninger, M., et al.: Ontologies: principles, methods and applications. Knowl. Eng. Rev. **11**(2), 93–136 (1996)

30. Whetzel, P.L., Parkinson, H.E., Causton, H.C., Fan, L., Fostel, J., Fragoso, G., Game, L., Heiskanen, M., Morrison, N., Rocca-Serra, P., Sansone, S., Taylor, C.F., White, J., Stoeckert, C.J.: The MGED ontology: a resource for semantics-based description of microarray experiments. Bioinformatics **22**(7), 866–873 (2006)
31. Zemmouchi-Ghomari, L., Ghomari, A.R.: Translating natural language competency questions into SPARQL queries: a case study. In: The First International Conference on Building and Exploring Web Based Environments, WEB 2013, pp. 81–86 (2013)
32. Zuber, R., Zuber, R.: Non-declarative Sentences. John Benjamins Publishing, Amsterdam (1983)

Matching Web Tables with Knowledge Base Entities: From Entity Lookups to Entity Embeddings

Vasilis Efthymiou[1]([✉]), Oktie Hassanzadeh[2], Mariano Rodriguez-Muro[2], and Vassilis Christophides[3]

[1] ICS-FORTH & University of Crete, Heraklion, Greece
vefthym@ics.forth.gr
[2] IBM Research, New York, USA
[3] INRIA Paris-Rocquencourt, Paris, France

Abstract. Web tables constitute valuable sources of information for various applications, ranging from Web search to Knowledge Base (KB) augmentation. An underlying common requirement is to annotate the rows of Web tables with semantically rich descriptions of entities published in Web KBs. In this paper, we evaluate three unsupervised annotation methods: (a) a *lookup-based* method which relies on the minimal entity context provided in Web tables to discover correspondences to the KB, (b) a *semantic embeddings* method that exploits a vectorial representation of the rich entity context in a KB to identify the most relevant subset of entities in the Web table, and (c) an *ontology matching* method, which exploits schematic and instance information of entities available both in a KB and a Web table. Our experimental evaluation is conducted using two existing benchmark data sets in addition to a new large-scale benchmark created using Wikipedia tables. Our results show that: (1) our novel lookup-based method outperforms state-of-the-art lookup-based methods, (2) the semantic embeddings method outperforms lookup-based methods in one benchmark data set, and (3) the lack of a rich schema in Web tables can limit the ability of ontology matching tools in performing high-quality table annotation. As a result, we propose a hybrid method that significantly outperforms individual methods on all the benchmarks.

1 Introduction

A large amount of data is published on the World Wide Web as structured data, embedded in HTML pages. A study by Cafarella et al. [9] estimated that Google's index of English documents contains 154 million high-quality relational tables, which constitute a valuable source of facts about real-world entities (e.g., persons, places, products). On the other hand, a great variety of real-world entities are described on the Web as Linked Data. Only the English version of

---

V. Efthymiou—Work done while at IBM Research.

C. d'Amato et al. (Eds.): ISWC 2017, Part I, LNCS 10587, pp. 260–277, 2017.
DOI: 10.1007/978-3-319-68288-4_16

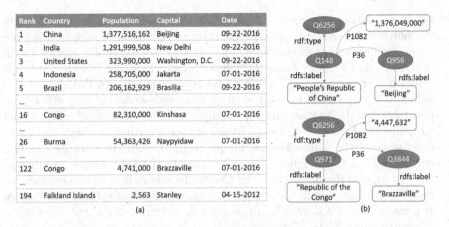

Fig. 1. (a) An example of a Web table describing countries ranked by population (b) parts of two of those countries' descriptions from Wikidata.

DBpedia [8] describes 6.2M entities using 1.1B triples, including 1.6M persons, 800K places, 480K works (e.g., films, music albums), 267K organizations, 293K species, and 5K diseases.

In this paper, we study the problem of interpreting the rows of Web tables and matching them to semantically rich descriptions of entities published in Web KBs. *Web table annotation* [20,23] (or interpretation [25,39]) is a prerequisite for a number of applications, such as Web table search [6,35] or KB augmentation [11,13,29,30,37,38]. We focus only on the evaluation of instance-level matching (table rows to KB entities) and leave the evaluation of schema-level matching (table columns to KB properties) outside the scope of this work.

Example 1. Figures 1(a) and (b) contain the descriptions of countries, as they can be found in a Web table and in Wikidata [4]. The header row (in gray color), gives the property names of the described entities. Each row in the table describes a real-world entity (e.g., the second row describes China), and each column contains the value of the corresponding property, e.g., ("Population", "1,377,516,162"), ("Capital", Beijing)[1]. Graph-based descriptions of the same entities are available in the KB, e.g., China is described by node Q148, which is of type country (node Q6256) and has a label "People's Republic of China". Entity Q148 (China) is related with Q956 (Beijing) by the property P36 (capital).

There are several key challenges in Web table annotation:

1. The *types* of the entities described in a table are *not known in advance*, and the entities described may correspond to more than one type in the

---

[1] This model is only applicable to horizontal relational tables, leaving out vertical tables such as Wikipedia infoboxes. Turning vertical tables to horizontal, identifying sub-tables, grouped columns, etc. are challenges beyond the scope of this work.

target KB. Most of the entities described in the table of Fig. 1(a), can uniquely be matched to an entity of type country in Wikidata. However, there are some exceptions. For example, "China" is also the name of a city in Japan (Q932423) and a city in Texas (Q288864)[2]. Also, "Falkland Islands" is of type "British overseas territory" and not "country" according to Wikidata.

2. Which *columns* should be used to check for *correspondences may differ* from one table row to another. In our example, column "Country" can be used to uniquely identify the names of the entities described in the table. However, some of the values are not unique: e.g., "Congo" in rows 16 and 122, corresponds to two neighbor countries, namely the Democratic Republic of the Congo, and the Republic of the Congo. To successfully match entities, we need to compare descriptions using a *variable* subset of columns/properties per entity (e.g., "Country" only is enough for most rows, but for Congo, "Country" and "Capital" are required).

3. The names of an entity described both in a Web table and in a KB, may significantly differ. This implies that high string similarity of entity labels does not provide sufficient matching evidence and additional information, such as relations to other entities, might be needed as well. For example, the entity described in row 26 of Fig. 1(a) has name "Burma" (the old name of the country), which is different from label "Myanmar" used in Wikidata. However, those descriptions can be matched, based on their capital Naypyidaw, which has the same name both in Wikidata and the table.

Clearly, the quality of the entity mapping process depends on the richness of the context (e.g., types, names, relationships) exploited to establish the mappings between Web tables and KBs. In this work, we benchmark three alternative unsupervised approaches for matching entities whose contextual information may vary from poor (in Web tables) to rich (in KBs).

First, we examine a *lookup-based* method, which exploits the columns of the Web tables recognized as entity names. It essentially detects correspondences using the *minimal contextual information* available in Web tables, which is then refined (based on frequently occurring terms in entity descriptions) or enriched (by exploiting relationships with other entities) with respect to the context of entities available in the KB. In the opposite direction, we can exploit a *semantic embeddings* method that exploits a vectorial representation of the rich entity context in a KB to identify the most relevant subset of entities in the Web table. In-between, we explore an *ontology matching* approach, which exploits schematic and instance information of entities available both in a KB and a Web table.

In summary, the contributions of our work are as follows:

– We *experimentally evaluate* the effectiveness of different Web table annotation methods on gold standards exhibiting different data characteristics (varying number of rows and columns, the existence of related entities, etc.).

---

[2] Note that although the column header may indicate the right type for the column contents, the majority of tables on the Web have missing or obscure headers [6].

- We provide a *new Web table annotation gold standard*, which is the largest in the literature (by 3 orders of magnitude in the number of tables and 2 orders of magnitude in the number of rows and provided matches), while it contains the greatest diversity on Web table sizes in both rows and columns. We show that this gold standard is more challenging than other gold standards used in this field, due to its structure, diversity, and size.
- We introduce a *novel lookup-based method* that exploits entity relations and frequent words in the values of entity descriptions, outperforming the accuracy of state-of-the-art lookup method by up to 15% in F-score.
- We propose a *hybrid method* for Web table annotation, which outperforms existing methods on all benchmarks, by up to 16% in F-score, while it is able to discover up to 14% more annotations than the individual methods it is composed of.

Outline. In what follows, we first discuss the scope of our study and position our work in the literature (Sect. 2). In Sect. 3, we introduce the three classes of annotation methods. In Sect. 4, we present our experimental evaluation using existing gold standards, as well as our Wikipedia-based gold standard, and finally, we conclude our paper in Sect. 5.

2   Background and Related Work

In this section, we position our work in the literature, with respect to the different tasks on which the Web table annotation problem is decomposed. While there has been some remarkable work on supervised Web table annotation (e.g., [7,23, 32]), here we focus on unsupervised and scalable methods, which do not require training sets of annotated tables, or any kind of human interaction (e.g., [18]). Our motivation for this focus is our use case in designing a fully unsupervised and generic cloud API, making no assumptions about the input corpus and availability of training data. Our aim is not an exhaustive evaluation of every possible method, such as supervised (e.g., [7,23,32]) or less scalable (e.g., [19]) methods.

Interpretation of Web tables. Our goal is to map each Web table row to an entity described in a KB, unlike related works [7,23,39] treating individual cells as entities. The attribute values for an entity described in a row, are given by the contents of the cells for each column of the row, following the definition of entity descriptions in the Web of data as sets of attribute-value pairs [10].

Label column detection. The vast majority of Web tables contain a column, whose values serve as the names of the described entities [6]. Rather than supervised learning [6], we rely on a heuristic method: the *label column* is defined as the leftmost column with the maximum number of distinct (non-numeric) values [28]. In other words, the label of an entity (given by the label column) is the most important attribute of an entity (described as a table row).

Lookup. Recent works follow an iterative approach between instance- and schema-level refinements, until convergence. The first step for such refinements is to look up the contents of the label column in a KB index and get a list of first, unrefined candidate matches. For instance, Ritze et al. [28] use the DBpedia lookup service [1], while Zhang [39] uses the Freebase lookup service as baselines. In our experiments, we also use the unrefined results of *DBpedia lookup* as a baseline. In our lookup-based approach, we use our own generic search index over Wikidata entities that we refer to as *FactBase*. Another interesting approach is to use a trained text classifier to extract the entity types from the snippets of Google search results, given the content of the cell which has been inferred to contain the entity name [27].

Relations extraction. Relationships between entities described in the same row of a Web table can be induced by a probabilistic model built from a Web document corpus and natural language processing [6,30]. Our relationship extraction method is inspired by Venetis et al. [35], which consults an isA database and a relations database to identify binary relations in Web tables. Instead, we exploit the information contained in the target KB, and the unambiguous entity mappings that have been already identified.

Ontology matching and link discovery tools. There is a large body of work on Ontology Matching [33]. LogMap [22] is a logic-based tool for matching semantically rich ontologies. It iteratively explores new correspondences, based on a first list of lexicographically and structurally similar entities and the ontologies' class hierarchies, which are then searched for logical inconsistencies. It has been evaluated as one of the best and most efficient publicly available ontology matching tools [12]. PARIS [34] is an iterative probabilistic tool, that defines a normalized similarity score between the entities described in two ontologies, representing how likely they are to match. This similarity depends on the similarity of their neighbors, and is obtained by first initializing the scores on literal values, and then propagating the updates through a relationship graph, using a fixed point iteration. We have chosen these tools based on their popularity and availability, while we are planning to extend our experiments with other ontology matching tools such as RiMOM-IM [31] and SERIMI [5], which have also shown good results in the recent OAEI [2] benchmarks.

Link discovery tools (e.g., [26,36]) have a similar goal, but their applicability to our problem is limited as they require linkage rules that are manually-specified, or learned from training data [21].

Entity matching context. T2K [28] annotates Web tables by mapping their columns to DBpedia properties, and their rows to DBpedia entities, associating the whole table with a DBpedia class. The initial candidate instance mappings stem from a lexicographical comparison between the labels used in the table and those of the entities described in DBpedia, which allows a first round of property mapping. The results of property mapping can then be used to refine the instance mappings, and this process continues until convergence. Our lookup-based method uses a similar candidate generation phase, and then exploits entity types, relations and frequent terms in the descriptions of candidate matches to refine or even expand the candidate matches.

TableMiner [39] maps columns to ontology classes and single cells to entities, following a two-phase process. In the first sampling phase, it searches for candidate matches, which are ranked based on similarity computations using the contents of the table, as well as the page title, surrounding paragraphs and table caption. Then, it scans the table row-by-row, until a dynamic confidence value for the type of each column has been reached. In the second phase, it uses the class mappings of the first phase to refine the candidate instance mappings. Although new candidate matches can be provided in the second phase, convergence is usually reached from the first iteration. We use a similar sampling phase to detect the entity types in a table (using the label column).

Gold standards. T2D [28] consists of a schema-level gold standard of 1,748 Web tables, manually annotated with class- and property-mappings, as well as an entity-level gold standard of 233 Web tables. Limaye [23] consists of 400 manually annotated Web tables with entity-, class-, and property-level correspondences, where single cells (not rows) are mapped to entities. We have adapted the corrected version of this gold standard [7] to annotate rows with entities, from the annotations of the label column cells. Finally, Bhagavatula et al. [7] use a gold standard extracted from 3,000 Wikipedia tables, using the hyperlinks of cells to Wikipedia pages. In this paper, we introduce a new, instance-level gold standard from 485K Wikipedia tables, the biggest that exists in the literature, in which we use the links in the label column to infer the annotation of a row to a DBpedia entity. Overall, those gold standards exhibit a variety in their sizes, existence of relations, and sparseness, helping us show how these characteristics affect the quality of different annotation methods.

3 Matching Algorithms

In this section, we describe three different individual methods for the problem of Web table annotation, as well as a hybrid solution, built on them.

3.1 Lookup Method

The lookup-based method tries to match the poor information for entities offered by Web tables to the rich information offered for those entities in a KB. In order to search for the closest possible result in the KB to the contents of a Web table, it uses a lookup service on the target KB.

Refined lookup. In this baseline, we keep the type of the top lookup result for each label column cell in a first scan of the table and then store the top-5 most frequent types for each column as acceptable types[3]. Then, we perform a second lookup, but this time, we restrict the results to those of an acceptable type.

---

[3] We assume entities described in the same column to be of the same conceptual type, which can be expressed by different OWL classes, not considering class hierarchies.

We select the top result from the refined lookup as the annotation of each row. This method tries to increase the cohesiveness of the results, by filtering lookup results which do not fit well with the rest. As an example, consider that many lookup results are returned for the query "China", but we only want to restrict our results to those of an acceptable type (e.g., country, populated place).

FactBase lookup. The lookup method that we introduce, identifies and exploits frequent terms in the description of an entity, as well as entity relations. We build on a generic indexing mechanism over a KB with IDs and textual descriptions, and call the generated index *FactBase*. FactBase offers a lookup service, allowing the retrieval of entities with a specific label, or any given attribute-value pair. The pseudocode of FactBase lookup can be found in Algorithm 1.

Algorithm 1. FactBase lookup.

Data: Table T
Result: Annotated table T'
1 $T' \leftarrow T$;
2 allTypes $\leftarrow \emptyset$;   /* a multiset of types */
3 descriptionTokens $\leftarrow \emptyset$;   /* a multiset of tokens */
   /* samplePhase   */
4 labelColumn $\leftarrow$ getLabelColumn(T);
5 referenceColumns $\leftarrow$ getReferenceColumns(T);
6 **for** *each row i of T* **do**
7 | label $\leftarrow$ $T.i.labelColumn$;
8 | results $\leftarrow$ search(label);
9 | **if** *results.size > 0* **then**
10 | | topResult $\leftarrow$ results.get(0);
11 | | allTypes.addAll(topResult.getTypes());
12 | | tokens $\leftarrow$ topResult.getDescriptionTokens();
13 | | descriptionTokens.addAll(tokens);
14 | | **if** *results.size = 1* **then**
15 | | | annotate($T'.i$, topResult);
16 | | | **for** *each column j of referenceColumns* **do**
17 | | | | $v \leftarrow T.i.j$;
18 | | | | **if** *topResult.containsFact(a,v)* **then** /* v is the value of a relation a */
19 | | | | | candidateRelations.add(j,a);
20 acceptableTypes $\leftarrow$ allTypes.get5MostFrequent();
21 descriptionTokens $\leftarrow$ descriptionTokens.getMostFrequent();
22 **for** *each column j of referenceColumns* **do**
23 | relations[j] $\leftarrow$ candidateRelations.get(j).getFirst();
   /* annotation phase   */
24 **for** *each row i of T* **do**
25 | **if** *isAnnotated(T'.i)* **then** continue;
26 | label $\leftarrow$ $T.i.labelColumn$;
27 | results $\leftarrow$ search_strict(label, acceptableTypes, descriptionTokens);
28 | **if** *results.size > 0* **then**
29 | | topResult $\leftarrow$ results.get(0);
30 | | annotate($T'.i$, topResult);
31 | | continue ;   /* go to the next row */
32 | **for** *each column j in relations* **do**
33 | | $r \leftarrow$ relations[j];
34 | | results $\leftarrow$ search_loose(label,r,$T.i.j$);
35 | | **if** *results.size > 0* **then**
36 | | | topResult $\leftarrow$ results.get(0);
37 | | | annotate($T'.i$, topResult);
38 | | | break ;   /* go to the next row */

We perform a first scan of the Web table similar to the refined lookup method (Lines 6−19). In addition to frequent types, in this method, we also extract the most frequent words, excluding stopwords, used in the values of rdfs:description. Another feature that we extract in the first scan, is the set of binary relations between the entity described in a table row and entities mentioned in the same row, as part of its description (Lines 16−19). To identify binary relations, we build on the observation that when the lookup result is unique, it is in most cases a correct annotation. For the unique results, we further examine if any of their attribute-value pairs have the same value with any of the cells of the current row marked as entity references. If that is the case, then we add the attribute of the attribute-value pair as a candidate binary relation expressed by the column of this cell. After a small number of agreements on the same attribute for a column (5 agreements in our experiments), we use this attribute as the final extracted relation expressed in this column. Finally, we use the unique lookup result for a row as the annotation of this row, skipping the next phase (Lines 15, 25).

After the first scan, many rows are now annotated with a unique lookup result[4]. For the rest of the rows, either many results were returned, i.e., a more fine-grained lookup is needed (disambiguation), or no results were returned, so a more coarse-grained lookup is needed. For the first case, we perform a new, refined lookup (*search_strict*), restricting the results to those of an acceptable type, having one of the most frequent tokens in their rdfs:description values, if applicable (Lines 28 − 31). For the second case, we perform a new, looser lookup (*search_loose*) in the labels, allowing a big margin of edit distance (Levenshtein), restricting the results to have in their facts one of the binary relations that we have extracted (Lines 32 − 38). Allowing a big margin of edit distance offers a tolerance to typos, nicknames, abbreviations, etc., while relating to the same, third entity, in the same way (i.e., using the same relationship) is a positive evidence for two entities to match [15]. The final annotation is the lookup result with the most similar label.

For example, in Fig. 1, if many results for the query term "China" are returned, we keep those with an acceptable type (e.g., country, populated place) and having the most frequent words (e.g., "country", "state") in their description. If no results are returned for the query "China", then we perform a new query, restricting the results to only those whose capital is called "Beijing", even if their label is not exactly "China", but something as close to that as possible.

3.2   Entity Embeddings Method

The approach we now describe is a variation of a linking approach for text disambiguation. We considered this approach promising for table annotation because its core hypothesis is compatible with the task. The technique is an instance of a family of techniques called *global disambiguation* techniques, which assume that the entities that appear in sentences or paragraph tend to form *coherent*

---

[4] We assume that some of the results will be unique, but this is not a requirement. If it holds, it only speeds up the process and helps in identifying binary relations.

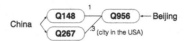

Fig. 2. Disambiguation graph for two terms. China candidates are the country or the city. Edges stand for the topic similarity score between the candidate objects.

sets with respect to the topic being discussed in the text. For example, consider two terms, *China* and *Beijing*, as shown in Fig. 2. There are two candidates for China, either the city or the country. However, a global approach would annotate "China" with the country (Q148) because it has a stronger connection to the city of Beijing (Q956). This assumption also applies to entities described in tables, where columns are usually strongly typed, and hence coherent at least with respect to types and topics.

We base our work on the global disambiguation technique used in the DoSeR framework [40], where similarity between entities is computed as the *cosine distance* between their vector representations. These vectors, called *embeddings*, are a continuous-space representation of the entities in the target KB (e.g., DBpedia), that capture the structure of the neighborhood of each node. In DoSeR, embeddings are computed using *word2vec* [24], an embedding algorithm for text that is known for its performance and scalability in computing embeddings for words. While graphs are clearly different than text, e.g., they have no clear start or end, DoSeR uses a novel approach to apply word2vec that has shown good results in terms of scalability and performance of the resulting embeddings. We will now describe this approach and the way we apply it for table disambiguation, which we divide in two stages, *off-line* and a *on-line*.

During the *off-line* stage, we first create a *surface form index* that maps each entity e of the KB to a set of known names for the entity $m(e)$. It is collected from properties in the KB that are known to contain *common names* for entities, e.g., rdfs:label, skos:altLabel, etc. In the case of DBpedia, we also use the property dbo:wikiPageWikiLinkText, which contains the anchor text used in Wikipedia to refer to the wiki page of e. Second, we compute *entity embeddings* using word2vec as follows: given the target KB, we generate a text document d by performing a random walk over the neighborhood of each entity in the KB and at each step of the walk, we append the visited node URIs to d. The resulting text document d is now used as input to word2vec which produces the embeddings for all words (node URIs) in the corpus in the standard way.

During the *on-line* stage, we use the embeddings and the surface form index to annotate tables. We consider only columns with text values, and regard each string value as an entity mention e. Then, given a set of entity mentions E, we annotate each entity $e \in E$ as follows. First, we create a *disambiguation graph* where the set of vertices V is the union of all candidates entities $m(e)$ (obtained from the surface form index) for all mentions $e \in E$. For each pair for vertices $v_1, v_2 \in V$ such that the vertices are not candidates for the same mention, i.e., there is no $e \in E$ such that $v_1, v_2 \in m(e)$, we add a weighted directed edge

$(v_1, v_2, etp(v_1, v_2))$, where $etp(v_1, v_2)$ is the normalized cosine similarity between the embeddings $emb(v_1)$, $emb(v_2)$ of v_1, v_2, respectively, computed as follows:

$$etp(v_1, v_2) = \frac{cos(emb(v_1), emb(v_2))}{\sum_{k \in V} cos(emb(v_1), emb(k))}.$$

Finally, we create an assignment for each node by applying a weighted PageRank algorithm [40] that allows us to compute the relevance of each node. We use 50 iterations for PageRank and select the nodes with the highest score from the set of candidates for each mention.

3.3   Ontology Matching Method

In this section, we briefly describe an ontology matching framework for annotating Web tables. Our framework provides the required input to any ontology matching tool, resulting in Web table annotations. Our candidate mapping selection enables even the less scalable ontology matching tools to provide annotations to large-scale KBs. For this approach, we require the existence of a header row, since each cell of this row defines the name of a property, and the cell of the label column in the header row defines the name of the table's class. For more details and preliminary results of this method, please refer to our previous work [17].

TBox. The values of an entity description can be literals, i.e., the column property is a datatype property, or references to other entities, i.e., the column property is an object property. We distinguish them by a pre-processing scan of the table and by sampling the data types of each column. To identify columns with entity references, we perform a small number of lookups in FactBase using the first few values from this column, if we have not already assigned it a numeric or date type. If most of those lookups return any result, we mark this column as an object property. The same scan also identifies the label column.

ABox. We perform a second scan, in which we create a new instance of the table class for each row. The label and URI suffix assigned to each instance are determined by the label column cell. The values of this instance for the property of each column, are the cell contents of this row for the respective column.

In Fig. 1, the header row defines the class of the table, *Country*, and the properties *Population*, *Capital*, and *Date*, all having the domain *Country*. *Capital* is an object property with range *Capital*. For the first row of the table in Fig. 1, we create an instance of the class *Country*, having the label "China", the value 1,377,516,162 for the property *Population*, the value *Beijing* for the property *Capital*, and the value 09-22-2016 for the property *Date*.

Blocking. To enable ontology matching tools that do not scale well be applicable in this framework, and to improve the efficiency of matching tools that do scale, we have applied a pre-processing step of candidate mappings selection, known as *blocking* [10]. Specifically, we retain only the DBpedia instances whose labels have at least one common token with the labels of our ontology's instances.

Finally, we call an ontology matching tool with the table ontology and the DBpedia ontology after blocking, as input, and return the mapping results.

3.4 Hybrid

We introduce two simple hybrid methods, to explore the benefits of combining FactBase lookup and embeddings, in the following way:

Hybrid I. If FactBase lookup provides a mapping for the entity of a row, then this hybrid method keeps this mapping. Otherwise, it uses the annotation provided by the embeddings for this row, if one exists.

Hybrid II. Same as Hybrid I in inverse order, i.e., using the embeddings first, before FactBase lookup.

The motivation is that individual methods handle different aspects of the contextual information that is offered in Web tables. As our experiments show, where one approach fails to perform correct annotations, the other approach often succeeds. This approach can only improve the recall of its first component (i.e., FactBase lookup for Hybrid I and embeddings for Hybrid II), since it returns all the annotations of the first component, plus additional annotations from the second component, if the first fails.

4 Experiments

Settings. For our experiments, we use MapReduce for annotating and evaluating multiple tables in parallel, and a key-value store as our index. We do not report run times for each experiment as they depend on the cluster configuration and other settings. Our experiments on smaller datasets take only a few minutes on our cluster of 16 medium-sized nodes, while experiments on larger datasets take several hours to finish. Our *FactBase* index implementation uses a 2016 dump of Wikidata, with entities linked to corresponding DBpedia entities. Hence, FactBase lookup results using gold standards annotated with older versions of DBpedia may slightly underestimate its accuracy. The datasets generated or used are made publicly available [16] along with implementation details: http://ibm.biz/webtables.

4.1 Datasets

In our experiments, we use three gold standards, whose characteristics are summarized in Table 1. Rows per table show the min, max and average number of rows per table in each gold standard. The same holds for columns per table. For the number of tables featuring entity relations, we applied the relation detection method from *FactBase lookup*. For a measure of cell completeness, we use *structuredness* as defined in [14]. In this context, we compute the percentage of cells in a table that are not empty (or "NULL" or "-"), as the structuredness of a table. Then, the overall structuredness of a gold standard is a weighted sum of each table's structuredness, where the weight of each table is based on its sum of columns and rows, normalized by the total sum of columns and rows in this gold standard. Intuitively, a structuredness value of 1 indicates that no cells are empty and 0 structuredness represents that all cells are empty.

Table 1. Characteristics of the gold standards. All are made publicly available [16].

Name	Tables	Rows	Matches	Rows per table (av.)	Columns per table (av.)	Tables with relations	Structuredness
T2D	233	28,647	26,124	6 - 586 (123)	3 - 14 (4.95)	108 (46%)	0.97
Limaye	296	8,670	5,278	6 - 465 (29)	2 - 6 (3.79)	78 (26%)	0.59
Wikipedia	485,096	7,437,606	4,453,329	2 - 3,505 (15)	1 - 76 (5.58)	24,628 (5%)	0.85

T2D [3] consists of 233 Web tables, manually annotated with instances from the 2014 version of DBpedia. It has the highest average number of rows per table (123), and the highest ratio of tables with relations (46%). It is also the gold standard with the highest structuredness (0.97), meaning that very few cells are empty in this corpus.

The updated version of the *Limaye* gold standard [23] published by Bhagavatula et al. [7], annotates cells with Wikipedia pages. We have replaced Wikipedia annotations with the corresponding entities from the October 2015 version of DBpedia. To make this gold standard applicable to our model, we have kept only one annotation per row, the one assigned to the cell of the label column, in 296 Web tables for which a label column could be detected. This is the gold standard with the lowest number of columns per table on average (3.79), still, one out of four tables (26%) contains entity relations. Due to a big number of empty cells, it presents the lowest structuredness (0.59), while it also contains a big number of empty rows. Missing data have a negative impact in the quality of the annotations for some systems, such as *T2K*. This dataset could not be used in the evaluation of ontology matching methods, as it misses header rows, thus no meaningful property and class names could be created for a table ontology.

Finally, we have created our own *Wikipedia* gold standard, by extracting the hyperlinks of existing Wikipedia tables to Wikipedia pages, which we have replaced with annotations to the corresponding entities from the October 2015 version of DBpedia. Since the header rows in Wikipedia tables are not linked to properties, our gold standard does not contain schema-level mappings. For the needs of our experiments, we only consider one mapping per row to evaluate the different methods, using the annotations for the label column. This gold standard is much more noisy than the other two, as it contains unannotated rows, multi-column and multi-row cells, which we split and replicate to avoid empty cells, and cells whose contents are entity labels with additional information for an entity (e.g., the cell "George Washington February 22, 1732 - December 14, 1799 (aged 67)", refers to George Washington), which makes the annotation task more difficult, as such labels are very dissimilar to the corresponding entity labels in a KB. Finally, even if the average number of rows (15) is much smaller than in the other two gold standards, we note that it contains almost 800 tables with more than 1,000 rows and the largest table consists of 3.5K rows. This gold standard contains the lowest ratio of tables with detected relations (only 5%), while it exhibits the highest average number of columns per table (5.58). Its structuredness is high (0.85), thus, only a few cells are empty.

4.2   Evaluation

In Table 2, we present the experimental results over the three gold standards, with respect to micro-averaged recall, precision, and F-score. The micro-averaged values over a set of tables are acquired by using the sums of true positives, false positives, true negatives and false negatives from each table, as if they were a single test. Different methods are separated by double horizontal lines.

Table 2. Results over T2D, Limaye, and Wikipedia Gold Standards.

Method	T2D gold standard			Limaye gold standard			Wikipedia gold standard		
	Re	Pr	F1	Re	Pr	F1	Re	Pr	F1
DBpedia lookup	0.73	0.79	0.76	0.73	0.79	0.76	-	-	-
DBpedia refined	0.76	0.86	0.81	0.68	0.73	0.71	-	-	-
T2K	0.76	**0.90**	0.82	0.63	0.70	0.66	0.22	**0.70**	0.34
FactBase lookup	**0.78**	0.88	**0.83**	**0.78**	**0.84**	**0.81**	0.50	**0.70**	0.58
Embeddings	0.77	0.86	0.81	0.65	**0.84**	0.73	**0.53**	**0.70**	**0.60**
Blocking	0.71	0.32	0.44	-	-	-	0.39	0.16	0.23
LogMap	0.57	0.89	0.70	-	-	-	0.29	0.34	0.32
PARIS	0.04	0.42	0.07	-	-	-	-	-	-
Hybrid I	**0.83**	0.87	**0.85**	0.79	0.84	0.81	0.57	0.66	0.61
Hybrid II	0.81	0.85	0.83	**0.79**	**0.84**	**0.82**	**0.60**	0.69	**0.64**

Results over T2D Gold Standard. As the results in Table 2 show, a simple *DBpedia lookup* without any schema-level refinements has very good results, verifying the numbers reported in [28]. Moreover, the *DBpedia lookup refined* is almost as good as state-of-the-art methods. *FactBase lookup* is the overall winner in this gold standard, having a slightly better recall than *T2K* (+2%) and a slightly worse precision (−2%). The *embeddings* are also better than *T2K* with respect to recall (+1%), but worse overall (−1% in F-score), showing almost the same results as the *DBpedia lookup refined* baseline. *The almost perfect structuredness value of T2D provides the ideal conditions for methods that exploit all the columns of a table for their annotations, such as T2K.*

The *ontology matching* tools exhibit much worse results, mainly in recall. For a fair comparison between the methods, we have included the results of *blocking*, which the ontology matching tools use as input. It is important to note that the recall of *blocking* is the upper recall threshold that an ontology matching tool can achieve and in this case, it is already lower than the recall of the other methods. Still, the difference between the recall of *blocking* and the recall of *LogMap* [22] (−14%) and *PARIS* [34] (−73%), is substantial. Most ontology matching tools are not designed to provide mappings between such heterogeneous ontologies with respect to the information richness and diversity they contain, like the ones we produce. The number of attributes (i.e., columns) used to describe entities in a Web table are quite different than the respective information in the ontology of a KB. Efthymiou et al. [15] show that an average entity description in DBpedia uses 11.44 attributes, whereas the number of attributes used in a Web table corpus is typically between 4 and 6 (Table 1). Furthermore, Duan et al. [14] show that unlike Web tables, KBs such as DBpedia are of very low structuredness.

The effectiveness of lookup-based methods heavily relies on the lookup service that is employed. Thus, lookup-based annotations could be used as an evaluation of such services. For example, when substituting *DBpedia lookup* with an unrefined version of FactBase lookup, the results were 0.57 recall, 0.62 precision, and 0.59 F-measure, as opposed to the T2D results for the DBpedia lookup (0.73 recall, 0.79 precision, and 0.76 F-measure). This shows that the DBpedia lookup service is much better than the FactBase lookup service, as FactBase lookup is still in the development phase. This difference is observed, mainly due to the different ranking of the results in those two services. DBpedia lookup service exploits the in-degree of entities in its returned rankings, whereas the lookup service of FactBase only considers the label similarity to the query.

Results over Limaye Gold Standard. As shown in Table 2, *FactBase lookup* outperforms other approaches with a difference of +8% in F-score from the second best technique, the *embeddings*, even if they are both tied at the highest precision. The difference in recall from the second best method *DBpedia lookup* is +5%. As we can see in Table 1, even if this gold standard contains more tables than *T2D,* the number of rows in those tables is significantly lower. Thus, *methods that rely on a sampling phase (e.g., FactBase lookup), or on a set of coherent results (e.g., embeddings), perform worse than in datasets with bigger tables,* which is also the reason why DBpedia lookup performs better than DBpedia refined in this gold standard. Nonetheless, even if this gold standard contains small and sparse tables (0.59 structuredness), there is a decent percentage (26%) of tables with entity relations, which *FactBase lookup* can exploit to achieve a much better performance than *embeddings*. The recall values of *DBpedia lookup* and *DBpedia lookup refined* are close to those of *embeddings*, while the latter show a much better precision. Due to the missing rows in this gold standard, *T2K* may disregard some tables as of low quality. It may also detect a different label column than the one *FactBase lookup* detects. This also explains the worse performance of *T2K* compared to *DBpedia lookup*. *FactBase lookup* yields a 15% higher F-score than *T2K*, showing that it can better handle tables of low structuredness, i.e., with many missing values.

Results over Wikipedia Gold Standard. As shown in Table 2, the *embeddings* show the best results for the *Wikipedia* gold standard, with *FactBase lookup* following (−4% in F-score) with worse recall (−6%) and equally good precision. Ontology matching is again worse than the other methods, even from the step of blocking (we excluded PARIS from this experiment given its poor performance on T2D). As expected, the results presented in this table are much worse than the other two gold standards, which can be justified by the noisiness of this dataset, as explained in Sect. 4.1. *Noisiness seems to favor the* *embeddings over the other methods, since it can better handle ambiguous mentions to entities in a textual context.* Another challenge in this gold standard is the small number of rows, which makes it more difficult for *FactBase lookup* and *embeddings* to have a decent sample for type refinements and relations extraction, and provide a set of coherent results, respectively. For the same reason, due its strict matching policy favoring precision over recall - at least 50% of the rows must be mapped to KB entities of the same type - *T2K* managed to annotate only 119K out of the 485K Web tables, resulting in a very low recall, presenting an overall performance close to that of *LogMap*. *DBpedia lookup* could not be applied to this gold standard, as the public server hosting it could not handle such a large amount of queries.

Hybrid Methods. As shown in Table 2, the hybrid methods seem to improve the results of their constituent methods, by enhancing recall, with a minor impact on precision. In *T2D*, *Hybrid I* exhibits an important improvement of the quality results over either of its constituent methods. Its recall is 5% better than that of *FactBase lookup*, while its precision is only 1% lower, resulting in a 2% higher F-score. *Hybrid II* is also better than its constituent methods, but slightly worse than *Hybrid I*. In *T2D*, the individual methods that constitute the hybrid have a 76% Jaccard similarity in the table rows that they annotate correctly, while their recall values are very close. An ideal solution that always chooses the correct annotation among the annotations provided by those methods would yield a recall of 0.88 for *T2D*.

In the *Limaye* gold standard, the benefit of using a hybrid method is not as significant as in *T2D*, but it is still the best-performing method. This is due to the fact that *FactBase lookup* performs much better than the *embeddings*, so the latter has little to offer in their combination. Still, the recall of their combination is better than that of *FactBase lookup* by 1% and the precision is the same as that of both methods (0.84). The two hybrid methods are almost identical, with *Hybrid II* showing a slightly better F-score (+1%). Again, the Jaccard similarity of correctly annotated rows in the constituent methods is 75%, while an ideal combination of those methods would yield a recall of 0.81.

In the *Wikipedia* gold standard, the hybrid methods significantly outperform the individual methods, as both of the constituent methods have a good precision and modest recall, which is the ideal case for such hybrids. Intuitively, in such cases the first constituent method has given only few annotations, still they are mostly correct. Thus, it has skipped to annotate many rows, which can be annotated by the second constituent method, mostly with a correct KB entity (good precision). Specifically, the recall of *Hybrid II* is better than that of the *embeddings* (+7%), while its precision is worse by only 1%, yielding an F-score that is 4% better than the *embeddings*. The difference to the *FactBase lookup* results is even bigger (+10% recall and +6% F-score). *Hybrid II* is much better than *Hybrid I* (+3% F-score) in this gold standard, since it exploits the better performance of *embeddings*.

Lessons Learned. The following are the key lessons learned from our results: (1) Both *FactBase lookup* and *embeddings* work better with tables of many rows. In tables with few rows (less than 5), *embeddings* provide better annotations than *FactBase lookup*. (2) When the Web tables contain entity relations, *FactBase lookup* provides the best annotation results. (3) *Embeddings* can cope with noise in the string similarity of labels better than the other methods. (4) Most ontology matching tools are not suited to match a flat ontology to another which has a rich structure. (5) Hybrid methods work better when the constituent methods have modest recall and good precision.

5 Conclusion and Future Work

In this paper, we performed a thorough evaluation of three different families of methods to annotate Web tables, and discussed key lessons learned from our experiments. We introduced a new benchmark and a hybrid approach that outperforms individual methods by up to 16% in F-score. In the future, we plan to expand our evaluation of ontology matching tools and propose a new track for the upcoming OAEI campaign to encourage the community to use and extend ontology matching tools as knowledge base population systems.

Acknowledgments. We would like to thank the authors of T2K [28], LogMap [22], and TabEL [7] (TabEL results not included in our experiments as it was not yet functional at the time of writing this manuscript, missing some custom resources.) for sharing their code and their assistance.

References

1. DBpedia Lookup. http://wiki.dbpedia.org/projects/dbpedia-lookup. Accessed 27 July 2017
2. Ontology Alignment Evaluation Initiative. http://oaei.ontologymatching.org/. Accessed 27 July 2017
3. T2D Gold Standard for Matching Web Tables to DBpedia. http://webdatacommons.org/webtables/goldstandard.html. Accessed 27 July 2017
4. Wikidata. http://www.wikidata.org. Accessed 27 July 2017
5. Araújo, S., Tran, D.T., de Vries, A.P., Schwabe, D.: SERIMI: class-based matching for instance matching across heterogeneous datasets. IEEE TKDE **27**(5), 1397–1440 (2015)
6. Balakrishnan, S., Halevy, A.Y., Harb, B., Lee, H., Madhavan, J., Rostamizadeh, A., Shen, W., Wilder, K., Wu, F., Yu, C.: Applying webtables in practice. In: CIDR (2015)
7. Bhagavatula, C.S., Noraset, T., Downey, D.: TabEL: entity linking in web tables. In: Arenas, M., Corcho, O., Simperl, E., Strohmaier, M., d'Aquin, M., Srinivas, K., Groth, P., Dumontier, M., Heflin, J., Thirunarayan, K., Staab, S. (eds.) ISWC 2015. LNCS, vol. 9366, pp. 425–441. Springer, Cham (2015). doi:10.1007/978-3-319-25007-6_25. http://websail-fe.cs.northwestern.edu/

8. Bizer, C., Lehmann, J., Kobilarov, G., Auer, S., Becker, C., Cyganiak, R., Hellmann, S.: DBpedia - a crystallization point for the web of data. JWS **7**(3), 154–165 (2009)
9. Cafarella, M.J., Halevy, A.Y., Wang, D.Z., Wu, E., Zhang, Y.: WebTables: exploring the power of tables on the web. PVLDB **1**(1), 538–549 (2008)
10. Christophides, V., Efthymiou, V., Stefanidis, K.: Entity Resolution in the Web of Data. Morgan & Claypool Publishers, San Rafael (2015)
11. Dalvi, B.B., Cohen, W.W., Callan, J.: WebSets: extracting sets of entities from the web using unsupervised information extraction. In: WSDM (2012)
12. Daskalaki, E., Flouris, G., Fundulaki, I., Saveta, T.: Instance matching benchmarks in the era of linked data. Web Semant. Sci. Serv. Agents World Wide Web **39**, 1–14 (2016)
13. Dong, X., Gabrilovich, E., Heitz, G., Horn, W., Lao, N., Murphy, K., Strohmann, T., Sun, S., Zhang, W.: Knowledge vault: a web-scale approach to probabilistic knowledge fusion. In: KDD (2014)
14. Duan, S., Kementsietsidis, A., Srinivas, K., Udrea, O.: Apples and oranges: a comparison of RDF benchmarks and real RDF datasets. In: SIGMOD (2011)
15. Efthymiou, V., Stefanidis, K., Christophides, V.: Big data entity resolution: from highly to somehow similar entity descriptions in the web. In: IEEE Big Data (2015)
16. Efthymiou, V., Hassanzadeh, O., Rodrguez-Muro, M., Christophides, V.: Evaluating Web Table Annotation Methods: From Entity Lookups to Entity Embeddings. figshare (2017). https://doi.org/10.6084/m9.figshare.5229847
17. Efthymiou, V., Hassanzadeh, O., Sadoghi, M., Rodriguez-Muro, M.: Annotating web tables through ontology matching. In: OM (2016)
18. Fan, J., Lu, M., Ooi, B.C., Tan, W., Zhang, M.: A hybrid machine-crowdsourcing system for matching web tables. In: ICDE (2014)
19. Guo, X., Chen, Y., Chen, J., Du, X.: ITEM: extract and integrate entities from tabular data to rdf knowledge base. In: Du, X., Fan, W., Wang, J., Peng, Z., Sharaf, M.A. (eds.) APWeb 2011. LNCS, vol. 6612, pp. 400–411. Springer, Heidelberg (2011). doi:10.1007/978-3-642-20291-9_45
20. Hassanzadeh, O., Ward, M.J., Rodriguez-Muro, M., Srinivas, K.: Understanding a large corpus of web tables through matching with knowledge bases: an empirical study. In: OM (2015)
21. Isele, R., Bizer, C.: Learning expressive linkage rules using genetic programming. PVLDB **5**(11), 1638–1649 (2012)
22. Jiménez-Ruiz, E., Grau, B.C.: LogMap: logic-based and scalable ontology matching. In: Aroyo, L., Welty, C., Alani, H., Taylor, J., Bernstein, A., Kagal, L., Noy, N., Blomqvist, E. (eds.) ISWC 2011. LNCS, vol. 7031, pp. 273–288. Springer, Heidelberg (2011). doi:10.1007/978-3-642-25073-6_18
23. Limaye, G., Sarawagi, S., Chakrabarti, S.: Annotating and searching web tables using entities, types and relationships. PVLDB **3**(1), 1338–1347 (2010)
24. Mikolov, T., Chen, K., Corrado, G., Dean, J.: Efficient estimation of word representations in vector space. CoRR abs/1301.3781 (2013)
25. Mulwad, V., Finin, T., Syed, Z., Joshi, A.: Using linked data to interpret tables. In: COLD (2010)
26. Ngomo, A.C.N., Auer, S.: LIMES - a time-efficient approach for large-scale link discovery on the web of data. In: IJCAI (2011)
27. Quercini, G., Reynaud, C.: Entity discovery and annotation in tables. In: EDBT (2013)
28. Ritze, D., Lehmberg, O., Bizer, C.: Matching HTML tables to DBpedia. In: WIMS (2015)

29. Ritze, D., Lehmberg, O., Oulabi, Y., Bizer, C.: Profiling the potential of web tables for augmenting cross-domain knowledge bases. In: WWW (2016)
30. Sekhavat, Y.A., Paolo, F.D., Barbosa, D., Merialdo, P.: Knowledge base augmentation using tabular data. In: LDOW (2014)
31. Shao, C., Hu, L., Li, J., Wang, Z., Chung, T.L., Xia, J.: RiMOM-IM: a novel iterative framework for instance matching. J. Comput. Sci. Technol. **31**(1), 185–197 (2016)
32. Shen, W., Wang, J., Luo, P., Wang, M.: LIEGE: link entities in web lists with knowledge base. In: KDD (2012)
33. Shvaiko, P., Euzenat, J.: Ontology matching: state of the art and future challenges. IEEE TKDE **25**(1), 158–176 (2013)
34. Suchanek, F.M., Abiteboul, S., Senellart, P.: PARIS: probabilistic alignment of relations, instances, and schema. PVLDB **5**(3), 157–168 (2011). http://webdam.inria.fr/paris/
35. Venetis, P., Halevy, A.Y., Madhavan, J., Pasca, M., Shen, W., Wu, F., Miao, G., Wu, C.: Recovering semantics of tables on the web. PVLDB **4**(9), 528–538 (2011)
36. Volz, J., Bizer, C., Gaedke, M., Kobilarov, G.: Silk - a link discovery framework for the web of data. In: LDOW, April 2009
37. Wang, J., Wang, H., Wang, Z., Zhu, K.Q.: Understanding tables on the web. In: Atzeni, P., Cheung, D., Ram, S. (eds.) ER 2012. LNCS, vol. 7532, pp. 141–155. Springer, Heidelberg (2012). doi:10.1007/978-3-642-34002-4_11
38. Yakout, M., Ganjam, K., Chakrabarti, K., Chaudhuri, S.: InfoGather: entity augmentation and attribute discovery by holistic matching with web tables. In: SIGMOD (2012)
39. Zhang, Z.: Towards efficient and effective semantic table interpretation. In: Mika, P., Tudorache, T., Bernstein, A., Welty, C., Knoblock, C., Vrandečić, D., Groth, P., Noy, N., Janowicz, K., Goble, C. (eds.) ISWC 2014. LNCS, vol. 8796, pp. 487–502. Springer, Cham (2014). doi:10.1007/978-3-319-11964-9_31
40. Zwicklbauer, S., Seifert, C., Granitzer, M.: DoSeR - a knowledge-base-agnostic framework for entity disambiguation using semantic embeddings. In: Sack, H., Blomqvist, E., d'Aquin, M., Ghidini, C., Ponzetto, S.P., Lange, C. (eds.) ESWC 2016. LNCS, vol. 9678, pp. 182–198. Springer, Cham (2016). doi:10.1007/978-3-319-34129-3_12

Learning Commonalities in SPARQL

Sara El Hassad, François Goasdoué$^{(\boxtimes)}$, and Hélène Jaudoin

IRISA, Univ. Rennes 1, Lannion, France
{sara.el-hassad,fg,helene.jaudoin}@irisa.fr

Abstract. Finding the commonalities between descriptions of data or knowledge is a foundational reasoning problem of Machine Learning. It was formalized in the early 70's as computing a *least general generalization* (lgg) of such descriptions. We revisit this well-established problem in the SPARQL query language for RDF graphs. In particular, and by contrast to the literature, we address it for the *entire* class of conjunctive SPARQL queries, a.k.a. Basic Graph Pattern Queries (BGPQs), and crucially, when *background knowledge* is available as RDF Schema ontological constraints, we take advantage of it to devise much more precise lggs, as our experiments on the popular DBpedia dataset show.

Keywords: BGP queries · RDF · RDFS · Least general generalization

1 Introduction

Finding the commonalities between descriptions of data or knowledge is a fundamental Machine Learning problem, which was formalized in the early 70's as computing a *least general generalization* (lgg) of such descriptions [21]. Since then, it has also received consideration in the Knowledge Representation field, where least general generalizations were rebaptized *least common subsumers* [5], in Description Logics [1,5,14,27] and in Conceptual Graphs [3]. More recently, this problem started being investigated in RDF [7,9] and its associated SPARQL query language [2,10,16], the two prominent Semantic Web standards by W3C.

Motivations. We study this old reasoning problem in the *SPARQL* setting (contributions to be outlined shortly), i.e., when input descriptions are SPARQL queries. Solutions to this problem can be applied to a variety of useful important applications, ranging from *optimization* to *exploration* and *recommendation* in RDF data management systems or in SPARQL endpoints. For instance, an lgg of incoming queries characterizes the largest set of their commonalities whose processing may be shared in *multi-query optimization* [15]. Similarly, lggs of subsets of a query workload correspond to candidate views that may be recommended for materialization in *view selection* [11], a typical optimization for data warehouses [6], and among which can be selected those that allow rewriting (partially or totally) the workload while minimizing a combination of rewriting processing, view storage and view maintenance costs. Also, *clustering user queries* found in system logs, based on their lggs, may help classifying the

© Springer International Publishing AG 2017
C. d'Amato et al. (Eds.): ISWC 2017, Part I, LNCS 10587, pp. 278–295, 2017.
DOI: 10.1007/978-3-319-68288-4_17

queries and identifying the kind of data each category accesses [4]. Finally, finding the relevant user query cluster for an incoming query may help recommending *similar and complementary searches* [13].

Contributions. We bring the following contributions to the problem of finding an lgg of SPARQL queries:

1. We carefully study a novel notion of lgg for the popular conjunctive fragment of SPARQL (Sect. 3), a.k.a. Basic Graph Pattern Queries (BGPQs). Our definition, which we briefly outlined in [10], significantly departs from the literature by (*i*) considering *general* BGPQs, instead of *unary tree-shaped* ones [2,16], and crucially by (*ii*) taking advantage of *background knowledge* formalized as RDF Schema (RDFS) ontological constraints. Furthermore, to establish this definition of an lgg, we revise the standard generalization/specialization relation (a.k.a. entailment) between BGPQs in order to devise a *well-founded* entailment relation that allows comparing BGPQs *w.r.t. extra RDFS constraints*, i.e., the counterpart to *subsumption between concepts w.r.t. a terminology* in Description Logics and to *containment between queries w.r.t. constraints* in Databases.
2. We provide a solution to the above problem (Sect. 4), which technically differs from the state of the art [2,16] in that it cannot exploit the (imposed) tree-shape of the input BGPQs to compute their lgg through a simultaneous root-to-leaves traversal. Instead, our solution traverses blindly the general (hence arbitrary-shaped) input BGPQs and builds their lgg using the notion of *least general anti-unification* of atoms [21,23], which is dual to the well-known notion of most general unification of atoms [22,23]. Also, to take into account background knowledge, we define a *well-founded* notion of *saturation of BGPQs w.r.t. extra RDFS constraints*, which we devise inspired by that of RDF graphs.
3. We report on experiments made to assess the added-value of considering background knowledge when computing lggs of BGPQs (Sect. 5). Notably, we use real data from DBpedia to show how much more precise lggs are when background knowledge is considered, by measuring the *gain in precision* it yields.

Organization. Following the presentation of [8–10], we first recall the basics of RDF and SPARQL in Sect. 2. Then, we detail the above contributions. Finally, we discuss related work and conclude in Sect. 6.

Supplementary material (proofs of our technical results, implemented algorithms, additional experiments, etc) is available in our online research report [8].

2   Preliminaries

2.1   The Resource Description Framework (RDF)

RDF Graphs. The RDF data model allows specifying *RDF graphs*. An RDF graph is a set of *triples* of the form (s, p, o). A triple states that its *subject* s

Table 1. RDF & RDFS statements.

RDF statement	Triple
Class assertion	$(s, \text{rdf:type}, o)$
Property assertion	(s, p, o) with $p \neq \text{rdf:type}$
RDFS statement	**Triple**
Subclass	$(s, \text{rdfs:subClassOf}, o)$
Subproperty	$(s, \text{rdfs:subPropertyOf}, o)$
Domain typing	$(s, \text{rdfs:domain}, o)$
Range typing	$(s, \text{rdfs:range}, o)$

Table 2. Sample RDF entailment rules.

Rule [25]	Entailment rule
rdfs2	$(p, \hookleftarrow_d, o), (s_1, p, o_1) \rightarrow (s_1, \tau, o)$
rdfs3	$(p, \hookrightarrow_r, o), (s_1, p, o_1) \rightarrow (o_1, \tau, o)$
rdfs5	$(p_1, \preceq_{sp}, p_2), (p_2, \preceq_{sp}, p_3) \rightarrow (p_1, \preceq_{sp}, p_3)$
rdfs7	$(p_1, \preceq_{sp}, p_2), (s, p_1, o) \rightarrow (s, p_2, o)$
rdfs9	$(s, \preceq_{sc}, o), (s_1, \tau, s) \rightarrow (s_1, \tau, o)$
rdfs11	$(s, \preceq_{sc}, o), (o, \preceq_{sc}, o_1) \rightarrow (s, \preceq_{sc}, o_1)$
ext1	$(p, \hookleftarrow_d, o), (o, \preceq_{sc}, o_1) \rightarrow (p, \hookleftarrow_d, o_1)$
ext2	$(p, \hookrightarrow_r, o), (o, \preceq_{sc}, o_1) \rightarrow (p, \hookrightarrow_r, o_1)$
ext3	$(p, \preceq_{sp}, p_1), (p_1, \hookleftarrow_d, o) \rightarrow (p, \hookleftarrow_d, o)$
ext4	$(p, \preceq_{sp}, p_1), (p_1, \hookrightarrow_r, o) \rightarrow (p, \hookrightarrow_r, o)$

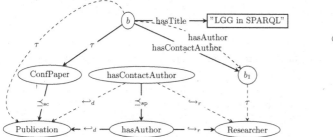

Fig. 1. Sample RDF graph $\mathcal{G}$.   **Fig. 2.** Sample RDF graph $\mathcal{G}'$.

has the *property* p, the value of which is the *object* o. Triples are built using three pairwise disjoint sets: a set $\mathcal{U}$ of *uniform resources identifiers (URIs)*, a set $\mathcal{L}$ of *literals* (constants), and a set $\mathcal{B}$ of *blank nodes* allowing to support *incomplete information*. Blank nodes are identifiers for missing values (unknown URIs or literals). *Well-formed triples*, as per the RDF specification [24], belong to $(\mathcal{U} \cup \mathcal{B}) \times \mathcal{U} \times (\mathcal{U} \cup \mathcal{L} \cup \mathcal{B})$; we only consider such triples hereafter.

Notations. We use s, p, o in triples as placeholders. We note $\text{Val}(\mathcal{G})$ the set of *values* occurring in an RDF graph $\mathcal{G}$, i.e., the URIs, literals and blank nodes; we note $\text{Bl}(\mathcal{G})$ the set of blank nodes occurring in $\mathcal{G}$. A blank node is written b possibly with a subscript, and a literal is a string between quotes. For instance, the triples $(b, \text{hasTitle})$, "LGG in SPARQL" and $(b, \text{hasContactAuthor}, b_1)$ mean: *something (b) entitled "LGG in SPARQL" has somebody (b_1) as contact author.*

A triple models an assertion, either for a *class* (unary relation) or for a *property* (binary relation). Table 1 (top) shows the use of triples to state such assertions. The RDF standard [24] provides built-in classes and properties, as URIs within the rdf and rdfs pre-defined namespaces, e.g., rdf:type which can be used to state that the above b is a conference paper with the triple $(b, \text{rdf:type}, \text{ConfPaper})$.

Adding Ontological Knowledge to RDF Graphs. An essential feature of RDF is the possibility to enhance the descriptions in RDF graphs by declaring *ontological constraints* between the classes and properties they use. This is achieved with *RDF Schema (RDFS)* statements, which are triples using particular built-in properties. Table 1 (bottom) lists the allowed constraints and the triples to state them; *domain* and *range* denote respectively the first and second attribute of every property. For example, the triple (ConfPaper, rdfs:subClassOf, Publication) states that *conference papers are publications*, the triple (hasContactAuthor, rdfs:subPropertyOf, hasAuthor) states that *having a contact author is having an author*, the triple (hasAuthor, rdfs:domain, Publication) states that *only publications may have authors*, and the triple (hasAuthor, rdfs:range, Researcher) states that *only researchers may be authors of something*.

Notations. For conciseness, we use the following shorthands for RDFS built-in properties: τ for rdf:type, $\preceq_{sc}$ for rdfs:subClassOf, $\preceq_{sp}$ for rdfs:subPropertyOf, $\hookrightarrow_d$ for rdfs:domain, and $\hookrightarrow_r$ for rdfs:range.

Figure 1 displays the usual representation of the RDF graph $\mathcal{G}$ made of the seven above-mentioned triples, which are called the *explicit triples* of $\mathcal{G}$. A triple (s, p, o) corresponds to a p-labeled directed edge from the s node to the o node: $s \xrightarrow{p} o$. Explicit triples are shown as solid edges, while the *implicit ones*, which are derived using ontological constraints (see below), are shown as dashed edges.

Importantly, it is worth noticing the deductive nature of ontological constraints, which begets implicit triples within an RDF graph. For instance, in Fig. 1, the constraint (hasContactAuthor, $\preceq_{sp}$, hasAuthor) together with the triple $(b, \text{hasContactAuthor}, b_1)$ imply the implicit triple $(b, \text{hasAuthor}, b_1)$, which, further, with the constraint (hasAuthor, $\hookrightarrow_r$, Researcher) yields another implicit triple $(b_1, \tau, \text{Researcher})$.

Deriving the Implicit Triples of an RDF Graph. The RDF standard defines a set of *entailment rules* in order to derive automatically *all* the triples that are implicit to an RDF graph. Table 2 shows the strict subset of these rules that we will use to illustrate important notions as well as our contributions in the next sections; importantly, our contributions hold for the entire set of entailment rules of the RDF standard, and any subset of thereof. The rules in Table 2 concern the derivation of implicit triples using ontological constraints (i.e., *RDFS statements*). They encode the *propagation* of assertions through constraints (rdfs2, rdfs3, rdfs7, rdfs9), the *transitivity* of the $\preceq_{sp}$ and $\preceq_{sc}$ constraints (rdfs5, rdfs11), the *complementation* of domains or ranges through $\preceq_{sc}$ (ext1, ext2), and the *inheritance* of domains and of ranges through $\preceq_{sp}$ (ext3, ext4).

The *saturation (or closure)* of an RDF graph $\mathcal{G}$ w.r.t. a set $\mathcal{R}$ of RDF entailment rules (a.k.a. entailment regime) is the RDF graph $\mathcal{G}^{\infty}$ obtained by adding to $\mathcal{G}$ *all* the implicit triples that follow from $\mathcal{G}$ and $\mathcal{R}$. Roughly speaking, the saturation $\mathcal{G}^{\infty}$ *materializes* the semantics of $\mathcal{G}$. It corresponds to the fixpoint reached by repeatedly applying the rules in $\mathcal{R}$ to $\mathcal{G}$ in a forward-chaining fashion, while adding to $\mathcal{G}$ the triples they derive. In RDF, the saturation is *finite, unique* (up to blank node renaming), and can be *computed in polynomial time* [25].

The saturation of the RDF graph $\mathcal{G}$ shown in Fig. 1 corresponds to the RDF graph $\mathcal{G}^\infty$ in which all the $\mathcal{G}$ implicit triples (dashed edges) are made explicit (solid edges). It is worth noting how, starting from $\mathcal{G}$, applying RDF entailment rules *mechanizes* the construction of $\mathcal{G}^\infty$. For instance, recall the reasoning sketched above for deriving the triple $(b_1, \tau, \text{Researcher})$. This is automated by the following sequence of applications of RDF entailment rules: $(\text{hasContactAuthor}, \preceq_{sp}, \text{hasAuthor})$ and $(b, \text{hasContactAuthor}, b_1)$ trigger `rdfs7` that adds $(b, \text{hasAuthor}, b_1)$ to the RDF graph. In turn, this new triple together with $(\text{hasAuthor}, \hookrightarrow_r, \text{Researcher})$ triggers `rdfs3` that adds $(b_1, \tau, \text{Researcher})$.

Comparing RDF Graphs. The RDF standard defines a generalization/specialization relationship between two RDF graphs, called *entailment between graphs*. Roughly speaking, an RDF graph $\mathcal{G}$ is more specific than another RDF graph $\mathcal{G}'$, or equivalently $\mathcal{G}'$ is more general than $\mathcal{G}$, whenever there is an embedding of $\mathcal{G}'$ into the *saturation* of $\mathcal{G}$, i.e., the complete set of triples that $\mathcal{G}$ models.

More formally, given any subset $\mathcal{R}$ of RDF entailment rules, an RDF graph $\mathcal{G}$ *entails* an RDF graph $\mathcal{G}'$, denoted $\mathcal{G} \models_\mathcal{R} \mathcal{G}'$, iff there exists an homomorphism ϕ from $\text{Bl}(\mathcal{G}')$ to $\text{Val}(\mathcal{G}^\infty)$ such that $[\mathcal{G}']_\phi \subseteq \mathcal{G}^\infty$, where $[\mathcal{G}']_\phi$ is the RDF graph obtained from $\mathcal{G}'$ by replacing every blank node b by its image $\phi(b)$.

Figure 2 shows an RDF graph $\mathcal{G}'$ entailed by the RDF graph $\mathcal{G}$ in Fig. 1 w.r.t. the entailment rules displayed in Table 2. In particular, $\mathcal{G} \models_\mathcal{R} \mathcal{G}'$ holds for the homomorphism ϕ such that: $\phi(b) = b$ and $\phi(b_2) = $ "LGG in SPARQL". By contrast, when $\mathcal{R}$ is empty, this is not the case (i.e., $\mathcal{G} \not\models_\mathcal{R} \mathcal{G}'$), as the dashed edges in $\mathcal{G}$ are not materialized by saturation, hence the $\mathcal{G}'$ triple $(b, \tau, \text{Publication})$ cannot have an image in $\mathcal{G}$ through some homomorphism.

Notations. When relevant to the discussion, we designate by $\mathcal{G} \models_\mathcal{R}^\phi \mathcal{G}'$ the fact that the entailment $\mathcal{G} \models_\mathcal{R} \mathcal{G}'$ holds due to the graph homomorphism ϕ. Also, when RDF entailment rules are disregarded, i.e., $\mathcal{R} = \emptyset$, we note the entailment relation $\models$ (without indicating the rule set at hand).

Importantly, from the definition of entailment between two RDF graphs [24, 25], the following holds:

Property 1. Given two RDF graphs $\mathcal{G}, \mathcal{G}'$ and a set $\mathcal{R}$ of RDF entailment rules, (*i*) $\mathcal{G}$ and $\mathcal{G}^\infty$ are equivalent ($\mathcal{G} \models_\mathcal{R} \mathcal{G}^\infty$ and $\mathcal{G}^\infty \models_\mathcal{R} \mathcal{G}$ hold), noted $\mathcal{G} \equiv_\mathcal{R} \mathcal{G}^\infty$, and (*ii*) $\mathcal{G} \models_\mathcal{R} \mathcal{G}'$ holds iff $\mathcal{G}^\infty \models \mathcal{G}'$ holds.

From a practical viewpoint, Property 1 points out that checking $\mathcal{G} \models_\mathcal{R} \mathcal{G}'$ can be done in two steps: a reasoning step that computes the saturation $\mathcal{G}^\infty$ of $\mathcal{G}$, followed by a standard graph homomorphism step that checks if $\mathcal{G}^\infty \models \mathcal{G}'$ holds.

2.2   SPARQL Conjunctive Queries

Basic Graph Pattern Queries. The well-established conjunctive fragment of SPARQL queries, a.k.a. *Basic Graph Pattern queries (BGPQs)*, is the counterpart of the select-project-join queries for databases; it is the most widely used subset of SPARQL queries in real-world applications [19].

A *Basic Graph Pattern (BGP)* is a set of *triple patterns*, or simply triples by a slight abuse of language. They generalize RDF triples by allowing the use of variables. Given a set $\mathcal{V}$ of variables, pairwise disjoint with $\mathcal{U}$, $\mathcal{L}$ and $\mathcal{B}$, triple patterns belong to: $(\mathcal{V} \cup \mathcal{U} \cup \mathcal{B}) \times (\mathcal{V} \cup \mathcal{U}) \times (\mathcal{V} \cup \mathcal{U} \cup \mathcal{L} \cup \mathcal{B})$.

Notations. We adopt the usual conjunctive query notation $q(\bar{x}) \leftarrow t_1, \ldots, t_\alpha$, where $\{t_1, \ldots, t_\alpha\}$ is a BGP. The *head* of q, noted $head(q)$, is $q(\bar{x})$, and the *body* of q, noted $body(q)$, is the BGP $\{t_1, \ldots, t_\alpha\}$ the cardinality of which is the *size* of q. The query head variables $\bar{x}$ are called *answer variables*, and form a subset of the variables occurring in $t_1, \ldots, t_\alpha$; for Boolean queries, $\bar{x}$ is empty. The cardinality of $\bar{x}$ is the *arity* of q. We use x and y in queries, possibly with subscripts, for answer and non-answer variables respectively. Finally, we note $\mathtt{VarBl}(q)$ the set of variables *and* blank nodes occurring in the query q, and $\mathtt{Val}(q)$ the set of all its values, i.e., URIs, blank nodes, literals and variables.

Entailing and Answering Queries. Two related important notions characterize how an RDF graph contributes to a query.

The weaker notion, called *query entailment*, indicates whether or not an RDF graph holds some answer(s) to a query. It generalizes entailment between RDF graphs, to account for the presence of variables in the query body, for establishing whether an RDF graph entails a query, i.e., whether the query embeds in that graph. Formally, given a BGPQ q, an RDF graph $\mathcal{G}$ and a set $\mathcal{R}$ of RDF entailment rules, $\mathcal{G}$ *entails* q, noted $\mathcal{G} \models_{\mathcal{R}} q$, iff $\mathcal{G} \models_{\mathcal{R}} body(q)$ holds, i.e., there exists a homomorphism ϕ from $\mathtt{VarBl}(q)$ to $\mathtt{Val}(\mathcal{G}^\infty)$ such that $[body(q)]_\phi \subseteq \mathcal{G}^\infty$.

The RDF graph $\mathcal{G}$ in Fig. 1 entails the query $q(x_1, x_2) \leftarrow (x_1, \tau, x_2)$ asking for all the resources and their classes for instance, because of the homomorphism ϕ such that $\phi(x_1) = b$ and $\phi(x_2) = \mathrm{ConfPaper}$. Observe that this entailment holds for any subset of RDF entailment rules, since the above homomorphism ϕ already holds for $\mathcal{R} = \emptyset$, i.e., considering only the explicit triples in Fig. 1.

Notations. Similarly to entailment between RDF graphs, we denote by $\mathcal{G} \models_{\mathcal{R}}^{\phi} q$ that the entailment $\mathcal{G} \models_{\mathcal{R}} q$ holds due to the homomorphism ϕ.

The stronger notion characterizing how an RDF graph contributes to a query, called *query answering*, identifies *all* the query answers that this graph holds. Formally, given a BGPQ q with set $\bar{x}$ of answer variables, the *answer set of q against $\mathcal{G}$* is $q(\mathcal{G}) = \{(\bar{x})_\phi \mid \mathcal{G} \models_{\mathcal{R}}^{\phi} body(q)\}$, where $(\bar{x})_\phi$ is the tuple of $\mathcal{G}^\infty$ values obtained by replacing every answer variable $x_i \in \bar{x}$ by its image $\phi(x_i)$. In case of a Boolean query, q is false iff $q(\mathcal{G}) = \emptyset$; otherwise q is true and $q(\mathcal{G}) = \{\langle\rangle\}$ where $\langle\rangle$ denotes the empty tuple.

The answer set to the above query $q(x_1, x_2) \leftarrow (x_1, \tau, x_2)$ against the RDF graph $\mathcal{G}$ in Fig. 1 is:

- $\{\langle b, \mathrm{ConfPaper}\rangle, \langle b, \mathrm{Publication}\rangle, \langle b_1, \mathrm{Researcher}\rangle\}$ for $\mathcal{R}$ the set of entailment rules in Table 2, i.e., considering the explicit *and* implicit triples in Fig. 1;
- $\{\langle b, \mathrm{ConfPaper}\rangle\}$ for $\mathcal{R} = \emptyset$, i.e., considering only the explicit triples in Fig. 1.

Importantly, from the definition of answer set of a SPARQL query against an RDF graph [26], the following holds:

Property 2. Given an RDF graph $\mathcal{G}$, a set $\mathcal{R}$ of entailment rules and a BGPQ q, (i) $\mathcal{G} \models_{\mathcal{R}} q$ holds iff $\mathcal{G}^{\infty} \models q$ holds, and (ii) $q(\mathcal{G}) = q(\mathcal{G}^{\infty})$ holds.

From a practical viewpoint, Property 2 points out that query entailment $\mathcal{G} \models_{\mathcal{R}} q$, respectively query answering $q(\mathcal{G})$, can be done in two steps: a reasoning step that computes the saturation $\mathcal{G}^{\infty}$ of $\mathcal{G}$, followed by a standard graph homomorphism step that checks if $\mathcal{G}^{\infty} \models^{\phi} q$ holds for some homomorphism ϕ, respectively enumerates all the homomorphisms ϕ for which $\mathcal{G}^{\infty} \models^{\phi} q$ holds.

Comparing Queries. Similarly to RDF graphs, queries can be compared through the generalization/specialization relationship of *entailment between queries*.

Let q, q' be BGPQs with the *same* arity, whose heads are $q(\bar{x})$ and $q'(\bar{x}')$, and $\mathcal{R}$ the set of RDF entailment rules under consideration. q *entails* q', denoted $q \models_{\mathcal{R}} q'$, iff $body(q) \models^{\phi}_{\mathcal{R}} body(q')$ *with* $(\bar{x}')_{\phi} = \bar{x}$ holds. Here, $body(q) \models^{\phi}_{\mathcal{R}} body(q')$ is the adaptation of the above-mentioned entailment relationships between RDF graphs to the fact that the query bodies may feature variables, i.e., ϕ is a homomorphism from $\mathtt{VarBl}(body(q'))$ to $\mathtt{Val}(body(q)^{\infty})$ such that $[body(q')]_{\phi} \subseteq body(q)^{\infty}$; the saturation of a BGP body, here $body(q)^{\infty}$, is the obvious generalization of RDF graph saturation that treats variables as blank nodes, since they both equivalently model unknown information within BGPs [26].

For instance, the query $q_1(x) \leftarrow (x, \tau, \mathrm{ConfPaper})$, $(x, \mathrm{hasContactAuthor}, y)$ entails the query $q_2(x) \leftarrow (x, \tau, y)$ with $\phi(x) = x$, $\phi(y) = \mathrm{ConfPaper}$ and any set of entailment rules.

We remark that entailment between queries, query entailment and query answering (obviously) relate as follows:

Property 3. Given an RDF graph $\mathcal{G}$, a set $\mathcal{R}$ of entailment rules and two BGPQs q, q' such that $q \models_{\mathcal{R}} q'$, (i) if $\mathcal{G} \models_{\mathcal{R}} q$ holds then $\mathcal{G} \models_{\mathcal{R}} q'$ holds, and (ii) $q(\mathcal{G}) \subseteq q'(\mathcal{G})$ holds.

Finally, query entailment, query answering and entailment between queries *treat blank nodes in queries exactly as non-answer variables* [26]. Hence, hereafter, we assume *without loss of generality* that queries do not use blank nodes.

3 Problem Statement

A *least general generalization* (lgg) of n descriptions $d_1, \ldots, d_n$ is a most specific description d generalizing $d_1, \ldots, d_n$ for some generalization/specialization relation [21]. In our SPARQL setting, we may use off-the-shelf BGPQs as descriptions and entailment between BGPQs as generalization/specialization relation:

Definition 1 (lgg of BGPQs). *Let* $q_1, \ldots, q_n$ *be BGPQs with the same arity and* $\mathcal{R}$ *a set of RDF entailment rules.*

- A generalization of $q_1, \ldots, q_n$ is a BGPQ q_g such that $q_i \models_{\mathcal{R}} q_g$ for $1 \leq i \leq n$.
- A least general generalization of $q_1, \ldots, q_n$ is a generalization q_{lgg} of $q_1, \ldots, q_n$ such that for any other generalization q_g of $q_1, \ldots, q_n$: $q_{\text{lgg}} \models_{\mathcal{R}} q_g$.

Unfortunately, this straightforward definition is of limited practical interest as the next example shows. Consider the BGPQs q_1 and q_2 in Fig. 3, which respectively ask for *the conference papers having some contact author*, and for *the journal papers having some author*. Clearly, with the RDF entailment rules shown in Table 2, an lgg of q_1 and q_2 is the *very* general BGPQ $q_{\text{lgg}}(x) \leftarrow (x, \tau, y)$ asking for *the resources having some type*.

We argue that the value of lggs could be significantly augmented by taking into account some *background knowledge* formalized as ontological constraints. For example, if we consider the RDFS statements shown in Fig. 3 that hold in the scientific publication domain, a more precise lgg for the above-mentioned q_1, q_2 would be $q_{\text{lgg}}(x) \leftarrow (x, \tau, \text{Publication}), (x, \text{hasAuthor}, y), (y, \tau, \text{Researcher})$ asking for *the publications having some researcher as author*, since (i) having a contact author is having an author, (ii) only publications have authors, (iii) only researchers are authors, and (iv) conference and journal papers are publications.

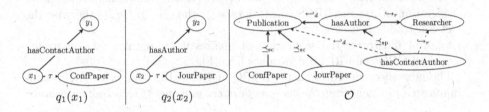

Fig. 3. Sample BGPQs q_1 and q_2; sample set $\mathcal{O}$ of RDFS ontological constraints.

To define such more precise lggs and state our learning problem in Sect. 3.2, we start by generalizing the standard specialization/generalization relation of *entailment between BGPQs* in Sect. 3.1, in order to allow comparing BGPQs w.r.t. an extra set of RDFS ontological constraints. In particular, this novel relation (i) *coincides with the standard one* when extra constraints are unavailable and (ii) *behaves like the standard one* w.r.t. the central reasoning tasks of query entailment and of query answering when extra constraints are available.

3.1   Comparing Queries w.r.t. Ontological Constraints

Our new entailment relation between queries builds on the following notion, which leverages the relevant background knowledge to complement a query:

Definition 2 (BGPQ saturation w.r.t. RDFS constraints). *Let $\mathcal{R}$ be a set of RDF entailment rules, $\mathcal{O}$ a set of RDFS statements, and q a BGPQ. The saturation of q w.r.t. $\mathcal{O}$, noted $q_{\mathcal{O}}^{\infty}$, is the BGPQ with the same answer variables as q and whose body, noted $body(q_{\mathcal{O}}^{\infty})$, is the maximal subset of $(body(q) \cup \mathcal{O})^{\infty}$ such that for any of its subset S: if $\mathcal{O} \models_{\mathcal{R}} S$ holds then $body(q) \models_{\mathcal{R}} S$ holds.*

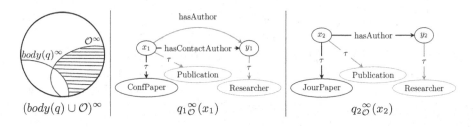

Fig. 4. Characterization of the body of a saturated BGPQ q w.r.t. a set $\mathcal{O}$ of RDFS constraints (left), and saturations of q_1 and of q_2 w.r.t. $\mathcal{O}$ from Fig. 3 (center and right respectively); triples shown in gray are added by saturation.

In essence, the saturation of a BGPQ comprises all the triples in the saturation of its body together with the RDFS constraints, from which are pruned out the triples derived solely from the constraints, i.e., which are not related to what the query is asking for. This corresponds exactly to the *non-hatched* subset of $(body(q)\cup\mathcal{O})^\infty$ shown in Fig. 4: $body(q_\mathcal{O}^\infty) = (body(q)\cup\mathcal{O})^\infty \setminus (\mathcal{O}^\infty \setminus body(q)^\infty)$. Of course, such a saturation is pertinent just in case the RDF entailment rules under consideration utilize the RDFS constraints, e.g., those in Table 2; otherwise the set of constraints is useless.

Figure 4 illustrates the saturation of queries w.r.t. ontological constraints using the BGPQs and RDFS contraints from Fig. 3.

The next theorem states that a BGPQ and its saturation w.r.t. RDFS constraints are *equivalent from the query entailment and query answering viewpoints*:

Theorem 1. *Let $\mathcal{R}$ be a set of RDF entailment rules, $\mathcal{O}$ a set of RDFS statements, and q a BGPQ whose saturation w.r.t. $\mathcal{O}$ is $q_\mathcal{O}^\infty$. For any RDF graph $\mathcal{G}$ whose set of RDFS statements is $\mathcal{O}$, (i) $\mathcal{G} \models_\mathcal{R} q$ holds iff $\mathcal{G} \models_\mathcal{R} q_\mathcal{O}^\infty$ holds, and (ii) $q(\mathcal{G}) = q_\mathcal{O}^\infty(\mathcal{G})$ holds.*

We can now endow entailment between queries with background knowledge:

Definition 3 (Entailment between BGPQs w.r.t RDFS constraints).
Given a set $\mathcal{R}$ of RDF entailment rules, a set $\mathcal{O}$ of RDFS statements, and two BGPQs q and q' with the same arity, q entails q' w.r.t. $\mathcal{O}$, denoted $q \models_{\mathcal{R},\mathcal{O}} q'$, iff $q_\mathcal{O}^\infty \models q'$ holds.

Using the set $\mathcal{R}$ of entailment rules in Table 2, the above mentioned BGPQ $q_{1gg}(x) \leftarrow (x, \tau, \text{Publication}), (x, \text{hasAuthor}, y), (y, \tau, \text{Researcher})$ is *neither* entailed by q_1 *nor* by q_2 from Fig. 3, while it *is* entailed by both of them w.r.t. the set $\mathcal{O}$ of constraints displayed in the same Figure, i.e., it is entailed *in the standard fashion* by their saturations shown in Fig. 4: $q_{1\mathcal{O}}^\infty \models^{\phi_1} q$ holds for $\phi_1(x) = x_1$ and $\phi_1(y) = y_1$, and $q_{2\mathcal{O}}^\infty \models^{\phi_2} q$ holds for $\phi_2(x) = x_2$ and $\phi_2(y) = y_2$.

Clearly, the above definition *coincides* with standard RDF entailment between BGPQs when $\mathcal{O}$ is empty (recall Sect. 2). Further, the main theorem below states the *required behaviour* for a query entailed by another w.r.t. onto-logical constraints, i.e., the counterpart of Property 3 in Sect. 2: *the former generalizes the latter from the query entailment and query answering viewpoints*:

Theorem 2. *Let $\mathcal{R}$ be a set of RDF entailment rules, $\mathcal{O}$ a set of RDFS statements, and two BGPQs q and q' such that $q \models_{\mathcal{R},\mathcal{O}} q'$. For any RDF graph $\mathcal{G}$ whose set of RDFS statements is $\mathcal{O}$, (i) if $\mathcal{G} \models_{\mathcal{R}} q$ holds then $\mathcal{G} \models_{\mathcal{R}} q'$ holds, and (ii) $q(\mathcal{G}) \subseteq q'(\mathcal{G})$ holds.*

3.2   Learning lggs w.r.t. Ontological Contraints

In the light of the preceding results, we revise/generalize Definition 1 as follows:

Definition 4 (lgg of BGPQs w.r.t RDFS constraints). *Let $\mathcal{R}$ be a set of RDF entailment rules, $\mathcal{O}$ a set of RDFS statements, and $q_1, \ldots, q_n$ BGPQs with the same arity.*

- *A generalization of $q_1, \ldots, q_n$ w.r.t. $\mathcal{O}$ is a BGPQ q_g such that $q_i \models_{\mathcal{R},\mathcal{O}} q_g$ for $1 \leq i \leq n$.*
- *A least general generalization of $q_1, \ldots, q_n$ w.r.t. $\mathcal{O}$ is a generalization q_{lgg} of $q_1, \ldots, q_n$ w.r.t. $\mathcal{O}$ such that for any other generalization q_g of $q_1, \ldots, q_n$ w.r.t. $\mathcal{O}$: $q_{\text{lgg}} \models_{\mathcal{R},\mathcal{O}} q_g$.*

By constrast with an lgg of RDF graphs that always exists [9], we found:

Theorem 3. *An lgg of BGPQs w.r.t. RDFS statements may not exist for some set of RDF entailment rules; when it exists, it is unique up to entailment ($\models_{\mathcal{R},\mathcal{O}}$).*

Indeed, consider the BGPQs $q_1(x_1) \leftarrow (x_1, \text{hasAuthor}, y_1)$ asking for the resources having some author, and $q_2(x_2) \leftarrow (y_2, \text{hasAuthor}, x_2)$ asking for the authors of some resource. Clearly, when the set $\mathcal{R}$ of entailment rules is empty or comprises the rules in Table 2, *no* BGPQ can generalize q_1 and q_2, hence there is *no* lgg of them. By contrast, if we use the complete set of RDF entailment rules, an lgg of q_1 and q_2 is $q_{\text{lgg}}(x) \leftarrow (x, \tau, \text{rdf:Resource})$, since every RDF value is an instance of the built-in class rdf:Resource. Also, when an lgg of BGPQs w.r.t. RDFS constraints exists, it is unique up to entailment, i.e., is semantically unique, because $q_{\text{lgg}} \models_{\mathcal{R},\mathcal{O}} q_g$ holds for any q_g in Definition 1. If it were that queries have *multiples* lggs *incomparable* w.r.t. entailment, say the BGPQs $\text{lgg}_1(\bar{x}), \ldots, \text{lgg}_m(\bar{x})$, the BGPQ defined as $q_{\text{lgg}}(\bar{x}) \leftarrow body(\text{lgg}_1) \cup \cdots \cup body(\text{lgg}_m)$ would be a *single strictly more specific* lgg, a contradiction.

Though unique up to entailment, there exist many syntactic variants (an infinity actually) of an lgg due to *redundant* triples, i.e., triples entailed by others within the lgg. For example, think of an lgg $q_{\text{lgg}}(x) \leftarrow (x, \tau, A), (x, \tau, B), (x, y, z)$ w.r.t. the set of constraints $\mathcal{O} = \{(A, \preceq_{\text{sc}}, B), (B, \preceq_{\text{sc}}, A)\}$, which asks for resources of types A and B that are somehow related to some resource, and it is known that A and B are equivalent classes. Clearly, different equivalent and minimal variants (w.r.t. the number of triples) of this lgg are $q_{\text{lgg}}(x) \leftarrow (x, \tau, A)$ and $q_{\text{lgg}}(x) \leftarrow$

(x, τ, B), since (x, y, z) is entailed by each of the two other triples, and (x, τ, B) is entailed by (x, τ, A) w.r.t. $\mathcal{O}$, and vice versa, because A and B are equivalent. Importantly, redundancy of triples is not specific to lggs of BGPQs w.r.t. RDFS constraints, since obviously any BGPQ may feature redundancy. The detection and elimination of such redundancy have been studied in the literature [18,20], hence we focus in this work on learning *some* lgg of BGPQs w.r.t. RDFS constraints; learning as minimal as possible lggs is a perspective of this work discussed in Sect. 6.

Based on the above discussion, the learning problem we propose to study is:

Problem 1. Given a set $\mathcal{R}$ of RDF entailment rules, a set $\mathcal{O}$ of RDFS statements, and the BGPQs $q_1, \ldots, q_n$ with the same arity, find an lgg of $q_1, \ldots, q_n$ w.r.t. $\mathcal{O}$.

Importantly, the proposition below shows that an lgg of $n \geq 3$ BGPQs can be inductively defined, hence computed, as a sequence of $n - 1$ lggs of *two* BGPQs. That is, assuming that $\ell_{k \geq 2}$ is an operator computing an lgg of k input BGPQs, the next proposition establishes that:

$$[\text{basis}] \quad \ell_3(q_1, q_2, q_3) \equiv_{\mathcal{R}, \mathcal{O}} \ell_2(\ell_2(q_1, q_2), q_3)$$
$$[\text{induction}] \quad \ell_n(q_1, \ldots, q_n) \equiv_{\mathcal{R}, \mathcal{O}} \ell_2(\ell_{n-1}(q_1, \ldots, q_{n-1}), q_n)$$
$$\equiv_{\mathcal{R}, \mathcal{O}} \ell_2(\ell_2(\cdots \ell_2(\ell_2(q_1, q_2), q_3) \cdots, q_{n-1}), q_n)$$

Proposition 1. *Let $q_1, \ldots, q_{n \geq 3}$ be n BGPQs, $\mathcal{O}$ a set of RDFS statements and $\mathcal{R}$ a set of RDF entailment rules. q_{lgg} is an lgg of $q_1, \ldots, q_n$ w.r.t. $\mathcal{O}$ iff q_{lgg} is an lgg w.r.t. $\mathcal{O}$ of an lgg of $q_1, \ldots, q_{n-1}$ w.r.t. $\mathcal{O}$ and q_n.*

Based on the above result, *without loss of generality*, we study in the next Section the particular instance of our learning problem for $n = 2$.

4 Computing lggs of Queries w.r.t. Ontological Constraints

Our solution to the above learning problem (Problem 1) builds on the notion of *least general anti-unifier of two atoms* [21,23], which is dual to the well-known notion of *most general unifier of two atoms* [22,23]. We use it to devise the *cover query* of two BGPQs q_1 and q_2 (to be defined shortly, Definition 5 below), which is an lgg of q_1 and q_2 *just in case* both RDF entailment rules and ontological constraints are ignored (Theorem 4). Further, we show (Theorem 5) that an lgg of q_1 and q_2 as defined in Definition 4, i.e., when RDF entailment rules and ontological constraints are taken into consideration, is the cover query of the saturations of q_1 and of q_2 with the RDF entailment rules and ontological constraints at hand (Definition 2). We also provide the size of these cover query-based lggs (i.e., number of triples), as well as the time to compute them.

Definition 5 (Cover query). *Let q_1, q_2 be two BGPQs with the same arity n. If there exists the BGPQ q such that*

- *$head(q_1) = q(x_1^1, \ldots, x_1^n)$ and $head(q_2) = q(x_2^1, \ldots, x_2^n)$ iff $head(q) = q(v_{x_1^1 x_2^1}, \ldots, v_{x_1^n x_2^n})$*

– $(t_1, t_2, t_3) \in body(q_1)$ and $(t_4, t_5, t_6) \in body(q_2)$ iff $(t_7, t_8, t_9) \in body(q)$ with, for $1 \leq i \leq 3$, $t_{i+6} = t_i$ if $t_i = t_{i+3}$ and $t_i \in \mathcal{U} \cup \mathcal{L}$, otherwise t_{i+6} is the variable $v_{t_i t_{i+3}}$

then q is the cover query of q_1, q_2.

The rationale behind the above definition of cover query is that (i) q's head is defined as the _least general anti-unifier_ of the heads of q_1 and q_2 (first item above) and (ii) each q triple is defined as a _least general anti-unifier_ of an _explicit_ q_1 triple and an _explicit_ q_2 triple (second item above), so that, when the cover query exits (If . . . then . . . above), it is a _generalization_ of q_1 and q_2 just in case RDF entailment rules and ontological constraints are _not considered_ (first item in Definition 4 with $\mathcal{R} = \emptyset$ and $\mathcal{O} = \emptyset$). Moreover, crucially, (iii) the variables used to generalize pairs of distinct values _across all_ the anti-unifications begetting q are _consistently named_: each time the distinct values α from q_1 and β from q_2 are generalized by a variable across these anti-unifications, it is _always_ by the _same_ q variable $v_{\alpha\beta}$. This naming scheme enforces _joins_ between q triples, which capture the common join structure within q_1 and q_2, so that q is not only a generalization of q_1 and q_2 but also a _least general generalization_ of them (second item in Definition 4 with $\mathcal{R} = \emptyset$ and $\mathcal{O} = \emptyset$).

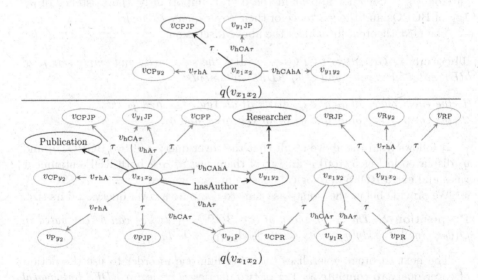

Fig. 5. Cover queries of the BGPQs q_1 and q_2 in Fig. 3 (top) and of their saturations $q_1^\infty_\mathcal{O}$ and $q_2^\infty_\mathcal{O}$ in Fig. 4 (bottom). Triples in grey are redundant w.r.t. those in black.

The cover query q of the BGPQs q_1 and q_2 is displayed in Fig. 5 (top). Its triple $(v_{x_1 x_2}, \tau, v_{\text{CPJP}})$ results from anti-unifying the q_1 triple $(x_1, \tau, \text{ConfPaper})$ and the q_2 triple $(x_2, \tau, \text{JourPaper})$; the variable $v_{x_1 x_2}$ is the least general value for the subject values x_1 and x_2, the URI τ is that for the property values τ

(because a constant is the least generalization of itself), and the variable v_{CPJP} is that for the object values ConfPaper and JourPaper. This q triple captures that q_1 and q_2 both ask for resources having some type. Here, the fact this type is related to scientific publications is missed, due to the absence of background knowledge relating conference papers, journal papers and scientific publications. Similarly, the q triple $(v_{x_1 x_2}, v_{\mathrm{hCAhCA}}, v_{y_1 y_2})$ results from anti-unifying the q_1 triple $(x_1, \mathrm{hasContactAuthor}, y_1)$ and the q_2 triple $(x_2, \mathrm{hasAuthor}, y_2)$. Because of our consistent naming of variables within q, this q triple and the preceding one join on $v_{x_1 x_2}$. Unfortunately, this second triple does not enhance the description of $v_{x_1 x_2}$ in q, since it generalizes, hence is redundant with, the preceding one. It only captures from q_1 and q_2 that q asks for resources having somehow related to something. Here again, the fact that this relationship is to have some author is missed due to the absence of background knowledge. The two other anti-unifications begetting q's body also produce redundant triples.

As mentioned earlier, the cover query q of two BGPQs q_1 and q_2 may not exist. This happens when q, as defined in Definition 5, has its head *not compatible* with its body: some required answer variable(s) cannot be supplied by q's body. For instance, recall the BGPQs q_1 and q_2 used in Sect. 3.2 to point out that an lgg may no exist. Their cover query does not exist either, because Definition 5 leads to $q(v_{x_1 x_2}) \leftarrow (v_{x_1 y_2}, \mathrm{hasAuthor}, v_{y_1 x_2})$, which is *not* a BGPQ (the answer variable $v_{x_1 x_2}$ does not appear in the body). Importantly, the existence of an lgg of BGPQs and the existence of their cover query *coincide*.

The next theorem formalizes the above discussion:

Theorem 4. *Given two BGPQs q_1, q_2 with the same arity and empty sets $\mathcal{R}$ of RDF entailment rules and $\mathcal{O}$ of RDFS statements:*

1. *the cover query of q_1 and q_2 exists iff an lgg of q_1 and q_2 exists;*
2. *the cover query of q_1 and q_2 is an lgg of q_1 and q_2.*

It follows from the above result that the cover query q of two BGPQs q_1 and q_2 displayed in Fig. 5 (top) is an lgg of them *just in case* both RDF entailment rules and extra RDFS óntological constraints are ignored.

We provide below the worst-case time to compute a cover query, and its size.

Proposition 2. *The cover query of two BGPQs q_1 and q_2 can be computed in $O(|body(q_1)| \times |body(q_2)|)$; its size is $|body(q_1)| \times |body(q_2)|$.*

The next theorem generalizes the preceding one in order to use the notion of cover query to compute an lgg of two queries *w.r.t. extra RDFS ontological constraints* and *any* set of RDF entailment rules.

Theorem 5. *Given a set $\mathcal{R}$ of RDF entailment rules, a set $\mathcal{O}$ of RDFS statements and two BGPQs q_1, q_2 with the same arity,*

1. *the cover query q of $q_1{}^\infty_{\mathcal{O}}, q_2{}^\infty_{\mathcal{O}}$ exists iff an lgg of q_1, q_2 w.r.t. $\mathcal{O}$ exists;*
2. *the cover query q of $q_1{}^\infty_{\mathcal{O}}, q_2{}^\infty_{\mathcal{O}}$ is an lgg of q_1, q_2 w.r.t. $\mathcal{O}$.*

As an immediate consequence of the above results, we get the following worst-case time to compute an $\texttt{lgg}$ of two BGPQs q_1 and q_2, and its size. We assume given the saturation $q_1{}_{\mathcal{O}}^{\infty}$ and $q_2{}_{\mathcal{O}}^{\infty}$ w.r.t. the sets $\mathcal{O}$ of RDFS constraints and $\mathcal{R}$ of RDF entailment rules under consideration, as the times to compute $q_1{}_{\mathcal{O}}^{\infty}$ and $q_2{}_{\mathcal{O}}^{\infty}$, and their sizes, depend on the particular sets $\mathcal{O}$ and $\mathcal{R}$ at hand.

Corollary 1. *A cover query-based* $\texttt{lgg}$ *of two BGPQs* q_1 *and* q_2 *is computed in* $O(|body(q_1{}_{\mathcal{O}}^{\infty})| \times |body(q_2{}_{\mathcal{O}}^{\infty})|)$ *and its size is* $|body(q_1{}_{\mathcal{O}}^{\infty})| \times |body(q_2{}_{\mathcal{O}}^{\infty})|$.

Figure 5 (bottom) displays the cover query of the BGPQs $q_1{}_{\mathcal{O}}^{\infty}$ and $q_2{}_{\mathcal{O}}^{\infty}$ shown in Fig. 4. It is therefore (Theorem 5) an $\texttt{lgg}$ of the BGPQs q_1 and q_2 w.r.t. the set $\mathcal{O}$ of RDFS constraints, all shown in Fig. 3, using the RDF entailment rules shown in Table 2.

Figure 5 exemplifies the benefits of taking into account extra ontological constraints modeling background knowledge when identifying the commonalities between queries, thus of endowing the RDF relation of generalization/specialization between queries with such knowledge. When background knowledge is ignored (top), we only learn that both q_1 and q_2 ask for *the resources having some type*. In contrast, when we do consider background knowledge (bottom), we further learn that these resources, which both q_1 and q_2 ask for, are *publications, which have some researcher as author*.

5   Experiments

Goal. We study the added-value of considering background knowledge when learning $\texttt{lgg}$s of queries. As Proposition 3 shows below, this amounts to measuring *how much more precise* is an $\texttt{lgg}$ of queries that considers background knowledge *than* an $\texttt{lgg}$ of the same queries that ignores background knowledge:

Proposition 3. *Given a set* $\mathcal{R}$ *of RDF entailment rules, a set* $\mathcal{O}$ *of RDFS statements, two BGPQs* q_1, q_2 *with the same arity, an* $\texttt{lgg}$ $q_{\texttt{lgg}}$ *of* q_1, q_2 *(Definition 1) and an* $\texttt{lgg}$ $q_{\texttt{lgg}}^{\mathcal{O}}$ *of* q_1, q_2 *w.r.t.* $\mathcal{O}$ *(Definition 4),* $q_{\texttt{lgg}}^{\mathcal{O}} \models_{\mathcal{R}} q_{\texttt{lgg}}$ *holds.*

Intuitively, this result follows from the fact that (*i*) $q_{\texttt{lgg}}$ is *equivalent* to the cover query-based $\texttt{lgg}$ q of the saturations of q_1 and of q_2 w.r.t. the empty set of RDFS constraints, (*ii*) $q_{\texttt{lgg}}^{\mathcal{O}}$ is *equivalent* to the cover query-based $\texttt{lgg}$ q' of the saturations of q_1 and of q_2 w.r.t. $\mathcal{O}$, and (*iii*) by *definition* of a cover query (Definition 5), q and q' have the same heads and the body of q is a subset of that q', thus $q' \models_{\mathcal{R}} q$ holds, hence $q_{\texttt{lgg}}^{\mathcal{O}} \models_{\mathcal{R}} q_{\texttt{lgg}}$ holds.

From this result and Property 3 (Sect. 2.2), $q_{\texttt{lgg}}^{\mathcal{O}}(\mathcal{G}) \subseteq q_{\texttt{lgg}}(\mathcal{G})$ holds for any RDF graph $\mathcal{G}$, and clearly the more $q_{\texttt{lgg}}^{\mathcal{O}}$ is specific w.r.t. $q_{\texttt{lgg}}$, the smaller the subset $q_{\texttt{lgg}}^{\mathcal{O}}(\mathcal{G})$ of $q_{\texttt{lgg}}(\mathcal{G})$ is, i.e., the smaller $|q_{\texttt{lgg}}^{\mathcal{O}}(\mathcal{G})|$ is w.r.t. $|q_{\texttt{lgg}}(\mathcal{G})|$. Therefore, as a practical metric for measuring the semantic distance between $q_{\texttt{lgg}}^{\mathcal{O}}$ and $q_{\texttt{lgg}}$ through $\models_{\mathcal{R}}$, we compute the *gain in precision* in (%) that background knowledge yields *w.r.t. query answering* as:

gain in precision $= 1 - \frac{|q_{1gg}^{\mathcal{O}}(\mathcal{G}) \cap q_{1gg}(\mathcal{G})|}{|q_{1gg}(\mathcal{G})|} = 1 - \frac{|q_{1gg}^{\mathcal{O}}(\mathcal{G})|}{|q_{1gg}(\mathcal{G})|}$ since $q_{1gg}^{\mathcal{O}}(\mathcal{G}) \subseteq q_{1gg}(\mathcal{G})$.

Prototype. We implemented our technical contributions in Java 1.8, on top of the Jena 3.0.1 RDF reasoner and of a PostgreSQL 9.3.11 server, all used with default settings; our implemented algorithms are detailed in [8].

We used Jena to compute the *saturation of an RDF graph*, against which queries must be evaluated to obtained their *complete* answer sets (Sect. 2.1). We also used Jena to compute the *saturation $q_{\mathcal{O}}^{\infty}$ of a BGPQ q w.r.t. a set $\mathcal{O}$ of RDFS constraints* (Definition 2): we rely on Jena's saturation, union and difference operators to compute $q_{\mathcal{O}}^{\infty}$'s body as described in Sect. 3.1.

We used PostgreSQL to evaluate *SQLized* BGPQs against a *saturated* RDF graph stored in a `Triple(s,p,o)` table.

We deployed our prototype on an Intel Xeon X5550 2.67 GHz machine with 32 GB of RAM, running Ubuntu 14.04.3 64bits; times reported below are in ms.

Setting. We conducted experiments using *real DBpedia data* [17] and *synthetic LUBM data* [12]. For space reasons, we present only our DBpedia experiments; LUBM ones can be found in [8] and allow drawing similar conclusions.

We used the subset of standard RDF entailment rules in Table 2, which fully allows exploiting RDFS ontological constraints, i.e., background knowledge.

From the DBpedia dataset, we picked four complementary files[1] to build the RDF graph $\mathcal{G}_{\texttt{DBpedia}}$ comprising 41.18M triples, whose subset $\mathcal{O}_{\texttt{DBpedia}}$ of 30.31k RDFS constraints represents DBpedia's background knowledge. The saturation of $\mathcal{G}_{\texttt{DBpedia}}$ comprises 78.14M triples and takes about 30 min to be computed.

Finally, we defined 42 test BGPQs, among which we picked 8 representative ones with 2 variables; they can be found in [8]. Table 3 displays their characteristics (top), as well as their saturation size and time (bottom): the size augments from ×3.16 for Q_2 up to ×4.75 for Q_3; the time is 692 ms on average. Also, importantly, queries Q_1–Q_4 (left) are heterogeneous in the sense that they differ significantly both on their structure and the kind of information they ask for, hence use many distinct classes, properties and URI values, while Q_4–Q_8 (right) are homogeneous and only differ in some classes, properties and URI values.

Table 3. Characteristics of our test BGPQs (top) and of their saturations (bottom).

Query $Q_{1 \leq i \leq 8}$:	Q_1	Q_2	Q_3	Q_4	Q_5	Q_6	Q_7	Q_8
Q_i's shape	tree	tree	tree	graph	graph	graph	graph	graph
$|body(Q_i)|$	4	6	4	6	4	6	6	6
Number of URI/variable occurrence in Q_i	7/5	9/9	5/7	7/11	5/7	9/9	9/9	9/9
$|Q_i(\mathcal{G}_{\texttt{DBpedia}})|$	77	0	41,695	13	6	0	1	0
$|body(Q_i {}_{\mathcal{O}_{\texttt{DBpedia}}}^{\infty})|$	16	19	19	23	16	23	23	23
Time to compute $Q_i {}_{\mathcal{O}_{\texttt{DBpedia}}}^{\infty}$	666	643	677	734	681	706	697	736

---

[1] We use the `dbpedia_2015-10.nt` RDF Schema file and the `instance_types_en.ttl`, `mappingbased_literals_en.ttl` and `mappingbased_objects_en.ttl` RDF data files.

Table 4. Characteristics of cover query-based lggs of test queries, w/ or w/o using the DBpedia RDFS constraints.

lgg of:	Q_1Q_2	Q_1Q_3	Q_1Q_4	Q_2Q_3	Q_4Q_5	Q_5Q_6	Q_5Q_7	Q_7Q_8
Time to compute q_{lgg}	3	3	5	4	4	5	6	5
$\lvert q_{\mathrm{lgg}}(\mathcal{G}_{\mathrm{DBpedia}})\rvert$	477,455	34,747,102	34,901,117	60,356,807	1,977	1,221	35	70
Time to compute $q_{\mathrm{lgg}}^{\mathcal{O}_{\mathrm{DBpedia}}}$	13	14	14	15	15	14	17	18
$\lvert q_{\mathrm{lgg}}^{\mathcal{O}_{\mathrm{DBpedia}}}(\mathcal{G}_{\mathrm{DBpedia}})\rvert$	10,637	7,874,768	456,690	7,874,768	1,701	780	34	36
Gain in precision	98	77	99	87	14	36	3	49

Results. First, as Table 4 (lines 1 and 3) shows, the cover query-based lggs of test queries are always computed fast whether or not the DBpedia constraints are considered: from 3 to 6 ms when ignored, to 13 to 18 ms when considered.

Table 4 (lines 2 and 4) also shows that the answer set of an lgg is significantly larger when DBpedia constraints are not taken into account: the size difference goes from a small ×1.02 for the homogeneous queries Q_5, Q_7 up to a striking ×76.42 for the heterogeneous queries Q_1, Q_4, with a significant average of ×17.38 (×33.34 for the heterogeneous queries and ×1.42 for the homogeneous ones). This translates into the precision gains shown at line 5: 58% overall, 90% for the heterogeneous queries, and 25% for the homogeneous ones.

These results confirm our claim that *taking into account background knowledge yields more precise lggs*. Indeed, ontological constraints help finding *common super-* classes and properties to be used in lggs in place of the different ones used in input queries; when constraints are ignored, these can just be generalized using *variables*. Therefore, the more heterogeneous input queries are, the more such common super-classes and properties are used in their lgg instead of variables, and the more the gain in precision of their lgg is high. For homogeneous input queries, while less striking, the gain in precision is significant in general.

6 Related Work and Conclusion

The reasoning problem of learning lggs has been studied in various formalisms, e.g., Conceptual Graphs (CGs), Description Logics (DLs), RDF and SPARQL.

Most of the solutions exploit the (underlying) *structure* of the input descriptions, like *trees* for DL formulae (e.g., [1,14,27]) and for unary tree-shaped BGPQs [2,16], and *directed single-root graphs* for the RDF *r*-graphs of [7]. Roughly speaking, they all consist in a simultaneous traversal of the input descriptions, starting from their roots, while incrementally computing their lgg. In contrast, when the input descriptions do not have a particular (or imposed) structure, solutions need to blindly traverse them while still being able to compute their lgg. They rely on standard *categorial graph product* for the so-called *simple* (i.e., purely conjunctive) CGs [3], on *anti-unifications of triples* for *general* RDF graphs [9], and on *anti-unifications of query heads and of query body triples* for the *general* BGPQs considered in this paper. Further, while (some of) the above solutions take into account background knowledge in CGs, DLs, and RDF, this is not the case for the state of the art in SPARQL [2,16]: unary tree-shaped BGPQs are solely compared based on standard graph homomorphism ($\models_\emptyset$).

Our results significantly advance the state of the art [2,16] by considering (*i*) *general BGPQs* and (*ii*) *background knowledge* to obtain more precise lggs, as our experiments showed. Next, we plan studying heuristics that prune out as much as possible redundant triples, *while computing* lggs. Indeed, as Fig. 5 shows, our cover query-based lggs may contain redundant triples. This would allow having more compact lggs, as well as reducing the a posteriori elimination effort of redundant triples using standard technique from the literature.

References

1. Baader, F., Sertkaya, B., Turhan, A.Y.: Computing the least common subsumer w.r.t. a background terminology. J. Appl. Logic **5**(3), 392–420 (2007)
2. Bühmann, L., Lehmann, J., Westphal, P.: DL-Learner - a framework for inductive learning on the Semantic Web. J. Web Semant. **39**, 15–24 (2016)
3. Chein, M., Mugnier, M.: Graph-Based Knowledge Representation - Computational Foundations of Conceptual Graphs. Springer, London (2009)
4. Chuang, S.L., Chien, L.F.: Towards automatic generation of query taxonomy: a hierarchical query clustering approach. In: ICDM (2002)
5. Cohen, W.W., Borgida, A., Hirsh, H.: Computing least common subsumers in description logics. In: AAAI (1992)
6. Colazzo, D., Goasdoué, F., Manolescu, I., Roatis, A.: RDF analytics: lenses over semantic graphs. In: WWW (2014)
7. Colucci, S., Donini, F.M., Giannini, S., Sciascio, E.D.: Defining and computing least common subsumers in RDF. J. Web Semant. **39**, 62–80 (2016)
8. El Hassad, S., Goasdoué, F., Jaudoin, H.: Learning commonalities in RDF and SPARQL (research report) (2016). https://hal.inria.fr/hal-01386237
9. El Hassad, S., Goasdoué, F., Jaudoin, H.: Learning commonalities in RDF. In: Blomqvist, E., Maynard, D., Gangemi, A., Hoekstra, R., Hitzler, P., Hartig, O. (eds.) ESWC 2017. LNCS, vol. 10249, pp. 502–517. Springer, Cham (2017). doi:10. 1007/978-3-319-58068-5_31
10. El Hassad, S., Goasdoué, F., Jaudoin, H.: Towards learning commonalities in SPARQL. In: d'Amato, C., et al. (eds.) ESWC 2017. LNCS, vol. 10587, pp. 278–295. Springer, Cham (2017)
11. Goasdoué, F., Karanasos, K., Leblay, J., Manolescu, I.: View selection in semantic web databases. PVLDB **5**(2), 97–108 (2011)
12. Guo, Y., Pan, Z., Heflin, J.: LUBM: a benchmark for OWL knowledge base systems. J. Web Semant. **3**(2–3), 158–182 (2005)
13. Huang, Z., Cautis, B., Cheng, R., Zheng, Y.: KB-enabled query recommendation for long-tail queries. In: CIKM (2016)
14. Küsters, R.: Non-Standard Inferences in Description Logics. Lecture Notes in Computer Science, vol. 2100. Springer, Heidelberg (2001)
15. Le, W., Kementsietsidis, A., Duan, S., Li, F.: Scalable multi-query optimization for SPARQL. In: ICDE (2012)
16. Lehmann, J., Bühmann, L.: AutoSPARQL: let users query your knowledge base. In: Antoniou, G., Grobelnik, M., Simperl, E., Parsia, B., Plexousakis, D., Leenheer, P., Pan, J. (eds.) ESWC 2011. LNCS, vol. 6643, pp. 63–79. Springer, Heidelberg (2011). doi:10.1007/978-3-642-21034-1_5

17. Lehmann, J., Isele, R., Jakob, M., Jentzsch, A., Kontokostas, D., Mendes, P.N., Hellmann, S., Morsey, M., van Kleef, P., Auer, S., Bizer, C.: DBpedia. Semant. Web **6**(2), 167–195 (2015)
18. Meier, M.: Towards rule-based minimization of RDF graphs under constraints. In: Calvanese, D., Lausen, G. (eds.) RR 2008. LNCS, vol. 5341, pp. 89–103. Springer, Heidelberg (2008). doi:10.1007/978-3-540-88737-9_8
19. Picalausa, F., Luo, Y., Fletcher, G.H.L., Hidders, J., Vansummeren, S.: A structural approach to indexing triples. In: Simperl, E., Cimiano, P., Polleres, A., Corcho, O., Presutti, V. (eds.) ESWC 2012. LNCS, vol. 7295, pp. 406–421. Springer, Heidelberg (2012). doi:10.1007/978-3-642-30284-8_34
20. Pichler, R., Polleres, A., Skritek, S., Woltran, S.: Complexity of redundancy detection on RDF graphs in the presence of rules, constraints, and queries. Semant. Web **4**(4), 351–393 (2013)
21. Plotkin, G.D.: A note on inductive generalization. Mach. Intell. **5**, 153–163 (1970)
22. Robinson, J.A.: A machine-oriented logic based on the resolution principle. J. ACM **12**(1), 23–41 (1965)
23. Robinson, J.A., Voronkov, A. (eds.): Handbook of Automated Reasoning. Elsevier and MIT Press, Amsterdam and Cambridge (2001)
24. Resource description framework 1.1. https://www.w3.org/TR/rdf11-concepts
25. RDF 1.1 semantics. https://www.w3.org/TR/rdf11-mt/
26. SPARQL 1.1. https://www.w3.org/TR/sparql11-query/
27. Zarrieß, B., Turhan, A.: Most specific generalizations w.r.t. general EL-TBoxes. In: IJCAI (2013)

Meta Structures in Knowledge Graphs

Valeria Fionda[1] and Giuseppe Pirrò[2(✉)]

[1] DeMaCS, University of Calabria, Rende, Italy
fionda@mat.unical.it
[2] Institute for High Performance Computing and Networking,
ICAR-CNR, Rende, Italy
pirro@icar.cnr.it

Abstract. This paper investigates meta structures, schema-level graphs that abstract connectivity information among a set of entities in a knowledge graph. Meta structures are useful in a variety of knowledge discovery tasks ranging from relatedness explanation to data retrieval. We formalize the meta structure computation problem and devise efficient automata-based algorithms. We introduce a meta structure-based relevance measure, which can retrieve entities related to those in input. We implemented our machineries in a visual tool called MEKoNG. We report on an extensive experimental evaluation, which confirms the suitability of our proposal from both the efficiency and effectiveness point of view.

1 Introduction

Knowledge Graphs (KGs) are becoming a common support in many application domains including information retrieval, recommendation, clustering, entity resolution, and generic exploratory search. One fundamental task underpinning these applications is the extraction of connectivity structures such as paths or graphs between entities. At the data level, these structures reflect fine-grained semantic associations like: K. Knuth award Turing Award award^{-1} John Hopcroft; the abstraction of these structures by using schema information (e.g., typing, domain and range) allows to capture meta information (e.g., Scientist award Prize award^{-1} Scientist). Most of current efforts focus on finding simple connectivity structures like (meta) paths between *a pair* of entities [2,17]. This has several limitations: (i) paths are not enough to capture complex relationships; (ii) limiting the input to a pair of entities does not allow to find refined associations both at the data and schema level; (iii) enumerating paths is a computationally hard problem. Recent approaches (e.g., [1]) focus on finding richer structures *only* but do not report on their usage in knowledge discovery tasks (see Sect. 5).

In this paper we focus on *meta structures*, schema-level graphs that abstract connectivity information among a set of entities in a knowledge graph. We study the problem of both finding *meta structures* and computing *meta structure-based relevance* and define: (a) efficient algorithms to isolate the subgraph connecting the input entities *without enumerating paths*; (b) techniques to pick the *most relevant portion of this subgraph*; (c) techniques to *abstract* data level information

C. d'Amato et al. (Eds.): ISWC 2017, Part I, LNCS 10587, pp. 296–312, 2017.
DOI: 10.1007/978-3-319-68288-4_18

into a meta structure; (d) *relevance measures* based on meta structures; (f) *user supports*. The contributions of this paper are as follows:

- Automata-based algorithms to find a subgraph connecting a set of entities.
- Layered-Tuple-Relevance (LTR), a meta structure-based relevance measure.
- A visual tool called MEKoNG implementing our approach.
- An experimental evaluation, which shows the efficiency of our proposal both in terms of running time and in concrete knowledge discovery tasks.

The goal of this paper is on the efficient computation of meta structures and their usage for relevance computation; the effectiveness from the user point of view of several types of connectivity structures has been investigated in [17].

Meta structures are useful in a variety of tasks ranging from finding/visualizing connectivity among entities to recommender systems (e.g., by computing the relevance between items already purchased and new items). In Sect. 1.1, we describe an instantiation of our proposal in the MEKoNG tool, useful to both discover entity relatedness and recommend related entities; other applications of our framework (e.g., entity resolution) are considered in Sect. 4. The paper is organized as follows. Section 2 describes the problem and the algorithms. Meta structure-based relevance is discussed in Sect. 3. Experiments are discussed in Sect. 4. We review related work in Sect. 5 and conclude in Sect. 6.

1.1 Running Example

We now illustrate MEKoNG, a tool that leverages the low-level services provided by our framework. We consider the tuple (A. Aho, J. Hopcroft, D. Knuth) as input and focus on the following tasks: (i) retrieve and explore a meta structure and its instances; (ii) retrieve the top-5 relevant entities.

Figure 1 (a) shows a meta structure retrieved for this entity tuple; we can see that it is a graph including three entities of type Scientist and two entities of type Award. In particular, one of the scientist has been a doctoral student of a second Scientist; note also that all three scientist share the same Award and that two of them also share a second award. The level of expressiveness of this meta structure goes beyond the expressiveness of its (meta) paths taken separately. In fact by using meta paths only it would not have been possible to capture constraints like the common Award. MEKoNG allows to explore a meta structure and its instances giving insights about the relatedness among the input entities. This is extremely useful in large KGs as it allows to find out previously unknown knowledge that is of relevance and understand how it is of relevance. We can see (Fig. 1 (b)) that the Award that the three Scientist share is the IEEE von Neumann Medal and that D. Knuth and J. Hopcroft share the Turing Award.

Building upon meta structures, MEKoNG allows to assess entity relevance. This occurs by replacing nodes in a meta structure with source entities and picking one of the remaining nodes as target. In the example (see Fig. 1 (c)) A. Aho and J. Hopcroft are used as seed entities thus replacing the leftmost Scientist nodes in Fig. 1 (a) and the target is the remaining Scientist. The top-5

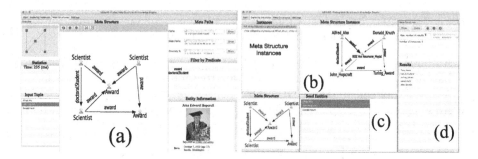

Fig. 1. The MEKoNG system.

more relevant entities, ranked according to the LTR relevance measure presented in Sect. 3, are shown in Fig. 1 (d). The top relevant result is T. Hoare followed by I. Sutherland. We can explain this ranking with the fact that LTR when using the seed entities A. Aho and J. Hopcroft and the meta structure in Fig. 1 (a) can both discover Award entities and take into account their *specificity* (i.e., how many other scientists have a particular Award). I. Sutherland and T. Hoare are ranked higher than, for instance, J. Ullman that share more awards, because the former share the Turing Award with J. Hopcroft and this award is less common than the ACM Fellowship shared with J. Ullman.

2 Discovering Meta Structures

In this section we introduce our approach to find meta structures. We start with some preliminaries and formalize the problem in Sect. 2.1. Then, we introduce algorithms to find a meta structure instance for an input tuple in Sect. 2.2. In Sect. 2.3 we discuss how to abstract a meta structure instance.

2.1 Problem Formalization

A Knowledge Graph (KG) is a heterogeneous network where nodes are entities of different types and edges model different types of semantic relationships. Yago, DBpedia, and Freebase are a few examples of popular KGs available in the RDF standard data format. Due to the generality of our approach, in what follows we provide a general notation that models graph data. A KG is a directed node and edge labeled graph $G = (V, E)$ with two node mapping functions $\phi_i : V \rightarrow \mathcal{L}_v$, which assigns to each node a unique *id* and $\phi_t : V \rightarrow 2^{\mathcal{L}_s}$, which assigns to each node a set of types in $\mathcal{L}_s$. An edge mapping function $\varphi : E \rightarrow \mathcal{L}_e$ associates to each edge a type from $\mathcal{L}_e$. To structure knowledge, KGs resort to an underlying schema, which is defined in terms of entity *types* and their links.

Definition 1 (Knowledge Graph Schema). Given a KG G and its mapping functions $\phi_t : V \rightarrow 2^{\mathcal{L}_s}$ and $\varphi : E \rightarrow \mathcal{L}_e$, the schema T_G of G is a directed graph defined over $\mathcal{L}_s$ and $\mathcal{L}_e$, that is, $T_G = (\mathcal{L}_s, \mathcal{L}_e)$.

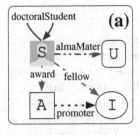
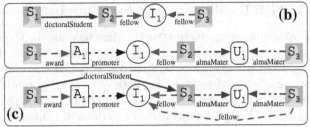

Fig. 2. A KG schema (a); some meta paths (b); a meta structure (c). Edge types/colors represent different kinds of relationships; node shapes represent different entity types. (Color figure online)

An example of KG schema is reported in Fig. 2 (a); it allows to abstract and define data and their compatibility (e.g., *fellow* links Scientist and Association).

Given a KG, a meta path is essentially an abstract data representation, which uses schema information. Examples of meta paths are shown in Fig. 2 (b). Meta paths can only capture simple relationship between entities, while meta structures, being modeled as graphs, allow to capture more complex relationships. As an example, the meta structure in Fig. 2 (c), can model the fact that the Association I_1 *is shared* between the Scientists S_3, S_2, and the Award A_1. This aspect cannot be modeled by using the two meta paths in Fig. 2 (b). We now introduce the notion of m-meta structure, which generalizes the notion of meta structure, defined for a pair of entities [10], to a tuple of arbitrary length.

Definition 2 (m-**Meta Structure**). *Given a KG schema $T_G = (\mathcal{L}_s, \mathcal{L}_e)$ and an entity tuple $t = \langle e_1, ..., e_m \rangle$, an m-meta structure for t is a graph $S = (N, M, T_s)$, where $N \subseteq \mathcal{L}_s$ is a set of entity type nodes, M a set of edges and $T_s = \langle T_1, ..., T_m \rangle \subseteq N$ is a set of entity types each corresponding to an input entity. For any edge $(u, v) \in M$ we have that $(u, v) \in \mathcal{L}_e$.*

Definition 3 (m-**Meta Structure Instance**). *An instance of an m-meta structure $S = (N, M, T_s)$ for $t = \langle e_1, ..., e_m \rangle$ on a KG G, is a subgraph $s = (N_s, M_s)$ of G such that there exists a mapping for s, $h_s : N_s \rightarrow N$ satisfying the following constraints: (i) for any entity $v \in N_s$ its type $h_s(v) \in \phi_t(v)$; (ii) for any edge $(u, v) \in (\notin) M_s$ we have that $(h_s(u), h_s(v)) \in (\notin) M$.*

The first goal of this paper is to tackle the problem of computing an m-meta structure given a knowledge graph G, its schema T_G and an input tuple $\langle e_1, ..., e_m \rangle$. This goal can be formalized via the following general problem:

> **Problem:** m-METASTRUCTURECOMPUTATION
> **Input:** A KG G, a KG schema T_G, an entity tuple $\langle e_1, ..., e_m \rangle$
> **Output:** An m-meta structure S

To solve m-METASTRUCTURECOMPUTATION we address two subproblems: **SP1**, which focuses on building an m-meta structure instance s (Sect. 2.2); and, **SP2**, which is about abstracting s by using the KG schema T_G (Sect. 2.3).

2.2 SP1: Building m-Meta Structure Instances

In computing an m-meta structure instance for the input tuple $t = \langle e_1, ..., e_m \rangle$, our algorithm sets a horizon h; this parameter bounds the portion of the graph considered where entities in t are connected. If one were not to limit the search horizon, then paths connecting entities in t can potentially span over large portions of G. These generic paths would be not informative as they fail to capture the essential relationships between entities in t. Indeed, if a too large horizon is considered then the whole G (more precisely, the connected component where entities in t lie) can trivially become the sought m-meta structure instance.

In what follows, we refer to the problem of computing an m-meta structure instance that connects the m entities in input as m-METASTRINSTCOMP. One way to approach the above problem could be to compute paths of length at most h interlinking the entities in $t = \langle e_1, ..., e_m \rangle$ and then merging them to obtain the m-meta structure instance. Some existing approaches (e.g., [2,17]) obtain paths via SPARQL queries and then merge (a subset of) them according to different strategies. From a computational point of view, materializing paths and merging them is not an efficient choice. This is because the number of paths can be exponential, thus requiring both exponential space (to store them) and exponential time (to iterate over them). In what follows we give an algorithm showing that m-MetaStrInstComp can be efficiently solved.

Proposition 4. m-METASTRINSTCOMP can be solved in time $\mathcal{O}(m \times h \times |G|)$

To prove the above result, we provide an algorithm based on automata theory. The algorithm encodes the input entity tuple $t = \langle e_1, ..., e_m \rangle$ as a regular expression having the form $e_t = (\bullet)^*/[e_2]/.../(\bullet)^*/[e_{m-1}]/(\bullet)^*/[e_m]$; here, $\bullet$ is a wild-card, representing a generic edge label in $\mathcal{L}_e$ and the notation $[e_i]$ encodes a test, which checks whether an edge endpoint is equals to e_i, one of the entities in $t = \langle e_1, ..., e_m \rangle$; such kind of regular expression can be represented via a NFA [5] over the alphabet $\bigcup_{i=1}^{m}\{[e_i]\} \cup \{\bullet\}$ with state transitions occurring when finding an input entity. We refer to this automaton as *tuple automaton* A_t (see Fig. 3). The set of strings obtained by concatenating the edge labels of paths passing through $e_1, ..., e_m$ are the set of strings generated by the language corresponding to e_t and recognized by A_t.

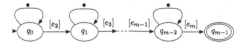

Fig. 3. Tuple-automaton.

Base Algorithm. We are now ready to present the algorithm to compute the m-meta structure instance linking entities in $t = \langle e_1, ..., e_m \rangle$. The algorithm includes two main steps: (i) building a directed label graph $G \times A_t$ (see Algorithm 1); (ii) filtering the portion of the input KG G that should not be part of the m-meta structure instance identified in the first step (see Algorithm 3). The graph $G \times A_t$ is built via the procedure reported in Algorithm 1 that performs an optimized Breadth-First Search on the graph G, according to the automaton A_t.

Input : KG G, tuple $t = \langle e_1, ..., e_m \rangle$, horizon h
Output: $G \times A_t = (V', E')$ /* marking of G with states of A_t */
 1: $A_t =$ buildTupleAutomaton(t) /* build the tuple automaton for the tuple t */
 2: $V' = \{(e_1, q_0, 0)\}$; $E' = \emptyset$ /* 0 is the starting depth and q_0 the initial state of A_t */
 3: $toVisit = visited = \{(e_1, q_0, 0)\}$
 4: **while** $toVisit \neq \emptyset$ **do**
 5:    $(v, q_i, d) =$ extract$(toVisit)$ /* remove the pair inserted first */
 6:    **for all** $\langle (v', q_j), p \rangle$ in expandState$((v, q_i), G, A_t)$ **do**
 7:       **if** $((v', q_j, d + 1) \notin visited)$ and $(d < h)$ and $(|t| \text{-} j \text{-} 1) < (h \text{-} d))$ **then**
 8:          $toVisit$.add$((v', q_j, d + 1))$
 9:          $visited$.add$((v', q_j, d + 1))$
10:          $V' = V' \cup \{(v', q_j, d + 1)\}$
11:          $E' = E' \cup \{((v, q_i, d), p, (v', q_j, d + 1))\}$
12: **return** $G \times A_t$

Algorithm 1. buildMarkedGraph(G, t, l)

Input : node-state pair (v, q), KG G, tuple-automaton A_t
Output: $\langle (node, state), edgeLabel \rangle$ pairs L
 1: $L = \emptyset$
 2: **for all** $(v, p, v') \in G$ **do**
 3:    **if** $(q, [v'], q') \in A_t$ **then**
 4:       L.add$(\langle (v', q'), p \rangle)$
       else L.add$(\langle (v', q), p \rangle)$
 5: **for all** $(v', p, v) \in G$ **do**
 6:    **if** $(q, [v'], q') \in A_t$ **then**
 7:       L.add$(\langle (v', q'), p^- \rangle)$
       else L.add$(\langle (v', q), p^- \rangle)$
 8: **return** L

Algorithm 2. expandState$((v, q), G, A_t)$.

Input : $G \times A_t$: Marking of G with states of A_t
Output: $s = (N_s, M_s) \subseteq G$: m-meta structure Instance
 1: $toVisit = visited = \{(e_m, q_{m-1}, k) \mid (e_m, q_{m-1}, k) \in G \times A_t\}$
 2: $N_s = \emptyset$, $M_s = \emptyset$
 3: **while** $toVisit \neq \emptyset$ **do**
 4:    $(v, q, d) =$ extract$(toVisit)$
 5:    $N_s = N_s \cup \{v\}$
 6:    **for all** $((v', q', d - 1), p, (v, q, d))$ in $G \times A_t$ **do**
 7:       $N_s = N_s \cup \{v'\}$
 8:       $M_s = M_s \cup \{(v', p, v)\}$
 9:       **if** $(v', q', d - 1) \notin visited$ **then**
10:          $toVisit$.add$((v', q', d - 1))$
11:          $visited$.add$((v', q', d - 1))$
12: **return** s

Algorithm 3. filterMetaStructureInstance$(G \times A_t)$

The first step is the construction of the tuple-automaton $A_t = \langle Q, \Sigma, q_0, \{q_{m-1}\}, \delta \rangle$ associated to e_t (line 1) and reported in Fig. 3; here, Q is the set of states, Σ is the alphabet, q_0 the initial state, $\{q_{m-1}\}$ is the set of final states, and δ the transition function. The size of A_t linear in the size of the input tuple, that is, $|A_t| = \mathcal{O}(m)$. A_t is used to build the labeled graph $G \times A_t$ whose nodes are a subset of $V \times Q \times \{0, ..., h\}$. $G \times A_t$ contains an edge from the node (v, q, d) to the node $(v', q', d+1)$ labeled with $p \in \mathcal{L}_e$ (resp., p^-) if, and only if: (i) G contains an edge (v, v') (resp., (v', v)) labeled by p; (ii) the transition function δ contains the triple $(q, [v'], q')$, and (iii) the node v has been visited at depth d. If δ does not contain the triple $(q, [v'], q')$ then the edge from (v, q, d) to $(v', q, d+1)$ labeled with $p \in \mathcal{L}_e$ (resp., p^-) is added to $G \times A_t$. The selection of the edges of G to be traversed and the nodes/edges to be added to $G \times A_t$ is made at lines 6–11. The function expandState (see Algorithm 2) (lines 3, 6) drives the traversal of the data graph according to the transitions of the automaton A_t.

Note that an early termination condition is implemented in Algorithm 1 line 7 by: *(i)* limiting the horizon of the traversal to h and *(ii)* stopping the traversal in advance as soon as some node is reached at a depth that does not allow to reach all the remaining entities of the input tuple. Indeed when the state q_j is reached, it is necessary to perform at least m-1-j additional traversals to reach the final state, and thus the entity e_m. It is easy to see that the size of $G \times A_t$ is linear both in the size of G, the size of the tuple-automaton and the horizon h, i.e., $|G \times A_t| = \mathcal{O}(|G| \times |A_t| \times h) = \mathcal{O}(|G| \times m \times h)$.

Lemma 5. There exists a path of length at most h connecting e_1 to e_m in G and passing, in order, through $e_2, ..., e_{m-1}$, if, and only if, there exists a path from $(e_1, q_0, 0)$ to (e_m, q_{m-1}, l) in the graph $G \times A_t$ such that $l \leq h$.

By leveraging the above property, Algorithm 3 uses $G \times A_t$ to build the m-meta structure instance s. The idea is to start with an empty m-meta structure instance and navigate $G \times A_t$ backward (from (e_m, q_{m-1}, l) to $(e_1, q_0, 0)$) by adding nodes and edges to s (lines 5, 7 and 8). Each node and each edge of $G \times A_t$ (in the opposite direction) is visited at most once with cost $\mathcal{O}(|G \times A_t|) = O(|G| \times |A_t| \times h) = O(m \times h \times |G|)$. Thus, the total cost, when also considering the cost of building $G \times A_t$, is $O(m \times h \times |G|)$.

The above algorithm uses a horizon h to only consider paths of length at most h interlinking the entities in t. We now discuss a variant, which introduces a generic top-k path filtering mechanism based on an edge weighting function.

Edge weighting function. To filter the m-meta structure instance found by the base algorithm described above we use an approach that assigns to each edge label a weight. Weights can be assigned according to several strategies; in this paper we use informativeness, and specifically we build upon the notion of Inverse Triple Frequency (ITF) introduced and evaluated in our previous work [16]. Basically, the less frequent an edge label is the more it is informative thus getting a higher weight. More formally, for an edge label p in G we have that $\text{ITF}(p, G) = log \frac{|\mathcal{E}|}{|\mathcal{E}|_{\pi(p)}}$, where $|\mathcal{E}|_{\pi(p)}$ is the number of statements in G where p appears. Note that ITF values can be precomputed offline. Since our top-k

Input : $G \times A_t$: Marking of G with states of A_t, integer k
Output: $s = (N_s, M_s) \subseteq G$: m-meta structure Instance
1: $H = []$ /* Heap used to store prioritized paths */
2: $N_s = M_s = \emptyset$
3: **for all** (v, q, i) in $G \times A_t$ **do**
4:    $count_{(v,q,i)} = 0$ /* number of times a node (v, q, i) in $G \times A_t$ is visited */
5: $P_{(e_1, q_0, i)} = \{(e_1, q_0, i)\}$
6: $H.\text{add}(P_{(e_1, q_0, i)}, 0)$ /* the initial total weight of the path is 0 */
7: **while** $H \neq \emptyset$ and $\sum_i count_{(e_m, q_{m-1}, i)} < k$ **do**
8:    $(P_{(v,q,i)}, C) = H.\text{extractMinCost}()$ /* extract the path with minimum cost C */
9:    $count_{(v,q,i)} = count_{(v,q,i)} + 1$
10:    **if** $v = e_m$ and $q = q_{m-1}$ **then**
11:       $s.\text{add}(P_{(v,q,i)})$
12:    **else if** $count_{(u,q,i)} \leq k$ **then**
13:       **for all** $((v, q, i), p, (v', q', j))$ in $G \times A_t$ **do**
14:          **if** $(v', q', j) \notin P_{(v,q,i)}$ **then**
15:             $P_{(v',q',j)} = \text{concatenatePath}(P_{((v,q,i))}((v, q, i), p, (v', q', j)))$
16:             $H.\text{add}(P_{(v',q',j)}, C + \text{ITF}(p, G)$ /* insert the path */
Algorithm 4. $\text{selectTopK}(G \times A_t, k)$

algorithm works by extracting minimum cost paths, we assign lower ITF values to more informative edge labels.

Edge Weight Based Algorithm. We describe a variant of the base algorithm that exploits edge label informativeness. After building the m-meta structure instance via the base algorithm, selectTopK (Algorithm 4) is used to build the top-k m-meta structure instance as the graph obtained by considering the top-k *most informative paths* between $(e_1, q_0, 0)$ and (e_m, q_{m-1}, l) (line 11). Algorithm 4 is an adaptation of Eppstein's algorithm [3] to find k shortest paths in a graph, where each node can be visited at most k times.

Lemma 6. Algorithm 4 runs in $\mathcal{O}(|edges(G \times A_t)| + k \times |nodes(G \times A_t)| \times \log |nodes(G \times A_t)|) = \mathcal{O}(k \times m \times h \times |G| \times \log(m \times h \times |G|))$ where $nodes(G)$ is the set of nodes in G and $edges(G)$ the set of edges.

2.3 SP2: Abstracting Meta Structure Instances

The second step to solve the m-METASTRUCTURECOMPUTATION is the abstraction of an instance s into an m-meta structure S by using the KG schema T_G. We considered typing information (the type) of the nodes in the m-meta structure instance. Existing methods (e.g., [12,21]) often assume that each node in a KG G belongs to exactly one class; hence, to abstract s it is enough to substitute to each node in s its class. However, in complex and real KGs, nodes can belong to multiple classes. Hence, our approach assign to each node in s the Lowest Common Ancestor (LCA) of all its types in the type hierarchy. We also considered another strategy based on the domain and range of edge labels. Given a node $n \in s$, we consider all its incoming and outgoing edges; then, by considering their

range and **domain**, we obtain a set of types. The type of n in the meta structure S will be the LCA of the types in this set.

3   Meta Structure Based Relevance

This section outlines an m-meta structure-based relevance measure called Layered Tuple Relevance (LTR). Given a KG $G = (V, E)$ and an m-meta structure S including Q nodes, the relevance between a tuple including *at most* Q-1 distinct entities and a target entity e_Q is defined as follow:

$$\mathcal{R}[(e_1, e_2, ..e_{Q-1}), e_Q \mid S] = \sum_{s \text{ instance of } S} f[(e_1, e_2, ..e_{Q-1}), e_Q \mid s]$$

where f is a relevance measure and s is an instance of the m-meta structure S (see Definition 3). One basic form of $\mathcal{R}$ would be to simply *count* the number of instances that the tuple $(e_1, e_2, ..e_{Q-1})$ and the target entity e_Q share; f would simply return 1 for each instance s of S matching the tuple $(e_1, e_2, ..e_Q)$. For instance, $\mathcal{R}[(\text{A. Aho, J. Hopcroft}), \text{D.Knuth} \mid S]$ where S is shown in Fig. 1 (a) gives 11 instances; apart from the Turing Award, shown in the instance in Fig. 1 (b), there are 10 more awards, among which the Faraday Medal and Kyoto Prize. Other entities that are relevant to the input tuple (A. Aho, J. Hopcroft) are I. Sutherland, J. Ullman and T. Hoare, for which there are 16, 12, and 9 instances, respectively. Using count leads to biased results for two main reasons: (i) count is not bound, so it is difficult to have an objective way of interpreting relevance; (ii) count favors popular objects, as objects with large degrees lead to a larger number of instances. LTR is bound between 0 and 1 and takes into account the specificity of m-meta structure instances in the relevance assessment.

LTR splits a m-meta structure S in two parts S_l and S_r. S_l considers the subgraph of S obtained by removing the node where the target entity e_Q is mapped and its edges; besides, in S_l the Q-1 entities in input are used in lieu of their types. S_r only retains the node (i.e., the type) where e_Q is mapped and its immediate neighbors. Splitting S in this way models the fact that we are interested in the relevance between at most Q-1 entities whose structural information is captured by S_l and a target entity e_Q whose structural information is captured by S_r. We sketch the rationale behind LTR via an example.

Consider the m- meta structure S_t in Fig. 1 (a) including $Q = 5$ nodes. We are interested in measuring the relevance between the pair A. Aho (aa), J. Hopcroft (jh) and an instance et of Scientist (i.e., S_3 in Fig. 4), that is, $\mathcal{R}_{\text{LTR}}[(\text{aa, jh}), \text{et} \mid S_t] = \sum_s \text{LTR}[(\text{aa, jh}), \text{et} \mid s]$ with s being an instance of S_t. Here, we are instantiating 2 out of the 4 possible nodes in the m-meta structure. Although in this example we focus on aa and jh we may use *any pair of entities* (or tuple of at most 4 entities) that conform to the m-meta structure in Fig. 1 (a). Figure 4 (a) shows S_l (dotted blue line) and S_r (dotted orange line) while Fig. 4 (b) shows instances of both Award and Scientist; entities for the relevance assessment are instances of the node S3. LTR leverages the tree structure shown in Fig. 4 (c). The root (level 0) is S_l and is used to start the traversal of the

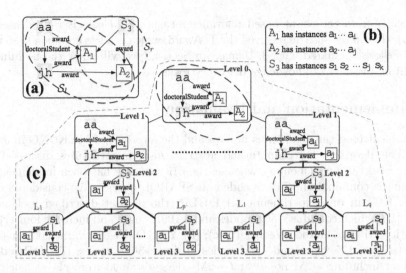

Fig. 4. Computing meta structure-based relevance via LTR. (Color figure online)

KG by creating at level 1, for each possible pair of instances of A_1 and A_2, a new child node; anecdotally there are 10 children in this example; IEEE J. von Neumann Medal and Turing Award, are examples of instances of A_1 and A_2, respectively. Each child node gives a new instance of the (sub)-meta structure S_l. For each mapping a_1 and a_2 of A_1 and A_2, a new child node is created at level 2 by instantiating these mappings into S_r. Leaves (level 3) are created by instantiating into S_3 the instances $s_1, ...,s_k$ obtained again by traversing the KG (level 2). As an example, for the leftmost node at level 2, S_3 has p instances and thus the corresponding subtree has p leaves. Note that level 1 and level 3 contain data triples only, while level 0 and level 2 have the placeholders A_1, A_2 and S_3, respectively. These can be basically treated as variables with a typing constraint (e.g., S_3 is a Scientist). The relevance between the pair (aa,jh) and a target entity et is computed starting from the leaves of the tree (level 3) and checking for each leaf whether et appears. As an example, if et $= s_3$, the second leftmost leaf and the central leaf from the right hand side subtree receive a value 1; all the others receive 0. Relevance is assessed via Eq. 1, where N_i is the number of nodes at level i, N_n is the number of nodes in the subtree rooted at n (excluding n), and $N_{n|1}$ is the number of nodes in the subtree rooted at n having value 1 (excluding n).

$$R_{\text{LTR}} = \frac{\sum_{n \in level2} \Theta(n)}{N_1} \quad \text{with} \quad \Theta(n) = \frac{N_{n|1}}{N_n} \tag{1}$$

When traveling up the tree starting from the leaves, each node n at level 2, receives the value $N_{n|1}/N_n$. Relevance is computed at the root by summing values of nodes at level 2 and dividing by the number of children at level 1. This guarantees that target entities sharing with the other entities of the tuple less frequent objects (i.e., an Award a_i) are ranked higher. Hence, we have that differently from the count based relevance measure, T. Hoare is ranked higher than J. Ullman because he received the T. Award, which is a less common than the ACM Fellowship shared with J. Ullman. In Sect. 4.2 we will show the usefulness of LTR in a variety of knowledge discovery tasks.

4   Implementation and Evaluation

We implemented the algorithms in Java and the interface of MEKoNG in Java FX. The algorithm to compute and abstract m-meta structures discussed in Sect. 2 works in main memory whereas the LTR measure has been implemented by using a combination of Java code and SPARQL queries. We considered different KGs in our experiments; (i) **DBLP**: the dataset described in Huang et al. [10], which contains ~50K nodes and ~100K edges and includes four types of entities (Paper, Author, Venue, Topic); (ii) **YAGO**: Yago core, which consists of 5M edges, 125 types and ~2M nodes having ~365K types; (iii) **DBpedia**: a subset including ~2M nodes and ~5M edges obtained from classes such as Person, Location, and City. For the experiments about relevance (Sect. 4.2) the full datasets have been accessed via their SPARQL endpoints. Experiments have been performed on a MacBook Pro with a 2.8 GHz i5 CPU and 16 GBs RAM. Results are the average of 5 runs. We abstract m-meta structure instances using the LCA of the types of each entity.

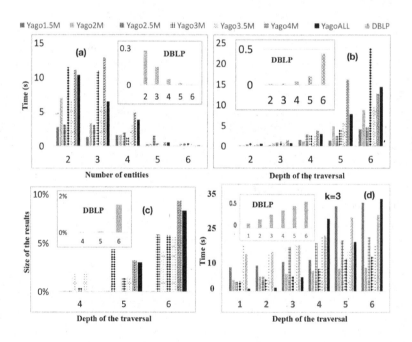

Fig. 5. Results about efficiency.

4.1 Efficiency

To test efficiency we used increasing subsets of Yago (from 1.5M of edges to the full dataset) and the full DBLP. Entities are randomly chosen for each run. Figure 5 (a) reports the average running time when varying the number of input entities n_e w.r.t. the depth spanning from n_e-1 to 6.

We observe that in general the running time does not strictly depend on the size of the dataset; it actually depends from the size of the input tuple with lower values being responsible for higher running times. The reason is that the early stopping condition in Algorithm 1 (line 7) is satisfied more frequently when the number of input entities increases (for a given depth). Figure 5 (b) reports the average running times when varying the depth d of the traversal w.r.t. the number of entities spanning from 2 to d+1. The running time increases with the depth (as one would expect); it reaches its maximum value for the subset of Yago including 3M of edges. Figure 5 (c) reports the size of results as a function of the depth of the traversal. The size is measured as the % of the triples in the whole dataset that belong to the m-meta structure discovered. We note that the higher the depth the larger the m-meta structure discovered. Nevertheless, the size always remains below 10%. Results for depth equals to 2 and 3 are not reported as they approach zero.

As for the algorithm that considers top-k paths only, Fig. 5 (d) reports the average running times as a function of the depth d of the traversal for a fixed k w.r.t. the number of entities spanning from 2 to d+1. Running times are higher than those in Fig. 5 (b) since the algorithm requires a further step to find the top-k most informative paths. In particular, for depth equals to 6 the running time is ~35 s (it was 25 s without the application of the top-k algorithm). Using the top-k algorithm allows to obtain significantly smaller and more understandable m-meta structures As an example, for 3 entities and depth 6, the m-meta structure instance on DBLP has 390 nodes and 928 edges when using the base algorithm; the number of nodes is 10 and the number of edges is 11 when using the top-k algorithm instead. On the whole Yago dataset, for the same depth and number of entities, the number of nodes and edges is ~8K and ~15K, respectively, for the base algorithm; these numbers become 8 and 10 for the top-k. Running times for DBpedia are not reported since they showed similar trend to that of Yago. Overall, the base algorithm is able to retrieve an m-meta structure instance linking the input tuple in a reasonable amount of time (considering the size of the dataset and the depth); however, the size of such m-meta structure instance can become prohibitively large. On the other hand, the top-k requires a slightly larger running time (with an increase of about 30% on average) but allows to obtain smaller and more useful m-meta structure instances.

4.2 Effectiveness

We now compare the performance of LTR with the approach that count meta structure instances (referred to as StrCnt) and SCSE and BSCSE [10]; SCSE performs subgraph expansion (from a source entity) by restricting the traversal of a KG to $\mathcal{S}$) and BSCSE combines and generalizes StrCnt and SCSE. In this case we consider tuples consisting of two entities. Figure 6 reports some of the meta structures used to test the effectiveness of the LTR measure. Besides meta structures we also considered (combinations of) some of their constituent meta paths.

Entity Resolution. We used LTR to identify entities in a KG that refer to the same person. In order to construct the ground-truth, we used the entity tuple (Barack Obama, Republican Party, Presidency of Barack Obama) to obtain the meta structure in Fig. 6 (a) using data from DBpedia. The meta structure tells us that two entities of type Person (i.e., P_1 and P_2) are both married to the same person P and member of the same Organization (i.e., O); Fig. 6 (a) also shows (dotted lines) two meta paths $\mathcal{P}_1$ and $\mathcal{P}_2$.

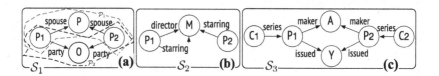

Fig. 6. Meta structures used in the experiments.

By using this meta structure we obtained a set of 558 entity pairs; then, we manually inspected these results to discover 124 pairs of entities that refer to the same person (e.g., Barack Obama, Presidency of Barack Obama). As for Yago, we used the ground-truth constructed by Huang et al. [10] including 44 positive pairs and 2967 negative ones. The meta structure used in Yago is slightly different; it uses marriedTo in lieu of spouse and affiliatedTo in lieu of party. We compared the performance of LTR, StrCnt, SCSE, BSCSE on the two meta paths $\mathcal{P}_1$ and $\mathcal{P}_2$ taken separately and their (optimal) linear combination. Results are shown in Table 1. Using meta paths alone gives the lowest performance, while their combination brings slightly better results on DBpedia. The reason is that meta paths fail in capturing complex relationships that meta structures can capture using shared nodes. StrCnt gave better results but it favors popular objects thus giving higher relevance to pairs of entities sharing more meta structure instances. LTR performs better as it is able to perform a deeper assessment of relevance by considering the specificity of entities shared (e.g., P and O) in a meta structure. SCSE/BSCSE work on main memory and could not handle DBpedia because of a memory overflow. On Yago, the trend of results remains the same as DBpedia with LTR reporting slightly lower performance than SCSE/BSCSE. We can explain this behavior by the fact that SCSE/BSCSE perform a finer-grained layered structural analysis of a meta structure; however, they assume that the meta structure itself is a DAG. LTR does not impose this constraint and performs a higher level analysis by splitting a meta structure in two parts (see Sect. 3). Nevertheless, LTR brings the following advantages over SCSE/BSCSE:

Table 1. AUC for the Entity Resolution Experiment.

Dataset	P_1	P_2	$\alpha P_1 + (1-\alpha)P_2$	StrCnt	SCSE	BSCSE	LTR
Yago	0.223	0.115	0.298	0.495	0.534	0.543	0.512
DBpedia	0.167	0.118	0.213	0.314	–	–	0.498

(i) it can work on any existing KG exposed via SPARQL, while SCSE/BSCSE require preprocessing and index building/maintenance; (ii) it can work with arbitrarily-shaped meta structures and not only DAGs; (iii) LTR is built given a *tuple of entities* while SCSE/BSCSE assume meta structures are given.

Ranking. We now discuss relevance in different domains. The meta structure in Fig. 6 (b) models relevance with a person (P_1) that has acted and directed movies (M) where also acted a different persons (P_2). The meta structure in Fig. 6 (c) is used to asses relevance on DBLP based on the fact that authors (A) have published two papers (P_1 and P_2) in two venues (C_1, C_2) in the same year (Y). Table 2 reports the top-5 relevant entities for different source entities (i.e., instantiations of nodes in a meta structure).

Table 2. Top-5 relevant entities using different meta structures and source entities.

	Meta Structure			
	S_2 (Fig. 6 (b))	S_2 (Fig. 6 (b))	S_3 (Fig. 6 (c))	S_3 (Fig. 6 (c))
Rank	$P_1 = $ Q. Tarantino	$P_1 = $ C. Eastwood	$C_1 = $ ISWC, Y $= 2010$	$C_1 = $ ISWC, Y $= 2016$
1	H. Keitel	S. Locke	ESWC	ESWC
2	S. L. Jackson	K. Costner	EKAW	WWW
3	M. Madsen	M. Freeman	WWW	JIST
4	T. Roth	M. Hill	Description Logics	EKAW
5	U. Thurman	J. Walter	I-Semantics	swat4ls

As for S_2, in DBpedia Q. Tarantino is highly related to H. Keitel and S. L. Jackson. On Yago (full ranking not reported) we have that S. L. Jackson is ranked higher than H. Keitel and that L. Bender enters the top-5. By changing the source entities to C. Eastwood, on DBpedia we get S. Locke and then K. Costner while in Yago (ranking not reported) we have M. Freeman ranked second and A. Her entering the ranking. S_3 uses two entities as source (a venue C_1 and a year Y) and retrieve the top-k most related venues (instances of C_2). In 2010, ESWC is the most relevant and I-Semantics is the least relevant according to the meta structure S_3. Interestingly, when changing year we can see that WWW becomes more relevant and that JIST in included in the top-5. LTR offers a flexible way of assessing relevance by allowing to fix a subset of entities in a tuple. Fixing two entities allowed to obtain a more refined (venue-year-centric) ranking than fixing only the venue. In this latter case the ranking would have been different: OWLED would have entered the ranking in lieu of swat4ls. As an example, by using StrCnt in 2016 we would have obtained BigData instead of swat4ls, although the latter (Semantic Web Applications and Tools for Life Science) is clearly more relevant. Overall, LTR coupled with meta structures offers flexibility in two respects: (i) it can be applied in a variety of KGs thanks to its SPARQL-based implementation; (ii) an arbitrary subset of nodes in a meta structure (e.g., a venue and a year) can be chosen as a source for relevance wrt a target node (e.g., another venue).

5   Related Work

Connectivity Structures. The problem of finding connectivity structures in graphs has been studied in different fields [19]. Hintsanen [9] focused on finding the most reliable subgraph in a graph subject to edge and node failures. Ramakrishnan et al. [18] focused on finding the most informative entity-relationship subgraphs in a given graph. A variant of this problem has been studied by Mendes et al. [14]. Other approaches have focused on determining specific substructures such as the minimum spanning tree or approximations (e.g., STAR [11]). Neither the above approaches focus on finding meta structures (schema graphs) given a tuple of entities nor on using meta structures for relevance computation. A number of approaches (e.g., [2,4,6,8,17]) have reduced the problem of finding paths (and meta paths) between entities to that of directly querying a KG by fixing a maximum path length and then displaying/abstracting (a subset of) the paths found. Beside the fact that these approaches neither focus on meta structure nor on relevance computation, their major drawback is that they require to enumerate paths first. A few approaches focused on finding meta paths; Lao et al. [12] tackle this problem by using constrained random walks. AMIE [7] is a system to mine association rules from KG. The difference with meta paths algorithms, and with our meta structure finding algorithm, is that AMIE does not find associations by taking into account the user input (i.e., a tuple of entities). Meng et al. [15], focuses on meta paths while we focus on meta structures. A recent approach [1] focuses on finding associations given a tuple of entities. Our work differs in several respects: (i) we control the size of the subgraph linking the input tuple by including top-k informative paths since this subgraph can be very large and thus difficult to visualize (e.g., for relatedness explanation) and reuse (e.g., for relevance computation); (ii) we do not focus on trees as meta structures are graphs; (iii) we introduce a novel meta structure-based relevance measure and show its usefulness in a variety of tasks. Overall, we tackle a more comprehensive problem: *finding meta structures given a tuple of entities as input, meta structure-based relevance,* and *user supports* (via MEKoNG).

Relevance Measures. Several measures have been proposed to compute relevance; examples include: (i) measure based on the graph structure (e.g., common neighbors), Jaccards coefficient or based on random walks [12]; (ii) schema-based measures based on meta-paths (e.g., [20]); (iii) Huang et al. [10] define relevance based on meta structures. Our work differs from (i) in the fact that LTR leverages schema information and from (ii) because we use meta structures instead of meta paths. As for (iii), the underlying assumption that meta structures are already available may be not realistic for a number of reasons: manually defining meta structures can be tedious and difficult when dealing with complex KGs like Yago/DBpedia; and complex meta structures can be difficult to discover, especially if this is done without automation. Our work is more comprehensive as it deals with both meta structure finding and relevance computation. Finally, differently from (i), (ii), and (iii) we focus on entity tuples and not just pairs.

6   Concluding Remarks and Future Work

We discussed an approach to compute meta structures combining an automata-based algorithm and its variant, which considers the most informative top-k paths. As our algorithm to find meta structures works in main memory, it cannot deal with very large KGs. To address this limitation we plan to consider the vertex-centric Gather Apply Scatter (GAS) paradigm [13] in the future. We have shown how meta structure-based relevance is useful in a variety of task (e.g., entity resolution, ranking). Our implementation of LTR, by a combination of Java code and SPARQL queries, makes it readily available on any SPARQL endpoint. Testing LTR in other domains is in our research agenda.

References

1. Cheng, G., Liu, D., Qu, Y.: Efficient algorithms for association finding and frequent association pattern mining. In: Groth, P., Simperl, E., Gray, A., Sabou, M., Krötzsch, M., Lecue, F., Flöck, F., Gil, Y. (eds.) ISWC 2016. LNCS, vol. 9981, pp. 119–134. Springer, Cham (2016). doi:10.1007/978-3-319-46523-4_8
2. Cheng, G., Zhang, Y., Qu, Y.: Explass: Exploring associations between entities via Top-K ontological patterns and facets. In: Mika, P., et al. (eds.) ISWC 2014. LNCS, vol. 8797, pp. 422–437. Springer, Cham (2014). doi:10.1007/978-3-319-11915-1_27
3. Eppstein, D.: Finding the k Shortest Paths. SIAM J. Comp. **28**(2), 652–673 (1998)
4. Fionda, V., Pirrò, G., Gutierrez, C.: Building knowledge maps of web graphs. Artif. Intell. **239**, 143–167 (2016)
5. Fionda, V., Pirrò, G., Gutierrez, C.: NautiLOD: A formal language for the web of data graph. ACM Trans. Web **9**(1), 5 (2015)
6. Fionda, V., Pirrò, G., Consens, M., Paths, E.P.: Writing more SPARQL queries in a succinct way. In: AAAI (2015)
7. Galárraga, L.A., Teflioudi, C., Hose, K., Suchanek, F.: AMIE: Association rule mining under incomplete evidence in ontological knowledge bases. In: WWW, pp. 413–422 (2013)
8. Heim, P., Hellmann, S., Lehmann, J., Lohmann, S., Stegemann, T.: RelFinder: Revealing relationships in RDF knowledge bases. In: Chua, T.-S., Kompatsiaris, Y., Mérialdo, B., Haas, W., Thallinger, G., Bailer, W. (eds.) SAMT 2009. LNCS, vol. 5887, pp. 182–187. Springer, Heidelberg (2009). doi:10.1007/978-3-642-10543-2_21

9. Hintsanen, P.: The most reliable subgraph problem. In: Kok, J.N., Koronacki, J., Lopez de Mantaras, R., Matwin, S., Mladenič, D., Skowron, A. (eds.) PKDD 2007. LNCS (LNAI), vol. 4702, pp. 471–478. Springer, Heidelberg (2007). doi:10.1007/978-3-540-74976-9_48

10. Huang, Z., Zheng, Y., Cheng, R., Sun, Y., Mamoulis, N., Li, X., Structure, M.: Computing relevance in large heterogeneous information networks. In: KDD, pp. 1595–1604 (2016)

11. Kasneci, G., Ramanath, M., Sozio, M., Suchanek, F.M., Weikum, G.: STAR: Steiner-tree approximation in relationship graphs. In: ICDE, pp. 868–879 (2009)

12. Lao, N., Cohen, W.W.: Relational retrieval using a combination of path-constrained random walks. Mach. Learn. 81(1), 53–67 (2010)

13. Grzegorz. M., Austern, M., et al.: Pregel: a System for Large-Scale Graph Processing. In: SIGMOD, pp. 135–146 (2010)

14. Mendes, P.N., Kapanipathi, P., Cameron, D., Sheth, A.P.: Dynamic associative relationships on the linked open data web. In: Web Science Conference (2010)

15. Meng, C., Cheng, R., Maniu, S., Senellart, P., Zhang, W.: Discovering meta-paths in large heterogeneous information networks. In: WWW, pp. 754–764 (2015)

16. Pirrò, G.: REWOrD: Semantic relatedness in the web of data. In: AAAI (2012)

17. Pirró, G.: Explaining and suggesting relatedness in knowledge graphs. In: Arenas, M., et al. (eds.) ISWC 2015. LNCS, vol. 9366, pp. 622–639. Springer, Cham (2015). doi:10.1007/978-3-319-25007-6_36

18. Ramakrishnan, C., Milnor, W.H., Perry, M., Sheth, A.P.: Discovering informative connection subgraphs in multi-relational graphs. SIGKDD Newsl. 7(2), 56–63 (2005)

19. Sheth, A., et al.: Semantic association identification and knowledge discovery for national security applications. JDBM 16(1), 33–53 (2005)

20. Shi, C., Kong, X., Huang, Y., Yu, P.S., Wu, B.: HeteSim: A general framework for relevance measure in heterogeneous networks. TKDE 26(10), 2479–2492 (2014)

21. Sun, Y., Han, J., Yan, X., Yu, P.S., PathSim, T.: Meta Path-based top-k Similarity Search in Heterogeneous Information Networks. In: PVLDB (2011)

Challenges of Source Selection in the WoD

Tobias Grubenmann$^{(\boxtimes)}$ ⓘ, Abraham Bernstein ⓘ, Dmitry Moor ⓘ,
and Sven Seuken ⓘ

Department of Informatics, University of Zurich, Zurich, Switzerland
{grubenmann,bernstein,dmoor,seuken}@ifi.uzh.ch

Abstract. Federated querying, the idea to execute queries over several
distributed knowledge bases, lies at the core of the semantic web vision.
To accommodate this vision, SPARQL provides the SERVICE keyword
that allows one to allocate sub-queries to servers. In many cases, however,
data may be available from multiple sources resulting in a combinatori-
ally growing number of alternative allocations of subqueries to sources.
Running a federated query on all possible sources might not be very
lucrative from a user's point of view if extensive execution times or fees
are involved in accessing the sources' data. To address this shortcoming,
federated join-cardinality approximation techniques have been proposed
to narrow down the number of possible allocations to a few most promising (or results-yielding) ones.

In this paper, we analyze the usefulness of cardinality approximation
for source selection. We compare both the runtime and accuracy of Bloom
Filters empirically and elaborate on their suitability and limitations for
different kind of queries. As we show, the performance of cardinality
approximations of federated SPARQL queries degenerates when applied
to queries with multiple joins of low selectivity. We generalize our results
analytically to any estimation technique exhibiting false positives. These
findings argue for a renewed effort to find novel join-cardinality approximation techniques or a change of paradigm in query execution to settings,
where such estimations play a less important role.

Keywords: Approximate query processing · Bloom Filter · Federated
SPARQL · Source selection · Web of Data

1 Introduction

At the core of the Semantic Web vision lies the possibility to ubiquitously access
distributed, machine-readable, linked data. This Web of Data (WoD) relies on
the notion of being able to access partial information from a variety of sources
that then gets combined to an integrated answer.

One major approach to achieving this functionality in a distributed fashion is federated querying [2,3,7,14,18,24,25]. It relies on traditional database
approaches to join partial results from multiple sources into a combined answer.
Specifically, it divides a query into subqueries and delegates the execution of

ⓒ Springer International Publishing AG 2017
C. d'Amato et al. (Eds.): ISWC 2017, Part I, LNCS 10587, pp. 313–328, 2017.
DOI: 10.1007/978-3-319-68288-4_19

each of these subqueries to one or more remote databases, which on the WoD are called endpoints. A query execution plan assigns the subqueries to a certain set of endpoints and determines the order of the subquery execution. Hereby, results from one subquery can vastly reduce the computational effort of answering another. One major problem of querying the Web of Data is *source selection*, which is deciding which subqueries should be delegated to which SPARQL endpoints during query execution and which endpoints should not be considered for query execution at all. We will focus in this paper on the cardinality of the query answer as the metric to evaluate the worthiness of including certain sources into query execution.

Ideally, a user would be able to estimate the cardinality of the query answer for any subset of all relevant sources. Given the knowledge about the resulting cardinality for different combinations of sources, a user could make an informed decision whether a certain source should be included into the federated query execution or not. By an informed decision we mean deciding whether selecting and accessing a certain subset of all available endpoints is worth the time and, potentially, fees which are associated with accessing these endpoints.

In this paper, we argue that **the performance of *cardinality* approximations of federated SPARQL queries degenerates when applied to queries with multiple joins having low join selectivities**. This means that such approximations are not sufficiently precise to allow a user to make an informed decision. As a consequence, a user who cannot afford to query all relevant sources for a given query must blindly exclude some relevant sources risking low cardinality or empty query answers, even though solutions to the query would be available on the WoD. Specifically, our contributions are:

- We show empirically that the *cumulative error of cardinality estimation techniques based on Bloom Filters explodes* in the combinatorial distributed setting of the WoD, which questions its usefulness for informed source selection.
- We show empirically that the explosion of the *cumulative error often makes join-cardinality estimation slower than executing the actual query*. Hence, using such a technique may not only lead to suboptimal results but even slow down the query execution process, which is exactly the opposite of the goal of source selection.
- Using a theoretical analysis of the problem, we explain why these *negative results necessarily occur when using any estimation technique exhibiting false positives* in combination with queries having low join selectivities.

The remainder of this paper is organized as follows. First, we succinctly discuss the most relevant related work. Next, Sect. 3 provides empirical evidence of our claims about the limited usefulness of join approximation techniques using Bloom Filters, which is followed by a discussion of the results. In Sect. 4, we present our main result: a theoretical analysis which explains the cumulative error and associated runtime behavior that federated cardinality approximation techniques face in the WoD. We close with some conclusions.

2   Related Work

Federated SPARQL querying and source selection: Different approaches have been proposed to query RDF data in a federated setting. Mediator systems like FedX [24] and DARQ [20] allow a user to query a federation of endpoints in a transparent way while incorporating all known SPARQL endpoints into the query answer. The federation appears to the user as one big SPARQL endpoint holding the data of all the members of the federation. Once the members are specified and initialized, the user can issue SPARQL queries against the mediator without having to adapt the query for federated execution or providing any additional information about the federation members.

Avalanche [3] and ANAPSID [2] propose different, more dynamic systems where they relax the requirement of complete results and allow certain endpoints to fail. Their systems focus on robustness of query execution in the Web. Avalanche [3] executes all possible queries (i.e., all combinations of possible endpoints) in parallel eventually timing out a query when the rate of incoming results slows down. In queries with many combinations this may lead to a very high network load and a significant time between querying and query completion. ANAPSID [2], in contrast, runs only one query plan and dispatches each sub-query to every possible endpoint using a mediator. This results in a highly robust execution but again, faces the danger of including a very large number of endpoints if no sensible source-selection approach is available.

SPLENDID [9] proposed to exploit service descriptions and VoID statistics about each endpoint to perform source selection and query optimization. HiBISCuS [21] uses join-aware techniques to select relevant sources for federated query execution. HiBISCuS maintains an index which stores the authorities of certain URIs. [27] introduced Fed-DSATUR, an algorithm for SPARQL query decomposition in federated settings. They do not use statistics, indices, or estimates for source selection.

The SPARQL 1.1 Federated Query extension [10] follows a different approach: a user must explicitly specify which part of the query should be executed on which server. The extension requires the user to know which SPARQL endpoint can provide data for which subquery and rewrite the query accordingly using a special SERVICE-clause.

Duplicate aware source selection [22] tries to eliminate sources with duplicate data using Min-Wise Independent Permutations. [11] used Bloom Filters for source selection of RDF sources and investigated the number of requests needed for an approximation to achieve a certain recall.

Good estimates of the contribution of different sources towards a query answer plays an important role in [16,17], where users have to pay for accessing the selected sources.

In contrast to the work presented so far, we perform an empirical and theoretical analysis of the error behavior for the problem of source selection when the cardinality of the result is used as the deciding factor.

Cardinality Estimation Techniques: In the traditional database domain, join approximation has been used as a suitable technique for approximate query processing [8]. The goal of approximate query processing is to compute an answer that approximates the query answer without having to execute the query. Join approximations can be used to calculate the expected cardinality and the join selectivity of a specific query.

. A variety of approaches provide *data synopses* (i.e., summaries of the data) for join approximation. Histograms [13] and Wavelets [8] have been used to approximate the distribution of a dataset over a given domain. Also, Bloom Filters were first proposed as a space-efficient probabilistic data structure to approximate sets [5]. The advantage of Bloom Filters is that they allow to specify the desired false-positive rate for set-membership checking without leading to false-negatives. Given that they also allow intersections between bloom-filtered sets they have become a de-facto standard for join approximations. Q-Trees [19] were introduced as a special data summary technique for RDF data. [26] compared the runtime and space complexity of indexing techniques, multidimensional histograms, and Q-Trees and evaluated, in particular, their usefulness for source selection and highlighted the superiority of Q-Trees over the others.

Sampling methods [15] do not rely on a synopsis but on a selection of the data. Hence, they do not produce false positive matches but might produce false negatives. Sampling methods provide a lower bound on the cardinality of a join.

Join synopses [1] are special summary structures built for join approximation. They are constructed for specific, ex-ante known join operations and are therefore not suitable to the purely ad-hoc federated settings. They are, however, useful when one knows that certain joins are likely to occur.

Finally, [12] studied the propagation of errors in the size of the join result. In this paper, we will extend the analysis done by [12] to the domain of SPARQL queries.

3   Experimental Evaluation of the Cumulative Join Estimation Error

The goal of this section is to show the relative error and runtime behavior of join cardinality approximation using Bloom Filters, which motivated our theoretical analysis of the problem and our conclusion that join approximation techniques are problematic for source selection. We used Bloom Filters for the approximation as they provide an easy and straightforward way to encode strings like IRIs and Literals.

In the following, we will first describe the experimental setup, including the query approximation engine and the data we used before presenting the results.

3.1   Query Approximation Engine

We implemented a query engine that allows us to execute joins over federated SPARQL endpoints on dynamically generated data synopses. The query engine accepts a query consisting of basic graph patterns using the SPARQL 1.1 SERVICE-clause to allocate a certain Basic Graph Pattern (BGP), called *service pattern*, to specified endpoints. Our approximation engine currently does not yet support UNION-clauses, OPTIONAL-clauses and filters outside of service patterns.

To approximate a join between two service patterns, a data synopsis of the data matching the first service pattern is generated by the responsible endpoint. This synopsis summarizes the bindings of the joining variables for each solution of the assigned service pattern. The data synopsis is generated by inserting the string representation of the bindings of a solution into a Bloom Filter. If multiple variables are joining, the bindings are combined into one string using a special delimiter. The endpoint responsible for the second SERVICE-clause receives the data synopsis and does a membership check on the string representation of the bindings of the joining variables of its assigned service pattern. The bindings for which the membership check is positive form the basis for the *join synopsis*. The join synopsis summarizes the bindings of those variables which are joining with the next service pattern and is used as input for the next join approximation step.

To illustrate the approximation process, Fig. 1 shows how the query in Listing 1 would be approximated. First, ep1.com receives the first service pattern, consisting of only one triple pattern ?a ex:p ?x, and creates a list of bindings for variable ?a (① in Figure). These bindings get approximated by an appropriate data synopsis ②. The synopsis is joined with the bindings provided by endpoint ep2.com for the second service pattern ?a ex:p ?b ③. Note that only variable ?a is involved in the join while a synopsis for the corresponding bindings for variable ?b is created ④. The second synopsis is joined with the bindings for the third service pattern ?y ex:p ?b ⑤. Since this clause is the last one, there is no further synopsis needed. Instead, we count the number of bindings that join with this last synopsis ⑥. This number is the estimated cardinality of the join between the three service patterns when they are assigned to the sources according to the federated query in Listing 1.

Listing 1. A SPARQL query with 3 Service Patterns, each consisting of 1 Triple Pattern.

```
PREFIX ex: <http://example.com/>
SELECT * WHERE {
   SERVICE <http://ep1.com> {
      ?a ex:p ?x . }
   SERVICE <http://ep2.com> {
      ?a ex:q ?b . }
   SERVICE <http://ep3.com> {
      ?y ex:r ?b . }
}
```

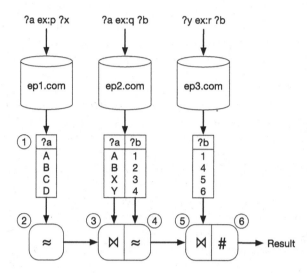

Fig. 1. Approximating the query in Listing 1 using our approximation engine.

3.2   Experimental Setup

For our evaluation, we investigated the scenario where each triple pattern must be sent to a different source. This means that it is not possible to form exclusive groups to speed up query processing/approximation, as proposed by [24].

For the evaluation, we used FedBench [23] as a benchmark. FedBench consists of 25 queries and more than 200 million triples distributed over 9 datasets. Since we do not support UNION or OPTIONAL-clauses at the moment, we removed queries containing those clauses from our evaluations. To give a baseline for the execution time of the different approximation techniques, we executed each query using the query engine Jena ARQ[1]. We used the SERVICE-clause to direct each triple pattern to a separate SPARQL endpoint. We used Blazegraph[2] as a triple store. Table 1 shows the queries used, their runtime in milliseconds when using Jena ARQ, the actual cardinality of the query answer, and the number of triple patterns in the query.

We simulated both, query execution using Jena ARQ and the approximations using Bloom Filters, with a network speed of 10 Mbps, which is around the average speed of the top 10 countries in the world [4]. For the query execution, we adapted Jena ARQ to do block-nested-loop joins with a block size of 500 bindings to reduce the number of HTTP-connections, which have a negative impact on the runtime behavior of federated query execution. In addition, we optimized the join order of the different queries using simple heuristics to keep query execution in a reasonable time-frame. The query execution and all query approximations used the same join ordering to keep the results comparable.

---

[1] https://jena.apache.org.
[2] https://www.blazegraph.com.

For the Bloom Filter implementation, we used the Guava Google Core Library for Java[3].

Table 1. The execution time, count, and number of triple patterns of the different queries.

Query	Time [ms]	Cardinality	Triple patterns
CD3	2.50E+03	2	5
CD4	3.90E+02	1	5
CD5	4.80E+02	2	4
CD6	1.30E+03	11	4
CD7	5.70E+02	1	4
LS3	3.80E+04	9054	5
LS4	5.20E+02	3	7
LS5	1.02E+02	393	6
LS6	4.40E+05	28	5
LD1	6.90E+02	308	3
LD2	4.70E+02	185	3
LD3	7.60E+02	159	4
LD4	3.10E+03	50	5
LD5	3.00E+02	28	3
LD6	6.20E+02	39	5
LD7	1.50E+03	1216	2
LD8	5.90E+02	22	5
LD9	3.20E+02	1	3
LD10	2.90E+02	3	3
LD11	2.00E+03	376	5

3.3   Results

Figure 2 shows the absolute value of the *relative* error and the *relative* execution time of the approximation both computed with respect to the actual runtime and count when running the query in a federated fashion using Jena ARQ.

The relative error e_{rel} is defined as

$$e_{rel} = \frac{card_{est} - card_{actual}}{card_{actual}},$$

where $card_{est}$ is the estimated cardinality of the query answer based on the approximation and $card_{actual}$ is the actual cardinality of the query answer.

---

[3] https://github.com/google/guava.

The relative execution time t_{rel} is defined as

$$t_{rel} = \frac{t_{est}}{t_{actual}} \, ,$$

where t_{est} is the runtime of the approximation technique and t_{actual} is the runtime of the query execution using Jena ARQ.

Clearly, a relative runtime of less than 1 is desirable, as otherwise it would be faster to execute the query and get the actual cardinality. For the relative error, it is not so clear what kind of error would still be in an acceptable range.

Each plot in Fig. 2 shows the relative error (solid line) and relative execution time (dashed line). We measured the error and execution time for false positive rates of $fpp = 0.1, 0.01, 10^{-4}, 10^{-8}$.

As we can see in Fig. 2, the runtime of the Bloom Filter approximation is very often disappointing. The approximation tends to require considerably more time for the approximation than the actual query execution. Surprisingly, the execution time for those approximations often improves when increasing the size of the underlying data synopsis. The discussions in Sect. 4 provide a good explanation for this behavior: the more accurate the synopsis, the less false positives must be processed. The overhead in processing more false positives seem to have a bigger negative impact on the runtime than the reduction of the size of the synopsis. *This behavior somewhat counteracts the actual purpose of a data synopsis to provide a trade-off between less accurate information and reduced processing time.*

Discussion of selected queries: The Bloom Filter approximation shows good results for the runtime of queries LS3, LS5, LS6, LD2, and LD4. Also, the error is comparably low and most of the time below 1. For those queries, the approximation can be considered successful: the approximation is able to return a reasonable approximation of the result size while running considerably faster than the actual query execution.

Queries CD7, LS4, and LD11 show worse approximation for a false positive probability of 10^{-8} than for a probability of 10^{-4}. One likely explanation for this is the fact that the original false positive analysis done by [5] is incomplete and only gives a lower bound on the false positive rate. Indeed, as [6] points out, the actual false positive rate might be worse than expected when a small value for the false-positive probability is chosen as a parameter and a large number of hash functions have to be used in the filters.

The approximation yields a relative error of 0 for the query LD9. The reason for this behavior is that the last triple pattern only matches one single triple. Thus, our approximation engine predicts a cardinality of at most 1, because the prediction is based on the number of those triples matching the last triple pattern which also join the synopsis of the previous joins, which can never be larger than the number of triples matching the last triple pattern. At the same time, the actual result of the query is also 1. Hence, approximation technique which overestimate the cardinality will yield a perfect prediction, necessarily. However, the relative runtime of the approximation methods is around 1.

The query LD4 is another one where the last triple pattern only matches one single triple. Again, our approximation engine predicts a cardinality of at most 1. But this time, the actual result is not 1 but 50. In fact, all 50 different results have the same binding for the last joining variable. As the Bloom Filter does not account for duplicated values the approximation wrongly predicts 1 instead of 50. At the same time, the approximation speed profits slightly from this error by yielding a faster execution time.

4   Theoretical Analysis of the Cumulative Join Estimation Error

In this section, we investigate to theoretical foundations which can explain the disapointing performance of our Bloom Filter join approximation. We will estimate the cumulative error for WoD queries for approximation techniques that overestimate the results due to false positives, which includes all data synopses which are not based on sampling, in particular, our Bloom Filter-based method. Such overestimating data synopses can lead to false-positive matches (i.e., the prediction of a match where there is none) due to loss of information. When approximating multiple joins, the result of the first join (including its false positives) is again encoded as a data synopsis passed to the second join, which will now attempt to match all encoded elements including the false-positives. Hence, the error of the synopsis gets propagated through each join and accumulates [12].

We now formally discuss the propagation of the error in a multi-join, that is, a sequence of joins where the output of one join is an input for the next join. For this we extend the formula for the error derived by [12] by analyzing the relation between the rate of false positive matches and the join selectivity based on the following assumption:

Assumption 1. *All joins are equality inner-joins.*

Assumption 1 is motivated by the fact that we do not consider filter expressions in our evaluation and hence, we only support equality joins. We will not discuss outer joins because their cardinality estimation is trivial.

Assume we want to approximate the join result of joining $m + 1$ basic graph patterns $bgp_0, \ldots, bgp_m$. We define n_i for $i \in \{0, \ldots, m\}$ as the number of results selected by BGP bgp_i from the corresponding dataset. Let n_i^{FP} be the number of false positives at step i, which is the number of elements that are wrongly classified as a match given the synopsis from the previous joins. We define the false positive rate fpr_i as the ratio between n_i^{FP} and n_i.

Let $prop_i^{FP}$ for $i \in \{1, \ldots, m\}$ be the *propagation rate* of the false positives in the synopsis for the join approximation between $bgp_0, \ldots, bgp_{i-1}$. The propagation rate indicates how many false-positives matches are produced *on average* by a single false-positive propagated from previous join approximations.

The expected number of false positives FP_k for the approximation of the join of $bgp_0, \ldots, bgp_k$ is the number of false positives introduced by fpr_k for bgp_k plus

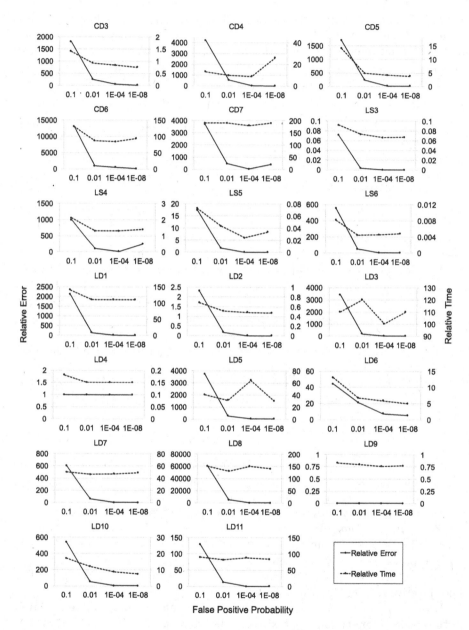

Fig. 2. Relative error (left vertical axis) and relative execution time (right vertical axis) for different false positive probabilities.

the false-positives given the false-positives FP_{k-1} of the approximation of the join of $bgp_0, \ldots, bgp_{k-1}$:

$$FP_k = \underbrace{fpr_k \cdot n_k}_{\text{synopsis error}} + \underbrace{prop_k^{FP} \cdot FP_{k-1}}_{\text{propagated error}} . \tag{1}$$

We define $FP_0 := 0$, as there is no propagated error influencing the first join operation. Applying Eq. 1 recursively gives the following formula for the number of false positives FP_m of the approximation of the join of $bgp_0, \ldots, bgp_m$:

$$FP_m = \sum_{i=1}^{m} fpr_i \cdot n_i \cdot \prod_{j=i+1}^{m} prop_j^{FP} . \tag{2}$$

To compare the number of false positive matches with the number of true positive matches, we analogously compute the number of true positives TP_m. To do that we define the propagation rate of the true-positives $prop_i^{TP}$ for the join between $bgp_0, \ldots, bgp_{i-1}$ (just like we defined the propagation rate $prop_i^{FP}$ for false-positives). Using this definition, the number of true positives TP_k of joining $bgp_0, \ldots, bgp_k$ is:

$$TP_k = n_0 \cdot \prod_{j=1}^{k} prop_j^{TP} . \tag{3}$$

To continue our analysis, we introduce the following assumption:

Assumption 2. *False-positive matches and true-positive matches have the same propagation rate, i.e. $prop_j^{FP} = prop_j^{TP} =: prop_j$.*

Assumption 2 is motivated by the fact that the propagation rate of both, true positives and false positives, are influenced by the type of URI and not by the fact whether they are false or true positive. For example, there is an average number of addresses joining with a person, independent of whether the person is true or false positive. Hence, we assume that there is no bias which would cause that a true positive match has, on average, a lower/higher propagation rate than a false positive match.

Under Assumption 2, we get the following formula for the relative error E of the approximation:

$$E = \frac{FP_m}{TP_m} = \frac{\sum\limits_{i=1}^{m} fpr_i \cdot n_i \cdot \prod\limits_{j=i+1}^{m} prop_j}{n_0 \cdot \prod\limits_{j=1}^{m} prop_j} \tag{4}$$

$$= \sum_{i=1}^{m} \frac{fpr_i \cdot n_i}{n_0 \cdot \prod\limits_{j=1}^{i} prop_j} .$$

We define the selectivity $sel_{bgp_0,\ldots,bgp_j}$ of the join between $bgp_0,\ldots,bgp_j$ as the number of results of the join divided by the product $n_0 \cdots n_j$, i.e. the cardinality of the cross product of all results for $bgp_0,\ldots,bgp_j$. It follows that:

$$n_0 \cdot \prod_{j=1}^{i} prop_j = sel_{bgp_0,\ldots,bgp_j} \cdot \prod_{j=0}^{i} n_j \tag{5}$$

and consequently:

$$E = \sum_{i=1}^{m} \frac{fpr_i}{sel_{bgp_0,\ldots,bgp_i} \cdot \prod_{j=0}^{i-1} n_j} \ . \tag{6}$$

Equation 6 shows that the higher the number of joins and the lower the join-selectivities $sel_{bgp_0,\ldots,bgp_j}$ are, the smaller the false positive rate fpr_i of the approximation must be to produce a reasonably small estimation error. Thus, the *approximation error is determined by the **ratio between the false positive rate and selectivity*** and not "just" the false positive rate. In addition, this error does not only lead to inaccurate results but *also has a negative impact on the execution time* of the approximation: If the selectivities are low and the false-positive rates relatively high, it can happen that the query approximation mainly processes false-positives and that the data synopses based on these false-positives are larger than the actual data of all true-positives. Thus, the *query approximation might take longer than the actual query execution.*

Note that these theoretical findings should be cause for concern for building federated query systems in the light of false positive baring data synopses. In the next section, we will explore if these theoretical considerations apply to the practical Web of Data setting that we are currently exploring in federated querying.

Verification of the Analysis: We want to verify that our theoretical analysis indeed serves as an explanation of the error and runtime behavior that we observed in Sect. 3. For this, we compared the estimated error predicted by our analysis with the actual error which we observed in our evaluation. Figure 3 plots the estimated error based on Eq. 6 against the actual relative error measured for the Bloom Filter approximation in a log-log scale (as the values include both very small and very large numbers). Figure 3 suggests a very strong correlation between relative error of the estimation and the predicted error by our analysis. Indeed, both the Pearson correlation coefficient $R^2 = 0.81$ and the Spearman's Rank Correlation $\rho = 0.76$ between the actual (non-log) numbers indicate a strong correlation between the theoretical estimation of the error and the actual evaluation. Not included in the figure, but included in the calculation of the correlation coefficients are those estimates that produced a relative error of 0, which could not be drawn in the log-log scale plot.

The figure shows that for a false positive probability of 10^{-8} (indicated by little pluses "+" mostly at the top left of the Figure) the actual error is not as small as one might expect. One likely explanation for this is the fact that the

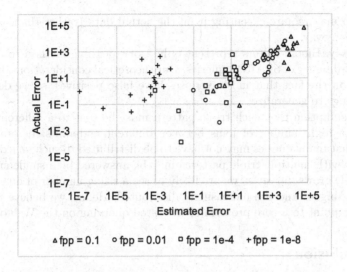

Fig. 3. Estimated error plotted against actual error.

specified false positive rate only gives a lower bound on the actual false positive rate, as we already discussed in Sect. 3.

Overall, Fig. 3 confirms the theoretical analysis of the error accumulation in Eq. 6, which indicates that *SPARQL queries require data synopses with very low false-positive rates to produce reasonably accurate results – an effect which is much more pronounced for queries with a low selectivity, as we have shown in Eq. 6.* This, in turn, might require specific implementations of Bloom Filters that can handle such low probabilities. However, the need for such accurate synopses make it questionable whether join approximations that produce false positives are suitable for such tasks, in general.

5   Limitations and Future Work

In this paper, we focused our evaluations on queries which did not include UNION, OPTIONALs, and FILTERs outside of service patterns. However, we think, given the performance of our Bloom Filter approximation in this simpler setting, one cannot expect the approximations to perform better when extending the evaluation to include more complex queries. In particular, joins over multiple variables are likely to further constrain a join offering even more potential for synopses to generate false positives. UNIONS can be seen as a conjunction of multiple queries, which does not pose a significantly different setting. We will have to consider OPTIONALs in future work, though our intuition indicates that they can be seen as a combination of two different queries, which should not impact our results. FILTER expressions are more complex and warrant future work, as they might impact synopses construction. In particular, when a filter compares two bindings from different sources it can only be applied after the join, which may require executing it on the actual data (rather than only on a synopsis), anyway.

Obviously, Bloom Filters represent only a one possible method to estimate the join-cardinality of SPARQL queries. Our theoretical considerations, however, are based on the fact that most synopses have false positives, so we do expect these findings to generalize.

Our assumption that each triple pattern must be sent to a different source results in a high number of joins between different endpoints. In practice, it could be that many queries may not have to be distributed to such an extent and subqueries with multiple triple patterns may be answered by a single endpoint. As the WoD grows, however, we are likely to see a rising number of queries that are getting bigger and are increasingly distributed. Hence, we believe that our findings do point to a core problem of federated querying on the Web of Data.

6   Conclusion

This paper set out to investigate the applicability of query approximation for source selection. We hypothesized that the performance of cardinality approximations of federated SPARQL queries degenerates when applied to queries with multiple joins of low selectivity. Indeed, both our empirical evaluation and our theoretical considerations indicate that data synopses are not suitable for this task due to their cumulative error, which also substantially slows down the estimation process. Based on our analysis, one can only expect good approximation performance if (1) the number of joins is low, (2) the join-selectivity is high, and/or (3) there is a bias which causes true positive matches to have a much higher propagation rate than false positive matches. These findings seriously hamper the usefulness of current selectivity estimation techniques for domains such as the WoD, where the number of joins involved in the estimation process is high. Indeed, our focus on a setting with many joins pinpointed a deficit in the generalizability of selectivity estimation techniques which came from a domain where usually only few inter-domain-joins are to be expected.

It is important to note that whilst this paper focused on federated SPARQL-querying in the context of the WoD our findings generalize to any federated conjunctive querying setting where join estimates cannot be precomputed.

The consequence of our work is twofold: First, to fulfil the Semantic Web vision via federated querying requires a *renewed effort to find suitable join-approximations for federated SPARQL queries.* As the WoD progresses, we will require more sophisticated approximation techniques, which are more adapted to the WoD: i.e., the need to be able to handle many inter-source joins and low selectivity better. Note, however, that no matter what new technique gets introduced, in the presence of low selectivity, our analysis of the error propagation adds a limit to what can be achieved by join-approximations that cause false-positives.

Second, if the community does not manage to drastically improve approximation techniques, *there might be a need to consolidate datasets from different sources into more centralized structures to reduce the number of endpoints that must be accessed during federated query execution.* This centralization will allow computing better estimations or incorporating them into the indices.

In conclusion, our findings showed that we may have to rethink well-known techniques such as the concept of join-approximation when applying them to the WoD. Doing so, will both advance our understanding of these techniques and may cause us to rethink the structure of the Web of Data as a whole.

Acknowledgments. This work was partially supported by the Swiss National Science Foundation under grant #153598.

References

1. Acharya, S., Gibbons, P.B., Poosala, V., Ramaswamy, S.: Join synopses for approximate query answering. In: Proceedings of the 1999 ACM SIGMOD International Conference on Management of Data, pp. 275–286 (1999)
2. Acosta, M., Vidal, M.-E., Lampo, T., Castillo, J., Ruckhaus, E.: ANAPSID: an adaptive query processing engine for SPARQL endpoints. In: Aroyo, L., Welty, C., Alani, H., Taylor, J., Bernstein, A., Kagal, L., Noy, N., Blomqvist, E. (eds.) ISWC 2011. LNCS, vol. 7031, pp. 18–34. Springer, Heidelberg (2011). doi:10.1007/978-3-642-25073-6_2
3. Basca, C., Bernstein, A.: Querying a messy web of data with Avalanche. J. Web Semant. **26**, 1–28 (2014)
4. Belson, D.: Akamai's [state of the internet]. Q3 2015 report. Technical report, Akamai Technologies (2015)
5. Bloom, B.H.: Space/time trade-offs in hash coding with allowable errors. Commun. ACM **13**, 422–426 (1970)
6. Bose, P., Guo, H., Kranakis, E., Maheshwari, A., Morin, P., Morrison, J., Smid, M., Tang, Y.: On the false-positive rate of Bloom Filters. Inf. Process. Lett. **108**(4), 210–213 (2008)
7. Buil-Aranda, C., Arenas, M., Corcho, O., Polleres, A.: Federating queries in SPARQL 1.1: syntax, semantics and evaluation. Web Semant. Sci. Serv. Agents World Wide Web **18**(1), 1–17 (2013)
8. Chakrabarti, K., Garofalakis, M., Rastogi, R., Shim, K.: Approximate query processing using Wavelets. VLDB J. **10**, 199–223 (2001)
9. Görlitz, O., Staab, S.: SPLENDID: SPARQL endpoint federation exploiting VoID descriptions. In: Proceedings of the 2nd International Workshop on Consuming Linked Data, vol. 782, pp. 13–24. Bonn, Germany (2011). http://uni-koblenz.de/~goerlitz/publications/GoerlitzAndStaab_COLD2011.pdf
10. Harris, S., Seaborne, A.: SPARQL 1.1 query language, March 2013. https://www.w3.org/TR/sparql11-query/
11. Hose, K., Schenkel, R.: Towards benefit-based RDF source selection for SPARQL queries. In: SWIM 2012 Proceedings of the 4th International Workshop on Semantic Web Information Management, Scottsdale, Arizona (2012)
12. Ioannidis, Y.E., Christodoulakis, S.: On the propagation of errors in the size of join results. In: Proceedings of ACM SIGMOD Conference, pp. 268–277 (1991)
13. Ioannidis, Y.E., Poosala, V.: Histogram-based approximation of set-valued query answers. In: Proceedings of the 25th International Conference on Very Large Data Bases, pp. 174–185 (1999)

14. Kossmann, D.: The state of the art in distributed query processing. ACM Comput. Surv. **32**(4), 422–469 (2000)
15. Lipton, R.J., Naughton, J.F., Schneider, D.A.: Practical selectivity estimation through adaptive sampling. In: Proceedings of the 1990 ACM SIGMOD International Conference on Management of Data, pp. 1–11 (1990)
16. Moor, D., Grubenmann, T., Seuken, S., Bernstein, A.: A double auction for querying the web of data. In: The Third Conference on Auctions, Market Mechanisms and Their Applications (2015)
17. Moor, D., Seuken, S., Grubenmann, T., Bernstein, A.: Core-selecting payment rules for combinatorial auctions with uncertain availability of goods. In: Twenty-Fifth International Joint Conference on Artificial Intelligence, pp. 424–432 (2016)
18. Ozsu, T., Valduriez, P.: Principles of Distributed Database Systems, 2nd edn. Prentice Hall, New Jersey (1999). http://www.citeulike.org/user/zflavio/article/379597
19. Prasser, F., Kemper, A., Kuhn, K.A.: Efficient distributed query processing for autonomous RDF databases. In: Proceedings of the 15th International Conference on Extending Database Technology - EDBT 2012, pp. 372–383 (2012)
20. Quilitz, B., Leser, U.: Querying distributed RDF data sources with SPARQL. In: Bechhofer, S., Hauswirth, M., Hoffmann, J., Koubarakis, M. (eds.) ESWC 2008. LNCS, vol. 5021, pp. 524–538. Springer, Heidelberg (2008). doi:10.1007/978-3-540-68234-9_39
21. Saleem, M., Ngonga Ngomo, A.-C.: HiBISCuS: hypergraph-based source selection for SPARQL endpoint federation. In: Presutti, V., d'Amato, C., Gandon, F., d'Aquin, M., Staab, S., Tordai, A. (eds.) ESWC 2014. LNCS, vol. 8465, pp. 176–191. Springer, Cham (2014). doi:10.1007/978-3-319-07443-6_13
22. Saleem, M., Ngonga Ngomo, A.-C., Xavier Parreira, J., Deus, H.F., Hauswirth, M.: DAW: Duplicate-AWare federated query processing over the web of data. In: Alani, H., et al. (eds.) ISWC 2013. LNCS, vol. 8218, pp. 574–590. Springer, Heidelberg (2013). doi:10.1007/978-3-642-41335-3_36
23. Schmidt, M., Görlitz, O., Haase, P., Ladwig, G., Schwarte, A., Tran, T.: FedBench: a benchmark suite for federated semantic data query processing. In: Aroyo, L., Welty, C., Alani, H., Taylor, J., Bernstein, A., Kagal, L., Noy, N., Blomqvist, E. (eds.) ISWC 2011. LNCS, vol. 7031, pp. 585–600. Springer, Heidelberg (2011). doi:10.1007/978-3-642-25073-6_37
24. Schwarte, A., Haase, P., Hose, K., Schenkel, R., Schmidt, M.: FedX: optimization techniques for federated query processing on linked data. In: Aroyo, L., Welty, C., Alani, H., Taylor, J., Bernstein, A., Kagal, L., Noy, N., Blomqvist, E. (eds.) ISWC 2011. LNCS, vol. 7031, pp. 601–616. Springer, Heidelberg (2011). doi:10.1007/978-3-642-25073-6_38
25. Sheth, A.P., Larson, J.A.: Federated database systems for managing distributed, heterogeneous, and autonomous databases. ACM Comput. Surv. **22**(3), 183–236 (1990)
26. Umbrich, J., Hose, K., Karnstedt, M., Harth, A., Polleres, A.: Comparing data summaries for processing live queries over linked data. World Wide Web **14**(5), 495–544 (2011)
27. Vidal, M.-E., Castillo, S., Acosta, M., Montoya, G., Palma, G.: On the selection of SPARQL endpoints to efficiently execute federated SPARQL queries. In: Hameurlain, A., Küng, J., Wagner, R. (eds.) Transactions on Large-Scale Data- and Knowledge-Centered Systems XXV. LNCS, vol. 9620, pp. 109–149. Springer, Heidelberg (2016). doi:10.1007/978-3-662-49534-6_4

AMUSE: Multilingual Semantic Parsing for Question Answering over Linked Data

Sherzod Hakimov[✉], Soufian Jebbara, and Philipp Cimiano

Semantic Computing Group, Cognitive Interaction Technology – Center of Excellence
(CITEC), Bielefeld University, 33615 Bielefeld, Germany
{shakimov,sjebbara,cimiano}@cit-ec.uni-bielefeld.de

Abstract. The task of answering natural language questions over RDF
data has received wide interest in recent years, in particular in the context of the series of QALD benchmarks. The task consists of mapping a
natural language question to an executable form, e.g. SPARQL, so that
answers from a given KB can be extracted. So far, most systems proposed are (i) monolingual and (ii) rely on a set of hard-coded rules to
interpret questions and map them into a SPARQL query. We present
the first multilingual QALD pipeline that induces a model from training
data for mapping a natural language question into logical form as probabilistic inference. In particular, our approach learns to map universal
syntactic dependency representations to a language-independent logical form based on DUDES (Dependency-based Underspecified Discourse
Representation Structures) that are then mapped to a SPARQL query
as a deterministic second step. Our model builds on factor graphs that
rely on features extracted from the dependency graph and corresponding
semantic representations. We rely on approximate inference techniques,
Markov Chain Monte Carlo methods in particular, as well as Sample
Rank to update parameters using a ranking objective. Our focus lies on
developing methods that overcome the lexical gap and present a novel
combination of machine translation and word embedding approaches for
this purpose. As a proof of concept for our approach, we evaluate our
approach on the QALD-6 datasets for English, German & Spanish.

Keywords: Question answering · Multilinguality · QALD · Probabilistic graphical models · Factor graphs

1 Introduction

The task of Question Answering over Linked Data (QALD) has received
increased attention over the last years (see the surveys [14,36]). The task consists
in mapping natural language questions into an executable form, e.g. a SPARQL
query in particular, that allows to retrieve answers to the question from a given

© Springer International Publishing AG 2017
C. d'Amato et al. (Eds.): ISWC 2017, Part I, LNCS 10587, pp. 329–346, 2017.
DOI: 10.1007/978-3-319-68288-4_20

knowledge base. Consider the question: *Who created Wikipedia?*, which can be interpreted as the following SPARQL query with respect to DBpedia[1]:

```
SELECT DISTINCT ?uri WHERE { dbr:Wikipedia dbo:author ?uri .}
```

An important challenge in mapping natural language questions to SPARQL queries lies in overcoming the so called *'lexical gap'* (see [13,14]). The lexical gap makes interpreting the above mentioned question correctly challenging, as there is no surface relation between the query string *created* and the URI local name *author*. To bridge the lexical gap, systems need to infer that *create* should be interpreted as author in the above case.

The lexical gap is only exacerbated when considering multiple languages as we face a cross-lingual gap that needs to be bridged. Consider for instance the question: *Wer hat Wikipedia gegründet?*, which involves mapping *gründen* to author to successfully interpret the question.

Addressing the lexical gap in question answering over linked data, we present a new system we call AMUSE that relies on probabilistic inference to perform structured prediction in the search space of possible SPARQL queries to predict the query that has the highest probability of being the correct interpretation of the given query string. As the main contribution of the paper, we present a novel approach to question answering over linked data that relies on probabilistic inference to determine the most probable meaning of a question given a model. The parameters of the model are optimized on a given training dataset consisting of natural language questions with their corresponding SPARQL queries as provided by the QALD benchmark. The inference process builds on approximate inference techniques, Markov Chain Monte Carlo in particular, to assign knowledge base (KB) Identifiers as well as meaning representations to every node in a dependency tree representing the syntactic dependency structure of the question. On the basis of these assigned meaning representations to every node, a full semantic representation can be computed relying on bottom-up semantic composition along the parse tree. As a novelty, our model can be trained on different languages by relying on universal dependencies. To our knowledge, this is the first system for question answering over linked data that can be trained to perform on different languages (three in our case) without the need of implementing any language-specific heuristics or knowledge. To overcome the cross-lingual lexical gap, we experiment with automatically translated labels and rely on an embedding approach to retrieve similar words in the embedding space. We show that by using word embeddings one can effectively contribute to reducing the lexical gap compared to a baseline system where only known labels are used.

2   Approach

Our intuition in this paper is that the interpretation of a natural language question in terms of a SPARQL query is a compositional process in which partial

---

[1] The prefixes dbo and dbr stand for the namespaces http://dbpedia.org/ontology and http://dbpedia.org/resource/, respectively.

semantic representations are combined with each other in a bottom-up fashion along a dependency tree representing the syntactic structure of a given question. Instead of relying on hand-crafted rules guiding the composition, we rely on a learning approach that can infer such 'rules' from training data. We employ a factor graph model that is trained using a ranking objective and SampleRank as training procedure to learn a model that learns to prefer good over bad interpretations of a question. In essence, an interpretation of a question represented as a dependency tree consists of an assignment of several variables: (i) a KB Id and semantic type to every node in the parse tree, and (ii) an argument index (1 or 2) to every edge in the dependency tree specifying which slot of the parent node, subject or object, the child node should be applied to. The input to our approach is thus a set of pairs (q, sp) of question q and SPARQL query sp. As an example, consider the following questions in English, German & Spanish : *Who created Wikipedia? Wer hat Wikipedia gegründet? Quién creó Wikipedia?* respectively. Independently of the language they are expressed in, the threes question can be interpreted as the same SPARQL query from the introduction.

Our approach consists of two inference layers which we call L2KB and QC. Each of these layers consists of a different factor graph optimized for different subtasks of the overall task. The first inference layer is trained using an entity linking objective that learns to link parts of the query to KB Identifiers. In particular, this inference step assigns KB Identifiers to open class words such as nouns, proper nouns, adjectives and verbs etc. In our case, the knowledge base is DBpedia. We use Universal Dependencies[2] [28] to get dependency parse trees for 3 languages. The second inference layer is a query construction layer that takes the top k results from the L2KB layer and assigns semantic representations to closed class words such as question pronouns, determiners, etc. to yield a logical representation of the complete question. The approach is trained on the QALD-6 train dataset for English, German & Spanish questions to optimize the parameters of the model. The model learns mappings between the dependency parse tree for a given question text and RDF nodes in the SPARQL query. As output, our system produces an executable SPARQL query for a given NL question. All data and source code are freely available[3]. As semantic representations, we rely on DUDES, which are described in the following section.

2.1 DUDES

DUDES (*Dependency-based Underspecified Discourse Representation Structures*) [9] is a formalism for specifying meaning representations and their composition. They are based on *Underspecified Discourse Representation Theory* (UDRT) [10, 33], and the resulting meaning representations. Formally, a DUDE is defined as follows:

Definition 1. *A DUDE is a 5-tuple $(v, vs, l, drs, slots)$ where*

---

[2] http://universaldependencies.org/v2, 70 treebanks, 50 languages.
[3] https://github.com/ag-sc/AMUSE.

– *v is the* main variable *of the DUDES*
– *vs is a (possibly empty) set of variables, the* projection variables
– *l is the label of the* main DRS
– *drs is a DRS (the main semantic content of the DUDE)*
– *slots is a (possibly empty) set of semantic dependencies*

The core of a DUDES is thus a *Discourse Representation Structure* (DRS) [15]. The main variable represents the variable to be unified with variables in slots of other DUDES that the DUDE in question is inserted into. Each DUDE captures information about which semantic arguments are required for a DUDE to be complete in the sense that all slots have been filled. These required arguments are modeled as set of slots that are filled via (functional) application of other DUDES. The projection variables are relevant in meaning representations of questions; they specify which entity is asked for. When converting DUDES into SPARQL queries, they will directly correspond to the variables in the SELECT clause of the query. Finally, slots capture information about which syntactic elements map to which semantic arguments in the DUDE.

As basic units of composition, we consider 5 pre-defined DUDES types that correspond to data elements in RDF datasets. We consider *Resource DUDES* that represent resources or individuals denoted by proper nouns such as *Wikipedia* (see 1st DUDES in Fig. 1). We consider *Class DUDES* that correspond to sets of elements, i.e. classes, for example the class of *Persons* (see 2nd DUDES in Fig. 1). We also consider *Property DUDES* that correspond to object or datatype properties such as *author* (see 3rd DUDES in Fig. 1). We further consider restriction classes that represent the meaning of intersective adjectives such as *Swedish* (see 4th DUDES in Fig. 1). Finally, a special type of DUDES can be used to capture the meaning of question pronouns, e.g. *Who* or *What* (see 5th DUDES in Fig. 1).

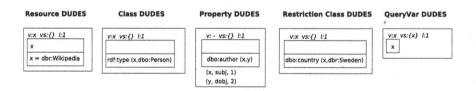

Fig. 1. Exampeles for the 5 types of DUDES

When applying a DUDE d_2 to d_1 where d_1 subcategorizes a number of semantic arguments, we need to indicate which argument d_2 fills. For instance, applying the 1st DUDES in Fig. 1 to the 3rd DUDES in Fig. 1 at argument index 1 yields the following DUDE:

2.2 Imperatively Defined Factor Graphs

In this section, we introduce the concept of factor graphs [19], following the notations in [17,41]. A factor graph $\mathcal{G}$ is a bipartite graph that defines a probability distribution π. The graph consists of variables V and factors Ψ. Variables can be further divided into sets of *observed* variables X and *hidden* variables Y. A factor Ψ_i connects subsets of observed variables x_i and hidden variables y_i, and computes a scalar score based on the exponential of the scalar product of a feature vector $f_i(x_i, y_i)$ and a set of parameters θ_i: $\Psi_i = e^{f_i(x_i,y_i)\cdot\theta_i}$. The probability of the hidden variables given the observed variables is the product of the individual factors:

$$\pi(y|x;\theta) = \frac{1}{Z(x)} \prod_{\Psi_i \in \mathcal{G}} \Psi_i(x_i, y_i) = \frac{1}{Z(x)} \prod_{\Psi_i \in \mathcal{G}} e^{f_i(x_i,y_i)\cdot\theta_i} \tag{1}$$

where $Z(x)$ is the partition function. For a given input consisting of a dependency parsed sentence, the factor graph is rolled out by applying template procedures that match over parts of the input and generate corresponding factors. The templates are thus imperatively specified procedures that roll out the graph. A template $T_j \in \mathcal{T}$ defines the subsets of observed and hidden variables (x', y') with $x' \in X_j$ and $y' \in Y_j$ for which it can generate factors and a function $f_j(x', y')$ to generate features for these variables. Additionally, all factors generated by a given template T_j share the same parameters θ_j. With this definition, we can reformulate the conditional probability as follows:

$$\pi(y|x;\theta) = \frac{1}{Z(x)} \prod_{T_j \in \mathcal{T}} \prod_{(x',y') \in T_j} e^{f_j(x',y')\cdot\theta_j} \tag{2}$$

Input to our approach is a pair (W, E) consisting of a sequence of words $W = \{w_1, \ldots, w_n\}$ and a set of dependency edges $E \subseteq W \times W$ forming a tree. A state $(W, E, \alpha, \beta, \gamma)$ represents a partial interpretation of the input in terms of partial semantic representations. The partial functions $\alpha : W \to KB$, $\beta : W \to \{t_1, t_2, t_3, t_4, t_5\}$ and $\gamma : E \to \{1, 2\}$ map words to KB identifiers, words to the five basic DUDES types, and edges to indices of semantic arguments, with 1 corresponding to the subject of a property and 2 corresponding to the object, respectively. Figure 2 shows a schematic visualization of a question along with its factor graph. Factors measure the compatibility between different assignments of observed and hidden variables. The interpretation of a question is the one that maximizes the posterior of a model with parameters θ: $y^* = argmax_y \pi(y|x;\theta)$.

2.3 Inference

We rely on an approximate inference procedure, Markov Chain Monte Carlo in particular [1]. The method performs iterative inference for exploring the state space of possible question interpretations by proposing concrete changes to sets of variables that define a proposal distribution. The inference procedure performs an iterative local search and can be divided into (i) generating possible

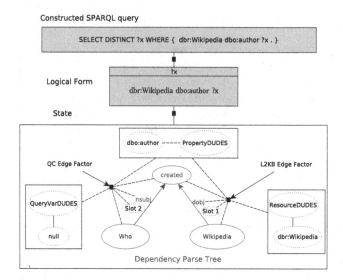

Fig. 2. Factor graph for the question: *Who created Wikipedia?*. Observed variables are depicted as bubbles with straight lines; hidden variables as bubbles with dashed lines. Black boxes represent factors.

successor states for a given state by applying changes, (ii) scoring the states using the model score, and (iii) deciding which proposal to accept as successor state. A proposal is accepted with a probability that is proportional to the likelihood assigned by the distribution π. To compute the logical form of a question, we run two inference procedures using two different models. The first model L2KB is trained using a linking objective that learns to map open class words to KB identifiers. The MCMC sampling process is run for m steps for the L2KB model; the top k states are used as an input for the second inference model called QC that assigns meanings to closed class words to yield a full fledged semantic representation of the question. Both inference strategies generate successor states by exploration based on edges in the dependency parse tree. We explore only the following types of edges: *Core arguments, Non-core dependents, Nominal dependents* defined by Universal Dependencies[4] and nodes that have the following POS tags: NOUN, VERB, ADJ, PRON, PROPN, DET. In both inference models, we alternate across iterations between using the probability of the state given the model and the objective score to decide which state to accept. Initially, all partial assignments $\alpha_0, \beta_0, \gamma_0$. are empty.

We rely on an inverted index to find all KB IDs for a given query term. The inverted index maps terms to candidate KB IDs for all 3 languages. It has been created taking into account a number of resources: names of DBpedia resources, Wikipedia anchor texts and links, names of DBpedia classes, synonyms for DBpedia classes from WordNet [16,26], as well as lexicalizations of properties

---

[4] http://universaldependencies.org/u/dep/index.html.

and restriction classes from DBlexipedia [40]. Entries in the index are grouped by DUDES type, so that it supports type-specific retrieval. The index stores the frequency of the mentions paired with KB ID. During retrieval, the index returns a normalized frequency score for each candidate KB ID.

L2KB: Linking to Knowledge Base. Proposal Generation: The L2KB proposal generation proposes changes to a given state by considering single dependency edges and changing: (i) the KB IDs of parent and child nodes, (ii) the DUDES type of parent and child nodes, and (iii) the argument index attached to the edge. The Semantic Type variables range over the 5 basic DUDES types defined, while the argument index variable ranges in the set $\{1,2\}$. The resulting partial semantic representations for the dependency edge are checked for satisfiability with respect to the knowledge base, pruning the proposal if it is not satisfiable. Figure 3 depicts the local exploration of the *dobj*-edge between *Wikipedia* and *created*. The left image shows an initial state with empty assignments for all hidden variables. The right image shows a proposal that is changed the KB IDs and DUDE types of the nodes connects by the *dobj* edge. The inference process has assigned the KB ID *dbo:author* and the *Property DUDES* type to the *created* node. The *Wikipedia* nodes gets assigned the type *Resource DUDES* as well as the KB ID *dbr:Wikipedia*. The dependency edge gets assigned the argument index 1, representing that *dbr:Wikipedia* should be inserted at the subject position of the *dbo:author* property. The partial semantic representation represented by this edge is the one depicted at the end of Sect. 2.2. As it is satisfiable, it is not pruned. In contrast, a state in which the edge is assigned the argument index 2 would yield the following non-satisfiable representation, corresponding to things that were authored by *Wikipedia* instead of things that authored *Wikipedia*:

$$v:-\ vs:\{\}\ l:1$$
$$1:\ \boxed{\texttt{dbo:author}(y,\ dbr:Wikipedia)}$$
$$(y,\ a_2,\ 2)$$

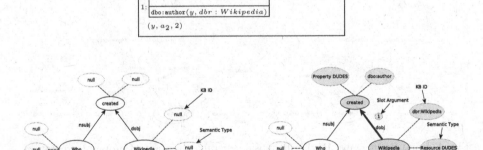

Fig. 3. Left: Initial state based on dependency parse where each node has empty KB ID and Semantic Type. **Right**: Proposal generated by the LKB proposal generation for the question *Who created Wikipedia?*

Objective Function: As objective for the L2KB model we rely on a linking objective that calculates the overlap between inferred entity links and entity links in the gold standard SPARQL query.

All generated states are ranked by the objective score. Top-k states are passed to the next sampling step. In the next iteration, the inference is performed on these k states. Following this procedure for m iterations yields a sequence of states $(s_0, \ldots, s_m)$ that are sampled from the distribution defined by the underlying factor graphs.

QC: Query Construction. Proposal Generation: Proposals in this inference layer consist of assignments of the type *QueryVar DUDES* to nodes for class words, in particular determiners, that could fill the argument position of a parent with unsatisfied arguments.

Objective Function: As objective we use an objective function that measures the (graph) similarity between the inferred SPARQL query and the gold standard SPARQL query.

Figure 4 shows an input state and a sampled state for the QC inference layer of our example query: *Who created Wikipedia?*. The initial state (see Left) has Slot 1 assigned to the edge *dobj*. Property DUDES have 2 slots by definition. The right figure shows a proposed state in which the argument slot 2 has been assigned to the nsubj edge and the *QueryVar DUDES* type has been assigned to node *Who*. This corresponds to the representation and SPARQL queries below:

```
SELECT DISTINCT ?y WHERE { dbr:Wikipedia dbo:author ?y .}
```

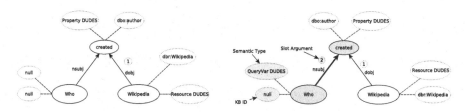

Fig. 4. Left: Input state; **Right**: Proposal generated by the QC proposal generation for the question *Who created Wikipedia?*

2.4   Features

As features for the factors, we use conjunctions of the following information: (i) lemma of parent and child nodes, (ii) KB Ids of parent and child nodes, (iii) POS tags of parent and child nodes, (iv) DUDE type of parent and child, (v) index of argument at edge, vi) dependency relation of edge, (vii) normalized frequency score for retrieved KB Ids, (viii) string similarity between KB Id and lemma of node, (ix) rdfs:domain and rdfs:range restrictions for the parent KB Id (in case of being a property).

2.5   Learning Model Parameters

In order to optimize parameters θ, we use an implementation of the SampleRank [41] algorithm. The SampleRank algorithm obtains gradients for these parameters from pairs of consecutive states in the chain based on a preference function $\mathbb{P}$ defined in terms of the objective function $\mathbb{O}$ as follows:

$$\mathbb{P}(s', s) = \begin{cases} 1, & \text{if } \mathbb{O}(s') > \mathbb{O}(s) \\ 0, & \text{otherwise} \end{cases} \tag{3}$$

We have observed that accepting proposals only on the basis of the model score requires a large number of inference steps. This is due to the fact that the exploration space is huge considering all the candidate resources, predicates, classes etc. in DBpedia. To guide the search towards good solutions, we switch between model score and objective score to compute the likelihood of acceptance of a proposal. Once the training procedure switches the scoring function in the next sampling step, the model uses the parameters from the previous step to score the states.

2.6   Addressing the Lexical Gap

A key component in the proposed question answering pipeline is the L2KB layer. This layer is responsible for proposing possible KB identifiers for parts of the question. Consider the question *Who is the writer of The Hunger Games?* It seems to be a trivial task to link the query word *writer* to the appropriate identifier dbo:author, however it still requires prior knowledge about the semantics of the query word and the KB entry (e.g. that the writer of a book is the author).

To address the lexical gap, we rely on the one hand on lexicalizations of DBpedia properties as extracted by M-ATOLL [39,40] for multiple languages[5]. In particular for Spanish and German, however, M-ATOLL produces very sparse results. We propose two solutions to overcome the lexical gap by using machine translation to translate English labels into other languages as well as using word embeddings to retrieve candidate properties for a given mention text.

Machine Translations. We rely on the online dictionary Dict.cc[6] as our translation engine. We query the web service for each available English label and target language and store the obtained translation candidates as new labels for

---

[5] M-ATOLL currently provides lexicalizations for English, German and Spanish.
[6] http://www.dict.cc.

the respective entity and language. While these translations are prone to be noisy without a proper context, we receive a reasonable starting point for the generation of candidate lexicalizations, especially in combination with the word embedding approach.

Word Embedding Retrieval. Many word embedding methods such as the skip-gram method [25] have been shown to encode useful semantic and syntactic properties. The objective of the skip-gram method is to learn word representations that are useful for predicting context words. As a result, the learned embeddings often display a desirable linear structure that can be exploited using simple vector addition. Motivated by the compositionality of word vectors, we propose a measure of semantic relatedness between a mention m and a DBpedia entry e using the cosine similarity between their respective vector representations $\boldsymbol{v}_m$ and $\boldsymbol{v}_e$. For this we follow the approach in [5] to derive entity embedding vectors from word vectors: We define the vector of a mention m as the sum of the vectors of its tokens[7] $\boldsymbol{v}_m = \sum_{t \in m} \boldsymbol{v}_t$, where the $\boldsymbol{v}_t$ are raw vectors from the set of pretrained skip-gram vectors. Similarly, we derive the vector representation of a DBpedia entry e by adding the individual word vectors for the respective label l_e of e, thus $\boldsymbol{v}_e = \sum_{t \in l_e} \boldsymbol{v}_t$.

As an example, the vector for the mention text *movie director* is composed as $\boldsymbol{v}_{movie\ director} = \boldsymbol{v}_{movie} + \boldsymbol{v}_{director}$. The DBpedia entry `dbo:director` has the label *film director* and is thus composed of $\boldsymbol{v}_{dbo:director} = \boldsymbol{v}_{film} + \boldsymbol{v}_{director}$.

To generate potential linking candidates given a mention text, we can compute the cosine similarity between $\boldsymbol{v}_m$ and each possible $\boldsymbol{v}_e$ as a measure of semantic relatedness and thus produce a ranking of all candidate entries. By pruning the ranking at a chosen threshold, we can control the produced candidate list for precision and recall.

For this work, we trained 3 instances of the skip-gram model with each 100 dimensions on the English, German and Spanish Wikipedia respectively. Following this approach, the top ranking DBpedia entries for the mention text *total population* are listed below:

Mention	DBpedia entry	Cos. Similarity
Total population	`dbo:populationTotal`	1.0
	`dbo:totalPopulation`	1.0
	`dbo:agglomerationPopulationTotal`	0.984
	`dbo:populationTotalRanking`	0.983
	`dbo:PopulatedPlace/areaTotal`	0.979

A more detailed evaluation is conducted in Sect. 3 where we investigate the candidate retrieval in comparison to an M-ATOLL baseline.

---

[7] We omit all stopword tokens.

3   Experiments and Evaluation

We present experiments carried out on the QALD-6 dataset comprising of English, German & Spanish questions. We train and test on the multilingual subtask. This yields a training dataset consisting of 350 and 100 test instances. We train the model with 350 training instances for each language from QALD-6 train dataset by performing 10 iterations over the dataset with learning rate set to 0.01 to optimize the parameters. We set k to 10. We perform a preprocessing step on the dependency parse tree before running through the pipeline. This step consists of merging nodes that are connected with compound edges. This results in having one node for compound names and reduces the traversing time and complexity for the model. The approach is evaluated on two tasks: a linking task and a question answering task. The linking task is evaluated by comparing the proposed KB links to the KB elements contained in the SPARQL question in terms of F-Measure. The question answering task is evaluated by executing the constructed SPARQL query over the DBpedia KB, and comparing the retrieved answers with answers retrieved for the gold standard SPARQL query in terms of F-Measure.

Before evaluating the full pipeline on the QA task, we evaluate the impact of using different lexical resources including the word embedding to infer unknown lexical relations.

3.1   Evaluating the Lexicon Generation

We evaluate the proposed lexicon generation methods using machine translation and embeddings with respect to a lexicon of manual annotations that are obtained from the training set of the QALD-6 dataset. The manual lexicon is a mapping of mention to expected KB entry derived from the (question-query) pairs in QALD-6 dataset. Since M-ATOLL only provides DBpedia ontology properties, we restrict our word embedding approach to also only produce this subset of KB entities. Analogously, the manual lexicon is filtered such that it only contains word-property entries for DBpedia ontology properties to prevent the unnecessary distortion of the evaluation results due to unsolvable query terms.

The evaluation is carried out with respect to the number of generated candidates per query term using the Recall@k measure. Focusing on the recall is a reasonable evaluation metric since the considered manual lexicon is far from exhaustive, but only reflects a small subset of possible lexicalizations of KB properties in natural language questions. Furthermore, the L2KB component is responsible for producing a set of linked candidate states which act as starting points for the second layer of inference, the QC layer. Providing a component with a high recall in this step of the pipeline is crucial for the query construction component.

Figure 5 visualizes the retrieval performance using the Recall@k metric. We can see a large increase in recall across languages when generating candidates using the word embedding method. Combining the M-ATOLL candidates with

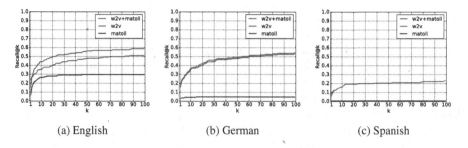

(a) English   (b) German   (c) Spanish

Fig. 5. Retrieval performance with respect to the manual lexicon.

the word embedding candiates yields the strongest recall performance. The largest absolute increase is observed for German.

3.2 Evaluating Question Answering

In order to contextualise our results, we provide an upper bound for our approach, which consists of running over all instances in test using 1 epoch and accepting states according to objective score only, thus yielding an oracle-like approach. We report Macro F-Measures for this oracle in Table 1 together with the actual results on test when optimizing parameters on training data. We evaluate different configurations of our system in which we consider (i) a name dictionary derived only from DBpedia labels (DBP), (ii) additional dictionary entries derived from DBLexipedia (DBLex), (iii) a manually created dictionary (Dict), and (iv) entries inferred using cosine similarity in embedding space (Embed). It is important to note that even the oracle does not get perfect results, which is due to the fact that the lexical gap still persists and some entries can not be mapped to the correct KB Ids. Further, errors in POS tagging or in the dependency tree prevent the inference strategy to generate the correct proposals.

We see that in all configurations, results clearly improve when using additional entries from DBLexipedia (DBLex) in comparison to only using labels from DBpedia. The results further increase by adding lexical entries inferred via similarity in embedding space (+Embed), but are still far from the results with manually created dictionary (Dict), showing that addressing the lexical gap is an important issue to increase performance of question answering systems over linked data.

On the linking task, while the use of embeddings increases performance as seen in the DBP + DBLex + Embed vs. DBP + DBLex condition, there is still a clear margin to the DBP + DBLex + Dict condition (English 0.16 vs. 0.22, German 0.10 vs. 0.27, Spanish 0.04 vs. 0.30).

On the QA task, adding embeddings on top of DBP + DBLex also has a positive impact, but is also lower compared to the DBP + DBLex + Dict condition (English 0.26 vs. 0.34, German 0.16 vs. 0.37, Spanish 0.20 vs. 0.42). Clearly, one can observe that the different between the learned model and the oracle diminishes the more lexical knowledge is added to the system.

Table 1. Macro F1-scores on test data for the linking and question answering tasks using different configurations

Language	Task	DBP	DBP + DBLex	DBP + DBLex + Embed	DBP + DBLex + Dict
Oracle					
EN	Linking	0.05	0.22	0.46	0.59
EN	QA	0.05	0.21	0.30	**0.51**
DE	Linking	0.01	0.01	0.10	0.48
DE	QA	0.04	0.04	0.18	**0.44**
ES	Linking	0.02	0.04	0.10	0.51
ES	QA	0.04	0.06	0.22	**0.52**
Test					
EN	Linking	0.05	0.13	0.16	0.22
EN	QA	0.05	0.20	**0.26**	**0.34**
DE	Linking	0.01	0.01	0.10	0.27
DE	QA	0.04	0.04	**0.16**	**0.37**
ES	Linking	0.02	0.02	0.04	0.30
ES	QA	0.04	0.04	**0.20**	**0.42**

3.3 Error Analysis

An error analysis revealed the following four common errors that prevented the system from finding the correct interpretation: (i) wrong resource (30% of test questions), as in *When did the Boston Tea Party take place?* where *Boston Tea Party* is not mapped to any resource, (ii) wrong property (48%), as in the question *Who wrote the song Hotel California?* where our system infers the property dbpedia:musicalArtist for *song* instead of the property dbpedia:writer, (iii) wrong slot (10%), as in *How many people live in Poland?*, where Poland is inferred to fill the 2nd slot instead of the 1st slot of dbepdia:populationTotal and (iv) incorrect query type (12%), as in *Where does Piccadilly start?* where our approach wrongly infers that this is an ASK-query.

4 Related Work

There is a substantial body of work on semantic parsing for question answering. Earlier work addressed the problem using statistical machine translation methods [42] or inducing synchronous grammars [43]. Recent work has framed the task as the one of inducing statistical lexicalized grammars; most of this work has relied on CCG as grammar theory and lambda calculus for semantic representation and semantic composition [2–4,18,20–22,35,46]. In contrast to the above work, we assume that a syntactic analysis of the input in the form of a dependency tree is available and we learn a model that assigns semantic representations to each node in the tree. Most of earlier work in semantic parsing has concentrated on very specific domains with a very restricted semantic vocabulary. More recently, a number of researchers have considered this challenge and focused on open-domain QA datasets such as WebQuestions, which relies on Freebase [6–8,30–32,34,44,45].

Our approach bears some relation to the work of Reddy et al. [31] in the sense that we both start from a dependency tree (or ungrounded graph in their terminology) and the goal is to ground the ungrounded relations in a KB. We use a different learning approach and model as well as a different semantic representation formalism (DUDES vs. lambda expressions). More recently, Reddy et al. [32] have extended their method to produce general logical forms relying on Universal Dependencies, independent of the application, that is question answering. They evaluate their approach both on the WebQuestions as well as Graphqueries. While the datasets they use have thousands of training examples, we have shown that we can train a model using only 350 questions as training data.

The work of Freitas et al. [12] employs a distributional structured vector space, the τ-Space, to bridge the lexical gap between queries and KB in order to map query terms to corresponding properties and classes in the underlying KB. Further, Freitas et al. [11] studied different distributional semantic models in combination with machine translation. Their findings suggest that combining machine translation with a Word2Vec approach achieves the best performance for measuring semantic relatedness across multiple languages.

Denis et al. [23] have proposed an end-to-end QALD model exploiting neural networks. The approach works well for answering simple questions and has been trained on a dataset with 100.000 training instances. In contrast, QALD-6 benchmarks have less data (350 instances) and questions include more difficult questions requiring aggregation and comparison. Neelakantan et al. [27] have proposed an approach based on neural model that achieves comparable results to the state-of-art non-neural semantic parsers on WikiTableQuestions [29] dataset, which includes questions with aggregation.

The best performing system on the QALD-6 benchmark [36] was the one by [24], achieving an F-measure of 89%. However, the approach relies on a controlled natural language approach in which queries have been manually reformulated so that the approach can parse them. The only system that is able to perform on three languages as ours is the UTQA system [38]. The UTQA system achieves much higher results compared to our system, reaching F-measures of 75% (EN), 68% (ES) and 61% (Persian). The approach relies on a pipeline of several classifiers performing keyword extraction, relation and entity linking as well as answer-type detection. All these steps are performed jointly in our model.

Höffner et al. [14] recently surveyed published approaches on QALD benchmarks, analysed the differences and identified seven challenges. Our approach addresses four out of these seven challenges: multilingualism, ambiguity, lexical gap and templates. Our probabilistic model performs implicit disambiguation and performs semantic interpretation using a traditional bottom-up semantic composition using state-of-the-art semantic representation formalisms and thus does not rely on any fixed templates. We have proposed how to overcome the lexical gap using an approach to induce lexical relations between surface mentions and entities in the knowledge base using a representational learning approach. Multilinguality is addressed by building on universal dependencies and our methodology which allows to train models for different languages.

5 Conclusion

We have presented a multilingual factor graph model that can map natural language input into logical form relying on DUDES as semantic formalism. Given dependency-parsed input, our model infers both a semantic type and KB entity to each node in the dependency tree and computes an overall logical form by bottom-up semantic composition. We have applied our approach to the task of question answering over linked data, using the QALD-6 dataset. We show that our model can learn to map questions into SPARQL queries by training on 350 instances only. We have shown that our approach works for multiple languages, English, German and Spanish in particular. We have also shown how the lexical gap can be overcome by using word embeddings increasing performance beyond using explicit lexica produced by lexicon induction approaches such as M-ATOLL. As a future work, we will extend our approach to handle questions with other filtering operations. We will also make our system available on GERBIL [37] to support the direct comparison to other systems.

Acknowledgements. This work was supported by the Cluster of Excellence Cognitive Interaction Technology 'CITEC' (EXC 277) at Bielefeld University, which is funded by the German Research Foundation (DFG).

References

1. Andrieu, C., de Freitas, N., Doucet, A., Jordan, M.I.: An introduction to MCMC for machine learning. Mach. Learn. **50**, 5–43 (2003)
2. Artzi, Y., Lee, K., Zettlemoyer, L.: Broad-coverage CCG semantic parsing with AMR. In: Proceedings of EMNLP, pp. 1699–1710 (2015)
3. Artzi, Y., Zettlemoyer, L.S.: Bootstrapping semantic parsers from conversations. In: Proceedings of ACL, pp. 421–432 (2011)
4. Baldridge, J., Kruijff, G.J.M.: Coupling ccg and hybrid logic dependency semantics. In: Proceedings of ACL, pp. 319–326. Association for Computational Linguistics (2002)
5. Basile, V., Jebbara, S., Cabrio, E., Cimiano, P.: Populating a knowledge base with object-location relations using distributional semantics. In: Blomqvist, E., Ciancarini, P., Poggi, F., Vitali, F. (eds.) EKAW 2016. LNCS (LNAI), vol. 10024, pp. 34–50. Springer, Cham (2016). doi:10.1007/978-3-319-49004-5_3
6. Berant, J., Chou, A., Frostig, R., Liang, P.: Semantic parsing on freebase from question-answer pairs. In: Proceedings of EMNLP, 1533–1544, October 2013
7. Berant, J., Liang, P.: Semantic Parsing via Paraphrasing. In: ACL (Figure 1), pp. 1415–1425 (2014)
8. Berant, J., Liang, P.: Imitation learning of agenda-based semantic parsers. Trans. Assoc. Comput. Linguist. **3**, 545–558 (2015)

9. Cimiano, P.: Flexible semantic composition with dudes. In: Proceedings of the 8th International Conference on Computational Semantics (IWCS), pp. 272–276 (2009)

10. Cimiano, P., Frank, A., Reyle, U.: UDRT-based semantics construction for LTAG - and what it tells us about the role of adjunction in LTAG. In: Proceedings of the 7th International Workshop on Computational Semantics (IWCS), pp. 41–52 (2007)

11. Freitas, A., Barzegar, S., Sales, J.E., Handschuh, S., Davis, B.: Semantic relatedness for all (languages): a comparative analysis of multilingual semantic relatedness using machine translation. In: Blomqvist, E., Ciancarini, P., Poggi, F., Vitali, F. (eds.) EKAW 2016. LNCS (LNAI), vol. 10024, pp. 212–222. Springer, Cham (2016). doi:10.1007/978-3-319-49004-5_14

12. Freitas, A., Curry, E.: Natural language queries over heterogeneous linked data graphs: a distributional-compositional semantics approach. In: Proceedings of the 19th International Conference on Intelligent User Interfaces, pp. 279–288. ACM (2014)

13. Hakimov, S., Unger, C., Walter, S., Cimiano, P.: Applying semantic parsing to question answering over linked data: addressing the lexical gap. In: Biemann, C., Handschuh, S., Freitas, A., Meziane, F., Métais, E. (eds.) NLDB 2015. LNCS, vol. 9103, pp. 103–109. Springer, Cham (2015). doi:10.1007/978-3-319-19581-0_8

14. Höffner, K., Walter, S., Marx, E., Usbeck, R., Lehmann, J., Ngonga Ngomo, A.C.: Survey on challenges of question answering in the semantic web. Semantic Web (Preprint), 1–26 (2016)

15. Kamp, H., Reyle, U.: From Discourse to Logic. Introduction to the Modeltheoretic Semantics of Natural Language. Kluwer, Dordrecht (1993)

16. Kilgarriff, A., Fellbaum, C.: Wordnet: an electronic lexical database (2000)

17. Klinger, R., Cimiano, P.: Joint and pipeline probabilistic models for fine-grained sentiment analysis: extracting aspects, subjective phrases and their relations. In: Proceedings of ICDMW, pp. 937–944 (2013)

18. Krishnamurthy, J., Mitchell, T.M.: Joint syntactic and semantic parsing with combinatory categorial grammar. In: Proceedings of ACL, pp. 1188–1198 (2014)

19. Kschischang, F.R., Frey, B.J., Loeliger, H.A.: Factor graphs and sum product algorithm. IEEE Trans. Inf. Theory **47**(2), 498–519 (2001)

20. Kwiatkowski, T., Choi, E., Artzi, Y., Zettlemoyer, L.: Scaling semantic parsers with on-the-fly ontology matching. In: Proceedings of EMNLP, pp. 1545–1556, October 2013

21. Kwiatkowski, T., Zettlemoyer, L., Goldwater, S., Steedman, M.: Inducing probabilistic CCG grammars from logical form with higher-order unification. In: Proceedings of EMNLP, pp. 1223–1233, October 2010

22. Lee, K., Lewis, M., Zettlemoyer, L.: Global neural CCG parsing with optimality guarantees. In: Proceedings of EMNLP pp. 2366–2376 (2015)

23. Lukovnikov, D., Fischer, A., Lehmann, J., Auer, S.: Neural network-based question answering over knowledge graphs on word and character level. In: Proceedings of the 26th International Conference on World Wide Web, pp. 1211–1220. International World Wide Web Conferences Steering Committee (2017)

24. Mazzeo, G.M., Zaniolo, C.: Answering controlled natural language questions on RDF knowledge bases. In: Proceedings of the 19th International Conference on Extending Database Technology, pp. 608–611 (2016)

25. Mikolov, T., Sutskever, I., Chen, K., Corrado, G.S., Dean, J.: Distributed representations of words and phrases and their compositionality. In: Advances in Neural Information Processing Systems, pp. 3111–3119 (2013)

26. Miller, G.A.: Wordnet: a lexical database for english. Commun. ACM **38**(11), 39–41 (1995)
27. Neelakantan, A., Le, Q.V., Abadi, M., McCallum, A., Amodei, D.: Learning a natural language interface with neural programmer. In: International Conference on Learning Representations (2017)
28. Nivre, J., et al.: Universal dependencies 2.0. LINDAT/CLARIN digital library at the Institute of Formal and Applied Linguistics, Charles University (2017). http://hdl.handle.net/11234/1-1983
29. Pasupat, P., Liang, P.: Compositional semantic parsing on semi-structured tables. In: ACL (2015)
30. Reddy, S., Lapata, M., Steedman, M.: Large-scale semantic parsing without question-answer pairs. Trans. ACL **2**, 377–392 (2014)
31. Reddy, S., Täckström, O., Collins, M., Kwiatkowski, T., Das, D., Steedman, M., Lapata, M.: Transforming dependency structures to logical forms for semantic parsing. Trans. ACL **4**, 127–140 (2016)
32. Reddy, S., Täckström, O., Petrov, S., Steedman, M., Lapata, M.: Universal semantic parsing. In: Proceedings of EMNLP (2017)
33. Reyle, U.: Dealing with ambiguities by underspecification: construction, representation and deduction. J. Semant. **10**(2), 123–179 (1993)
34. Rockt, T., Riedel, S.: Injecting logical background knowledge into embeddings for relation extraction. In: NAACL, pp. 1119–1129 (2014)
35. Steedman, M.: The syntactic process. Comput. Linguist. **131**(1), 146–148 (2000)
36. Unger, C., Ngomo, A.-C.N., Cabrio, E.: 6th open challenge on question answering over linked data (QALD-6). In: Sack, H., Dietze, S., Tordai, A., Lange, C. (eds.) SemWebEval 2016. CCIS, vol. 641, pp. 171–177. Springer, Cham (2016). doi:10.1007/978-3-319-46565-4_13
37. Usbeck, R., Röder, M., Ngonga Ngomo, A.C., Baron, C., Both, A., Brümmer, M., Ceccarelli, D., Cornolti, M., Cherix, D., Eickmann, B., et al.: Gerbil: general entity annotator benchmarking framework. In: Proceedings of the 24th International Conference on World Wide Web, pp. 1133–1143. International World Wide Web Conferences Steering Committee (2015)
38. Veyseh, A.P.B.: Cross-lingual question answering using common semantic space. In: TextGraphs@ NAACL-HLT, pp. 15–19 (2016)
39. Walter, S., Unger, C., Cimiano, P.: M-ATOLL: a framework for the lexicalization of ontologies in multiple languages. In: Mika, P., et al. (eds.) ISWC 2014. LNCS, vol. 8796, pp. 472–486. Springer, Cham (2014). doi:10.1007/978-3-319-11964-9_30
40. Walter, S., Unger, C., Cimiano, P.: Dblexipedia: A nucleus for a multilingual lexical semantic web. In: Proceedings of 3th International Workshop on NLP and DBpedia, co-located with the 14th International Semantic Web Conference (ISWC 2015), USA, 11–15 October 2015
41. Wick, M., Rohanimanesh, K., Culotta, A., McCallum, A.: SampleRank. Learning preferences from atomic gradients. In: NIPS Workshop on Advances in Ranking, pp. 1–5 (2009)
42. Wong, Y.W., Mooney, R.J.: Learning for semantic parsing with statistical machine translation. In: Proceedings of the main conference on Human Language Technology Conference of the North American Chapter of the ACL, pp. 439–446. ACL (2006)
43. Wong, Y.W., Mooney, R.J.: Learning synchronous grammars for semantic parsing with lambda calculus. In: Proceedings of ACL, vol. 45, p. 960 (2007)

44. Xu, K., Reddy, S., Feng, Y., Huang, S., Zhao, D.: Question answering on freebase via relation extraction and textual evidence. In: Proceedings of ACL, pp. 2326–2336 (2016)
45. Yih, W.T., Chang, M.W., He, X., Gao, J.: Semantic parsing via staged query graph generation: question answering with knowledge base. In: ACL, pp. 1321–1331 (2015)
46. Zettlemoyer, L.S., Collins, M.: Learning to map sentences to logical form: structured classification with probabilistic categorial grammars. In: 21st Conference on Uncertainty in Artificial Intelligence (2005)

Computing FO-Rewritings in $\mathcal{EL}$ in Practice: From Atomic to Conjunctive Queries

Peter Hansen and Carsten Lutz[(✉)]

University of Bremen, Bremen, Germany
{hansen,clu}@informatik.uni-bremen.de

Abstract. A prominent approach to implementing ontology-mediated queries (OMQs) is to rewrite into a first-order query, which is then executed using a conventional SQL database system. We consider the case where the ontology is formulated in the description logic $\mathcal{EL}$ and the actual query is a conjunctive query and show that rewritings of such OMQs can be efficiently computed in practice, in a sound and complete way. Our approach combines a reduction with a decomposed backwards chaining algorithm for OMQs that are based on the simpler atomic queries, also illuminating the relationship between first-order rewritings of OMQs based on conjunctive and on atomic queries. Experiments with real-world ontologies show promising results.

1 Introduction

One of the most important tools in ontology-mediated querying is *query rewriting*: reformulate a given ontology-mediated query (OMQ) in an equivalence-preserving way in a query language that is supported by a database system used to store the data. Since SQL is the dominating query language in conventional database systems, rewriting into SQL and into first-order logic (FO) as its logical core has attracted particularly much attention [3–7,10,12,15]. In fact, the DL-Lite family of description logics (DLs) was invented specifically with the aim to guarantee that FO-rewritings of OMQs (whose ontology is formulated in DL-Lite) always exist [1,7], but is rather restricted in expressive power. For essentially all other DLs, there are OMQs which cannot be equivalently rewritten into an FO query. However, ontologies used in real-world applications tend to have a very simple structure and, consequently, one may hope that FO-rewritings of practically relevant OMQs exist in the majority of cases. This hope was confirmed in an experimental evaluation carried out in the context of the $\mathcal{EL}$ family of description logics where less than 1% of the considered queries was found not to be FO-rewritable [12]; moreover, most of the negative cases seemed to be due to modeling mistakes in the ontology.

In this paper, we focus on the description logic $\mathcal{EL}$, which can be viewed as a logical core of the OWL EL profile of the OWL 2 ontology language [19]. We use $(\mathcal{L}, \mathcal{Q})$ to denote the OMQ language that consists of all OMQs where the ontology is formulated in the description logic $\mathcal{L}$ and the actual query is formulated in

© Springer International Publishing AG 2017
C. d'Amato et al. (Eds.): ISWC 2017, Part I, LNCS 10587, pp. 347–363, 2017.
DOI: 10.1007/978-3-319-68288-4_21

the query language $\mathcal{Q}$. Important choices for $\mathcal{Q}$ include *atomic queries (AQs)* and the much more expressive *conjunctive queries (CQs)*. It has been shown in [6] that for OMQs from $(\mathcal{EL}, \mathrm{AQ})$, it is EXPTIME-complete to decide FO-rewritability. Combining the techniques from [6] and the backwards chaining approach to query rewriting brought forward e.g. in [8,15], a practical algorithm for computing FO-rewritings of OMQs from $(\mathcal{EL}, \mathrm{AQ})$ was then developed in [12]. This algorithm is based on a *decomposed version* of backwards chaining that implements a form of structure sharing. It was implemented in the *Grind* system and shown to perform very well in practice [12]. It is important to remark that the algorithm is *complete*, that is, it computes an FO-rewriting whenever there is one and reports failure otherwise.

The aim of this paper is to devise a way to efficiently compute FO-rewritings of OMQs from $(\mathcal{EL}, \mathrm{CQ})$, and thus the challenge is to deal with conjunctive queries instead of only with atomic ones. Note that, as shown in [5], FO-rewritability in $(\mathcal{EL}, \mathrm{CQ})$ is still EXPTIME-complete. Our approach is to combine a reduction with the decomposed algorithm from [12], also illuminating the relationship between first-order rewritings of OMQs based on CQs and on AQs. It is worthwhile to point out that naive reductions of FO-rewritability in $(\mathcal{EL}, \mathrm{CQ})$ to FO-rewritability in $(\mathcal{EL}, \mathrm{AQ})$ fail. In particular, FO-rewritability of all AQs that occur in a CQ q are neither a sufficient nor a necessary condition for q to be FO-rewritable. As a simple example, consider the OMQ that consists of the ontology and query

$$\mathcal{O} = \{\exists r.A \sqsubseteq A, \ \exists s.\top \sqsubseteq A\} \quad \text{and} \quad q(x) = \exists y \, (A(x) \wedge s(x, y))$$

and which is FO-rewritable into $\exists y \, s(x, y)$, but the only AQ $A(x)$ that occurs in q is not FO-rewritable in the presence of $\mathcal{O}$.[1] In fact, it is not clear how to attain a reduction of FO-rewritability in $(\mathcal{EL}, \mathrm{CQ})$ to FO-rewritability in $(\mathcal{EL}, \mathrm{AQ})$, and even less so a polynomial time one. This leads us to considering mildly restricted forms of CQs and admitting reductions that make certain assumptions on the algorithm used to compute FO-rewritings in $(\mathcal{EL}, \mathrm{AQ})$—all of them are satisfied by the decomposed backwards chaining algorithm implemented in Grind.

We first consider the class of *tree-quantified CQs (tqCQs)* in which the quantified parts of the CQ form a collection of directed trees. In this case, we indeed achieve a polynomial time reduction to FO-rewritability in $(\mathcal{EL}, \mathrm{AQ})$. To also transfer actual FO-rewritings from the OMQ constructed in the reduction to the original OMQ, we make the assumption that the rewriting of the former takes the form of a UCQ (union of conjunctive queries) in which every CQ is tree-shaped and that, in a certain sense made precise in the paper, atoms are never introduced into the rewriting 'without a reason'. Both conditions are very natural in the context of backwards chaining and satisfied by the decomposed algorithm.

---

[1] OMQs also allow to fix the signature (set of concept and role names) that can occur in the ABox. In this example, we do not assume any restriction on the ABox signature.

We then move to *rooted CQs (rCQs)* in which every quantified variable must be reachable from some answer variable (in an undirected sense, in the query graph). We consider this a mild restriction and expect that almost all queries in practical applications will be rCQs. In the rCQ case, we do not achieve a 'black box' reduction. Instead, we assume that FO-rewritings of the constructed OMQs from $(\mathcal{EL}, \text{AQ})$ are obtained from a certain straightforward backwards chaining algorithm or a refinement thereof as implemented in the Grind system. We then show how to combine the construction of (several) OMQs from $(\mathcal{EL}, \text{AQ})$, similar to those constructed in the tqCQ case, with a modification of the assumed algorithm to decide FO-rewritability in $(\mathcal{EL}, \text{rCQ})$ and to construct actual rewritings. The approach involves exponential blowups, but only in parameters that we expect to be very small in practical cases and that, in particular, only depend on the actual query contained in the OMQ but not on the ontology.

We have implemented our approach in the Grind system and carried out experiments on five real-world ontologies with 10 hand-crafted CQs for each. The average runtimes are between 0.5 and 19s (depending on the ontology), which we consider very reasonable given that we are dealing with a complex static analysis problem.

Proofs are deferred to the appendix, which is made available at http://www. cs.uni-bremen.de/tdki/research/papers.html.

Related Work. We directly build on our prior work in [12] as discussed above, and to a lesser degree also on [5,6]. The latter line of work has recently been picked up in the context of existential rules [3]. The distinguishing features of our work are that (1) our algorithms are sound, complete, and terminating, that is, they find an FO-rewriting if there is one and report failure otherwise, and (2) we rely on the decomposed calculus from [12] that implements structure sharing for constructing small rewritings and achieving practical feasibility. We are not aware of other work that combines features (1) and (2) and is applicable to OMQs based on $\mathcal{EL}$. In the context of the description logic DL-Lite, though, the construction of small rewritings has received a lot of attention, see e.g. [11,13,21,22]. Producing small rewritings of OMQs whose ontology is a set of existential rules has been studied in [14], but there are no termination guarantees. Constructing small *Datalog*-rewritings of OMQs based on $\mathcal{EL}$, which are guaranteed to always exist, was studied e.g. in [9,20,24,25]. A different approach to answering $\mathcal{EL}$-based OMQs using SQL databases is the combined approach where the consequences of the ontology are materialized in the data [18,23].

2   Preliminaries

Let N_C, N_R, and N_I be countably infinite sets of *concept names*, *role names*, and *individual names*. An $\mathcal{EL}$-*concept* is formed according to the syntax rule

$$C, D ::= \top \mid A \mid C \sqcap D \mid \exists r.C$$

where A ranges over N_C and r over N_R. An $\mathcal{EL}$-*TBox* $\mathcal{T}$ is a finite set of *concept inclusions* $C \sqsubseteq D$, with C and D $\mathcal{EL}$-concepts. Throughout the paper, we use

$\mathcal{EL}$-TBoxes as ontologies. An *ABox* is a finite set of *concept assertions* $A(a)$ and *role assertions* $r(a, b)$ where a and b range over $\mathsf{N_I}$. We use $\mathsf{Ind}(\mathcal{A})$ to denote the set of individual names in the ABox $\mathcal{A}$. A *signature* is a set of concept and role names. When an ABox uses only symbols from a signature Σ, then we call it a Σ-*ABox*. To emphasize that a signature Σ is used to constrain the symbols admitted in ABoxes, we sometimes call Σ an *ABox signature*.

The semantics of concepts, TBoxes, and ABoxes is defined in the usual way, see [2]. We write $\mathcal{T} \models C \sqsubseteq D$ if the concept inclusion $C \sqsubseteq D$ is satisfied in every model of $\mathcal{T}$; when $\mathcal{T}$ is empty, we write $\models C \sqsubseteq D$. As usual in ontology-mediated querying, we make the *standard names assumption*, that is, an interpretation $\mathcal{I}$ satisfies a concept assertion $A(a)$ if $a \in A^{\mathcal{I}}$ and a role assertion $r(a, b)$ if $(a, b) \in r^{\mathcal{I}}$.

A *conjunctive query (CQ)* takes the form $q(\mathbf{x}) = \exists \mathbf{y}\, \varphi(\mathbf{x}, \mathbf{y})$ with $\mathbf{x}, \mathbf{y}$ tuples of variables and φ a conjunction of atoms of the form $A(x)$ and $r(x, y)$ that uses only variables from $\mathsf{var}(q) = \mathbf{x} \cup \mathbf{y}$. The variables $\mathbf{x}$ are the *answer variables* of q, denoted $\mathsf{avar}(q)$, and the *arity* of q is the length of $\mathbf{x}$. Unless noted otherwise, we allow equality in CQs, but we assume w.l.o.g. that equality atoms contain only answer variables, and that when $x = y$ is an equality atom in q, then y does not occur in any other atoms in q. Other occurrences of equality can be eliminated by identifying variables. An *atomic query (AQ)* is a conjunctive query of the form $A(x)$. A *union of conjunctive queries (UCQ)* is a disjunction of CQs that share the same answer variables.

An *ontology-mediated query (OMQ)* is a triple $Q = (\mathcal{T}, \Sigma, q)$ where $\mathcal{T}$ is a TBox, Σ an ABox signature, and q a CQ. We use $(\mathcal{EL}, \mathrm{AQ})$ to denote the set of OMQs where $\mathcal{T}$ is an $\mathcal{EL}$-TBox and q is an AQ, and similarly for $(\mathcal{EL}, \mathrm{CQ})$ and so on. We do generally not allow equality in CQs that are part of an OMQ. Let $Q = (\mathcal{T}, \Sigma, q)$ be an OMQ, $\mathcal{A}$ a Σ-ABox and $\mathbf{a} \subseteq \mathsf{Ind}(\mathcal{A})$. We write $\mathcal{A} \models Q(\mathbf{a})$ if $\mathcal{I} \models q(\mathbf{a})$ for all models $\mathcal{I}$ of $\mathcal{T}$ and $\mathcal{A}$. In this case, $\mathbf{a}$ is a *certain answer* to Q on $\mathcal{A}$.

Example 1. Consider an example from the medical domain. The following ABox holds data about patients and diagnoses:

$$\mathcal{A} = \{\mathsf{Person}(a), \mathsf{hasDisease}(a, oca_1), \mathsf{Albinism}(oca_1)\}$$

A TBox $\mathcal{T}_1$ is used to make domain knowledge available:

$$\mathcal{T}_1 = \{\mathsf{Albinism} \sqsubseteq \mathsf{HereditaryDisease},$$
$$\mathsf{Person} \sqcap \exists \mathsf{hasDisease}.\mathsf{HereditaryDisease} \sqsubseteq \mathsf{GeneticRiskPatient}\}$$

Let Q_1 be the OMQ $(\mathcal{T}_1, \Sigma_{\mathsf{full}}, q_1(x))$, where $q_1(x) = \mathsf{GeneticRiskPatient}(x)$, and Σ_{full} contains all concept and role names. It can be verified that $\mathcal{A} \models Q_1(a)$. ⊣

We do not distinguish between a CQ and the set of atoms in it and associate with each CQ q a directed graph $G_q := (\mathsf{var}(q), \{(x, y) \mid r(x, y) \in q\})$ (equality atoms are not reflected). A CQ q is *tree-shaped* if G_q is a directed tree and $r(x, y), s(x, y) \in q$ implies $r = s$. A *tree CQ (tCQ)* is a tree-shaped CQ with the root the only answer variable and a *tree UCQ (tUCQ)* is a disjunction of tree CQs. Every $\mathcal{EL}$-concept can be viewed as a tree-shaped CQ and vice versa; for example, the $\mathcal{EL}$-concept $A \sqcap \exists r.(B \sqcap \exists s.A)$ corresponds to the CQ $q(x) = \exists y, z\, A(x) \wedge r(x,y) \wedge B(y) \wedge s(y,z) \wedge A(z)$. We will not always distinguish between the two representations and even mix them. We might thus write $\exists r.q$ to denote an $\mathcal{EL}$-concept when q is a tree-shaped CQ; if $q(x)$ is as in the example just given, then $\exists r.q$ is the $\mathcal{EL}$-concept $\exists r.(A \sqcap \exists r.(B \sqcap \exists s.A))$. If convenient, we also view a CQ q as an ABox $\mathcal{A}_q$ which is obtained from q by dropping equality atoms and then replacing each variable with an individual (not distinguishing answer variables from quantified variables). A *rooted CQ (rCQ)* is a CQ q such that in the undirected graph induced by G_q, every quantified variable is reachable from some answer variable. A *tree-quantified CQ (tqCQ)* is an rCQ q such that after removing all atoms $r(x,y)$ with $x,y \in \mathsf{avar}(q)$, we obtain a disjoint union of tCQs. We call these tCQs the *tCQs in q*. For example, $q(x_1,x_2) = \exists y_1, y_2\, r(x_1,x_2) \wedge r(x_2,x_1) \wedge r(x_1,y_1) \wedge s(x_2,y_2)$ is a tqCQ and the tCQs in q are $\exists y_1\, r(x_1,y_1)$ and $\exists y_2\, s(x_2,y_2)$; by adding to q the atom $r(y_1,y_2)$, we obtain an rCQ that is not a tqCQ.

An OMQ $Q = (\mathcal{T}, \Sigma, q)$ is *FO-rewritable* if there is a first-order (FO) formula φ such that $\mathcal{A} \models Q(\mathbf{a})$ iff $\mathcal{A} \models \varphi(\mathbf{a})$ for all Σ-ABoxes $\mathcal{A}$. In this case, φ is an *FO-rewriting* of Q. When φ happens to be a UCQ, we speak of a *UCQ-rewriting* and likewise for other classes of queries. It is known that FO-rewritability coincides with UCQ-rewritability for OMQs from $(\mathcal{EL}, \mathrm{CQ})$ [4,6]; note that equality is important here as, for example, the OMQ $(\{B \sqsubseteq \exists r.A\}, \{B,r\}, q)$ with $q(x,y) = \exists z(r(x,z) \wedge r(y,z) \wedge A(z))$ rewrites into the UCQ $q \vee (B(x) \wedge x = y)$, but not into an UCQ that does not use equality.

Example 2. We extend the TBox $\mathcal{T}_1$ from Example 1 to additionally describe the hereditary nature of genetic defects:

$$\mathcal{T}_2 := \mathcal{T}_1 \cup \{\mathsf{Person} \sqcap \exists\mathsf{hasParent}.\mathsf{GeneticRiskPatient} \sqsubseteq \mathsf{GeneticRiskPatient}\}.$$

The OMQ $Q_1' = (\mathcal{T}_2, \Sigma_{\mathsf{full}}, q_1(x))$ with $q_1(x)$ as in Example 1, is not FO-rewritable, intuitively because it expresses unbounded reachability along the hasParent role. In contrast, consider the OMQ $Q_2 = (\mathcal{T}_2, \Sigma_{\mathsf{full}}, q_2(x))$ where $q_2(x) = \exists y\, \mathsf{GeneticRiskPatient}(x) \wedge \mathsf{hasDisease}(x,y) \wedge \mathsf{Albinism}(y)$. Even though q_2 is an extension of q_1 with additional atoms, Q_2 is FO-rewritable, with $\varphi(x) = q_2(x) \vee (\exists y\, \mathsf{Person}(x) \wedge \mathsf{hasDisease}(x,y) \wedge \mathsf{Albinism}(y))$ a concrete rewriting. $\dashv$

We shall sometimes refer to the problem of *(query) containment* between two OMQs $Q_1 = (\mathcal{T}_1, \Sigma, q_1)$ and $Q_2 = (\mathcal{T}_2, \Sigma, q_2)$; we say Q_1 *is contained in* Q_2 if $\mathcal{A} \models Q_1(\mathbf{a})$ implies $\mathcal{A} \models Q_2(\mathbf{a})$ for all Σ-ABoxes $\mathcal{A}$ and $\mathbf{a} \subseteq \mathsf{Ind}(\mathcal{A})$. If both OMQs are from $(\mathcal{EL}, \mathrm{rCQ})$ and $\mathcal{T}_1 = \mathcal{T}_2 = \mathcal{T}$, then we denote this with $q_1 \subseteq_{\mathcal{T}} q_2$.

We now introduce two more technical notions that are central to the constructions in Sect. 4. Both notions have been used before in the context of ontology-mediated querying, see for example [16,17]. They are illustrated in Example 3 below.

Definition 1 (Fork rewriting). *Let q_0 be a CQ. Obtaining a CQ q from q_0 by fork elimination means to select two atoms $r(x_0, y)$ and $r(x_1, y)$ with y an existentially quantified variable, then to replace every occurrence of x_{1-i} in q with x_i, where $i \in \{0, 1\}$ is chosen such that x_i is an answer variable if any of x_0, x_1 is an answer variable, and to finally add the atom $x_i = x_{1-i}$ if x_{1-i} is an answer variable. When q can be obtained from q_0 by repeated (but not necessarily exhaustive) fork elimination, then q is a fork rewriting of q_0.*

For a CQ q and $V \subseteq \mathsf{var}(q)$, we use $q|_V$ to denote the restriction of q to the variables in V, that is, $q|_V$ is the set of atoms in q that use only variables from V.

Definition 2 (Splitting). *Let $\mathcal{T}$ be an $\mathcal{EL}$-TBox, q a CQ, and $\mathcal{A}$ an ABox. A splitting of q w.r.t. $\mathcal{A}$ and $\mathcal{T}$ is a tuple $\Pi = \langle R, S_1, \ldots, S_\ell, r_1, \ldots, r_\ell, \mu, \nu \rangle$, where $R, S_1, \ldots, S_n$ is a partitioning of $\mathsf{var}(q)$, $r_1, \ldots, r_\ell$ are role names, $\mu : \{1, \ldots, \ell\} \to R$ assigns to each set S_i a variable from R, $\nu : R \to \mathsf{Ind}(\mathcal{A})$ assigns to each variable from R and individual name from $\mathcal{A}$, and the following conditions are satisfied:*

1. *$\mathsf{avar}(q) \subseteq R$ and $x = y \in q$ implies $\nu(x) = \nu(y)$;*
2. *if $r(x, y) \in q$ with $x, y \in R$, then $r(\nu(x), \nu(y)) \in \mathcal{A}$;*
3. *$q|_{S_i}$ is tree-shaped and can thus be seen as an $\mathcal{EL}$-concept $C_{q|S_i}$, for $1 \le i \le \ell$;*
4. *if $r(x, x') \in q$ then either (i) x, x' belong to the same set $R, S_1, \ldots, S_\ell$, or (ii) $x \in R$ and, for some i, $r = r_i$ and x' root of $q|_{S_i}$.*

The following lemma illustrates the combined use and raison d'être of both fork rewritings and splittings. A proof is standard and omitted, see for example [17]. It does rely on the existence of *forest models* for ABoxes and $\mathcal{EL}$-TBoxes, that is, for every ABox $\mathcal{A}$ and TBox $\mathcal{T}$, there is a model $\mathcal{I}$ whose shape is that of $\mathcal{A}$ with a directed (potentially infinite) tree attached to each individual.

Lemma 1. *Let $Q = (\mathcal{T}, \Sigma, q_0)$ be an OMQ from $(\mathcal{EL}, CQ)$, $\mathcal{A}$ a Σ-ABox, and $\mathbf{a} \subseteq \mathsf{Ind}(\mathcal{A})$. Then $\mathcal{A} \models Q(\mathbf{a})$ iff there exists a fork rewriting q of q_0 and a splitting $\langle R, S_1, \ldots, S_\ell, r_1, \ldots, r_\ell, \mu, \nu \rangle$ of q w.r.t. $\mathcal{A}$ and $\mathcal{T}$ such that the following conditions are satisfied:*

1. *$\nu(\mathbf{x}) = \mathbf{a}$, $\mathbf{x}$ the answer variables of q_0;*
2. *if $A(x) \in q$ and $x \in R$, then $\mathcal{A}, \mathcal{T} \models A(\nu(x))$;*
3. *$\mathcal{A}, \mathcal{T} \models \exists r_i . C_{q|S_i}(\nu(\mu(i)))$ for $1 \le i \le \ell$.*

Example 3. To illustrate the described notions, consider the following CQ.

$$q_3(x) = \exists y_1, y_2, z \; \mathsf{Person}(x) \wedge$$
$$\mathsf{hasDisease}(x, y_1) \wedge \mathsf{MelaminDeficiency}(y_1) \wedge \mathsf{causedBy}(y_1, z) \wedge$$
$$\mathsf{hasDisease}(x, y_2) \wedge \mathsf{ImpairedVision}(y_2) \wedge \mathsf{causedBy}(y_2, z) \wedge$$
$$\mathsf{GeneDefect}(z)$$

It asks for persons suffering from two conditions connected with the same gene defect. Let the ABox $\mathcal{A}$ consist only of the assertion $\mathsf{OCA1aPatient}(a)$. We extend the TBox $\mathcal{T}_2$ from Example 2, as follows:

$$\mathcal{T}_3 := \mathcal{T}_2 \cup \{\mathsf{OCA1aPatient} \sqsubseteq \mathsf{Person} \sqcap \mathsf{hasDisease.OCA1aAlbinism}$$
$$\mathsf{OCA1aAlbinism} \sqsubseteq \mathsf{ImpairedVision} \sqcap \mathsf{MelaninDeficiency}$$
$$\mathsf{OCA1aAlbinism} \sqsubseteq \exists \mathsf{causedBy.GeneDefect}\}$$

Let $Q = (\mathcal{T}_3, \Sigma_{\mathsf{full}}, q_3(x))$. It can be verified that $\mathcal{A} \models Q(a)$. By Lemma 1, this is witnessed by a fork rewriting and a splitting Π. The fork rewriting is

$$q_3'(x) = \exists y_1, z\, \mathsf{Person}(x) \wedge$$
$$\mathsf{hasDisease}(x, y_1) \wedge \mathsf{MelaminDeficiency}(y_1) \wedge \mathsf{ImpairedVision}(y_1) \wedge$$
$$\mathsf{causedBy}(y_1, z) \wedge \mathsf{GeneDefect}(z)$$

The splitting $\Pi = \langle R, S_1, r_1, \mu, \nu \rangle$ of q_3' wrt. $\mathcal{A}$ and $\mathcal{T}_3$ is defined by setting

$$R = \{x\},\ S_1 = \{y_1, z\},\ r_1 = \mathsf{hasDisease},\ \mu(1) = x,\ \nu = (x \mapsto a)$$

It can be verified that the conditions given in Lemma 1 are satisfied.   ⊣

3 Tree-Quantified CQs

We reduce FO-rewritability in $(\mathcal{EL}, \mathrm{tqCQ})$ to FO-rewritability in $(\mathcal{EL}, \mathrm{AQ})$ and, making only very mild assumptions on the algorithm used for solving the latter problem, show that rewritings of the OMQs produced in the reduction can be transformed in a straightforward way into rewritings of the original OMQ. The mild assumptions are that the algorithm produces a tUCQ-rewriting and that, informally, when constructing the tCQs of the tUCQ-rewriting it never introduces atoms 'without a reason'—this will be made precise later.

Let $Q = (\mathcal{T}, \Sigma, q_0)$ be from $(\mathcal{EL}, \mathrm{tqCQ})$. We can assume w.l.o.g. that q_0 contains only answer variables: every tCQ in q with root x can be represented as an $\mathcal{EL}$-concept C and we can replace the tree with the atom $A_C(x)$ (unless it has only a single node) and extend $\mathcal{T}$ with $C \sqsubseteq A_C$ where A_C is a fresh concept name that is not included in Σ. Clearly, the resulting OMQ is equivalent to the original one.

Let Q be an OMQ from $(\mathcal{EL}, \mathrm{tqCQ})$. We show how to construct an OMQ $Q' = (\mathcal{T}', \Sigma', q_0')$ from $(\mathcal{EL}, \mathrm{AQ})$ with the announced properties; in particular, Q is FO-rewritable if and only if Q' is. Let $\mathsf{CN}(\mathcal{T})$ and $\mathsf{RN}(\mathcal{T})$ denote the set of concept names and role names that occur in $\mathcal{T}$, and let sub_L denote the set of concepts that occur on the left-hand side of a concept inclusion in $\mathcal{T}$, closed under subconcepts. Reserve a fresh concept name A^x for every $A \in \mathsf{CN}(\mathcal{T})$ and $x \in \mathsf{avar}(q_0)$, and a fresh role name r^x for every $r \in \mathsf{RN}(\mathcal{T})$ and $x \in \mathsf{avar}(q_0)$. Set

$$\Sigma' = \Sigma \cup \{A^x \mid A \in \mathsf{CN}(\mathcal{T}) \cap \Sigma \text{ and } x \in \mathsf{avar}(q_0)\}$$
$$\cup \{r^x \mid r \in \mathsf{RN}(\mathcal{T}) \cap \Sigma \text{ and } x \in \mathsf{avar}(q_0)\}.$$

Additionally reserve a concept name $A^x_{\exists r.E}$ for every concept $\exists r.E \in \mathsf{sub}_L(\mathcal{T})$ and every $x \in \mathsf{avar}(q_0)$. Define

$$\mathcal{T}' := \mathcal{T} \cup \{C^x_L \sqsubseteq D^x_R \mid x \in \mathsf{var}(q_0) \text{ and } C \sqsubseteq D \in \mathcal{T}\}$$
$$\cup \{\exists r^x.C \sqsubseteq A^x_{\exists r.C} \mid x \in \mathsf{var}(q_0) \text{ and } \exists r.C \in \mathsf{sub}_L(\mathcal{T})\}$$
$$\cup \{C^y_L \sqsubseteq A^x_{\exists r.C} \mid r(x,y) \in q_0 \text{ and } \exists r.C \in \mathsf{sub}_L(\mathcal{T})\}$$
$$\cup \{\underset{A(x)\in q_0}{\sqcap} A^x \sqsubseteq N\}$$

where for a concept $C = A_1 \sqcap \cdots \sqcap A_n \sqcap \exists r_1.E_1 \sqcap \cdots \sqcap \exists r_m.E_m$, the concepts C^x_L and C^x_R are given by

$$C^x_L = A^x_1 \sqcap \cdots \sqcap A^x_n \sqcap A^x_{\exists r_1.E_1} \sqcap \cdots \sqcap A^x_{\exists r_m.E_m}$$
$$C^x_R = A^x_1 \sqcap \cdots \sqcap A^x_n \sqcap \exists r^x_1.E_1 \sqcap \cdots \sqcap \exists r^x_m.E_m$$

Moreover, set $q'_0 := N(x)$.

Example 4. Consider the OMQ $Q = (\mathcal{T}_1, \Sigma_{\mathsf{full}}, q(x,y))$ with $\mathcal{T}_1$ as in Example 1 and let $q(x,y)$ the following tqCQ:[2]

$$q(x,y) = \exists z\, \mathsf{GeneticRiskPatient}(x) \wedge \mathsf{hasDisease}(x,y) \wedge$$
$$\mathsf{Disease}(y) \wedge \mathsf{hasDisease}(x,z) \wedge \mathsf{Albinism}(z)$$

We first remove quantified variables: all atoms that contain the variable z are replaced by $A_{\exists\mathsf{hasDisease.Albinism}}(y)$, and the TBox is extended with the inclusion $\exists\mathsf{hasDisease.Albinism} \sqsubseteq A_{\exists\mathsf{hasDisease.Albinism}}$. We then construct $\mathcal{T}'_1$, which we give here only partially. The final concept inclusion in $\mathcal{T}_1$ is

$$\mathsf{GeneticRiskPatient}^x \sqcap \mathsf{Disease}^y \sqcap A^x_{\exists\mathsf{hasDisease.Albinism}} \sqsubseteq N,$$

representing the updated query without role atoms; for example, the concept name $\mathsf{Disease}^y$ stands for the atom $\mathsf{Disease}(y)$. Among others, $\mathcal{T}'_1$ contains the further concept inclusions

$$\exists\mathsf{hasDisease}^x.\mathsf{HereditaryDisease} \sqsubseteq A^x_{\exists\mathsf{hasDisease.HereditaryDisease}}$$
$$\mathsf{HereditaryDisease}^y \sqsubseteq A^x_{\exists\mathsf{hasDisease.HereditaryDisease}}$$

where, intuitively, the lower concept inclusion captures that case that the truth of the concept $\exists\mathsf{hasDisease.HereditaryDisease}$ is witnessed at y (the role atom $\mathsf{hasDisease}(x,y)$ from q is only implicit here) while the upper concept inclusion deals with other witnesses.   ⊣

Before proving that the constructed OMQ Q' behaves in the desired way, we give some preliminaries. It is known that, if an OMQ from $(\mathcal{EL}, \mathsf{AQ})$ has an FO-rewriting, then it has a tUCQ-rewriting, see for example [6,12]. A tCQ q is *conformant* if it satisfies the following properties:

---

[2] We only use here that $\mathcal{T}_1$ contains the concept $\exists\mathsf{hasDisease.HereditaryDisease}$ on the left-hand side of a concept inclusion.

1. if $A(x)$ is a concept atom, then either A is of the form B^y and x is the answer variable or A is not of this form and x is a quantified variable;
2. if $r(x, y)$ is a role atom, then either r is of the form s^z and x is the answer variable or r is not of this form and x is a quantified variable.

A *conformant tUCQ* is then defined in the expected way. The notion of conformance captures what we informally described as never introducing atoms into the rewriting 'without a reason'. By the following lemma, FO-rewritability of the OMQs constructed in our reduction implies conformant tUCQ-rewritability, that is, there is indeed no reason to introduce any of the atoms that are forbidden in conformant rewritings.

Lemma 2. *Let Q be from $(\mathcal{EL}, tqCQ)$ and Q' the OMQ constructed from Q as above. If Q' is FO-rewritable, then it is rewritable into a conformant tUCQ.*

When started on an OMQ produced by our reduction, the algorithms presented in [12] and implemented in the Grind system produce a conformant tUCQ-rewriting. Indeed, this can be expected of any reasonable algorithm based on backwards chaining. Let q' be a conformant tUCQ-rewriting of Q'. The *corresponding UCQ for Q* is the UCQ q obtained by taking each CQ from q', replacing every atom $A^x(x_0)$ with $A(x)$ and every atom $r^x(x_0, y)$ with $r(x, y)$, and adding all atoms $r(x, y)$ from q_0 such that both x and y are answer variables. The answer variables in q are those of q_0. Observe that q is a union of tqCQs.

Proposition 1. *Q is FO-rewritable iff Q' is FO-rewritable. Moreover, if q' is a conformant tUCQ-rewriting of Q' and q the corresponding UCQ for Q, then q is a rewriting of Q.*

The proof strategy is to establish the 'moreover' part and to additionally show how certain UCQ-rewritings of Q can be converted into UCQ-rewritings of Q'. More precisely, a CQ q is a *derivative* of q_0 if it results from q_0 by exchanging atoms $A(x)$ for $\mathcal{EL}$-concepts C, seen as tree-shaped CQs rooted in x. We are going to prove the following lemma in Sect. 4.

Lemma 3. *If an OMQ $(\mathcal{T}, \Sigma, q_0)$ from $(\mathcal{EL}, tqCQ)$ is FO-rewritable, then it has a UCQ-rewriting in which each CQ is a derivative of q_0.*

Let q be a UCQ in which every CQ is a derivative of q_0. Then the *corresponding UCQ for Q'* is the UCQ q' obtained by taking each CQ from q, replacing every atom $A(x)$, x answer variable, with $A^x(x_0)$, every atom $r(x, y)$, x answer variable and y quantified variable, with $r^x(x_0, y)$, and deleting all atoms $r(x_1, x_2)$, x_1, x_2 answer variables. The answer variable in q' is x_0. Note that q' is a tUCQ. To establish the "only if" direction of Proposition 1, we show that when q is a UCQ-rewriting of Q in which every CQ is a derivative of the query q_0, then the corresponding UCQ for Q' is a rewriting of Q'.

4   Rooted CQs

We consider OMQs based on rCQs, a strict generalization of tqCQs. In this case, we are not going to achieve a 'black box' reduction, but rely on a concrete algorithm for solving FO-rewritability in $(\mathcal{EL}, \mathrm{AQ})$. This algorithm is a straightforward and not necessarily terminating backwards chaining algorithm or a (potentially terminating) refinement thereof, as implemented in the Grind system. We show how to combine the construction of (several) OMQs from $(\mathcal{EL}, \mathrm{AQ})$ with a modification of the assumed algorithm to decide FO-rewritability in $(\mathcal{EL}, \mathrm{rCQ})$ and to construct actual rewritings.

We start with introducing the straightforward backwards chaining algorithm mentioned above which we refer to as $\mathsf{bc_{AQ}}$. Central to $\mathsf{bc_{AQ}}$ is a backwards chaining step based on concept inclusions in the TBox used in the OMQ. Let C and D be $\mathcal{EL}$-concepts, $E \sqsubseteq F$ a concept inclusion, and $x \in \mathsf{var}(C)$ (where C is viewed as a tree-shaped CQ). Then D is *obtained from C by applying $E \sqsubseteq F$ at x* if D can be obtained from C by

- removing $A(x)$ for all concept names A with $\models F \sqsubseteq A$;
- removing $r(x, y)$ and the tree-shaped CQ G rooted at y when $\models F \sqsubseteq \exists r.G$;
- adding $A(x)$ for all concept names A that occur in E as a top-level conjunct (that is, that are not nested inside existential restrictions);
- adding $\exists r.G$ as a CQ with root x, for each $\exists r.G$ that is a top-level conjunct of E.

Let C and D be $\mathcal{EL}$-concepts. We write $D \prec C$ if D can be obtained from C by removing an existential restriction (not necessarily on top level, and potentially resulting in $D = \top$ when C is of the form $\exists r.E$). We use $\prec^*$ to denote the reflexive and transitive closure of $\prec$ and say that D is $\prec$-*minimal with* $\mathcal{T} \models D \sqsubseteq A_0$ if $\mathcal{T} \models D \sqsubseteq A_0$ and there is no $D' \prec D$ with $\mathcal{T} \models D' \sqsubseteq A_0$.

Now we are in the position to describe algorithm $\mathsf{bc_{AQ}}$. It maintains a set M of $\mathcal{EL}$-concepts that represent tCQs. Let $Q = (\mathcal{T}, \Sigma, A_0)$ be from $(\mathcal{EL}, \mathrm{AQ})$. Starting from the set $M = \{A_0\}$, it exhaustively performs the following steps:

1. find $C \in M$, $x \in \mathsf{var}(C)$, a concept inclusion $E \sqsubseteq F \in \mathcal{T}$, and D, such that D is obtained from C by applying $E \sqsubseteq F$ at x;
2. find $D' \prec^* D$ that is $\prec$-minimal with $\mathcal{T} \models D' \sqsubseteq A_0$, and add D' to M.

Application of these steps might not terminate. We use $\mathsf{bc_{AQ}}(Q)$ to denote the potentially infinitary UCQ $\bigvee M|_\Sigma$ where M is the set obtained in the limit and $q|_\Sigma$ denotes the restriction of the UCQ q to those disjuncts that only use symbols from Σ. Note that, in Point 2, it is possible to find the desired D' in polynomial time since the subsumption '$\mathcal{T} \models D' \sqsubseteq A_0$' can be decided in polynomial time. The following is standard to prove, see [12, 15] and Lemma 5 below for similar results.

Lemma 4. *Let Q be an OMQ from $(\mathcal{EL}, \mathrm{AQ})$. If $\mathsf{bc}_{AQ}(Q)$ is finite, then it is a UCQ-rewriting of Q. Otherwise, Q is not FO-rewritable.*

Example 5. Consider the TBox

$$\mathcal{T} = \{\text{Person} \sqcap \exists \text{hasParent.GeneticRiskPatient} \sqsubseteq \text{GeneticRiskPatient}\}$$

and let $Q = (\mathcal{T}, \Sigma, \text{GeneticRiskPatient}(x))$ with $\Sigma = \{\text{Person}, \text{GeneticRiskPatient}\}$. Note that the role name hasParent does not occur in Σ. Even though the set M generated by bc_{AQ} (in the limit of its non-terminating run) is infinite, $\text{bc}_{\text{AQ}}(Q) = \text{GeneticRiskPatient}(x)$ is finite and a UCQ-rewriting of Q. ⊣

The algorithm for deciding FO-rewritability in $(\mathcal{EL}, \text{AQ})$ presented in [12] and underlying the Grind system can be seen as a refinement of bc_{AQ}. Indeed, that algorithm always terminates and returns $\bigvee M|_\Sigma$ if that UCQ is finite and reports non-FO-rewritability otherwise. Moreover, the UCQ-rewriting is represented in a decomposed way and output as a non-recursive Datalog program for efficiency and succinctness. For our purposes, the only important aspect is that, when started on an FO-rewritable OMQ, it computes (a non-recursive Datalog program that is equivalent to) the UCQ-rewriting $\bigvee M|_\Sigma$.

We next introduce a generalized version bc_{AQ}^+ of bc_{AQ} that takes as input an OMQ $Q = (\mathcal{T}, \Sigma, A_0)$ from $(\mathcal{EL}, \text{AQ})$ and an additional $\mathcal{EL}$-TBox $\mathcal{T}^{\min}$, such that termination and output of bc_{AQ}^+ agrees with that of bc_{AQ} when the input satisfies $\mathcal{T}^{\min} = \mathcal{T}$. Starting from $M = \{A_0\}$, algorithm bc_{AQ}^+ exhaustively performs the following steps:

1. find $C \in M$, $x \in \text{var}(C)$, a concept inclusion $E \sqsubseteq F \in \mathcal{T}$, and D, such that D is obtained from C by applying $E \sqsubseteq F$ at x;
2. find $D' \prec^* D$ that is $\prec$-minimal with $\mathcal{T}^{\min} \models D' \sqsubseteq A_0$, and add D' to M.

We use $\text{bc}_{\text{AQ}}^+(Q, \mathcal{T}^{\min})$ to denote the potentially infinitary UCQ $\bigvee M|_\Sigma$, M obtained in the limit. Note that bc_{AQ}^+ uses the TBox $\mathcal{T}$ for backwards chaining and $\mathcal{T}^{\min}$ for minimization while bc_{AQ} uses $\mathcal{T}$ for both purposes. The refined version of bc_{AQ} implemented in the Grind system can easily be adapted to behave like a terminating version of bc_{AQ}^+.

Our aim is to convert an OMQ $Q = (\mathcal{T}, \Sigma, q_0)$ from $(\mathcal{EL}, \text{rCQ})$ into a set of pairs $(Q', \mathcal{T}^{\min})$ with Q' an OMQ from $(\mathcal{EL}, \text{AQ})$ and $\mathcal{T}^{\min}$ an $\mathcal{EL}$-TBox such that Q is FO-rewritable iff $\text{bc}_{\text{AQ}}^+(Q', \mathcal{T}^{\min})$ terminates for all pairs $(Q', \mathcal{T}^{\min})$ and, moreover, if this is the case, then the resulting UCQ-rewritings can straightforwardly be converted into a rewriting of Q.

Let $Q = (\mathcal{T}, \Sigma, q_0)$. We construct one pair $(Q_{q_r}, \mathcal{T}_{q_r}^{\min})$ for each fork rewriting q_r of q_0. We use $\text{core}(q_r)$ to denote the minimal set V of variables that contains all answer variables in q_r and such that after removing all atoms $r(x,y)$ with $x, y \in V$, we obtain a disjoint union of tree-shaped CQs. We call these CQs the *trees in* q_r. Intuitively, we separate the tree-shaped parts of q_r from the cyclic part, the latter identified by $\text{core}(q_r)$. This is similar to the definition of tqCQs where, however, cycles cannot involve any quantified variables. In a forest model of an ABox and a TBox as mentioned before Lemma 1, the variables in $\text{core}(q_r)$

must be mapped to the ABox part of the model (rather than to the trees attached to it). Now $(Q_{q_r}, \mathcal{T}_{q_r}^{\min})$ is defined by setting $Q_{q_r} = (\mathcal{T}_{q_r}, \Sigma_{q_r}, N(x))$ and

$$\mathcal{T}_{q_r} = \mathcal{T} \cup \{C_R^x \sqsubseteq D_R^x \mid x \in \mathsf{core}(q_r), C \sqsubseteq D \in \mathcal{T}\}$$
$$\cup \{\underset{C(x) \text{ a tree in } q_r}{\bigsqcap} C_R^x \sqsubseteq N\}$$

where C_R^x is defined as in Sect. 3, and Σ_{q_r} is the extension of Σ with all concept names A^x and role names r^x used in $\mathcal{T}_{q_r}$ such that $A, r \in \Sigma$.

It remains to define $\mathcal{T}_{q_r}^{\min}$, which is $\mathcal{T}_{q_r}$ extended with one concept inclusion for each fork rewriting q of q_0 and each splitting $\Pi = \langle R, S_1, \ldots, S_\ell, r_1, \ldots, r_\ell, \mu, \nu \rangle$ of q w.r.t. $\mathcal{A}_{q_r}$, as follows. For each $x \in \mathsf{avar}(q_r)$, the equality atoms in q_r give rise to an equivalence class $[x]_{q_r}$ of answer variables, defined in the expected way. We only consider the splitting Π of q if it preserves answer variables modulo equality, that is, if $x \in \mathsf{avar}(q)$, then there is a $y \in [x]_{q_r}$ such that $\nu(x) = y$. We then add the inclusion

$$\left(\underset{\substack{A(x) \in q \\ \text{with } x \in R}}{\bigsqcap} A^{\nu(x)} \right) \sqcap \left(\underset{1 \leq i \leq \ell}{\bigsqcap} \exists r_i^{\nu(\mu(i))}.C_{q|S_i} \right) \sqsubseteq N$$

It can be shown that, summing up over all fork rewritings and splittings, only polynomially many concepts $\exists r_i^{\nu(\mu(i))}.C_{q|S_i}$ are introduced (this is similar to the proof of Lemma 6 in [17]). Note that we do not introduce fresh concept names of the form $A_{\exists r.C}^x$ as in Sect. 3. This is not necessary here because of the use of fork rewritings and splittings in $\mathcal{T}^{\min}$.

Example 6. Consider query q_3 from Example 3 and TBox $\mathcal{T}_1$ from Example 1. Constructing $\mathcal{T}_{q_3}$ (thus considering q_3 as a fork rewriting of itself) would add concept inclusions like

$$\mathsf{Person}^x \sqcap \exists \mathsf{hasDisease}^x.\mathsf{HereditaryDisease} \sqsubseteq \mathsf{GeneticRiskPatient}^x$$

The final concept inclusion added is the following, listing concepts needed at x, y_1, y_2, and z that result in a match of q_3:

$$\mathsf{Person}^x \sqcap \mathsf{MelaminDeficiency}^{y_1} \sqcap \mathsf{ImpairedVision}^{y_2} \sqcap \mathsf{GeneDefect}^z \sqsubseteq N$$

When building the TBox $\mathcal{T}_{q_3}^{\min}$, it is necessary to look for matches of q_3 by a splitting Π of a fork rewriting of q_3 w.r.t. $\mathcal{A}_{q_3}$ and $\mathcal{T}_1$. We consider here the splitting $\Pi = \langle R, S_1, r_1, \mu, \nu \rangle$ of the fork rewriting q_3' of q_3 given in Example 3, defined by setting

$$R = \{x\}, \ S_1 = \{y_1, z\}, \ r_1 = \mathsf{hasDisease}, \ \mu(1) = x, \ \nu = (x \mapsto x)$$

For Π, the following concept inclusion is added to $\mathcal{T}_{q_3}^{\min}$:

$$\mathsf{Person}^x \sqcap \exists \mathsf{hasDisease}^x.(\mathsf{MelaminDeficiency} \sqcap \mathsf{ImpairedVision} \sqcap$$
$$\mathsf{causedBy}.\mathsf{GeneDefect}) \sqsubseteq N \qquad \dashv$$

It can be seen that when $\mathrm{bc}^+_{\mathrm{AQ}}(Q_{q_r}, \mathcal{T}^{\min}_{q_r})$ is finite, then it is a conformant tUCQ in the sense of Sect. 3. Thus, we can also define a *corresponding UCQ q for Q* as in that section, that is, q is obtained by taking each CQ from q', replacing every atom $A^x(x_0)$ with $A(x)$ and every atom $r^x(x_0, y)$ with $r(x, y)$, and adding all atoms $r(x, y)$ from q_r such that $x, y \in \mathsf{core}(q_r)$. The answer variables in q are those of q_0.

Proposition 2. *Let $Q = (\mathcal{T}, \Sigma, q_0)$ be an OMQ from $(\mathcal{EL}, r\mathrm{CQ})$. If $\mathrm{bc}^+_{\mathrm{AQ}}(Q_{q_r}, \mathcal{T}^{\min}_{q_r})$ is finite for all fork rewritings q_r of q_0, then $\bigvee_{q_r} \widehat{q}_{q_r}$ is a UCQ-rewriting of Q, where $\widehat{q}_{q_r}$ is the UCQ for Q that corresponds to $\mathrm{bc}^+_{\mathrm{AQ}}(Q_{q_r}, \mathcal{T}^{\min}_{q_r})$. Otherwise, Q is not FO-rewritable.*

To prove Proposition 2, we introduce a backwards chaining algorithm $\mathrm{bc}_{r\mathrm{CQ}}$ for computing UCQ-rewritings of OMQs from $(\mathcal{EL}, r\mathrm{CQ})$ that we refer to as $\mathrm{bc}_{r\mathrm{CQ}}$. In a sense, $\mathrm{bc}_{r\mathrm{CQ}}$ is the natural generalization of $\mathrm{bc}_{\mathrm{AQ}}$ to rCQs. We then show a correspondence between the run of $\mathrm{bc}_{r\mathrm{CQ}}$ on the input OMQ Q from $(\mathcal{EL}, r\mathrm{CQ})$ and the runs of $\mathrm{bc}^+_{\mathrm{AQ}}$ on the constructed inputs of the form $(Q_{q_r}, \mathcal{T}^{\min}_{q_r})$.

On the way, we also provide the missing proof for Lemma 3, which in fact is a consequence of the correctness of $\mathrm{bc}_{r\mathrm{CQ}}$ (stated as Lemma 5 in the appendix) and the observation that, when $Q = (\mathcal{T}, \Sigma, q_0)$ is from $(\mathcal{EL}, \mathrm{tqCQ})$, then $\mathrm{bc}_{r\mathrm{CQ}}(Q)$ contains only derivatives of q_0. The latter is due to the definition of the $\mathrm{bc}_{r\mathrm{CQ}}$ algorithm, which starts with a set of minimized fork rewritings of q_0, and the fact that the only fork rewriting of a tqCQ is the query itself.

There are two exponential blowups in the presented approach. First, the number of fork rewritings of q_0 might be exponential in the size of q_0. We expect this not to be a problem in practice since the number of fork rewritings of realistic queries should be fairly small. And second, the number of splittings can be exponential and thus the same is true for the size of each $\mathcal{T}^{\min}_{q_r}$. We expect that also this blowup will be moderate in practice. Moreover, in an optimized implementation one would not represent $\mathcal{T}^{\min}_{q_r}$ as a TBox, but rather check the existence of fork rewritings and splittings that give rise to concept inclusions in $\mathcal{T}^{\min}_{q_r}$ in a more direct way. This involves checking whether concepts of the form $\exists r_i^{\nu(\mu(i))}.C_{q'|_{S_i}}$ are derived, and the fact that there are only polynomially many different such concepts should thus be very relevant regarding performance.

5   Experiments

We have extended the *Grind* system [12] to support OMQs from $(\mathcal{EL}, \mathrm{tqCQ})$ and $(\mathcal{EL}, r\mathrm{CQ})$ instead of only from $(\mathcal{EL}, \mathrm{AQ})$, and conducted experiments with real-world ontologies and hand-crafted conjunctive queries. The system can be downloaded from http://www.cs.uni-bremen.de/~hansen/grind, together with the ontologies and queries, and is released under GPL. It outputs rewritings in the form of non-recursive Datalog queries. We have implemented the following optimization: given $Q = (\mathcal{T}, \Sigma, q_0)$, first compute all fork rewritings of q_0, rewrite away all variables outside of the core (in the same way in which tree parts of the query are removed in Sect. 3) to obtain a new OMQ $(\mathcal{T}', \Sigma, q_0')$, and then test for each atom $A(x) \in q_0'$ whether $(\mathcal{T}', \Sigma, A(x))$ is FO-rewritable. It can be shown that, if this is the case, then Q is FO-rewritable, and it is also possible to transfer the actual rewritings. If this check fails, we go through the full construction described in the paper.

Experiments were carried out on a Linux (3.2.0) machine with a 3.5 GHz quad-core processor and 8 GB of RAM. For the experiments, we use (the $\mathcal{EL}$ part of) the ontologies ENVO, FBbi, SO, MOHSE, and not-galen. The first three ontologies are from the biology domain, and are available through Bioportal[3]. MOHSE and not-galen are different versions of the GALEN ontology[4], which describes medical terms. Some statistics is given in Table 1, namely the number of concept inclusions (CI), concept names (CN), and role names (RN) in each ontology. For each ontology, we hand-crafted 10 conjunctive queries (three tqCQs and seven rCQs), varying in size from 2 to 5 variables and showing several different topologies (see Fig. 1 for a sample).

Table 1. TBox information and results of experiments

TBox	CI	CN	RN	Min CQ	Avg CQ	Max CQ	Avg AQ	Aborts
ENVO	1942	1558	7	0.2 s	1.5 s	7 s	1 s	0
FBbi	567	517	1	0.05 s	0.5 s	3 s	0.3 s	0
MOHSE	3665	2203	71	2 s	10 s	40 s	6 s	0
not-galen	4636	2748	159	6 s	9 s	28 s	25 s	2
SO	3160	2095	12	1 s	19 s	2 min 23 s	4 s	1

The runtimes are reported in Table 1. Only three queries did not terminate in 30 min or exhausted the memory. For the successful ones, we list fastest (Min CQ), slowest (Max CQ), and average runtime (Avg CQ). For comparison, the Avg AQ column lists the time needed to compute FO-rewritings for all queries $(\mathcal{T}, \Sigma, A(x))$ with $A(x)$ an atom in q_0. This check is of course incomplete for FO-rewritability of Q, but can be viewed as a lower bound. A detailed picture of individual runtimes is given in Fig. 2.

In summary, we believe that the outcome of our experiments is promising. While runtimes are higher than in the AQ case, they are still rather small given that we are dealing with an intricate static analysis task and that many parts of our system have not been seriously optimized. The queries with long runtimes or timeouts contain AQs that are not FO-rewritable which forces the decomposed algorithm implemented in Grind to enter a more expensive processing phase.

---

[3] https://bioportal.bioontology.org.
[4] http://www.opengalen.org/.

$$q_1(x, y) = \text{Patient}(x) \wedge \text{shows}(x, y) \wedge \text{Endocarditis}(y)$$
$$
\begin{aligned}
q_2(w, x, y, z) = {} & \text{Doctor}(w) \wedge \text{hasPersonPerforming}(x, w) \wedge \text{Surgery}(x) \wedge \\
& \text{actsOn}(x, y) \wedge \text{Tissue}(y) \wedge \text{actsOn}(x, z) \wedge \\
& \text{InternalOrgan}(z) \wedge \text{hasAlphaConnection}(y, z)
\end{aligned}
$$
$$
\begin{aligned}
q_7(x) = {} & \exists y, z\ \text{Protein}(x) \wedge \text{contains}(x, y) \wedge \text{Tetracycline}(y) \wedge \\
& \text{InternalOrgan}(z) \wedge \text{isActedOnSpecificallyBy}(z, y)
\end{aligned}
$$
$$
\begin{aligned}
q_8(x) = {} & \exists v, w, y, z\ \text{Sulphonamide}(v) \wedge \text{serves}(v, w) \wedge \text{TumorMarkerRole}(w) \wedge \\
& \text{NamedEnzyme}(x) \wedge \text{serves}(x, w) \wedge \text{actsOn}(x, z) \wedge \text{Liver}(z) \wedge \\
& \text{TeichoicAcid}(y) \wedge \text{actsOn}(y, z)
\end{aligned}
$$
$$
\begin{aligned}
q_{10}(x) = {} & \exists y, z\ \text{BodyStructure}(x) \wedge \text{isBetaConnectionOf}(x, y) \wedge \text{Brain}(y) \wedge \\
& \text{IntrinsicallyNormalBodyStructure}(z) \wedge \text{isBetaConnectionOf}(z, y)
\end{aligned}
$$

Fig. 1. Examplary queries used for experiments with TBox not-galen.

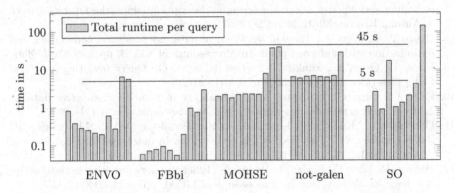

Fig. 2. Runtimes for individual OMQs, showing only non-aborting runs.

6 Conclusion

We remark that our approach can also be used to compute FO-rewritings of OMQs from $(\mathcal{EL}, \text{CQ})$ even if the CQs are not rooted, as long as they are not Boolean (that is, as long as they contain at least one answer variable) and an algorithm for query containment in $(\mathcal{EL}, \text{CQ})$ is also available. This follows from (a minor variation of) an observation from [5]: FO-rewritability of non-Boolean OMQs from $(\mathcal{EL}, \text{CQ})$ can be polynomially reduced to a combination of containment in $(\mathcal{EL}, \text{CQ})$ and FO-rewritability in $(\mathcal{EL}, \text{rCQ})$. As future work, it would be interesting to extend our approach to UCQs, to the extension of $\mathcal{EL}$ with role hierarchies and domain and range restrictions, or even to the extension $\mathcal{ELI}$ of $\mathcal{EL}$ with inverse roles.

Acknowledgements. We acknowledge support by ERC grant 647289 'CODA'.

References

1. Artale, A., Calvanese, D., Kontchakov, R., Zakharyaschev, M.: The DL-Lite family and relations. J. Artif. Intell. Res. **36**, 1–69 (2009)
2. Baader, F., Horrocks, I., Lutz, C., Sattler, U.: An Introduction to Description Logics. Cambridge University Press, Cambridge (2017)
3. Barceló, P., Berger, G., Pieris, A.: Containment for rule-based ontology-mediated queries, 19 April 2017. https://arxiv.org/abs/1703.07994 [cs.DB]
4. Bienvenu, M., ten Cate, B., Lutz, C., Wolter, F.: Ontology-based data access: a study through disjunctive datalog, CSP, and MMSNP. J. ACM Trans. Database Syst. **39**(4), 33:1–33:44 (2014)
5. Bienvenu, M., Hansen, P., Lutz, C., Wolter, F.: First order-rewritability and containment of conjunctive queries in Horn description logics. In: Proceedings of IJCAI, pp. 965–971 (2016)
6. Bienvenu, M., Lutz, C., Wolter, F.: First order-rewritability of atomic queries in Horn description logics. In: Proceedings of IJCAI, pp. 754–760 (2013)
7. Calvanese, D., De Giacomo, G., Lembo, D., Lenzerini, M., Rosati, R.: Tractable reasoning and efficient query answering in description logics: the DL-Lite family. J. Autom. Reason. **39**(3), 385–429 (2007)
8. Deutsch, A., Popa, L., Tannen, V.: Physical data independence, constraints, and optimization with universal plans. In: Proceedings of VLDB, pp. 459–470 (1999)
9. Eiter, T., Ortiz, M., Simkus, M., Tran, T., Xiao, G.: Query rewriting for Horn-SHIQ plus rules. In: Proceedings of AAAI (2012)
10. Feier, C., Lutz, C., Kuusisto, A.: Rewritability in monadic disjunctive datalog, MMSNP, and expressive description logics. In: Proceedings of ICDT (2017)
11. Gottlob, G., Kikot, S., Kontchakov, R., Podolskii, V.V., Schwentick, T., Zakharyaschev, M.: The price of query rewriting in ontology-based data access. J. Artif. Intell. **213**, 42–59 (2014)
12. Hansen, P., Lutz, C., Seylan, I., Wolter, F.: Efficient query rewriting in the description logic EL and beyond. In: Proceedings of IJCAI, pp. 3034–3040 (2015)
13. Kikot, S., Kontchakov, R., Zakharyaschev, M.: Conjunctive query answering with OWL 2 QL. In: Proceedings of KR (2012)
14. König, M., Leclère, M., Mugnier, M.: Query rewriting for existential rules with compiled preorder. In: Proceedings of IJCAI, pp. 3106–3112 (2015)
15. König, M., Leclère, M., Mugnier, M., Thomazo, M.: Sound, complete and minimal UCQ-rewriting for existential rules. Semant. Web **6**(5), 451–475 (2015)
16. Lutz, C.: The complexity of conjunctive query answering in expressive description logics. In: Armando, A., Baumgartner, P., Dowek, G. (eds.) IJCAR 2008. LNCS (LNAI), vol. 5195, pp. 179–193. Springer, Heidelberg (2008). doi:10.1007/978-3-540-71070-7_16
17. Lutz, C.: Two upper bounds for conjunctive query answering in SHIQ. In: Proceedings of DL (2008)
18. Lutz, C., Toman, D., Wolter, F.: Conjunctive query answering in the description logic EL using a relational database system. In: Proceedings of IJCAI, pp. 2070–2075 (2009)
19. Motik, B., Cuenca Grau, B., Horrocks, I., Wu, Z., Fokoue, A., Lutz, C.: OWL 2 web ontology language: profiles. W3C recommendation, 11 December 2012. http://www.w3.org/TR/owl2-profiles/
20. Pérez-Urbina, H., Motik, B., Horrocks, I.: Tractable query answering and rewriting under description logic constraints. J. Appl. Logic **8**(2), 186–209 (2010)

21. Rodriguez-Muro, M., Calvanese, D.: High performance query answering over DL-Lite ontologies. In: Proceedings of KR (2012)
22. Rosati, R., Almatelli, A.: Improving query answering over DL-Lite ontologies. In: Proceedings of KR (2010)
23. Stefanoni, G., Motik, B.: Answering conjunctive queries over EL knowledge bases with transitive and reflexive roles. In: Proceedings of AAAI, pp. 1611–1617 (2015)
24. Stefanoni, G., Motik, B., Horrocks, I.: Small datalog query rewritings for EL. In: Proceedings of DL (2012)
25. Trivela, D., Stoilos, G., Chortaras, A., Stamou, G.B.: Optimising resolution-based rewriting algorithms for OWL ontologies. J. Web Semant. **33**, 30–49 (2015)

A Formal Framework for Comparing Linked Data Fragments

Olaf Hartig[1]([⊠]), Ian Letter[2], and Jorge Pérez[3]([⊠])

[1] Department of Computer and Information Science (IDA), Linköping University,
Linköping, Sweden
olaf.hartig@liu.se
[2] Departamento de Ingeniería Matemática, Universidad de Chile, Santiago, Chile
iletter@dim.uchile.cl
[3] Department of Computer Science, Universidad de Chile, Santiago, Chile
jperez@dcc.uchile.cl

Abstract. The Linked Data Fragment (LDF) framework has been proposed as a uniform view to explore the trade-offs of consuming Linked Data when servers provide (possibly many) different interfaces to access their data. Every such interface has its own particular properties regarding performance, bandwidth needs, caching, etc. Several practical challenges arise. For example, before exposing a new type of LDFs in some server, can we formally say something about how this new LDF interface compares to other interfaces previously implemented in the same server? From the client side, given a client with some restricted capabilities in terms of time constraints, network connection, or computational power, which is the best type of LDFs to complete a given task? Today there are only a few formal theoretical tools to help answer these and other practical questions, and researchers have embarked in solving them mainly by experimentation.

In this paper we propose the *Linked Data Fragment Machine* (LDFM) which is the first formalization to model LDF scenarios. LDFMs work as classical Turing Machines with extra features that model the server and client capabilities. By proving formal results based on LDFMs, we draw a fairly complete *expressiveness lattice* that shows the interplay between several combinations of client and server capabilities. We also show the usefulness of our model to formally analyze the fine-grain interplay between several metrics such as the number of requests sent to the server, and the bandwidth of communication between client and server.

1 Introduction

The idea behind Linked Data Fragments (LDFs) is that different Semantic Web servers may provide (possibly many) different interfaces to access their datasets allowing clients to decide which interface better satisfies a particular need. Every such interface provides a particular type of so-called "fragments" of the underlying dataset [13]. Moreover, every interface has its own particular properties regarding performance, bandwidth needs, cache effectiveness, etc. Clients can

© Springer International Publishing AG 2017
C. d'Amato et al. (Eds.): ISWC 2017, Part I, LNCS 10587, pp. 364–382, 2017.
DOI: 10.1007/978-3-319-68288-4_22

analyze the trade-offs when using one of these interfaces (or a combination of them) for completing a specific task. There are a myriad of possible interfaces in between SPARQL endpoints and RDF data dumps. Some interfaces that have already been proposed in the literature include Linked Data Documents [4,5], Triple Pattern Fragments (TPF) [13], and Bindings-Restricted Triple Pattern Fragments (brTPF) [7]. Different options for LDF interfaces are shown in Fig. 1.

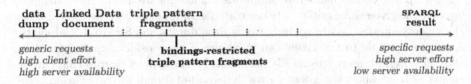

Fig. 1. Unidimensional view of Linked Data Fragments (figure taken from [7,13])

LDFs have already had a considerable practical impact. For instance, since the proposal of the TPF interface, the LOD Laundromat Website has published more than 650,000 datasets on the Web with this interface [3]. Moreover, DBpedia has also published a TPF interface which had an uptime of 99.99% during its first nine months [13]. Up to now, the research and development of LDFs has produced interesting practical results, but the studied interfaces are definitely not the final answer to querying semantic data on the Web, and one may expect that many new interfaces with different trade-offs can be made available by Semantic Web data servers in the near future.

Several practical challenges arise. On the server side, developers need to construct LDF interfaces that ensure a good cost/performance trade-off. Before implementing a new interface in some server, can we formally say something about the comparison of this new type of LDFs with earlier-proposed types? If the new interface is somehow subsumed in capabilities and cost by previously implemented interfaces (or by a simple combination of them), then there might be no reason to implement it. Answering this question requires an answer to the more general question on how to formally compare the properties of two different LDF interfaces given only their specifications.

On the client side, developers need to efficiently use and perhaps combine LDF interfaces. Thus, an interesting problem is the following: given a client with some restricted capabilities (in terms of time constraints, small budget, little computational power, restricted local expressiveness, etc.) and a task to be completed, which is the best interface that can be used to complete the task? Or even more drastically, can the task be completed at all given the restrictions on the client and a set of LDF interfaces to choose from? Today there are only a few formal tools to help answer the previously described questions, and researchers have embarked in solving them mainly by experimentation. The main goal of this paper is to help fill this gap by developing solid theoretical foundations for studying and comparing LDF interfaces.

It is not difficult to see that one can compare LDF interfaces in different ways. For instance, in Fig. 1 (taken from [7,13]) three criteria are considered: (1) general vs. specific requests, (2) client vs. server effort, and (3) high vs. low availability. We note however that this figure is not meant to provide an accurate account of the trade-offs of the included interfaces but to highlight the existence of such trade-offs. To this end, the figure has been kept deliberately simplistic by organizing the criteria and the interfaces along a single axis. While serving the intended purpose, this deliberate simplification has the disadvantage of suggesting that the given three criteria are correlated and, for example, the Linked Data Documents interface is always in between data dumps and SPARQL endpoints. A counterexample to the latter can be shown if we consider expressiveness as another criterion; more specifically, lets consider the type of queries that can be answered if we allow the client to use full computational power (Turing complete) to process data after making as many requests to the server as it needs. Assume that we have a server that provides data dumps, Linked Data Documents, and a SPARQL endpoint. Then, one can formally prove that the client is strictly less expressive when accessing the Linked Data Documents instead of the data dump or the SPARQL endpoint. To see this, consider a query of the following form:

$Q1$: "Give me all the subjects and objects of RDF triples whose predicate is rdf:type."

This query cannot be answered completely over a dataset by using the Linked Data Document interface no matter how many requests the client sends to the server [6]. On the other hand, it is not difficult to show that both, data dumps and SPARQL endpoints, can answer the query completely. Thus, when considering the expressiveness dimension, Linked Data Documents are not longer in between data dumps and SPARQL endpoints.

Consider another scenario in which one wants to measure only the number of requests that the client sends to the server in order to answer a specific query. Lets assume this time that the server provides a data dump, a SPARQL endpoint, and a TPF interface, and consider the following query.

$Q2$: "Give me all the persons reachable from Peter by following two foaf:knows links."

It is straightforward to see that a client using either the data dump or the SPARQL endpoint can answer this query by using a single request to the server, while a TPF client needs at least two requests. Thus, in this case, data dumps are more efficient than TPFs in terms of number of server requests. On the other hand it is clear that in terms of the amount of data transferred, TPFs are more desirable for $Q2$ than data dumps.

Although the two examples described above are very simple, they already show that the comparison of LDF interfaces is not always one-dimensional. Moreover, the comparison can quickly become more complex as we want to analyze and compare more involved scenarios. For instance, in both cases above we just analyzed a single query. In general, one would like to compare LDF interfaces in terms of classes of queries. Another interesting dimension is client-side computational power. In both cases above we assumed that the client is Turing complete, and thus the client is able to apply any computable function to the fragments obtained from an LDF interface. However, one would like to consider also clients with restricted capabilities (e.g., in terms of computational power or storage). Moreover, other dimensions such as bandwidth from client to server, bandwidth from server to client, time complexity on the server, cacheability of results, and so on, can substantially add difficulty to the formal analysis. In this paper we embark on the formal study of Linked Data Fragments by proposing a framework in which several of the aforementioned issues can be formally analyzed.

Main contributions and organization of the paper: As our main conceptual contribution we propose the *Linked Data Fragment Machine* (LDFM). LDFMs work as classical Turing Machines with some extra features that model the server and client capabilities in an LDF scenario. Our machine model is designed to clearly separate three of the main tasks done when accessing a Linked Data Fragment server: (1) the computation that plans and drives the overall query execution process by making requests to the server, (2) the computation that the server needs to do in order to answer requests issued by the client, and (3) the computation that the client needs to do to create the final output from the server responses. These design decisions allow us to have a model that is powerful enough to capture several different scenarios while simple enough to allow us to formally prove properties about it. The LDFM model is presented in Sect. 2.

As one of our main technical contributions, we use our machine to formalize the notion of *expressiveness* of an LDF scenario and we draw a fairly complete *lattice* that shows the interplay between several combinations of client and server capabilities. While expressiveness is studied in Sect. 3, in Sect. 4 we analyze LDF scenarios in terms of classical computational complexity. Moreover, our machine model also allows us to formally analyze LDFs in terms of two additional important metrics, namely, the number of requests sent to the server, and the bandwidth of communication between the server and the client. Both notions are formalized as specific computational-complexity measures over LDFMs. We present formal results comparing different scenarios and demonstrate the suitability of our proposed framework to also analyze the fine-grain interplay between complexity metrics. These results are presented in Sect. 5.

For the sake of space most of the details on the proofs have been omitted but can be found in the appendix at http://dcc.uchile.cl/~jperez/ldfm-ext.pdf.

2   Linked Data Fragment Machine

This section introduces our abstract machine model that captures possible client-server systems that execute user queries, issued at the client side, over a server-side dataset.

Informally, the machine in our model captures the whole of a client-server system (i.e., both, the server and the client). However, the program of the machine can be considered to be executed on the client side. To communicate with the server the machine uses a *server language*, $\mathcal{L}_S$, which essentially represents the type of requests that the server interface is able to answer. Additionally, the machine is also in charge of producing the result of the given user query by combining the responses from the server. The corresponding result-construction capability is captured by a *response-combination language*, $\mathcal{L}_C$, which is an algebra over the server responses. To answer a user query the machine performs the following general process: The machine begins by creating requests for the server in the form of $\mathcal{L}_S$ queries. After issuing such a request, the corresponding response becomes available in an internal *result container*. Then, the machine can decide to continue with this process by issuing another request. Every response from the server is stored in a different result container, and moreover, a result container cannot be modified after it is filled with a server response (i.e., it can only be read by the machine). In the final step, the machine uses the response-combination language $\mathcal{L}_C$ to create a query over the result containers. The execution of this $\mathcal{L}_C$-query produces the final output of the process (that is, the result of the user query). In the following, we define the machine formally. We first formally capture the different types of query languages involved and next we provide the formal definition of the machine; thereafter, we describe the rationale of the different parts of the machine and we introduce notions of computability and expressiveness based on the machine.

2.1 Preliminaries

Our model assumes the following three types of queries.

User queries are queries that are issued at the client side and that the client-server system (captured by our machine) executes over the server-side dataset. We assume that this dataset is represented as an RDF graph without blank nodes. Then, a possible class of user queries could be SPARQL queries. However, to make our model more general we allow user queries to be expressed also in other query languages. To this end, for our model we introduce the abstract notion of an *RDF query*. Formally, an RDF query is an expression q for which there exists an evaluation function that is defined for every RDF graph G and that returns a set of SPARQL solution mappings, denoted by $[\![q]\!]_G$.

Requests are queries that the client sends to the server during the execution of a user query. The form of these requests depends on the type of interface provided by the server. We capture such interface types (and, thus, the possible requests) by introducing the notion of a *server language*; that is, a language $\mathcal{L}_S$ that is associated with an evaluation function that, for every query $q_R \in \mathcal{L}_S$ and every RDF graph G, returns a set of SPARQL solution mappings, which we denote by $[\![q_R]\!]_G$. Examples of server languages considered in this paper are given as follows:

– CORESPARQL is the core fragment of SPARQL that considers triple patterns, AND, OPT, UNION, FILTER, and SELECT. Due to space limitations, we refer to [2, 10] for a formal definition of this fragment and its evaluation function.

- BGP is the basic graph pattern fragment of SPARQL (i.e., triple patterns and AND).
- TPF is the language composed of queries that are a single triple pattern. Hence, this language captures servers that support the triple pattern fragments interface [13].
- TPF+FILTER is the language composed of queries of the form $(tp$ FILTER $\theta)$ where tp is a triple pattern and θ is a SPARQL built-in condition as defined in [10].
- BRTPF is the language composed of queries of the form (tp, Ω), where tp is a triple pattern and Ω is a set of solution mappings. This language captures the bindings-restricted triple pattern interface [7]. The evaluation function is defined such that for every RDF graph G it holds that $[\![(tp, \Omega)]\!]_G = \pi_{\mathrm{vars}(tp)}([\![tp]\!]_G \bowtie \Omega)$ where π is the projection operator [11], $\mathrm{vars}(tp)$ is the set of variables in tp, $[\![tp]\!]_G$ is the evaluation of tp over G [10], and $\bowtie$ is the join operator [10]. For simplicity we assume that a triple pattern tp is also a BRTPF query in which case the evaluation function is simply $[\![tp]\!]_G$.
- DUMP is the language that has a single expression only, namely the triple pattern $(?s, ?p, ?o)$ where $?s$, $?p$, and $?o$ are different variables. This language captures interfaces for downloading the complete server-side dataset.

For any two server languages $\mathcal{L}_S$ and $\mathcal{L}'_S$ we write $\mathcal{L}_S \subseteq \mathcal{L}'_S$ if every query in $\mathcal{L}_S$ is also in $\mathcal{L}'_S$. For instance, DUMP $\subseteq$ TPF $\subseteq$ BGP $\subseteq$ CORESPARQL.

Response-combination queries are queries that describe how the result of a user query can be produced from the server responses. Since each server response in our model is a set of solution mappings, and so is the result of any user query, we assume that response-combination queries can be expressed using languages that resemble an algebra over sets of solution mappings. We call such a language a *response-combination language*. In this paper we denote such response-combination languages by the set of algebra operators that they implement. For instance, the response-combination language denoted by the set $\{\bowtie, \pi\}$ can be used to combine multiple sets $\Omega_1, \ldots, \Omega_n$ of solution mappings by applying the aforementioned join and projection operators in an arbitrary manner. Other algebra operators that we consider in this paper are the union and the left outer join [2], denoted by $\cup$ and $\bowtie$, respectively. Note that based on our notation, the empty operator set $(\emptyset)$ also denotes a response-combination language. This language can be used only to simply select one Ω_i out of multiple given sets $\Omega_1, \ldots, \Omega_n$ of solution mappings (i.e., without being able to modify Ω_i).

2.2 Formalization

A *Linked Data Fragment Machine* (LDFM) M is a multi-tape Turing Machine with the following special features. In addition to several ordinary *working tapes*, M has five special tapes: a *query tape* $\mathcal{T}_Q$, a *data tape* $\mathcal{T}_D$, a *server-request tape* $\mathcal{T}_R$, a *client tape* $\mathcal{T}_C$, and an *output tape* $\mathcal{T}_O$. Tapes $\mathcal{T}_Q$ and $\mathcal{T}_D$ are read-only tapes, while $\mathcal{T}_R$, $\mathcal{T}_C$, and $\mathcal{T}_O$ are write-only tapes. As another special component,

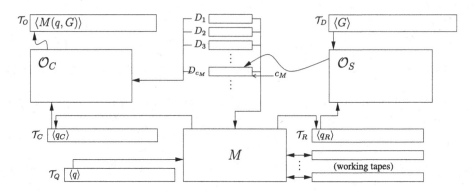

Fig. 2. $(\mathcal{L}_C, \mathcal{L}_S)$-LDFM M

the machine has an unbounded sequence $D_1, D_2, \ldots, D_k, \ldots$ of *result containers* (which can also be considered as read-only tapes), and a counter c_M, called the *result counter*, that defines the last used result container. M also has four different *modes*: *computing the next server request* (R), *waiting for response* (W), *computing client query* (C), and *done* (F). In all these modes the machine may use the full power of a standard Turing Machine. Additionally, M has access to two *oracle machines*: a *server oracle* $\mathcal{O}_S$, which is associated with a server language $\mathcal{L}_S$, and a *client oracle* $\mathcal{O}_C$, associated with a response-combination language $\mathcal{L}_C$.

An LDFM M receives as input an RDF query q and an RDF graph G. Before the computation begins, q is assumed to be in tape $\mathcal{T}_Q$ and G is assumed to be in tape $\mathcal{T}_D$. All other tapes as well as the result containers are initially empty, the counter c_M is 0, and the machine is in mode R. Then, during the computation, the machine can use its ordinary working tapes arbitrarily (read/write). However, the access to the special tapes is restricted. That is, tape $\mathcal{T}_R$ can be used by the machine only when it is in mode R, and tape $\mathcal{T}_C$ can be used only in mode C. Moreover, the machine does not have direct access to the tapes $\mathcal{T}_D$ and $\mathcal{T}_O$; instead, the read-only tape $\mathcal{T}_D$ can be accessed only by the oracle $\mathcal{O}_S$, and the write-only tape $\mathcal{T}_O$ can be accessed only by oracle $\mathcal{O}_C$. Regarding the result containers, M is only able to read from them, and only oracle $\mathcal{O}_S$ can write in them. Figure 2 illustrates an LDFM and Fig. 3 shows the possible state transitions.

The computation of an LDFM M works as follows. While in mode R, the machine can construct a query $q_R \in \mathcal{L}_S$ and write it in tape $\mathcal{T}_R$. When the machine is finished writing q_R, it may change to mode W, which is a call to oracle $\mathcal{O}_S$. The oracle then increments the counter c_M, deletes the content of tape $\mathcal{T}_R$, and writes the set of mappings $[\![q_R]\!]_G$ in the container D_{c_M}. Next, the computation continues, M changes back to mode R, and the previous process may be repeated. Alternatively, at any point when in mode R, the machine may decide to change to mode C. In this mode, M constructs a query $q_C \in \mathcal{L}_C$, writes it in tape $\mathcal{T}_C$, and changes to mode F, which is a call to oracle $\mathcal{O}_C$. Then,

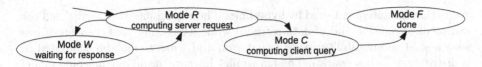

Fig. 3. Possible state transitions of an LDFM

oracle $\mathcal{O}_C$ evaluates q_C over data $D_1, \ldots, D_{c_M}$, and writes the result of this evaluation in tape $\mathcal{T}_O$ which is the final output of M. Hence, at this point the computation terminates. We denote the final output as $M(q, G)$.

Example 1. A typical SPARQL endpoint based client-server scenario may be captured by an LDFM M whose server language $\mathcal{L}_S$ is CORESPARQL and the response-combination language $\mathcal{L}_C$ is $\emptyset$. For any user query q, assuming q is in CORESPARQL, the machine simply copies q into tape $\mathcal{T}_R$ and enters mode W. After obtaining $[\![q]\!]_G$ from oracle $\mathcal{O}_S$ in result container D_1, the machine enters mode C, writes D_1 (as an expression in $\mathcal{L}_C = \emptyset$) in tape $\mathcal{T}_C$, and changes to mode F. Then, oracle $\mathcal{O}_C$ writes the query result $[\![q]\!]_G$ from D_1 to the output tape.

Example 2. Let M be an LDFM such that $\mathcal{L}_S = $ BRTPF and $\mathcal{L}_C = \{\bowtie, \cup\}$. Hence, M has access to a server capable of handling BRTPF requests, and M can do joins and unions to construct the final output. Assume now that a user wants to answer a SPARQL query q of the form $((?X, a, ?Y)$ AND $(?X, b, ?Y))$, which is initially in tape $\mathcal{T}_Q$. Then, to evaluate q over a graph G (in tape $\mathcal{T}_D$), M may work as follows: First, M writes query $(?X, a, ?Y)$ in tape $\mathcal{T}_R$ and calls $\mathcal{O}_S$ by entering mode W. After this call we have that $D_1 = [\![(?X, a, ?Y)]\!]_G$. Now, M can write $(?X, b, ?Y)$ in tape $\mathcal{T}_R$, which is another call to $\mathcal{O}_S$ that produces $D_2 = [\![(?X, b, ?Y)]\!]_G$. Finally, M writes query $D_1 \bowtie D_2$ in tape $\mathcal{T}_C$ and calls $\mathcal{O}_C$, which produces the output, $M(q, G)$, in tape $\mathcal{T}_O$. It is not difficult to see that $M(q, G) = [\![q]\!]_G$. We may have an alternative LDFM M' that computes q as follows. Initially, M' calls the server oracle $\mathcal{O}_S$ with query $(?X, a, ?Y)$ to obtain $D_1 = [\![(?X, a, ?Y)]\!]_G$. Next, M' performs the following iteration: for every mapping $\mu \in D_1$ it writes the BRTPF query $((?X, b, ?Y), \{\mu\})$ in $\mathcal{T}_R$ and calls the oracle $\mathcal{O}_S$ to produce $[\![((?X, b, ?Y), \{\mu\})]\!]_G = [\![(?X, b, ?Y))]\!]_G \bowtie \{\mu\}$ in one of its result containers. After all these calls, M' writes query $(D_2 \cup D_3 \cup \cdots \cup D_k)$ in tape $\mathcal{T}_C$, where $k = c_{M'}$ is the index of the last used result container. The oracle $\mathcal{O}_C$ then produces the final output $M'(q, G)$. In this case we also have that $M'(q, G) = [\![q]\!]_G$.

2.3 Rationale and Limitations of LDFMs

Machine models to formalize Web querying have been previously proposed in the literature [1,6,9]. Most of the early work in this context is based on an understanding of the Web as a distributed hypertext system consisting of Web pages that are interconnected by hyperlinks. These machines then formalized the notion of navigation and of data retrieval while navigating, and their focus was on classical computability issues (what can, and what cannot be computed in a distributed Web scenario). Though similar in motivation, our machine model in contrast formalizes a different approach to access and to query Web data. In this section we explain the rationale behind our design.

The perhaps most important characteristic of our model is that it separates the computation that creates the final output (as done by the client oracle $\mathcal{O}_C$) from the computation that plans and drives the overall query execution process (as done by the LDFM itself). Hence, the expressive power of the response-combination language $\mathcal{L}_C$ only determines how the query result to be returned to the user can be computed by using the result containers, but it does not have any impact whatsoever on the computations that the machine can do when it generates any of the server requests (in mode R) or when it generates the final $\mathcal{L}_C$-query (in mode C). This separation allows us to precisely pinpoint the computational power needed for the latter without mixing it up with the power needed for constructing the output (and vice versa). Of course, in practice the two tasks do not need to be separated into two consecutive phases as suggested by our model. In fact, an alternative version of our model could allow the machine to use oracle $\mathcal{O}_C$ multiple times to produce the first elements of the complete output as early as possible.

Another separation, which is perhaps more natural because it also exists in practice, is the delegation of the computation of the server responses to the server oracle $\mathcal{O}_S$. Besides also avoiding a mix-up when analyzing required computational power, this separation additionally allows us to prevent the LDFM from accessing the data tape $\mathcal{T}_D$ directly. This features captures the fact that, in practice, a client also has to use the server interface instead of being able to directly access the server-side dataset.

The result containers $(D_1, D_2, \ldots)$, with their corresponding result counter (c_M), provide us with an abstraction based on which notions of network cost of different pairs of client/server capabilities can be quantified. We shall use this abstraction to define network-related complexity measures in Sect. 5.

While our notion of the LDFM provides us with a powerful model to formally study many phenomena of LDF-based client-server settings, there are a few additional factors in practice that are not captured by the model in its current form. In particular, the model does not capture the option for the server to (i) decide to split responses into pages (that have to be requested separately) and (ii) send metadata with its responses that clients can use to adapt their query execution plans. Additionally, in practice there may be a cache located between the server and the client, which might have to be captured to study metrics related to server load (given that such a cache is not equally effective for different LDF interfaces [7,13]). We deliberately ignored these options to keep our model sufficiently simple. However, corresponding features may be added to our notion of an LDFM if useful for future analyses.

2.4 Computability and Expressiveness for LDFMs

We conclude the introduction of our machine model by defining notions of computability and expressiveness based on LDFMs.

The most basic notion of computability for LDFMs is that of a computable query. We say that an RDF query q *is computable under an LDFM M* if for every RDF graph G it holds that $M(q, G) = [\![q]\!]_G$. That is, q is computable under M if, with (q, G) as input, M produces $[\![q]\!]_G$ as output, for every possible graph G. We can also extend this notion to classes of queries. Formally, the *class of queries computed by* an LDFM M, denoted by $\mathcal{C}(M)$, is the set of all RDF queries that are computable under M.

Notice that every LDFM comes with a response-combination language and a server language, and thus we can also define classes of LDFMs in terms of the languages that they use. In particular, we say that an LDFM M is an $(\mathcal{L}_C, \mathcal{L}_S)$-LDFM if the response-combination language of M is $\mathcal{L}_C$ and the server language of M is $\mathcal{L}_S$. Now, we can define our main notion of computability.

Definition 1. *Let $\mathcal{L}_C$ be a response-combination language and $\mathcal{L}_S$ be a server language. A class $\mathcal{C}$ of RDF queries is* computable under $(\mathcal{L}_C, \mathcal{L}_S)$ *if there exists an $(\mathcal{L}_C, \mathcal{L}_S)$-LDFM M such that every query q in $\mathcal{C}$ is computable under M.*

Definition 1 is our main building block to compare different combinations of client and server languages independent of the possible LDFMs that use these languages. The following definition formalizes our main comparison notion.

Definition 2. *Let $\mathcal{L}_1$ and $\mathcal{L}'_1$ be response-combination languages, and $\mathcal{L}_2$ and $\mathcal{L}'_2$ be server languages. Then, $(\mathcal{L}'_1, \mathcal{L}'_2)$ is* at least as expressive as $(\mathcal{L}_1, \mathcal{L}_2)$, *denoted by $(\mathcal{L}_1, \mathcal{L}_2) \preceq_e (\mathcal{L}'_1, \mathcal{L}'_2)$, if every class of queries that is computable under $(\mathcal{L}_1, \mathcal{L}_2)$ is also computable under $(\mathcal{L}'_1, \mathcal{L}'_2)$.*

We use $(\mathcal{L}_1, \mathcal{L}_2) \equiv_e (\mathcal{L}'_1, \mathcal{L}'_2)$ to denote that $(\mathcal{L}_1, \mathcal{L}_2)$ and $(\mathcal{L}'_1, \mathcal{L}'_2)$ are *equally expressive*, that is, $(\mathcal{L}_1, \mathcal{L}_2) \preceq_e (\mathcal{L}'_1, \mathcal{L}'_2)$ and $(\mathcal{L}'_1, \mathcal{L}'_2) \preceq_e (\mathcal{L}_1, \mathcal{L}_2)$. As usual, we write $(\mathcal{L}_1, \mathcal{L}_2) \prec_e (\mathcal{L}'_1, \mathcal{L}'_2)$ to denote that $(\mathcal{L}_1, \mathcal{L}_2) \preceq_e (\mathcal{L}'_1, \mathcal{L}'_2)$ and $(\mathcal{L}'_1, \mathcal{L}'_2) \npreceq_e (\mathcal{L}_1, \mathcal{L}_2)$.

Example 3. It is easy to show that $(\emptyset, \text{DUMP}) \prec_e (\emptyset, \text{TPF})$. That is, whenever you have a server that can only provide a DUMP of its dataset and you do not have any additional power in the client, then you can accomplish strictly less tasks compared with the case in which you have access to a server that can answer TPF queries. In the next section we prove more such relationships (including less trivial ones).

3 Expressiveness Lattice

In this section we show the relationships between different pairs of client and server capabilities in terms of expressiveness. In particular, we establish a lattice that provides a full picture of many combinations of the server languages mentioned in Sect. 2.1 with almost every possible response-combination language constructed by using some of the algebra operators in $\{\bowtie, \cup, \bowtie, \pi\}$. Figure 4 illustrates this expressiveness-related lattice. As we will show, some of the equivalences and separations in this lattice do not necessarily follow from standard expressiveness results in the query language literature. In particular, the lattice highlights the expressive power of using the BRTPF interface [7]. It should be noticed that several other combinations of response-combination languages and server languages might have been considered. We plan to cover more of them as part of our future work. Before going into the results, we make the following simple observation about the expressiveness of LDFMs.

Note 1. Let $(\mathcal{L}_1, \mathcal{L}_2)$ and $(\mathcal{L}_1', \mathcal{L}_2')$ be arbitrary pairs of response-combination/server languages s.t. $\mathcal{L}_1 \subseteq \mathcal{L}_1'$ and $\mathcal{L}_2 \subseteq \mathcal{L}_2'$. Then, it is easy to prove that $(\mathcal{L}_1, \mathcal{L}_2) \preceq_e (\mathcal{L}_1', \mathcal{L}_2')$.

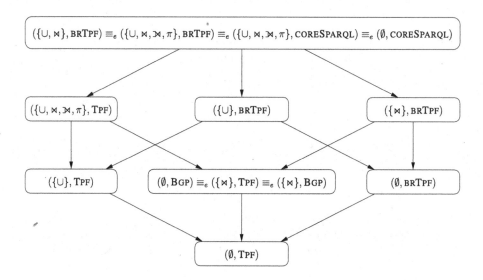

Fig. 4. Expressiveness lattice for LDFMs

3.1   The Expressiveness of Using the BRTPF Interface

We begin with a result that shows that BRTPF in combination with join and union in the client side is as expressive as server-side CORESPARQL with $\{\bowtie, \cup, \bowtie, \pi\}$ in the client.

Theorem 1. $(\{\cup, \bowtie\}, \text{BRTPF}) \equiv_e (\{\bowtie, \cup, \bowtie, \pi\}, \text{CORESPARQL})$.

The result, that might seem surprising, follows from two facts: (1) an LDFM can use unbounded computational power to issue server requests, and (2) a BRTPF server can accept arbitrary solutions mappings to be joined with triple patterns in the server side. The proof is divided in several parts and exploits a trick that is used in practice to avoid client-side joins when accessing a BRTPF interface. We illustrate the main idea with an example. Assume that one wants to compute a SPARQL query P of the form $(t_1\mathrm{OPT}t_2)$ over G where t_1 and t_2 are triple patterns. Since $[\![P]\!]_G = [\![t_1]\!]_G \bowtie [\![t_2]\!]_G$, one can easily evaluate P with a $(\{\bowtie, \cup, \bowtie, \pi\}, \mathrm{CORESPARQL})$-LDFM by just evaluating t_1 and t_2 separately in the server, and then using $\bowtie$ in the client to construct the final output. On the other hand, one can use the following strategy to evaluate P with a $(\{\cup, \bowtie\}, \mathrm{BRTPF})$-LDFM M. Recall that

$$[\![t_1]\!]_G \bowtie [\![t_2]\!]_G = ([\![t_1]\!]_G \bowtie [\![t_2]\!]_G) \cup ([\![t_1]\!]_G \setminus [\![t_2]\!]_G),$$

where $[\![t_1]\!]_G \setminus [\![t_2]\!]_G$ is the set of all mappings in $[\![t_1]\!]_G$ that are not compatible with any mapping in $[\![t_2]\!]_G$ [2]. We can first evaluate t_1 in the server to obtain $[\![t_1]\!]_G$ as one of M's result containers, say D_1. Next, M can use D_1 to construct the BRTPF query $(t_2, [\![t_1]\!]_G)$, which can be evaluated in the server and stored in the next container D_2. Notice that D_2 now contains all mappings in $[\![t_2]\!]_G$ that can be joined with some mapping in $[\![t_1]\!]_G$. Now M can use its internal computational power to produce the following set of queries: for every mapping μ in D_1 that is not compatible with any mapping in D_2, M constructs the BRTPF query $(t_1, \{\mu\})$, sends it to the server, and stores the result in one of the result containers, starting in container D_3. Notice that M is essentially mimicking the difference operator $\setminus$ using one mapping at a time. After all these requests, M has all the mappings of the set $[\![t_1]\!]_G \setminus [\![t_2]\!]_G$ stored in its containers, every mapping in a different container. Moreover, given that $D_1 \bowtie D_2 = [\![t_1]\!]_G \bowtie [\![t_2]\!]_G$, M can generate the client query $(D_1 \bowtie D_2) \cup D_3 \cup \cdots \cup D_{c_M}$ which will give exactly $[\![t_1]\!]_G \bowtie [\![t_2]\!]_G$. A similar strategy can be used to compute all other operators.

It is not difficult to prove that when having CORESPARQL for server requests, the operators $\{\bowtie, \cup, \bowtie, \pi\}$ on the client do not add any expressiveness. Moreover, from proving Theorem 1 it is easy to also obtain that $(\{\cup, \bowtie\}, \mathrm{BRTPF}) \equiv_e (\{\bowtie, \cup, \bowtie, \pi\}, \mathrm{BRTPF})$. Thus, we have that all the following four settings are equivalent in expressiveness:

$$(\{\cup, \bowtie\}, \mathrm{BRTPF}) \equiv_e (\{\cup, \bowtie, \bowtie, \pi\}, \mathrm{BRTPF})$$
$$\equiv_e (\{\bowtie, \cup, \bowtie, \pi\}, \mathrm{CORESPARQL}) \equiv_e (\emptyset, \mathrm{CORESPARQL}).$$

These equivalences are shown at the top of the lattice in Fig. 4.

Theorem 1 has several practical implications. One way to read this result is that whenever a BRTPF interface is available, a machine having operators $\{\bowtie, \cup, \bowtie, \pi\}$ in the client has plenty of options to produce *query execution plans* to answer user queries. In particular, for user queries needing $\bowtie$ or π, the machine may decide if some of these operators are evaluated in the client or part of them are evaluated in the server. What Theorem 1 does not state is an estimation of the cost of executing these different plans. In Sect. 5 we shed some light on this issue, in particular, we study the additional cost payed when using different server interfaces in terms of the number of requests sent to the server and the size of the data transferred between server and client.

The following result shows that union in the client is essential to obtain Theorem 1.

Theorem 2. $(\{\bowtie\}, \text{BRTPF}) \prec_e (\{\cup, \bowtie\}, \text{BRTPF})$.

It should be noticed that this result does *not* directly follow from the fact that $\cup$ cannot be expressed using $\bowtie$ since, as we have shown, a BRTPF interface is very expressive when queried with unbounded computational power. Towards proving Theorem 2, it is clear that $(\{\bowtie\}, \text{BRTPF}) \preceq_e (\{\cup, \bowtie\}, \text{BRTPF})$. Thus, to prove the theorem it only remains to show that $(\{\cup, \bowtie\}, \text{BRTPF}) \npreceq_e (\{\bowtie\}, \text{BRTPF})$. The following lemma proves something that, by Note 1 above, is actually stronger.

Lemma 1. $(\{\cup\}, \text{TPF}) \npreceq_e (\{\bowtie, \bowtie\!\!\!\bowtie, \pi\}, \text{BRTPF})$.

Consider the CORESPARQL query $q = ((?X, a, 2) \text{UNION} (3, b, 4))$. It is clear that q is computable by a $(\{\cup\}, \text{TPF})$-LDFM. It can be proved that q is not computable by a $(\{\bowtie, \bowtie\!\!\!\bowtie, \pi\}, \text{BRTPF})$-LDFM.

The following result proves that join is also needed to obtain Theorem 1.

Theorem 3. $(\{\cup\}, \text{BRTPF}) \prec_e (\{\cup, \bowtie\}, \text{BRTPF})$.

As for Theorem 2, we only need to prove that $(\{\cup, \bowtie\}, \text{BRTPF}) \npreceq_e (\{\cup\}, \text{BRTPF})$ which follows from the next, stronger result.

Lemma 2. $(\{\bowtie\}, \text{TPF}) \npreceq_e (\{\cup, \pi\}, \text{BRTPF})$.

The lemma follows from the fact that a $(\{\bowtie\}, \text{TPF})$-LDFM can produce solution mappings with an unbounded number of variables in its domain while, given the restrictions of the BRTPF interface, every solution mapping in the output of a $(\{\cup, \pi\}, \text{BRTPF})$-LDFM has at most three variables in its domain.

3.2   The Expressiveness of Using the TPF Interface

One interesting point is the comparison between TPF and BRTPF. The first important question is whether Theorem 1 can be obtained by considering TPF instead of BRTPF. Our next result provides a negative answer.

Theorem 4. $(\{\bowtie, \cup, \bowtie\!\!\!\bowtie, \pi\}, \text{TPF}) \prec_e (\{\cup, \bowtie\}, \text{BRTPF})$.

We have that $(\{\bowtie, \cup, \bowtie\!\!\!\bowtie, \pi\}, \text{TPF}) \preceq_e (\{\bowtie, \cup, \bowtie\!\!\!\bowtie, \pi\}, \text{CORESPARQL})$ because it holds that $\text{TPF} \subseteq \text{CORESPARQL}$. By combining this with Theorem 1 we obtain that $(\{\bowtie, \cup, \bowtie\!\!\!\bowtie, \pi\}, \text{TPF}) \preceq_e (\{\cup, \bowtie\}, \text{BRTPF})$. Thus, to prove Theorem 4 it remains to show that $(\{\cup, \bowtie\}, \text{BRTPF}) \npreceq_e (\{\bowtie, \cup, \bowtie\!\!\!\bowtie, \pi\}, \text{TPF})$. We prove something stronger:

Lemma 3. $(\emptyset, \text{BRTPF}) \npreceq_e (\{\bowtie, \cup, \bowtie\!\!\!\bowtie, \pi\}, \text{TPF})$.

It turns out that FILTER is all that one needs to add to TPF to make it comparable with BRTPF. In fact, in terms of expressive power of LDFMs, TPF with FILTER and BRTPF are equivalent regardless of the client language.

Proposition 1. $(\mathcal{L}, \mathrm{BRTPF}) \equiv_e (\mathcal{L}, \mathrm{TPF} + \mathrm{FILTER})$ *holds for every response-combination language* $\mathcal{L}$.[1]

Given Proposition 1, in every combination in the lattice of Fig. 4 we can replace BRTPF by TPF+FILTER and the relationships still hold.

The next result shows an equivalence concerning TPF and BGP.

Proposition 2. $(\emptyset, \mathrm{BGP}) \equiv_e (\{\bowtie\}, \mathrm{TPF}) \equiv_e (\{\bowtie\}, \mathrm{BGP})$

Our final result in this section is a set of incompatibilities for TPF and BRTPF which follow from our previous results.

Corollary 1. *The following relationships hold.*

1. $(\{\bowtie, \cup, \bowtie, \pi\}, \mathrm{TPF})$ *and* $(\emptyset, \mathrm{BRTPF})$ *are not comparable in terms of* $\preceq_e$.
2. $(\{\cup\}, \mathrm{TPF})$ *and* $(\{\bowtie\}, \mathrm{BRTPF})$ *are not comparable in terms of* $\preceq_e$.
3. $(\{\bowtie\}, \mathrm{TPF})$ *and* $(\{\cup\}, \mathrm{BRTPF})$ *are not comparable in terms of* $\preceq_e$.

The lattice of the expressiveness of LDFMs shown in Fig. 4 is constructed by composing all the results in this section.

4 Comparisons Based on Classical Complexity Classes

Besides expressiveness, another classical measure is the (computational) complexity of query evaluation. In this section we present a simple analysis to provide a comparison of LDFs settings in terms of the complexity of the query evaluation problem for the server and response-combination languages. In particular, we focus on the *combined complexity* that measures the complexity of problems for which a query and a dataset are both assumed to be given as input [12]. We begin by defining two new comparison notions.

Definition 3. *We say that* $(\mathcal{L}_1, \mathcal{L}_2)$ *is at most as server-power demanding as* $(\mathcal{L}'_1, \mathcal{L}'_2)$, *denoted by* $(\mathcal{L}_1, \mathcal{L}_2) \preceq_{sp} (\mathcal{L}'_1, \mathcal{L}'_2)$, *if the combined complexity of the evaluation problem for* $\mathcal{L}_2$ *is at most as high as the combined complexity of the evaluation problem for* $\mathcal{L}'_2$. *Similarly,* $(\mathcal{L}_1, \mathcal{L}_2)$ *is at most as result-construction demanding as* $(\mathcal{L}'_1, \mathcal{L}'_2)$, *denoted by* $(\mathcal{L}_1, \mathcal{L}_2) \preceq_{rc} (\mathcal{L}'_1, \mathcal{L}'_2)$, *if the combined complexity of the evaluation problem for* $\mathcal{L}_1$ *is at most as high as the combined complexity of the evaluation problem for* $\mathcal{L}'_1$.

---

[1] This result and the next are given as propositions instead of theorems because they are simple to prove with standard notions of logic (as detailed in the aforementioned appendix of this paper) and they do not add an important separation in the expressiveness lattice (Fig. 4).

We write $(\mathcal{L}_1, \mathcal{L}_2) \equiv_c (\mathcal{L}_1', \mathcal{L}_2')$ if $(\mathcal{L}_1, \mathcal{L}_2) \preceq_c (\mathcal{L}_1', \mathcal{L}_2')$ and $(\mathcal{L}_1', \mathcal{L}_2') \preceq_c (\mathcal{L}_1, \mathcal{L}_2)$, for $c \in \{sp, rc\}$. The next result follows trivially from the results of Pérez et al. [10] and Schmidt et al. [11] that show that for the AND-fragment and the UNION-fragment of SPARQL, the evaluation problem is in PTIME, respectively, for the AND-UNION-fragment it is NP-complete, and for fragments containing OPT it is PSPACE-complete.

Corollary 2. *For any server language $\mathcal{L}_S$, the following properties hold:*

1. $(\emptyset, \mathcal{L}_S) \equiv_{rc} (\{\bowtie\}, \mathcal{L}_S) \equiv_{rc} (\{\cup\}, \mathcal{L}_S)$
2. $(\emptyset, \mathcal{L}_S) \preceq_{rc} (\{\bowtie, \cup\}, \mathcal{L}_S) \preceq_{rc} (\{\bowtie\}, \mathcal{L}_S)$
3. $(\{\bowtie\}, \mathcal{L}_S) \equiv_{rc} (\{\bowtie, \bowtie\}, \mathcal{L}_S) \equiv_{rc} (\{\bowtie, \bowtie, \cup\}, \mathcal{L}_S) \equiv_{rc} (\{\bowtie, \bowtie, \cup, \pi\}, \mathcal{L}_S)$

Moreover, for any response-combination language $\mathcal{L}_C$, the following properties hold:

4. $(\mathcal{L}_C, \text{BGP}) \equiv_{sp} (\mathcal{L}_C, \text{BRTPF}) \equiv_{sp} (\mathcal{L}_C, \text{TPF}) \equiv_{sp} (\mathcal{L}_C, \text{DUMP})$
5. $(\mathcal{L}_C, \text{BGP}) \preceq_{sp} (\mathcal{L}_C, \text{CORESPARQL})$

Notice that the pairs of response-combination and server languages mentioned in the corollary can be organized into two additional lattices along the lines of the expressiveness lattice in Fig. 4. That is, Properties 1–3 in Corollary 2 establish a *result-construction demand lattice*, and Properties 4 and 5 establish a *server-power demand lattice*. However, both of these lattices consist of only a single path from top to bottom.

5   Additional Complexity Measures

In the previous sections we provide a base for comparing different combinations of client/server capabilities considering expressiveness and complexity. While these comparisons are a necessary starting point, from a practical point of view one would also want to compare the computational resources that have to be payed when using one LDF interface or another. More specifically, assume that you have two combinations of client and server capabilities that are equally expressive, that is, $(\mathcal{L}_1, \mathcal{L}_2) \equiv_e (\mathcal{L}_1', \mathcal{L}_2')$. Then, we know that every task that can be completed in $(\mathcal{L}_1, \mathcal{L}_2)$ can also be completed in $(\mathcal{L}_1', \mathcal{L}_2')$. The question however is: are we paying an additional cost when using one setting or the other? Or more interestingly, is any of the two strictly better than the other in terms of some of the resources needed to answer queries? In this section we show the suitability of our proposed framework to also analyze this aspect of LDFs.

We begin this section with a definition that formalizes two important resources used when consuming Linked Data Fragments, namely, the number of requests sent to the server, and the total size of the data transferred from the server to the client.

Definition 4. *For an LDFM M, an RDF query q, and an RDF graph G, we define the number of requests of M with input (q, G), denoted by $r_M(q, G)$, as* *the final value of counter c_M during the computation of M with input (q, G). Similarly, the amount of data transferred by M with input (q, G), denoted by $t_M(q, G)$, is defined as the value $|D_1| + |D_2| + \cdots + |D_{r_M(q,G)}|$.*

We can now define the request and transfer complexity of classes of RDF queries.

Definition 5. *Let f be a function from the natural numbers. A class $\mathcal{C}$ of RDF queries has* request complexity *at most f under $(\mathcal{L}_1, \mathcal{L}_2)$ if there exists an $(\mathcal{L}_1, \mathcal{L}_2)$-LDFM M that computes every query $q \in \mathcal{C}$ such that for every $q \in \mathcal{C}$ and RDF graph G it holds that $r_M(q, G) \leq f(|q| + |G|)$. Similarly we say that $\mathcal{C}$ has* transfer complexity *at most f under $(\mathcal{L}_1, \mathcal{L}_2)$ if there exists an $(\mathcal{L}_1, \mathcal{L}_2)$-LDFM M that computes every $q \in \mathcal{C}$ such that $t_M(q, G) \leq f(|q| + |G|)$ for every $q \in \mathcal{C}$ and RDF graph G.*

We now have all the necessary to present our main notions to compare different classes of RDF queries in terms of the resources needed to compute them with LDFMs.

Definition 6. *Let $\mathcal{L}_1, \mathcal{L}_1'$ be response-combination languages and $\mathcal{L}_2, \mathcal{L}_2'$ be server languages. Then, $(\mathcal{L}_1, \mathcal{L}_2)$ is* at most as request demanding as *$(\mathcal{L}_1', \mathcal{L}_2')$, denoted by $(\mathcal{L}_1, \mathcal{L}_2) \preceq_r (\mathcal{L}_1', \mathcal{L}_2')$, if the following condition holds: For every function f and every class $\mathcal{C}$ of RDF queries expressible in both $(\mathcal{L}_1, \mathcal{L}_2)$ and $(\mathcal{L}_1', \mathcal{L}_2')$, if $\mathcal{C}$ has request complexity at most f under $(\mathcal{L}_1', \mathcal{L}_2')$, then $\mathcal{C}$ has request complexity at most f under $(\mathcal{L}_1, \mathcal{L}_2)$. We similarly define the notions of being at most as* data-transfer demanding, *and denote it using $\preceq_t$.*

Regarding the notions in Definition 6 we make the following general observation.

Note 2. Let $(\mathcal{L}_1, \mathcal{L}_2)$ and $(\mathcal{L}_1', \mathcal{L}_2')$ be arbitrary pairs of response-combination/ server languages s.t. $\mathcal{L}_1 \subseteq \mathcal{L}_1'$ and $\mathcal{L}_2 \subseteq \mathcal{L}_2'$. Since $(\mathcal{L}_1, \mathcal{L}_2) \preceq_e (\mathcal{L}_1', \mathcal{L}_2')$, any $(\mathcal{L}_1', \mathcal{L}_2')$-LDFM that can be used to compute the class of RDF queries computable under $(\mathcal{L}_1', \mathcal{L}_2')$ can also be used to compute every RDF query that is computable under $(\mathcal{L}_1, \mathcal{L}_2)$. Therefore, it follows trivially that $(\mathcal{L}_1', \mathcal{L}_2') \preceq_r (\mathcal{L}_1, \mathcal{L}_2)$ and $(\mathcal{L}_1', \mathcal{L}_2') \preceq_t (\mathcal{L}_1, \mathcal{L}_2)$.

We next show some (less trivial) results that provide more specific comparisons with respect to the above introduced notions. To this end, we write $(\mathcal{L}_1, \mathcal{L}_2) \prec_c (\mathcal{L}_1', \mathcal{L}_2')$ to denote that $(\mathcal{L}_1, \mathcal{L}_2) \preceq_c (\mathcal{L}_1', \mathcal{L}_2')$ and $(\mathcal{L}_1', \mathcal{L}_2') \not\preceq_c (\mathcal{L}_1, \mathcal{L}_2)$, for $c \in \{r, t\}$.

Recall that $(\emptyset, \text{BGP})$, $(\{\bowtie\}, \text{TPF})$, and $(\{\bowtie\}, \text{BGP})$ are all equivalent in terms of expressive power. The next result proves formally that, in terms of the data transferred, they can actually be separated.

Proposition 3. *It holds that $(\{\bowtie\}, \text{BGP}) \prec_t (\{\bowtie\}, \text{TPF})$. Moreover, $(\{\bowtie\}, \text{TPF})$ and $(\emptyset, \text{BGP})$ are not comparable in terms of $\preceq_t$. Regarding the number of requests it holds that $(\{\bowtie\}, \text{BGP}) \equiv_r (\emptyset, \text{BGP}) \prec_r (\{\bowtie\}, \text{TPF})$.*

To see why the $\preceq_t$ incomparability result holds, consider the class $\mathcal{C}_1$ of SPARQL queries of the form $((?X_1, ?Y_1, ?Z_1)$ AND $(?X_2, ?Y_2, ?Z_2))$. It can be shown that any $(\emptyset, \text{BGP})$-LDFM M that computes $\mathcal{C}_1$ is such that $t_M(q, G)$, as a function, is in $\Omega(|G|^2)$. On the other hand there exists a $(\{\bowtie\}, \text{TPF})$-LDFM M' such that $t_{M'}(q, G)$ is in $O(|G|)$. This shows that $(\emptyset, \text{BGP}) \npreceq_t$ $(\{\bowtie\}, \text{TPF})$. Consider now the class $\mathcal{C}_2$ of SPARQL queries of the form $((a_1, b_1, c_1)$ AND $\cdots$ AND $(a_k, b_k, c_k))$. One can show that any $(\{\bowtie\}, \text{TPF})$-LDFM M that computes $\mathcal{C}_2$ is such that $t_M(q, G)$ is in $\Omega(|q|)$ in the worst case. On the other hand, $\mathcal{C}_2$ can be computed with a $(\emptyset, \text{BGP})$-LDFM that, in the worst case, transfers a single mapping (the complete query result) thus showing that $(\{\bowtie\}, \text{TPF}) \npreceq_t (\emptyset, \text{BGP})$. Class $\mathcal{C}_2$ can also be used to show that $(\emptyset, \text{BGP}) \prec_r$ $(\{\bowtie\}, \text{TPF})$. Our final result shows that even though $(\{\cup, \bowtie\}, \text{BRTPF})$ is very expressive, one may need to pay an extra overhead in terms of transfer and request complexity compared with a setting with a richer response-combination language.

Theorem 5. *The following strict relationships hold.*

1. $(\{\cup, \bowtie, \bowtie, \pi\}, \text{BRTPF}) \prec_t (\{\cup, \bowtie\}, \text{BRTPF})$
2. $(\{\cup, \bowtie, \bowtie, \pi\}, \text{BRTPF}) \prec_r (\{\cup, \bowtie\}, \text{BRTPF})$

The first point of this last theorem can be intuitively read as follows: in terms of bandwidth, the best possible query plans for an LDFM that access a BRTPF interface and then construct the output using operators in $\{\cup, \bowtie, \bowtie, \pi\}$, are strictly better than the best possible query plans that access a BRTPF interface and then construct the output using operators in $\{\cup, \bowtie\}$. The second point has a similar interpretation regarding the best possible query plans in terms of the number of requests sent to the server.

Although in this section we did not present a complete lattice as for the case of expressiveness in Sect. 3, these results show the usefulness of our framework to formally compare different options of Linked Data Fragments.

6   Concluding Remarks and Future Work

In this paper we have presented LDFMs, the first formalization to model LDF scenarios. By proving formal results based on LDFMs we show the usefulness of our model to analyze the fine-grain interplay between several metrics. We think that our formalization is a first step towards a theory to compare different access protocols for Semantic Web data. We next describe some possible directions for future research regarding LDFMs, extensions to the model, and its usage in some alternative scenarios.

In this paper we consider a specific set of client and server capabilities but our framework is by no means tailored to them. In particular, it would be really interesting to consider more expressive operators in the client languages and also new LDF interfaces, and compare them with the ones presented in this paper. One notable interface that is widely used in practice and that we plan to integrate in our study is the URI-lookup interface to retrieve Linked Data documents [4,5].

Besides the classical metrics (expressiveness and computational complexity), in this paper we considered only the number of requests sent to the server and the data transferred from server to client. It is easy to include other practical metrics in our framework. One important practical metric might be the amount of data transferred from the client to the server. In particular this metric might be very important for the BRTPF interface which requires sending solution mappings from the client to the server. Notice that this metric can be formalized by simply considering the space complexity on the request tape T_R of an LDFM. Similarly, if we consider the space complexity of the client query tape T_C, then we can restrict the size of the output query which makes sense as a restriction for clients with local memory constraints.

Finally, our model and results can be used as a first step towards a foundation for the theoretical study of Semantic Web query planning; more specifically, we would like to compile into our model already proposed languages for querying Linked Data, and to formally study what are the server interfaces and client capabilities needed to execute queries expressed in these languages, considering also the cost of compilation and execution according to our formal metrics. One possible starting point would be to study languages designed for live queries on the Web of Linked Data. For instance, we have recently proposed LDQL [8], which is a navigational language designed to query Semantic Web data based on the URI-lookup interface. Although we have presented a fairly complete formal analysis of LDQL [8], the computational complexity considered was only a classical analysis that disregards some important features of querying the Web such as server communication, latency, etc. Our machine model plus the results on comparisons of different LDFs can help to derive a more realistic complexity analysis for languages such as LDQL. We plan to tackle this problem in our future work.

Acknowledgements. Hartig's work has been funded by the CENIIT program at Linköping University (project no. 17.05). Pérez is supported by the Millennium Nucleus Center for Semantic Web Research NC120004, and ENLACE-Fondecyt VID-UChile.

References

1. Abiteboul, S., Vianu, V.: Queries and computation on the web. Theor. Comput. Sci. **239**(2), 231–255 (2000)
2. Arenas, M., Gutierrez, C., Miranker, D.P., Pérez, J., Sequeda, J.: Querying semantic data on the web. SIGMOD Rec. **41**(4), 6–17 (2012)
3. Beek, W., Rietveld, L., Bazoobandi, H.R., Wielemaker, J., Schlobach, S.: LOD laundromat: a uniform way of publishing other people's dirty data. In: Mika, P., et al. (eds.) ISWC 2014. LNCS, vol. 8796, pp. 213–228. Springer, Cham (2014). doi:10.1007/978-3-319-11964-9_14
4. Berners-Lee, T.: Design issues: linked data, July 2006
5. Bizer, C., Heath, T., Berners-Lee, T.: Linked data - the story so far. Int. J. Semant. Web Inf. Syst. **5**(3), 1–22 (2009)

6. Hartig, O.: SPARQL for a web of linked data: semantics and computability. In: Simperl, E., Cimiano, P., Polleres, A., Corcho, O., Presutti, V. (eds.) ESWC 2012. LNCS, vol. 7295, pp. 8–23. Springer, Heidelberg (2012). doi:10.1007/978-3-642-30284-8_8

7. Hartig, O., Buil-Aranda, C.: Bindings-restricted triple pattern fragments. In: Debruyne, C., Panetto, H., Meersman, R., Dillon, T., Kühn, E., O'Sullivan, D., Ardagna, C.A. (eds.) OTM 2016. LNCS, vol. 10033, pp. 762–779. Springer, Cham (2016). doi:10.1007/978-3-319-48472-3_48

8. Hartig, O., Pérez, J.: LDQL: a query language for the web of linked data. J. Web Semant. **41**, 9–29 (2016)

9. Mendelzon, A.O., Milo, T.: Formal models of web queries. Inf. Syst. **23**(8), 615–637 (1998)

10. Pérez, J., Arenas, M., Gutierrez, C.: Semantics and complexity of SPARQL. ACM Trans. Database Syst. **34**(3), 16:1–16:45 (2009)

11. Schmidt, M., Meier, M., Lausen, G.: Foundations of SPARQL query optimization. In: Proceedings of the 13th International Conference on Database Theory (ICDT) (2010)

12. Vardi, M.Y.: The complexity of relational query languages. In: STOC (1982)

13. Verborgh, R., Sande, M.V., Hartig, O., Herwegen, J.V., Vocht, L.D., Meester, B.D., Haesendonck, G., Colpaert, P.: Triple pattern fragments: a low-cost knowledge graph interface for the web. J. Web Semant. **37–38**, 184–206 (2016)

Language-Agnostic Relation Extraction from Wikipedia Abstracts

Nicolas Heist and Heiko Paulheim$^{(\boxtimes)}$

Data and Web Science Group, University of Mannheim, Mannheim, Germany
`heiko@informatik.uni-mannheim.de`

Abstract. Large-scale knowledge graphs, such as DBpedia, Wikidata, or YAGO, can be enhanced by relation extraction from text, using the data in the knowledge graph as training data, i.e., using *distant supervision*. While most existing approaches use language-specific methods (usually for English), we present a language-agnostic approach that exploits background knowledge from the graph instead of language-specific techniques and builds machine learning models only from language-independent features. We demonstrate the extraction of relations from Wikipedia abstracts, using the twelve largest language editions of Wikipedia. From those, we can extract 1.6M new relations in DBpedia at a level of precision of 95%, using a RandomForest classifier trained only on language-independent features. Furthermore, we show an exemplary geographical breakdown of the information extracted.

1 Introduction

Large-scale knowledge graphs, like DBpedia [16], Freebase [3], Wikidata [30], or YAGO [17], are usually built using heuristic extraction methods, e.g., from Wikipedia infoboxes, by exploiting crowd-sourcing processes, or both. These approaches can help creating large-scale public cross-domain knowledge graphs, but are prone both to errors as well as incompleteness. Therefore, over the last years, various methods for refining those knowledge graphs have been developed [22]. For filling missing relations (e.g., the missing birthplace of a person), *relation extraction* methods are proposed. Those can be applied to fill in relations for entities derived from Wikipedia pages without or with only sparsely filled infoboxes.

Most methods for relation extraction work on text and thus usually have at least one component which is explicitly specific for the language at hand (e.g., stemming, POS tagging, dependency parsing), like, e.g., [10,27,35], or implicitly exploits some characteristics of that language [2]. Thus, adapting those methods to work with texts in different natural languages is usually not a straight forward process.

In this paper, we propose a language-agnostic approach. Instead of knowledge about the language, we take background knowledge from the DBpedia knowledge graph into account. With that, we try to discover certain patterns in how Wikipedia abstracts are written. For example, in many cases, any genre mentioned in the abstract about a band is usually a genre of that band, the first

© Springer International Publishing AG 2017
C. d'Amato et al. (Eds.): ISWC 2017, Part I, LNCS 10587, pp. 383–399, 2017.
DOI: 10.1007/978-3-319-68288-4_23

city mentioned in an abstract about a person is that person's birthplace, and so on. In that case, the linguistic assumptions that we make about a language at hand are quite minimal. In fact, we only assume that for each language edition of Wikipedia, there are certain ways to structure an abstract of a given type of entity, in terms of what aspect is mentioned where (e.g., the birth place is the first place mentioned when talking about a person). Thus, the approach can be considered as language-independent (see [2] for an in-depth discussion).

The choice for Wikipedia abstracts as a corpus mitigates one of the common sources of errors in the relation extraction process, i.e., the entity linking. Since Wikipedia articles can be unambiguously related to an instance in a knowledge base, and Wikipedia page links contained in Wikipedia abstracts are mostly free from noise, the corpus at hand can be directly exploited for relation extraction without the need for an upfront potentially noisy entity linking step.

By applying the exact same pipeline without any modifications to the twelve largest languages of Wikipedia, which encompass languages from different language families, we demonstrate that such patterns can be extracted from Wikipedia abstracts in arbitrary languages. We show that it is possible to extract valuable information by combining the information extracted from different languages.

The rest of this paper is structured as follows. In Sect. 2, we review related work. We introduce our approach in Sect. 3, and discuss various experiments in Sect. 4. We conclude with a summary and an outlook on future work.

2   Related Work

Various approaches have been proposed for relation extraction from text, in particular from Wikipedia. In this paper, we particularly deal with *closed* relation extraction, i.e., extracting new instantiations for relations that are defined a priori (by considering the schema of the knowledge graph at hand, or the set of relations contained therein).

Using the categorization introduced in [22], the approach proposed in this paper is an *external* one, as it uses Wikipedia as an external resource in addition to the knowledge graph itself. While internal approaches for relation prediction in knowledge graphs exist as well, using, e.g., association rule mining, tensor factorization, or graph embeddings, we restrict ourselves to comparing the proposed approach to other external approaches.

Most of the approaches in the literature make more or less heavy use of language-specific techniques. Distant supervision is proposed by [19] as a means to relation extraction for Freebase from Wikipedia texts. The approach uses a mixture of lexical and syntactic features, where the latter are highly language-specific. A similar approach is proposed for DBpedia in [1]. Like the Freebase-centric approach, it uses quite a few language-specific techniques, such as POS tagging and lemmatization. While those two approaches use Wikipedia as a corpus, [13] compare that corpus to a corpus of news texts, showing that the usage of Wikipedia leads to higher quality results.

Nguyen et al. [20] introduce an approach for mining relations from Wikipedia articles which exploits similarities of dependency trees for extracting new relation instances. In [34], the similarity of dependency trees is also exploited for clustering pairs of concepts with similar dependency trees. The construction of those dependency trees is highly language specific, and consequently, both approaches are evaluated on the English Wikipedia only.

An approach closely related to the one discussed in this paper is *iPopulator* [15], which uses Conditional Random Fields to extract patterns for infobox values in Wikipedia abstracts. Similarly, *Kylin* [33] uses Conditional Random Fields to extract relations from Wikipedia articles and general Web pages. Similarly to the approach proposed in this paper, *PORE* [31] uses information on neighboring entities in a sentence to train a support vector machine classifier for the extraction of four different relations. The papers only report results for English language texts.

Truly language-agnostic approaches are scarce. In [8], a multi-lingual approach for open relation extraction is introduced, which uses Google translate to produce English language translations of the corpus texts in a preprocessing step, and hence exploits externalized linguistic knowledge. In the recent past, some approaches based on deep learning have been proposed which are reported to or would in theory also work on multi-lingual text [21,29,36,37]. They have the advantages that (a) they can compensate for shortcomings in the entity linking step when using arbitrary text and (b) that explicit linguistic feature engineering is replaced by implicit feature construction in deep neural networks. In contrast to those works, we work with a specific set of texts, i.e., Wikipedia abstracts. Here, we can assume that the entity linking is mostly free from noise (albeit not complete), and directly exploit knowledge from the knowledge graph at hand, i.e., in our case, DBpedia.

In contrast to most of those works, the approach discussed in this paper works on Wikipedia abstracts in *arbitrary* languages, which we demonstrate in an evaluation using the twelve largest language editions of Wikipedia. While, to the best of our knowledge, most of the approaches discussed above are only evaluated on one or at maximum two languages, this is the first approach to be evaluated on a larger variety of languages.

3 Approach

Our aim is to identify and exploit typical patterns in Wikipedia abstracts. As a running example, we use the *genre* relation which may hold between a music artist and a music genre. Figure 1 depicts this example with both an English and a French Wikipedia abstract. As our aim is to mine relations for the canonical DBpedia, extracted from the (largest) English language Wikipedia, we inspect all links in the abstract which have a corresponding entity in the main DBpedia knowledge base created from the English Wikipedia.[1] For other languages, we take one intermediate step via the interlanguage links in Wikipedia, which are extracted as a part of DBpedia [16].

3.1   Overall Approach

For 395 relations that can hold between entities, the ontology underlying the DBpedia knowledge graph[2] defines an explicit domain and range, i.e., the types of objects that are allowed in the subject and object position of this relation.[3] Each Wikipedia page also maps to an entity in the DBpedia knowledge graph, some of which are typed. We consider a pair of a Wikipedia page p_0 and a Wikipedia page p_1 linked from the abstract of p_0 as a *candidate* for a relation R if the corresponding DBpedia entities e_0 and e_1 have types that are equal to the domain and range of R. In that case, $R(e_0, e_1)$ is considered a candidate axiom to be included in the DBpedia knowledge graph. In the example in Fig. 1, given that the *genre* relation holds between musical artists and genres, and the involved entities are of the matching types, one candidate each is generated from both the English and the French DBpedia.[4]

We expect that candidates contain a lot of false positives. For example, for the *birthplace* relation holding between a person and a city, all cities linked from the person's web page would be considered candidates. However, cities may be referred to for various different reasons in an abstract about a person (e.g., they may be their death place, the city of their alma mater, etc.). Thus, we require additional evidence to decide whether a candidate actually represents a valid instantiation of a relation.

For taking that decision, we train a *machine learning model*. For each abstract of a page for which a given relation is present in the knowledge base, we use the *partial completeness assumption* [11] or *local closed world assumption* [7], i.e., we consider the relation to be complete. Hence, all candidates for the relation created from the abstract which are contained in the knowledge base are considered as *positive* training examples, all those which are not contained are considered as *negative* training examples. In the example in Fig. 1, *Industrial Rock* would be considered a positive example for the relation *genre*, whereas the genre *Rock*, if it were linked in the abstract, would be considered a negative example, since it is not linked as a genre in the DBpedia knowledge graph.

---

[1] For this work, we use the 2014 version of DBpedia, which was the most recent release available at the time the experiments were conducted. This version is available at http://oldwiki.dbpedia.org/Downloads2014. All statements made in this paper about the size etc. of DBpedia correspond to that version.

[2] http://dbpedia.org/services-resources/ontology.

[3] Note that the underlying OWL ontology distinguishes *object properties* that hold between entities, and *datatype properties* that hold between an entity and a literal value. Here, we only regard the former case.

[4] Prefixes used in this paper: dbr=http://dbpedia.org/, dbf=http://fr.dbpedia.org/, dbo=http://dbpedia.org/ontology/.

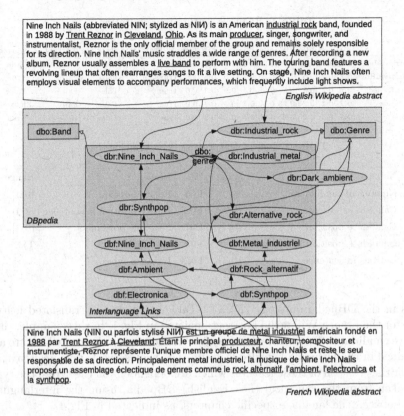

Fig. 1. Approach illustrated with extraction from English (above) and French (below) Wikipedia abstract

3.2 Feature Engineering

For training a classifier, both positive and negative examples need to be described by *features*. Table 2 sums up the features used by the classifiers proposed in this paper.

We use features related to the actual candidates found in the abstract (i.e., entities whose type matches the range of the relation at hand), i.e., the total number of candidates in the abstract (F00) and the candidate's sentence (F01), the position of the candidate w.r.t. all other candidates in the abstract (F02) and the candidate's sentence (F03), as well as the position of the candidate's sentence in the abstract (F07). The same is done for all entities, be it candidates or not (F04, F05, F06). Since all of those measures yield positive integers, they are normalized to (0, 1] by using their inverse.

Further features taken into account are the existence of a back link from the candidate's page to the abstract's page (F08), and the vector of all the candidate's

Table 1. Example feature representation

Instance	F00	F01	F02	F03	F04	F05	F06	F07	F08	dbo:MusicGenre	dbo:Place	dbo:Band	...	Correct
Industrial_Metal	0.2	1.0	1.0	1.0	0.25	1.0	1.0	1.0	1.0	True	False	False	...	True
Alternative_Rock	0.2	0.2	0.5	1.0	0.25	0.2	1.0	0.3	1.0	True	False	False	...	True
Ambient_music	0.2	0.2	0.3	0.5	0.25	0.1	0.5	0.3	0.0	True	False	False	...	False
Electronica	0.2	0.2	0.25	0.25	0.3	0.1	0.3	0.3	0.0	True	False	False	...	False
Synthpop	0.2	0.2	0.2	0.25	0.25	0.1	0.25	0.3	0.0	True	False	False	...	True

Table 2. List of features used by the classifier

ID	Name	Range	ID	Name	Range
F00	Number of candidates	(0, 1]	F05	Entity position	(0, 1]
F01	Candidates in sentence	(0, 1]	F06	Entity position in sentence	(0, 1]
F02	Candidate position	(0, 1]	F07	Sentence position	(0, 1]
F03	Candidate position in sentence	(0, 1]	F08	Back link	T/F
F04	Entities in sentence	(0, 1]	FXX	Instance types	T/F

types in the DBpedia ontology (FXX).[5] Table 1 depicts the translated feature table for the French Wikipedia abstract depicted in Fig. 1. In this example, there are five candidates (i.e., entities of type dbo:MusicGenre), three of which are also contained in the DBpedia knowledge graph (i.e., they serve as true positives).

For the creation of those features which are dependent on the types, the types are taken from the canonical (i.e., English) DBpedia, using the interlanguage links between the language specific chapters, as indicated in Fig. 1.

With the help of a feature vector representation, it is possible to learn fine-grained classification models, such as *The first three genres mentioned in the first or second sentence of a band abstract are genres of that band.*

3.3 Machine Learning Algorithms

Initially, we experimented with a set of five classification algorithms, i.e., Naive Bayes, RIPPER [5], Random Forest (RF) [4], Neural Networks [14] and Support Vector Machines (SVM) [6]. For all those classifiers, we used the implementation in *RapidMiner*[6], and, for the preliminary evaluation, all classifiers were used in their standard setup.

For those five classifiers, we used samples of size 50,000 from the ten most frequent relations in DBpedia, the corresponding English language abstracts, and performed an experiment in ten-fold cross validation. The results are depicted in Table 3. We can observe that the best results in terms of F-measure are achieved by Random Forests, which has been selected as the classifier to use in the subsequent experiments.

---

[5] The subject's types are not utilized. For DBpedia, they only exist if the subject has an infobox, which would make the approach infeasible to use for long tail entities for which the Wikipedia page does not come with an infobox.

[6] http://www.rapidminer.com/.

Table 3. Pre-study results on five machine learning algorithms

Relation	Naive Bayes			Rand.For.			RIPPER			Neural Net			SVM		
	P	R	F	P	R	F	P	R	F	P	R	F	P	R	F
dbo:birthPlace	.69	.65	.67	.69	.76	.72	.72	.73	.72	.61	.75	.67	.72	.74	.73
dbo:family	.55	.93	.69	.87	.83	.85	.85	.83	.84	.77	.83	.80	.87	.83	.85
dbo:deathPlace	.42	.30	.35	.51	.30	.38	.64	.18	.28	.61	.19	.29	.66	.20	.31
dbo:producer	.35	.55	.43	.35	.14	.20	.47	.04	.07	.23	.10	.14	.48	.05	.09
dbo:writer	.55	.61	.58	.62	.55	.58	.64	.54	.59	.52	.51	.51	.67	.53	.59
dbo:subsequentWork	.11	.21	.14	.35	.10	.16	.42	.02	.04	.21	.07	.11	.61	.06	.11
dbo:previousWork	.18	.43	.25	.39	.18	.25	.59	.05	.09	.57	.08	.14	.60	.10	.17
dbo:artist	.94	.94	.94	.94	.95	.94	.95	.96	.95	.95	.86	.90	.95	.89	.92
dbo:nationality	.76	.90	.82	.76	.92	.83	.77	.91	.83	.72	.81	.76	.77	.92	.84
dbo:formerTeam	.79	.74	.76	.85	.88	.86	.85	.88	.86	.82	.77	.79	.85	.89	.87
Average	.53	.63	.56	.63	.56	.58	.69	.51	.53	.60	.50	.51	.72	.52	.55

Furthermore, we compared the machine learning approach to four simple baselines using the same setup:

Baseline 1. The first entity with a matching type is classified as a positive relation, all others as negative.

Baseline 2. All entities with a matching type are classified as positive relations.

Baseline 3. The first entity with a matching ingoing edge is classified as a positive relation. For example, when trying to extract relations for dbo:birth-Place, the first entity which already has one ingoing edge of type dbo:birth-Place would be classified as positive.

Baseline 4. All entities with a matching ingoing edge are classified as positive relations.

Table 4. Pre-study results on the four baselines

Relation	Baseline 1			Baseline 2			Baseline 3			Baseline 4		
	P	R	F	P	R	F	P	R	F	P	R	F
dbo:birthPlace	.47	.99	.64	.46	1.00	.63	.49	.98	.66	.48	.99	.65
dbo:family	.18	.85	.30	.17	1.00	.29	.87	.84	.86	.86	1.00	.92
dbo:deathPlace	.28	.97	.43	.27	1.00	.43	.30	.93	.46	.30	.96	.46
dbo:producer	.17	.93	.29	.15	1.00	.26	.33	.80	.47	.32	.87	.46
dbo:writer	.41	.69	.52	.19	1.00	.32	.56	.59	.58	.45	.86	.59
dbo:subsequentWork	.02	1.00	.04	.02	1.00	.04	.02	.19	.03	.02	.19	.03
dbo:previousWork	.04	1.00	.08	.04	1.00	.08	.04	.20	.06	.03	.20	.06
dbo:artist	.31	.99	.47	.27	1.00	.42	.57	.87	.69	.53	.87	.66
dbo:nationality	.73	.96	.83	.64	1.00	.78	.74	.96	.84	.64	1.00	.78
dbo:formerTeam	.35	.72	.47	.40	1.00	.57	.78	.70	.74	.81	.98	.89
Average	.30	.91	.41	.26	1.00	.38	.47	.71	.54	.44	.79	.55

The results of the baseline evaluations are depicted in Table 4. We can observe that in terms of F-measure, they are outperformed by RandomForest. Although the margin seems small, the baseline approaches usually have a high recall, but low precision. In fact, none of them reaches a precision above 0.5, which means that by applying such approaches, at least half of the relations inserted into a knowledge graph would be noise.

4   Experiments

We conducted different experiments to validate the approach. First, we analyzed the performance of the relation extraction using a RandomForest classifier on the English DBpedia only. Here, we follow a two-fold approach: for once, we use a cross-validated silver standard evaluation, where we evaluate how well existing relations can be predicted for instances already present in DBpedia. Since such a silver-standard evaluation can introduce certain biases [22], we additionally validate the findings on a subset of the extracted relations in a manual retrospective evaluation.

In a second set of experiments, we analyze the extraction of relations on the twelve largest language editions of Wikipedia, which at the same time are those with more than 1M articles, i.e., English, German, Spanish, French, Italian, Dutch, Polish, Russian, Cebuano, Swedish, Vietnamese, and Waray.[7,8] Note that this selection of languages does not only contain Indo-European, but also two Austroasiatic and an Austronesian language.

In addition, we conduct further analyses. First, we investigate differences of the relations extracted for different languages with respect to topic and locality. For the latter, the hypothesis is that information extracted, e.g., for places from German abstracts is about places in German speaking countries.

4.1   Pre-study on English Abstracts

In a first set of experiments, we analyzed the performance of our method on English abstracts only. Since we aim at augmenting the DBpedia knowledge graph at a reasonable level of precision, our aim was to learn models which reach a precision of at least 95%, i.e., that add statements with no more than 5% noise to the knowledge graph. Out of the 395 relations under inspection, the RandomForest classifier could learn models with a precision of 95% or higher for 99 relations. For the 99 models that RF could extract with a minimum precision of 95%, the macro (micro) average recall and precision are 31.5% (30.6%) and 98.2% (95.7%), respectively.

---

[7] According to http://wikistats.wmflabs.org/display.php?t=wp, as of December 2015.

[8] The datasets of the extracted relations for all languages can be found online at http://dws.informatik.uni-mannheim.de/en/research/language-agnostic-relation-extraction-from-wikipedia-abstracts.

By applying the 99 models to all candidates, a total of 998,993 new relation instances could be extracted, which corresponds to roughly 5% of all candidates. Figure 2 depicts the 20 relations for which most instances are extracted.

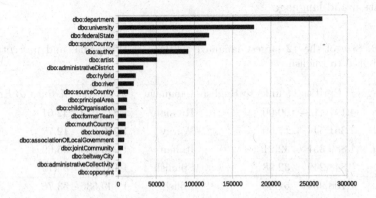

Fig. 2. 20 most frequent relations extracted from English abstracts

For validating the precision and recall scores computed on the existing relation instances, we sampled each 200 *newly* generated from five relations (i.e., 1,000 in total) and validated them manually. For the selection of entities, we aimed at a wider coverage of common topics (geographic entities, people, books, music works), as well as relations which can be validated fairly well without the need of any specific domain knowledge. The results are depicted in Table 5. It can be observed that the precision values obtained in cross-validation are rather reliable (i.e., the deviation from the estimate is 3% on average), while the recall values are less reliable (with a deviation of 9% on average). The first observation is crucial, as it allows to create new relations for the knowledge graph at a reasonable level of precision, i.e., the amount of noise introduced is strictly controlled.

Table 5. Results of the manual verification of precision and recall scores computed on the existing relation instances. R_e and P_e denotes the recall and precision of the models computed on the existing relation instances, while R_m and P_m denotes those verified by manual computation.

Relation	R_e	P_e	R_m	P_m
dbo:musicalBand	96.2	95.1	87.9	96.7
dbo:author	68.2	95.2	53.4	91.9
dbo:department	64.5	99.5	53.5	93.7
dbo:sourceCountry	98.9	98.0	98.8	97.8
dbo:saint	41.2	100	53.25	95.5

4.2   Cross-Lingual Relation Extraction

In the next experiment, we used the RandomForests classifier to extract models for relations for the top 12 languages, as depicted in Table 6. One model is trained per relation and language.

Table 6. Size of the 12 largest language editions of Wikipedia, and percentage of articles linked to English.

Language	# Entities	% links to English	Language	# Entities	% links to English
English	4,192,414	100.00	Russian	1,277,074	42.61
Swedish	2,351,544	17.60	Waray	1,259,540	12.77
German	1,889,351	42.21	Italian	1,243,586	55.69
Dutch	1,848,249	32.98	Spanish	1,181,096	54.72
French	1,708,934	51.48	Polish	1,149,530	53.70
Cebuano	1,662,301	5.67	Vietnamese	1,141,845	28.68

As a first result, we look at the number of relations for which models can be extracted at 95% precision. While it is possible to learn extraction models for 99 relations at that level of precision for English, that number almost doubles to 187 when using the top twelve languages, as depicted in Fig. 3. These results show that it is possible to learn high precision models for relations in other languages for which this is not possible in English.

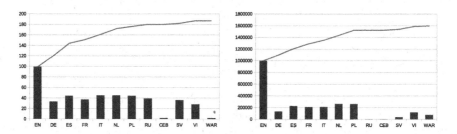

Fig. 3. Number of relations (left) and statements (right) extracted at 95% precision in the top 12 languages. The bars show the number of statements that could be extracted for the given language, the line depicts the accumulated number of statements for the top N languages.

When extracting new statements (i.e., instantiations of the relations) using those models, our goal is to extract those statements in the canonical DBpedia knowledge base, as depicted in Fig. 1. The number of extracted statements per language, as well as cumulated statements, is depicted in Fig. 3.

At first glance, it is obvious that, although a decent number of models can be learned for most languages, the number of statements extracted are on average an order of magnitude smaller than the number of statements that are extracted for English. However, the additional number of extracted relations is considerable: while for English only, there is roughly 1M relations, 1.6M relations can be extracted from the top 12 languages, which is an increase of about 60% when stepping from an English-only to a multi-lingual extraction. The graphs in Fig. 3 also shows that the results stabilize after using the seven largest language editions, i.e., we do not expect any significant benefits from adding more languages with smaller Wikipedias to the setup.

As can be observed in Fig. 3, the number of extracted statements is particularly low for Russian and Cebuano. For the latter, the figure shows that only a small number of high quality models can be learned, mostly due to the low number of inter-language links to English, as depicted in Table 6. For the former, the number of high quality models that can be learned is larger, but the models are mostly unproductive, since they are learned for rather exotic relations. In particular, for the top 5 relations in Fig. 2, no model is learned for Russian.

It is evident that the number of extracted statements is not proportional to the relative size of the respective Wikipedia, as depicted in Table 6. For example, although the Swedish Wikipedia is more than half the size of the English one, the number of extracted statements from Swedish is by a factor of 28 lower than those extracted from English. At first glance, this may be counter intuitive.

The reason for the number of statements extracted from languages other than English is that we only generate candidates if both the article at hand and the entity linked from that article's abstract have a counterpart in the canonical English DBpedia. However, as can be seen from Table 6, those links to counterparts are rather scarce. For the example of Swedish, the probability of an entity being linked to the English Wikipedia is only 0.176. Thus, the probability for a candidate that both the subject and object are linked to the English Wikipedia is $0.176 \times 0.176 = 0.031$. This is pretty exactly the ratio of statements extracted from Swedish to statements extracted from English (0.036). In fact, the number of extracted statements per language and the squared number of links between the respective language edition and the English Wikipedia have a Pearson correlation coefficient of 0.95. This shows that the low number of statements is mainly an effect of missing inter-language links in Wikipedia, rather than a shortcoming of the approach as such.[9]

4.3 Topical and Geographical Analysis by Language

To further analyze the extracted statements, we look at the topical and geographical coverage for the *additional* statements (i.e., statements that are

---

[9] If we were interested in extending the coverage of DBpedia not only w.r.t. relations between existing entities, but also adding *new* entities (in particular: entities which only exist in language editions of Wikipedia other than English), then the number of statements would be larger. However, this was not in the focus of this work.

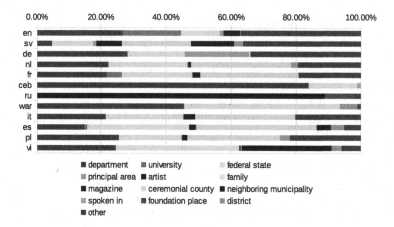

Fig. 4. Distribution of relations in the different language extractions

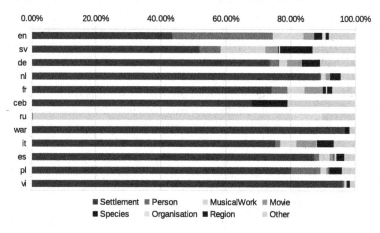

Fig. 5. Distribution of subject types in the different language extractions

not yet contained in DBpedia) that are extracted for the twelve languages at hand. First, we depict the most frequent relations and subject classes for the statements. The results are depicted in Figs. 4 and 5. It can be observed that the majority of statements is related to geographical entities and their relations. The Russian set is an exception, since most extracted relations are about musical works, in contrast to geographic entities, as for the other languages. Furthermore, the English set has the largest fraction of person related facts.

We assume that the coverage of Wikipedia in different languages is, to a certain extent, biased towards places, persons, etc. from countries in which the respective language is spoken.[10] Thus, we expect that, e.g., for relations

---

[10] See, e.g., http://geography.oii.ox.ac.uk/?page=geographic-intersections-of-languages-in-wikipedia for evidence.

extracted about places, we will observe that the distribution of countries to which entities are related differs for the various language editions.

To validate this hypothesis, we determine the country to which a statement is related as follows: given a statement s in the form

```
s p o .
```

we determine the set of pairs $P_s := <r, c>$ of relations and countries that fulfill

```
s r c .
c a dbo:Country .
```

and

```
o r c .
c a dbo:Country .
```

For all statements S extracted from a language, we sum up the relative number of relations of a country to each statement, i.e., we determine the weight of a country C as

$$w(C) := \sum_{s=1}^{|S|} \frac{|\{<r,c> \in P_s | c = C\}|}{|P_s|} \tag{1}$$

The analysis was conducted using the RapidMiner Linked Open Data Extension [25].

Figure 6 depicts the distributions for the countries. We can observe that while in most cases, facts about US related entities are the majority, only for Polish, entities related to Poland are the most frequent. For Swedish, German, French, Cebuano and Italian, the countries with the largest population speaking those languages (i.e., Sweden, Germany, France, Philippines, and Italy, respectively),

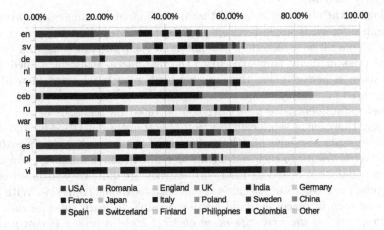

Fig. 6. Distribution of locality in the different language extractions

are at the second position. For Spanish, Spain is at the second position, despite Mexico and Colombia (rank 11 and 6, respectively) having a larger population. For the other languages, a language-specific effect is not observable: for Dutch, the Netherlands are at rank 8, for Vietnamese, Vietnam is at rank 34, for Waray, the Philippines are at rank 7. For Russian, Russia is on rank 23, preceded by Soviet Union (sic!, rank 15) and Belarus (rank 22).

The results show that despite the dominance of US-related entities, there is a fairly large variety in the geographical coverage of the information extracted. This supports the finding that adding information extracted from multiple Wikipedia language editions helps broadening the coverage of entities.

5   Conclusion and Outlook

Adding new relations to existing knowledge graphs is an important task in adding value to those knowledge graphs. In this paper, we have introduced an approach that adds relations to DBpedia using abstracts in Wikipedia. Unlike other works in that area, the approach presented in this paper uses background knowledge from DBpedia, but does not rely on any language-specific techniques, such as POS tagging, stemming, or dependency parsing. Thus, it can be applied to Wikipedia abstracts in any language.

While we have worked with DBpedia only in this paper, the approach can be applied to other cross-domain knowledge graphs, such as YAGO or Wikidata, as well, since they also link to DBpedia. Furthermore, for a significant portion of Semantic Web datasets, links to DBpedia exist as well [26], so that the approach can be applied even to such domain-specific datasets.

The experimental results show that the approach can add a significant amount of new relations to DBpedia. By extending the set of abstracts from English to the most common languages, the coverage both of relations for which high quality models can be learned, as well as of instantiation of those relations, significantly increases.

Following the observation in [29] that multi-lingual training can improve the performance for each single language, it might be interesting to apply models also on languages on which they had not been learned. Assuming that certain patterns exist in many languages (e.g., the first place being mentioned in an article about a person being the person's birth place), this may increase the amount of data extracted.

In our experiments, we have only concentrated on relations between entities so far. However, a significant fraction of statements in DBpedia and other knowledge graphs also have literals as objects. That said, it should be possible to extend the framework to such statements as well. Although numbers, years, and dates are usually not linked to other entities, they are quite easy to detect using, e.g., regular expressions or specific taggers such as *HeidelTime* [28]. With such a detection step in place, it would also be possible to learn rules for datatype properties, such as: *the first date in an abstract about a person is that person's birthdate*, etc.

Furthermore, our focus so far has been on adding missing relations. A different, yet related problem is the detection of wrong relations [22–24]. Here, we could use our approach to gather *evidence* for relations in different language editions of Wikipedia. Relations for which there is little evidence could then be discarded (similar to DeFacto [12]). While for adding knowledge, we have tuned our models towards *precision*, such an approach, however, would require a tuning towards *recall*. In addition, since there are also quite a few errors in numerical literals in DBpedia [9,32], an extension such as the one described above could also help detecting such issues.

So far, we have worked on one genre of text, i.e., abstracts of encyclopedic articles. However, we are confident that this approach can be applied to other genres of articles as well, as long as those follow typical structures. Examples include, but are not limited to: extracting relations from movie, music, and book reviews, from short biographies, or from product descriptions. All those are texts that are not strictly structured, but expose certain patterns. While for the Wikipedia abstracts covered in this paper, links to the DBpedia knowledge graph are implicitly given, other text corpora would require entity linking using tools such as DBpedia Spotlight [18].

In summary, we have shown that Wikipedia abstracts are a valuable source of knowledge for extending knowledge graphs such as DBpedia. Those abstracts expose patterns which can be captured by language-independent features, thus allowing for the design of language-agnostic systems for relation extraction from such abstracts.

References

1. Aprosio, A.P., Giuliano, C., Lavelli, A.: Extending the coverage of DBpedia properties using distant supervision over Wikipedia. In: NLP & DBpedia. CEUR Workshop Proceedings, vol. 1064 (2013)
2. Bender, E.M.: Linguistically naïve != language independent: why NLP needs linguistic typology. In: EACL 2009 Workshop on the Interaction Between Linguistics and Computational Linguistics: Virtuous, Vicious or Vacuous? pp. 26–32 (2009)
3. Bollacker, K., Evans, C., Paritosh, P., Sturge, T., Taylor, J.: Freebase: a collaboratively created graph database for structuring human knowledge. In: 2008 ACM SIGMOD International Conference on Management of Data, pp. 1247–1250. ACM (2008)
4. Breiman, L.: Random forests. Mach. Learn. **45**(1), 5–32 (2001). http://dx.doi.org/10.1023/A:1010933404324
5. Cohen, W.W.: Fast effective rule induction. In: Machine Learning, Twelfth International Conference on Machine Learning, Tahoe City, CA, USA, pp. 115–123, 9–12 July 1995
6. Cristianini, N., Shawe-Taylor, J.: An Introduction to Support Vector Machines and Other Kernel-Based Learning Methods. Cambridge University Press, Cambridge (2010)
7. Dong, X.L., Murphy, K., Gabrilovich, E., Heitz, G., Horn, W., Lao, N., Strohmann, T., Sun, S., Zhang, W.: Knowledge vault: a web-scale approach to probabilistic knowledge fusion. In: 20th ACM SIGKDD International Conference on Knowledge Discovery and Data Mining, pp. 601–610 (2014)

8. Faruqui, M., Kumar, S.: Multilingual open relation extraction using cross-lingual projection. arXiv preprint arXiv:1503.06450 (2015)
9. Fleischhacker, D., Paulheim, H., Bryl, V., Völker, J., Bizer, C.: Detecting errors in numerical linked data using cross-checked outlier detection. In: Mika, P., et al. (eds.) ISWC 2014. LNCS, vol. 8796, pp. 357–372. Springer, Cham (2014). doi:10.1007/978-3-319-11964-9_23
10. Fundel, K., Küner, R., Zimmer, R.: RelEx—relation extraction using dependency parse trees. Bioinformatics 23(3), 365–371 (2007)
11. Galárraga, L.A., Teflioudi, C., Hose, K., Suchanek, F.: AMIE: association rule mining under incomplete evidence in ontological knowledge bases. In: 22nd International Conference on World Wide Web, pp. 413–422 (2013)
12. Gerber, D., Esteves, D., Lehmann, J., Bühmann, L., Usbeck, R., Ngomo, A.C.N., Speck, R.: DeFacto - temporal and multilingual deep fact validation. Web Semant. Sci. Serv. Agents World Wide Web 35(2), 85–101 (2015)
13. Gerber, D., Ngomo, A.C.N.: Bootstrapping the linked data web. In: Workshop on Web Scale Knowledge Extraction (2011)
14. Kubat, M.: Neural networks: a comprehensive foundation by Simon Haykin, Macmillan, 1994. ISBN 0-02-352781-7. Knowl. Eng. Rev. 13(4) 409–412 (1999). http://journals.cambridge.org/action/displayAbstract?aid=71037
15. Lange, D., Böhm, C., Naumann, F.: Extracting structured information from Wikipedia articles to populate infoboxes. In: 19th ACM Conference on Information and Knowledge Management (CIKM), pp. 1661–1664. ACM (2010)
16. Lehmann, J., Isele, R., Jakob, M., Jentzsch, A., Kontokostas, D., Mendes, P.N., Hellmann, S., Morsey, M., van Kleef, P., Auer, S., Bizer, C.: DBpedia - a large-scale, multilingual knowledge base extracted from Wikipedia. Semant. Web J. 6(2), 167–195 (2013)
17. Mahdisoltani, F., Biega, J., Suchanek, F.M.: YAGO3: a knowledge base from multilingual Wikipedias. In: Conference on Innovative Data Systems Research (2015)
18. Mendes, P.N., Jakob, M., García-Silva, A., Bizer, C.: DBpedia spotlight: shedding light on the web of documents. In: 7th International Conference on Semantic Systems (2011)
19. Mintz, M., Bills, S., Snow, R., Jurafsky, D.: Distant supervision for relation extraction without labeled data. In: Joint Conference of the 47th Annual Meeting of the ACL and the 4th International Joint Conference on Natural Language Processing of the AFNLP, pp. 1003–1011. Association for Computational Linguistics (2009)
20. Nguyen, D.P., Matsuo, Y., Ishizuka, M.: Relation extraction from Wikipedia using subtree mining. In: National Conference on Artificial Intelligence, vol. 22, p. 1414 (2007)
21. Nguyen, T.H., Grishman, R.: Relation extraction: perspective from convolutional neural networks. In: Proceedings of NAACL-HLT, pp. 39–48 (2015)
22. Paulheim, H.: Knowledge graph refinement: a survey of approaches and evaluation methods. Semant. Web 8, 489–508 (2017)
23. Paulheim, H., Bizer, C.: Improving the quality of linked data using statistical distributions. Int. J. Semant. Web Inf. Syst. (IJSWIS) 10(2), 63–86 (2014)
24. Paulheim, H., Gangemi, A.: Serving DBpedia with DOLCE – more than just adding a cherry on top. In: Arenas, M., et al. (eds.) ISWC 2015. LNCS, vol. 9366, pp. 180–196. Springer, Cham (2015). doi:10.1007/978-3-319-25007-6_11
25. Ristoski, P., Bizer, C., Paulheim, H.: Mining the web of linked data with rapidminer. Web Semant. Sci. Serv. Agents World Wide Web 35, 142–151 (2015)

26. Schmachtenberg, M., Bizer, C., Paulheim, H.: Adoption of the linked data best practices in different topical domains. In: Mika, P., et al. (eds.) ISWC 2014. LNCS, vol. 8796, pp. 245–260. Springer, Cham (2014). doi:10.1007/978-3-319-11964-9_16
27. Schutz, A., Buitelaar, P.: *RelExt*: a tool for relation extraction from text in ontology extension. In: Gil, Y., Motta, E., Benjamins, V.R., Musen, M.A. (eds.) ISWC 2005. LNCS, vol. 3729, pp. 593–606. Springer, Heidelberg (2005). doi:10.1007/11574620_43
28. Strötgen, J., Gertz, M.: HeidelTime: high quality rule-based extraction and normalization of temporal expressions. In: 5th International Workshop on Semantic Evaluation, pp. 321–324 (2010)
29. Verga, P., Belanger, D., Strubell, E., Roth, B., McCallum, A.: Multilingual relation extraction using compositional universal schema. arXiv preprint arXiv:1511.06396 (2015)
30. Vrandečić, D., Krötzsch, M.: Wikidata: a free collaborative knowledge base. Commun. ACM **57**(10), 78–85 (2014)
31. Wang, G., Yu, Y., Zhu, H.: PORE: positive-only relation extraction from Wikipedia text. In: Aberer, K., et al. (eds.) ASWC/ISWC 2007. LNCS, vol. 4825, pp. 580–594. Springer, Heidelberg (2007). doi:10.1007/978-3-540-76298-0_42
32. Wienand, D., Paulheim, H.: Detecting incorrect numerical data in DBpedia. In: Presutti, V., d'Amato, C., Gandon, F., d'Aquin, M., Staab, S., Tordai, A. (eds.) ESWC 2014. LNCS, vol. 8465, pp. 504–518. Springer, Cham (2014). doi:10.1007/978-3-319-07443-6_34
33. Wu, F., Hoffmann, R., Weld, D.S.: Information extraction from Wikipedia: moving down the long tail. In: 14th ACM SIGKDD International Conference on Knowledge Discovery and Data Mining, pp. 731–739. ACM (2008)
34. Yan, Y., Okazaki, N., Matsuo, Y., Yang, Z., Ishizuka, M.: Unsupervised relation extraction by mining wikipedia texts using information from the web. In: Joint Conference of the 47th Annual Meeting of the ACL and the 4th International Joint Conference on Natural Language Processing of the AFNLP, ACL 2009, vol. 2, pp. 1021–1029. Association for Computational Linguistics (2009)
35. Zelenko, D., Aone, C., Richardella, A.: Kernel methods for relation extraction. J. Mach. Learn. Res. **3**, 1083–1106 (2003)
36. Zeng, D., Liu, K., Chen, Y., Zhao, J.: Distant supervision for relation extraction via piecewise convolutional neural networks. In: 2015 Conference on Empirical Methods in Natural Language Processing (EMNLP), Lisbon, Portugal, pp. 17–21 (2015)
37. Zeng, D., Liu, K., Lai, S., Zhou, G., Zhao, J., et al.: Relation classification via convolutional deep neural network. In: COLING, pp. 2335–2344 (2014)

Alignment Cubes: Towards Interactive Visual Exploration and Evaluation of Multiple Ontology Alignments

Valentina Ivanova[1], Benjamin Bach[2], Emmanuel Pietriga[3],
and Patrick Lambrix[4(✉)]

[1] Swedish e-Science Research Centre and Linköping University, Linköping, Sweden
Valentina.Ivanova@liu.se
[2] University of Edinburgh, Edinburgh, UK
[3] INRIA, LRI (Univ Paris-Sud & CNRS), Université Paris-Saclay, Orsay, France
[4] Department of Computer and Information Science,
Linköping University, 58183 Linköping, Sweden
patrick.lambrix@liu.se

Abstract. Ontology alignment is an area of active research where many algorithms and approaches are being developed. Their performance is usually evaluated by comparing the produced alignments to a reference alignment in terms of precision, recall and F-measure. These measures, however, only provide an overall assessment of the quality of the alignments, but do not reveal differences and commonalities between alignments at a finer-grained level such as, e.g., regions or individual mappings. Furthermore, reference alignments are often unavailable, which makes the comparative exploration of alignments at different levels of granularity even more important. Making such comparisons efficient calls for a "human-in-the-loop" approach, best supported through interactive visual representations of alignments. Our approach extends a recent tool, Matrix Cubes, used for visualizing dense dynamic networks. We first identify use cases for ontology alignment evaluation that can benefit from interactive visualization, and then detail how our *Alignment Cubes* support interactive exploration of multiple ontology alignments. We demonstrate the usefulness of Alignment Cubes by describing visual exploration scenarios, showing how Alignment Cubes support common tasks identified in the use cases.

Keywords: Ontology alignment evaluation · Visual exploration · Multiple alignment comparison

1 Introduction

The need for automatic alignment of ontologies has sparked the development of a growing number of tools and algorithms. A comprehensive literature review can be found in [18]. It has also led to the creation of an annual event, the Ontology

© Springer International Publishing AG 2017
C. d'Amato et al. (Eds.): ISWC 2017, Part I, LNCS 10587, pp. 400–417, 2017.
DOI: 10.1007/978-3-319-68288-4_24

Alignment Evaluation Initiative (OAEI)[1], where alignments computed by the participating tools are compared against *reference alignments* (RA). In most cases the quality of these alignments is measured in terms of precision, recall, and F-measure. Precision is the ratio of correct suggested mappings over all suggested mappings. Recall is the ratio of correct suggested mappings over all correct mappings. F-measure is a harmonic mean between precision and recall. These measures give a good overall assessment of the quality of alignments in terms of the ratio of found mappings, missed mappings and wrongly suggested mappings. However, they do not allow for comparing alignments of specific parts of ontologies, or for comparing alignments to each other and to the RA at the detailed level of concepts and relations. Without means to compare the tools and algorithms at a detailed level, their strengths and weaknesses cannot be easily revealed and understood.

Furthermore, RAs are often not available, as their development is time and effort consuming and requires domain expertise. As a consequence, the quality of alignments is difficult to measure. In the absence of RA, the evaluation of alignments requires the exploration and comparison of multiple alignments, which involves expert users (analysts) performing tasks at different levels of granularity [1,8,20]: determining regions with similar or different number of mappings between the alignments, determining common or rarely found mappings, characterizing mappings as correct or incorrect. However, there is currently little support for performing these tasks in an interactive and flexible manner. Analysts are relying on custom scripts, which can be error-prone and require time to develop and fine-tune.

This work presents the following contributions to the ontology alignment field: (i) we identify several use cases that would benefit from comparative assessment of several alignments at different level of detail; we discuss their shared analytical tasks and identify features that would benefit from visual support. (ii) To address these use cases and tasks, we propose an interactive visual environment for the simultaneous comparative exploration and evaluation of multiple alignments at different levels of granularity. While visualizing even a single alignment is still a challenge due to the size and complexity of the ontologies, we provide a compact way to visualize multiple alignments. Instead of depicting all mappings together in a single representation, which would cause visual clutter and information overload, we provide an interactive visualization that supports multiple complementary views, and overview and detail techniques to explore alignments at different levels of granularity. We interpret an alignment as a bipartite graph (bi-graph), i.e., a network where links exist only between nodes of different sets (ontologies), and draw from the literature in the field of network visualization (e.g., [3,22]). We identify Matrix Cubes [2], a novel technique introduced for the interactive visual exploration of dynamic networks, as a promising visual approach to serve as a foundation for our tool - *Alignment Cubes*. Alignment Cubes significantly extend Matrix Cubes in order to make it applicable to the visualization of multi-level ontology alignment networks in the form of bi-graphs.

---

[1] http://oaei.ontologymatching.org.

This article is structured as follows: Sect. 2 presents the use cases and their shared tasks, and discusses existing approaches for visualizing multiple alignments. Section 3 describes Matrix Cubes, and Sect. 4 describes the Alignment Cubes we derived from them. We explain how users interact with Alignment Cubes using an example scenario in Sect. 5, discuss lessons learned and future extensions in Sect. 6, and conclude in Sect. 7.

2   Ontology Alignment Evaluation

The interactive exploration and evaluation of several alignments is only rarely considered in the literature. In [1] several analytic tasks have been identified and supported through multiple connected views, while [15, 19, 20] focus more on the alignment computation than their presentation. We thus first identify several evaluation use cases and discuss shared activities that could be efficiently supported through interactive visualization in Subsect. 2.1. In Subsect. 2.2 we connect this discussion with work about cognitive support for ontology mapping [9], requirements and evaluation of user interfaces in ontology alignment systems [7, 12], and review capabilities for simultaneous visualization of several alignments in existing systems. In Subsect. 2.3, we study the visualization approaches taken in alignment evaluation frameworks.

2.1   Evaluation Use Cases

The following use cases would benefit from users being able to simultaneously explore and evaluate several alignments interactively:

(UC1) **Selecting, combining and fine tuning alignment algorithms and tools:** OAEI editions, and [8, 21] among others, have shown that matchers and tools do not necessarily find the same correct mappings, and may compute different erroneous mappings too. Thus, selecting and combining matchers and tools requires examination of overlapping and divergent mappings to understand the differences in the underlying algorithms. It also includes assessing the impact of parameter changes on single similarity values and parts of the alignments for fine-tuning.

(UC2) **Matchers development:** Developers alter their algorithms according to some observations. Examining the outcome of such changes over other parts of the alignment and comparing to previous versions at different levels of granularity helps them assess the consequences of these changes.

(UC3) **Ontology alignment evolution:** Alignments are used for, e.g., data integration, merging ontologies, and database annotation. Changes in the alignments may influence the applications employing them. Understanding how alignments differ will facilitate the assessment of the impact of changes on their client applications [14, 23].

(UC4) **Validating and debugging of ontology alignments and RA:** Analyzing several alignments at the same time may reveal parts with large variations in the number of mappings or similarity values, and help in identifying potential errors and their sources during diagnosis. Developing and debugging RAs is a laborious and error-prone task. Recently, several works have found problems in the OAEI Anatomy track's RA [8]. Manual mapping validation requires a detailed view of each mapping and its context [9]. Understanding consequences of user validations and exploring what-if scenarios are also important [12].

(UC5) **Collaborative ontology alignment:** Collaborators need to understand the current state of an alignment, where and why their peers have introduced changes in comparison to previous revisions. This is especially needed when collaborative work happens over a long time period, or in distributed teams.

These use cases share common analytic tasks at *different granularity levels*; identifying parts of the alignment covered or not covered by all alignments, agreement or disagreement between matchers, determining incorrect, missed or always found mappings—which could be efficiently supported through interactive visualizations. Without measures to provide well-defined quantitative outputs, and with only high-level goals and questions, e.g., which threshold to choose and why (UC1), which version of my algorithm is better and why (UC2), what has been changed between two revisions and why (UC3, UC5), all of the use cases above are exploratory in their nature. They aim to find relevant information and answer questions not known in advance.

These are typical scenarios in which visual and interactive representations can be of help. In a visual environment exploration activities are supported by interactively varying parameters and thresholds to estimate the impact of changes, changing visual encodings to highlight different aspects, and reordering elements to facilitate trend and pattern discovery. Interactive exploration at different granularity levels reveals *regions of interest* to guide further exploration and help in identifying *patterns in and among different regions of interest* which may reveal similarities and dissimilarities between the respective alignments. These benefits directly apply to our case, where analysts are faced with the problem of exploring and visualizing multiple alignments.

Our use cases UC1–UC5 involve numerous *compare and contrast tasks* to select a threshold (UC1), an alignment to use (UC2 and UC4), for diagnosis and to identify outliers (UC4), common trends and regions (UC1, UC2), and for identifying changes (UC3, UC5). According to [1], diagnosis is a complex activity which is composed of iterative sequences of exploration and comparison, analyses of clusters of mappings, and comparative evaluation of matchers' performance.

2.2 Existing Approaches

Two recent studies review exploratory features in the user interfaces of ontology alignment systems [7,12]. Only one of the tools [5] (including its recent extensions [1,17]) provides support for visualization and exploration of several alignments together after discussing the need for such in connection to analytic tasks identified in interviews with alignment experts. Navigation and exploration in ontologies and just a single alignment have been highlighted in the context of discovering mappings and verification in [9], through the *inspection* dimension defined in [12], and by the 7 information seeking tasks and visual analytics from [7]. Another desirable functionality identified by alignment experts in [1] is the clustering of mappings according to different statistics in order to analyze each cluster separately. Several other works have also emphasized the importance of visually identifying dense regions in single alignments: for planning manual validation and identifying the most similar areas of the ontologies [9], as part of alignment inspection [12], and grouping to help identifying patterns [7]. Small-world graphs were used to present clusters in a single alignment at different granularity levels [16].

The exploration and comparison task functionality identified by experts in [1], is supported through comparative views by showing juxtaposed matrices computed by a combination of different matchers in the system. An additional matrix highlights variations in computed mappings between the matchers. RAs can be overlaid on top of each matcher's matrix. This approach is similar to one of the views in our approach using Matrix Cubes [2]—small multiples—but in comparison to our work, it forgoes the structure of the ontologies which is shown in another view. Similar to our approach, previous work [6,13] has presented the structure of ontologies as indented trees on the sides of a matrix, but only focused on a single alignment. One of them [6] provides support for reordering and depicts several types of mappings as well as derived and asserted mappings. Recent work [20] takes another approach to simultaneously visualizing several (externally-generated) alignments, employing linked indented lists and color-coding to depict the edges belonging to different alignments. The authors emphasize that with their tool *"[...] users can better compare and analyze alignments (i.e., parts of the ontologies which are covered for most alignments and those which are not, consensus between alignments, etc.)"*. Although filtering by threshold and mapping type is supported, the view quickly becomes cluttered as the size of ontologies and the number of alignments involved grow.

2.3   Frameworks for Ontology Alignment Evaluation

A few ontology alignment evaluation frameworks, SEALS[2], KitAMO [15] and AMC [19], provide rich back-end infrastructures for configuring (to a different extent), executing and storing the results from the execution of alignment components (matchers, filters and combination algorithms). In SEALS, used in OAEI, the alignments computed by the tools are compared to RA and evaluated in terms of precision, recall, F-measure, run time, coherence and number of requests to an oracle. The results are presented in sortable tables, after analysis with custom scripts. In KitAMO [15], probably the earliest system, the results are presented in the form of sortable tables containing either the mappings with their similarity values computed by each component, or aggregated data

---

[2] http://seals-project.eu—Semantic Evaluation At Large Scale.

(number of correct, incorrect and inferred mappings) in comparison to another component. In AMC [19], linked indented lists are used together with sortable tables as well. It additionally introduces a cube view which presents a single alignment where two of the dimensions depict the source and target ontologies, and the third dimension shows similarity values as bars—taller bars representing higher similarity values.

While all three frameworks provide rich back-end infrastructures for configuring and executing alignment algorithms, the tabular views are too limited to adequately address the simultaneous interactive comparison of several alignments and provide visual exploration at different granularity levels. The third framework devotes more attention to the visual presentation of the results, but it only depicts one alignment at a time. In comparison, our work focuses on the user interface and allows users to visually explore multiple alignments together. It can thus be seen as complementary to the back-end functionalities offered by these frameworks.

3 Matrix Cubes and the Cubix Interface

Alignment Cubes are adapted from earlier work that introduced *Matrix Cubes* [2] as an interactive visualization metaphor for the comparison of multiple time steps in dynamic networks. Here, we briefly summarize Matrix Cubes and *Cubix*, the interactive interface prototype used to manipulate and explore Matrix Cubes, and refer readers to [2].

Dynamic networks are networks whose topology and attributes change over time. The general idea of Matrix Cubes is to represent the different states (time steps) of a dynamic network as adjacency matrices, one matrix showing the state of the network at one given point in time. Each adjacency matrix is organized as follows (Fig. 1-a): nodes are the row and column headers, and cells represent the links between nodes. A cell at the intersection of a given row and column will only be filled if there is a link between the two corresponding nodes. Attributes of such links can be encoded visually inside the matrix cells', using variables such as, e.g., color hue or saturation, texture, and glyph size.

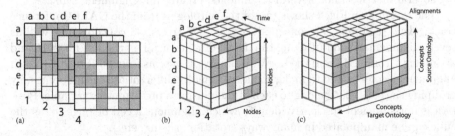

Fig. 1. From dynamic networks to Matrix Cubes and Alignment Cubes. (a) Adjacency matrices stacked to form a (b) 3-dimensional space-time cube (Matrix Cube). (c) Translation of the concept of Matrix Cubes to ontology alignment.

All adjacency matrices corresponding to the individual states of the network over time are then stacked, forming a cube (Fig. 1-b). The resulting 3D visualization acts mainly as a pivot and metaphor. Users manipulate the cube interactively to derive multiple meaningful 2D projections of the cube or its content, better suited to their visual analysis tasks. Manipulations include slicing the cube along different dimensions, rotating slices or the entire cube, juxtaposing slices to obtain small-multiple views, playing with cells' transparency to enable detailed compare & contrast tasks between slices.

As shown in Fig. 1-b, Matrix Cubes hold the network's nodes along two of the cube's three dimensions, the last dimension representing time, i.e., the different states of the network over time. As detailed below, instead of representing time on the cube's third dimension, our Alignment Cubes represent the different alignments being compared thus opening analysis opportunities for other dimensions than time.

An interactive visualization environment for Matrix Cubes, called Cubix, has been developed in Java + OpenGL by the authors of [2]. Our prototype Alignment Cube visualization tool is derived from the Cubix implementation. While Matrix Cubes are the general visualization structure (i.e., the 3D cube consisting of matrices) and Cubix is the interactive interface, the term *Alignment Cubes* refers to both; a specialization of Matrix Cubes *and* the name of our interface.

4   Alignment Cubes

This section details our extensions and adaptations of Matrix Cubes and describes our tool, Alignment Cubes[3], in connection to the discussion in Sect. 2.

4.1   From Matrix Cubes to Alignment Cubes

Two ontologies and their alignment can be seen as a bipartite network of mappings between individual concepts in the two ontologies. A matrix represents a single alignment between two ontologies. The rows hold the concepts from one ontology, the columns hold the concepts from the other ontology. Cells denote existing mappings between concepts in the respective rows and columns. Stacking several matrices, i.e., several alignments, creates an Alignment Cube.

The example in Fig. 2 shows two of the ontologies from the OAEI Conference track, *ekaw* (columns, 77 concepts) and *confOf* (rows, 38 concepts), as well as seven alignments (laid out along the depth dimension), i.e., the RA for 2016 and alignments from AML and the LogMap-family of systems from 2011 to 2013. Each alignment is color-coded to make it easy to visually differentiate the mappings, by grouping the cells that belong to each of them using a pre-attentive variable. Position is not sufficient to clearly identify which alignment a cell belongs to, as the cube can be manipulated in many ways (rotation, slicing, etc.).

---

[3] http://www.ida.liu.se/~patla00/publications/ISWC17 provides supplemental material: all figures from the paper in higher resolution, a screencast of the tool, and a downloadable version of the tool itself.

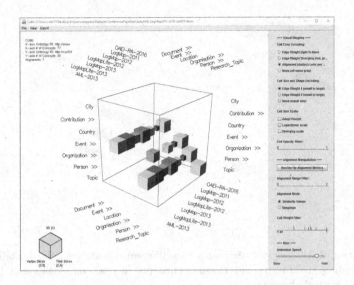

Fig. 2. Default view of Alignment Cubes in *similarities* mode. Rows and columns of the cube represent ontology concepts, individual cells inside the cube represent mapping relationships. Each alignment, corresponding to a slice in the third dimension, is assigned a different color. Widgets (sliders, button groups, etc.) mentioned in the text are referred to directly using their name. (Color figure online)

Concepts in ontologies often form a taxonomic hierarchy, but as Matrix Cubes do not support hierarchical networks, we extended the original framework. With Alignment Cubes, we represent the ontologies as indented lists with collapsible rows and columns. Figure 2 depicts the first level in both ontologies. Concepts that feature sub-concepts display the ≫ symbol after the concept label (e.g., *Event*, present in both ontologies, features sub-concepts). Clicking on a concept label expands the corresponding row or column. Expanded concepts then show the > symbol, and sub-concepts are indented according to their level in the hierarchy (Fig. 3-*a*). Concepts that have multiple parents appear under each parent, i.e., potentially multiple times in the hierarchy.

4.2 Granularity Levels

As discussed in Sect. 2, we aim to support views at different levels of granularity—from an overall view to regions based on the is-a hierarchy, and down to single mappings. To do so we introduce *alignment modes*. In *similarities* mode (Fig. 2), a filled cell represents an existing mapping between a pair of concepts. In *mappings* mode (Figs. 3-a and 4), a filled cell indicates that there is at least one existing mapping between a pair of concepts or their descendants. The cell weight represents either the similarity value (in the former case), or the number of mappings (in the latter case). Each mode is focused on performing one of two tasks: to compare similarity values for a pair of concepts, and to identify

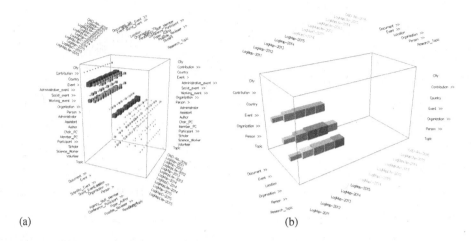

(a)   (b)

Fig. 3. Views of Alignment Cubes with two different cell weight color encodings: (a) after expanding the *Events* and *Persons* concepts in both ontologies and (b) after filtering out several alignments.

regions in the alignments with few or many mappings. The latter task provides a starting point for exploration and highlights regions of interest where many or few mappings have been calculated. When a concept is expanded in *mappings* mode, a cell is shown for both the concept itself and its sub-concepts. This forms regions in the cube (as in Fig. 3-a) where smaller cells indicate mappings deeper in the hierarchy.

4.3   Interactive Visual Exploration

The Alignment Cubes user interface provides a variety of interactions for visual exploration, shown in Fig. 2: changing alignment modes (see above), cell color and size encodings, switching between individual views, adapting cell transparency, brushing and linking, as well as alignment slice reordering. The cubelet widget (bottom left corner in Fig. 2) allows for a quick navigation between a set of predefined views by clicking or dragging the mouse on its faces. For example, cells can be filtered out by specifying minimum or maximum value thresholds using a range slider. This also allows to simulate different thresholds and explore what-if questions and cases. Entire alignments can be hidden. To support pattern discovery, the order of alignments (slices) in the cube can be changed to facilitate comparison. A specific order can be calculated based on measures of precision, recall and F-measure between the ontologies, or based on alphanumeric label sorting (labels representing matcher, tool or alignment name). After sorting by label, matchers from one family are displayed together next to each other.

4.4   Compare and Contrast

As with Matrix Cubes, Alignment Cubes provide several views onto the data, resulting from manipulations of the 3D cube. The individual views are: (a) 3D view, (b) 2D projection on 2 of the orthogonal cube faces, (c) side-by-side layout (small-multiples view) of the cube's slices (along 2 of the orthogonal dimensions). The 3D cube provides an overview of the number of alignments, number, size, and distribution of cells (mappings). It helps identify regions of interest and thus drive the initial exploration phase, and can possibly yield some high-level insights (Fig. 3-a). It allows for interactive rotation and zoom but suffers from the typical drawbacks of 3D visualization, including occlusion and perspective distortion. Projection views allow for a clutter-free aggregated view on all alignments by orthogonally overlapping cells (Fig. 6). Side-by-side views provide the most detailed view onto the data by entirely decomposing the view and showing each alignment in detail (Fig. 5). Individual views, together with the ability to vary cell size, color, and translucency, allow for flexible multi-perspective exploration of the entire data set.

Each of the two projections (alignment topology and concepts network) is paired with its respective small-multiples view. Both projections/small-multiple pairs allow for investigating the behavior of matchers—the alignment topology pair focuses on the similarities and differences between the alignments as a whole, while the concepts network pair allows for analyzing the behavior of matchers for a particular concept.

5   Use Cases Support

This section revisits the tasks and use cases identified in Sect. 2 and demonstrates how our tool supports interactive visual exploration and comparative evaluation of multiple alignments in Subsect. 5.1. We further show that Alignment Cubes satisfy requirements for ontology alignment evaluation systems in Subsect. 5.2.

5.1   Comparing Alignments, Systems and Support for Comparative Evaluation

We demonstrate how the tasks discussed in Subsect. 2.1 can be performed with our tool by conducting a walk-through scenario. As the evaluation of interactive visualization tools is challenging [4], methods such as case studies and usage scenario, are often employed [4,10] as they are more likely to provide insightful observations than traditional controlled experiments. In this scenario we aim to answer analytical questions including the following: Are the same regions covered in all alignments? Do matchers agree or disagree? Are there consistently stable and changing regions? Do similarity values differ? Are there missing and wrong mappings? Could we obtain other insights? These analytical questions are shared by all use cases. We focus on observations which would be problematic to obtain without a visual representation of the alignments, as was the case in, e.g., [8].

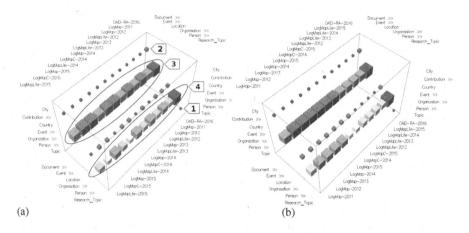

Fig. 4. 3D view in mappings mode: (a) initial view and (b) after reordering by name.

Dataset: We use the same two ontologies from the example in Sect. 4, but this time with a different set of alignments. We downloaded the alignments for the LogMap-family of systems between 2011 and 2015, and the RA for 2016. During this period, LogMap contributed three different versions: LogMapLite 2012–2015, LogMapC 2014–2015, and LogMap 2011–2015. Matrices for the alignment (Figs. 5 and 6) appear sparse since the respective alignments are the final alignments for the OAEI evaluation campaign, and thresholds have already been applied to remove mappings with a low similarity value. Note that in the process of matcher development, selection and fine tuning (see UC1 and UC2), the matrices would often be denser since more potential mappings would be considered. Alignment Cubes would scale to such higher-density matrices, as the technique was designed for dense dynamic networks in the first place [2].

Exploration: Our exploration starts with the initial 3D cube view in *mappings* mode (Fig. 4-a). The colors and sizes of cells show that most of the mappings (large red cells) are concentrated around the two sets of concepts between *Person* (④) and *Event* (③). In contrast, few mappings have been found between *Organization* and *confOf:Contribution-ekaw:Document*. To see the subconcepts of *Person* and *Event*, we expand these two concepts in both ontologies (Fig. 3-a). After expanding these concepts, as the visualization is in *mappings* mode, the cells that appear smaller and lighter (because of this particular color scheme) indicate under which subconcepts the single mappings are located. We now collapse these concepts and return to the view in Fig. 4-a. We see that all matchers have computed similar numbers for the *Event* concept pair, as the size of cells is more or less constant along the mapping dimension (cube depth).

However, somewhat larger differences in cell size can be observed along the depth dimension (across alignments) for the *Person* concept pair, which indicates a lower level of agreement across matching algorithms in this case. Hovering the respective cells with the mouse reveals that numbers vary between 4 and 8.

Apparently, only RA (the last, backmost slice) contains a mapping between *con-fOf:Topic* & *ekaw:Research Topic*, meaning that we found a missing mapping: the single cell not aligned with others (Fig. 4-a ①).

For further exploration, we investigate different alignment orderings (by interactively reordering alignment slices). Reorder-by-name (Fig. 4-b) clearly separates the three versions of the LogMap-family systems and allows to compare the performance for each version during the years. LogMap performs consistently better in terms of number of mappings found between 2012 and 2015 than in 2011, as visually indicated by the larger and more saturated (red) cells. To see if the same is true for similarity values, we switch to the *similarities* mode: if both modes show a similar picture, the system likely has used the same combination of alignment algorithms. To focus only on the LogMap alignments, we filter out all other alignments in Fig. 3-b, leaving the cube half-empty. The similarity values computed by LogMap vary between the years (Fig. 3-b), but not for its lightweight version, LogMapLite (not shown due to the filtering).

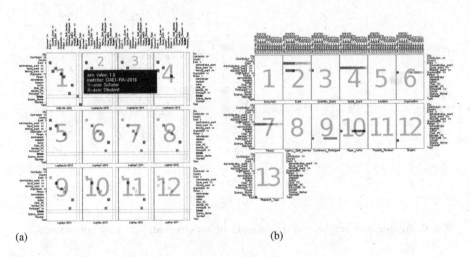

(a)   (b)

Fig. 5. Small-multiples views: (a) alignment topology (b) concept networks. Gray numbers have been added manually to the figure.

Focusing on the regions with many mappings, we expand the respective concepts in both ontologies and switch to the small-multiples view that shows alignment topology (Fig. 5-a). In both modes the patterns for each of the versions are clearly noticeable. The lightweight LogMapLite in all four years (matrices ②–⑤) consistently finds fewer mappings than the versions of LogMap between 2012 and 2015 (matrices ⑧–⑪). LogMap 2011's pattern (matrix ⑫) is closer to the LogMapLite alignments than to the rest of the LogMaps. We may conclude that LogMapLite reuses LogMap 2011 algorithms and settings, and that there were likely significant changes in algorithms or their settings between LogMap 2011 and the following LogMaps. Further evidence about this can be found in the small-multiples view that shows concept-networks (Fig. 5-b). Looking at the Event matrix (②), all LogMapLites and LogMap 2011 have computed an *incorrect* mapping between *confOf:Working Event* & *ekaw:Event*, and behave similarly in the *ekaw:Conference Participant* and *ekaw:Paper Author* matrices (⑨,⑩). Additionally, when observing alignment matrices, we can easily see that the following two mappings are missing from all LogMap-family alignments: *confOf:Scholar* & *ekaw:Student* in the alignment topology small-multiples view (on Fig. 5-a the labeled cell on matrix ① does not exist in the other matrices) and *confOf:Working Event* & *ekaw:Scientific Event* in the concept-networks small-multiples view (matrix ③ on Fig. 5-b). We can also observe on Fig. 5-b two of the missing mappings noticed before, *confOf:Scholar* & *ekaw:Student* (matrix ⑫), and *confOf:Topic* & *ekaw:Research Topic* (matrix ⑬).

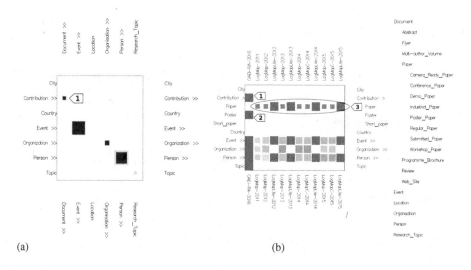

(a)   (b)

Fig. 6. Aggregated projections: (a) alignment topology and (b) concept networks.

Going back to the initial 3D cube view in *mappings* mode (Fig. 4-a), we make another observation: the cell in the top-left corner seems larger than the other cells aligned with it (Fig. 4-a ②). We switch to the alignment topology view, change the cell color encoding to a uniform color (gray) and decrease transparency using the cell-opacity slider. In this aggregated view (Fig. 6-a), cells that appear nested within each other (cells still have different sizes) indicate that the different matchers have computed different values for the same pair of concepts (Fig. 6-a). This is the case with the top-left corner cell we noticed earlier. There are at least two nested cells between *confOf:Contribution* & *ekaw:Document* (Fig. 6-a ①).

We expand both the *confOf:Contribution* and *ekaw:Document* concepts, as well as *ekaw:Paper*, which is a subconcept of *ekaw:Document*. We then switch to the concept networks projection view in *similarities* mode (Fig. 6-b). We can now explore the matchers' behavior (matchers have become columns in this view) while hovering over the concepts from the *ekaw* ontology on the right of the matrix. Observing the mappings in RA (the left-most column) around *confOf:Contribution*, we can see that the mappings for *confOf:Contribution* (①) and *confOf:Poster* (②) are only found in RA, and that there is no mapping under *confOf:Paper* (③) in RA (while it is found by all other matchers). To better observe where these mappings are, we switch to the concept-networks small-multiples view (not shown) and can see that the missing mappings are *confOf:Poster* & *ekaw:Poster Paper* and *confOf:Contribution* & *ekaw:Paper*. The wrong mapping is *confOf:Paper* & *ekaw:Paper*.

5.2 Ontology Alignment Evolution

We now describe how Alignment Cubes satisfy requirements for ontology alignment evolution systems (closely connected to UC3).

A five-steps process for ontology evolution was proposed in [23]. It can be generalized to ontology alignment evolution. The first step of the process focuses on the exploration of the ontologies. This is where an interactive visualization tool is most needed. Requirements to support the first step have been identified in [14]. In Table 1, we show an adaptation of these requirements for step 1, targeted at the alignment evolution. The category indicates whether we deal with inspection (I) or explanation (E).

Table 1. Functionality for alignment evolution systems.

Category	Functionality	
I	F1	Show an alignment version
I, E	F2	Show different alignments in evolution graph
I, E	F3	Show changes/diff between alignments (with change types)
I	F4	Show summary of changes
I	F5	Show specialized view of changes
I	F6	Show change history of a mapping / concept in mappings
I, E	F7	Show provenance information
I	F8	Show information about/context of concepts in mappings
I, E	F9	Compare different alignment versions
I	F10	Search and query alignment
I	F11	Query old versions using terminology of new version
I, E	F12	Discover trends
I, E	F13	Discover volatile and stable regions

Alignment Cubes address requirements F1–F9, F12–F13. It visualizes every alignment (F2) as a separate, labeled (F1) matrix showing both ontologies on its sides (F8). The cube, projections and small multiple views support visual identification and comparison of alignment revisions (F9), trends (F12), volatile and stable regions (F13) and changes between alignments (F3). The latter allows for deriving a history of changes made to mappings (F6). The alignment topology projection can be particularly useful for showing a summary of changes (F4). Additional matrices or small-multiples views can be introduced to show specialized views of changes (F5) and provenance information (F7).

6   Discussion and Future Work

Validation of the Approach: We demonstrated some of the analytic tasks that Alignment Cubes support by describing a scenario in Sect. 5.1. Making such observations took only a couple of minutes with Alignment Cubes. We could identify the common trends between 12 alignments, and found five mappings missing from all 11 alignments and one wrong mapping in all 11 alignments. Furthermore, we found one incorrect mapping in five alignments (LogMap2011 and LogMapLite2012–2015). While we could likely have found missing and incorrect mappings via other means, this was achieved here easily, and in a very short time. The conclusions we draw come from integrating several observations, including all alignments after an exploration guided by the observed regions. Some observations could be made in more than one view, which allowed interpreting them in different contexts, and yielded additional opportunities to observe them if we had missed them earlier.

In Sect. 5.2, we showed that Alignment Cubes address many of the requirements expressed about understanding the evolution of ontology alignments. Alignment Cubes also support requirements in the *inspection* and *partial explanation* dimensions from [12]: representing dense regions, ontologies, mappings and mapping suggestions, filtering, and providing a starting point for exploration. It also covers visual analytics and grouping aspects from [7]. It could further support the analytic tasks identified in [1]—evaluation of matcher performance, exploration and comparison, and diagnosis (which comprises iterations of the other tasks).

User Evaluation: Matrix Cubes have been evaluated with domain experts in Astronomy and Neurosciences, and have been found to be understandable after some initial learning [2]. We have performed pilot tests with ontology alignment experts using the smallest task in the LargeBio track in the OAEI[4] and are currently planning more extensible usability tests with experts in ontology alignment in order to identify further use cases and to inform the design and development of future features.

Scalability: The ontologies in this paper contained less than 100 concepts, and individual alignments had no more than 20 mappings. The tool was successfully

---

[4] http://www.cs.ox.ac.uk/isg/projects/SEALS/oaei/2016/.

tested using the ontologies (3696 and 6488 concepts in each) and all 12 alignments from the smallest task in the LargeBio track in the OAEI. Alignment Cubes have provided a compact overview for all of our examples, and should remain relatively compact with a higher number of mappings. Interactively collapsing and expanding concepts has proven useful to cope with the size of the ontologies and the mappings. Due to the size and depth of the ontologies, the small-multiples views required some pan and zoom on a regular workstation monitor. This can be addressed by filtering, or to some extent by using a large very-high-resolution display. Using larger display surfaces to show multiple views simultaneously is one of the directions identified in [11].

Generalizability and Availability: Though we developed Alignment Cubes for ontology alignment, our adaptations to the original Matrix Cubes are generalizable to any (un)directed bi-graph. Examples include networks connecting authors to their publications, or documents to keywords, or proteins to certain biological functions.

Future Features: Drawing from our experience with the tool so far, we have identified several directions for future extensions. Immediate improvements to consider include: adding visual support for different types of mappings (subsumptions, asserted, derived, etc.); exploring clustering and reordering algorithms to further support trend and pattern discovery; further supporting comparisons by visualizing the results of set operations (union, intersection, complement) as matrices. As discussed in [7,12], providing explanations about why and how a mapping has been computed supports decision making. We thus plan to explore different ways to compactly present such information to users.

In the longer term, we are interested in investigating the integration of Alignment Cubes with the SEALS platform used in OAEI. This will also open the stage for investigating advantages, drawbacks and methodological issues around the two evaluation approaches: comparative visual exploration at a detailed level, and overall assessment of the quality of alignments.

7   Conclusions

This work aims to take the evaluation of ontology alignments' quality beyond general measures such as precision, recall and F-measure. It identifies several use cases and shared tasks where comparison and exploration of multiple alignments at a high level of detail is needed. As the number of approaches and algorithms grows, capturing and analyzing their similarities and differences at varying levels of granularity will facilitate the understanding of their features, and provide additional means for alignment evaluation, hopefully contributing to driving the field forward. We see the evaluation of ontology alignments as an exploratory task, and discuss several activities that could be efficiently supported by an interactive tool—interactive visual exploration at different levels of granularity to perform compare & contrast tasks. Drawing from the field of data visualization, we significantly adapt and extend a technique for dynamic network visualization. Our approach, *Alignment Cubes*, enables the interactive visual exploration of alignments and supports views at different levels of detail. We show their usefulness for the purpose of exploration of multiple alignments by describing a scenario where, in only a few minutes, we could identify several missing and incorrect mappings. This initial experience with the tool is encouraging, and we strongly believe that alignment evaluation should consider other means beyond precision, recall and F-measure, including visual exploration. We hope to integrate this tool with the SEALS platform used in the OAEI campaigns and evaluate its usefulness with developers and researchers involved and participating in them.

Acknowledgements. This work has been supported by the Swedish e-Science Research Centre (SeRC), the Swedish national graduate school in computer science (CUGS) and the EU project VALCRI (FP7-IP-608142).

References

1. Aurisano, J., Nanavaty, A., Cruz, I.: Visual analytics for ontology matching using multi-linked views. In: VOILA, pp. 25–36 (2015)
2. Bach, B., Pietriga, E., Fekete, J.-D.: Visualizing dynamic networks with matrix cubes. In: CHI, pp. 877–886 (2014)
3. Beck, F., Burch, M., Diehl, S., Weiskopf, D.: The state of the art in visualizing dynamic graphs. In: EuroVis STAR 2 (2014)
4. Carpendale, S.: Evaluating information visualizations. In: Kerren, A., Stasko, J.T., Fekete, J.-D., North, C. (eds.) Information Visualization. LNCS, vol. 4950, pp. 19–45. Springer, Heidelberg (2008). doi:10.1007/978-3-540-70956-5_2
5. Cruz, I., Stroe, C., Palmonari, M.: Interactive user feedback in ontology matching using signature vectors. In: ICDE, pp. 1321–1324 (2012)
6. Dang, T., Franz, N., Ludäscher, B., Forbes, A.G.: Provenancematrix: a visualization tool for multi-taxonomy alignments. In: VOILA, pp. 13–24 (2015)
7. Dragisic, Z., Ivanova, V., Lambrix, P., Faria, D., Jiménez-Ruiz, E., Pesquita, C.: User validation in ontology alignment. In: Groth, P., Simperl, E., Gray, A., Sabou, M., Krötzsch, M., Lecue, F., Flöck, F., Gil, Y. (eds.) ISWC 2016. LNCS, vol. 9981, pp. 200–217. Springer, Cham (2016). doi:10.1007/978-3-319-46523-4_13
8. Dragisic, Z., Ivanova, V., Li, H., Lambrix, P.: Experiences from the anatomy track in the ontology alignment evaluation initiative (2017, submitted)
9. Falconer, S.M., Storey, M.-A.: A cognitive support framework for ontology mapping. In: Aberer, K., et al. (eds.) ASWC/ISWC 2007. LNCS, vol. 4825, pp. 114–127. Springer, Heidelberg (2007). doi:10.1007/978-3-540-76298-0_9
10. Isenberg, T., Isenberg, P., Chen, J., Sedlmair, M., Möller, T.: A systematic review on the practice of evaluating visualization. IEEE TVCG **19**(12), 2818–2827 (2013)
11. Ivanova, V.: Applications of large displays: advancing user support in large scale ontology alignment. In: Doctoral Consortium @ ISWC 2016, pp. 50–57 (2016)
12. Ivanova, V., Lambrix, P., Åberg, J.: Requirements for and evaluation of user support for large-scale ontology alignment. In: Gandon, F., Sabou, M., Sack, H., d'Amato, C., Cudré-Mauroux, P., Zimmermann, A. (eds.) ESWC 2015. LNCS, vol. 9088, pp. 3–20. Springer, Cham (2015). doi:10.1007/978-3-319-18818-8_1
13. El Jerroudi, Z., Ziegler, J.: iMERGE: interactive ontology merging. In: EKAW, pp. 52–56 (2008)

14. Lambrix, P., Dragisic, Z., Ivanova, V., Anslow, C.: Visualization for ontology evolution. In: VOILA, pp. 54–67 (2016)
15. Lambrix, P., Tan, H.: A tool for evaluating ontology alignment strategies. J. Data Semant. **VIII**, 182–202 (2007)
16. Lanzenberger, M., Sampson, J., Rester, M.: Ontology visualization: tools and techniques for visual representation of semi-structured meta-data. J. UCS **16**(7), 1036–1054 (2010)
17. Li, Y., Stroe, C., Cruz, I.F.: Interactive visualization of large ontology matching results. In: VOILA, pp. 37–48 (2015)
18. Otero-Cerdeira, L., Rodríguez-Martínez, F.J., Gómez-Rodríguez, A.: Ontology matching: a literature review. Expert Syst. Appl. **42**(2), 949–971 (2015)
19. Peukert, E., Eberius, J., Rahm, E.: AMC-a framework for modeling and comparing matching systems as matching processes. In: ICDE, pp. 1304–1307 (2011)
20. Severo, B., Trojahn, C., Vieira, R.: A GUI for visualising and manipulating multiple ontology alignments. In: ISWC (Posters & Demos), pp. 37–48 (2015)
21. Shvaiko, P., Euzenat, J.: Ontology matching: state of the art and future challenges. J. Knowl. Data Eng. **25**(1), 158–176 (2013)
22. Von Landesberger, T., Kuijper, A., Schreck, T., Kohlhammer, J., van Wijk, J.J., Fekete, J.D., Fellner, D.W.: Visual analysis of large graphs: state-of-the-art and future research challenges. In: Computer Graphics Forum, vol. 30, pp. 1719–1749. Wiley Online Library (2011)
23. Zablith, F., Antoniou, G., d'Aquin, M., Flouris, G., Kondylakis, H., Motta, E., Plexousakis, D., Sabou, M.: Ontology evolution: a process-centric survey. Knowl. Eng. Rev. **30**, 45–75 (2013)

Attributed Description Logics: Ontologies for Knowledge Graphs

Markus Krötzsch$^{(\boxtimes)}$ ⓘ, Maximilian Marx$^{(\boxtimes)}$ ⓘ, Ana Ozaki$^{(\boxtimes)}$ ⓘ,
and Veronika Thost$^{(\boxtimes)}$ ⓘ

Center for Advancing Electronics Dresden (cfaed), TU Dresden, Dresden, Germany
{markus.krotzsch,maximilian.marx,ana.ozaki,veronika.thost}@tu-dresden.de

Abstract. In modelling real-world knowledge, there often arises a need to represent and reason with meta-knowledge. To equip description logics (DLs) for dealing with such ontologies, we enrich DL concepts and roles with finite sets of attribute–value pairs, called annotations, and allow concept inclusions to express constraints on annotations. We show that this may lead to increased complexity or even undecidability, and we identify cases where this increased expressivity can be achieved without incurring increased complexity of reasoning. In particular, we describe a tractable fragment based on the lightweight description logic $\mathcal{EL}$, and we cover $\mathcal{SROIQ}$, the DL underlying OWL 2 DL.

1 Introduction

Modern data management has re-discovered the power and flexibility of graph-based representation formats, and so-called *knowledge graphs* are now used in many practical applications, e.g., in companies such as Google or Facebook. The shift towards graphs is motivated by the need for integrating knowledge from a variety of heterogeneous sources into a common format.

Description logics (DLs) seem to be an excellent fit for this scenario, since they can express complex schema information on graph-like models, while supporting incomplete information via the open world assumption. Ontology-based query answering has become an important research topic, with many recent results and implementations, and the W3C OWL and SPARQL standards provide a basis for practical adoption. One would therefore expect to encounter DLs in many applications of knowledge graphs.

However, this is not the case. While OWL is often used in RDF-based knowledge graphs developed in academia, such as DBpedia [4] and Bio2RDF [3], it has almost no impact on other applications of graph-structured data. This might in part be due to a format mismatch. Like DLs, many knowledge graphs use directed, labelled graph models, but unlike DLs they often add *(sets of) annotations* to vertices and edges. For example, the fact that Liz Taylor married

---

M. Krötzsch—The author thanks the competent and friendly staff of trauma surgery ward OUC-S2 at the University Hospital *Carl Gustav Carus*, Dresden, where some of this research has been executed.

C. d'Amato et al. (Eds.): ISWC 2017, Part I, LNCS 10587, pp. 418–435, 2017.
DOI: 10.1007/978-3-319-68288-4_25

Richard Burton can be described by an assertion spouse(taylor, burton), but in practice we may also wish to record that they married in 1964 in Montreal, and that the marriage ended in 1974. We may write this as follows:

$$\text{spouse(taylor, burton)@[start : 1964, location : Montreal, end : 1974]} \qquad (1)$$

Such annotated graph edges today are widespread in practice. Prominent representatives include *Property Graph*, the data model used in many graph databases [19], and *Wikidata*, the knowledge graph used by Wikipedia [24]. Looking at Wikidata as one of the few freely accessible graphs outside academia, we obtain several requirements:

- *No single purpose.* Annotations are used for many modelling tasks. Expected cases such as validity time and provenance are important, but are by far not the only uses, as (1) (taken from Wikidata) illustrates. Besides *start*, *end*, and *location*, over 150 other attributes are used at least 1000 times as annotations on Wikidata.
- *Multi-graphs.* It can be necessary to include the same assertion multiple times with different annotations. For example, Wikidata in addition to (1) also includes the assertion spouse(taylor, burton)@[start : 1975, end : 1976]. Such multi-graphs are also supported by Property Graph, but not by logics with functional annotations, such as semi-ring approaches [9,22] and aRDF [23].
- *Multi-attribute annotations.* Wikidata (but not Property Graph) further supports annotations where the same attribute has more than one value. Among others, Wikidata includes, e.g., the assertion castMember(Sesame_Street, Frank_Oz)@[role : Bert, role : Cookie_Monster, role : Grover].

One can encode annotated (multi-)graphs as directed graphs, e.g., using reification [8], but DLs cannot express much over such a model. For example, one cannot say that the spouse relation is symmetric, where annotations are the same in both directions [16]. Other traditional KR formalisms are similarly challenged in this situation.

In a recent work, we have therefore proposed to develop logics that support sets of attribute–value annotations natively [16]. The according generalisation of first-order logic, called *multi-attribute predicate logic* (MAPL), is expressive enough to capture weak second-order logic, making reasoning non-semi-decidable. For that reason, we have developed the Datalog-like *MAPL rule language* (MARPL) as a decidable fragment.

In this paper, we explore the use of description logics as a basis for decidable, and even tractable, fragments of MAPL. The resulting family of *attributed DLs* allows statements such as $\text{spouse@}X \sqsubseteq \text{spouse}^-\text{@}X$ to say that spouse is symmetric. We introduce set variables (X in the example) to refer to annotations. We refer to variables to express constraints over annotations and to compare attribute values between them. A challenge is to add functionality of this type without giving up the nature of a DL.

Another challenge is that these extensions may greatly increase the complexity of DLs. We show that reasoning becomes 2ExpTime-complete for attributed $\mathcal{ALCH}$, a prototypical DL; ExpTime-complete for attributed $\mathcal{EL}$, a DL close to OWL 2 EL; and N2ExpTime-complete for attributed $\mathcal{SROIQ}$, the DL underlying OWL 2 DL. Slight extensions of our DLs even lead to undecidability. We develop syntactic constraints to recover lower complexities, including PTime-completeness for attributed $\mathcal{EL}$.

For readability, some proofs are only sketched out in this paper or have been omitted entirely. Full versions can be found in the technical report [14].

2   Attributed Description Logics

We introduce attributed description logics by defining the syntax and semantics of attributed $\mathcal{ALCH}$, denoted $\mathcal{ALCH}_{@+}$. This allows us to illustrate the central ideas without having to deal with the full generality of $\mathcal{SROIQ}$, which we introduce in Sect. 6. We note that fact entailment can be polynomially reduced in the DLs we study.

2.1   Syntax and Intuition

We first give the syntax and intuitive semantics of $\mathcal{ALCH}_{@+}$; the semantics will be formalised thereafter.

Example 1. We start with a guiding example, which will be formally explained when we define $\mathcal{ALCH}_{@+}$. Wikidata contains assertions of the form educatedAt(a_person, a_university)@[start : 2005, end : 2009, degree : master]. This motivates the following $\mathcal{ALCH}_{@+}$ axiom:

$$X : \lfloor \text{degree} : \text{master} \rfloor \quad \left(\exists \text{educatedAt}@X.\text{University} \sqsubseteq \text{MSc}@[\text{start} : X.\text{end}] \right) \tag{2}$$

The underlying DL axiom is $\exists \text{educatedAt}.\text{University} \sqsubseteq \text{MSc}$, stating that anybody educated at some university holds an M.Sc. Axiom (2) restricts this to educatedAt assertions whose annotations X specify the degree to be a master, where X may contain further attribute–value pairs. Indeed, if X specifies an end date for the education, then this is used as a start for the entailed MSc assertion. Similarly, we may express that a person that was educatedAt some institution (where the degree attribute has some value) obtained a degree from this institution:

$$\text{educatedAt}@\lfloor \text{degree} : + \rfloor \sqsubseteq \text{obtainedDegreeFrom} \tag{3}$$

Attributed DLs are defined over the usual DL signature with sets of *concept names* N_C, *role names* N_R, and *individual names* N_I. In OWL terminology, concepts correspond to classes, roles correspond to properties, and individual names correspond to individuals. We consider an additional set N_V of *(set) variables*. Following the definition of multi-attributed predicate logic (MAPL, [16]), we define annotation sets as finite binary relations, understood as sets of attribute–value pairs. In particular, *attributes* refer to domain elements and are syntactically denoted by individual names. To describe annotation sets, we introduce *specifiers*. The set **S** of specifiers contains the following expressions:

- set variables $X \in N_V$;
- *closed specifiers* $[a_1 : v_1, \ldots, a_n : v_n]$; and
- *open specifiers* $\lfloor a_1 : v_1, \ldots, a_n : v_n \rfloor$,

where $a_i \in N_I$ and v_i is either $+$, an individual name in N_I, or an expression of the form $X.c$, with X a set variable in N_V and c an individual name in N_I. Intuitively, closed specifiers define specific annotation sets whereas open specifiers merely provide lower bounds. We use $+$ for "one or more" values, while $X.c$ refers to the (finite, possibly empty) set of all values of attribute c in an annotation set X. A *ground specifier* is a specifier that does not contain expressions of the form $X.c$.

Example 2. The open specifier $\lfloor \mathsf{degree} : \mathsf{master} \rfloor$ in Example 1 describes all annotation sets with at least the given attribute–value pair. The closed specifier $[\mathsf{start} : X.\mathsf{end}]$ denotes the (unique) annotation set with start as the only attribute, having exactly the values given for attribute end in X.

The set **R** of $\mathcal{ALCH}_{@+}$ *role expressions* contains all expressions $r@S$ with $r \in N_R$ and $S \in \mathbf{S}$. The set **C** of $\mathcal{ALCH}_{@+}$ *concept expressions* is defined as follows

$$\mathbf{C} ::= \top \mid \bot \mid \mathsf{N_C}@\mathbf{S} \mid \neg\mathbf{C} \mid \mathbf{C} \sqcap \mathbf{C} \mid \mathbf{C} \sqcup \mathbf{C} \mid \exists\mathbf{R}.\mathbf{C} \mid \forall\mathbf{R}.\mathbf{C} \qquad (4)$$

An $\mathcal{ALCH}_{@+}$ *concept* (or *role*) *assertion* is an expression $A(a)@S$ (or $r(a,b)@S$), with $A \in N_C$ (or $r \in N_R$), $a, b \in N_I$, and $S \in \mathbf{S}$ a specifier that is not a set variable. An $\mathcal{ALCH}_{@+}$ *concept inclusion* is an expression of the form

$$X_1 : S_1, \ldots, X_n : S_n \quad (C \sqsubseteq D), \qquad (5)$$

where $C, D \in \mathbf{C}$ are $\mathcal{ALCH}_{@+}$ concept expressions, $S_1, \ldots, S_n \in \mathbf{S}$ are specifiers, and $X_1, \ldots, X_n \in N_V$ are set variables occurring in C, D or in $S_1, \ldots, S_n$. $\mathcal{ALCH}_{@+}$ *role inclusions* are defined analogously, but with role expressions instead of the concept expressions. An $\mathcal{ALCH}_{@+}$ *ontology* is a set of $\mathcal{ALCH}_{@+}$ assertions, and role and concept inclusions.

To simplify notation, we omit the specifier $\lfloor\rfloor$ (meaning "any annotation set") in role or concept expressions, as done for University in Example 1. In this sense, any $\mathcal{ALCH}$ axiom is also an $\mathcal{ALCH}_{@+}$ axiom. Moreover, we omit prefixes of the form $X : \lfloor\rfloor$, which merely state that X might be any annotation set.

We follow the usual DL notation for referring to other attributed DLs, where we add symbols to the DL name to indicate additional features, and remove symbols to indicate restrictions. Thus, $\mathcal{ALC}_{@+}$ denotes $\mathcal{ALCH}_{@+}$ without role hierarchies, and $\mathcal{ALCH}_{@}$ corresponds to the fragment of $\mathcal{ALCH}_{@+}$ that disallows $+$ in specifiers.

2.2 Formal Semantics

As usual in DLs, an interpretation $\mathcal{I} = \langle \Delta^{\mathcal{I}}, \cdot^{\mathcal{I}} \rangle$ consists of a domain $\Delta^{\mathcal{I}}$ and an interpretation function $\cdot^{\mathcal{I}}$. Individual names $c \in \mathsf{N}_\mathsf{I}$ are interpreted as elements $c^{\mathcal{I}} \in \Delta^{\mathcal{I}}$. Concepts and roles are interpreted as relations that here include annotation sets:

- $A^{\mathcal{I}} \subseteq \Delta^{\mathcal{I}} \times \mathcal{P}_{\mathsf{fin}}\left(\Delta^{\mathcal{I}} \times \Delta^{\mathcal{I}}\right)$ for a concept $A \in \mathsf{N}_\mathsf{C}$, and
- $r^{\mathcal{I}} \subseteq \left(\Delta^{\mathcal{I}} \times \Delta^{\mathcal{I}}\right) \times \mathcal{P}_{\mathsf{fin}}\left(\Delta^{\mathcal{I}} \times \Delta^{\mathcal{I}}\right)$ for a role $r \in \mathsf{N}_\mathsf{R}$,

where $\mathcal{P}_{\mathsf{fin}}\left(\Delta^{\mathcal{I}} \times \Delta^{\mathcal{I}}\right)$ denotes the set of all finite binary relations over $\Delta^{\mathcal{I}}$. Expressions with free set variables are interpreted using variable assignments $\mathcal{Z} : \mathsf{N}_\mathsf{V} \to \mathcal{P}_{\mathsf{fin}}\left(\Delta^{\mathcal{I}} \times \Delta^{\mathcal{I}}\right)$. For an interpretation $\mathcal{I}$ and a variable assignment $\mathcal{Z}$, we define the semantics of specifiers as follows:

$$
\begin{aligned}
X^{\mathcal{I},\mathcal{Z}} &:= \{\mathcal{Z}(X)\}, \\
[a : b]^{\mathcal{I},\mathcal{Z}} &:= \{\{\langle a^{\mathcal{I}}, b^{\mathcal{I}} \rangle\}\}, \\
[a : X.b]^{\mathcal{I},\mathcal{Z}} &:= \{\{\langle a^{\mathcal{I}}, \delta \rangle\} \mid \text{there is } \delta \in \Delta^{\mathcal{I}} \text{ such that } \langle b^{\mathcal{I}}, \delta \rangle \in \mathcal{Z}(X)\}, \\
[a : +]^{\mathcal{I},\mathcal{Z}} &:= \{\{\langle a^{\mathcal{I}}, \delta_1 \rangle, \ldots, \langle a^{\mathcal{I}}, \delta_\ell \rangle\} \mid \ell \geq 1 \text{ and } \delta_i \in \Delta^{\mathcal{I}}\}, \\
[a_1 : v_1, \ldots, a_n : v_n]^{\mathcal{I},\mathcal{Z}} &:= \left\{ \textstyle\bigcup_{i=1}^n \Psi_i \mid \Psi_i \in [a_i : v_i]^{\mathcal{I},\mathcal{Z}} \right\}, \\
\lfloor a_1 : v_1, \ldots, a_n : v_n \rfloor^{\mathcal{I},\mathcal{Z}} &:= \left\{ \Psi \in \mathcal{P}_{\mathsf{fin}}\left(\Delta^{\mathcal{I}} \times \Delta^{\mathcal{I}}\right) \mid \Psi \supseteq \Phi \right. \\
&\qquad \left. \text{for some } \Phi \in [a_1 : v_1, \ldots, a_n : v_n]^{\mathcal{I},\mathcal{Z}} \right\},
\end{aligned}
$$

where $X \in \mathsf{N}_\mathsf{V}$, $a, a_i, b \in \mathsf{N}_\mathsf{I}$, and v_i is $+$, an element of N_I, or of the form $X.a$. We can now define the semantics of concept and role expressions:

$$
A @ S^{\mathcal{I},\mathcal{Z}} := \{\delta \in \Delta^{\mathcal{I}} \mid \langle \delta, \Psi \rangle \in A^{\mathcal{I}} \text{ for some } \Psi \in S^{\mathcal{I},\mathcal{Z}}\} \tag{6}
$$

$$
r @ S^{\mathcal{I},\mathcal{Z}} := \{\langle \delta_1, \delta_2 \rangle \in \Delta^{\mathcal{I}} \times \Delta^{\mathcal{I}} \mid \langle \delta_1, \delta_2, \Psi \rangle \in r^{\mathcal{I}} \text{ for some } \Psi \in S^{\mathcal{I},\mathcal{Z}}\} \tag{7}
$$

Observe that we quantify existentially over admissible annotations here ("some $\Psi \in S^{\mathcal{I},\mathcal{Z}}$"). However, variables and closed specifiers without $+$ are interpreted as singleton sets, so true existential quantification only occurs if S is an open specifier or if it contains $+$. All other DL constructs can now be defined as usual, e.g., $(C \sqcap D)^{\mathcal{I},\mathcal{Z}} = C^{\mathcal{I},\mathcal{Z}} \cap D^{\mathcal{I},\mathcal{Z}}$, $(\exists r.C)^{\mathcal{I},\mathcal{Z}} = \{\delta \mid \text{there is } \langle \delta, \epsilon \rangle \in r^{\mathcal{I},\mathcal{Z}} \text{ with } \epsilon \in C^{\mathcal{I},\mathcal{Z}}\}$, and $(\neg C)^{\mathcal{I},\mathcal{Z}} = \Delta^{\mathcal{I}} \setminus C^{\mathcal{I},\mathcal{Z}}$. Note that we do not include annotations on $\top$, i.e. $\top^{\mathcal{I},\mathcal{Z}} = \Delta^{\mathcal{I}}$, and similarly for $\bot^{\mathcal{I},\mathcal{Z}} = \emptyset$.

Now $\mathcal{I}$ *satisfies* an $\mathcal{ALCH}_{@+}$ concept inclusion α of the form (5), written $\mathcal{I} \models \alpha$, if for all variable assignments $\mathcal{Z}$ such that $\mathcal{Z}(X_i) \in S_i^{\mathcal{I},\mathcal{Z}}$ for all $i \in \{1, \ldots, n\}$, we have $C^{\mathcal{I},\mathcal{Z}} \subseteq D^{\mathcal{I},\mathcal{Z}}$. Satisfaction of role inclusions is defined analogously. Moreover, $\mathcal{I}$ satisfies an $\mathcal{ALCH}_{@+}$ concept assertion $A(a) @ S$ if $\langle a^{\mathcal{I}}, \Psi \rangle \in A^{\mathcal{I}}$ for some $\Psi \in S^{\mathcal{I}}$ (the latter is well-defined since S contains no variables). $\mathcal{I}$ satisfies an ontology if it satisfies all of its axioms. Based on this model theory, logical entailment is defined as usual.

Example 3. Consider the concept inclusion α of Example 1 and the interpretation $\mathcal{I}$ over domain $\Delta^{\mathcal{I}} = \{\text{Mary}, \text{John}, \text{TUD}, \text{start}, \text{end}, 2017, 2018, \text{master}, \text{degree}\}$, given by

$$\text{MSc}^{\mathcal{I}} = \{\langle \text{Mary}, \{\langle \text{start}, 2016 \rangle\}\rangle, \langle \text{John}, \{\langle \text{start}, 2017 \rangle\}\rangle\},$$

$$\text{educatedAt}^{\mathcal{I}} = \{\langle \text{Mary}, \text{TUD}, \{\langle \text{degree}, \text{master} \rangle, \langle \text{end}, 2016 \rangle\}\rangle,$$

$$\langle \text{John}, \text{TUD}, \{\langle \text{degree}, \text{master} \rangle, \langle \text{end}, 2017 \rangle\}\rangle\}, \text{ and}$$

$$\text{University}^{\mathcal{I}} = \{\langle \text{TUD}, \{\}\rangle\}.$$

Then $\mathcal{I} \models \alpha$, i.e., $\mathcal{I}$ satisfies α.

3 Expressivity of Attributed Description Logics

In this section, we clarify some basic semantic properties of attributed DLs and the general relation of attributed DLs to other logical formalisms. As a first observation, we note that already $\mathcal{ALC}_{@+}$ is too expressive to be decidable:

Theorem 1. *Satisfiability of attributed DLs with $+$ is undecidable, even if the DL only supports $\sqcap$, and supports either only open specifiers or only closed specifiers.*

Proof. We reduce from the query answering problem for existential rules, i.e., first-order formulae of the form

$$\forall \boldsymbol{x}. p_1(x_1^1, \ldots, x_{\mathsf{ar}(p_1)}^1) \wedge \ldots \wedge p_n(x_1^n, \ldots, x_{\mathsf{ar}(p_n)}^n) \rightarrow \exists \boldsymbol{y}. p(z_1, \ldots, z_{\mathsf{ar}(q)}), \quad (8)$$

where the variables x_j^i occur among the universally quantified variables, i.e., $x_j^i \in \boldsymbol{x}$, and variables z_i might be universally or existentially quantified, i.e., $z_i \in \boldsymbol{x} \cup \boldsymbol{y}$. We require that each universally quantified variable occurs in some atom in the premise of the rule (safety), and that each existentially quantified variable occurs only once per rule. The latter is without loss of generality since rules that violate this restriction can be split into two rules using an auxiliary predicate. A fact is a formula of the form $q(c_1, \ldots, c_{\mathsf{ar}(q)})$ with constants c_i. Entailment of facts from given sets of facts and existential rules is known to be undecidable [2,7].

To translate an existential rule of the form (8), we consider DL concept names $P_{(i)}$ for each predicate symbol $p_{(i)}$, and individual names $a_1, \ldots, a_\ell$, where ℓ is the maximal arity of any such predicate. For each universally quantified variable x, let $\pi_x = \langle p_i, k \rangle$ be an (arbitrary but fixed) position at which x occurs, i.e., for which $x = x_k^i$. The rule can now be rewritten to the attributed DL axiom

$$X_1 : S_1, \ldots, X_n : S_n \quad (P_1 @ X_1 \sqcap \ldots \sqcap P_n @ X_n \sqsubseteq P @ T),$$

where the specifiers are defined as $S_i = [a_j : X_m.a_k \mid 1 \leq j \leq \mathsf{ar}(p_i)$ and $\pi_{x_j^i} = \langle p_m, k \rangle]$ and $T = [a_j : + \mid z_j \in \boldsymbol{y}] \cup [a_j : X_m.a_k \mid z_j \in \boldsymbol{x}$ and $\pi_{z_j} = \langle p_m, k \rangle]$

(note that we slightly abuse | and ∪ here for a simpler presentation). For example, the rule $\forall xy.p_1(x,y) \land p_2(y,x) \rightarrow \exists z.p(x,z)$ is translated into the concept inclusion $X_1 : S_1, X_2 : S_2 \; (P_1@X_1 \sqcap P_2@X_2 \sqsubseteq P@[a_1 : X_1.a_1, a_2 : +])$, where $S_1 = [a_1 : X_1.a_1, a_2 : X_2.a_1]$ and $S_2 = [a_1 : X_2.a_1, a_2 : X_1.a_1]$. Observe that the specifier S_i for X_i may contain assignments of the form $a_j : X_i.a_j$: by our semantics, this merely states that a_j may have zero or more values. Facts of the form $q(c_1, \ldots, c_m)$ can be translated into assertions $Q(b)@[a_1 : c_1, \ldots, a_m : c_m]$ for an individual name b that is used in all such assertions.

Entailment of facts is preserved in this translation. Correctness is retained if we replace all closed by open specifiers, since the translated ontology admits a least model where all annotation sets are interpreted as the smallest possible sets. □

In Sects. 4 and 5, we present two approaches for overcoming the undecidability of Theorem 1, namely to exclude + from attributed DLs, and to restrict the use of expressions of the form $X.a$.

Example 4. It follows from Theorem 1 that $\mathcal{ALC}_{@+}$ ontologies may require models with annotation sets of unbounded size. To see this, consider the following ontology:

$$A(b)@\lfloor c : c \rfloor \tag{9}$$

$$A@X \sqsubseteq \exists r.A@\lfloor c : +, p : X.c, p : X.p \rfloor \tag{10}$$

$$A@X \sqcap A@\lfloor p : X.c \rfloor \sqsubseteq \bot \tag{11}$$

Axiom (9) defines an initial A member. Axiom (10) states that all A members have an r successor that is in A, annotated with some value for c ("current"), and values for p ("previous") that include all of its predecessor's c and p values. Axiom (11) requires that no individual in A may have a set of p values that include all of its c values. It is not hard to see that all models of this ontology include an infinite r-chain with arbitrarily large (but finite) A-related annotations sets.

It is interesting to discuss Theorem 1 in the context of our previous work on multi-attributed predicate logic (MAPL), which generalises first-order logic with annotation sets for arbitrary predicates. Indeed, our interpretations for attributed DLs are a special case of *multi-attributed relational structures* (MARS), though we do not make the unique name assumption here, since it is not common for the DLs we consider. Otherwise, attributed DLs are fragments of MAPL. Our notation $X.a$ is new, but it can be simulated in MAPL, e.g., by using function definitions [16].

MAPL is not semi-decidable, and we have proposed *MAPL rules* (MARPL) as a decidable fragment. MARPL supports + without restrictions, and it includes arbitrary predicate arities and more expressive specifiers (with some form of negation). In contrast, attributed DLs add the ability to quantify existentially over annotations, and therefore to derive partially specified annotation sets, which is the main reason for Theorem 1. In general, attributed DLs are based on the open world assumption, whereas MARPL could equivalently be interpreted under a closed world, least model semantics. Nevertheless, even without $+$ the translation from the proof of Theorem 1 allows attributed DLs to capture rule languages, as the following result shows. Here, by *Datalog* we mean first-order Horn logic without existential quantifiers.

Theorem 2. *Attributed DLs can capture Datalog in the sense that every set $\mathbb{P}$ of Datalog rules and fact $q(c_1, \ldots, c_m)$ can be translated in linear time into an attributed DL ontology $KB_{\mathbb{P}}$ and assertion $Q(b)@S$, such that $\mathbb{P} \models q(c_1, \ldots, c_m)$ iff $KB_{\mathbb{P}} \models Q(b)@S$. This translation requires just $\sqcap$, no $+$, and either only open or only closed specifiers.*

The ability to capture Datalog reminds us of *nominal schemas*, the extension of DLs with "variable nominals" [13, 15]. Indeed, this extension can also be captured in attributed DLs (we omit the details here). The converse is not true, e.g., since nominal schemas cannot encode annotation sets on role assertions. Role inclusion axioms such as $\mathsf{spouse}@X \sqsubseteq \mathsf{spouse}^-@X$ are therefore impossible. Another related formalism is DL-Lite$_A$, which supports (data) annotations on domain elements and pairs of domain elements [5]. This extension of DLs supports some forms of ternary relations. Nevertheless, the use case and complexity properties of DL-Lite$_A$ are different from the logics we study here, and it remains for future work to further explore attributed DL-Lite in more detail.

4   Reasoning in $\mathcal{ALCH}_@$

We first focus on $\mathcal{ALCH}_@$, for which we show reasoning to be decidable, albeit at a higher complexity. For a first positive result, we consider *ground $\mathcal{ALCH}_@$*, where ontologies do not contain any set variables. We show that we can translate any ground $\mathcal{ALCH}_@$ ontology into an equisatisfiable $\mathcal{ALCH}$ ontology by introducing fresh names for annotated concept and role names. This *renaming* is one of the key ingredients in obtaining decision procedures for attributed DLs.

Theorem 3. *Satisfiability of ground $\mathcal{ALCH}_@$ ontologies is* ExpTime-*complete.*

Proof. Hardness is immediate since $\mathcal{ALCH}_@$ generalises $\mathcal{ALCH}$. For membership, we reduce $\mathcal{ALCH}_@$ satisfiability to $\mathcal{ALCH}$ satisfiability. Given an $\mathcal{ALCH}_@$ ontology KB, let $KB^\dagger$ denote the $\mathcal{ALCH}$ ontology that is obtained by replacing each annotated concept name $A@S$ with a fresh concept name A_S, and each annotated role name $r@S$ with a fresh role name r_S, respectively. We then extend $KB^\dagger$ by all axioms

$$A_S \sqsubseteq A_T, \quad \text{where } A_S \text{ and } A_T \text{ occur in translated axioms of } KB^\dagger, \text{ and} \quad (12)$$

$$r_S \sqsubseteq r_T, \quad \quad \text{where } r_S \text{ and } r_T \text{ occur in translated axioms of } KB^\dagger \quad (13)$$

such that T is an open specifier, and the set of attribute–value pairs $a : b$ in S is a superset of the set of attribute–value pairs in T. We show that KB is satisfiable iff $KB^\dagger$ is satisfiable. The claim then follows from the well-known ExpTime-completeness of satisfiability checking in $\mathcal{ALCH}$. Given an $\mathcal{ALCH}_@$ model $\mathcal{I}$ of KB, we directly obtain an $\mathcal{ALCH}$ interpretation $\mathcal{J}$ over $\Delta^\mathcal{I}$ by undoing the renaming and applying $\mathcal{I}$, i.e., by mapping $A_S \in \mathsf{N_C}$ to $A@S^\mathcal{I}$, $r_S \in \mathsf{N_R}$ to $r@S^\mathcal{I}$, and $a \in \mathsf{N_I}$ to $a^\mathcal{I}$. Clearly, $\mathcal{J} \models KB^\dagger$. Conversely, given an $\mathcal{ALCH}$ model $\mathcal{J}$ of $KB^\dagger$, we construct an $\mathcal{ALCH}_@$-interpretation $\mathcal{I}$ over domain $\Delta^\mathcal{I} = \Delta^\mathcal{J} \cup \{\star\}$, where $\star$ is a fresh individual name, and define $a^\mathcal{I} := a^\mathcal{J}$ for all $a \in \mathsf{N_I}$. For a ground closed specifier $S = [a_1 : b_1, \ldots, a_n : b_n]$, we set $\Psi_S := S^\mathcal{I}$. Similarly, for a ground open specifier $S = \lfloor a_1 : b_1, \ldots, a_n : b_n \rfloor$, we define $\Psi_S := S^\mathcal{I} \cup \{\langle \star, \star \rangle\}$. Furthermore, let $A^\mathcal{I} := \{\langle a, \Psi_S \rangle \mid a \in A_S^\mathcal{J}$ for some specifier $S\}$ and $r^\mathcal{I} := \{\langle a, b, \Psi_S \rangle \mid \langle a, b \rangle \in r_S^\mathcal{J}$ for some specifier $S\}$. Then $\mathcal{I} \models KB$, where $\star$ ensures that axioms such as $\top \sqsubseteq A@\lfloor a : b \rfloor \sqcap \neg A@[a : b]$ remain satisfiable. $\qquad\square$

The other important technique for dealing with attributed DLs is *grounding*, where we eliminate set variables from an ontology, thus transforming it into a ground ontology. As illustrated by the next result, this grounding may lead to an ontology of exponentially larger size, resulting in an increased complexity of reasoning.

Theorem 4. *Satisfiability of $\mathcal{ALCH}_@$ ontologies is in* 2ExpTime.

Proof. Let KB be an $\mathcal{ALCH}_@$ ontology, and let $\mathsf{N_I}^{KB}$ the set of individual names occurring in KB, extended by one fresh individual name x. The grounding $\mathsf{ground}(KB)$ of KB consists of all assertions in KB, together with grounded versions of inclusion axioms. Let $\mathcal{I}$ be an interpretation over domain $\Delta^\mathcal{I} = \mathsf{N_I}^{KB}$ satisfying $a^\mathcal{I} = a$ for all $a \in \mathsf{N_I}^{KB}$, and $\mathcal{Z} : \mathsf{N_V} \to \mathcal{P}_\mathsf{fin}\left(\Delta^\mathcal{I} \times \Delta^\mathcal{I}\right)$ be a variable assignment. Consider a concept inclusion α of the form $X_1 : S_1, \ldots, X_n : S_n$ $(C \sqsubseteq D)$. We say that $\mathcal{Z}$ is *compatible with* α if $\mathcal{Z}(X_i) \in S_i^{\mathcal{I}, \mathcal{Z}}$ for all $1 \leq i \leq n$. In this case, the $\mathcal{Z}$-*instance* $\alpha_\mathcal{Z}$ of α is the concept inclusion $C' \sqsubseteq D'$ obtained by

- replacing each variable X_i with $[a : b \mid \langle a, b \rangle \in \mathcal{Z}(X_i)]$, and
- replacing every assignment $a : X_i.b$ occurring in some specifier by all assignments $a : c$ such that $\langle b, c \rangle \in \mathcal{Z}(X_i)$.

Then $\mathsf{ground}(KB)$ contains all $\mathcal{Z}$-instances $\alpha_\mathcal{Z}$ for all concept inclusions α in KB and all compatible variable assignments $\mathcal{Z}$; and analogous axioms for role inclusions. In general, there may be exponentially many different instances for each terminological axiom in KB, thus $\mathsf{ground}(KB)$ is of exponential size. We conclude the proof by showing that KB is satisfiable iff $\mathsf{ground}(KB)$ is satisfiable, the result then follows from Theorem 3. By construction, we have $KB \models \mathsf{ground}(KB)$, i.e., any model of KB is also a model of $\mathsf{ground}(KB)$. Conversely, let $\mathcal{I}$ be a model of $\mathsf{ground}(KB)$. Without loss of generality, assume that $x^\mathcal{I} \neq a^\mathcal{I}$ for all $a \in \mathsf{N_I}^{KB}\backslash\{x\}$ (it suffices to add a fresh individual since x does not occur in KB). For an annotation set $\Psi \in \mathcal{P}_\mathsf{fin}\left(\Delta^\mathcal{I} \times \Delta^\mathcal{I}\right)$, we define $\mathsf{rep}_x(\Psi)$ to be the annotation obtained from Ψ by replacing any individual $\delta \notin \mathcal{I}(\mathsf{N_I}^{KB})$ in Ψ by $x^\mathcal{I}$. We let $\sim$ be the equivalence relation induced by $\mathsf{rep}_x(\Psi) = \mathsf{rep}_x(\Phi)$ and define an interpretation $\mathcal{J}$ over domain $\Delta^\mathcal{J} := \Delta^\mathcal{I}$, where $A^\mathcal{J} := \{\langle \delta, \Phi \rangle \mid \langle \delta, \Psi \rangle \in A^\mathcal{I}$ and $\Psi \sim \Phi\}$ for

$A \in N_C$, $r^{\mathcal{J}} := \{\langle \delta, \epsilon, \Phi \rangle \mid \langle \delta, \epsilon, \Psi \rangle \in r^{\mathcal{I}} \text{ and } \Psi \sim \Phi\}$ for $r \in N_R$, and $a^{\mathcal{J}} := a^{\mathcal{I}}$ for all individual names $a \in N_I$. It remains to show that $\mathcal{J}$ is indeed a model of KB. Suppose for a contradiction that there is a concept inclusion α that is not satisfied by $\mathcal{J}$ (the case for role inclusions is analogous). Then we have some compatible variable assignment $\mathcal{Z}$ that leaves α unsatisfied. Let $\mathcal{Z}_x$ be the variable assignment $X \mapsto \text{rep}_x(\mathcal{Z}(X))$ for all $X \in N_V$. Clearly, $\mathcal{Z}_x$ is also compatible with α. But now we have $C^{\mathcal{J}, \mathcal{Z}} = C^{\mathcal{I}, \mathcal{Z}_x}$ for all $\mathcal{ALCH}_@$ concepts C, yielding the contradiction $\mathcal{I} \not\models \alpha_{\mathcal{Z}_x}$. $\qquad \square$

We regain decidability for $\mathcal{ALC}_{@+}$ by disallowing expressions of the form $X.a$.

Theorem 5. *Satisfiability of $\mathcal{ALCH}_{@+}$ ontologies without expressions of the form $X.a$ is in* 2ExpTime.

Proof. We reduce satisfiability in $\mathcal{ALCH}_{@+}$ (without expressions of the form $X.a$) to satisfiability in $\mathcal{ALCH}$, similar to the proof of Theorem 4. Consider an $\mathcal{ALCH}_{@+}$ ontology KB that contains the individual names N_I^{KB}, along with two fresh individual names x and x_+. The grounding proceeds as in the proof of Theorem 4, except that for $\mathcal{Z}$-instances $\alpha_{\mathcal{Z}}$ of concept inclusions α, we additionally replace each assignment $a : +$ occurring in some specifier by the assignment $a : x_+$. The exponentially large grounding again yields containment in 2ExpTime. From a model $\mathcal{J}$ of KB, we obtain a model $\mathcal{I}$ of $\text{ground}(KB)$ by setting $\Delta^{\mathcal{I}} := N_I^{KB}$, $a^{\mathcal{I}} := a^{\mathcal{J}}$ for $a \in N_I \setminus \{x, x_+\}$, $x^{\mathcal{I}} := x$, $x_+^{\mathcal{I}} := x_+$, $A^{\mathcal{I}} := \{\langle \delta, \Psi \cup \Phi \rangle \mid \langle \delta, \Psi \rangle \in A^{\mathcal{J}}, \Phi \in \mathcal{P}\left(\{\langle a, x_+ \rangle \mid \langle a, b \rangle \in \Psi\}\right)\}$ for $A \in N_C$, and $r^{\mathcal{I}} := \{\langle \delta, \epsilon, \Psi \cup \Phi \rangle \mid \langle \delta, \epsilon, \Psi \rangle \in A^{\mathcal{J}}, \Phi \in \mathcal{P}\left(\{\langle a, x_+ \rangle \mid \langle a, b \rangle \in \Psi\}\right)\}$ for $r \in N_R$. Clearly, if $\mathcal{J}$ satisfies a concept inclusion in KB, then $\mathcal{I}$ satisfies a corresponding concept inclusion in $\text{ground}(KB)$. Similarly, any concept inclusion satisfied by $\mathcal{I}$ must correspond to a concept inclusion satisfied by $\mathcal{J}$ since x_+ does not occur in KB. The converse direction follows immediately from the proof of Theorem 4. $\quad \square$

Both of these upper bounds are tight, as the next theorem shows:

Theorem 6. *Checking satisfiability of $\mathcal{ALC}_@$ ontologies without expressions of the form $X.a$ is* 2ExpTime-*hard.*

Proof (sketch). We reduce the word problem for exponentially space-bounded alternating Turing machines (ATMs) [6] to the entailment problem for $\mathcal{ALC}_@$ ontologies. We construct the tree of all configurations reachable from the initial configuration, encoding the transitions in the edges of the tree, i.e., each configuration is represented by an individual. The tape cells are represented as concepts carrying an annotation encoding the cell content and position (as a binary number). We mark the current head position with an additional concept, allowing us to copy each non-head position of the tape to successors in the configuration tree, while changing the tape cell at the head position and moving the head depending on the transition from the preceding configuration. As acceptance of a given configuration depends solely on the state and the successor configurations, we can propagate acceptance backwards from the leaves of the configuration tree to the initial configuration. $\quad \square$

5 Tractable Reasoning in Attributed $\mathcal{EL}$

In this section, we investigate $\mathcal{ALC}_@$ fragments based on the $\mathcal{EL}$ family of description logics. This family includes $\mathcal{EL}^{++}$, which forms the logical foundation of the OWL 2 EL profile and is widely used in applications such as in SNOMED CT [21], a clinical terminology with global scope. SNOMED CT also features a compositional syntax [20], which has recently been augmented with attribute sets allowing arbitrary concrete values. While concept expressions in either of the syntaxes can be translated into the other, $\mathcal{EL}^{++}$ provides no such attributes (i.e., concepts with attribute sets have to be represented by introducing new concept names). We can not only capture these attributes using our attribute–value sets, but also include them into the reasoning process. As a (simplified) example, the concept of a 500 mg Paracetamol tablet could be annotated with

$$\lfloor \mathsf{strengthMagnitude} : 500, \mathsf{tradeName} : \mathsf{PANADOL} \rfloor.$$

The basic logic is $\mathcal{EL}_@$, the fragment of $\mathcal{ALC}_@$ which uses only $\exists$, $\sqcap$, $\top$ and $\bot$ in concept expressions. Unfortunately, Theorem 2 shows that $\mathcal{EL}_@$ is ExpTime-complete, even with severe syntactic restrictions. To overcome this source of complexity, we impose a bound on the number of set variables per concept inclusion and exclude $X.a$:

Theorem 7. *Let $\ell \in \mathbb{N}$. Checking satisfiability of $\mathcal{EL}_@$ ontologies with at most ℓ variables per axiom, and without expressions of the form $X.a$ is* PTime-*complete.*

Proof. Hardness follows from the PTime-hardness of $\mathcal{EL}$ [1]. For membership, we polynomially reduce $\mathcal{EL}_@$ satisfiability to $\mathcal{ELH}$ satisfiability. Indeed, the grounding used in Theorem 4 can be restricted to annotation sets that are described in (ground) specifiers that are found in the ontology, since no new sets can be derived without $X.a$. The bounded number of variables then ensures that the grounding remains polynomial. Since neither grounding nor renaming introduce negation, the resulting ontology belongs to the $\mathcal{ELH}$ fragment of $\mathcal{ALCH}$. □

Observe that we can allow some uses of $X.a$, given that we obey certain restrictions:

Theorem 8. *Let $\ell, k \in \mathbb{N}$. Checking satisfiability of $\mathcal{EL}_@$ ontologies is* PTime-*complete if all of the following conditions are satisfied:*

(A) axioms contain at most ℓ variables,
(B) any closed or open specifier contains at most k expressions of the form $X.a$, and,
(C) if any specifier contains an assignment $a : X.b$, then it does not contain any other assignment for attribute a.

Proof. As in the proof of Theorem 7, we can obtain a polynomial grounding, but we may need to consider annotation sets that are not explicitly specified in the original ontology. But, due to condition (C), as the set of values for any attribute we only need to consider one of the polynomially many sets of values given explicitly through ground assignments in specifiers. Considering any combination of these value sets for any of the at most k attributes that use $X.a$ in assignments results in polynomially many annotation sets.   □

We now show that violating any of these conditions makes satisfiability intractable.

Theorem 9. *Let KB be an $\mathcal{EL}_@$ ontology and consider conditions (A)–(C) of Theorem 8 with $\ell = 1$ and $k = 2$. Then deciding satisfiability of KB is*

(1) ExpTime-hard if KB satisfies only conditions (B) and (C),
(2) ExpTime-hard if KB satisfies only conditions (A) and (C), and
(3) PSpace-hard if KB satisfies only conditions (A) and (B).

It is an open question whether the PSpace bound in the third case is tight. Nevertheless, it implies intractability for this case. Finally, we show that also $\mathcal{EL}_{@+}$ (without $X.a$) is intractable (recall that $\mathcal{EL}_{@+}$ with $X.a$ is already undecidable by Theorem 1).

Theorem 10. *Checking satisfiability of $\mathcal{EL}_{@+}$ ontologies without expressions of the form $X.a$ is ExpTime-complete.*

Proof. ExpTime-hardness follows from Theorem 9. From the proof of Theorem 5, we obtain an exponentially large grounding, which, together with the PTime complexity of $\mathcal{ELH}$, yields the ExpTime upper bound.   □

6   Attributed OWL

In this section, we consider attributed DLs with further expressive features, so that in particular we can cover all of the expressivity of the OWL 2 DL ontology language [17]. The underlying DL is $\mathcal{SROIQ}_@$, which we introduce next by slightly extending our earlier definition of $\mathcal{ALCH}_@$. The set $\mathbf{R}$ of $\mathcal{SROIQ}_@$ *role expressions* contains all expressions $r@S$ and $r^-@S$ with $r \in \mathsf{N_R}$ and $S \in \mathbf{S}$. The set $\mathbf{C}$ of $\mathcal{SROIQ}_@$ *concept expressions* is defined as follows

$$\mathbf{C} ::= \top \mid \bot \mid \mathsf{N_C}@S \mid \{\mathsf{N_I}\} \mid \neg\mathbf{C} \mid \mathbf{C} \sqcap \mathbf{C} \mid \mathbf{C} \sqcup \mathbf{C} \mid \exists \mathbf{R}.\mathbf{C} \mid \forall \mathbf{R}.\mathbf{C} \mid \leqslant n\,\mathbf{R}.\mathbf{C} \mid \geqslant n\,\mathbf{R}.\mathbf{C} \tag{14}$$

The new features are *nominals* $\{c\}$, which denote concepts containing one individual, and number restrictions $\leqslant n\,R.C$ and $\geqslant n\,R.C$, which express concepts of elements with at most/at least $n \geq 0$ R-successors in C. Note that we do not include annotations on nominals. This is no real restriction, since one can use axioms such as $\{c\} \equiv A_c@\bigsqcup$ to introduce a concept name A_c that may hold such annotations. This allows us to use the same notion of interpretation as for $\mathcal{ALCH}_@$. Assertions, concept and role inclusions are defined as before, based on these extended sets of expressions. In addition, $\mathcal{SROIQ}_@$ supports complex role inclusion axioms of the form

$$X_1 : S_1, \ldots, X_n : S_n \quad (R_1 \circ \ldots \circ R_\ell \sqsubseteq T), \tag{15}$$

where $R_i, T \in \mathbf{R}$ are $\mathcal{SROIQ}_@$ role expressions, $S_1, \ldots, S_n \in \mathbf{S}$ are specifiers, and $X_1, \ldots, X_n \in \mathsf{N_V}$ are set variables occurring among $R_i, T, S_1, \ldots, S_n$. A $\mathcal{SROIQ}_@$ *ontology* is a set of $\mathcal{SROIQ}_@$ assertions, and role and concept inclusions.

The semantics of these constructs and axioms is defined as usual [10], where the interpretation of roles and concepts takes annotations into account as in Sect. 2. For instance, we may express that any drug, such as a Paracetamol tablet, that contains at most one active ingredient and a certain amount of some such ingredient, such as 500 mg of Acetaminophen, has the same dose:

$$X : \bigsqcup \; \mathsf{Drug} \sqcap \leqslant 1 \, \mathsf{hasActiveIngredient}.\top \sqcap \exists \mathsf{hasActiveIngredient}@X.\top \sqsubseteq$$
$$\mathsf{Drug}@\lfloor \mathsf{strengthMagnitude} : X.\mathsf{strengthMagnitude} \rfloor$$

To ensure decidability of reasoning, $\mathcal{SROIQ}$ imposes two additional restrictions on ontologies: *simplicity* and *regularity* [10]. We adopt them to $\mathcal{SROIQ}_@$ as follows.

Simplicity is defined as in $\mathcal{SROIQ}$, ignoring the annotations. The set of *non-simple roles* $\mathsf{N_R^n} \subseteq \mathsf{N_R}$ w.r.t. a $\mathcal{SROIQ}_@$ ontology is defined recursively: $t \in \mathsf{N_R^n}$ if t occurs on the right of an axiom of form (15) and either (1) $\ell > 1$ or (2) some non-simple role $s \in \mathsf{N_R^n}$ occurs on the left of the axiom. All other role names are *simple*. We now require that only simple roles occur in R in number restrictions $\leqslant n \, R.C$ and $\geqslant n \, R.C$.

A $\mathcal{SROIQ}_@$ ontology is *regular* if there is a strict partial order $\prec$ on the set $\mathsf{N_R^\pm} = \mathsf{N_R} \cup \{r^- \mid r \in \mathsf{N_R}\}$, such that

(1) for all $R \in \mathsf{N_R^\pm}$ and $s \in \mathsf{N_R}$, we have $s \prec R$ iff $s^- \prec R$, and
(2) for all role inclusion axioms of form (15), the inclusion $R_1 \circ \ldots \circ R_\ell \sqsubseteq T$ has one of the following forms:

$$T@S \circ T@S \sqsubseteq T@S \qquad R_1 \circ \ldots \circ R_{\ell-1} \circ T@S \sqsubseteq T@S \qquad r^-@S \sqsubseteq r@S$$
$$R_1 \circ \ldots \circ R_\ell \sqsubseteq T@S \qquad T@S \circ R_2 \circ \ldots \circ R_\ell \sqsubseteq T@S$$

where $S \in \mathbf{S}$, $T \in \mathsf{N_R^\pm}$, $r \in \mathsf{N_R}$, and $R_1, \ldots, R_\ell \in \mathbf{R}$ are of form $R_1@S_1, \ldots, R_\ell@S_\ell$ such that $R_i \prec T$ for all $i \in \{1, \ldots, \ell\}$.

Note that we adopt the usual conditions from $\mathcal{SROIQ}$ for (inverted) role names, and further require that cases with the same role T on both sides use the same specifier S. As for $\mathcal{SROIQ}$, this condition can be verified in polynomial time by computing a minimal relation $\prec$ that satisfies the conditions and checking if it is a strict partial order.

For reasoning, the step from $\mathcal{ALCH}_@$ to $\mathcal{SROIQ}_@$ leads to several difficulties. First, nominals and cardinality restrictions may lead to the entailment of equalities $a \approx b$, which has consequences on annotation sets (e.g.,

$A@\lfloor c : a \rfloor \equiv A@\lfloor c : b \rfloor$ in this case). For obtaining complexity upper bounds by transformation to standard DLs as in Sect. 4, we need to axiomatise such relationships. Second, nominals may be used to restrict the overall size of the domain, e.g., when stating $\top \sqsubseteq \{a\}$. Besides the entailment of further equalities, this also changes the semantics of open specifiers (e.g., we obtain $A@\lfloor a : a \rfloor \sqsubseteq A@\lceil a : a \rceil$ in this case). As before, this requires suitable axiomatisation in $\mathcal{SROIQ}$. Either of these two effects may require exponentially many auxiliary axioms, leading to an N3ExpTime upper bound even for ground $\mathcal{SROIQ}_@$. However, we will show an N2ExpTime upper bound as for $\mathcal{SROIQ}$, which is tight.

Theorem 11. *Satisfiability of ground* $\mathcal{SROIQ}_@$ *ontologies is in* N2ExpTime.

To prove this theorem, we first translate ground $\mathcal{SROIQ}_@$ into an auxiliary DL, called $\mathcal{SROIQ}_\approx$, and then show how to reason in this DL by an exponential reduction to $\mathcal{C}^2$, the two-variable fragment with counting [18], which yields the desired N2ExpTime upper bound. The second part of the proof is split over several lemmas.

$\mathcal{SROIQ}_\approx$, in addition to the usual $\mathcal{SROIQ}$ axioms, supports concept inclusions of the form $a \approx b \Rightarrow C \sqsubseteq D$ and role inclusions of the form $a \approx b \Rightarrow R_1 \circ \ldots \circ R_\ell \sqsubseteq T$. An axiom $a \approx b \Rightarrow \alpha$ is satisfied by interpretation $\mathcal{I}$ if either $a^\mathcal{I} \neq b^\mathcal{I}$ or $\mathcal{I} \models \alpha$.

The translation from a ground $\mathcal{SROIQ}_@$ ontology KB to a $\mathcal{SROIQ}_\approx$ ontology $KB^\ddagger$ now proceeds as for ground $\mathcal{ALCH}_@$, by replacing annotated concept names $A@S$ by new names A_S, and likewise for roles. However, we now introduce names $A_S \in \mathsf{N_C}$ and $r_S \in \mathsf{N_R}$ for all possible open and closed ground specifiers over the set of individual names in KB, as opposed to only those occurring in KB. We then add two families of axioms for capturing the aforementioned effects. First, to handle individual equality, for each $A \in \mathsf{N_C}$ and $r \in \mathsf{N_R}$, we add axioms $a \approx b \Rightarrow A_S \sqsubseteq A_T$ and $a \approx b \Rightarrow r_S \sqsubseteq r_T$ for every pair S, T of ground specifiers that are either both open or both closed, and where the sets of pairs in S and T are the same when replacing each occurrence of a by b. Second, to handle bounded domain size, we consider an individual name z not occurring in KB. Entailments of the form $z \approx a$ will be used to detect the bounded domain case. We can formalise this effect by axioms $z \approx a \Rightarrow \top \sqsubseteq \bigsqcup_{c \in \mathsf{N}_\mathsf{I}^{KB}} \{c\}$, where $\mathsf{N}_\mathsf{I}^{KB}$ is the set of individual names occurring in KB for all $a \in \mathsf{N}_\mathsf{I}^{KB}$. To handle specifiers in this situation, we add axioms of the form

$$z \approx a \Rightarrow A_S \sqsubseteq \bigsqcup_{T \supseteq_c S} A_T \qquad \text{for all } A \in \mathsf{N_C} \text{ in } KB \text{ and } a \in \mathsf{N}_\mathsf{I}^{KB} \qquad (16)$$

where S is a ground open specifier and $T \supseteq_c S$ holds whenever T is a ground closed specifier that contains all attribute–value pairs in S. We would need a similar axiom as (16) for roles, but this would require disjunctions of arbitrary roles, which is not supported in $\mathcal{SROIQ}$. However, since these axioms only are necessary when all elements in the domain of interpretation are the interpretation of some individual name in N_I^{KB}, we can instead use concept inclusions as follows:

$$z \approx a \Rightarrow \{b\} \sqcap \exists r_S.\{c\} \sqsubseteq \bigsqcup_{T \sqsupseteq_c S} \exists r_T.\{c\} \quad \text{for all } r \in N_R \text{ in } KB \text{ and } a, b, c \in N_I^{KB}$$

$$(17)$$

where S and T are as above. Intuitively, this axiom states that any fact $r_S(b,c)$ entails some fact of the form $r_T(b,c)$. Finally, as previously for $\mathcal{ALCH}_{@}$, we also add all axioms of the form (12) and (13). This finishes our construction of $KB^{\ddagger}$.

Lemma 1. *For any ground $\mathcal{SROIQ}_{@}$ ontology KB, the $\mathcal{SROIQ}_{\approx}$ ontology $KB^{\ddagger}$ is equisatisfiable and can be constructed in exponential time.*

The proof is analogous to the proof of Theorem 3 with one exception: when constructing models we do not introduce a fresh, unnamed domain element $\star$, but rather use $z^{\mathcal{J}}$ instead (which may or may not be named).

To complete the proof of Theorem 11, it remains to show that satisfiability checking for the exponentially larger $KB^{\ddagger}$ can still be done in nondeterministic double exponential time w.r.t. the size of KB. To this end, we can define simplicity and regularity for $\mathcal{SROIQ}_{\approx}$ as for $\mathcal{SROIQ}_{@}$, by ignoring the additional $\approx$-prefixes and disregarding any condition related to annotations. In particular, we obtain a strict partial order $\prec$, as before, and, since $KB^{\ddagger}$ only contains role inclusions translated directly from those in KB, it also satisfies the regularity restrictions. We define the $\circ$-*depth* of a regular $\mathcal{SROIQ}_{\approx}$ ontology $KB_{\approx}$ to be the maximal number k for which there is a chain of (inverted) roles $R_1 \prec R_1' \prec \ldots \prec R_k \prec R_k'$, such that $KB_{\approx}$ contains complex role inclusions with R_i occurring as one of several roles on the left and R_i' on the right. Intuitively speaking, the $\circ$-depth bounds the number of axioms with $\circ$ along paths of $\prec$. Clearly, the $\circ$-depth of $KB^{\ddagger}$ is the same as for KB, in spite of the exponential increase in the number of axioms.

Lemma 2. *Checking satisfiability of a $\mathcal{SROIQ}_{\approx}$ ontology $KB_{\approx}$ of size s and $\circ$-depth d is possible in NTIME $(2^{p(s \cdot 2^{q(d)})})$, where p, q are some fixed polynomial functions.*

In particular, if an ontology is of size $O(2^n)$ but retains a $\circ$-depth in $O(n)$, then reasoning is still in N2ExpTime. To show this, we adapt the translation from $\mathcal{SROIQ}$ to $\mathcal{SHOIQ}$ as given by Kazakov [12], which is based on representing the effects of complex role inclusion axioms using concept inclusions. As a first step, one constructs, for any non-simple role expression R, a nondeterministic finite automaton $\mathcal{B}_R$ that describes the regular language of all sequences of roles that entail R [10]. We modify the known construction for $\mathcal{SROIQ}_{\approx}$ by allowing transitions in this automaton to be labelled not just by role expressions S, but also by conditional expressions $a \approx b \Rightarrow S$. The idea is that these transitions are only available if the precondition holds. By a slight adaptation of a similar observation of Horrocks and Sattler [11, Lemma 11], we obtain:

Lemma 3. *For a $\mathcal{SROIQ}_\approx$ ontology $KB_\approx$ and a role expression R, the size of $\mathcal{B}_R$ is bounded exponentially in the $\circ$-depth of $KB_\approx$.*

Kazakov considers a normal form of axioms, which we can construct analogously for $\mathcal{SROIQ}_\approx$ [12, Table 1]. We can ensure that conditions $a \approx b$ occur in concept inclusions only if they have the form $a \approx b \Rightarrow A \sqsubseteq B$ with $A, B \in \mathsf{N_C}$. The automaton $\mathcal{B}(R)$ is then used to replace every axiom of the form $A \sqsubseteq \forall R.B$ (which never has $\approx$-conditions) by the following axioms:

$$A \sqsubseteq A_q^R \qquad\qquad q \text{ starting state of } \mathcal{B}(R) \qquad (18)$$

$$a \approx b \Rightarrow A_{q_1}^R \sqsubseteq \forall S.A_{q_2}^R \qquad q_1 \xrightarrow{a\approx b\Rightarrow S} q_2 \text{ a transition of } \mathcal{B}(R) \qquad (19)$$

$$A_q^R \sqsubseteq B \qquad\qquad q \text{ a final state of } \mathcal{B}(R) \qquad (20)$$

where the condition $a \approx b$ in axioms (19) can be omitted if it is not given. The resulting $\mathcal{SROIQ}_\approx$ ontology still contains axioms with preconditions $a \approx b$, but no more $\circ$. Every normalised $\mathcal{SROIQ}$ axiom α can be translated into a $\mathcal{C}^2$ formula $\mathsf{c2}(\alpha)$ as shown in [12, Table 1]. A $\mathcal{SROIQ}_\approx$ axiom of the form $a \approx b \Rightarrow \alpha$ accordingly can be translated as $(\exists^{=1}x.A_a(x) \wedge A_b(x)) \to \mathsf{c2}(\alpha)$. This completes the proof of Theorem 11.

We can lift this result to non-ground ontologies without increasing complexity:

Theorem 12. *Satisfiability of $\mathcal{SROIQ}_@$ ontologies is N2ExpTime-complete.*

Proof. Hardness is immediate given the hardness of $\mathcal{SROIQ}$. The proof of membership uses the same grounding approach as the proof of Theorem 4, which is easily seen to be correct. This grounded ontology $\mathsf{ground}(KB)$ is exponentially larger than the input KB, but the regularity conditions for $\mathcal{SROIQ}_@$ ensure that it has the same (linearly bounded) $\circ$-depth. Moreover, while the transformation used for axiomatising ground $\mathcal{SROIQ}_@$ ontologies is also exponential, it is polynomial in the number of possible ground annotation sets; this number remains single exponential w.r.t. the size of KB, even when considering $\mathsf{ground}(KB)$. Therefore, we find that the auxiliary $\mathcal{SROIQ}_\approx$ ontology $\mathsf{ground}(KB)^\ddagger$ is still only exponential w.r.t. KB while having a polynomial $\circ$-depth. The claimed complexity therefore follows from Lemma 2. $\qquad\qquad\square$

7 Conclusion

Current graph-based knowledge representation formalisms suffer from an inability to handle meta-data in the form of sets of attribute–value pairs. These limitations show up even when dealing with purely abstract data and are orthogonal to datatype support in the formalisms. We therefore believe that KR formalisms must urgently take up the challenge of incorporating annotation structures into their expressive repertoire.

Our family of attributed description logics represents a potential solution in the context of DLs, and covers attributed $\mathcal{SROIQ}$, the DL underlying

OWL 2 DL. In contrast to our recent findings on rule-based logics supporting similar annotations, attributed DLs often incur an increased reasoning complexity due to the open-world nature of DLs. We have presented a grounding-
based decision procedure and identified the special cases of ground ontologies
and structural restrictions on axioms, for which this overhead can be avoided.
In particular, this ensures the tractability of attributed $\mathcal{EL}$.

More work is now needed regarding practical reasoning algorithms in
attributed DLs. We believe that similar approaches to those used for reasoning with nominal schemas might be effective here. A related practical issue is
the syntactic integration of the new features in OWL. The existing annotation
mechanism of OWL 2 [17] can be used to store attribute-value sets, e.g., of assertions, but is not general enough to capture our extended syntax for arbitrary
axioms. Finally, there are certainly many further expressive mechanisms related
to modelling with annotations that should be considered and investigated in
future studies of this new field.

Acknowledgements. This work is partly supported by the German Research Foundation (DFG) in CRC 912 (HAEC) and in Emmy Noether grant KR 4381/1-1.

References

1. Baader, F., Brandt, S., Lutz, C.: Pushing the $\mathcal{EL}$ envelope. In: Kaelbling, L.,
   Saffiotti, A. (eds.) Proceeding of 19th International Joint Conference on Artificial Intelligence (IJCAI 2005), pp. 364–369. Professional Book Center (2005)
2. Beeri, C., Vardi, M.Y.: The implication problem for data dependencies. In: Even,
   S., Kariv, O. (eds.) ICALP 1981. LNCS, vol. 115, pp. 73–85. Springer, Heidelberg
   (1981). doi:10.1007/3-540-10843-2_7
3. Belleau, F., Nolin, M., Tourigny, N., Rigault, P., Morissette, J.: Bio2RDF: Towards
   a mashup to build bioinformatics knowledge systems. J. of Biomed. Inf. **41**(5), 706–
   716 (2008)
4. Bizer, C., Lehmann, J., Kobilarov, G., Auer, S., Becker, C., Cyganiak, R.,
   Hellmann, S.: DBpedia - A crystallization point for the Web of Data. J. Web
   Semant. **7**(3), 154–165 (2009)
5. Calvanese, D., De Giacomo, G., Lembo, D., Lenzerini, M., Poggi, A., Rosati, R.:
   Linking data to ontologies: The description logic DL-Lite$_A$. In: Proceedings of the
   OWLED 2006 Workshop on OWL: Experiences and Directions, 10–11 November
   2006, Athens, Georgia, USA (2006)
6. Chandra, A.K., Kozen, D.C., Stockmeyer, L.J.: Alternation. J. ACM **28**(1), 114–
   133 (1981)
7. Chandra, A.K., Lewis, H.R., Makowsky, J.A.: Embedded implicational dependencies and their inference problem. In: Proceeding of the 13th Annual ACM Symposium on Theory of Computation (STOC 1981), pp. 342–354. ACM (1981)
8. Erxleben, F., Günther, M., Krötzsch, M., Mendez, J., Vrandečić, D.: Introducing
   wikidata to the linked data web. In: Mika, P., et al. (eds.) ISWC 2014. LNCS, vol.
   8796, pp. 50–65. Springer, Cham (2014). doi:10.1007/978-3-319-11964-9_4
9. Green, T.J., Karvounarakis, G., Tannen, V.: Provenance semirings. In: Proceedings
   of the Twenty-Sixth ACM SIGACT-SIGMOD-SIGART Symposium on Principles
   of Database Systems, 11–13 June 2007, Beijing, China, pp. 31–40 (2007)

10. Horrocks, I., Kutz, O., Sattler, U.: The even more irresistible $\mathcal{SROIQ}$. In: Doherty, P., Mylopoulos, J., Welty, C.A. (eds.) Proceeding of 10th International Conference on Principles of Knowledge Representation and Reasoning (KR 2006), pp. 57–67. AAAI Press (2006)

11. Horrocks, I., Sattler, U.: Decidability of $\mathcal{SHIQ}$ with complex role inclusion axioms. Artif. Intell. **160**(1), 79–104 (2004)

12. Kazakov, Y.: $\mathcal{RIQ}$ and $\mathcal{SROIQ}$ are harder than $\mathcal{SHOIQ}$. In: Brewka, G., Lang, J. (eds.) Proceeding of 11th International Conference on Principles of Knowledge Representation and Reasoning (KR 2008), pp. 274–284. AAAI Press (2008)

13. Krötzsch, M., Maier, F., Krisnadhi, A.A., Hitzler, P.: A better uncle for OWL: Nominal schemas for integrating rules and ontologies. In: Proceeding of 20th International Conference on World Wide Web (WWW 2011), pp. 645–654. ACM (2011)

14. Krötzsch, M., Marx, M., Ozaki, A., Thost, V.: Attributed description logics: Ontologies for knowledge graphs. Technical report, TU Dresden (2017). https://iccl.inf.tu-dresden.de/web/AtDLs/en

15. Krötzsch, M., Rudolph, S.: Nominal schemas in description logics: Complexities clarified. In: Baral, C., De Giacomo, G., Eiter, T. (eds.) Proceeding of 14th International Conference on Principles of Knowledge Representation and Reasoning (KR 2014), pp. 308–317. AAAI Press (2014)

16. Marx, M., Krötzsch, M., Thost, V.: Logic on MARS: Ontologies for generalised property graphs. In: Proceeding of 26th International Joint Conference on Artificial Intelligence (IJCAI 2017). AAAI Press (2017, to appear) https://iccl.inf.tu-dresden.de/web/MARS/en

17. OWL Working Group, W: OWL 2 Web Ontology Language: Document Overview. W3C Recommendation (27 October 2009). http://www.w3.org/TR/owl2-overview/

18. Pratt-Hartmann, I.: Complexity of the two-variable fragment with counting quantifiers. J. Logic Lang. Inf. **14**, 369–395 (2005)

19. Rodriguez, M.A., Neubauer, P.: Constructions from dots and lines. Bull. Am. Soc. Inf. Sci. Technol. **36**(6), 35–41 (2010)

20. SNOMED CT: Compositional Grammar Specification and Guide v2.02. IHTSDO (22 May 2015). http://doc.ihtsdo.org/download/doc_CompositionalGrammarSpecificationAndGuide_Current-en-US_INT_20150522.pdf. Accessed 27 Jul 2017

21. Spackman, K.A., Campbell, K.E., Côté, R.A.: SNOMED RT: A reference terminology for health care. In: Masys, D.R. (ed.) Proceeding 1997 AMIA Annual Fall Symposium, pp. 640–644. Journal of the American Medical Informatics Association, Symposium Supplement, Hanley & Belfus (1997)

22. Straccia, U., Lopes, N., Lukacsy, G., Polleres, A.: A general framework for representing and reasoning with annotated semantic web data. In: Fox, M., Poole, D. (eds.) Proceeding of 24th AAAI Conference on Artificial Intelligence (AAAI 2010). AAAI Press (2010)

23. Udrea, O., Recupero, D.R., Subrahmanian, V.S.: Annotated RDF. ACM Trans. Comput. Logic **11**(2), 10:1–10:41 (2010)

24. Vrandečić, D., Krötzsch, M.: Wikidata: A free collaborative knowledgebase. Commun. ACM **57**(10), 78–85 (2014)

Reliable Granular References to Changing Linked Data

Tobias Kuhn[1](✉), Egon Willighagen[2], Chris Evelo[2], Núria Queralt-Rosinach[3],
Emilio Centeno[4], and Laura I. Furlong[4]

[1] Department of Computer Science,
Vrije Universiteit Amsterdam, Amsterdam, Netherlands
t.kuhn@vu.nl
[2] Department of Bioinformatics, NUTRIM,
Maastricht University, Maastricht, Netherlands
[3] Department of Integrative Structural and Computational Biology,
The Scripps Research Institute, La Jolla, USA
[4] Research Group on Integrative Biomedical Informatics (GRIB),
Institut Hospital Del Mar D'Investigacions Mèdiques (IMIM),
Universitat Pompeu Fabra (UPF), Barcelona, Spain

Abstract. Nanopublications are a concept to represent Linked Data in
a granular and provenance-aware manner, which has been successfully
applied to a number of scientific datasets. We demonstrated in previous
work how we can establish reliable and verifiable identifiers for nanopublications and sets thereof. Further adoption of these techniques, however,
was probably hindered by the fact that nanopublications can lead to an
explosion in the number of triples due to auxiliary information about the
structure of each nanopublication and repetitive provenance and metadata. We demonstrate here that this significant overhead disappears once
we take the version history of nanopublication datasets into account,
calculate incremental updates, and allow users to deal with the specific
subsets they need. We show that the total size and overhead of evolving
scientific datasets is reduced, and typical subsets that researchers use for
their analyses can be referenced and retrieved efficiently with optimized
precision, persistence, and reliability.

1 Introduction

Datasets in general and Linked Data resources in particular play an increasingly
important role in data-driven research, as exemplified by the datasets provided
by WikiPathways [20] and DisGeNET [32], and overarching initiatives such as
Bio2RDF [3]. Reproducibility and persistence have been ongoing concerns in this
regard, as dataset identification and access has often been brittle and unreliable.
Datasets based on Linked Data, as most types of datasets, are typically quite
dynamic and change over time [9,36], and capturing the data's provenance [24]
is crucial for their proper interpretation and reuse. Moreover, as we will show,
scientific data analyses typically use relatively small subsets of Linked Data
resources, but we currently lack reliable methods to refer to such subsets.

© Springer International Publishing AG 2017
C. d'Amato et al. (Eds.): ISWC 2017, Part I, LNCS 10587, pp. 436–451, 2017.
DOI: 10.1007/978-3-319-68288-4_26

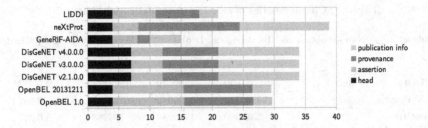

Fig. 1. Average triple counts of existing nanopublication datasets.

In the context of the recent initiatives to promote FAIR data publishing [41], Linked Data can contribute to the requirement of interoperability across datasets. We argue that researchers should—in papers as well as the software code for computational analyses—be able to exactly specify what dataset they are using as input. Currently, the best researchers can do is to provide version numbers and bibliographic references in papers, like "we used DisGeNET-RDF version 4.0 [32]", and to make the downloaded dataset explicit in the source code of their computational analyses, like in the following line of a Unix script:

```
wget http://rdf.disgenet.org/download/v4.0.0/geneDiseaseAssociation.ttl.gz
# Run analysis here
```

We can therefore identify the following two problems with the current practice of dataset references: (1) Researchers can only specify at the dataset level which data they use as input. They cannot reliably point to the exact subset that is needed for a given analysis. And (2) researchers cannot reliably refer to specific versions of evolving datasets; even with version numbers included, researchers cannot be sure that others can later retrieve exactly the same dataset to replicate the results. We argue that we can address both problems with an approach of incremental dataset definitions based on the technologies of nanopublications and trusty URIs.

Nanopublications [23] are tiny packages of Linked Data that come with provenance and metadata attached [12]. In previous work, we showed how identifers based on cryptographic hashes, called trusty URIs [18,19], can be used in combination with nanopublications to make them (and their entire reference trees) immutable and verifiable, two important properties for scientific data. In contrast to other proposals for data citations [29], such a cryptography-empowered approach can provide us with strong technical—rather than weaker organizational—guarantees with respect to the integrity and original state of datasets.

Fine-grained and provenance-aware approaches like nanopublications, however, come at a cost. The internal structure of each nanopublication has to be defined, and the provenance and metadata has to be repeated even if it is virtually identical for a large number of them. This effect can be seen in Fig. 1 for a number of existing dataset that use the nanopublication format: LIDDI [2], neXtProt [6], GeneRIF-AIDA [15], three versions of DisGeNET [31], and two

Table 1. Characteristics of existing nanopublication datasets.

Dataset	Nanopublications	Total triples	Triples outside of head (t)	Decontextualized triples (d)	Ratio d/t
LIDDI	98085	2051959	1659619	1364314	0.8221
neXtProt	4025981	156263513	140159589	76722914	0.5474
GeneRIF-AIDA	156026	2340390	1716286	733208	0.4272
DisGeNET v4.0.0.0	1414902	48106668	38202354	5390141	0.1411
DisGeNET v3.0.0.0	1018735	34636990	27505845	3908268	0.1421
DisGeNET v2.1.0.0	940034	31961156	25380918	3667767	0.1445
OpenBEL 20131211	74173	2186874	1890182	1308625	0.6923
OpenBEL 1.0	50707	1502574	1299746	903066	0.6948

versions of a dataset extracted from OpenBEL[1]. We see that the nanopublication format implies a significant overhead in terms of number of triples. The main content of a nanopublication in the assertion graph account for just a minority of the total triples. While the provenance and publication info graphs provide additional context for the assertion triples, the head graph's sole purpose is to link to the other graphs and thereby to hold the nanopublication together.

While the provenance and publication information contents are by no means useless and therefore not purely an overhead, they tend to be quite repetitive. This is at least partly caused by the fact that most existing nanopublication datasets are extracted from "non-nano" datasets that do not capture granular metadata, and therefore no granular metadata is available for export. The overhead is in any case significant for existing datasets, as shown in Table 1. Even when disregarding the triples of the head graph, the numbers of triples is significantly larger than what we get if we "decontextualize" the triples to attach provenance and metadata only to the entire dataset and remove all duplicates. A decontexualized dataset, for example, would state that a given publication was the source of some entries in the dataset, but not refer to these exact entries, as enforced with nanopublications. We will use this method of *decontextualization* also below for our analyses. DisGeNET is an extreme example here, with the number of decontextualized triples making up only 14% of the number of nanopublication triples, caused by the repetition of triples across nanopublications.

This significant overhead that comes with the nanopublication technology might have been a hindrance in its further adoption. We show here, however, that nanopublications together with an approach to represent and construct

---

[1] https://github.com/tkuhn/bel2nanopub.

incremental datasets and subsets thereof lead to a situation where the benefits of the fine-grained nanopublication structure offset the costs, even for the most extreme case of the DisGeNET dataset.

2 Background

Versioning and capturing the evolution of Linked Data has been a concern and research area for many years. While the early work focused on capturing the changes in ontologies [1,39], later work included approaches to combine RDF versioning with web archiving [37], long-term observation of the dynamics of Linked Data [13], and efficient archiving of dynamic Linked Data [9]. There have also been a few approaches that deal with access and versions of *subsets* of Linked Data resources [34,35].

Providing version indicators for datasets is considered common best practice[2], but version numbers cannot guarantee that data providers do not violate a dataset version's immutability. To provide such kinds of strong technical guarantees, approaches inspired by the Git versioning system have been proposed [11,38] that involve cryptographic hash values to enforce immutable versions. Similar approaches to reliable incremental Linked Data versioning have been developed by others [10,21], including applications to Big Data environments [5]. Outside of the Linked Data world, approaches for cryptographically strong data archiving have been proposed for decentralized systems like Bitcoin [22] and BitTorrent [7].

In our own previous work, we showed how nanopublications with trusty URIs can make data publishing verifiable and reliable, without depending on a central server or trusted authority [16]. In the same work, we also proposed a method to describe datasets as nanopublications themselves, thereby making references to entire sets of nanopublications verifiable through recursive hashing.

While a number of approaches exist on each of (1) Linked Data versioning, (2) cryptographically reliable dataset identifiers, and (3) references to subsets of larger datasets, and while these aspects are covered by the data citation recommendations of the Research Data Alliance [33], there are currently no concrete solutions that combine them all. In other words, existing approaches do not allow for cryptographically reliable references at high granularity in terms of both, time (i.e. versions) and space (i.e. subsets). We will present and evaluate such an approach below.

3 Approach

Our approach consists of the following three aspects: (1) We use the nanopublication concept to model datasets and their versions, (2) provide a method to create incremental datasets, and (3) connect these components to allow for flexible and reliable references to subsets of data resources.

---

[2] See e.g. [33] and https://www.w3.org/TR/dwbp/#dataVersioning.

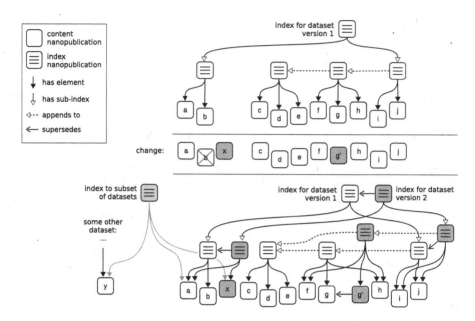

Fig. 2. Schematic depiction of a dataset specified with nanopublication indexes (top), the occurred content changes (middle), and their result as a new dataset version that reuses as much as possible. The blue index shows a subset definition.

3.1 Incremental Datasets with Nanopublications

Figure 2 schematically depicts the gist of our approach. It is based on our previous proposal to define sets of nanopublications as nanopublications themselves [17]. We call these set-defining nanopublications *index nanopublications*, as they consist of direct and indirect links to the nanopublications they contain as elements. An index nanopublication can directly link to elements via links of the type *has element* (these elements are marked with lowercase letters in Fig. 2), but can also point to subsets in the form of other indexes via links of the type *has sub-index*. Sub-indexes can be used, for example, to partition a dataset into different parts each containing a particular type of data. Finally, for nanopublication sets that are large but have no such partitioning, we need a method to ensure that all these index nanopublications remain small, as this is a core feature of the nanopublication concept. For that reason, we introduce relations of the type *appends to* that allows for more nanopublications being added in a new index, once an index is full. The size limit of a nanopublication index is set to 1000 entries (either elements or sub-indexes). All these links are established via the trusty URIs of the referred nanopublication, and thereby the whole reference tree can be cryptographically verified from just the URI of the top index nanopublication [19]. We will come back below to the issue of how to retrieve such sets of nanopublications.

Because of its granularity, this approach provides excellent opportunities to reuse parts of a dataset for a new version in an incremental manner. In general, there are three kinds of changes that can happen: A nanopublication can be removed from a dataset (such as b in Fig. 2); a nanopublication can be added (x); and a nanopublication can be changed and replaced by a new version (g being replaced by g'). All remaining nanopublications remain unchanged and can thereby be reused, i.e. linked from an index nanopublication belonging to the new version of the dataset. Moreover, we might also be able to reuse some of the nanopublication indexes, namely the ones representing subsets that didn't change. For both, content and index nanopublications, we can furthermore establish *supersedes* links to the respective previous versions, to allow users to navigate back in time through the version history.

It is important to note that the previous version remains untouched: None of the existing nanopublications are changed (trusty URIs in fact enforce this) and by starting from the URI of the previous version and follow its links, the existence of the new version is not even noticed. Turning this property around implies that defining sets of nanopublications in this way does not require any control over the contained elements. Everybody can define after the fact (i.e. after the release of a dataset) arbitrary subsets by creating the appropriate index nanopublications. These subsets are maximally flexible in the sense that they can reuse any possible subset, be augmented with new nanopublications, and even combine subsets of different datasets, as illustrated by the blue index nanopublication in Fig. 2. In such a case, one has to publish the new index nanopublications to be able to publicly refer to the specified subset, but no part of the content needs to be republished, and its original state is easy to verify.

We base our implementation and evaluation on the specific technologies and formats underlying Linked Data and nanopublications, but our general approach is portable to any type of knowledge representation with declarative monotonic semantics, which by their nature allow for subdividing representations into small independent pieces.

3.2 From Snapshots to Incremental Datasets

To actually generate an incremental dataset for a nanopublication-based resource, one has to ideally record all changes when they occur and build the proper index structure accordingly. However, such a direct construction is often non-trivial to integrate in existing data production pipelines, which is why first producing a full new snapshot and then calculating an incremental update is often more practical, in particular for smaller datasets. We therefore present such an approach here and apply it in the evaluations described below.

To calculate incremental updates of nanopublications, we apply the two concepts of *fingerprints* and *topics*. These two concepts establish identity relations that are weaker than the one that is enforced by trusty URIs. With trusty URIs, any tiny change in a nanopublication, such as a new timestamp, leads to a new URI and therefore to a new nanopublication. In contrast to trusty URIs, neither fingerprints nor topics are visible to the users of the dataset, but are merely a method to calculate incremental updates from dataset snapshots.

Fingerprints—like trusty URIs—correspond to a cryptographic hash value that is based on the RDF content of nanopublication, but consider only a subset of the triples and may apply preprocessing and normalization. In the simplest case, a fingerprint ignores the content of the timestamp found in the publication info graph. Other variants are possible, such as ignoring the entire publication info graph, and this can be configured for a given dataset and the intended use of its incremental versioning. The purpose of these fingerprints is to decide whether a new nanopublication (i.e. a nanopublication that would get a new trusty URI) is "new enough" to warrant an update, or whether a nanopublication from the previous version of the dataset can be reused.

Topics are similar to fingerprints, but normally correspond to a URI instead of a hash. A new nanopublication with an existing topic *is* included in the new dataset version, but the new nanopublication will be marked as an update of the old. The addition of *supersedes*-links as shown in Fig. 2 thereby provides users a access to the version history on the level of individual nanopublications. By default, the topic is calculated to be the URI that has the highest occurrence in the subject position of the assertion triples, but this can be configured to match the characteristics of a given dataset.

It is worth noting that the matching of fingerprints and topics comes at a cost, in particular the cost of keeping a mapping table during the process. For large datasets, it can therefore pay off to record changes as they happen, which eliminates the need to reconstruct changes with fingerprints or topics.

3.3   Granular and Reliable Retrieval

So far we have only described our approach from a conceptual level assuming a reliable method to follow links. The most straight-forward approach to actually do this is the "follow your nose" principle[3] of URI dereferencing, which however is in general not reliable and can be very slow, depending on web servers a user has no control over. This problem is particularly grave for large datasets and those spanning multiple web domains. We also need to provide convenient methods for users to make their own subset definitions publicly available.

We address these problems by applying and using the decentralized server network that we demonstrated in previous work, based on nanopublications and trusty URIs [17]. With this network, we do not have to assume that URIs are efficiently resolvable, but we can instead rely on the redundancy of the network and the verifiability of trusty URIs. This nanopublication network has grown in the last months and years, consisting now of 15 server instances on 10 distinct physical servers in 8 countries.[4] Our approach relies on this server network to let data producers publish incremental datasets, and to allow researchers to publish index nanopublications to precisely specify the subsets of existing Linked Data resources they are using for their analyses.

---

[3] https://www.w3.org/wiki/FollowYourNose.

[4] http://purl.org/nanopub/monitor.

4   Implementation and Methods

We implemented our approach in a command line tool, and evaluated it with two studies. We performed a technical study covering the publishing aspect to find out about the overall data volume for changing datasets with our approach and to compare it to idealized alternative approaches of decontextualized triples. We then performed a second study to investigate how our approach performs on typical subsets of datasets that are used in scientific studies.

4.1   Nanopublication Operation Tool: *npop*

Based on our existing *nanopub-java* library[5] [14], we implemented a command line tool that we call *npop* (standing for *nano*publication *op*erations). The following commands are relevant to the work presented here:

- `count` can be used to count nanopublications and their triples from a file or stream. It is therefore like a `wc` command for nanopublications.
- `filter` reads nanopublications from a file or stream and filters them by given URIs or literals. It is therefore like a `grep` command for nanopublications.
- `extract` retrieves triples from the different nanopublication graphs.
- `reuse` takes a dataset snapshot and its previous version, and generates an incremental update from it. Nanopublications from the previous version with a matching fingerprint are reused, and for those with a matching topic (but not a matching fingerprint) a *supersedes*-link is introduced.
- `ireuse` does the same as `reuse` but for index nanopublications.
- `fingerprint` calculates the fingerprints for nanopublications following a specified configuration.
- `topic` calculates the topics according to a specified configuration.
- `decontext` produces decontextualized triples for given nanopublications, for comparative studies such as the ones presented in this paper.

These commands, together with the commands from the underlying *nanopub-java* library (such as `get` to retrieve nanopublications and `publish` to upload them to the network), allowed us to perform the studies to be described below, and they are available for other data producers to apply to their own datasets.

4.2   Evaluation on Data Publishing

The first evaluation was performed on WikiPathways, a community-curated open database of biological pathways [20], with the aim to find out whether our approach is beneficial on the data producer side. Recently, the RDF export of the WikiPathways database was established [40], making the content of the database much easier to integrate. This RDF export contains information from the original WikiPathways and Reactome pathways [4,8]. Using a number of SPARQL CON-STRUCT queries, three types of nanopublications are generated:[6] interactions,

---

[5] https://github.com/Nanopublication/nanopub-java.
[6] https://github.com/wikipathways/nanopublications.

complex participation, and pathway participation. Importantly, only nanopublications are generated for statements if the fact is supported by a publication, marked with a PubMed database identifier. Overall, the dataset currently consists of a bit over 10 000 nanopublications.

For this evaluation, we retroactively generated nanopublication snapshots from old data dumps, corresponding to 11 monthly builds between June 2016 to May 2017 (January 2017 is missing). For these we built an incremental dataset using the *npop* tool. We can then compare the size of the resulting cumulative dataset, growing over 11 months, with the size of the nanopublication snapshots as well as decontextualized versions thereof, to evaluate whether incremental versioning can indeed offset the increased space needs of nanopublications.

This is not a very fair comparison, of course, because nanopublications come with valuable context-dependent information on the one hand and because incremental versioning could just as well be applied to decontextualized data on the other. We will keep the first point in mind when interpreting the results, and to address the second point we calculate an incremental version for the decontextualized case too. Three general approaches exist for versioning of arbitrary RDF data [9,36]: independent copies, change-based approach, and timestamp-based approach. Independent copies correspond to what we called dataset snapshots, i.e. non-incremental versions. The change-based approach keeps separate lists of added and removed triples for each version after the first, whereas the timestamp-based approach keeps all triples in the same collection but attaches timestamps of their addition or removal. While the latter two have different advantages and shortcomings, they lead to the same overall triple count (if we require a triple to be duplicated to acquire more than one timestamp). As a further point of comparison for our study, we therefore use this overall triple count for an incremental decontextualized dataset according to the change-based or timestamp-based approach.

4.3   Evaluation on Data Analyses

With the second evaluation we wanted to find out whether our approach is beneficial on the consumer end. It was performed on DisGeNET [30], one of the most comprehensive databases on human diseases and their genes that is publicly available. DisGeNET is available in RDF [32] and nanopublication [31] formats. There are currently three releases of the DisGeNET nanopublication dataset (version 2.1 with 940 034 nanopublications, version 3.0 with 1 018 735 nanopublications, and version 4.0 with 1 414 902 nanopublications), which correspond to three most recent releases of the database. The releases differ mainly in data content due to the incremental update of the database, the incorporation of new data sources for the gene-disease associations, and the incorporation of new data attributes.

To find out about the use of this dataset by researchers, we looked at the publications that cited one of the DisGeNET papers during 2017 (31 publications as of 5 May 2017). We were interested in studies that included the DisGeNET dataset or subsets thereof in their analyses, but closer inspection revealed that six of these publications did not actually use the data (but only mentioned Dis-GeNET as related work) and another five of them used the data but did not include them in any analyses (e.g. describing a tool that imported the data). For the remaining 20 publications, we manually determined whether the authors used the whole dataset or specific subsets. If the study used a specific subset, we looked for information about how this selection was performed (e.g. based on a particular disease or a family of genes, or using a pre-defined value of some of the DisGeNET data attributes as such as the DisGeNET score, among others). Finally, we matched these subsets to the corresponding subsets of our incremental nanopublication-based dataset to find out what set of nanopublications they *would have* used if they had followed our proposed approach.

From this empirical collection of used subsets, we can then investigate the typical size of such database subsets used for scientific analyses. We can also compare the size of these subsets to the decontextualized version of DisGeNET to find out whether the overhead of nanopublications is actually still an overhead once we look at specific subsets. We can reliably refer to such subsets with nanopublications, but we have to refer to (and therefore handle) the entire dataset for data based on regular (decontextualized) triples.

Finally, to measure the practicality of retrieving subsets from the server network, we also measure the time it takes to do so for a typical subset. To put that into perspective, we also measure the time needed to download the entire dataset from the `disgenet.org` website.

5   Results

Table 2 gives an overview of the structure of the incremental dataset for WikiPathways, showing the number of nanopublications for each release, the number of reused nanopublications from the previous version (by fingerprint matching), and the number of new nanopublications. The right-hand side of the table shows how many of the new ones were updates of nanopublications from the previous version (by topic matching). We see that the datasets underwent fundamental changes in the first two months, with a majority of nanopublications being replaced. Afterwards, the changes are much less drastic, in the sense that the majority of nanopublications are reused and often a majority of the new ones can be linked to previous nanopublications of the same topic.

Figure 3 shows the gains from the incremental approach to nanopublication-based versioning (light blue line). After the first two tumultuous months, the gain in number of triples to the cumulative nanopublication-based snapshots (dark blue line) quickly widens. In the end, we only need 23% (0.78M/3.38M) of the triples to express the same version history. Comparing the two to our main reference point—cumulative snapshots of decontextualized triples (dark red line)—we see that the overhead of the nanopublication snapshots is in the end 54% (1 − 1.55M/3.38M), meaning that we could drop 54% of the triples if we weren't interested in the fine-grained context. With the incremental nanopublication datasets, however, this overhead turns into a "negative overhead" of

Table 2. Overview of the incremental dataset generated for WikiPathways.

Version	Nanopublications	Reused (%)		New (%)		Update (%)		Addition (%)	
20160610	9018	0	(0.0)	9018	(100.0)	0	(0.0)	9018	(100.0)
20160710	10173	1405	(13.8)	8768	(86.2)	3	(0.0)	8765	(100.0)
20160810	10123	3836	(37.9)	6287	(62.1)	0	(0.0)	6287	(100.0)
20160910	10124	9838	(97.2)	286	(2.8)	0	(0.0)	286	(100.0)
20161010	10127	9620	(95.0)	507	(5.0)	16	(3.2)	491	(96.8)
20161110	13958	10041	(71.9)	3917	(28.1)	18	(0.5)	3899	(99.5)
20161210	13975	13794	(98.7)	181	(1.3)	152	(84.0)	29	(16.0)
20170210	14323	13743	(96.0)	580	(4.0)	176	(30.3)	404	(69.7)
20170310	14319	13938	(97.3)	381	(2.7)	230	(60.4)	151	(39.6)
20170410	14323	13972	(97.5)	351	(2.5)	317	(90.3)	34	(9.7)
20170510	14323	13980	(97.6)	343	(2.4)	340	(99.1)	3	(0.9)

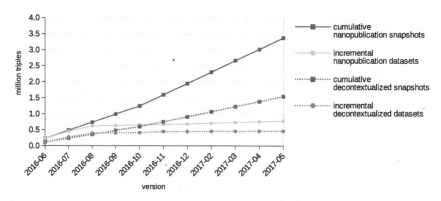

Fig. 3. Overall size of the evolving WikiPathways version history (Color figure online).

98% $(1 - 1.55M/0.78M)$, meaning that we needed 98% more triples if we were to switch to decontextualized snapshots. We see that the overhead of nanopublications has indeed turned into a gain.

As we noted above, this comparison is not perfectly fair on either side. Still keeping in mind that decontextualized triples carry less information, we can compare our incremental nanopublication-based approach to what could be ideally achieved with a change-based or timestamp-based approach on decontextualized triples (light red line). The overhead of our approach to this idealized setting is 41% $(1 - 0.46M/0.78M)$. The fact that this is again an actual overhead is not surprising, as it is always possible to handle *less* information more efficiently. We will show below, however, that even this overhead is in fact turned into a gain when we look at the side of data consumers and the typical subsets they use.

Table 3 shows the result of the second empirical study on the subsets of DisGeNET used and reported in scientific papers from 2017. Only three out of the 20 papers used the entire dataset. The distribution of the subset sizes is also

Table 3. DisGeNET subsets used and reported in papers, sorted by ascending size.

DOI of paper	nanopub- lication count	triple count	rel. size to full dataset	rel. size to decontext. version
10.21873/cgp.20028	14	476	0.00001	0.00009
10.3892/ijmm.2017.2853	482	16388	0.00034	0.00304
10.1007/s12539-017-0213-z	533	18122	0.00038	0.00336
10.1038/srep46760	782	26588	0.00055	0.00493
10.1016/j.preteyeres.2017.02.001	1711	58174	0.00121	0.01079
10.1101/gr.210740.116	2014	68476	0.00142	0.01270
10.1186/s12920-017-0259-0	2158	73372	0.00153	0.01361
10.1016/j.jprot.2017.03.015	4859	165206	0.00343	0.03065
10.1016/j.neuron.2017.01.033	18098	615332	0.01279	0.11416 *
10.1021/acs.jcim.6b00725	21336	725424	0.01508	0.13458
10.1101/119099	31105	1057570	0.02198	0.19620
10.1002/jcb.25799	61198	2080732	0.04325	0.38603
10.3390/ncrna3020020	78742	2677228	0.05565	0.49669
10.1007/978-1-4939-6843-5_13	83771	2848214	0.05921	0.52841
10.1038/srep43632	101297	3444098	0.07159	0.63896
10.1016/j.dib.2017.04.001	196108	6667672	0.13860	1.23701
10.1186/s13148-017-0336-4	326472	11100048	0.23074	2.05932
10.1038/srep40154	1414902	48106668	1.00000	8.92494
10.1038/srep42638	1414902	48106668	1.00000	8.92494
10.1002/pmic.201700056	1414902	48106668	1.00000	8.92494
average:	258769	8798156	0.18289	1.63227
median:	26221	891497	0.01853	0.16539
average of proper subsets:	54746	1861360	0.03869	0.34533
median of proper subsets:	18098	615332	0.01279	0.11416

shown in Fig. 4 as a histogram. The two peaks indicate that researchers tend to use a dataset either entirely or only a very small subset of it. For 40% of the papers we studied (8 out of 20), less than 1% of the dataset was used. The largest proper subset used consisted of just 23% of the data.

We can again compare these numbers to the idealized setting without nanopublications where triples are decontextualized and where reliable identifiers only exist at the dataset level. In comparison to such a decontextualized snapshot, 15 out of the 20 studied subsets have a lower triple count (green). For a typical subset, the overhead of nanopublications in terms of number of triples is therefore again turned into a gain (in addition to the gains with respect to precision, verifiability and fine-grained provenance and metadata). We should also remember that DisGeNET is an extreme case in terms of triple overhead.

Finally, Fig. 5 shows the results for the retrieval times of a typical subset (the subset with the median size value of the proper subsets, marked with * in Table 3). We see that the retrieval via the server network takes about the same time as downloading the whole dataset from disgenet.org (both roughly

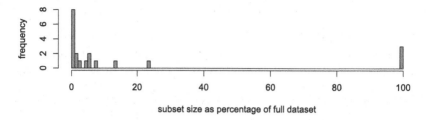

subset size as percentage of full dataset

Fig. 4. Histogram of the subset sizes (in triples) in relation to the entire dataset.

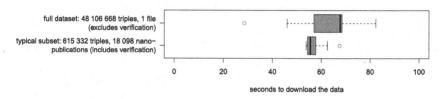

seconds to download the data

Fig. 5. Download times for the full DisGeNET dataset (v4.0.0.0) and a typical subset (marked with * in Table 3; $n=10$ in both cases; whiskers show $+/-$ 1.5 IQR).

around 60 seconds). Instead of just downloading a single file, the subset retrieval consists of requesting 18 098 individual nanopublications and verifying their content against their trusty URIs. Despite the resulting lower throughput in terms of triples per second, we can efficiently retrieve the specific subset of data.

The code used for these studies and the resulting data can be found online.[7]

6   Discussion and Conclusions

Data providers and data consumers have to pay a price for granular and precise references to subsets of datasets, to make these references cryptographically strong, and to verify the integrity of retrieved data. We showed, however, that this price is offset by the benefits of incremental versioning and by being able to refer to exactly the needed subset of a given dataset, on top of the gains from cryptographically strong verifiability. Data providers should take into account the gain in storage overhead and the benefits of reproducibility and verifiability—and thus better FAIR publishing—of evolving datasets that our incremental nanopublication approach provides. Also, it allows data publishers to reliably check and record how their data evolves from version to version.

To come back to the examples of dataset references, we can now refer to our datasets in papers with references that include the trusty URI of the nanopublication index of the appropriate version and subset, such as the incremental DisGeNET datasets [25–27] and the incremental WikiPathways dataset [28] we

---

[7] See https://doi.org/10.6084/m9.figshare.5230639 and https://bitbucket.org/tkuhn/nanodiff-exp/.

cite in this paper. For integration in the code to perform computational analyses, we can now use the np command provided by the *nanopub-java* library to reliably download a precisely specified set of nanopublications:

```
np get -c -o data.trig
http://purl.org/np/RAxMyDRaM8RmKGNiEe7dQPRUTuz616iI-N2T-H3MPYmXk
# Run analysis here
```

We now get cryptographic guarantees on the retrieved content, and we can rely on an entire network of nanopublication servers and therefore do not depend on the uptime of individual servers.

As future work, we will keep providing incremental updates for the nanopublication datasets we presented here. We will also investigate how we can reduce the overhead present in DisGeNET nanopublications for future releases. The most obvious improvement is the reduction of the number of head triples from 7 to the mandatory minimum of 4. This alone will reduce the overall triple count by 9%. Further improvements can probably be achieved—without substantial negative side effects—by reducing the redundancy in the provenance and publication info graphs, and possibly also in the assertion graph.

To conclude, we demonstrated how our approach can contribute to the verifiability and granular accessibility of scientific Linked Data resources. As such, we think that it can put many other Linked Data solutions that require precise and reliable data publishing and consumption onto a solid technical basis.

Acknowledgments. We would like to thank Javier D. Fernández for valuable input and discussions on RDF versioning. L.I. Furlong and E. Centeno received support from ISCIII-FEDER (PI13/00082, CP10/00524, CPII16/00026), the EU H2020 Programme 2014-2020 under grant agreements no. 634143 (MedBioinformatics) and no. 676559 (Elixir-Excelerate).

References

1. Auer, S., Herre, H.: A versioning and evolution framework for RDF knowledge bases. In: Virbitskaite, I., Voronkov, A. (eds.) PSI 2006. LNCS, vol. 4378, pp. 55–69. Springer, Heidelberg (2007). doi:10.1007/978-3-540-70881-0_8

2. Banda, J.M., Kuhn, T., Shah, N.H., Dumontier, M.: Provenance-centered dataset of drug-drug interactions. In: Arenas, M., et al. (eds.) ISWC 2015. LNCS, vol. 9367, pp. 293–300. Springer, Cham (2015). doi:10.1007/978-3-319-25010-6_18

3. Belleau, F., Nolin, M.-A., Tourigny, N., Rigault, P., Morissette, J.: Bio2RDF: towards a mashup to build bioinformatics knowledge systems. J. Biomed. Inf. **41**(5), 706–716 (2008)

4. Bohler, A., Wu, G., Kutmon, M., Pradhana, L.A., Coort, S.L., Hanspers, K., Haw, R., Pico, A.R., Evelo, C.T.: Reactome from a WikiPathways perspective. PLoS Comput. Biol. **12**(5), e1004941 (2016)

5. Chard, K., D'Arcy, M., Heavner, B., Foster, I., Kesselman, C., Madduri, R., Rodriguez, A., Soiland-Reyes, S., Goble, C., Clark, K., et al.: I'll take that to go: Big data bags and minimal identifiers for exchange of large, complex datasets. In: IEEE International Conference on Big Data, pages 319–328. IEEE (2016)

6. Chichester, C., Karch, O., Gaudet, P., Lane, L., Mons, B., Bairoch, A.: Converting nextprot into linked data and nanopublications. Semant. Web **6**(2), 147–153 (2015)
7. Cohen, J.P., Lo, H.Z.: Academic torrents: A community-maintained distributed repository. In: Proceedings of XSEDE 2014, p. 2. ACM (2014)
8. Fabregat, A., et al.: The reactome pathway knowledgebase. Nucleic Acids Res. **44**(D1), D481–D487 (2016)
9. Fernández, J.D. Polleres, A., Umbrich, J.: Towards efficient archiving of dynamic linked open data. In: DIACRON@ESWC, pp. 34–49 (2015)
10. Frommhold, M., Piris, R.N., Arndt, N., Tramp, S., Petersen, N., Martin, M.: Towards versioning of arbitrary RDF data. In: Proceedings of the 12th International Conference on Semantic Systems, pp. 33–40. ACM (2016)
11. Graube, M. Hensel, S., Urbas, L.: R43ples: revisions for triples. In Proceedings of the 1st Workshop on Linked Data Quality. Citeseer (2014)
12. Groth, P., Gibson, A., Velterop, J.: The anatomy of a nanopublication. Inf. Serv. Use **30**(1–2), 51–56 (2010)
13. Käfer, T., Abdelrahman, A., Umbrich, J., O'Byrne, P., Hogan, A.: Observing linked data dynamics. In: Cimiano, P., Corcho, O., Presutti, V., Hollink, L., Rudolph, S. (eds.) ESWC 2013. LNCS, vol. 7882, pp. 213–227. Springer, Heidelberg (2013). doi:10.1007/978-3-642-38288-8_15
14. Kuhn, T.: Nanopub-java: a java library for nanopublications. In: Proceedings of the 5th Workshop on Linked Science (LISC 2015) (2015)
15. Kuhn, T., Barbano, P.E., Nagy, M.L., Krauthammer, M.: Broadening the scope of nanopublications. In: Cimiano, P., Corcho, O., Presutti, V., Hollink, L., Rudolph, S. (eds.) ESWC 2013. LNCS, vol. 7882, pp. 487–501. Springer, Heidelberg (2013). doi:10.1007/978-3-642-38288-8_33
16. Kuhn, T., Chichester, C., Krauthammer, M., Dumontier, M.: Publishing Without publishers: a decentralized approach to dissemination, retrieval, and archiving of data. In: Arenas, M., et al. (eds.) ISWC 2015. LNCS, vol. 9366, pp. 656–672. Springer, Cham (2015). doi:10.1007/978-3-319-25007-6_38
17. Kuhn, T., Chichester, C., Krauthammer, M., Queralt-Rosinach, N., Verborgh, R., Giannakopoulos, G., Ngomo, A.-C.N., Viglianti, R., Dumontier, M.: Decentralized provenance-aware publishing with nanopublications. PeerJ Comput. Sci. **2**, e78 (2016)
18. Kuhn, T., Dumontier, M.: Trusty URIs: verifiable, immutable, and permanent digital artifacts for linked data. In: Presutti, V., d'Amato, C., Gandon, F., d'Aquin, M., Staab, S., Tordai, A. (eds.) ESWC 2014. LNCS, vol. 8465, pp. 395–410. Springer, Cham (2014). doi:10.1007/978-3-319-07443-6_27
19. Kuhn, T., Dumontier, M.: Making digital artifacts on the web verifiable and reliable. IEEE Trans. Knowl. Data Eng. **27**(9), 2390–2400 (2015)
20. Kutmon, M., et al.: WikiPathways: capturing the full diversity of pathway knowledge. Nucleic Acids Res. **44**(D1), D488–D494 (2016)
21. Meinhardt, P., Knuth, M., Sack, H.: TailR: a platform for preserving history on the web of data. In: Proceedings of the 11th International Conference on Semantic Systems, pp. 57–64. ACM (2015)
22. Miller, A., Juels, A., Shi, E., Parno, B., Katz, J.: Permacoin: repurposing Bitcoin work for data preservation. In: Proceedings of the IEEE Symposium on Security and Privacy (SP), pp. 475–490. IEEE (2014)
23. Mons, B., et al.: The value of data. Nat. Genet. **43**(4), 281–283 (2011)
24. Moreau, L., Groth, P.: Provenance: an introduction to prov. Synth. Lect. Semant. Web Theor. Technol. **3**(4), 1–129 (2013)

25. Nanopubs extracted from DisGeNET v2.1.0.0, incremental dataset. Nanop-ublication index, 9 May 2017. http://purl.org/np/RADYX-ia_TZYAw_eZD0-2oGGA7gnMxOnVj-Gh8wdJgAzI

26. Nanopubs extracted from DisGeNET v3.0.0.0, incremental dataset. Nanopublication index, 9 May 2017. http://purl.org/np/RAufQaKzv1pZlMhZo2eBuZtx9vuugLBJsrs4ZkvR53xzw

27. Nanopubs extracted from DisGeNET v4.0.0.0, incremental dataset. Nanopublication index, 9 May 2017. http://purl.org/np/RAu0PUrg-M8HxkOiYRXkTg7r9fgOIzFZNINj8q7ywNrdM

28. Nanopublications extracted from WikiPathways, incremental dataset, 20170510. Nanopublication index, 11 May 2017. http://purl.org/np/RAKz0OQ3Dq8dDWqF7SIY4TgYcZRX4d2TnmLUEbOwnaGmQ

29. Task Group on Data Citation Standards and Practices.: Out of cite, out of mind: The current state of practice, policy, and technology for the citation of data. In: Data Sci. J. **12**, pp. CIDCR1-CIDCR75 (2013)

30. Piñero, J., Bravo, À., Queralt-Rosinach, N., Gutiérrez-Sacristán, A., Deu-Pons, J., Centeno, E., García-García, J., Sanz, F., Furlong, L.I.: DisGeNET: a comprehensive platform integrating information on human disease-associated genes and variants. Nucleic Acids Res. **45**, D833–D839 (2016)

31. Queralt-Rosinach, N., Kuhn, T., Chichester, C., Dumontier, M., Sanz, F., Furlong, L.I.: Publishing DisGeNET as nanopublications. Semant. Web **7**(5), 519–528 (2016)

32. Queralt-Rosinach, N., Piñero, J., Bravo, À., Sanz, F., Furlong, L.I.: DisGeNET-RDF: harnessing the innovative power of the semantic web to explore the genetic basis of diseases. Bioinformatics **32**, 2236–2238 (2016)

33. Rauber, A., Asmi, A., van Uytvanck, D., Pröll, S.: Identification of reproducible subsets for data citation, sharing and re-use. Bull. IEEE Tech. Comm. Digit. Libr. **12**(1), 6–15 (2016)

34. Schandl, B.: Replication and versioning of partial RDF graphs. In: Aroyo, L., Antoniou, G., Hyvönen, E., ten Teije, A., Stuckenschmidt, H., Cabral, L., Tudorache, T. (eds.) ESWC 2010. LNCS, vol. 6088, pp. 31–45. Springer, Heidelberg (2010). doi:10.1007/978-3-642-13486-9_3

35. Silvello, G.: A methodology for citing linked open data subsets. D-Lib Magazine, **21**(1/2) (2015)

36. Tzitzikas, Y., Theoharis, Y., Andreou, D.: On storage policies for semantic web repositories that support versioning. In: Bechhofer, S., Hauswirth, M., Hoffmann, J., Koubarakis, M. (eds.) ESWC 2008. LNCS, vol. 5021, pp. 705–719. Springer, Heidelberg (2008). doi:10.1007/978-3-540-68234-9_51

37. Van de Sompel, H., Sanderson, R., Nelson, M.L., Balakireva, L.L., Shankar, H., Ainsworth, S.: An HTTP-based versioning mechanism for linked data (2010). arXiv:1003.3661

38. Vander Sande, M., Colpaert, P., Verborgh, R., Coppens, S., Mannens, E., Van de Walle, R.: R&Wbase: git for triples. In: LDOW (2013)

39. Volkel, M., Winkler, W., Sure, Y., Kruk, S.R., Synak, M.: Semversion: A versioning system for RDF and ontologies. In: Proceedings of ESWC (2005)

40. Waagmeester, A., Kutmon, M., Riutta, A., Miller, R., Willighagen, E.L., Evelo, C.T., Pico, A.R.: Using the semantic web for rapid integration of WikiPathways with other biological online data resources. PLoS Comput. Biol. **12**(6), e1004989 (2016)

41. Wilkinson, M.D., Dumontier, M., et al.: The FAIR guiding principles for scientific data management and stewardship. Sci. data **3**, 160018 (2016)

Cost-Driven Ontology-Based Data Access

Davide Lanti, Guohui Xiao$^{(\boxtimes)}$, and Diego Calvanese

KRDB Research Centre for Knowledge and Data,
Free University of Bozen-Bolzano, Bolzano, Italy
{dlanti,xiao,calvanese}@inf.unibz.it

Abstract. SPARQL query answering in ontology-based data access (OBDA) is carried out by translating into SQL queries over the data source. Standard translation techniques try to transform the user query into a union of conjunctive queries (UCQ), following the heuristic argument that UCQs can be efficiently evaluated by modern relational database engines. In this work, we show that translating to UCQs is not always the best choice, and that, under certain conditions on the interplay between the ontology, the mappings, and the statistics of the data, alternative translations can be evaluated much more efficiently. To find the best translation, we devise a cost model together with a novel cardinality estimation that takes into account all such OBDA components. Our experiments confirm that *(i)* alternatives to the UCQ translation might produce queries that are orders of magnitude more efficient, and *(ii)* the cost model we propose is faithful to the actual query evaluation cost, and hence is well suited to select the best translation.

1 Introduction

The paradigm of Ontology-based Data Access (OBDA) [17] presents to the end-users a convenient *virtual RDF graph* [13] view of the data stored in a relational database. Such RDF graph is realized by means of the *TBox of an OWL2 QL ontology* [16] connected to the data source through declarative *mappings* [7]. SPARQL query answering [10] over the RDF graph is not carried out by actually materialising the data according to the mappings, but rather by first *rewriting* the user query with respect to the TBox, and then *translating* the rewritten query into an SQL query over the data.

In state-of-the-art OBDA systems [5], such SQL translation is the result of *structural optimizations*, which aim at obtaining a *union of conjunctive queries* (UCQ). Such an approach is claimed to be effective because *(i)* joins are over database values, rather than over URIs constructed by applying mapping definitions; *(ii)* joins in UCQs are performed by directly accessing (usually, indexed) database tables, rather than materialized and non-indexed intermediate views. However, the requirement of generating UCQs comes at the cost of an exponential blow-up in the size of the user query.

A more subtle, *sometimes* critical issue, is that the UCQ structure accentuates the problem of redundant data, which is particularly severe in OBDA

© Springer International Publishing AG 2017
C. d'Amato et al. (Eds.): ISWC 2017, Part I, LNCS 10587, pp. 452–470, 2017.
DOI: 10.1007/978-3-319-68288-4_27

where the focus is on retrieving *all* the answers implied by the data and the TBox: each CQ in the UCQ can be seen as a different attempt of enriching the set of retrieved answers, without any guarantee on whether the attempt will be successful in retrieving new results. In fact, it was already observed in [2] that generating UCQs is sometimes counter-beneficial (although that work was focusing on a substantially different topic).

As for the rewriting step, Bursztyn et al. [3,4] have investigated a space of alternatives to UCQ rewritings, by considering *joins of UCQs* (JUCQs), and devised a cost-based algorithm to select the best alternative. However, the scope of their work is limited to the simplified setting in which there are no mappings and the extension of the predicates in the ontology is directly stored in the database. Moreover, they use their algorithm in combination with traditional cost models from the database literature of query evaluation costs, which, according to their experiments, provide estimations close to the native ones of the PostgreSQL database engine.

In this work we study the problem of alternative translations in the general setting of OBDA, where the presence of mappings needs to be taken into account. To do so, we first study the problem of translating JUCQ rewritings such as those from [3], into SQL queries that preserve the JUCQ structure while maintaining property *(i)* above, i.e., the ability of performing joins over database values, rather than over constructed URIs. We also devise a cost model based on a *novel cardinality estimation*, for estimating the cost of evaluating a translation for a UCQ or JUCQ over the database. The novelty in our cardinality estimation is that it exploits the interplay between the components of an OBDA instance, namely ontology, mappings, and statistics of the data, so as to better estimate the number of non-duplicate answers.

We carry out extensive and in-depth experiments based on a synthetic scenario built on top of the *Winsconsin Benchmark* [8], a widely adopted benchmark for databases, so as to understand the trade-off between a translation for UCQs and JUCQs. In these experiments we observe that: *(i)* factors such as the number of mapping assertions, also affected by the number of axioms in the ontology, and the number of redundant answers are the main factors for deciding which translation to choose; *(ii)* the cost model we propose is faithful to the actual query evaluation cost, and hence is well suited to select the best alternative translation of the user query; *(iii)* the cost model implemented by PostgreSQL performs surprisingly poorly in the task of estimating the best translation, and is significantly outperformed by our cost model. The main reason for this is that PostgreSQL fails at recognizing when different translations are actually equivalent, and may provide for them cardinality estimations that differ by several orders of magnitude.

In addition, we carry out an evaluation on a real-world scenario based on the NPD benchmark for OBDA [14]. Also in these experiments we confirm that alternative translations to the UCQ one may be more efficient, and that the same factors already identified in the Winsconsin experiments determine which choice is best.

The rest of the paper is structured as follows. Section 2 introduces the relevant technical notions underlying OBDA. Section 3 provides our characterization for SQL translations of JUCQs. Section 4 presents our novel model for cardinality estimation, and Sect. 5 the associated cost model. Section 6 provides the evaluation of the cost model on the Wisconsin and NPD Benchmarks. Section 7 concludes the paper. Due to space limitation, more details of the techniques, proofs and experiments are provided in an online report [15]. The materials to reproduce the experiments are available online (https://github.com/ontop/ontop-examples/tree/master/iswc-2017-cost).

2 Preliminaries

In this work, we use the **bold** font to denote tuples (when convenient we might treat tuples as sets). Given a tuple of function symbols $\mathbf{f} = (f_1, \ldots, f_n)$ and of variables $\mathbf{x}$, we denote by $\mathbf{f}(\mathbf{x})$ a tuple of terms of the form $(f_1(\mathbf{x_1}), \ldots, f_n(\mathbf{x_n}))$, with $\mathbf{x_i} \subseteq \mathbf{x}$, $1 \leq i \leq n$. We assume some familiarity with basic notions from probability calculus and statistics. We rely on the OBDA framework of [17], which we formalize here through the notion of *OBDA specification*, which is a triple $\mathcal{S} = (\mathcal{T}, \mathcal{M}, \Sigma)$ where $\mathcal{T}$ is an *ontology TBox*, $\mathcal{M}$ is a set of *mappings*, and Σ is the schema of a relational database.

We assume that ontologies are formulated in *DL-Lite$_\mathcal{R}$* [6], which is the DL providing the formal foundations for OWL 2 QL, the W3C standard ontology language for OBDA [16]. A *DL-Lite$_\mathcal{R}$ TBox* $\mathcal{T}$ is a finite set of axioms of the form $C \sqsubseteq D$ or $P \sqsubseteq R$, where C, D are *DL-Lite$_\mathcal{R}$* concepts and P, R are *roles*, following the *DL-Lite$_\mathcal{R}$* grammar. A *DL-Lite$_\mathcal{R}$ ABox* $\mathcal{A}$ is a finite set of assertions of the form $A(a)$, $P(a, b)$, where A is a concept name, P a role name, and a, b *individuals*. We call the pair $\mathcal{O} = (\mathcal{T}, \mathcal{A})$ a *DL-Lite$_\mathcal{R}$ ontology*.

We consider here *first-order (FO) queries* [1], and we use $q^{\mathcal{D}}$ to denote the evaluation of a query q over a database $\mathcal{D}$. We use the notation $q^{\mathcal{A}}$ also for the evaluation of q over the ABox $\mathcal{A}$, viewed as a database. For an ontology $\mathcal{O}$, we use $cert(q, \mathcal{O})$ to denote the *certain answers* of q over $\mathcal{O}$, which are defined as the set of tuples $\mathbf{a}$ of individuals such that $\mathcal{O} \models q(\mathbf{a})$ (where $\models$ denotes the *DL-Lite$_\mathcal{R}$* entailment relation). We consider also various fragments of FO queries, notably *conjunctive queries* (CQs), *unions of CQs* (UCQs), and *joins of UCQs* (JUCQs) [1].

Mappings specify how to populate the concepts and roles of the ontology from the data in the underlying relational database. A *mapping* m is an expression of the form $L(\mathbf{f}(\mathbf{x})) \leftsquigarrow q_m(\mathbf{x})$: the *target part* $L(\mathbf{f}(\mathbf{x}))$ of m is an atom over function symbols[1] $\mathbf{f}$ and variables $\mathbf{x}$ whose predicate name L is a concept or role name; the *source part* $q_m(\mathbf{x})$ of m is a FO query with output variables[2] $\mathbf{x}$. We say that

---

[1] For conciseness, we use here abstract function symbols in the mapping target. We remind that in concrete mapping languages, such as R2RML [7], such function symbols correspond to IRI templates used to generate object IRIs from database values.

[2] In general, the output variables of the source query might be a superset of the variables in the target, but for our purposes we can assume that they coincide.

the *signature* $sign(m)$ of m is the pair $(L, \mathbf{f})$, and that m *defines* L. We also define $sign(\mathcal{M}) = \{sign(m) \mid m \in \mathcal{M}\}$.

Following [9], we split each mapping $m = L(\mathbf{f}(\mathbf{x})) \leftsquigarrow q_m(\mathbf{x})$ in $\mathcal{M}$ into two parts by introducing an intermediate view name V_m for the FO query $q_m(\mathbf{x})$. We obtain a *low-level* mapping of the form $V_m(\mathbf{x}) \leftsquigarrow q_m(\mathbf{x})$, and a *high-level* mapping of the form $L(\mathbf{f}(\mathbf{x})) \leftsquigarrow V_m(\mathbf{x})$. In the following, we abstract away the low-level mapping parts, and we consider $\mathcal{M}$ as consisting directly of the high-level mappings. In other words, we directly consider the intermediate view atoms V_m as the source part, with the semantics $V_m^{\mathcal{D}} = q_m^{\mathcal{D}}$, for each database instance $\mathcal{D}$. We denote by $\Sigma_{\mathcal{M}}$ the *virtual schema* consisting of the relation schemas whose names are the intermediate view symbols V_m, with attributes given by the answer variables of the corresponding source queries.

From now on we fix an OBDA specification $\mathcal{S} = (\mathcal{T}, \mathcal{M}, \Sigma)$. Given a database instance $\mathcal{D}$ for Σ, we call the pair $(\mathcal{S}, \mathcal{D})$ an *OBDA instance*. We call the set of assertions $\mathcal{A}_{(\mathcal{M}, \mathcal{D})} = \{L(\mathbf{f}(\mathbf{a})) \mid L(\mathbf{f}(\mathbf{x})) \leftsquigarrow V(\mathbf{x}) \in \mathcal{M} \text{ and } \mathbf{a} \in V(\mathbf{x})^{\mathcal{D}}\}$ the *virtual ABox exposed by* $\mathcal{D}$ *through* $\mathcal{M}$. Intuitively, such an ABox is obtained by evaluating, for each (high level) mapping m, its source view $V(\mathbf{x})$ over the database $\mathcal{D}$, and by using the returned tuples to instantiate the concept or role L in the target part of m. The *certain answers* $cert(q, (\mathcal{S}, \mathcal{D}))$ to a query q over an OBDA instance $(\mathcal{S}, \mathcal{D})$ are defined as $cert(q, (\mathcal{T}, \mathcal{A}_{(\mathcal{M}, \mathcal{D})}))$.

In the virtual approach to OBDA, such answers are computed without actually materializing $\mathcal{A}_{(\mathcal{M}, \mathcal{D})}$, by transforming the query q into a FO query q_{fo} formulated over the database schema Σ such that $q_{fo}^{\mathcal{D}'} = cert(q, (\mathcal{S}, \mathcal{D}'))$, for every OBDA instance $(\mathcal{S}, \mathcal{D}')$. To define the query q_{fo}, we introduce the following notions:

- A query q_r is a *perfect rewriting* of a query q' with respect to a TBox $\mathcal{T}$, if $cert(q', (\mathcal{T}, \mathcal{A})) = q_r^{\mathcal{A}}$ for every ABox $\mathcal{A}$ [6].
- A query q_t is an $\mathcal{M}$-*translation* of a query q', if $q_t^{\mathcal{D}} = q'^{\mathcal{A}_{(\mathcal{M}, \mathcal{D})}}$, for every database $\mathcal{D}$ for Σ [17].

Notice that, by definition, all perfect rewritings (resp., translations) of q' with respect to $\mathcal{T}$ (resp., $\mathcal{M}$) are equivalent. Consider now a perfect rewriting $q_{\mathcal{T}}$ of q with respect to $\mathcal{T}$, and then a translation $q_{\mathcal{T}, \mathcal{M}}$ of $q_{\mathcal{T}}$ with respect to $\mathcal{M}$. It is possible to show that such a $q_{\mathcal{T}, \mathcal{M}}$ satisfies the condition stated above for q_{fo}.

Many different algorithms have been proposed for computing perfect rewritings of UCQs with respect to $DL\text{-}Lite_{\mathcal{R}}$ TBoxes, see, e.g., [6,11]. As for the translation, [17] proposes an algorithm that is based on non-recursive *Datalog* [1], extended with function symbols in the head of rules, with the additional restriction that such rules never produce nested terms. We consider Datalog queries of the form (G, Π), where G is the answer atom, and Π is a set of Datalog rules following the restriction above. We abbreviate a Datalog query of the form $(q(\mathbf{x}), \{q(\mathbf{x}) \leftarrow B_1, \ldots, B_n\})$, corresponding to a CQ (possibly with function symbols), as $q(\mathbf{x}) \leftarrow B_1, \ldots, B_n$, and we also call it q.

Definition 1 (Unfolding of a UCQ [17]). *Let* $q(\mathbf{x}) \leftarrow L_1(\mathbf{v}_1), \ldots, L_n(\mathbf{v}_n)$ *be a CQ. Then, the* unfolding $unf(q, \mathcal{M})$ *of* q *w.r.t.* $\mathcal{M}$ *is the Datalog query*

$(q_{unf}(\mathbf{x}), \Pi)$, where Π is a (up to variable renaming) minimal set of rules having the following property:

If $((m_1, \ldots, m_n), \sigma)$ is a pair such that $\{m_1, \ldots, m_n\} \subseteq \mathcal{M}$, and

- $m_i = L_i(\mathbf{f}_i(\mathbf{x}_i)) \rightsquigarrow V_i(\mathbf{z}_i)$, for each $1 \leq i \leq n$, and
- σ is a most general unifier for the set of pairs $\{(L_i(\mathbf{v}_i), L_i(\mathbf{f}_i(\mathbf{x}_i))) \mid 1 \leq i \leq n\}$,

then the query $q_{unf}(\sigma(\mathbf{x})) \leftarrow V_1(\sigma(\mathbf{z}_1)), \ldots, V_n(\sigma(\mathbf{z}_n))$ belongs to Π.
The unfolding of a UCQ q is the union of the unfoldings of each CQ in q.

It has been proved in [17] that, for a UCQ q, $unf(q, \mathcal{M})$ is an $\mathcal{M}$-translation.

3   Cover-Based Translation in OBDA

We first introduce some terminology from [3], that we use in our technical development. Let q be a query consisting of atoms $\mathcal{F} = \{L_1, \ldots, L_n\}$. A cover for q is a collection $C = \{f_1, \ldots, f_m\}$ of non-empty subsets of $\mathcal{F}$, called fragments, such that (i) $\bigcup_{f_i \in C} f_i = \mathcal{F}$ and (ii) no fragment is included into another one. Given a cover C for a query $q(\mathbf{x})$, the fragment query $q|_f(\mathbf{x}_f)$, for $f \in C$, is the query whose body consists of the atoms in f and whose answer variables $\mathbf{x}_f$ are given by the answer variables $\mathbf{x}$ of q that appear in the atoms of f, union the existential variables in f that are shared with another fragment $f' \in C$, with $f' \neq f$. Consider the query $q_C(\mathbf{x}) \leftarrow \bigwedge_{f \in C} q_{|_f}^{ucq}(\mathbf{x}_f)$, where $q_{|_f}^{ucq}(\mathbf{x}_f)$, for each $f \in C$, is a CQ-to-UCQ perfect rewriting of the query $q_{|f}$ w.r.t. $\mathcal{T}$. Then q_C is a cover-based JUCQ perfect rewriting of q w.r.t. $\mathcal{T}$ and C, if it is a perfect rewriting of q w.r.t. $\mathcal{T}$.

Authors in [3] have shown that, in $DL\text{-}Lite_{\mathcal{R}}$, not every cover leads to a cover-based perfect rewriting. Thus, they introduced the notion of safe covers, which are covers that guarantee the existence of a cover-based perfect rewriting.

For the remaining part of the section, we fix a query $q(\mathbf{x})$ and a (safe) cover C for it, as well as its cover-based JUCQ perfect rewriting $q_C(\mathbf{x}) \leftarrow \bigwedge_{f \in C} q_{|_f}^{ucq}$ w.r.t $\mathcal{T}$ and C. We introduce two different characterizations of unfoldings of q_C, which produce $\mathcal{M}$-translations of q. The first characterization relies on the intuition of joining the unfoldings of each fragment query in q_C.

Definition 2 (Unfolding of a JUCQ 1). *For each $f \in C$, let Aux_f be an auxiliary predicate for $q_{|_f}^{ucq}(\mathbf{x}_f)$, and let U_f be a view symbol for the unfolding $unf(q_{|_f}^{ucq}(\mathbf{x}_f), \mathcal{M})$, for each $f \in C$. Consider the set of mappings $\mathcal{M}^{aux} = \{Aux_f(\mathbf{x}_f) \rightsquigarrow U_f(\mathbf{x}_f) \mid f \in C\}$ associating the auxiliary predicates to the auxiliary view names. Then, we define the unfolding $unf(q_C, \mathcal{M})$ of q_C with respect to $\mathcal{M}$ as $unf(q_C^{aux}(\mathbf{x}) \leftarrow \bigwedge_{f \in C} Aux_f(\mathbf{x}_f), \mathcal{M}^{aux})$.*

Theorem 1 (Translation 1). *The query $unf(q_C, \mathcal{M})$ is an $\mathcal{M}$-translation for q_C.*

The above unfolding characterization for JUCQs corresponds to a translation containing SQL joins over URIs resulting from the application of function symbols to database values, rather than over (indexed) database values themselves (see [15]). In general, such joins cannot be evaluated efficiently by RDBMSs [19]. We introduce a second, less trivial, unfolding characterization that guarantees that joins are performed only over database values. For this we first need to introduce a number of auxiliary notions and results.

Definition 3. *Let $(L, \mathbf{f}) \in sign(\mathcal{M})$ be a signature in $\mathcal{M}$. Then, the restriction $\mathcal{M}|_{(L,\mathbf{f})}$ of $\mathcal{M}$ w.r.t. the signature $(L, \mathbf{f})$ is the set of mappings $\mathcal{M}|_{(L,\mathbf{f})} = \{m \in \mathcal{M} \mid m = L(\mathbf{f}(\mathbf{v})) \leftsquigarrow V(\mathbf{v})\}$.*

Definition 4 (Wrap). *Let $\mathcal{M}|_{(L,\mathbf{f})} = \{L(\mathbf{f}(\mathbf{v}_i)) \leftsquigarrow V_i(\mathbf{v}_i) \mid 1 \leq i \leq n\}$ be the restriction of $\mathcal{M}$ w.r.t. the signature $(L, \mathbf{f})$, and $\mathbf{f}(\mathbf{v})$ be a tuple of terms over fresh variables $\mathbf{v}$. Then, the wrap of $\mathcal{M}|_{(L,\mathbf{f})}$ is the (singleton) set of mappings $wrap(\mathcal{M}|_{(L,\mathbf{f})}) = \{L(\mathbf{f}(\mathbf{v})) \leftsquigarrow W(\mathbf{v})\}$ where W is a fresh view name for the Datalog query $(W(\mathbf{v}), \{W(\mathbf{v}_i) \leftarrow V_i(\mathbf{v}_i) \mid 1 \leq i \leq n\})$.*
The wrap of $\mathcal{M}$ is the set $wrap(\mathcal{M}) = \bigcup_{(L,\mathbf{f}) \in sign(\mathcal{M})} wrap(\mathcal{M}|_{(L,\mathbf{f})})$ of mappings.

The wrap operation groups the mappings for a signature into a single mapping. We now introduce an operation that *splits* a mapping according to the function symbols adopted on its source part.

Definition 5 (Split). *Let $m = L(\mathbf{x}) \leftsquigarrow U(\mathbf{x})$ be a mapping where U is the name for the query $(U(\mathbf{x}), \{U(\mathbf{f}_i(\mathbf{x}_i)) \leftarrow V_i(\mathbf{x}_i) \mid 1 \leq i \leq n\})$. Then, the split of m is the set $split(m) = \{L(\mathbf{f}_i(\mathbf{x}_i)) \leftsquigarrow V_i(\mathbf{x}_i) \mid 1 \leq i \leq n\}$ of mappings. We denote by $split(\mathcal{M})$ the split of the set $\mathcal{M}$ of mappings.*

Definition 6 (Unfolding of a JUCQ 2). *Let q_C^{aux} be a query and $\mathcal{M}^{aux}$ a set of mappings as in Definition 2. Then, the optimized unfolding $unf_{opt}(q_C(\mathbf{x}), \mathcal{M})$ of q_C w.r.t. $\mathcal{M}$ is defined as $unf(q_C^{aux}(\mathbf{x}), wrap(split(\mathcal{M}^{aux})))$.*

Theorem 2 (Translation 2). *The query $unf_{opt}(q_C, \mathcal{M})$ is an $\mathcal{M}$-translation for q_C.*

Observe that the optimized unfolding of a JUCQ is a *union of JUCQs* (UJUCQ). Moreover, where each JUCQ produces answers built from a *single* tuple of function symbols, if all the attributes are kept in the answer. The next example, aimed at clarifying the notions introduced so far, illustrates these.

Example 1. Let $q(x, y, z) \leftarrow P_1(x, y), C(x), P_2(x, z)$, and consider a cover $\{f_1, f_2\}$ generating fragment queries $q|_{f_1} = q(x, y) \leftarrow P_1(x, y), C(x)$ and $q|_{f_2} = q(x, z) \leftarrow P_2(x, z)$. Consider the set of mappings

$$\mathcal{M} = \left\{ \begin{array}{ll} P_1(f(a), g(b)) \leftsquigarrow V_1(a, b) & P_1(f(a), g(b)) \leftsquigarrow V_2(a, b) \\ P_1(h(a), i(b)) \leftsquigarrow V_3(a, b) & C(f(a)) \quad\quad\quad \leftsquigarrow V_4(a) \\ P_2(f(a), k(b)) \leftsquigarrow V_5(a, b) & P_2(f(a), h(b)) \leftsquigarrow V_6(a, b) \end{array} \right\}$$

Translation I. According to Definition 2, the JUCQ $q(x, y, z) \leftarrow q|_{f_1}(x, y), q|_{f_2}(x, z)$ can be rewritten as the auxiliary query $q^{aux}(x, y, z) = Aux_1(x, y), Aux_2(x, z)$ over mappings

$$\mathcal{M}^{aux} = \{ \; Aux_1(x, y) \leftsquigarrow U_1(x, y) \qquad Aux_2(x, z) \leftsquigarrow U_2(x, z) \; \}$$

where U_1 is a view name for $unf(q|_{f_1}(x, y), \mathcal{M}) = (U_1(x, y), \Pi_1)$, and U_2 is a view name for $unf(q|_{f_2}(x, z), \mathcal{M}) = (U_2(x, z), \Pi_2)$, such that

$$\Pi_1 = \left\{ \begin{array}{l} U_1(f(a), g(b)) \leftarrow V_1(a, b), V_4(a) \\ U_1(f(a), g(b)) \leftarrow V_2(a, b), V_4(a) \end{array} \right\} \qquad \Pi_2 = \left\{ \begin{array}{l} U_2(f(a), k(b)) \leftarrow V_5(a, b) \\ U_2(f(a), h(b)) \leftarrow V_6(a, b) \end{array} \right\}$$

Translation II. By Definition 5, we compute the split of $\mathcal{M}^{aux}$:

$$split(\mathcal{M}^{aux}) = \left\{ \begin{array}{ll} Aux_1(f(a), g(b)) \leftsquigarrow V_1(a, b), V_4(a) & Aux_2(f(a), k(b)) \leftsquigarrow V_5(a, b) \\ Aux_1(f(a), g(b)) \leftsquigarrow V_2(a, b), V_4(a) & Aux_2(f(a), h(b)) \leftsquigarrow V_6(a, b) \end{array} \right\}$$

By Definition 4, we compute the wrap of $split(\mathcal{M}^{aux})$:

$$wrap(split(\mathcal{M}^{aux})) = \left\{ \begin{array}{ll} Aux_1(f(a), g(b)) \leftsquigarrow W_3(a, b) & Aux_2(f(a), k(b)) \leftsquigarrow W_4(a, b) \\ & Aux_2(f(a), h(b)) \leftsquigarrow W_5(a, b) \end{array} \right\}$$

where $W_3(a, b)$, $W_4(a, b)$, $W_5(a, b)$ are Datalog queries whose programs are respectively

$$\Pi_3 = \left\{ \begin{array}{l} W_3(a, b) \leftarrow V_1(a, b), V_4(a) \\ W_3(a, b) \leftarrow V_2(a, b), V_4(a) \end{array} \right\} \qquad \begin{array}{l} \Pi_4 = \{ W_4(a, b) \leftarrow V_5(a, b) \} \\ \Pi_5 = \{ W_5(a, b) \leftarrow V_6(a, b) \} \end{array}$$

Finally, by Definition 6 we compute the optimized unfolding of q_C w.r.t. $\mathcal{M}$:

$$unf_{opt}(q_C(x, y, z), \mathcal{M}) = unf(q^{aux}(x, y, z), wrap(split(\mathcal{M}^{aux}))) = (q^{aux}_{unf}(x, y, z), \Pi_{unf})$$

where

$$\Pi_{unf} = \left\{ \begin{array}{l} q^{aux}_{unf}(f(a), g(b), k(b')) \leftarrow W_3(a, b), W_4(a, b') \\ q^{aux}_{unf}(f(a), g(b), h(b')) \leftarrow W_3(a, b), W_5(a, b') \end{array} \right\}$$

Observe that $unf_{opt}(q_C(x, y, z), \mathcal{M})$ is a UJUCQ. Moreover, each of the two JUCQs in q^{aux}_{unf} contributes with answers built out of a specific tuple of function symbols. ∎

4   Unfolding Cardinality Estimation

For convenience, in this section, we use relational algebra notation [1] for CQs. To deal with multiple occurrences of the same predicate in a CQ, the corresponding algebra expression would contain renaming operators. However, in our cardinality estimations we need to understand when two attributes actually refer to the same relation, and this information is lost in the presence of renaming.

Instead of introducing renaming, we first explicitly replace multiple occurrences of the same predicate name in the CQ by aliases (under the assumption that aliases for the same predicate name are interpreted as the same relation). Specifically, we use alias $V_{[i]}$ to represent the i-th occurrence of predicate name V in the CQ. Then, when translating the aliased CQ to algebra, we use *fully qualified attribute names* (i.e., each attribute name is prefixed with the (aliased) predicate name). So, to reconstruct the relation name V to which an attribute $V_{[i]}.x$ refers, it suffices to remove the occurrence information $_{[i]}$ from the prefix $V_{[i]}$. When the actual occurrence of V is not relevant, we use $V_{[\cdot]}$ to denote the alias.

Moreover, in the following, we consider only the restricted form of CQs, which we call *basic CQs*, whose algebra expression is of the form

$$E = V_{[\cdot]}^0 \bowtie_{\theta_1} V_{[\cdot]}^1 \bowtie_{\theta_2} \cdots \bowtie_{\theta_n} V_{[\cdot]}^n,$$

where, the V^is denote predicate names, and for each $i \in \{1, \ldots, n\}$, the join condition θ_i is of the form $V_{[\cdot]}^j.\mathbf{x} = V_{[\cdot]}^i.\mathbf{y}$, for some $j < i$. Arbitrary CQs, allowing for projections and arbitrary joins, are considered in the extended version of this work [15].

Given a basic CQ E as above, we denote by $E^{(m)}$, for $1 \leq m \leq n$, the subexpression of E up to the m-th join operator, namely $E^{(m)} = V_{[\cdot]}^0 \bowtie_{\theta_1} V_{[\cdot]}^1 \bowtie_{\theta_2} \cdots \bowtie_{\theta_m} V_{[\cdot]}^m$.

In the following, in addition to an OBDA specification, we also fix a database instance $\mathcal{D}$ for Σ. We use V and W to denote relation names (with an associated relation schema) in the virtual schema $\mathcal{M}_\Sigma$, whose associated relations consist of (multi)sets of labeled tuples (see the *named perspective* in [1]). Given a relation S, we denote by $|S|$ the number of (distinct) tuples in S, by $\pi_L(S)$ the *projection* of S over attributes L (under *set-semantics*), and by $\pi_{L_1}(S_1) \cap \pi_{L_2}(S_2)$ intersection of relations disregarding attribute names, i.e., $\pi_{L_1}(S_1) \cap \rho_{L_2 \mapsto L_1}(\pi_{L_2}(S_2))$. We also use the classical notation $P(\alpha)$ to denote the probability that an event α happens.

Background on Cardinality Estimation. We start by recalling some assumptions that are commonly made by models of cardinality estimation proposed in the database literature (e.g., see [20]): *(i)* For each relation column C, values are *uniformly distributed across* C; intuitively, for a column C of integers, $P(C < v) = (v - \min(C))/(\max(C) - \min(C))$, for each value $v \in C$. *(ii)* There is a *uniform distribution across distinct values*, i.e., $P(C = v_1) = P(C = v_2)$, for all values $v_1, v_2 \in C$. *(iii)* The distributions in different colums are independent, i.e., $P(C_1 = v_1 | C_2 = v_2) = P(C_1 = v_1)$, for all values $v_1 \in C_1$ and $v_2 \in C_2$. *(iv)* Columns in a join condition match "as much as possible", i.e., given a join $V \bowtie_{\mathbf{x}=\mathbf{y}} W$, it is assumed that $|\pi_\mathbf{x}(V^\mathcal{D}) \cap \pi_\mathbf{y}(W^\mathcal{D})| = \min(|\pi_\mathbf{x}(V)|, |\pi_\mathbf{y}(W)|)$.

Given the assumptions, the cardinality of a join $V \bowtie_{\mathbf{x}=\mathbf{y}} W$ is estimated [21] as:

$$k_\mathcal{D}(V \bowtie_{\mathbf{x}=\mathbf{y}} W) \cdot |V^\mathcal{D}| / dist_\mathcal{D}(V, \mathbf{x}) \cdot |W^\mathcal{D}| / dist_\mathcal{D}(W, \mathbf{y}) \tag{1}$$

where $k_\mathcal{D}$ is an estimation of the number of distinct values satisfying the join condition (i.e., $k_\mathcal{D}$ estimates $|\pi_\mathbf{x}(V^\mathcal{D}) \cap \pi_\mathbf{y}(W^\mathcal{D})|$, and $dist_\mathcal{D}(V, \mathbf{x})$ (resp., $dist_\mathcal{D}(W, \mathbf{y})$) corresponds to the estimation of $|\pi_\mathbf{x}(V^\mathcal{D})|$ (resp., $|\pi_\mathbf{y}(W^\mathcal{D})|$), both calculated according to the aforementioned assumptions. Note that the fractions such as $\frac{|V^{\mathcal{D}}|}{dist_{\mathcal{D}}(V,\mathbf{x})}$ estimate the number of tuples associated to each value that satisfies the join condition.

Of the assumptions *(i)–(iv)* above, we maintain only *(ii)* and *(iii)* in our cardinality estimator, while we drop *(i)* and *(iv)* due to the additional information given by the structure of the mappings. In the following, we will show how even under these conditions we can use Formula (1), to estimate the cardinality of conjunctive queries.

Basic CQ Cardinality Estimation. We first generalize Formula (1) to basic CQs.

Cardinality Estimator. Given a basic CQ E', $f_{\mathcal{D}}(E')$ estimates the number $|E'^{\mathcal{D}}|$ of distinct results in the evaluation of E' over $\mathcal{D}$. We define it as

$$f_{\mathcal{D}}(E \bowtie_{V_{[p]}.\mathbf{x}=W_{[q]}.\mathbf{y}} W_{[q]}) = \begin{cases} \left\lceil \dfrac{k_{\mathcal{D}}(V_{[p]} \bowtie_{V_{[p]}.\mathbf{x}=W_{[q]}.\mathbf{y}} W_{[q]}) \cdot |V^{\mathcal{D}}| \cdot |W^{\mathcal{D}}|}{dist_{\mathcal{D}}(V,V_{[p]}.\mathbf{x}) \cdot dist_{\mathcal{D}}(W,W_{[q]}.\mathbf{y})} \right\rceil, & \text{if } E = V \\[2em] \left\lceil \dfrac{k_{\mathcal{D}}(E \bowtie_{V_{[p]}.\mathbf{x}=W_{[q]}.\mathbf{y}} W_{[q]}) \cdot f_{\mathcal{D}}(E) \cdot |W^{\mathcal{D}}|}{dist_{\mathcal{D}}(E,V_{[p]}.\mathbf{x}) \cdot dist_{\mathcal{D}}(W,V_{[p]}.\mathbf{y})} \right\rceil, & \text{otherwise.} \end{cases}$$
$$(2)$$

Our cardinality estimator exploits assumptions *(ii)* and *(iii)* above, and relies on our definitions of the *facing values estimator* $k_{\mathcal{D}}$ and of the *distinct values estimator* $dist_{\mathcal{D}}$, which are based on additional statistics collected with the help of the mappings, instead of being based on assumptions *(i)* and *(iv)*, as in Formula (1).

Facing Values Estimator. Given a basic CQ $E' = E \bowtie_{V_{[p]}.\mathbf{x}=W_{[q]}.\mathbf{y}} W_{[q]}$, the estimation $k_{\mathcal{D}}(E')$ of the cardinality $|\pi_{V.\mathbf{x}}(E^{\mathcal{D}}) \Cap \pi_{W.\mathbf{y}}(W^{\mathcal{D}})|$ is defined as

$$k_{\mathcal{D}}(E \bowtie_{V_{[p]}.\mathbf{x}=W_{[q]}.\mathbf{y}} W_{[q]}) = \begin{cases} |\pi_{\mathbf{x}}(V^{\mathcal{D}}) \Cap \pi_{\mathbf{y}}(W^{\mathcal{D}})|, & \text{if } E = V \\[1em] \left\lceil |\pi_{\mathbf{x}}(V^{\mathcal{D}}) \Cap \pi_{\mathbf{y}}(W^{\mathcal{D}})| \cdot \dfrac{dist_{\mathcal{D}}(E,V_{[p]}.\mathbf{x})}{dist_{\mathcal{D}}(V,V_{[p]}.\mathbf{x})} \right\rceil, & \text{otherwise,} \end{cases} \quad (3)$$

where $|\pi_{\mathbf{x}}(V^{\mathcal{D}}) \Cap \pi_{\mathbf{y}}(W^{\mathcal{D}})|$ is assumed to be a statistic available after having analyzed the mappings together with the data instance. The fraction $\frac{dist_{\mathcal{D}}(E,V_{[p]}.\mathbf{x})}{dist_{\mathcal{D}}(V,V_{[p]}.\mathbf{x})}$ is a scaling factor relying on assumption *(ii)*.

Distinct Values Estimator. Let Q be a set of qualified attributes, and E be basic CQ. We define the set $ea(E,Q)$ of equivalent attributes of Q in E as $\bigcup_{i>0} C_i$, where *(i)* $C_1 := \{Q\}$ *(ii)* $C_{n+1} := C_n \cup \{Q' \mid \exists Q'' \in C_n \text{ s.t. } Q' = Q'' \text{ or } Q'' = Q' \text{ is a join condition in } E\}$, $n \geq 1$. Given a basic CQ E and a set $V_{[p]}.\mathbf{x}$ of qualified attributes, the expression $se(E,V_{[p]}.\mathbf{x})$ denotes the longest sub-expression $E^{(n)}$ in E, for some $n > 1$, such that $E^{(n)} = E^{(n-1)} \bowtie_{W_{[q]}.\mathbf{y}=U_{[r]}.\mathbf{z}} U_{[r]}$, for some relation name W, tuples of attributes $\mathbf{y}$ and $\mathbf{z}$ such that $U_{[r]}.\mathbf{z} \in ea(E,V_{[p]}.\mathbf{x})$, if $E^{(n)}$ exists, and $\bot$ otherwise. For

E and $V_{[p]}.\mathbf{x}$, the estimation $dist_{\mathcal{D}}(E, V_{[p]}.\mathbf{x})$ of the cardinality $|\pi_{V_{[p]}.\mathbf{x}}(E^{\mathcal{D}})|$ is defined as

$$
dist_{\mathcal{D}}(E, V_{[p]}.\mathbf{x}) = \begin{cases} |\pi_{\mathbf{x}}(V^{\mathcal{D}})|, & \text{if } E = V \\ \min\left\{ \left\lceil k_{\mathcal{D}}(E') \cdot \dfrac{f_{\mathcal{D}}(E)}{f_{\mathcal{D}}(E')} \right\rceil, k_{\mathcal{D}}(E') \right\}, & \text{if } se(E, V_{[p]}.\mathbf{x}) = E' \neq \bot \\ \min\left\{ \left\lceil |\pi_{\mathbf{x}}(V^{\mathcal{D}})| \cdot \dfrac{f_{\mathcal{D}}(E)}{|V^{\mathcal{D}}|} \right\rceil, |\pi_{\mathbf{x}}(V^{\mathcal{D}})| \right\}, & \text{otherwise.} \end{cases} \quad (4)
$$

where $|\pi_{\mathbf{x}}(V^{\mathcal{D}})|$ is assumed to be a statistic available after having analyzed the mappings together with the data instance. Observe that the fractions $\frac{f_{\mathcal{D}}(E)}{f_{\mathcal{D}}(E')}$ and $\frac{f_{\mathcal{D}}(E)}{|V^{\mathcal{D}}|}$ are again scaling factors relying on assumption (ii). Also, $dist_{\mathcal{D}}(E, V.\mathbf{x})$ must not increase when the number of joins in E increases, which explains the use of min for the case where the number of distinct results in E increases with the number of joins.

Fig. 1. Data instance $\mathcal{D}$.

Example 2. Consider the data instance $\mathcal{D}$ from Fig. 1. Relevant statistics are:

- $|T_1^{\mathcal{P}}| = 5$, $|T_2^{\mathcal{P}}| = |T_3^{\mathcal{P}}| = 10$
- $|\pi_{\mathrm{a}}(T_1^{\mathcal{P}})| = |\pi_{\mathrm{d}}(T_2^{\mathcal{P}})| = 5$, $|\pi_{\mathrm{c}}(T_2^{\mathcal{P}})| = |\pi_{\mathrm{f}}(T_3^{\mathcal{P}})| = |\pi_{\mathrm{e}}(T_3^{\mathcal{P}})| = 10$,
- $|\pi_{\mathrm{a}}(T_1^{\mathcal{P}}) \cap \pi_{\mathrm{c}}(T_2^{\mathcal{P}})| = 3$, $|\pi_{\mathrm{d}}(T_2^{\mathcal{P}}) \cap \pi_{\mathrm{e}}(T_3^{\mathcal{P}})| = 5$, $|\pi_{\mathrm{a}}(T_1^{\mathcal{P}}) \cap \pi_{\mathrm{f}}(T_3^{\mathcal{P}})| = 1$.

We calculate $f_{\mathcal{D}}(E)$ for the basic CQ $E = T_1 \bowtie_{T_1.\mathrm{a}=T_2.\mathrm{c}} T_2 \bowtie_{T_2.\mathrm{d}=T_3.\mathrm{e}} T_3 \bowtie_{T_1.\mathrm{a}=T_3'.\mathrm{f}} T_3'$, where T_3' is an alias (written in this way for notational convenience) for the table T_3. To do so, we first need to calculate the estimations $f_{\mathcal{D}}(E^{(1)})$ and $f_{\mathcal{D}}(E^{(2)})$.

$$
f_{\mathcal{D}}(E^{(1)}) = f_{\mathcal{D}}(T_1 \bowtie_{T_1.\mathrm{a}=T_2.\mathrm{c}} T_2) = \left\lceil \frac{k_{\mathcal{D}}(T_1 \bowtie_{T_1.\mathrm{a}=T_2.\mathrm{c}} T_2) \cdot |T_1^{\mathcal{P}}| \cdot |T_2^{\mathcal{P}}|}{dist_{\mathcal{D}}(T_1, \mathrm{a}) \cdot dist_{\mathcal{D}}(T_2, \mathrm{c})} \right\rceil
$$

$$
= \left\lceil \frac{|\pi_{\mathrm{a}}(T_1^{\mathcal{P}}) \cap \pi_{\mathrm{c}}(T_2^{\mathcal{P}})| \cdot |T_1^{\mathcal{P}}| \cdot |T_2^{\mathcal{P}}|}{|\pi_{\mathrm{a}}(T_1^{\mathcal{P}})| \cdot |\pi_{\mathrm{c}}(T_2^{\mathcal{P}})|} \right\rceil = \lceil (3 \cdot 5 \cdot 10)/(5 \cdot 10) \rceil = 3
$$

$$
f_{\mathcal{D}}(E^{(2)}) = f_{\mathcal{D}}(E^{(1)} \bowtie_{T_2.\mathrm{d}=T_3.\mathrm{e}} T_3) = \left\lceil \frac{k_{\mathcal{D}}(E^{(1)} \bowtie_{T_2.\mathrm{d}=T_3.\mathrm{e}} T_3) \cdot f_{\mathcal{D}}(E^{(1)}) \cdot |T_3^{\mathcal{P}}|}{dist_{\mathcal{D}}(E^{(1)}, T_2.\mathrm{d}) \cdot dist_{\mathcal{D}}(T_3, \mathrm{e})} \right\rceil
$$

$$(5)$$

By Formula (4), $dist_\mathcal{D}(E^{(1)}, T_2.d)$ in Formula (5) can be calculated as

$$dist_\mathcal{D}(E^{(1)}, T_2.d) = \min\left\{\left\lceil \frac{|\pi_d(T_2^\mathcal{D})|}{|T_2^\mathcal{D}|} \cdot f_\mathcal{D}(E^{(1)})\right\rceil, |\pi_d(T_2^\mathcal{D})|\right\}$$

$$= \min\left\{\left\lceil \frac{5}{10} \cdot 3\right\rceil, 5\right\} = \left\lceil \frac{3}{2}\right\rceil = 2$$

By Formula (3), $k_\mathcal{D}(E^{(1)} \bowtie_{T_2.d=T_3.e} T_3)$ in Formula (5) can be calculated as

$$k_\mathcal{D}(E^{(1)} \bowtie_{T_2.d=T_3.e} T_3) = \left\lceil \frac{k_\mathcal{D}(T_2 \bowtie_{T_2.d=T_3.e} T_3)}{dist_\mathcal{D}(T_2, d)} \cdot dist_\mathcal{D}(E^{(1)}, T_2.d)\right\rceil$$

$$= \left\lceil \frac{|\pi_d(T_2^\mathcal{D}) \cap \pi_e(T_3^\mathcal{D})|}{|\pi_d(T_2^\mathcal{D})|} \cdot dist_\mathcal{D}(E^{(1)}, T_2.d)\right\rceil = \left\lceil \frac{5}{5} \cdot 2\right\rceil = 2$$

By plugging the values for $k_\mathcal{D}$ and $dist_\mathcal{D}$ in Formula (5), we obtain

$$f_\mathcal{D}(E^{(2)}) = \lceil(2 \cdot 3 \cdot 10)/(2 \cdot 10)\rceil = 3$$

We are now ready to calculate the cardinality of E, which is given by the formula

$$f_\mathcal{D}(E) = f_\mathcal{D}(E^{(2)} \bowtie_{T_1.a=T_3'.f} T_3') = \left\lceil \frac{k_\mathcal{D}(E^{(2)} \bowtie_{T_1.a=T_3'.f} T_3') \cdot f_\mathcal{D}(E^{(2)}) \cdot |T_3^\mathcal{D}|}{dist_\mathcal{D}(E^{(2)}, T_1.a) \cdot dist_\mathcal{D}(T_3, f)}\right\rceil \tag{6}$$

By Formula (4), $dist_\mathcal{D}(E^{(2)}, T_1.a)$ in Formula (6) can be computed as

$$dist_\mathcal{D}(E^{(2)}, T_1.a) = \min\left\{\left\lceil \frac{k_\mathcal{D}(E^{(1)})}{f_\mathcal{D}(E^{(1)})} \cdot f_\mathcal{D}(E^{(2)})\right\rceil, k_\mathcal{D}(E^{(1)})\right\} = \min\left\{\left\lceil \frac{3}{3} \cdot 3\right\rceil, 3\right\} = 3$$

Then, by Formula (3), $k_\mathcal{D}(E^{(2)} \bowtie_{T_1.a=T_3'.f} T_3')$ in Formula (6) can be computed as

$$k_\mathcal{D}(E^{(2)} \bowtie_{T_1.a=T_3'.f} T_3') = \left\lceil \frac{k_\mathcal{D}(T_1 \bowtie_{T_1.a=T_3'.f} T_3')}{dist_\mathcal{D}(T_1, a)} \cdot dist_\mathcal{D}(E^{(2)}, T_1.a)\right\rceil = \left\lceil \frac{3}{5}\right\rceil = 1$$

By plugging the values for $k_\mathcal{D}$ and $dist_\mathcal{D}$ in (6), we finally obtain

$$f_\mathcal{D}(E) = \lceil(1 \cdot 3 \cdot 10)/(3 \cdot 10)\rceil = 1$$

Observe that, in this example, our estimation is exact, that is, $f_\mathcal{D}(E) = |E^\mathcal{D}|$. ∎

Collecting the Necessary Statistics. The estimators introduced above assume a number of statistics to be available. We now show how to compute such statistics on a data instance by analyzing the mappings. Consider a set of mappings $\mathcal{M} = \{L_i(\mathbf{f_i(v_i)}) \leadsto V_i(\mathbf{v_i}) \mid 1 \leq i \leq n\}$ and a data instance $\mathcal{D}$. We store the statistics:

S_1 $|V_i^{\mathcal{D}}|$, for each $i \in \{1, \ldots, n\}$;

S_2 $|\pi_{\mathbf{x}}(V_i^{\mathcal{D}})|$, if $f(\mathbf{x})$ is a term in $\mathbf{f_i}(\mathbf{v_i})$, for some function symbol f and $i \in \{1, \ldots, n\}$;

S_3 $|\pi_{\mathbf{x}}(V_i^{\mathcal{D}}) \cap \pi_{\mathbf{y}}(V_j^{\mathcal{D}})|$, if $f(\mathbf{x})$ is a term in $\mathbf{f_i}(\mathbf{v_i})$, and $f(\mathbf{y})$ is a term in $\mathbf{f_j}(\mathbf{v_j})$, for some function symbol f and $i, j \in \{1, \ldots, n\}$, $i \neq j$.

Statistics S_1 and S_2 are required by all three estimators that we have introduced, and can be measured directly by evaluating source queries on $\mathcal{D}$. Statistics S_3 can be collected by first iterating over the function symbols in the mappings, and then calculating the cardinalities for joins over pairs of source queries whose corresponding mapping targets have a function symbol in common. It is easy to check that Statistics S_1–S_3 suffice for our estimation, since all joins in a CQ are between source queries, and moreover, every translation calculated according to Definition 1 contains only joins between pairs of source queries considered by Statistics S_3.

Unfolding Cardinality Estimator. We now show how to estimate the cardinality of an unfolding by using the Formulas (2), (3), and (4) introduced for cardinality estimation. The next theorem shows that such estimation can be calculated by summing-up the estimated cardinalities for each CQ in the unfolding of the input query, provided that *(i)* the unfolding is being calculated over *wrap* mappings, and *(ii)* the query to unfold is a CQ.

Theorem 3. *Consider a CQ $q(\mathbf{x}) \leftarrow L_1(\mathbf{v_1}), \ldots, L_n(\mathbf{v_n})$ such that $\mathbf{x} = \bigcup_{i=1}^n \mathbf{v_i}$. Then*

$$|unf(q(\mathbf{x}), \mathcal{M})^{\mathcal{D}}| = \sum_{q_u \in unf(q, wrap(\mathcal{M}))} |q_u(\mathbf{x})^{\mathcal{D}}|$$

The previous theorem states that the cardinality of the unfolding of a query over a wrap mapping corresponds to the sum of the cardinalities of each CQ in the unfolding, under the assumption that all the attributes are kept in the answer. Intuitively, the proof [15] relies on the fact that, when wrap mappings are used, each CQ in the unfolding returns answer variables built using a specific combination of function names. Hence, to calculate the cardinality of a CQ q, it suffices to collect statistics as described in the previous paragraph, but over $wrap(\mathcal{M})$ rather than $\mathcal{M}$, and sum up the estimations for each CQ in $unf(q, wrap(\mathcal{M}))$.

The method above might overestimate the actual cardinality if the input CQ contains non-answer variables. In [15] we show how to address this limitation by storing, for each property in the mappings, the probability of having duplicate answers if the projection operation is applied to one of the (two) arguments of that property. Also, the method above assumes a CQ as input to the unfolding, whereas a rewriting is in general a UCQ. This is usually not a critical aspect, especially in practical applications of OBDA. By using saturated (or T-)mappings [18] $\mathcal{M}_{\mathcal{T}}$ in place of $\mathcal{M}$, in fact, the rewriting of an input CQ q

almost always [12] coincides with q itself[3]. Hence, in most cases we can directly use in Theorem 3 the input query q, if we use $wrap(\mathcal{M}_\mathcal{T})$ instead of $wrap(\mathcal{M})$. A fully detailed example on how this is done is provided in [15].

5   Unfolding Cost Model

We are now ready to estimate the actual costs of evaluating UJUCQ and UCQ unfoldings, by exploiting the cardinality estimations from the previous section. Our cost model is based on traditional textbook-formulae for query cost estimation [20]. We here provide the high-level view of the cost model, and leave the details in [15].

Cost for the Unfolding of a UCQ. Recall from Sect. 3 that the unfolding of a UCQ produces a UCQ translation $q^{ucq} = \bigvee_i q_i^{cq}$. We estimate the cost of evaluating q^{ucq} as

$$c(q^{ucq}) \;=\; \sum_i c(q_i^{cq}) + c_u(q^{ucq})$$

where

- $c(q_i^{cq})$ is the cost of evaluating each q_i^{cq} in q^{ucq};
- $c_u(q^{ucq})$ is the cost of removing duplicate results.

Cost for the Unfolding of a JUCQ. Recall from Sect. 3 that the optimized unfolding of a JUCQ produces a UJUCQ. We estimate the cost of a single JUCQ $q^{jucq} = \bigwedge_i q_i^{ucq}$ in the unfolding as

$$c(q^{jucq}) \;=\; \sum_i c(q_i^{ucq}) + \sum_{i \neq k} c_{mat}(q_i^{ucq}) + c_{mj}(q^{jucq}) + c_u(q^{jucq})$$

where

- $c(q_i^{ucq})$ is the cost of evaluating each UCQ component q_i^{ucq};
- $\sum_{i \neq k} c_{mat}(q_i^{ucq})$ is the cost of materializing the intermediate results from q_i^{ucq}, where the k-th UCQ is assumed to be *pipelined* [20] and not materialized;
- $c_{mj}(q^{jucq})$ is the cost of a merge join over the materialized intermediate results;
- $c_u(q^{jucq})$ is the cost of removing duplicate results.

The cost for a UJUCQ $q^{ujucq} = \bigvee_i q_i^{jucq}$, if all the attributes are kept in the answer, is simply the sum $\sum_i c(q_i^{jucq})$, since the results of all JUCQs are disjoint (c.f., Sect. 3). Otherwise, we need to consider the cost of eliminating duplicate results.

---

[3] *Always*, if the CQ is interpreted as a SPARQL query and evaluated according to the OWL 2 QL entailment regime, or if the CQ does not contain existentially quantified variables.

6   Experimental Results

In this section, we provide an empirical evaluation that compares unfoldings for UCQs and (optimized) unfoldings for JUCQs, as well as the estimated costs and the actual time needed to evaluate the unfoldings. We ran the experiments on an HP Proliant server with 2 Intel Xeon X5690 Processors (each with 12 logical cores at 3.47 GHz), 106 GB of RAM and five 1TB 15K RPM HDs. As RDBMS we have used PostgreSQL 9.6. In the extended version [15] of this work we provide the material to replicate our experiments.

Wisconsin Experiment. This experiment is based on the *Wisconsin Benchmark* [8], which allows for in-detail analyses w.r.t. parameters such as join selectivities. We created several copies of the Wisconsin table, and populated each of them with 1M rows. Our test is on 84 queries, instantiations of the following template:

```
SELECT DISTINCT * WHERE {?x :MmRrProp1 ?y1; :JjMmRrProp2 ?y2; :JjMmRrProp3
    ?y3}
```

where $j \in \{5, 10, 15, 20\}$ denotes the selectivity of the join between the first property and each of the remaining two, expressed as a percentage of the number of retrieved rows for each mapping defining the property (each mapping retrieves 200 k tuples); $m \in \{1, \dots, 6\}$ denotes the number of mappings defining the property (all such mappings have the same signature), and $r \in \{0, \dots, m-1\}$ denotes the number of *redundant* mappings, that is, the number of mappings assertions retrieving the same results of another mapping definining the property, minus one.

For each query, we have tested a correspondent cover query of two fragments f_1, f_2, where each fragment is an instantiation of the following templates:

```
f1: SELECT DISTINCT ?x ?y1 ?y2 WHERE { ?x :MmRrProp1 ?y1; :JjMmRrProp2 ?y2.
    }
f2: SELECT DISTINCT ?x ?y3 WHERE { ?x a :MmRrProp1; ?x :JjMmRrProp3 ?y3. }
```

We have implemented our cost model in a Python script. For each SPARQL query, we compute the estimation of the costs of both unfoldings for UCQs and JUCQs, and evaluate these unfoldings over the PostgreSQL database with a timeout of 20 min.

In Fig. 2, we present the cost estimation and the actual running time for each query. We have the following observations:

- In this experiment, for the considered cover, JUCQs are generally faster than UCQs. In fact, out of the 84 SPARQL queries, only one JUCQ was timed out, while 16 UCQs were timed out. The mean running time of successful UCQs and JUCQs are respectively 160 s and 350 s.
- In Fig. 2a, where the fitted lines are obtained by applying linear regression over successful UCQ and JUCQ evaluations, we observe a strong linear correlation between our estimated costs and real running times. Moreover, the coefficients (b_1 and b_0) for UCQs and JUCQs are rather close. This empirically shows that our cost model can estimate the real running time well.

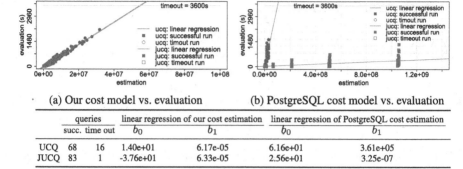

(a) Our cost model vs. evaluation   (b) PostgreSQL cost model vs. evaluation

	queries		linear regression of our cost estimation		linear regression of PostgreSQL cost estimation	
	succ.	time out	b_0	b_1	b_0	b_1
UCQ	68	16	1.40e+01	6.17e-05	6.16e+01	3.61e+05
JUCQ	83	1	-3.76e+01	6.33e-05	2.56e+01	3.25e-07

(c) Results of linear regressions ($evaluation = b_0 + b_1 \times estimation$)

Fig. 2. Cost estimations vs evaluation running times

- Fig. 2b shows that the PostgreSQL cost model assigns the same estimation to many queries having different running times. Moreover, the linear regressions for UCQs and JUCQs are rather different, which suggests that PostgreSQL is not able to recognize when two translations are semantically equivalent. Hence, PostgreSQL is not able to estimate the cost of these queries properly.

In Fig. 3, we visualize the performance gain of JUCQs compared with UCQs. The four subgraphs correspond to four different join selectivities. Each subgraph is a matrix in which each cell shows the value of the performance gain $g = 1 - \text{jucq\_time/ucq\_time}$. When $g > 0$, we apply the red color; otherwise framed-blue. These graphs clearly show that when there is a large number of mappings and there is high redundancy, we have better performance gains. When the redundancy is low (0 or 1), and the number of mapping axioms is large, the join selectivity plays an important role in the performance gain, as discussed in [3]; in other cases, the impacts are non-significant.

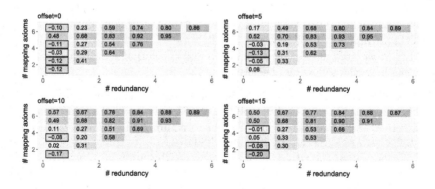

Fig. 3. Performance gain of JUCQ compared with UCQ

Figures 4 and 5 report the cardinalities estimated by PostgreSQL divided by the actual sizes of the query answers for all UCQ and JUCQ queries. For UCQs, it shows that PostgreSQL normally underestimates the cardinalities, but it overestimates them when the redundancies are high. As for JUCQS, PostgreSQL always overestimates the cardinalities, ranging from 40 to 200 K times. These numbers partially explain why PostgreSQL estimate the costs of both UCQs and JUCQs so badly in Fig. 2b.

We obtained similar conclusions for a query with four atoms, and a cover of three fragments. For more details, refer to the extended version [15] of this work.

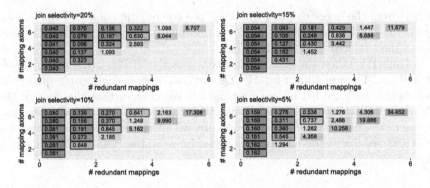

Fig. 4. UCQs: (PostgreSQL estimated cardinality)/(real cardinality)

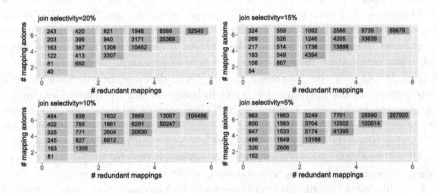

Fig. 5. JUCQs: (PostgreSQL estimated cardinality)/(real cardinality)

NPD Experiment. The goal of this experiment is to verify that cost-based techniques can improve the performance of query answering over real-world queries and instances. This test is carried on the original real-world instance (as opposed to the scaled data instances) of the NPD benchmark [14] for OBDA systems. We pick the three most challenging UCQ queries (namely q_6, q_{11}, q_{12},

Table 1. Evaluation over the NPD benchmark

SPARQL query		Unfolding for UCQs		Unfolding for JUCQs		
Name	# Triple patterns	time (s)	# CQs	Time (s)	# Frags	# CQs
q_6	7	2.18	48	1.20	2	14
q_{11}	8	3.39	24	0.40	2	12
q_{12}	10	6.67	48	0.47	2	14
q_{31}	10	54.27	3840	1.58	2	327

and q_{31}) from the query catalog, where q_{31} is a combination of queries q_6 and q_9, created during this work, which retrieves information regarding wellbores (from q_6) and their related facilities (from q_9).

In Table 1, we show the evaluation results over the NPD benchmark for UCQs and JUCQs. The unfoldings for JUCQs are constructed using cover queries of 2 fragments, each guided by our cost model. We observe that the sizes of the unfoldings for JUCQs, measured in number of CQs, are sensibly smaller than the size of the unfoldings for UCQs. Finally, we observe that the unfoldings for the JUCQ version of the considered queries improve the running times up to a factor of 34.

7 Conclusion and Future Work

In this paper, we have studied the problem of finding efficient alternative translations of a user query in OBDA. Specifically, we introduced a translation for JUCQ queries that preserves the JUCQ structure while maintaining the possibility of performing joins over database values, rather than URIs constructed by applying mappings definitions. We devised a cost model based on a novel cardinality estimation, for estimating the cost of evaluating a translation for a UCQ or JUCQ over the database. We compared different translations on both a synthetic and fully customizable scenario based on the Wisconsin Benchmark and on a real-world scenario from the NPD Benchmark. In these experiments we have observed that (i) our approach based on JUCQ queries can produce translations that are orders of magnitude more efficient than traditional translations into UCQs, and that (ii) the cost model we devised is faithful to the actual query evaluation cost, and hence is well suited to select the best translation.

As future work, we plan to implement our techniques in the state-of-the-art OBDA system *Ontop* and to integrate them with existing optimization strategies. This will allow us to test our approach in more and diversified settings. We also plan to explore alternatives beyond JUCQs. Finally, we plan to work on the problem of relaxing the uniformity assumption made in our cost estimator, by integrating our model with existing techniques based on histograms.

References

1. Abiteboul, S., Hull, R., Vianu, V.: Foundations of Databases. Addison-Wesley Publishing Co., Boston (1995)
2. Bienvenu, M., Ortiz, M., Simkus, M., Xiao, G.: Tractable queries for lightweight description logics. In: Proceedings of IJCAI, IJCAI/AAAI (2013)
3. Bursztyn, D., Goasdoué, F., Manolescu, I.: Efficient query answering in DL-Lite through FOL reformulation (extended abstract). In: Proceedings of DL, vol. 1350. CEUR, CEUR-WS.org (2015). http://ceur-ws.org/Vol-1350/paper-15.pdf
4. Bursztyn, D., Goasdoué, F., Manolescu, I.: Reformulation-based query answering in RDF: alternatives and performance. PVLDB **8**(12), 1888–1891 (2015). http://www.vldb.org/pvldb/vol8/p1888-bursztyn.pdf
5. Calvanese, D., Cogrel, B., Komla-Ebri, S., Kontchakov, R., Lanti, D., Rezk, M., Rodriguez-Muro, M., Xiao, G.: Ontop: answering SPARQL queries over relational databases. Semant. Web J. **8**(3), 471–487 (2017). http://dx.doi.org/10.3233/SW-160217
6. Calvanese, D., De Giacomo, G., Lembo, D., Lenzerini, M., Rosati, R.: Tractable reasoning and efficient query answering in description logics: the DL-Lite family. JAR **39**(3), 385–429 (2007)
7. Das, S., Sundara, S., Cyganiak, R.: R2RML: RDB to RDF mapping language. W3C Recommendation, W3C, September 2012. http://www.w3.org/TR/r2rml/
8. DeWitt, D.J.: The Wisconsin benchmark: past, present, and future. In: Gray, J. (ed.) The Benchmark Handbook for Database and Transaction Systems, 2nd edn. Morgan Kaufmann, San Mateo (1993)
9. Di Pinto, F., Lembo, D., Lenzerini, M., Mancini, R., Poggi, A., Rosati, R., Ruzzi, M., Savo, D.F.: Optimizing query rewriting in ontology-based data access. In: Proceedings of EDBT, pp. 561–572. ACM Press and Addison Wesley (2013)
10. Harris, S., Seaborne, A.: SPARQL 1.1 query language. W3C Recommendation, W3C, March 2013. http://www.w3.org/TR/sparql11-query
11. Kikot, S., Kontchakov, R., Podolskii, V., Zakharyaschev, M.: Exponential lower bounds and separation for query rewriting. In: Czumaj, A., Mehlhorn, K., Pitts, A., Wattenhofer, R. (eds.) ICALP 2012. LNCS, vol. 7392, pp. 263–274. Springer, Heidelberg (2012). doi:10.1007/978-3-642-31585-5_26
12. Kikot, S., Kontchakov, R., Zakharyaschev, M.: Conjunctive query answering with OWL 2 QL. In: Proceedings of KR, pp. 275–285 (2012)
13. Klyne, G., Carroll, J.J.: Resource Description Framework (RDF): concepts and abstract syntax. W3C Recommendation, W3C, February 2004. http://www.w3.org/TR/rdf-concepts/
14. Lanti, D., Rezk, M., Xiao, G., Calvanese, D.: The NPD benchmark: reality check for OBDA systems. In: Proceedings of EDBT, pp. 617–628 (2015). http://openproceedings.org/
15. Lanti, D., Xiao, G., Calvanese, D.: Cost-driven ontology-based data access (extended version). CoRR abs/1707.06974 (2017). http://arxiv.org/abs/1707.06974
16. Motik, B., Cuenca Grau, B., Horrocks, I., Wu, Z., Fokoue, A., Lutz, C.: OWL 2 Web Ontology Language Profiles, 2nd edn. W3C Recommendation, W3C, December 2012. http://www.w3.org/TR/owl2-profiles/
17. Poggi, A., Lembo, D., Calvanese, D., De Giacomo, G., Lenzerini, M., Rosati, R.: Linking data to ontologies. In: Spaccapietra, S. (ed.) Journal on Data Semantics X. LNCS, vol. 4900, pp. 133–173. Springer, Heidelberg (2008). doi:10.1007/978-3-540-77688-8_5

18. Rodriguez-Muro, M., Calvanese, D.: High performance query answering over DL-Lite ontologies. In: Proceedings of KR, pp. 308–318 (2012)
19. Rodriguez-Muro, M., Rezk, M.: Efficient SPARQL-to-SQL with R2RML mappings. J. Web Semant. **33**, 141–169 (2015)
20. Silberschatz, A., Korth, H.F., Sudarshan, S.: Database System Concepts, 5th edn. McGraw-Hill Book Company, Boston (2005)
21. Swami, A., Schiefer, K.B.: On the estimation of join result sizes. In: Jarke, M., Bubenko, J., Jeffery, K. (eds.) EDBT 1994. LNCS, vol. 779, pp. 287–300. Springer, Heidelberg (1994). doi:10.1007/3-540-57818-8_58

The *Odyssey* Approach for Optimizing Federated SPARQL Queries

Gabriela Montoya[1]([✉]), Hala Skaf-Molli[2], and Katja Hose[1]

[1] Aalborg University, Aalborg, Denmark
{gmontoya,khose}@cs.aau.dk
[2] Nantes University, Nantes, France
hala.skaf@univ-nantes.fr

Abstract. Answering queries over a federation of SPARQL endpoints requires combining data from more than one data source. Optimizing queries in such scenarios is particularly challenging not only because of (i) the large variety of possible query execution plans that correctly answer the query but also because (ii) there is only limited access to statistics about schema and instance data of remote sources. To overcome these challenges, most federated query engines rely on heuristics to reduce the space of possible query execution plans or on dynamic programming strategies to produce optimal plans. Nevertheless, these plans may still exhibit a high number of intermediate results or high execution times because of heuristics and inaccurate cost estimations. In this paper, we present *Odyssey*, an approach that uses statistics that allow for a more accurate cost estimation for federated queries and therefore enables *Odyssey* to produce better query execution plans. Our experimental results show that *Odyssey* produces query execution plans that are better in terms of data transfer and execution time than state-of-the-art optimizers. Our experiments using the FedBench benchmark show execution time gains of at least 25 times on average.

1 Introduction

Federated SPARQL query engines [1,4,7,14,17] answer SPARQL queries over a federation of SPARQL endpoints. Query optimization is a particularly complex and challenging task in a federated setting. The query optimizer minimizes processing and communication costs by selecting only relevant sources for a query. It decomposes the query into subqueries, and produces a query execution plan with good join ordering and physical operators. With limited access to statistics, however, most federated query engines rely on heuristics [1,17] to reduce the huge space of possible plans or on dynamic programming (DP) [5,7] to produce optimal plans. However, these plans may still exhibit a high number of intermediate results or high execution times because of inadequate heuristics or inaccurate estimations of cost functions [8].

In this paper, we propose *Odyssey*, a cost-based query optimization approach for federations of SPARQL endpoints. *Odyssey* defines statistics for representing

© Springer International Publishing AG 2017
C. d'Amato et al. (Eds.): ISWC 2017, Part I, LNCS 10587, pp. 471–489, 2017.
DOI: 10.1007/978-3-319-68288-4_28

entities inspired by [12] and statistics for representing links among datasets while guaranteeing result completeness. In a federated setting, computing statistics naturally requires access to more than one dataset. To reduce the overhead, *Odyssey* uses entity synopsis to identify links among datasets. This comes at the risk of losing some accuracy in the link identification but still guarantees that no links will be missed during query optimization, i.e., there is a small risk that more sources are queried than strictly necessary but the query result will be complete.

Odyssey uses the computed statistics to estimate the sizes of intermediate results and dynamic programming to produce an efficient query execution plan with a low number of intermediate results. In summary, this paper makes the following contributions:

- Concise statistics of adequate granularity representing entities and describing links among datasets while guaranteeing result completeness.
- A lightweight technique to compute federated statistics in a federated setup that relies on entity synopsis.
- A query optimization algorithm based on dynamic programming using our statistics to find the best plan.
- Extensive evaluation using a well-accepted standard benchmark for federated query processing [16], including comparison against a broad range of state-of-the-art related work [5,7,15,17]. The results show *Odyssey*'s superiority with a speed-up of up to 126 times and a reduction of transferred data of up to 118 times on average.

This paper is organized as follows. Section 2 presents related work, Sect. 3 describes the *Odyssey* approach and its algorithms. Section 4 discusses our experimental results. Finally, conclusions and future work are outlined in Sect. 5.

2   Related Work

Query optimization in state-of-the-art federated query engines, such as FedX [17] and ANAPSID [1], relies on heuristics. For instance, FedX [17] integrates the variable counting heuristic, where relative selectivity of triple patterns is heuristically estimated according to the presence of constants and variables in the triple patterns. These heuristics are lightweight but might not lead to the best query execution plan [18]. To find an optimal plan, several approaches [5,7,14,19] rely on dynamic programming. However, given the high number of alternative query plans for SPARQL queries with many triple patterns, dynamic programming is very expensive [8]. Another important factor of query optimization is source selection. Several approaches [1,7,15,17,19] try to determine the relevance of a source by sending ASK queries, which increases the costs for a single query but might amortize in large federations for an overlapping query load. Another technique is to estimate whether combining the data of multiple sources can lead to any join results, e.g., by computing the intersection of the sources' URI authorities [15] or detailed statistics [10,13].

Federated query optimization can also rely on cardinality estimations based on statistics and used, for instance, to reduce sizes of intermediate results. Most available statistics [3] use the Vocabulary of Interlinked Datasets voiD [2], which describes statistics at dataset level (e.g., the number of triples), at the property level (e.g., for each property, its number of different subjects), and at the class level (e.g., the number of instances of each class). However, approaches based on voiD [5,7,9] and other statistics, such as QTrees [10] and PARTrees [13], share the drawback of missing the best query execution plans because of errors in estimating cardinalities caused by relying on assumptions that often do not hold for arbitrary RDF datasets [12], e.g., a uniform data distribution and that the results of triple patterns are independent.

Characteristic sets (CS) [6,12] aim at solving this problem in centralized systems by capturing statistics about sets of entities having the same set of properties. This information can then be used to accurately estimate the cardinality and join ordering of star-shaped queries. Typically, any set of joined triple patterns in a query can be divided into connected star-shaped subqueries. Subqueries in combination with the predicate that links them, define a characteristic pair (CP) [8,11]. Statistics about such CPs can then be used to estimate the selectivity of two star-shaped subqueries. Such cardinality estimations can be combined with dynamic programming on a reduced space of alternative query plans. Whereas existing work on CSs and CPs were developed for centralized environments, this paper proposes a solution generalizing these principles for federated environments.

3 The *Odyssey* Approach

Inspired by the latest advances in statistics for centralized triple stores [8,11,12], *Odyssey* uses statistics about individual datasets to derive detailed statistics for optimizing federated queries. In the following, we first describe the foundations of our statistics on individual datasets (Sect. 3.1) and then propose a novel method for computing such statistics in a federated environment based on entity descriptions (Sect. 3.2). As the detailed entity descriptions cause too much overhead in a federated setup, we propose a method for reducing the sizes of the descriptions (Sect. 3.3). Finally, we present the *Odyssey* approach for query optimization and its main steps (Sect. 3.4): source selection, join ordering, and query decomposition.

3.1 Dataset Statistics on Individual Datasets

Star-Shaped Subqueries. To estimate the cardinality and costs of BGPs sharing the same subject (or object), i.e., *star-shaped subqueries*, we exploit the principle that entities sharing the same set of properties are similar. In this context, we refer to the set of an entity's properties as its characteristic set (CS) and use $cs_s(e)$ to denote the CS of entity e in dataset s or $cs(e)$ if s is clear from the context. For instance, in DBpedia 3.5.1 $cs(dbr{:}Gary\_Goetzman) = C_1 = \{dbo{:}birthDate, \; foaf{:}name, \; rdf{:}type, \; dbo{:}activeYearsStartYear, \; rdfs{:}label, \; skos{:}subject\}$. In total, 260 entities share this set of properties and therefore CS C_1.

Listing 1.1. Statistics for CS C_1

```
{ count :  260,
  elems :
  {{ pred :  dbo : birthDate ,  ocurrences  :  260 },
   { pred :  foaf : name,  ocurrences :  326 },
   { pred :  rdf : type ,  ocurrences :  1023 },
   { pred :  dbo : activeYearsStartYear ,  ocurrences :  260 },
   { pred :  rdfs : label ,  ocurrences :  260 },
   { pred :  skos : subject ,  ocurrences :  1336 }}}
```

CSs can be computed by scanning once a dataset's triples sorted by subject; after all the entity properties have been scanned, the entity's CS is identified. For each CS C, we compute statistics, i.e., the number of entities sharing C ($count(C)$) and the number of triples with predicate p occurring with these entities ($occurrences(p,\, C)$). Listing 1.1 shows the statistics for the above mentioned example CS C_1. Entities of C_1 occur on average in 1 triple with property $dbo{:}birthDate$ and in 3.94 triples with property $rdf{:}type$.

For a star-shaped query, only CSs including all of the query's properties are relevant as entities that only satisfy a subset of these properties cannot contribute to the answer.

Listing 1.2. Find persons that have been active

```
SELECT DISTINCT ?person WHERE {
  ?person dbo : birthDate ?date .          (tp1)
  ?person dbo : activeYearsStartYear ?sy . (tp2)
  ?person foaf : name ?name                (tp3)
}
```

For star-shaped queries asking for the set of unique entities described by some properties (query with DISTINCT modifier), the exact number of answers can be determined precisely (no estimation). For example, the cardinality of the query given in Listing 1.2 can be obtained by adding up the $count(C)$ of all CSs containing the properties $dbo{:}birthDate$, $dbo{:}activeYearsStartYear$, and $foaf{:}name$. In DBpedia 3.5.1, there are 7,059 CSs that include these three properties, and the total number of entities with these CSs is 83,438. Formally, the number of entities for a given set of properties P, $cardinality(P)$, is computed based on the CSs C_j that include all the properties in P as:

$$cardinality(P) = \sum_{P \subseteq C_j} count(C_j) \qquad (1)$$

For queries without the DISTINCT modifier, we need to account for duplicates by considering the number of triples with predicate $p_i \in P$ that an entity is associated with on average:

$$estimatedCardinality(P) = \sum_{P \subseteq C_j} \left(count(C_j) * \prod_{p_i \in P} \frac{ocurrences(p_i, C_j)}{count(C_j)} \right) \qquad (2)$$

In DBpedia 3.5.1, as mentioned above, there are 7,059 CSs relevant for the query in Listing 1.2 with 83,438 entities as answer. These 83,438 entities are described by 109,830 triples with predicate *foaf:name*, 83,448 with predicate *dbo:birthDate*, and 110,460 with predicate *dbo:activeYearsStartYear*. If the query is considered without the DISTINCT modifier, i.e., considering duplicated results, we estimate: 148,486 matching entities in the result, which is very close to the real number (149,440).

Once the relevant CSs for a query have been identified, they can be used to find the join order minimizing the sizes of intermediate results. For the query in Listing 1.2, we start by estimating the cardinalities for each subquery with two out of the three triple patterns using Formula 1: {tp1, tp2}: 98,281, {tp1, tp3}: 209,731, and {tp2, tp3}: 127,712. The triple pattern not included in the cheapest subquery ({tp1, tp2}) is executed last (tp3). We proceed recursively with the cheapest subquery and determine the cardinalities for its subsets: {tp1}: 232,608 and {tp2}: 143,004. Again, the triple pattern not included in the cheapest subquery (tp1) will be executed last of the currently considered set of triple patterns. As a result, we will execute the join between tp2 and tp1 first and afterwards compute the join with tp3. We also get the order in which the triple patterns should be evaluated for the first join: first tp2 and then tp1.

Arbitrary Queries. To estimate the cardinality for queries with more complex shapes, we need to consider the connections (links) between entities with different CSs. Entity *dbr:Evan_Almighty*, for example, is linked to *dbr:Tom_Shadyac* via property *dbo:director* by triple *(dbr:Evan_Almighty, dbo:director, dbr:Tom_Shadyac)*.

The links between CSs via properties can formally be described by characteristic pairs (CPs), they are defined as $(cs_s(e1), cs_s(e2), p)$ for entities e1 and e2 if $(e1, p, e2) \in s$. The statistics – $count((C_i, C_j, p))$ – capture the number of links between a pair of CSs (C_i and C_j) using a particular property p. For example, given the CSs of *dbr:Evan_Almighty* and *dbr:Tom_Shadyac* as C_1 and C_2 the number of links via property *dbo:director* is given by: $count((C_1, C_2, dbo:director))$.

Listing 1.3. Find movies and their directors

```
SELECT DISTINCT ?film ?director WHERE {
    ?film  dbo:runtime ?runtime .              (tp1)
    ?film  dbo:director ?director .            (tp2)
    ?film  dbo:budget ?budget .                (tp3)
    ?director  dbo:birthDate ?date .           (tp4)
    ?director  dbo:activeYearsStartYear ?sy .  (tp5)
    ?director  foaf:name ?name                 (tp6)
}
```

The number of unique results (pairs of entities with set of properties P_k and P_l, query with DISTINCT modifier) can be exactly computed (not estimated) using the formula:

$$cardinality((P_k, P_l, p)) = \sum_{P_k \subseteq C_i \wedge P_l \subseteq C_j} count((C_i, C_j, p)) \qquad (3)$$

For the query in Listing 1.3 property *dbo:director* links several pairs of CSs representing movies and actors. Hence, we need to compute $\Sigma_{f_1 \wedge f_2}\ count((C_i, C_j, dbo:director))$, where f_1 is ($\{dbo:runtime,\ dbo:director,\ dbo:budget\} \subseteq C_i$) and f_2 is ($\{dbo:birthDate,\ dbo:activeYearsStartYear,\ foaf:name\} \subseteq C_j$); one of the operands of this sum is $count((C_1, C_2, dbo:director))$ mentioned in the example above. For this query, DBpedia 3.5.1 contains 1,509 CPs linking entities from two CSs via property *dbo:director*.

If a query does not involve the DISTINCT modifier, result cardinality estimation considers the property occurrences in the CSs:

$$estimatedCardinality((P_k, P_l, p)) = \sum_{P_k \subseteq C_i \wedge P_l \subseteq C_j} \left(count((C_i, C_j, p)) \right.$$

$$\left. * \prod_{p_k \in P_k - \{p\}} \left(\frac{ocurrences(p_k, C_i)}{count(C_i)} \right) * \prod_{p_l \in P_l} \left(\frac{ocurrences(p_l, C_j)}{count(C_j)} \right) \right)$$

$$(4)$$

Assuming that the order of joins within star-shaped subqueries has already been optimized based on the CSs as described above, we treat each star-shaped subquery as a single meta-node to reduce complexity. We estimate the cardinalities of joins between the meta-nodes using the statistics on CPs and use dynamic programming (DP) to determine the optimal join order that minimizes the sizes of intermediate results. Although the presentation in this section focuses on subject-subject joins, the same principle can be applied to other types of joins, e.g., object-object.

3.2   Federated Statistics

In general, entities might occur in multiple datasets in a federation S. Hence, we define a *federated characteristic set* (FCS) as follows: $fcs_S(e) = \bigcup_{s \in S} cs_s(e)$, S might be omitted if clear from the context. However, triples describing the same entity are typically part of a single dataset so that most CSs can be computed

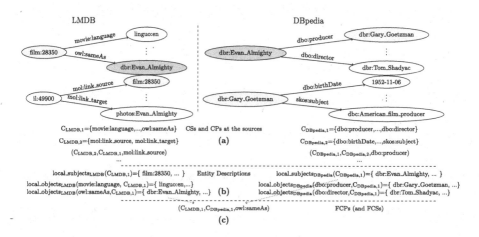

Fig. 1. Federated computation of statistics

over each dataset independently from the others[1]. The *federated characteristic pair* (FCP) of entities *e1* and *e2* via property p in federation S is defined as $(fcs_S(e1), fcs_S(e2), p)$. For FCSs FC_i and FC_j and property p, we compute statistics $count(FC_i)$, $occurrences(p, FC_i)$, and $count((FC_i, FC_j, p))$ as before for CSs and CPs. For simplicity, the following sections focus on FCPs connecting CSs instead of FCSs. The generalization using FCSs is straightforward.

Whereas single dataset statistics can be computed once and provided by the sources in the same way they currently provide voiD statistics [2], FCSs and FCPs require more effort and centralized knowledge about all entities in the considered datasets. A naive way to compute FCSs and FCPs is evaluating expensive SPARQL queries with FILTER expressions involving NOT EXISTS, but this can take weeks for a dataset with thousands of CSs. It is much more efficient if the sources directly share information about local subjects and objects with the federated query engine: $local\_subjects_s(C)$ contains the IRIs of entities with CS C for source s, while $local\_objects_s(p, C)$ contains the IRIs of entities linked via predicate p to subjects with CS C. Such information can, for instance, be obtained efficiently while computing CSs and CPs locally and then shared with the federated query engine.

The federated query engine can then use this information to compute FCSs and FCPs. Consider, for instance, the two datasets LMDB and DBpedia in Fig. 1; based on the CSs (Fig. 1(a)), the sources compute *entity descriptions* ($local\_subjects_i$ and $local\_objects_i$ in Fig. 1(b)). Entity *film:28350* has properties {movie:language, ..., owl:sameAs} = $C_{\text{LMDB},1}$. Hence, *film:28350* $\in$ $local\_subjects_{LMDB}(C_{\text{LMDB},1})$. There is a triple with *dbr:Evan_Almighty* as value of property *owl:sameAs* for an entity with CS $C_{\text{LMDB},1}$ (*film:28350*) so *dbr:Evan_Almighty* $\in$ $local\_objects_{LMDB}(owl:sameAs, C_{\text{LMDB},1})$ (Fig. 1(b)). The overlap between the set of entities $local\_subjects_{DBpedia}(C_{\text{DBpedia},1})$ and $local\_objects_{LMDB}(owl:sameAs, C_{\text{LMDB},1})$ represent linked entities between LMDB and DBpedia via property owl:sameAs. Hence, we obtain FCP $(C_{\text{LMDB},1}, C_{\text{DBpedia},1}, owl:sameAs)$ (Fig. 1(c)). $count((C_{\text{LMDB},1}, C_{\text{DBpedia},1}, owl:sameAs))$ corresponds to the cardinality of the intersection between all the $local\_objects_{DBpedia}$ and $local\_subjects_{LMDB}$ linked by property owl:sameAs.

Algorithm 1 describes in more detail how to compute FCPs only based on the pre-computed statistics $local\_objects_{d1}$ and $local\_subjects_{d2}$ (newFunction(0) returns a new function with default value 0). First, all common entities in $local\_objects_{d1}$ and $local\_subjects_{d2}$ are identified in line 7. These common entities represent links between CSs $C_{d1,i}$ and $C_{d2,j}$ via property p and are captured by a FCP (lines 9–10).

Listing 1.4. Find LMDB movies that are also DBpedia movies

```
SELECT ?film ?movie WHERE {
  ?film dbo:budget ?budget .
  ?film dbo:director ?director .
  ?movie owl:sameAs ?film .
  ?movie lmdb:sequel ?seq
}
```

---

[1] FCSs describing entities across multiple datasets are very rare. In FedBench, for instance, they affect less than 0.5% of all CSs.

Algorithm 1. Compute FCPs Algorithm

Input: $local\_objects_{d1}$ and $local\_subjects_{d2}$ for datasets $d1$ and $d2$
Output: A set of FCPs (*FCPs*) with links from $d1$ to $d2$; $count$(fcp) for each fcp in FCPs
1: **function** COMPUTEFCPS($local\_subjects_{d2}$, $local\_objects_{d1}$)
2:     FCPs ← { }
3:     count ← newFunction(0)
4:     **for** (p, $C_{d1,i}$) ∈ domain($local\_objects_{d1}$) **do**
5:         entities ← $local\_objects_{d1}$(p,$C_{d1,i}$)
6:         **for** $C_{d2,j}$ ∈ domain($local\_subjects_{d2}$) **do**
7:             entities ← entities ∩ $local\_subjects_{d2}$($C_{d2,j}$)
8:             **if** entities ≠ ∅ **then**
9:                 FCPs ← FCPs ∪ { ($C_{d1,i}$, $C_{d2,j}$, p) }
10:                count(($C_{d1,i}$, $C_{d2,j}$, p)) ← count(($C_{d1,i}$, $C_{d2,j}$, p)) + cardinality(entities)
11:            **end if**
12:        **end for**
13:    **end for**
14:    **return** CPs, count
15: **end function**

FCPs can be used for cardinality estimation and join ordering using the same principles as described in Sect. 3.1. Consider a federation consisting of DBpedia (160,061 CSs) and LMDB (8,466 CSs) with 22,592 FCPs and query in Listing 1.4. We can use Formula 4 with the FCPs connecting LMDB to DBpedia via the owl:sameAs property to estimate the result cardinality: 171. This is close to the real cardinality (293).

3.3 Reducing the Sizes of Entity Descriptions

As the entity descriptions ($local\_subjects_d$ and $local\_objects_d$) introduced above are often very expensive to compute, maintain, and exchange, we propose a technique to reduce their sizes. We organize the entity descriptions in a tree structure that summarizes the entities used as subject or object in any of the dataset's triples. Inspired by [10,13,15], we factorize common prefixes, transform suffixes into integers, and summarize sets of integers in buckets, i.e., a set synopsis consisting of minimum value (mn), maximum value (mx), [mn, mx], number of elements, num, and their set of two least significant bytes (lsb). lsb(i) is computed as i **mod** 2^{16} and is included to improve the synopsis' accuracy.

The tree structure is organized in three levels. The top level summarizes the prefixes of entity IRIs occurring as subjects and objects in the dataset. Suffixes are mapped to integers using a hash function, these integers are summarized in the middle and bottom levels. The middle level includes buckets where parent nodes subsume the synopsis of their children (containment relationship between parent and child ranges and summation between parent and child num) and aids in efficiently accessing the bottom level. The bottom level (leaves) stores (in $local\_subjects$ and $local\_objects$) only the integer's lsb to reduce the storage space while improving the synopsis' accuracy.

In Fig. 2 we present a fragment of the reduced descriptions for LMDB. The reduced descriptions include all the entities that are subject or object in the dataset's triples. In particular, it includes the entity with IRI http://data.linkedmdb.org/resource/film/28350 (Fig. 2(c)). This IRI prefix identifies the subtree that summarizes the entity (light gray ellipses in Fig. 2(a)), while the hash code of its suffix (resource/film/28350), 1093595742, is used to identify the leaf that includes its lsb (−3490), i.e., with 1093595742 between its minimum and maximum values (gray rectangle in Fig. 2(b)). Its lsb is in $local\_subjects(C_{LMDB,1})$ and $local\_objects(mol{:}link\_source, C_{LMDB,2})$ in the identified leaf (trapezium in Fig. 2(b)). This tree structure exhibits size reduction and eases the computation of FCPs by allowing to discard large portions of the descriptions contrary to descriptions in Fig. 1(b), where all the $local\_subjects$ and $local\_objects$ need to be pair-wise tested for overlap.

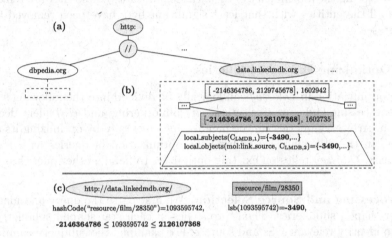

Fig. 2. Reduced entity descriptions for LMDB in Fig. 1. The tree factorizes common prefixes in the top level (in the ellipses) and summarizes the suffixes in the middle (in the rectangles) and bottom (in the trapezium) levels

Computation costs are greatly reduced by pruning large portions of the tree and comparing only a few pairs of leaves, the ones that have common prefixes and overlapping representation of the suffixes. An important feature of these summaries is that entities present in more than one dataset are always detected.

These trees are considerably lighter than the entity descriptions discussed in Sect. 3.2, but they might reduce accuracy. For FedBench's DBpedia 3.5.1 subset, a dataset with 43,126,772 triples that occupies 6.1 GB, the $local\_subjects$ and $local\_objects$ occupy 1.37 GB and the tree occupies only 68 MB[2]. They have compression ratios of 4.45 and 91.86, respectively. Regarding the quality, the tree summary allows for computing all the FCSs and FCPs.

To reduce the resources used by the tree, we have reduced the number of CSs as suggested in [8, 12] to 10,000. Only the CSs that are shared by the largest number of entities are kept, and the others are removed and merged into the remaining CSs if possible. For instance, by selecting from the remaining CSs

---

[2] Implementation based on Java's HashSet and HashMap was used to measure their sizes.

that include all the properties of the removed CS, the one with the smallest number of properties and combining their *count* and *ocurrences*, or by splitting the removed CS into two disjoint property sets that can be merged with other CSs. This may reduce the accuracy of the query cardinality estimation, but it allows to bound the resources used to store and access these statistics.

Entity summaries can be kept up-to-date in two ways. For datasets that are rarely updated, the subtree representing the entities with the prefix affected by the updates, e.g., Fig. 2(b) in our example, can be re-computed. For datasets that are often updated, leaves should support removal of entities, this can easily be done by storing the multiplicity of each least significant byte so they are removed only if all the entities with that least significant byte have been removed from the dataset.

3.4   Optimizing Federated Queries

Query optimization in *Odyssey* can logically be divided into the following steps: *(i)* preprocessing and source selection, *(ii)* join ordering, and *(iii)* query decomposition. Arbitrary queries can be handled incrementally by optimizing its subqueries. In the following, we address the optimization of queries with bound predicates, *Odyssey* relies on existing optimizers to handle other queries.

Preprocessing and Source Selection. We first parse the query and identify its star-shaped subqueries. Then, properties in each star-shaped subquery are used to identify relevant CSs and sources. For example, the subquery composed by tp3 and tp4 in Fig. 3(a) has relevant CSs that include both owl:sameAs and movie:sequel. In the FedBench federation described in Table 1, these CSs are only part of LMDB. Therefore, LMDB is the only relevant source for this subquery. Afterwards, we use CPs/FCPs to identify relevant sources for the links between the star-shaped subqueries.

Join Ordering. Once we have identified the set of relevant sources, we can estimate cardinalities of subqueries and find the best join ordering. We first optimize the order of joins and triple patterns within each star-shaped subquery

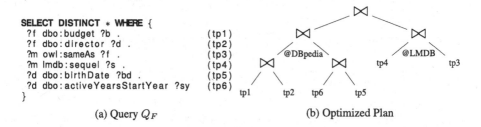

(a) Query Q_F (b) Optimized Plan

Fig. 3. Query Q_F and its optimized plan

using CS statistics ($count(C_i)$ and $occurrences(p, C_i)$) as explained in Sect. 3.1. Afterwards, as described in Sect. 3.1, each subquery is treated as a meta-node and we estimate cardinalities of the joins between these meta-nodes using the formulas presented in Sect. 3.1 to estimate subquery costs and apply DP. For Q_F (Fig. 3(a)), three star-shaped subqueries are identified and treated as meta-nodes to estimate the cardinalities of their joins (Fig. 4, left). Figure 4 (right) shows the estimated cardinality and cost of the subqueries, solid arrows indicate which smaller subqueries were combined by the DP algorithm to form larger subqueries. As the number of subqueries is usually considerably lower than the number of triple patterns, applying DP becomes affordable.

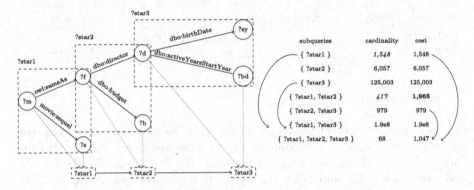

Fig. 4. Example query optimization

In our current implementation, the cost function is solely defined on the cardinalities of intermediate results and how many results need to be transferred from endpoints during execution. This favors query plans with selective subqueries. For instance, the cost of the join between meta-nodes ?star1 and ?star2 (**1,965**) includes the result size (*417*) and the sum of all transferred intermediate results (*1,548*). This cost function assumes that all endpoints have the same characteristics. We can easily extend this cost function by additional parameters that can be fine-tuned to represent the characteristics of each endpoint individually, e.g., communication delays, response times, etc.

Query Decomposition. Finally, we optimize the SPARQL queries that are actually sent to the endpoints and try to minimize their number. For instance, we combine all triple patterns and logical subqueries to a particular endpoint into a single SPARQL query to a particular endpoint whenever possible. For instance, meta-nodes ?star2 and ?star3 in Fig. 4 are combined into one subquery (Fig. 3(b)) and evaluated by the DBpedia endpoint.

Table 1. FedBench [16] dataset statistics: number of distinct triples (#DT), predicates (#P), CSs (#CS), and CPs (#CP); computation time in seconds of *Odyssey*, HiBISCuS, and voiD statistics

Dataset	#DT	#P	# CS	#CP	#FCP	*Odyssey*	HiBISCuS	voiD
ChEBI	4,772,706	28	978	9,958	19,360	82.91	96.02	73.89
KEGG	1,090,830	21	67	239	13,822	30.15	95.23	12.84
Drugbank	517,023	119	3,419	12,589	103,070	1,299.9	76.4	6.98
DBpedia subset	42,855,253	1,063	10,000	1,069,431	6,583	2,739	770.48	1,465.36
Geonames	107,949,927	26	673	7,707	322,672	1,885.97	609.52	39,694.07
Jamendo	1,049,647	26	42	190	1,259	31.25	99.17	14.66
SWDF	103,595	118	547	6,713	17,557	7.27	69.21	2.03
LMDB	6,147,916	222	8,466	94,188	359,340	947.16	317.21	355.45
NYTimes	335,119	36	47	158	3.96	10.01	72.56	4.22
Federated						620.35		
Total						7,654.27	2,205.8	41,629.5

4   Evaluation

In this section, we present the results of our experimental study that compares our approach, *Odyssey*, with state-of-the-art federated query engines: HiBIS-CuS (FedX-HiBISCuS, cold and warm cache) [15], SemaGrow [5], FedX (cold and warm cache) [17], and SPLENDID [7]. Full implementations, statistics, and results are available at https://github.com/gmontoya/federatedOptimizer.

Datasets and Queries: We use the real datasets and queries proposed in the FedBench benchmark [16]. Queries are divided into three groups Linked Data (LD1-LD11), Cross Domain (CD1-CD7), and Life Science (LS1-LS7). They have 2–7 triple patterns and star and hybrid shapes. They have between 1 and 9,054 answers. Basic statistics about the datasets are listed in Table 1. We ran each query ten times and report the averages over the last nine runs. Standard deviation is included as error bars on the plots.

Implementation: *Odyssey* is implemented in Java using the Jena library to parse and transform queries into queries with SPARQL 1.1 service clauses. Our implementation uses the FedX 3.1 framework with deactivated native optimization to execute *Odyssey*'s query plans.

Hardware Configuration: For our experiments we used virtual machines (VMs). A VM using up to 4 GB of RAM to run the federated query engine and nine VMs with 2 processors, 8 GB of RAM and CPU 2294.250 MHz to host Virtuoso endpoints with the datasets described in Table 1 (one dataset and endpoint per VM).

Statistics Computation: As DBpedia has a very high number of CSs (160,061), we reduced them to 10,000 by merging (as suggested in [8,12] and explained in Sect. 3.3) without significant losses in the quality of estimations. Details on creation times of statistics are listed in Table 1. *Odyssey*'s statistics

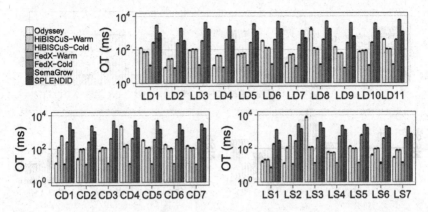

Fig. 5. Optimization time in ms (OT, log scale). CD1 and LS2 have variable predicates and *Odyssey* relies on FedX to find plan.

can be more expensive to compute for datasets with more than 3,419 CSs and cheaper than HiBISCuS's for datasets with less than 67 CSs. In total, *Odyssey*'s statistics are computed five times faster than voiD's.

Evaluation Metrics: *(i) Optimization time (OT):* is the elapsed time since the query is issued until the optimized query plan is produced, *(ii) number of selected sources (NSS):* is the number of sources that have been selected to answer a query, *(iii) number of subqueries (NSQ):* is the number of subqueries that are included in the query plan, *(iv) execution time (ET):* is the time elapsed since the evaluation of the query plan starts until the complete answer is produced (with a timeout of 1,800 s), *(v) number of transferred tuples (NTT):* is the number of tuples transferred from all the endpoints to the query engine during query evaluation.

Result Completeness: All approaches produce the complete result set for non-timed out queries, except SPLENDID for query LS7.

4.1 Experimental Results

Optimization Time. Figure 5 shows the optimization time (OT) for the studied approaches. Because of the detailed statistics and dynamic programming, one might expect *Odyssey* to suffer from a considerable overhead in OT. As our experimental results show, however, *Odyssey*'s query planner is competitive to most other approaches with a slight advantage for FedX-Warm as this system has cached information about the query relevant sources. For instance, *Odyssey* is up to 69 times faster (SemaGrow) than other approaches on average.

Number of Selected Sources. As Fig. 6 shows, *Odyssey* selects only a small number of relevant sources; for instance, at least 1.81 times less (FedX-Cold/Warm and SemaGrow) and up to 1.93 times less (HiBISCuS-Cold/Warm)

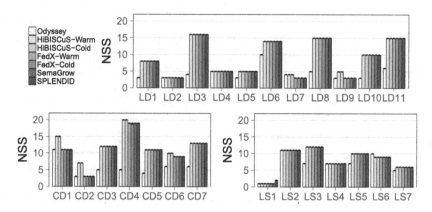

Fig. 6. Number of selected sources (NSS)

on average. For some queries, e.g., LS4, existing approaches already select the optimal number of sources. For LD7, *Odyssey* selects a larger number of sources than the optimum because our approach does not perform ASK queries during execution to prune irrelevant sources. Sometimes *Odyssey* overestimates the set of relevant sources – but on the other hand it never misses any relevant sources. For LS1, most approaches select just one (10^0) source because there is only one dataset that has triples with the predicate in the query.

Number of Subqueries. As Fig. 7 shows, *Odyssey* uses considerably fewer subqueries than other approaches, at least 2.62 times less (HiBISCuS-Cold/Warm) and up to 3.41 times less (SPLENDID) on average. The fact that Odyssey always produces the correct and complete answers confirms that *Odyssey* correctly identifies and exploits cases for which it is advantageous to combine subqueries. *Odyssey*'s reduction of the number of relevant sources has a positive

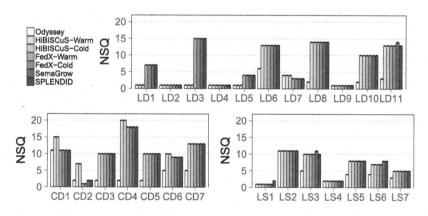

Fig. 7. Number of subqueries (NSQ)

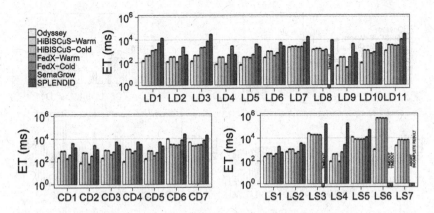

Fig. 8. Execution time in ms (ET, log scale)

impact on the number of subqueries (NSQ), *Odyssey*'s pruning of non-relevant sources allows for combining triple patterns into subqueries without affecting the result completeness. Some queries, like LD2, LD4, and LD9, include triple patterns that can be evaluated by a unique endpoint of the federation and existing approaches already decompose the query into the optimal NSQ. Only for LD7, FedX-Cold/Warm, SPLENDID, and SemaGrow decompose the query into fewer subqueries than *Odyssey*, this is because they use ASK queries to assess a source's relevance. *Odyssey* could be enhanced with this strategy.

Execution Time. Some approaches failed to answer all queries before the time-out (1,800s): SPLENDID (2 queries) and SemaGrow (4 queries). Even when considering only those queries that completed before the timeout, *Odyssey* is on average 126.26 times faster than SPLENDID and 28.30 times faster than SemaGrow. Figure 8 shows the execution times (ET) for the studied approaches. *Odyssey* is on average at least 25.46 times faster (FedX-Warm). Only for a few queries *Odyssey* is (slightly) slower than other approaches, e.g., LS3. As for the other metrics, *Odyssey*'s ET can be improved if ASK queries were used during query execution to further reduce the relevant sources similarly as it is done by other approaches. For five of the queries, *Odyssey* is one of the fastest approaches and for 11 queries, *Odyssey* is the fastest approach. *Odyssey*'s achieved reductions on the NSS and NSQ have a positive impact on the ET; as fewer endpoints are queried fewer times, *Odyssey* produces results faster than most approaches in most cases.

Number of Transferred Tuples. Figure 9 shows the number of transferred tuples (NTT) for the studied approaches. *Odyssey* transfers fewer tuples than other approaches. Even when considering only those queries that completed before the timeout, *Odyssey* transfers on average 1.15 times fewer tuples faster than SemaGrow and 108.4 times fewer tuples than SPLENDID. For the

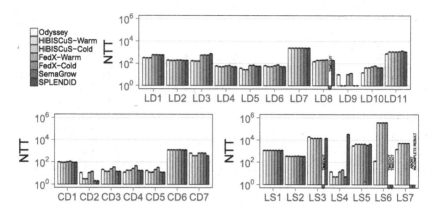

Fig. 9. Number of transferred tuples (NTT, log scale, $10^0 = 1$)

approaches that completed all the queries, *Odyssey* transfers at least 117.55 fewer tuples (HiBISCuS-Cold/Warm) on average. Most approaches are competitive in terms of NTT. The largest difference is observed for LS6, where *Odyssey* clearly outperforms the other approaches transferring 500 times fewer tuples. In contrast to other approaches, *Odyssey* not only reduces the number of requests sent to the endpoints but also avoids non-selective subqueries, which significantly reduces network traffic and the local query load at the endpoints.

4.2 Combining *Odyssey* with Existing Optimizers

We have also integrated *Odyssey* techniques directly into the FedX optimizer and obtained:

- *Odyssey*-FedX-Cold, which relies on CSs and CPs to select sources and decomposes the query but uses FedX join ordering.
- FedX-Cold-*Odyssey*, which relies on the FedX optimizer for source selection but uses *Odyssey* for query decomposition and join ordering.

Figure 10 compares the execution times (ET) of these two implementations with *Odyssey*, FedX-Cold, and FedX-Warm. In most cases the combined approaches are considerably faster than native FedX. In a few cases, however, their ET can increase considerably. In these cases, queries include a highly selective subquery with one triple pattern and using FedX's heuristic to execute subqueries with more than one triple pattern first leads to plans that are more expensive than others. On average, the combined approaches are 26.86 and 3.99 times faster than FedX-Cold.

For query LD7, *Odyssey* and FedX-Cold/Warm exhibit similar ETs whereas FedX-Cold-*Odyssey* is considerably faster. For this query it happens that the advantages of both *Odyssey* and FedX coincide, i.e., we can take advantage of the good join ordering by *Odyssey* but also of the additional pruning based on ASK queries by FedX.

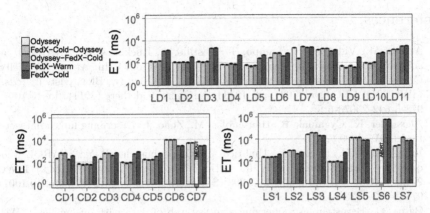

Fig. 10. Execution time in ms (ET, log scale) of query plans optimized using Odyssey and FedX

Even if *Odyssey*'s OT can be higher in comparison to existing approaches, *Odyssey* produces better plans composed of fewer subqueries and fewer selected sources per triple pattern without compromising result completeness. Benefits of these features have been evidenced with significantly faster ETs and less transferred data from endpoints to the federated query engine.

5 Conclusion

In this paper, we have presented *Odyssey*, an approach for optimizing federated SPARQL queries based on statistics. These statistics detail information about the data provided by remote endpoints as well as the links between them. This enables more accurate cost estimations, query optimization, and selection of relevant sources. Our extensive experimental evaluation shows that *Odyssey* produces query execution plans that are better in terms of data transfer and execution time than state-of-the-art optimizers. In our future work, we plan to further improve *Odyssey* by considering in which situations exactly it is worthwhile to use additional aspects of other optimizers, such as ASK queries and associated statistics. Another interesting direction of future work is to further reduce the computation time and sizes of the entity descriptions and provide efficient strategies to update the descriptions and statistics.

Acknowledgments. This research was partially funded by the Danish Council for Independent Research (DFF) under grant agreement no. DFF-4093-00301.

References

1. Acosta, M., Vidal, M.-E., Lampo, T., Castillo, J., Ruckhaus, E.: ANAPSID: an adaptive query processing engine for SPARQL endpoints. In: Aroyo, L., Welty, C., Alani, H., Taylor, J., Bernstein, A., Kagal, L., Noy, N., Blomqvist, E. (eds.) ISWC 2011. LNCS, vol. 7031, pp. 18–34. Springer, Heidelberg (2011). doi:10.1007/978-3-642-25073-6_2
2. Alexander, K., Cyganiak, R., Hausenblas, M., Zhao, J.: Describing linked datasets. In: LDOW 2009 (2009)
3. Buil-Aranda, C., Hogan, A., Umbrich, J., Vandenbussche, P.-Y.: SPARQL web-querying infrastructure: ready for action? In: Alani, H., et al. (eds.) ISWC 2013. LNCS, vol. 8219, pp. 277–293. Springer, Heidelberg (2013). doi:10.1007/978-3-642-41338-4_18
4. Basca, C., Bernstein, A.: Querying a messy web of data with avalanche. J. Web Semant. **26**, 1–28 (2014)
5. Charalambidis, A., Troumpoukis, A., Konstantopoulos, S.: SemaGrow: optimizing federated SPARQL queries. In: SEMANTICS 2015, pp. 121–128 (2015)
6. Du, F., Chen, Y., Du, X.: Partitioned indexes for entity search over RDF knowledge bases. In: Lee, S., Peng, Z., Zhou, X., Moon, Y.-S., Unland, R., Yoo, J. (eds.) DASFAA 2012. LNCS, vol. 7238, pp. 141–155. Springer, Heidelberg (2012). doi:10.1007/978-3-642-29038-1_12
7. Görlitz, O., Staab, S.: SPLENDID: SPARQL endpoint federation exploiting VOID descriptions. In: COLD 2011 (2011)
8. Gubichev, A., Neumann, T.: Exploiting the query structure for efficient join ordering in SPARQL queries. In: EDBT 2014, pp. 439–450 (2014)
9. Hagedorn, S., Hose, K., Sattler, K., Umbrich, J.: Resource planning for SPARQL query execution on data sharing platforms. In: COLD, pp. 49–60 (2014)
10. Harth, A., Hose, K., Karnstedt, M., Polleres, A., Sattler, K., Umbrich, J.: Data summaries for on-demand queries over linked data. In: WWW 2010, pp. 411–420 (2010)
11. Meimaris, M., Papastefanatos, G., Mamoulis, N., Anagnostopoulos, I.: Extended characteristic sets: graph indexing for SPARQL query optimization. In: ICDE 2017 (2017)
12. Neumann, T., Moerkotte, G.: Characteristic sets: accurate cardinality estimation for RDF queries with multiple joins. In: ICDE 2011, pp. 984–994 (2011)
13. Prasser, F., Kemper, A., Kuhn, K.A.: Efficient distributed query processing for autonomous RDF databases. In: EDBT 2012, pp. 372–383 (2012)
14. Quilitz, B., Leser, U.: Querying distributed RDF data sources with SPARQL. In: Bechhofer, S., Hauswirth, M., Hoffmann, J., Koubarakis, M. (eds.) ESWC 2008. LNCS, vol. 5021, pp. 524–538. Springer, Heidelberg (2008). doi:10.1007/978-3-540-68234-9_39
15. Saleem, M., Ngonga Ngomo, A.-C.: HiBISCuS: hypergraph-based source selection for SPARQL endpoint federation. In: Presutti, V., d'Amato, C., Gandon, F., d'Aquin, M., Staab, S., Tordai, A. (eds.) ESWC 2014. LNCS, vol. 8465, pp. 176–191. Springer, Cham (2014). doi:10.1007/978-3-319-07443-6_13
16. Schmidt, M., Görlitz, O., Haase, P., Ladwig, G., Schwarte, A., Tran, T.: FedBench: a benchmark suite for federated semantic data query processing. In: Aroyo, L., Welty, C., Alani, H., Taylor, J., Bernstein, A., Kagal, L., Noy, N., Blomqvist, E. (eds.) ISWC 2011. LNCS, vol. 7031, pp. 585–600. Springer, Heidelberg (2011). doi:10.1007/978-3-642-25073-6_37

17. Schwarte, A., Haase, P., Hose, K., Schenkel, R., Schmidt, M.: FedX: optimization techniques for federated query processing on linked data. In: Aroyo, L., Welty, C., Alani, H., Taylor, J., Bernstein, A., Kagal, L., Noy, N., Blomqvist, E. (eds.) ISWC 2011. LNCS, vol. 7031, pp. 601–616. Springer, Heidelberg (2011). doi:10.1007/978-3-642-25073-6_38
18. Stocker, M., Seaborne, A., Bernstein, A., Kiefer, C., Reynolds, D.: SPARQL basic graph pattern optimization using selectivity estimation. In: WWW 2008, pp. 595–604 (2008)
19. Wang, X., Tiropanis, T., Davis, H.C.: LHD: optimising linked data query processing using parallelisation. In: LDOW (2013)

Automated Fine-Grained Trust Assessment in Federated Knowledge Bases

Andreas Nolle[1]([⊠]), Melisachew Wudage Chekol[2], Christian Meilicke[2], German Nemirovski[1], and Heiner Stuckenschmidt[2]

[1] Albstadt-Sigmaringen University, Albstadt, Germany
{nolle,nemirovskij}@hs-albsig.de
[2] Research Group Data and Web Science, University of Mannheim, Mannheim, Germany
{mel,christian,heiner}@informatik.uni-mannheim.de

Abstract. The federation of different data sources gained increasing attention due to the continuously growing amount of data. But the more data are available from heterogeneous sources, the higher the risk is of inconsistency. To tackle this challenge in federated knowledge bases we propose a fully automated approach for computing trust values at different levels of granularity. Gathering both the conflict graph and statistical evidence generated by inconsistency detection and resolution, we create a Markov network to facilitate the application of Gibbs sampling to compute a probability for each conflicting assertion. Based on which, trust values for each integrated data source and its respective signature elements are computed. We evaluate our approach on a large distributed dataset from the domain of library science.

1 Introduction

The permanent growing amount of data published in the Linked Open Data (LOD) cloud opens new challenges in data integration. Additionally the use of different schema makes the task of federating several data sources a difficult problem. The federation of various data sources implies typically the amalgamation of ambiguous and possibly conflicting information and often leads to inconsistencies. The resolution of conflicts in federated large scale knowledge bases (KBs) is studied in [17]. Their approach is based on the generation and evaluation of federated clash queries, which are known to be complete for inconsistency detection in *DL-Lite$_A$* KBs. They apply a majority voting scheme to determine a partial repair. This approach does not aim at finding a global optimal repair, but applies an efficient heuristic where each step in the algorithm corresponds to a reasonable decision.

However, resolving conflicts by removing (or ignoring) a subset of the given assertions may result in loss of information. An alternative approach is to determine the trustworthiness of *individual assertions*, data source specific *signature*

We refer the interested reader to an extended version of this paper available at http://www.researchgate.net/publication/318722371.

C. d'Amato et al. (Eds.): ISWC 2017, Part I, LNCS 10587, pp. 490–506, 2017.
DOI: 10.1007/978-3-319-68288-4_29

elements (concept, role, or attribute names) and *data sources* integrated in the federated KB. Grandison and Sloman [8] define "trust as the belief in the competence of an entity to act dependably, securely, and reliably within a specified context". In our work we are concerned with data sources and their competences to provide reliably information with respect to a given assertion or with respect to the set of all assertions that have the same predicate (signature element of the TBox) in common. In that sense our definition of trust also builds on the notion of context dependency, while we understand context as reference to a given fact or reference to a predicate.[1]

We use the statistical evidence gathered by calculating a repair, as prior knowledge for the calculation of trust values at different levels of granularity. In particular, we consider the conflict graph, generated by clashing assertions, as a Markov network that can be used to determine the probability for each conflicting assertion via Gibbs sampling. With the aid of these probabilities, specific trust values for signature elements and data sources can be computed to estimate the probabilities of non-conflicting assertions. Consequently, our approach requires neither a full trusted data source (as in [5]) nor any manual assignments (or user interactions) and relies solely on the identified conflicts. Unlike other approaches [7,12–14,20,22] that in principle rely on the determination of source reliability, we additionally compute individual trust measures on the assertion and signature level of each integrated data source. Our main contribution is a fully automated approach of fine-grained trust assessment and consequently the transformation of a conventional (federated) KB into a probabilistic one.

In Sect. 2 we briefly introduce some fundamental terms and definitions. After introducing the generation of a conflict graph and its repair in Sect. 3 we propose our approach for assessing fine-grained trust values in Sect. 4. Subsequently, we present and discuss results of our experiments in Sect. 5. Before concluding in Sect. 7, we discuss related work in Sect. 6.

2 Preliminaries

We briefly introduce the definition of federated $DL\text{-}Lite_{\mathcal{A}}$ KBs, basic notions related to inconsistency in description logic (DL) KBs, and Markov networks.

2.1 Federated $DL\text{-}Lite_{\mathcal{A}}$ Knowledge Bases

$DL\text{-}Lite$ is a family of languages in which checking KB satisfiability can be done in PTime in the size of the TBox and query answering in AC^0 in the size of the ABox. We consider the subfamily $DL\text{-}Lite_{\mathcal{A}}$, which has been designed for efficiently dealing with huge amounts of extensional information (ABox). We refer the reader to [3,18] for a detailed discussion of the syntax and semantics. In general, subsumption axioms in $DL\text{-}Lite_{\mathcal{A}}$ can be normalized, i.e., each axiom

---

[1] The measure of trust essentially indicates the probability of an assertion to be true. While the term trust is used more on the data source level, probability is more often used with respect to a specific assertion. We use both terms interchangeably.

comprise only one element on the left of the subsumption relation ($\sqsubseteq$) and one element on the right hand side.

The signature Σ (also known as alphabet or vocabulary) of a KB is a finite set of concept, role and attribute names. Furthermore, for ABox assertions of the form $A(x)$, $R(x,y)$ and $U(x,v)$ we refer to the concept, role and attribute names of assertions, i.e., $A, R, U \in \Sigma$, as *signature elements*. In the context of federated KBs, where each integrated data source uses different terminologies (signatures) that are linked by an intermediary (central) schema, we can define a federated *DL-Lite$_{\mathcal{A}}$* KB as well as federated ABox assertions as follows.

Definition 1. *A federated DL-Lite$_{\mathcal{A}}$ knowledge base is a DL-Lite$_{\mathcal{A}}$ knowledge base $\mathcal{K}$ with $\mathcal{K} = \langle \mathcal{T}_c \cup \bigcup_{i \in \mathbb{F}} \mathcal{T}_i, \bigcup_{i \in \mathbb{F}} \mathcal{A}_i \rangle$ where $\mathcal{T}_c$ is a central TBox, each $\mathcal{T}_i$ is a TBox and $\mathcal{A}_i$ is an ABox in data source i and $\mathbb{F}$ is a set of indices that refers to the federated data sources. A federated ABox assertion is a pair $\langle \alpha, i \rangle$ where α denotes an ABox assertion stated in $\mathcal{A}_i$.*

For compact presentation we write $\mathcal{T}$ instead of $\mathcal{T}_c \cup \bigcup_{i \in \mathbb{F}} \mathcal{T}_i$ and $\mathcal{A}$ instead of $\bigcup_{i \in \mathbb{F}} \mathcal{A}_i$. Besides, without loss of generality, in the remainder of this paper we assume that there is only one central schema $\mathcal{T}$ which might be the union of some data source specific schema and an intermediary one comprising mappings between the data source specific vocabularies. Furthermore, we do not address integration problems related to incoherency, i.e., we assume that $\mathcal{T}$ is coherent. Note that there are other works that deal with debugging issues on the terminological level, e.g., [9].

2.2   Inconsistency in Description Logics

In DL, an interpretation $\mathcal{I}$ that satisfies all assertions in $\mathcal{T} \cup \mathcal{A}$ of KB $\mathcal{K}$ is called a *model*. The set of all models for $\mathcal{K}$ is denoted by $Mod(\mathcal{K})$. $\mathcal{K}$ is called *satisfiable* or *consistent*, if $Mod(\mathcal{K}) \neq \emptyset$ [2,6]. Otherwise $\mathcal{K}$ is called *inconsistent*. $\mathcal{K} \models \phi$ denotes that $\mathcal{K}$ logically entails or satisfies a closed first-order logic sentence (formula) ϕ, provided that $\phi^{\mathcal{I}}$ is true for every $\mathcal{I} \in Mod(\mathcal{K})$. If a set F of closed sentences is entailed by $\mathcal{K}$, we can also write $\mathcal{K} \models F$ [19].

An *explanation* (or justification) for $\mathcal{K} \models \phi$ is a subset $\mathcal{K}'$ of $\mathcal{K}$ such that $\mathcal{K}' \models \phi$ while $\mathcal{K}'' \not\models \phi$ for all $\mathcal{K}'' \subset \mathcal{K}'$ [10]. Consequently, an explanation can be interpreted as a minimal reason that explains why ϕ follows from $\mathcal{K}$. Given an inconsistent KB $\mathcal{K}$, an explanation for the inconsistency is called a minimal inconsistent subset (*MIS*) and is denoted by the subset $\mathcal{K}'$ of $\mathcal{K}$ such that $\mathcal{K}'$ is inconsistent while $\mathcal{K}''$ is consistent for all $\mathcal{K}'' \subset \mathcal{K}'$. A subset $\mathcal{R} \subseteq \mathcal{K}$ is called a *repair* (or repair plan) of an inconsistent KB $\mathcal{K}$, if $\mathcal{K} \setminus \mathcal{R}$ is consistent.

Assuming that all of the terminological axioms are (semantically) *correct*, we are only interested in the subset of a MIS that comprises only ABox assertions. We refer to such a subset of a MIS as a MISA (minimal inconsistency preserving sub-ABox). Please notice that in *DL-Lite$_{\mathcal{A}}$* each MISA comprise at most two ABox assertions due to the normalized form of subsumption axioms (see Sect. 2.1). As we will show in Sect. 4.2, the conflict graph obtained from the MISAs can be represented as a Markov network.

2.3 Markov Networks

Graphical models are used to compactly describe a complex distribution over a multi-dimensional space as a graph and provide a central framework to reason on uncertain information. A *Markov network* or *Markov random field* is a probabilistic model that represents the joint probability distribution over a set of random variables $X = (x_1, x_2, ..., x_n)$ as an undirected graph [11]. Each variable is represented by a node and a direct probabilistic interaction between two nodes is represented by an edge. For each clique D comprising the set of nodes X_D there exists a real-valued weight w_D and a feature f_D mapping a possible state $\mathbf{x}_D$ of that clique to a real value. A clique of a graph is a set of nodes which are fully connected. The joint distribution of a Markov network can be defined as a log-linear model of the form

$$p(X = \mathbf{x}) = \frac{1}{Z} \exp\left(\sum_D w_D f_D(\mathbf{x}_D) \right),\tag{1}$$

where $\mathbf{x}$ is a vector, comprising the state of the variables X and Z is a normalization constant, called partition function. The *Markov blanket* B_x of a variable (node) x is defined as the minimal set of variables (nodes) that renders x independent from the rest of the graph, which is simply all neighboring nodes of x. We consider binary discrete variables, hence, the *state* of a variable is its truth value, i.e., either 1 or 0. The conditional probability of a variable x when its Markov blanket B_x is in a state $\mathbf{b}_x$ is given by:

$$p(x = \mathbf{x} | B_x = \mathbf{b}_x) \tag{2}$$
$$= \frac{\exp\left(\sum_{f_x \in F_x} w_x f_x(x = \mathbf{x}, B_x = \mathbf{b}_x) \right)}{\exp\left(\sum_{f_x \in F_x} w_x f_x(x = 0, B_x = \mathbf{b}_x) \right) + \exp\left(\sum_{f_x \in F_x} w_x f_x(x = 1, B_x = \mathbf{b}_x) \right)},$$

where $\mathbf{b}_x$ is a vector that denotes the state of the Markov blanket B_x of node x, F_x is the set of features in which x appears and the feature f_x is a real value of the state, given $\mathbf{x}$ and $\mathbf{b}_x$. In this paper we focus on binary features $f(\mathbf{x}) \in \{0, 1\}$. We will use formula (2) to compute the probabilities of conflicting assertions as shown in Sect. 4.2.

3 Conflict Graph and Repair Generation

To illustrate how MISAs are used to generate a conflict graph, we introduce an example that is used throughout the remainder of this paper. Let $\mathcal{T}$ be a central schema that comprises the following axioms.

$$Book \sqcup Paper \sqsubseteq Publication \qquad\qquad Paper \sqsubseteq \neg Book$$
$$Proceedings \sqsubseteq Book \qquad\qquad Publication \sqsubseteq \neg SlideSet$$
$$\exists isPartOf \sqsubseteq Paper \qquad\qquad \exists isPartOf^- \sqsubseteq Proceedings$$
$$\exists hasSlideSet \sqsubseteq Paper \qquad\qquad \exists hasSlideSet^- \sqsubseteq SlideSet$$

And let $\mathcal{A}_1$, $\mathcal{A}_2$, and $\mathcal{A}_3$ denote three distributed data sources that contain assertions shown in the following table.

$\mathcal{A}_1$		$\mathcal{A}_2$		$\mathcal{A}_3$	
$Paper(\mathbf{I1})$	(α_1)	$Paper(\mathbf{I1})$	(β_1)	$SlideSet(\mathbf{I1})$	(γ_1)
$isPartOf(\mathbf{I1},\mathbf{C1})$	(α_2)	$Proceedings(\mathbf{I1})$	(β_2)	$SlideSet(\mathbf{I2})$	(γ_2)
$Paper(\mathbf{I2})$	(α_3)	$isPartOf(\mathbf{C1},\mathbf{I1})$	(β_3)	$hasSlideSet(\mathbf{I3},\mathbf{I2})$	(γ_3)
$Paper(\mathbf{I4})$	(α_4)	$isPartOf(\mathbf{I4},\mathbf{C2})$	(β_4)	$SlideSet(\mathbf{I4})$	(γ_4)
$isPartOf(\mathbf{C2},\mathbf{I5})$	(α_5)	$Proceedings(\mathbf{C2})$	(β_5)	$hasSlideSet(\mathbf{C2},\mathbf{I4})$	(γ_5)
$isPartOf(\mathbf{I6},\mathbf{C3})$	(α_6)	$isPartOf(\mathbf{I6},\mathbf{C3})$	(β_6)	$Proceedings(\mathbf{C3})$	(γ_6)
$Paper(\mathbf{I6})$	(α_7)	$Proceedings(\mathbf{C3})$	(β_7)	$Proceedings(\mathbf{C4})$	(γ_7)
$Paper(\mathbf{I7})$	(α_8)	$Paper(\mathbf{C4})$	(β_8)	$hasSlideSet(\mathbf{I6},\mathbf{C4})$	(γ_8)

For example, the assertion that **I1** is a *Paper* (α_1 in $\mathcal{A}_1$) and the assertion that **I1** is a *SlideSet* (γ_1 in $\mathcal{A}_3$) are obviously in contradiction due to the axiom $Paper \sqsubseteq \neg SlideSet$ originated from the axiom $Publication \sqsubseteq \neg SlideSet$ in $\mathcal{T}$. In addition, as the assertion $Paper(\mathbf{I1})$ is also found in $\mathcal{A}_2$ (β_1), it is also contradictory to $\mathcal{A}_3$. Furthermore, we can entail this assertion in $\mathcal{A}_1$ from $isPartOf(\mathbf{I1},\mathbf{C1})$ (α_2) and the axiom $\exists isPartOf \sqsubseteq Paper$ in $\mathcal{T}$.

Note that our example can easily be extended to the case where the integrated data sources use different terminologies that are linked by equivalence or subsumption axioms by an intermediary schema. Relying on a previous work [17], we can efficiently detect and resolve inconsistency in federated *DL-Lite$_\mathcal{A}$* KBs. The complete set of conflicts respectively the corresponding MISAs is generated by so-called federated clash queries. Hence, for the above KB, the complete set $\mathcal{C}$ of identified conflicts (MISAs) is given by $\{ \{\alpha_1,\beta_2\}, \{\alpha_1,\beta_3\}, \{\alpha_1,\gamma_1\}, \{\alpha_2,\beta_2\},$ $\{\alpha_2,\beta_3\}, \{\alpha_2,\gamma_1\}, \{\beta_1,\beta_2\}, \{\beta_1,\beta_3\}, \{\beta_1,\gamma_1\}, \{\beta_2,\gamma_1\}, \{\beta_3,\gamma_1\}, \{\alpha_3,\gamma_2\},$ $\{\alpha_3,\gamma_3\}, \{\alpha_4,\gamma_4\}, \{\alpha_4,\gamma_5\}, \{\alpha_5,\beta_4\}, \{\alpha_5,\beta_5\}, \{\alpha_5,\gamma_5\}, \{\beta_4,\gamma_4\}, \{\beta_4,\gamma_5\},$ $\{\beta_5,\gamma_5\}, \{\beta_8,\gamma_7\}, \{\beta_8,\gamma_8\}, \{\gamma_7,\gamma_8\} \}$. The corresponding conflict graph comprising four independent subgraphs is shown in Fig. 1. Each federated assertion is represented by a node and a contradiction between two assertions is represented by an edge.

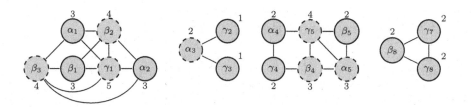

Fig. 1. Conflict graph

Majority Voting Approach. Once all logical conflicts have been collected, the resolution of the identified contradictions is based on the assumption that the more data sources are integrated, the higher is the probability that correct assertions occur redundantly. Conversely, the probability that an assertion is incorrect correlates with the number of contradictions in which the assertion is involved. Based on this assumption, a majority voting scheme is applied on the assertion cardinalities, which are given by the number of involved MISAs for each assertion as illustrated in Fig. 1. MISAs comprising assertions with different cardinalities are iteratively resolved by adding the assertion with higher cardinality to the repair. Note that MISAs with minimum cardinality are resolved first, to reduce the impact (of wrong decisions) on subsequent decisions. Applying this heuristic to the conflict graph of our example will produce the repair $\{\beta_2, \beta_3, \gamma_1, \alpha_3, \alpha_5, \beta_4, \gamma_5\}$, depicted as dashed nodes.

Obviously, this heuristic may not resolve all logical conflicts, i.e., MISAs whose assertions having the same cardinalities (like β_8, γ_7 and γ_8). As a consequence, the heuristic generates a unique but not a full nor a global optimal repair. The application of this approach to a federated setting comprising four LOD data sources has shown that 39.5% of the detected conflicts could be solved with a precision up to 97% [17]. One possibility to get a full repair leading to a consistent KB could be for example to choose a random repair for all remaining contradictions. However, the resolution of conflicts implies the removal of all assertions that are part of the repair. To avoid loss of information we will now use the result of this approach to compute trust values respectively probabilities for individual assertions as well as for each data source and its individual signature elements.

4   Fine-Grained Trust Assessment

Since the evaluation of the approach for inconsistency resolution shows a high precision, we use the gathered statistical evidence as a basis for a fine-grained assessment of trust values at the level of assertions, signatures and data sources.

4.1   Signature Accuracy

We determine the *signature accuracy*[2] for each signature element with respect to a data source based on conflicting assertions and assertions that are 'correct'. Correct means in this case solely assertions whose individuals occur in a non-conflicting assertion in at least one other integrated data source. The set of conflicting assertions and correct assertions can be treated as an adequate sample of all assertions that use the same signature element. Furthermore, conflicting assertions can be defined into the following three subcategories:

– likely false assertions (assertions that are in the majority voting based repair),

---

[2] We intentionally avoid here the terms 'trust' or 'probability' to prevent any confusion with the calculated signature trusts later on.

- likely true assertions (conflicting assertions that would become conflict-free if the repair is removed),
- always conflicting assertions (assertions that are part of unresolvable MISAs).

Accordingly, we can define the accuracy for an signature element $\sigma \in \Sigma$ of a specific data source i formally as follows:

Definition 2. *Given a federated knowledge base* $\mathcal{K} = \langle \mathcal{T}, \bigcup_{i \in \mathbb{F}} \mathcal{A}_i \rangle$, *the set* X *of all conflicting assertions and the set* $C = \{c_1, ..., c_n\}$ *of all conflicts (MISAs) in* $\mathcal{K}$ *with* $c := \{x_k, x_l\}$, $k \neq l$ *and* $x_k, x_l \in X$, *a repair* $\mathcal{R}$ *computed by a majority voting approach, and the set* $\mathcal{G}$ *of non-conflicting assertions comprising individuals that occur in more than one data source (correct assertions). Let* σ *be either a concept, a property or an attribute in the signature* Σ *of* $\mathcal{K}$, *and let* $\Psi \subseteq \bigcup_{i \in \mathbb{F}} \mathcal{A}_i$ *be a set of federated assertions, then* $sas(\sigma, \Psi, i)$ *is defined as the subset of assertions in* Ψ *that use* σ *and originate from* $\mathcal{A}_i$. *The signature accuracy acc of* σ *with respect to* $\mathcal{A}_i$ *is defined as*

$$acc(\sigma, i) = 1 - \frac{|sas(\sigma, \mathcal{R}, i)| + \displaystyle\sum_{x \in sas(\sigma, a \in c:c \in C; c \cap \mathcal{R} = \emptyset, i)} \dfrac{1}{|c \in C : x \in c|}}{|sas(\sigma, X \cup \mathcal{G}, i)|}, \qquad (3)$$

where x *is an assertion in* $\mathcal{A}_i$ *that uses the signature element* σ *and is part of a MISA not resolved by* $\mathcal{R}$. *The accuracy of a signature is between 0 and 1, i.e.,* $0 < acc(\sigma, i) < 1$. *Accuracy values that are outside of this range, i.e., for* $acc(\sigma, i) = 0$ *and* $ar(\sigma, i) = 1$, *the accuracy is set to a fixed value: 0.001 and 0.999 respectively.*

Informally, the accuracy for a signature element of a specific data source is defined by '$1-$ the ratio of incorrect assertions with respect to the total number of conflicting assertions and correct assertions'. The numerator in formula (3) is the number of incorrect assertions. It is given by the number of likely false assertions ($|sas(\sigma, \mathcal{R}, i)|$) and the probability of being true for each always conflicting assertion, which in turn is given by 1 divided by the number of contradicting assertions (number of involved conflicts).

Example 1. From the example of Sect. 3, the set of conflicting assertions comprises α_1, α_3 and α_4 with respect to the signature element *Paper* in data source $\mathcal{A}_1$, where only α_3 is part of the repair. On the other hand, α_7 is a correct assertion because it is verified by β_6 and not in conflict with any other assertion. Further, α_8 is neither a correct assertion nor part of any MISA. According to Definition 2 the accuracy for signature element *Paper* in data source $\mathcal{A}_1$ is given by $acc(Paper, 1) = 1 - \frac{1+0}{4} = 0.75$. The accuracy values for all signature elements are shown below.

$acc(Paper, 1) = 0.75$	$acc(Paper, 2) = 0.33$	$acc(SlideSet, 3) = 0.67$
$acc(isPartOf, 1) = 0.67$	$acc(Proceedings, 2) = 0.67$	$acc(hasSlideSet, 3) = 0.44$
	$acc(isPartOf, 2) = 0.67$	$acc(Proceedings, 3) = 0.67$

Based on the above definition, we can now use the calculated signature accuracy for a specific signature element with respect to a data source, to compute precise probabilities for conflicting assertions.

4.2 Assertion Trusts

We consider a conflict graph as a Markov network, where $X = \{x_1, \ldots, x_m\}$ represents the set of all federated assertions that are involved in some conflict and $C = \{c_1, \ldots, c_n\}$ the set of all conflicts (edges) with $c := \{x_k, x_l\}$, $k \neq l$. Since the edges in the conflict graph are undirected, we have chosen Markov Network as undirected graphical model. Each assertion x represents a binary random variable $x \in \{0, 1\}$, i.e., either true ($x = 1$) or false ($x = 0$). For each assertion x we have a feature $f_a \in F$ such that $f_a(x = 0) = 0$ and $f_a(x = 1) = 1$, i.e., $f_a(x) = x$. Moreover, in order to obtain a consistent *possible world* the condition $!(\bigwedge_{x \in c} x)$ has to be satisfied for each conflict $c \in C$. A possible world is an assignment of truth values to all the variables. Consequently, each such condition is also treated as a feature $f_c \in F$ such that the Markov network specifies a probability distribution over all possible worlds $\mathcal{X}$.

Since each condition f_c is a hard constraint that has to be satisfied in each possible world $\mathbf{x} \in \mathcal{X}$, the corresponding weight is $w_c \to \infty$. If any constraint is violated, the joint distribution (given by Eq. (1)) is $\lim_{w \to \infty} p(X = \mathbf{x}) = 0$. Further, if at least one variable $b_x \in B_x$ in the Markov blanket of x is true, the conditional probability (given by Eq. (2)) of x is $\lim_{w \to \infty} p(x = 0 | B_x = \mathbf{b}_x) = 1$ and $\lim_{w \to \infty} p(x = 1 | B_x = \mathbf{b}_x) = 0$. This is because, the feature $f_x(x = 0, B_x = \mathbf{b}_x)$ (resp. $f_x(x = 1, B_x = \mathbf{b}_x)$) can only be true (resp. false) iff all its neighbors $b_x \in B_x$ are false, i.e., $b_x = 0$ (resp. true $b_x = 1$).

In order to compute the marginal probability of an assertion that uses signature element σ with respect to a data source i, we make use of the calculated signature accuracies. Hence we determine the weight w_a of a feature f_a for an assertion x in $\mathcal{A}_i$ as the log odds between a world in which an assertion x of $\mathcal{A}_i$ that uses σ is true and a world in which it is false, given by

$$w_a = \ln\left(\frac{acc(\sigma(x), i)}{1 - acc(\sigma(x), i)}\right), \tag{4}$$

where $\sigma(x)$ is the signature element of assertion x.

The complexity of computing the marginal probabilities is time exponential in the number of nodes. Thus, to perform approximate inference in Markov networks, Markov chain Monte Carlo (MCMC) particularly Gibbs sampling [11] is one of the most commonly used methods. In Gibbs sampling each node is sampled randomly in turn, given its Markov blanket using Eq. (2). An approximation of the marginal probabilities, which is also called marginal inference, can be done by simply counting over the samples. Flipping the state of a node (e.g., changing its truth value from true to false) can be treated as a 'transition' between different worlds $\mathbf{x} \in \mathcal{X}$ (possible worlds of X). Because of the conditions $f_c \in F$, a change of the state of an assertion x according to its conditional probability is only performed, iff all its neighbors $b_x \in B_x$ are false, i.e.,

$b_x = 0$ (denoted by $B_x = 0$ for short) and consequently the flip would not lead to an inconsistent world. Otherwise the state of an assertion remains unchanged. Given that $B_x = 0$, in Eq. (2) all constraint features f_c in which x appears are zero ($f_c = 0$) and there remains one feature $f_a(x)$ whose value depends on the state of x. As we have already computed a possible repair based on a majority voting approach, we use it as a starting point for the Gibbs sampling. However, as there is no guarantee that all conflicts are resolved, a repair for all remaining contradictions is chosen randomly. Provided that we jump only between consistent possible worlds, there remain solely two cases for the conditional probability of node x, representing an assertion in $\mathcal{A}_i$ from which we have to sample:

1. if the current world contains $x = 0$ and $B_x = 0$, then the probability that x is true in the next possible world is given by:

$$p(x = 1 | B_x = 0) = \frac{\exp\left(\ln\left(\frac{acc(\sigma(x), i)}{1 - acc(\sigma(x), i)}\right)\right)}{\exp(0) + \exp\left(\ln\left(\frac{acc(\sigma(x), i)}{1 - acc(\sigma(x), i)}\right)\right)} = acc(\sigma(x), i), \quad (5)$$

2. if the current world contains $x = 1$ and $B_x = 0$, the probability that x is false in the next possible world is given by:

$$p(x = 0 | B_x = 0) = \frac{\exp(0)}{\exp(0) + \exp\left(\ln\left(\frac{acc(\sigma(x), i)}{1 - acc(\sigma(x), i)}\right)\right)} = 1 - acc(\sigma(x), i). \quad (6)$$

Consequently, the calculated accuracy of a signature element σ is exactly the conditional (prior) probability of an assertion $x \in \mathcal{A}_i$ comprising σ, given that all neighbors (contradicting assertions) are false. Since we start with a consistent world and ensure that an inconsistent world is never reached, the flipping of states causes that in some circumstances too many assertions are false (part of the repair), which is absolutely legitimate in terms of an acceptable repair. In terms of performance optimization, the sampling is applied to each independent subgraph of the conflict graph in parallel. After the sampling the approximate marginal probability (trust) of each assertion x can be calculated according to the following definition:

Definition 3. *Given a federated knowledge base $\mathcal{K} = \langle \mathcal{T}, \bigcup_{i \in \mathbb{F}} \mathcal{A}_i \rangle$, the set X of all conflicting assertions in $\mathcal{K}$, the set $\mathcal{G}$ of (non-conflicting) correct assertions and the set M containing, for each conflicting assertion $x \in X$, the number of Gibbs sampling states in which $x = 1$. Then, the assertion trust $p(x)$ for each federated assertion x in $\mathcal{A}$ of $\mathcal{K}$ is given by*

$$p(x) = \begin{cases} 1.0, & x \in \mathcal{G}, \\ \frac{M_{x=1}}{N}, & x \in X, \\ \varnothing, & otherwise, \end{cases} \quad (7)$$

where $M_{x=1}$ is the number of states in which $x = 1$, N is the number of samples and $\varnothing$ denotes undefined.

Probabilities cannot be assessed for all assertions in $\mathcal{A}$ of $\mathcal{K}$, i.e., for those assertions that are not correct and are not involved in some MISAs. For such assertions, we determine (in Sect. 4.3) trust values for different signature elements with respect to a specific data source, called *signature trusts*.

Example 2. From the example in Sect. 3, $\alpha_6, \alpha_7, \beta_6, \beta_7$ and γ_6 are correct assertions and hence get a probability of 1.0. Using the accuracies of Example 1 and calculating assertion trusts using Gibbs sampling with $N = 10,000$ as described above, will result in the following assertion trusts:

$$p(\alpha_1) = 0.66 \quad p(\alpha_5) = 0.31 \quad p(\beta_1) = 0.58 \quad p(\beta_5) = 0.41 \quad p(\gamma_1) = 0.05 \quad p(\gamma_5) = 0.07$$
$$p(\alpha_2) = 0.58 \quad p(\alpha_6) = 1.0 \quad p(\beta_2) = 0.07 \quad p(\beta_6) = 1.0 \quad p(\gamma_2) = 0.42 \quad p(\gamma_6) = 1.0$$
$$p(\alpha_3) = 0.37 \quad p(\alpha_7) = 1.0 \quad p(\beta_3) = 0.03 \quad p(\beta_7) = 1.0 \quad p(\gamma_3) = 0.28 \quad p(\gamma_7) = 0.34$$
$$p(\alpha_4) = 0.48 \quad p(\alpha_8) = \varnothing \quad p(\beta_4) = 0.15 \quad p(\beta_8) = 0.35 \quad p(\gamma_4) = 0.32 \quad p(\gamma_8) = 0.14$$

Only for assertion α_8 no probability is assessed ($\varnothing$), because it is not part of any conflict nor is correct.

4.3 Signature Trusts

Based on the previously computed probabilities of assertions, we can now define the trust for a signature element σ of a specific data source i as shown below.

Definition 4. *Given a federated knowledge base $\mathcal{K} = \langle \mathcal{T}, \bigcup_{i \in \mathbb{F}} \mathcal{A}_i \rangle$, the set X of all conflicting assertions in $\mathcal{K}$ and the set $\mathcal{G}$ of correct assertions in $\mathcal{K}$. Then, the signature trust $p(\sigma, i)$, for each signature element $\sigma \in \mathcal{A}_i$ of data source i in $\mathcal{K}$, is given by*

$$p(\sigma, i) = \begin{cases} \dfrac{\sum\limits_{a \in sas(\sigma, X \cup \mathcal{G}, i)} p(a)}{|sas(\sigma, X \cup \mathcal{G}, i)|}, & sas(\sigma, X, i) \neq \emptyset, \\ \varnothing, & otherwise. \end{cases} \tag{8}$$

Roughly, the signature trust with respect to a data source is defined by the average of all its assertion trusts. As a result we can now use the calculated signature trusts as the probability of assertions for which no trust value is assessed.

Example 3. In order to calculate the trust value of the signature element *Paper* in data source $\mathcal{A}_1$, we have to consider the probabilities of $\alpha_1, \alpha_3, \alpha_4$ and α_7. Following Definition 4, the signature trust of *Paper* is given by $p(Paper, 1) = \frac{0.66 + 0.37 + 0.48 + 1.0}{4} = 0.63$. Since for α_8 no assertion trust was computed, the signature trust of *Paper* in data source $\mathcal{A}_1$ is used as its probability. The calculated trusts for all signature elements with respect to the corresponding data sources are shown below:

$$p(Paper, 1) = 0.63 \qquad p(Paper, 2) = 0.47 \qquad p(SlideSet, 3) = 0.26$$
$$p(isPartOf, 1) = 0.63 \quad p(Proceedings, 2) = 0.49 \quad p(hasSlideSet, 3) = 0.16$$
$$p(isPartOf, 2) = 0.39 \quad p(Proceedings, 3) = 0.67$$

4.4   Data Source Trusts

Obviously, if there is no conflicting assertion that uses the signature element σ in a specific data source i, the signature trust value for σ with respect to data source i cannot be assessed. For this reason we in turn determine trust values for each data source in $\mathcal{K}$. Based on the definition of signature trusts, the trust value for a specific data source can be formally defined as:

Definition 5. *Given a federated knowledge base* $\mathcal{K} = \langle \mathcal{T}, \bigcup_{i \in \mathbb{F}} \mathcal{A}_i \rangle$, *the signature* Σ *of* $\mathcal{K}$ *and the complete set* X *of conflicting assertions in* $\mathcal{K}$. *Then, the trust value* $p(i)$ *for data source* i *in* $\mathcal{K}$ *is given by*

$$
p(i) = \begin{cases} \dfrac{\displaystyle\sum_{\sigma \in \Sigma : sas(\sigma, X, i) \neq \emptyset} p(\sigma, i) * |sas(\sigma, \mathcal{A}_i, i)|}{\displaystyle\sum_{\sigma \in \Sigma : sas(\sigma, X, i) \neq \emptyset} |sas(\sigma, \mathcal{A}_i, i)|}, & \text{if } \mathcal{A}_i \cap X \neq \emptyset, \\[4mm] \varnothing, & \text{otherwise.} \end{cases} \tag{9}
$$

Roughly, the trust in data source i is given by the average of the weighted sum of its signature trusts. Each signature trust is weighted by the number of assertions that uses the corresponding signature element in data source i. As there still might be some signature elements and consequently some assertions without an assessed probability, the trust value of the respective data source is used instead. Of course, if a data source contains no conflicting assertions the trust value for this data source cannot be computed. In this case a default or user-defined trust value could be used.

Example 4. With respect to the calculated signature trusts of Example 3 and using Definition 5, the data source trust for $\mathcal{A}_1$ is given by $p(\mathcal{A}_1) = \frac{0.63 * 5 + 0.63 * 3}{8} = 0.63$. The calculation of the data source trusts for $\mathcal{A}_2$ and $\mathcal{A}_3$ yields $p(\mathcal{A}_2) = 0.45$ and $p(\mathcal{A}_3) = 0.33$ respectively. If $\mathcal{A}_1$ would contain an additional assertion $SlideSet(\mathbf{I8})$, the signature trust of $SlideSet$ with respect to $\mathcal{A}_1$ and consequently the assertion trust for $SlideSet(\mathbf{I8})$ would be the data source trust $p(\mathcal{A}_1) = 0.63$.

5   Experimental Evaluation

In order to evaluate our approach we have used a large distributed LOD dataset from the domain of library science, comprising four LOD data sources. Namely, FacetedDBLP ($\mathcal{A}_1$), BibSonomy ($\mathcal{A}_2$), RKB Explorer ePrints Open Archives ($\mathcal{A}_3$), and RKB Explorer DBLP ($\mathcal{A}_4$). Since the OWL 2 QL profile is based on *DL-Lite*, we have used it as specification language of our central TBox that includes the TBoxes of each data source. In order to ensure that the federated TBox is coherent and to gain a higher overlapping of the data sources, we have applied some small modifications of the data source specific TBoxes as well as its datasets (ABoxes). For more detail, we refer the interested reader to [17]. The collection of the central TBox as well as the referenced TBoxes is available online[3]. For legal reasons we are currently not able to publish the final dataset of each integrated data source. Please contact us if you are interested in these datasets. We run the implementation of our trust assessment approach on a CentOS 6.7 virtual machine consisting of 6x Intel Xeon CPUs (à 4 cores @ 2.50 GHz) and 128 GB of RAM.

Accuracy and Trust Computation. The federated KB contains 284,355,894 assertions. The evaluation of 44,072 generated clash queries resulted in 18,146,950 MISAs[4]. The majority voting approach proposed in [17] could resolve 7,166,005 (39.5%) MISAs and generated a repair of 1,993,136 assertions. Note that the number of resolved MISAs is significantly higher than the size of the repair and indicates a high overlap of the MISAs. Based on this repair, the signature accuracy values are calculated using the formula in Definition 2. The distribution of the resulting values are depicted in Fig. 2(a). As shown in the figure, there exist one signature element with an accuracy <0.1 with respect to $\mathcal{A}_1$ and $\mathcal{A}_3$. We had already observed that assertions involving the attribute *volume* are misused in $\mathcal{A}_1$ and $\mathcal{A}_3$, i.e., *volume* attributes are in both data sources not used at the level of collections like proceedings, journals or books, but on the level of articles published in a collection. Hence, it is not surprising that we get a low signature accuracy <0.1 for *volume* with respect to $\mathcal{A}_1$ and $\mathcal{A}_3$.

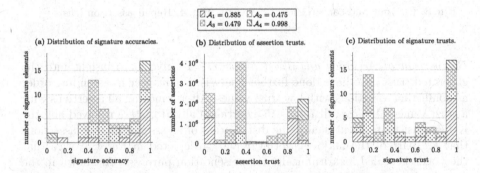

Fig. 2. Signature accuracy and trust values of assertions and signature elements.

Since the generated repair resolves only 39.5% of the conflicts, we choose randomly a repair for all the remaining conflicts such that the starting point of the Gibbs sampling represents a possible world. The application of our approach for fine-grained trust assessment based on this repair and the calculated signature accuracy values result in the data source trusts, distributions of assertion trusts and signature trusts depicted in Fig. 2(b) and (c). In Fig. 2(c), if we consider data source $\mathcal{A}_4$, we see that it contains two signature trusts >0.9 (for the signature elements *article-of-journal* and *Journal*); and one trust <0.1 (for signature

---

[3] http://www.researchgate.net/publication/299852903.
[4] Clashes of incorrect datatypes are not considered since its resolution is trivial.

element *title*). Due to the negligible number of assertions in $\mathcal{A}_4$ with a low trust, the trust value of this data source is close to 1.0. Nevertheless, we cannot trust $\mathcal{A}_4$ with respect to the signature element *title*.

Runtime and Convergence Performance. The runtime, with increasing samples N (with a step size of 200) as well as the corresponding convergence of the trust values, is shown in Fig. 3. After a burn-in period of 1,000 samples in which the variables state may not exactly represent the desired distribution, the runtime increases linearly with the number of samples. After sampling each node 10,000 times, the maximal deviation of a trust value compared to the previous sample is 0.019. Thus, the probabilities converge towards their true values as N increases.

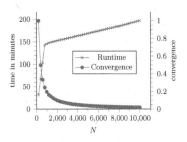

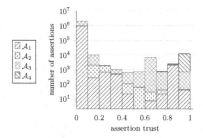

Fig. 3. Runtime and convergence.   **Fig. 4.** Repair assertion trusts.

Comparison of Accuracy and Trust Measures. To give more insight into the generated trusts, we have done further analysis. We inspect in ascending order all conflicting assertions with low trust values. After removing all assertions with a trust value ≤ 0.5 (overall 7,465,415 assertions) all MISAs are resolved and the KB is consistent. Additionally, the distribution of assessed trusts for assertions that are part of the majority voting repair is depicted in Fig. 4. Notice that the y-axis is scaled logarithmically for presentation purposes. As shown in the figure, solely 22,497 (1.13%) assertions of the repair have trust values ≥ 0.5. This indicates that our approach performs very well (which is in line with the high precision (97%) of the repair shown in [17]).

Comparing the calculated signature accuracy values with the assessed signature trusts shows that the prior probabilities comprise 20 signature elements with a value ≤ 0.5 whereas the signature trusts have 30 elements. Table 1 shows the top 5 signature elements with a high deviation between the signature accuracy and the signature trust. For example, if we look at the signature element *Proceedings* of data source $\mathcal{A}_1$ and $\mathcal{A}_2$, it shows that most of the MISAs are not resolved by the majority voting. Moreover, the signature elements of conflicting assertions in resolved MISAs are in many cases different from the signature elements of conflicting assertions in unresolved MISAs. Since the accuracy for signature element *Proceedings* is less than the accuracy of conflicting signature elements in unresolved MISAs, the resulting trust for assertions that use *Proceedings* is low.

Table 1. Top 5 of signature elements with high deviation

Data source	$\sigma \in \Sigma$	Signature accuracy	Signature trust
$\mathcal{A}_1$	http://swrc.ontoware.org/ontology#Proceedings	0.761	0.029
$\mathcal{A}_2$	http://swrc.ontoware.org/ontology#Proceedings	0.578	0.178
$\mathcal{A}_3$	http://purl.org/ontology/bibo/EditedBook	0.591	0.224
$\mathcal{A}_3$	http://purl.org/ontology/bibo/Book	0.534	0.185
$\mathcal{A}_3$	http://purl.org/ontology/bibo/Website	0.500	0.163

Qualitative Analysis of Trust Values. To evaluate the quality of assessed assertion trusts, we randomly selected 100 assertions from the repair with a trust
≥ 0.8, representing a set of assertions that are probably mistaken for being part
of the repair by the majority voting. Because of the already evaluated high precision of the repair, we omit the evaluation of assertions from the repair with
a low trust value. The selected subset of assertions is manually evaluated by a
domain expert. Since 81% of the assertions are annotated as correct, the evaluation indicates a high precision of the assessed probabilities and substantiate that
the approach is reasonable. Besides, this precision score confirms that the calculation of signature accuracy values used as prior probability is a valid premise
and enables a high precision of the assessed trust values.

6 Related Work

The notion of trust has been used in a heterogeneous way within the semantic
web community (surveyed in [1]). The referred works are often based on the
assumption that an external criteria is used to estimate trusts or that initial
trust estimations are already given. Contrary to that, our work is based on the
assumption that each data source and each assertion has the same level of trust
prior to the majority voting. Moreover, our method is based on the idea that we
have to readjust the initial assumption by analyzing and leveraging the logical
contradictions of given assertions. Note also, that we could extend our approach,
by starting with varying trust values based on an analysis of data provenance.

Beside addressing issues like the correction of mistakes that stem from the
knowledge extraction process or with the aggregation of different values, dealing with contradictory assertions is one of the central tasks of knowledge fusion
[4]. Given an inconsistent KB, one possible approach is to resolve all conflicts
by eliminating at least one of the conflicting statements. However, conflict resolution often results in loss of information. Contrary to this, paraconsistent
(inconsistency-tolerant) logics are used for reasoning in KBs that contain conflicts. To represent and reason on uncertain (i.e., imprecise) knowledge, there
exist several approximation approaches. An overview of such approaches is for
example given in [15].

In addition to paraconsistent logics, one straightforward approach is to eliminate conflicts by applying a majority voting scheme as shown in [17]. In order to
consider the quality of different data sources, truth discovery techniques are proposed in [7,12,14,20,22]. A comprehensive survey on truth discovery is given by

Li et al. [13]. The principle of truth discovery is to estimate the reliability of each source, i.e., the more frequently true information is provided, the higher is the trust in that source. Consequently, the information of a reliable source is considered as trustworthy. One shortcoming of (most of) these approaches is that they do not asses the quality of a data source with respect to some specific information or information type (signature element). As a consequence, all assertions of a data source have the same probability, yet assertions with respect to a specific signature element whose trust differ widely from the data source trust are neglected. So the trust calculation for an assertion on which the truth discovery is based upon is computed by means of the assumed data source trust (top-down), whereas in our approach the data source trust is determined by the signature trust and consequently by the individual assertion trusts (bottom-up). Another approach proposed by Ma et al. [16] considers the varying reliability of sources among different topics by automatically assigning topics to a question and estimating the topic-specific expertise of a source. Closer to our approach is the work proposed by Zhao et al. [23], since they calculate probabilistic values on facts (assertions) by using a Bayesian model and Gibbs sampling. Contrary to our approach, Zhao et al. base their notion of conflicting facts on direct contradictions that origin from a closed-world assumption instead of using a TBox that allows to find both explicit and implicit conflicts while still preserving the assumption that non-stated facts do not correspond to the claim of their negation.

In addition to the estimation of source reliability only by the accuracy of the provided information, there exist methodologies and frameworks for assessing data quality respectively its source by considering diverse quality dimensions and metrics, e.g., accessibility, performance, reputation, timeliness and others. Zaveri et al. [21] proposed a systematic review of such approaches that evaluate the quality of LOD sources and provide under a common classification scheme a comprehensive list of dimensions and metrics.

Our proposed approach is different from the approaches mentioned above in two aspects. First, we exploit the composition of the conflict graph, which is constructed based on a well-defined semantics, as well as the statistical evidence, gathered by inconsistency resolution, to compute individual probabilities for conflicting assertions. Second, the intention is not to use the computed probabilities for truth discovery but to enable the representation of uncertain knowledge and thereby the application of probabilistic reasoning and paraconsistent logics as well as the computation of the most probable consistent KB. To the best of our knowledge there is currently no other approach in this direction.

7   Conclusion

In this paper we proposed an automated approach for fine-grained trust assessment at different levels of granularity. In particular, by exploiting the statistical evidence generated by inconsistency resolution via majority voting and considering the conflict graph as a Markov network, we facilitate the application of Gibbs sampling to compute a probability for each conflicting assertion. Based on which, specific trust values for signature elements and data sources are computed to estimate the probabilities of non-conflicting assertions. We evaluated our approach on a large distributed dataset and could measure a high precision of the calculated probabilities.

Beside an evaluation against related truth discovery approaches, one further aspect will be to examine whether and to what extent it is possible to improve the calculated probabilities, by considering the entailment relation between several assertions (according to the given TBox) within the Gibbs sampling.

References

1. Artz, D., Gil, Y.: A survey of trust in computer science and the semantic web. Web Semant. Sci. Serv. Agents WWW **5**(2), 58–71 (2007)
2. Baader, F.: The Description Logic Handbook: Theory, Implementation, and Applications. Cambridge University Press, Cambridge (2003)
3. Calvanese, D., De Giacomo, G., Lembo, D., Lenzerini, M., Rosati, R.: Tractable reasoning and efficient query answering in description logics: the DL-Lite family. J. Autom. Reason. **39**(3), 385–429 (2007)
4. Dong, X.L., Gabrilovich, E., Heitz, G., Horn, W., Murphy, K., Sun, S., Zhang, W.: From data fusion to knowledge fusion. PVLDB **7**(10), 881–892 (2014)
5. Dong, X.L., Gabrilovich, E., Murphy, K., Dang, V., Horn, W., Lugaresi, C., Sun, S., Zhang, W.: Knowledge-based trust: estimating the trustworthiness of web sources. PVLDB **8**(9), 938–949 (2015)
6. Flouris, G., Huang, Z., Pan, J.Z., Plexousakis, D., Wache, H.: Inconsistencies, negations and changes in ontologies. In: AAAI 21, vol. 2, 1295–1300 (2006)
7. Galland, A., Abiteboul, S., Marian, A., Senellart, P.: Corroborating information from disagreeing views. In: WSDM, pp. 131–140. ACM (2010)
8. Grandison, T., Sloman, M.: A survey of trust in internet applications. IEEE Commun. Surv. Tutor. **3**(4), 2–16 (2000)
9. Ji, Q., Haase, P., Qi, G., Hitzler, P., Stadtmüller, S.: RaDON — repair and diagnosis in ontology networks. In: Aroyo, L., et al. (eds.) ESWC 2009. LNCS, vol. 5554, pp. 863–867. Springer, Heidelberg (2009). doi:10.1007/978-3-642-02121-3_71
10. Kalyanpur, A., Parsia, B., Horridge, M., Sirin, E.: Finding all justifications of OWL DL entailments. In: Aberer, K., et al. (eds.) ASWC/ISWC -2007. LNCS, vol. 4825, pp. 267–280. Springer, Heidelberg (2007). doi:10.1007/978-3-540-76298-0_20
11. Koller, D., Friedman, N.: Probabilistic Graphical Models: Principles and Techniques. MIT Press, Cambridge (2009)
12. Li, X., Dong, X.L., Lyons, K., Meng, W., Srivastava, D.: Truth finding on the deep web: is the problem solved? PVLDB **6**(2), 97–108 (2012)
13. Li, Y., Gao, J., Meng, C., Li, Q., Su, L., Zhao, B., Fan, W., Han, J.: A survey on truth discovery. SIGKDD Explor. Newsl. **17**(2), 1–16 (2016)
14. Liu, W., Liu, J., Duan, H., Hu, W., Wei, B.: Exploiting source-object networks to resolve object conflicts in linked data. In: Blomqvist, E., Maynard, D., Gangemi, A., Hoekstra, R., Hitzler, P., Hartig, O. (eds.) ESWC 2017. LNCS, vol. 10249, pp. 53–67. Springer, Cham (2017). doi:10.1007/978-3-319-58068-5_4
15. Lukasiewicz, T., Straccia, U.: Managing uncertainty and vagueness in description logics for the semantic web. J. Web Semant. **6**(4), 291–308 (2008)

16. Ma, F., Li, Y., Li, Q., Qiu, M., Gao, J., Zhi, S., Su, L., Zhao, B., Ji, H., Han, J.: FaitCrowd: fine grained truth discovery for crowdsourced data aggregation. In: ACM SIGKDD, pp. 745–754. ACM (2015)
17. Nolle, A., Meilicke, C., Chekol, M.W., Nemirovski, G., Stuckenschmidt, H.: Schema-based debugging of federated data sources. In: ECAI, pp. 381–389 (2016)
18. Poggi, A., Lembo, D., Calvanese, D., De Giacomo, G., Lenzerini, M., Rosati, R.: Linking data to ontologies. In: Spaccapietra, S. (ed.) Journal on Data Semantics X. LNCS, vol. 4900, pp. 133–173. Springer, Heidelberg (2008). doi:10.1007/ 978-3-540-77688-8_5
19. Rudolph, S.: Foundations of description logics. In: Polleres, A., d'Amato, C., Arenas, M., Handschuh, S., Kroner, P., Ossowski, S., Patel-Schneider, P. (eds.) Reasoning Web 2011. LNCS, vol. 6848, pp. 76–136. Springer, Heidelberg (2011). doi:10.1007/978-3-642-23032-5_2
20. Yin, X., Han, J., Philip, S.Y.: Truth discovery with multiple conflicting information providers on the web. IEEE TKDE **20**(6), 796–808 (2008)
21. Zaveri, A., Rula, A., Maurino, A., Pietrobon, R., Lehmann, J., Auer, S.: Quality assessment for linked data: a survey. Semant. Web **7**(1), 63–93 (2016)
22. Zhao, B., Han, J.: A probabilistic model for estimating real-valued truth from conflicting sources. In: Proceedings of QDB (2012)
23. Zhao, B., Rubinstein, B., Gemmell, J., Han, J.: A bayesian approach to discovering truth from conflicting sources for data integration. PVLDB **5**(6), 550–561 (2012)

Completeness-Aware Rule Learning
from Knowledge Graphs

Thomas Pellissier Tanon[1]([✉]), Daria Stepanova[1]([✉]), Simon Razniewski[2],
Paramita Mirza[1], and Gerhard Weikum[1]

[1] Max Planck Institute of Informatics, Saarbrücken, Germany
{tpelliss,dstepano,paramita,weikum}@mpi-inf.mpg.de
[2] Free University of Bozen-Bolzano, Bolzano, Italy
razniewski@inf.unibz.it

Abstract. Knowledge graphs (KGs) are huge collections of primarily encyclopedic facts. They are widely used in entity recognition, structured search, question answering, and other important tasks. Rule mining is commonly applied to discover patterns in KGs. However, unlike in traditional association rule mining, KGs provide a setting with a high degree of *incompleteness*, which may result in the wrong estimation of the quality of mined rules, leading to erroneous beliefs such as all artists have won an award, or hockey players do not have children.

In this paper we propose to use (in-)completeness meta-information to better assess the quality of rules learned from incomplete KGs. We introduce completeness-aware scoring functions for relational association rules. Moreover, we show how one can obtain (in-)completeness metadata by learning rules about numerical patterns of KG edge counts. Experimental evaluation both on real and synthetic datasets shows that the proposed rule ranking approaches have remarkably higher accuracy than the state-of-the-art methods in uncovering missing facts.

1 Introduction

Motivation. Advances in information extraction have led to general-purpose knowledge graphs (KGs) containing billions of positive facts about the world (e.g., [1–3, 21]). KGs are widely applied in semantic web search, question answering, web extraction and many other tasks. Unfortunately, due to their wide scope, KGs are generally incomplete. To account for the incompleteness, KGs typically adopt the Open World Assumption (OWA) under which missing facts are treated as unknown rather than false.

An important task over KGs is rule learning, which is relevant for a variety of applications ranging from knowledge graph curation (completion, error detection) [10, 12, 24] to data mining and semantic culturonomics. However, since such rules are learned from incomplete data, they might be erroneous and might make incorrect predictions on missing facts. E.g., r_1 : $hasChild(X, Y) \leftarrow worksAt(X, Z), educatedAt(Y, Z)$ could be mined from the KG in Fig. 1, stating that workers of certain institutions often have children

© Springer International Publishing AG 2017
C. d'Amato et al. (Eds.): ISWC 2017, Part I, LNCS 10587, pp. 507–525, 2017.
DOI: 10.1007/978-3-319-68288-4_30

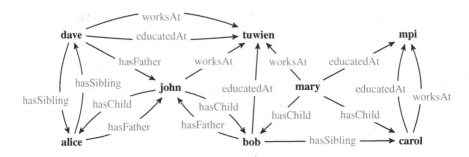

Fig. 1. Example KG

among the people educated there, as this is frequently the case for popular scientists. While r_1 is clearly not universal and should be ranked lower than the rule $r_2 : hasSibling(X, Z) \leftarrow hasFather(X, Y), hasChild(Y, Z)$, standard rule measures like confidence (i.e., conditional probability of the rule's head given its body) incorrectly favor r_1 over r_2 for the given KG.

Recently, efforts have been put into detecting the concrete numbers of facts of certain types that hold in the real world (e.g., *"Einstein has 3 children"*) by exploiting Web extraction and crowd-sourcing methods [23, 26]. Such metadata provides a lot of hints about the topology of KGs, and reveals parts that should be especially targeted by rule learning methods. However, surprisingly, despite its obvious importance, to date, no systematic way of making use of such information in rule learning exists.

In this work we propose to exploit meta-data about the expected number of edges in KGs to better assess the quality of learned rules. To further facilitate this approach, we discuss a method for learning edge count information by extracting rules like *"If a person has more than 2 siblings, then his parents are likely to have more than 3 children."*

State of the art and its limitations. In [12] a completeness-aware rule scoring based on the partial completeness assumption (PCA) was introduced. The idea of PCA is that whenever at least one object for a given subject and a predicate is in a KG (e.g., *"Eduard is Einstein's child"*), then all objects for that subject-predicate pair (*Einstein's children*) are assumed to be known. This assumption was taken into account in rule scoring, and empirically it turned out to be indeed valid in real-world KGs for some topics. However, it does not universally hold, and treats cases inappropriately when edges in a graph are randomly missing. Similarly, whether to count absence of contradiction as confirmation for default rules was discussed in [8]. In [11] new completeness data was learned from a KG by taking as ground truth completeness data obtained via crowd-sourcing. The acquired statements were then used in a post-processing step of rule learning to filter out predictions that violate these statements. However, this kind of filtering does not have any impact on the quality of the mined rules and the incorrect predictions for instances about which no completeness information exists.

Contributions. This work presents the first proper investigation of how meta-information about (in-)completeness, more specifically, about the number of edges that should exist for a given subject-predicate pair in a KG, can be used to improve rule learning. The salient contributions of our work are as follows:

1. We present an approach that accounts for meta-data about the number of edges that should exist for given subject-predicate pairs in the ranking stage of rule learning.
2. We discuss a method for the automated acquisition of approximate upper and lower bounds on the number of edges that should exist in KGs.
3. We implement the proposed rule ranking measures and evaluate them both on real-world and synthetic dataset, showing that they outperform existing measures both with respect to the quality of the mined rules and the predictions they produce.[1]

2 Related Work

Rule learning. The problem of automatically learning patterns from KGs has gained a lot of attention in the recent years. Some relevant works are [12,28], which focus on learning Horn rules and either ignore completeness information, or make use of completeness by filtering out predicted facts violating completeness in a post-processing step. On the contrary we aim at injecting the statements into the learning process.

In the context of inductive and abductive logic programming, learning rules from incomplete interpretations given as a set of positive facts along with a possibly incomplete set of negative ones was studied, e.g., in [18]. In contrast to our approach, this work does not exploit knowledge about the number of missing facts, and neither do the works on terminology induction, e.g., [27]. Learning nonmonotonic rules in the presence of incompleteness was studied in hybrid settings [16,20], where a background theory or a hypothesis can be represented as a combination of an ontology and Horn or nonmonotonic rules. The main point in these works is the assumption that there might be potentially missing facts in a given dataset. However, it is not explicitly mentioned which parts of the data are (in)complete like in our setting. Moreover, the emphasis of these works is on the complex reasoning interaction between the components, while we are more concerned with techniques for deriving rules with high predictive quality from large KGs. Recent work by d'Amato et al. [4] shows how in the presence of ontologies that allow to determine incorrect facts, rules can be ranked by the ratio of correct versus incorrect predictions. In contrast to our scenario of interest, in this work, the knowledge about exact numbers of missing KG facts has not been exploited.

There are also a number of less relevant statistical approaches to completing knowledge graphs based on, e.g., low-dimensional embeddings [30] or tensor factorization [29].

---

[1] The extended version of this paper is available as a technical report at https://raw. githubusercontent.com/Tpt/CARL/master/technical_report.pdf.

Completeness information. The idea of bridging the open and closed world assumption by using completeness information was first introduced in the database world in [9,19], and later adapted to the Semantic Web in [5]. For describing such settings, the common approach is to fix the complete parts (and assume that the rest is potentially incomplete).

Recent work [11] has extended the rule mining system AMIE to mine rules about completeness, that predict in which parts a knowledge graph may be complete or incomplete. The focus of the work is on the learning of association rules like *"If someone has a date of birth but no place of birth, then the place of birth is missing."* In contrast, we reason about the missing edges trying to estimate the exact number (bounds on the number) of edges that should be present in a KG. In [11] it has also been shown that completeness information can be used to improve the accuracy of fact prediction, by pruning out in a post-processing step those facts that are predicted in parts expected to be complete. In the present paper, we take a more direct approach and inject completeness information already into the rule acquisition phase, in order to also prune away problematic rules, not only individual wrong predictions.

Our cardinality statements (e.g., John has 3 children) encode knowledge about parts of a KG that are (un)known, and thus should have points of contact with operators from epistemic logic; we leave the extended discussion on the matter for future work.

3   Preliminaries

Knowledge graphs. Knowledge graphs (KG) represent interlinked collections of factual information, and they are often encoded using the RDF data model [17]. The content of KGs is a set of ⟨*subject predicate object*⟩ triples, e.g., ⟨*john hasChild alice*⟩. For encyclopedic knowledge graphs on the semantic web, usually the open world assumption (OWA) is employed, i.e., these graphs contain only a subset of the true information.

In the following we take the unique name assumption, and for simplicity, write triples using binary predicates, like $hasChild(john, alice)$. A signature of a KG $\mathcal{G}$ is $\Sigma_{\mathcal{G}} = \langle \mathbf{R}, \mathcal{C} \rangle$, where $\mathbf{R}$ is the set of binary predicates and $\mathcal{C}$ is the set of constants appearing in $\mathcal{G}$. Following [5], we define the gap between the available graph $\mathcal{G}^a$ and the ideal graph $\mathcal{G}^i$, which contains all correct facts over $\mathbf{R}$ and $\mathcal{C}$ that hold in the real world.

Definition 1 (Incomplete data source). *An incomplete data source is a pair* $G = (\mathcal{G}^a, \mathcal{G}^i)$ *of two KGs, where* $\mathcal{G}^a \subseteq \mathcal{G}^i$ *and* $\Sigma_{\mathcal{G}^a} = \Sigma_{\mathcal{G}^i}$.

Note that the ideal graph $\mathcal{G}^i$ is an imaginary construct whose content is generally not known. What is known instead is to which extent the available graph approximates/lacks information wrt. the ideal graph, e.g., *"Einstein is missing 2 children and Feynman none"*. We formalize this knowledge as cardinality assertions in Sect. 4.

Rule learning. Association rule learning concerns the discovery of frequent patterns in a data set and the subsequent transformation of these patterns into rules. Association rules in the relational format have been subject of intensive research in ILP (see, e.g., [7] as the seminal work in this direction) and more recently in the KG community (see [12] as the most prominent work). In the following, we adapt basic notions in relational association rule mining to our case of interest.

A *conjunctive query* Q over $\mathcal{G}$ is of the form $Q(\boldsymbol{X}) :- p_1(\boldsymbol{X_1}), \dots, p_m(\boldsymbol{X_m})$. Its right-hand side (i.e., body) is a finite set of atomic formulas over $\Sigma_{\mathcal{G}}$, while the left-hand side (i.e., head) is a tuple of variables occurring in the body. The *answer* of Q on $\mathcal{G}$ is the set $Q(\mathcal{G}) = \{\nu(\boldsymbol{X}) \mid \nu$ is a function from variables to $\mathcal{C}$ and $\forall i : p_i(\nu(\boldsymbol{X_i})) \in \mathcal{G}\}$. As in [7], the *support* of Q in $\mathcal{G}$ is the number of distinct tuples in the answer of Q on $\mathcal{G}$.

An *association rule* is of the form $Q_1 \Rightarrow Q_2$, such that Q_1 and Q_2 are both conjunctive queries and $Q_1 \subseteq Q_2$, i.e., $Q_1(\mathcal{G}') \subseteq Q_2(\mathcal{G}')$ for any possible KG $\mathcal{G}'$. In this work we exploit association rules for reasoning purposes, and thus (with some abuse of notation) treat them as logical rules, i.e., for $Q_1 \Rightarrow Q_2$ we write $Q_2 \backslash Q_1 \leftarrow Q_1$, where $Q_2 \backslash Q_1$ refers to the set difference between Q_2 and Q_1 seen as sets of atoms.

Classical scoring of association rules is based on *rule support, body support* and *confidence*, which in [12] for a rule $r : \boldsymbol{H} \leftarrow \boldsymbol{B}$ with $\boldsymbol{H} = h(X, Y)$ are defined as:

$$supp(r) := \#(x, y) : \exists \boldsymbol{Z} : \boldsymbol{B} \wedge h(x, y) \tag{1}$$

$$supp(\boldsymbol{B}) := \#(x, y) : \exists \boldsymbol{Z} : \boldsymbol{B} \tag{2}$$

$$conf(r) := \frac{supp(r)}{supp(\boldsymbol{B})} \tag{3}$$

where $\#\alpha : \mathcal{A}$ denotes the number of α that fulfill the condition $\mathcal{A}$, and $conf(r) \in [0, 1]$. As in [12] we compute the support of the rule (body) w.r.t. to the head variables.

Example 1. Consider the KG in Fig. 1 and the rules r_1 and r_2 mined from it:

- $r_1 : hasChild(X, Y) \leftarrow worksAt(X, Z), educatedAt(Y, Z)$
- $r_2 : hasSibling(X, Z) \leftarrow hasFather(X, Y), hasChild(Y, Z)$

The body and rule supports of r_1 over the KG are $supp(\boldsymbol{B}) = 8$ and $supp(r_1) = 2$ respectively. Hence, we have $conf(r_1) = \frac{2}{8}$. Analogously, $conf(r_2) = \frac{1}{6}$. □

Support and confidence were originally developed for scoring rules over complete data. If data is missing, their interpretation is not straightforward and they can be misleading. In [12], *confidence under the Partial Completeness Assumption* (PCA) has been proposed as a measure, which guesses negative facts by assuming that data is usually added to KGs in batches, i.e., if at least one child of John is known then most probably all John's children are present in the KG. The *PCA confidence* is defined as

$$conf_{pca}(r) := \frac{supp(r)}{\#(x,y) : \exists \boldsymbol{Z} : \boldsymbol{B} \wedge \exists y' : h(x,y') \in \mathcal{G}^a} \tag{4}$$

Example 2. We obtain $conf_{pca}(r_1) = \frac{2}{4}$. Indeed, since *carol* and *dave* are not known to have any children in the KG, four existing body substitutions are not counted in the denominator. Meanwhile, we have $conf_{pca}(r_2) = \frac{1}{6}$, since all people that are predicted to have siblings by r_2 already have siblings in the available graph. □

Given a rule r and a KG $\mathcal{G}$ the application of r on $\mathcal{G}$ results in a rule-based graph completion defined relying on the Answer Set semantics (see [13] for details), which for positive programs coincides with the least model datalog semantics.

Definition 2 (Rule-based KG completion). *Let $\mathcal{G}$ be a KG over the signature $\Sigma_{\mathcal{G}} = \langle \mathbf{R}, \mathcal{C} \rangle$ and let r be a rule mined from $\mathcal{G}$, i.e. a rule over $\Sigma_{\mathcal{G}}$. Then the completion of $\mathcal{G}$ is a graph $\mathcal{G}_r$ constructed from the answer set of $r \cup \mathcal{G}$.*

Example 3. We have $\mathcal{G}^a_{r_1} = \mathcal{G} \cup \{hasChild(john, dave), hasChild(carol, mary), hasChild(dave, dave), hasChild(carol, carol), hasChild(dave, bob), hasChild(mary, dave)\}$. □

Note that $\mathcal{G}^i$ is the perfect completion of $\mathcal{G}^a$, i.e., it is supposed to contain all correct facts with entities and relations from $\Sigma_{\mathcal{G}^a}$ that hold in the current state of the world. The goal of rule-based KG completion is to extract from $\mathcal{G}^a$ a set of rules $\mathcal{R}$ such that $\cup_{r \in \mathcal{R}} \mathcal{G}^a_r$ is as close to $\mathcal{G}^i$ as possible.

4   Completeness-Aware Rule Scoring

Scoring and ranking rules are core steps in association rule learning. A variety of measures for ranking rules have been proposed, with prominent ones being confidence, conviction and lift. The existing (in-)completeness-aware rule measure in the KG context (the PCA confidence (4)) has two apparent shortcomings: First, it only counts as counterexamples those pairs (x, y) for which at least one $h(x, y')$ is in $\mathcal{G}^a$ for some y' and a rule's head predicate h. Thus, it may incorrectly give high scores to rules predicting facts for very incomplete relations, e.g., *place of baptism*. Second, it is not suited for data in non-functional relations that is not added in batches, such as awards, where the important ones are added instantly, while others much slower or even possibly never.

Thus, in this work we focus on the improvements of rule scoring functions by making use of the extra (in-)completeness meta-data. Before dwelling into the details of our approach we discuss the formal representation of such meta-data.

Cardinality statements. Overall, one can think of 6 different cardinality templates obtained by fixing subject, predicate or object in a triple and report the number of respective facts that hold in $\mathcal{G}^i$. E.g., for $\langle john\ hasChild\ mary \rangle$ we can count (1) children of $john$; (2) edges from $john$ to $mary$; (3) incoming edges to $mary$; (4) facts with $john$ as a subject; (5) facts over $hasChild$ relation; (6) facts with $mary$ as an object.

In practice, numerical statements for templates (1) and (3) can be obtained using web extraction techniques [23], from functional properties of relations or from crowd-sourcing. For other templates things get trickier; one might be able to learn them from the data or they could be defined by domain experts in topic-specific KGs. We leave this issue for future work, and focus here only on templates (1) and (3), which could be rewritten as the instances of the template (1) provided that inverse relations can be expressed in a KG. For instance, $\#s : hasChild(s, john) = \#o : hasParent(john, o)$ for the predicates $hasChild$ and $hasParent$, which are inverses of one another.

We represent the (in)completeness meta-data using cardinality statements by reporting (the numerical restriction on) the absolute number of facts over a certain relation in the ideal graph $\mathcal{G}^i$. More specifically, we define the partial function num that takes as input a predicate p and a constant s and outputs a natural number corresponding to the number of facts in $\mathcal{G}^i$ over p with s as the first argument:

$$num(p, s) := \#o : p(s, o) \in \mathcal{G}^i \tag{5}$$

Naturally, the number of missing facts for a given p and s can be obtained as

$$miss(p, s) := num(p, s) - \#o : p(s, o) \in \mathcal{G}^a \tag{6}$$

Example 4. Consider the KG in Fig. 1. and the following cardinality statements for it:

- $num(hasChild, john) = num(hasChild, mary) = 3$; $num(hasChild, alice) = 1$; $num(hasChild, carol) = num(hasChild, dave) = 0$;
- $num(hasSibling, bob) = 3$; $num(hasSibling, alice) = num(hasSibling, carol) = num(hasSibling, dave) = 2$.

We then have:

- $miss(hasChild, mary) = miss(hasChild, john) = miss(hasChild, alice) = 1$; $miss(hasChild, carol) = miss(hasChild, dave) = 0$;
- $miss(hasSibling, bob) = miss(hasSibling, carol) = 2$; $miss(hasSibling, alice) = miss(hasSibling, dave) = 1$. □

We are now ready to define the *completeness-aware rule scoring problem.* Given a KG and a set of cardinality statements, *completeness-aware rule scoring* aims to score rules not only by their predictive power on the known KG, but also wrt. the number of wrongly predicted facts in complete areas and the number of newly predicted facts in known incomplete areas.

In the following we discuss and compare three novel approachses for completeness-aware rule scoring. These are (i) the *completeness confidence*, (ii) *completeness precision* and *recall*, and (iii) *directional metric*. Henceforth, all examples consider the KG in Fig. 1, rules from Example 1, and cardinality statements described in Example 4.

4.1   Completeness Confidence

In this work we propose to explicitly rely on incompleteness information in determining whether to consider an instance as a counterexample for a rule at hand or not.

To do that, we first define two indicators for a given rule $r : h(X, Y) \leftarrow B$, reflecting the number of new predictions made by r in incomplete ($npi(r)$) and, respectively, complete ($npc(r)$) KG parts:

$$npi(r) := \sum_x min(\#y : h(x, y) \in \mathcal{G}_r^a \backslash \mathcal{G}^a, miss(h, x)) \quad (7)$$

$$npc(r) := \sum_x max(\#y : h(x, y) \in \mathcal{G}_r^a \backslash \mathcal{G}^a - miss(h, x), 0) \quad (8)$$

Note that summation is done exactly over those entities for which *miss* is defined. Exploiting these additional indicators for $r : h(X, Y) \leftarrow B$ we obtain the following *completeness-aware confidence*:

$$conf_{comp}(r) := \frac{supp(r)}{supp(B) - npi(r)} \quad (9)$$

Example 5. Obviously, the rule r_2 should be preferred over r_1. For our novel completeness confidence, we get $conf_{comp}(r_1) = \frac{2}{6}$ and $conf_{comp}(r_2) = \frac{1}{2}$, resulting in the desired rule ordering, which is not achieved by existing measures (see Examples 1 and 2). □

Our completeness confidence generalizes both the standard and the PCA confidence:

Proposition 1. *For every KG $\mathcal{G}$ and rule r it holds that*

(i) under the Closed World Assumption (CWA) $conf_{comp}(r) = conf(r)$;
(ii) under the Partial Completeness Assumption (PCA) $conf_{comp}(r) = conf_{pca}(r)$.

In other words, if the graph is known to be fully complete, i.e., for all $p \in \mathbf{R}, s \in \mathcal{C}$ we have $miss(p, s) = 0$, then $conf_{comp}$ is the same as the standard confidence. Similarly, if $miss(p, s) = 0$ for such p, s pairs that at least one fact $p(s, \_) \in \mathcal{G}^a$ exists and $miss(p, s) = +\infty$ for the rest, then $conf_{comp}$ is the same as the PCA confidence.

4.2   Completeness Precision and Recall

Further developing the idea of scoring rules based on their predictions in complete and incomplete KG parts, we propose to consider the notions of *completeness precision* and *recall*[2] for rules defined in the spirit of information retrieval. Intuitively, rules having high precision are rules that predict few facts in complete parts, while rules having high recall are rules that predict many facts in incomplete ones. Rule scoring could then be based on any weighted combination of these two metrics.

Formally, we define the precision and recall of a rule $r : h(X, Y) \leftarrow \boldsymbol{B}$ as follows:

$$precision_{comp}(r) = 1 - \frac{npc(r)}{supp(\boldsymbol{B})} \tag{10}$$

$$recall_{comp}(r) = \frac{npi(r)}{\sum_s miss(h, s)} \tag{11}$$

The *recall measure* is similar to classical support measures, but now expresses how many facts on KG parts known to be incomplete, are generated by the rule (the more the better). The *precision measure*, in turn, assesses how many of the generated facts are definitely wrong, namely those in complete parts (the more of these, the worse the rule). In fact, this is an upper bound on the precision, as the other facts cannot be evaluated.

Example 6. It holds that $npi(r_1) = 2$, $npc(r_1) = 4$, while $npi(r_2) = 4$, $npc(r_2) = 1$, resulting in $precision_{comp}(r_1) = 0.5$, $recall_{comp}(r_1) \approx 0.67$, and $precision_{comp}(r_2) \approx 0.83$, $recall_{comp}(r_2) \approx 0.67$, which lead to the expected relative rule ordering.   □

Limitations. While precision and recall are insightful when there are sufficiently many predictions made in (in-)complete parts, they fail when the number of (in-)completeness statements in comparison with the KG size is small. Consider, for instance, a rule that predicts 1000 new facts over *hasChild* relation, out of which 2 are in complete, and 2 are in incomplete parts, and overall 1 million children are missing. This would imply a precision of 99.8%, and a recall of 0.0002%, both of which are not very informative.

Therefore, next we propose to look at the difference between expected numbers of predictions in complete and incomplete parts, or simply at their ratio.

4.3   Directional Bias

If rule mining does make use of completeness information, and both do not exhibit any statistical bias, then intuitively the rule predictions and the (in)complete areas should be statistically independent. On the other hand, correlation between the two indicates that the rule-mining is *(in)completeness-aware*.

---

[2] For brevity we skip the word "completeness" if clear from the context.

Example 7. Suppose in total a given KG stores 1 million humans, and we know that 10,000 (1%) of these are missing some children (incompleteness information), while we also know that 1000 of the persons are definitely complete for children (0.1%). Let the set of rules mined from a KG predict 50,000 new facts for the *hasChild* relation. Assuming independence between predictions and (in)completeness statements, we would expect 1% out of 50,000, i.e., 500 facts to be predicted in the incomplete areas and 0.1%, i.e., 50 in the complete KG parts. If instead we find 1000 children predicted for people that are missing correspondingly many children, and 10 for people that are not missing these, the former deviates from the expected value by a factor of 2, and the latter by a factor of 5.

Following the intuition from the above example, we propose to look at the extent of the non-independence to quantify the (in)completeness-awareness of rule mining. Let us consider predictions made by rules in a given KG, where $E(\#facts)$ is the expected number of predictions and $\alpha = 0..1$ is the weight given to completeness versus incompleteness. Then the directional coefficient of a rule r is defined as follows:

$$direct\_coef(r) := \alpha \cdot \frac{E(npc(r))}{npc(r)} + (1 - \alpha) \cdot \frac{npi(r)}{E(npi(r))} \qquad (12)$$

Unlike the other measures that range from 0 to 1, the directional coefficient takes values between 0 and infinity, where 1 is the default. If the ratio between the KG size and the size of the (in)complete parts is the same as the ratio between the predictions in the (in)complete parts and their total number, i.e., if the directional coefficient is 1, then the statements do not influence the rule at all. The higher is the *directional coefficient*, the more "*completeness-aware*" the rules are.

In practice, expected values might be difficult to compute, and statistical independence is a strong assumption. An alternative that does not require knowledge about expected values is to directly measure the proportion between predictions in complete and incomplete parts. We call this the *directional metric*, which is computed as

$$direct\_metric(r) := \frac{npi(r) - npc(r)}{2 \cdot (npi(r) + npc(r))} + 0.5 \qquad (13)$$

The metric is based on the same ideas as the directional coefficient, but does not require knowledge about the expected number of predictions in complete/incomplete KG parts. It is designed to range between 0 and 1 again, thus allowing convenient weighting with other $[0, 1]$ measures. The directional metric of a rule that predicts the same number of facts in incomplete as in complete parts is 0.5, a rule that predicts twice as many facts in incomplete parts has a value of 0.66, and so on.

Since the real-world KGs are often highly incomplete, it might be reasonable to put more weight on predictions in complete parts. This can be done by multiplying predictions made in complete parts by a certain factor. We propose to consider the combination of a weighted existing association rule measure, e.g., confidence or conviction and the directional metric, with the weighting factor $\beta = 0..1$. Using confidence, we obtain

$$weighted\_dm(r) = \beta \cdot conf(r) + (1 - \beta) \cdot direct\_metric(r) \qquad (14)$$

Example 8. We get $direct\_metric(r_1) \approx 0.33$ and $direct\_metric(r_2) = 0.8$. For $\beta' = 0.5$ and confidence from Example 1, $weighted\_dm(r_1) \approx 0.29$ and $weighted\_dm(r_2) \approx 0.48$.   □

5   Acquisition of Numerical Statements

As we have shown, exploitation of numerical (in-)completeness statements is very beneficial for rule quality assessment. A natural question is where to acquire such statements from in real-world settings. Various works have shown that numerical assertions can be frequently found on the Web [5], obtained via crowd-sourcing [6], text mining [22] or completeness rule mining [11]. We believe that mining numerical correlations concerning KG edges and then assembling them into rules is a valuable and a modular approach to obtain further completeness information, which we sketch in what follows.

We start with an available KG $\mathcal{G}^a$ and some statements of the form (5).

Step 1. For every cardinality $num(p, s) = k$, we create the facts $p_{\leq k}(s)$ and $p_{\geq k}(s)$. For the pairs $p \in \mathbf{R}, s \in \mathcal{C}$ with no available cardinality statements we construct the facts $p_{\geq \#o:p(s,o) \in \mathcal{G}^a}(s)$, encoding that outgoing p-edges from s might be missing in $\mathcal{G}^a$, as the graph is believed to be incomplete by default. Here, p_{card} with $card \in \{\leq \_, \geq \_\}$ are fresh unary predicates not present in $\Sigma_{\mathcal{G}^a}$, which describe (bounds on) the number of outgoing p-edges for a given constant. We store all constructed facts over p_{card} in $\mathcal{S}$.

We then complete the domain of each p_{card} predicate as follows. For every $p_{\leq k}(s) \in \mathcal{S}$, if $p_{\leq k'}(s') \in \mathcal{S}$ for some $s' \in \mathcal{C}$ and $k' > k$, we construct the rule $p_{\leq k'}(X) \leftarrow p_{\leq k}(X)$. Similarly, for every $p_{\geq k}(s) \in \mathcal{S}$, if $p_{\geq k'}(s') \in \mathcal{S}$ where $k' < k$, we create $p_{\geq k'}(X) \leftarrow p_{\geq k}(X)$. The constructed rules are then applied to the facts in $\mathcal{S}$ to obtain an extended set $\mathcal{G}^{card}$ of facts over p_{card}. The latter step is crucial when using a rule mining system that is not doing arithmetic inferences (like $x > 4$ implies $x > 3$).

Step 2. We then use such a standard rule learning system, AMIE [12], on $\mathcal{G}^a \cup \mathcal{G}^{card}$ to mine rules like:

(1) $p_{card}(X) \leftarrow p'_{card}(X)$
(2) $p_{card}(X) \leftarrow p'_{card}(X), p''_{card}(X)$
(3) $p_{card}(X) \leftarrow p'_{card}(X), r(X, Y)$
(4) $p_{card}(X) \leftarrow p'_{card}(X), r(X, Y), p''_{card}(Y)$
(5) $p_{card}(X) \leftarrow r(X, Y), p''_{card}(Y)$

We rank the obtained rules based on confidence and select the top ones into the set $\mathcal{R}$.

Step 3. Finally, in the last step we use the obtained ruleset $\mathcal{R}$ to derive further numerical statements together with weights assigned to them. For that we compute $\mathcal{G}' = \bigcup_{r \in \mathcal{R}} \{\mathcal{G}^{card} \cup \mathcal{G}^a\}_r$. The weights of the statements are inherited from the rules that derived them. We then employ two simple heuristics: (i) Given multiple rules predicting the same fact, the highest weight for it is kept. We then post-process predictions made by different rules for the same subject-predicate pair as follows. (ii) If $p_{\leq k}(s), p_{\geq k'}(s) \in \mathcal{G}'$ for $k' > k$, we remove from $\mathcal{G}'$ predictions with the lowest weight thus resolving the conflict on the numerical bounds.

From the obtained graph we reconstruct cardinality statements as follows.

- Given $p_{\leq k}(s), p_{\geq k}(s) \in \mathcal{G}'$ with weights w and w' we create a cardinality statement $num(p, s) = k$ with the weight $min(w, w')$.
- If $p_{\leq k}(s), p_{\geq k'}(s) \in \mathcal{G}'$ for $k' < k$, then we set $k' \leq num(p, s) \leq k$.
- Among two facts $p_{\leq k}(s), p_{\leq k'}(s)$ (resp. $p_{\geq k}(s), p_{\geq k'}(s)$) with $k < k'$ (resp. $k > k'$) the first ones are kept and represented similar to 5.

Regular facts in $\mathcal{G}'$ are similarly translated into their numerical representations.

Example 9. Consider the KG in Fig. 1 and the following cardinality statements for it: $num(hasChild, john) = num(hasSibling, bob) = 3$. Among others, $\mathcal{G}^{card}$ contains the facts: $hasChild_{\geq 3}(john), hasSibling_{\geq 3}(bob), hasChild_{\geq 2}(mary),$ $hasChild_{\geq 2}(john), hasSibling_{\geq 2}(bob), hasSibling_{\geq 1}(dave),$ and $hasSibling_{\geq 1}$ (*alice*). On the graph $\mathcal{G}^a \cup \mathcal{G}^{card}$, the confidence of $hasSibling_{\geq 2}(X) \leftarrow$ $hasFather(X, Y), hasChild_{\geq 3}(Y)$ is $\frac{1}{3}$ and 1 for $hasSibling_{\geq 1}(X) \leftarrow hasFather$ $(X, Y), hasChild_{\geq 3}(Y)$. □

Ideally, provided that sufficiently many similar numerical correlations about edge numbers are extracted, one can induce more general hypothesis involving arithmetic functions like the number of person's siblings is bounded by the number of his parents' children plus 1 or the sum of person's brothers and sisters equals the number of his siblings. We leave these more complex generalizations for future work. Similarly, the employed heuristics provide potential for more advanced voting/weighting schemes and inconsistency resolution in the case of conflicting cardinality assertions.

6   Evaluation

6.1   Completeness-Aware Rule Learning

We have implemented our completeness-aware rule learning approach into a C++ system prototype CARL[3], following a standard relational learning

---

[3] The source code and all the data are available at https://github.com/Tpt/CARL.

algorithm implementation such as [14]. While our general methodology can be applied to mining rules of arbitrary form, in the evaluation we focus only on rules of the form

$$r(X, Z) \leftarrow p(X, Y), q(Y, Z) \tag{15}$$

We aim at comparing the predictive quality of the top k rules mined by our completeness-aware approach with the ones learned by standard rule learning methods: (1) AMIE [12] (PCA confidence) and (2) WarmeR [14] (standard confidence).

Dataset. We used two datasets for the evaluation: (i) *WikidataPeople*, which is a dataset we have created from the Wikidata knowledge graph, containing 2.4M facts over 9 predicates[4] about biographical information and family relationships of people; and (ii) *LUBM*, which is a synthetic dataset describing the structure of a university [15].

For the WikidataPeople dataset, the approximation of the ideal KG ($\mathcal{G}^i$) is obtained by exploiting available information about inverse relations (e.g., *hasParent* is the inverse of *hasChild*), functional relations (e.g., *hasFather, hasMother*) as well as manually hand-crafted solid rules from the family domain like[5]

$$hasSibling(X, Y) \leftarrow hasParent(X, Z), hasParent(Y, Z), X \neq Y.$$

From WikidataPeople $\mathcal{G}^i$ containing 5M facts, we acquired cardinality statements by exploiting properties of functional relations, e.g., *hasBirthPlace*, *hasFather*, *hasMother* must be uniquely defined, and everybody with a *hasDeathDate* has a *hasDeathPlace*. For the other relations, the PCA [12] is used. This resulted in 10M cardinality statements.

LUBM $\mathcal{G}^i$, with 1.2M facts, was constructed by running the LUBM data generator for 10 universities, removing all `rdf:type` triples and introducing inverse predicates. 464K cardinality statements were obtained by counting the number of existing objects for each subject-predicate pair, i.e., assuming the PCA on the whole dataset.

Experimental setup. To assess the effect of our proposed measures, we first construct versions of the available KG ($\mathcal{G}^a$) by removing parts of the data from $\mathcal{G}^i$ and introducing a synthetic bias in the data (i.e., leaving many facts in $\mathcal{G}^a$ for some relations and few for others). The synthetic bias is needed to simulate our scenario of interest, where some parts of $\mathcal{G}^a$ are very incomplete while others are fairly complete, which is indeed the case in real world KGs. In Wikidata, for instance, only for 3% of non-living people sibling information is reported, while children data is known for 4%.

We proceed in two steps: First, we define a *global ratio*, which determines a uniform percentage of data retained in the available graph. To further refine this, we then factor a *predicate ratio* individually for each predicate.

---

[4] *hasFather, hasMother, hasStepParent, hasSibling, hasSpouse, hasChild, hasBirthPlace, hasDeathPlace*, and *hasNationality*.

[5] See https://github.com/Tpt/CARL/tree/master/eval/wikidata for details.

For the WikidataPeople KG, this ratio is chosen as *(i)* 0.8 for *hasFather* and *hasMother*; *(ii)* 0.5 for *hasSpouse*, *hasStepParent*, *hasBirthPlace*, *hasDeathPlace* and *hasNationality*; *(iii)* 0.2 for *hasChild*; and *(iv)* 0.1 for *hasSibling*. For the LUBM dataset, the predicate ratio is uniformly defined as 1 for regular predicates and 0.5 for inverse predicates.

For a given predicate, the final ratio of facts in $\mathcal{G}^a$ retained from those in $\mathcal{G}^i$ is then computed as $min(1, 2 * k * n)$, where k is the predicate ratio and n is the global ratio.

The assessment of the rules learned from different versions of the available KG is performed by comparing rule predictions with the approximation of $\mathcal{G}^i$. More specifically, every learned rule is assigned a *quality score*, defined as the ratio of the number of predictions made by the rule in $\mathcal{G}^i \setminus \mathcal{G}^a$ over the number of all predictions outside $\mathcal{G}^a$.

$$quality\_score(r) = \frac{|\mathcal{G}^a_r \cap \mathcal{G}^i \setminus \mathcal{G}^a|}{|\mathcal{G}^a_r \setminus \mathcal{G}^a|} \qquad (16)$$

This scoring naturally allows us to control the percentage of rule predictions that hit our approximation of $\mathcal{G}^i$, similar to standard recall estimation in machine learning.

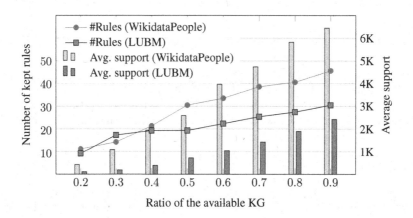

Fig. 2. Number of kept rules (#Rules) and their average support for WikidataPeople and LUBM datasets

Results. From every version of the available KG we have mined rules of the form (15) and kept only rules r with $conf(r) \geq 0.001$ and $supp(r) \geq 10$, whose *head coverage*[6] is greater than 0.001. Figure 2 shows the number of kept rules and their average support (1) for each global ratio used for generating $\mathcal{G}^a$.

---

[6] *Head coverage* is the ratio of the number of predicted facts that are in $\mathcal{G}^a$ over the number of facts matching the rule head.

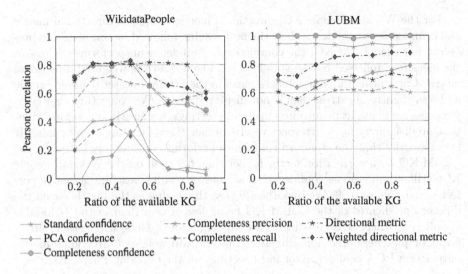

Fig. 3. Evaluation results for WikidataPeople and LUBM datasets

Evaluation results for WikidataPeople and LUBM datasets are in Fig. 3. The horizontal axis displays the global ratio used for generating $\mathcal{G}^a$. We compared different rule ranking methods as previously discussed, including standard confidence (3), PCA confidence (4), completeness confidence (9), completeness precision (10), completeness recall (11), directional metric (13) and weighted directional metric ($\beta = 0.5$) (14). The Pearson correlation factor[7] (vertical axis) between each ranking measure and the rules quality score (16) is used to evaluate the measures' effectiveness. We measured the Pearson correlation, as apart from the ranking order (captured by, e.g., the Spearman's rank correlation), the absolute values of the measures are also insightful for our setting.

Since facts are randomly missing in the considered versions of $\mathcal{G}^a$, the PCA confidence performs worse than the standard confidence for given datasets, while our completeness confidence significantly outperforms both (see Table 1 for examples).

Table 1. Example of rules mined from WikidataPeople with global ratio of 0.5

Rule r	$conf(r)$	$conf_{pca}(r)$	$conf_{comp}(r)$	$dir\_metric(r)$
$hasSibling(X, Z) \leftarrow hasSibling(X, Y),$ $hasSibling(Y, Z)$	0.10	0.10	0.89	0.98
$hasStepParent(X, Z) \leftarrow hasMother(X, Y),$ $hasSpouse(Y, Z)$	0.0015	0.48	0.0015	0.38

---

[7] The Pearson correlation factor between two variables X and Y is defined by $\rho_{X,Y} = \frac{cov(X,Y)}{\sigma_X \sigma_Y}$ with cov being the covariance and σ the standard deviation.

For the WikidataPeople KG, directional metric, weighted directional metric and completeness confidence show the best results, followed by completeness precision. For the LUBM KG, the completeness confidence outperforms the rest of the measures, followed by the standard confidence and the weighted directional metric. Correlation for completeness recall in the LUBM dataset behaved erratic and was slightly negative, thus is not displayed at all. We conjecture that completeness recall might be unsuited in certain settings, because it may reward rules that predict many facts, irrespective of whether these facts are true or false. It is noteworthy that the standard confidence performs considerably better on the LUBM KG with correlation factor higher than 0.9 than on the WikidataPeople KG. Still, completeness confidence shows better results, reaching a nearly perfect correlation of 0.99. We hypothesize that this is due to the bias between the different predicates of the LUBM KG being less strong than in the WikidataPeople KG, where some predicates are missing a lot of facts, while others just a few. Completeness precision, directional metric and weighted directional metric outperform PCA confidence for most settings on the WikidataPeople KG.

6.2 Automated Acquisition of Cardinality Statements

To evaluate our method for automated acquisition of cardinality statements from a KG we reused the WikidataPeople dataset–without completing the data.

Dataset. We have collected around 282K cardinality statements from various sources:

- Wikidata schema, i.e., *hasFather*, *hasMother*, *hasBirthPlace*, and *hasDeathPlace* are functional properties and, thus, should have at most one value.
- The 7.5K values of the Wikidata predicate *numberOfChildren*;
- 663 *novalue* statements from Wikidata;
- 86K cardinality statements from [23] for the *hasChild* predicate of Wikidata;
- 182K cardinality statements are extracted from human-curated and complete Freebase facts (1.6M). The mapping to Wikidata has been done using tools from [25].

Experimental setup. We set aside random 20% of the cardinality statements as validation set, while the rest were incorporated into the WikidataPeople KG, as explained in Sect. 5. We then ran our rule learning algorithm to mine cardinality rules. Rules with support less than 200 or confidence smaller than 0.01 were pruned out. Examples of mined rules along with their standard confidences include

- $hasSibling_{\geq 3}(x) \leftarrow hasSibling(x, y), hasSibling_{\geq 4}(y)$: 0.97
- $hasChild_{\geq 3}(x) \leftarrow hasFather(y, x), hasSibling(y)_{\geq 4}(y)$: 0.90.

The learned rules were then applied to the enriched WikidataPeople KG to retrieve new exact cardinalities $num(p, s)$ by only keeping (p, s) pairs where the higher and lower bounds matched. The minimum of the standard confidence of the best rules used to get the upper and lower bounds were assigned as the final confidence of each $num(p, s)$.

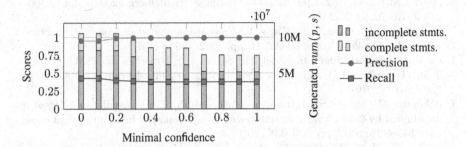

Fig. 4. Number of (in-)complete statements for generated cardinalities $num(p, s)$, and quality of predicted cardinalities.

Results. We aim to evaluate whether we can accurately recover the cardinality statements in the validation set–as the gold standard–by utilizing the learned cardinality rules. For different minimal confidence thresholds, the quality of the predicted cardinalities is measured with standard precision and recall, which is presented in Fig. 4. We get a nearly perfect precision and a fair recall (around 40%) for the generated cardinalities, which amount to 7.5M-10M depending on the threshold. Around one third of $num(p, s)$ statements indicate completeness of the KG for given (p, s) pairs. If we remove the schema information from the KG, we get lower precision (around 70%) and recall (around 1%) before a minimal confidence of 0.6, and similar values after.

7 Conclusion and Future Work

We have defined the problem of learning rules from incomplete KGs enriched with the exact numbers of missing edges of certain types, and proposed three novel rule ranking measures that effectively make use of the meta-knowledge about complete and incomplete KG parts: *completeness confidence, precision/recall* and the (weighted) *directional metric*. Our measures have been injected in the rule learning prototype CARL and evaluated on real-world and synthetic KGs, demonstrating significant improvements both w.r.t. the quality of mined rules and predictions they produce. Moreover, we have proposed a method for acquiring cardinality meta-data about edge counts from KGs.

For future work, we plan to encode the cardinality information into background knowledge, e.g., using qualified role restrictions in OWL ontologies and exploit it to get rid of faulty rules that introduce inconsistencies. Another interesting further direction is to learn general correlations about edge counts that include mathematical functions, e.g., the number of siblings should be equal to the sum of the number of sisters and brothers.

References

1. Auer, S., Bizer, C., Kobilarov, G., Lehmann, J., Cyganiak, R., Ives, Z.: DBpedia: a nucleus for a web of open data. In: Aberer, K., et al. (eds.) ASWC/ISWC - 2007. LNCS, vol. 4825, pp. 722–735. Springer, Heidelberg (2007). doi:10.1007/978-3-540-76298-0_52

2. Bollacker, K.D., Cook, R.P., Tufts, P.: Freebase: a shared database of structured general human knowledge. In: AAAI, pp. 1962–1963 (2007)

3. Carlson, A., Betteridge, J., Kisiel, B., Settles, B., Hruschka Jr., E.R., Mitchell, T.M.: Toward an architecture for never-ending language learning. In: AAAI, pp. 2302–2310 (2010)

4. d'Amato, C., Staab, S., Tettamanzi, A.G., Minh, T.D., Gandon, F.: Ontology enrichment by discovering multi-relational association rules from ontological knowledge bases. In: SAC, pp. 333–338 (2016)

5. Darari, F., Nutt, W., Pirrò, G., Razniewski, S.: Completeness statements about RDF data sources and their use for query answering. In: Alani, H., et al. (eds.) ISWC 2013. LNCS, vol. 8218, pp. 66–83. Springer, Heidelberg (2013). doi:10.1007/978-3-642-41335-3_5

6. Darari, F., Razniewski, S., Prasojo, R.E., Nutt, W.: Enabling fine-grained RDF data completeness assessment. In: Bozzon, A., Cudre-Maroux, P., Pautasso, C. (eds.) ICWE 2016. LNCS, vol. 9671, pp. 170–187. Springer, Cham (2016). doi:10.1007/978-3-319-38791-8_10

7. Dehaspe, L., De Raedt, L.: Mining association rules in multiple relations. In: Lavrač, N., Džeroski, S. (eds.) ILP 1997. LNCS, vol. 1297, pp. 125–132. Springer, Heidelberg (1997). doi:10.1007/3540635149_40

8. Doppa, J.R., Sorower, S., NasrEsfahani, M., Orr, J.W., Dietterich, T.G., Fern, X., Tadepalli, P., Irvine, J.: Learning rules from incomplete examples via implicit mention models. In: ACML, pp. 197–212 (2011)

9. Etzioni, O., Golden, K., Weld, D.S.: Sound and efficient closed-world reasoning for planning. AI **89**(1–2), 113–148 (1997)

10. Gad-Elrab, M.H., Stepanova, D., Urbani, J., Weikum, G.: Exception-enriched rule learning from knowledge graphs. In: Groth, P., Simperl, E., Gray, A., Sabou, M., Krötzsch, M., Lecue, F., Flöck, F., Gil, Y. (eds.) ISWC 2016. LNCS, vol. 9981, pp. 234–251. Springer, Cham (2016). doi:10.1007/978-3-319-46523-4_15

11. Galárraga, L., Razniewski, S., Amarilli, A., Suchanek, F.M.: Predicting completeness in knowledge bases. In: WSDM, pp. 375–383 (2017)

12. Galárraga, L., Teflioudi, C., Hose, K., Suchanek, F.M.: Fast rule mining in ontological knowledge bases with AMIE+. VLDB **24**, 707–730 (2015)

13. Gelfond, M., Lifschitz, V.: The stable model semantics for logic programming. In: Proceedings of ICLP/SLP, pp. 1070–1080 (1988)

14. Goethals, B., Van den Bussche, J.: Relational association rules: getting WARMER. In: Hand, D.J., Adams, N.M., Bolton, R.J. (eds.) Pattern Detection and Discovery. LNCS, vol. 2447, pp. 125–139. Springer, Heidelberg (2002). doi:10.1007/3-540-45728-3_10

15. Guo, Y., Pan, Z., Heflin, J.: LUBM: a benchmark for owl knowledge base systems. Web Semant. Sci. Serv. World Wide Web **3**(2–3), 158–182 (2011)

16. Józefowska, J., Lawrynowicz, A., Lukaszewski, T.: The role of semantics in mining frequent patterns from knowledge bases in description logics with rules. TPLP **10**(3), 251–289 (2010)

17. Lassila, O., Swick, R.R.: Resource description framework (RDF) model and syntax specification (1999)
18. Law, M., Russo, A., Broda, K.: Inductive learning of answer set programs. In: Fermé, E., Leite, J. (eds.) JELIA 2014. LNCS, vol. 8761, pp. 311–325. Springer, Cham (2014). doi:10.1007/978-3-319-11558-0_22
19. Levy, A.Y.: Obtaining complete answers from incomplete databases. VLDB **96**, 402–412 (1996)
20. Lisi, F.A.: Inductive logic programming in databases: from Datalog to DL+log. TPLP **10**(3), 331–359 (2010)
21. Mahdisoltani, F., Biega, J., Suchanek, F.M.: YAGO3: a knowledge base from multilingual Wikipedias. In: CIDR (2015)
22. Mirza, P., Razniewski, S., Darari, F., Weikum, G.: Cardinal virtues: extracting relation cardinalities from text. ACL (2017)
23. Mirza, P., Razniewski, S., Nutt, W.: Expanding Wikidata's parenthood information by 178%, or how to mine relation cardinality information. In: ISWC 2016 Posters & Demos (2016)
24. Paulheim, H.: Knowledge graph refinement: a survey of approaches and evaluation methods. Semant. Web **8**(3), 489–508 (2017)
25. Pellissier Tanon, T., Vrandečić, D., Schaffert, S., Steiner, T., Pintscher, L.: From Freebase to Wikidata: the great migration. In: Proceedings of WWW, pp. 1419–1428 (2016)
26. Prasojo, R.E., Darari, F., Razniewski, S., Nutt, W.: Managing and consuming completeness information for Wikidata using COOL-WD. In: COLD@ISWC (2016)
27. Sazonau, V., Sattler, U., Brown, G.: General terminology induction in OWL. In: ISWC, pp. 533–550 (2015)
28. Wang, Z., Li, J.: RDF2Rules: learning rules from RDF knowledge bases by mining frequent predicate cycles. CoRR abs/1512.07734 (2015)
29. Nickel, M., Tresp, V., Kriegel, H.P.: Factorizing YAGO: scalable machine learning for linked data. In: WWW, pp. 271–280 (2012)
30. Wang, Z., et al.: Knowledge graph embedding by translating on hyperplanes. In: AAAI, pp. 1112–1119 (2014)

Entity Comparison in RDF Graphs

Alina Petrova[(✉)], Evgeny Sherkhonov, Bernardo Cuenca Grau,
and Ian Horrocks

University of Oxford, Oxford, UK
alina.petrova@cs.ox.ac.uk

Abstract. In many applications, there is an increasing need for the new types of RDF data analysis that are not covered by standard reasoning tasks such as SPARQL query answering. One such important analysis task is entity comparison, i.e., determining what are similarities and differences between two given entities in an RDF graph. For instance, in an RDF graph about drugs, we may want to compare Metamizole and Ibuprofen and automatically find out that they are similar in that they are both analgesics but, in contrast to Metamizole, Ibuprofen also has a considerable anti-inflammatory effect. Entity comparison is a widely used functionality available in many information systems, such as universities or product comparison websites. However, comparison is typically domain-specific and depends on a fixed set of aspects to compare. In this paper, we propose a formal framework for domain-independent entity comparison over RDF graphs. We model similarities and differences between entities as SPARQL queries satisfying certain additional properties, and propose algorithms for computing them.

1 Introduction

The Resource Description Framework (RDF) is the standard format for representing and integrating information on the Web. The canonical reasoning task over RDF data exploited in applications is query answering, where SPARQL is the standard query language developed for that purpose [10]. There is, however, an increasing need in many applications for non-standard analysis tasks that do not directly correspond to SPARQL query answering. One such important task is *entity comparison*—that is, to determine what are the similarities and differences between the information about two given entities in an RDF graph.

Let us consider two example use cases. In the first one, a startup company is developing a toolkit for analysing widely-used biomedical RDF repositories, such as Bio2RDF [5]. The tool being developed should provide a drug comparison functionality; in particular, when given two drugs described in an RDF graph from the repository, such as Ibuprofen and Metamizole, the tool should be able to automatically report that "both drugs are analgesics and can reduce fever;

Work supported by the Royal Society under a University Research Fellowship and the EPSRC under an IAA award and the projects DBOnto, MaSI[3], ED[3], and VADA(EP/M025268/1).

C. d'Amato et al. (Eds.): ISWC 2017, Part I, LNCS 10587, pp. 526–541, 2017.
DOI: 10.1007/978-3-319-68288-4_31

however, Metamizole can also act as a spasm reliever, whereas Ibuprofen has an anti-inflammatory function". The second use case concerns the development of an analysis tool on top of IMDB data; such tool should allow users to compare arbitrary aspects of movie-making, such as directors, producers, actors and so on. For example, when comparing Quentin Tarantino to Martin Scorsese, the tool should report that they are similar in that they are both male directors who won both an Oscar and a Golden Globe and who have also acted in their own movies; in turn, they are different in that Tarantino won the Palme d'Or at the Cannes Film Festival, while Scorsese won an Emmy award, to which Tarantino was only nominated.

Entity comparison is conventionally seen in the Information Retrieval community as a type of exploratory search [15,22]. It is an important task which is implemented in a wide range of tools and web portals, in domains as diverse as hotels,[1] cars,[2] universities,[3] or online shopping[4]. Existing entity comparison tools typically perform a side-by-side comparison of items based on a fixed (often hard-coded) template of features to compare (e.g., price, location, rating, and so on in the case of hotels). Relying on a fixed set of features is a reasonable solution for tabular, domain specific data whose structure is relatively rigid and stable. It is even appropriate in the context of graph data, provided that a limited set of relevant features can be specified beforehand; for instance, Facebook Friendship pages allow for the comparison of two Facebook users by displaying their shared information based on a limited set of features specific to social networks (e.g., "likes", mutual friends, relationship status).

A more flexible approach to entity comparison is, however, needed in the context of Linked Data, where loosely structured RDF graphs (often describing overlapping domains) are merged and updated. Up to now, such approaches have mainly been based on the structure of the graph, e.g., finding a path that connects the two entities (see Sect. 7 for a discussion of related work). In this paper we propose a novel approach based on the semantics of the graph.

In Sect. 3 we propose a logical framework for our approach, where similarities and differences between entities are formalised as conjunctive SPARQL queries. Specifically, a *similarity query* (resp. a *difference query*) for given entities in an RDF graph is a query having both entities as answers (resp. having one entity as answer but not the other). In the case of similarity queries, we are interested in the *most specific ones*, e.g., knowing that Tarantino and Scorsese are both American-born film directors is more informative than reporting only that they are both film directors. In turn, in the case of difference queries we are interested in the *most general ones*, e.g., knowing that Brad Pitt is an actor, whereas George Lucas is a producer is more informative than knowing that the former is an American actor while the latter is an American producer, since being American is irrelevant to differentiating them.

---

[1] http://www.flightnetwork.com/pages/hotel-comparison-tool/.
[2] http://www.cars.com/go/compare/modelCompare.jsp.
[3] http://colleges.startclass.com/.
[4] http://www.intel.co.uk/content/www/uk/en/products/compare-products.html.

In Sect. 4, we focus on similarities, and propose a polynomial-time algorithm for computing a most specific similarity query. As a by-product of the properties of our algorithm, we are also able to show that most specific similarity queries for two given entities in an RDF graph are unique modulo equivalence. The problem we consider in this section is strongly related to the *Query Reverse Engineering problem* in RDF [2], as well as to that of computing *Least Common Subsumers* in Description Logic ontologies [3].

In Sect. 5, we focus on difference queries. We first argue that this is a hard problem; specifically, we argue that simply checking existence of a difference query for two given entities in a graph is CONP-complete. We then propose an exponential-time algorithm for computing a most general difference query, should one exist.

Finally, we describe a prototype implementation of the algorithm for computing a most specific similarity query and present a proof of concept case study using the data from Wikipedia infoboxes.

2   Preliminaries

We follow [16] in the definition of RDF graphs and triple patterns. Let $\mathbf{U}$, $\mathbf{L}$ and $\mathbf{B}$ be pairwise disjoint, countably infinite sets of URIs, literals and blank nodes, respectively. An *RDF triple* (or simply a *triple*) is a tuple $(s, p, o) \in (\mathbf{U} \cup \mathbf{B}) \times \mathbf{U} \times (\mathbf{U} \cup \mathbf{L} \cup \mathbf{B})$. In such a triple, s is the *subject*, p the *predicate* and o the *object*. An *RDF graph* G is a finite set of triples. Any URI or literal from G is called an *entity*.

Let $\mathbf{V}$ be a countably infinite set of variables disjoint from $\mathbf{U}$ and $\mathbf{L}$. A *term* is an element from $\mathbf{U} \cup \mathbf{L} \cup \mathbf{V}$. The basic building block of our queries is a *triple pattern*, which is an element from $(\mathbf{U} \cup \mathbf{V}) \times (\mathbf{U} \cup \mathbf{V}) \times (\mathbf{U} \cup \mathbf{L} \cup \mathbf{V})$. A *basic graph pattern* is a non-empty finite set P of triple patterns. For any basic graph pattern P, we denote with $\mathsf{term}(P)$ and $\mathsf{var}(P)$ the sets of terms and variables occurring in P, respectively.

We define a *query* Q as a pair $(\bar{X}, P)$, where P is a basic graph pattern and $\bar{X} \subseteq \mathsf{var}(P)$ is the set of *answer variables* of Q. Such queries capture the fragment of SPARQL queries of the form SELECT $?\bar{X}$ WHERE P, with P a basic graph pattern. We define $\mathsf{term}(Q) = \mathsf{term}(P)$ and $\mathsf{var}(Q) = \mathsf{var}(P)$. We say that Q is *monadic* if its set of answer variables is a singleton. A basic graph pattern P is *connected* if for every $t, t' \in \mathsf{term}(P)$ there is a sequence of triple patterns $tp_1, \ldots, tp_n$ in P such that $t \in \mathsf{term}(tp_1)$, $t' \in \mathsf{term}(tp_n)$ and $\mathsf{term}(tp_i) \cap \mathsf{term}(tp_{i+1}) \neq \emptyset$, for $1 \leq i < n$. Query $Q = (\bar{X}, P)$ is *connected* if so is P. For brevity, in examples we will write a query $Q = (\bar{X}, P)$ simply as P and adopt the convention that $X_{(i)}$ represent answer variables, whereas $Y_{(j)}$ represent the remaining variables.

We next recapitulate the semantics of queries. A *valuation* over variables $\bar{X}$ is a mapping ν from $\bar{X}$ to $\mathbf{U} \cup \mathbf{L} \cup \mathbf{B}$. For ν a valuation over $\bar{X}$ and $\bar{Y} \subseteq \bar{X}$, let $\nu|_{\bar{Y}}$ be the restriction of ν to $\bar{Y}$. Valuations are applied to triple patterns and basic graph patterns in the obvious way. Let $Q = (\bar{X}, P)$ be a query, let G be an RDF graph, and ν a valuation over $\bar{X}$. Then, G *satisfies* Q *under* ν, denoted $G, \nu \models Q$ if $\nu = \mu|_{\bar{X}}$ for some valuation μ over $\mathsf{var}(Q)$ satisfying $\mu(P) \subseteq G$. The semantics $[Q]_G$ of a query $Q = (\bar{X}, P)$ over G is

$$[Q]_G = \{\nu(\bar{X}) \mid G, \nu \models Q \text{ and } \nu \text{ is a valuation over } \bar{X}\}.$$

Let G be an RDF graph. The *canonical graph pattern* of G is the set $\mathsf{Can}(G)$ of triple patterns (X_s, X_p, X_o) for each triple (s, p, o) in G, where X_s, X_p and X_o are variables uniquely assigned to s, p and o in G. A *canonical query* of G is any query of the form $(\bar{X}, \mathsf{Can}(G))$.

Let $Q_1 = (\bar{X}_1, P_1)$ and $Q_2 = (\bar{X}_2, P_2)$ be queries. We say that Q_1 is *subsumed* by Q_2, denoted as $Q_1 \sqsubseteq Q_2$, if $[Q_1]_G \subseteq [Q_2]_G$ for every RDF graph G. The subsumption relation between two queries with equal number of answer variables can be characterised by existence of a homomorphism—a mapping $h : \mathsf{term}(Q_2) \rightarrow \mathsf{term}(Q_1)$ that is the identity on URIs, literals and answer variables and satisfying $(h(t_s), h(t_p), h(t_o)) \in P_1$ whenever $(t_s, t_p, t_o) \in P_2$ and $h(\bar{X}_2) = \bar{X}_1$. It is well-known that $Q_1 \sqsubseteq Q_2$ if and only if there exists a homomorphism from Q_2 to Q_1. Subsumption allows us to compare queries relative to their specificity. We say that Q_1 is *more specific than* Q_2 if $Q_1 \sqsubseteq Q_2$; it is *strictly more specific*, denoted as $Q_1 \sqsubset Q_2$, if $Q_1 \sqsubseteq Q_2$ and $Q_2 \not\sqsubseteq Q_1$. Finally, Q_1 and Q_2 are *equivalent*, denoted $Q_1 \equiv Q_2$, if $Q_1 \sqsubseteq Q_2$ and $Q_2 \sqsubseteq Q_1$.

3   A Framework for Entity Comparison

In this section, we present our formalisation of entity comparison. As a running example, consider a small subset G_{mov} of the YAGO graph [18] about the movie industry depicted in Fig. 1. In our example, we would like to compare Quentin Tarantino and Martin Scorsese. By inspecting G_{mov} we can observe, for instance, that Tarantino and Scorsese are similar in that both of them are male, they both won an Academy Award and a Golden Globe Award, and they both acted in some of their own movies. In turn, they are different in that Tarantino directed *Reservoir Dogs*, whereas Scorsese directed *Taxi Driver*; furthermore, unlike Scorsese, Tarantino also won the Palme d'Or at the Cannes Film Festival, while Scorsese won an Emmy award, to which Tarantino was only nominated.

How can we formalise and automatically identify such similarities and differences? There has been significant recent work in the literature on discovering relationships between entities in an RDF graph [7,11,14]. Existing approaches describe such relationships by means of explicit paths in the graph, which are then grouped and ranked. Using such an approach, we could view a similarity between entities as paths originating in those entities and converging into the same node; for instance, we could justify as a similarity the fact that both Tarantino and Scorsese are male by two paths leading to the node for male and starting from the nodes for Scorsese and Tarantino, respectively. In turn, we could justify a difference through the absence of such paths; for instance, the node for Emmy Award is reachable from the node for Scorsese but not from that for Tarantino. An important limitation of existing approaches, however, is that

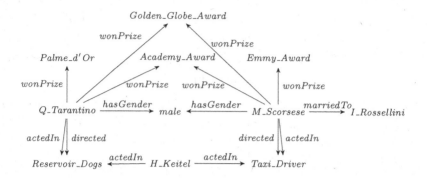

Fig. 1. An example RDF graph G_{mov}.

they cannot capture comparison at a *higher level of abstraction*; for instance, we cannot justify by means of explicit converging paths in a graph the fact that both Scorsese and Tarantino participated in a film as both actors and directors, where the specific names of those films are irrelevant.

In our framework we propose to capture similarities and differences using *queries* rather than explicit paths, where the presence of variables allows us to represent information at a higher level of abstraction. We start by formalising similarities. Given two entities in a graph, we view a similarity as a query having both entities as answers.

Definition 1 (Similarity query). *A* similarity query *for entities a and b in an RDF graph G is a monadic connected query Q satisfying* $\{a, b\} \subseteq [Q]_G$.

For instance, the following queries Q_1–Q_3 are similarity queries for Tarantino and Scorsese in our example graph G_{mov}:

$$Q_1(X) = \{(X, wonPrize, Academy\_Award)\};$$
$$Q_2(X) = \{(X, hasGender, male), (X, wonPrize, Academy\_Award)\};$$
$$Q_3(X) = \{(X, directed, Y), (X, actedIn, Y), (H\_Keitel, actedIn, Y)\}.$$

These similarity queries can be interpreted as follows: Q_1 says that both Scorsese and Tarantino received an Academy award, whereas Q_2 additionally states that they are both male; in turn, Q_3 states that they are both directors who acted in their own movies, in which Harvey Keitel was also part of the cast.

We next formalise the notion of a difference. Intuitively, given two entities in an RDF graph, a difference is a query having one of the entities as answer, but not the other. Furthermore, we are specially interested in differences that are *relevant to an identified similarity*, in the sense that they distinguish the entities based on an aspect that they have in common.

Definition 2 (Difference query). *Let a and b be entities in an RDF graph G. A* difference query *for a relative to b is a monadic connected query Q satisfying* $a \in [Q]_G$ *and* $b \notin [Q]_G$.

Additionally, let Q' be a similarity query for a and b in G. Then, we say that Q is a difference query modulo Q' if Q is a difference query for a relative to b and it holds that $Q \subseteq Q'$.

For instance, the following query $Q_4(X)$ is a difference query for Scorsese relative to Tarantino and modulo the similarity query $Q_1(X)$ given before.

$$Q_4(X) = \{(X, wonPrize, Academy\_Award), (X, wonPrize, Emmy\_Award)\}.$$

In turn, the following query is also a difference query for Scorsese relative to Tarantino, but it does not relate to any (non-trivial) similarity between them.

$$Q_5(X) = \{(X, marriedTo, Y)\}.$$

As we can see from the aforementioned examples, there may be multiple (even infinitely many) similarity and difference queries for a given pair of entities. Some of them are, however, more informative than others. In the case of similarity queries, it is natural to expect more specific queries to be more informative; for instance, it is natural to prefer our example query Q_2 over Q_1 since it better differentiates Tarantino and Scorsese from other directors, by ruling out those who won an Emmy but are female. In contrast, in the case of difference queries it is natural to favour more general queries over more specific ones; for instance, Q_5 is more informative that the following query Q_6 since it conveys the information that Scorsese is married, but Tarantino is not (or at least not known to be).

$$Q_6(X) = \{(X, marriedTo, I\_Rossellini)\}.$$

We now define these notions formally.

Definition 3. *Query Q is a most specific similarity query (MSSQ) for a and b in G if Q is a similarity query for a and b in G, and there is no similarity query Q' for a and b in G such that $Q' \subset Q$.*

Query Q is a most general difference query (MGDQ) for a relative to b in G if Q is a difference query for a relative to b in G, and there is no difference query Q' for a relative for b in G such that $Q \subset Q'$. This definition extends to the notion of difference query modulo a similarity query in the obvious way.

Intuitively, given two similarity queries Q and Q' for the same pair of entities, their conjunction is also a similarity query that is more specific than both of them. We will show in the following section that MSSQs for given entities and graph are unique modulo equivalence over the given input graph. As an example, consider the following query, which combines Q_2 and Q_3; it can be checked that it is a MSSQ for Scorsese and Tarantino in G_{mov}:

$$Q_7(X) = \{(X, hasGender, male), (X, wonPrize, Academy\_Award),$$
$$(X, wonPrize, Golden\_Globe\_Award), (X, actedIn, Y),$$
$$(X, directed, Y), (H\_Keitel, actedIn, Y)\}.$$

Indeed, query $Q_8 = Q_7 \cup \{(X, actedIn, Z)\}$ is also a MSSQ but it is equivalent to Q_7. In turn, both query Q_5 and the following query Q_9 are both MGDQs for Scorsese relative to Tarantino:

$$Q_9(X) = \{(X, Y, Emmy\_Award)\}.$$

Furthermore, they are incomparable with respect to subsumption and hence, in contrast to MSSQs, we cannot formulate a uniqueness result for MGDQs.

4   Computing a Most Specific Similarity Query

In this section, we tackle the problem of computing a most specific similarity query. In particular, we present a polynomial time algorithm and then show, as a byproduct of the correctness proof, that MSSQs are unique up to equivalence.

Our algorithm relies on the notion of the *(tensor) product graph*, which is commonly exploited in Graph Theory and in Databases (under the name of *direct product* [19]). Given graphs G_1 and G_2, the product $G_1 \otimes G_2$ is a graph whose vertex set is the cartesian product of the vertices of G_1 and G_2, and where two vertices in the product graph are connected by an edge if and only if their component elements are also related by an edge in the original graph. We next adapt the standard notion of product to RDF graphs. Intuitively, given entities a, b and graph G, the connected subgraph of the product $G \otimes G$ of G with itself represents the "largest common pattern" in the neighbourhoods of a and b.

Definition 4 (Product graph). *Let* $t_1 = (s_1, p_1, o_1)$ *and* $t_2 = (s_2, p_2, o_2)$ *be triples. The* product *of* t_1 *and* t_2, *denoted as* $t_1 \otimes t_2$, *is the triple*

$$(\langle s_1, s_2 \rangle, \langle p_1, p_2 \rangle, \langle o_1, o_2 \rangle).$$

The product graph $G_1 \otimes G_2$ *of RDF graphs* G_1 *and* G_2 *is the set*

$$\{t_1 \otimes t_2 \mid t_1 \in G_1 \text{ and } t_2 \in G_2\}.$$

For instance, the self-product $G_{mov} \otimes G_{mov}$ of our example graph G_{mov} contains triples such as the following:[5]

$$(\langle Q\_Tarantino, M\_Scorsese \rangle,$$
$$\langle wonPrize, wonPrize \rangle,$$
$$\langle Palme\_d'Or, Emmy\_Award \rangle)$$

which is the product of triples $(Q\_Tarantino, wonPrize, Palme\_d'Or)$ and $(M\_Scorsese, wonPrize, Emmy\_Award)$.

---

[5] Note that the product graph is strictly speaking not an RDF graph, but this is a technicality that is not important for our purposes.

Algorithm 1. COMPUTE-MSSQ

Input: an RDF graph G and two entities a and b from G.
Output: a MSSQ for a and b.
1 Compute $G \otimes G$;
2 **if** $\langle a, b \rangle$ *does not occur in a triple in* $G \otimes G$ **then**
3 $\quad \lfloor$ **return** *fail;*
4 Let G' be the connected component in $G \otimes G$ that contains $\langle a, b \rangle$;
5 Construct the canonical query Q of G' with the answer variable $X_{\langle a,b \rangle}$;
6 Replace each variable $X_{\langle c,c \rangle}$ in Q with c;
7 **return** Q.

We are now ready to describe our algorithm (see Algorithm 1). Given a, b and G as input, the first step is to compute the product graph $G \otimes G$ and check whether $\langle a, b \rangle$ occurs in a triple; if it doesn't then the algorithm fails and we can conclude that there is no query having both a and b as answers. If $\langle a, b \rangle$ occurs in the product graph, then the algorithm computes the connected component G' in which it occurs. Given G', we are interested in its canonical query having as answer variable the variable $X_{\langle a,b \rangle}$ corresponding to $\langle a, b \rangle$ in $\mathsf{Can}(G')$. The result of this step is already a similarity query. In the last step, the algorithm grounds all variables $X_{\langle c,c \rangle}$ corresponding to nodes $\langle c, c \rangle$ to c itself; this step is essential to ensure that the output similarity query is a most specific one.

Correctness of the algorithm follows from the following lemma.

Lemma 1. *Algorithm* COMPUTE-MSSQ *satisfies the following properties on input a, b and G:*

1. *It fails if and only if there is no similarity query for a and b in G.*
2. *The output query Q is a similarity query for a and b in G such that any similarity query Q' for a, b and G is homomorphically embeddable into Q.*

Proof. 1. It is easy to see that a similarity query for a and b exists if and only if a and b appear as subjects, properties, or objects at the same time in G. This is equivalent to the fact that $\langle a, b \rangle$ appears in a triple in $G \otimes G$. COMPUTE-MSSQ returns "fail" iff the latter is not the case.

2. We first show that $\{a, b\} \subseteq [Q]_G$. Define two valuations over $\mathsf{var}(Q)$, ν_1 and ν_2, as follows: for every variable $X_{\langle c,c' \rangle}$ in Q, $\nu_1(X_{\langle c,c' \rangle}) = c$, and $\nu_2(X_{\langle c,c' \rangle}) = c'$. We now show that G satisfies Q under both ν_1 and ν_2. Let $(X_{\langle s_1,s_2 \rangle}, X_{\langle p_1,p_2 \rangle}, X_{\langle o_1,o_2 \rangle})$ be in Q, then it follows by definition of Q that $(\langle s_1, s_2 \rangle, \langle p_1, p_2 \rangle, \langle o_1, o_2 \rangle) \in G'$. Then by construction of G' we know that both (s_1, p_1, o_1) and $(s_2, p_2, o_2) \in G$. We then obtain that by definition of ν_1 and ν_2: $(\nu_i(X_{\langle s_1,s_2 \rangle}), \nu_i(X_{\langle p_1,p_2 \rangle}), \nu_i(X_{\langle o_1,o_2 \rangle}))) \in G$, for $i = 1, 2$. Hence, ν_1 and ν_2 are satisfying for Q in G. We have $\nu_1(X_{\langle a,b \rangle}) = a$ and $\nu_2(X_{\langle a,b \rangle}) = b$. Therefore, $\{a, b\} \subseteq [Q]_G$.

Let $Q'(X)$ be an arbitrary similarity query for a and b. There are two satisfying valuations ν_1 and ν_2 over $\mathsf{var}(Q')$ for Q' in G that map X to a and b

respectively. We define $\nu(Y) = \langle \nu_1(Y), \nu_2(Y) \rangle$ for Y a variable and $\nu(e) = \langle e, e \rangle$ for e an entity. Since Q' is connected and $\nu(X) = \langle a, b \rangle$, the image of Q' under ν is a connected subgraph in $G \otimes G$ and thus is contained in G'. Since G' and Q are isomorphic, ν can be considered as a homomorphism from Q' to Q.   □

Clearly, our algorithm works in polynomial time; in particular the size of the product graph $G \otimes G$ is cubic in the size of G. Hence, using the previous Lemma we conclude the following.

Theorem 1. Compute-MSSQ *is a polynomial time algorithm that returns a MSSQ for its input if one exists, and "fail" otherwise.*

Finally, note that the second statement in Lemma 1 ensures that the return query is, in fact, more specific than *any other* similarity query. Thus, it also follows from the lemma that MSSQs are unique up to equivalence.

Corollary 1. *If Q and Q' are MSSQs for a and b in RDF graph G, then $Q \equiv Q'$.*

We conclude by observing that the algorithm Compute-MSSQ will compute, on our running example, a query that is significantly larger than (yet equivalent to) Q_7 in the previous section. Indeed, Q_7 is a *core* query in the sense that it cannot be further minimised while preserving equivalence.

5   Computing Most General Difference Queries

We now turn our attention to MGDQs. As already pointed out, MGDQs are not unique modulo equivalence and hence we focus on providing an algorithm that computes one of them.

In contrast to the case of computing MSSQs, we will not be able to provide a polynomial-time algorithm. In fact, we show that the associated decision problem of checking whether a MGDQ exists is CONP-complete. This result stems from a characterisation of existence of MGDQs in terms of (non-)existence of homomorphisms.

In what follows we fix arbitrary entities a and b in an arbitrary RDF graph G. We denote with Q_b to be the query $(X_b, \mathsf{Can}(G))$ and Q_a to be the query (X_a, P_{X_a}) with P_{X_a} the connected component of $\mathsf{Can}(G)$ containing X_a.

Lemma 2. *A difference query for a relative to b in G exists if and only if there is no homomorphism from Q_a to Q_b.*

Proof. ($\Leftarrow$). The following properties hold for Q_a. It is (1) connected and (2) $a \in [Q_a]_G$. Moreover, since there is no homomorphism from Q_a to Q_b, it holds that (3) $b \notin [Q_a]_G$. Indeed, otherwise a satisfying valuation ν for Q_a over $\mathsf{var}(Q_a)$ with $\nu(X_a) = b$ can be seen as a homomorphism from Q_a to Q_b, as $\mathsf{Can}(G)$ and G are isomorphic. Thus, Q_a is a difference query for a relative to b in G.

($\Rightarrow$). Let $Q(X)$ be a difference query for a relative to b in G. It implies there is a satisfying valuation ν over $\mathsf{var}(Q)$ for Q in G which can be regarded as a homomorphism from Q to Q_a (since Q is connected) with $\nu(X) = X_a$. For the sake of contradiction, suppose there is a homomorphism h from Q_a to Q_b. This homomorphism can be regarded as a satisfying valuation for Q_a in G with $h(X_a) = b$. Hence, the mapping $h \circ \nu$ is a satisfying valuation for $Q(X)$ in G with $h \circ \nu(X) = b$ which implies $b \in [Q]_G$, a contradiction with the fact that Q is a difference query for a relative to b in G.   □

Since homomorphism checking is a well-known NP-complete problem, the following result follows.

Theorem 2. *The problem of checking whether a difference query for a relative to b in G exists is* CONP*-complete.*

Proof. It is known that checking existence of a homomorphism is in NP. Together with Lemma 2 it implies that existence of a difference query can be checked in CONP. We show the lower bound by reducing from the homomorphism problem for graphs to the complement of our problem. Let $\mathsf{G}_1 = (V_1, E_1)$ and $\mathsf{G}_2 = (V_2, E_2)$ be graphs which we can assume to be disjoint. We then construct an RDF graph G over the set of URIs $V_1 \cup V_2 \cup \{a, b, e, e'\}$, where $\{a, b, e, e'\} \cap V_i = \emptyset, i = 1, 2$, as the following set:

$$G = \{(u, e, v) \mid \langle u, v \rangle \in E_1 \cup E_2\} \cup \{(a, e', u) \mid u \in V_1\} \cup \{(b, e', v) \mid v \in V_2\}.$$

It is straightforward to show that there exists a homomorphism from G_1 to G_2 if and only there is a homomorphism from Q_a to Q_b (note that this homomorphism must map X_a to X_b). Lemma 2 implies that this is equivalent to non-existence of a difference query for a relative to b in G.   □

In light of this result, there is no hope for a polynomial time algorithm for computing a MGDQ unless PTIME = NP. Therefore, we present a naive, non-deterministic algorithm COMPUTE-MGDQ for acyclic graphs. In the first step, the algorithm computes Q_a (feasible in polynomial time). Then, it checks (using the oracle as per Lemma 2) whether Q_a is already a difference query. If it is not, then none can exist. If it is, then it may not be a most general one. Hence, the algorithm tries to make it more general by relaxing the query while checking (again using the oracle as per Lemma 2) whether the result is still a difference query. Correctness is established in the following theorem.

Theorem 3. *Algorithm* COMPTUTE-MGDQ *returns a MGDQ if one exists, and "fail" otherwise.*

Proof. The algorithm fails if and only if there is a homomorphism from Q_a to Q_b. By Lemma 2 this is equivalent to the fact that no (most general) difference query for a relative to b exists.

Let Q be the output of COMPTUTE-MGDQ different from "fail". The for-loop on Line 5 tries to greedily relax the query. Namely, for each variable Y we introduce a set of fresh variables Y_i that replace Y in Q (thus relaxing it) as long as the result is still a difference query for a relative to b. Note that

---

Algorithm 2. COMPUTE-MGDQ

Input: an RDF graph G and two entities a and b from G.
Output: a MGDQ for a and b.

1 Compute $Q_a = (X_a, P_{X_a})$;
2 **if** *there exists a homomorphism from Q_a to Q_b* **then**
3 | **return** *fail;*

4 Let $Q = Q_a$;
5 **foreach** *variable $Y \neq X_a$ in Q* **do**
6 | Let Occ be the set of all occurrences of Y in Q;
7 | Guess a number $1 < N \leq |Occ|$ and a partition $Occ = \cup_{i=1}^{N} Occ_i$ with each $Occ_i \neq \emptyset$;
8 | Let $Y_i, i = 1, \ldots, N$, be a fresh variable for each Occ_i;
9 | In Q, replace each occurrence of Y that is in Occ_i by Y_i;
10 | Let Q' be the connected component of X_a in Q;
11 | **if** *there is no homomorphism from Q' to Q_b* **then**
12 | | Update $Q := Q'$;

13 **return** Q.

---

for each intermediate query Q' it holds $a \in [Q']_G$ since the result of Line 9 is homomorphically embeddable into the original query. Therefore, we have $a \in [Q]_G$. The if-condition ensures that $b \notin [Q]_G$ as per Lemma 2. Therefore, Q is a difference query for a relative to b.

Suppose there is a difference query Q'' for a relative to b that is strictly more general than Q. This means there is a homomorphism h from Q'' to Q but not vice versa. If h is injective, then there is a triple pattern in Q that is not in the image of Q'' under h but connected to it. But then the commands in the for-loop are applicable to a variable Y that connects the image of Q'' and the triple pattern (with the following partition: the occurrence of Y replaced with Y_1 and the occurrence of Y in the triple pattern with Y_2), a contradiction. Now suppose h is not injective. Then let $\{Z_1, \ldots, Z_n\}$ be variables in Q'' that are mapped by h to the same variable Y in Q. We claim that the for-loop in Line 5 is applicable to Y with $\{Z_1, \ldots, Z_n\}$ defining a partition, a contradiction. $\square$

6 Case Study

We have implemented a prototype system in Java that implements our Algorithm 1 for computing MSSQs. As a proof of concept, we have run the algorithm on a fragment of DBpedia [13] that captures the information corresponding to Wikipedia infoboxes—tables with a fixed structure used in Wikipedia to present the key information about an entity in a concise and structured way.[6] Infoboxes are located on the right-hand-side of Wikipedia pages that correspond to certain categories, such as people, organisations or geographical locations.

---

[6] https://en.wikipedia.org/wiki/Help:Infobox.

Entity comparison in Wikipedia could be implemented by comparing their infoboxes directly; such a tool would provide analogous functionality to that in existing comparison tools in Web portals, in the sense that the features to compare would be considered fixed. Figure 2 displays side by side the infoboxes corresponding to Brad Pitt and Tom Cruise, which are both fairly detailed. We can observe similarities such as their occupations and country of birth, or the fact that they have both been married and have children.

		Born	Thomas Cruise Mapother IV
Born	William Bradley Pitt December 18, 1963 (age 53) Shawnee, Oklahoma, U.S.		July 3, 1962 (age 54) Syracuse, New York, U.S.
		Occupation	Actor, producer
Occupation	Actor · producer	**Years active**	1981–present
Years active	1987–present	**Spouse(s)**	Mimi Rogers (m. 1987; div. 1990)
Works	Filmography		Nicole Kidman (m. 1990; div. 2001)
Home town	Springfield, Missouri		
Spouse(s)	Jennifer Aniston (m. 2000; div. 2005) Angelina Jolie (m. 2014; separated 2016)		Katie Holmes (m. 2006; div. 2012)
		Children	3
Children	6	**Relatives**	William Mapother (cousin)
Relatives	Douglas Pitt (brother)	**Website**	tomcruise.com🔗

Fig. 2. Wikipedia infoboxes for actors Brad Pitt (left) and Tom Cruise (right).

We tried our algorithm for Brad Pitt and Tom Cruise and the aforementioned fragment of DBpedia. We observed that the computed MSSQ provides much richer information than what can be obtained by direct inspection of the infoboxes. Since the resulting MSSQ is rather large, we concentrate on its subqueries of special interest. First, we notice that we generated all the aforementioned similarities that could be obtained by manual inspection of the infoboxes. In particular, we found that both Brad Pitt and Tom Cruise are:

– both actors and producers, as witnessed by the subquery

$$\{(X, occupation, Actor), (X, occupation, Producer)\};$$

– were born in the U.S., as witnessed by

$$\{(X, birth\_place, Y_1), (Y_1, country, United\_States)\};$$

– were married, have kids and relatives, as witnessed by

$$\{(X, children, Y_2), (X, spouse, Y_3), (X, relatives, Y_4)\}.$$

However, the computed MSSQ also contains plenty of additional useful information. For instance, both Pitt and Cruise:

– were married to U.S. actresses, as witnessed by

$$\{(X, spouse, Y_3), (Y_3, nationality, United\_States), (Y_3, occupation, Actress)\};$$

– were born in cities that are both the administrative centers and largest cities of their respective counties:

$$\{(X, birth\_place, Y_1), (Y_1, county, Y_5),$$
$$(Y_5, largest\_city, Y_1), (Y_5, seat, Y_1), (Y_1, settlement\_type, City)\};$$

– were married to actresses who were also married to musicians:

$$\{(X, spouse, Y_3), (Y_3, occupation, Actress),$$
$$(Y_3, spouse, Y_6), (Y_6, occupation, Musician)\};$$

To sum up, even using only DBpedia data capturing Wikipedia infoboxes, we are able to significantly enhance the explicit contents of fairly comprehensive infoboxes and exploit the graph nature of the data to discover "deeper-level" similarities between the entities of interest. We envision that our approach could even be more useful if the whole of DBpedia had been considered, especially in the case where the infoboxes corresponding to the entities of interest are rather minimalistic and hence do not provide sufficiently many features to compare.

7 Related Work

There is a growing interest in techniques for discovering and explaining relationships between entities in an RDF graph [7,11,14]. These approaches are based on computing paths in the input graph connecting the input entities. Such paths are first computed via standard graph traversal algorithms, and then ranked according to certain structural and/or statistical measures [7]. We note that the problem of finding connections between entities is orthogonal to that of computing similarities and differences between them. Furthermore, as already argued, the natural adaptations of such techniques to our setting do not allow for entity comparison at a sufficiently high level of abstraction.

Computation of both similarity and difference queries can be seen as an instance of the more general problem of *Query Reverse Engineering (QRE)* in databases. An input to QRE is a database instance, a set of *positive examples* (i.e., elements that must be in the query result) and also in some cases a set of *negative examples* (i.e., elements that must not be included in the query result). The QRE problem for a query language $\mathcal{L}$ is to decide whether an $\mathcal{L}$-query exists whose answers satisfy the given constraints imposed by positive and negative examples over the input database instance. This problem has been studied for regular languages over strings [1], queries over relational databases [20,21,23,25],

XML queries [9,17], graph database queries [6] and SPARQL queries over RDF graphs [2]. QRE is known to be CONEXPTIME-complete for conjunctive queries over relational databases [4,19]. When applied to our setting, this result implies CONEXPTIME-completeness of the following problem: given an RDF graph, and sets of entities A and B in G, does there exist a difference query for A relative to B in G, where the definition of a difference query is extended to sets of entities in the obvious way. QRE for RDF graphs was first studied in [2], where the complexity analysis of different variations of the problem is provided for SPARQL queries allowing for the AND, FILTER and OPT operators.

Computing MSSQs is also related to (a variant of) the problem of computing the *Least Common Subsumer* between concepts in Description Logics (DLs) [3]. Specifically, given entities a and b, we could cast our problem as that of finding the least (i.e., most specific modulo subsumption) DL concept that contains both a and b as instances. An important difference with our setting is that DL concepts in logics such as $\mathcal{EL}$ and $\mathcal{ALC}$ can only capture conjunctive queries that are both constant-free and tree-shaped. In this sense, our query language is more expressive, as it allows for arbitrarily-shaped connected CQs. The additional expressivity turns out to be critical: while a least DL concept may not exist (e.g., if the input graph has cycles then the least concept could be infinite), our algorithm in Sect. 4 ensures that a MSSQ is always finite and can be computed in polynomial time.

Finally, it is worth mentioning that there has been a lot of work on *similarity measures* for computing a numeric score that estimates how similar two entities in a graph are [8,12,24]; this has applications, for instance, in discovering entities that are similar to a given one (i.e., those with the highest similarity score). Please note that we are considering a very different problem since our focus is on *describing* similarities and differences in a declarative way.

8   Conclusion and Future Work

We have investigated the problem of entity comparison over RDF graphs and proposed a logical framework that models comparison through similarity and difference queries. In particular, we have studied most specific similarity queries (MSSQs) and most general difference queries (MGDQs) as the most informative such queries. We have shown that, for a given graph and a pair of entities, there always exists a unique MSSQ modulo equivalence, which can be computed in polynomial time. In contrast, computing MGDQs is a harder problem; indeed, the underpinning decision problem is CONP-hard. Finally, we have discussed an initial implementation of the algorithm that computes a MSSQ.

An immediate step of future research would be to extend the prototype implementation of the framework into a comprehensive entity comparison tool that would account for both similarity and difference queries. This would imply, firstly, creating practical algorithms for computing MGDQs, possibly of bounded size. As for MSSQs, a practical implementation of the tool would effectively address the problem of large-sized MSSQs and how they can be presented to a user in an easy-to-read manner. One possible solution would be to split the output MSSQs into comprehensible subqueries (similar to the ones presented in Sect. 6); another solution would involve partially verbalizing MSSQs into natural language explanations. For example, a query $\{(X, livesIn, London), (X, friendsWith, Y), (Y, worksAt, Oracle)\}$ could be transformed into a natural language explanation *"Both input entities live in London and are friends with someone who works at Oracle"*. In addition, an interesting problem would be to consider more expressive query languages, in particular conjunctive queries with inequalities and numeric comparisons. As the example infoboxes from Sect. 6 suggests, such extensions to the query language would allow for similarity queries such as *"Both Brad Pitt and Tom Cruise have at least 3 children"*. Lastly, our approach to entity comparison should be thoroughly evaluated.

References

1. Angluin, D.: Queries and concept learning. Mach. Learn. **2**(4), 319–342 (1988)
2. Arenas, M., Diaz, G.I., Kostylev, E.V.: Reverse engineering SPARQL queries. In: Proceedings of the 25th International Conference on World Wide Web, pp. 239–249. International World Wide Web Conferences Steering Committee (2016)
3. Baader, F., Turhan, A.-Y.: On the problem of computing small representations of least common subsumers. In: Jarke, M., Lakemeyer, G., Koehler, J. (eds.) KI 2002. LNCS, vol. 2479, pp. 99–113. Springer, Heidelberg (2002). doi:10.1007/3-540-45751-8_7
4. Barcelo, P., Romero, M.: The complexity of reverse engineering problems for conjunctive queries. In: Proceedings of the 20th International Conference on Database Theory. Schloss Dagstuhl-Leibniz-Zentrum fuer Informatik (to appear, 2017)
5. Belleau, F., Nolin, M.-A., Tourigny, N., Rigault, P., Morissette, J.: Bio2RDF: towards a mashup to build bioinformatics knowledge systems. J. Biomed. Inf. **41**(5), 706–716 (2008)
6. Bonifati, A., Ciucanu, R., Lemay, A.: Learning path queries on graph databases. In: 18th International Conference on Extending Database Technology (EDBT) (2015)
7. Cheng, G., Zhang, Y., Qu, Y.: Explass: exploring associations between entities via top-K ontological patterns and facets. In: Mika, P., et al. (eds.) ISWC 2014. LNCS, vol. 8797, pp. 422–437. Springer, Cham (2014). doi:10.1007/978-3-319-11915-1_27
8. Choi, S.-S., Cha, S.-H., Tappert, C.C.: A survey of binary similarity and distance measures. J. Syst. Cybern. Inf. **8**(1), 43–48 (2010)
9. Cohen, S., Weiss, Y.Y.: Learning tree patterns from example graphs. In: LIPIcs-Leibniz International Proceedings in Informatics, vol. 31. Schloss Dagstuhl-Leibniz-Zentrum fuer Informatik (2015)
10. Harris, S., Seaborne, A.: SPARQL 1.1 query language. W3C proposed recommendation, 21 March 2013. World Wide Web Consortium (2013). https://www.w3.org/TR/sparql11-query/. Accessed 1 October 2016
11. Heim, P., Hellmann, S., Lehmann, J., Lohmann, S., Stegemann, T.: RelFinder: revealing relationships in RDF knowledge bases. In: Chua, T.-S., Kompatsiaris, Y., Mérialdo, B., Haas, W., Thallinger, G., Bailer, W. (eds.) SAMT 2009. LNCS, vol. 5887, pp. 182–187. Springer, Heidelberg (2009). doi:10.1007/978-3-642-10543-2_21
12. Huang, A.: Similarity measures for text document clustering. In: Proceedings of the Sixth New Zealand Computer Science Research Student Conference (NZCSRSC2008), Christchurch, New Zealand, pp. 49–56 (2008)

13. Lehmann, J., Isele, R., Jakob, M., Jentzsch, A., Kontokostas, D., Mendes, P., Hellmann, S., Morsey, M., van Kleef, P., Auer, S., Bizer, C.: DBpedia - a large-scale, multilingual knowledge base extracted from wikipedia. Semant. Web J. **6**, 167–195 (2014)

14. Lehmann, J., Schüppel, J., Auer, S.: Discovering unknown connections-the dbpedia relationship finder. CSSW **113**, 99–110 (2007)

15. Marchionini, G.: Exploratory search: from finding to understanding. Commun. ACM **49**(4), 41–46 (2006)

16. Pérez, J., Arenas, M., Gutierrez, C.: Semantics and complexity of SPARQL. ACM Trans. Database Syst. (TODS) **34**(3), 16 (2009)

17. Staworko, S., Wieczorek, P.: Learning twig and path queries. In: Proceedings of the 15th International Conference on Database Theory, pp. 140–154. ACM (2012)

18. Suchanek, F.M., Kasneci, G., Weikum, G.: YAGO: a large ontology from Wikipedia and Wordnet. Web Semant. Sci. Serv. Agents World Wide Web **6**(3), 203–217 (2008)

19. ten Cate, B., Dalmau, V.: The product homomorphism problem and applications. In: 18th International Conference on Database Theory (ICDT 2015), pp. 161–176 (2015)

20. Tran, Q.T., Chan, C.-Y., Parthasarathy, S.: Query by output. In: Proceedings of the 2009 ACM SIGMOD International Conference on Management of Data, pp. 535–548. ACM (2009)

21. Tran, Q.T., Chan, C.-Y., Parthasarathy, S.: Query reverse engineering. VLDB J. **23**(5), 721–746 (2014)

22. White, R.W., Roth, R.A.: Exploratory search: beyond the query-response paradigm. Synth. Lect. Inf. Concepts Retr. Serv. **1**, 1–98 (2009)

23. Zhang, M., Elmeleegy, H., Procopiuc, C.M., Srivastava, D.: Reverse engineering complex join queries. In: Proceedings of the 2013 ACM SIGMOD International Conference on Management of Data, pp. 809–820. ACM (2013)

24. Zhao, P., Han, J., Sun, Y.: P-rank: a comprehensive structural similarity measure over information networks. In: Proceedings of the 18th ACM Conference on Information and Knowledge Management, pp. 553–562. ACM (2009)

25. Zloof, M.M.: Query-by-example: a data base language. IBM Syst. J. **16**(4), 324–343 (1977)

Provenance Information in a Collaborative Knowledge Graph: An Evaluation of Wikidata External References

Alessandro Piscopo[✉], Lucie-Aimée Kaffee, Chris Phethean, and Elena Simperl

University of Southampton, Southampton, UK
{A.Piscopo,Kaffee,C.J.Phethean,E.Simperl}@soton.ac.uk

Abstract. Wikidata is a collaboratively-edited knowledge graph; it expresses knowledge in the form of subject-property-value triples, which can be enhanced with references to add provenance information. Understanding the quality of Wikidata is key to its widespread adoption as a knowledge resource. We analyse one aspect of Wikidata quality, provenance, in terms of relevance and authoritativeness of its external references. We follow a two-staged approach. First, we perform a crowdsourced evaluation of references. Second, we use the judgements collected in the first stage to train a machine learning model to predict reference quality on a large-scale. The features chosen for the models were related to reference editing and the semantics of the triples they referred to. 61% of the references evaluated were relevant and authoritative. Bad references were often links that changed and either stopped working or pointed to other pages. The machine learning models outperformed the baseline and were able to accurately predict non-relevant and non-authoritative references. Further work should focus on implementing our approach in Wikidata to help editors find bad references.

Keywords: Wikidata · Provenance · Collaborative knowledge graph

1 Introduction

Wikidata is a collaborative knowledge graph started in 2012 by the Wikimedia foundation. It supplies data to other Wikimedia projects (including Wikipedia), as well as anyone else who wants to use it, under a public license. Wikidata already has a broad coverage, with data covering more than 24M abstract and concrete entities, gathered by a user pool of around 17,000 monthly active users. This data has already been encoded in RDF and connected to the Linked Data Web [7]. All these features have drawn the attention of researchers and practitioners alike. Following its elder sister Wikipedia, Wikidata requires all information to be verifiable, but goes a step further. It is a secondary database and as such its aim is not to state facts about the world, but to report claims from primary sources [26]. Each claim must be supported by a source and linked to it.

© Springer International Publishing AG 2017
C. d'Amato et al. (Eds.): ISWC 2017, Part I, LNCS 10587, pp. 542–558, 2017.
DOI: 10.1007/978-3-319-68288-4_32

While most work around Wikidata focuses on the quality of its triples [4] or analyses its community dynamics [20], to the best of our knowledge no studies have investigated provenance quality. Little is known about the quality of the sources included to support claims, although this is a key issue for Wikidata. Provenance facilitates the reuse of data by improving error-detection and decision-processes based on the information source [16]. The lack of provenance information or the use of poor sources may affect its trustworthiness and hinder the reuse of its data for business and other purposes [12]. Additionally, the availability of provenance information can increase trust in the project, as noted in Wikipedia [17]. On a practical side, a method to detect bad external sources would support editors in maintaining Wikidata knowledge graph.

This paper proposes an approach to analyse quality of provenance information in Wikidata. We define quality in terms of relevance and authoritativeness of the external sources used in Wikidata references. To assess these, we use two complementary methods: microtask crowdsourcing and machine learning. Crowdsourcing is used to collect judgements about relevance and authoritativeness of sources. These judgements are successively utilised to train machine learning models to predict problematic references on a large-scale.

2   Background and Related Work

Wikidata consists of *items*—representing concrete (such as the Colosseum) or abstract things (e.g. humans)—and *properties* which express relationships between items or between items and values. Items and properties are identified by URIs, starting respectively with 'Q' or 'P'. Relationships are encoded via *claims*, which can be enriched by adding qualifiers (to provide contextual information) and/or references to form a *statement*. Statements are maintained by the Wikidata community. Beyond human editors, who can be registered or contribute anonymously, pieces of software called *bots* carry out a broad range of tasks, adding and maintaining content. Whereas human editors are the main contributors to the conceptual structure of Wikidata [18], bots perform more when it comes to adding and modifying content and can often add large batches of statements in one go [24]. No study has examined yet the differences between bot and human contributions in Wikidata in terms of quality. This would be relevant, considering the difference between the contribution patterns of these two user types. Bots author the majority of revisions in Wikidata and the sources on which their edits are based belong to a predetermined set of domains, thus they focus on fewer types of statements compared to human editors. We analysed external reference quality on Wikidata overall and separately by bot or human editor to provide insights into the outcome of the work of each user type.

2.1   Provenance in Wikidata

Provenance information may be either recorded at the moment of data creation (*eager* approach) or computed upon request (*lazy* approach) [11]. Wikidata adopts the former approach and editors are asked to add sources to the statements that they create. Provenance in Wikidata can be added by enriching claims with references. Most types of statements require a reference, otherwise they are deemed unverified and should be removed [28]. However, community-generated policies define some statement types that are exempt from this rule, such as undisputed claims (e.g. *Earth, instance of, planet*) [27]. The sources used as references can either be internal (an item already in Wikidata), or external, i.e. linking to a URL [27]. Statements that are not exempt must be verifiable by consulting a referenceable primary source. This must be **accessible** 'by at least some' Wikidata contributors to confirm the source firsthand [28]. A good reference must also be **relevant**—it must provide evidence for the claim it is linked to. Additionally, good references must be **authoritative** or 'deemed trustworthy, up-to-date, and free of bias for supporting a particular statement' [28].

2.2 Authoritativeness in Wikidata

Wikidata defines authoritative sources by describing suitable types of publisher and author. This is also the approach of Wikipedia, whose policy Wikidata redirects to. Specifically, the term 'source' has three meanings in Wikipedia [29]: the *type of work* itself, the *author* of the work, and the *publisher* of the work. Wikidata's policy specifies types of sources that are authoritative: books; academic, scientific and industry publications; policy and legislation documents; news and media sources. These must have a corresponding entity in Wikidata, linked to claims through property P248 (*stated in*). Databases and web pages may also be authoritative. Databases require a corresponding property already defined in the knowledge graph, pointing to an entry in the database. Authoritativeness of web pages, referenced through property P854 (*reference URL*), depends on their author and publisher type. Authors may be *individuals* (one or more identifiable persons), *organisations*, or *collective* (a number of individuals who often utilise a username and whose contribution is voluntary). Sources whose author is unknown should be avoided, as well as user-generated sources, e.g. forums or social review sites. Regarding publishers, sources with no editorial oversight and relying on rumours and personal opinions are not generally considered authoritative. Authoritative publishers are government agencies, companies and organisations, and academic institutions [28]. Self-published sources are generally not accepted, nor are websites with promotional purposes or those affected by political, financial, or religious bias. Wikipedia pages are not good references because they are not primary sources and are collectively created. Table 1 shows publisher types. Combinations of author and publisher types are in Table 2.

2.3 Evaluating Provenance

Literature about authoritativeness on the Web can be roughly divided into two approaches. The first uses automated methods to analyse the hyperlinked structure of the Web to generate link-based metrics to gauge the authoritativeness of pages. As an example, in [15] authority measures are generated using interlinks within sub-graphs of the Web. A similar approach is followed by works

Table 1. Types of publisher in the classification used. On the right column, sub-types or, when these are missing, definitions of higher-level types.

Academic and scientific organisations	*Academic and research institutions* (e.g. universities and research centres, but not museums and libraries); *Academic publishers*; *Other academic organisations*
Companies or organisations	*Vendors and e-commerce companies*; *Political or religious organisations*; *Cultural institutions*; *Other types of company*
Government agencies	Any governmental institution, national or supranational
News and media outlets	*Traditional news and media* (e.g. news agencies, broadcasters); *Non-traditional news and media* (e.g. online magazines, platforms to collaboratively create news)
Self-published sources	Any sources that does not belong to any organisation/company, maintained by authors themselves

Table 2. Authoritativeness of sources (ticks indicate authoritative)

Publisher	Author		
	Individual	Organisation	Collective
Academic and research institution	✓	✓	✗
Academic publisher	✓	✓	✗
Other academic	✓	✓	✗
Government agency	✓	✓	✗
Vendor or e-commerce company	✗	✗	✗
Political or religious organisation	✗	✗	✗
Cultural institution	✓	✓	✗
Other type of company	✓	✓	✗
Traditional news and media	✓	✓	✗
Non-traditional news and media	✓	✗	✗
Self-published source	✗	✗	✗

that investigate automatic source retrieval. DeFacto [16] uses machine learning and NLP to produce scores about the likelihood of a web page to contain specific pieces of information and about its trustworthiness. Fetahu et al. also apply machine learning to assess web pages and find sources that are authoritative and relevant for statements within Wikipedia articles [8]. Other methods focus on evaluating provenance through similarity and distance metrics computed across different databases [5]. These models did not apply to Wikidata as this quantitative approach differs from the focus on principles such as type, author, and publisher that Wikidata follows. Furthermore, Wikidata external sources have diverse formats including web pages, PDFs, or csv files, which may be problematic to evaluate for completely automated systems such as [8] or [16]. DeFacto's measure of trustworthiness would need extensive testing in order to understand how it matches the definition of authoritativeness used by Wikidata.

The second group of approaches, followed by Wikidata, manually identifies principles to define credible and authoritative web sources. A small sample of Wikipedia citations have been evaluated by analysing their author, publisher, and document types in [9]. Crowdsourcing has been used to evaluate page relevance with faster completion times compared to expert-run experiments or online surveys, and low cost, whilst yielding high quality results [2].

3   Methods

We developed an approach that evaluates Wikidata references in terms of relevance and authoritativeness. We aimed to carry out a large-scale scale evaluation of Wikidata provenance, and adopted a two-staged approach relying on two complementary methods: microtask crowdsourcing and machine learning. Because of the advantages outlined above, we performed a crowdsourced evaluation of references, which was used to train a machine learning model to predict their quality. Machine learning can be easily applied on a large-scale and is virtually costless. We evaluated only external references, which were 6% of the total. In our analysis, we distinguished between bots and people because of their different roles in maintaining the knowledge graph. We posed these research questions:

RQ1 To what extent are Wikidata external references relevant?
RQ2 To what extent are Wikidata external reference authoritative?
RQ3 To what extent can non-relevant and non-authoritative references be predicted in Wikidata?

3.1   Source Evaluation

We designed three crowdsourcing tasks to assess reference quality, which were carried out on CrowdFlower[1]. All tasks included one type of microtask, except one, which included two. In order to increase the clarity of microtasks, we refined their design by launching test runs of small samples (between 50–100) of references to be evaluated. User behaviour (number of missed questions and completion time) was observed to understand microtask clarity.

Relevance. The first task (**T1**) was designed to assess relevance by asking users to find the pieces of information composing a statement within its source. Each microtask in T1 evaluated a reference, i.e. a statement with its attached source.

---

[1] https://www.crowdflower.com/.

In order to decrease the cognitive burden on workers, we structured microtasks along three questions, one for each element of a statement (subject, property, object). For each of these, we asked whether the source provided information about it. Users were prompted the successive questions only if they responded positively to the prior one (we asked about the property of a statement only if evidence about its subject was found in the source). English labels were shown for each statement's part, instead of their URIs. In the case of pages not working or requiring a log in, or for pages not in English, users could select the appropriate responses. Figure 1 illustrates an example of T1 microtask.

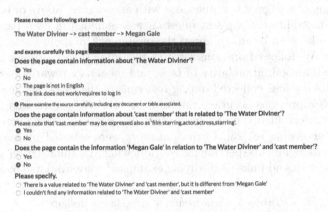

Fig. 1. A HIT from T1

Authoritativeness. A similar concept to authoritativeness—credibility—is consistently assessed under a positive bias by web users [13]. Hence, instead of directly questioning users about the authoritativeness of a source, which would have likely given overly subjective responses, we tested whether sources matched the types specified by Wikidata policy and asked the crowd to classify them, similar to the approach followed for Wikipedia in [9].

Author type was assessed in **T2.** Microtasks in T2 asked users to indicate the most appropriate author type for a source. Users were shown only the source, rather than the whole reference. Therefore, T2 included only unique web pages.

Task 3 (T3) evaluated publisher type. We assumed that pages belonging to the same domain had the same publisher. Hence, we collected judgements for unique domains, rather than for each single reference. **T3.A** included only higher-level types of publisher: *academic and scientific organisations, companies and organisations, government institutions, news and media,* and *self-published sources.* It consisted of a multiple choice question to select the most appropriate type of publisher. **T3.B** collected judgements related to the sub-types in Table 1. In T3.B users were asked whether the publisher type obtained from the previous task was appropriate for the source, in order to test contributors' performance and verify the results of T3.A. If users answered positively, they were asked to classify the sub-type of the source publisher. User pools of T3.A and T3.B were independent from each other. Responses for pages not working or requiring log in, or pages not in English were included in T2, T3.A, and T3.B.

Quality Assurance. Crowdsourcing is vulnerable to users who perform poorly due to lack of skills, malicious behaviour, or distraction [6]. We adopted various strategies to tackle this issue. We added gold standard questions to tasks and excluded workers whose performance fell under a certain threshold, which we set to 80% in all tasks. Tasks were structured in pages, each containing a number of microtasks varying according to the task. Workers were first required to pass a test consisting of a page of test questions with an accuracy above or equal to the threshold set. Additionally, a test question was included in each page of work. Users had to keep an accuracy above the minimum threshold throughout their contribution. We followed previous research regarding the experimental design of workers' qualification, granularity of task, and monetary rewards (see Table 3). Based on observations collected during test runs of the tasks, we accepted only workers with a previous accuracy rate of 85%—the highest allowed by Crowd-Flower[2]—to select highly performing users [6]. Payments per microtask were determined according to [23]. Correct answers were selected by majority voting over five assignments per microtask, following [1]. Information on how to complete the task and links to clarifying examples[3] were available on each page.

Table 3. Crowdsourcing experiment design

	T1	T2	T3.A	T3.B
Worker qualification	≥85%	≥85%	≥85%	≥85%
Granularity (microtasks per page)	10	8	8	8
Monetary reward (per microtasks)	$0.08	$0.06	$0.05	$0.05
Assignments	5	5	5	5
Min. worker accuracy	80%	80%	80%	80%

3.2 Automatic Evaluation Model

We used a machine learning classifier to identify not relevant or not authoritative sources. We trained a supervised algorithm for each outcome variable, using the labels obtained through the crowdsourcing experiment. Both relevance and authoritativeness models included features concerning the source itself and the semantics and editing activity of the statement it referred to. We assumed more frequently used sources are more likely to be checked by several users and therefore to be trusted. Regarding statement semantics, the rationale was that if a

---

[2] http://crowdflowercommunity.tumblr.com/post/108559336035/new-performance-level-badge-requirements.

[3] Examples were provided for T2, T3.A, and T3.B: https://wdref-author-evaluation.000webhostapp.com/, https://wdref-evaluation.000webhostapp.com/.

reference is good for a statement, it might be good for similar statements as well. Activity metrics were added as users with a larger number of edits may be more trustworthy, according to previous findings [21]. We included the same features in both models, as they could contribute to various extents to their accuracy.

URL reference uses. Number of times a URL has been used as a reference.
Domain reference uses. Number of times a domain has been used.
Source HTTP code. HTTP response code given by the source link.
Statement property. The property used in the statement.
Statement item. The item subject of the statement, represented as a vector of its structured components, i.e. labels and aliases were excluded.
Statement object. The object of the statement represented as a vector.
Subject parent class. Item parent class, i.e. object of property P279 (*subclass of*) or P31 (*instance of*).
Property parent class. Property parent class, i.e. object of P279 or P31.
Object parent class. Item parent class, i.e. object of P279 or P31.
Author type. Anonymous, bot, or registered human.
Author activity. Total number of revisions carried out by the reference creator, prior to adding it.
Author activity concerning references. Proportion between number of reference edits and total number of edits carried out by the author of the reference. Editors who are more active on references are more likely to add good sources.

We tested three different algorithms that previously performed well for different tasks, Naive Bayes, SVM, and Random Forests. Models were trained using the python library `scikit-learn` [19].

4   Evaluation

4.1   Data

Wikidata Corpus. We used the complete edit history of Wikidata updated to the 1st October 2016. We extracted all statements containing external references, excluding those pointing to a Wikimedia link and those not requiring any reference, according to Wikidata policy [27]. This gave $1,629,102$ references, of which $1,449,295$ pointed to two domains (uniprot.org and ebi.ac.uk). Around 98% of these were added by one bot and each of their domains was successively assigned a database property, therefore we removed them from the sample. Only references in English were selected; we dropped all references whose source did not have an international top-level domain or one from an English-speaking country[4]. $83,215$ references remained, from which we extracted 2586 (99% confidence level, 2.5% margin of error; further details in Table 4). We wanted our

---

[4] We kept the following top-level domains: tv, au, gov, com, net, org, info, edu, uk, mt, eu, ca, mil, wales, nz, ph, euweb, ie, id, info, ac, za, int, london, museum.

Table 4. Sample characteristics. Humans include registered and anonymous users.

	Total instances	Total items	Total statements	Total properties	Total URLs	Total domains	Avg. domains per property	Avg. edits per reference
All	2586	2372	2583	182	1674	345	3	1.03
Added by bots	1175	1108	1,175	30	486	38	3	1
Added by humans	1411	1269	1408	173	1189	325	2.7	1.2

sample to reflect the different subject-object relations supported by references. Therefore, the sample was drawn in order to reflect the proportion of property uses from the larger dataset. We automatically tested the validity of each link by querying its HTTP code with the python library **requests**. Pages that returned a 404 code or timed out were flagged as not working and not submitted to the crowd. One link[5], used in several references (512, 19.8%), redirected to another page which did not contain the data initially hosted by the link and was judged as not relevant. Two more links[6] (282 uses, 11% of the total) pointed to csv files that were automatically checked. Both links were classified as relevant and not submitted to the crowd. Other pages belonged to research projects which explicitly stated their authors. We labelled their author type as 'individual' and did not submit them for evaluation. After this filtering, the datasets submitted to the crowd included 1701 references (T1), 1178 unique URLs (T2), and 335 unique domains (T3.A and T3.B)[7].

Crowdsourcing Gold Standard. Two of the researchers independently created the gold standard for each task, manually labelling random samples of each of the datasets submitted to the crowd. The size of the annotated samples were determined to ensure that workers would not respond twice to the same question (sample size: T1:333; T2:116; T3.A and T3.B:67). Inter-rater agreement of gold standard questions (using Cohen's kappa) was between moderate and substantial for the four tasks: T1:0.447; T2:0.802; T3.A:0.587; T3.B:0.545. Divergent judgements were settled by mutual agreement. Furthermore, sources assessed in T1 had varying levels of difficulty. In some the information sought could be easily found, whereas others were very technical or contained long text. To better assess the crowd's performance, we labelled each reference in T1 gold standard as 'easy' or 'hard'. We found 239 easy and 94 hard references.

Machine Learning Data. We aimed to build binary classifiers to predict relevance and authoritative of sources. Hence, we converted the judgements collected into binary labels for each of these two outcome variables,

---

[5] http://www.census.gov/popest/data/counties/totals/2013/files/CO-EST2013-Alldata.csv.

[6] https://figshare.com/articles/GRID_release_2015_12_14/2010108, https://figshare.com/articles/GRID_release_2016-05-31/3409414.

[7] Data and code available at https://github.com/Aliossandro/WD_references_analysis.

i.e. relevant vs. non-relevant and authoritative vs. non-authoritative. We followed Wikidata and Wikipedia verifiability policies to identify the combinations of author and publisher types corresponding to authoritative sources (Table 2). Wikidata contemplates exceptions for sources generally considered as 'bad', e.g. self-published sources are acceptable in references regarding their author. For the purpose of analysis, we classified these types of sources as always not authoritative. We deemed not relevant, nor authoritative, sources with non-working links or that required log in as these were not accessible. We also excluded all references classified as not in English by crowdworkers. After this filtering, the dataset used to train the models had 2550 instances (1781 relevant vs. 769 non-relevant; 1610 authoritative vs. 940 non-authoritative).

4.2 Metrics

Crowdsourcing Experiment. CrowdFlower provides a full report for each task, which includes every response, plus several details about workers, e.g. id, country, and their previous accuracy rate. We extracted from this data the metrics we used to evaluate the performance of crowdworkers. For each task, we measured the percentage of correct answers to test questions, inter-rater agreement (measured as Fleiss' kappa [1]), and completion time.

Predictive Models. We evaluated the performance of the predictive models by comparing them to a baseline. For the relevance model, the baseline was generated by matching English labels of subject and object of a statement in the source text. A match of both would correspond to a relevant source. In case of labels composed of several words, if any of them were found in a page, we considered that a match. For authoritativeness, a blacklist of deprecated domains has been compiled within the *primary sources tool* project [25]. This list is currently used to exclude non-authoritative sources, thus we judged it as a meaningful term of comparison for an approach assessing reference authoritativeness. We deemed not authoritative all sources whose domain was not included in this blacklist.

4.3 Crowdsourcing Experiment Evaluation

The accuracy of trusted workers, i.e. contributors whose accuracy did not drop under 80%, was higher than that threshold (around 90%) and their responses had Fleiss' kappa between 0.335 and 0.534, indicating fair to moderate agreement. These figures suggest that judgements collected had good quality (see Table 5).

More than half of participants who worked on T1 were discarded due to a low accuracy rate. However, this was the task with the highest rate of microtasks completed per hour (37), i.e. the average number of microtasks successfully completed by the minimum number of workers (5) per hour. Furthermore, workers' accuracy was high on both easy (91.5%) and hard (89.7%) references.

Table 5. Task statistics (includes test questions)

Task	Microtasks	Total judgements	Trusted judgements	Total workers	Trusted workers	Trusted workers accuracy	Fleiss' k	Time	Cost
T1	1701	13, 330	9671	457	218	0.335	87.4%	45 h	$858
T2	1178	14, 340	9170	749	322	0.534	80.9%	90 h	$500
T3.A	345	4325	1950	322	60	0.435	76.9%	81 h	$116
T3.B	345	3622	2555	239	116	0.391	68.2%	24 h	$119

T2 took longer to complete (90 h), although not by microtasks/hour (13). The accuracy rate of all contributors to T2 was lower than T1 (72% vs. 75%). Task 3.A appeared to be the most difficult. The accuracy of its overall user pool (including trusted and non-trusted workers) was the lowest, with 66% of correct responses to test questions. Consequently, a high number of contributors were expelled from the task, leading to very long completion times. However, responses to T3.A had a moderate inter-rater agreement (0.435). 94.8% of the responses were confirmed by the first question of T3.B.

4.4   Relevance Evaluation

The ensuing sections report the findings of the reference evaluation. The results presented include both references assessed through crowdsourcing and those previously evaluated by the researchers (see Sect. 4.1).

The majority (67.2%) of sources evaluated in T1 were relevant (see Table 6) (**RQ1**). Non-relevant sources (23.8%) primarily did not support the subject of the statements (20.9% of the total). 7.5% of the pages assessed were not working. Only 1.5% of sources were found to not be in English, meaning that the approach followed to select only English-language pages worked well. Registered and anonymous human users were counted together, as the number of references added by anonymous users in our sample was not sufficient to draw sound conclusions. Overall, human editors added more relevant references than bots (90% vs. 43.8%). Evaluation results by type of user are shown in Table 6.

Table 6. Percentage of relevant sources by type of user

	Humans	Bots	All Users
Relevant	90	30.3	67.1
Not relevant	3.1	58.5	23.9
Page not working	4.9	11.1	7.5
Page not in English	2	0.1	1.5

4.5 Authoritativeness Evaluation

Concerning publisher type, the majority of references pointed to sources published by government agencies (37.5%). Academic institutions were the second most common type (around 24%). This changes if we look at the occurrences of unique web domains. In this case, government agencies slip to 5.8%, whereas 'other companies or organisations' become the most used sources with 19.9%. Regarding editor types, governments were still the most common among both bots and humans. However, the situation differs depending on whether all references are considered or unique domains. This is common to other publisher types and affects especially bot-added sources. Table 7 shows percentages of publisher type by user type, for all references and unique domains.

Table 7. Percentage of sources by type of publisher

	Sources			Unique domains		
	Humans	Bots	All users	Humans	Bots	All users
Governmental agencies	32.7	44.4	37.5	34.2	1.5	5.8
Other companies & organisations	15.3	12.6	14.4	17.6	27	19.9
Academic & research institutions	13	12.6	12.4	15.3	28.2	7.8
Other academic organisations	10.3	12.6	11.2	0.4	1.2	1.2
Cultural institutions	7.7	11.9	15	8.6	28.8	15
Vendors & e-commerce companies	7.3	1.8	5.4	8.6	1	15.9
Non-traditional news & media	3.7	1.2	2.5	4.3	2.9	10.1
Self-published	3	0.2	1.6	2.5	0.1	5.4
Traditional news & media	2	0	1.1	2.4	0	5.2
Political or religious institutions	0.9	4.6	1.2	0.9	4.6	1.7
Academic publishers	0.4	0	0.2	0.5	0	1.1
Others	0.1	0	0.1	0.1	0	0.3

Organisation staff were by far the most common author type (78%) overall, and both among bot- and human-added references (see Table 8). Sources created by identifiable individuals followed (7.9%) and appear to be reused less often than those authored by organisation (12.5% of unique URLs). Collectively-authored sources represented only 2.9% of our sample. Whereas these were only 0.2% of bot-added pages, they were 5.3% of those created by human users. Finally, applying the criteria in Table 2, 63.7% of the references were classified as authoritative (**RQ2**). We summarised results about reference quality in Table 9.

Table 8. Percentage of sources by type of author

	Sources			Unique domains		
	Humans	Bots	All users	Humans	Bots	All users
Organisation	75.7	81.4	78.2	72.4	50.5	65.8
Individual	10.8	4.5	7.9	11.8	13.1	12.5
Collective	5.3	0.2	2.9	6.1	0.6	4.5
Page not working	3.9	0.2	2.1	4.9	0.6	3.7
Page not in English	4.3	13.7	3.7	4.9	35.2	13.4

Table 9. Percentage of sources by relevance and authoritativeness

	Humans	Bots	All users
Relevant & authoritative	78.2	41.1	60.8
Relevant & not authoritative	14	2.5	9
Not relevant & authoritative	3.7	2.3	0.7
Not relevant & not authoritative	4.1	55.7	27.8

4.6 Quality Prediction Models

The trained models were binary classifiers aiming to predict non-relevant and non-authoritative references. We used stratified 10-folds cross-validation to estimate the algorithms' performance. Stratified cross-validation ensures outcome classes have the same distribution in the subsets selected in each fold and improves the comparability of different algorithms [10]. The F_1 measure was computed on true and false positive over all folds, providing a more unbiased estimate compared to other methods [10]. We used Matthews correlation coefficient (MCC) to estimate the level of agreement between predicted and observed labels. MCC has values between -1 and $+1$, with higher values indicating better agreement [3]. Class unbalance was addressed by adjusting prediction weights in SVM and Random Forest [19]. Further details about implementation and hyperparameters of the models are provided in the above cited GitHub repository.

The **relevance** baseline was good at predicting non-relevant sources ($F_1 = 0.84$, MCC = 0.68), although it was outperformed by all models. Random Forest provided the best scores. The **authoritativeness** baseline gave worse results ($F_1 = 0.53$, MCC = 0.15). All trained models outperformed the baseline, with Random Forest yielding the highest F_1 (0.89) and MCC (0.83). Results for both models are shown in Table 10.

Table 10. Performance of prediction models for relevance and authoritativeness

		P	R	F$_1$	AUC-PR	MCC
Relevance	Baseline	0.88	0.83	0.84	0.81	0.68
	Naive Bayes	0.94	0.94	0.90	0.92	0.86
	Random Forest	0.95	0.95	**0.92**	0.94	**0.89**
	SVM	0.94	0.94	0.91	0.94	0.87
Authoritativeness	Baseline	0.71	0.65	0.53	0.62	0.16
	Naive Bayes	0.90	0.90	0.86	0.88	0.78
	Random Forest	0.93	0.92	**0.89**	0.93	**0.83**
	SVM	0.90	0.90	0.89	0.90	0.79

5 Discussion

The crowdsourced experiment provided accurate results, as shown by the level of agreement between workers and the percentage of correct responses to test questions. Task completion times differed greatly, probably due to the task type. T1 asked users to find a piece of information within a web page and seemed to be straightforward. Conversely, the classification tasks T3.A and T3.B were harder. This may be due to the classification system used appearing unclear for workers, or clashing with their prior knowledge, leading to erroneous responses, similar to what has been noted before in taxonomy creation tasks [14]. Nevertheless, the judgements collected in T3.B largely confirmed T3.A.

The majority of references examined included relevant sources, although those added by humans and bots diverged considerably. This (see Table 6) may have been caused by a link to a US census dataset that was redirected to another page, which did not contain relevant data anymore. We believe this is not an isolated case. Bots add large numbers of statements in batch, including references. References pointing to invalid URLs may become outdated or invalid. Continuous control from the community is required—the eyeballs required to make all bugs shallow [22]—or a method to automatically check sources.

Government agencies are the most common publisher type, both among human- and bot-added references. Sources are generally authored by organisation staff and not by individuals. Two classes of publisher showed large differences between percentage of references and percentage of unique domains (Table 7). In both categories, the skewness is likely to be determined by the massive automatic generation of statements by bots. This led us to hypothesise that typical bot editing patterns may result in a lower degree of diversity of source types. The data confirmed this: in spite of similar numbers of references by bots and humans (46.3% vs 53.6%), bots used 36 web domains, compared to 295 by humans. This analysis should increase awareness about the current limitations of using bots to add references, and in turn help design bots that follow a more nuanced approach to reference selection.

The distribution of author and publisher types for references did not match Wikipedia [9], despite the partial overlap of the two communities [20]. Almost no news sources are used as sources in Wikidata, compared to the online encyclopedia. Whereas Wikidata recommends primary sources as references, Wikipedia asks editors to use secondary sources and officially disapproves of primary ones, in line with the rule that the encyclopedia cannot contain original research.

Sources are generally split between 'good' and 'bad' (Table 9). Few references are relevant but not authoritative; even fewer are not relevant but authoritative. Accessibility was required, therefore several were classified as neither relevant nor authoritative because they were not working or required to log in. Some pages redirected to a new one, which often was not relevant. These were possibly valid at the time of addition, but subsequently changed. A frequent check of URL validity may be effective to spot those that have become bad.

The predictive models for relevance and authoritativeness performed well, which may support our intuition that sources from a website that are good for a type of statement, i.e. using a determined property with defined domain and range, are likely to be good for similar statements. Another explanation may regard the characteristics of references in Wikidata. From a total of around 2000 properties, only about 200 have references. Sources from the same web domain tend to have the same level of quality. On the other hand, the number of domains per property is low. As a consequence, the algorithm may find 'easy' to assess combination of properties and domains. If the number of properties with references and the diversity of web domains used will increase, further research should evaluate how this affects the performance of predictive models of reference quality. It should also seek to understand how to adapt these models to be implemented in Wikidata, to help editors find bad references.

6   Conclusions and Future Work

The contribution of this paper is twofold. First, this is the first study to evaluate provenance quality in Wikidata. Second, we tested a two-staged approach to evaluate Wikidata references, combining microtask crowdsourcing and machine learning. Crowdsourcing provided accurate evaluation of external references, which were mostly relevant and authoritative. A continuous check by users may be needed to address the issue of links becoming non-valid. Models to predict non-relevant or non-authoritative references may also be useful. With respect to that, our results were encouraging. Our models outperformed the baseline, which motivates towards further work to integrate them in Wikidata. Future work should validate whether our results hold true for non-English sources. Besides using outgoing links, Wikidata expresses provenance by means of internal connections, which were not examined in this study. These are a substantial part of Wikidata references and should be examined in the future, in order to achieve a comprehensive evaluation of provenance quality in Wikidata.

Acknowledgement. This project is supported by funding received from the European Union's Horizon 2020 research and innovation programme under the Marie Skłodowska-Curie grant agreement No. 642795 (WDAqua ITN).

References

1. Acosta, M., Zaveri, A., Simperl, E., Kontokostas, D., Auer, S., Lehmann, J.: Crowdsourcing linked data quality assessment. In: Alani, H., et al. (eds.) ISWC 2013. LNCS, vol. 8219, pp. 260–276. Springer, Heidelberg (2013). doi:10.1007/978-3-642-41338-4_17
2. Alonso, O., Rose, D.E., Stewart, B.: Crowdsourcing for relevance evaluation. SIGIR Forum **42**(2), 9–15 (2008)
3. Baldi, P., Brunak, S., Chauvin, Y., Andersen, C.A.F., Nielsen, H.: Assessing the accuracy of prediction algorithms for classification: an overview. Bioinformatics **16**(5), 412–424 (2000)
4. Brasileiro, F., Almeida, J.P.A., de Carvalho, V.A., Guizzardi, G.: Applying a multi-level modeling theory to assess taxonomic hierarchies in Wikidata. In: Proceedings of the 25th International Conference on World Wide Web, WWW 2016, Montreal, Canada, 11–15 April 2016, Companion Volume, pp. 975–980 (2016)
5. Dai, C., Lin, D., Bertino, E., Kantarcioglu, M.: An approach to evaluate data trustworthiness based on data provenance. In: Jonker, W., Petković, M. (eds.) SDM 2008. LNCS, vol. 5159, pp. 82–98. Springer, Heidelberg (2008). doi:10.1007/978-3-540-85259-9_6
6. Eickhoff, C., de Vries, A.P.: Increasing cheat robustness of crowdsourcing tasks. Inf. Retr. **16**(2), 121–137 (2013)
7. Erxleben, F., Günther, M., Krötzsch, M., Mendez, J., Vrandečić, D.: Introducing Wikidata to the linked data web. In: Mika, P., et al. (eds.) ISWC 2014. LNCS, vol. 8796, pp. 50–65. Springer, Cham (2014). doi:10.1007/978-3-319-11964-9_4
8. Fetahu, B., Markert, K., Nejdl, W., Anand, A.: Finding news citations for Wikipedia. In: Proceedings of the 25th ACM International on Conference on Information and Knowledge Management, CIKM 2016, Indianapolis, IN, USA, 24–28 October 2016, pp. 337–346. ACM (2016)
9. Ford, H., Sen, S., Musicant, D.R., Miller, N.: Getting to the source: where does Wikipedia get its information from? In: Proceedings of the 9th International Symposium on Open Collaboration, Hong Kong, China, 05–07 August 2013, pp. 9:1–9:10 (2013)
10. Forman, G., Scholz, M.: Apples-to-apples in cross-validation studies: pitfalls in classifier performance measurement. SIGKDD Explor. **12**(1), 49–57 (2010)
11. Hartig, O.: Provenance information in the web of data. In: Proceedings of the WWW 2009 Workshop on Linked Data on the Web, LDOW 2009, Madrid, Spain, 20 April 2009. CEUR Workshop Proceedings, vol. 538. CEUR-WS.org (2009)
12. Hartig, O., Zhao, J.: Using web data provenance for quality assessment. In: Proceedings of the First International Workshop on the Role of Semantic Web in Provenance Management (SWPM 2009), Collocated with the 8th International Semantic Web Conference (ISWC-2009), Washington DC, USA, 25 October 2009. CEUR Workshop Proceedings, vol. 526. CEUR-WS.org (2009)
13. Kakol, M., Jankowski-Lorek, M., Abramczuk, K., Wierzbicki, A., Catasta, M.: On the subjectivity and bias of web content credibility evaluations. In: 22nd International World Wide Web Conference, WWW 2013, Rio de Janeiro, Brazil, 13–17 May 2013, Companion Volume, pp. 1131–1136. International World Wide Web Conferences Steering Committee/ACM (2013)
14. Karampinas, D., Triantafillou, P.: Crowdsourcing taxonomies. In: Simperl, E., Cimiano, P., Polleres, A., Corcho, O., Presutti, V. (eds.) ESWC 2012. LNCS, vol. 7295, pp. 545–559. Springer, Heidelberg (2012). doi:10.1007/978-3-642-30284-8_43

15. Kleinberg, J.M.: Authoritative sources in a hyperlinked environment. J. ACM **46**(5), 604–632 (1999)
16. Lehmann, J., Gerber, D., Morsey, M., Ngonga Ngomo, A.-C.: DeFacto - deep fact validation. In: Cudré-Mauroux, P., et al. (eds.) ISWC 2012. LNCS, vol. 7649, pp. 312–327. Springer, Heidelberg (2012). doi:10.1007/978-3-642-35176-1_20
17. Lucassen, T., Schraagen, J.M.: Trust in Wikipedia: how users trust information from an unknown source. In: Proceedings of the 4th ACM Workshop on Information Credibility on the Web, WICOW 2010, Raleigh, North Carolina, USA, 27 April 2010, pp. 19–26. ACM (2010)
18. Müller-Birn, C., Karran, B., Lehmann, J., Luczak-Rösch, M.: Peer-production system or collaborative ontology engineering effort: what is Wikidata? In: Proceedings of the 11th International Symposium on Open Collaboration, San Francisco, CA, USA, 19–21 August 2015, pp. 20:1–20:10. ACM (2015)
19. Pedregosa, F., Varoquaux, G., Gramfort, A., Michel, V., Thirion, B., Grisel, O., Blondel, M., Prettenhofer, P., Weiss, R., Dubourg, V., Vanderplas, J., Passos, A., Cournapeau, D., Brucher, M., Perrot, M., Duchesnay, E.: Scikit-learn: machine learning in Python. J. Mach. Learn. Res. **12**, 2825–2830 (2011)
20. Piscopo, A., Phethean, C., Simperl, E.: Wikidatians are born: paths to full participation in a collaborative structured knowledge base. In: 50th Hawaii International Conference on System Sciences, HICSS 2017, Hilton Waikoloa Village, Hawaii, USA, 4–7 January 2017. AIS Electronic Library (AISeL) (2017)
21. Potthast, M., Stein, B., Gerling, R.: Automatic vandalism detection in Wikipedia. In: Macdonald, C., Ounis, I., Plachouras, V., Ruthven, I., White, R.W. (eds.) ECIR 2008. LNCS, vol. 4956, pp. 663–668. Springer, Heidelberg (2008). doi:10.1007/978-3-540-78646-7_75
22. Raymond, E.S.: The Cathedral and the Bazaar - Musings on Linux and Open Source by an Accidental Revoltionary, Rev. edn. O'Reilly, Sebastopol (2001)
23. Snow, R., O'Connor, B., Jurafsky, D., Ng, A.Y.: Cheap and fast - but is it good? Evaluating non-expert annotations for natural language tasks. In: 2008 Conference on Empirical Methods in Natural Language Processing, EMNLP 2008, Proceedings of the Conference, 25–27 October 2008, Honolulu, Hawaii, USA, A Meeting of SIGDAT, A Special Interest Group of the ACL. pp. 254–263. ACL (2008)
24. Steiner, T.: Bots vs. Wikipedians, Anons vs. Logged-Ins (Redux): a global study of edit activity on Wikipedia and Wikidata. In: Proceedings of the International Symposium on Open Collaboration, OpenSym 2014, Berlin, Germany, 27–29 August 2014, pp. 25:1–25:7. ACM (2014)
25. Tanon, T.P., Vrandecic, D., Schaffert, S., Steiner, T., Pintscher, L.: From freebase to Wikidata: the great migration. In: Proceedings of the 25th International Conference on World Wide Web, WWW 2016, Montreal, Canada, 11–15 April 2016, pp. 1419–1428 (2016)
26. Vrandecic, D., Krötzsch, M.: Wikidata: a free collaborative knowledge base. Commun. ACM **57**(10), 78–85 (2014)
27. Wikidata: Wikidata: Sources – Wikidata, the free knowledge base (2017). https://www.wikidata.org/wiki/Help:Sources. Accessed 09 Apr 2017
28. Wikidata: Wikidata: Verifiability – Wikidata, the free knowledge base (2017). https://www.wikidata.org/wiki/Wikidata:Verifiability. Accessed 07 Apr 2017
29. Wikipedia: Wikipedia: Verifiability – Wikipedia, the free encyclopedia (2017). https://en.wikipedia.org/wiki/Wikipedia:Verifiability. Accessed 07 Apr 2017

Strider: A Hybrid Adaptive Distributed RDF Stream Processing Engine

Xiangnan Ren[1,2] and Olivier Curé[2(✉)]

[1] ATOS, 80 Quai Voltaire, 95870 Bezons, France
xiang-nan.ren@atos.net
[2] LIGM (UMR 8049), CNRS, UPEM, 77454 Marne-la-vallée, France
olivier.cure@u-pem.fr

Abstract. Real-time processing of data streams emanating from sensors is becoming a common task in Internet of Things scenarios. The key implementation goal consists in efficiently handling massive incoming data streams and supporting advanced data analytics services like anomaly detection. In an on-going, industrial project, a 24/7 available stream processing engine usually faces dynamically changing data and workload characteristics. These changes impact the engine's performance and reliability. We propose Strider, a hybrid adaptive distributed RDF Stream Processing engine that optimizes logical query plan according to the state of data streams. Strider has been designed to guarantee important industrial properties such as scalability, high availability, fault tolerance, high throughput and acceptable latency. These guarantees are obtained by designing the engine's architecture with state-of-the-art Apache components such as Spark and Kafka. We highlight the efficiency (*e.g.*, on a single machine machine, up to 60x gain on throughput compared to state-of-the-art systems, a throughput of 3.1 million triples/second on a 9 machines cluster, a major breakthrough in this system's category) of Strider on real-world and synthetic data sets.

Keywords: RDF stream processing · SPARQL · Adaptive query processing · Distributed computing · Apache spark

1 Introduction

With the growing use of Semantic Web Technology in Internet of Things (IoT) contexts, *e.g.*, for data integration and reasoning purposes, the requirement for almost real-time platforms that can efficiently adapt to large scale data streams, *i.e.*, continuous SPARQL query processing, is gaining more and more attention. In the context of the FUI (Fonds Unique Interministeriel) Waves project[1], we are processing data streams emanated from sensors distributed over the drinking water distribution network of a resource management international company. For France alone, this company distributes water to over 12 million clients through

---

[1] http://www.waves-rsp.org/.

© Springer International Publishing AG 2017
C. d'Amato et al. (Eds.): ISWC 2017, Part I, LNCS 10587, pp. 559–576, 2017.
DOI: 10.1007/978-3-319-68288-4_33

a network of more than 100.000 km equipped with thousands (and growing) of sensors. Obviously, our RDF Stream Processing (RSP) engine should satisfy some common industrial features, e.g., high throughput, high availability, low latency, scalability and fault tolerance.

Querying over RDF data streams can be quite challenging. Due to fast generation rates and schema free natures of RDF data streams, a continuous SPARQL query usually involves intensive join tasks which may rapidly become a performance bottleneck. Existing centralized RSP systems like C-SPARQL [4], CQELS [13] and ETALIS [3] are not capable of handling massive incoming data streams, as they do not benefit from task parallelism and the scalability of a computing cluster. Besides, most streaming systems are operating 24/7 with patterns, i.e., stream graph structures, that may change overtime (in terms of graph shapes and sizes). This can potentially have a performance impact on query processing since in most available distributed RDF streaming systems, e.g., CQELSCloud [17] and Katts [9], the logical query plan is determined at compile time. Such a behavior can hardly promise long-term efficiency and reliability, since there is no single query plan that is always optimal for a given query.

A general approach for large scale data stream processing is performed over a distributed setting. Such systems are better designed and operated upon when implemented on top of robust, state-of-the-art engines, e.g., Kafka [10] and Spark [26,27]. Moreover, the system has to adapt to unpredictable input data streams and to dynamically updated execution plans while ensuring optimal performance. A time-driven/batch-driven [5] approach could be a solution for adaptive streaming query. In that context, it becomes possible to reconstruct the logical plan for each query execution. Furthermore, compared to data-driven systems [5], time-driven/batch-driven provides a more coarse operation granularity. Although this mechanism inevitably causes higher query latency, it also brings high system throughput, inexpensive cost and low latency to achieve fault tolerance and system adaptivity [27].

Our system, Strider, possesses the aforementioned characteristics. In this paper, we present three main contributions concerning this system: (1) the design and implementation of a production-ready RSP engine for large scale RDF data streams processing which is based on the state-of-the-art distributed computing frameworks (i.e., Spark and Kafka). (2) Strider integrates two forms of adaptation. In the first one, for each execution of a continuous query, the system decides, based on incoming stream volumes, to use either a query compile-time (rule-based) or query run-time (cost-based) optimization approach. The second one concerns the run-time approach and decides when the query plan is optimized (either at the previous query window or at the current one). (3) an evaluation of Strider over real-world and synthetic data sets.

2   Background Knowledge

Strider follows a classical streaming system approach with a messaging component for data flow management and a computing core for real-time data analytics.

In this section, we present and motivate the use of Spark Streaming and Kafka as these two components. Then, we consider streaming models and adaptive query processing.

Kafka and Spark Streaming. Kafka is a distributed message queue which aims to provide a unified, high-throughput, low-latency real-time data management. Intuitively, producers emit messages which are categorized into adequate *topics*. The messages are partitioned among a cluster to support parallelism of upstream/downstream operations. Kafka uses *offsets* to uniquely identify the location of each message within the partition.

Spark is a MapReduce-like cluster-computing framework that proposes a parallelized fault tolerant collection of elements called Resilient Distributed Dataset (RDD) [26]. An RDD is divided into multiple partitions across different cluster nodes such that operations can be performed in parallel. Spark enables parallel computations on unreliable machines and automatically handles locality-aware scheduling, fault-tolerant and load balancing tasks. Spark Streaming extends RDD to Discretized Stream (DStream) [27] and thus enables to support near real-time data processing by creating *micro-batches* of duration T. DStream represents a sequence of RDDs where each RDD is assigned a timestamp. Similar to Spark, Spark Streaming describes the computing logics as a template of RDD Directed Acyclic Graph (DAG). Each batch generates an instance according to this template for later job execution. The micro-batch execution model provides Spark Streaming second/sub-second latency and high throughput. To achieve continuous SPARQL query processing on Spark Streaming, we bind the SPARQL operators to the corresponding Spark SQL relational operators. Moreover, the data processing is based on DataFrame (DF), an API abstraction derived from RDD.

Streaming Models. At the physical level, a computation model for stream processing has two principle classes: Bulk Synchronous Parallel (BSP) and Record-at-a-time [25]. From a logical level perspective, a streaming model uses the concept of a *Tick* to drive the system in taking actions over input streams. [5] defines a Tick in three ways: data-driven (DD), time-driven (TD) and batch-driven (BD). In general, the physical BSP is associated to the TD and/or BD models, *e.g.*, Spark Streaming [27] and Google DataFlow with FlumeJava [1] adopt this approach by creating a micro-batch of a certain duration T. That is data are cumulated and processed through the entire DAG within each batch. The record-at-a-time model is usually associated to the logical DD model (although TD and BD are possible) and prominent examples are Flink [6] and Storm [23]. The record-at-a-time/DD model provides lower latency than BSP/TD/BD model for typical computation. On the other hand, the record-at-a-time model requires state maintenance for all operators with record-level granularity. This behavior obstructs system throughput and brings much higher latencies when recovering after a system failure [25]. For complex tasks involving lots of aggregations and iterations, the record-at-a-time model could be less efficient, since it introduces an overhead for the launch of frequent tasks. Given these properties and the fact that in [7], the authors emphasize that latencies in the order of few seconds is enough for most extreme use cases at Facebook, we have decided to use Spark Streaming.

Adaptive Query Processing (AQP) is recognized as a complex task, especially in the streaming context [8]. Moreover, AQP for continuous SPARQL query needs to cope with some cross-field challenges such as SPARQL query optimization, stream processing, *etc.*. Due to structure unpredictability, schema-free and real-time features of RDF data streams, conventional optimizations for static RDF data processing through data pre-processing, *e.g.*, triple indexing and statistic summarizing, become impractical. However, the perspectives from [16,21] show that most parts of RDF graphs have tabular structure, especially in the IoT domain. This opens up several perspectives concerning selectivity/-cardinality estimation and the possibility to use Dynamic Programming (DP) approaches. Inspired by [11,14,22,24,25], we propose a novel AQP optimizer for RDF stream processing.

3   Strider Overview

In this section, we first present a Strider query example, then we provide a system's overview, detail the data flow and query optimization components.

3.1   Continuous Query Example

Listing 1.1 introduces a running scenario that we will use throughout this paper. The example corresponds to a use case encountered in the Waves project, *i.e.*, query Q_8 continuously processes the messages of various types of sensor observations.

We introduce new lexical rules for continuous SPARQL queries which are tailored to a micro-batch approach. The STREAMING keyword initializes the application context of Spark Streaming and the windowing operator. More precisely, WINDOW and SLIDE respectively indicate the size and sliding parameter of a time-based window. The novelty comes from the BATCH clause which specifies the micro-batch interval of discretized stream for Spark Streaming. Here, a sliding window consists of one or multiple micro-batches.

```
STREAMING { WINDOW [10\,s] SLIDE [10\,s] BATCH [5\,s] }
REGISTER { QUERYID [Q8] SPARQL [
  prefix rdf: <http://www.w3.org/1999/02/22-rdf-syntax-ns#>
  prefix ssn: <http://purl.oclc.org/NET/ssnx/ssn/>
  prefix cuahsi: <http://www.cuahsi.org/waterML/>
  SELECT ?s ?o1 ?o2 ?o3
  WHERE {    ?s ssn:hasValue ?o1 (tp1); ssn:hasValue ?o2 (tp2);
             ssn:hasValue ?o3 (tp3).
          ?o1 rdf:type cuahsi:flow (tp4).
          ?o2 rdf:type cuahsi:temperature (tp5).
          ?o3 rdf:type cuahsi:chlorine    (tp6). }] }
```

Listing 1.1. Strider's query example (Q_8)

The REGISTER clause is used to register standard SPARQL queries. Each query is identified by an identifier. The system allows to register several queries simultaneously in a thread pool. By sharing the same application context and cluster resources, Strider launches all registered continuous SPARQL queries asynchronously by different threads.

3.2 Architecture

Strider contains two principle modules: (1) data flow management. In order to ensure high throughput, fault-tolerance, and easy-to-use features, Strider uses Apache Kafka to manage input data flow. The incoming RDF streams are categorized into different *message topics,* which practically represent different types of RDF events. (2) Computing core. Strider core is based on the Spark programming framework. Spark Streaming receives, maintains messages emitted from Kafka in parallel, and generates data processing pipeline.

Figure 1 gives a high-level overview of the system's architecture. The upper part of the figure provides details on the application's data flow management. In a nutshell, data sources (IoT sensors) are sending messages to a publish-subscribe layer. This layer emits messages for the streaming layer which executes registered queries. The sensor's metadata are converted into RDF events for data integration purposes. We use Kafka to design the system's data flow management. Kafka is connected to Spark Streaming using a *Direct Approach*[2]

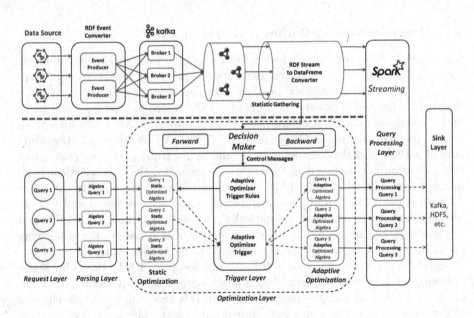

Fig. 1. Strider architecture

---

[2] https://spark.apache.org/docs/latest/streaming-kafka-integration.html.

to guarantee exactly-once semantics and parallel data feeding. The input RDF event streams are then continuously transformed to DataFrames.

The lower part of Fig. 1 presents components related to the implementation of the computing core. The Request layer registers continuous queries. Currently, we consider that the input queries are independent, thus a multi-query optimization approach (e.g., sub-query sharing) is not in the scope of the current state of Strider. These queries are later sent to the Parsing layer to compute a first version of a query plan. These new plans are pushed to the Optimization layer which consists of four collaborating sub-components: static and adaptive optimizations as well as a trigger mechanism and a Decision Maker for adaptation strategy. Finally, the Query Processing layer sets the query execution off right after the optimized logical plan takes place.

4   Strider's Continuous SPARQL Processing

In this section, we detail the components of the Strider's optimizer layer. Two optimization components are proposed, i.e., static and adaptive, which are respectively based on heuristic rules and (stream-based) statistics. The trigger layer decides whether the query processing adopts a static or an adaptive approach. Two strategies are proposed for AQP: backward (B-AQP) and forward (F-AQP). They mainly differ on when, i.e., at the previous or current window, the query plan is computed.

4.1   Query Processing Outline and Trigger Layer

Intuitively, Strider's optimizers search for the optimal join ordering of triple patterns based on collected statistics. Both static (query compile-time) and adaptive (query run-time) optimizations are processed using a graph $G^U = (V, E)$, denoted Undirected Connected Graph (UCG) [22] where vertices represent triple patterns and edges symbolize joins between triple patterns. Naturally, for a given query q and its query graph $G^Q(q)$, $G^U(q) \subseteq G^Q(q)$. A UCG showcases the structure of a BGP and the join possibilities among its triple patterns. That query representation is considered to be more expressive [14] than the classical RDF query graph. The weight of UCG's vertices and edges correspond to the selectivity of triple patterns and joins, respectively. Once the weights of an UCG are initialized, the query planner automatically generates an optimal logical plan and triggers a query execution. For the sake of a better explanation, the windowing operator involved in this section is considered as a tumbling window.

Strider's static optimization retains the philosophy of [24]. Basically, static optimization implies a heuristics-based query optimization. It ignores data statistics and leads to a static query planner. In this case, unpredictable changes in data stream structures may incur a bad query plan. The static optimization layer aims at giving a basic performance guarantee. The predefined heuristic rules set empirically assign the weights for UCG vertices and edges. Next, the query planner determines the shortest traversal path in the current UCG and generates the logical plan for query execution. The obtained logical plan represents the query execution pipeline which is permanently kept by the system. More details about UCG creation and query logical plan generation are given in Sect. 4.2.

The Trigger layer supports the transition between the stages of static optimization and adaptive optimization. In a nutshell, that layer is dedicated to notify the system whether it is necessary to proceed with an adaptive optimization. Our adaptation strategy requires collecting statistical information and generating an execution logical plan. The overhead coming with such actions is not negligible in a distributed environment. The Strider prototype provides a set of straightforward trigger rules, *i.e.*, the adaptive algebra optimization is triggered by a configurable workload threshold. The threshold refers to two factors: (1) the input number of RDF events/triples; (2) the fraction of the estimated input data size and the allocated executors' heap memory.

4.2 Run-Time Query Plan Generation

Here, we first briefly introduce how we collect stream statistics and construct query plan. Then, we give an insight into the AQP optimization, which is essentially a cardinality-based optimization.

Unlike systems based on greedy and left-deep tree generation, *e.g.*, [13,22], Strider makes a full usage of CPU computing resources and benefits from parallel hardware settings. It thus creates query logical plans in the form of general (bushy) directed trees. Hence, the nodes with the same height in a query plan p_n can be asynchronously computed in a non-blocking way (in the case where computing resources are allowed). Coming back to our Listing 1.1 example, Fig. 2 refines the procedure of query processing (F-AQP) at w_n, $n \in N$. If w_n contains multiple RDDs (micro-batches), the system performs the union all RDDs and generates a new combined RDD. Note that the union operator has a very low-cost in Spark. Afterward, the impending query plan optimization follows three steps: (a) UCG (weight) initialization; (b) UCG path cover finding; (c) query plan generation.

UCG weight initialization is briefly described in Algorithm 1 and Fig. 3 (step (a), step (b)). Since triple patterns are located at the bottom of a query tree, the query evaluation is performed in a bottom-up fashion and starts with the selection of triple patterns $\sigma(tp_i)$, $1 \le i \le I$ (with I the number of triple patterns in the query's BGP). The system computes $\sigma(tp_i)$ asynchronously for each i and temporally caches the corresponding results $(R^\sigma(tp_i))$ in memory. $Card(tp_i)$, *i.e.*, the cardinality of $R^\sigma(tp_i)$, is computed by a Spark count action. Thence, we can directly assign the weight of vertices in $G^U(Q)$. Note that the estimation of $Card(tp_i)$ is exact.

Once all vertices are set up, the system predicts the weight of edges (*i.e.*, joined patterns) in $G^U(q)$. We categorize two types of joins (edges): (i) star join, includes two sub-types, *i.e.*, star join without bounded object and star join with bounded object; (ii) non-star join. To estimate the cardinality of join

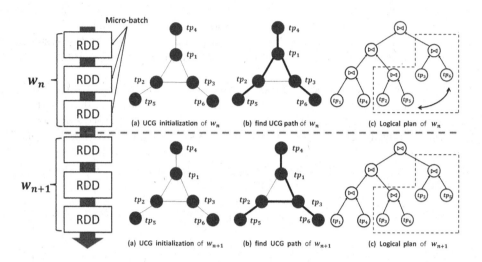

Fig. 2. Dynamic query plan generation for Q_8

patterns, we make a trade-off between accuracy and complexity. The main idea is inspired by a research conducted in [11,14,22]. However, we infer the weight of an edge from its connected vertices, *i.e.*, no data pre-processing is required. The algorithm begins by iteratively traversing $G^U(q)$ and identifies each vertex $v \in V$ and each edge $e \in E$. Then we can decompose $G^U(q)$ into the disjoint star-shaped joins and their interconnected chains (Fig. 3, step (b)). The weight of an edge in a star join shape is estimated by the function getStarJoinWeight. The function first estimates the upper bound of each star join output cardinality $(e.g., , Card(tp_1 \bowtie tp_2 \bowtie tp_3))$, then assigns the weight edge by edge. Every time the weight of the current edge e is assigned, we mark e as visited. This process repeats until no more star join can be found. Then, the weight of unvisited non-star join shapes is estimated by the function getNonStarJoinWeight. It lookups the two vertices of the current edge, and chooses the one with smaller weight to estimate the edge cardinality. The previous processes are repeated until all the edges have been visited in $G^U(q)$.

UCG path cover finding and Query plan generation. Figure 3 step (c) introduces path cover finding and query plan generation. The system starts by finding the path cover in $G^U(q)$ right after $G^U(q)$ is prepared. Intuitively, we search the undirected path cover which links all the vertices of $G^U(q)$ with a minimum total edge weight. The path searching is achieved by applying Floyd-Warshall algorithm iteratively. The extracted path $Card(G^U(q)) \subseteq G^U(q)$, is regarded as the candidate for the logical plan generation. Finally, we construct p_n, the logical plan of $G^U(q)$ at w_n, in a top-down manner (Fig. 3, step (c)). Note that path finding and plan generation are both computed on the driver node and are not expensive operations (around 2–4 ms in our case).

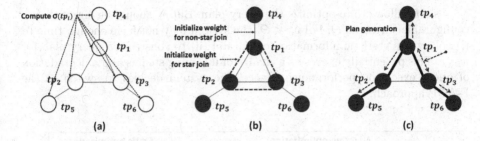

Fig. 3. Initialized UCG weight, find path cover and generate query plan

---

Algorithm 1. UCG weight initialization

Input: query q, $G^U(q) = (V, E) \subseteq G^Q(q)$, current buffered window w_n
Output: $G^U(q)$ with weight-assigned

1 **while** $\exists v$ *unvisited* $\in V$ **do**
2   mark v as visited, $R^\sigma(v) \leftarrow$ compute (v) ;
3   buffer $(v, R^\sigma(v)) \wedge v$.weight $\leftarrow Card(v)$;

4 **while** $\exists e$ *unvisited* $\in E$ **do**
5   mark e as visited ;
6   **if** *($\exists$ star join S_J) $\wedge e \cap S_J \neq \emptyset$* **then**
7   locate each $S_J \in G^U(q)$
8   **foreach** $\forall e_S \in S_J$ **do**
9   mark e_S as visited ;
10   e_S.weight $\leftarrow$ getStarJoinWeight(S_J, e_S.vertices) ;

11   **else** e.weight $\leftarrow$ getNonStarJoinWeight(S_J);

4.3 B-AQP and F-AQP

We propose a dual AQP strategy, namely, **backward** (B-AQP) and **forward** (F-AQP). B/F-AQP depict two philosophies for AQP, Fig. 4 roughly illustrates how B/F-AQP switching is decided at run-time, *i.e.*, this is the responsibility of the Decision Maker component. Generally, B-AQP and F-AQP are using similar techniques for query plan generation. Compared to F-AQP, B-AQP delays the process for query plan generation.

Our B-AQP strategy is inspired by [25]'s pre-scheduling. Backward implies gathering, feeding back the statistics to the optimizer on the current window, then the optimizer constructs the query plan for the next window. That is the system computes the query plan p_{n+1} of a window w_{n+1} through the statistics of a previous window w_n. Strider possesses a time-driven execution mechanism, the query execution is triggered periodically with a fixed update frequency s (*i.e.*, sliding window size). Between two consecutive windows w_n and w_{n+1}, there is a computing barrier to reconstruct the query plan for w_{n+1} based on the collected statistics from a previous window w_n. Suppose the query execution of w_n consumes a time t_n (*e.g.*, in seconds), then for all $t_n < s$, the idle duration

$\delta_n = s - t_n$ allows to re-optimize the query plan. But δ_n should be larger than a configurable threshold Θ. For $\delta_n < \Theta$, the system may not have enough time to (i) collect the statistic information of w_n and (ii) to construct a query plan for w_{n+1}. This potentially expresses a change of incoming steams and a degradation of query execution performance. Hence, the system decides to switch to the F-AQP approach.

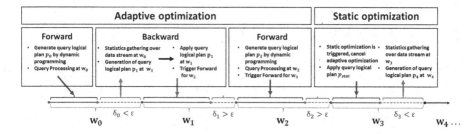

Fig. 4. Decision maker of adaptation strategy

F-AQP applies a DP strategy to find the optimal logical query plan for the current window w_n. The main purpose of F-AQP is to adjust the system state as soon as possible. The engine executes a query, collects statistics and computes the logical query plan simultaneously. Here, the statistics are obtained by counting intermediate query results, which causes data shuffling and DAG interruption, *i.e.*, the system has to temporally cut the query execution pipeline. In Spark, such suspending operation is called an *action*, which immediately triggers a job submission in Spark application. However, a frequent job submission may bring some side effects. The rationale is, for a master-slave based distributed computing framework (*e.g.*, Spark, Storm) uses a master node (*i.e.*, driver) to schedule jobs. The driver locally computes and optimizes each submitted DAG and returns the control messages to each worker node for parallel processing. Although the "count" action itself is not expensive, the induced side effects (*e.g.*, driver job-scheduling/submission, communication of control message between driver and workers) will potentially impact the system's stability. For instance, based on our experience, F-AQP's frequent job submission and intermediate data persistence/unpersistence put a great pressure on the JVM's Garbage Collector (GC), *e.g.*, untypical GC pauses are observed from time to time in our experiment.

Decision Maker. Through experimentations of different Strider configurations, we understood the complementarity of both the B-AQP and F-AQP approaches. Real performance gains can be obtained by switching from one approach to another. This is mainly due to their properties which are summarized in Table 1.

We designed a decision maker to automatically select the most adapted strategy for each query execution. The decision maker takes into account two parameters: a configurable switching threshold $\Theta \in \,]0,1[$; $\gamma_n = \frac{t_n}{s}$, the fraction of

Table 1. B/F-AQP summarization

Strategy	Advantage	Drawback
B-AQP	No dynamic programming overhead	Approximate query plan generation through previously-collected statistics
F-AQP	Query plan generation through real-time collected statistics	Overhead for dynamic programming, side-effects caused by pipeline interruption

query execution time t over windowing update frequency s. For the query execution at w_n, if $\gamma_n < \Theta$, the system updates the query plan from p_n to p_{n+1} for the next execution. Otherwise, the system recomputes p_{n+1} by DP at w_{n+1} (see Algorithm 2). We empirically set $\Theta = 0.7$ by default.

Algorithm 2. B-AQP and F-AQP Switching in Decision Maker

Input: query q, switching threshold Θ, sliding window $W = \{w_n\}_{n \in N}$,
        update frequency s of W

1   **foreach** $w_n \in W$ **do**
2     $t_n \leftarrow$ getRuntime { execute (q) } // executionTime ;
3     $\lambda_n \leftarrow$ getAdaptiveStrategy (Θ, t_n, s) // adaptiveStrategy;
4   **if** $\lambda_n == Backward$ **then**
5   update query plan p_n of q at w_n
6       $p_{n+1} \leftarrow$ update (p_n);
7   **if** $\lambda_n == Forward$ **then** Recompute p_{n+1} at w_{n+1};

The decision maker plays a key role for maintaining the stability of the system's performance. Our experiment (Sect. 5.3) shows that, the combination of F/B-AQP through decision maker is able to prevent the sudden performance declining during a long running time.

5 Evaluation

5.1 Implementation Details

Strider is written in Scala, the code source can be found here[3]. To enable SPARQL query processing on Spark, Strider parses a query with Jena ARQ and obtains a query algebra tree in the Parsing layer. The system reconstructs the algebra tree into a new Abstract Syntax Tree (AST) based on the Visitor model. Basically, the AST represents the logical plan of a query execution. Once the AST is created, it is pushed into the algebra Optimization layer. By traversing the AST, we bind the SPARQL operators to the corresponding Spark SQL relational operators for query evaluation.

---

[3] https://github.com/renxiangnan/strider.

5.2 Experimental Setup

We test and deploy our engine on Amazon EC2/EMR cluster of 9 computing nodes and Yarn resource management. The system holds 3 nodes of m4.xlarge for data flow management (*i.e.*, Kafka broker and Zookeeper [12]). Each node has 4 CPU virtual cores of 2.4 GHz Intel Xeon E5-2676, 16 GB RAM and 750 MB/s bandwidth. We use Apache Spark 2.0.2, Scala 2.11.7 and Java 8 as baselines for our evaluation. The Spark (Streaming) cluster is configured with 6 nodes (1 master, 5 workers) of type c4.xlarge. Each one has 4 CPU virtual cores of 2.9 GHz Intel Xeon E5-2666, 7.5 GB RAM and 750 MB/s. The experiments of Strider on local mode, C-SPARQL and CQELS are all performed on a single instance of type c4.xlarge.

Datasets and Queries. We evaluated our system using two datasets that are built around real world streaming use cases: *SRBench* [28] and *Waves*. SRBench, one of the first available RSP benchmarks, comes with 17 queries on LinkedSensorData. The datasets consists of weather observations about hurricanes and blizzards in the United States (from 2001 to 2009). Another dataset considered in our evaluation comes from aforementioned project Waves. The dataset describes different water measurements captured by sensors. Values of flow, water pressure and chlorine levels are examples of these measurements. The value annotation uses three popular ontologies: SSN, CUAHSI-HIS and QUDT. Each sensor observes and records at least one physical phenomenon or a chemical property, and thus generates RDF data stream through Kafka producer. Our micro-benchmark contains 9 queries, denoted from Q_1 to Q_9[4]. The road map of our evaluation is designed as follow: (1) injection of structurally stable stream for experiment of Q_1 to Q_6. Q_1 to Q_3 are tested by SRBench datasets. Here, a comparison between Strider and the state of the art RSP systems *e.g.*, C-SPARQL and CQELS are also provided. Then we perform Q_4 to Q_6 based on Waves dataset. (2) Injection of structurally unstable stream. We generate RDF streams by varying the proportion of different types of Kafka messages (*i.e.*, sensor observations). For this part of the evaluation, queries Q_7 to Q_9 are considered.

Performance criteria. In accordance with *Benchmarking Streaming Computation Engines at Yahoo!*[5], we choose the system throughput and query latency as two primary performance metrics. Throughput indicates how many data can be processed in a unit of time. Throughput is denoted as "triples per second" in our case. Latency means how long does the RSP engine consumes between the arrival of an input and the generation of its output. The reason why we abandoned existing RSP performance benchmarking systems [2,18] is that, none of them is tailored for massive data stream. This limitation is contrary to our original intention of using distributed stream processing framework to cope with massive RDF stream. We did not record the latency of

---

[4] Check the wiki of our github page for more details of the queries and datasets.
[5] https://yahooeng.tumblr.com/post/135321837876/benchmarking-streaming-computation-engines-at.

C-SPARQL, CQELS and Strider in local mode for two reasons: (1) given the scalability limitation of C-SPARQL, we have to control input stream rate within a low level to ensure the engine can run normally [18]. (2) due to its design, based on a so-called eager execution mechanism and *DStream* R2S operator, the measure of latencies in CQELS is unfeasible [18]. Moreover, given reasons provided in Sect. 4.3, we have not done any comparisons of B/F-AQP versus F-AQP approaches.

Performance tuning on Spark is quite difficult. Inappropriate cluster configuration may seriously hinder engine performance. So far we can only empirically configure Spark cluster and tune the cluster settings step by step. We briefly list some important performance settings based on our experience. First of all, we apply some basic optimization techniques. *e.g.*, using Kryo serializer to reduce the time for task/data serialization. Besides, we generally considered adjustments of Spark configuration along three control factors to achieve better performance. The first factor is the size of micro-batch intervals. Smaller batch sizes can better meet real-time requirements. However, it also brings frequent job submissions and job scheduling. The performance of a BSP system like Spark is sensitive to the chosen size of batch intervals. The second factor is GC tuning. Set appropriately, the GC strategy (*e.g.*, using Concurrent Mark-Sweep) and storage/shuffle fraction may efficiently reduce GC pressure. The third factor is the parallelism level. This includes the partition number of Kafka messages, the partition number of RDD for shuffling, and the upper/lower bound for concurrent job submissions, *etc.*

5.3   Evaluation Results and Discussions

Figures 5 and 6 respectively summarize the RSP engines throughput and latency. Note that CQELS gives a parsing error for Q_5. This is due, at least for the version that we have evaluated, to the lack of support for the UNION operator in the source code. In view of the centralized designs of C-SPARQL and CQELS, a direct performance comparison to Strider with distributed hardware settings seems unfair. So we also evaluated Strider in local mode, *i.e.*, running the system on a single machine (although it should not be its forte, Strider still gets an advantage from the multi-core processor). Based on this preliminary evaluation, we try to give an intuitive impression and reveal our findings about these three RSP systems.

In Fig. 5, we observe that Strider generally achieves million/sub-million-level throughput under our test suite. Note that both Q_1 and Q_4 have only one join, *i.e.*, optimization is not needed. Most tested queries scale well in Strider. Adaptive optimization generates query plans based on the workload statistics. In total, it provides a more efficient query plan than static optimization. But the gain of AQP for the simple queries that have less join tasks (*e.g.*, Q_1, Q_5) becomes insubstantial. We also found out that, even if Strider runs on a single machine, it still provides up to 60x gain on throughput compared to C-SPARQL and CQELS. Figure 6 shows Strider attains a second/sub-second delay. Obviously,

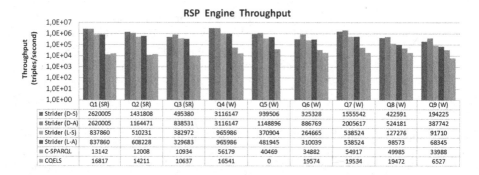

Fig. 5. RSP engine throughput (triples/second). **D/L-S:** Distributed/Local mode Static Optimization. **D/L-A:** Distributed/Local mode Adaptive Optimization. **SR:** Queries for SRBench dataset. **W:** Queries for Waves dataset.

for queries with 2 triple patterns in the query's BGP, we can observe the same latency between static and adaptive optimizations, Q_1 and Q_4. Query Q_2 is the only query where the latency of the adaptive approach is higher than the static one. This is due to the very simple structure of the BGP (2 joins in the BGP). In this situation, the overhead of DP covers the gain from AQP. For all other queries, the static latency is higher than the adaptive one. This is justified by more complex BGP structures (more than 5 triple patterns per BGP) or some union of BGPs.

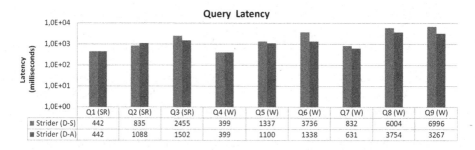

Fig. 6. Query latency (milliseconds) for strider (in distributed mode)

On the contrary, the average throughput of C-SPARQL and CQELS is maintained in the range of 6.000 and 50.000 triples/second. The centralized designs of C-SPARQL and CQELS limit the scalability of the systems. Beyond the implementation of query processing, the reliability of data flow management on C-SPARQL and CQELS could also cause negative impact on system robustness. Due to the lack of some important features for streaming system (*e.g.*, back pressure, checkpoint and failure recovery) once input stream rate reaches to certain scale, C-SPARQL and CQELS start behaving abnormally, *e.g.*, data loss, exponential increasing latency or query process interruption [18,19]. Moreover, we have also observed that CQELS' performance is insensitive to the changing of computing resources. We tested CQELS on different EC2 instance types, *i.e.*, with 2, 4 and 8 cores, and the results evaluation variations were negligible.

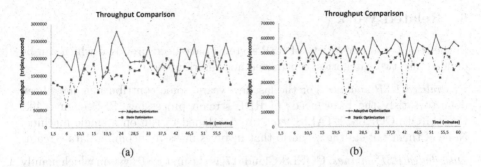

(a)   (b)

Fig. 7. Record of throughput on strider. (a)-throughput for q_7; (b)-throughput for q_8.

Figures 7 and 8 concern the monitoring of Strider's throughput for Q_7 to Q_9. We recorded the changes of throughput over a continuous period of time (one hour). The source stream produces the messages with different types of sensor observations. The stream is generated by mixing temperature, flow and chlorine-level measurement with random proportions. The red and blue curves denote query with respectively static and adaptive logical plan optimization. For Q_7 and Q_8 (Fig. 7), except when some serious throughput drops have been observed in Fig. 7b, static and adaptive planners return a close throughput trend. For a more complex query Q_9 (Fig. 8), which contains 9 triple patterns and 8 join operators. Altering logical plans on Q_9 causes significant impact on engine performance. Consequently, our adaptive strategy is capable to handle the structurally unstable RDF stream. Thus the engine can avoid a sharp performance degradation.

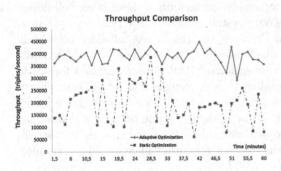

Fig. 8. Throughput for q_9 on strider.

Through this experiment, we identified some shortcomings in Strider that will be addressed in future work: (1) the data preparation on Spark Streaming is relatively expensive. It costs around 0.8 to 1 s to initialize before triggering the query execution in our experiment. (2) Strider has a more substantial throughput decreasing with an increasing number of join tasks. In order to alleviate this effect, the possible solution is enlarging the cluster scale or choosing a more powerful driver node. (3) Strider does not support well high concurrent requests, although this is not at the moment one of our system design goals. *E.g.*, some use cases demand to process a big amount of concurrent queries. Even through Strider allows to perform multiple queries asynchronously, it could be less efficient.

6   Related Work

In the recent years, a variety of RSP systems have been proposed which can be divided into two categories: centralized and distributed.

Centralized RSP engines. For the last few years, some contributions have been done to satisfy the basic needs of RDF stream processing. RSP engines like C-SPARQL, CQELS, ETALIS, *etc.*, are developed to run on a single machine. None of them targets the scenario that involves massive incoming data stream.

Distributed RSP engines. CQELS-Cloud [17].is the first RSP system which mainly focuses on the engine elasticity and scalability. The whole system is based on Apache Storm. Firstly, CQELS-Cloud compresses the incoming RDF streams by dictionary encoding in order to reduce the data size and the communication in the computing cluster. The query logical plan is mapped to a Storm topology, and the evaluation is done through a series of SPARQL operators located on the vertex of the topology. Then, to overcome the performance bottlenecks on join tasks, the authors propose a *parallel multiway join* based on probing sequence. From the aspect of implementation, CQELS-Cloud is designed as the streaming service for high concurrent requests. The capability of CQELS-Cloud to cope with massive incoming RDF data streams is still missing. Furthermore, to the best of our knowledge, CQELS-Cloud is not open source, customized queries and data feeding are not feasible. Katts is another RSP engine based on Storm. The implementation of Katts [9] is relatively primitive, it is more or less a platform for algorithm testing but not an RSP engine. The main goal of Katts is designed to verify the efficiency of graph partitioning algorithm for cluster communication reduction.

Although the SPARQL query optimization techniques have been well developed recently, CQELS is still the only system which considers query optimization to process RDF data stream. However, the greedy-like left-deep plan leads to sequential query evaluation, which makes CQELS benefit from few additional computing resources. The conventional SPARQL optimization for static data processing can be hardly applied in a streaming context. Recent efforts [14,15,20,22] possess long data preprocessing stage before launching the query execution. The proposed solutions do not meet real-time or near real-time use cases. The heuristic-based query optimization in [24] totally ignores data statistics and thus does not promise the optimal execution plan for 24×7 running streaming service.

7   Conclusion and Future Work

In this paper, we present Strider, a distributed RDF batch stream processing engine for large scale data stream. It is built on top of Spark Streaming and Kafka to support continuous SPARQL query evaluation and thus possesses the characteristics of a production-ready RSP. Strider comes with a set of hybrid

AQP strategies: *i.e.*, static heuristic rule-based optimization, forward and backward adaptive query processing. We insert the trigger into the optimizer to attain the automatic strategy switching at query runtime. Moreover, with its micro-batch approach, Strider fills a gap in the current state of RSP ecosystem which solely focuses on record-at-a-time. Through our micro-benchmark based on real-word datasets, Strider provides a million/sub-million-level throughput and second/sub-second latency, a major breakthrough in distributed RSPs. And we also demonstrate the system reliability which is capable to handle the structurally instable RDF streams.

There is still room for improving the system's implementation. As future work, we aim to add stream reasoning capacities and the ability of combining static data.

References

1. Akidau, T., Bradshaw, R., Chambers, C., Chernyak, S., Fernández-Moctezuma, R.J., Lax, R., McVeety, S., Mills, D., Perry, F., Schmidt, E., Whittle, S.: The dataflow model: A practical approach to balancing correctness, latency, and cost in massive-scale, unbounded, out-of-order data processing. PVLDB **8**, 1792–1803 (2015)

2. Ali, M.I., Gao, F., Mileo, A.: CityBench: A configurable benchmark to evaluate RSP engines using smart city datasets. In: Arenas, M., et al. (eds.) ISWC 2015. LNCS, vol. 9367, pp. 374–389. Springer, Cham (2015). doi:10.1007/978-3-319-25010-6_25

3. Anicic, D., Rudolph, S., Fodor, P., Stojanovic, N.: Stream reasoning and complex event processing in ETALIS. Semant. web **3**, 397–407 (2012)

4. Barbieri, D.F., et al.: C-SPARQL: SPARQL for continuous querying. In: WWW (2009)

5. Botan, I., Derakhshan, R., Dindar, N., Haas, L., Miller, R.J., Tatbul, N.: Secret: A model for analysis of the execution semantics of stream processing systems. PVLDB **3**, 232–243 (2010)

6. Carbone, P., Katsifodimos, A., Ewen, S., Markl, V., Haridi, S., Tzoumas, K.: Apache flink^{TM}: Stream and batch processing in a single engine. IEEE Data Eng. Bull. **38**, 28–38 (2015)

7. Chen, G.J., Wiener, J.L., Iyer, S., Jaiswal, A., Lei, R., Simha, N., Wang, W., Wilfong, K., Williamson, T., Yilmaz, S.: Realtime data processing at facebook. In: SIGMOD (2016)

8. Deshpande, A., Ives, Z.G., Raman, V.: Adaptive query processing. Found. Trends Databases **1**, 1–140 (2007)

9. Fischer, L., et al.: Scalable linked data stream processing via network-aware workload scheduling. In: SSWS@ISWC (2013)

10. Goodhope, K., Koshy, J., Kreps, J., Narkhede, N., Park, R., Rao, J., Ye, V.Y.: Building linkedin's real-time activity data pipeline. IEEE Data Eng. Bull. **35**, 33–45 (2012)

11. Gubichev, A., Neumann, T.: Exploiting the query structure for efficient join ordering in SPARQL queries. EDBT **14**, 439–450 (2014)

12. Hunt, P., Konar, M., Junqueira, F.P., Reed, B.: Zookeeper: Wait-free coordination for internet-scale systems. In: USENIX (2010)

13. Le-Phuoc, D., Dao-Tran, M., Xavier Parreira, J., Hauswirth, M.: A native and adaptive approach for unified processing of linked streams and linked data. In: Aroyo, L., Welty, C., Alani, H., Taylor, J., Bernstein, A., Kagal, L., Noy, N., Blomqvist, E. (eds.) ISWC 2011. LNCS, vol. 7031, pp. 370–388. Springer, Heidelberg (2011). doi:10.1007/978-3-642-25073-6_24

14. Neumann, T., Moerkotte, G.: Characteristic sets: Accurate cardinality estimation for RDF queries with multiple joins. In: ICDE (2011)

15. Neumann, T., Weikum, G.: Scalable join processing on very large RDF graphs. In: SIGMOD (2009)

16. Pham, M.-D., Boncz, P.: Exploiting emergent schemas to make rdf systems more efficient. In: Groth, P., Simperl, E., Gray, A., Sabou, M., Krötzsch, M., Lecue, F., Flöck, F., Gil, Y. (eds.) ISWC 2016. LNCS, vol. 9981, pp. 463–479. Springer, Cham (2016). doi:10.1007/978-3-319-46523-4_28

17. Le-Phuoc, D., Nguyen Mau Quoc, H., Le Van, C., Hauswirth, M.: Elastic and scalable processing of linked stream data in the cloud. In: Alani, H., et al. (eds.) ISWC 2013. LNCS, vol. 8218, pp. 280–297. Springer, Heidelberg (2013). doi:10. 1007/978-3-642-41335-3_18

18. Le-Phuoc, D., Dao-Tran, M., Pham, M.-D., Boncz, P., Eiter, T., Fink, M.: Linked stream data processing engines: facts and figures. In: Cudré-Mauroux, P., et al. (eds.) ISWC 2012. LNCS, vol. 7650, pp. 300–312. Springer, Heidelberg (2012). doi:10.1007/978-3-642-35173-0_20

19. Ren, X., Khrouf, H., Kazi-Aoul, Z., Chabchoub, Y., Curé, O.: On measuring performances of C-SPARQL and CQELS. In: SWIT@ISWC (2016)

20. Schätzle, A., Przyjaciel-Zablocki, M., Skilevic, S., Lausen, G.: S2RDF: RDF querying with sparql on spark. PVLDB 9, 804–815 (2016)

21. Siow, E., Tiropanis, T., Hall, W.: SPARQL-to-SQL on internet of things databases and streams. In: Groth, P., Simperl, E., Gray, A., Sabou, M., Krötzsch, M., Lecue, F., Flöck, F., Gil, Y. (eds.) ISWC 2016. LNCS, vol. 9981, pp. 515–531. Springer, Cham (2016). doi:10.1007/978-3-319-46523-4_31

22. Stocker, M., Seaborne, A., Bernstein, V., Kiefer, C., Reynolds, D.: SPARQL basic graph pattern optimization using selectivity estimation. In: WWW (2008)

23. Toshniwal, A., Taneja, S., Shukla, A., Ramasamy, K., Patel, J.M., Kulkarni, S., Jackson, J., Gade, K., Fu, M., Donham, J., Bhagat, N., Mittal, S., Ryaboy, D.: Storm@twitter. In: SIGMOD (2014)

24. Tsialiamanis, P., Sidirourgos, L., Fundulaki, I., Christophides, V., Boncz, P.: Heuristics-based query optimisation for SPARQL. In: EDBT (2012)

25. Venkataraman, S., Panda, A., Ousterhout, K., Ghodsi, A., Franklin, M.J., Recht, B., Stoica, I.: Drizzle: Fast and adaptable stream processing at scale. In: Spark Summit (2016)

26. Zaharia, M., Chowdhury, M., Das, T., Dave, A., Ma, J., McCauley, M., Franklin, M.J., Shenker, S., Stoica, I.: Resilient distributed datasets: A fault-tolerant abstraction for in-memory cluster computing. In: NSDI (2012)

27. Zaharia, M., Das, T., Li, H., Hunter, T., Shenker, S., Stoica, I.: Discretized streams: Fault-tolerant streaming computation at scale. In: SOSP (2013)

28. Zhang, Y., Duc, P.M., Corcho, O., Calbimonte, J.-P.: SRBench: A streaming RDF/SPARQL benchmark. In: Cudré-Mauroux, P., et al. (eds.) ISWC 2012. LNCS, vol. 7649, pp. 641–657. Springer, Heidelberg (2012). doi:10.1007/ 978-3-642-35176-1_40

Mining Hypotheses from Data in OWL: Advanced Evaluation and Complete Construction

Viachaslau Sazonau[✉] and Uli Sattler

The University of Manchester, Oxford Road, Manchester M13 9PL, UK
{sazonauv,sattler}@cs.manchester.ac.uk

Abstract. Automated acquisition (learning) of ontologies from data has attracted research interest because it can complement manual, expensive construction of ontologies. We investigate the problem of General Terminology Induction in OWL, i.e. acquiring general, expressive TBox axioms (hypotheses) from an ABox (data). We define novel measures designed to rigorously evaluate the quality of hypotheses while respecting the standard semantics of OWL. We propose an informed, data-driven algorithm that constructs class expressions for hypotheses in OWL and guarantees completeness. We empirically evaluate the quality measures on two corpora of ontologies and run a case study with a domain expert to gain insight into applicability of the measures and acquired hypotheses. The results show that the measures capture different quality aspects and not only correct hypotheses can be interesting.

1 Introduction

In computer science, an *ontology* is a machine-processable representation of knowledge about some domain. Ontologies are encoded in ontology languages, such as the expressive Web Ontology Language [11] (OWL) based on Description Logics [3] (DLs). An ontology is a set of logical statements, called *axioms*. Axioms can be universal statements or specific facts. The set of universal statements of an ontology is called the *TBox* and represents schema-level conceptual relationships, or *terminology*. The set of facts of an ontology is called the *ABox* and represents instance-level class and property assertions, or *data*. Besides simple "SubClassOf" relationships and class definitions, OWL allows for encoding complex TBox axioms such as general class inclusions (GCIs) where complex class expressions occur on both sides, e.g. $\exists hasChild.\top \sqsubseteq Mother \sqcup Father$ states that "having a child implies being a mother or father".

Since manual engineering of TBoxes is a difficult, time-consuming task, automated acquisition of them from data has attracted research attention. In this paper, we investigate learning expressive TBox axioms (hypotheses) from a given ABox (data). Our contributions are as follows:

- definitions of novel quality measures that can rigorously evaluate expressive GCIs in OWL respecting its semantics;

© Springer International Publishing AG 2017
C. d'Amato et al. (Eds.): ISWC 2017, Part I, LNCS 10587, pp. 577–593, 2017.
DOI: 10.1007/978-3-319-68288-4_34

- an informed, bottom-up algorithm that efficiently constructs complex class expressions (and thus GCIs) in OWL and guarantees completeness;
- an empirical analysis of the relationships between the quality measures via mutual correlations;
- the design and execution of a case study which confirms the ability of our approach to generate three different kinds of interesting hypotheses and gains insight into relationships of the measures with hypothesis validity and interestingness.

2   Preliminaries

We assume the reader to be familiar with DLs [3] and OWL [11]. We denote an ontology as $\mathcal{O} := \mathcal{T} \cup \mathcal{A}$, where $\mathcal{T}$ and $\mathcal{A}$ are its TBox and ABox, respectively. An *axiom* is denoted as α or η. A general class inclusion (GCI) is an axiom of the form $C \sqsubseteq D$, where C and D are (possibly complex) class expressions, and corresponds to a "SubClassOf" axiom in OWL. An object property inclusion (OPI) is an axiom of the form $R \sqsubseteq S$, where R and S are (possibly complex) object property expressions, and corresponds to a "SubObjectPropertyOf" axiom in OWL. A *hypothesis* is a TBox axiom (GCI or OPI). An ABox axiom, called *fact*, is an assertion of the form $C(a)$ or $R(a,b)$, where C is a class expression, R an object property, a, b individuals. The set of all terms occurring in an ontology $\mathcal{O}$ is called the *signature* of $\mathcal{O}$ and denoted as $\widetilde{\mathcal{O}}$ ($\widetilde{\mathcal{T}}$ is the signature of $\mathcal{T}$). We denote the set of all individuals occurring in $\mathcal{O}$ as $in(\mathcal{O})$. We use $\models$ to denote the usual entailment relation and $\equiv$ to denote logical equivalence. The function $\ell(C)$ returns the usual syntactic length [3,13] of a class expression C, e.g. $\ell(\exists R.A \sqcap \forall R.(\neg B \sqcup \exists S.B)) = 9$; $\ell(C \sqsubseteq D) = \ell(C) + \ell(D)$; $\ell(\mathcal{O}) = \sum_{\alpha \in \mathcal{O}} \ell(\alpha)$.

3   Related Work

There are different approaches to acquiring TBox axioms from data. The common approach is Class Description Learning [5,7,14–16,18] (CDL) which aims at inducing a description (class expression) C of a given class name A using a set of positive and negative training examples. Statistical Schema Induction [22] uses Association Rules Mining (ARM) to generate and evaluate candidate axioms using off-the-shelf quality measures [10]. BelNet [23] learns a Bayesian Network from data and uses its structure to generate the corresponding TBox. In contrast to CDL, the last two approaches are not restricted to learning only class descriptions and can generate GCIs with complex class expressions on both sides. However, they require specifying shapes of generated axioms and have so far been considerably limited in *expressivity*, i.e. richness of knowledge that generated axioms are able to capture. Moreover, they tend to view a given ABox (data) under the Closed Word Assumption (CWA) or some form of it [9]. This is unnatural for the standard semantics of OWL allowing for the Open World Assumption (OWA), i.e. *incomplete information*. In addition, the approaches usually ignore the given TBox while generating candidate axioms.

Like ARM-based approaches, we focus on learning GCIs rather than class expressions. The rationale is that the former can express arbitrary implications, e.g. "people who pay dog tax also buy dog food", while the latter cannot since it captures commonalities in the given group of individuals (as positive or negative examples), e.g. "people who pay dog tax". Thus, the goals of learning GCIs and learning class expressions are rather different. To draw further similarities between our approach and ARM, we can view an individual as a transaction that contains class expressions as its items. A class expression is included in the transaction if and only if the individual is an instance of that class expression. However, in contrast to items in ARM, class expressions can be logically related to each other (in light of the TBox) and it can be unknown whether a class expression is in the transaction or not because of the OWA. In addition, unlike items in ARM, class expressions are not usually known in advance and naive generation of them is infeasible in all but trivial cases.

4   Advanced Evaluation of Hypotheses

A candidate axiom, or *hypothesis*, can be evaluated by different quality criteria. One can use the usual axiom *length* and *depth* [3,4,13] to evaluate readability. As we suggested in [20], logical quality can be evaluated by *consistency, informativeness, and logical strength (weakness)*: an axiom α is called *consistent* with an ontology $\mathcal{O}$ if $\mathcal{O} \cup \{\alpha\}$ is consistent; α is called *informative* for a TBox $\mathcal{T}$ if $\mathcal{T} \not\models \alpha$; α is said to be *weaker* than another axiom α' if $\alpha' \models \alpha$ and $\alpha \not\models \alpha'$. Statistical quality can be evaluated by *fitness* and *braveness* [20]. Intuitively, fitness counts the number of facts entailed by a hypothesis and braveness counts the number of "guesses" of a hypothesis.

Definition 1 (fitness, braveness). *Let $\mathcal{O} := \mathcal{T} \cup \mathcal{A}$ be an ontology, $\mathbb{C}$ a set of class expressions with their negations included, α a GCI consistent with $\mathcal{O}$. Then, the fitness and braveness of α are defined as follows:*

$$fit(\alpha, \mathcal{O}, \mathbb{C}) := dlen(\pi(\mathcal{O}, \mathbb{C}), \mathcal{T}) - dlen(\pi(\mathcal{O}, \mathbb{C}), \mathcal{T} \cup \{\alpha\})$$
$$bra(\alpha, \mathcal{O}, \mathbb{C}) := dlen(\psi(\alpha, \mathcal{O}, \mathbb{C}), \mathcal{O})$$

where $\pi(\mathcal{O}, \mathbb{C}) := \{C(a) \mid \mathcal{O} \models C(a), C \in \mathbb{C}, a \in in(\mathcal{O})\}$,[1] $\psi(\alpha, \mathcal{O}, \mathbb{C}) := \pi(\mathcal{O} \cup \{\alpha\}, \mathbb{C}) \setminus \pi(\mathcal{O}, \mathbb{C})$, $dlen(\mathcal{B}, \mathcal{O}) := min\{\ell(\mathcal{B}') \mid \mathcal{B}' \cup \mathcal{O} \equiv \mathcal{B} \cup \mathcal{O}\}$.

4.1   New Logical Measures

To capture further aspects of logical quality, we propose new logical measures: dissimilarity and complexity. These are *numeric* logical measures (compare to consistency, informativeness, and logical strength mentioned above).

Dissimilarity. Given a GCI $C \sqsubseteq D$, one can measure how "dissimilar" C and D are with respect to the TBox. Intuitively, the more dissimilar they are, the more

---

[1] It is the result of retrieving instances of every $C \in \mathbb{C}$.

"surprising" the axiom is for the TBox. We adapt the class similarity measure from [2].

Definition 2 (Dissimilarity). *Let* $\mathcal{O} := \mathcal{T} \cup \mathcal{A}$ *be an ontology,* $\mathbb{C}$ *a set of class expressions,* $subs(C, \mathbb{C}, \mathcal{T}) := \{C' \in \mathbb{C} \cup \{C\} \mid \mathcal{T} \models C \sqsubseteq C'\}$. *The dissimilarity of* $\alpha := C \sqsubseteq D$ *is defined as follows:*

$$dsim(\alpha, \mathbb{C}, \mathcal{T}) := 1 - \frac{|subs(C, \mathbb{C}, \mathcal{T}) \cap subs(D, \mathbb{C}, \mathcal{T})|}{|subs(C, \mathbb{C}, \mathcal{T}) \cup subs(D, \mathbb{C}, \mathcal{T})|}.$$

Informally, given a TBox $\mathcal{T}$, the dissimilarity of a GCI $C \sqsubseteq D$ measures how many common subsumers the class expressions C and D have in a set $\mathbb{C}$ of class expressions.

Example 1. Consider the following TBox:

$$\mathcal{T} := \{C_1 \sqsubseteq B_1,\ B_1 \sqsubseteq A_1,\ A_1 \sqsubseteq A,$$
$$C_2 \sqsubseteq B_2,\ B_2 \sqsubseteq A_2,\ A_2 \sqsubseteq A\}.$$

Given $\mathbb{C} := \widetilde{\mathcal{T}}$ (all classes of $\mathcal{T}$), the dissimilarity of $\alpha_1 := C_1 \sqsubseteq C_2$ is higher than the one of $\alpha_2 := A_1 \sqsubseteq C_2$:

$$dsim(\alpha_1, \mathbb{C}, \mathcal{T}) = 1 - \frac{|\{A\}|}{|\{A, A_1, B_1, C_1, A_2, B_2, C_2\}|} = \frac{6}{7}$$

$$dsim(\alpha_2, \mathbb{C}, \mathcal{T}) = 1 - \frac{|\{A\}|}{|\{A, A_1, A_2, B_2, C_2\}|} = \frac{4}{5}$$

The dissimilarity of an OPI is defined analogously and omitted for the sake of brevity. The minimal (maximal) value of dissimilarity implies that all subsumers are the same (different). Dissimilarity is a *symmetric* measure, i.e.

$$dsim(C \sqsubseteq D,\ \mathbb{C}, \mathcal{T}) = dsim(D \sqsubseteq C,\ \mathbb{C}, \mathcal{T}).$$

Complexity. Given an axiom α, we can compare the *complexity* of the new theory $\mathcal{T} \cup \{\alpha\}$ with the complexity of the old theory $\mathcal{T}$ by quantifying how many *new entailments* the new theory has. As the set of new entailments is infinite in general, we only consider a finite subset of them.

Definition 3 (Complexity). *Let* $\mathcal{O} := \mathcal{T} \cup \mathcal{A}$ *be an ontology,* $\mathbb{C}$ *a set of class expressions. The complexity of* $\alpha := C \sqsubseteq D$ *is defined as follows:* $com(\alpha, \mathbb{C}, \mathcal{T}) := |\{\eta \mid \mathcal{T} \cup \{\alpha\} \models \eta,\ \mathcal{T} \not\models \eta,\ \eta = C_1 \sqsubseteq C_2,\ C_1, C_2 \in \mathbb{C}\}|.$

Thus, we only count new entailments that are subsumptions between class expressions from a fixed set $\mathbb{C}$. The complexity of an OPI is defined analogously and omitted for the sake of brevity. In contrast to dissimilarity, complexity is *asymmetric*. They are rather independent measures, see Example 2.

Example 2. Let us calculate the complexity of the axioms α_1 and α_2 from Example 1:

$$com(\alpha_1, \mathbb{C}, \mathcal{T}) = |\{C_1 \sqsubseteq C_2, C_1 \sqsubseteq B_2, C_1 \sqsubseteq A_2\}| = 3,$$
$$com(\alpha_2, \mathbb{C}, \mathcal{T}) = |\{C_1 \sqsubseteq C_2, C_1 \sqsubseteq B_2, C_1 \sqsubseteq A_2,$$
$$B_1 \sqsubseteq C_2, B_1 \sqsubseteq B_2, B_1 \sqsubseteq A_2,$$
$$A_1 \sqsubseteq C_2, A_1 \sqsubseteq B_2, A_1 \sqsubseteq A_2\}| = 9.$$

Thus, α_1 has lower complexity than α_2 but higher dissimilarity. In addition, consider the axiom $\alpha_3 := B_1 \sqcap C_2 \sqsubseteq A_1$: $com(\alpha_3, \mathbb{C}, \mathcal{T}) = 0$ since $\mathcal{T} \models \alpha_3$ but

$$dsim(\alpha_3, \mathbb{C}, \mathcal{T}) = 1 - \frac{|\{A, A_1\}|}{|\{A, B_1, A_1, C_2, B_2, A_2\}|} = \frac{2}{3}.$$

4.2 New Statistical Measures

We propose new statistical measures that capture further aspects of statistical quality while respecting the standard semantics of OWL and given TBox. They are based on *counting instances* of certain kinds.

Definition 4 (Instance function). *Let $\mathcal{O}$ be an ontology; $\mathring{C} \in \{C, {}_?C\}$, where C is a class expression. The* instance function *is defined as follows:*

$$inst(\mathring{C}, \mathcal{O}) := \begin{cases} \{a \in in(\mathcal{O}) \mid \mathcal{O} \models C(a)\} & \text{if } \mathring{C} = C \\ \{a \in in(\mathcal{O}) \mid \mathcal{O} \not\models C(a) \wedge \mathcal{O} \not\models \neg C(a)\} & \text{if } \mathring{C} = {}_?C \end{cases}$$

Basic Measures. Let us consider a GCI $C \sqsubseteq D$. The axiom states that all instances of C are also instances of D. Given an ontology $\mathcal{O} := \mathcal{T} \cup \mathcal{A}$, we can check *how well* the data in $\mathcal{A}$ supports this statement taking the background knowledge in $\mathcal{T}$ into account.

Definition 5 (Basic measures). *Given an ontology $\mathcal{O}$, the* basic coverage, support, contradiction, assumption *of $\alpha := C \sqsubseteq D$ are defined, respectively, as follows:*

$$bcov(\alpha, \mathcal{O}) := |inst(C, \mathcal{O})| \qquad bsup(\alpha, \mathcal{O}) := |inst(C \sqcap D, \mathcal{O})|$$
$$bcnt(\alpha, \mathcal{O}) := |inst(C \sqcap \neg D, \mathcal{O})| \quad basm(\alpha, \mathcal{O}) := |inst(C, \mathcal{O}) \cap inst({}_?D, \mathcal{O})|$$

Support is presumably a *positive* measure, i.e. higher values indicate better quality, while contradiction and assumption are presumably *negative* ones, i.e. lower values indicate better quality. Coverage is neither positive nor negative as it is the sum of support, contradiction, and assumption. Support is a symmetric measure, while others are not. The basic measures respect the OWA via distinguishing assumption and contradiction.

Example 3. Consider the ontology $\mathcal{O} := \mathcal{T} \cup \mathcal{A}$ that models family relations, where the TBox $\mathcal{T}$ and ABox $\mathcal{A}$ are as follows (*hc, mt* stand for *hasChild, marriedTo*).

$$\mathcal{T} = \{Father \sqsubseteq Man,\ Mother \sqsubseteq Woman,\ Man \sqsubseteq \neg Woman,\ mt \sqsubseteq mt^-\},$$
$$\mathcal{A} = \{Man(Arthur),\ Father(Chris),\ Father(James),\ Woman(Charlotte),$$
$$Woman(Margaret),\ Mother(Penelope),\ Mother(Victoria),$$
$$hc(James, Charlotte),\ hc(Victoria, Charlotte),\ hc(Chris, Victoria),$$
$$hc(Penelope, Victoria),\ hc(Chris, Arthur),\ hc(Penelope, Arthur),$$
$$mt(Chris, Penelope),\ mt(James, Victoria),\ mt(Arthur, Margaret)\}.$$

Consider the following axioms:

$$\alpha_1 := \exists mt.\top \sqsubseteq Mother, \qquad \alpha_2 := \exists hc.\top \sqsubseteq Mother.$$

Their basic measures are calculated as follows:

$$bsup(\alpha_1, \mathcal{O}) = 2 \quad bcnt(\alpha_1, \mathcal{O}) = 3 \quad basm(\alpha_1, \mathcal{O}) = 1 \quad bcov(\alpha_1, \mathcal{O}) = 6$$
$$bsup(\alpha_2, \mathcal{O}) = 2 \quad bcnt(\alpha_2, \mathcal{O}) = 2 \quad basm(\alpha_2, \mathcal{O}) = 0 \quad bcov(\alpha_2, \mathcal{O}) = 4$$

Thus, α_2 is better than α_1 because its support is the same but its contradiction and assumption are lower.

The basic measures can be defined for an OPI $R \sqsubseteq S$ in the same way as for a GCI $C \sqsubseteq D$. The only difference is that, instead of returning instances of a class expression C, the instance function would return instances of an object property expression R, i.e. individual pairs (a, b) which are entailed to be connected by R. Please note that assumption resembles braveness [20] but counts "guesses" of a hypothesis in a more straightforward way since it depends only on a hypothesis and ontology.

Main Measures. The basic measures only consider the "forward" direction of a GCI $C \sqsubseteq D$. According to the semantics of OWL, $C \sqsubseteq D$ has also the "backward" direction. Formally, $C \sqsubseteq D \equiv \neg D \sqsubseteq \neg C$ which is called the law of *contraposition*, where $\neg D \sqsubseteq \neg C$ is called the *contrapositive* of $C \sqsubseteq D$. Thus, $C \sqsubseteq D$ not only implies that all instances of C are instances of D but also implies that all instances of $\neg D$ are instances of $\neg C$. We refine the basic measures using a syntactic trick to "merge" a GCI and its contrapositive into a single GCI.

Definition 6 (Main Measures). *Let $\mathcal{O}$ be an ontology, $\alpha := C \sqsubseteq D$, and $\overline{\alpha} := C \sqcup \neg D \sqsubseteq \neg C \sqcup D$. The main coverage, support, contradiction, assumption of α are defined, respectively, as follows:*

$$cov(\alpha, \mathcal{O}) := bcov(\overline{\alpha}, \mathcal{O}) \qquad sup(\alpha, \mathcal{O}) := bsup(\overline{\alpha}, \mathcal{O})$$
$$cnt(\alpha, \mathcal{O}) := bcnt(\overline{\alpha}, \mathcal{O}) \qquad asm(\alpha, \mathcal{O}) := basm(\overline{\alpha}, \mathcal{O})$$

In comparison to the basic measures, see Definition 5, their respective main measures additionally count individuals relevant for the contrapositive. Example 4 shows how a main measure can differ from its basic measure.

Example 4. In Example 3, we evaluate $\alpha_2 := \exists hc.\top \sqsubseteq Mother$ via the basic measures. Its basic assumption is $basm(\alpha_2, \mathcal{O}) = 0$, i.e. α_2 makes no "guesses". However, its main assumption is $asm(\alpha_2, \mathcal{O}) = 1$. Indeed, as *Arthur* is an instance of $\neg Mother$, the axiom α_2 assumes that *Arthur* has no children, i.e. he is an instance of $\neg(\exists hc.\top)$.

In contrast to the basic measures, the main measures always return the same values for an axiom and its contrapositive. Thus, they respect the semantics of OWL better than the basic measures. The main measures of an axiom can be represented via the basic measures of that axiom and its contrapositive. These properties are stated by Lemma 1.

Lemma 1. *Let $\mathcal{O}$ be an ontology, $\alpha := C \sqsubseteq D$, and $\alpha' := \neg D \sqsubseteq \neg C$. Then*

$$cov(\alpha, \mathcal{O}) = cov(\alpha', \mathcal{O}) = bcov(\alpha, \mathcal{O}) + bcov(\alpha', \mathcal{O}) - bcnt(\alpha, \mathcal{O})$$
$$sup(\alpha, \mathcal{O}) = sup(\alpha', \mathcal{O}) = bsup(\alpha, \mathcal{O}) + bsup(\alpha', \mathcal{O})$$
$$cnt(\alpha, \mathcal{O}) = cnt(\alpha', \mathcal{O}) = bcnt(\alpha, \mathcal{O}) = bcnt(\alpha', \mathcal{O})$$
$$asm(\alpha, \mathcal{O}) = asm(\alpha', \mathcal{O}) = basm(\alpha, \mathcal{O}) + basm(\alpha', \mathcal{O})$$

Proof. Follows from Definitions 4, 5, and 6, see [19] for details.

Clearly, the basic and main measures coincide if $\neg C$ and $\neg D$ have no instances in $\mathcal{O}$, e.g. C and D are $\mathcal{EL}$ class expressions and $\mathcal{O}$ is in $\mathcal{EL}$. Example 5 illustrates how evaluating a disjointness axiom under the OWA differs from evaluating it under the CWA which is commonly made for learning disjointness axioms, see e.g. [8].

Example 5. Consider the ontology

$$\mathcal{O} := \{A(a_1), \ldots, A(a_m), \; B(b_1), \ldots, B(b_n)\}.$$

Under the CWA, the absence of information in $\mathcal{O}$ is treated as negation:

$$\mathcal{O}^- := \mathcal{O} \cup \{\neg B(a_1), \ldots, \neg B(a_m), \; \neg A(b_1), \ldots, \neg A(b_n)\}.$$

Consider the disjointness axiom $\alpha := A \sqsubseteq \neg B$. Under the CWA, it is assumed, perhaps wrongly, to be of high quality: $sup(\alpha, \mathcal{O}^-) = m + n$, $asm(\alpha, \mathcal{O}^-) = 0$. In contrast, under the OWA, its evaluation better reflects the state of knowledge in $\mathcal{O}$: $sup(\alpha, \mathcal{O}) = 0$, $asm(\alpha, \mathcal{O}) = m + n$.

Composite Measures. As an axiom $C \sqsubseteq D$ in OWL is similar to an association rule $X \Rightarrow Y$ in ARM, rule measures [10] can be adapted to OWL. The challenge is to respect the OWA, i.e. consider that there is $?C$, see Definition 4, in addition to C and $\neg C$. Given a rule measure $f(X, Y)$, we suggest to translate it as follows. First, substitute each positive occurrence of a variable X (Y) in $f(X,Y)$ with a class expression C (D). If neither X nor Y occurs negatively in $f(X,Y)$, then the translation is finished and results in the axiom measure $f(C,D)$. Otherwise, obtain two axiom measures as follows: substitute each negative occurrence $\neg X$ $(\neg Y)$ in $f(X,Y)$ with $\neg C$ $(\neg D)$, resulting in $f^{\neg}(C,D)$, and with $?C$ $(?D)$, resulting in $f^{?}(C,D)$. Following this procedure, we translate the standard rule measures: confidence, lift, and conviction.

Definition 7 (Composite basic measures). *Let $\mathcal{O}$ be an ontology; $\mathring{C} \in \{C, ?C\}$, where C is a class expression;*

$$\mathbf{P}_{\mathcal{O}}(\mathring{C}_1, \ldots, \mathring{C}_k) := \frac{1}{|in(\mathcal{O})|} | \bigcap_{i=1}^{k} inst(\mathring{C}_i, \mathcal{O})|.$$

The basic confidence, lift, negated and assumed conviction of $\alpha := C \sqsubseteq D$ are defined, respectively, as follows:

$$bconf(\alpha, \mathcal{O}) := \frac{\mathbf{P}_{\mathcal{O}}(C,D)}{\mathbf{P}_{\mathcal{O}}(C)} \qquad blift(\alpha, \mathcal{O}) := \frac{\mathbf{P}_{\mathcal{O}}(C,D)}{\mathbf{P}_{\mathcal{O}}(C) \cdot \mathbf{P}_{\mathcal{O}}(D)}$$

$$bconv^{\neg}(\alpha, \mathcal{O}) := \frac{\mathbf{P}_{\mathcal{O}}(C) \cdot \mathbf{P}_{\mathcal{O}}(\neg D)}{\mathbf{P}_{\mathcal{O}}(C, \neg D)} \qquad bconv^{?}(\alpha, \mathcal{O}) := \frac{\mathbf{P}_{\mathcal{O}}(C) \cdot \mathbf{P}_{\mathcal{O}}(?D)}{\mathbf{P}_{\mathcal{O}}(C, ?D)}$$

The OWA is taken into consideration via distinguishing negated and assumed conviction. The composite basic measures can be rewritten using the basic coverage, support, contradiction, and assumption, see [19] for details.

Example 6. We calculate the composite basic measures of the axioms α_1 and α_2 in Example 3. We first calculate the required probabilities (M stands for *Mother*): $\mathbf{P}_{\mathcal{O}}(M) = \frac{2}{7}$, $\mathbf{P}_{\mathcal{O}}(\neg M) = \frac{3}{7}$, $\mathbf{P}_{\mathcal{O}}(?M) = \frac{2}{7}$. Then, we use them along with the basic measures calculated in Example 3:

$bconf(\alpha_1, \mathcal{O}) = \frac{2}{6} = \frac{1}{3}$, $blift(\alpha_1, \mathcal{O}) = \frac{2}{6 \cdot \frac{2}{7}} = \frac{7}{6}$, $bconv^{\neg}(\alpha_1, \mathcal{O}) = \frac{6 \cdot \frac{3}{7}}{3}$

$= \frac{6}{7}$, $bconv^{?}(\alpha_1, \mathcal{O}) = \frac{6 \cdot \frac{2}{7}}{1} = \frac{12}{7}$; $bconf(\alpha_2, \mathcal{O}) = \frac{2}{4} = \frac{1}{2}$, $blift(\alpha_2, \mathcal{O}) = \frac{2}{4 \cdot \frac{4}{7}}$

$= \frac{7}{4}$, $bconv^{\neg}(\alpha_2, \mathcal{O}) = \frac{4 \cdot \frac{3}{7}}{2} = \frac{6}{7}$, $bconv^{?}(\alpha_2, \mathcal{O}) = \frac{4 \cdot \frac{2}{7}}{0} = \infty$.

The composite basic measures can be refined to treat GCIs according to the standard semantics of OWL, i.e. as being equivalent to their contrapositives.

Definition 8 (Composite main measures). *Let $\mathcal{O}$ be an ontology, $\alpha := C \sqsubseteq D$, and $\overline{\alpha} := C \sqcup \neg D \sqsubseteq \neg C \sqcup D$. The main confidence, lift, negated and assumed conviction of α are defined, respectively, as follows:*

$$conf(\alpha, \mathcal{O}) := bconf(\overline{\alpha}, \mathcal{O}) \qquad lift(\alpha, \mathcal{O}) := blift(\overline{\alpha}, \mathcal{O})$$

$$conv^{\neg}(\alpha, \mathcal{O}) := bconv^{\neg}(\overline{\alpha}, \mathcal{O}) \qquad conv^{?}(\alpha, \mathcal{O}) := bconv^{?}(\overline{\alpha}, \mathcal{O})$$

A lemma analogous to Lemma 1 holds for the composite main measures, i.e. they treat a GCI as being equivalent to its contrapositive and can be rewritten using the main measures and hence the basic measures [19].

5   Complete Construction of Hypotheses

We reduce the problem of constructing hypotheses to the problem of constructing class (and property) expressions. Indeed, given a set $\mathbb{C}$ of class expressions of interest, we can generate all possible GCIs using class expressions from $\mathbb{C}$ as a left-hand side or right-hand side, i.e. $\{C \sqsubseteq D \mid C, D \in \mathbb{C}\}$. Thus, the number of generated GCIs is quadratic in the size of $\mathbb{C}$. As we suggested in [20], class expressions $\mathbb{C}$ can be generated from some "seed" signature Σ using certain construction rules (templates), e.g. all pairwise conjunctions, simple existential restrictions, etc. However, it is generally hard to know which templates are likely to produce useful class expressions. Moreover, a brute-force procedure that generates *all* class expressions is doomed even for inexpressive DLs, e.g. $\mathcal{EL}$. For example, given n class and m object property names, a number of all $\mathcal{EL}$ class expressions of length up to 5 grows as fast as $O(n^3 + n^2 \cdot m^2 + n \cdot m^4)$.

We propose an informed, bottom-up algorithm that constructs *all* class expressions $\mathbb{C}$ of length up to ℓ_{max} in a given $\mathcal{DL}$ that have at least s_{min} instances, i.e. sufficient evidence in data. Importantly, the algorithm avoids considering all other class expressions that are numerous, e.g. all class expressions without instances (and many others). We integrate two ideas in one algorithm: enumerating class expressions via a *refinement operator* [7,14,16] and pruning unpromising (insufficiently supported by data) class expressions from the search a priori. A *downward* refinement operator[2] ρ for $\mathcal{DL}$ specifies a set $\rho(C)$ of specialisations of a class expression C in that $\mathcal{DL}$. Refinement operators normally use the classic subsumption $\sqsubseteq$ as an ordering on class expressions. Thus, $C' \in \rho(C)$ implies $C' \sqsubseteq C$.[3]

Example 7. Given the terms M, W, hc (standing for $Man, Woman, hasChild$) from Example 3, the refinement operator ρ can be used to traverse the space of $\mathcal{EL}$ class expressions as follows:

$$\rho(\top) = \{M, W, \exists hc.\top\}$$
$$\rho(M) = \{M \sqcap M, M \sqcap W, M \sqcap \exists hc.\top\}$$

$$\rho(W) = \{W \sqcap M, W \sqcap W, W \sqcap \exists hc.\top\}$$
$$\rho(\exists hc.\top) = \{\exists hc.M, \exists hc.W, \exists hc.\exists hc.\top, \exists hc.\top \sqcap M, \exists hc.\top \sqcap W, \exists hc.\top \sqcap \exists hc.\top\}$$

...

The mechanics of refinement operators allows for pruning unpromising class expressions from the search without even generating them (and hence without checking their instances). Indeed, a specialisation of a class expression cannot have more instances than the class expression itself has, see Lemma 2.

Lemma 2 (Anti-monotone property of specialisations). *Let $\mathcal{O}$ be an ontology, C a class expression, ρ a (downward) refinement operator. Then, $C' \in \rho(C)$ implies $|inst(C', \mathcal{O})| \leq |inst(C, \mathcal{O})|$.*

---

[2] It is sufficient to consider only downward refinement operators.
[3] The statement $C' \sqsubseteq C$ is the abbreviation of $\emptyset \models C' \sqsubseteq C$.

Lemma 2 implies that if C has an insufficient number of instances, then so do all its further specialisations. It is essentially the anti-monotone property of itemsets used in the APRIORI algorithm [1] which we have defined for OWL class expressions. Due to this similarity, we call our algorithm of constructing class expressions DL-APRIORI, see Algorithm 1.

Algorithm 1. DL-APRIORI $(\mathcal{O}, \Sigma, \mathcal{DL}, \ell_{max}, s_{min})$

1: **inputs**
2:    $\mathcal{O} := \mathcal{T} \cup \mathcal{A}$: an ontology
3:    Σ: a finite set of terms such that $\top \in \Sigma$
4:    $\mathcal{DL}$: a DL for class expressions
5:    ℓ_{max}: a maximal length of a class expression such that $1 \leq \ell_{max} < \infty$
6:    s_{min}: a minimal instance threshold (support) such that $0 < s_{min} \leq |in(\mathcal{O})|$
7: **outputs**
8:    $\mathbb{C}$: the set of all class expressions satisfying the input constraints
9: **do**
10:    $\mathbb{C} \leftarrow \emptyset$ % initialise the final set of class expressions
11:    $\mathbb{D} \leftarrow \{\top\}$ % initialise the set of class expressions yet to be specialised
12:    $\rho \leftarrow getOperator(\mathcal{DL}, \Sigma, \ell_{max}, \mathcal{T})$ % initialise a refinement operator ρ
13:    **while** $\mathbb{D} \neq \emptyset$ **do**
14:       $C \leftarrow pick(\mathbb{D})$ % pick a class expression C to be specialised
15:       $\mathbb{D} \leftarrow \mathbb{D} \backslash \{C\}$ % remove C from $\mathbb{D}$
16:       $\mathbb{C} \leftarrow \mathbb{C} \cup \{C\}$ % add C to $\mathbb{C}$
17:       $\mathbb{C}' \leftarrow specialise(C, \rho)$ % specialise C using ρ
18:       $\mathbb{D}_C \leftarrow \{D \in urc(\mathbb{C}') \mid \nexists D' \in \mathbb{C} \cup \mathbb{D} : D' \equiv D\}$ % discard syntactic variations
19:       $\mathbb{D} \leftarrow \mathbb{D} \cup \{D \in \mathbb{D}_C \mid |inst(D, \mathcal{O})| \geq s_{min}\}$ % add suitable specialisations
20:    **end while**
21:    **return** $\mathbb{C}$

DL-APRIORI operates as follows. First, we initialise the refinement operator ρ (see Line 12) with the given logic $\mathcal{DL}$, signature Σ, maximal length ℓ_{max}, and TBox $\mathcal{T}$ such that it only constructs specialisations satisfying the constraints and takes $\mathcal{T}$ into consideration, e.g. its class hierarchy. The construction starts from $\top$, see also Example 7. The operator repeatedly specialises every expression picked from the set $\mathbb{D}$ of candidates and adds its suitable specialisations to $\mathbb{D}$ (see Line 14 – 19). A specialisation is suitable if it is not a syntactic variation of an already constructed one (see Line 18 where the function $urc(\mathbb{C}')$ returns unique representatives of logically equivalent class expressions in a set $\mathbb{C}'$) and satisfies the minimal support s_{min} (see Line 19). Once the set $\mathbb{D}$ is empty, the algorithm terminates. Intuitively, s_{min} acts as a "noise threshold" that prunes expressions with insufficient evidence and therefore should be sufficiently small to avoid missing useful expressions.

Given $\mathcal{DL} \leq \mathcal{SROI}$, DL-APRIORI always *terminates*, guarantees to return all class expressions *modulo equivalence* satisfying the input constraints, i.e. it is *complete*, and only expressions satisfying the constraints, i.e. it is *correct*, see [19] for details. Completeness of DL-APRIORI ensures that no class expression (and thus no GCI) satisfying the input constraints is missed, i.e. all suitable class expressions (modulo equivalence) are returned. Of course, one should specify input constraints cautiously (which is rather easy to do) to avoid missing useful class expressions.

Correctness, completeness, and termination of DL-APRIORI can be proved for DLs with number restrictions $\geq k.C$ and $\leq k.C$, e.g. $\mathcal{SROIQ}$. This would require either making the function $\ell(C)$ (the length of a class expression C) dependent on k or introducing the parameter k_{max} which bounds k. Both ways regain the properties of DL-APRIORI for $\mathcal{SROIQ}$ but complicate the presentation.

6   Empirical Evaluation

We have implemented all presented techniques in a system called DL-MINER (see the source code[4] and demo interface[5]), as it is aimed at *mining*, i.e. constructing and evaluating, axioms in DLs and OWL, see [19]. We use Java (version 8.91), the OWL API [12] (version 3.5.0), and PELLET [21] (version 2.3.1) as a reasoner. All experiments are executed on the following machine: Linux Ubuntu 14.04.2 LTS (64 bit), Intel Core i5-3470 3.20 GHz, 8 GB RAM.

6.1   Mutual Correlations of Hypothesis Quality Measures

It is worthwhile to investigate whether the quality measures indeed capture different aspects of hypothesis quality. This can be clarified by examining their mutual correlations. We investigate the following research question:

RQ. Do related measures strongly correlate? Do unrelated measures not correlate?

The experimental data consists of two corpora of ontologies. The first corpus, called *handpicked*, consists of 16 ontologies hand-picked from related work, e.g. from [7,15]. The second corpus, called *principled*, comprises all BioPortal[6] ontologies taken from [17] which contain some data (at least 100 individuals and 100 facts). It consists of 21 ontologies. In the handpicked and principled corpus, 9 and 14 ontologies, respectively, are at least as expressive as $\mathcal{ALC}$. With regard to the size, 3 and 0 ontologies, respectively, contain less than 100 individuals; 8 and 9 ontologies contain from 100 to 1000 individuals; 5 and 12 ontologies contain more than 1000 individuals. Both corpora are made publicly available [19]. We run the experiment on each corpus independently.

For each ontology $\mathcal{O}$, we run DL-APRIORI, see Algorithm 1, with $\mathcal{DL} := \mathcal{ALC}$, $\ell_{max} := 4$, $s_{min} := 10$. Since $\widetilde{\mathcal{O}}$ can contain many irrelevant terms, the seed signature is selected using the modular structure of the ontology as follows [20]:

---

[4] https://github.com/slava-sazonau/dlminer.

[5] http://www.dlminer.io.

[6] http://bioportal.bioontology.org.

$\Sigma := crn(\mathcal{M}) \cup \{\top\}$, where $\mathcal{M} := \bot\text{-}module(\mathcal{O}, crn(\mathcal{A}))$ [6] and $crn(\mathcal{O})$ returns the set of all class and property names occurring in $\mathcal{O}$. Then, we generate all possible GCIs (which can thus have length up to 8) from the constructed class expressions and OPIs with inverse properties and property chains. Using the proposed quality measures and measures from [20], we evaluate 500 randomly selected hypotheses per ontology. Then, we compute mutual correlations of the quality measures across all hypotheses in a corpus. We present the results, see Fig. 1, in the form of a *correlation matrix*, which is a symmetric matrix of (Pearson's) correlation coefficients. For each correlation, we additionally run a statistical significance test with significance level 0.05.

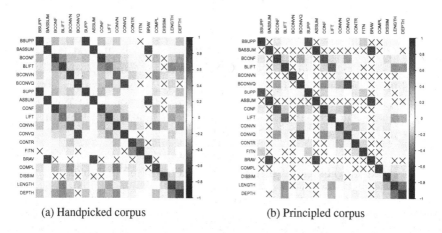

(a) Handpicked corpus   (b) Principled corpus

Fig. 1. Mutual correlations of quality measures for handpicked (a) and principled (b) corpus: positive correlations are in blue, negative correlations are in red, crosses mark statistically insignificant correlations (significance level 0.05). The abbreviations are as follows: (B)SUPP – (basic) support, (B)ASSUM – (basic) assumption, (B)CONF – (basic) confidence, (B)LIFT – (basic) lift, (B)CONVN – (basic) negated conviction, (B)CONVQ – (basic) assumed conviction, CONTR – contradiction, FITN – fitness, BRAV – braveness, COMPL – complexity, DISSIM – dissimilarity. (Color figure online)

First, we note that all main measures, except negated conviction for the principled corpus, strongly and positively correlate with their basic counterparts (please notice lines of dark blue squares parallel to the main diagonal in Fig. 1). This result is expected because the basic measures are approximations of the respective main measures. All the differences are due to the presence of negative information in the ontologies. Another strong and positive correlation occurs between assumption and braveness which is also expected since these measures count (though differently) "guesses" of a hypothesis. Among other observations are the positive correlations between conviction and confidence, particularly in the principled corpus, that capture similar aspects of quality. Interestingly, lift positively correlates with length and depth, i.e. longer hypotheses are likely to be of higher quality as measured by lift. Thus, we can answer RQ as follows:

related measures do correlate significantly, while unrelated measures mostly do not. In other words, the measures do capture different aspects of quality.

In addition, we have examined the acquired hypotheses by eyeballing them. Table 1 shows some high-quality hypotheses (please notice two property chains).

Table 1. Examples of acquired hypotheses

$\exists hasBond.\top \sqsubseteq \exists hasAtom.\top$
$AssociateProfessor \sqsubseteq \exists teaches.TeachingCourse$
$Patient \sqcap \exists hasShape.Irregular \sqsubseteq \exists hasDensity.Illdefined$
$\forall siblingof.Human \sqsubseteq Human$
$OKRunningLoan \sqsubseteq \exists hasLoanStatusValue.(\neg ProblemStatus)$
$married \circ hasChild \sqsubseteq hasChild$
$Movie \sqsubseteq \exists cast.Actor$
$BetaSugar \sqcap \exists hasRingForm.\top \sqsubseteq Pyranose$
$clinicallySimilar \circ hasSeverity \sqsubseteq hasSeverity$
$PlanetaryLayer \sqsubseteq \exists hasAstronomicalBody.\top$

6.2   A Case Study

In order to receive human feedback, we run a preliminary case study with one domain expert. The subject of the study is the ontology,[7] in the following called ntds, created using data from the US National Transgender Discrimination Survey[8] and curated by the domain expert. The ontology is in $\mathcal{SROIQ}$ and contains 169,058 individuals. We investigate the following research questions:

RQ1. What kinds of interesting hypotheses (if any) can we mine for the domain expert?
RQ2. Which measures (if any) are indicators of interestingness of a hypothesis?

To answer the research questions, we ask the domain expert to judge a hypothesis by validity and interestingness (which are different notions):

- *Validity* shows whether a hypothesis captures a general truth about the domain and can be perceived as an axiom to be added to the ontology.
- *Interestingness* shows how interesting a hypothesis is for a domain expert, i.e. evaluates her curiosity and attention that she pays to a hypothesis.

The domain expert assesses validity of a hypothesis by choosing one of the following three options: *"correct"*, *"wrong"*, *"don't know"*. Interestingness of a hypothesis is rated on the linear scale from 0 (lowest) to 4 (highest). We collect

---

[7] The ontology is not public yet.
[8] http://www.ustranssurvey.org/.

feedback using an online survey. To make a survey, we generate hypotheses as above. Since purely random sampling is likely to result in few (or no) promising hypotheses, we randomly select 30 hypotheses whose confidence exceeds 0.9 and 30 from all the rest to ensure variability of hypothesis quality in the survey which thus consists of 60 hypotheses.

The survey was completed by one domain expert. In the feedback that we received, the domain expert expressed interest in reviewing additional hypotheses and gave us *focus terms*, i.e. class and property names of a certain topic. We ran another survey of 60 hypotheses made analogously but using only the focus terms instead of the (almost) entire signature. The survey was completed by the same domain expert. Thus, 120 hypotheses were judged in total. In the following, we refer to the initial, unfocused survey as *Survey 1* and the follow-up, focused survey as *Survey 2*, see Table 2.

Table 2. Assessment of hypotheses acquired for ntds ("-" denotes zero)

	Validity	Interestingness				
		0	*1*	*2*	*3*	*4*
Survey 1 (unfocused)	*Wrong*	6	11	30	-	-
	Don't know	-	1	-	2	4
	Correct	-	-	-	6	-
Survey 2 (focused)	*Wrong*	1	-	1	-	5
	Don't know	-	-	-	-	49
	Correct	-	-	-	-	4

According to Table 2, in Survey 1, unknown and correct hypotheses are rated to be much more interesting than wrong ones: all of them, except one, have high values of interestingness. Amongst those, unknown hypotheses are marked to be the most interesting and, according to the expert's response, require further analysis. The results of Survey 2 are much different from the results of Survey 1. All hypotheses, except two, are marked by the highest value of interestingness, including wrong ones. Moreover, the domain expert informed us in her response that one of the wrong hypotheses not only indicated data bias but revealed an *error in the ontology*.

Thus, a mined hypothesis can be interesting regardless of its validity. More specifically, there are three kinds of interesting hypotheses: a correct hypothesis reflects known domain knowledge which is not yet captured in the ontology (enriches the TBox); an unknown hypothesis captures possibly true but yet unknown domain knowledge worthy of further enquiry; a wrong hypothesis indicates a modelling error or data bias. This answers RQ1 and confirms our observations made in [20].

We now turn our attention to RQ2, i.e. compare measures with expert's judgements. Figure 2 shows correlations between the quality measures and expert's judgements. Dissimilarity, confidence, length, and depth are the strongest positive indicators of validity, see Fig. 2a. Lift turns from a non-indicator in Survey 1 to a positive indicator in Survey 2. The strongest negative indicators of validity are complexity, support, and assumption. The result that support is a negative indicator is rather unexpected, considering its definition. A possible explanation is that hypotheses with more evidence seem to be easier to reject for the domain expert because "counterexamples" are easier to recall.

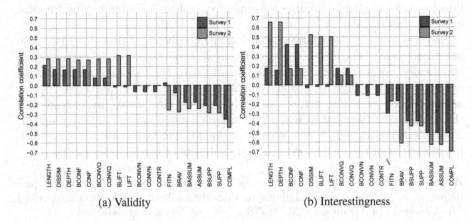

(a) Validity   (b) Interestingness

Fig. 2. Correlations (in descending order) between hypothesis quality measures (abbreviated as in Fig. 1) and expert's judgements: validity (a) and interestingness (b).

As Fig. 2b shows, confidence is a positive indicator of interestingness in Survey 1. However, it is not in Survey 2: length, depth, dissimilarity, and lift have significantly stronger positive correlations. Thus, lift and dissimilarity turn from non-indicators of interestingness in Survey 1 to its positive indicators in Survey 2. Moreover, length and depth become strong positive indicators of interestingness showing that longer hypotheses are likely to be more interesting. This is not surprising because longer hypotheses are capable of capturing phenomena that shorter ones cannot capture, i.e. they are more *powerful*. Of course, a hypothesis can be "too long" for a domain expert to perceive. As for validity, the strongest negative indicators of interestingness are complexity, assumption, and support. Support appears to be a negative indicator of interestingness because hypotheses with high support are likely to be familiar to the expert since they reflect easily seen patterns in the data. Overall, the results in Fig. 2 show that there is *no* single best indicator of hypothesis quality. This further supports our view that we need to consider multiple quality measures to identify promising hypotheses.

7   Future Work

The defined quality measures do not form the "complete list" of hypothesis quality measures. Clearly, there are other possible measures. In particular, additional rule measures can be adapted to OWL, e.g. cosine, Gini index, J-measure [10]. Such adaptation can respect the standard OWL semantics and its OWA using the procedure of translating rule measures into axiom measures presented in this paper.

Our implementation, DL-MINER, currently supports constructing GCIs for $\mathcal{ALC}$ (as well as complex property hierarchies and inverses). It relies on the availability of suitable refinement operators that are currently proposed for $\mathcal{ALC}$ [16]. In order to construct class expressions beyond $\mathcal{ALC}$ while preserving completeness, we need to design suitable refinement operators for more expressive DLs, e.g. $\mathcal{SROIQ}(\mathcal{D})$ [11].

Besides sequentially examining acquired hypotheses, a domain expert can potentially use them for *interactive ontology completion and debugging*. More specifically, approved hypotheses can be added to the ontology which is then used to mine new hypotheses and the step is repeated. Within such an iterative process, modelling errors can be identified using wrong hypotheses and then repaired. After that, a user can continue completing the ontology until it is sufficiently enriched or new errors are found. This scenario and additional investigations of the quality measures are subjects of further case studies.

Acknowledgements. We thank Amanda Hicks (the University of Florida) for participating in our case study and giving us valuable feedback and Michael Rutherford (the University of Arkansas for Medical Sciences) for translating data into OWL.

References

1. Agrawal, R., Srikant, R.: Fast algorithms for mining association rules in large databases. In: Proceedings of the 20th International Conference on Very Large Data Bases (VLDB 1994), pp. 487–499. Morgan Kaufmann, Santiago de Chile, September 1994

2. Alsubait, T., Parsia, B., Sattler, U.: Measuring similarity in ontologies: a new family of measures. In: Janowicz, K., Schlobach, S., Lambrix, P., Hyvönen, E. (eds.) EKAW 2014. LNCS, vol. 8876, pp. 13–25. Springer, Cham (2014). doi:10.1007/978-3-319-13704-9_2

3. Baader, F., Calvanese, D., McGuinness, D., Nardi, D., Patel-Schneider, P.F. (eds.): The Description Logic Handbook: Theory, Implementation, and Applications, 2nd edn. Cambridge University Press, New York (2010)

4. Baader, F., Sertkaya, B., Turhan, A.: Computing the least common subsumer w.r.t. a background terminology. J. Appl. Logic 5(3), 392–420 (2007)

5. Cohen, W.W., Hirsh, H.: Learning the CLASSIC description logic: theoretical and experimental results. In: Proceedings of the 4th International Conference on Principles of Knowledge Representation and Reasoning (KR 1994), pp. 121–133. Morgan Kaufmann, Bonn, May 1994

6. Del Vescovo, C., Klinov, P., Parsia, B., Sattler, U., Schneider, T., Tsarkov, D.: Empirical study of logic-based modules: cheap is cheerful. In: Alani, H., Kagal, L., Fokoue, A., Groth, P., Biemann, C., Parreira, J.X., Aroyo, L., Noy, N., Welty, C., Janowicz, K. (eds.) ISWC 2013. LNCS, vol. 8218, pp. 84–100. Springer, Heidelberg (2013). doi:10.1007/978-3-642-41335-3_6

7. Fanizzi, N., d'Amato, C., Esposito, F.: DL-FOIL concept learning in description logics. In: Železný, F., Lavrač, N. (eds.) ILP 2008. LNCS, vol. 5194, pp. 107–121. Springer, Heidelberg (2008). doi:10.1007/978-3-540-85928-4_12

8. Fleischhacker, D., Völker, J.: Inductive learning of disjointness axioms. In: Meersman, R., Dillon, T., Herrero, P., Kumar, A., Reichert, M., Qing, L., Ooi, B.-C., Damiani, E., Schmidt, D.C., White, J., Hauswirth, M., Hitzler, P., Mohania, M. (eds.) OTM 2011. LNCS, vol. 7045, pp. 680–697. Springer, Heidelberg (2011). doi:10.1007/978-3-642-25106-1_20

9. Galárraga, L.A., Teflioudi, C., Hose, K., Suchanek, F.: AMIE: association rule mining under incomplete evidence in ontological knowledge bases. In: Proceedings of the 22nd International World Wide Web Conference (WWW 2013), pp. 413–422. International World Wide Web Conferences Steering Committee/ACM, Rio de Janeiro (2013)

10. Geng, L., Hamilton, H.J.: Interestingness measures for data mining: a survey. ACM Comput. Surv. **38**(3), 9 (2006)

11. Grau, B.C., Horrocks, I., Motik, B., Parsia, B., Patel-Schneider, P., Sattler, U.: OWL 2: the next step for OWL. J. Web Semant. **6**(4), 309–322 (2008)

12. Horridge, M., Bechhofer, S.: The OWL API: a java API for OWL ontologies. Semant. Web **2**(1), 11–21 (2011)

13. Horridge, M., Parsia, B., Sattler, U.: Laconic and precise justifications in OWL. In: Sheth, A., Staab, S., Dean, M., Paolucci, M., Maynard, D., Finin, T., Thirunarayan, K. (eds.) ISWC 2008. LNCS, vol. 5318, pp. 323–338. Springer, Heidelberg (2008). doi:10.1007/978-3-540-88564-1_21

14. Iannone, L., Palmisano, I., Fanizzi, N.: An algorithm based on counterfactuals for concept learning in the semantic web. Appl. Intell. **26**(2), 139–159 (2007)

15. Lehmann, J., Auer, S., Bühmann, L., Tramp, S.: Class expression learning for ontology engineering. J. Web Semant. **9**(1), 71–81 (2011)

16. Lehmann, J., Hitzler, P.: Concept learning in description logics using refinement operators. Mach. Learn. **78**(1–2), 203–250 (2010)

17. Matentzoglu, N., Parsia, B.: BioPortal Snapshot 27.01.2015, February 2015. https://doi.org/10.5281/zenodo.15667

18. Ratcliffe, D., Taylor, K.: Closed-world concept induction for learning in OWL knowledge bases. In: Janowicz, K., Schlobach, S., Lambrix, P., Hyvönen, E. (eds.) EKAW 2014. LNCS, vol. 8876, pp. 429–440. Springer, Cham (2014). doi:10.1007/978-3-319-13704-9_33

19. Sazonau, V.: General Terminology Induction in Description Logics. Technical report, The University of Manchester (2017). https://doi.org/10.5281/zenodo.579593

20. Sazonau, V., Sattler, U., Brown, G.: General terminology induction in OWL. In: Arenas, M., Corcho, O., Simperl, E., Strohmaier, M., d'Aquin, M., Srinivas, K., Groth, P., Dumontier, M., Heflin, J., Thirunarayan, K., Staab, S. (eds.) ISWC 2015. LNCS, vol. 9366, pp. 533–550. Springer, Cham (2015). doi:10.1007/978-3-319-25007-6_31

21. Sirin, E., Parsia, B., Grau, B.C., Kalyanpur, A., Katz, Y.: Pellet: a practical OWL-DL reasoner. J. Web Semant. **5**(2), 51–53 (2007)

22. Völker, J., Niepert, M.: Statistical schema induction. In: Antoniou, G., Grobelnik, M., Simperl, E., Parsia, B., Plexousakis, D., De Leenheer, P., Pan, J. (eds.) ESWC 2011. LNCS, vol. 6643, pp. 124–138. Springer, Heidelberg (2011). doi:10.1007/978-3-642-21034-1_9

23. Zhu, M., Gao, Z., Pan, J.Z., Zhao, Y., Xu, Y., Quan, Z.: TBox learning from incomplete data by inference in BelNet+. Knowl. Based Syst. **75**, 30–40 (2015)

Semantic Faceted Search with Aggregation and Recursion

Evgeny Sherkhonov$^{(\boxtimes)}$, Bernardo Cuenca Grau, Evgeny Kharlamov, and Egor V. Kostylev

University of Oxford, Oxford, UK
{evgeny.sherkhonov,bernardo.cuenca.grau,evgeny.kharlamov,
egor.kostylev}@cs.ox.ac.uk

Abstract. Faceted search is the de facto approach for exploration of data in e-commerce: it allows users to construct queries in an intuitive way without a prior knowledge of formal query languages. This approach has been recently adapted to the context of RDF. Existing faceted search systems however do not allow users to construct queries with aggregation and recursion which poses limitations in practice. In this work we extend faceted search over RDF with these functionalities and study the corresponding query language. In particular, we investigate complexity of the query answering and query containment problems.

1 Introduction

Faceted search is a prominent search and data exploration paradigm in Web applications, where users can progressively narrow down the search results by applying filters, called *facets* [28]. Faceted search has also been proposed in the Semantic Web context as a suitable paradigm for exploring and querying RDF graphs, and a number of RDF-based faceted search systems have been developed in recent years [1,4,8,12,14–17,20,25].

The theoretical underpinnings of faceted search in the Semantic Web context were first studied in [10,23,30] and more recently in [1], where the authors identified a class of first-order *faceted queries* providing a balance between expressivity of the query language and complexity of query answering. On the one hand, faceted queries naturally capture the core functionality of faceted query interfaces as implemented in existing systems; on the other hand, in contrast to arbitrary first-order queries, their restrictions ensure that they can be answered in polynomial time in the combined size of the input RDF graph and query [1].

Faceted queries as defined in [1], however, do not capture some of the functionality needed for applications. We discuss this missing functionality on an example of a marketing company recording different kinds of information about products using an RDF graph. In enterprise data management such graphs

Work supported by the Royal Society under a University Research Fellowship and the EPSRC under an IAA award and the projects DBOnto, MaSI^3, ED^3, and VADA(EP/M025268/1).

C. d'Amato et al. (Eds.): ISWC 2017, Part I, LNCS 10587, pp. 594–610, 2017.
DOI: 10.1007/978-3-319-68288-4_35

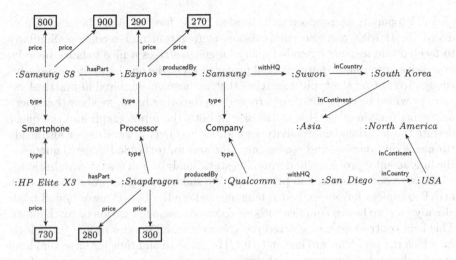

Fig. 1. Example RDF graph about products

are often the result of data integration, where data from disparate sources are exported into RDF for sharing and analysis purposes. An excerpt of our example graph is shown in Fig. 1. The graph describes mobile phones such as "Samsung S8" by providing information such as their price as advertised by different sellers, their parts (e.g., processors), or the country where phones and their parts were produced. The expert users working for the company would want to exploit faceted search to enable sophisticated searches such as the following ones:

(S1) find smartphones with price between £500 and £900;
(S2) find companies producing at least ten different models of smartphones; or
(S3) find smartphones with processors produced by North American companies.

To capture search (S1), a faceted search system should support *numeric value ranges*; in particular, this requires the underpinning query language to allow for comparisons between variables and numbers. Search (S2) requires a form of *aggregation* since it involves counting the number of smartphone models produced by each company. Search (S3) is rather cumbersome to perform in a typical RDF faceted search system, where facets are generated by "following" the explicit links in the input graph. In particular, one would typically search for smartphones first, then select the relevant processor (note the direct link between phones and processors via the hasPart relation), then select relevant cities and subsequently countries, until eventually reaching the selection for continents. Furthermore, by the time users are asked to select processors or even cities, they are unlikely to know whether these are related at all to North America. Thus, in many applications it is useful for faceted interfaces to provide "shortcuts" that would allow, for instance, a selection for continent without the need for first selecting processors, cities, or countries. Supporting such shortcuts requires a form of reachability (i.e., *recursion*) in the underpinning query language.

In this paper, we propose an extension of the faceted query language introduced in [1] with numeric comparisons, aggregation and recursion. Similarly to faceted queries, our extended query language strikes a nice balance between expressive power and computational properties. On the one hand, it is expressive enough to capture the typical searches that we have encountered in practical use cases provided by our industrial partners. On the other hand, we show that query answering remains tractable in the size of both the input graph and the query despite the additional expressivity. In addition to query answering, we also study the *query containment* and *equivalence problems* for (extended) faceted queries—the fundamental problems underpinning static analysis and query optimisation—which were not considered in prior work. We show that these problems are both CONP-complete for our extended language, where the CONP lower bound holds already for core faceted queries without comparisons, aggregation or reachability. This is in contrast to unrestricted positive existential queries in first-order logic for which the problems are known to be Π_2^p-complete and thus in the second level of the polynomial hierarchy. Furthermore, we propose a practical fragment of our extended query language for which the problems become tractable. Finally, we have extended the faceted search system SemFacet[1] to support numeric value ranges and aggregation, and we are currently working on extending the system to further support the aforementioned reachability features.

2   Preliminaries

We assume a vocabulary consisting of pairwise disjoint countably infinite sets of *individuals* $\mathbf{I}$, *numeric literals* $\mathbf{NL}$ (which we assume to correspond to the rational numbers), *classes* $\mathbf{C}$—that is, unary predicates that range over $\mathbf{I}$, *object properties* $\mathbf{OP}$—that is, binary predicates with both arguments ranging over $\mathbf{I}$, and *datatype properties* $\mathbf{DP}$—that is, binary predicates with the first argument ranging over $\mathbf{I}$ and the second over $\mathbf{NL}$. We also consider a countably infinite set $\mathbf{V}$ of variables, which is pairwise disjoint with all the aforementioned sets.

A *fact* is an expression of the form $A(c)$ with $A \in \mathbf{C}$ and $c \in \mathbf{I}$, $P(c_1, c_2)$ with $P \in \mathbf{OP}$ and $c_1, c_2 \in \mathbf{I}$, or $D(c, n)$ with $D \in \mathbf{DP}$, $c \in \mathbf{I}$ and $n \in \mathbf{NL}$. In the context of this paper, we define an *RDF graph* as a finite set of facts. The *active domain* $\mathsf{ADom}(G)$ of an RDF graph G is the set of all its individuals and numeric literals. Note that our formalisation captures RDF datasets corresponding to sets of OWL 2 DL assertions—that is, the datasets that can be seamlessly used in conjunction with OWL 2 DL ontologies.

A *relational atom* is an expression of the form $A(x)$ with $A \in \mathbf{C}$ and $x \in \mathbf{V}$ or $R(x_1, x_2)$ with $R \in \mathbf{OP} \cup \mathbf{DP}$ and $x_1, x_2 \in \mathbf{V}$. An *equality atom* is an expression of the form $x = a$, where $x \in \mathbf{V}$ and $a \in \mathbf{I} \cup \mathbf{NL}$.

A *positive existential query* $Q(\bar{x})$ is a first-order logic formula with free variables $\bar{x}$, denoted $\mathsf{fvar}(Q)$, built from relational and equality atoms using disjunction $\vee$, conjunction $\wedge$, and existential quantification $\exists$. We assume all positive existential queries to be *rectified*—that is, without different quantifications of

---

[1] https://www.cs.ox.ac.uk/isg/tools/SemFacet/.

the same variable, and denote PEQ the set of all such queries. A positive existential query is a *conjunctive query* if it is $\vee$-free. We denote CQ the set of all
conjunctive queries. A query Q is *monadic* if it has exactly one free variable.

We next define the semantics of PEQ. Let G be an RDF graph. A *valuation*
over variables $\bar{x}$ is a mapping $\nu : \bar{x} \to \mathsf{ADom}(G)$. For ν a valuation over $\bar{x}$ and
variables $\bar{y} \subseteq \bar{x}$, we denote $\nu|_{\bar{y}}$ the restriction of ν to $\bar{y}$. Let $Q \in$ PEQ, and ν be
a valuation over $\mathsf{fvar}(Q)$. Then, G *satisfies* Q *under* ν, denoted $G, \nu \models Q$, if

- Q is an atom $R(\bar{x})$ and $R(\nu(\bar{x})) \in G$;
- Q is an atom $x = a$ and $\nu(x) = a$;
- $Q = Q_1 \wedge Q_2$, $G, \nu|_{\mathsf{fvar}(Q_1)} \models Q_1$, and $G, \nu|_{\mathsf{fvar}(Q_2)} \models Q_2$;
- $Q = Q_1 \vee Q_2$ and either $G, \nu|_{\mathsf{fvar}(Q_1)} \models Q_1$ or $G, \nu|_{\mathsf{fvar}(Q_2)} \models Q_2$; or
- $Q = \exists y. Q'$ and $G, \nu \cup \{y \mapsto c\} \models Q'$ for some $c \in \mathbf{I} \cup \mathbf{NL}$.

The *semantics* $[Q]_G$ of a query $Q(\bar{x})$ (in PEQ or its extension) over an RDF
graph G is the following set of tuples of elements in $\mathbf{I} \cup \mathbf{NL}$:

$$\{\nu(\bar{x}) \mid G, \nu \models Q \text{ and } \nu \text{ is a valuation over } \bar{x}\}.$$

The *query answering problem* is to compute $[Q]_G$ given Q and G.

A query Q is *contained* in a query Q', written $Q \subseteq Q'$ if $[Q]_G \subseteq [Q']_G$ holds
for every RDF graph G. They are *equivalent*, written $Q \equiv Q'$, if $[Q]_G = [Q']_G$ for
every G. The *query containment problem* is to determine, given queries Q and
Q' as input, whether $Q \subseteq Q'$. The *query equivalence problem* is to determine
whether $Q \equiv Q'$. Note that these problems are easily reducible to each other for
all query languages considered in this paper: $Q \equiv Q'$ if and only if $Q \subseteq Q'$ and
$Q' \subseteq Q$, while $Q \subseteq Q'$ if and only if $Q \wedge Q' \equiv Q$.

When talking about complexity of algorithms, we assume the usual binary
representation of graphs and queries; in particular, rational numbers are represented by pairs of an integer and a positive integer in binary, one for the numer-
ator and the other for the denominator. This representation size of a graph G
should be distinguished from the number of facts in G, which is denoted as $|G|$.

3   Faceted Queries

In this section, we recapitulate the language of faceted queries as proposed in
[1] and justify its main features using the example faceted interface on the left-
hand-side of Fig. 2.[2] Our treatment is by no means comprehensive, and we refer
the interested reader to the aforementioned papers for additional details.

The front-end of a typical RDF faceted search system provides *(1)* a *search
text box*, where users can enter keywords; *(2)* a *faceted interface*, which contains facets and their possible values; and *(3)* a *results pane*, where the search
results are provided. The keywords entered in the search box are used, on the
one hand, to obtain an initial set of results (using standard information-retrieval

---

[2] The figure is based on the front-end of the SemFacet system.

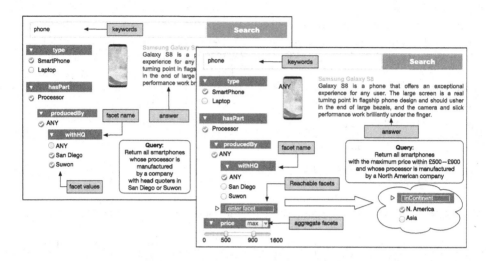

Fig. 2. Example faceted query interfaces over RDF data

techniques) and, on the other hand, to construct an initial faceted interface without selected values, which constitutes the starting point for faceted navigation. The set of values selected by users in the faceted interface are compiled into a query, which is then issued to a triple store holding the input RDF graph. The answers to the query are finally depicted in the results pane.

The basic element of a faceted interface is a *facet*, which consists of a facet name and a set of values (see Fig. 2). The special *type* facet is used to select the categories (classes) to which the results must belong. Facets can be conjunctive or disjunctive, depending on whether the selection of different values is interpreted disjunctively or conjunctively. For instance, the facet *withHQ*, which indicates the headquarters of companies, is disjunctive in the sense that selecting both *Suwon* and *San Diego* as values would result in a query asking for companies with headquarters in either of the aforementioned cities. In contrast to conventional faceted search systems, where the underpinning data has a simple "flat" structure, systems based on RDF must be able to search through complex graph data, and as a result *facet nesting* becomes an important feature. For instance, the *producedBy* facet in Fig. 2 (left) is nested under the *hasPart* facet, which indicates that the values of the facet refer to the companies that produce phone parts, rather than those producing phones themselves.

The queries obtained as a result of compiling user value selections in a faceted interface are referred to as *faceted queries*. We next discuss the intuition behind such compilation; a formal treatment can be found in [1].

Selections in the special facet *type* are interpreted as conjunctions (or disjunctions) of unary relational atoms over the same variable. Selections on any other facet yield either a binary relational atom whose second argument is existentially quantified (if the special value *Any* is selected), or in a conjunction (disjunction) of binary relational atoms having as second argument a constant or a variable belonging to a unary relational atom. Facet nesting involves a "shift" of variable from the parent facet to the nested facet as well as to the introduction of fresh existentially quantified variables. As a result, faceted queries can be seen as positive existential queries satisfying the following restrictions:

(R1) they are *monadic* since query answers displayed in a system's results pane are individual objects, rather than tuples of objects;

(R2) they are *tree-shaped* since existentially quantified variables introduced by facet nesting are always fresh; and

(R3) all disjuncts of a disjunctive (sub-)query are also monadic, with the same free variable shared across all their disjuncts.

For instance, the user selections on the left-hand side of Fig. 2 are compiled into the following faceted query $Q_1^{ex}(x)$ asking for smartphones whose processor is produced by any company with headquarters in either Suwon or San Diego:

$$\mathsf{Smartphone}(x) \land \exists y. \,(\mathsf{hasPart}(x, y) \land \mathsf{Processor}(y) \land$$
$$(\exists z_1. \,(\mathsf{producedBy}(y, z_1) \land \exists w_1. \,\mathsf{withHQ}(z_1, w_1) \land (w_1 = :\!Suwon)) \lor$$
$$(\exists z_2. \,(\mathsf{producedBy}(y, z_2) \land \exists w_2. \,\mathsf{withHQ}(z_2, w_2) \land (w_2 = :\!San\ Diego)))). \quad (1)$$

Note that query Q_1^{ex} has a single free variable x and hence satisfies restriction (R1). Furthermore, it has no cyclic dependencies between its variables and hence satisfies restriction (R2). Finally, the disjuncts in the only disjunctive subquery of Q_1^{ex} share their only free variable y, and hence the query satisfies (R3). Restrictions (R1)–(R3) are formalised in the following definitions.

Definition 1. *The* graph *of $Q \in \mathsf{PEQ}$ is the directed labeled graph such that*

- *its nodes are the variables mentioned in Q;*
- *its edges are the pairs (x_1, x_2) with relational atoms $P(x_1, x_2)$ in Q; and*
- *the label of (x_1, x_2) is the set of all properties P with $P(x_1, x_2)$ in Q.*

A monadic query $Q(x) \in \mathsf{PEQ}$ is tree-shaped *if its graph is a directed tree rooted at x and the label of each edge is a singleton.*

Definition 2. *A (core)* faceted query *Q is a monadic, tree-shaped query in PEQ satisfying the following additional property: if $Q_1 \lor Q_2$ is a sub-query of Q, then $\mathsf{fvar}(Q_1) = \mathsf{fvar}(Q_2) = \{x\}$ for some variable x. We denote with FQ and CFQ the classes of all faceted queries and all conjunctive faceted queries, respectively.*

The restrictions in this definition are sufficient for an existence of a polynomial-time query answering algorithm [1].

4   Extended Faceted Queries

In this section, we present our extension of core faceted queries. We consider as a running example the faceted interface depicted on the right-hand-side of Fig. 2. Intuitively, the user selections in the figure represent a search for all smartphones with maximum price amongst all sellers comprised between £500 and £900, and whose processor has been manufactured by a North American company. The interface on the right-hand side of the figure extends that on the left-hand side with two additional elements:

- an *aggregate facet* consisting of a selection for an aggregate and a numeric range slider, and which establishes the relevant restriction on the maximum smartphone price;
- a special facet with a search box which allows users to search for "reachable" facets, thus providing a shortcut for the relevant continent selection.

To capture such new elements, we extend the query language in Sect. 4 with three new types of atoms, namely *(i)* *comparison atoms*, extending equality atoms and capture numeric comparisons between a variable and a numeric literal; *(ii)* *aggregate atoms*, capturing aggregation; and *(iii)* *reachability atoms*, representing a limited form of recursion sufficient to capture the shortcuts.

We start by defining comparison atoms and their semantics.

Definition 3. *A* comparison atom *is an expression of the form* x op a, *where* $x \in \mathbf{V}$, op $\in \{=, \leq, \geq, <, >\}$, *and* $a \in \mathbf{I} \cup \mathbf{NL}$ *if* op *is* $=$ *and* $a \in \mathbf{NL}$ *otherwise. An RDF graph* G *satisfies a comparison atom* x op a *under a valuation* ν *over* x, *written* $G, \nu \models x$ op a, *if and only if* $\nu(x)$ op a *holds under the conventional built-in meaning of comparison predicates (assuming that* $\nu(x)$ op a *is false if* $\nu(x) \notin \mathbf{NL}$ *and* op *is not* $=$).

Note that each equality atom is a comparison atom by definition.

For instance, the following query uses comparison atoms to ask for all smartphones with price range between £500 and £900:

$$Q_2^{\text{ex}}(x) = \text{Smartphone}(x) \wedge \exists y. \left(\text{price}(x, y) \wedge (y \geq 500) \wedge (y \leq 900)\right).$$

Aggregate atoms in our language provide a restricted form of aggregation over what is available in standard query languages such as SPARQL 1.1 [13,18]. An important restriction is that the value computed by the corresponding *aggregate function* is immediately compared to a constant and thus the atom is evaluated to either true or false in any given graph and valuation. This is in contrast to SPARQL 1.1, where the value computed by an aggregate function can be assigned to a variable which can then occur in other parts of the query. Another restriction is that *grouping* is always performed over the first argument of an object or datatype property and, as a result, the collection of values over which the aggregate function is evaluated cannot contain duplicates and thus can be seen as a set rather than a multiset.

Definition 4. *An* aggregate function *is a function* $\mathsf{f} : 2^{\mathbf{I} \cup \mathbf{NL}} \to \mathbf{NL} \cup \{\text{undef}\}$, *where* undef *is a special symbol. We concentrate on several specific aggregate functions, defined as follows, for* $S \subseteq \mathbf{I} \cup \mathbf{NL}$:

- count(S) *is the cardinality of* S;
- min(S) *is the minimum in* S *if* $S \subseteq \mathbf{NL}$ *and* $S \neq \emptyset$, *and it is* undef *otherwise;*
- max(S) *is the maximum in* S *if* $S \subseteq \mathbf{NL}$ *and* $S \neq \emptyset$, *and* undef *otherwise;*
- sum(S) *is the sum of literals in* S *if* $S \subseteq \mathbf{NL}$, *and it is* undef *otherwise;*
- avg(S) *is* sum(S)/count(S) *if* sum(S) $\neq$ undef *and* count(S) $\notin \{0, \text{undef}\}$, *and it is* undef *otherwise.*

An aggregate atom *is an expression of the form* $\mathsf{Agg}(x, R, \mathsf{f})$ op n, *where* f *is one of the aforementioned aggregate functions,* R *is a property that is datatype if* $\mathsf{f} \neq$ count, x *is a variable,* op $\in \{=, \leq, \geq, <, >\}$, *and* $n \in \mathbf{NL}$. *An RDF graph* G *satisfies an* aggregate atom $\mathsf{Agg}(x, R, \mathsf{f})$ op n *under a valuation* ν *over* x, *written* $G, \nu \models \mathsf{Agg}(x, R, \mathsf{f})$ op n, *if and only if* $\mathsf{f}(\{a \mid R(\nu(x), a) \in G\})$ op n *(assuming that all comparison operators return false if the first argument is* undef *).*

For instance, the following query relies on aggregate atoms to ask for smartphones with average price across all sellers greater than £500:

$$Q_3^{\text{ex}}(x) = \mathsf{Smartphone}(x) \land (\mathsf{Agg}(x, \mathsf{price}, \mathsf{avg}) \geq 500).$$

We next define reachability atoms, capturing the shortcuts in navigation.

Definition 5. *A* reachability atom *is an expression of the form* $\mathsf{Next}(x_1, x_2)$ *or* $\mathsf{Next}^+(x_1, x_2)$ *with* $x_1, x_2 \in \mathbf{V}$. *An RDF graph* G *satisfies a* reachability atom α *under a valuation* ν, *denoted* $G, \nu \models \alpha$, *if*

- $\alpha = \mathsf{Next}(x_1, x_2)$ *and there is a property* R *such that* $G, \nu \models R(x_1, x_2)$; *or*
- $\alpha = \mathsf{Next}^+(x_1, x_2)$ *and there exist* $a^1, \dots, a^n$, $n \geq 1$, *in* $\mathbf{I} \cup \mathbf{NL}$ *such that* $\nu(x_1) = a^1$, $\nu(x_2) = a^n$, *and, for each* $i = 1, \dots, n-1$, *there is a property* R_i *such that* $R_i(a^i, a^{i+1}) \in G$.

Our example search on the right-hand side of Fig. 2 can be captured by the following faceted query $Q_4^{\text{ex}}(x)$, involving aggregate and reachability atoms:

$\mathsf{Smartphone}(x) \land (\mathsf{Agg}(x, \mathsf{price}, \mathsf{max}) \geq 500) \land (\mathsf{Agg}(x, \mathsf{price}, \mathsf{max}) \leq 900)$

$\land \exists y. (\mathsf{hasPart}(x, y) \land \mathsf{Processor}(y) \land \exists z.(\mathsf{producedBy}(y, z)$

$\land \exists v. \mathsf{Next}^+(z, v) \land \exists u. \mathsf{inContinent}(v, u) \land (u = :\!North\ America))).$

The languages of positive existential queries and faceted queries are extended in the obvious way by allowing for the new types of atoms (i.e., comparison, aggregate and reachability) in addition to relational atoms.

Definition 6. Extended positive existential queries *are defined in the same way as positive existential queries, except that they allow for not only relational and equality, but also (arbitrary) comparison, aggregate, and reachability atoms as building blocks.* Extended faceted queries *are also defined in the same way as core faceted queries; in this case, the graph of the query takes into account binary relational atoms and reachability atoms (but not comparison or aggregate ones). We denote with* $\mathcal{L}[\mathcal{O}]$, *for* $\mathcal{L} \in \{\mathsf{PEQ}, \mathsf{CQ}, \mathsf{FQ}, \mathsf{CFQ}\}$ *and* $\mathcal{O} \subseteq \{Comp, Agg, Next, Next^+\}$ *the language obtained by extending* $\mathcal{L}$ *with atoms specified in* $\mathcal{O}$ *as follows: comparison if* $Comp \in \mathcal{O}$, *aggregate if* $Agg \in \mathcal{O}$, Next *if* $Next \in \mathcal{O}$, *and* Next^+ *if* $Next^+ \in \mathcal{O}$.

It is known that core faceted queries are expressible in the standard RDF query language SPARQL [1]. Similarly, extended faceted queries allow for a direct translation to the current version of this language, SPARQL 1.1 [13,18]. In particular, it has aggregation functionality, which captures aggregate atoms in faceted queries, and property paths, which capture reachability atoms.

5   Answering Extended Faceted Queries

In [1] it was shown that core faceted queries (i.e., faceted queries without comparison, aggregate, and reachability atoms) can be answered in polynomial time. This is in contrast to unrestricted positive existential (or even conjunctive) queries, where evaluation problem is well-known to be NP-complete.

Tractability of core faceted query answering relies on two key observations [1]. First, answering monadic tree-shaped conjunctive queries is a well-known tractable problem; thus, the only possible source of intractability is the presence of disjunction. Second, disjunctive subqueries in a faceted query can be answered in a bottom-up fashion: to compute the answers to $Q_1(x) \vee Q_2(x)$ it suffices to answer $Q_1(x)$ and $Q_2(x)$ independently and "store" the answers as new unary relational facts in the input RDF graph using a fresh class $C_{Q_1 \vee Q_2}$ uniquely associated to $Q_1(x) \vee Q_2(x)$. The polynomial time algorithm in [1] stems from a direct application of these observations, and relies on an oracle for answering monadic tree-shaped conjunctive queries.

In this section, we study the problem of answering extended faceted queries over RDF graphs. Specifically, we propose a polynomial time query answering algorithm that generalises that in [1] to account for the additional features of the query language. We proceed in the following two steps.

1. In the first step we show that comparison and aggregate atoms can be encoded away by a polynomial time rewriting of the input query and RDF graph; the correctness of this rewriting is independent from the special properties of faceted queries, and thus it equivalently transforms any query in PEQ[$Comp, Agg, Next, Next^+$] into PEQ[$Next, Next^+$].
2. In the second step we show that, analogously to core faceted queries, any query in FQ[$Next, Next^+$] can be efficiently answered in a bottom-up fashion while "storing" the results of disjunctive subqueries in the RDF graph. In contrast to the algorithm in [1], which relies on an oracle for answering monadic tree-shaped conjunctive queries, our extended algorithm relies on the existence of a polynomial time procedure for answering a special type of *conjunctive regular path queries* (*CRPQs*) [2].

In the intermediate steps of the algorithms in this and the following sections we operate with graphs and queries that allow for generalised predicates: a *heterogeneous class* is a unary predicate that ranges over $\mathbf{I} \cup \mathbf{NL}$, and a *heterogeneous property* is a binary predicate with the first argument ranging over $\mathbf{I}$ and the second over $\mathbf{I} \cup \mathbf{NL}$. For brevity, we assume that such graphs are RDF graphs and such queries belong to the corresponding languages (e.g., FQ).

For the first step, consider a query $Q(x)$ in $\mathsf{PEQ}[Comp, Agg, Next, Next^+]$ and an RDF graph G. For every comparison or aggregate atom α in Q, we introduce a fresh heterogeneous class C_α. Let $\tilde{Q}$ be the query in $\mathsf{PEQ}[Next, Next^+]$ obtained from Q by replacing each comparison or aggregate atom α with the free variable x by $C_\alpha(x)$. Note that if Q is in $\mathsf{FQ}[Comp, Agg, Next, Next^+]$, then $\tilde{Q}$ is in $\mathsf{FQ}[Next, Next^+]$. Let also $\tilde{G}$ be the union of G and the following graphs:

$$\{C_{x\,op\,a}(a') \mid x \text{ op } a \text{ is atom in } Q,\ a' \in \mathsf{ADom}(G), \text{ and } a' \text{ op } a\},$$
$$\{C_{\mathsf{Agg}(x,R,\mathsf{f})\,op\,n}(a) \mid \mathsf{Agg}(x, R, \mathsf{f}) \text{ op } n \text{ is atom in } Q,\ a \in \mathsf{ADom}(G), \text{ and }$$
$$G, \{x \mapsto a\} \models \mathsf{Agg}(x, R, \mathsf{f}) \text{ op } n\}.$$

The following lemma establishes the correctness of the transformation.

Lemma 1. *Given a query Q in $\mathsf{PEQ}[Comp, Agg, Next, Next^+]$ and an RDF graph G, query $\tilde{Q}$ and RDF graph $\tilde{G}$ can be computed in polynomial time in the sizes of binary representations of Q and G. Moreover, $[Q]_G = [\tilde{Q}]_{\tilde{G}}$.*

Note that, in particular, the number N of atoms in $\tilde{Q}$ is the same as in Q, and $|\tilde{G}| \leq |G| + N \cdot |\mathsf{ADom}(G)|$.

Having Lemma 1 at hand, it is enough to define a polynomial-time procedure for answering queries in $\mathsf{FQ}[Next, Next^+]$, which we do in the second step. To this end, we first note that tree-shaped queries in $\mathsf{CQ}[Next, Next^+]$ can be directly translated into *strongly acyclic CRPQs*, which can be answered in linear time both in the size of the query and the RDF graph [2].

Lemma 2. *Computing $[Q]_G$ for a monadic tree-shaped query Q in the class $\mathsf{CQ}[Next, Next^+]$ and a generalised RDF graph G can be done in $O(n \cdot m)$, where n and m are the sizes of binary representations of Q and G, respectively.*

We next present Algorithm 1, which computes $[Q]_G$ for a query $Q(x) \in \mathsf{FQ}[Comp, Agg, Next, Next^+]$ and an RDF graph G. First, the algorithm eliminates comparison and aggregation atoms on the basis of Lemma 1. Then, analogously to the algorithm in [1], it iterates, in a bottom-up manner, over all disjunctive subqueries of Q: each disjunctive-free subquery is dealt with using the procedure ANSWER-SACRPQ for answering strongly acyclic CRPQs on the basis of Lemma 2, while the disjunctive subquery is replaced with the atom $C_{Q_1 \vee Q_2}(x)$ in Q (for $C_{Q_1 \vee Q_2}$ a fresh heterogeneous class), and the graph is extended by atoms $C_{Q_1 \vee Q_2}(a)$ for all a returned by the call to ANSWER-SACRPQ. The correctness of Algorithm 1 leads to our main result in this section.

Theorem 1. *Query answering in $\mathsf{FQ}[Comp, Agg, Next, Next^+]$ can be solved in polynomial time.*

6   Query Containment and Equivalence

In this section we consider the containment and equivalence problems for faceted queries. These are fundamental problems for static analysis and query optimisation and, to the best of our knowledge, have not been considered in prior work on faceted search in the Semantic Web context.

Algorithm 1. ANSWER-FQ[$Comp, Agg, Next, Next^+$]

INPUT   : Q a query in FQ[$Comp, Agg, Next, Next^+$], G an RDF graph
OUTPUT: $[Q]_G$

1 $Q := \tilde{Q}$ and $G := \tilde{G}$
2 **while** Q has a disjunctive subquery **do**
3 $\quad$ pick a subquery $Q_1(x) \vee Q_2(x)$ in Q with Q_1 and Q_2 disjunction-free
4 $\quad$ **for each** $1 \leq i \leq 2$ **do**
5 $\quad\quad$ $Ans_i :=$ ANSWER-SACRPQ(Q_i, G)
6 $\quad$ replace $Q_1(x) \vee Q_2(x)$ in Q with $C_{Q_1 \vee Q_2}(x)$ for heterogeneous class $C_{Q_1 \vee Q_2}$
7 $\quad$ $G := G \cup \{C_{Q_1 \vee Q_2}(a) \mid a \in Ans_1 \cup Ans_2\}$
8 **return** ANSWER-SACRPQ(Q, G)

We concentrate on containment: as argued in Sect. 2, containment and equivalence are polynomially inter-reducible. We start by showing that containment is CONP-complete for FQ[$Comp, Agg, Next, Next^+$], and the hardness holds even for FQ and for CFQ[$Next, Next^+$]. Then, we establish tractability of containment for practically important subclasses of faceted queries, namely CFQ[$Comp, Agg, Next$] and CFQ[$Comp, Agg, Next^+$]. Finally, we show that the requirement on disjunction in the definition of faceted queries has a significant impact on complexity: containment of monadic tree-shaped PEQ (without any additional restriction on disjunctive subformulas) is Π_2^p-complete, and hence as hard as containment for unrestricted PEQ.

First we show a CONP upper bound for FQ[$Comp, Agg, Next, Next^+$]. We start with several definitions.

Let Q and Q' be FQ[$Comp, Agg, Next, Next^+$] queries, and let N and N^+ be fresh heterogeneous properties. We first show how to eliminate reachability atoms and fractional numbers from Q and Q'. Consider all the numeric literals $a_1, \ldots, a_n$ in the comparison and aggregate atoms of Q and Q' except aggregate atoms over count, as well as integers $b_1, \ldots, b_n$ that are numerators of rational numbers obtained from $a_1, \ldots, a_n$ by bringing them to the smallest common denominator. Denote $\tilde{Q}$ and $\tilde{Q}'$ the queries in FQ[$Comp, Agg$] obtained from Q and Q', respectively, by replacing

1. each a_i in comparison and non-count aggregate atoms by b_i; and
2. each atom $Next(x_1, x_2)$ by $N(x_1, x_2)$ and each $Next^+(x_1, x_2)$ by $N^+(x_1, x_2)$.

The size of binary representation of $\tilde{Q}$ and $\tilde{Q}'$ is polynomial in the size of Q and Q', and $\tilde{Q}$ and $\tilde{Q}'$ can be constructed efficiently, in polynomial time. As we will see later, containment of Q in Q' can be reduced to containment of $\tilde{Q}$ in $\tilde{Q}'$.

A *generalised RDF graph* G is a set of facts enriched, for each constant $c \in \mathbf{I}$,

- by a non-negative integer $Val(c, R, \mathsf{count})$ for each $R \in \mathbf{OP} \cup \mathbf{DP}$, and
- by rational numbers $Val(c, D, \mathsf{f})$ for all $\mathsf{f} \in \{\mathsf{min}, \mathsf{max}, \mathsf{sum}\}$ and all $D \in \mathbf{DP}$.

Graph G is *realisable* if there is an RDF graph G' such that all facts of G are also in G', and $\mathsf{f}(\{a \mid R(c, a) \in G'\}) = Val(c, R, \mathsf{f})$ for all $Val(c, R, \mathsf{f})$ in G.

The *semantics* $[Q]_G$ of a query $Q(\bar{x})$ over a generalised RDF graph G is defined in the same way as over a usual one, except that, when evaluating aggregate atoms, aggregation values are not computed on the facts, but taken from the corresponding $Val(c, R, f)$ (assuming $Val(c, R, \mathsf{avg}) = Val(c, R, \mathsf{sum})/Val(c, R, \mathsf{count})$ for uniformity).

Intuitively, the generalised RDF graph G represents (a part of) the usual RDF graph G' witnessing its realisability: numbers $Val(c, R, f)$ describe the values of aggregates f for c and R in G' in a concise way. Note, however, that the size of a binary representation of G may be exponentially smaller than that of G', because for some constants c and properties R graph G may store only the number of R-successors of c in binary instead of listing them one by one (of course, some parts of G' may also be not represented in G at all). If fact, as we will see soon, in search for a witness for non-containment, we can restrict ourselves to generalised graphs with polynomially-sized binary representation, while the corresponding witnessing usual graph may be necessarily exponential. But before formalising this, we show how to modify the graph to deal correctly with reachability.

A generalised RDF graph G is *reachability-closed* if

- $N(a_1, a_2) \in G$ if and only if $R(a_1, a_2) \in G$ for some $R \notin \{N, N^+\}$; and
- $N^+(a_1, a_2) \in G$ if and only if there is a directed path from a_1 to a_2 in G via properties different from N and N^+.

Lemma 3. *Given queries Q and Q' in FQ[Comp, Agg, Next, Next$^+$], $Q \not\sqsubseteq Q'$ if and only if there exists a realisable generalised reachability-closed RDF graph G' with binary representation of polynomial size in the sizes of representations of Q and Q' such that $[\tilde{Q}]_{G'} \not\subseteq [\tilde{Q'}]_{G'}$.*

The final key observation is that Theorem 1, which ensures that the query evaluation is feasible, applies to generalised graphs with minor modifications of justifying Algorithm 1, while realisability can also be easily checked.

Lemma 4. *Containment is in* CONP *for* FQ[Comp, Agg, Next, Ñext$^+$].

We now move on to the CONP lower bound which, as we show next, holds already for rather restricted languages.

Lemma 5. *Containment is* CONP-*hard for both* FQ *and* CFQ[Next, Next$^+$].

Proof (Sketch). We start with a reduction of 3SAT to the complement of the containment for FQ. Let φ be a propositional formula in 3CNF over m variables u_i, $i = 1, \ldots, m$, with n clauses $\gamma_j = \ell_j^1 \vee \ell_j^2 \vee \ell_j^3$, $j = 1, \ldots, n$. For each $i = 1, \ldots, m$, let T_i and F_i be classes, and, for each $j = 1, \ldots, n$, let $Q_j(x) = V_j^1(x) \vee V_j^2(x) \vee V_j^3(x)$, where V_j^k, for $k = 1, 2, 3$, is T_i if $\ell_j^k = u_i$ and F_i if $\ell_j^k = \neg u_i$.
Consider the following queries in FQ:

$$Q(x) = \bigwedge_{i=1}^{m} (T_i(x) \vee F_i(x)) \wedge \bigwedge_{j=1}^{n} Q_j(x) \quad \text{and} \quad Q'(x) = \bigvee_{i=1}^{m} (T_i(x) \wedge F_i(x)).$$

Intuitively, Q encodes the fact that for every $i = 1, \ldots, m$ either u_i or $\neg u_i$ must be true and that every clause γ_j, $1 \le j \le n$, must be true as well. Negation of Q' encodes the fact that u_i and $\neg u_i$ cannot be true at the same time. We claim that φ is satisfiable if and only if $Q \not\subseteq Q'$.

The coNP-hardness for CFQ[$Next, Next^+$] can be proved in a similar way as the hardness of containment of tree patterns over trees in [22]. □

Lemmas 4 and 5 give us the following theorem.

Theorem 2. *Containment is* coNP-*complete for any query language between* FQ *and* FQ[$Comp, Agg, Next, Next^+$] *as well as for any query language between* CFQ[$Next, Next^+$] *and* FQ[$Comp, Agg, Next, Next^+$].

This theorem leaves open the question what faceted queries have tractable containment. Next we show that it is true for conjunctive faceted queries that use either only Next or only $Next^+$. We start with some definitions.

Consider a query Q in CFQ[$Comp, Agg, Next$] or in CFQ[$Comp, Agg, Next^+$]. A variable x in Q is *domain-inconsistent* if Q has an atom of the form $C(x)$ with $C \in \mathbf{C}$, $R(x, y)$ with $R \in \mathbf{OP} \cup \mathbf{DP} \cup \{Next, Next^+\}$, $P(x', x)$ with $P \in \mathbf{OP}$, x op a with $a \in \mathbf{I}$, or $Agg(x, R, f)$ op n, as well as an atom of the form $D(x', x)$ with $D \in \mathbf{DP}$ or x op n with $n \in \mathbf{NL}$. Intuitively, domain-consistency ensures that no variable is required to match both a constant and a numeric literal.

For each variable x in Q, let $\Sigma_{Comp}(x, Q)$ be the set of all comparison atoms in Q where x appears. Then, for any variables x and y, denote $x \sim_Q y$ the fact that $\Sigma_{Comp}(x, Q)$ and $\Sigma_{Comp}(y, Q)$ imply $x = y$. Finally, for each x and property R, let $\Sigma_{Agg}(x, R, Q)$ be the set of constraints

$$\{x_f \text{ op } n \mid Agg(y, R, f) \text{ op } n \text{ is an aggregate atom in } Q \text{ and } x \sim_Q y\}$$
$$\cup \{x_{\mathsf{min}} \le x_{\mathsf{avg}}, x_{\mathsf{avg}} \le x_{\mathsf{max}}, x_{\mathsf{count}} \times x_{\mathsf{avg}} = x_{\mathsf{sum}}\},$$

where, for each aggregate function f, x_f is a fresh variable. Query Q is *consistent* if $\Sigma_{Comp}(x, Q)$ has a solution for any x in Q, $\Sigma_{Agg}(x, R, Q)$ has a solution for any x and any $R \in \mathbf{OP} \cup \mathbf{DP}$, and Q has no domain-inconsistent variable.

Given queries $Q(x)$ and $Q'(x)$ both either in CFQ[$Comp, Agg, Next$] or in CFQ[$Comp, Agg, Next^+$], a *homomorphism* from Q' to Q is a mapping h from variables of Q' to variables of Q such that $h(x) = x$ and, for every relational atom $R(x'_1, \ldots, x'_n) \in Q'$, there exists $R(x_1, \ldots, x_n) \in Q$ with $h(x'_i) \sim_Q x_i$ for every i. Homomorphism h is *comparison-preserving* if $\Sigma_{Comp}(h(x'), Q)$ implies $\Sigma_{Comp}(x', Q')$ for any variable x' of Q'. It is *aggregation-preserving* if $\Sigma_{Agg}(h(x'), R, Q)$ implies $\Sigma_{Agg}(x', R, Q')$ for any variable x' of Q' and any R. It is $Next$-*preserving* if, for every atom $Next(x'_1, x'_2)$ in Q', there is $R(x_1, x_2) \in Q$ with $R \in \mathbf{OP} \cup \mathbf{DP} \cup \{Next\}$, $h(x'_1) \sim_Q x_1$, and $h(x'_2) \sim_Q x_2$. It is $Next^+$-*preserving* if for every $Next^+(x'_1, x'_2)$ in Q' there are $R_1(y_1, z_1), \ldots, R_n(y_n, z_n)$, $n \ge 1$, in Q with all $R_i \in \mathbf{OP} \cup \mathbf{DP} \cup \{Next^+\}$, such that $h(x'_1) \sim_Q y_1$, $h(x'_2) \sim_Q z_n$, and $z_i \sim_Q y_{i+1}$ for each $i = 1, \ldots, n-1$.

Proposition 1. *Let Q and Q' be queries in* CFQ[$Comp, Agg, \mathcal{N}$], *where $\mathcal{N} \in \{Next, Next^+\}$. Then, $Q \subseteq Q'$ if and only if either Q is not consistent or there is a comparison-, aggregation- and $\mathcal{N}$-preserving homomorphism from Q' to Q.*

Checking for existence of a comparison-, aggregation- and $\mathcal{N}$-preserving homomorphism for tree-shaped queries can be done in polynomial time using standard techniques for tree homomorphisms (see, e.g., [22]), while checking for consistency is straightforward. So, we have the following theorem.

Theorem 3. *The containment problem both for* CFQ[$Comp, Agg, Next$] *and for* CFQ[$Comp, Agg, Next^+$] *is in* PTIME.

We conclude by showing that the requirement on disjunction in the definition of faceted queries makes a difference, and containment for monadic tree-shaped PEQ is Π_2^p-complete. The following theorem can be proved by a reduction of $\forall\exists$3SAT; the matching upper complexity bound is inherited from arbitrary PEQ.

Theorem 4. *Containment is* Π_2^p*-hard for monadic tree-shaped* PEQ.

7 Related Work

To the best of our knowledge, there is no theoretical study on extensions of faceted search with numeric value ranges, aggregation, and reachability. On the system side, we are not aware of any RDF-based faceted search system that currently supports aggregation (see [29] for a comprehensive survey). Aggregation in faceted search has so far been considered only in the context of conventional data models [3,7], which are not graph-based; in that setting, the focus was on improved indexing schemes to optimise interface computation and update. A limited form of recursion is supported by the */facet* system [15], where the transitive closure of transitive properties is precomputed and explicitly stored in the RDF graph. Finally, numeric value ranges have been implemented in several systems [12,27] and their implementation is similar to ours in SemFacet.

Query containment is a classical problem in database theory. Containment of acyclic conjunctive queries is tractable [11,31] which implies tractability of core conjunctive faceted queries that are tree-shaped and thus acyclic. Containment for (unions of) conjunctive queries is NP-complete [5]. It is also known that containment is Π_2^p-complete for PEQ [24], while our results show that hardness already holds for tree-shaped PEQ.

For CQ it is known that adding comparison atoms changes complexity of containment from NP-complete to Π_2^p-complete [9,19,21] and the known proofs of the lower bound either rely on ternary relations, or they exploit atoms that compare two variables. Our results show that adding comparison atoms of the form x op a (for a a constant) does not increase the complexity of containment, which remains in coNP. Moreover, containment for tree-shaped conjunctive queries with comparison atoms of the form x op a is tractable [26], and thus the containment is also tractable for core conjunctive faceted queries with comparisons.

When aggregates are added to CQ or PEQ, the complexity of containment becomes dependent on the supported aggregate functions [6]. Notably, most complexity upper bounds in the literature are formulated for queries containing a specific aggregate function only. In contrast, in this paper we allow for arbitrary combinations of aggregate functions in queries, while at the same time restricting other aspects of aggregation as discussed in Sect. 4.

A number of languages with recursive navigational features have been considered in the context of graph databases, including regular path queries (RPQs) and conjunctive regular path queries (CRPQs). These languages are very expressive and, as a result, containment becomes computationally expensive: it is EXPSPACE-complete for CRPQs, where the lower bound already holds for acyclic CRPQs [2]. In contrast, the form of recursion provided by our query language is rather limited, and does not result in a complexity jump when added to faceted queries. Conjunctive faceted queries also resemble XML tree patterns, where the *descendant axis* in tree patterns is akin to our reachability atoms interpreted over XML trees. Containment of tree patterns is CONP-complete [22], and we used a similar idea to establish a CONP lower bound for conjunctive faceted queries with reachability atoms.

8   Conclusion and Future Work

In this paper we have extended existing faceted query languages with new features important in applications. We have shown that, despite the additional expressivity, query answering remains tractable in the combined size of the input query and RDF graph. We have also studied the query containment problem and established complexity bounds for a number of practically relevant fragments of our query language. From a practical point of view, we have extended the faceted search system SemFacet to support numeric value ranges and aggregation, and are currently working on extending it to also support reachability.

We see many directions for future work. From a theoretical perspective, we are planning to study extensions of faceted queries with additional features suggested by practical use cases, and in particular with a form of *negation*. Furthermore, we are also planning to study the computational properties of extended faceted queries in the presence of an ontology. From a practical perspective, we are working closely with our collaborators at EDF Energy on the development of a Semantic Search tool combining SemFacet and their in-house visualisation tool SemVue. The initial results of this collaboration have been very encouraging.

References

1. Arenas, M., Cuenca Grau, B., Kharlamov, E., Marciuška, Š., Zheleznyakov, D.: Faceted search over RDF-based knowledge graphs. J. Web Semant. **37**, 55–74 (2016)
2. Barceló, P.: Querying graph databases. In: Proceedings of PODS (2013)
3. Ben-Yitzhak, O., Golbandi, N., Har'El, N., Lempel, R., Neumann, A., Ofek-Koifman, S., Sheinwald, D., Shekita, E., Sznajder, B., Yogev, S.: Beyond basic faceted search. In: Proceedings of WSDM (2008)
4. Berners-Lee, T., Hollenbach, J., Lu, K., Presbrey, J., Prudhommeaux, E., Schraefel, M.C.: Tabulator redux: browsing and writing linked data. In: LDOW (2008)

5. Chekuri, C., Rajaraman, A.: Conjunctive query containment revisited. Theor. Comput. Sci. **239**(2), 211–229 (2000)
6. Cohen, S.: Containment of aggregate queries. SIGMOD Rec. **34**(1), 77–85 (2005)
7. Dash, D., Rao, J., Megiddo, N., Ailamaki, A., Lohman, G.: Dynamic faceted search for discovery-driven analysis. In: Proceedings of CIKM (2008)
8. Fafalios, P., Tzitzikas, Y.: X-ENS: semantic enrichment of Web search results at real-time. In: Proceedings of SIGIR (2013)
9. Farré, C., Nutt, W., Teniente, E., Urpí, T.: Containment of conjunctive queries over databases with null values. In: Proceedings of ICDT (2007)
10. Ferré, S., Hermann, A.: Semantic search: reconciling expressive querying and exploratory search. In: Aroyo, L., Welty, C., Alani, H., Taylor, J., Bernstein, A., Kagal, L., Noy, N., Blomqvist, E. (eds.) ISWC 2011. LNCS, vol. 7031, pp. 177–192. Springer, Heidelberg (2011). doi:10.1007/978-3-642-25073-6_12
11. Gottlob, G., Leone, N., Scarcello, F.: The complexity of acyclic conjunctive queries. J. ACM **48**(3), 431–498 (2001)
12. Hahn, R., Bizer, C., Sahnwaldt, C., Herta, C., Robinson, S., Bürgle, M., Düwiger, H., Scheel, U.: Faceted Wikipedia search. In: Proceedings of BIS (2010)
13. Harris, S., Seaborne, A.: SPARQL 1.1 query language. W3C recommendation, W3C, March 2013
14. Heim, P., Ziegler, J., Lohmann, S.: gFacet: a browser for the Web of Data. In: Proceedings of IMC-SSW (2008)
15. Hildebrand, M., van Ossenbruggen, J., Hardman, L.: /facet: a browser for heterogeneous semantic web repositories. In: Cruz, I., Decker, S., Allemang, D., Preist, C., Schwabe, D., Mika, P., Uschold, M., Aroyo, L.M. (eds.) ISWC 2006. LNCS, vol. 4273, pp. 272–285. Springer, Heidelberg (2006). doi:10.1007/11926078_20
16. Huynh, D., Mazzocchi, S., Karger, D.R.: Piggy bank: experience the semantic web inside your web browser. J. Web Sem. **5**(1), 16–27 (2007)
17. Huynh, D.F., Karger, D.R.: Parallax and companion: set-based browsing for the Data Web (2013). www.davidhuynh.net
18. Kaminski, M., Kostylev, E.V., Cuenca Grau, B.: Semantics and expressive power of subqueries and aggregates in SPARQL 1.1. In: Proceedings of WWW (2016)
19. Klug, A.C.: On conjunctive queries containing inequalities. J. ACM **35**(1), 146–160 (1988)
20. Kobilarov, G., Dickinson, I.: Humboldt: exploring linked data. In: LDOW (2008)
21. van der Meyden, R.: The complexity of querying indefinite data about linearly ordered domains. J. Comput. Syst. Sci. **54**(1), 113–135 (1997)
22. Miklau, G., Suciu, D.: Containment and equivalence for a fragment of XPath. J. of the ACM **51**(1), 2–45 (2004)
23. Oren, E., Delbru, R., Decker, S.: Extending faceted navigation for RDF data. In: Cruz, I., Decker, S., Allemang, D., Preist, C., Schwabe, D., Mika, P., Uschold, M., Aroyo, L.M. (eds.) ISWC 2006. LNCS, vol. 4273, pp. 559–572. Springer, Heidelberg (2006). doi:10.1007/11926078_40
24. Sagiv, Y., Yannakakis, M.: Equivalences among relational expressions with the union and difference operators. J. ACM **27**(4), 633–655 (1980)
25. Schraefel, M.C., Smith, D.A., Owens, A., Russell, A., Harris, C., Wilson, M.L.: The evolving mSpace platform: leveraging the Semantic Web on the trail of the Memex. In: Proceedings of Hypertext (2005)
26. Sherkhonov, E., Marx, M.: Containment of acyclic conjunctive queries with negated atoms or arithmetic comparisons. Inf. Process. Lett. **120**, 30–39 (2017)

27. Soylu, A., Giese, M., Schlatte, R., Jiménez-Ruiz, E., Kharlamov, E., Özçep, Ö.L., Neuenstadt, C., Brandt, S.: Querying industrial stream-temporal data: an ontology-based visual approach. J. AISE **9**(1), 77–95 (2017)
28. Tunkelang, D.: Faceted Search. Synthesis Lectures on Information Concepts, Retrieval, and Services. Morgan & Claypool Publishers, Burlington (2009)
29. Tzitzikas, Y., Manolis, N., Papadakos, P.: Faceted exploration of RDF/S datasets: a survey. J. Intell. Inf. Syst. **48**, 329–364 (2017)
30. Wagner, A., Ladwig, G., Tran, T.: Browsing-oriented semantic faceted search. In: Proceedings of DEXA (2011)
31. Yannakakis, M.: Algorithms for acyclic database schemes. In: Proceedings of VLDB (1981)

Investigating Learnability, User Performance, and Preferences of the Path Query Language SemwidgQL Compared to SPARQL

Timo Stegemann[✉] and Jürgen Ziegler

University of Duisburg-Essen, Duisburg, Germany
timo.stegemann@uni-due.de
http://interactivesystems.info

Abstract. In this paper, we present an empirical comparison of user performance and perceived usability for SPARQL versus SemwidgQL, a path-oriented RDF query language. We developed SemwidgQL to facilitate the formulation of RDF queries and to enable non-specialist developers and web authors to integrate Linked Data and other semantic data sources into standard web applications. We performed a user study in which participants wrote a set of queries in both languages. We measured both objective performance as well as subjective responses to a set of questionnaire items. Results indicate that SemwidgQL is easier to learn, more efficient, and preferred by learners. To assess the applicability of SemwidgQL in real applications, we analyzed its expressiveness based on a large corpus of observed SPARQL queries, showing that the language covers more than 90% of the typical queries performed on Linked Data.

1 Introduction

The wealth of Linked Data published on the open Web [15] offers a wide range of opportunities that are to date still underexploited in practical applications. Integrating Linked Data from different sources into standard web sites, blogs or other web applications would enable web authors and developers to reuse the vast amount of information already available and create additional value by enriching their content or by syndicating different data sources. However, a more widespread use of textual and multimedia resources from Linked Data and, even more so, of time-dependent data from the Internet of Things is currently significantly hindered by their complexity. It thus seems important to lower the threshold for users such as web developers or even normal web authors by providing techniques for using Linked Data without requiring complicated technical installations or the knowledge of powerful yet complex query languages such as SPARQL.

To alleviate the problems involved in using linked data, we have developed a JavaScript-based environment, that facilitates the integration of Linked Data in web pages. A main component of this environment is the path query language SemwidgQL that is intended to be significantly easier to use than standard SPARQL. A first overview of the SemwidgJS environment was presented

© Springer International Publishing AG 2017
C. d'Amato et al. (Eds.): ISWC 2017, Part I, LNCS 10587, pp. 611–627, 2017.
DOI: 10.1007/978-3-319-68288-4_36

in [16]. In this current paper, we focus on the path query language developed and provide a description of its novel extensions. We further present a comprehensive empirical user study comparing SPARQL and SemwidgQL. The goal of this study is to explore SemwidgQL's effectiveness, efficiency, learnability for users, and user preference in comparison to SPARQL. The study supports our claim that SemwidgQL is easier to learn, more efficient, and preferred by the learners. To investigate how well SemwidgQL covers the range of SPARQL queries used in practice, we further analyzed several hundred thousand log entries of public SPARQL endpoints. Results indicate that SemwidgQL can cover most of the requests that are currently made with SPARQL.

2   Related Work

Several approaches to support querying, exploring and displaying Linked Open Data have been described in literature so far. Many of these approaches are specialized on browsing (e.g. [2,7]) and visualizing queried data values or sub graphs (e.g. [8]) respectively, which is generating revealing insights but can only be reused on other websites with large effort.

FSL [11] and LDPath [14] are path query languages for RDF data inspired by XPath for XML. LDPath is part of the Apache Marmotta platform for Linked Data. One drawback of these languages is that they can only return single result lists but not lists of results sets, which is necessary when querying a set of different properties at once. Requesting coherent values from different properties require distinct queries that request each property separately. Therefore, it is not provided that these values stay connected, since the respective order can be different, or values can be added to or removed from the data set between requests. Rules for a translation into SPARQL do not exist for these languages and therefore they require direct access to the data or a special interface on the server side. Language extensions for SPARQL such as C-SPARQL [1] and SPARQLStream [5] facilitate the usage of queries over streams of RDF data. Time windows that restrict the queried data to a period of time can be specified in a special FROM STREAM statement.

The performance of users for different query languages has already been evaluated in pre-SQL times [12]. However, since the effort is very high, user studies that compare different query languages are rarely conducted. Participants require an extensive introduction to be able to use a query language at a satisfying level. Mostly this happens in the context of a lecture. We are not aware of any user study that compares the participants' performance with SPARQL and another query language of the Linked Data area.

3   SemwidgQL

SemwidgQL is a path query language that transcompiles to SPARQL. In contrast to queries formulated in other Linked Data path query languages, such as LDPath [14] or FSL [11], SemwidgQL can therefore be used to query any public

SPARQL endpoint without further special requirements. Unlike these languages, SemwidgQL is also capable of querying sets of different properties at once, by adding all properties of interest to the SELECT statement of its SPARQL translation. Ultimately, SemwidgQL aims to combine the benefits of SPARQL (such as its prevalence in the Linked Open Data area or its ability of returning lists of result sets) with the simplicity of path query languages.

In the following section, we give an overview of SemwidgQL's core features that have been described in more detail in a previous publication [16]. SemwidgQL has been significantly extended since then and we present further features that were added to facilitate among others the querying of time-sequential data, such as sensor data, and give experienced users more control over the generated SPARQL queries via filters and pseudo-filters. Specifications of time windows are comparable to the approaches of SPARQL streaming extensions. In contrast to these extensions, SemwidgQL is compatible with regular SPARQL endpoints and requires no additional execution environment.

3.1 Core Features

As a path query language, SemwidgQL traverses RDF graphs. The traversal is indicated by the dot notation, which is reminiscent of the well-known syntax used in object-oriented programming. Figure 1 shows the simplified basic structure of a SemwidgQL query. Usually a query starts with a resource followed by one or more properties. To further filter the result set, properties can be restricted. Filters are enclosed in parentheses and are appended the property they restrict. The left-hand side of a filter expression is typically a property (or a property path) that refers to the property to restrict outside of the parentheses. The right-hand side specifies a filter value that can be a literal, IRI, or even a nested query. Between them stands a relational operator. Several filter expressions can

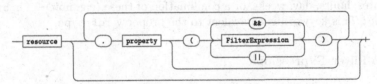

Fig. 1. Basic structure of a SemwidgQL query.

Table 1. Basic SemwidgQL queries and their meanings.

SemwidgQL query	Technique	Meaning
dbr:Vienna.rdfs:comment	Path Expression	Textual description of Vienna
dbr:Vienna.^dbo:capital	Inverse Property	Country, where Vienna is the capital
dbr:Vienna.^dbo:birthPlace ↪ (rdf:type = dbo:SoccerPlayer)	Filter	Soccer players, who were born in Vienna

be combined by logical operators. Furthermore, SemwidgQL allows wildcard selectors, inverse property selections, and multiple property selections. Table 1 shows some exemplary SemwidgQL queries.

3.2 Advanced Features

In addition to SemwidgQL's core features, we have implemented several filter and pseudo-filter keywords that, among others, simplify restricting language of string literals or allow aggregation of results. Also, they facilitate querying of time-sequential data with flexibly specified sampling intervals. Filter and pseudo-filter keyword expressions can be combined with normal SemwidgQL filter expressions and with each other as well. While filter expressions in SemwidgQL result in filter expressions in SPARQL, pseudo-filter expressions can have an impact on' different parts of the translated query. An overview of these expressions is given below.

Filter Expressions

@lang: With this keyword the language of the property can be filtered by the given language code.

@self: This keyword refers to the property to restrict itself. Instead of filtering a property that is related to the property to restrict, it can be filtered directly.

@timestart/@timeend: These keywords allow the filtering of values after, before, or (when combined) between two points of time. The right-hand side of the expression can be an absolute date or a relative point in time, depending on the time of the query execution. The expression is parsed as an equation, whose first part is a timestamp or the term now followed by the amount of time that has to be added or subtracted. This can be expressed in seconds, minutes, hours, day, weeks, or a combination of these (e.g. now - 1 h 5 min).

@type: This keyword is equivalent to the property rdf:type.

Pseudo-Filter Expressions

@aggregate: This keyword allows to apply an aggregate function to the variable of the property within the SELECT statement. Allowed values are COUNT, SUM, MIN, MAX, AVG, and SAMPLE.

@hide: If set to true, the variable of the property will not be part of the SELECT statement.

@optional: If set to true, the triple pattern, in which the property is created, will be enclosed in an OPTIONAL statement.

@predicate: Typically, the predicate of a triple pattern is not part of the SELECT statement. If set to true, the predicate of the triple pattern, in which the property is created, will be added to the SELECT statement.

@timeinterval: This keyword is used to group and aggregate time-sequential values. On the right-hand side of the expression, a sampling interval can be defined. All returned values within this interval will be aggregated. By default, the SAMPLE aggregate function will be applied to all variables, but different functions can be specified by the @aggregate keyword. Similar to @timestart and @timeend, the length of the interval can be expressed in seconds, minutes, hours, day, weeks, or a combination of these.

```
*(ip:sensor = ir:TH_LF285 && ip:type = 'Temperature').[ip:value(@aggregate = 'AVG'),
ip:measuredAt(@timeinterval = '60 min' && @timestart = 'now - 7 days' && @aggregate = 'MIN')]
                                    ⇓
        SELECT DISTINCT SAMPLE(?wildcard) AS ?wildcard
            AVG(?value) AS ?value MIN(?measuredAt) AS ?measuredAt
        WHERE {
          ?wildcard ip:value ?value .
          ?wildcard ip:measuredAt ?measuredAt .
          ?wildcard ip:sensor ?sensor .
          ?wildcard ip:type ?type .
          FILTER (
              ?sensor = ir:TH_LF285_01 && STR(?type) = "Temperature"
          )
          FILTER (
              xsd:dateTime(?measuredAt) >= now() - 604800
          )
          BIND(FLOOR((xsd:dateTime(?measuredAt) -
              xsd:dateTime("1970-01-01T00:00:00")) / (3600)
              ) AS ?measuredAt_timeinterval)
        }
        GROUP BY ?measuredAt_timeinterval
        ORDER BY DESC(?measuredAt_timeinterval)
```

Fig. 2. A SemwidgQL query and the corresponding SPARQL query that requests the average temperature measurements that were made by a specific sensor during the last week, aggregated on an hourly base.

A SemwidgQL query and its rather complex translation into SPARQL is shown in Fig. 2. The query contains normal SemwidgQL filter expressions combined with previously presented filter and pseudo-filter keyword expressions. It requests the average temperature measurements that were made by a specific sensor (located in our office) during the last week, aggregated on an hourly base.

4   Empirical User Study

We conducted an empirical user study comparing SPARQL and SemwidgQL. SemwidgQL was developed to be effective, efficient, and easy to learn by non-expert users. The goal of our study is to explore whether SemwidgQL can fulfill these requirements in comparison to SPARQL. In addition we want to investigate the users' satisfaction. At the beginning of this section, we will describe the design of the study and its procedure. Afterwards, we will present the results. In conclusion, we interpret and discuss these results.

4.1   Method

Design: We conducted an empirical user study with a mixed methods design and repeated measures, combining objective performance measures and a subjective questionnaire. For the performance measure, participants had to complete several query interpretation and formulation tasks. Effectiveness was measured by the number of correct answers of all query tasks.

Efficiency was measured by the participants' performance measures for the query formulation tasks. We investigated these tasks regarding nine dependent variables, i.e. (a) *number of keystrokes* (number of keystrokes made by a participant, including deletion and substitution of characters), (b) *number of corrections* (number of correcting keystrokes made by a participant, such as backspace, delete, replacing several selected characters etc.), (c) *number of conjunct corrections* (a coherent sequence of correcting keystrokes forms a conjunct correction, e.g. multiple backspaces in succession; typing of a character ends a conjunct correction), (d) *number of pauses* (number of pauses taken by a participant; a pause starts after two seconds without a keystroke; a pause might be an indicator for that a participant requires some time to think about further actions that are required to solve the task), (e) *time of pauses* (accumulated time of pauses in seconds taken by a participant during a task; operationalizes thinking time), (f) *time on task* (processing time of a task in seconds), (g) *number of requests* (number of requests a participant made to the SPARQL endpoint), (h) *fraction of erroneous requests* (fraction of requests that could not be executed due to parser errors etc.), (i) *display time of solutions* (time in seconds that a participant inspected the sample solution; a high display time might be an indicator that participants are uncertain about their solutions and therefore compare their own and the model solution more thoroughly).

Learnability was evaluated by comparing the results of the query formulation tasks from the initial and repeated measures regarding the above listed variables.

User preferences were measured through the answers from the questionnaire. The questionnaire asked to rate six characteristics of SPARQL and SemwidgQL on the basis of an equidistant five-point numerical rating scale. The minimum value always had a negative and the maximum value always had a positive connotation. These items were related to the subjective assessment of SPARQL's and SemwidgQL's learnability, intuitiveness, logical structure, comprehensibility, writing effort, and sophistication. Also, the participants were explicitly asked for their personally preferred language and a brief explanation for their decision.

Participants: The study was attended by seven students (one female), all enrolled on master courses in computer science at our University. The age of the participants was between 23 and 28 years ($M = 25.57$; $SD = 2.07$). Three participants had already gathered previous experience in Linked Data and Semantic Web from different courses, and one student had already worked with RDF and SPARQL as part of his bachelor thesis.

Procedure: The user study took place in the context of the introductory session of a seminar on "Semantic Web Technologies and Applications" for graduate students in the field of computer science. At the beginning of the seminar, the participants were handed a three-page handout[1], which contained an overview of relevant SPARQL and SemwidgQL commands, as well as a small RDF graph that was used for all examples and tasks of the presentation and evaluation. The graph contained, among other things, some information about cities in the region, such as label, population, districts, class, but also temperature measurements of sensors. The data were chosen in such a way that the participants could compensate for misunderstandings through their personal context knowledge.

The introductory session consisted of a three-hour lecture which was divided into three one-hour sections. In the first section, the participants were taught the basic ideas, techniques and formats on which Linked Data and the Semantic Web are built. In the second section, the participants were given an introduction to SPARQL and in the third section an introduction to SemwidgQL. As far as it was possible, the procedure corresponded to the procedure of the previous section. Care was taken to explain both languages to a similar extent and it was ensured that the participants understood both languages at a comparable level.

Afterwards, the participants had to complete a set of twelve query tasks. In the first three tasks, they had to interpret predefined SPARQL and SemwidgQL queries. In the following nine tasks, they had to query predetermined information using SPARQL and SemwidgQL. Each task had to be processed with both languages. Namespace definitions were predefined for both languages. The order of the query languages changed at each task. At any time, participants could query the SPARQL endpoint and validate their queries and results. They could quit tasks at any time and move on to the next one. No time limit was set for solving a task. After each task, a model solution was presented.

Subsequently, the participants filled out a questionnaire in which they should specify socio-demographic information and previous experiences with Semantic Web and Linked Data techniques. Then they evaluated SPARQL and SemwidgQL regarding the above mentioned characteristics. One week after the introductory session, the study was repeated.

Data Collection: The data of the interpretation and formulation of queries were automatically collected via the specially prepared website on which the participants had to solve their tasks. Each keystroke was recorded and stored together with a time stamp in a central database. It was also recorded when the SPARQL endpoint was queried and it was recorded whether the query was valid or contained errors. The time stamps, at which the participants started or ended a task, the model solution was displayed, and a task was marked as successfully completed or marked as canceled by the participants, were recorded as well. The questionnaire data were collected via the online survey portal SoSci Survey[2].

---

[1] Handouts and tasks: https://semwidg.org/files/share/iswc2017_appendix.pdf.
[2] https://www.soscisurvey.de/.

4.2   Results

Correctness of Answers: Answers were divided into three categories. Correct answers, answers with minor errors, and incorrect answers. Answers with minor errors are syntactically correct and close to the model solutions, but can contain minor inaccuracies, such as queries that contain a triple pattern for requesting a desired property but do not contain the corresponding variable in the SELECT statement. Incorrect answers are syntactically incorrect, do not fulfill the requirements given in the task description, or the task was aborted by the user.

In total, we evaluated results of 147 tasks per language. From these results 21 belong to the query interpretation tasks and 126 belong to the query formulation tasks. The participants performed slightly better, when interpreting SemwidgQL queries compared to interpreting SPARQL tasks. Regarding SemwidgQL, 86% of the tasks were solved correctly, 14% of the solutions had minor errors. Regarding SPARQL, 76% of the tasks were solved correctly, and 24% of the solutions had minor errors. There were no incorrect answers in terms of the query interpretation tasks. With regard to the query formulation tasks, the participants achieved almost equally good results with both languages. Regarding SPARQL, 90% of the tasks were solved correctly, 6% of the solutions contained minor errors and 4% were incorrect. Regarding SemwidgQL, 89% of the tasks were solved correctly, 7% of the solutions contained minor errors and 4% were incorrect.

Query Formulation Tasks: In the following subsections, we will describe the results of the nine query formulation tasks (tasks 4–12), the participants had to solve during the evaluation. For each of the following statistical tests, we compared the participants' performance regarding the nine dependent variables listed in the study design subsection. For the subsequent tests, we restrict the examined data to pairs of correct answers or answers with minor errors, since data from incorrect or canceled solution would doubtlessly distort the results.

Analysis of Mean Performance: We compared the participants' performance regarding the above-mentioned dependent variables by calculating multiple dependent t-tests for paired samples. The further described results are presented in detail in Table 2. SemwidgQL's values regarding six of all nine dependent variables were significantly better compared to SPARQL. The *number of conjunct corrections (c)* was descriptively better regarding SemwidgQL compared to SPARQL. However, this difference is not statistically significant. The *number of requests (g)* and the *fraction of erroneous requests (h)* were better in SPARQL compared to SemwidgQL. These differences are also not statistically significant.

Analysis of Learning Effects: We evaluated, how the participants performance changed between the first and second pass of the user study. We also compared the differences between SPARQL and SemwidgQL during these two

Table 2. Differences between SPARQL and SemwidgQL.

	SPARQL		SemwidgQL		t-test		
	M	SD	M	SD	$t(124)$	p	
(a) number of keystrokes	136.32	58.90	74.56	55.02	14.33	<.001	***
(b) number of corrections	15.10	16.49	12.15	16.10	2.04	.044	*
(c) number of conjunct corrections	6.02	5.27	5.10	6.63	1.72	.088	
(d) number of pauses	11.06	7.95	7.57	7.36	5.82	<.001	***
(e) time of pauses (s)	99.82	122.89	67.84	73.91	2.99	.003	**
(f) time on task (s)	152.26	117.81	109.44	89.85	4.60	<.001	***
(g) number of requests	3.54	4.51	4.26	5.78	−1.45	.150	
(h) fraction of erroneous requests	0.19	0.27	0.21	0.27	−0.56	.578	
(i) display time of solutions (s)	7.56	10.75	4.67	4.60	2.83	.005	**

$*p < .05, **p < .01, ***p < .001$

passes. Again, we calculated multiple dependent t-tests for paired samples. Differences between SPARQL and SemwidgQL at each pass are presented in Table 3 and Fig. 3. Differences between the first and second pass for each language are shown in Table 4 and Fig. 3, in combination with the results of the previous tests.

In the first pass, results in terms of SemwidgQL were significantly better regarding four of the nine dependent variables compared to SPARQL, and descriptively but not significantly better regarding two further dependent variables. The participants never performed significantly better with SPARQL. In the second pass, results regarding SemwidgQL became significantly better at all but one dependent variable compared to the first pass. Results regarding SPARQL became significantly better regarding four dependent variables. All other results became descriptively but not significantly better. In comparison to SPARQL, participants performed significantly better with SemwidgQL regarding five of all nine dependent variables. Again, the participants never performed significantly better with SPARQL.

Complexity-Dependent Analysis: We compared the performance of the participants for SPARQL and SemwidgQL regarding a task's complexity. We assume that complexity of a task is a predictor for the measured responses. For this purpose, we conducted several linear regression analyses for the previously mentioned dependent variables and the complexity of a task as predictor variable.

In various works to determine the difficulty of SPARQL (e.g. [10]) or other (database) queries (e.g. [3,9]) Halstead's complexity measure [6] has been used. This measure is based on the number of distinct operators and operands as well as the total number of operands of a query or piece of source code. Halstead's complexity measure tends to produce comparatively high values when SPARQL queries contain filter expressions because the number of operators increases noticeably. Thus, it seems to overrate the influence of filter expressions on complexity. Because of this limitation, we developed an alternative complexity

Table 3. Differences between SPARQL and SemwidgQL per pass.

	Pass	SPARQL M	SD	SemwidgQL M	SD	t-test $t(56)$	p	
(a) number of keystrokes	1	143.74	71.14	83.65	66.78	2.54	.014	*
	2	126.33	44.41	63.39	38.50	2.68	.010	**
(b) number of corrections	1	17.14	20.00	15.95	20.55	1.96	.056	
	2	12.28	11.28	7.74	8.81	3.40	.001	**
(c) number of conjunct corrections	1	6.09	6.05	6.44	8.82	0.71	.483	
	2	5.60	3.65	3.61	3.33	2.90	.005	**
(d) number of pauses	1	12.49	9.52	9.21	8.89	3.57	<.001	***
	2	8.79	4.87	5.54	5.03	4.00	<.001	***
(e) time of pauses (s)	1	102.98	120.26	79.85	84.21	1.03	.309	
	2	80.88	115.70	49.39	50.57	3.58	<.001	***
(f) time on task (s)	1	166.33	140.71	125.51	103.54	2.84	.006	**
	2	118.67	53.56	85.65	61.55	3.85	<.001	***
(g) number of requests	1	3.82	5.25	4.77	6.53	1.42	.161	
	2	2.89	2.66	3.11	3.18	2.53	.014	*
(h) fraction of erroneous requests	1	0.21	0.27	0.27	0.28	0.90	.374	
	2	0.17	0.26	0.12	0.22	3.77	<.001	***
(i) display time of solutions (s)	1	10.40	14.60	4.58	4.63	3.33	.002	**
	2	4.04	3.20	4.40	4.50	0.30	.765	

$^{*}p < .05, ^{**}p < .01, ^{***}p < .001$

Table 4. Differences between first and second pass per language.

	Lang[a]	1st pass M	SD	2nd pass M	SD	t-test $t(56)$	p	
(a) number of keystrokes	A	143.74	71.14	126.33	44.41	2.54	<.001	***
	B	83.65	66.78	63.39	38.50	2.68	<.001	***
(b) number of corrections	A	17.14	20.00	12.28	11.28	1.96	.641	
	B	15.95	20.55	7.74	8.81	3.40	.004	**
(c) number of conjunct corrections	A	6.09	6.05	6.44	3.65	0.71	.717	
	B	6.44	8.82	3.61	3.33	2.90	<.001	***
(d) number of pauses	A	12.49	9.52	8.79	4.87	3.57	.003	**
	B	9.21	8.89	5.54	5.03	4.00	<.001	***
(e) time of pauses (s)	A	102.98	120.26	80.88	115.70	1.03	.109	
	B	79.85	84.21	49.39	50.57	3.58	.051	
(f) time on task (s)	A	166.33	140.71	118.67	53.56	2.84	.012	*
	B	125.51	103.54	85.65	61.55	3.85	<.001	***
(g) number of requests	A	3.82	5.25	2.89	2.66	1.42	.264	
	B	4.77	6.53	3.11	3.18	2.53	.650	
(h) fraction of erroneous requests	A	0.21	0.27	0.17	0.26	0.90	.223	
	B	0.27	0.28	0.12	0.22	3.77	.266	
(i) display time of solutions (s)	A	10.40	14.60	4.04	3.20	3.33	.005	**
	B	4.58	4.63	4.40	4.50	0.30	.613	

[a] A: SPARQL, B: SemwidgQL
$^{*}p < .05, ^{**}p < .01, ^{***}p < .001$

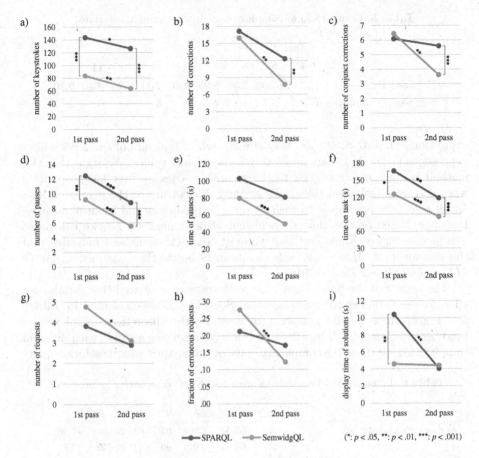

Fig. 3. Differences between SPARQL and SemwidgQL per pass, and differences between first and second pass per language.

measure, which is based on the number of nodes of a query in SPARQL Syntax Expressions (SSE) notation[3]. Later on, we show that the empirical data are better represented by the alternative SSE based complexity measure.

To calculate the SSE based complexity measure, we summed up the number of nodes of the SSE syntax tree, but combined all nodes which were required for matching the language in a filter expression into one. Since the participants were taught this filter as a fixed expression in both languages, we assumed that writing this expression requires no additional mental effort than a normal filter expression. Also, we did not count the first projection node (i.e. SELECT), which occurs in all SELECT queries. Table 5 shows the complexity values of the SPARQL sample solutions of each task in comparison, calculated according to Halstead's D as well as the SSE based complexity c. D and c values of tasks without filter

---

[3] https://jena.apache.org/documentation/notes/sse.html.

Table 5. Comparison of complexity of SPARQL sample solutions.

	Task								
	4	5	6	7	8	9	10	11	12
Halstead D	2.67	4.00	3.50	8.25	3.60	7.71	3.75	8.40	9.10
SSE based complexity c	2	3	3	4	3	6	3	5	8

expressions (4, 5, 6, 8, 10) are very similar, while D values of tasks with filter expressions (7, 9, 11, 12) are noticeably higher than c values. We argue that this method is much closer aligned to the mental processes a user has to perform when solving a task than Halstead's method. We calculated the regression lines for all response variables with each D and c as predictors and SPARQL as query language. Based on the yielded coefficient of determination R^2, we calculated a Wilcoxon Signed-Rank Test that supports our statement and indicates that the median for c, $Mdn = .86$, was significantly better than the median for D, $Mdn = .56$ ($z = -2.35$, $p = .016$).

The results of the linear regression analyses with c as predictor variable for all response variables with SPARQL and SemwidgQL are presented in Table 6 and Fig. 4. Since we did not want to compare the theoretical complexity of SPARQL and SemwidgQL but their practical performance at tasks with different complexities, we chose the complexity value of the SPARQL sample solution query

Table 6. Linear regression analyses with SSE based complexity as predictor.

	Lang[a]	$F(1,7)$	p	R^2	f	$f_i(c)$[b]
(a) number of keystrokes	$\mathcal{A}$	92.43	<.001	.93	3.63	$23.90c + 41.98$
	$\mathcal{B}$	64.04	<.001	.90	3.02	$21.32c - 9.57$
(b) number of corrections	$\mathcal{A}$	36.93	.001	.84	2.30	$4.00c - 1.30$
	$\mathcal{B}$	24.22	.002	.78	1.86	$4.33c - 4.95$
(c) number of conjunct corrections	$\mathcal{A}$	42.98	<.001	.86	2.48	$1.67c - 0.77$
	$\mathcal{B}$	25.06	.002	.78	1.89	$1.82c - 2.13$
(d) number of pauses	$\mathcal{A}$	156.63	<.001	.96	4.73	$3.08c - 0.72$
	$\mathcal{B}$	81.27	<.001	.92	3.41	$3.24c - 5.02$
(e) time of pauses (s)	$\mathcal{A}$	34.19	.001	.83	2.21	$39.51c - 50.15$
	$\mathcal{B}$	60.02	<.001	.90	2.93	$36.70c - 71.90$
(f) time on task (s)	$\mathcal{A}$	92.33	<.001	.93	3.63	$46.19c - 31.83$
	$\mathcal{B}$	57.90	<.001	.89	2.88	$40.24c - 47.17$
(g) number of requests	$\mathcal{A}$	18.27	.004	.72	1.62	$2.54c - 5.95$
	$\mathcal{B}$	59.15	<.001	.89	2.91	$2.18c - 3.41$
(h) fraction of erroneous requests	$\mathcal{A}$	2.05	.195	.23	0.54	$0.05c + 0.07$
	$\mathcal{B}$	0.52	.494	.07	0.27	$0.02c + 0.23$
(i) display time of solutions (s)	$\mathcal{A}$	19.27	.003	.73	1.66	$2.27c - 1.64$
	$\mathcal{B}$	7.41	.030	.51	1.03	$1.33c - 0.53$

[a]$\mathcal{A}$: SPARQL, $\mathcal{B}$: SemwidgQL
[b]Linear regression equation, i: measured response, c: complexity

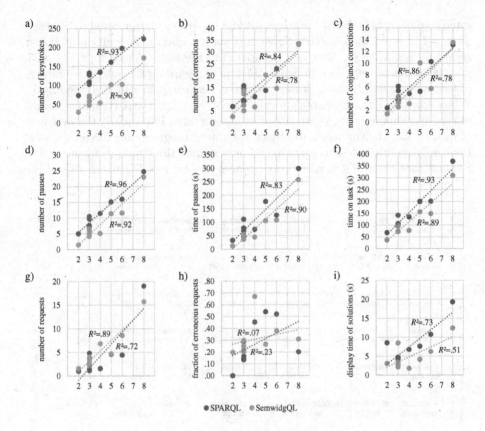

Fig. 4. Linear regression analyses with task complexity as predictor.

as complexity value for the corresponding tasks. Results indicate that there is a significant association between complexity c and all response variables except for *fraction of erroneous requests (h)*. The corresponding regression equations have very high R^2 values (one third of them $\geq$ .90) and the effect sizes f are also high, according to Cohen [4].

The regression lines for the values of SemwidgQL in the examined range of c are in all cases, except *number of requests (g)* and *fraction of erroneous requests (h)*, below the regression lines for the values of SPARQL. In four of these seven cases, the slopes of the SemwidgQL lines are less steep than the slopes of the SPARQL lines, suggesting that SemwidgQL will perform better then SPARQL at more complex tasks. In the remaining three cases, the lines intersect at complexity values above the investigated range.

Subjective Evaluation by the Participants: In the following subsection, we will present the results of the questionnaire, the participants completed after the query tasks. We calculated multiple Wilcoxon Signed-Rank Tests to compare the participants' subjective ratings for SPARQL and SemwidgQL. *Writing effort* was rated significantly better regarding SemwidgQL, $Mdn = 4$, compared to SPARQL, $Mdn = 2$ ($z = -3.03$, $p = .001$). *Sophistication* was also rated significantly better regarding SemwidgQL, $Mdn = 4$, compared to SPARQL, $Mdn = 2$ ($z = -3.23$, $p < .001$). There were no significant differences regarding the subjective ratings of *learnability*, *intuitiveness*, *logical structure*, and *comprehensibility* (see Fig. 5). When asked for advantages of SemwidgQL over SPARQL, the participants named nine unique characteristics with 30 occurrences in total. Particularly the shortness of queries and the similarity to object orientated programming languages were frequently mentioned. The participants only named three unique advantages of SPARQL over SemwidgQL with 5 occurrences in total (see Fig. 6). In 79% of the

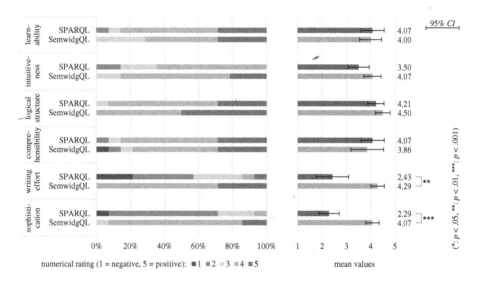

Fig. 5. Subjective evaluation of SPARQL and SemwidgQL.

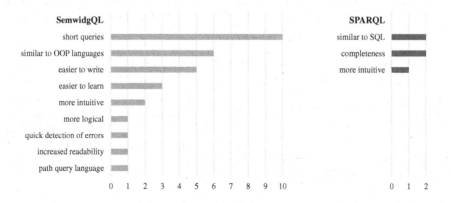

Fig. 6. Cumulative numbers of stated advantages of SPARQL and SemwidgQL.

answers SemwidgQL was named as the preferred query language. Accordingly, SPARQL was only preferred in 21% of the answers.

4.3 Discussion

The user study showed that the participants performed significantly better with SemwidgQL regarding most of the evaluated dependent variables compared to SPARQL. Especially the time on task, the number of corrections, and the number and time of pauses that the participants took to think about the correct solution of the task indicate that SemwidgQL is easier to use than SPARQL.

After the introductory session, the participants achieved better results with SemwidgQL than with SPARQL regarding most of the evaluated dependent variables. They improved significantly in the second pass in all but one area with SemwidgQL. Most of the improvements with SPARQL were not significant. The participants had already performed better in the first pass with SemwidgQL, and had improved even more in the second pass compared to SPARQL. The results suggest that SemwidgQL is easier to learn.

The reason for the better results with SemwidgQL was not that some already simple tasks were made even easier. The linear regression analyses indicate that the good results with SemwidgQL were achieved at all evaluated complexity levels. Some regression lines predict that even more complex tasks than that we have evaluated can be solved better with SemwidgQL. However, it should also be noted that some regression lines indicate that users will perform worse with SemwidgQL at tasks with higher complexity levels than evaluated. Since continuously written SemwidgQL queries can become very unwieldy at a certain length, this is to be expected.

The good results of the objective measures are supported by the participants' subjective evaluation, the number of mentioned advantages and, of course, the explicit personal preference for SemwidgQL of 79%.

5   Evaluation of SemwidgQL's Expressiveness

To investigate how well SemwidgQL covers the range of SPARQL queries used in practice we analyzed to what extent our language is able to express the queries that occur in the Linked SPARQL Queries Dataset (LSQ), collected by Saleem et al. [13]. We extracted 636,876 unique SELECT queries with 1,526,804 executions and then transformed them into a parameterized form. We mapped all IRIs, variables, literals and language tags of each query to a generic format (e.g. SELECT ?v2 WHERE {<i1> ?v1 ?v2}), and replaced all wildcards in SELECT statements with the corresponding list of variables from the WHERE statement and harmonized language filter expressions. Completely identically parameterized queries were merged automatically. We were able to manually merge further pattern that were not syntactically but semantically identical (e.g. queries with the same triple patterns in their WHERE clauses, but in different order, or queries with and without the DISTINCT keyword, where the DISTINCT keyword is not able to reduce the result set). Finally, we obtained 1619 unique query patterns where the first 120 patterns of the most frequently executed queries represent 99% of the SELECT queries executed overall in the LSQ dataset.

Based on these 120 query patterns, we evaluated how well SemwidgQL covers the range of SPARQL queries used in practice. From these patterns 66, representing 91% of the overall executed queries, can be directly expressed in SemwidgQL without any limitations. In contrast, 15 of these patterns, representing only 2% of the overall executed queries, can not be expressed. These patterns contain GROUP BY expressions or function calls, such as bound or isLiteral, which are not implemented in SemwidgQL. The remaining 39 patterns, representing 6% of the queries executed overall, make use of UNION graph patterns. SemwidgQL does not provide an equivalent for these constructs. Nevertheless, some of these patterns can be expressed without UNION but with FILTER expressions. Additionally, SemwidgQL allows the declaration of multiple queries in a single statement. These queries are translated into separate SPARQL queries. Combining their results is up to the processing program.

We calculated the SSE based complexity measure for the 120 most frequently used query patterns. Most of the requests made (89%) have a c value below or equal to 8 and thus lay in the evaluated range of our user study. One third of them have a c value of 2 or 3. Few query patterns have c values above 20 (up to 58). However, these patterns only represent less than 3% of the requests made.

6   Conclusion

We have presented SemwidgQL, a path query language for RDF data that transcompiles to SPARQL. Our empirical user study indicates that SemwidgQL is easier to learn, more efficient, and preferred by the learners compared to SPARQL. An additional evaluation of the LSQ dataset indicates that SemwidgQL, despite its limited expressiveness, is capable of querying most of the data that is currently queried with SPARQL. Also, the queries we used in the user study have a comparable complexity to queries that are used in practice. SemwidgQL is not intended as a replacement for SPARQL but rather as a more light-weight language that lowers the entry barriers to the Semantic Web and Linked Data area. Results indicate that SemwidgQL is suitable for this purpose.

References

1. Barbieri, D.F., Braga, D., Ceri, S., Grossniklaus, M.: An execution environment for C-SPARQL queries. In: Proceedings of the 13th International Conference on Extending Database Technology, EDBT 2010, pp. 441–452. ACM, New York (2010)
2. Berners-Lee, T., Chen, Y., Chilton, L., Connolly, D., Dhanaraj, R., Hollenbach, J., Lerer, A., Sheets, D.: Tabulator: exploring and analyzing linked data on the semantic web. In: Proceedings of the 3rd International Semantic Web User Interaction Workshop (2006)
3. Casterella, G.I., Vijayasarathy, L.: An experimental investigation of complexity in database query formulation tasks. J. Inf. Syst. Educ. **24**(3), 211 (2013)

4. Cohen, J.: A power primer. Psychol. Bull. **112**(1), 155 (1992)
5. Corcho, O., Calbimonte, J.P., Jeung, H., Aberer, K.: Enabling query technologies for the semantic sensor web. Int. J. Semant. Web Inf. Syst. **8**(1), 43–63 (2012)
6. Halstead, M.H.: Elements of Software Science, vol. 7. Elsevier, New York (1977)
7. Harth, A.: VisiNav: a system for visual search and navigation on web data. Web Semant. Sci. Serv. Agents World Wide Web **8**(4), 348–354 (2010)
8. Heim, P., Hellmann, S., Lehmann, J., Lohmann, S., Stegemann, T.: RelFinder: revealing relationships in RDF knowledge bases. In: Chua, T.-S., Kompatsiaris, Y., Mérialdo, B., Haas, W., Thallinger, G., Bailer, W. (eds.) SAMT 2009. LNCS, vol. 5887, pp. 182–187. Springer, Heidelberg (2009). doi:10.1007/978-3-642-10543-2_21
9. Lassila, M., Junkkari, M., Kekäläinen, J.: Comparison of two XML query languages from the perspective of learners. J. Inf. Sci. **41**(5), 584–595 (2015)
10. Leinberger, M., Scheglmann, S., Lämmel, R., Staab, S., Thimm, M., Viegas, E.: Semantic web application development with LITEQ. In: Mika, P., et al. (eds.) ISWC 2014. LNCS, vol. 8797, pp. 212–227. Springer, Cham (2014). doi:10.1007/978-3-319-11915-1_14
11. Pietriga, E., Bizer, C., Karger, D., Lee, R.: Fresnel: a browser-independent presentation vocabulary for RDF. In: Cruz, I., Decker, S., Allemang, D., Preist, C., Schwabe, D., Mika, P., Uschold, M., Aroyo, L.M. (eds.) ISWC 2006. LNCS, vol. 4273, pp. 158–171. Springer, Heidelberg (2006). doi:10.1007/11926078_12
12. Reisner, P., Boyce, R.F., Chamberlin, D.D.: Human factors evaluation of two data base query languages: square and sequel. In: Proceedings of the National Computer Conference and Exposition, AFIPS 1975, pp. 447–452. ACM, New York, 19–22 May 1975
13. Saleem, M., Ali, M.I., Hogan, A., Mehmood, Q., Ngomo, A.-C.N.: LSQ: the linked SPARQL queries dataset. In: Arenas, M., et al. (eds.) ISWC 2015. LNCS, vol. 9367, pp. 261–269. Springer, Cham (2015). doi:10.1007/978-3-319-25010-6_15
14. Schaffert, S., Bauer, C., Kurz, T., Dorschel, F., Glachs, D., Fernandez, M.: The linked media framework: Integrating and interlinking enterprise media content and data. In: Proceedings of the 8th International Conference on Semantic Systems, pp. 25–32. I-SEMANTICS 2012. ACM, New York (2012)
15. Schmachtenberg, M., Bizer, C., Paulheim, H.: Adoption of the linked data best practices in different topical domains. In: Mika, P., et al. (eds.) ISWC 2014. LNCS, vol. 8796, pp. 245–260. Springer, Cham (2014). doi:10.1007/978-3-319-11964-9_16
16. Stegemann, T., Ziegler, J.: SemwidgJS: a semantic widget library for the rapid development of user interfaces for linked open data. In: Plödereder, E., Grunske, L., Schneider, E., Ull, D. (eds.) 44. Jahrestagung der Gesellschaft für Informatik GI, Informatik 2014. LNI, vol. 232, pp. 479–490 (2014)

Cross-Lingual Entity Alignment via Joint Attribute-Preserving Embedding

Zequn Sun[1], Wei Hu[1(⊠)], and Chengkai Li[2]

[1] State Key Laboratory for Novel Software Technology,
Nanjing University, Nanjing, China
zqsun.nju@gmail.com, whu@nju.edu.cn
[2] Department of Computer Science and Engineering,
University of Texas at Arlington, Arlington, TX, USA
cli@uta.edu

Abstract. Entity alignment is the task of finding entities in two knowledge bases (KBs) that represent the same real-world object. When facing KBs in different natural languages, conventional cross-lingual entity alignment methods rely on machine translation to eliminate the language barriers. These approaches often suffer from the uneven quality of translations between languages. While recent embedding-based techniques encode entities and relationships in KBs and do not need machine translation for cross-lingual entity alignment, a significant number of attributes remain largely unexplored. In this paper, we propose a joint attribute-preserving embedding model for cross-lingual entity alignment. It jointly embeds the structures of two KBs into a unified vector space and further refines it by leveraging attribute correlations in the KBs. Our experimental results on real-world datasets show that this approach significantly outperforms the state-of-the-art embedding approaches for cross-lingual entity alignment and could be complemented with methods based on machine translation.

Keywords: Cross-lingual entity alignment · Knowledge base embedding · Joint attribute-preserving embedding

1 Introduction

In the past few years, knowledge bases (KBs) have been successfully used in lots of AI-related areas such as Semantic Web, question answering and Web mining. Various KBs cover a broad range of domains and store rich, structured real-world facts. In a KB, each fact is stated in a triple of the form $(entity, property, value)$, in which $value$ can be either a literal or an entity. The sets of entities, properties, literals and triples are denoted by E, P, L and T, respectively. Blank nodes are ignored for simplicity. There are two types of properties—relationships (R) and attributes (A)—and correspondingly two types of triples, namely relationship triples and attribute triples. A relationship triple $tr \in E \times R \times E$ describes the relationship between two

© Springer International Publishing AG 2017
C. d'Amato et al. (Eds.): ISWC 2017, Part I, LNCS 10587, pp. 628–644, 2017.
DOI: 10.1007/978-3-319-68288-4_37

entities, e.g. ($Texas, hasCapital, Austin$), while an attribute triple $tr \in E \times A \times L$ gives a literal attribute value to an entity, e.g. ($Texas, areaTotal,$ "696241.0").

As widely noted, KBs often suffer from two problems: (i) Low coverage. Different KBs are constructed by different parties using different data sources. They contain complementary facts, which makes it imperative to integrate multiple KBs. (ii) Multi-linguality gap. To support multi-lingual applications, a growing number of multi-lingual KBs and language-specific KBs have been built. This makes it both necessary and beneficial to integrate cross-lingual KBs.

Entity alignment is the task of finding entities in two KBs that refer to the same real-world object. It plays a vital role in automatically integrating multiple KBs. This paper focuses on cross-lingual entity alignment. It can help construct a coherent KB and deal with different expressions of knowledge across diverse natural languages. Conventional cross-lingual entity alignment methods rely on machine translation, of which the accuracy is still far from perfect. Spohr et al. [21] argued that the quality of alignment in cross-lingual scenarios heavily depends on the quality of translations between multiple languages.

Following the popular translation-based embedding models [1,15,22], a few studies leveraged KB embeddings for entity alignment and achieved promising results [5,11]. Embedding techniques learn low-dimensional vector representations (i.e., embeddings) of entities and encode various semantics (e.g. types) into them. Focusing on KB structures, the embedding-based methods provide an alternative for cross-lingual entity alignment without considering their natural language labels.

There remain several challenges in applying embedding methods to cross-lingual entity alignment. First, to the best of our knowledge, most existing KB embedding models learn embeddings based solely on relationship triples. However, we observe that attribute triples account for a significant portion of KBs. For example, we count triples of infobox facts from English DBpedia (2016-04),[1] and find 58,181,947 attribute triples, which are three times as many as relationship triples (the number is 18,598,409). Facing the task of entity alignment, attribute triples can provide additional information to embed entities, but how to incorporate them into cross-lingual embedding models remains largely unexplored. Second, thanks to the Linking Open Data initiative, there exist some aligned entities and properties between KBs, which can serve as bridge between them. However, as discovered in [5], the existing alignment between cross-lingual KBs usually accounts for a small proportion. So how to make the best use of it is crucial for embedding cross-lingual KBs.

To deal with the above challenges, we introduce a joint attribute-preserving embedding model for cross-lingual entity alignment. It employs two modules, namely structure embedding (SE) and attribute embedding (AE), to learn embeddings based on two facets of knowledge (relationship triples and attribute triples) in two KBs, respectively. SE focuses on modeling relationship structures of two KBs and leverages existing alignment given beforehand as bridge to overlap their structures. AE captures the correlations of attributes (i.e. whether these

---

[1] http://wiki.dbpedia.org/downloads-2016-04.

attributes are commonly used together to describe an entity) and clusters entities based on attribute correlations. Finally, it combines SE and AE to jointly embed all the entities in the two KBs into a unified vector space $\mathbb{R}^d$, where d denotes the dimension of the vectors. The aim of our approach is to find latent cross-lingual target entities (i.e. truly-aligned entities that we want to discover) for a source entity by searching its nearest neighbors in $\mathbb{R}^d$. We expect the embeddings of latent aligned cross-lingual entities to be close to each other.

In summary, the main contributions of this paper are as follows:

- We propose an embedding-based approach to cross-lingual entity alignment, which does not depend on machine translation between cross-lingual KBs.
- We jointly embed the relationship triples of two KBs with structure embedding and further refine the embeddings by leveraging attribute triples of KBs with attribute embedding. To the best of our knowledge, there is no prior work learning embeddings of cross-lingual KBs while preserving their attribute information.
- We evaluated our approach on real-world cross-lingual datasets from DBpedia. The experimental results show that our approach largely outperformed two state-of-the-art embedding-based methods for cross-lingual entity alignment. Moreover, it could be complemented with conventional methods based on machine translation.

The rest of this paper is organized as follows. We discuss the related work on KB embedding and cross-lingual KB alignment in Sect. 2. We describe our approach in detail in Sect. 3, and report experimental results in Sect. 4. Finally, we conclude this paper with future work in Sect. 5.

2   Related Work

We divide the related work into two subfields: KB embedding and cross-lingual KB alignment. We discuss them in the rest of this section.

2.1   KB Embedding

In recent years, significant efforts have been made towards learning embeddings of KBs. TransE [1], the pioneer of translation-based methods, interprets a relationship vector as the translation from the head entity vector to its tail entity vector. In other words, if a relationship triple (h, r, t) holds, $\mathbf{h} + \mathbf{r} \approx \mathbf{t}$ is expected. TransE has shown its great capability of modeling 1-to-1 relations and achieved promising results for KB completion. To further improve TransE, later work including TransH [22] and TransR [15] was proposed. Additionally, there exist a few non-translation-based approaches to KB embedding [2,18,20].

Besides, several studies take advantage of knowledge in KBs to improve embeddings. Krompaß et al. [13] added type constraints to KB embedding models and enhanced their performance on link prediction. KR-EAR [14] embeds attributes additionally by modeling attribute correlations and obtains good results on predicting entities, relationships and attributes. But it only learns attribute embeddings in a single KB, which hinders its application to cross-lingual cases. Besides, KR-EAR focuses on the attributes whose values are from a small set of entries, e.g. values of "gender" are {Female, Male}. It may fail to model attributes whose values are very sparse and heterogeneous, e.g. "name", "label" and "coordinate". RDF2Vec [19] uses local information of KB structures to generate sequences of entities and employs language modeling approaches to learn entity embeddings for machine learning tasks. For cross-lingual tasks, [12] extends NTNKBC [4] for cross-lingual KB completion. [7] uses a neural network approach that translates English KBs into Chinese to expand Chinese KBs.

2.2   Cross-Lingual KB Alignment

Existing work on cross-lingual KB alignment generally falls into two categories: cross-lingual ontology matching and cross-lingual entity alignment. For cross-lingual ontology matching, Fu et al. [8,9] presented a generic framework, which utilizes machine translation tools to translate labels to the same language and uses monolingual ontology matching methods to find mappings. Spohr et al. [21] leveraged translation-based label similarities and ontology structures as features for learning cross-lingual mapping functions by machine learning techniques (e.g. SVM). In all these works, machine translation is an integral component.

For cross-lingual entity alignment, MTransE [5] incorporates TransE to encode KB structures into language-specific vector spaces and designs five alignment models to learn translation between KBs in different languages with seed alignment. JE [11] utilizes TransE to embed different KBs into a unified space with the aim that each seed alignment has similar embeddings, which is extensible to the cross-lingual scenario. Wang et al. [23] proposed a graph model, which only leverages language-independent features (e.g. out-/inlinks) to find cross-lingual links between Wiki knowledge bases. Gentile et al. [10] exploited embedding-based methods for aligning entities in Web tables. Different from them, our approach jointly embeds two KBs together and leverages attribute embedding for improvement.

3   Cross-Lingual Entity Alignment via KB Embedding

In this section, we first introduce notations and the general framework of our joint attribute-preserving embedding model. Then, we elaborate on the technical details of the model and discuss several key design issues.

We use lower-case bold-face letters to denote the vector representations of the corresponding terms, e.g., $(\mathbf{h}, \mathbf{r}, \mathbf{t})$ denotes the vector representation of triple (h, r, t). We use capital bold-face letters to denote matrices, and we use superscripts to denote different KBs. For example, $\mathbf{E}^{(1)}$ denotes the representation matrix for entities in KB_1 in which each row is an entity vector $\mathbf{e}^{(1)}$.

3.1   Overview

The framework of our joint attribute-preserving embedding model is depicted in Fig. 1. Given two KBs, denoted by KB_1 and KB_2, in different natural languages and some pre-aligned entity or property pairs (called seed alignment, denoted by superscript $^{(1,2)}$), our model learns the vector representations of KB_1 and KB_2 and expects the latent aligned entities to be embedded closely.

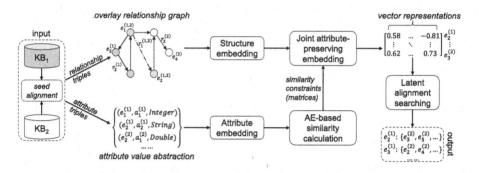

Fig. 1. Framework of the joint attribute-preserving embedding model

Following TransE [1], we interpret a relationship as the translation from the head entity to the tail entity, to characterize the structure information of KBs. We let each pair in the seed alignment share the same representation to serve as bridge between KB_1 and KB_2 to build an overlay relationship graph, and learn representations of all the entities jointly under a unified vector space via structure embedding (SE). The intuition is that two alignable KBs are likely to have a number of aligned triples, e.g. $(Washington, capitalOf, America)$ in English and its correspondence $(Washington, capitaleDes, États-Unis)$ in French. Based on this, SE aims at learning approximate representations for the latent aligned triples between the two KBs.

However, SE only constrains that the learned representations must be compatible within each relationship triple, which causes the disorganized distribution of some entities due to the sparsity of their relationship triples. To alleviate this incoherent distribution, we leverage attribute triples for helping embed entities based on the observation that the latent aligned entities usually have a high degree of similarity in attribute values. Technically, we overlook specific attribute values by reason of their complexity, heterogeneity and cross-linguality. Instead, we abstract attribute values to their range types, e.g. $(Tom, age, "12")$ to $(Tom, age, Integer)$, where $Integer$ is the abstract range type of value "12". Then, we carry out attribute embedding (AE) on abstract attribute triples to capture the correlations of cross-lingual and mono-lingual attributes, and calculate the similarities of entities based on them. Finally, the attribute similarity constraints are combined with SE to refine representations by clustering entities with high attribute correlations. In this way, our joint model preserves both relationship and attribute information of the two KBs.

With entities represented as vectors in a unified embedding space, the alignment of latent cross-lingual target entities for a source entity can be conducted by searching the nearest cross-lingual neighbors in this space.

3.2 Structure Embedding

The aim of SE is to model the geometric structures of two KBs and learn approximate representations for latent aligned triples. Formally, given a relationship triple $tr = (h, r, t)$, we expect $\mathbf{h} + \mathbf{r} = \mathbf{t}$. To measure the plausibility of tr, we define the score function $f(tr) = \|\mathbf{h} + \mathbf{r} - \mathbf{t}\|_2^2$. We prefer a lower value of $f(tr)$ and want to minimize it for each relationship triple.

Figure 2 gives an example about how SE models the geometric structures of two KBs with seed alignment. In Phase (1), we initialize all the vectors randomly and let each pair in seed alignment overlap to build the overlay relationship graph. In order to show the triples intuitively in the figure, we regard an entity as a point in the vector space and move relationship vectors to start from their head entities. Note that, currently, entities and relationships distribute randomly. In Phase (2), we minimize scores of triples and let vector representations compatible within each relationship triple. For example, the relationship *capitalOf* would tend to be close to *capitaleDes* because they share the same head entity and tail entity. In the meantime, the entity *America* and its correspondence *États-Unis* would move closely to each other due to their common head entity and approximate relationships. Therefore, SE is a dynamic spreading process. The ideal state after training is shown as Phase (3). We can see that the latent aligned entities *America* and *États-Unis* lie together.

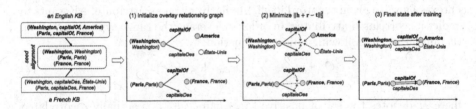

Fig. 2. An example of structure embedding

Furthermore, we detect that negative triples (a.k.a. corrupted triples), which have been widely used in translation-based embedding models [1,15,22], are also valuable to SE. Considering that another English entity *China* and its latent aligned French one *Chine* happen to lie closely to *America*, SE may take the *Chine* as a candidate for *America* by mistake due to their short distance. Negative triples would help reduce the occurrence of this coincidence. If we generate a negative triple $tr' = (Washington, capitalOf, China)$ and learn a high score for tr', *China* would keep a distance away from *America*. As we enforce the length of any embedding vector to 1, the score function f has a constant maximum. Thus, we would like to minimize $-f(tr')$ to learn a high score for tr'.

In summary, we prefer lower scores for existing triples (positives) and higher scores for negatives, which leads to minimize the following objective function:

$$\mathcal{O}_{SE} = \sum_{tr \in T} \sum_{tr' \in T'_{tr}} \big(f(tr) - \alpha f(tr') \big), \tag{1}$$

where T denotes the set of all positive triples and T'_{tr} denotes the associated negative triples for tr generated by replacing either its head or tail by a random entity (but not both at the same time). α is a ratio hyper-parameter that weights positive and negative triples and its range is $[0, 1]$. It is important to remember that each pair in the seed alignment share the same embedding during training, in order to bridge two KBs.

3.3 Attribute Embedding and Entity Similarity Calculation

Attribute Embedding. We call a set of attributes correlated if they are commonly used together to describe an entity. For example, attributes *longitude*, *latitude* and *place_name* are correlated because they are widely used together to describe a place. Moreover, we want to assign a higher correlation to the pair of *longitude* and *latitude* because they have the same range type. We use seed entity pairs to establish correlations between cross-lingual attributes. Given an aligned entity pair $(e^{(1)}, e^{(2)})$, we regard the attributes of $e^{(1)}$ as correlated ones for each attribute of $e^{(2)}$, and vice versa. We expect attributes with high correlations to be embedded closely.

To capture the correlations of attributes, AE borrows the idea from Skip-gram [16], a very popular model that learns word embeddings by predicting the context of a word given the word itself. Similarly, given an attribute, AE wants to predict its correlated attributes. In order to leverage the range type information, AE minimizes the following objective function:

$$\mathcal{O}_{AE} = -\sum_{(a,c) \in H} w_{a,c} \cdot \log p(c|a), \tag{2}$$

where H denotes the set of positive (a, c) pairs, i.e., c is actually a correlated attribute of a, and the term $p(c|a)$ denotes the probability. To prevent all the vectors from having the same value, we adopt the negative sampling approach [17] to efficiently parameterize Eq. (2), and $\log p(c|a)$ is replaced with the term as follows:

$$\log \sigma(\mathbf{a} \cdot \mathbf{c}) + \sum_{(a,c') \in H'_a} \log \sigma(-\mathbf{a} \cdot \mathbf{c'}), \tag{3}$$

where $\sigma(x) = \frac{1}{1+e^{-x}}$. H'_a is the set of negative pairs for attribute a generated according to a log-uniform base distribution, assuming that they are all incorrect.

We set $w_{a,c} = 1$ if a and c have different range types, otherwise $w_{a,c} = 2$ to increase their probability of tending to be similar. In this paper, we distinguish four kinds of abstract range types, i.e., *Integer, Double, Datetime* and *String* (as default). Note that it is easy to extend to more types.

Entity Similarity Calculation. Given attribute embeddings, we take the representation of an entity to be the normalized average of its attribute vectors, i.e., $\mathbf{e} = [\sum_{a \in A_e} \mathbf{a}]_1$, where A_e is the set of attributes of e and $[.]_1$ denotes the normalized vector. We have two matrices of vector representations for entities in two KBs, $\mathbf{E}_{AE}^{(1)} \in \mathbb{R}^{n_e^{(1)} \times d}$ for KB_1 and $\mathbf{E}_{AE}^{(2)} \in \mathbb{R}^{n_e^{(2)} \times d}$ for KB_2, where each row is an entity vector, and $n_e^{(1)}$, $n_e^{(2)}$ are the numbers of entities in KB_1, KB_2, respectively.

We use the cosine distance to measure the similarities between entities. For two entities e, e', we have $\text{sim}(e, e') = \cos(\mathbf{e}, \mathbf{e}') = \frac{\mathbf{e} \cdot \mathbf{e}'}{\|\mathbf{e}\| \|\mathbf{e}'\|} = \mathbf{e} \cdot \mathbf{e}'$, as the length of any embedding vector is enforced to 1. The cross-KB similarity matrix $\mathbf{S}^{(1,2)} \in \mathbb{R}^{n_e^{(1)} \times n_e^{(2)}}$ between KB_1 and KB_2, as well as the inner similarity matrices $\mathbf{S}^{(1)} \in \mathbb{R}^{n_e^{(1)} \times n_e^{(1)}}$ for KB_1 and $\mathbf{S}^{(2)} \in \mathbb{R}^{n_e^{(2)} \times n_e^{(2)}}$ for KB_2, are defined as follows:

$$\mathbf{S}^{(1,2)} = \mathbf{E}_{AE}^{(1)} \mathbf{E}_{AE}^{(2)\top}, \quad \mathbf{S}^{(1)} = \mathbf{E}_{AE}^{(1)} \mathbf{E}_{AE}^{(1)\top}, \quad \mathbf{S}^{(2)} = \mathbf{E}_{AE}^{(2)} \mathbf{E}_{AE}^{(2)\top}. \tag{4}$$

A similarity matrix $\mathbf{S}$ holds the cosine similarities among entities and $\mathbf{S}_{i,j}$ is the similarity between the i-th entity in one KB and the j-th entity in the same or the other KB. We discard lower values of $\mathbf{S}$ because a low similarity of two entities indicates that they are likely to be different. So, we set the entry $\mathbf{S}_{i,j} = 0$ if $\mathbf{S}_{i,j} < \tau$, where τ is a threshold and can be set based on the average similarity of seed entity pairs. In this paper, we fix $\tau = 0.95$ for inner similarity matrices and 0.9 for cross-KB similarity matrix, to achieve high accuracy.

3.4 Joint Attribute-Preserving Embedding

We want similar entities across KBs to be clustered to refine their vector representations. Inspired by [25], we use the matrices of pairwise similarities between entities as supervised information and minimize the following objective function:

$$\mathcal{O}_S = \|\mathbf{E}_{SE}^{(1)} - \mathbf{S}^{(1,2)} \mathbf{E}_{SE}^{(2)}\|_F^2$$
$$+ \beta(\|\mathbf{E}_{SE}^{(1)} - \mathbf{S}^{(1)} \mathbf{E}_{SE}^{(1)}\|_F^2 + \|\mathbf{E}_{SE}^{(2)} - \mathbf{S}^{(2)} \mathbf{E}_{SE}^{(2)}\|_F^2), \tag{5}$$

where β is a hyper-parameter that balances similarities between KBs and their inner similarities. $\mathbf{E}_{SE} \in \mathbb{R}^{n_e \times d}$ denotes the matrix of entity vectors for one KB in SE with each row an entity vector. $\mathbf{S}^{(1,2)} \mathbf{E}_{SE}^{(2)}$ calculates latent vectors of entities in KB_1 by accumulating vectors of entities in KB_2 based on their similarities. By minimizing $\|\mathbf{E}_{SE}^{(1)} - \mathbf{S}^{(1,2)} \mathbf{E}_{SE}^{(2)}\|_F^2$, we expect similar entities across KBs to be embedded closely. The two inner similarity matrices work in the same way.

To preserve both the structure and attribute information of two KBs, we jointly minimize the following objective function:

$$\mathcal{O}_{joint} = \mathcal{O}_{SE} + \delta \mathcal{O}_S, \tag{6}$$

where δ is a hyper-parameter weighting $\mathcal{O}_S$.

3.5   Discussions

We discuss and analyze our joint attribute-preserving embedding model in the following aspects:

Objective Function for Structure Embedding. SE is translation-based embedding model but its objective function (see Eq. (1)) does not follow the margin-based ranking loss function below, which is used by many previous KB embedding models [1]:

$$\mathcal{O} = \sum_{tr \in T} \sum_{tr' \in T'_{tr}} \max[\gamma + f(tr) - f(tr'), 0]. \tag{7}$$

Equation (7) aims at distinguishing positive and negative triples, and expects that their scores can be separated by a large margin. However, for the cross-lingual entity alignment task, in addition to the large margin between their scores, we also want to assign lower scores to positive triples and higher scores to negative triples. Therefore, we choose Eq. (1) instead of Eq. (7).

In contrast, JE [11] uses the margin-based ranking loss from TransE [1], while MTransE [5] does not have this as it does not use negative triples. However, as explained in Sect. 3.2, we argue that negative triples are effective in distinguishing the relations between entities. Our experimental results reported in Sect. 4.4 also demonstrate the effectiveness of negative triples.

Training. We initialize parameters such as vectors of entities, relations and attributes randomly based on a truncated normal distribution, and then optimize Eqs. (2) and (6) with a gradient descent optimization algorithm called AdaGrad [6]. Instead of directly optimizing $\mathcal{O}_{joint}$, our training process involves two optimizers to minimize $\mathcal{O}_{SE}$ and $\delta\mathcal{O}_S$ independently. At each epoch, the two optimizers are executed alternately. When minimizing $\mathcal{O}_{SE}$, $f(tr)$ and $-\alpha f(tr')$ can also be optimized alternately.

The length of any embedding vector is enforced to 1 for the following reasons: (i) this constraint prevents the training process from trivially minimizing the objective function by increasing the embedding norms and shaping the embeddings, (ii) it limits the randomness of entity and relationship distribution in the training process, and (iii) it fixes the mismatch between the inner product in Eq. (3) and the cosine similarity to measure embeddings [24].

Our model is also scalable in training. The structure embedding belongs to the translation-based embedding models, which have already been proved to be capable of learning embeddings at large scale [1]. We use sparse representations for matrices in Eq. (5) for saving memory. Additionally, the memory cost to compute Eq. (4) can be reduced using a divide-and-conquer strategy.

Parameter Complexity. The parameter complexity of our joint model is $O\big(d(n_e + n_r + n_a)\big)$, where n_e, n_r, n_a are the numbers of entities, relationships and attributes, respectively. d is the dimension of the embeddings. Considering that $n_r, n_a \ll n_e$ in practice and the seed alignment share vectors in training, the complexity of the model is roughly linear to the number of total entities.

Searching Latent Aligned Entities. Because the length of each vector always equals 1, the cosine distance between entities of the two KBs can be calculated as $\mathbf{D} = \mathbf{E}_{SE}^{(1)}\mathbf{E}_{SE}^{(2)\top}$. Thus, the nearest entities can be obtained by simply sorting each row of $\mathbf{D}$ in descending order. For each source entity, we expect the rank of its truly-aligned target entity to be the first few.

4 Evaluation

In this section, we report our experiments and results on real-world cross-lingual datasets. We developed our approach, called JAPE, using TensorFlow[2]—a very popular open-source software library for numerical computation. Our experiments were conducted on a personal workstation with an Intel Xeon E3 3.3 GHz CPU and 128 GB memory. The datasets, source code and experimental results are accessible at this website[3].

4.1 Datasets

We selected DBpedia (2016-04) to build three cross-lingual datasets. DBpedia is a large-scale multi-lingual KB including inter-language links (ILLs) from entities of English version to those in other languages. In our experiments, we extracted 15 thousand ILLs with popular entities from English to Chinese, Japanese and French respectively, and considered them as our reference alignment (i.e., gold standards). Our strategy to extract datasets is that we randomly selected an ILL pair s.t. the involved entities have at least 4 relationship triples and then extracted relationship and attribute infobox triples for selected entities. The statistics of the three datasets are listed in Table 1, which indicate that the number of involved entities in each language is much larger than 15 thousand, and attribute triples contribute to a significant portion of the datasets.

4.2 Comparative Approaches

As aforementioned, JE [11] and MTransE [5] are two representative embedding-based methods for entity alignment. In our experiments, we used our best effort to implement the two models as they do not release any source code or software currently. We conducted them on the above datasets as comparative approaches. Specifically, MTransE has five variants in its alignment model, where the fourth performs best according to the experiments of its authors. Thus, we chose this variant to represent MTransE. We followed the implementation details reported

---

[2] https://www.tensorflow.org/.
[3] https://github.com/nju-websoft/JAPE.

Table 1. Statistics of the datasets

Datasets		Entities	Relationships	Attributes	Rel. triples	Attr. triples
DBP15K$_{\text{ZH-EN}}$	Chinese	66,469	2,830	8,113	153,929	379,684
	English	98,125	2,317	7,173	237,674	567,755
DBP15K$_{\text{JA-EN}}$	Japanese	65,744	2,043	5,882	164,373	354,619
	English	95,680	2,096	6,066	233,319	497,230
DBP15K$_{\text{FR-EN}}$	French	66,858	1,379	4,547	192,191	528,665
	English	105,889	2,209	6,422	278,590	576,543

in [5, 11] and complemented other unreported details with careful consideration. For example, we added a strong orthogonality constraint for the linear transformation matrix in MTransE to ensure the invertibility, because we found it leads to better results. For JAPE, we tuned various parameter values and set $d = 75, \alpha = 0.1, \beta = 0.05, \delta = 0.05$ for the best performance. The learning rates of SE and AE were empirically set to 0.01 and 0.1, respectively.

4.3 Evaluation Metrics

Following the conventions [1,5,11], we used $Hits@k$ and $Mean$ to assess the performance of the three approaches. $Hits@k$ measures the proportion of correctly aligned entities ranked in the top k, while $Mean$ calculates the mean of these ranks. A higher $Hits@k$ and a lower $Mean$ indicate better performance. It is a phenomenon worth noting that the optimal $Hits@k$ and $Mean$ usually do not come at the same epoch in all the three approaches. For fair comparison, we did not fix the number of epochs but used early stopping to avoid overtraining. The training process is stopped as long as the change ratio of $Mean$ is less than 0.0005. Besides, the training of AE on each dataset takes 100 epochs.

4.4 Experimental Results

Results on DBP15K. We used a certain proportion of the gold standards as seed alignment while left the remaining as testing data, i.e., the latent aligned entities to discover. We tested the proportion from 10% to 50% with step 10%, and Table 2 lists the results using 30% of the gold standards. The variation of $Hits@k$ with different proportions will be shown shortly. For relationships and attributes, we simply extracted the property pairs with exactly the same labels, which only account for a small portion of the seed alignment.

Table 2 indicates that JAPE largely outperformed JE and MTransE, since it captures both structure and attribute information of KBs. For JE, it employs TransE as its basic model, which is not suitable to be directly applied to entity alignment as discussed in Sect. 3.5. Besides, JE does not give a mandatory constraint on the length of vectors. Instead, it only minimizes $\|\mathbf{v}\|_2^2 - 1$ to restrain vector length and brings adverse effect. For MTransE, it models the structures

Table 2. Result comparison and ablation study

DBP15K$_{ZH-EN}$		ZH → EN				EN → ZH			
		Hits@1	*Hits@10*	*Hits@50*	*Mean*	*Hits@1*	*Hits@10*	*Hits@50*	*Mean*
JE		21.27	42.77	56.74	766	19.52	39.36	53.25	841
MTransE		30.83	61.41	79.12	154	24.78	52.42	70.45	208
JAPE	SE w/o neg	38.34	68.86	84.07	103	31.66	59.37	76.33	147
	SE	39.78	72.35	87.12	84	32.29	62.79	80.55	109
	SE + AE	**41.18**	**74.46**	**88.90**	**64**	**40.15**	**71.05**	**86.18**	**73**
DBP15K$_{JA-EN}$		JA → EN				EN → JA			
		Hits@1	*Hits@10*	*Hits@50*	*Mean*	*Hits@1*	*Hits@10*	*Hits@50*	*Mean*
JE		18.92	39.97	54.24	832	17.80	38.44	52.48	864
MTransE		27.86	57.45	75.94	159	23.72	49.92	67.93	220
JAPE	SE w/o neg	33.10	63.90	80.80	114	29.71	56.28	73.84	156
	SE	34.27	66.39	83.61	104	31.40	60.80	78.51	127
	SE + AE	**36.25**	**68.50**	**85.35**	**99**	**38.37**	**67.27**	**82.65**	**113**
DBP15K$_{FR-EN}$		FR → EN				EN → FR			
		Hits@1	*Hits@10*	*Hits@50*	*Mean*	*Hits@1*	*Hits@10*	*Hits@50*	*Mean*
JE		15.38	38.84	56.50	574	14.61	37.25	54.01	628
MTransE		24.41	55.55	74.41	139	21.26	50.60	69.93	156
JAPE	SE w/o neg	29.55	62.18	79.36	123	25.40	56.55	74.96	133
	SE	29.63	64.55	81.90	95	26.55	60.30	78.71	107
	SE + AE	**32.39**	**66.68**	**83.19**	**92**	**32.97**	**65.91**	**82.38**	**97**

of KBs in different vector spaces, and information loss happens when learning the translation between vector spaces.

Additionally, we divided JAPE into three variants for ablation study, and the results are shown in Table 2 as well. We found that involving negative triples in structure embedding reduces the random distribution of entities, and involving attribute embedding as constraint further refines the distribution of entities. The two improvements demonstrate that systematic distribution of entities makes for the cross-lingual entity alignment task.

It is worth noting that the alignment direction (e.g. ZH → EN vs. EN → ZH) also causes performance difference. As shown in Table 1, the relationship triples in a non-English KB are much sparser than those in an English KB, so that the approaches based on the relationship triples cannot learn good representations to model the structures of non-English KBs, as restraints for entities are relatively insufficient. When performing alignment from an English KB to a non-English KB, we search for the nearest non-English entity as the aligned one to an English entity, the sparsity of the non-English KB leads to the disorganized distribution of its entities, which brings negative effects on the task. However, it is comforting to see that the performance difference becomes narrower when involving attribute embedding, because the attribute triples provide additional information to embed entities, especially for sparse KBs.

Figure 3 provides the visualization of sample results for entity alignment and attribute correlations. We projected the embeddings of aligned entity pairs and

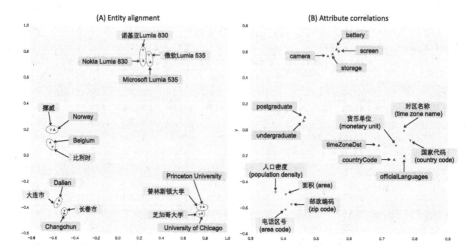

Fig. 3. Visualization of results on DBP15K$_{\text{ZH-EN}}$

involved attribute embeddings to two dimensions using PCA. The left part indicates that universities, countries, cities and cellphones were divided widely while aligned entities from Chinese to English were laid closely, which met our expectation of JAPE. The right part shows our attribute embedding clustered three groups of monolingual attributes (about cellphones, cities and universities) and one group of cross-lingual ones (about countries).

Sensitivity to Proportion of Seed Alignment. Figure 4 illustrates the change of $Hits@k$ with varied proportion of seed alignment. In accordance with our expectation, the results on all the datasets become better with the increase of the proportion, because more seed alignment can provide more information to overlay the two KBs. It can be seen that, when using half of the gold standards as seed alignment, JAPE performed encouragingly, e.g. $Hits@1$ and $Hits@10$ on DBP15K$_{\text{ZH-EN}}$ are 53.27% and 82.91%, respectively. Moreover, even with a very small proportion of seed alignment like 10%, JAPE still achieved promising results, e.g. $Hits@10$ on DBP15K$_{\text{ZH-EN}}$ reaches 55.04% and on DBP15K$_{\text{JA-EN}}$ reaches 44.69%. Therefore, it is feasible to deploy JAPE to various entity alignment tasks, even with limited seed alignment.

Combination with Machine Translation. Since machine translation is often used in cross-lingual ontology matching [9,21], we designed a machine translation based approach that employs Google Translate to translate the labels of entities in one KB and computes similarities between the translations and the labels of entities in the other KB. For similarity measurement, we chose Levenshtein distance because of its popularity in ontology matching [3].

We chose DBP15K$_{\text{ZH-EN}}$ and DBP15K$_{\text{JA-EN}}$, which have big barriers in linguistics. As depicted in Table 3, machine translation achieves satisfying results,

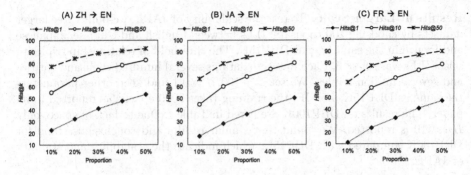

Fig. 4. *Hits@k* w.r.t. proportion of seed alignment

especially for *Hits@1*, and we think that it is due to the high accuracy of Google Translate. However, the gap between machine translation and JAPE becomes smaller for *Hits@10* and *Hits@50*. The reason is as follows. When Google misunderstands the meaning of labels (e.g. polysemy), the top-ranked entities are all very likely to be wrong. On the contrary, JAPE relies on the structure information of KBs, so the correct entities often appear slightly behind. Besides, we found that translating from Chinese (or Japanese) to English is more accurate than the reverse direction.

To further investigate the possibility of combination, for each latent aligned entities, we considered the lower rank of the two results as the combined rank. It is surprising to find that the combined results are significantly better, which reveals the mutual complementarity between JAPE and machine translation. We believe that, when aligning entities between cross-lingual KBs where the quality of machine translation is difficult to guarantee, or many entities lack meaningful labels, JAPE can be a practical alternative.

Table 3. Combination of machine translation and JAPE

DBP15K$_{ZH-EN}$	ZH → EN				EN → ZH			
	Hits@1	*Hits@10*	*Hits@50*	*Mean*	*Hits@1*	*Hits@10*	*Hits@50*	*Mean*
Machine translation	55.76	67.61	74.30	820	40.38	54.27	62.27	1,551
JAPE	41.18	74.46	88.90	64	40.15	71.05	86.18	73
Combination	**73.09**	**90.43**	**96.61**	**11**	**62.70**	**85.21**	**94.25**	**26**
DBP15K$_{JA-EN}$	JA → EN				EN → JA			
	Hits@1	*Hits@10*	*Hits@50*	*Mean*	*Hits@1*	*Hits@10*	*Hits@50*	*Mean*
Machine translation	74.64	84.57	89.13	333	61.98	72.07	77.22	1,095
JAPE	36.25	68.50	85.35	99	38.37	67.27	82.65	113
Combination	**82.84**	**94.65**	**98.31**	**9**	**75.94**	**90.70**	**96.04**	**25**

˙**Results at Larger Scale.** To test the scalability of JAPE, we built three larger datasets by choosing 100 thousand ILLs between English and Chinese, Japanese and French in the same way as DBP15K. The threshold of relationship triples to select ILLs was set to 2. Each dataset contains several hundred thousand entities and several million triples. We set $d = 100, \beta = 0.1$ and keep other parameters the same as DBP15K. For JE, the training takes 2000 epochs as reported in its paper. The results on DBP100K are listed in Table 4. Due to lack of space, only *Hits*@10 is reported. We found that similar results and conclusions stand for DBP100K compared with DBP15K, which indicate the scalability and stability of JAPE.

Table 4. *Hits*@10 comparison on DBP100K

DBP100K	ZH → EN	EN → ZH	JA → EN	EN → JA	FR → EN	EN → FR
JE	16.95	16.63	21.17	20.98	22.98	22.63
MTransE	34.31	29.18	33.93	27.22	44.84	39.19
JAPE	**41.75**	**40.13**	**42.00**	**39.30**	**53.64**	**50.51**

Furthermore, the performance of all the methods decreases to some extent on DBP100K. We think that the reasons are twofold: (i) DBP100K contains quite a few "sparse" entities involved in a very limited number of triples, which affect embedding the structure information of KBs; and (ii) as the number of latent aligned entities in DBP100K are several times larger than DBP15K, the TransE-based models suffer from the increased occurrence of multi-mapping relations as explained in [22]. Nevertheless, JAPE still outperformed JE and MTransE.

5   Conclusion and Future Work

In this paper, we introduced a joint attribute-preserving embedding model for cross-lingual entity alignment. We proposed structure embedding and attribute embedding to represent the relationship structures and attribute correlations of KBs and learn approximate embeddings for latent aligned entities. Our experiments on real-world datasets demonstrated that our approach achieved superior results than two state-of-the-art embedding approaches and could be complemented with conventional methods based on machine translation.

In future work, we look forward to improving our approach in several aspects. First, the structure embedding suffered from multi-mapping relations, thus we plan to extend it with cross-lingual hyperplane projection. Second, our attribute embedding discarded attribute values due to their diversity and cross-linguality, which we want to use cross-lingual word embedding techniques to incorporate. Third, we would like to evaluate our approach on more heterogeneous KBs developed by different parties, such as between DBpedia and Wikidata.

Acknowledgements. This work is supported by the National Natural Science Foundation of China (Nos. 61370019, 61572247 and 61321491).

References

1. Bordes, A., Usunier, N., Garcia-Duran, A., Weston, J., Yakhnenko, O.: Translating embeddings for modeling multi-relational data. In: NIPS, pp. 2787–2795 (2013)
2. Bordes, A., Weston, J., Collobert, R., Bengio, Y.: Learning structured embeddings of knowledge bases. In: AAAI, pp. 301–306 (2011)
3. Cheatham, M., Hitzler, P.: String similarity metrics for ontology alignment. In: Alani, H., et al. (eds.) ISWC 2013. LNCS, vol. 8219, pp. 294–309. Springer, Heidelberg (2013). doi:10.1007/978-3-642-41338-4_19
4. Chen, D., Socher, R., Manning, C.D., Ng, A.Y.: Learning new facts from knowledge bases with neural tensor networks and semantic word vectors (2013). arXiv:1301.3618
5. Chen, M., Tian, Y., Yang, M., Zaniolo, C.: Multi-lingual knowledge graph embeddings for cross-lingual knowledge alignment. In: IJCAI (2017)
6. Duchi, J., Hazan, E., Singer, Y.: Adaptive subgradient methods for online learning and stochastic optimization. J. Mach. Learn. Res. **12**(7), 2121–2159 (2011)
7. Feng, X., Tang, D., Qin, B., Liu, T.: English-Chinese knowledge base translation with neural network. In: COLING, pp. 2935–2944 (2016)
8. Fu, B., Brennan, R., O'Sullivan, D.: Cross-lingual ontology mapping - an investigation of the impact of machine translation. In: Gómez-Pérez, A., et al. (eds.) ASWC, pp. 1–15 (2009)
9. Fu, B., Brennan, R., O'Sullivan, D.: Cross-lingual ontology mapping and its use on the multilingual semantic web. In: WWW Workshop on Multilingual Semantic Web, pp. 13–20 (2010)
10. Gentile, A.L., Ristoski, P., Eckel, S., Ritze, D., Paulheim, H.: Entity matching on web tables : a table embeddings approach for blocking. In: EDBT, pp. 510–513 (2017)
11. Hao, Y., Zhang, Y., He, S., Liu, K., Zhao, J.: A joint embedding method for entity alignment of knowledge bases. In: Chen, H., Ji, H., Sun, L., Wang, H., Qian, T., Ruan, T. (eds.) CCKS 2016. CCIS, vol. 650, pp. 3–14. Springer, Singapore (2016). doi:10.1007/978-981-10-3168-7_1
12. Klein, P., Ponzetto, S.P., Glavaš, G.: Improving neural knowledge base completion with cross-lingual projections. In: EACL, pp. 516–522 (2017)
13. Krompaß, D., Baier, S., Tresp, V.: Type-Constrained Representation Learning in Knowledge Graphs. In: Arenas, M., et al. (eds.) ISWC 2015. LNCS, vol. 9366, pp. 640–655. Springer, Cham (2015). doi:10.1007/978-3-319-25007-6_37
14. Lin, Y., Liu, Z., Sun, M.: Knowledge representation learning with entities, attributes and relations. In: IJCAI, pp. 2866–2872 (2016)
15. Lin, Y., Liu, Z., Sun, M., Liu, Y., Zhu, X.: Learning entity and relation embeddings for knowledge graph completion. In: AAAI, pp. 2181–2187 (2015)
16. Mikolov, T., Chen, K., Corrado, G., Dean, J.: Efficient estimation of word representations in vector space (2013). arXiv:1301.3781
17. Mikolov, T., Sutskever, I., Chen, K., Corrado, G.S., Dean, J.: Distributed representations of words and phrases and their compositionality. In: NIPS, pp. 3111–3119 (2013)
18. Nickel, M., Tresp, V., Kriegel, H.: A three-way model for collective learning on multi-relational data. In: ICML, pp. 809–816 (2011)

19. Ristoski, P., Paulheim, H.: RDF2Vec: RDF graph embeddings for data mining. In: Groth, P., Simperl, E., Gray, A., Sabou, M., Krötzsch, M., Lecue, F., Flöck, F., Gil, Y. (eds.) ISWC 2016. LNCS, vol. 9981, pp. 498–514. Springer, Cham (2016). doi:10.1007/978-3-319-46523-4_30

20. Socher, R., Chen, D., Manning, C.D., Ng, A.Y.: Reasoning with neural tensor networks for knowledge base completion. In: NIPS, pp. 926–934 (2013)

21. Spohr, D., Hollink, L., Cimiano, P.: A machine learning approach to multilingual and cross-lingual ontology matching. In: Aroyo, L., Welty, C., Alani, H., Taylor, J., Bernstein, A., Kagal, L., Noy, N., Blomqvist, E. (eds.) ISWC 2011. LNCS, vol. 7031, pp. 665–680. Springer, Heidelberg (2011). doi:10.1007/978-3-642-25073-6_42

22. Wang, Z., Zhang, J., Feng, J., Chen, Z.: Knowledge graph embedding by translating on hyperplanes. In: AAAI, pp. 1112–1119 (2014)

23. Wang, Z., Li, J., Wang, Z., Tang, J.: Cross-lingual knowledge linking across wiki knowledge bases. In: WWW, pp. 459–468 (2012)

24. Xing, C., Wang, D., Liu, C., Lin, Y.: Normalized word embedding and orthogonal transform for bilingual word translation. In: HLT-NAACL, pp. 1006–1011 (2015)

25. Zou, W.Y., Socher, R., Cer, D.M., Manning, C.D.: Bilingual word embeddings for phrase-based machine translation. In: EMNLP, pp. 1393–1398 (2013)

Blockchain Enabled Privacy Audit Logs

Andrew Sutton[✉] and Reza Samavi

Department of Computing and Software, McMaster University,
1280 Main St. West, Hamilton, ON L8S 4K1, Canada
{suttonad,samavir}@mcmaster.ca

Abstract. Privacy audit logs are used to capture the actions of participants in a data sharing environment in order for auditors to check compliance with privacy policies. However, collusion may occur between the auditors and participants to obfuscate actions that should be recorded in the audit logs. In this paper, we propose a Linked Data based method of utilizing blockchain technology to create tamper-proof audit logs that provide proof of log manipulation and non-repudiation. We also provide experimental validation of the scalability of our solution using an existing Linked Data privacy audit log model.

Keywords: Blockchain · Privacy audit log · RDF signatures · Bitcoin · Tamper-proof · Linked Data · Semantic Web · DSA · Privacy

1 Introduction

Protecting the privacy of individuals who contribute their data to a collaborative service or research environment is becoming more challenging. This becomes apparent as an individual's personal information is passed between different organizations that might operate under different jurisdictions and governing bodies. Data sharing agreements (DSA) are legally binding documents established between organizations that detail the policies and conditions related to the sharing of personal data [1]. The scenario in Fig. 1 demonstrates a collaborative research environment where the research teams must comply with the DSAs and are monitored for their compliance through the use of privacy audit logs. Auditors are responsible for checking compliance with the DSA by examining the privacy logs generated by the research teams [2].

In the scenario in Fig. 1, there is a problem in the trust placed in an auditor and the audit log itself. If the auditor works for the organization that they are auditing then the quality of the audit depends on influencing factors between the organization and the auditor [3]. Collusion can occur between individuals in the organization, such as researchers in the research teams, and the auditor to obfuscate or modify the integrity of the generated logs. The resulting degraded trust placed in the auditing process is a problem that needs to be solved in order to prove that organizations are responsible for privacy breaches resulting from non-compliant actions or to prove that they are compliant with the policies.

© Springer International Publishing AG 2017
C. d'Amato et al. (Eds.): ISWC 2017, Part I, LNCS 10587, pp. 645–660, 2017.
DOI: 10.1007/978-3-319-68288-4_38

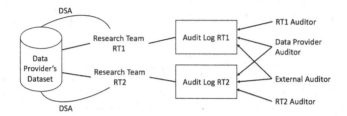

Fig. 1. Example privacy auditing scenario in a data sharing environment [5]

In order to combat the potential modification of the logs due to collusion, a mechanism to provide tamper-proof audit logs is needed [3,4].

In this paper, we propose a Linked Data-based [6] model for creating tamper-proof privacy audit logs and provide a mechanism for log integrity and authenticity verification that auditors can execute in conjunction with performing compliance checking queries. The Linked Data-based L2TAP (Linked Data Log to Transparency, Accountability, and Privacy) audit log framework [5] is used as the underlying log framework. We leverage theories and technologies stemming from blockchain technology [3,4,7–9], Linked Data graph signatures [10–13], and Linked Data graph digest computation [12,14] to create non-repudiable log events and utilize the distributed and immutable properties of blockchain technology to make the audit logs tamper-proof. We experimentally verify that the log integrity verification process scales linearly.

The structure of the paper and the contributions of our work are as follows. Section 2 presents how privacy audit logs are generated and the design requirements of our model. Our solution to generate tamper-proof privacy audit logs is described in Sect. 3. Section 4 presents a SPARQL-based solution to perform log integrity verification. In Sect. 5, the results of an experiment to validate the scalability of our method is given. Section 6 provides an investigation of the related work. Concluding remarks are discussed in Sect. 7.

2   Characteristics of Tamper-Proof Privacy Logs

Privacy auditing addresses three characteristics of information accountability: validation, attribution, and evidence [15,16]. Validation verifies a posteriori if a participant has performed the tasks as expected, whereas attribution and evidence deal with finding the responsible participants for non-compliant actions and producing supporting evidence, respectively [15,16]. To address these characteristics, privacy audit logs need to capture events with deontic modalities, such as capturing privacy policies, purpose of data usage, obligations of parties, and data access activities. A privacy audit log generation process is depicted in Fig. 2a. The process is composed of a logger producing log events of promised and performed privacy acts and storing them in an audit log accessible to auditors. The logger generates multiple privacy log events (e_1 to e_n) over time (e.g., expressing privacy policies, requesting access and access activities). An auditor

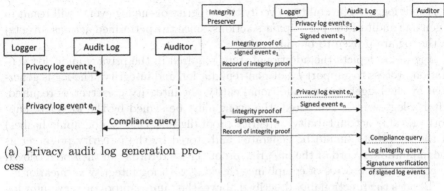

(a) Privacy audit log generation process

(b) Tamper-proof log generation process

Fig. 2. Privacy audit log generation comparison

can then perform compliance queries against the audit log to determine if the performed acts are in compliance with the polices in the governing DSA (e.g., the scenario in Fig. 1) [5].

There are a number of proposals on logs for supporting privacy auditing [18–20]. In this research, we utilize the L2TAP privacy audit log because it provides an infrastructure to capture all relevant privacy events and provides SPARQL solutions for major privacy processes such as obligation derivation and compliance checking [5]. The L2TAP model follows the principles of Linked Data to publish the logs. By leveraging a Linked Data infrastructure and expressing the contents of the logs using dereferenceable URIs, the L2TAP audit log supports extensibility and flexibility in a web-scale environment [5]. In this research we extend the L2TAP ontology to support non-repudiation and log event integrity.

2.1   Tamper-Proof Privacy Audit Log Desiderata

An event in a privacy audit log needs to be non-repudiable so that the performed act cannot be denied and the authenticity of the event can be provably demonstrated. For example, in the scenario in Fig. 1, if an auditor determines that the researchers have performed non-compliant actions, there is no provable method of holding the researchers accountable for their performed acts. Furthermore, after being logged, log events should not be altered by any participant, including the logger and auditor. If the researchers and auditors act in collusion to hide non-compliant acts in the log to avoid consequential actions, the resulting log does not represent the true events. Without a mechanism to provably demonstrate that the integrity of the log is intact, there will be a significant lack of confidence in the auditing process [3,4]. The privacy audit log should enable the logger to digitally sign an event to support non-repudiation. The log should also offer a mechanism to preserve the integrity of log events (e.g., hashing or encryption). Verifying the signature of an event will prove the authenticity of the event logger. The ability to verify the integrity of the log events will result in a genuine audit of the participant's actions, since the performed actions (events) in the log are proven to be authentic.

Figure 2b depicts the additional steps required in the privacy audit log generation process to support event non-repudiation and integrity. The log is generated by the logger, but an additional entity, the integrity preserver, is required. After a log event is generated, the event must be signed by the logger to support provable accountability. Integrity proof digests (i.e. cryptographic hashes) of the log events should be generated and stored by the integrity preserver as the immutable record of the integrity proof. These records can then be retrieved to enhance the process of compliance checking with log integrity verification.

Besides the functionality described above, the tamper-proof privacy audit log should preserve the extensibility, flexibility and scalability of the underlying logging framework (i.e. L2TAP). We achieve flexibility through the Linked Data and SPARQL based solution for the log verification. The extensibility is addressed by a limited extension of the L2TAP ontology and using other external ontologies through the modular structure of L2TAP. As demonstrated in [5], the L2TAP privacy audit log is scalable. The additional verification processes introduced in this paper to make the log tamper-proof should preserve the scalability.

3 Blockchain Enabled Privacy Audit Logs

In situations where a central authority has control over information resources, the trust placed in that authority to maintain correct and accurate information is reduced because there is no provable mechanism for external entities to verify the state of the resources. Blockchain technology solves the trust problem by maintaining records and transactions of information resources through a distributed network, rather than a central authority [21,22]. The use of blockchain technology to create an immutable record of transactions is analogous to the auditing problem we are trying to solve; the need for the immutable storage of information that is not governed by a central authority. In this section, we present how our blockchain enabled privacy audit log model works. We start with a brief background on the blockchain technology leveraged by our model, the Bitcoin blockchain, in Sect. 3.1. We describe the architecture of our model in Sect. 3.2. Sections 3.3 and 3.4 present the signature graph and block graph generation components of our model, respectively.

3.1 Bitcoin Blockchain

The Bitcoin system [23] is a cryptocurrency scheme based on a decentralized and distributed consensus network. Transactions propagate through the Bitcoin peer-to-peer network in order to be verified and stored in a blockchain. A blockchain is a decentralized database comprised of a continuously increasing amount of records, or blocks, that represents an immutable digital ledger of transactions [7].

Distributed ledgers allow for a shared method of record keeping where each participant has a copy of the ledger, meaning that each node on the network will have to be
in collusion to modify the records in the blockchain. Each block in the blockchain is
composed of a header containing a hash of the previous block in the chain (forming
a chain of blocks) and a payload of transactions.

Transactions are written to the blockchain through data structures that contain an input(s) and output(s). Monetary value is transferred between the transaction input and output, where the input defines where the value is coming
from and the output defines the destination. The Bitcoin blockchain allows a
small amount of data to be stored in a transaction output using a special transaction opcode that makes the transaction provably non-spendable [8]. Using
the OP_RETURN opcode available through Bitcoin's transaction scripting language[1] allows up to 80 bytes of additional storage to a transaction output [24].
Changes to the state of the blockchain are achieved through a consensus mechanism called Proof of Work. Transactions are propagated through the Bitcoin
network and specialized nodes, called miners, validate the transactions. These
miners generate new blocks on the blockchain by solving a hard cryptographic
problem and the other nodes on the network verify and mutually agree that the
solution is correct. As more transactions and blocks are generated, the difficulty
of the cryptographic problem rises, which makes the tampering of data written in
the blocks very difficult. A blockchain explorer application programming interface (API) is required to query transaction information on the Bitcoin network.
A blockchain explorer is a web application that acts as a Bitcoin search engine,
allowing users to query the transactions and blocks on the blockchain [24]. We
utilize this queryable special transaction to store an integrity proof of privacy
audit logs on the Bitcoin blockchain.

3.2   Architectural Components

A blockchain is well suited to fill the role of the integrity preserver in the tamper-
proof log generation process in Fig. 2b. We use the capabilities provided by the
Bitcoin blockchain to store an immutable record of the log integrity proofs.
The logger generates privacy log events and signs these events. After producing
integrity proofs of the signed events, each of the proofs will be written to the
Bitcoin blockchain through a series of transactions. The immutable record of the
integrity proofs on the blockchain will be retrieved using a blockchain explorer.
The components for signing log events and creating Bitcoin transactions are
signature graph generation and *block graph generation* illustrated in Fig. 3 and
described below.

The signature graph generation component is responsible for capturing the
missing non-repudiation property of the L2TAP audit log framework. An L2TAP
audit log is composed of various privacy events such as data access requests and
responses. The log events consist of a header that captures the provenance of an
event and a body containing information about the event, such as what data is

---

[1] https://en.bitcoin.it/wiki/Script.

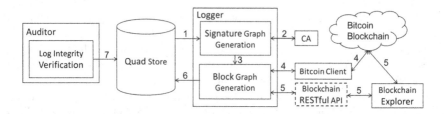

Fig. 3. The architecture of the model

being accessed by whom. URIs are used to identify a set of statements in the header and body to form RDF named graphs stored in a quad store [25]. We generate a new named graph, called the *signature graph*, that contains assertions about the event's signature. The event that will be signed is pulled from the quad store and signed by the logger (flow 1). There needs to be a public key infrastructure (PKI) with certificate authorities (CA) in place where the logger has a generated key pair used for digital signatures (flow 2). The computed signature and signature graph will be passed to the block graph generation component to be part of the integrity proof digest computation (flow 3).

The block graph generation component conducts transactions on the Bitcoin network to write the integrity proof digest to the blockchain. The logger uses a Bitcoin client to create a transaction containing the integrity proof digest (flow 4). After the transaction is written to the blockchain, the transaction data is queried through a RESTful request [26] to a blockchain explorer API (flow 5). The queried data is parsed to an RDF named graph, called the *block graph*. The block graph contains the integrity proof digest and information identifying the block containing the transaction on the blockchain. After the block graph has been generated, it is stored in a quad store in order for an auditor to perform log event integrity and signature verification queries (flows 6' and 7, respectively). Generating a block graph reduces the burden on the auditor when performing log integrity verification since all of the event integrity proofs are stored in a quad store. Without the block graphs, the auditor would have to search the *entire* Bitcoin blockchain for the integrity proof digests. Since the Bitcoin blockchain is a public ledger, there are many transactions unrelated to the auditor's search, which would make this method of searching inefficient. An alternative approach is to use a full Bitcoin client to download the entire blockchain, however in this case the required network bandwidth and local computing power are major limitations.

The signature graph and block graph generation components require two ontology modules to be added to the modular structure of the L2TAP ontology. The Signing Framework signature ontology [13] expresses all of the necessary algorithms and methods required for verifying a signature. The BLONDiE [27, 28] ontology semantically represents the Bitcoin blockchain. We also need to extend the L2TAP ontology to capture the signature graph and the signed log event. The new `hasSignedGraph` property in the L2TAP-participant module links the signature graph and signed event graph. An L2TAP log event body is dereferenced in the corresponding event header through the L2TAP eventData property. The signature graph just needs to reference the event header since there is an assertion between the body and header that the two graphs belong to the same event. The existing structure of L2TAP allows other components of the tamper-proof auditing to be asserted when a new log is initiated. For example, if a log uses Symantec[2] as the CA this can be included as a triple in the body of the log initialization event. The extended ontology is available on the tamper-proof audit log section of the L2TAP ontology website[3].

3.3   Signature Graph Generation

The process that the logger of an event has to take to compute a signature and generate a signature graph is formalized in Algorithm 1. The input parameters are the log event i header RDF graph, hg_i, body, bg_i, and the logger's private key, sk. Our algorithm follows the process of signing graph data in [11], which includes: canonicalization, serialization, hash, signature, and assembly [10,11]. We can omit the canonicalization and serialization steps as we can assume our graphs are in canonicalized form and are serialized in the TriG syntax [29].

Data: Event header graph: hg_i, event body graph: bg_i, private key: sk
Result: Signature graph: sg_i
1 $Triples \leftarrow (\text{extractTriples}(hg_i) \cup \text{extractTriples}(bg_i))$;
2 $Hash \leftarrow \prod_{j=1}^{|Triples|} h(t_j \in Triples)\text{mod}(p)$;
3 $Sig \leftarrow \text{Sign}(Hash, sk)$;
4 $sg_i \leftarrow \text{assembly}(Sig)$;
5 **return** sg_i

Algorithm 1. Signature graph generation algorithm

The first step in Algorithm 1 is to compute the hash of the input event header, hg_i, and body, bg_i. We use incremental cryptography and the graph digest algorithm [14] to compute the digest of hg_i and bg_i. Since the ordering of triples in the RDF graph is undefined, the graph digest computation involves segmenting the input into pieces, using a hash function on each piece, and combining the results [14]. In line 1 we extract the triples from hg_i and bg_i into the set of triples, $Triples$, so that incremental cryptography can be performed on each triple. In line 2, a set hash over all of the triples in $Triples$ is computed using a cryptographically secure hash function (e.g., SHA-256) to produce a hash of each triple [14]. This triple hash is reduced using the modulo operation by a sufficiently large prime number, p (the level of security depends on the size of the prime number [14]). Each of the triple hashes are multiplied together, producing the $Hash$ value in line 2 as the resulting header and body graph digest. After constructing the graph digest, the logger generates a signature, Sig, by signing the digest using the Elliptic Curve Digital Signature Algorithm (ECDSA) in

---

[2] https://www.symantec.com.
[3] http://l2tap.org.

line 3. ECDSA uses smaller keys to achieve the same level of security as other algorithms (such as RSA), resulting in a faster signing algorithm. In the final step we generate the triples of the signature graph as a new named graph using the *assembly* function. The triples in this graph contain the signature value and algorithms for verifying the signature [11].

Listing 1.1 illustrates an example signature graph generated using Algorithm 1. Analogous to work presented in [10], we also use the Signing Framework signature ontology [13]. Lines 5–8 in this listing contain the signature triples. Line 6 contains the WebID [30] where the signer's public key can be acquired [10]. The log event signature, *Sig*, is identified in line 7. Line 8 references the log event header that is signed. The signature graph also contains triples describing the algorithms required to verify the signature (omitted here).

```
1 @prefix sig: <http://icp.it-risk.iwvi.uni-koblenz.de/ontologies/signature.owl#> .
2 @prefix l2tapp: <http://purl.org/l2tapp#> .
3 _:log-sig-1 {
4    # triples omitted describing graph signing methods
5    _:log-sig-1 a sig:Signature ;
6       sig:hasVerificationCertificate <signer/WebID/URI> ;
7       sig:hasSignatureValue "MEUCIQC44Qy2O8Mx..."^^xsd:string ;
8       l2tapp:hasSignedGraph _:log_h1 . }
```

Listing 1.1. Signature graph

3.4 Block Graph Generation

Algorithm 2 inputs an event's signature (sg_i), header (hg_i) and body (bg_i) graphs to compute and write an integrity proof digest to the Bitcoin blockchain and generate a block graph. Analogous to Algorithm 1, the triples are extracted from the input graphs into the set of triples, *Triples* (line 1), so that incremental cryptography can be used to compute the integrity proof digest, *H* (line 2).

Data: Signature graph: sg_i, event header graph: hg_i, event body graph: bg_i
Result: Block graph: $BlockGraph_i$
1 $Triples \leftarrow (\text{extractTriples}(sg_i) \cup \text{extractTriples}(hg_i) \cup \text{extractTriples}(bg_i))$;
2 $H \leftarrow \prod_{j=1}^{|Triples|} h(t_j \in Triples) mod(p)$;
3 Write H to Bitcoin blockchain (using Bitcoin client) ;
4 $md \leftarrow$ query block metadata (using blockchain API) ;
5 $BlockGraph_i \leftarrow \text{assembly}(md, H)$;
6 **return** $BlockGraph_i$

Algorithm 2. Block graph generation algorithm

The next step is to create a Bitcoin transaction using a Bitcoin client[4] to write the integrity proof to the Bitcoin blockchain (line 3). An audit log requires one transaction per event. The Bitcoin client validates transactions by executing a script written in Bitcoin's transaction scripting language. The language provides the *scriptPubKey* output and the *scriptSig* input scripts[5] to

---

[4] https://blockchain.info/wallet/#/.

[5] https://en.bitcoin.it/wiki/Script#Provably_Unspendable.2FPrunable_Outputs.

validate transactions. A transaction in our model contains the OP_RETURN opcode in the *scriptPubKey* output (*scriptPubKey* = *OP_RETURN* + *H*) and the logger's signature and public key in the *scriptSig* input (*scriptSig* = *signature* + *publicKey*). We store the integrity proof digest in the 80-byte data segment of the OP_RETURN transaction output. The transaction is propagated through the Bitcoin network for verification.

After the transaction containing the integrity proof digest has been stored on the Bitcoin blockchain, two queries are performed to retrieve the metadata of the transaction using the Bitcoin blockchain data API[6] provided by the *blockchain.info* blockchain explorer (line 4). The first query is an HTTP GET request to https://blockchain.info/rawaddr/$bitcoin_address, where *$bitcoin_address* is the logger's Bitcoin address used to create the transaction. JSON data is returned containing an array of transactions made from the specified Bitcoin address. The JSON data is parsed to find the block height of the block containing the integrity proof digest transaction. The block height is the number of blocks between the first block in the Bitcoin blockchain and the current block. The block height can be found in the transaction array using the transaction's *scriptSig* value. The second query is an HTTP GET request to https://blockchain.info/block-height/$block_height?format=json, where *$block_height* is the retrieved block height. This query returns the block metadata needed to assemble the block graph, such as the hash of the previous block and timestamp. This information is necessary to build a complete representation of the block and allow for the block graph data to be easily verified.

The final step in the algorithm is to use the *assembly* function to create a new named graph, called the block graph, that describes the metadata about the block containing the integrity proof digest transaction. Listing 1.2 illustrates an example of a block graph output by Algorithm 2, serialized in TriG. We use the BLONDiE [27] ontology to generate the triples in this listing. The object of each triple is populated with the values extracted from the *blockchain.info* queries. Lines 5–9 describe the integrity proof transaction. The *scriptSig* value is captured in Line 8 and the hash of the transaction in line 7. Line 9 holds the integrity proof digest of the event and signature graphs (in hexadecimal). This value is what an auditor will be querying when conducting log integrity verification. Additional triples that describe the block header and payload are omitted to save space.

```
1  @prefix blo: <http://www.semanticblockchain.com/Blondie.owl#> .
2  _:exlog-block-1 {
3    _:exlog-block-1 a blo:BitcoinBlock ;
4    # triples omitted describing block header and payload
5    blo:BitcoinTransaction blo:hasBitcoinTransactionInput blo:BitcoinTransactionInput ;
6      blo:hasBitcoinTransactionOutput blo:BitcoinTransactionOutput .
7    blo:BitcoinTransactionInput blo:hashBitcoinTransactionInput "1a2...3fc"^^xsd:string ;
8      blo:scriptSignBitcoinTransactionInput "4730440...41d6e6"^^xsd:string .
9    blo:BitcoinTransactionOutput blo:scriptPubkeyBitcoinTransactionOutput "6a2848...e46e65"^^
         xsd:string . }
```

Listing 1.2. Block graph

---

[6] https://blockchain.info/api/blockchain_api.

4   Log Integrity Verification

The goal of an auditor in a privacy auditing scenario is to check the compliance of participants' actions with respect to the privacy policies. The authors in [5] described a SPARQL-based solution for compliance checking; i.e. answering the question of, for a given access request and its associated access activities, have the data holders followed the access policies? This section describes our extended SPARQL-based solution to enhance the compliance checking queries described in [5] to include the integrity and authenticity verification of log events.

For a given L2TAP log, the process of verifying the log integrity and authenticity and compliance checking can be performed in a sequence; i.e. for all events in the log, first ensure the integrity and authenticity of all events and then execute the compliance queries for the interested access request. However, in practice this approach is not desirable as for a fast growing log, verifying the entire log for each audit query is very expensive (see our experiment in Sect. 5). Alternatively, we can devise an algorithm that verifies the integrity and authenticity of a small subset of the event graphs for a given access request. The L2TAP ontology provides compliance checking of a subset of events through SPARQL queries [2], which the following algorithm can leverage to reduce the runtime.

Data: Event header graph: hg_i, event body graph: bg_i, signature graph: sg_i
Result: Boolean verification value: v_i

1 $Triples \leftarrow$ (extractTriples(hg_i) $\cup$ extractTriples(bg_i) $\cup$ extractTriples(sg_i)) ;

2 $H \leftarrow \prod\limits_{j=1}^{|Triples|} h(t_j \in Triples)mod(p)$;

3 $URI \leftarrow$ Query block graphs for H (Listing 1.3) ;
4 **if** $URI \neq \emptyset$ **then**
5 | $v_i \leftarrow$ verifySignature(sg_i, hg_i, bg_i) ;
6 **else**
7 | $v_i \leftarrow$ false ;
8 **end**
9 **return** v_i

Algorithm 3. Verification algorithm

Algorithm 3 formalizes the steps an auditor takes to verify the integrity of a log event and the event signature prior to checking compliance. The input parameters are the event header (hg_i), body (bg_i), and signature (sg_i) graphs, for an event i in the subset of events related to an access request. Assuming a cryptographically secure hash function is used to recompute the digest, any modification of the graphs will result in a different digest. If the search of the block graphs is successful and the computed digest is found, then the log event must have remained unmodified [3]. Therefore, the first step in the algorithm is to recompute the integrity proof digest of the log event. We originally used incremental cryptography to calculate the integrity proof digest, so the same method must be used again for computing consistent digests. In lines 1 and 2, we first extract the triples of the input graphs and compute the integrity proof digest, H, similar to what we described in Sect. 3.4. The SPARQL query in Listing 1.3 is executed against the block graphs to find a matching digest in the `scriptPubkeyBitcoinTransactionOutput` relation (line 3). This query is parameterized with the integrity proof digest, H (`@integrityProofDigest`). If the query returns the URI of a block graph containing the integrity proof digest, we proceed to verify the signature in the signature graph (lines 4 and 5). Otherwise, if no matching value is found in the block graphs, we conclude that the integrity of the log event has been compromised.

```
1 PREFIX blo: <http://www.semanticblockchain.com/Blondie.owl#> .
2 SELECT ?g WHERE {
3   GRAPH ?g { ?s blo:scriptPubkeyBitcoinTransactionOutput @integrityProofDigest }}
```

Listing 1.3. SPARQL query for integrity verification

The signature graph of the event can be found through the `hasSignedGraph` property. The algorithms used to verify the signature are extracted from the signature graph triples containing the hashing (i.e. SHA-256) and signing algorithms (i.e. ECDSA). The public key of the logger is retrieved by following the WebID URL in the `hasVerificationCertificate` property of the signature graph. If the signature verification process in line 5 fails, the algorithm returns `false`. In the case of no matching integrity proof digest or signature verification failure, the auditor will know which event has been modified and who the logger of the event is. However, the auditor will not know *what* the modification is, only that a modification *has occurred*. Therefore, proof of malicious interference would need further investigation.

Despite the process in this section supporting the confidentiality, authenticity and integrity of a privacy log, the approach is susceptible to an *internal* attack to subvert the verification process. However, to be successful, an attacker would have to generate and sign a *fake* log event, store the event in the quad store, calculate an integrity proof, store the proof on the blockchain, and finally generate a block graph pointing to the fake integrity proof block.

5   Experimental Evaluation

This section presents a scalability evaluation of our blockchain enabled privacy audit log model from the perspective of an auditor. In the experiment, we ran our integrity checking algorithm on increasingly sized L2TAP privacy audit logs. Section 5.1 describes the synthetic audit log used in the experiment. In Sect. 5.2, we illustrate the details of the test environment. The results of the experiment are discussed in Sect. 5.3.

5.1   Dataset

To simulate the process of an auditor checking the integrity of an audit log, we generated synthetic L2TAP logs[7]. A basic log consists of eight events: log

---

[7] Datasets are available in the figshare repository: https://doi.org/10.6084/m9.figshare.5234770.

initialization, participants registration, privacy preferences and policies, access request, access response, obligation acceptance, performed obligation, and actual access. The actual contents of these events can be found in [5]. To create a larger audit log, we repeatedly generate the access request events. Our largest synthetic log, composed of 9998 events, contains a total of 989,589 triples: 84 triples from the first three events of log initialization, participants registration, and privacy preferences and policies, and 989,505 triples generated from 9995 additional access request events where each access request leads to the generation of the five remaining events with a total of 99 triples.

The signature and block graph for each event needs to be generated for the auditor to perform the integrity verification procedure. A log containing 9998 events would generate the same number of signature graphs, block graphs, and Bitcoin transactions. In this case, the total size of the dataset that the auditor would need to process is 39,992 graphs. The initial state of the experiment is an audit log containing n events (composed of $2n$ header and body graphs) with n generated signature graphs and n generated block graphs. All of these graphs ($4n$) would be stored on a server in a quad store prior to measuring the scalability of the integrity verification solution. Figure 4 illustrates the log sizes used for the experiment, which range from a log containing 98 events to 9998 events.

5.2   Test Environment

The experiment was run by executing the SPARQL queries on a Virtuoso [31] server and quad store deployed on a Red Hat Enterprise Linux Server release 7.3 (Maipo) with two CPUs (both 2 GHz Intel Xeon) and 8 GB of memory. The RDF graph processing and hash computations in Algorithm 3 were run on a MacBook Pro with a 2.9 GHz Intel Core i7 processor and 8 GB of memory. The Java method used to measure the elapsed execution time of the experiment is *System.nanoTime()*. The execution time is measuring the time difference between sending the queries to the quad store on the server over HTTP and verifying the integrity proof digest and the signature. The recorded time does not take into account the time to generate the signature and block graphs (these were pre-computed before the experiment) or the time needed to write the data to the Bitcoin blockchain. To account for variability in the testing environment, each reported elapsed time is the average of five independent executions.

5.3   Experimental Results

In practice, an auditor would operate on a subset of events in the log based on the results from compliance queries for a given access request. We have opted to demonstrate a worst-case scenario by verifying the integrity and authenticity of an *entire* log rather than a subset of the events. This will also demonstrate the execution time of large subsets of events that are the size of the entire logs we conducted the experiment on.

The experiment consisted of retrieving all of the log events and their corresponding signature graphs from a quad store deployed on the server. Each set

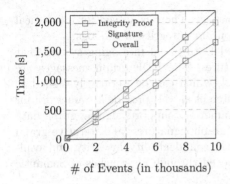

# of Events	# of Graphs for Hashing	Execution Time (s)
98	294	23.19
1998	5994	432.15
3998	11994	851.28
5998	17994	1311.51
7998	23994	1743.78
9998	29994	2191.06

Fig. 4. Elapsed execution times for integrity and signature verification

of graphs were input to Algorithm 3, which computes the integrity proof digest and executes the query in Listing 1.3 to determine if the integrity proof could be found in a block graph in the quad store. This procedure was executed on an audit log that contained a number of events ranging from 98 to 9998, as shown in Fig. 4. Figure 4 also illustrates the number of graphs that were input to the integrity proof digest computation in line 2 of Algorithm 3. A log consisting of 9998 events requires 29,994 (9998 header, 9998 body, 9998 signature graphs) graph digest calculations. A log of this size will generate 9998 block graphs as well, which will need to be searched for the integrity proof.

The elapsed execution time is plotted in Fig. 4. The graph illustrates the execution time of verifying the signature, computing and verifying the integrity of the events, and the overall process. The experiment validates the linear time growth for the entire integrity checking procedure. It can be seen that an increase of about 2000 events results in an increase of approximately 7 min to the integrity verification procedure. The reported results can be extrapolated to predict that a log containing an extreme case of one million events will take approximately 48 hours to perform an integrity check. This time is relatively small considering the vast amount of triples that would need to be processed from the event header and body, signature and block graphs (>100 million triples). The results of the experiment validate the scalability of our blockchain solution and demonstrates that the solution can perform efficiently at the task of verifying the integrity and signature of the audit log events.

6   Related Work

There are a number of proposals that provide a mechanism for verifying the integrity of an audit log [17,32]. Butin et al. [19] address the issues of log design for accountability, such as determining what the log should include so auditors can perform meaningful a posteriori compliance analysis. Tong et al. [20] propose a method of providing role-based access control auditability in audit logs to prevent the misuse of data. These solutions only address the integrity of privacy audit logs and miss the non-repudiation aspect. There is a need for a practical solution for supporting the non-repudiation *and* integrity of the logs.

Kleedorfer et al. [10] propose a Linked Data based messaging system that verifies conversations using digital signatures. The RDF graph messages are signed and a signature graph is produced, which can be iteratively signed as the messages pass between recipients. Kasten et al. [11] provide a framework for computing RDF graph signatures. This framework supports signing graph data at different levels of granularity, multiple graph signatures, and iterative graph signatures [11]. Kasten [12] discusses how the confidentiality, integrity, and availability of Semantic Web data can be achieved through approaches of Semantic Web encryption and signatures.

Use of blockchain technology in the auditing of financial transactions have been investigated [3] after the repercussions of the Enron Scandal in 2001, where auditor fraud was the source of public distrust [4]. Anderson [3] proposes a method of verifying the integrity of files using a blockchain. Similar to our approach, Cucurull et al. [8] present a method for enhancing the security of logs by utilizing the Bitcoin blockchain. Our approach differs by providing a model to create tamper-proof logs in a highly scalable Linked Data environment.

7 Conclusions

In this paper we presented a method for utilizing blockchain technology to provide tamper-proof privacy audit logs. The provided solution applies to Linked Data based privacy audit logs, in which lacked a mechanism to preserve log integrity. SPARQL queries and graph generation algorithms are presented that a log generator can perform to write log events to a blockchain and auditors can perform to verify the integrity of log events. The model can be used by loggers to generate tamper-proof privacy audit logs whereas the integrity queries can be used by external auditors to check if the logs have been modified for nefarious purposes. The paper includes an experimental evaluation that demonstrates the scalability of the audit log integrity verification procedure. Based on our experimental results, the solution scales linearly with increasingly sized privacy audit logs.

There are a number of directions for future work. First, we acknowledge Bitcoin's limitations in terms of cost, speed, and scalability [33]. We utilized Bitcoin since it provides an established storage mechanism suitable for integrity proofs and to demonstrate the feasibility of our solution applied to Linked Data. For an optimized implementation, other blockchain technologies, such as Ethereum [34], should be compared in terms of transaction fee, scalability, and smart contract and private ledger support. Second, a log containing thousands of events will require thousands of transactions and occupy a large space on the blockchain. Using Merkle trees [8,35] can reduce the storage and transaction requirements by writing the root of the tree (composed of multiple integrity proofs) to the blockchain. However, this will increase the work for an auditor to verify the log integrity since more hash value computations are required to reconstruct the hash tree. Formalizing the trade-offs between hash trees and the verification effort is an interesting optimization problem to investigate.

Acknowledgments. Financial support from NSERC and SOSCIP are greatly acknowledged.

References

1. Swarup, V., Seligman, L., Rosenthal, A.: A data sharing agreement framework. In: Bagchi, A., Atluri, V. (eds.) ICISS 2006. LNCS, vol. 4332, pp. 22–36. Springer, Heidelberg (2006). doi:10.1007/11961635_2
2. Samavi, R., Consens, M.P.: L2TAP+SCIP: an audit-based privacy framework leveraging Linked Data. In: 8th International Conference on Collaborative Computing: Networking, Applications and Worksharing, CollaborateCom 2012, pp. 719–726. IEEE (2012)
3. Anderson, N.: Blockchain Technology: A Game-Changer in Accounting? Deloitte (2016)
4. Spoke, M.: How blockchain tech will change auditing for good. CoinDesk (2015). http://www.coindesk.com/blockchains-and-the-future-of-audit/. Accessed Feb 2017
5. Samavi, R., Consens, M.P.: Publishing L2TAP logs to facilitate transparency and accountability. In: Proceedings of the Workshop on Linked Data on the Web Co-located with the 23rd International World Wide Web Conference (WWW), Seoul, Korea, vol. 1184. CEUR-WS (2014)
6. Heath, T., Bizer, C.: Linked Data: Evolving the Web into a Global Data Space. Synthesis Lectures on the Semantic Web: Theory and Technology, 1st edn., vol. 1, pp. 1–136. Morgan & Claypool, San Rafael (2011)
7. Pilkington, M.: Blockchain Technology: Principles and Applications. Research Handbook on Digital Transformations. Edward Elgar, Northampton (2016)
8. Cucurull, J., Puiggalí, J.: Distributed immutabilization of secure logs. In: Barthe, G., Markatos, E., Samarati, P. (eds.) STM 2016. LNCS, vol. 9871, pp. 122–137. Springer, Cham (2016). doi:10.1007/978-3-319-46598-2_9
9. Haber, S., Stornetta, W.S.: How to time-stamp a digital document. In: Menezes, A.J., Vanstone, S.A. (eds.) CRYPTO 1990. LNCS, vol. 537, pp. 437–455. Springer, Heidelberg (1991). doi:10.1007/3-540-38424-3_32
10. Kleedorfer, F., Panchenko, Y., Busch, C.M., Huemer, C.: Verifiability and traceability in a linked data based messaging system. In: Proceedings of the 12th International Conference on Semantic Systems, SEMANTiCS 2016, pp. 97–100. ACM, Leipzig (2016)
11. Kasten, A., Scherp, A., Schauß, P.: A framework for iterative signing of graph data on the web. In: Presutti, V., d'Amato, C., Gandon, F., d'Aquin, M., Staab, S., Tordai, A. (eds.) ESWC 2014. LNCS, vol. 8465, pp. 146–160. Springer, Cham (2014). doi:10.1007/978-3-319-07443-6_11
12. Kasten, A.: Secure semantic web data management: confidentiality, integrity, and compliant availability in open and distributed networks. Doctoral Dissertation, Universität Koblenz-Landau, Germany (2016)
13. Kasten, A.: A software framework for iterative signing of graph data. GitHub repository (2016). https://github.com/akasten/signingframework. Accessed Jan 2017
14. Sayers, C., Karp, A.H.: Computing the digest of an RDF graph. Technical report, Mobile and Media Systems Laboratory, HP Laboratories, HPL-2003-235, Palo Alto, USA (2004)
15. Weitzner, D.J., Abelson, H., Berners-Lee, T., Feigenbaum, J., Hendler, J., Sussman, G.J.: Information accountability. Commun. ACM **51**, 82–87 (2008)

16. Castelluccia, C., Druschel, P., Hübner, S., Pasic, A., Preneel, B., Tschofenig, H.: Privacy, Accountability and Trust - Challenges and Opportunities. Technical report, ENISA (2011)
17. Accorsi, R.: Log data as digital evidence: what secure logging protocols have to offer?. In: Proceeding of 33rd Annual IEEE International Computer Software and Applications Conference, vol. 2, pp. 398–403. IEEE (2009)
18. Agrawal, R., Evfimievski, A., Kiernan, J., Velu, R.: Auditing disclosure by relevance ranking. In: Proceedings of the 2007 ACM SIGMOD International Conference on Management of Data, pp. 79–90 (2007)
19. Butin, D., Chicote, M., Le Metayer, D.: Log design for accountability. In: Security and Privacy Workshops (SPW), pp. 1–7. IEEE (2013)
20. Tong, Y., Sun, J., Chow, S.S.M., Li, P.: Cloud-assisted mobile-access of health data with privacy and auditability. IEEE J. Biomed. Health Inform. 18, 419–429 (2014). IEEE
21. Kehoe, L., Dalton, D., Leonowicz, C., Jankovich, T.: Blockchain Disrupting the Financial Services Industry? Deloitte (2015)
22. Libert, B., Beck, M., Wind, J.: How blockchain technology will disrupt financial services firms. Knowledge@Wharton, Wharton University of Pennsylvania (2016). http://knowledge.wharton.upenn.edu/article/blockchain-technology-will-disrupt-financial-services-firms/. Accessed May 2017
23. Nakamoto, S.: Bitcoin: A Peer-to-Peer Electronic Cash System (2008)
24. Antonopoulos, A.M.: Mastering Bitcoin: Unlocking Digital Cryptocurrencies. O'Reilly Media Inc., Sebastopol (2014)
25. Carroll, J.J., Bizer, C., Hayes, P., Stickler, P.: Named graphs. In: Web Semantics: Science, Services and Agents on the World Wide Web, vol. 3, pp. 247–267 (2005)
26. A. Rodriguez, "Restful web services: The basics", IBM developerWorks, 2008
27. English, M., Auer, S., Domingue, J.: Block chain technologies & the semantic web: a framework for symbiotic development. In: Computer Science Conference for University of Bonn Students, Germany, pp. 47–61 (2016)
28. Ugarte R, H.E.: BLONDiE - blockchain ontology with dynamic extensibility. GitHub repository (2016). https://github.com/hedugaro/Blondie. Accessed Feb 2017
29. Bizer, C., Cyganiak, R.: TriG: RDF dataset language. W3C (2013). http://www.w3.org/TR/trig/. Accessed May 2017
30. Sambra, A., Story, H., Berners-Lee, T.: WebId 1.0: web identity and discovery (2014). https://www.w3.org/2005/Incubator/webid/spec/identity/. Accessed Mar 2017
31. Virtuoso Universal Server, OpenLink Software. https://virtuoso.openlinksw.com. Accessed Feb 2017
32. Stathopoulos, V., Kotzanikolaou, P., Magkos, E.: Secure log management for privacy assurance in electronic communications. Comput. Secur. 27, 298–308 (2008)
33. Manu, S.: Building better blockchains. In: Linked Data in Distributed Ledgers Workshop Keynote, WWW 2017 (2017)
34. Buterin, V.: Ethereum white paper. GitHub repository (2013). https://github.com/ethereum/wiki/wiki/White-Paper. Accessed July 2017
35. Merkle, R.C.: Protocols for public key cryptosystems. In: 1980 IEEE Symposium on Security and Privacy, pp. 122–133. IEEE (1980)

VICKEY: Mining Conditional Keys
on Knowledge Bases

Danai Symeonidou[1(✉)], Luis Galárraga[2], Nathalie Pernelle[3], Fatiha Saïs[3],
and Fabian Suchanek[4]

[1] INRA, Montpellier, France
danai.symeonidou@inra.fr
[2] Aalborg University, Aalborg, Denmark
[3] LRI, Orsay, France
[4] Télécom ParisTech, Paris, France

Abstract. A conditional key is a key constraint that is valid in only a
part of the data. In this paper, we show how such keys can be mined
automatically on large knowledge bases (KBs). For this, we combine
techniques from key mining with techniques from rule mining. We show
that our method can scale to KBs of millions of facts. We also show that
the conditional keys we mine can improve the quality of entity linking
by up to 47% points.

1 Introduction

Recent years have seen the rise of large knowledge bases (KBs), such as
YAGO [26], Wikidata [29], and DBpedia [18] on the academic side, and the
Google Knowledge Graph [7] or Microsoft's Satori graph on the commercial
side. These KBs contain millions of entities (such as people, places, or organizations), and millions of facts about them. This knowledge is typically expressed
in RDF [19], i.e., as triples of the form ⟨*Einstein, won, NobelPrize*⟩. A key constraint on such data specifies that no two distinct entities can share a certain
set of properties (e.g., no two people share given name, family name, and birthdate). Key constraints are used for applications such as knowledge base fusion [8],
knowledge base enrichment [22] and data linking [1,9,23].

It is impractical to specify keys manually for large KBs (with millions of triples and hundreds or thousands of properties). Therefore, several
approaches [4,21,25,27] have been developed to automatically discover keys from
RDF data. However, these works have also shown that for several datasets, there
are no or only few keys that are valid in the entire dataset. This is the reason
why we aim to mine *conditional keys* in this paper, i.e., keys that are valid in
only a part of the data.

A conditional key is an axiom saying that under particular conditions, no
two distinct entities can have the same values on a particular set of properties.
For example, we can say that at a German university, no two professors can
advise the same doctoral student. The situation might be different at a French or

© Springer International Publishing AG 2017
C. d'Amato et al. (Eds.): ISWC 2017, Part I, LNCS 10587, pp. 661–677, 2017.
DOI: 10.1007/978-3-319-68288-4_39

American university – hence the key is "conditional" to German universities. In this paper, we distinguish conditional keys from classical keys, which hold for an atomic class (or for every tuple of a table in a relational database). Conditional keys can express constraints on entities and are strictly more expressive than classical keys. Therefore, they can be more productive in tasks such as entity linking – as we show in our experiments. Apart from this, conditional keys carry knowledge in themselves. For example, it is interesting to know that France allows several advisors, while Germany does not.

Mining conditional keys automatically from the data is a challenging endeavor, for several reasons. First, the KBs we consider here contain only binary relations, which means that keys usually do not live in a single table, but can be a join of up to a dozen relations. Second, KBs are usually incomplete [12]. If a student at a German university has only one advisor in the KB, she could still have several in real life. Thus, any approach that automatically mines conditional keys risks being misled. Finally, the challenge is to scale: Today's KBs contain millions of statements. This means that there are billions of possible conditions and property combinations that could define a conditional key. In the example, professors could be distinguished by their doctoral students, but also by their given and family name or by their discipline and birthdate. These keys could hold only for German professors, only for Danish ones, only for professors at a certain university in Mexico, or only for professors born in a certain city in Iowa. This huge search space is one of the main reasons why there is today no approach that could mine conditional keys on KBs.

Our proposal is to combine key mining techniques [27] with techniques from rule mining [13]. More precisely, VICKEY discovers first the set of maximal non-keys from which the conditional keys can be computed. Thus, the search space can be significantly reduced while avoiding to scan all the data. Secondly, VICKEY applies a breadth-first strategy to discover frequent candidate conditional keys and efficiently check their validity. More precisely, our contributions are as follows:

- We develop an algorithm that can mine conditional keys efficiently.
- We show that our method scales gracefully to KBs of millions of facts.
- We show that the use of our conditional keys improves the F1 measure of KB linking by up to 47% points over the use of classical keys.

The rest of this paper is structured as follows. We discuss related work in Sect. 2, and introduce preliminaries in Sect. 3. In Sect. 4 we present our approach. Section 5 showcases our experiments, before Sect. 6 concludes.

2   Related Work

Relational Databases. Two types of key discovery approaches have been proposed for relational databases [16,24]: data-driven [24], where keys are discovered from the tuples in a table, and schema-based [16], where property combinations of a certain size are generated and then checked on the tuples. Such approaches cannot be applied directly to KBs, because they are geared towards relations that contain one single value for each subject. In KBs, in contrast, a relation can contain several objects for the same subject.

Knowledge Bases. Approaches for KBs [3,4,21,25,27] can be roughly classified into two groups, depending on how they deal with multivalued properties [2]: The *forall-key approaches* [4,25] discover keys that fire when two entities share *all* values for each property. In [4], the authors have developed a level-wise schema-based approach based on TANE [17], to discover pseudo-keys (keys with exceptions). Rocker [25] is a refinement-operator-based approach that efficiently discovers pseudo-keys using a top-down strategy guided by a discriminability score function designed for forall-keys. The *some-key approaches* [3,21,27], on the other hand, discover keys that fire as soon as two entities share *at least one* value for each property. Some-keys can be particularly useful under the Open World Assumption (OWA), where the KB may not contain all relevant facts. Thus, it is for example sufficient that two researchers share their last name, their first name, and one of their publications in order for them to be linked – even if the KB does not know all of their publications. [3] discovers discriminative combinations of corresponding properties that can be used to link two datasets with different schemas. KD2R [21] extends the relational data-driven approach of [24] in order to exploit ontology axioms (such as the subsumption relation) and considers multivalued properties. SAKey [27] introduces additional filtering and pruning techniques to discover efficiently some-keys with exceptions. To avoid scanning the entire dataset, both KD2R and SAKey discover first the maximal non-keys and then derive the keys from this set. Yet, none of these approaches is able to mine the *conditional keys* that we aim at in this paper.

Conditional Functional Dependency Mining. A conditional functional dependency (CFD) expresses a functional dependency between two sets of attributes that holds on a subset of tuples [6]. For example, a CFD could state that when two customers are based in the UK, the zipcode uniquely determines the city. A conditional key is a particular type of CFD, where the second set of attributes is a unique identifier for a record in the database. CFD discovery has been addressed in [6,10,15]. The work of [6] uses a breadth-first strategy inspired by the schema-based approach TANE [17]. FastCFD [10] finds a canonical cover of all minimal CFDs that satisfy a given support using a depth-first strategy. Compared to [6] (which works well when the number of tuples is large), FastCFD [10] is efficient when the number of attributes is large. Nevertheless, none of these approaches is able to discover conditional keys in KBs, because they cannot efficiently deal with multivalued properties and would require a post-processing to mine conditional keys from the obtained CFDs.

Rule Mining. Finally, one possibility to find conditional keys would be to use rule mining approaches. AMIE [13], e.g., can learn logical rules with up to 4 atoms on KBs that contain millions of facts. However, even relatively simple conditional keys can easily contain five or more atoms. This leads to an exponential increase of the search space that such rule mining approaches cannot handle – as we show in our experiments. In [5], the authors propose a more efficient rule mining approach that implements a series of parallelization and pruning techniques. However, it focuses only on Horn rules with ungrounded atoms. Thus, it cannot be applied for conditional key discovery. In [11], the authors propose to apply, first, a rule mining tool like [5,13] and then refine the obtained rules by adding negated atoms. However, the result are rules with negations, not conditional keys. In this paper, we propose a method called VICKEY, which we believe is the first approach to mine conditional keys efficiently on large KBs.

3   Preliminaries

Knowledge Bases. The knowledge bases that we consider here [18,26,29] use a set $\mathcal{I}$ of instances (such as a researcher identified as $r1$), a set $\mathcal{L}$ of literals, a set $\mathcal{P}$ of properties (such as *nationality*), and a set $\mathcal{C}$ of class names (such as *country*). A fact is a triple of a subject $s \in \mathcal{C} \cup \mathcal{I}$, a property $p \in \mathcal{P}$, and an object $o \in \mathcal{C} \cup \mathcal{I} \cup \mathcal{L}$, which we write as $p(s,o)$. Every instance is typically associated to one or more classes by the *type* property, and these classes can be arranged in a hierarchy by the *subclassOf* property. A set of such facts constitutes a knowledge base (KB)[1]. Given a KB $\mathcal{K}$, a *dataset* $\mathcal{D}$ for a class c of $\mathcal{K}$ is the set of all facts that have as subject an instance of c or of a subclass of c. Table 1 shows an example dataset[2] about researchers $r1, ..., r7$, each having the properties *firstName*, *lastName*, *gender*, *lab*, and *nationality* – with one or more objects for each property. When $\mathcal{D}$ is given, we write $p(x,y)$ to mean $p(x,y) \in \mathcal{D}$.

Keys. In our setting, a key is defined as follows [21,27].

Table 1. Example dataset

	FirstName	LastName	Gender	Lab	Nationality
r1	Claude	Dupont	Female	Paris-Sud	France
r2	Claude	Dupont	Male	Paris-Sud	Belgium
r3	Juan	Rodríguez	Male	INRA	Spain, Italy
r4	Juan	Salvez	Male	INRA	Spain
r5	Anna	Georgiou	Female	INRA	Greece, France
r6	Pavlos	Markou	Male	Paris-Sud	Greece
r7	Marie	Legendre	Female	INRA	France

---

[1] The KBs considered in this work do not contain blank nodes.
[2] For readability, the table does not distinguish literals and instances.

Definition 1 *(Key)*. *A key in a dataset $\mathcal{D}$ is a set of properties $p_1, \ldots, p_n$ of $\mathcal{D}$ such that:*

$$\forall x, y, \, u_1, \ldots, u_n \left(\bigwedge_{i=1\ldots n} p_i(x, u_i) \wedge p_i(y, u_i) \Rightarrow x = y \right)$$

In our example, the property set {*lastName, gender*} is a key while {*lab, nationality*} is not a key, because $r3$ and $r4$ are both *Spanish*. Note that {*lab, nationality*} is a forall-key since no two people share the lab and the entire set of nationalities.

Definition 2 *(Maximal non-key)*. *A maximal non-key for a dataset $\mathcal{D}$ is a set of properties P of $\mathcal{D}$ such that P is not a key, and the addition of any other property makes P a key.*

In our example, {*firstName, lastName, lab*} is a maximal non-key, because adding any other property makes the set a key.

Key Discovery. To discover the keys of a dataset automatically, a naive algorithm would have to compare all subjects of the dataset to all other subjects – which is prohibitively expensive. To avoid this complexity, the SAKey algorithm [27] first finds maximal non-keys. This is more efficient, because to verify that a set of properties is a non-key, it suffices to find two subjects that share values for these properties. SAKey starts with property combinations that contain only a single property, and incrementally adds more and more properties until it arrives at maximal non-keys. When it has found all non-keys, all other property combinations must be keys – which is what SAKey outputs.

Conditional Keys. Our example in Table 1 shows two researchers with the last name Dupont. Therefore the property *lastName* is not a key. The combination {*firstName, lastName*} is not a key either, because there are two researchers with the same first and last names. However, when we restrict our set of researchers to those working at INRA, the property *lastName* identifies researchers uniquely. In contrast, this is not true for the researchers in Paris-Sud. Thus, {*lastName, lab*} is not a key in general. We say that *lastName* is a *conditional key* for people working at INRA. In this work, we chose to focus on conditions that can be expressed using constraints on property values. More formally, a condition is a pair composed of a property p and an object o, written $p = o$ (e.g., $lab = INRA$). A condition cd with property p and object o holds for a subject x, written $cd(x)$, if $p(x, o)$. In the example, the condition $lab = INRA$ holds for $r3$, $r4$, $r5$ and $r7$.

Definition 3 *(Conditional key)*. *A conditional key for a dataset $\mathcal{D}$ is a non-empty set of conditions $\{cd_1, \ldots, cd_n\}$ and a non-empty set of properties $\{p_1, \ldots, p_m\}$ of $\mathcal{D}$ (disjoint from the properties in the conditions), such that:*

$$\forall x, y, \, u_1, \ldots, u_m \left(\bigwedge_{i=1..n} (cd_i(x) \wedge cd_i(y)) \wedge \bigwedge_{i=1..m} (p_i(x, u_i) \wedge p_i(y, u_i)) \Rightarrow x = y \right)$$

Definition 4 *(Minimal conditional key)*. *A conditional key with conditions CD and properties P is minimal, if the removal of a condition in CD, the removal of a property from P, or the transfer of a property p from CD to P (with the corresponding removal of the condition), all result in something that is neither a conditional key nor a key.*

In our example, *lastName* is a conditional key with condition *nationality = Spanish ∧ lab = INRA*, but this conditional key is not minimal, because there exists a simpler version of the key with fewer conditions, namely *nationality = Spanish*. In the same vein, {*lastName*} with the condition *gender = male* is not a minimal conditional key, because {*lastName, gender*} is a key.

The *support* of a conditional key with properties $\{p_1, ..., p_m\}$ and conditions $\{cd_1, ..., cd_n\}$ is the number of subjects x such that $\bigwedge_{i=1..m} \exists u_i : p_i(x, u_i)$ and $\bigwedge_{i=1..n} cd_i(x)$. A proportional version of the support, which we call the *coverage*, measures the ratio of subjects in the dataset identified by the conditional key. In our example, the support of the key {*lastName*} under the condition *lab = INRA* is 4, and the coverage is $\frac{4}{7}$, since there are 7 subjects.

Keys in OWL. Conditional keys can be defined in the ontology language OWL2 [20]. OWL2 allows defining keys not just on atomic classes (such as *researcher*), but also on more complex class expressions. We can define, e.g., the class "Researchers who work at INRA" as $c = Researcher \sqcap \exists lab.\{INRA\}$. Then, {*lastName*} is a key on the dataset of c according to Definition 1.

4   Mining Conditional Keys

We now present our approach to automatically discover conditional keys on a dataset. To learn conditional keys under the Open World Assumption, we assume that all instances in a dataset refer to distinct real world objects, and that all unknown values are different from the existing ones in the dataset [7,13,14,21,27]. The discovery of simple keys alone already requires checking a large number of property combinations (of which there are $2^{|\mathcal{P}|}$ in total, where $\mathcal{P}$ is the set of properties). Discovering conditional keys is even more complex, since the search space is in the order of $O(|\mathcal{V}|^{|\mathcal{P}|})$, where $\mathcal{V}$ is the set of objects in the dataset. Our algorithm can discover conditional keys efficiently in spite of this large search space. Our method takes as input a dataset $\mathcal{D}$ and a threshold θ for the minimal support of the discovered keys. We proceed in three phases:

(1) *Discovery of non-keys*: Instead of exploring the whole set of combinations of properties, we focus our search on those combinations that are not keys.
(2) *Generation of Conditional Key Graphs*: We use the non-keys to generate candidate keys, which we store in conditional key graphs.
(3) *Mining of Conditional Key Graphs*: The conditional key graphs are then mined for minimal conditional keys.

4.1   Discovery of Non-keys

The naive method to mine conditional keys explores all possible combinations of properties and conditions in the input KB and verifies whether they fulfill Definition 3. Such an approach is infeasible on large datasets. Our main idea (the key insight, so to speak) is the following (see [28] for more details):

Observation 1 *(Conditional Keys and Non-Keys). Given a minimal conditional key for a dataset $\mathcal{D}$ with properties P and conditions $\{p_1 = o_1, ..., p_n = o_n\}$, the set of properties $P \cup \{p_1, ..., p_n\}$ must be a non-key for $\mathcal{D}$.*

This follows from Definition 4. In our example from Table 1, $\{firstName\}$ is a minimal conditional key with condition $gender = Female$, and $\{gender, firstName\}$ is a non-key. Thus, if we want to mine the complete set of minimal conditional keys, it suffices to consider only the property combinations given by non-keys. Since maximal non-keys are super-sets of all other non-keys (Definition 2), it is sufficient to explore only property combinations given by maximal non-keys. The maximal non-keys in the input dataset can be mined efficiently with the SAKey algorithm [27] (Sect. 3). Thus, we concentrate in the following on mining the conditional keys from these maximal non-keys. As a running example, consider again the dataset in Table 1. It contains two maximal non-keys: $\{firstName, lastName, lab\}$ and $\{firstName, gender, lab, nationality\}$.

4.2   Generation of Conditional Key Graphs

Our method for discovering conditional keys from non-keys relies on a modifiable data structure that we call a *conditional key graph*. Such a graph is a tuple $\langle P^k, P^c, cond, G \rangle$ with the following components:

- P^k and P^c are disjoint sets of properties, called *key properties* and *condition properties*, respectively.
- *cond* is a set of conditions on P^c.
- G is a directed graph. Each node v is associated to a set $v.p \subseteq P^k$ and to a boolean flag $v.explore$ set by default to true. There is a directed edge from u to v if $u.p \subset v.p$ and $|u.p| = |v.p| - 1$.

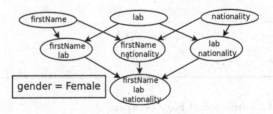

Fig. 1. Example of a conditional key graph with $P^k = \{firstName, lab, nationality\}$, $P^c = \{gender\}$, $cond = \{gender = Female\}$.

We construct the initial conditional key graphs with Algorithm 1. This algorithm takes as input the dataset, the support threshold θ, and the non-keys discovered in Sect. 4.1. We first construct all possible conditions $p = a$ that combine a property p from the non-keys with an instance or literal a from the dataset (Lines 2–3). Conditions with support less than θ are not considered (Line 4). We then look at all non-keys N in which p appears (Line 5). The conditional key graph for the condition $p = a$ will contain as nodes all subsets of $N \setminus \{p\}$ (Line 6) except the empty set (Line 7). As an example, let us consider again the dataset of Table 1 and its two maximal non-keys $\{firstName, lastName, lab\}$ and $\{firstName, gender, lab, nationality\}$. Figure 1 depicts the conditional key graph associated to the condition $gender = Female$ constructed by Algorithm 1.

Lemma 1 (Graph Construction). *If Algorithm 1 is given a dataset $\mathcal{D}$, a complete set of maximal non-keys $\mathcal{N}$ for $\mathcal{D}$ and a support threshold θ, then for each conditional key of $\mathcal{D}$ with a single condition and with at least support θ, there is a graph in the output that contains the key condition and a node with the key properties.*

Lemma 1 follows from the fact that Algorithm 1(a) iterates over all conditions $p = o$ with a least support θ and (b) considers *all* the possible subsets of properties $2^{N \setminus \{p\}}$ with $N \in \mathcal{N}$ (except for $\emptyset$). From Observation 1 we recall that for any conditional key with properties P and condition $p = o$, the set of properties $P \cup \{p\}$ must be a non-key. Thus, from the completeness of our set of maximal non-keys, it follows that our graph contains in its nodes all possible keys with support higher than θ for a given condition $p = o$.

Algorithm 1. ConstructGraphs

Input: dataset $\mathcal{D}$, min. support θ, set of non-keys $\mathcal{N}$
Output: set of conditional key graphs $\mathcal{G}$

1 $\mathcal{G} \leftarrow \emptyset$
2 **for** $p \in \bigcup_{N \in \mathcal{N}} N$ **do**
3   **for** $a \in \mathcal{I} \cup \mathcal{L}$ such that $\exists x : p(x, a) \in \mathcal{D}$ **do**
4   **if** *number of x with $p(x, a)$ is at least θ* **then**
5           $V \leftarrow \emptyset$
6   **for** $N \in \mathcal{N}$ where $p \in N$ **do** $V \leftarrow V \cup 2^{N \setminus \{p\}}$
7           $V \leftarrow V \setminus \emptyset$
8   **for** $v \in V$ **do** $v.explore = true$
9           $E \leftarrow \{u, v \in V : u.p \subset v.p \wedge |u.p| = |v.p| - 1\}$
10          $P^k = \bigcup_{v \in V} v.p$
11          $P^c = \{p\}$
12          $cond = \{p = a\}$
13          $\mathcal{G} \leftarrow \mathcal{G} \cup \{\langle P^k, P^c, cond, (V, E)\rangle\}$

14 **return** $\mathcal{G}$

4.3   Mining of Conditional Key Graphs

Mining conditional keys. We mine the conditional key graphs for keys with Algorithm 2. It takes as input a dataset, a support threshold, and the set of conditional key graphs constructed in the previous phase. All these conditional key graphs have conditions of size 1 (see Algorithm 1). The algorithm proceeds in batches, looking first at the graphs with condition size 1, then size 2, etc. (Lines 2–3). For each batch, it mines the conditional keys (Line 6). The graphs in one batch are then post-processed (Line 7) to give rise to new graphs with conditions of larger size. The algorithm iterates until all sizes are processed (Line 4).

Algorithm 2. ConditionalKeyDiscovery

Input: dataset $\mathcal{D}$, minimum support θ, set of conditional key graphs $\mathcal{G}$
Output: set of minimal conditional keys CKs

1 $CKs \leftarrow \emptyset$
2 **for** $size = 1$ *to* ∞ **do**
3 | $\mathcal{G}' \leftarrow \{g \in \mathcal{G} : |g.cond| = size\}$
4 | **if** $\mathcal{G}' = \emptyset$ **then return** CKs
5 | **for** $\langle P^k, P^c, cond, G \rangle \in \mathcal{G}'$ **do**
6 | | $CKs \leftarrow CKs \cup MineGraph(\mathcal{D}, \theta, \langle P^k, P^c, cond, G \rangle, CKs)$
7 | $\mathcal{G} \leftarrow newConditions(size, \mathcal{G}, \theta, \mathcal{D})$

Mining a conditional key graph. Let us now discuss how one conditional key graph can be mined for keys (Line 7 in Algorithm 2). This task is done by Algorithm 3. This algorithm takes as input a dataset, the support threshold, a conditional key graph, and the set of conditional keys found so far. The algorithm proceeds in levels, looking first at the nodes that contain one property, then two properties, etc. For each level, we consider every node *cand*. If the node is still marked for exploration (Line 3), we construct a candidate conditional key, with the input conditions as condition part, and the properties in *cand.p* as the key part (Line 4). We then verify if the candidate key (a) meets the definition of a conditional key and (b) is minimal with respect to the other keys that have already been mined (Lines 5–6). If that is the case, the conditional key is added to the output (Line 7). If the key is a minimal key, then any extension of the key with more properties in the key part must be non-minimal and can safely be abandoned. Likewise, if the support of the candidate key is below the given threshold, so are its refinements. In both cases, we can prune the node and all descendants (Lines 8–11).

As an example, let us consider again the data from Table 1, with the condition *gender = Female* and the maximal non-key {*firstName, gender, lab, nationality*}. The corresponding conditional key graph after scanning the first level is shown in Fig. 2(a). Nodes with the *explore* flag set to false are greyed out. At the end of this step, only the property *firstName* is discovered as a key, since first names are unique among female researchers. It follows that nodes containing this property in the next levels of the graph define non-minimal keys. They are therefore discarded for further exploration (the *explore* flag is set to false). The search for conditional keys is then applied to the nodes on levels 2 and 3, for which the *explore* flag is still true.

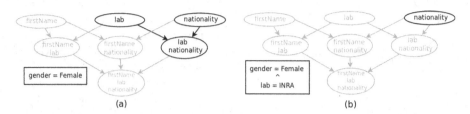

(a)   (b)

Fig. 2. (a) Keys of size 1 explored for the condition *gender* = *Female*. (b) Example of a merged graph with condition {*gender* = *Female*, *lab* = *INRA*}

Algorithm 3. MineGraph

Input: dataset $\mathcal{D}$, minimum support θ,
conditional key graph $\langle P^k, P^c, cond, G = (V, E)\rangle$,
set of conditional keys found so far CKs
Output: modified CKs

1 **for** $level = 1$ *to* $max_{v \in V}|v.p|$ **do**
2 ⎸ `for` $cand \in V$ *where* $|cand.p| = level$ **do**
3 ⎸ ⎸ **if** $cand.explore$ **then**
4 ⎸ ⎸ ⎸ $ck \leftarrow \langle cond, cand.p \rangle$
5 ⎸ ⎸ ⎸ $isMinimal \leftarrow ck$ is a minimal key w.r.t CKs
6 ⎸ ⎸ ⎸ **if** $isMinimal \wedge support(ck, \mathcal{D}) \geq \theta$ **then**
7 ⎸ ⎸ ⎸ ⎸ $CKs = CKs \cup \{ck\}$
8 ⎸ ⎸ ⎸ **if** $isMinimal \vee support(ck, \mathcal{D}) < \theta$ **then**
9 ⎸ ⎸ ⎸ ⎸ $cand.explore \leftarrow false$
10 ⎸ ⎸ ⎸ ⎸ **for** $child \in descendants(cand, G)$ **do**
11 ⎸ ⎸ ⎸ ⎸ ⎸ $child.explore \leftarrow false$

12 **return** CKs

Lemma 2 *(Graph Mining)*. *Given a conditional key graph $\langle P^k, P^c, cond, G \rangle$ for a dataset $\mathcal{D}$ and a threshold θ, Algorithm 3 will ensure that the result set CKs contains all minimal conditional keys for the condition set cond whose key properties are given by one of the nodes in G, and whose support is at least θ.*

This lemma holds because Algorithm 3 traverses all nodes in the conditional key graph, and checks each of them for being a conditional key. It excludes only (a) those nodes whose ancestors already had a support smaller than θ, in which case the node itself must also have a support smaller than θ, and (b) the nodes that lead to non-minimal keys.

Merging conditions. Let us now look at the process of generating more complex conditions (Line 8 in Algorithm 2). This work is done by Algorithm 4. It takes as input a set of conditional key graphs, a support threshold, a dataset, and a size parameter. It looks at all conditional key graphs that have a condition set of the given size (Lines 2–3). For each of them, it constructs a clone (Line 4). It then adds one more condition to the condition set of the clone. This new condition consists of a property and a constant (Sect. 3). The property is taken from a node of size 1 having its *explore* flag still set to true (Lines 5–6). The constant is taken from the constants that appear with that property in the conditional key graphs of size 1 (Line 9). If the new combined condition has a support that is large enough (Line 10), the conditional key graph of the singleton condition is merged with the clone and added to the output set.

Algorithm 4. newConditions

Input: size of condition set *size*
set of conditional key graphs $\mathcal{G}$
support threshold θ, dataset $\mathcal{D}$
Output: modified set of conditional key graphs $\mathcal{G}$
1 $\mathcal{G}_1 \leftarrow \{g \in \mathcal{G} : |g.cond| = 1\}$
2 $\mathcal{G}_{size} \leftarrow \{g \in \mathcal{G} : |g.cond| = size\}$
3 **for** $g \in \mathcal{G}_{size}$ **do**
4    $g \leftarrow clone(g)$
5   **for** $v \in g.V$ *where* $|g.V.p| = 1$ **do**
6   **if** $v.explore$ **then**
7          $v.explore \leftarrow false$
8   **for** $v' \in g.descendants(v)$ **do** $v'.explore \leftarrow false$
9   **for** $g_1 \in \mathcal{G}_1$ *where* $g_1.P^c = v.p$ **do**
10   **if** $support(g.cond \wedge g_1.cond, \mathcal{D}) \geq \theta$ **then** $\mathcal{G} \leftarrow \mathcal{G} \cup merge(g, g_1)$

11 **return** $\mathcal{G}$

The *merge* operation between two conditional key graphs $\langle P_1^k, P_1^c, cond_1, (V_1, E_1)\rangle$ and $\langle P_2^k, P_2^c, cond_2, (V_2, E_2)\rangle$ with $P_1^c \cap P_2^c = \emptyset$, produces a new conditional graph $\langle P^k, P^c, cond, (V, E)\rangle$ with:

- $P^k = P_1^k \cap P_2^k$ and $P^c = P_1^c \cup P_2^c$.
- $cond = cond_1 \cup cond_2$
- $V = \{\langle v.p, v.explore\rangle : \exists v_1 \in V_1, v_2 \in V_2 : v_1.p = v_2.p = v.p \ \wedge \ v.explore = (v_1.explore \wedge v_2.explore)\}$
- $E = \{u, v \in V : u.p \subset v.p \wedge |u.p| = |v.p| - 1\}$

As an example, Fig. 2(b) shows the conditional graph with the set of conditions $\{gender = Female, lab = INRA\}$ produced by Algorithm 4 from the conditional graphs with conditions $gender = Female$ and $lab = INRA$. This graph is a clone of the graph with the condition $gender = Female$. A node is marked to be explored only if it was marked to be explored in both of the original graphs.

Lemma 3 (New Conditions). *Given a dataset $\mathcal{D}$, a set of conditional key graphs $\mathcal{G}$, a size parameter size, and a threshold θ, Algorithm 4 produces all conditional key graphs that contain condition sets of size size+1. Each of those graphs contains all the conditional keys for the given condition.*

We can prove Lemma 3 by induction. For $size = 0$, Lemma 1 guarantees that Algorithm 4 starts with all conditional key graphs for conditions of size 1.

For $size > 0$, we need to show that (a) Algorithm 4 generates all conditional key graphs of size $size+1$ and (b) each of these graphs contains all minimal conditional keys for their condition.

We start by showing (b), that is, the merge operation between two conditional key graphs $G_1 = \langle P_1^k, P_1^c, cond_1, (V_1, E_1) \rangle$ and $G_2 = \langle P_2^k, P_2^c, cond_2, (V_2, E_2) \rangle$ does not skip any minimal conditional key for the new condition. There are only two ways a node can be excluded from exploration in the merge operation: (1) the node is explicitly marked for non-exploration and (2) the node does not occur in one of the conditional key graphs. Case (1) occurs when the corresponding nodes are below the support threshold θ or they define non-minimal keys. In Case (2), the claim follows from the fact that if a node v is not contained in one of the graphs (e.g., $v \notin V_1$), then $v.p \cup P_1^c$ must be a key, i.e., it is not contained in any maximal non-key. This rationale applies analogously if $v \notin V_2$.

To show (a) we need to prove that our conditions are complete and correct. To show completeness we observe that Algorithm 4 builds conditions with $|cond| = size + 1$ based on the complete set of conditions with $|cond| = size$ and $|cond| = 1$. From the monotonicity of support, it follows that all conditions with $|cond| = size + 1$ with support greater than θ can be computed from these sets. To show correctness we note that for each graph with condition $cond = \{p_1 = o_1, \ldots, p_{size} = o_{size}\}$ and key properties P^k, Algorithm 4 will merge the graph with all conditions of the form $p_{size} = o_{size}$ where $p_{size} \in P^k$ (conditions of size 1, Line 5). This will produce graphs with conditions of the form $\{p_1 = o_1, \ldots, p_{size-1} = o_{size-1}, p_{size} = o_{size}\}$ with key part $P^k \setminus \{p_{size}\}$ with support greater than θ. (a) follows from Observation 1, since we have just transferred a property from the key part to the condition part.

Theorem 1 *(Conditional Key Discovery). Given a dataset $\mathcal{D}$, a set of conditional key graphs $\mathcal{G}$, and a threshold θ, Algorithm 2 produces all conditional keys whose properties are a subset of the properties of any node in any graph in $\mathcal{G}$, whose conditions are built from conditions or properties in $\mathcal{G}$, and whose support is at least θ.*

This theorem follows from the fact that Algorithm 2 calls Algorithm 3 for all sizes between 1 and the maximal number of property combinations. Lemma 2 makes sure that all possible graphs are generated. Lemma 3 ensures that all possible combinations of conditions are treated.

Corollary 1 *(Conditional Key Mining). Our method for conditional key mining is complete and correct.*

The correctness follows from the fact that Algorithm 3 adds a new key if and only if it is a key (Line 5). The completeness follows from Observation 1 and Theorem 1.

4.4   Implementation

Our method, VICKEY, is implemented in Java 7. The conditional key graphs have large condition sets and large associated graphs. Therefore, we do not store the graphs in memory, but rather generate them on the fly when they are accessed [28]. Furthermore, we parallelize the algorithm: the set of input non-keys is split into batches containing up to 50 (potentially non-distinct) properties. The batches are then scheduled to threads in the system, each one running Algorithms 1 and 2. This may lead to mining the same non-key multiple times, and therefore we perform a de-duplication before reporting the final results.

5 Experiments

We evaluate VICKEY in two series of experiments. First, we show the ability of VICKEY to discover conditional keys in large datasets with millions of triples. We compare the runtime of VICKEY to a generic rule mining approach, AMIE [13]. Then, we evaluate the utility of conditional keys for the task of data linking. We compare the conditional keys mined by VICKEY to the classical keys mined by SAKey [27].

5.1 Runtime Experiments

Setting. To evaluate the performance of VICKEY and AMIE [13], we adapt AMIE to mine rules of the form: $P_c \land P_k \Rightarrow x = y$. Here, $P_c = \bigwedge_{1..n} pc_i(x, A_i) \land pc_i(y, A_i)$ corresponds to the condition part of a key expression, and $P_k = \bigwedge_{1..m} pk_i(x, u_i) \land pk_i(y, u_i)$ represents the key part. Both AMIE and VICKEY take as input a set of maximal non-keys. These non-keys are obtained from the input dataset using SAKey [27]. Like VICKEY, our adapted variant of AMIE uses the non-keys to restrict the search space by pruning the combinations of properties that do not occur in the non-keys. Unlike VICKEY, AMIE searches exhaustively for all rules that define conditional keys in the input dataset, regardless of their minimality. AMIE therefore requires a post-processing phase where all non-minimal conditional keys are removed. Both AMIE and VICKEY are run with a coverage threshold of 1%. We set the confidence threshold of AMIE to 100%, so that VICKEY and the modified AMIE mine exactly the same set of conditional keys. As datasets, we have used nine classes from DBpedia [18], covering different domains such as people, organizations, and locations. All experiments are run on a server with an AMD Opteron 6376 Processor (2.40 GHz), 8 cores, and 128 GB of RAM under Ubuntu Server 16.04.

Results. Our results are shown in Table 2. The first three columns show some statistics about the testing datasets, followed by the number of discovered non-keys (NKs), the runtimes of both VICKEY and AMIE and finally the number of obtained conditional keys (CKs). We observe that a generic rule mining solution cannot handle some of the input datasets in less than 1 day. VICKEY, in contrast, runs on the smaller datasets *Actor*, *Mountain*, *Museum* and *Scientist* in less than 1 h. This is because VICKEY's strategy prunes the search space much more effectively by avoiding candidate CKs that are not minimal. Other classes, such as *University* and *Organization*, are more challenging because they have many long non-keys (up to 15 properties). The longer the non-keys, the

Table 2. VICKEY vs AMIE on DBpedia

Class	Triples	Inst.	#Pro	#NKs	VICKEY	AMIE	#CKs
Actor	57.2k	5.8k	71	137	4.52 m	12.58 h	311
Album	786.1k	85.3k	39	68	1.53 h	3.90 h	304
Book	258.4k	30.0k	51	95	11.84 h	> 1 d	419
Film	832.1k	82.6k	74	132	1.37 h	3.64 h	185
Mount.	127.8k	16.4k	58	47	2.86 m	23.57 m	257
Museum	12.9k	1.9k	65	17	1.46 s	6.45 s	58
Organiz.	1.82M	178.7k	553	3221	26.32 h	> 36 h	28
Scientist	258.5k	19.7k	73	309	27.67 m	> 1 d	582
Univ.	85.8k	8.7k	89	140	14.45 h	> 1 d	941

Table 3. Linked classes stats

Class	#Pro	#Ks	#NKs	#CKs
Actor	16	93	22	748
Album	5	1	2	5864
Book	7	5	2	538
Film	9	14	13	26750
Mount	5	3	2	775
Museum	7	14	5	80
Organiz.	17	149	3	9737
Scientist	10	22	8	407
Univ.	9	5	5	449

larger the number of property combinations in the search space. For example, for the class *Album*, AMIE explores more than 12.3k rules (including intermediate rules), where 6.4k rules correspond to potential conditional keys. In contrast, VICKEY explores only 4.1k candidates. This shows that VICKEY's strategy indeed prunes the search space much more effectively. It can mine conditional keys on hundreds of thousands of facts in a matter of minutes.

5.2 Extrinsic Evaluation

Setting. One of the primary application areas of keys is the discovery of equivalent entities across two KBs: If some combination of properties is a key, and if an entity in one KB shares values of these properties with an entity in the other KB, then the two entities must be the same. In this section we investigate the performance of conditional keys with respect to classical keys for this task. We emphasize that entity linking is not the primary goal of this paper. Instead, we want to show the potential of conditional keys, introduced in this paper, over classical keys introduced by other approaches such as SAKey [27]. Entity linking is only an example setting to this end.

As KBs, we chose DBpedia [18] and YAGO [26], because there is a gold standard available for the entity links on the YAGO Web page. We have used the same set of classes as for the runtime experiments. As this type of entity linking assumes that the properties have been aligned, we mapped the properties of these classes manually, and rewrote the properties of YAGO using its DBpedia counterparts. We ran SAKey [27] and VICKEY on DBpedia to find standard and conditional keys, respectively. Table 3 shows the number of common properties, the number of keys (Ks), non-keys (NKs) and conditional keys (CKs) in each DBpedia class. Among others, VICKEY finds that *motto* is a key for universities in Italy and some other countries – but not in all countries; and that the name is a key for organizations in certain places – but not all places. To link the datasets, we use a simple algorithm [27]: For each key, we iterate over the entities in DBpedia that have the key properties. If there is an entity in YAGO that shares at least one value for every of these properties, we link the two. For conditional keys, we also check whether the conditions of the key are fulfilled in both datasets.

Table 4. Linking results with classical keys (Ks), conditional keys (CKs), and both.

Class		Recall	Precision	F1	
Actor	Ks [27]	0.27	0.99	0.43	
	CKs	0.57	0.99	0.73	× 1.75
	Ks+CKs	0.60	0.99	**0.75**	
Album	Ks [27]	0.00	1	**0.00**	
	CKs	0.15	0.99	0.26	× 869
	Ks+CKs	0.15	0.99	**0.26**	
Book	Ks [27]	0.03	1	**0.06**	
	CKs	0.11	0.99	0.20	× 3.48
	Ks+CKs	0.13	0.99	**0.23**	
Film	Ks [27]	0.04	0.99	**0.08**	
	CKs	0.38	0.96	0.54	× 7.1
	Ks+CKs	0.39	0.98	**0.55**	
Mountain	Ks [27]	0.00	1	**0.00**	
	CKs	0.28	0.99	0.44	× 101
	Ks+CKs	0.29	0.99	**0.45**	
Museum	Ks [27]	0.12	1	**0.21**	
	CKs	0.25	1	0.40	× 2.19
	Ks+CKs	0.31	1	**0.47**	
Organization	Ks [27]	0.01	1	**0.02**	
	CKs	0.14	0.98	0.24	× 11
	Ks+CKs	0.14	0.99	**0.24**	
Scientist	Ks [27]	0.05	0.98	**0.11**	
	CKs	0.16	0.99	0.28	× 2.96
	Ks+CKs	0.19	0.99	**0.32**	
University	Ks [27]	0.09	0.99	**0.16**	
	CKs	0.22	0.99	0.36	× 2.44
	Ks+CKs	0.25	0.99	**0.40**	

Results. Table 4 shows the precision, recall and F1 measure of the entity linking task using (a) classical keys mined by SAKey [27], (b) conditional keys alone and (c) both types of keys (VICKEY). We first observe that the precision is always over 98%. Conversely, the recall is low in some cases. This happens mainly due to our simple linking method, which uses a strict string equality when comparing the values of properties, and also due to the incompleteness of the data in both YAGO and DBpedia. However, even with this simple method, the use of conditional keys can lead to a significant increase in recall – with a negligible impact on precision. For example, for the class *Film*, recall increases from 4% to 38% when conditional keys are considered. Furthermore, when combining classic keys and conditional keys, the recall improves further. Overall, we observe an average increase of 21% points in recall, and of 29 points in F1 when both standard keys and conditional keys are used to link the data. The average drop in precision is only 0.5% points. This shows that conditional keys can significantly increase the performance of entity linking.

6   Conclusion

We have presented VICKEY, an approach to mine conditional keys on knowledge bases. Our approach overcomes the complexity of the search space by restricting it to the non-keys found by SAKey [27], and by pruning it smartly. This allows VICKEY to mine minimal conditional keys in datasets of up to 1.8M triples.

In an extrinsic evaluation, we have shown that conditional keys can increase the recall of entity linking by up to 34% points. As future work we plan to extend VICKEY by exploiting ontological classes and axioms, to discover more expressive conditional keys. The VICKEY system, as well as the datasets and evaluations, are available at https://github.com/lgalarra/vickey.

Acknowledgments. This research was supported by the grants ANR-11-LABEX-0045-DIGICOSME and ANR-16-CE23-0007-01 ("DICOS"), by the Chair "Machine Learning for Big Data" of Télécom ParisTech, and by the AGINFRA+ project (Grant Agreement no. 731001).

References

1. Al-Bakri, M., Atencia, M., David, J., Lalande, S., Rousset, M.-C.: Uncertainty-sensitive reasoning for inferring sameAs facts in linked data. In: ECAI (2016)
2. Atencia, M., Chein, M., Croitoru, M., David, J., Leclère, M., Pernelle, N., Saïs, F., Scharffe, F., Symeonidou, D.: Defining key semantics for the RDF datasets: experiments and evaluations. In: Hernandez, N., Jäschke, R., Croitoru, M. (eds.) ICCS 2014. LNCS, vol. 8577, pp. 65–78. Springer, Cham (2014). doi:10.1007/978-3-319-08389-6_7
3. Atencia, M., David, J., Euzenat, J.: Data interlinking through robust linkkey extraction. In: ECAI, Czech Republic (2014)
4. Atencia, M., David, J., Scharffe, F.: Keys and pseudo-keys detection for web datasets cleansing and interlinking. In: ten Teije, A., Völker, J., Handschuh, S., Stuckenschmidt, H., d'Acquin, M., Nikolov, A., Aussenac-Gilles, N., Hernandez, N. (eds.) EKAW 2012. LNCS, vol. 7603, pp. 144–153. Springer, Heidelberg (2012). doi:10.1007/978-3-642-33876-2_14
5. Chen, Y., Goldberg, S.L., Wang, D.Z., Johri, S.S.: Ontological pathfinding. In: SIGMOD (2016)
6. Chiang, F., Miller, R.J.: Discovering data quality rules. In: VLDB (2008)
7. Dong, X., Gabrilovich, E., Heitz, G., Horn, W., Lao, N., Murphy, K., Strohmann, T., Sun, S., Zhang, W.: Knowledge vault: a web-scale approach to probabilistic knowledge fusion. In: KDD (2014)
8. Dong, X.L., Gabrilovich, E., Heitz, G., Horn, W., Murphy, K., Sun, S., Zhang, W.: From data fusion to knowledge fusion, In: VLDB (2014)
9. Fan, W., Fan, Z., Tian, C., Dong, X.L.: Keys for graphs. In: VLDB (2015)
10. Fan, W., Geerts, F., Li, J., Xiong, M.: Discovering conditional functional dependencies. IEEE Trans. Knowl. Data Eng. **23**, 683–698 (2011)
11. Gad-Elrab, M.H., Stepanova, D., Urbani, J., Weikum, G.: Exception-enriched rule learning from knowledge graphs. In: Groth, P., Simperl, E., Gray, A., Sabou, M., Krötzsch, M., Lecue, F., Flöck, F., Gil, Y. (eds.) ISWC 2016. LNCS, vol. 9981, pp. 234–251. Springer, Cham (2016). doi:10.1007/978-3-319-46523-4_15
12. Galarraga, L., Razniewski, S., Amarilli, A., Suchanek, F.M.: Predicting completeness in knowledge bases. In: WSDM (2017)
13. Galárraga, L., Teflioudi, C., Hose, K., Suchanek, F.M.: AMIE: association rule mining under incomplete evidence in ontological knowledge bases. In: WWW (2013)
14. Galárraga, L., Teflioudi, C., Hose, K., Suchanek, F.M.: Fast rule mining in ontological knowledge bases with AMIE+. VLDB J. **24**(6), 707–730 (2015)

15. Golab, L., Karloff, H., Korn, F., Srivastava, D., Yu, B.: On generating near-optimal tableaux for conditional functional dependencies. VLDB **1**, 376–390 (2008)
16. Heise, A., Quiane-Ruiz, J.-A., Abedjan, Z., Jentzsch, A., Naumann, F.: Scalable discovery of unique column combinations. In: VLDB (2013)
17. Huhtala, Y., Kärkkäinen, J., Porkka, P., Toivonen, H.: TANE: an efficient algorithm for discovering functional and approximate dependencies. Comput. J. **42**(2), 100–111 (1999)
18. Lehmann, J., Isele, R., Jakob, M., Jentzsch, A., Kontokostas, D., Mendes, P.N., Hellmann, S., Morsey, M., van Kleef, P., Auer, S., Bizer, C.: DBpedia - a large-scale, multilingual knowledge base extracted from wikipedia. Semant. Web J. **6**(2), 167–195 (2015)
19. Manola, F., Miller, E.: RDF primer. W3C recommendation. W3C, February 2004. http://www.w3.org/TR/2004/REC-rdf-primer-20040210/
20. Patel-Schneider, P., Parsia, B., Rudolph, S., Krötzsch, M., Hitzler, P.: OWL 2 web ontology language primer. W3C recommendation. W3C, October 2009. http://www.w3.org/TR/2009/REC-owl2-primer-20091027/
21. Pernelle, N., Saïs, F., Symeonidou, D.: An automatic key discovery approach for data linking. J. Web Semant. **23**, 16–30 (2013)
22. Preda, N., Kasneci, G., Suchanek, F.M., Neumann, T., Yuan, W., Weikum, G.: Active knowledge: dynamically enriching RDF knowledge bases by web services. In: SIGMOD (2010)
23. Saïs, F., Pernelle, N., Rousset, M.C.: Combining a logical and a numerical method for data reconciliation. J. Data Semant. **12**, 69–94 (2009)
24. Sismanis, Y., Brown, P., Haas, P.J., Reinwald, B.: GORDIAN: efficient and scalable discovery of composite keys. In: VLDB (2006)
25. Soru, T., Marx, E., Ngonga Ngomo, A.-C.: ROCKER: a refinement operator for key discovery. In: WWW (2015)
26. Suchanek, F.M., Kasneci, G., Weikum, G.: Yago: a core of semantic knowledge. In: WWW (2007)
27. Symeonidou, D., Armant, V., Pernelle, N., Saïs, F.: SAKey: scalable almost key discovery in RDF data. In: Mika, P., et al. (eds.) ISWC 2014. LNCS, vol. 8796, pp. 33–49. Springer, Cham (2014). doi:10.1007/978-3-319-11964-9_3
28. Symeonidou, D., Galarrága, L., Pernelle, N., Saïs, F., Suchanek, F.: VICKEY: mining conditional keys on RDF datasets. Technical report (2017). https://doi.org/10.5281/zenodo.835647
29. Vrandečić, D., Krötzsch, M.: Wikidata: a free collaborative knowledgebase. Commun. ACM **57**(10), 78–85 (2014)

Ontolex JeuxDeMots and Its Alignment to the Linguistic Linked Open Data Cloud

Andon Tchechmedjiev$^{(\boxtimes)}$, Théophile Mandon, Mathieu Lafourcade,
Anne Laurent, and Konstantin Todorov

University of Montpellier / LIRMM, Montpellier, France
{andon.tchechmedjiev,theophile.mandon,mathieu.lafourcade,
anne.laurent,konstantin.todorov}@lirmm.fr

Abstract. JeuxDeMots (JdM) is a rich collaborative lexical network in French, built on a crowdsourcing principle as a game with a purpose, represented in an ad-hoc tabular format. In the interest of reuse and interoperability, we propose a conversion algorithm for JdM following the Ontolex model, along with a word sense alignment algorithm, called JdMBabelizer, that anchors JdM sense-refinements to synsets in the *lemon* edition of BabelNet and thus to the Linguistic Linked Open Data cloud. Our alignment algorithm exploits the richness of JdM in terms of weighted semantic-lexical relations—particularly the inhibition relation between senses—that are specific to JdM. We produce a reference alignment dataset for JdM and BabelNet that we use to evaluate the quality of our algorithm and that we make available to the community. The obtained results are comparable to those of state of the art approaches.

Keywords: LLOD · Lexical resources · Lexical data linking · Ontolex · JdM

1 Introduction

The availability of large lexical-semantic resources (LSRs) is of central importance for a variety of natural language processing and semantic web applications. The lack of interoperability between these resources, as well as their limited coverage—most world languages are under-resourced to date—have been a significant hindrance to progress in the field.

JeuxDeMots (JdM) [1] is a collaborative lexical network of French terms built on a crowdsourcing principle as a game with a purpose (GWAP). JdM is very successful and has currently produced a network of over 1 million terms, more than 75 million relations of around 100 types, and around 70,000 word senses for polysemous entries. Beyond its importance for French, JdM is a generic platform that can be adapted to other languages that critically require the production of LSRs. It is, therefore, an effective answer to the knowledge acquisition bottleneck.

C. d'Amato et al. (Eds.): ISWC 2017, Part I, LNCS 10587, pp. 678–693, 2017.
DOI: 10.1007/978-3-319-68288-4_40

However, JdM uses an ad-hoc tabulated data format, with a custom representation formalism that is different from typical (lexical architecture as opposed to cognitive architecture) LSRs. Therefore, using JdM in conjunction with other resources is non-trivial and both JdM and its applications would benefit from being made interoperable.

With the advent of semantic web technologies, the Linguistic Linked Open Data (LLOD) [2], based on the *lemon* and Ontolex ontologies, is becoming a *de facto* standard for the access, interoperability and interlinking of language resources. Major state of the art LSRs such as BabelNet [3], Uby [4], many WordNets and DBnary [5] now exist as *lemon*/Ontolex[1] together with numerous alignments to other LSR datasets from the LLOD cloud.[2]

In light of the above, we address the problem of converting the JdM model to Ontolex and aligning it to the LLOD cloud. We use the core Ontolex model to represent entries and sense refinements (word senses), and the vartrans module of Ontolex to represent lexical and sense relations, to which we add a custom weight property. Given that JdM senses do not possess definitions (only word associations), linking JdM to another resource from the LLOD that is rich in definitions, would allow us to project the definitions back to JdM so as to enrich the network. We chose BabelNet as a target for the alignment as there already exist alignments between JdM and BabelNet at the lexical entry level. Additionally, BabelNet is one of largest resources on the LLOD cloud, possessing rich sense definitions. Given the structures of JdM and BabelNet, we developed a Word Sense Alignment (WSA) algorithm that we called JdMBabelizer, using a threshold decision criterion based on a weighted Lesk overlap similarity, where the weights of JdM relations and the normalized relative word frequencies of BabelNet definitions are taken into account. The proposed method is generic and language agnostic. Beyond its application to the data of the French lexical network, it can be seamlessly applied to editions of JdM in any other language. Thus, we enable the production of LLOD resources for languages such as Khmer, Thaï, Bangali, and Comorian, for which the JdM GWAP model has already been used.[3]

For the purpose of evaluating the JdMBabelizer algorithm, we construct a custom reference dataset by adding an innovate feature: we propose a crowd-sourced gamified dataset creation, which considerably lowers the annotation burden. We make this benchmark dataset available to the community.

In the remainder of the paper, we first present JdM in detail followed by a related work review pertaining to the conversion of LSRs to *lemon*/Ontolex and to WSA techniques in the context of linking resources in the LLOD. Subsequently, we present the extended JdM/Ontolex model and the conversion algorithm, followed by a presentation of the WSA techniques applied. Before concluding, we evaluate the alignment with the help of our benchmark dataset.

---

[1] An exhaustive list of *lemon* resources: https://datahub.io/dataset?tags=lemon.

[2] http://linguistic-lod.org/llod-cloud.

[3] http://jeuxdemots.liglab.fr.

2   JeuxDeMots: A Lexical Network

JeuxDeMots[4] (*Eng., word plays*) is a large lexical-semantic network, composed of terms (nodes) and typed, weighted and possibly annotated relations [1]. It contains term refinements (acceptations or word-senses), organized hierarchically (senses can have sub-senses). By May 15, 2017, it consists of roughly $75,799,080$ relations between $1,058,530$ nodes. Around $26,000$ polysemous terms are refined into $71,276$ word senses (or related usages for some domains). More than $800,000$ relations have negative weights and can be used as inhibitory relations. JdM contains links to DBnary and BabelNet at the word-level (words with the same canonical form). However, few alignments exist at the sense-level, although a dedicated tool allows the JdM players to refine word-level alignments.

2.1   Construction of JdM

JdM is a two player GWAP, allowing to *earn* and *collect* words. It has the following driving mechanics. (**1.**) The system (S) or a challenger (C) picks a term (T) that is offered to a player (A) along with a particular relation (R) from a manually curated list of relations (synonymy, antonymy, etc.) The system only chooses from existing terms, while challengers can offer new ones. (**2.**) Player A has a limited amount of time to enter terms which, to her/his mind, are related to T via R. The term T, along with the same set of instructions, will be later given to another player, say B, with an identical protocol for consolidation. The two players score points for words they both choose. The more "original" the proposition given by both players, the higher the reward. (**3.**) For a term offered to the players, answers in common from both A and B are inserted to the database (if the contributed terms are new, the term and a new relation instance are created with a weight of 1, otherwise the existing weights are incremented). Answers given by only one of the players are not considered, which reduces noise.

The network is constructed by connecting terms by typed and weighted relations, validated by pairs of players. Several other games complement the main JdM game.[5] Their purpose is to cross validate information collected in the main game, or to accelerate the relation harvesting for specific relation types.

2.2   Relations

An instance of each JdM relation links two particular nodes and has an associated weight. Relations can link nodes of any type. Even word-senses are defined as regular nodes that are linked to their corresponding entry by a particular type of refinement relation. Some lexical functions such as Magn and antiMagn[6] are represented as associative relations as well as predicative relations and can be

---

[4] http://www.jeuxdemots.org.

[5] http://imaginat.name/JDM/Page_Liens_JDMv1.html.

[6] Magn. for *Magnification* and antiMagn. the inverse relation: e.g. Magn(big)=huge, Magn(smoker)=heavy smoker, antiMagn(big)=small.

in a sense equated to semantic frames. Although they represent the same type of information, they are encoded following the principles of the Meaning Text Theory (MTT) by Mel'čuk [6], rather than the semantic frame formalism (a conversion is non-trivial). The relations are not bound to grammatical categories (part of speech tags): grammatical categories are represented as separate nodes and linked to term (lexeme) nodes. The relations of JdM fall into one of the following categories.

- *Lexical relations:* synonymy, antonymy, expression, lexical family. This type of relations is about vocabulary and lexicalization.
- *Ontological relations:* hyperonymy, hyponymy, meronymy, holonymy, matter/substance, instances (named entities), typical location, characteristics and relevant properties, etc. These relations concern knowledge about world objects.
- *Associative relations:* free associations of feelings, meanings, similar objects, intensity (Magn and antiMagn). These relations are rather about subjective and global knowledge; some of them can be considered as phrasal associations.
- *Predicative relations:* typical agent, patient, instrument, or location of the action, typical manner, cause, or consequence. These relations are associated to a verb (or action noun) and to the values of its arguments (in a very wide sense).

Refinements. Word senses (or acceptations) of a given term node T (equivalent to a lexical entry) are represented as $T>gloss_1$, $T>gloss_2$, ..., $T>gloss_n$ nodes linked to the term node through REFINE(ment) relations. Glosses (following the lexicographical definition of gloss) are textual *annotations* that evoke the meaning of term T. For example, consider the French term *frégate (Eng., frigate)*. A frigate can be a ship or a bird (both English and French have the same ambiguity), and as a ship it can either be ancient (with sails) or modern (with missiles) (cf. upper part of Fig. 1 for an exmaple). Word refinements are structured, which, contrarily to a flat set of word meanings, has advantages for lexical disambiguation. Monosemous words do not have refinements as the term itself represents its only sense and requires no clarification.

Free Associations. The most common relation in the network, accounting for over 26% of all relations, is the free association relation (ASSOC), which for a given node provides cognitively related terms (mental associations). We make use of this relation to align JdM to other resources, as the terms related to a refinement through ASSOC form a sort of synset of words that allow humans to discriminate that particular meaning of the word and can thus be used as a substitution for definitions when overlap-based similarity measures are applied.

Inhibitory Relations. An inhibitory relation discriminates a specific refinement R_E of a top-level term E (equivalent to a lexeme/lexical entry) from another term T. Such a relation models the fact that if the term T negatively related to the R_E sense of E, appears in the same context as E (e.g. same sentence), then R_E is probably not the right sense for E in this context (relations of this type are extremely useful for Word Sense Disambiguation). Generally speaking, any relation between the refinement of a term and another term with a negative weight is inhibitory proportionally to its weight. However, there is also an explicit INHIB relation type, which indicates that the presence of the related term T formally implies (with absolute certainty) that E cannot be in its R_E sense in that particular context. INHIB relations are computed automatically through the application of the following rule: $\forall E \; \exists T, R_{E,1}, R_{E,2}$: REFINE$(E, R_{E,1}) \wedge$ REFINE$(E, R_{E,2}) \wedge$ ASSOC$(R_{E,1}, T) \wedge \nexists$ ASSOC$(R_{E,2}, T) \Rightarrow$ INHIB$(T, R_{E,2})$. If the entry term E has at least two refinements, $R_{E,1}$ and $R_{E,2}$, and if the first refinement is associated to a term T but not the second one, then T inhibits the second refinement.

3   Related Work

Since the very early years of the web data field, rich LSRs have been called upon to provide robust semantic similarity measures [7], to assist ontology matching and link discovery across highly heterogeneous and multilingual datasets [8,9], or to facilitate automatic question answering on large RDF graphs [10]. A crucial requirement to enable these applicatons is that these resources are interoperable. In this section, we focus on the conversion of LSRs to RDF Ontolex and their interlinking on the web of data.

3.1   The Ontolex Model

Ontolex has emerged as a standard for representing lexical data on the web. It builds around the core model of its predecessor *lemon*, introduced by McCrae, Aguado-de-Cea, Buitelaar, *et al.* [11] to represent LSRs and their alignments with ontologies (OWL) and terminologies (SKOS), inspired by the LMF ISO-24613:2008 standard [12]. Ontolex adds modules for the representation of various linguistic phenomena and features (Syntax and Semantics, Decomposition, Variation and Translation, Linguistic Metadata, Linguistic Description, Lexical Networks).

For the representation of the JdM data, we are concerned with the use of the core model together with the Variational Translation (vartrans) module.[7] The main classes of the Ontolex core model include `LexicalEntry` and `LexicalSense`, the former representing the entry point into the resource (lemmatized words, affixes or multi-word expressions) and the latter representing word senses or semantic refinements associated to lexical entries. The `LexicalConcept` class allows to represent concepts lexicalised by a set of lexical senses and is a subclass of `skos:Concept`. The synsets in cognitive architecture LSRs (WordNet and derivatives, including BabelNet) would typically be represented by lexical concepts in Ontolex. The core model does not include the notion of lexical-semantic relations and we have to turn to the vartrans module to represent relations from

---

[7] https://www.w3.org/community/ontolex/wiki/Final_Model_Specification.

resources such as BabelNet or JdM, through the reified `SenseRelation` class. Although `SenseRelation` does not have a weight data property, it is trivial to add one for the purpose of modeling the weights in JDM, for example.

Ontolex uses the `Form` class to describe the forms and representations of a `LexicalEntry`. Each lexical entry should have a canonical form, which is the lemmatisation of the term, and possibly other forms if any exist (e.g. morphological variants). Each form has a written representation datatype property that contains the terms. The linguistic meta-data module of Ontolex allows to encode useful information pertaining to lexical datasets, such as the language of lexical elements. The decomposition of multi-word expressions with relation to atomic lexical entries can be represented using the Decomposition module.

3.2   Converting Lexical Resources to Ontolex

Multiple LSRs built by professional linguists from scratch or by extending already exiting web resources have been successfully represented using lemon and its successor Ontolex, including Panlex [13], Parole [14], UBY [15], Eurosentiment [16] and Framebase [17]. In what follows, we focus on the main LSRs used in the web data field.

The well-known lexical database WordNet is composed of groups of quasi-synonyms called *synsets* with lexical relations linking synsets or words together. However, since the *lemon* model does not allow to represent synsets, in the *lemon* version of WordNet they have been represented as subclasses of `skos:Concept` linked to senses with the `lemon:reference` property [18]. Relations have been represented in the same way as in *lemon*UBY. Note that Ontolex now offers lexical concepts to represent synsets, while the vartrans module allows to describe relations directly (without using external vocabularies).

BabelNet [3], another well-established multilingual LSR, combines WordNet with Wikipedia (exploiting the multilingual information) and other resources (OmegaWiki, OpenMultilingualWordNet, etc.). Definitions in all languages are enriched through a machine translation of English definitions. The conversion of BabelNet to *lemon* [19] follows the same principle as that of WordNet, using the *lemon* vocabulary where possible along with other ontologies (*lime*, *lexvo*). The only custom class that had to be created in the conversion process is `BabelGloss`, representing the glosses bound to synsets.

Note that, unlike WordNet or BabelNet, JdM is created in a collaborative manner. Therefore, we pay close attention to DBnary [5], a LSR first modeled in lemon with custom properties, as it is also based on a collaborative resource (Wiktionary). We adopt a similar approach in the conversion of JdM to Ontolex and its alignment to the LLOD.

3.3   Word Sense Alignment Techniques for the LLOD Cloud

Although the LLOD cloud contains datasets represented as RDF graphs using the Ontolex ontology, aligning these resources is a substantially different problem as compared to standard data linking tasks on the larger LOD cloud. The problem we face here is that of aligning LSRs at the word sense level, known as Word Sense Alignment. Most linked resources in the LLOD cloud are aligned using techniques that are not specific to the LOD representation of the data, but to the pair of resources being aligned: there are no LOD specific algorithms for WSA.

WSA techniques use similarity between senses as a proxy for semantic equivalence across resources. The decision of whether to align two senses usually depends on an empirically determined threshold [20]. There are three main types of similarity computation approaches: lexical, structural, and hybrid. The field being vast, we only give several recent examples of applications relevant to this work. We refer the interested reader to [21].

Lexical similarity techniques exploit textual descriptions of lexical semantic elements (e.g. glosses or definitions) in LSRs. This is the most popular approach to WSA, as there are often definitions or some form of textual descriptions of senses in traditional LSRs (dictionaries). In recent applications, lexical similarity techniques have been applied (non exhaustively) to align the following resources (we provide the measures used and their performances in terms of precision (P), recall (R), F-score (F1) and accuracy(A) in brackets): Wiktionary and OmegaWiki (Personalized Page Rank (PPR) + Cosine (Cos) similarity, P 0.68, R 0.65, F1 0.66, A 0.78) [22]; WordNet and Wiktionary (PPR + Cos, P 0.67, R 0.64, F 0.66, A 0.91) [20]; GermaNet with Wiktionary (Lesk overlap measure, F1 0.84, A 0.91) [23]. Among the above-mentioned alignments, the most relevant to the present work is that of [23], as the authors apply an overlap-based measure using definitions. Moreover, one of their goals is to provide definitions to GermaNet from Wiktionary based on a projection through the alignments. Although the resources do not directly use lexical-semantic relations, these relations are present on Wiktionary pages and used to obtain extended textual representations for Wiktionary senses.

Structural similarity approaches exploit the topography of the graphs of the resources to determine whether two items should be aligned, by using classical graph search approaches and combinatorial graph metrics (path length, degrees, cycles, etc.). SSI-Dijkstra+ [24] has been applied to align WordNet and FrameNet (P 0.79, R 0.74, F1 0.75), while Dijkstra-WSA [22] — to align WordNet with Wikipedia (P 0.75, R 0.87, F1 0.81, A 0.95), as well as WordNet with Wiktionary (P 0.68, R 0.71, F1 0.69, A 0.92).

From a more general point of view, lexical and structural approaches can be combined in a *hybrid similarity framework*, by producing semantic signatures that include both definition-based and structural semantic information, normalized to live in the same space. This is the approach used to build resources such as BabelNet [3] or OpenMultilingualWordnet [25], formalized in an unified manner by [26]. The framework remains the same for any resource pair and only the construction of the semantic signatures differs. Our extended overlap measure also enters in this category, as we create weighted bags of words (signatures) that contain words from definitions in BabelNet, related terms in JdM and the weights on relations from both resources.

The evaluation of the alignment of resources is tricky, because the reference data must be specific to each pair. Additionally, parameters that work for one pair, rarely generalize well to others. The standard approach in the domain is to either use an existing dataset to realign resources that are already aligned, or manually produce an evaluation dataset from a sample of representative entries. We follow the latter approach, producing benchmark data in a novel crowd-sourced game-based manner.

4   Producing Ontolex JeuxDeMots

Let us describe the conversion of the JdM tabulated (relational) model to Ontolex.

Core Model. The main elements in the core Ontolex model are lexical entries and lexical senses. We first identify corresponding elements in JdM. All nodes that are sources of a REFINE relation became lexical entries[8] and all nodes that are its targets became lexical senses.[9] We link corresponding lexical senses to their lexical entries and create `ontolex:Form` instances as needed to represent the canonical forms of the lexical entries.[10] A custom `jdm:id` datatype property contains the original JdM node id. Note that the hierarchical sense distinctions of JdM cannot be directly represented in Ontolex. We, therefore, do not represent sub-senses in the Ontolex model, only keeping the first level (cf. Figure 1). For each lexical sense we create a lexical concept with a `lexinfo:gloss` property that contains the gloss from the JdM refinement/sense node (it will be enriched with `skos:definition` in future work). For each ASSOC relation leaving from JdM refinement/sense nodes, the lexical concept that corresponds to that sense node is linked to the lexical entries of the corresponding words though the

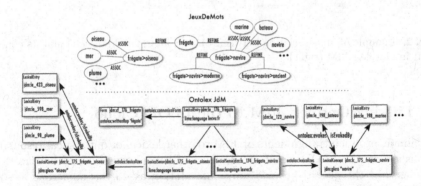

Fig. 1. An example of the conversion of term nodes and refinements to the Ontolex core model for the term *frigate*. Only first level senses are kept.

---

[8] URI scheme *jdm:le_term*, where term is the canonical form of the term node.

[9] URI scheme *jdm:ls_term_gloss*, where gloss is the gloss of the refinement node.

[10] URI scheme *jdm:cf_term*, where term is the canonical form of the term node.

`ontolex:evokes/ontolex:isEvokedBy` property. In JdM, parts of speech are represented as POS nodes linked to terms. We retrieve the POS nodes for each lexical entry and add the `lexinfo:partOfSpeech` property.

Relations and Vartrans. What remains to be modeled are the numerous specific relations found in JdM, from which we exclude relations encoding structural information, used in the previous section. For that task, we turn to the vartrans module of Ontolex. Each relation is represented as a sublcass of `ontolex:LexicalRelation` and/or `ontolex:SenseRelation` as there are relations at both levels.[11] Where possible, we also made the relations sub-classes of existing relations in DBnary or in SKOS (OWL allows multiple inheritance). We added a custom `jdm:weight` datatype property to relation instances to represent `jdm:weights`.[12] The ASSOC relations are represented by `ontolex:evokes` and `ontolex:isEvokedBy` but also have weights, which cannot be represented by `ontolex:LexicalRelation` nor by `ontolex:SenseRelation`. We reify the `ontolex:evokes/isEvokedBy` as a sub-class of `ontolex:LexicoSemanticRelation` directly, as the source and targets can be `LexicalSense/LexicalEntry` or the reverse. We also represent weights by the `jdm:weight` relation. Figure 2 illustrates how a lexical relation is represented in the original JdM data and in its Ontolex version. We make the converted JdM data available.[13]

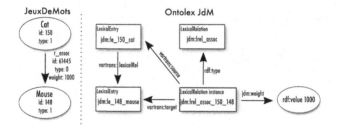

Fig. 2. Example of an association between *cat* and *mouse* in JdM (left) and its equivalent in Ontolex JdM (right).

5   Linking Ontolex JdM to the LLOD Cloud

We aim at producing alignments of JdM to other lexical or ontological resources published on the LLOD cloud at the level of lexical senses. JdM has no definitions, but the glosses provide some information as do the numerous ASSOC links that evoke the lexical senses. We can thus produce textual descriptions that capture the semantics of the lexical senses that can be used for WSA.

---

[11] URI scheme: *jdm:lr_relname* or *jdm:sr_relname*.

[12] URI scheme of relation instances: *lri_sourcenodeid_targetnodeid* or *sri_sourcenodeid_targetnodeid*.

[13] https://tinyurl.com/jdmbabelnetbench.

Algorithm 1. JdMBabelizer: the JdM/BabelNet alignment algorithm

function JDMBABELIZER(jdmLE, bnLE, inhib={None/Vt/Wgt}, θ)
2:     $alignedPairs \leftarrow \emptyset$
    for all $jdmS \in Senses(jdmLE)$ **do**
4:        **for all** $bnS \in Senses(bnLE)$ **do**
            $bnSig \leftarrow \emptyset$
6:            $AddToSig(bnSig, Words\{Def(bnS)\}, w = 1.5)$
            $AddToSig(bnSig, Lemma\{Senses(Synset(bnS))\}w = 2.0)$
8:            $AddToSig(bnSig, BibTaxonomy(bnS), updtW = 1.5)$
            $AddToSig(bnSig, Words\{Examples\{bnS\}\}, w = 0.75)$
10:            $jdmSig \leftarrow \emptyset$
            for all $evokedLe \in EvokedBy(jdmS)$ **do**
12:                $AddToSig(jdmSig, \{WrRep(evokeLe)\},$
                        $w = rWeight(jdmS, evokedLe))$
14:            **end for**
                                    ▷ Weight-based inhibition strategy
16:            **if** $inhib = Wgt$ **then**
                for all $inhibLe \in Inhib(jdmS)$ **do**
18:                    ▷ Adding term to signature with the largest negative weight
                    $AddToSig(jdmSig, \{CanWrRep(inhibLe)\}, w = -1000)$
20:                **end for**
            end if
22:                ▷ If there isn't an inhibition while in veto mode, we continue
                                ▷ Otherwise, we *veto* this pair of senses
24:            **if** $inhib \neq Vt \vee \nexists t \in bnSig \cap jdmSig : WrRep(Inhib(jdmS) = t)$ **then**
                $score \leftarrow 0$
26:                **for all** $\forall bnSigEl, jdmSigEl \in words(jdmSig) \cup words(bnSig)$ **do**
                    $score \leftarrow score + weight(bnSigEl) \times weight(jdmSigEl)$
28:                **end for**
                if $score > \theta$ **then**
30:                    $CreateAlignement(jdmS, bnS)$
                end if
32:            **end if**
        end for
34:    **end for**
end function

JdM already contains alignments at the lexical entry level to other LSRs (DBpedia, DBnary, BabelNet) and to certain medical ontologies (Radlex, UMLS) through ad-hoc approaches and in ad-hoc formats that are not interoperable with the LLOD cloud. We may thus reuse the alignments as a starting point to align the resources at the lexical sense level through explicit RDF statements so as to include JdM in the LLOD cloud.

As a first step, we endeavour to align JdM to BabelNet, as BabelNet has rich definitions in several languages, that we could project back unto JdM through the alignment. We start off at entry level alignments and then compare all (BabelSense, JdM LexicalSense) pairs to find the ones that are most likely to be equivalent. Algorithm 1, named JdMBabelizer, details the process, roughly following the approach formulated by Pilehvar and Navigli [26].

For each of the pairs, we create a weighted bag-of-words semantic signature for the BabelNet sense and another for the JdM sense. For the BabelNet sense, we build the signature from the words of the definition, the lemmas of the other senses corresponding to the synset of the sense, the category names from the the Wikipedia Bitaxonomy [27] and the words from the examples. We keep only unique words and increment the weight associated to each word (+1.5 if the word comes from a definition, +2.0 if the word comes from the lemmas of the synset senses, +1.5 for BibTaxonomy categories and +0.75 for words from the examples) by using the `AddToSig` function that takes the existing signature, a set of words to add and an update weight (lines 6 to 9). `AddToSig` filters stop words and lemmatizes the words to add before their addition.

We create the signature for JdM by taking all the canonical written representations of lexical entries that evoke the sense (initially, the ASSOC relation), where the weights of each word correspond to the normalized relation weight (a value between -1000 and 1000). We reuse the same `AddToSig` function (10–14). In the case of the weight-based inhibition strategy, we add each word stemming from an inhibition relation to the signature with the highest negative weight (-1000, lines 15–20).

If we are in a veto inhibition mode and if there is an inhibition relation that points to a lexical entry that has a written representation matching words from the BabelNet signature, we immediately discard the current pair of senses (line 24). Otherwise, we move on to the score computation: for each overlapping word between the BabelNet signature and the JdM signature, we increment the score by the multiplication of the weight for the word from the BabelNet signature and the weight for the word from the JdM signature (lines 25–28). This is a weighted Lesk overlap similarity measure [28]. If the score is higher than the threshold, we create the alignment by adding a triple to the RDF model (lines 29–32).

6   Evaluation of the Linking Algorithm

The current section presents an evaluation of our linking approach. We start by describing our benchmark data before presenting and analyzing our results.

6.1   Benchmark Construction

Due to the specificity of JdM, it is difficult to use off-the-shelf benchmark data to evaluate our linking algorithm. Therefore, we manually create our own benchmark (as is customary in the field), containing valid links between JdM and BabelNet. To this end, we created a new game within a crowdsourcing paradigm. For two corresponding entries in JdM and BabelNet (same lemmas), the game shows to the player all of the BabelNet senses and for each of them a list of possible sense refinements from JdM (word senses). The player can click on each of the JdM refinements to mark the correspondence as true, false or undefined.[14]

Since JdM, contrarily to BabelNet, has case sensitive entries, it is useful to be able to say that a given synset does not match the JdM entry. For that purpose, all synsets containing, e.g., "jade" will be returned for both "Jade" (with one sense being the first name), and "jade" (one sense of this being the gem). Approximately half of the benchmark dataset contains inhibition relations. We prioritize words with many senses and many matching BabelNet synsets (common words like "cat"). Since there are approximatively 25,000 polysemous words in JdM, we included the hardest cases in order to have an overview of the worst-case alignment scenarios. We also picked nouns with few outgoing relations, like the French "religieuse", which can both be a religious person and a kind of a pastry, to analyse the impact of a lack of information on the the alignment results.The resulting dataset contains 574 links between nouns, accounting for approximately 2.5% of all possible links. It is used for all of our experiments and made freely available.[15]

6.2   Experimental Protocol

We start by selecting all noun nodes in JdM that are not refinements and that have at least two distinct semantic refinements (senses). Then, we compare and decide whether to align the semantic refinements of each of these terms to all of the BabelNet senses of nouns that have the same written representation[16], through the application of the JDMBabelizer algorithm. Subsequently, we evaluate the results against our benchmark data.

We ran Algorithm 1 for the entire JdM on a Hitachi HTS547575A9E384 laptop, with 8G RAM and an i5-2450m 2.50 GHz processor. The final alignments, as well as both JdM and BabelNet Lucene indexes were stored on a mechanical hard-drive. There are 19782 polysemous nouns in JdM with a total of 51657 senses that we compare to 58816 tentative equivalent BabelSynsets. The entire alignment process took 4927597ms to run (approximately 1h21min). The solution space for the alignment is the union of Cartesian products of lexical senses for each pair of aligned lexical entries.

6.3   Results and Discussion

Threshold tuning. We start by estimating the optimal value of the cutoff threshold. We show the results for several threshold values in Table 1. Two scenarios stem from this experiment: (s1) favoring recall, with a corresponding threshold of 500 and (s2) favoring precision, with a threshold of 1,000. Although we give more importance to (s2) (ensuring that the established links are mostly

---

[14] A link to the game with an example of the word "chat" (*Fr.*, *cat*): http://www. jeuxdemots.org/aki_fech_babelnet_distrib.php?term=chat.

[15] https://tinyurl.com/jdmbabelnetbench.

[16] We used the BabelNet API http://babelnet.org/guide.

Table 1. Threshold variation.

Threshold	Precision	Recall	Accuracy
500	66%	80%	93%
750	68%	65%	93%
1,000	74%	51%	93%
1,250	74%	47%	91%

correct), we analyze both cases in detail below with regard to the effects of inhibition.

Impact of inhibition. The results of our experiments on both scenarios by using inhibitions as negative weights, using inhibition as a veto (if an inhibited word is found, the link is immediately discarded) and not using inhibition are shown in Table 2 in terms of Precision ($\frac{TP}{TP+FP}$), Recall ($\frac{TP}{TP+FN}$), F-measure (harmonic mean of P and R) and Accuracy ($\frac{TP+TN}{TP+FP+TN+FN}$). With a threshold of 500 (s1), we achieve an uninhibited Precision of 65% with a recall at 80% and a F-measure of 72%, which translates into an accuracy of 93%. With a threshold of 1,000 (s2), we achieve an uninhibited Precision of 73% with a recall at 52% and a F-measure of 60%, which translates into an accuracy of 92%. When we take inhibition into account as negative weights, we increase precision by 1%, while the other measures remain the same in both (s1) and (s2). When we take inhibition into account as a veto, we increase precision by 2% but decrease recall by 2% in (s2) and by 4% in (s1). For (s1), the F-measure decreases by 1% with no impact on accuracy, while in (s2) the F-measure remains unchanged, but the accuracy increases by 1%. All-in-all, the impact of inhibition appears to be much less significant than what we anticipated. However, in the interest of producing the most reliable alignment between JdM and BabelNet (at the price of lower recall), we identify the best configuration to be (s2) with a veto inhibition.

Table 2. Results of aligning JdM to BabelNet with and without using the inhibition relation and by using it as a veto.

Dataset	Threshold/Scenario	Precision	Recall	F-measure	Accuracy
NoInhib	500 / (s1)	65%	80%	72%	93%
Inhib	500 / (s1)	66%	80%	72%	93%
InhibVeto	500 / (s1)	67%	76%	71%	93%
NoInhib	1000 / (s2)	73%	51%	60%	92%
Inhib	1000 / (s2)	74%	51%	60%	93%
InhibVeto	1000 / (s2)	76%	49%	60%	93%

Error analysis. In order to better understand our results, we studied the false negatives and false positives produced by our algorithm. As expected, many false negatives are due to lack of information in JdM. For instance, one of the senses of the French word "baguette" is a rod used to push ammo for old firearms. The JdM entry contains only three outgoing relations, two of them being "military" and "history", while the BabelNet synset does not mention neither of these. Since JdM is constantly evolving thanks to the permanent contributions of its players, we can hope that this missing information will be filled in the future.

The participative nature of JdM has also its downsides. Certain false negatives are due to the fact that the BabelNet synsets tend to contain academic definitions, while the terms linked through the JdM associations are rather common or colloquial.

Another source of false positives lies in the fact that some synsets do not have French definitions and use English ones instead. Since JdM is only in French, we want the projected definitions to be in French, too. For that reason, we systematically discard links to definitions in other languages. However some of these links are still established by our algorithm, because certain words have the same written representation in both languages. For example, the English definition of "devil" contains "cruel" and "demon", both valid French words and present in the JdM relations.

Among the remaining false positives, we frequently encounter senses that are close but still distinct. For example, "copper" can be used to describe the metal, or the color. Since the color is called that way because it is the color of the metal, these senses are tightly related and mislead the similarity judgment. This problem could be resolved by using more specialized relations in both BabelNet and JdM, like the is_a relation.

Comparison to state of the art. Comparing WSA results directly to the state of the art is generally difficult, because each time a specific pair of resources are aligned, having specific properties and evaluated on different reference datasets. This difficulty is amplified in our case by the lack of definitions in JdM. Nonetheless, we note that the best results obtained for scenarios (s1) and (s2), respectively, outperform the average of the WSA approaches. In scenario (s2), we obtain significantly higher precision values than most established approaches. The benefits of using the inhibition relation become clear as it adds a combinatorial pruning constraint that improves precision, although it decreases recall. In turn, this explains why the impact of inhibition is marginal in scenario (s1).

7   Conclusion

This paper deals with the addition of JdM, a French lexical resource, to the linguistic web of data. We introduce a conversion scheme of JdM to RDF allowing to model weighted relations by using Ontolex along with an approach to link JdM to BabelNet and thus to the LLOD. These links can be used for automatic translation, or to help enrich BabelNet using the JdM data and vice versa, enabling the interoperability of the two resources. By adding JdM to the LLOD, we also contribute to the enrichment of non-English linguistic resources on the web. We construct a benchmark dataset in the form of a reference alignment between JdM and BabelNet on the basis of a crowdsourced game. We use this data for evaluating our approach and we share it along with all produced data and algorithms.

References

1. Lafourcade, M.: Making people play for lexical acquisition with the jeuxdemots prototype. In: SNLP2007: 7th International Symposium on Natural Language Processing, p. 7 (2007)
2. Chiarcos, C., Hellmann, S., Nordhoff, S.: Towards a linguistic linked open data cloud: the open linguistics working group. TAL **52**(3), 245–275 (2011)
3. Navigli, R., Ponzetto, S.P.: BabelNet: the automatic construction, evaluation and application of a wide-coverage multilingual semantic network. Artif. Intell. **193**, 217–250 (2012)
4. Eckle-Kohler, J., McCrae, J.P., Chiarcos, C.: LemonUBY a large, interlinked, syntactically-rich lexical resource for ontologies. Semant. Web **6**(4), 371–378 (2015)
5. Sérasset, G.: Dbnary: Wiktionary as a lemon-based multilingual lexical resource in rdf. Semant. Web **6**(4), 355–361 (2015)
6. Mel'čuk, I.: Lexical functions: a tool for the description of lexical relations in a lexicon. In: Wanner, L., Benjamins, J., (eds.) Lexical functions in lexicography and natural language processing, pp. 37–102 (1996)
7. Hulpuş, I., Prangnawarat, N., Hayes, C.: Path-based semantic relatedness on linked data and its use to word and entity disambiguation. In: Arenas, M., et al. (eds.) ISWC 2015. LNCS, vol. 9366, pp. 442–457. Springer, Cham (2015). doi:10.1007/978-3-319-25007-6_26
8. Shvaiko, P., Euzenat, J.: Ontology matching: state of the art and future challenges. IEEE Trans. Knowl. Data Eng. **25**(1), 158–176 (2013)
9. Tigrine, A.N., Bellahsene, Z., Todorov, K.: Light-weight cross-lingual ontology matching with LYAM++. In: Debruyne, C., et al. (eds.) On the Move to Meaningful Internet Systems: OTM 2015 Conferences. LNCS, vol. 9415, pp. 527–544. Springer, Cham (2015). doi:10.1007/978-3-319-26148-5_36
10. Unger, C., Freitas, A., Cimiano, P.: An introduction to question answering over linked data. In: Koubarakis, M., Stamou, G., Stoilos, G., Horrocks, I., Kolaitis, P., Lausen, G., Weikum, G. (eds.) Reasoning Web 2014. LNCS, vol. 8714, pp. 100–140. Springer, Cham (2014). doi:10.1007/978-3-319-10587-1_2
11. McCrae, J., Aguado-de-Cea, G., Buitelaar, P., Cimiano, P., Declerck, T., Góomez-Pérez, A., Gracia, J., Hollink, L., Montiel-Ponsoda, E., Spohr, D., Wunner, T.: Interchanging lexical resources on the semantic web. Lang. Resour. Eval. **46**(4), 701–719 (2012). doi:10.1007/s10579-012-9182-3. ISSN: 1574-0218
12. Francopoulo, G., Bel, N., George, M., Calzolari, N., Monachini, M., Pet, M., Soria, C.: Lexical markup framework (LMF) for NLP multilingual resources. In: Workshop on Multilingual Language Resources and Interoperability, pp. 1–8. ACL (2006)
13. Westphal, P., Stadler, C., Pool, J.: Countering language attrition with panlex and the web of data. Semant. Web **6**(4), 347–353 (2015)
14. Villegas, M., Bel, N.: Parole/simple lemon ontology and lexicons. Semant. Web **6**(4), 363–369 (2015)

15. Gurevych, I., Eckle-Kohler, J., Hartmann, S., Matuschek, M., Meyer, C.M., Wirth, C.: UBY—a large-scale unified lexical-semantic resource based on lmf. In: 13th Conference of the European Chapter of the Association for Computational Linguistics, pp. 580–590. Association for Computational Linguistics (2012)

16. Buitelaar, P., Arcan, M., Iglesias Fernandez, C.A., Sánchez Rada, J.F., Strapparava, C.: Linguistic linked data for sentiment analysis. In: 2nd Workshop on Linked Data in Linguistics: Representing and linking lexicons, terminologies and other language data, Telecomunicacion (2013)

17. Rouces, J., de Melo, G., Hose, K.: FrameBase: representing N-ary relations using semantic frames. In: Gandon, F., Sabou, M., Sack, H., d'Amato, C., Cudré-Mauroux, P., Zimmermann, A. (eds.) ESWC 2015. LNCS, vol. 9088, pp. 505–521. Springer, Cham (2015). doi:10.1007/978-3-319-18818-8_31

18. McCrae, J., Fellbaum, C., Cimiano, P.: Publishing and linking wordnet using lemon and rdf. In: 3rd Workshop on Linked Data in Linguistics (2014)

19. Ehrmann, M., Cecconi, F., Vannella, D., McCrae, J.P., Cimiano, P., Navigli, R.: Representing multilingual data as linked data: the case of babelnet 2.0. In: LREC, pp. 401–408 (2014)

20. Meyer C.M., Gurevych, I.: What psycholinguists know about chemistry: Aligning wiktionary and wordnet for increased domain coverage. In: 5th International Joint Conference on Natural Language Processing, pp. 883–892. Asian Federation of Natural Language Processing (2011)

21. Gurevych, I., Eckle-Kohler, J., Matuschek, M.: Linked Lexical Knowledge Bases: Foundations and Applications. Morgan & Claypool, San Rafael (2016)

22. Matuschek, M.: Word sense alignment of lexical resources. PhD thesis, Technische Universitat Darmstadt (2015)

23. Henrich, V., Hinrichs, E., Vodolazova, T.: Aligning GermaNet senses with wiktionary sense definitions. In: Vetulani, Z., Mariani, J. (eds.) LTC 2011. LNCS, vol. 8387, pp. 329–342. Springer, Cham (2014). doi:10.1007/978-3-319-08958-4_27

24. Laparra, E., Rigau, G., Cuadros, M.: Exploring the integration of wordnet and framenet. In: 5th Global WordNet Conference (2010)

25. Bond, F., Foster R.: Linking and extending an open multilingual wordnet. In: 51st Annual Meeting of the Association for Computational Linguistics, pp. 1352–1362. ACL (2013)

26. Pilehvar, M.T., Navigli, R.: A robust approach to aligning heterogeneous lexical resources. In: 52nd Annual Meeting of the Association for Computational Linguistics, pp. 468–478. ACL (2014)

27. Flati, T., Vannella, D., Pasini, T., Navigli, R.: Multiwibi: the multilingual wikipedia bitaxonomy project. Artif. Intell. **241**, 66–102 (2016)

28. Lesk, M.: Automatic sense disambiguation using machine readable dictionaries: how to tell a pine cone from an ice cream cone. In: 5th Annual International Conference on Systems Documentation, pp. 24–26 (1986)

Towards Holistic Concept Representations: Embedding Relational Knowledge, Visual Attributes, and Distributional Word Semantics

Steffen Thoma[(✉)], Achim Rettinger, and Fabian Both

Karlsruhe Institute of Technology (KIT), Karlsruhe, Germany
{steffen.thoma,rettinger}@kit.edu, fabian.both@student.kit.edu

Abstract. Knowledge Graphs (KGs) effectively capture explicit relational knowledge about individual entities. However, visual attributes of those entities, like their shape and color and pragmatic aspects concerning their usage in natural language are not covered. Recent approaches encode such knowledge by learning latent representations ('embeddings') separately: In computer vision, visual object features are learned from large image collections and in computational linguistics, word embeddings are extracted from huge text corpora which capture their distributional semantics. We investigate the potential of complementing the relational knowledge captured in KG embeddings with knowledge from text documents and images by learning a shared latent representation that integrates information across those modalities. Our empirical results show that a joined concept representation provides measurable benefits for (i) semantic similarity benchmarks, since it shows a higher correlation with the human notion of similarity than uni- or bi-modal representations, and (ii) entity-type prediction tasks, since it clearly outperforms plain KG embeddings. These findings encourage further research towards capturing types of knowledge that go beyond today's KGs.

Keywords: Knowledge fusion · Multimodality · Entity embeddings · Visual features · Distributional semantics · Entity-type prediction

1 Introduction

In recent years, several large, cross-domain, and openly available knowledge graphs (KGs) have been created. They offer an impressively large collection of cross-domain, general knowledge about the world, specifically instantiated relations between individual entities (statements). However, there is a lack of other types of information like visual object features or distributional semantics about the usage of those entities in the context of textual descriptions of real-world events.

Consider for instance the entity 'baseball' as depicted in Fig. 1: Images of baseballs provide basic visual information about the shape and color, something that is not present in KGs. While it is theoretically possible to make such information explicit with a graph-based formalism, it is not the obvious choice, since

C. d'Amato et al. (Eds.): ISWC 2017, Part I, LNCS 10587, pp. 694–710, 2017.
DOI: 10.1007/978-3-319-68288-4_41

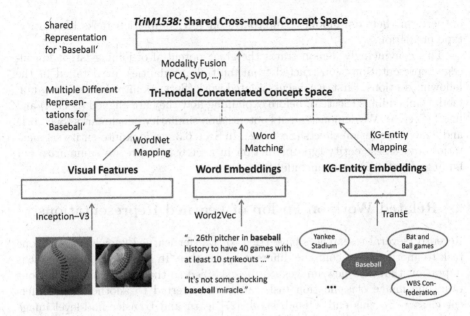

Fig. 1. Approach for extracting a shared cross-modal concept space from image, text and knowledge graph (aligned on word-level).

the detailed formal modelling of a shape or texture is far less efficient than capturing this with an unstructured representation like an image.

Similarly, text documents contain another type of essential information that is not available in KGs. Texts that mention 'baseball' typically comment or analyze baseball games and players. Since there is a huge number of examples on the actual usage of terms in text, this provides distributional context which is not available via the graph-neighborhood of the entity 'baseball' in a KG. KGs contain rather stable relations between individual entities, like attributes of baseball teams, their locations, equipment and abstract categorizations such as a 'Bat and Ball Game'.

It seems obvious that the three modalities (KGs, Text, Images) contribute different types of complementing information. Considering recent results in extraction of visual and textual content, that indicate an advantage of exploiting both modalities simultaneously to represent concepts [18], there also seems to be potential for tri-modal embeddings of textual context, visual information and relational knowledge of KG concepts.

This work investigates the influence of additional modalities on concept representations by means of a tri-modal embedding space that fuses information from text documents and image collections with knowledge graphs. When evaluating the resulting latent concept representation on standard similarity benchmarks, it indeed shows a higher correlation with the human notion of concept similarity than uni- (e.g., KG only) or bi-modal representations. Also, KG embeddings fused with embeddings trained on visual and textual documents clearly outperform their uni-modal counterparts on KG completion tasks like entity-type prediction.

This convincingly demonstrates the great potential of joining latent knowledge representations constructed from multiple modalities, as detailed in the following sections. First, we discuss related work (Sect. 2), introduce existing unimodal embeddings (Sect. 3), before explaining how they are aligned (Sect. 4) and fused (Sect. 5). We demonstrate its potential on similarity benchmarks (Sect. 6.1) and analyze its fusion effects (Sect. 6.2). In Sect. 6.3, we look into entity segmentation and assess entity-type prediction in Sect. 6.4, before we summarize our findings (Sect. 6.5) and conclude (Sect. 7).

2   Related Work on Fusion of Learned Representations

Recently, several researchers have tried to transfer learned knowledge from one task to another or to combine different approaches. In image classification, it is important that also new images can be classified so that visual representations from one image classification task can be transferred to another with different classes. To this end, Oquab et al. [27] learn and transfer mid-level image representations of CNNs. Kiela and Bottou [18] test the combination of visual and textual representations via vector stacking which is similar to [33] which uses a stacked auto-encoder to combine visual and textual input. In contrast to our approach they only evaluate simple vector stacking and neither evaluate more sophisticated combination techniques nor the incorporation of structured resources like KGs.

In contrast, Goikoetxea et al. [11] use textual information from a text corpus and WordNet. For this purpose, WordNet is transferred to text by performing random walks on the synset hierarchy and hereby storing the traversal path to text [12]. But, they neither use visual representations nor do they work with the information of an expressive KG directly. The transformation of a traversal path to text might lose characteristics of the underlying graph structure which is why we used latent vector representations from an explicit KG model, learned on a complete KG. Furthermore, they only combine vectors of equal size to circumvent the dimensionality bias while we introduce an appropriate normalization and weighting scheme.

Our approach also goes beyond current retrofitting ideas like [9]. They adjust learned word embeddings by incorporating information from lexical databases. Firstly, we do not slightly adapt one representation but learn a completely new combined representation. Secondly, we use much more information from a large expressive KG (DBpedia) instead of a smaller lexical database. Lastly, we also use visual information.

The closest work to our word-level alignment to concept space is [30][1]. They used autoencoders with rank 4 weight tensors to create vector representations

---

[1] Please note, that they did not consider any combinations with visual or KG embeddings.

for synsets and lexemes in WordNet for which there was no learned vector representation before. They achieve this by treating a word and a synset as the sum of its lexemes.

The closest work to our approach are [6,14]. Hill et al. [14] add explicit image tag information into the textual representation by adding the image tags into the training data. By placing the tags next to the words, they include the connection between word and its explicit visual features (tags). Then again, [6] concatenate and fuse latent 'visual words' and textual representations with singular value decomposition (SVD). Their results on bi-modal experiments indicate that multi-modal information is useful and can be harnessed. In addition to [6], we also consider relational knowledge from a KG, test further combination methods and evaluate on different tasks.

3 Uni-Modal Vector Representations

Latent vector representations of various types have become quite popular in recent years. The most common ones are latent *textual representations*, which are also referred to as *word embeddings, distributional word semantics* or *distributed word representations*. Created with unsupervised methods, they only rely on a huge text corpus as input. The information of co-occurrences with other words is encoded in a dense vector representation and by calculating the cosine similarity between two representations, a similarity score between two words is obtained. Examples for such *textual representations* are [2], SENNA [7], hierarchical log-bilinear models [24], word2vec [21–23], and GloVe [28]. Word embeddings are able to capture the *distributional knowledge* of how words are used across huge document collections.

Similarly, images can be encoded in a latent vector space. For *image representations*, deep convolutional neural networks (CNNs) have shown promising results in recent years. Deep CNNs transfer an image into a low dimensional vector space representation e.g. for image classification by applying a softmax function. The latent vector representation for images correspond to layers in the deep CNN before applying the softmax. For image classification with CNNs, Inception-V3 [34] which is used in TensorFlow [1] has shown good results on the ImageNet classification task [31]. Image embeddings are able to capture abstract *visual attributes* of objects, like their abstract shape.

The term 'Knowledge Graph' was revived by Google in 2012 and is since then used for any graph-based knowledge base, the most popular examples being DBpedia, Wikidata, and YAGO (see [8] for a survey). Similarly, *knowledge graph embeddings* can be learned on those graphs consisting of entities and typed predicates between entities and abstract concepts. These entities and predicates can be encoded in a low dimensional vector space, facilitating the computation of probabilities for relations within the knowledge graph which can be used for link prediction tasks [29]. Examples for learning latent vector representations of knowledge graphs are SE [5], RESCAL [26], LFM [17], TransE [4], SME [3], HolE [25], ComplEx [35], and the SUNS framework [16]. KG embeddings are obtained by collective learning which is able to capture the *relational structure* of related entities in a KG.

4   Tri-Modal Concatenated Concept Space

The aim of this paper is to assess the potential of integrating *distributional, visual,* and *relational knowledge* into one representation. For obtaining such a consolidated tri-modal space, an embedding across all modalities is needed. Most existing bi-modal approaches rely on manually aligned document collections. Thus, an explicit reference (i.e., DBpedia URI) to the mentioned or depicted concept cannot be established, since a whole document is embedded and no individual concepts. This is not suitable for our investigations, since we want to assess how representations of single concepts can benefit from multi-modal embeddings. Instead, we build on pre-trained uni-modal representations (KG entities, words and visual objects) and align them across modalities.

We chose the most established approaches from their respective fields[2]: For *textual embeddings* we picked the word2vec model and Inception-V3 for *visual embeddings*. For *knowledge graph embeddings*, we trained representations using the TransE model [19]. To establish which embeddings represent the same concept in the different modalities we align them on a word-level:

Matching of Word Embeddings: We identified the intersection of word2vec embeddings that are represented by all modalities.

Concept Mapping of KG Embeddings: The latent vectors of TransE are representing concepts in the DBpedia graph. Each concept is uniquely address-able through a DBpedia URI and several labels (surface forms) are provided. We use the most commonly used label for referring to the concept.

WordNet Mapping of Visual Objects: For visual representations, we use the images from *ImageNet 1k* [31] which consists of 1000 categories. Each category has a set of at least 1300 images for the respective concept and is linked to synsets in WordNet. By combining all image representations for a given synset, we obtain a visual representation for the synset. Alike to [18] we combine the image repre-sentations by taking the max-value for each vector index as this yielded better results compared to mean values. Additionally, we build more abstract synset representations by utilizing the WordNet hierarchy, e.g. an embedding of *'instru-ment'* can be created by combining embeddings of *'violin'*, *'harp'*, etc. We build hierarchical subtrees in WordNet for each missing synset in *ImageNet 1k*. All synset representations in such a subtree with a visual representation from *Ima-geNet 1k* are then combined with a feature-wise max operator to form an abstract synset representation. In total, we abstract 396 additional synset representations.

---

[2] Please note, that any other embedding approach (see Sect. 3), could be plugged into our approach. We are not aiming to compete on uni-modal benchmarks but investigate the impact of additional modalities regardless of the original embedding approach.

The alignment of the synset representations to a shared set of concepts are performed with the WordNet lexemes which are assigned to at least one synset in WordNet. In the end, we extract 2574 lexeme representations by averaging the synset representations related to a given lexeme.

The intersection of Inception-V3 with word2vec and TransE embeddings leads to an aligned tri-modal concept space containing 1538 concepts. For each shared concept, the representations from all modalities are concatenated so that fusion techniques for the resulting concept space *TriM1538* can be applied next (see Fig. 1).

5   Shared Cross-Modal Concept Space

For fusing *distributional, visual,* and *relational knowledge* from the respective modalities, we used several methods which are described in the following paragraphs. Apart from simple concatenation we build on methods like SVD and PCA by proposing a *normalization (N)* and *weighting (W)* scheme for embeddings from multiple modalities. Our tri-modal concept space of 1538 different concepts is represented in three matrices: text T, knowledge graph G, and visual V. For combination techniques, we use the whole information of all three modalities and define matrix $M \in \mathbb{R}^{(t+g+v) \times 1538}$ as the vertically stacked matrices of T, G, and V. The dimensionality of these three matrices varies drastically: *Visual representations* tend to have more than 1000 dimensions while *knowledge graph representations* typically have around 50 to 100 dimensions. Thus, the representations with higher dimensionalities tend to dominate the combination techniques. Furthermore, the value range of features can differ depending on the underlying training objective and method. To address these problems we propose pre-processing steps, comprising *normalization (N)* of each column vector of T, G, and V to unit length as well as *weighting (W)* of the normalized matrices with weights w_T, w_G, and w_V before stacking. Thus, we can take into account that certain representations are more informative and condensed than others.

AVG: The averaging method uses the cosine similarity of all three modalities which are calculated separately. By averaging these three values, we get a combined similarity measure which is also robust with respect to different vector dimensionalities.

CONC: The similarity for the concatenated vectors of the single representations can be calculated with the cosine similarity. The similarities of the following techniques are also calculated with cosine similarity.

SVD: Singular value decomposition factorizes the input matrix M into three matrices such that $M = U\Sigma V^T$. U and V are unitary matrices and Σ is a diagonal matrix with the singular values of M in descending order on its diagonal. By taking the first k columns of U and the k biggest singular values of Σ, we get a new combined k-dimensional representation: $M \leftarrow M_k = U_k\Sigma_k$.

PCA: Principal Component Analysis uses an orthogonal transformation to convert the correlated variables into linearly uncorrelated variables. Fixing the number of uncorrelated principal components results in a projection into a lower dimensional vector space. By taking the principal components with the highest variance, we create a representation with the most distinctive features. We also tested canonical correlation analysis (CCA) but in our tests PCA always performed superior which is consistent with [11]. Thus, we omitted further attempts based on CCA.

AUTO: Autoencoders are neural networks for learning efficient encodings (representations). Autoencoders consist of an encode and a decode function for transforming an input vector to a lower dimensional encoding which can be decoded again. The neural network variables are learned by reducing the reconstruction error between the encoded and subsequently decoded columns of M compared to its original column.

6   Experiments

To investigate if our joint embedding approach is able to integrate *distributional, visual,* and *relational knowledge* from the respective modalities and ultimately if common tasks benefit from that, we conducted qualitative and quantitative empirical tests. In our assessments, we use pre-trained representations for text and images as well as trained knowledge graph representations. For the *textual representation* we use word2vec[3]. Its vectors have 300 dimensions and were trained on the Google News corpus containing about 100 billion words. For *visual representations*, the Inception-V3 model[4], pre-trained on the *ImageNet 1k* classification task, was applied to compute representations with 2048 dimensions. *Knowledge graph representations* were obtained with the TransE model [4] which we trained by running TransE on DBpedia. We trained TransE with a local closed word assumption for type constraints, rank = 50, gamma = 0.3, learningrate-embeddings = 0.2 and learningrate-parameters = 0.5 on the latest DBpedia dump (April 2016). We made all used embeddings available online[5].

6.1   Word Similarity

For evaluating whether a joint embedding captures the human notion of similarity better than uni-modal embeddings, we utilize various word similarity datasets. These datasets were created by several persons that rated the similarity of word pairs like 'cheetah - lion'. Since *TriM1538* does not cover all words in

---

[3] https://code.google.com/archive/p/word2vec/.
[4] http://download.tensorflow.org/models/image/imagenet/inception-v3-2016-03-01. tar.gz.
[5] https://people.aifb.kit.edu/sto/TriM1538.

Table 1. Spearman's rank correlation on subsets and complete datasets for word2vec.

	MEN	WS-353	SimLex-999	MTurk-771	weighted ∅
Complete data	0.762	0.700	0.442	0.671	0.682
Subset	0.740	0.694	0.441	0.608	0.672

the evaluation datasets[6], we evaluate on the covered subsets and provide them online (See Footnote 5). To ensure that the subsets used for evaluation are not easier to align we compared the word2vec performance to the full set. Table 1 shows the performance of word2vec on the respective datasets *MEN* [6], *WS-353* [10], *SimLex-999* [15], and *MTurk-771* [13]. We also report the average performance over all evaluation datasets, weighted by their respective size. Table 1 confirms that similarities in the subsets are equally hard to predict.

In Table 2, the Spearman's rank correlation on all subsets for raw stacking, *normalization (N)* and *weighting (W)* is reported. Normalized representations allow for a fixed combination ratio, resembling an equal weight of information from all modalities. We conducted experiments with different dimension parameters for SVD, PCA, and AUTO. Our results indicate that 100 dimensions are sufficient to encode the information for the word similarity task. In case of simple stacking (second block in Table 2), none of the combination methods is significantly better than the uni-modal text representation on the *MEN*, *MTurk-771*, and *WS-353* subset. Also, combination methods with *normalization (N)* are not significantly and consistently outperforming the textual representation.

To investigate if modalities are equally informative or provide complementary information we use *weighting (W)* of representations after normalization in order to quantify the impact of different proportions of information induced by each representation. With grid search and a step size of 0.05 we investigated the modality composition on the weighted average of all evaluation sets. The optimal weights for (w_T, w_G, w_V) are: AVG (0.15, 0.05, 0.8), CONC (0.25, 0.15, 0.6), SVD (0.3, 0.05, 0.65), and PCA (0.25, 0.05, 0.7)[7]. While some of the weighting schemes only include small proportions of the KG representations, the extracted complementary information from KGs still improves the performance in every approach significantly. In Fig. 2, you can see the weighted average of Spearman's rank correlation scores for different weightings between normalized *visual, textual,* and *KG representations*. It clearly shows that the combination of the three fused and weighted modalities produces better results than any single modality[8]. Weighted combination methods substantially outperform uni- and bi-modal embeddings while best results are obtained with SVD and PCA. Applying the dimension reduction methods SVD and PCA (100 dimensions) only on the initial

---

[6] Naturally, the limiting factors are verbs, abstract words, and named entities (e.g. persons) for which no visual representation is available.

[7] Due to high computational costs we omitted the autoencoder.

[8] Otherwise the optimum (depicted with a black cross) would be in a corner (uni-modal) or edge (bi-modal) of the triangle.

Table 2. Spearman's rank correlation on subsets of evaluation datasets.

	MEN	WS-353	SimLex-999	MTurk-771	Weighted ∅
Visual	0.619	0.526	0.522	0.308	0.546
Textual	0.740	0.707	0.423	0.594	0.669
KG	0.452	0.433	0.284	0.097	0.369
AVG	0.738	0.595	0.460	0.485	0.643
CONC	0.620	0.520	0.518	0.317	0.546
SVD	0.739	0.646	0.591	0.352	0.646
PCA	0.710	0.595	0.663	0.354	0.634
AUTO	0.456	0.672	0.485	0.294	0.456
AVG-N	0.738	0.595	0.460	0.485	0.643
CONC-N	0.738	0.595	0.460	0.485	0.643
SVD-N	0.724	0.555	0.422	0.440	0.618
PCA-N	0.769	0.601	0.452	0.558	0.673
AUTO-N	0.742	0.607	0.473	0.527	0.655
AVG-W	0.795	0.726	0.592	0.577	0.724
CONC-W	0.795	0.726	0.598	0.574	0.724
SVD-W	0.826	0.722	0.633	**0.667**	**0.762**
PCA-W	**0.831**	**0.758**	**0.688**	0.567	0.760

uni-modal embeddings did show improvements for the visual embeddings to an averaged Spearman's rank of 0.619 (SVD) and 0.639 (PCA) (weighted average). For comparison, the best reported result for uni-modal models on SimLex-999 is [32] with Spearman's rank correlation of 0.563. The bi-modal approach [6] reported Spearman's rank correlations of 0.78 on MEN and 0.75 on WS-353 while their model covered 252 word pairs of WS-353. Please note, our results on subsets of *MEN*, *WS-353*, *SimLex-999*, and *MTurk-771* are competitive but not directly comparable to the numbers reported by state-of-the-art uni-modal approaches as they are evaluated on the complete datasets and ours cannot. However, since this paper is about relative performance gains through additional modalities we do not compete with, but are complementary to the state-of-the-art uni- and bi-modal approaches.

For combinations via AVG and CONC as shown in Fig. 2a and b, we observe similar behavior on all evaluation datasets in terms of optimal weights. SVD and PCA exploit information from KG representations with very low weight, but the combined representation of all three modalities is significantly better than a combination of only two modalities. The best bi-modal combinations were AVG (0.15, 0, 0.85) with 0.709, CONC (0.3, 0, 0.7) with 0.709, PCA (0.3, 0, 0.7) with 0.749, and SVD (0.3, 0, 0.7) with 0.759 Spearman's rank correlation (weighted average).

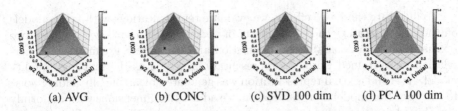

| (a) AVG | (b) CONC | (c) SVD 100 dim | (d) PCA 100 dim |

Fig. 2. Averaged plots over all evaluation datasets for weighting with normalization. The colorbar indicates Spearman's rank correlation and the black cross marks the optimum.

The key finding is, that optimal weights always include all three modalities, so indeed make use of *visual, distributional,* and *relational knowledge.* Further experiments with different TransE model parameterizations revealed that this finding is not depending on a specifically trained TransE embedding, but can be attributed to information extracted from the knowledge graph. Thus, we can improve concept representations from other modalities with complementary information encoded in Inception-V3, word2vec, and TransE embeddings.

6.2   Noise Induced Errors Vs. Complementary Information Gain

In a further step, we investigated the fusion effects in more detail. Every meaningful representation encodes useful information which is defined by the model's learning objective. Before combining models for a certain task, one has to verify that the model encodes information for that specific task. Also, the representation quality for a certain task might vary greatly. While complementary information of various models and modalities can lead to an improvement when combined, a weak model for the specific task might induce noise. Adding a model to a combined representation is only beneficial if the gain through complementary information is greater than the information loss induced by noise.

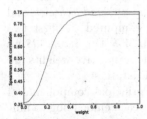
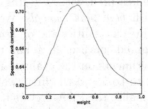
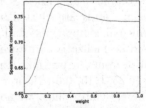

(a) No complementary information between noisy word2vec (w=0) and noise-free word2vec (w=1).

(b) Complementary information between visual (w=0) and noisy word2vec (w=1) representations.

(c) Superposition of both effects, visual (w=0) and noise-free word2vec (w=1).

Fig. 3. Concatenation effects

To illustrate these two effects, we evaluate representations with noisy models on the *MEN* dataset. To isolate effects of *noise induced errors*, we combine two textual representations after normalization and compute Spearman's rank correlations. Pre-trained word2vec representations served as the first high quality model. A second textual representation was generated by artificially adding noise to the word2vec model. For that reason, we added 100 dimensions with uniformly distributed random values and tuned representation quality by scaling the distribution interval. Following this procedure, we can observe the fusion effects between two concatenated representations with no complementary information in Fig. 3a.

For showing the information gain of *complementary information* in Fig. 3b, we combine Inception-V3 representations ($w = 0$) with another noisy word2vec version ($w = 1$). Following the procedure above, we added noise to the word2vec representations and scaled the distribution interval until performance was similar to Inception-V3. One can observe the performance peak close to a weighting ratio of 1:1 between visual and textual representations which indicates that the visual and textual embeddings indeed hold complementary information.

In Fig. 3c one can observe the superposition of both effects during concatenation. While the visual model performs worse than the textual model on its own, the information gain through complementary information is larger than the information loss due to noise. Understanding the exact position of the maximum requires further research. Overall, combining two representations via concatenation improves results, if the performance gap between both models is not too large and both models encode complementary information (which is the case in our experiments).

6.3 Entity Segmentation

Besides showing that a joint concept embedding comes closer to the human notion of similarity, we can also demonstrate improvements in semantic entity segmentation. In Fig. 4, we exemplarily show that the *TriM1538* space is better suited for segmenting entities when compared to the *textual, visual,* and *KG embedding space*. Entities represented with *red crosses* are *land vehicles* and various *birds* are plotted with *blue plus symbols*. We computed the first two principal components of all three modalities and of *TriM1538*. For *TriM1538* we used normalization with weighted concatenation and the respective weights are taken from our previous experiments on the evaluation datasets: (w_T, w_G, w_V) = (0.25, 0.15, 0.6). In order to compare the first two principal components of different embeddings, we normalize the PCA-vectors for each embedding to unit length. This is important since we are interested in a relative separation while the variance explained by the first two components might vary greatly between different representations.

All three single representations show the ability to separate the DBpedia categories *birds* from *land vehicles*. In the textual domain, clustering of *land vehicles* is clearly observable and *birds* are separated but do not show an equally

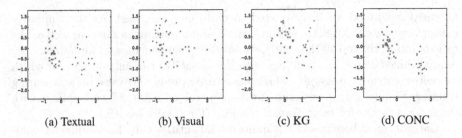

(a) Textual   (b) Visual   (c) KG   (d) CONC

Fig. 4. Segmentation results for birds (blue '+') and land vehicles (red 'x'). (Color figure online)

condensed cluster. Visually, *birds* are clustered relatively close together, but vehicles are mixed into the cluster.

Similarly to text, the KG separates *birds* and *land vehicles* almost perfectly, but does not create clean clusters. When combined in *TriM1538*, clustering and separation is better than in all others modalities. Apparently, exploiting *distributional*, *visual* and *relational knowledge* results in a clearer semantic entity segmentation.

6.4 Entity-Type Prediction

Finally, we show that established KG tasks can also benefit from embedding *distributional semantic* and *visual attributes* into *relational knowledge*. Entity-type prediction is such a common KG completion task, similar to link prediction [20].

In order to test our *TriM1538* embeddings in the context of entity-type prediction, we use the following experimental setup: for a given KG entity $e \in E$ and the set of available categories C, we predict to which of the categories $c \in C$ the entity belongs (e.g. http://dbpedia.org/page/Category:Mammals). We define the subgraph of DBpedia that contains entities covered by *TriM1538* and their relations as the *TriM-KG* and denote the complete set of KG entities as $E^* = C \cup E$. Overall, *TriM-KG* contains 3220 triples and 1955 entities of which 634 are categories and 1321 entities with multi-modal information. Embeddings trained on *TriM-KG* are named *locally* trained embeddings, while embeddings trained on the whole KG are referred to as *globally* trained. In the following, we refer to entity, predicate and category vector embeddings with e, p and c.

We utilize the standard link prediction procedure of TransE as a baseline: For an entity e of interest, we train TransE on *TriM-KG* and exclude all triples connecting that entity to its category in C. The training parameters are the same as for the *globally* trained TransE except for a reduced rank in order to circumvent overfitting. The translation operation of TransE is then defined as the vector operation:

$$sim(e, p, c) = \|c - (e + p)\|_2 \tag{1}$$

Similar to [19], we compute $sim(e, p, c)$ for all possible $c \in C$ and get the rank of the true triples by ignoring all other true triples to prevent distortion (since an entity might be correctly related to multiple categories). As the similarity measure we use the L2-norm within TransE and report mean ranks as well as the ratio of hits in the top 10 (hits@10). As an additional benchmark, we compare the *locally* trained TransE embeddings with the *global* TransE embeddings, for which the entity-category relations (which have to be predicted) were present during training. Finally, we report results for *locally* trained RESCAL embeddings with the same setup as for *local* TransE training (for details see [19]).

Category memberships of the multi-modal entities can also be directly computed with multi-modal embeddings of *TriM1538*. For this, we construct category embeddings from entity embeddings related to that category: For a given category, we compute its embedding with $\frac{1}{N} \cdot \sum_{i=1}^{N} e_i$ for all N multi-modal embeddings e_i related to category c. Please note, for predicting category memberships of an entity, that specific entity is not considered as being related to any category during the category construction process. Thus, we obtain different category embeddings for each related entity. In *TriM-KG*, all considered categories have connections to at least two different multi-modal entities to ensure the construction of the category embedding. We name this procedure *hierarchic construction (HC)* and use $d = \|e - c\|_2$ as the similarity measure.

Finally, we combine the entity-type prediction schemes from above. Since TransE performs superior to RESCAL (see Table 3), we introduce an enrichment procedure for TransE, which could similarly be adapted to RESCAL. We concatenate *locally* trained TransE representations e_{loc} with *TriM1538* entities e_{tri} after normalizing the respective embeddings to unit length. Similarly, we concatenate TransE category representations with embeddings obtained by *HC*. With these extended embeddings $e_{ext} = (e_{loc}, e_{tri})$, $c_{ext} = (c_{loc}, c_{tri})$ we reformulate Eqs. 1 to 2:

$$sim(e_{ext}, p, c_{ext}) = \|(c_{loc}, c_{tri}) - (e_{loc} + p, e_{tri})\|_2 \qquad (2)$$

For the fusion techniques, the modality weights have to be optimized. To this end, we create training and test sets with a 0.5:0.5 split of our data and optimize on the training set. This resulted in (w_T, w_G, w_V): PCA (0.2, 0.4, 0.4), SVD (0.45, 0.55, 0), and CONC (0.4, 0.6, 0) for *Trans* E_{loc}+ *HC* and PCA (0.2, 0.55, 0.25), SVD (0.4, 0.6, 0), and CONC (0.4, 0.6, 0) for *HC*. As we have discussed in Sect. 6.2, weighting is task and model dependent which implies that the usefulness of the different types of knowledge from the respective modalities varies across different tasks. Further, the performance of a model, which is enriched with multi-modal information, greatly impacts the optimal modality composition. Thus, adapting the modality composition for new tasks is necessary.

Results for all methods are shown in Table 3. Consistent with observations in [19], the TransE-based baseline performs better than RESCAL. Interestingly, the *globally* trained TransE embeddings perform worse than the *locally* trained TransE, although the links to be predicted were present during its training and it has more information available. However, this is not surprising when comparing the size of the concept space of DBpedia ($7 \cdot 10^6$ concepts) with *TriM-KG* (1955 concepts).

Table 3. Results for type predictions with multi-modal embeddings on the right side. Results for TransE$_{loc}$ enriched with multi-modal embeddings on the left side. *TransE*, *RESCAL*, and *Random* at the bottom are baseline predictors without any multi-modal information or enhanced construction scheme.

| | TransE$_{loc}$ + *HC* | | | | Hierarchic Construction | | | |
| | Train | | Test | | Train | | Test | |
	Mean rank	hits@10	mean rank	hits@10	Mean rank	hits@10	Mean rank	hits@10
PCA	**10.401**	**0.828**	**10.251**	**0.824**	**12.274**	**0.863**	**14.680**	**0.869**
SVD	14.310	0.749	14.637	0.716	17.424	0.762	19.420	0.762
CONC	14.086	0.765	13.696	0.742	17.254	0.807	19.595	0.806
Word	14.297	0.763	14.215	0.741	24.157	0.784	28.107	0.764
Visual	32.982	0.475	33.477	0.462	96.805	0.581	96.763	0.575
KG	15.609	0.744	14.009	0.730	33.129	0.671	30.732	0.699
	Baselines							
TransE$_{loc}$	35.641	0.442	36.408	0.422				
TransE$_{glob}$	58.493	0.382	57.075	0.392				
RESCAL$_{loc}$	116.640	0.286	115.275	0.261				
Random	317.000	0.016	317.000	0.016				

The *HC* method even yields good results for entity type-predictions with uni-modal embeddings as shown in Table 3. Visual attributes alone are obviously not suited for predictions of type relations within the KG. Consistent with our observations in the word similarity task, embeddings from different modalities incorporate complementary information which can be exploited. With our modality fusion techniques, we achieve substantially superior results compared to uni-modal embeddings. Further, PCA is the best suited method for incorporating the sparse and rather noisy visual information in this setup and shows a significant performance boost compared to CONC and SVD.

Combining TransE$_{loc}$ with *HC* improves the mean rank even further. Utilizing uni- and multi-modal information enhances the predictions while PCA dominates all other methods. Compared to the standard TransE predictions, we improve the mean rank by 255% with multi-modal enrichment via *HC*.

6.5   Key Findings

- All our empirical evidence suggests that each modality encodes complementing information that is conceptually different: text provides *distributional*, images *visual* and KGs *relational knowledge*. Information encoded in the structure of embeddings can be useful for vastly different tasks and training objectives, even in other domains, as long as concepts can be aligned.
- Complementing information can be embedded in a joint representation which is closer to the human notion of similarity (see Sect. 6.1), as well as the human intuition in entity segmentation tasks (see Sect. 6.3).
- When enriching KG embeddings with *distributional* and *visual* knowledge from text and images, the performance of entity-type predictions is considerably improved (see Sect. 6.4). This indicates that those types of knowledge

are missing in today's KGs and KGs would greatly benefit if this could be integrated.

- The weighting of the influence for each modality before joining them across modalities is crucial and task dependent since the type of knowledge needed for each task varies. For improved performance, the positive effects created by the complementarity of information has to outweigh negative effects induced by noise in the original embeddings (see Sect. 6.2).

7   Conclusion and Future Work

The intention of this research was to find out if essential types of information, like *distributional* and *visual knowledge*, are not sufficiently represented in today's KGs (here DBpedia). This was investigated by embedding knowledge from text corpora, image collection and KG entities into a joint concept space. Comparing the performance of the joint cross-modal representation to uni-modal representations on various benchmark tasks allowed a quantitative and qualitative assessment. Our proposed two-step approach starts with pre-trained uni-modal concept representations created with established embedding methods from computer vision, natural language processing and semantic technologies. Next, the obtained concept embeddings were aligned across the three modalities, normalization and weighting schemes were devised, before the embeddings were fused into one shared space. Our novel cross-modal concept representation was evaluated in four sets of experiments by comparing it to uni-modal representations.

The main finding of this work is that the fused tri-modal embeddings reliably outperform uni- and bi-modal embeddings. This indicates that complementing information is available in the three investigated content representations and that the types of knowledge represented in text and images is conceptually different (*distributional* and *visual*) to the knowledge represented in KGs (*relational*). On the one hand, the performance gains were observed in tasks that optimize for the human notion of semantic similarity. It appears that the more modalities are considered the closer the knowledge representations come to a human-like perception. On the other hand, we investigated type-prediction in KGs and outperformed existing uni-modal methods by 255%. Again, the shared concept representation performed best when information from all three modalities was included.

Our findings raise fundamental questions and open up a large number of future research directions. First and foremost, it became obvious that knowledge graphs, and likely any knowledge representation that aims to provide a holistic view on entities and concepts, would benefit from integrating distributional and visual knowledge. Fusing embeddings from multiple modalities is an initial step to achieve that. Our approach is currently limited to the concept intersection of all modalities. While we do not need aligned training data, the obtained multi-modal concept space is relatively small. The most pressing issue for future work is to find ways to scale to a larger number of entities e.g. by including visual representations of tagged images, and to include relations.

Investigating approaches which harness multi-modal information for concepts outside of this intersection is also part of our future research. Beyond knowledge representation and representation learning research, findings in this area would impact numerous cross-disciplinary fields like sensory neuroscience, philosophy of perception, and multimodality research.

References

1. Abadi, M., Agarwal, A., Barham, P., Brevdo, E., Chen, Z., Citro, C., Corrado, G.S., Davis, A., Dean, J., Devin, M., et al.: TensorFlow: Large-Scale Machine Learning on Heterogeneous Distributed Systems. arXiv preprint arXiv:1603.04467 (2016)
2. Bengio, Y., Ducharme, R., Vincent, P., Janvin, C.: A neural probabilistic language model. J. Mach. Learn. Res. **3**, 1137–1155 (2003)
3. Bordes, A., Glorot, X., Weston, J., Bengio, Y.: A semantic matching energy function for learning with multi-relational data. Mach. Learn. **94**(2), 233–259 (2014)
4. Bordes, A., Usunier, N., García-Durán, A., Weston, J., Yakhnenko, O.: Translating embeddings for modeling multi-relational data. In: NIPS 26, pp. 2787–2795 (2013)
5. Bordes, A., Weston, J., Collobert, R., Bengio, Y.: Learning structured embeddings of knowledge bases. In: AAAI 2011, pp. 301–306 (2011)
6. Bruni, E., Tran, N., Baroni, M.: Multimodal distributional semantics. J. Artif. Intell. Res. (JAIR) **49**, 1–47 (2014)
7. Collobert, R., Weston, J.: A unified architecture for natural language processing: deep neural networks with multitask learning. In: ICML 2008, pp. 160–167 (2008)
8. Färber, M., Bartscherer, F., Menne, C., Rettinger, A.: Linked Data Quality of DBpedia, Freebase, OpenCyc, Wikidata, and YAGO. Semant. Web J. (2017, to be published)
9. Faruqui, M., Dodge, J., Jauhar, S.K., Dyer, C., Hovy, E.H., Smith, N.A.: Retrofitting word vectors to semantic lexicons. In: NAACL HLT 2015, pp. 1606–1615 (2015)
10. Finkelstein, L., Gabrilovich, E., Matias, Y., Rivlin, E., Solan, Z., Wolfman, G., Ruppin, E.: Placing search in context: the concept revisited. In: WWW 2001, pp. 406–414 (2001)
11. Goikoetxea, J., Agirre, E., Soroa, A.: Single or multiple? combining word representations independently learned from text and WordNet. In: AAAI 2016, pp. 2608–2614 (2016)
12. Goikoetxea, J., Soroa, A., Agirre, E.: Random walks and neural network language models on knowledge bases. In: NAACL HLT 2015, pp. 1434–1439 (2015)
13. Halawi, G., Dror, G., Gabrilovich, E., Koren, Y.: Large-scale learning of word relatedness with Constraints. In: ACM SIGKDD 2012, pp. 1406–1414 (2012)
14. Hill, F., Korhonen, A.: Learning abstract concept embeddings from multi-modal data: since you probably can't see what i mean. In: EMNLP 2014, pp. 255–265 (2014)
15. Hill, F., Reichart, R., Korhonen, A.: SimLex-999: evaluating semantic models with (genuine) similarity estimation. Comput. Linguist. **41**(4), 665–695 (2015)
16. Huang, Y., Tresp, V., Nickel, M., Rettinger, A., Kriegel, H.: A scalable approach for statistical learning in semantic graphs. Semant. Web **5**(1), 5–22 (2014)
17. Jenatton, R., Roux, N.L., Bordes, A., Obozinski, G.: A latent factor model for highly multi-relational data. In: NIPS 25, pp. 3176–3184 (2012)

18. Kiela, D., Bottou, L.: Learning image embeddings using convolutional neural networks for improved multi-modal semantics. In: EMNLP 2014, pp. 36–45 (2014)
19. Krompaß, D., Baier, S., Tresp, V.: Type-constrained representation learning in knowledge graphs. In: Arenas, M., et al. (eds.) ISWC 2015. LNCS, vol. 9366, pp. 640–655. Springer, Cham (2015). doi:10.1007/978-3-319-25007-6_37
20. Lin, Y., Liu, Z., Sun, M., Liu, Y., Zhu, X.: Learning entity and relation embeddings for knowledge graph completion. In: AAAI 2015, pp. 2181–2187 (2015)
21. Mikolov, T., Chen, K., Corrado, G., Dean, J.: Efficient Estimation of Word Representations in Vector Space. arXiv preprint arXiv:1301.3781 (2013)
22. Mikolov, T., Sutskever, I., Chen, K., Corrado, G.S., Dean, J.: Distributed representations of words and phrases and their compositionality. In: NIPS 26, pp. 3111–3119 (2013)
23. Mikolov, T., Yih, W., Zweig, G.: Linguistic regularities in continuous space word representations. In: NAACL HLT 2013, pp. 746–751 (2013)
24. Mnih, A., Hinton, G.E.: A scalable hierarchical distributed language model. In: NIPS 21, pp. 1081–1088 (2008)
25. Nickel, M., Rosasco, L., Poggio, T.A.: Holographic embeddings of knowledge graphs. In: AAAI 2016, pp. 1955–1961 (2016)
26. Nickel, M., Tresp, V., Kriegel, H.: A three-way model for collective learning on multi-relational data. In: ICML 2011, pp. 809–816 (2011)
27. Oquab, M., Bottou, L., Laptev, I., Sivic, J.: Learning and transferring mid-level image representations using convolutional neural networks. In: CVPR 2014, pp. 1717–1724 (2014)
28. Pennington, J., Socher, R., Manning, C.D.: Glove: global vectors for word representation. In: EMNLP 2014, pp. 1532–1543 (2014)
29. Rettinger, A., Lösch, U., Tresp, V., d'Amato, C., Fanizzi, N.: Mining the semantic web - statistical learning for next generation knowledge bases. Data Min. Knowl. Discov. 24(3), 613–662 (2012)
30. Rothe, S., Schütze, H.: AutoExtend: extending word embeddings to embeddings for synsets and lexemes. In: ACL 2015, pp. 1793–1803 (2015)
31. Russakovsky, O., Deng, J., Su, H., Krause, J., Satheesh, S., Ma, S., Huang, Z., Karpathy, A., Khosla, A., Bernstein, M.S., Berg, A.C., Li, F.: ImageNet large scale visual recognition challenge. Int. J. Comput. Vis. 115(3), 211–252 (2015)
32. Schwartz, R., Reichart, R., Rappoport, A.: Symmetric pattern based word embeddings for improved word similarity prediction. In: CoNLL 2015, pp. 258–267 (2015)
33. Silberer, C., Lapata, M.: Learning grounded meaning representations with autoencoders. In: ACL 2014, pp. 721–732 (2014)
34. Szegedy, C., Vanhoucke, V., Ioffe, S., Shlens, J., Wojna, Z.: Rethinking the inception architecture for computer vision. In: CVPR 2016, pp. 2818–2826 (2016)
35. Trouillon, T., Welbl, J., Riedel, S., Gaussier, É., Bouchard, G.: Complex embeddings for simple link prediction. In: ICML 2016, vol. 48, pp. 2071–2080 (2016)

An Extension of SPARQL for Expressing Qualitative Preferences

Antonis Troumpoukis[1,2(✉)], Stasinos Konstantopoulos[1],
and Angelos Charalambidis[1]

[1] Institute and Informatics and Telecommunications, NCSR 'Demokritos',
Aghia Paraskevi 15310, Athens, Greece
{antru,konstant,acharal}@iit.demokritos.gr
[2] Department of Informatics and Telecommunications,
University of Athens, Athens, Greece

Abstract. In this paper we present SPREFQL, an extension of the
SPARQL language that allows appending a "PREFER" clause that
expresses 'soft' preferences over the query results obtained by the main
body of the query. The extension does not add expressivity and any
SPREFQL query can be transformed to an equivalent standard SPARQL
query. However, clearly separating preferences from the 'hard' patterns
and filters in the "WHERE" clause gives queries where the intention of the
client is more cleanly expressed, an advantage for both human readability and machine optimization. In the paper we formally define the syntax
and the semantics of the extension and we also provide empirical evidence
that optimizations specific to SPREFQL improve run-time efficiency by
comparison to the usually applied optimizations on the equivalent standard SPARQL query.

Keywords: SPARQL query processing · Expressing preferences · Query
execution optimization

1 Introduction

Preferences can be used in situations where, while looking for the best solution with respect to a set of criteria, we find out that too strict criteria might
not return any solutions, but relaxing them returns too many solutions to sift
through. The integration of preferences allows to view some constraints as soft
constraints that can be violated in the former case and return less-preferred
results, but will be enforced in the latter case to only return more-preferred
results.

Preferences have been explored in Artificial Intelligence [8], Database Systems [21], Programming Languages [7], and, more recently, enjoy a growing
interest in the area of the Semantic Web [17]. In the Semantic Web context,
preferences allow users to sift through data of varying trustworthiness, quality, and relevance from a specific end user's point of view [22]. As argued by

© Springer International Publishing AG 2017
C. d'Amato et al. (Eds.): ISWC 2017, Part I, LNCS 10587, pp. 711–727, 2017.
DOI: 10.1007/978-3-319-68288-4_42

Siberski et al. [20], the motivating example in the beginning of the seminal Semantic Web article [2] can be interpreted as a preference search.

Strictly speaking, preferences are not more expressive than standard SPARQL. Their most prominent feature, returning less-preferred binding sets in the absence of more-preferred ones, can be simulated with "NOT EXISTS" and, in general, with the syntax already offered by SPARQL. However, clearly separating preferences from the 'hard' patterns and filters in the "WHERE" clause gives us queries where the intention of the author is cleanly expressed and not obscured. This has advantages in both human readability and machine optimization.

In this paper, we first give a background on the treatment of preferences in databases (Sect. 2) and proceed to present our proposed SPREFQL syntax and semantics (Sect. 3). We then present our SPREFQL query processor implementations and our benchmarks on them (Sect. 4). These empirical results are used to support our claim above that optimizing directly at the SPREFQL syntax is more efficient than rewriting into standard SPARQL and passing the latter to an optimizing SPARQL query processor. We then present some related work on the Semantic Web and compare it with our approach (Sect. 5). We close the paper with conclusions and future research directions (Sect. 6).

2   Background

Preference representation formalisms are either *quantitative*, where preferences are represented by a preference value function [1,13], or *qualitative*, where preferences are expressed by directly defining a binary preference relation between objects [5,11]. In the example below:

Example 1. Show me Sci-fi movies, assuming I prefer longer movies.

there is a hard constraint for SciFi movies and a preference towards longer movies. Such a constraint can be represented both as a quantitative function of the movies' runtime and as a qualitative relation that compares movies' runtimes. With this example, however:

Example 2. Show me Sci-fi movies, assuming I prefer original movies to their sequels.

it becomes apparent that there are cases where not all objects are directly comparable, and therefore the total ordering implied by the preference value function cannot always be defined. In fact, Chomicki [5] argues that the qualitative approach is strictly more general than the quantitative approach, as not all preference relations can be expressed using a preference value function. In Chomicki's framework, *preference relations* are defined using first-order formulas:

Definition 1. *Given a relation schema $R(A_1, \ldots, A_n)$ such that U_i, $1 \leq i \leq n$, is the domain of the attribute A_i, a relation $\succ$ is a preference relation over R if it is a subset of $(U_1 \times \cdots \times U_n) \times (U_1 \times \cdots \times U_n)$. A result tuple t_1 is said to be dominated by t_2, if $t_2 \succ t_1$.*

This general preference relation is restricted into *intrinsic preference formulas* that do not rely on external information to compare two objects:

Definition 2. *Let t_1, t_2 denote tuples of a given database relation. A preference formula $P(t_1, t_2)$ is a first-order formula defining a preference relation $\succ_P$ in the standard sense, namely, $t_1 \succ_P t_2$ iff $P(t_1, t_2)$ holds. An* intrinsic preference formula *is a preference formula that uses only built-in predicates (i.e. equality, inequality, arithmetic comparison operations, and so on).*

Table 1. A sample movies relation.

ID	Title	Genre	Duration	Sequel
m_1	Star Wars Ep.IV: A New Hope	Sci-fi	121	m_2
m_2	Star Wars Ep.V: The Empire Strikes Back	Sci-fi	124	m_3
m_3	Star Wars Ep.VI: Return of the Jedi	Sci-fi	130	
m_4	Die Hard	Action	131	m_5
m_5	Die Hard with a Vengeance	Action	128	

Example 3. Consider the `movie(ID,Title,Genre,Duration)` relation shown in Table 1. Suppose that we have the following preference: 'I prefer one `movie` tuple over another iff their genre is the same and the first one runs longer'. The preference relation $\succ_P$ implied by the previous sentence can be defined using formula P:

$$(i, t, g, d) \succ_P (i', t', g', d') \equiv (g = g') \wedge (d > d').$$

Therefore, we prefer movie m_3 to m_2, movie m_2 to m_1, m_3 to m_1 and movie m_4 to m_5. Both conjuncts must be satisfied for the preference relation to hold, so there is no preference relation between movies from different genres regardless of their runtime.

A new relational algebra operator is introduced, called *winnow*. This operator takes two parameters, a database relation and a preference formula and selects from its argument relation the most preferred tuples according to the given preference relation.

Preference relations can be composed in order to form more complex ones. Since preference relations are defined through preference formulas, in order to combine two such relations one must combine their corresponding formulas. Given two preference relations $\succ_P, \succ_Q$, the most common composition operations are the following:

- *Boolean:* (e.g. intersection) $t_1 \succ_{P \wedge Q} t_2 \equiv (t_1 \succ_P t_2) \wedge (t_1 \succ_Q t_2)$,
- *Pareto:* $t_1 \succ_{P \otimes Q} t_2 \equiv ((t_1 \succ_P t_2) \wedge (t_2 \not\succ_Q t_1)) \vee ((t_1 \succ_Q t_2) \wedge (t_2 \not\succ_P t_1))$,
- *Prioritized:* $t_1 \succ_{P \triangleright Q} t_2 \equiv (t_1 \succ_P t_2) \vee ((t_1 \sim_P t_2) \wedge (t_1 \succ_Q t_2))$,

where $t_1 \not\succ_P t_2 \equiv \neg(t_1 \succ_P t_2)$ and $t_1 \sim_P t_2 \equiv (t_1 \not\succ_P t_2) \wedge (t_2 \not\succ_P t_1)$.

In order to select the 'best' tuples from a given relation r based on a preference formula P, the *winnow* operator is introduced:

Definition 3. *Let r be a relation and let P be a preference formula defining a preference relation $\succ_P$. The winnow operator is defined as*

$$w_P(r) = \{t \in r : \neg\exists t' \in r \text{ such that } t' \succ_P t\}.$$

Example 4. Given the relation `movie` in Table 1 and the preference formula C of Example 3, the result of the $w_P(\text{movie})$ operation is the movies with IDs m_3 and m_4. m_1 and m_2 are not included in the result because they are less preferred than m_3 and m_5 because it is less preferred than m_4. Since there is no preference relation between m_3 and m_4, they are both included in the result.

Although winnow can be expressed using standard relational algebra operators [5], there also exist algorithms that directly compute the result of the winnow operator $w_P(R)$. The most prominent such algorithms are the *Nested Loops (NL)* algorithm and the *Blocked Nested Loops (BNL)* algorithm. In NL, each tuple of R is compared with all tuples in R, therefore the complexity of NL is quadratic in the size of R. In BNL, a fixed amount of main memory (a *window*) is used, in order to keep a set of incomparable tuples, which at the end of the algorithm will become the dominating tuples of R. Even though the asymptotic time complexity of BNL is also quadratic, in practice BNL performs better than NL. Especially in the case that the result set of winnow fits into the window, the algorithm operates in one or two iterations (i.e. linear time to the size of R) [3]. Regarding the correctness of the result of each algorithm, NL produces the correct result for every preference relation (even in unintuitive cases such as preference relations in which a tuple is preferred to itself). On the other hand, BNL produces the correct result only if the preference relation $\succ$ is a *strict partial order* [5], that is to say iff the relation is (1) *irreflexive* $\neg(x \succ x)$ (2) *transitive* $(x \succ y) \wedge (x \succ z) \Rightarrow (x \succ z)$ and (3) *asymmetric* $(x \succ y) \Rightarrow \neg(y \succ x)$.

Example 5. Let us assume the relation `movie` in Table 1 and the following preference formula C':

'I prefer one `movie` tuple over another iff their genre is the same and the first one has the second as sequel.'

In this case, BNL is *not* guaranteed to produce the correct result because m_1 'sequel' m_2 and m_2 'sequel' m_3, but m_1 'sequel' m_3 is not asserted, making the 'sequel' property (and thus the whole preference relation) not transitive. The result of the BNL algorithm depends on the order in which pairs are tested: if m_2 is compared to m_1 before being compared to m_3, the first comparison will remove m_2 from the window making m_1 and m_3 incomparable and the result is $\{m_1, m_3, m_4\}$; if m_2 is compared to m_3 before being compared to m_1, then both m_3 and m_2 will be removed and the result is $\{m_1, m_4\}$.

3   The SPREFQL Language

In this section we introduce SPREFQL, which is an extension of SPARQL that supports the expression of qualitative preferences. User preferences are expressed as a new solution modifier which eliminates the solutions that are dominated by (i.e., are less preferred than) another solution. This modifier is similar to a preference formula in Chomicki's framework discussed above. In this section we present the syntax and the semantics of SPREFQL, discuss its expressive power, and we will give some examples of SPREFQL queries.

3.1 Syntax

We assume as a basis the EBNF grammar that defines SPARQL syntax [10, Sect. 19.8] and we extend it by changing the definition of the ⟨SolutionModifier⟩ non-terminal (Rule 18). The new definition adds a ⟨PreferClause⟩ non-terminal between the ⟨HavingClause⟩ and the ⟨OrderClause⟩ non-terminals. The rationale for this positioning is that:

- The prefer clause should be after the group-by/having clauses, as it would make sense to use in the former the aggregates computed by the latter.
- The prefer clause should be before the limit/offset clauses, as it would be counter-intuitive to miss preferred solutions because they have been limited out, so the limit should apply to the preferred solutions.
- The prefer clause could equivalently be either before or after the order-by clause, but there is no reason to sort solutions that are going to be discarded afterwards. Naturally an optimizer could also re-order these computations, but there is no reason why the default execution plan should not put these in the more efficient order already. A further advantage of placing the prefer clause before the order-by clause is that this avoids requiring from compliant SPREFQL implementations that they maintain the order of the result set.

The full EBNF grammar for SPREFQL is the result of starting with the grammar for SPARQL 1.1 [10, Section 19.8], replacing Rule 18 with the first rule below, and appending the rest of the rules below.

⟨SolutionModifier⟩	::=	[⟨GroupClause⟩] [⟨HavingClause⟩] [⟨PreferClause⟩]
		[⟨OrderClause⟩] [⟨LimitOffsetClauses⟩]
⟨PreferClause⟩	::=	'PREFER' ⟨VarList⟩ 'TO' ⟨VarList⟩ 'IF' ⟨ParetoPref⟩
⟨VarList⟩	::=	⟨Var⟩
	|	'(' ⟨Var⟩+ ')'
⟨ParetoPref⟩	::=	⟨PrioritizedPref⟩ ['AND' ⟨ParetoPref⟩]
⟨PrioritizedPref⟩	::=	⟨BasicPref⟩ ['PRIOR' 'TO' ⟨PrioritizedPref⟩]
⟨BasicPref⟩	::=	'(' ⟨ParetoPref⟩ ')'
	|	⟨SimplePref⟩
⟨SimplePref⟩	::=	⟨Constraint⟩

Fig. 1. The SPREFQL grammar.

Figure 1 gives the EBNF rules that define ⟨*PreferClause*⟩ and also re-
define ⟨*SolutionModifier*⟩. All non-terminals that are not defined in this
table are defined by standard SPARQL syntax: ⟨*GroupClause*⟩ (Rule 19),
⟨*HavingClause*⟩ (Rule 21), ⟨*OrderClause*⟩ (Rule 23), ⟨*LimitOffsetClauses*⟩
(Rule 25). ⟨*Constraint*⟩ (Rule 69), and ⟨*Var*⟩ (Rule 108). Note, in particular,
how basic preferences are a conjunction of the standard SPARQL ⟨*Constraint*⟩
used in the definitions of "HAVING" and "FILTER" clauses. This means that
preferences are expressed using the familiar syntax of SPARQL constraints.

In the remainder, we shall call *query base* $B(Q)$ the standard SPARQL query
that is derived from a SPREFQL query Q by removing the "PREFER" clause. We
shall also call *full result set* the result set of $B(Q)$ and *preferred result set* the
result set of Q. We continue with a simple example in SPREFQL.

Example 6. Suppose that we want to query an RDF database with movies and
we have the following preference:

> 'I prefer one movie to another iff their genre are the same and the first one
> runs longer.'

The size of the preferred result set is equal to the number of the available
genres in the dataset (since two films with different genre are incomparable).
For each genre, the selected film must be the one with the longest runtime. The
corresponding SPREFQL query is listed in Listing 1.

To express preference of one binding set over another, we first use the
"PREFER" clause to assign variable names to the bindings in the two binding
sets, so that the two binding sets can be distinguished from each other. We then
use the "IF" clause to express the conditions that make the first binding set
dominate the second one. In the query in Listing 1, for example, there are three
bindings in each result, (?title ?genre ?runtime). In order to compare two
binding sets, the "PREFER" clause assigns the bindings in the first result to the
variables (?title1 ?genre1 ?runtime1) and the bindings in the second result
to the variables (?title2 ?genre2 ?runtime2). These new variable names are
then used in the "IF" clause to specify when the first result dominates the second result. Notice that any name can be used for the variables in the "PREFER"
clause, and what maps them to the variables in the "SELECT" clause is the
order of appearance. For example, in this query, variables ?title1, ?title2
correspond to variable ?title, the variables ?genre1, ?genre2 correspond to
variable ?genre and so on. Note also that the names in the "PREFER" clause
need to be distinct from each other, but they do *not* need to be distinct from
the names in the "SELECT" clause. In this manner, the style shown in Listing 2
is also possible, if the query author prefers it.

Given the above, we define well-formed SPREFQL queries as follows:

Definition 4. Let Q = SELECT L WHERE P_1 PREFER L_1 TO L_2 IF P_2 *be a
SPREFQL query produced by the grammar of Fig. 1. Then, Q is well-formed iff
$|L| = |L_1| = |L_2|$ and all variables of L_1, L_2 are distinct.*

Listing 1. 'I prefer one movie over another iff their genre is the same and the duration of the first is longer'.

```
SELECT ?title ?genre ?runtime WHERE {
  ?s a :film. ?s :title ?title. ?s :genre ?genre. ?s :runtime ?runtime.
}
PREFER (?title1 ?genre1 ?runtime1) TO (?title2 ?genre2 ?runtime2)
IF (?genre1 = ?genre2 && ?runtime1 > ?runtime2)
```

Listing 2. 'I prefer one movie over another iff their genre is the same and the duration of the first is longer'.

```
SELECT ?title ?genre ?runtime WHERE {
  ?s a :film. ?s :title ?title. ?s :genre ?genre. ?s :runtime ?runtime.
}
PREFER (?t ?genre ?runtime) TO (?otherT ?otherGenre ?otherRuntime)
IF (?genre = ?otherGenre && ?runtime > ?otherRuntime)
```

Listing 3. 'Given two action movies, I prefer the longest one and more recent one with equal importance'.

```
SELECT ?title ?genre ?runtime WHERE {
  ?s a :film. ?s :genre :action.
  ?s :title ?title. ?s :runtime ?runtime. ?s :year ?year.
}
PREFER (?title1 ?runtime1 ?year1) TO (?title2 ?runtime2 ?year2)
IF (?runtime1 > ?runtime2) AND (?year1 > ?year2)
```

Listing 4. 'Given two action movies, I prefer the one that runs between 115 and 125 min. If they are the same to me according to this criterion, I prefer the ones that they are after 2005'.

```
SELECT ?title ?genre ?runtime WHERE {
  ?s a :film. ?s :genre :action.
  ?s :title ?title. ?s :runtime ?runtime. ?s :year ?year.
}
PREFER (?title1 ?run1 ?year1) TO (?title2 ?run2 ?year2)
IF ( ?run1 >= 115 && ?run1 <= 125 && (?run2 < 115 || ?run2 > 125) )
PRIOR TO (?year1 >= 2005 && ?year2 < 2005)
```

Listing 5. 'I want to watch a movie with "Mad Max" in the title, and I prefer original movies to their sequels'.

```
SELECT ?film ?title WHERE {
  ?film a :film . ?film :title ?title. FILTER regex(?title,"Mad Max").
}
PREFER (?film1 ?title1) TO (?film2 ?title2)
IF EXISTS { ?film1 :sequel ?film2 }
```

Listing 6. Rewrite of the "PREFER" clause in Listing 3 without using the "AND" combinator.

```
PREFER (?title1 ?runtime1 ?year1) TO (?title2 ?runtime2 ?year2)
IF ( ((?runtime1 > ?runtime2) && !(?year2 > ?year1))
  || ((?year1 > ?year2) && !(?runtime2 > ?runtime1)) )
```

Listing 7. Rewrite of the "PREFER" clause in Listing 4 without using the "PRIOR TO" combinator.

```
PREFER (?title1 ?run1 ?year1) TO (?title2 ?run2 ?year2)
IF ( (?run1 >= 115 && ?run1 <= 125 &&  (?run2 < 115 || ?run2 > 125))
     ||
     ( !(?run1 >= 115 && ?run1 <= 125 && (?run2 < 115 || ?run2 > 125)) &&
       !(?run2 >= 115 && ?run2 <= 125 && (?run1 < 115 || ?run1 > 125)) &&
       (?year1 >= 2005 && ?year2 < 2005)
     ) )
```

In Sect. 2 we presented some ways so that two preference relations can be combined into one more complex one. As in the framework of Chomicki, we can also use boolean operators to combine the individual boolean expressions (boolean composition). Besides logical operators, we offer the following two preference combinators for combining preference relations:

– Pareto composition: the "AND" combinator composes a relation from two preference relations that are of equal importance (cf. Listing 3). We follow previous work [12,20] in using "AND" for the Pareto combinator, noting that it should not be confused with the logical conjunction operator.
– Prioritized composition: the "PRIOR TO" combinator composes a preference relation where the less-important right-hand side argument is only applied if the more-important left-hand side argument does not impose any preference between two object (cf. Listing 4).

These combinations can be expressed within a simple constraint with the elaborate use of boolean operators. But this 'syntactic sugar' makes useful expressions a lot more readable. Compare, for example, the queries in Listings 3 and 4 with their equivalent queries without using the "AND" and "PRIOR TO" combinators, in Listings 6 and 7 respectively.

Since a basic simple preference is a *Constraint*, anything that can appear as a parameter in a SPARQL "FILTER" clause can be used as a simple basic user preference, and has the same meaning as in SPARQL "FILTER" clauses. This could be also an "EXISTS" expression, as it is shown in Listing 5. These type of preference relations are known as *extrinsic* preferences [5], and are not supported by Chomicki's framework. A preference relation is extrinsic if the decision of whether an element is preferred over another depends not only on the values of the elements themselves, but also on external factors (such as the the :sequel predicate in our example).

3.2   Semantics

In this section we will define the semantics of SPREFQL. Our semantics extend the standard semantics of SPARQL [10]. We assume basic familiarity of the semantics of SPARQL, but we will present some basic terminology when needed.

We denote by $\mathbf{T}$ the set of all *RDF terms* and by $\mathbf{V}$ the set of all *variables*. A *mapping* μ is a partial function $\mu : \mathbf{V} \to \mathbf{T}$. The *domain* of a mapping μ, denoted as $\text{dom}(\mu)$ is the subset of $\mathbf{V}$ where μ is defined. It is straightforward to see that mappings express variable bindings and that given a mapping μ it is always possible to construct a "VALUES" clause that expresses the same bindings as μ does.

Example 7. Let $\mu = \{(\mathsf{g}, \texttt{"Sci-fi"}), (\mathsf{r}, 121)\}$ Then μ expresses the same binding of variable "?g" as the clause "VALUES (?g ?r) { "Sci-fi"121 }".

Following Pérez et al. [16] we denote by $[\![\cdot]\!]_D$ the *evaluation* of a SPARQL query over a dataset D. If a query Q is a SELECT query, then $[\![Q]\!]_D$ is a set of mappings, which are the solutions that satisfy Q over D. If Q is an ASK query, then $[\![Q]\!]_D$ is equal to true if there exists any solution for Q in D, otherwise it is equal to false.

We will now continue with the semantics of the preference solution modifier. Firstly though, we have to include some preliminary definitions:

Definition 5. *Let* $L = (l_1, \ldots, l_n), B = (b_1, \ldots, b_n)$ *be two variable lists and* μ *be a mapping s.t.* $\text{dom}(\mu) = \mathcal{B}$, *where* $\mathcal{B}$ *is the set of all variables of B. Then, we denote by* $\mathsf{Rename}_{B \to L}(\mu)$ *a mapping that is created from μ by renaming variable* b_i *to* l_i, *for all* $i = 1, \ldots, n$.

Definition 6. *Let* L, L', B *be three variable lists, s.t.* $|L| = |L'| = |B|$ *and all variables that appear in* L, L' *are distinct. Also, let* μ, μ' *be two mappings s.t.* $\text{dom}(\mu) = \text{dom}(\mu') = \mathcal{B}$, *where* $\mathcal{B}$ *is the set of all variables of B. Then, we denote by* $\mathsf{ConstructMapping}_{B \to L, B \to L'}(\mu, \mu')$ *a mapping such that*

$$\mathsf{ConstructMapping}_{B \to L, B \to L'}(\mu, \mu') = \mathsf{Rename}_{B \to L}(\mu) \cup \mathsf{Rename}_{B \to L'}(\mu').$$

Definition 7. *Let C be a SPARQL Constraint and μ be a mapping. Then, we denote by* $\mathsf{ConstructQuery}(C, \mu)$ *a query of the form* "ASK { FILTER C S }" *where s is the SPARQL ValuesClause that corresponds to the mapping μ. Note: SPARQL Constraint and SPARQL ValuesClause as defined in the SPARQL specification [10].*

Example 8. Let $\mu = \{(\mathsf{g}, \texttt{"Sci-fi"}), (\mathsf{r}, 121)\}$, $\mu' = \{(\mathsf{g}, \texttt{"Sci-fi"}), (\mathsf{r}, 124)\}$, $B = (\mathsf{g}, \mathsf{r})$, $L = (\mathsf{g1}, \mathsf{r1})$, $L' = (\mathsf{g2}, \mathsf{r2})$ and $C = $ "(g1 = g2 && r1 > r2)". Then,

$$\mathsf{ConstructMapping}_{B \to L, B \to L'}(\mu, \mu') = \mu^* = \left\{ \begin{array}{l} (\mathsf{g1}, \texttt{"Sci-fi"}), (\mathsf{r1}, 121), \\ (\mathsf{g2}, \texttt{"Sci-fi"}), (\mathsf{r2}, 124) \end{array} \right\}$$

$$\text{ConstructQuery}(C, \mu^*) = \begin{array}{l} \texttt{"ASK \{ FILTER (?g1 = ?g2 \&\& ?r1 > ?r2)} \\ \texttt{VALUES (?g1 ?r1 ?g2 ?r2)} \\ \texttt{\{ ("Sci-fi"121"Sci-fi"124) \} \}"} \end{array}$$

As stated earlier, our preference solution modifier expresses a preference relation between the results of the query base, therefore the meaning of the "PREFER" clause is actually a binary predicate p such that $p(\mu, \mu')$ holds if μ is preferred over μ'. Hence, below, the *evaluation* $[\![\cdot]\!]_D$ of a "PREFER" clause takes two mappings as input. Recall that except from a simple *Constraint*, a preference relation can be expressed using the *Pareto* and *Prioritized* preference compositors.[1]

Definition 8. *Let D be a dataset. Also, let C be a constraint and L, L', B be three variable lists, s.t. $|L| = |L'| = |B|$ and all variables that appear in L, L' are distinct. Also, let μ, μ' be two mappings s.t. $\text{dom}(\mu) = \text{dom}(\mu') = \mathcal{B}$, where $\mathcal{B}$ is the set of all variables of B. Then,*

$$[\![\text{PREFER } L \text{ TO } L' \text{ IF } C]\!]_{D,B} = \{(\mu, \mu') : [\![\text{ConstructQuery}(C, \mu^*)]\!]_D = \text{true},$$
$$\mu^* = \text{ConstructMapping}_{B \to L, B \to L'}(\mu, \mu')\}$$

Composite clauses using the "PRIOR TO" and "AND" combinators are defined as follows:

1. $[\![\text{PREFER } L \text{ TO } L' \text{ IF } P \text{ PRIOR TO } Q]\!]_{D,B} = [\![\mathcal{P}]\!]_{D,B} \rhd [\![\mathcal{Q}]\!]_{D,B}$,
2. $[\![\text{PREFER } L \text{ TO } L' \text{ IF } P \text{ AND } Q]\!]_{D,B} = [\![P]\!]_{D,B} \otimes [\![Q]\!]_{D,B}$,

where $\mathcal{P} = \text{PREFER } L \text{ TO } L' \text{ IF } P$, $\mathcal{Q} = \text{PREFER } L \text{ TO } L' \text{ IF } Q$, C is a constraint expression and P, Q non-terminal symbols.

Notice that in Example 8, $[\![\text{PREFER } L \text{ TO } L' \text{ IF } C]\!]_D(\mu, \mu') = \text{true}$ for every dataset D, or in other words the evaluation of the corresponding preference predicate is independent from the dataset D. This is the case for all constraint expressions that use only built-ins. The reason why we use the construction of this ASK query, is in the case of preferences that are defined with the use of an EXISTS expression (see for example Listing 5). In that example, in order to check whether a mapping is preferred from another, one has to check the dataset D for the existence of the corresponding :sequel triple.

Having defined the meaning of preference relations, we can proceed to define how the preference solution modifier uses a preference relation to reduce the full result set of the query base into the preferred result set. For this, we refer to the *winnow* operator $w_P([\![Q]\!]_D)$ which outputs the preferred result set when given the preference relation P and the full result set $[\![Q]\!]_D$ (cf. Definition 3).

Definition 9. *Let Q be a SELECT query. Then, we denote by $\text{ProjVarList}(Q)$ the projection list in the same order that it appears in the SELECT clause.*

---

[1] We use a slightly different notation in the following definitions from the definitions in Sect. 2. Instead of writing $[\![\mu \succ_C \mu']\!]_{D,B}$ we write $[\![C]\!]_{D,B}(\mu, \mu') = \text{true}$. In addition, the operators $\rhd$ and $\otimes$ correspond to the Prioritized and Pareto compositions.

Definition 10. *Let D be a dataset, Q be a SELECT query and L, L' be two variable lists such that $|\mathsf{ProjVarList}(Q)| = |L| = |L'|$ and all variables that appear in L, L' are distinct. Then,*

$$[\![Q \textsf{ PREFER } L \textsf{ TO } L' \textsf{ IF } C]\!]_D = w_{[\![\textsf{PREFER } L \textsf{ TO } L' \textsf{ IF } C]\!]_{D,B}}([\![Q]\!]_D),$$

where $B = \mathsf{ProjVarList}(Q)$ and C be a non terminal symbol.

3.3 Expressive Power of SPREFQL

Winnow can be expressed using standard relational algebra operators [5]. Therefore, a SPREFQL query, which is essentially a SPARQL 1.1 query extended with a winnow operation, can be also expressed using standard SPARQL 1.1, using a "NOT EXISTS" query rewriting. Given a SPREFQL query of the form

SELECT L WHERE $\{\ P\ \}$ PREFER L_1 TO L_2 IF C

the preferred result set consists of the result mappings of the query base that are the most preferred ones, or equivalently all mappings in the full result set such that there does not exist any mapping that is more preferred. This fact can be expressed using a standard SPARQL query of the following form

SELECT L WHERE $\{\ P$ FILTER NOT EXISTS $\{\ P_{\{L/L_1\}}$ FILTER $C_{\{L_2/L\}}\ \}\ \}$

where $P_{\{L/L_1\}}$ is created by P by replacing all variable names of P that appear in L with its corresponding variable in L_1, and $C_{\{L_2/L\}}$ is created by C by replacing all variable names of C that appear in L_2 with its L. The remaining variables on the new constructions are replaced with fresh variables. If C is a Pareto or a Prioritized composition, we first apply the rewritings into their corresponding simple preferences (ref. Sect. 2, Listings 6 and 7). For example, the corresponding rewriting of Listing 1 is illustrated in Listing 8.

Comparing the two queries, we observe that the SPREFQL query is smaller (it contains half the number of triple patterns), and it separates the definition of preferences from the hard constraints. This separation alleviates the need for the query author to include in the query body the actual operation that performs the selection of the best solutions, and to express the desired definition of preferences is more clearly. Apart from the advantages in human readability, there exist advantages in machine optimization as well. It would be difficult for a general purpose SPARQL optimizer to find out that in the query in Listing 8 actually implements an operation that resembles a self-join and the result can be computed even in a single pass (as in BNL algorithm).

4   Experiments

4.1   Implementation and Experimental Setup

This section experimentally validates the idea that optimizations specific to SPREFQL (such as efficient implementations of the winnow operator) can improve the overall query performance in comparison to the equivalent standard SPARQL query and its standard optimizations. As a proof of concept, we provide an open source prototype implementation of SPREFQL.[2] Our implementation is developed in Java within the RDF4J framework,[3] and it includes two implementations of the winnow operator (i.e. using NL and BNL algorithms) and a query rewriter which transforms a SPREFQL query into the equivalent SPARQL query, using the "NOT EXISTS" transformation. Our evaluator has the ability to operate over a simple memory store using the standard RDF4J evaluation mechanism, or over a remote SPARQL endpoint, in which the query base is executed.

In this experiment we are performing SPREFQL queries on the LinkedMDB database.[4] Our query set contains 7 queries. The queries are: **Q1:** Listing 1, **Q2:** Listing 3, **Q3:** Listing 4, **Q4:** Listing 3 without genre restriction, **Q5:** Listing 4 without genre restriction, **Q6:** Listing 5 and **Q7:** Listing 5 without the FILTER, but for all movies that feature the character 'James Bond', instead.[5] Firstly, we issue the query bases for each SPREFQL query directly on the SPARQL endpoint, and then we evaluate all SPREFQL queries, using (i) the NL algorithm, (ii) the query rewriting method and (iii) the BNL algorithm. The window size for the BNL algorithm was set large enough to contain all results, since we know that BNL behaves better if the preferred result set fits entirely in the window. The experiment was performed on a Linux machine (Ubuntu 14.04 LTS) with a 4-core Intel(R) Xeon(R) CPU E31220 at 3.10 GHz and 30 GB RAM. The LinkedMDB dataset was loaded into a locally deployed Virtuoso SPARQL endpoint.[6]

Listing 8. Rewriting of Listing 1 into standard SPARQL.

```
SELECT ?title ?genre ?runtime
WHERE {
  ?s a :film. ?s :title ?title. ?s :genre ?genre.
  ?s :runtime ?runtime.
  FILTER NOT EXISTS {
    ?s_tmp a :film. ?s_tmp :title ?title1. ?s_tmp :genre ?genre1.
    ?s_tmp :runtime ?runtime1.
    FILTER (?genre1 = ?genre && ?runtime1 > ?runtime)  }
}
```

---

[2] cf. https://bitbucket.org/dataengineering/sprefql.
[3] cf. http://rdf4j.org.
[4] cf. http://www.linkedmdb.org.
[5] These listings are edited in the paper for conciseness. The exact queries used in the experiment can be found at our code repository, cf. Footnote 4.
[6] Community edition Version 7.1, cf. http://virtuoso.openlinksw.com.

4.2   Results

Table 2 gives the experimental results. We observe that NL has the worst query execution times, and its performance is quadratic in the execution time of the query base. On the first 6 queries, BNL performs better than rewriting. Since BNL was configured so that to perform at its best, the query execution time of BNL is in most cases almost equal to that of the query base. The difference between the execution times of BNL and the query base in Q4 and Q5, can be explained due to the fact that the full result set is larger and BNL has to make more comparisons to calculate the preferred result. The rewrite method in those cases performs much worse than BNL (but much better than NL). In Q7 though, where an extrinsic preference is expressed, we have a different situation. The comparisons that BNL has to make are not that many (they are at most $23 \cdot 22$), but here BNL has to consider the database each time in order to decide whether one solution is preferred over another. So, BNL issues a heavy load of ASK queries to the endpoint, and therefore rewriting outperforms BNL in Q7. This also explains why BNL has a comparable execution time for Q7 and Q1, although Q1 fetches and considers orders of magnitude more results than Q7. As Q6 also expresses an extrinsic preference, we would expect query rewriting to outperform BNL, but the base result set is very small and the cost to prepare the rewrite is not recuperated. Overall, in our experiments BNL performed better in intrinsic preferences while rewriting performed better in extrinsic preferences.

In the last two queries, we observe that the number of the results that BNL returns is greater than the expected result. This happens because here the preference relation (which is the same for Q6 and Q7) is not a transitive relation (the :sequel is not a transitive predicate). This is a known issue of BNL, since BNL returns the correct number of results only on preference relations that impose a *strict partial order* (cf. Sect. 2). Therefore, in terms of the correctness of the result, rewriting is better than BNL for non strict partial order intrinsic preferences (in extrinsic preferences, rewriting is preferred anyway due to time performance). Checking whether an intrinsic preference expression corresponds to a strict partial order relation is not computationally challenging, as it depends only the size of the expression itself [5, Sect. 3.1]. In extrinsic expressions, transitivity needs to be confirmed extensionally by issuing "ASK" queries.

Regarding the memory footprint of the BNL algorithm, since BNL only maintains the current set of undominated results it is expected to require considerably less space than the base result set. In most cases, the maximum number of results maintained in memory will be close to the final number of results. In our experiments, only Q2 and Q4 required a slight amount of extra space, which can happen when many results that do not dominate each other are received before a result that dominates them.

Table 2. Number of returned results and query execution time (in milliseconds) for NL, query rewriting, and BNL. For BNL, the number of binding sets that need to be maintained in memory is also given, and the total number of bindings in these sets.

	Query base		NL		Rewrite		BNL			
	Exec.	Num.	Exec.	Num.	Exec.	Num.	Exec.	Num.	Num.	Num.
	Time	Res.	Time	Res.	Time	Res.	Time	Bindsets	Bindings	Res.
Q1	556	6,955	1,613,515	36	4,750	36	812	36	108	36
Q2	52	390	9,124	5	188	5	65	6	18	5
Q3	52	390	10,530	8	254	8	91	8	24	8
Q4	872	9,612	3,272,789	8	197,044	8	1,238	9	27	8
Q5	872	9,612	3,452,048	108	193,338	108	2,370	108	324	108
Q6	135	4	794	1	296	1	170	2	4	2
Q7	85	23	1,276	2	93	2	820	8	16	8

5 Related Work

In the Semantic Web literature there have been proposed SPARQL extensions that feature the expression of preferences [17], typically transferring ideas and results from relational database frameworks much like the work presented here.

When it comes to quantitative preferences, prominent examples include the extensions proposed by Cheng et al. [4] and Magliacane et al. [15]. Closer to our work, influential databases research on *qualitative* preferences includes the work of Kießling [11,12]. This was used by Siberski et al. [20] to propose a SPARQL extension using a "PREFERRING" solution modifier. Contrary to our approach, these preferences are expressed using unary preference constructors. These constructors are of two types: *boolean preferences* where the preferred elements fulfill a specific boolean condition while the non-preferred do not; and *scoring preferences*, denoted with a "HIGHEST" or "LOWEST" keyword, where the preferred elements have a higher (or lower) value from the non preferred ones. Simple preferences expressed with these constructors can be further combined using Pareto and prioritized composition operators. Gueroussova et al. [9] further extended this language with an "IF-THEN-ELSE" clause which allows expressing *conditional preferences* that apply only if a condition holds. Conditional preferences allow several other 'syntactic sugar' preference constructors to be defined, such as "AROUND" and "BETWEEN".

By comparison, the work presented here is (to the best of our knowledge) the first one to transfer to the Semantic Web the more general framework by Chomicki [5], allowing the expression of extrinsic preferences. Each of the basic preference constructors (boolean, scoring and conditional preferences) as well as the compositions in the approaches by Siberski et al. [20] and Gueroussova et al. [9] can be transformed in SPREFQL. For example, a query of the form

```
SELECT ?s ?o WHERE {?s :p ?o} PREFERRING HIGHEST(?o)
```

can be transformed into SPREFQL:

```
SELECT ?s ?o WHERE {?s :p ?o} PREFER (?s1 ?o1) TO (?s2 ?o2) IF (?o1>?o2)
```

Since in SPREFQL the preference relation is expressed using a binary formula, the reverse translation is not always possible (for example in Listings 1 and 5).

6 Conclusions and Future Work

In this paper we propose SPREFQL, an extension of SPARQL that allows the query author to specify a preference that modifies the query solutions. Although a SPREFQL query can be transformed into standard SPARQL, standard SPARQL query processing misses opportunities to optimize execution by avoiding the exhaustive comparison of all solution pairs. Our experiments demonstrate that when the BNL algorithm is applicable, even for relatively small result sets of under 10k tuples its execution can be two orders of magnitude faster than that of state-of-art SPARQL query processors.

Our first future work direction will be to evaluate the mean gain that can be achieved on realistic workflows. We plan to achieve this by identifying potential test cases where the SPREFQL extensions can be used, so that we can estimate how often the BNL optimization is applicable. This will also help us further develop the language, identifying additional 'syntactic sugar' constructs that can hint at optimizations targeting intransitive relations that fall outside the scope of BNL. Further extensions could allow the client to refer to preferences and preference-related metadata within the knowledge base itself [14,18,19].

A more ambitious future extension is to allow the client application to not only request the most preferred results, but to also be able to request all results ordered in different 'layers' of preference. This is a more general solution than any quantitative preference ranking system, as it handles the full generality of partially ordered preferences. We plan to base this on graph-theoretic work in sequencing and scheduling, such as the Coffman-Graham algorithm [6] which is widely used to visualize graphs as layers panning out of a central vertex. By representing arbitrary (including partial-order) preference relations as a directed graph, we can use similar layering approaches to order results in such a way that no dominated tuple is returned before any of the tuples that dominate it.

Acknowledgements. The work described here has received funding from the European Union's Horizon 2020 research and innovation programme under grant agreement No. 644564. For more details, please visit https://www.big-data-europe.eu.

References

1. Agrawal, R., Wimmers, E.L.: A framework for expressing and combining preferences. In: Proceedings of the 2000 ACM SIGMOD International Conference on Management of Data, Dallas, Texas, USA, pp. 297–306, 16–18 May 2000
2. Berners-Lee, T., Hendler, J., Lassila, O.: The semantic web. Sci. Am. **284**(5), 28–37 (2001)

3. Börzsönyi, S., Kossmann, D., Stocker, K.: The skyline operator. In: Proceedings of the 17th International Conference on Data Engineering (ICDE 2001), Heidelberg, Germany, pp. 421–430, 2–6 April 2001

4. Cheng, J., Ma, Z.M., Yan, L.: f-SPARQL: a flexible extension of SPARQL. In: Bringas, P.G., Hameurlain, A., Quirchmayr, G. (eds.) DEXA 2010. LNCS, vol. 6261, pp. 487–494. Springer, Heidelberg (2010). doi:10.1007/978-3-642-15364-8_41

5. Chomicki, J.: Preference formulas in relational queries. ACM Trans. Database Syst. **28**(4), 427–466 (2003)

6. Coffman, E.G.J., Graham, R.L.: Optimal scheduling for two-processor systems. Acta Informatica **1**, 200–213 (1972). doi:10.1007/bf00288685

7. Delgrande, J.P., Schaub, T., Tompits, H., Wang, K.: A classification and survey of preference handling approaches in nonmonotonic reasoning. Comput. Intell. **20**(2), 308–334 (2004)

8. Domshlak, C., Hüllermeier, E., Kaci, S., Prade, H.: Preferences in AI: an overview. Artif. Intell. **175**(7–8), 1037–1052 (2011)

9. Gueroussova, M., Polleres, A., McIlraith, S.A.: SPARQL with qualitative and quantitative preferences. In: Proceedings of the 2nd International Workshop on Ordering and Reasoning (OrdRing 2013), at ISWC 2013, Sydney, Australia. CEUR Workshop Proceedings, vol. 1059, 22 October 2013

10. Harris, S., Seaborne, A.: SPARQL 1.1 Query Language. Recommendation, W3C, March 2013. https://www.w3.org/TR/sparql11-query

11. Kießling, W.: Foundations of preferences in database systems. In: Proceedings of 28th International Conference on Very Large Data Bases (VLDB 2002), Hong Kong, China, pp. 311–322, 20–23 August 2002

12. Kießling, W., Köstler, G.: Preference SQL - design, implementation, experiences. In: Proceedings of the 28th International Conference on Very Large Data Bases (VLDB 2002), Hong Kong, China, pp. 990–1001, 20–23 August 2002

13. Koutrika, G., Ioannidis, Y.E.: Personalization of queries in database systems. In: Proceedings of the 20th International Conference on Data Engineering (ICDE 2004), Boston, MA, USA, pp. 597–608, 30 March–2 April 2004

14. Lukasiewicz, T., Martinez, M.V., Simari, G.I.: Preference-based query answering in Datalog+/− ontologies. In: Proceedings of the 23rd International Joint Conference on Artificial Intelligence (IJCAI 2013), Beijing, China, pp. 1017–1023, 3–9 August 2013

15. Magliacane, S., Bozzon, A., Della Valle, E.: Efficient execution of top-K SPARQL queries. In: Cudré-Mauroux, P., Heflin, J., Sirin, E., Tudorache, T., Euzenat, J., Hauswirth, M., Parreira, J.X., Hendler, J., Schreiber, G., Bernstein, A., Blomqvist, E. (eds.) ISWC 2012. LNCS, vol. 7649, pp. 344–360. Springer, Heidelberg (2012). doi:10.1007/978-3-642-35176-1_22

16. Pérez, J., Arenas, M., Gutierrez, C.: Semantics and complexity of SPARQL. ACM Trans. Database Syst. **34**(3), 16:1–16:45 (2009). http://doi.acm.org/10.1145/1567274.1567278

17. Pivert, O., Slama, O., Thion, V.: SPARQL extensions with preferences: a survey. In: Ossowski, S. (ed.) Proceedings of the 31st Annual ACM Symposium on Applied Computing, Pisa, Italy, pp. 1015–1020. ACM, 4–8 April 2016

18. Polo, L., Mínguez, I., Berrueta, D., Ruiz, C., Gómez-Pérez, J.M.: User preferences in the web of data. Semant. Web **5**(1), 67–75 (2014). http://dx.doi.org/10.3233/SW-2012-0080

19. Rosati, J., Noia, T., Lukasiewicz, T., Leone, R., Maurino, A.: Preference queries with ceteris paribus semantics for linked data. In: Debruyne, C., Panetto, H., Meersman, R., Dillon, T., Weichhart, G., An, Y., Ardagna, C.A. (eds.) OTM 2015. LNCS, vol. 9415, pp. 423–442. Springer, Cham (2015). doi:10.1007/978-3-319-26148-5_28
20. Siberski, W., Pan, J.Z., Thaden, U.: Querying the semantic web with preferences. In: Cruz, I., Decker, S., Allemang, D., Preist, C., Schwabe, D., Mika, P., Uschold, M., Aroyo, L.M. (eds.) ISWC 2006. LNCS, vol. 4273, pp. 612–624. Springer, Heidelberg (2006). doi:10.1007/11926078_44
21. Stefanidis, K., Koutrika, G., Pitoura, E.: A survey on representation, composition and application of preferences in database systems. ACM Trans. Database Syst. **36**(3), 19:1–19:45 (2011)
22. Valle, E.D., Schlobach, S., Krötzsch, M., Bozzon, A., Ceri, S., Horrocks, I.: Order matters! Harnessing a world of orderings for reasoning over massive data. Semant. Web **4**(2), 219–231 (2013)

Encoding Category Correlations into Bilingual Topic Modeling for Cross-Lingual Taxonomy Alignment

Tianxing Wu[1(✉)], Lei Zhang[2], Guilin Qi[1], Xuan Cui[1], and Kang Xu[1]

[1] School of Computer Science and Engineering, Southeast University, Nanjing, China
{wutianxing,gqi,xcui,kxu}@seu.edu.cn
[2] Institute AIFB, Karlsruhe Institue of Technology, Karlsruhe, Germany
l.zhang@kit.edu

Abstract. Cross-lingual taxonomy alignment (CLTA) refers to mapping each category in the source taxonomy of one language onto a ranked list of most relevant categories in the target taxonomy of another language. Recently, vector similarities depending on bilingual topic models have achieved the state-of-the-art performance on CLTA. However, these models only model the textual context of categories, but ignore explicit category correlations, such as correlations between the categories and their co-occurring words in text or correlations among the categories of ancestor-descendant relationships in a taxonomy. In this paper, we propose a unified solution to encode category correlations into bilingual topic modeling for CLTA, which brings two novel category correlation based bilingual topic models, called **CC-BiLDA** and **CC-BiBTM**. Experiments on two real-world datasets show our proposed models significantly outperform the state-of-the-art baselines on CLTA (at least **+10.9%** in each evaluation metric).

1 Introduction

Over past decades, with the dramatic growth of multilingual knowledge on the Web, aligning knowledge of different languages becomes an important way of realizing globalization of information. Taxonomies are a kind of significant knowledge, which often refers to category hierarchies used for organizing and classifying multilingual big data, and are prevalent on the Web, such as Web site directories (e.g., Dmoz.org) and product catalogues (e.g., eBay product taxonomy). Due to the different grounded languages and intentions of usage, even cross-lingual taxonomies of the same genre are highly heterogenous in linguistics, structure and contents. Hence, to facilitate knowledge sharing across languages, cross-lingual taxonomy alignment (CLTA), which maps each category in the source taxonomy of one language onto a ranked list of most relevant categories in the target taxonomy of another language, is a critical task to solve.

Previous work [2,10,15] on CLTA relies on string similarities based on a translation tool and domain-specific information, such as book instances and financial

© Springer International Publishing AG 2017
C. d'Amato et al. (Eds.): ISWC 2017, Part I, LNCS 10587, pp. 728–744, 2017.
DOI: 10.1007/978-3-319-68288-4_43

calculation items. There are two limitations: 1) string similarities suffer from the vocabulary mismatch problem, i.e., translated texts might be semantically similar even though the specific terms used differ substantially; 2) domain-specific information is often unavailable when aligning cross-lingual and cross-domain taxonomies (e.g., Web site directories and product catalogues).

To overcome these two limitations, our previous work [18] on CLTA introduces a vector similarity based approach relying on bilingual topic models without using any domain-specific information and has achieved the state-of-the-art performance. However, the problem is that these bilingual topic models directly model textual context of categories without considering explicit category correlations. The first category correlation is **co-occurrence correlation**, which exists between the categories and their co-occurring words in text. Some studies such as [9,13] have shown that simultaneously modeling co-occurred metadata (e.g., tags and authors) and text can learn higher-quality topic vectors for many applications. Another important category correlation is **structural correlation**, which means the associations among categories of ancestor-descendant relationships in a taxonomy. The idea of using this kind of correlation is intuitive, that is, if two categories from different taxonomies have similar ancestors or descendants, they may be of high relevance. Thus, we argue that if the above two kinds of category correlations are directly neglected, the topic vector of each category generated by existing bilingual topic models is insufficient to CLTA.

In this paper, we aim to exploit the benefits from both vector similarities and explicit category correlations to deal with the problem of CLTA. Therefore, we try to encode co-occurrence correlations and structural correlations into bilingual topic modeling, which poses two challenges:

- **How to capture both co-occurrence correlations and structural correlations?**
- **How to integrate such explicit category correlations into bilingual topic modeling?**

To solve these challenges, we propose a unified solution to encode category correlations into existing bilingual topic models, i.e., Bilingual Latent Dirichlet Allocation (BiLDA) [17] and Bilingual Biterm Topic Model (BiBTM) [18]. Before applying our solution, we use the same way in [18] to acquire textual context of categories by querying each category with a search engine and constructing paired bilingual documents with a translation tool, which results in a corpus of paired bilingual documents containing all categories. Here, a *modeling object* is defined as a pair of bilingual documents composed of a set of words in BiLDA or a biterm constructed by two distinct words from a pair of bilingual documents in BiBTM. Our solution is to (1) transform the co-occurrence correlations and structural correlations into a prior category distribution of each modeling object, and (2) integrate all prior category distributions into bilingual topic modeling by designing general steps of generating a word in each modeling object. After applying our solution to BiLDA and BiBTM, we obtain two new category correlation based bilingual topic models, called CC-BiLDA and CC-BiBTM. With the topic vector of each category learned by these two models, we compute vector similarities between the categories of different languages for CLTA.

In summary, the main contributions of this paper are as follows:

- We propose a *unified solution* to encode category correlations into bilingual topic modeling for CLTA, which *leverages the benefits from both vector similarities and explicit category correlations.*
- We design two *new category correlation based bilingual topic models*, CC-BiLDA and CC-BiBTM, by extending BiLDA and BiBTM with our solution. To the best of our knowledge, they are the *first work* on bilingual topic modeling that *simultaneously models bilingual text and its co-occurring categories* to *learn the vector representation* for each category.
- We conduct *experiments* on two real-world datasets and the results show the *effectiveness* of our bilingual topic modes for CLTA, when compared with several state-of-the-art baselines (at least +10.9% in each evaluation metric).

The rest of this paper is organized as follows. Section 2 introduces the background of this work. Section 3 presents the details of two new bilingual topic models by applying our proposed solution. Section 4 gives the experimental results. Section 5 outlines some related work and we conclude in the last section.

2   Preliminaries

In this section, we firstly provide an overview of cross-lingual taxonomy alignment (CLTA) and then discuss the existing bilingual topic models.

2.1   Cross-Lingual Taxonomy Alignment

The wide variety of Web taxonomies from different domains and languages are usually organized in a tree or a directed acyclic graph with categories as nodes. Given two independently created taxonomies of different languages, CLTA aims to map each category in the source taxonomy of one language to the most relevant category in the target taxonomy of another language. The key to CLTA is to measure the relevance between each category in the source taxonomy and its candidate matched categories in the target taxonomy.

Since categories usually do not have textual information to describe themselves, some strategies can be used for getting the textual context of categories in different languages, e.g., by utilizing Wikipedia as an intermediate source and following the interwiki links from one language to another [2] or by querying each category using a search engine and constructing paired bilingual documents by a translation tool [18]. To measure the relevance between categories for CLTA, bilingual topic models, such as BiLDA [17] and BiBTM [18], have been introduced to learn the vector representations of categories from their textual context, which will be discussed in Sect. 2.2. After obtaining the topic distribution of each category, the relevance score between one category in the source taxonomy and another one in the target taxonomy can be computed based on the topic vectors of categories in the same topic space.

2.2 Bilingual Topic Modeling

BiLDA and BiBTM are two existing bilingual topic models and a main difference between them is their modeling objects. BiLDA models paired bilingual documents, each of which is a pair of documents of similar contents but in different languages, such as two Wikipedia articles in different languages interlinked by Wikipedia's language links or a document in one language and its translated version in another language. The generation of a word in a pair of bilingual documents is defined by firstly drawing a topic from a topic distribution of this pair of bilingual documents, and then drawing a word from the topic-word distribution of some language.

BiBTM was proposed to model paired bilingual short documents because BiLDA suffers from the data sparsity problem [6] when documents are short. The modeling objects in BiBTM are biterms, which are unordered word-pairs occurring in a pair of bilingual documents. Any two distinct words in a pair of bilingual documents compose a biterm. For example, given a pair of bilingual documents (d^s, d^t), in which d^s and d^t respectively consist of n distinct words of language s and m distinct words of language t, totally $C_n^2 + C_m^2 + m \times n$ biterms will be generated, where C_m^2 and C_n^2 represent the binomial coefficients. To generate a word in each biterm, BiBTM first draws a topic from a global topic distribution of all biterms, and then draws a word from the topic-word distribution of some language.

3 Models

In this section, we first present an overview of our unified solution to encode category correlations into bilingual topic modeling for CLTA, and then discuss the details of two novel category correlation based bilingual topic models CC-BiLDA and CC-BiBTM resulting from the proposed solution.

3.1 Overview

To perform CLTA, we first learn the vector representations of all categories in the two given taxonomies of different languages using bilingual topic models, where each category can be represented as a topic vector. Then we compute the relevance between each category in the source taxonomy and its candidate matched categories in the target taxonomy using the cosine similarity between the vectors in the same topic space. Since the training of topic models needs large-scale corpus, we apply the same strategy used in [18] to query each category with a search engine to acquire its textual context (i.e., returned snippets). After translating each snippet into another language with a translation tool, each category corresponds to a set of paired bilingual documents and each pair contains at least the given category (maybe more categories) in text. This results in a corpus of paired bilingual documents containing all categories.

Based on the corpus, the previous work [18] first learns the word distribution in BiLDA or the biterm distribution in BiBTM for each topic, and then perform an additional step of topic inference to derive the topic vector for each category. In contrast, we explicitly model each category such that it allows further encoding various category correlations into bilingual topic modeling. In this work, we mainly consider two types of correlations: (1) co-occurrence correlations between the categories and their co-occurring words in text; (2) structural correlations among the categories of ancestor-descendant relationships in a taxonomy.

To capture co-occurrence correlations, we denote each modeling object (i.e., a pair of bilingual documents in BiLDA or a biterm in BiBTM) as a mixture of categories when the words in the modeling object co-occur with these categories in paired bilingual documents. Such a mixture serves as a prior category distribution of each modeling object. Concerning structural correlations among categories, we leverage information content [14] and path length in the taxonomic structure to improve the prior category distribution (the details of computing the prior category distribution of each modeling object are given in Sect. 3.3).

With both co-occurrence correlations and structural correlations encoded in the prior category distribution of each modeling object, we then integrate them into bilingual topic modeling. Since we need to utilize the low-dimensional topic vector of each category for CLTA, connections between explicit categories and latent topics have been built by supposing there exists a probability distribution over topics for each category, i.e., each category is treated as a mixture of topics. Similar to existing methods, for each language, we represent each topic with a mixture of words in that language. Therefore, we design *general steps* of generating a word in each modeling object as follows:

(1) Drawing a category from the prior category distribution of a modeling object;
(2) Drawing a topic from the category-topic distribution;
(3) Drawing a word from the topic-word distribution of some language.

With the above solution, we obtain two novel category correlation based bilingual topic models, CC-BiLDA and CC-BiBTM, which will be discussed in detail in the following sections.

3.2 Generative Processes

Firstly, we introduce some notations and the generative processes of CC-BiLDA and CC-BiBTM.

Given a corpus $\mathbb{O}$, suppose it contains $|\mathbf{D}|$ pairs of bilingual documents, $|\mathbf{B}|$ biterms and C explicit categories from two taxonomies to be aligned, which are of different languages. All paired bilingual documents are denoted by $\mathbf{D} = \{d_j\}_{j=1}^{|\mathbf{D}|} = \{(d_j^s, d_j^t)\}_{j=1}^{|\mathbf{D}|}$, where d_j represents a pair of bilingual documents composed of document d_j^s of length L_j^s in language s and document d_j^t of length L_j^t in language t, and a word in position p of d_j^s (or d_j^t) is denoted by $w_{j,p}^s$ (or $w_{j,p}^t$). All biterms are denoted by $\mathbf{B} = \mathbf{B}^s \cup \mathbf{B}^{st} \cup \mathbf{B}^t = \{b_i^s\}_{i=1}^{|\mathbf{B}^s|} \cup \{b_i^{st}\}_{i=1}^{|\mathbf{B}^{st}|} \cup \{b_i^t\}_{i=1}^{|\mathbf{B}^t|}$, where $b_i^s = (w_{i,1}^s, w_{i,2}^s)$ contains two words in language s, $b_i^{st} = (w_{i,1}^s, w_{i,2}^t)$ contains two words in different languages s and t, $b_i^t = (w_{i,1}^t, w_{i,2}^t)$ contains two words in language t.

Algorithm 1. Generative Process of CC-BiLDA

---

initialize: (1) set the number of topics K;
  (2) set values for Dirichlet priors α and β;
foreach *topic* $k \in [1, K]$ **do**
 └ **sample:** $\varphi_k^s, \varphi_k^t \sim Dirichlet(\beta)$;
foreach *category* $c \in [1, C]$ **do**
 └ **sample:** $\theta_c \sim Dirichlet(\alpha)$;
foreach *pair of bilingual documents* $d_j = (d_j^s, d_j^t)$ **do**
  given the prior category distribution π_j,
  foreach *word position* $p \in d_j^s$ **do**
    sample: $x_{j,p}^s \sim Multinomial(\pi_j)$;
    sample: $z_{j,p}^s \sim Multinomial(\theta_{x_{j,p}^s})$;
    sample: $w_{j,p}^s \sim Multinomial(\varphi_{z_{j,p}^s}^s)$;

  foreach *word position* $p \in d_j^t$ **do**
    sample: $x_{j,p}^t \sim Multinomial(\pi_j)$;
    sample: $z_{j,p}^t \sim Multinomial(\theta_{x_{j,p}^t})$;
    sample: $w_{j,p}^t \sim Multinomial(\varphi_{z_{j,p}^t}^s)$;

Like BiLDA and BiBTM, the modeling objects in CC-BiLDA and those in CC-BiBTM are respectively paired bilingual documents and biterms. Since we define each modeling object as a mixture of categories, a pair of bilingual documents d_j is represented with a C-dimensional multinomial distribution $\pi_j = \{\pi_{j,c}\}_{c=1}^C$ and a biterm b_i is represented with a C-dimensional multinomial distribution $\pi_i = \{\pi_{i,c}\}_{c=1}^C$, also expressed as π_i^s, π_i^{st} and π_i^t to distinguish three kinds of biterms. π_j and π_i serve as the prior category distributions of each pair of bilingual documents d_j in CC-BiLDA and each biterm b_i in CC-BiBTM, respectively. Let $x \in [1, C]$ be the category indicator variable, which is denoted by x^s, x^{st} and x^t respectively for biterms (or words in paired bilingual documents) in language s, biterms composed of two words in different languages s and t, and biterms (or words in paired bilingual documents) in language t. Similarly, the topic indicator variable $z \in [1, K]$ is denoted by z^s, z^{st} and z^t. Then, each category is expressed over K latent topics, which are also expressed over W^s and W^t distinct words of language s and language t, respectively. We use a K-dimensional multinomial distribution $\theta_c = \{\theta_{c,k}\}_{k=1}^K$ to describe the topics of each category c. Regarding the word distributions of languages s and t for topic k, they are respectively represented by a W^s-dimensional multinomial distribution φ_k^s with entry $\varphi_{k,w^s}^s = P(w^s|z = k)$ and a W^t-dimensional multinomial distribution φ_k^t with entry $\varphi_{k,w^t}^t = P(w^t|z = k)$. Following the convention of bilingual topic modeling, the hyperparameters α and β are the symmetric Dirichlet priors.

With the summarized general steps of generating a word in each modeling object (introduced in Sect. 3.1), the generative processes of CC-BiLDA and CC-BiBTM are respectively given in Algorithms 1 and 2, and their graphical representations are shown in Fig. 1.

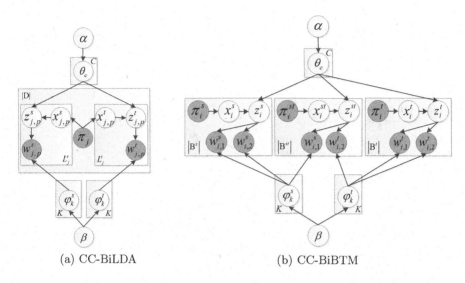

Fig. 1. Graphical representations of our models

Algorithm 2. Generative Process of CC-BiBTM

---

initialize: (1) set the number of topics K;
             (2) set values for Dirichlet priors α and β;
foreach *topic* $k \in [1, K]$ **do**
    sample: φ_k^s, $\varphi_k^t \sim Dirichlet(\beta)$;
foreach *category* $c \in [1, C]$ **do**
    sample: $\theta_c \sim Dirichlet(\alpha)$;
foreach *biterm* $b_i^s \in \mathbf{B}^s$ **do**
    given the prior category distribution $\boldsymbol{\pi}_i^s$,
    sample: $x_i^s \sim Multinomial(\boldsymbol{\pi}_i^s)$, $z_i^s \sim Multinomial(\theta_{x_i^s})$;
    sample: $w_{i,1}^s$, $w_{i,2}^s \sim Multinomial(\varphi_{z_i^s}^s)$;
foreach *biterm* $b_i^{st} \in \mathbf{B}^{st}$ **do**
    given the prior category distribution $\boldsymbol{\pi}_i^{st}$,
    sample: $x_i^{st} \sim Multinomial(\boldsymbol{\pi}_i^{st})$, $z_i^{st} \sim Multinomial(\theta_{x_i^{st}})$;
    sample: $w_{i,1}^s \sim Multinomial(\varphi_{z_i^{st}}^s)$, $w_{i,2}^t \sim Multinomial(\varphi_{z_i^{st}}^t)$;
foreach *biterm* $b_i^t \in \mathbf{B}^t$ **do**
    given the prior category distribution $\boldsymbol{\pi}_i^t$,
    sample: $x_i^t \sim Multinomial(\boldsymbol{\pi}_i^t)$, $z_i^t \sim Multinomial(\theta_{x_i^t})$;
    sample: $w_{i,1}^t$, $w_{i,2}^t \sim Multinomial(\varphi_{z_i^t}^t)$;

3.3   Computing Prior Category Distribution

Now we present our method to compute the prior category distribution $\boldsymbol{\pi}$ of each modeling object by leveraging different category correlations. With the strategy resulting in the corpus of paired bilingual documents as introduced in Sect. 3.1, each category from a taxonomy occurs in a set of paired bilingual documents. In other words, each modeling object corresponds to one or more categories, which are defined as the *co-occurring categories* of the modeling object. The category distribution over each modeling object reflects the co-occurrence correlation between all words in the modeling object and its co-occurring categories. Here, we simply assume that each co-occurring category of a modeling object has the same probability to be sampled. Given the jth modeling object R and the set of its co-occurring categories, denoted by $CC(R)$, the prior category probability $\pi_{j,c}^{CC}$ of each category $c \in [1, C]$ for R based on the co-occurrence correlation is computed as

$$\pi_{j,c}^{CC} = \begin{cases} \frac{1}{|CC(R)|}, & \text{if } c \in CC(R) \\ 0, & \text{otherwise} \end{cases} \tag{1}$$

where $|CC(R)|$ is the number of categories in $CC(R)$.

Besides the co-occurrence correlation between words and categories, we introduce two kinds of structural correlations among the categories of ancestor-descendant relationships in a taxonomy. The first structural correlation is based on information content [14]. The intuition is that co-occurring categories of a modeling object should have different importance since they may convey different amounts of information in a taxonomic structure. Similar to [12,14], we argue that the more abstract a category (i.e., more closer to the root of a taxonomy), the lower its information content, or there would be no need to further differentiate it with descendant categories. Thus, more specific co-occurring categories with more information content are more important for a modeling object. For jth modeling object R, we calculate the category probability $\pi_{j,c}$ of each category c by incorporating the intrinsic information content (IIC) measure [14] based on the set of descendants of c in the taxonomy T, denoted by $DES(c)$, as

$$\pi_{j,c} = IIC(c) \cdot \pi_{j,c}^{CC} \tag{2}$$

$$IIC(c) = 1 - \frac{\log(|DES(c)| + 1)}{\log N_T} \tag{3}$$

where $|DES(c)|$ is the number of categories in $DES(c)$ and N_T is the number of all categories in T. An imaginary root is created for each given taxonomy so as to avoid 0 IIC values of actual categories. We then normalize $\sum_c \pi_{j,c} = 1$.

The second structural correlation is based on path length. We find that the ancestors (in a taxonomy) of co-occurring categories for each modeling object might be also relevant to it. For example, if a pair of bilingual documents has category *"Computer Vision"*, its ancestor categories such as *"Artificial Intelligence"* are also relevant to this pair of bilingual documents. Hence, we treat the ancestors of co-occurring categories similarly w.r.t. a modeling object and also assign prior probabilities to them. Given the jth modeling object R, the intuition is that the greater distance in the taxonomy between a co-occurring category c_c and its ancestor c_a, the lower probability of c_a being a relevant category of R. Based on that, we use the shortest path length $SPL(c_c, c_a, T)$ (counted by

---

Algorithm 3. Prior Category Distribution Updating

Input: the jth modeling object R, its category distribution π_j, and the set of
co-occurring categories $CC(R)$
Output: updated π_j
Sort all categories $c_1, \cdots, c_{|CC(R)|}$ in $CC(R)$ as $c'_1, \cdots, c'_{|CC(R)|}$ in descending
order according to π_j;
for $i = 1, \cdots, |CC(R)|$ **do**
$\quad$ **foreach** ancestor c_a of c'_i **do**
$\quad\quad$ **if** $PP(c'_i, c_a) > \pi_{j,c_a}$ **then**
$\quad\quad\quad$ $\pi_{j,c_a} = PP(c'_i, c_a)$

Normalize $\sum_c \pi_{j,c} = 1$

---

edge numbers in the taxonomy T) between c_c and c_a to measure the propagation
probability (PP) from c_c to c_a as

$$PP(c_c, c_a) = \pi_{j,c_c} \cdot \frac{1}{SPL(c_c, c_a, T) + 1} \tag{4}$$

where π_{j,c_c} is the prior category probability of c_c for the jth modeling object.
As shown in Fig. 2, since an ancestor category 1 can get different propagation
probabilities (propagated from category 2, 4, 6), we decide to pick the highest
one propagated from all co-occurring categories, and if this propagation probability is higher than the current prior category probability of category 1, we will
make a replacement. However, a co-occurring category 2 also gets a propagation
probability (from category 4), which may be used to replace the current prior
category probability of category 2 with a higher value, thereby may lead to the
change of the highest propagation probability and prior category probability for
category 1. To ensure each ancestor category can get the highest prior category
probability, we first sort co-occurring categories by their current prior category
probabilities in descending order, then compute all propagation probabilities and
update the prior category probability for each ancestor of each co-occurring category in order. The details are given in Algorithm 3, which is used to update the
prior category distribution of each modeling object.

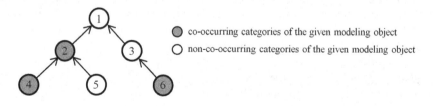

Fig. 2. An example of category locations in a taxonomy

3.4   Parameters Estimation

Since the coupled parameters $\boldsymbol{\theta}_c$, $\boldsymbol{\varphi}_k^s$ and $\boldsymbol{\varphi}_k^t$ in CC-BiLDA (or CC-BiBTM) are intractable to exactly solve, we follow BiLDA [17] and BiBTM [18] to utilize Gibbs Sampling [5] to perform approximate inference. Gibbs Sampling estimates the parameters with the samples drawn from the posterior distributions of latent variables sequentially, which are conditioned on the current values of all other variables and data. Here, we jointly sample latent variables x and z. Due to space limit, we only show the derived Gibbs Sampling formulas for CC-BiLDA and CC-BiBTM. For CC-BiLDA, given jth pair of bilingual documents $d_j = (d_j^s, d_j^t)$ in corpus $\mathbb{O}$, we sample the category c and topic k for the word in position p of document d_j^s in language s (or document d_j^t in language t) as follows:

$$P(x_{j,p}^s = c, z_{j,p}^s = k | x_{\neg(j,s,p)}, z_{\neg(j,s,p)}, \mathbb{O}) \propto$$
$$\pi_{j,c} \cdot \frac{(n_{\neg(j,s,p),k|c} + \alpha)}{(n_{\neg(j,s,p),\cdot|c} + K\alpha)} \cdot \frac{(n_{\neg(j,s,p),w_{j,p}^s|k} + \beta)}{(n_{\neg(j,s,p),\cdot^s|k} + W^s\beta)} \tag{5}$$

$$P(x_{j,p}^t = c, z_{j,p}^t = k | x_{\neg(j,t,p)}, z_{\neg(j,t,p)}, \mathbb{O}) \propto$$
$$\pi_{j,c} \cdot \frac{(n_{\neg(j,t,p),k|c} + \alpha)}{(n_{\neg(j,t,p),\cdot|c} + K\alpha)} \cdot \frac{(n_{\neg(j,t,p),w_{j,p}^t|k} + \beta)}{(n_{\neg(j,t,p),\cdot^t|k} + W^t\beta)} \tag{6}$$

In Eq. (5), $x_{j,p}^s$ and $z_{j,p}^s$ are respectively the category assignment and topic assignment for word $w_{j,p}^s$ in the current position. For all words in the corpus except the word in position p of document d_j^s, $x_{\neg(j,s,p)}$ is their category assignments and $z_{\neg(j,s,p)}$ is the topic assignments. $\pi_{j,c}$ means the prior probability of the pair of bilingual documents d_j assigned to category c. Also after excluding the word in position p of document d_j^s, $n_{\neg(j,s,p),k|c}$ is the number of words jointly assigned to category c and topic k, $n_{\neg(j,s,p),\cdot|c} = \sum_k n_{\neg(j,s,p),k|c}$, $n_{\neg(j,s,p),w_{j,p}^s|k}$ denotes the number of times for word $w_{j,p}^s$ assigned to topic k and $n_{\neg(j,s,p),\cdot^s|k} = \sum_{w^s} n_{\neg(j,s,p),w^s|k}$. In Eq. (6), all symbols have the same meaning as those in Eq. (5) after replacing language s with t.

With respect to CC-BiBTM, the Gibbs Sampling formulas for biterms $b_i^s \in \mathbf{B}^s$, $b_i^{st} \in \mathbf{B}^{st}$ and $b_i^t \in \mathbf{B}^t$ are as follows:

$$P(x_i^s = c, z_i^s = k | x_{\neg b_i^s}, z_{\neg b_i^s}, \mathbb{O}) \propto \pi_{i,c}^s \cdot \frac{(n_{\neg b_i^s, k|c} + \alpha)}{(n_{\neg b_i^s, \cdot|c} + K\alpha)} \cdot$$
$$\frac{(n_{\neg b_i^s, w_{i,1}^s|k} + \beta)(n_{\neg b_i^s, w_{i,2}^s|k} + \beta)}{(n_{\neg b_i^s, \cdot^s|k} + W^s\beta)(n_{\neg b_i^s, \cdot^s|k} + 1 + W^s\beta)} \tag{7}$$

$$P(x_i^{st} = c, z_i^{st} = k | x_{\neg b_i^{st}}, z_{\neg b_i^{st}}, \mathbb{O}) \propto \pi_{i,c}^{st} \cdot \frac{(n_{\neg b_i^{st}, k|c} + \alpha)}{(n_{\neg b_i^{st}, \cdot|c} + K\alpha)} \cdot$$
$$\frac{(n_{\neg b_i^{st}, w_{i,1}^s|k} + \beta)(n_{\neg b_i^{st}, w_{i,2}^t|k} + \beta)}{(n_{\neg b_i^{st}, \cdot^s|k} + W^s\beta)(n_{\neg b_i^{st}, \cdot^t|k} + W^t\beta)} \tag{8}$$

$$P(x_i^t = c, z_i^t = k | x_{\neg b_i^t}, z_{\neg b_i^t}, \mathbb{O}) \propto \pi_{i,c}^t \cdot \frac{(n_{\neg b_i^t, k|c} + \alpha)}{(n_{\neg b_i^t, \cdot|c} + K\alpha)} \cdot$$

$$\frac{(n_{\neg b_i^t, w_{i,1}^t|k} + \beta)(n_{\neg b_i^t, w_{i,2}^t|k} + \beta)}{(n_{\neg b_i^t, \cdot^t|k} + W^t\beta)(n_{\neg b_i^t, \cdot^t|k} + 1 + W^t\beta)} \tag{9}$$

where x and z are respectively current category assignment and topic assignment for the given biterm. For all biterms except biterm b, $x_{\neg b}$ is their category assignments and $z_{\neg b}$ denotes the topic assignments. $\pi_{i,c}$ represents the prior category probability of ith biterm $b_i^s \in \mathbf{B}^s$ or $b_i^{st} \in \mathbf{B}^{st}$ or $b_i^t \in \mathbf{B}^t$ assigned to category c. Under the condition of excluding biterm b, $n_{\neg b,k|c}$ is the number of biterms jointly assigned to category c and topic k, $n_{\neg b,\cdot|c} = \sum_k n_{\neg b,k|c}$, $n_{\neg b,w^s|k}$ is the number of times word w^s of language s assigned to topic k, $n_{\neg b,\cdot^s|k} = \sum_{w^s} n_{\neg b,w^s|k}$, $n_{\neg b,w^t|k}$ is the number of times word w^t of language t assigned to topic k, and $n_{\neg b,\cdot^t|k} = \sum_{w^t} n_{\neg b,w^t|k}$.

After a sufficient number of sampling iterations, we can estimate the parameters in CC-BiLDA and CC-BiBTM. Instead of computing all parameters like φ_k^s and φ_k^t, our solution to CLTA only needs $\boldsymbol{\theta}_c$, which is given as follows:

$$\theta_{c,k} = \frac{\alpha + n_{k|c}}{K\alpha + n_c} \tag{10}$$

where n_c is the number of words (or biterms) assigned to category c in CC-BiLDA (or CC-BiBTM), $n_{k|c}$ is the number of words (or biterms) simultaneously assigned to category c and topic k in CC-BiLDA (or CC-BiBTM).

With the topic distribution $\boldsymbol{\theta}_c$ obtained in CC-BiLDA and CC-BiBTM, we can represent categories from two taxonomies of different languages in the same topic space. The relevance score between each category in the source taxonomy and its candidate matched categories (identified with the same method in [18]) in the target taxonomy is computed as the cosine similarity between the topic vectors directly derived from $\boldsymbol{\theta}_c$.

4   Experiments

In this section, we evaluate CC-BiLDA and CC-BiBTM on two real-world datasets for CLTA. The source codes of these two models are publicly available[1].

4.1   Experiment Settings

(a) Datasets. We validated our models to CLTA on two public datasets[2] (also used in [18]), each of which consists of two cross-domain taxonomies of different languages and a set of labeled cross-lingual alignments. The taxonomies in one dataset are two product catalogues respectively extracted from JD.com (one of

---

[1] https://github.com/143230/CLTA.
[2] https://github.com/jxls080511/080424.

Table 1. Details of each taxonomy in each dataset

Taxonomy	JD.com	eBay.com	Chinese Dmoz.org	Yahoo! Directory
#category	7,741	7,782	2,084	2,353
#paired doc	67,594	72,979	19,277	21,467
#Chinese word	24,483	18,190	11,064	8,581
#English word	15,489	14,729	8,806	8,100

the largest Chinese B2C online retailers) and eBay.com, and those in another dataset are two Web site directories: Chinese Dmoz.org (the largest Chinese Web site directory) and Yahoo! Directory. We got a corpus of paired bilingual documents for each dataset with the strategy in [18], and processed them by word segmentation, stop words removal, stemming, etc. The details of each taxonomy and its extracted corpus of paired bilingual documents are given in Table 1.

(b) Baselines. We compared our models (i.e., CC-BiLDA and CC-BiBTM) with three kinds of baselines, which are existing bilingual topic models, variants of our models and cross-lingual ontology matching systems. Note that the hyperparameters α and β of all topic models are respectively set to $50/K$ (K is number of topics) and 0.1 according to [18]. All experiments were carried out on a Linux server with Intel Xeon E5-2630 v4 2.20 GHz CPU and 256 GB memory.

- **Existing Bilingual Topic Models:** They are BiLDA and BiBTM introduced in Sect. 2.2. To our knowledge, these two models are the state-of-the-art baselines for CLTA. In BiLDA and BiBTM, we respectively set the topic number K to 80 and 120 based on [18].
- **Variants of Our Models:** The full version of CC-BiLDA and that of CC-BiBTM apply three category correlations to category distribution computation. A kind of variants (denoted as CC-BiLDA (a) and CC-BiBTM (a)) of our models only utilize co-occurrence correlations. Another kind of variants (denoted as CC-BiLDA (b) and CC-BiBTM (b)) use information content based structural correlations besides co-occurrence correlations.
- **Cross-Lingual Ontology Matching Systems:** Although CLTA and cross-lingual ontology matching are different tasks, we can treat the taxonomies as a special kind of ontologies without formally defined properties, instances, axioms, etc. Thus, we took two state-of-the-art cross-lingual ontology matching systems (i.e., AML [4] and LogMap [7]) as the baselines.

(c) Evaluation Metrics. Similar to the work [2,10,15,18], we used MRR (Mean Reciprocal Rank) [3] and P@1 (precision for the top 1 ranking result) as the evaluation metrics because CLTA is seen as a ranking problem.

4.2 Parameter Tuning

Since different number of topics may lead to different performance in CLTA, we conducted an analysis by varying the number of topics K in our models and their variants. Figure 3 gives the alignment performance of CC-BiBTM, CC-BiLDA and their corresponding variants on each dataset when using different number of topics K. For CC-BiBTM and its variants, MRR or P@1 values reach the peak when K is from 100 to 120 on each dataset (in Fig. 3(a) and (c)), so K was set to 100 in these models for efficient training. For CC-BiLDA and its variants, most of their MRR and P@1 values are the highest when $K = 80$ (in Fig. 3(b) and (d)), so K was empirically set to 80 in these models.

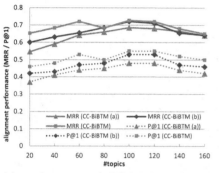

(a) performance of CC-BiBTM and its variants on product catalogues

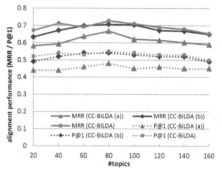

(b) performance of CC-BiLDA and its variants on product catalogues

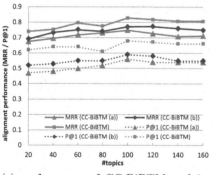

(c) performance of CC-BiBTM and its variants on Web site directories

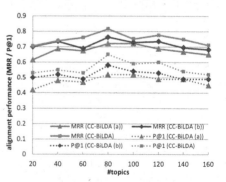

(d) performance of CC-BiLDA and its variants on Web site directories

Fig. 3. Alignment performance vs. number of topics K

4.3 Result Analysis

For each dataset, we trained all topic models with 500 iterations of Gibbs Sampling to converge. Table 2 gives the overall results of our proposed models and the baselines, and we can see that:

Table 2. Overall results

Approach	Product catalogues		Web site directories	
	MRR	P@1	MRR	P@1
AML	0.102	0.100	0.314	0.270
LogMap	0.105	0.100	0.265	0.250
BiLDA	0.553	0.390	0.679	0.480
CC-BiLDA (a)	0.667	0.480	0.721	0.520
CC-BiLDA (b)	0.706	0.540	0.763	0.580
CC-BiLDA	0.720	**0.550**	0.815	0.650
BiBTM	0.597	0.440	0.719	0.520
CC-BiBTM (a)	0.685	0.480	0.748	0.560
CC-BiBTM (b)	0.721	0.530	0.771	0.590
CC-BiBTM	**0.727**	**0.550**	**0.828**	**0.680**

- Our models CC-BiBTM and CC-BiLDA outperform all baselines, especially CC-BiBTM significantly improves the CLTA performance of the state-of-the-art baseline BiBTM (at least **+10.9%** in each evaluation metric). This reflects the value of our solution for encoding correlations into bilingual topic modeling, and the remarkable effects of category correlations on CLTA.
- Cross-lingual ontology matching systems have rather poor performance. Although they are not well tuned for the task of CLTA, it still shows that they cannot work well in real-world CLTA without internal features such as properties, instances and axioms available in ontologies.
- The performance of CLTA improves each time when we encoded one more kind of the proposed category correlations into bilingual topic modeling. It means that the co-occurrence correlations, structural correlations based on information content and those based on path length are all useful to CLTA.
- The performance of CC-BiLDA is close to that of CC-BiBTM. It reveals that although the training corpus are actually paired bilingual short documents, the data sparsity problem suffered by BiLDA has been greatly alleviated via the semantic information of category correlations.

Since the proposed models CC-BiLDA and CC-BiBTM have the best performance on MRR and P@1, we further compared their efficiency of model training by the average running time (per iteration) of CC-BiLDA and CC-BiBTM on

Table 3. Efficiency comparison of CC-BiLDA and CC-BiBTM

Model	Running time (seconds) per iteration		Time complexity per iteration
	Product catalogues	Web site directories	
CC-BiLDA	15.90	10.14	$O(K_1|D|\overline{L}_D\overline{C}_D)$
CC-BiBTM	453.31	251.39	$O(K_2|B|\overline{C}_B)$

the given datasets in Table 3. We can find that the running time of CC-BiBTM is about 25 times and 29 times of CC-BiLDA on Web site directories and product catalogues, respectively. The time complexity (per iteration) of each model is also shown in Table 3, where the topic number $K_1 = 80$ and $K_2 = 100$ according to Sect. 4.2; $|D|$ is the number of paired bilingual documents, each of which averagely contains $\overline{L}_D$ words and $\overline{C}_D$ co-occurring categories; and $|B|$ is the number of biterms, each of which averagely has $\overline{C}_B$ co-occurring categories. Suppose each document in each pair of bilingual documents averagely has $\overline{l}$ words ($\overline{l} \geq 2$), i.e., $\overline{L}_D \approx 2\overline{l}$, so $|B| \approx |D| \cdot (2 \cdot \frac{\overline{l}(\overline{l}-1)}{2} + \overline{l}^2)$. A biterm may have the co-occurring categories of more than one pair of bilingual documents, so $\frac{\overline{C}_B}{\overline{C}_D} \geq 1$. Since we have $\frac{K_2|B|\overline{C}_B}{K_1|D|\overline{L}_D\overline{C}_D} \approx \frac{5}{4} \cdot \frac{\overline{C}_B}{\overline{C}_D} \cdot (\overline{l} - \frac{1}{2})$, the time complexity of CC-BiBTM is much higher than that of CC-BiLDA. However, with the strategy in [18], the bilingual documents used for CLTA were actually extracted from the snippets (i.e., short documents) returned by a search engine, so the number of words in each document is small (e.g., $\overline{l} = 10.21$ for product catalogues and $\overline{l} = 9.73$ for Web site directories), and the running time of CC-BiBTM is still acceptable.

To sum up, for CLTA, if users have a high demand on accuracy and do not care about the efficiency, we suggest to use CC-BiBTM. If users care more about the efficiency and can accept a little lower accuracy, we recommend CC-BiLDA.

5   Related Work

5.1   Cross-Lingual Schema Matching

The problem of cross-lingual schema matching has been mainly studied in the area of ontology matching and taxonomy alignment. Some approaches or systems [4,7,16] for cross-lingual ontology matching mainly use the features based on string similarities after translation. The performance is often unsatisfactory due to the problems of vocabulary mismatch and improper translations. Different to ontologies, taxonomies do not always have logically rigorous structures with formally defined properties, instances and axioms to help solve matching tasks. Thus, several approaches have been especially designed to CLTA. Some of them [2,10,15] focus on aligning domain-specific taxonomies using string similarities based on a translation tool and domain-specific information. The most relevant work [18] also tries to align cross-lingual and cross-domain taxonomies with bilingual topic models. We improved this work by encoding different explicit category correlations into bilingual topic modeling for CLTA.

5.2   Metadata Topic Models

Topic models such as Latent Dirichlet Allocation (LDA) [1] and its numerous variants are well studied generative models for analysing latent semantic topics in text. Besides bilingual topic models BiLDA and BiBTM, metadata topic models are also related to our work. To simultaneously model the text and its metadata (e.g., authors and tags), a set of metadata topic models have been proposed including Author Topic Model [13], labeled-LDA [11], Tag-Weighted Topic Model [9], Tag-Weighted Dirichlet Allocation [8], etc. They denote each metadata as a mixture of topics or words, but cannot be applied to cross-lingual text mining. Our models CC-BiLDA and CC-BiBTM are the first work of cross-lingual metadata topic models, which already show the superiority in CLTA.

6   Conclusions and Future Work

In this paper, we proposed a unified solution to encode category correlations into bilingual topic modeling for CLTA. Our solution captures different category correlations with a prior category distribution of each modeling object, and integrates such distributions into bilingual topic modeling. This brings two novel category correlation based bilingual topic models CC-BiLDA and CC-BiBTM, which significantly outperform the state-of-the-art baselines on CLTA. In the future, we will apply our models to CLTA in knowledge graphs, to benefit cross-lingual knowledge graph fusion and cross-lingual semantic search.

Acknowledgements. This work is supported in part by the National Natural Science Foundation of China (Grant No. 61672153), the 863 Program (Grant No. 2015AA015406), the Fundamental Research Funds for the Central Universities and the Research Innovation Program for College Graduates of Jiangsu Province (Grant No. KYLX16_0295).

References

1. Blei, D.M., Ng, A.Y., Jordan, M.I.: Latent Dirichlet allocation. J. Mach. Learn. Res. **3**, 993–1022 (2003)
2. Boldyrev, N., Spaniol, M., Weikum, G.: ACROSS: a framework for multi-cultural interlinking of web taxonomies. In: WebSci, pp. 127–136 (2016)
3. Craswell, N.: Mean reciprocal rank. In: Liu, L., Tamer Özsu, M. (eds.) Encyclopedia of Database Systems, pp. 1703–1703. Springer, New York (2009). doi:10.1007/978-0-387-39940-9_488
4. Faria, D., Pesquita, C., Santos, E., Palmonari, M., Cruz, I.F., Couto, F.M.: The AgreementMakerLight ontology matching system. In: Meersman, R., Panetto, H., Dillon, T., Eder, J., Bellahsene, Z., Ritter, N., Leenheer, P., Dou, D. (eds.) OTM 2013. LNCS, vol. 8185, pp. 527–541. Springer, Heidelberg (2013). doi:10.1007/978-3-642-41030-7_38
5. Geman, S., Geman, D.: Stochastic relaxation, Gibbs distributions, and the Bayesian restoration of images. IEEE Trans. Pattern Anal. Mach. Intell. **6**, 721–741 (1984)

6. Hong, L., Davison, B.D.: Empirical study of topic modeling in Twitter. In: SOMA, pp. 80–88 (2010)
7. Jiménez-Ruiz, E., Cuenca Grau, B.: LogMap: logic-based and scalable ontology matching. In: Aroyo, L., Welty, C., Alani, H., Taylor, J., Bernstein, A., Kagal, L., Noy, N., Blomqvist, E. (eds.) ISWC 2011. LNCS, vol. 7031, pp. 273–288. Springer, Heidelberg (2011). doi:10.1007/978-3-642-25073-6_18
8. Li, S., Huang, G., Tan, R., Pan, R.: Tag-weighted Dirichlet allocation. In: ICDM, pp. 438–447 (2013)
9. Li, S., Li, J., Pan, R.: Tag-weighted topic model for mining semi-structured documents. In: IJCAI, pp. 2855–2861 (2013)
10. Prytkova, N., Weikum, G., Spaniol, M.: Aligning multi-cultural knowledge taxonomies by combinatorial optimization. In: WWW, pp. 93–94 (2015)
11. Ramage, D., Hall, D., Nallapati, R., Manning, C.D.: Labeled LDA: a supervised topic model for credit attribution in multi-labeled corpora. In: EMNLP, pp. 248–256 (2009)
12. Resnik, P.: Using information content to evaluate semantic similarity in a taxonomy. In: IJCAI, pp. 448–453 (1995)
13. Rosen-Zvi, M., Griffiths, T., Steyvers, M., Smyth, P.: The author-topic model for authors and documents. In: UAI, pp. 487–494 (2004)
14. Seco, N., Veale, T., Hayes, J.: An intrinsic information content metric for semantic similarity in WordNet. In: ECAI, pp. 1089–1090 (2004)
15. Spohr, D., Hollink, L., Cimiano, P.: A machine learning approach to multilingual and cross-lingual ontology matching. In: Aroyo, L., Welty, C., Alani, H., Taylor, J., Bernstein, A., Kagal, L., Noy, N., Blomqvist, E. (eds.) ISWC 2011. LNCS, vol. 7031, pp. 665–680. Springer, Heidelberg (2011). doi:10.1007/978-3-642-25073-6_42
16. Trojahn, C., Fu, B., Zamazal, O., Ritze, D.: State-of-the-art in multilingual and cross-lingual ontology matching. In: Buitelaar, P., Cimiano, P. (eds.) Towards the Multilingual Semantic Web, pp. 119–135. Springer, Heidelberg (2014). doi:10.1007/978-3-662-43585-4
17. Vulić, I., De Smet, W., Tang, J., Moens, M.F.: Probabilistic topic modeling in multilingual settings: an overview of its methodology and applications. Inf. Process. Manag. **51**(1), 111–147 (2015)
18. Wu, T., Qi, G., Wang, H., Xu, K., Cui, X.: Cross-lingual taxonomy alignment with bilingual biterm topic model. In: AAAI, pp. 287–293 (2016)

Cross-Lingual Infobox Alignment in Wikipedia Using Entity-Attribute Factor Graph

Yan Zhang, Thomas Paradis, Lei Hou, Juanzi Li[✉], Jing Zhang,
and Haitao Zheng

Knowledge Engineering Group, Tsinghua University, Beijing, China
{z-y14,jing-zha15}@mails.tsinghua.edu.cn, thomasparadis@126.com,
greener2009@gmail.com, lijuanzi@tsinghua.edu.cn,
zheng.haitao@sz.tsinghua.edu.cn

Abstract. Wikipedia infoboxes contain information about article entities in the form of attribute-value pairs, and are thus a very rich source of structured knowledge. However, as the different language versions of Wikipedia evolve independently, it is a promising but challenging problem to find correspondences between infobox attributes in different language editions. In this paper, we propose 8 effective features for cross lingual infobox attribute matching containing categories, templates, attribute labels and values. We propose entity-attribute factor graph to consider not only individual features but also the correlations among attribute pairs. Experiments on the two Wikipedia data sets of English-Chinese and English-French show that proposed approach can achieve high F1-measure: 85.5% and 85.4% respectively on the two data sets. Our proposed approach finds 23,923 new infobox attribute mappings between English and Chinese Wikipedia, and 31,576 between English and French based on no more than six thousand existing matched infobox attributes. We conduct an infobox completion experiment on English-Chinese Wikipedia and complement 76,498 (more than 30% of EN-ZH Wikipedia existing cross-lingual links) pairs of corresponding articles with more than one attribute-value pairs.

1 Introduction

With the rapid evolution of the Internet to be a world-wide global information space, sharing knowledge across different languages becomes an important and challenging task. Cross-lingual knowledge sharing not only benefits knowledge internationalization and globalization, but also has a very wide range of applications such as machine translation [20], information retrieval [19] and multilingual semantic data extraction [7,9]. Wikipedia is one of the largest multi-lingual encyclopedic knowledge bases on the Web and provides more than 25 million articles in 285 different languages. Therefore, many multilingual knowledge bases (KB) have been constructed based on Wikipedia, such as DBpedia [7], YAGO [9], Bablenet [11] and XLore [18]. Some approaches have been proposed to find cross-lingual links between Wiki articles, e.g., [15–17].

© Springer International Publishing AG 2017
C. d'Amato et al. (Eds.): ISWC 2017, Part I, LNCS 10587, pp. 745–760, 2017.
DOI: 10.1007/978-3-319-68288-4_44

There is a large amount of semantic information contained in Wikipedia *infoboxes*, which provide semi-structured, factual information in the form of attribute-value pairs. Attributes in infoboxes contain valuable semantic information, which play a key role in the construction of a coherent large-scale knowledge base [9]. However, each language version maintains its own set of infoboxes with their own set of attributes, as well as sometimes providing different values for corresponding attributes. Thus, attributes in different Wikipedia must be matched if we want to get coherent knowledge and develop some applications. For instance, inconsistencies among the data provided by different editions for corresponding attributes could be detected automatically. Furthermore, English Wikipedia is obviously larger and of higher quality than low resource languages, which is why we can use attribute alignments to expand and complete infoboxes in other languages, or at least help Wikipedia communities to do so. In addition, the number of existing attribute mappings is limited, e.g., there are more than 100 thousand attributes in English Wikipedia but only about 5 thousand (less than 5%) existing attribute mappings between English and Chinese.

Being aware of the importance of this problem, several approaches have been proposed to find new cross-lingual attribute mappings between Wikis. Bouma et al. [2] found alignments between English and Dutch infobox attributes based on values. Rinser et al. [13] proposed an instance-based schema matching approach to find corresponding attributes between different language infobox templates. Adar et al. [1] defined 26 features, such as equality, word, translation and n-gram features, then applied logistic regression to train a boolean classifier to detect whether two attributes are likely to be equivalent. These methods can be split into two categories: similarity-based and learning-based. Both of them mostly use the information of the attributes themselves and ignore the correlations among attributes within one knowledge base.

Based on our observation, there are several challenges involved in finding multilingual correspondences across infobox attributes. Firstly, there are Polysemy-Attributes (a given attribute can have different semantics, e.g., *country* can mean nationality of one person or place of a production) and Synonym-Attributes (different attributes can have the same meaning, e.g., *alias* and *other names*), which leads to worse performance on label similarity or translation based methods. Secondly, there also exist some problems in the values of attributes: 1. different measurement (e.g., *population* of *Beijing* is 21,700,000 in English edition and 2170 *ten thousand* in Chinese). 2. timeliness (e.g., *population* of *Beijing* is 21,150,000 (in 2013) in French edition). In this way, labels and values alone are not credible enough for cross-lingual attribute matching.

In order to solve above problems, we first investigate several effective features considering characteristics of cross-lingual attribute matching problem, and then propose an approach based on factor graph model [6]. The most significant advantage of this model is that it can formalize correlations between attributes explicitly, which is specified in Sect. 3. Specifically, our contributions include:

- We formulate the problem of attribute matching (attribute alignment) across Wikipedia knowledge bases in different language editions, and analyse several effective features based on categories, templates, labels and values.
- We present a supervised method based on an integrated factor graph model, which leverages information from a variety of sources and utilizes the correlations among attribute pairs.
- We conduct experiments to evaluate our approach on existing attribute mappings in the latest Wikipedia. It achieves a high F1-measure 85.5% between English and Chinese and 85.4% between English and French. Furthermore, we run our model on English, Chinese and French Wikipedia, and successfully identify 23,923 new cross-lingual attribute mappings between English and Chinese, 31,576 between English and French.

The rest of this paper is organized as follows, Sect. 2 defines the problem of attribute matching and some related concepts; Sect. 3 describes the proposed approach in detail; Sect. 4 presents the evaluation results; Sect. 5 discusses some related work and finally Sect. 6 concludes this work.

2   Problem Formulation

In this section, we formally define the problem of Wikipedia attribute (property) matching. We define the Wiki knowledge base and elements in it as follows.

Definition 1. Wiki Knowledge Base. *We consider each language edition of Wikipedia as a* **Wiki Knowledge Base***, which can be represented as*

$$K = \{A, P\}$$

where $A = \{a_i\}_{i=1}^n$ is the set of articles in K and n is the size of A, i.e., the number of articles. $P = \{p_i\}_{i=1}^r$ is the set of attributes in K and r is the size of P.

Definition 2. Wiki Article. *A* **Wiki Article** *can be formally defined as follows,*

$$a = (Ti(a), Te(a), Ib(a), C(a))$$

where

- *$Ti(a)$ denotes the title of the article a.*
- *$Te(a)$ denotes the unstructured text description of the article a, in other words, the free-text contents of the article a.*
- *$Ib(a)$ is the infobox associated with a; specifically, $Ib(a) = \{p_i, val_i\}_{i=1}^k$ represents the list of attribute-value pairs in this article's infobox, $P(a) = \{p_i\}_{i=1}^k$ represents the set of attributes which appear in Ib of a.*
- *$C(a)$ denotes the set of categories of the article a.*

Definition 3. Attribute. *According to the above definitions, an attribute can be defined as a 5-tuple,*

$$attr = (L(p), SO(p), AU(p), C(p), T(p))$$

where

- *$L(p)$ denotes the label of attribute p.*
- *$SO(p) = \{(a, val) \mid \forall a \in A, \exists (p, val) \in Ib(a)\}$ denotes a set which contains the subject-object pairs of the attribute. For example, in Fig. 1, attribute Alma_mater has a pair (Mark Zuckerberg, Harvard University) in $SO(p_{Alma\ mater})$.*
- *$AU(p) = \{a \mid \forall a, \exists (a, val) \in SO(p)\}$ denotes the set of articles which use attribute p.*
- *$C(p) = \bigcup\limits_{(p,o) \in Ib(a)} C(a)$ denotes a set of categories in which the attribute appears. For example, C of attribute Born contains a category People.*
- *$T(p) = \{p_i\}_{i=1}^m$ denotes the Infobox template to which the attribute p belongs.*

Definition 4. Attribute Matching (Property Matching). *Given two Wiki Knowledge Bases $K_1 = \{A_1, P_1\}$ and $K_2 = \{A_2, P_2\}$, attribute matching is a process of finding, for each attribute $p_i \in P_1$, one or more equivalent attributes in knowledge base K_2. When the two Wiki knowledge bases are in different languages, we call it the cross-lingual attribute matching (infobox alignment) problem. Generally, EL, EC and AL denote the existing cross-lingual links between articles, categories and attributes respectively between different language versions of Wikipedia.*

Here, we say two attributes are equivalent if they *semantically* describe the same type of information about an entity. Figure 1 shows an example of attribute

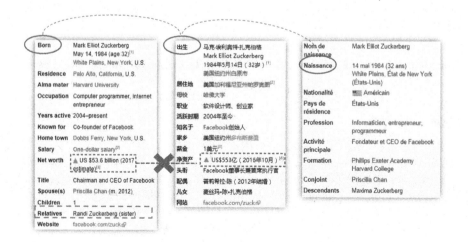

Fig. 1. An example of attribute matching

matching results concerning infoboxes of *Zuckerberg* (CEO of Facebook) in English, Chinese and French Wikipedia.

As shown in Fig. 1, *Born*, 出生 and *Naissance* are equivalent infobox attributes, which can be easily found according to the values using a translation tool. However, for attribute *Net worth* and its Chinese corresponding attribute 净资产 , they have different values because of timeliness, so we cannot find the alignment using value-based method. Furthermore, English Infobox (the left) has an attribute *Relatives*, which does not exist in other two versions. So we can complete the Chinese infobox of Zuckerberg if we find that 亲人 is the corresponding attribute of *Relatives* in Chinese.

3 The Proposed Approach

In this section, we first describe the motivation and overview of our approach, and then we introduce our proposed model in detail.

3.1 Overview

For the problem of Wikipedia attribute matching, existing works [1,2,13] mostly used label- and value-based features. Effectiveness of these direct features has been proved. However, as for cross-lingual attribute matching, text similarity cannot be computed directly and machine translation may induce more errors. In this way, only text feature is not enough. There are some works [15,17] on a similar problem, Wikipedia cross-lingual entity matching, and in these works some useful language-independent features are proposed, such as text hyperlinks. Furthermore, these works also provide large amounts of cross-lingual article links which are very valuable. Inspired by these works, we try to design a model leveraging text, article, category and template features simultaneously. Thus, there are two questions in front of us.

- How to use existing cross-lingual links as seeds to help us find more attribute mappings?
- How to use other information (e.g., article, category and external text) to deal with the lack of information in attribute itself?

3.2 Entity-Attribute Factor Graph Model

Factor graph model [6] has such an assumption that observation data depends on not only local features, but also on relationships with other instances. The characteristic of this model is fit for our problem intuitively, because:

- A pair of attributes is more likely equivalent if they co-occur with aligned attributes in a pair of equivalent articles.
- Template pairs which contain more equivalent attribute pairs tend to be more semantically similar, and other attribute pairs in such templates are more likely equivalent than the ones in other templates.
- Attribute pairs tend to be equivalent if their synonymous pairs are equivalent.

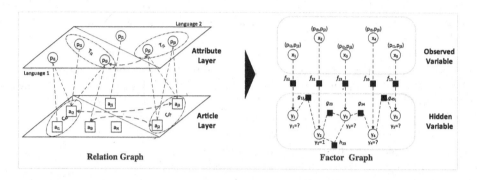

Fig. 2. An illustration of Entity-Attribute Factor Graph (EAFG) model

In this paper, using definitions in Sect. 2, we formalize the attribute matching problem into a model named Entity-Attribute Factor Graph (EAFG), which is shown in Fig. 2.

Figure 2 contains two parts, the left one is *relation graph*, which represents several relations in two editions of Wikipedia K_1 and K_2. Different language versions are separated by a diagonal line. The *attribute layer* contains the attributes and template relations among them. Similarly, the *article layer* contains the articles and category relations. The imaginary lines between the two layers denote the relation of usage between articles and attributes, and the red dashed lines denote the existing cross-lingual links. The right one is *factor graph*, the white nodes are *variables*, there are two types of variables, x_i and y_i. Each candidate pair is mapped to an observed variable x_i. The hidden variable y_i represents a Boolean label (equivalent or inequivalent) of the observed variable x_i. For example, x_2 in Fig. 2 corresponds to a candidate attribute pairs (p_{i3}, p_{j2}), and there exists a cross-lingual link between p_{i3} and p_{j2}, so the hidden variable y_2 equals to 1. The black nodes in *factor graph* are *factors*, there are three types, f, g, and h. Each type is associated with a kind of feature function which transforms relations into a computable feature.

Now, we define these feature functions in EAFG model in detail:

- **Local feature function:** $f(y_i, x_i)$ is a feature function which represents the posterior probability of label y_i given x_i; it describes local information and similarity on observed variables in EAFG;
- **Template feature function:** $g(y_i, CO(y_i))$ denotes the correlation between hidden variables according to template information. $CO(y_i)$ is the set of variables having template co-occurrence relation with y_i.
- **Synonym feature function:** $h(y_i, SY(y_i))$ denotes the correlation between hidden variables according to synonymous information. $SY(y_i)$ is the set of variables being semantically equivalent.

According to these feature functions, we can define joint distribution over the Y on our graph model as

$$p(Y) = \prod_i f(y_i, x_i)g(y_i, CO(y_i))h(y_i, SY(y_i)) \tag{1}$$

Then we introduce the definition of three feature functions in detail.

1. Local feature function

$$f(y_i, x_i) = \frac{1}{Z_\alpha}\exp\{\alpha^{\mathrm{T}}\mathbf{f}(y_i, x_i)\} \tag{2}$$

where $\mathbf{f}(y_i, x_i) = <f_{label}, f_{we}, f_{so}, f_{au}, f_{cate}>$ is a vector of features; α denotes the corresponding weights of these features; x_i is a variable corresponding to attribute pair (p_a, p_b). Then we describe these five features in detail.

(a) Label similarity feature: it computes the Levenshtein distance [3] after translating non-English attribute labels to English ones, and then get the similarity according to it.

$$f_{label} = 1 - \frac{Leven(L(p_a), L(p_b))}{\max(len(L(p_a)), len(L(p_b)))} \tag{3}$$

where $Leven(L(p_a), L(p_a))$ denotes the Levenshtein distance between two labels, and $len(L(p))$ denotes the length of the label of the attribute p.

Word embedding [10] represents each word as a vector and is able to grasp semantic information. We trained 100-dimension word embeddings on English Wikipedia text and represent each label as a vector (non-English labels are replaced by their translation result). Let $WE(p)$ be the word embedding (a 100-dimension vector) of the label of attribute p, we have

$$f_{we} = 1 - \frac{\arccos(\frac{WE(p_a)\cdot WE(p_b)}{\|WE(p_a)\|_2 \times \|WE(p_b)\|_2})}{\pi} \tag{4}$$

where $\|WE(p_a)\|_2$ denotes the Euclidean norm of the vector $WE(p_a)$, and f_{we} is the cosine similarity between word embeddings of p_a and p_b.

(b) Subject-object similarity feature: according to Definition 3, we can get a set SO for each attribute and compute the similarity between the two sets. First, we define an equivalence relation between subject-object pairs as

$$(s_i, o_i) \equiv (s_j, o_j) \iff (s_i, s_j) \in EL \wedge o_i \equiv o_j$$

it denotes pair (s_i, o_i) in SO_i is equivalent with (s_j, o_j) in SO_j if and only if there is a cross-lingual link between subjects, and objects are equivalent. The condition of objects being equivalent depends on the data type. For example, for type $Integer$, the objects should be equal, and for type $entity$, they should also have a cross-lingual link. f_{so} is defined as

$$f_{so} = \frac{2 \times |\{(s_i, o_i) \equiv (s_j, o_j) \mid (s_i, o_i) \in SO(p_a), (s_j, o_j) \in SO(p_b)\}|}{|SO(p_a)| + |SO(p_b)|} \tag{5}$$

(c) Article-usage feature: according to Definitions 3 and 4, we can define f_{au} as

$$f_{au} = \frac{2 \times |\{(a,b) \mid (a,b) \in EL, a \in AU(p_a), b \in AU(p_b)\}|}{|AU(p_a)| + |AU(p_b)|} \tag{6}$$

this feature represents the similarity between two article sets which contain the two attributes in their infoboxes respectively.

(d) Category similarity feature: similarly, we can define f_{cate} as

$$f_{cate} = \frac{2 \times |\{(c,c') \mid (c,c') \in EC, c \in C(p_a), c' \in C(p_b)\}|}{|C(p_a)| + |C(p_b)|} \tag{7}$$

where $C(p)$ is defined in Definition 3 and EC is defined in Definition 4. This feature represents the similarity between two category sets related to the two attributes.

2. **Template feature function**

$$g(y_i, CO(y_i)) = \frac{1}{Z_\beta} \exp\{ \sum_{y_j \in CO(y_i)} \beta^{\mathrm{T}} \mathbf{g}(y_i, y_j) \} \tag{8}$$

where β denotes the weight remaining to learn, and $\mathbf{g}(y_i, y_j)$ denotes a function to specify whether there exists a template sharing correlation between attribute pairs. Let (p_{a_i}, p_{b_i}) and (p_{a_j}, p_{b_j}) be the attribute pairs related with node y_i and y_j respectively in the factor graph. $\mathbf{g}(y_i, y_j) = 1$ if p_{a_i} and p_{a_j} appear in one common template, and so are p_{b_i} and p_{b_j}, otherwise 0. It should be noticed that this function is used to capture the relations between candidate attribute mappings.

3. **Synonym feature function**

$$h(y_i, SY(y_i)) = \frac{1}{Z_\gamma} \exp\{ \sum_{y_j \in S(y_i)} \gamma^{\mathrm{T}} \mathbf{h}(y_i, y_j) \} \tag{9}$$

where γ denotes the weight remaining to learn, and $\mathbf{h}(y_i, y_j)$ denotes the probability of semantically equivalence between y_i and y_j. First we define semantic relatedness between two attributes as,

$$SR(p_i, p_j) = \frac{2 \times |\{(c_i, c_j) \mid c_i \equiv c_j, c_i \in C(p_i), c_j \in C(p_j)\}|}{|C(p_i)| + |C(p_j)|} \tag{10}$$

which is similar with Eq. 7, except that p_i and p_j here are from the same language, thus the equivalence between category pairs can be derived directly. Then let (p_{a_i}, p_{b_i}) and (p_{a_j}, p_{b_j}) be the attribute pairs related with node y_i and y_j respectively, we have

$$\mathbf{h}(y_i, y_j) = SR(p_{a_i}, p_{a_j}) \times SR(p_{b_i}, p_{b_j}) \tag{11}$$

Therefore, the purpose of this feature function is to find more cross-lingual attribute mappings using information of synonym within one language edition of data set.

3.3   Learning and Inference

Given a set of labeled nodes (known attribute mappings) in the EAFG, learning the model is to estimate an optimum parameter configuration $\theta = (\alpha, \beta, \gamma)$ to maxmize the log-likelihood function of $p(Y)$. Based on Eqs. 1–11, the joint distribution $p(Y)$ can be denoted as

$$p(Y) = \frac{1}{Z} \prod_i \exp\{\theta^{\mathrm{T}}(\mathbf{f}(y_i, y_j), \sum_{y_j} \mathbf{g}(y_i, y_j), \sum_{y_j} \mathbf{h}(y_i, y_j))\} \qquad (12)$$

We use log-likelihood function $\log(p(Y^L))$ as the object function, where Y^L denotes the known labels. Then we apply a gradient descent method to estimate the parameter θ. After learning the optimal parameter θ, we can infer the unknown labels by finding a set of labels which maximizes the joint probability $p(Y)$.

4   Experiments

In this paper, the proposed approach is a general model (translation based features are optional), so we use the data from three language editions of Wikipedia (English, Chinese and French) to evaluate our proposed approach. First we evaluate EAFG model on existing cross-lingual attribute mappings, and then we use our approach to find English-Chinese and English-French mappings within Wikipedia.

4.1   Data Set

We construct two data sets (English-Chinese and English-French) from existing cross-lingual attribute links in Wikipedia. Table 1 shows the size of the 2 data sets. In each data set, we randomly select 2,000 corresponding attribute pairs which are labeled as positive instances. For each positive instance, we generate 5 negative instances by randomly replacing one of the attribute in the pairs with a wrong one.

Table 1. Size of the 2 data sets

Data set	#Attribute pairs	#Related articles	#Related categories
EN-ZH	2000	EN:96,331 ZH:54,195	EN:13,763 ZH:9,132
EN-FR	2000	EN:103,915 FR:89,012	EN:15,698 FR:12,371

4.2   Comparison Methods

We conduct four existing cross-lingual attribute matching methods. They are translation based method Label Matching (LM), Similarity Aggregation (SA) based method, classification based method Support Vector Matching (SVM) and another logistic regression based method (LR-ADAR) on the work of Adar [1]. As for our proposed approach, in order to evaluate the influence of translation tool, we conduct EAFG-NT (No Translation) which is same as EAFG except that it does not use translation-based features.

- **Label Matching (LM).** This method first uses Google Translation API to translate the labels of attributes in other languages into English, and then matches them. For each attribute pair, they are considered as equivalent attributes if they have strictly the same English labels.
- **Similarity Aggregation (SA).** This method aggregates several similarities of each attribute pair into a combined one averagely. Here, we compute 5 similarities same as **local feature function** in Sect. 3, namely label similarity, subject-object similarity, article-usage similarity, category similarity and word embedding similarity.

$$Sim(p_i, p_j) = \frac{1}{5}(f_{label} + f_{so} + f_{au} + f_{cate} + f_{we})$$

Then it selects pairs whose similarity is over a threshold ϕ as equivalent pairs. In our experiment, we test the parameter ϕ from 0.05 to 1.00 increasing by 0.05, and this method achieves the best F1-measure when $\phi = 0.75$ on EN-ZH data set, $\phi = 0.80$ on EN-FR data set.
- **Support Vector Machine (SVM).** This method first computes the five similarities in method SA, and then trains a SVM model [4]. Here, we use Scikit-Learn package [12] in our experiment with a linear kernel and parameter $C = 1.0$. Finally we predict the equivalence of new attribute pairs using this model. Compared with our approach, this method only uses similarities of attributes as features, and it does not take correlations among these instances into consideration.
- **Logistic Regression (LR-ADAR)** In [1], the author defined 26 features and trained a logistic regression model to solve this problem. They obtained good results in their experiments, so we implement this method as a comparison. Here we also use Scikit-Learn package to train a logistic regression model with 17 of their features (removing some language features because they are not suitable for Chinese). In our experiment, it achieves the best result when we use parameter $C = 10$ and L1-regularization.

4.3   Performance Metrics

We use *Precision*, *Recall* and *F1-measure* to evaluate different attribute matching methods. They are defined as usual: *Precision* is the percentage of correct discovered matched in all discovered matches; *Recall* is the percentage of correct discovered matches in all correct matches; *F1-Measure* is the harmonic mean of precision and recall. The data sets we use are described in Sect. 4.1.

4.4   Settings

For SVM, LR-ADAR and EAFG, we conduct 10-fold cross validation on the evaluation data set. EAFG uses 0.001 learning rate and runs 1000 iterations in all the experiments, and SVM and LR-ADAR runs with settings described in the above. As mentioned before, translation tool is optional in our approach, so we also implement method EAFG-NT for comparison. All experiments are carried out on a Ubuntu 14.04 server with 2.8 GHz CPU (8 cores) and 128 GB memory.

4.5   Results Analysis

Table 2 shows the performance of these 5 methods on English-Chinese (EN-ZH) and English-French (EN-FR) data sets. For EN-ZH data set, according to the results, the LM method gets a high precision of 97.3%, but its recall is only 26.1%. Apparently, the variety of translation results and too strict matching condition are the main reasons of the result. By using similarities on various information, SA improves recall significantly in comparison to LM, but it does not achieve good precision because averaging strategy is too simple. SVM and LR-ADAR are both learning-based methods. SVM method gets a precision of 87.5% with a recall 75.2%. Compared with SVM, LR-ADAR gets better precision but lower recall, and outperforms SVM by 1.0% in terms of F1-measure. Our method EAFG uses the same training data with SVM, and outperforms SVM by 4.6% in terms of F1-measure. EAFG get similar precision with LR-ADAR, but EAFG is able to discover more attribute mappings by considering the correlation between attribute pairs. EAFG-NT only uses language-independent features, although it does not work as well as EAFG, it still outperforms SVM by 0.5%, which indicates that correlations among attributes are helpful for the problem indeed. As for EN-FR data set, most of these methods get better precision than EN-ZH, and we think it is because English and French are both European languages. Correspondingly, we can get similar conclusions from the experiment on EN-FR data set.

Table 2. Perfomance of 5 methods on English-Chinese and English-French data sets.

Method	English-Chinese			English-French		
	Precision	Recall	F1-Measure	Precision	Recall	F1-Measure
LM	**0.973**	0.261	0.412	**0.982**	0.271	0.425
SA	0.749	0.673	0.709	0.764	0.662	0.709
SVM	0.875	0.752	0.809	0.883	0.755	0.814
LR-ADAR	0.907	0.746	0.819	0.917	0.739	0.818
EAFG(NT)	0.863	0.771	0.814	0.877	0.774	0.822
EAFG	0.911	**0.805**	**0.855**	0.913	**0.802**	**0.854**

4.6   Discovering New Cross-Lingual Attribute Mappings in Wikipedia

The motivation of this work is to find more attribute mappings among different language versions of Wikipedia. Therefore, we applied our proposed EAFG to align attributes in English, Chinese and French Wikipedia. First, we extract 107,302, 56,140 and 85,841 attributes from English, Chinese and French Wikipedia respectively. The existing attribute mappings are used for training, and the learned model is employed to predict the correspondence between cross-lingual attribute pairs. Both training and prediction are completed on a server with a 2.8 GHz CPU (32 cores) and 384 GB memory, and it costs 13 h and 21 h for EN-ZH and EN-FR data set respectively. Finally we get 23,923 new attribute mappings between English and Chinese Wikipedia, and 31,576 mappings between English and French. Table 3 presents a few examples of the discovered mappings.

Table 3. Examples of discovered attribute mappings

Classes	English	Chinese	French
Person	Alma mater	母校	Formation
	Spouse(s)	配偶	Conjoint
	Title	头衔	Activité principale
	Nationality	国籍	Nationalité
Location	Party Secretary	书记	Secrétaire du PCC
	Completed	竣工年份	Fin des travaux
	Population	人口	Population
	Mayor	市长	Maire
Film	Directed by	导演	Réalisation
	Screenplay by	编剧	Scénario
	Running time	片长	Durée
	Country	产地	Pays d'origine

4.7   Wikipedia Infobox Completion

Apparently, we can transfer infobox information that is missing in one language from other languages in which the information is already present, if we have the alignment of attributes. In this paper, we try to complement Chinese and English Wikipedia infoboxes from each other using the attribute alignments obtained above EAFG. Firstly, we extract 223,159 existing corresponding English-Chinese article pairs, and finally 76,498 article pairs are replenished by at least 1 attribute value. Figure 3 shows the number of added attribute values with respect to each article. The maximum number of added attribute values for one article is 34 and the average is 5.75, which indicates that infoboxes in Chinese and English both benefit a lot from the attribute alignments.

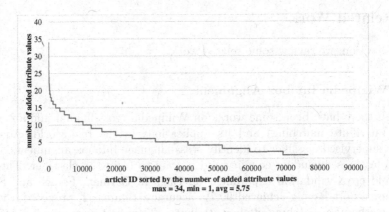

Fig. 3. Statistics of EN-ZH infobox complementing

We also count the times of each attribute being added into Chinese infoboxes, and list the top 20 attributes in Fig. 4. It should be noticed that most of the attributes are from these categories: *Person* (e.g., Born and Nationality), *Location* (e.g., time-zone and Original language) and *Film* (e.g., Director and Producer). The reason is that entities of these categories tend to have strong local features, and thus lead to imbalance of information among different language versions of Wikipedia. For example, a recent TV play *The Journey of Flower*[1] (花千骨[2] in Chinese) is very popular in China and its Chinese Wikipedia page contains elaborate information. In this experiment, we add 7 attribute values (such as (*editor*, Tianen Su), (*original channel*, Hunan Satellite)) from Chinese to English Wikipedia with respect to this entity (i.e., *The Journey of Flower*).

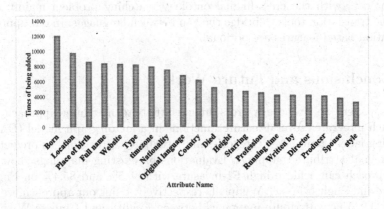

Fig. 4. Top 20 Attributes in EN-ZH infobox complementing

---

[1] https://en.wikipedia.org/wiki/The_Journey_of_Flower.
[2] https://zh.wikipedia.org/wiki/%E8%8A%B1%E5%8D%83%E9%AA%A8.

5   Related Work

In this section, we review some related work.

5.1   Wikipedia Infobox Alignment

Though there have been some works on Wikipedia cross-lingual infobox alignment (attribute matching) and its applications in the real world. Adar [1] used a supervised classifier to identify cross-language infobox alignments. They use 26 features, including equality and n-gram to train the classifier. Through a 10-fold cross-validation experiment on English, German, French and Spanish, they report having achieved 90.7% accuracy. Bouma [2] proposed a value-based method for matching infobox attributes. They first normalized all infobox attribute values, such as numbers, data formats and some units, and then matched the attributes according to the equality between English and Dutch Wikipedia. Rinser [13] proposed an instance-based attribute matching approach. They first matched entities in different language editions of Wikipedia, then they compared the values in attribute pairs and got final results using the entity mappings. However, these works did not consider the correlations among candidate attribute pairs, which is proved to be effective for attribute matching in our work.

5.2   Ontology Schema Matching

Ontology schema matching [14] is another related problem which mainly aims to get alignments of concepts and properties. Currently, some works focus on monolingual matching tasks, such as SOCOM [5] and RiMOM [8,21]. These systems deal with the cross-lingual ontology matching problem mainly using machine translation tools to bridge the gap between languages. In our approach, translation-based features are optional.

6   Conclusions and Future Work

In this paper, we propose a cross-lingual attribute matching approach. Our approach integrates several feature functions in a factor graph model (EAFG), including labels, templates, categories and attribute correlations to predict new cross-lingual attribute mappings. Evaluations on existing mappings show that our approach can achieve high F1-measure with 85.5% and 85.4% on English-Chinese and English-French Wikipedia respectively. Using our approach, we have found 23,923 new attribute mappings between English and Chinese Wikipedia and 31,576 between English and French. It is obvious that article and attribute mappings can benefit each other. Therefore, in the future, we are going to design a framework which can simultaneously and iteratively align all of the elements in Wikipedia.

Acknowledgments. The work is supported by 973 Program (No. 2014CB340504), NSFC key project (No. 61533018, 61661146007), Fund of Online Education Research Center, Ministry of Education (No. 2016ZD102), THUNUS NExT Co-Lab, National Natural Science Foundation of China (Grant No. 61375054), Natural Science Foundation of Guangdong Province (Grant No. 2014A030313745).

References

1. Adar, E., Skinner, M., Weld, D.S.: Information arbitrage across multi-lingual wikipedia. In: International Conference on Web Search and Web Data Mining, WSDM 2009, Barcelona, Spain, pp. 94–103, February 2009
2. Bouma, G., Duarte, S., Islam, Z.: Cross-lingual alignment and completion of wikipedia templates. In: Proceedings of the Third International Workshop on Cross Lingual Information Access: Addressing the Information Need of Multilingual Societies, pp. 21–29. Association for Computational Linguistics (2009)
3. Cohen, W.W., Ravikumar, P., Fienberg, S.E.: A comparison of string distance metrics for name-matching tasks 2003, pp. 73–78 (2003)
4. Cortes, C., Vapnik, V.: Support-vector networks. Mach. Learn. **20**(3), 273–297 (1995)
5. Fu, B., Brennan, R., O'Sullivan, D.: Cross-lingual ontology mapping – an investigation of the impact of machine translation. In: Gómez-Pérez, A., Yu, Y., Ding, Y. (eds.) ASWC 2009. LNCS, vol. 5926, pp. 1–15. Springer, Heidelberg (2009). doi:10. 1007/978-3-642-10871-6_1
6. Kschischang, F.R., Frey, B.J., Loeliger, H.A.: Factor graphs and the sum-product algorithm. IEEE Trans. Inf. Theory **47**(2), 498–519 (2001)
7. Lehmann, J., Isele, R., Jakob, M., Jentzsch, A., Kontokostas, D., Mendes, P.N., Hellmann, S., Morsey, M., Van Kleef, P., Auer, S., et al.: Dbpedia-a large-scale, multilingual knowledge base extracted from wikipedia. Semant. Web **6**(2), 167–195 (2015)
8. Li, J., Tang, J., Li, Y., Luo, Q.: Rimom: a dynamic multistrategy ontology alignment framework. IEEE Trans. Knowl. Data Eng. **21**(8), 1218–1232 (2009)
9. Mahdisoltani, F., Biega, J., Suchanek, F.: Yago3: a knowledge base from multilingual wikipedias. In: 7th Biennial Conference on Innovative Data Systems Research, CIDR Conference (2014)
10. Mikolov, T., Sutskever, I., Chen, K., Corrado, G.S., Dean, J.: Distributed representations of words and phrases and their compositionality. In: Advances in Neural Information Processing Systems, pp. 3111–3119 (2013)
11. Navigli, R., Ponzetto, S.P.: Babelnet: the automatic construction, evaluation and application of a wide-coverage multilingual semantic network. Artif. Intell. **193**, 217–250 (2012)
12. Pedregosa, F., Varoquaux, G., Gramfort, A., Michel, V., Thirion, B., Grisel, O., Blondel, M., Prettenhofer, P., Weiss, R., Dubourg, V.: Scikit-learn: machine learning in python. J. Mach. Learn. Res. **12**(10), 2825–2830 (2013)
13. Rinser, D., Lange, D., Naumann, F.: Cross-lingual entity matching and infobox alignment in wikipedia. Inf. Syst. **38**(6), 887–907 (2013)
14. Shvaiko, P., Euzenat, J.: Ontology matching: state of the art and future challenges. IEEE Trans. Knowl. Data Eng. **25**(1), 158–176 (2013)
15. Sorg, P., Cimiano, P.: Enriching the crosslingual link structure of wikipedia-a classification-based approach. In: Proceedings of the AAAI Workshop on Wikipedia & Artifical Intelligence (2008)

16. Wang, Z., Li, J., Tang, J.: Boosting cross-lingual knowledge linking via concept annotation. In: International Joint Conference on Artificial Intelligence, pp. 2733–2739 (2013)
17. Wang, Z., Li, J., Wang, Z., Tang, J.: Cross-lingual knowledge linking across wiki knowledge bases. In: International Conference on World Wide Web, pp. 459–468 (2012)
18. Wang, Z., Li, J., Wang, Z., Li, S., Li, M., Zhang, D., Shi, Y., Liu, Y., Zhang, P., Tang, J.: Xlore: a large-scale English-Chinese bilingual knowledge graph. In: Proceedings of the 2013th International Conference on Posters & Demonstrations Track, vol. 1035, pp. 121–124. CEUR-WS.org (2013)
19. Wang, Z., Li, Z., Li, J., Tang, J., Pan, J.Z.: Transfer learning based cross-lingual knowledge extraction for wikipedia. In: ACL (1), pp. 641–650 (2013)
20. Wentland, W., Knopp, J., Silberer, C., Hartung, M.: Building a multilingual lexical resource for named entity disambiguation, translation and transliteration. In: International Conference on Language Resources and Evaluation, LREC 2008, Marrakech, Morocco, 26 May–1 June 2008, pp. 3230–3237 (2008)
21. Zhang, Y., Li, J.: Rimom results for OAEI 2015. Ontol. Match. **185** (2015)

Author Index